WILEY PLUS

for *Introduction to Corporate Finance*

Check with your instructor to find out if you have access to *WileyPLUS!*

Study More Effectively with a Multimedia Text

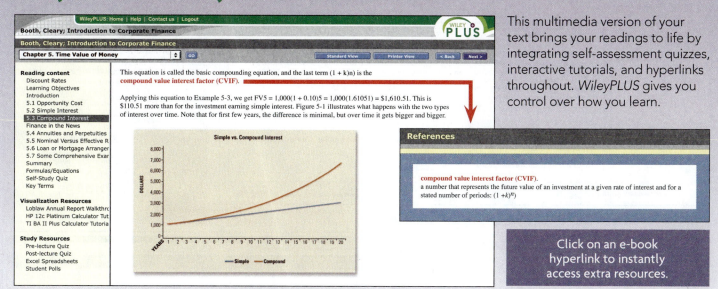

This multimedia version of your text brings your readings to life by integrating self-assessment quizzes, interactive tutorials, and hyperlinks throughout. *WileyPLUS* gives you control over how you learn.

Click on an e-book hyperlink to instantly access extra resources.

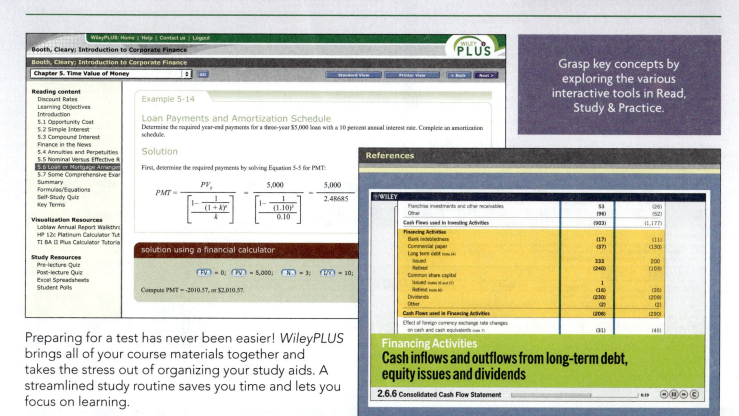

Grasp key concepts by exploring the various interactive tools in Read, Study & Practice.

Preparing for a test has never been easier! *WileyPLUS* brings all of your course materials together and takes the stress out of organizing your study aids. A streamlined study routine saves you time and lets you focus on learning.

John Wiley & Sons Canada, Ltd.

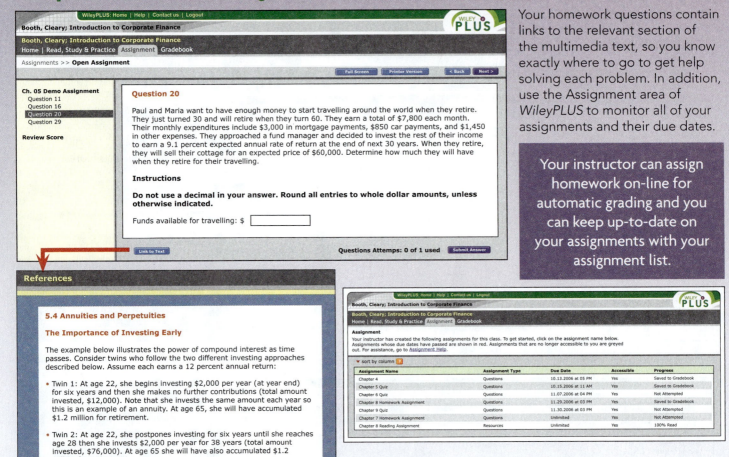
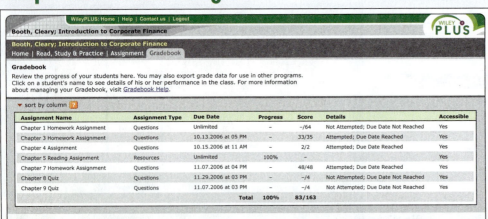

INTRODUCTION TO
CORPORATE
FINANCE

MANAGING CANADIAN FIRMS
IN A GLOBAL ENVIRONMENT

LAURENCE BOOTH
University of Toronto

W. SEAN CLEARY
Saint Mary's University

John Wiley & Sons Canada, Ltd.

Library and Archives Canada Cataloguing in Publication

Booth, Laurence D.
    Introduction to corporate finance / Laurence Booth, W. Sean Cleary.

ISBN 978-0-470-83780-1

    1. Corporations--Finance--Textbooks. 2. Business enterprises--Finance--Textbooks. I. Cleary, W. Sean
(William Sean), 1962- II. Title.

HG4026.B65 2007   658.15   C2007-902156-5

Production Credits

Acquisitions Editor: Darren Lalonde
Publishing Services Director: Karen Bryan
Editorial Manager: Karen Staudinger
Developmental Editor: Gail Brown
Marketing Manager: Aida Krneta
Editorial Assistant: Sheri Coombs
Editorial Assistant/Permissions Coordinator: Pauline Ricablanca
Media Editor: Elsa Passera Berardi
Design & Typesetting: Interrobang Graphic Design Inc.
Cover Photo: Joel Benard/Masterfile
Wiley Bicentennial Logo: Richard J. Pacifico
Printing & Binding: Quebecor World Inc.

Printed and bound in United States of America.
3 4 5 QW 11 10 09 08

John Wiley & Sons Canada, Ltd.
6045 Freemont Blvd.
Mississauga, Ontario L5R 4J3
Visit our website at: www.wiley.ca

WILEY

To all those I love, especially my parents
and my children.
—L. B.

To my children Jason, Brennan, Brigid, and
Siobhan—the joys of my life!
—S. C.

ABOUT THE AUTHORS

Laurence Booth D.B.A., M.B.A., M.A. (Indiana University); B.S. (London School of Economics) is Professor of Finance, holds the CIT chair in structured finance, and is the finance area coordinator at the Rotman School of Management at University of Toronto. His major research interests are in corporate finance and the behaviour of regulated industries. He has published over forty articles in numerous academic journals including the *Journal of Finance* and the *Journal of Financial and Quantitative Analysis*, co-authored a textbook on international business, and is on the editorial board of five academic journals.

At University of Toronto since 1978, Professor Booth has taught graduate courses in business finance, international financial management, corporate financing, mergers and acquisitions, financial management and financial theory, as well as short executive programs on money and foreign exchange markets, business valuation, mergers and acquisitions and financial strategy. His advice is frequently sought by the media and he has appeared as an expert

Sean Cleary (left) and Laurence Booth (right).

financial witness before the Ontario Securities Commission, the National Energy Board, the Canadian Radio-television and Telecommunications Commission (CRTC) as well as various regulatory tribunals in Canada.

W. Sean Cleary, CFA is Professor of Finance at Saint Mary's University in Halifax, Nova Scotia. Dr. Cleary graduated with his MBA from Saint Mary's University and with his PhD in finance from the University of Toronto. He was awarded the Chartered Financial Analyst (CFA) designation in 2001. He has also completed the Canadian Securities Course (CSC), the Professional Financial Planning course (PFPC), as well as the Investment Funds Institute of Canada (IFIC) Mutual Fund Course.

Dr. Cleary has taught numerous university finance courses, including investments, introductory finance, and corporate finance at Saint Mary's University, University of Toronto, Ryerson University, and University of Lethbridge over the past eight years. He has also taught seminars preparing students to write the Canadian Securities Course and all three levels of the CFA program for several years.

Dr. Cleary has published articles in numerous journals including *Journal of Finance, Journal of Financial and Quantitative Analysis, Journal of Banking and Finance, Journal of Multinational Financial Management*, and *Canadian Investment Review*, in addition to receiving major research grants from the Social Sciences and Humanities Research Council of Canada (SSHRC). He has also prepared chapters for professional courses offered by the Canadian Securities Institute. He is also the Canadian author of *Investments: Analysis and Management*, Second Canadian Edition and the *Canadian Securities Exam: Fast Track Study Guide*, both published by John Wiley & Sons Canada, Ltd.

PREFACE

In designing a textbook we have tried to answer the basic question: What do we want students to learn? In this respect we are very much aware that the target audience for this textbook is made up of bright students who seek careers in business and not academia. Further, they are predominantly already enrolled in a business or management program with the objective of working, initially at least, for a Canadian firm. This objective has dictated what is covered in the textbook and how we have tried to cover it.

Objective and Focus of the Textbook

A finance textbook designed for business students of necessity means that it should take a *managerial* focus. In this respect it is important to note that finance is built on three "legs":

* Accounting

* Law

* Economics

   Accounting is the language of business, and financial analysts must be able to understand a firm's financial statements. This is a prerequisite to understanding anything in finance. In fact for most non-financial companies, the terms 'finance' and 'accounting' are interchangeable. This is reflected in Chapters 3 and 4 of the textbook, where we review the basic features of financial statements and financial analysis. We do this by studying a real Canadian company, Rothmans Inc., and using its financial statements throughout the textbook to both illustrate and develop basic financial concepts. We chose to use the financial statements of Rothmans Inc. because its statements are uncomplicated and easy for a beginning student to understand. As well, the statements emphasize a key point for any financial manager: one must also read the notes that accompany any financial statement.

   However, if you go back fifty years you will discover that introductory finance textbooks were heavily based on *corporate and securities laws*. This is because financial securities are contracts and the terms of these contracts are partly determined by stature, while the ability to trade them in a securities market is determined by securities laws. Understanding the basics of the legal system is critical for understanding how finance works in practice. Notably, many of the best paid finance professionals, designing securities, advising on mergers and acquisitions, and running investment banks, are lawyers.

   The importance of the legal system permeates the whole text but the discussion of mergers and acquisitions in Chapter 15 and the discussion on securities issues and investment banking Chapter 17 requires at least some familiarity with the Canadian legal system since both involve the transfer of securities. Here it is important to understand that there are differences between the United States and Canada that flow from differences in the legal system. Coercive tender offers, for example, occur in the U.S. but not in Canada, while bought deal underwritings are common in Canada, but not the U.S. In both cases we cannot explain what we observe without understanding these legal issues.

While some may think of law as dry and boring, in fact the opposite is true. Behind most corporate and securities law there has been an action that has enriched one person at someone else's expense. While economists politely refer to these actions as "wealth transfers," more commonly they are referred to as fraud or at the very least ethical concerns. Here it is important to note that the legal system is simply the entrenchment of society's ethical or value system. For example, many of the accounting and securities frauds that we discuss in the text would have been viewed as ethical rather than legal issues 20 or 30 years ago! For this reason, the text includes a series of ethical issues for discussion and analysis at the end of most sections, to enhance our understanding of the legal system.

If accounting provides the data, and the legal system provides the constraints on what can be done, *economics* provides most of the principles on how to get things done. Understanding the workings of the economy—where we are in the business cycle, industry market structure, and the response of competitors—is all critical to understanding how financial markets behave and how firms manage their finances. However, this is not a financial economics textbook. We are not proving the existence of equilibrium, but rather we are **providing a framework to solve real problems**. We develop and use accounting, legal, and economic skills to solve financial problems faced every day by Canadians and Canadian firms

Organization of the Textbook

There is an artificial distinction that business finance is separate from personal finance. However, the truth is the exact opposite: many of the topics that we cover such as financial planning and analysis, financial leverage, and the valuation of financial securities are useful for all Canadians. There are underlying financial principles that every student of finance needs to know, and this text develops these principles first, and then applies them to business finance. However, some instructors may prefer to cover the material in different manner. To add flexibility we have designed the material in "parts."

Parts 1 and 2 are traditional. We start with an overview of the financial system and business finance, before reviewing basic financial statements and financial analysis. In Part 3 to 5 we deviate from the traditional structure by developing a general understanding of discounted cash flow models, modern portfolio theory, and options and futures. In our view, this is necessary to avoid undue duplication when discussing capital budgeting, corporate financing, and cost of capital. In particular, a general introduction to options and futures is useful for discussing real options in capital budgeting, as well as hybrid securities in corporate financing.

In Part 6 we then apply these ideas to the acquisition of long lived assets (capital budgeting); in Part 7 to corporate financing; in Part 8 to financial policy, and in Part 9 to working capital management. Furthermore, topics relating to international issues and ethics are integrated throughout the text. In this way, none of the topics are "add ons," pushed to the end of the textbook, to be rarely covered.

For those instructors who prefer a more traditional structure, the textbook is flexible enough that Part 6 on capital budgeting may easily be moved forward to follow Part 3 and the discussion of discounted cash flow models. The discussion of modern portfolio theory and Part 4 may then be developed in conjunction with risk analysis in capital budgeting. However, the disadvantage of this structure would be that Part 5, on futures and options, would be relegated to a special topic when in reality it is too important to be left to the end of the course.

Orientation

Finally, the textbook emphasizes that for students seeking careers in business management, in Canada or with Canadian firms, the focus must be on **Canadian content** and extensive **problem material**.

Many textbooks used in Canada are U.S. textbooks adapted for a Canadian market. In contrast, this text has been written from the ground up based on Canadian content and applications. Issues such as the day count, how to quote interest rates, takeover rules, and securities law continue to be different between Canada and the U.S. Canadians working for Canadian firms are expected to know what happens in Canada, as well as what happens in the United States.

However, Canadian content includes more than just describing different rules; it must also relate to current practice. We include news articles in the "Finance in the News" features, which bring to life the finance issues and topics covered in the textbook. Relating basic issues to Canadian examples makes the material more relevant to students. For example, it is more relevant to understand Research In Motion's option backdating issues than it is to understand Apple's.

On the other hand, in today's global business environment, what happens around the world impacts Canadian markets and Canadian firms. Therefore, it is important to consider how global factors influence the Canadian environment, and hence the decisions made by Canadian managers and investors. In fact, global influences are so great in Canada that all Canadian financial managers have to be aware of these issues. We address this by integrating international issues on a topic-by-topic basis, as they arise, rather than in a separate chapter where they are just "lumped together." In this way, awareness of international issues develops naturally.

Finally, finance is a ***how to*** subject. Students learn how to do things in a finance course, for example, how to evaluate securities, how to manage short term cash, how to evaluate a plant expansion, and how to build a portfolio. In developing these skills, this textbook has an extensive set of examples and problems worked out to show "how to" solve these problems in long hand or electronically using either a business calculator or spreadsheet. This approach is particularly important in the foundational Part 3, which deals with discounted cash flow valuation. This section develops the basics, and builds in a cumulative manner that allows the analysis of complex financial securities, while building student confidence in their ability to solve real problems.

We believe that this textbook will stimulate students to understand finance, as well as to apply it. After working through this textbook, we believe that students will be able to solve basic financial problems, add value to the firms for whom they will eventually work, and have the basic skills necessary to do more advanced work in finance. We hope this may then lead students to do even more advanced work in finance, and they will then share our enthusiasm for finance, which caused us to write this textbook. We know that these are high standards for a finance textbook; if you feel we have not met these objectives, we welcome your feedback.

Hallmark Features of this Textbook

Because students are motivated to learn finance if they are shown how it is relevant to their world, each chapter of *Introduction to Corporate Finance* is written with engaging real-world examples and a wealth of detail. The following features are included to further enhance this presentation:

finance INTHENEWS15-2

M&A MAY FUEL TSX INTO 2007

Halfway through the year, merger and acquisition activity in Canada is on track for its second-highest level on record, a frenzied pace of activity that has historically sparked gains on the Toronto Stock Exchange, according to data from Thomson First Call.

"If M&A activity is sustained throughout 2006 and into 2007, Canadian equities could see another strong year," Thomson First Call's research analyst Avita Sukhram said in a note to investors.

In the 212 days since the start of the year 893 corporate deals worth $100.6-billion have been unveiled. If this trend holds, 2006 could end with more than 1,700-making it the second-largest year when measured by number of deals.

However, "since 2000, the years with declines in M&A activity also saw decline in the TSX," said Thomson First Call.

The biggest year was 2000, when 2,118 transactions worth just over $201-billion helped drive stock prices higher.

"With only half of 2006 left to go, the dollar value of deals is just shy of the total in 2005," the report said. That year, 1,511 deals valued at $108-billion were made.

The flurry of consolidation shows no sign of abating, a good thing for Canadian stocks. Zinc and copper miner Teck Cominco Ltd. raised its bid for fellow Canadian nickel miner Inco Ltd. Monday, raising the stakes in a battle with Arizona copper producer Phelps Dodge Corp.

In the energy sector, Canadian Oil Sands Trust pushed back the deadline of its takeover offer for Canada Southern Petroleum Ltd. yesterday in order to give it more time to secure shareholder support. It is facing a competing bid from Canadian Superior Energy Inc.

Over the past 17 years, friendly and hostile takeovers, as well as mergers, have been dominated by Canadian materials and energy companies. Since 1990, energy has taken the top spot in the deal making eight times—while materials has stolen it seven times.

The rally in commodity prices has led to a surge of consolidation in the materials sector, with $66-billion in announced M&A activity so far in 2006.

In 2005, deals among materials companies reached $49-billion. The previous standout year for the sector was 1998, when the dollar value of activity was $14.9-billion.

The comparison of merger-and-acquisition activity and the TSX energy price index over the past 17 years suggests that as transactions increase or decrease, the energy sector index will follow suit, Thomson First Call said.

Source: Luciw, Roma, "M&A Fuel TSX into 2007," *Globe and Mail*, August 2, 2006, page B11. Reprinted with the permission of the *Globe and Mail*.

- **Finance in the News:** Each chapter includes at least one article or item from the financial press that is integrated into the main discussion of the chapter, to help students draw the connection between theory and application, and to highlight the relevance of the topic being discussed.

AUDIT OPTIONS POLICIES, CSA URGES

ethics AND CORPORATE GOVERNANCE 12-1

The Canadian Securities Administrators, or CSA, is recommending that all Canadian public companies assess their policies and controls for stock option grants to ensure they comply with legislation.

The notice comes as a scandal over backdated stock options continues to widen in the United States, where more than 40 companies have already said they will restate earnings or might do so once internal probes are completed. The restatements total at least $2.27 billion (U.S.).

Backdating occurs when a company sets the grant date for stock options retroactively, to a time when the company's stock price was lower, creating an instant paper gain for the executive or employee receiving the options.

Stock options allow recipients to buy shares at a future date, usually at the price on the day they were granted. They are given to managers as an incentive to find ways to boost the stock price.

A University of Michigan study released this week suggests shareholders bear the brunt of the practice, shouldering an average of $510 million per company in losses after the practice is made public. That far outweighs the average $600,000 annual gain for a company's executives.

"If CSA staff become aware, through disclosure reviews, tips or otherwise, of abuses by reporting issuers, they may take enforcement action against the issuers or their directors and officers," the administrators said yesterday.

Regulations in Canada may reduce the opportunity for companies to backdate options here, the CSA said.

Under Toronto Stock Exchange rules, the exercise price for options cannot be less than the market price of the stock when the options are granted, and the exercise price cannot be based on market prices that don't reflect undisclosed material information.

There are similar rules on the TSX Venture Exchange, except issuers are allowed to set the exercise price at a certain discount to the market price.

Securities legislation also requires company insiders to file an insider-trading report within 10 days of receiving options.

Directors are responsible for ensuring that a company prices and discloses options appropriately, the CSA said.

It suggested boards set up a compensation committee that follows national corporate governance guidelines. It also suggested they adopt corporate disclosure and insider-trading policies and establish blackout periods around earnings announcements.

In October, the TSX Group sent a notice to listed companies reminding them of the rules around options.

- **Ethics and Corporate Governance:** Found in the various parts in the text, this feature includes an item relating to ethics and corporate governance, and how these issues affect corporations today. These items are accompanied by questions to help launch in-class analysis and discussion.

- **Chapter-Opening Vignettes:** These introduce students to the main focus of the chapter through an interesting and relevant discussion, showing its real-world application.

Corporations

This chapter focuses on the different types of business organizations and what the role of one of these, the corporation, should be. These days, corporations are being called upon more than ever to act in a manner that is socially, economically, and environmentally responsible. However, being a good corporate citizen can put a firm at odds with its fundamental obligation, which is to maximize profits. Home Depot Canada has a solid track record of community involvement. The company uses its resources and expertise to build playgrounds and affordable housing and assists communities affected by natural disasters. It has also developed in-store programs that help customers to identify environmentally preferred products and to dispose of household materials safely.

Sources: Home Depot Canada website
http://www.homedepot.ca
Natural Resources Canada, Corporate Social Responsibility: Lessons Learned.
http://www.nrcan-rncan.gc.ca
Natural Resources Canada, Corporate Social Responsibility: Highlights of Company CSR Activities. http://www.nrcan.gc.ca

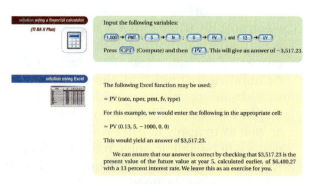

solution using a financial calculator
(TI BA II Plus)

Input the following variables:

$1,000 \rightarrow PMT$; $5 \rightarrow N$; $0 \rightarrow FV$; and $13 \rightarrow I/Y$

Press CPT (Compute) and then PV. This will give an answer of −3,517.23.

solution using Excel

The following Excel function may be used:

= PV (rate, nper, pmt, fv, type)

For this example, we would enter the following in the appropriate cell:

= PV (0.13, 5, −1000, 0, 0)

This would yield an answer of $3,517.23.

We can ensure that our answer is correct by checking that $3,517.23 is the present value of the future value at year 5, calculated earlier, of $6,480.27 with a 13 percent interest rate. We leave this as an exercise for you.

- **Financial Calculator Keystrokes:** All relevant demonstration problems include actual keystrokes for the TI BAII calculator.

- **Excel Spreadsheet Commands:** All relevant demonstration problems include Excel spreadsheet commands

Pedagogy to Enhance Student Understanding

Because an introductory finance course introduces students to many new concepts and constructs, this text features a rich array of study aids to enhance student understanding:

Learning Objectives: Listed at the start of each chapter, these focus students' attention on the key points of the chapter.

Running Glossary: Key terms are highlighted throughout each chapter, and are defined in the text margin for quick reference.

Concept Review Questions: At the end of each major topic, questions are provided to help students check of their understanding before moving on.

Examples: All examples in the text are numbered and labelled for easy reference, and include fully worked out solutions. Actual keystrokes for the TI BAII Plus financial calculator and Excel Spreadsheet commands are included for each relevant example. Spreadsheet templates and actual keystrokes for the other financial calculator recognized for the CFA exam, the Hewlett Packard 12C, is also included online.

Chapter Summary: Each chapter concludes with a summary of the key concepts covered in that chapter.

Equations Summary: All equations used in a chapter are listed and numbered for easy study reference at the end of that chapter.

Because students cannot learn finance unless they practice problems extensively, *Introduction to Corporate Finance* comes complete with WileyPLUS.

WileyPLUS is a unique, virtual learning environment, where students can practice algorithmically generated problems that include hints and that link directly to the relevant section of the e-text. For more information on WileyPLUS please see the front pages of the textbook.

Robust Instructor and Student Support Package

For Instructors:

Instructors Manual: Prepared by the text authors, the instructor's manual includes complete solutions to all of the questions and practice problems in the textbook; answers to the concept review questions; and additional Finance in the News and Ethics and Corporate Governance news articles with study questions. The news articles will be updated on the textbook's companion website twice a year by the authors, to keep these features current and relevant.

Test Bank: Test Bank: Written by Sandra Betton, John Molson School of Business, Concordia University, the Test Bank includes a rich selection of multiple choice, short answer, and practice problems, with full solutions. These are coded by difficulty and by knowledge level (skill, conceptual, analytical). A selection of questions will be offered in an algorithmic format, allowing instructors to create unique tests or quizzes.

PowerPoint: A full series of PowerPoint slides are included, which incorporate key points from each chapter, worked demonstration problems, and interesting web links to aid in-class presentations.

The supplements are available for download on the textbook's password protected instructor website.

WileyPLUS

- Assign automatically graded homework, practice problems, and quizzes from three sources of questions: end-of-chapter practice problems, test bank problems, or your own quiz questions.

- Track your students' progress in an instructor's grade book.

- Access all teaching and learning resources, including an electronic version of textbook and all instructor supplements, from one easy-to-use- website

- Create class presentations using Wiley-provided resources, with the ability to customize and add your own content.

For Students:

WileyPLUS

Within WileyPLUS, students will find a variety of interactive and media-rich study and learning tools. Some of these include:

Pre-and Post-Lecture Quizzes: Self-study practice questions, with immediate feedback, for every chapter of the textbook to help students gage their level of understanding as they prepare for class or a test.

Student Polls: Surveys are integrated throughout the e-text, providing students with the opportunity to register their opinion on a variety of ethical and corporate governance issues. After they have voted, they can compare their votes with those of other students taking this course across Canada.

Spreadsheet Templates and Financial Calculator Keystrokes: These are included for all worked out examples in the text, where relevant.

Flash Cards: These are included for key terms and their definitions

ACKNOWLEDGEMENTS

A large scale textbook project such as this one is not the work of single authors; rather it is the combined effort of many people whom we wish to acknowledge.We would first like to thank our many reviewers, listed below, who took the time to read and evaluate the draft manuscripts. Without their many helpful comments and their feedback, this textbook would not be what it is today.

Ashraf Al Zaman, St. Mary's University

Ben Amoako-Adu, Wilfrid Laurier University

Ata Assaf, University of Windsor

Larry Bauer, Memorial University of Newfoundland

David Birkett, University of Guelph

Edward Blinder, Ryerson University

Trevor W. Chamberlain, McMaster University

Chris Duff, Royal Roads University

Alex Faseruk, Memorial University of Newfoundland

Cameron Gall, Mount Royal College

Larbi Hammami, McGill University

Margery Heuser, Okanagan College

Robert Ironside, University of Lethbridge

Kurt Loescher, University of Saskatchewan

András Marosi, University of Alberta

Ian Rakita, Concordia University

Michael W. Reynolds, Carleton University

Wilf Roesler, University of Lethbridge

Shahbaz Sheikh, University of Western Ontario

David A. Stangeland, University of Manitoba

Thomas Walker, Concordia University

Eric Wang, Athabasca University

A special thank you to John Hull, who lent his expertise and keen eye to the derivatives section, and for being a good friend.

A number of other talented people made important contributions to the textbook. We would like to thank Sandra Otto for providing the interesting and thought provoking opening vignettes. We would also like to thank Grace Yu and Stephen C. Hiscock for providing additional problem material. Finally, we would especially like to single out the efforts of Sandra Betton who, we feel, has raised the bar with her contribution of practice problems and her authoring of the Test Bank materials.

Finally, we are grateful for the talented and dedicated individuals from John Wiley & Sons Canada, Ltd. our publisher, who helped to bring together the textbook you are now reading. They include: Darren Lalonde Acquisitions Editor; Karen Staudinger, Editorial Manager; Isabelle Moreau, Director of Marketing; Aida Krneta, Marketing Manager; Karen Bryan, Publishing Services Director;

Elsa Passera-Berardi, Media Editor; Gail Brown, Developmental Editor; Sheri Coombs, Editorial Assistant; and Christine Rae of Interrobang Graphic Design Inc., who designed and laid out the textbook. We would also like to thank copy editors Dawn Hunter and Laurel Hyatt, proof reader Sandra Otto, and checker Ross Meacher. We would particularly like to single out the efforts of our day-to-day 'boss,' Gail Brown. Her tireless efforts and long hours to keep the project on track went above and beyond the call of duty.

Laurence Booth   W. Sean Cleary
Toronto, Ontario   Halifax, Nova Scotia
May 2007

BRIEF TABLE OF CONTENTS

TABLE OF CONTENTS

PART 1

THE FINANCIAL ENVIRONMENT

What is business finance? In these opening chapters we examine the big picture in terms of the Canadian financial system, including the major actors in the system, the major securities that are issued, and the types of problems that are solved. We then discuss how business is organized and financed, and introduce the income trust sector, where billions of dollars in market value were wiped out overnight due to unexpected government policy changes. The role of management in dispersed firms is then developed with a discussion of key careers available to finance majors.

CHAPTER 1
An Introduction to Finance

CHAPTER 2
Business (Corporate) Finance

Canada's Balance Sheet

An introduction to basic finance concepts in this chapter includes a discussion of Canada's balance sheet. The debt on Canada's balance sheet is the accumulation of all budget deficits and surpluses since Confederation in 1867, when the debt was a mere $75 million. World War I pushed this number up to approximately $3 billion by 1920. In 1996–97, the debt had reached a high of $562.9 billion, with interest payments of around $45 billion. The debt was a whopping 68.4% of gross domestic product (GDP). Since then, efforts to eliminate budget deficits have resulted in a reduced debt and lower interest charges on the existing debt. The government has used the increased financial flexibility to invest in other long-term objectives and has set a target debt-to-GDP ratio of less than 20% by 2020.

Source: "Canada's Fiscal Progress," Department of Finance Canada website: <http://www.fin.gc.ca/ec2005/ec/ecc3e.html>, February 2, 2007.

"Government Budget." *Encyclopædia Britannica*. 2007. Encyclopædia Britannica Online. February 2, 2007. http://www.britannica.com/eb/article-26363

An Introduction to Finance

Learning Objectives

After reading this chapter, you should understand the following:

1. What finance is and what is involved in the study of finance

2. How financial securities can be used to provide financing for borrowers and simultaneously to provide investment opportunities for lenders

3. How financial systems work in general

4. The channels of intermediation and the role played by market and financial intermediaries within this system

5. The basic types of financial instruments that are available and how they are traded

6. The importance of the global financial system

INTRODUCTION

finance the study of how and under what terms savings (money) are allocated between lenders and borrowers

O ften, the first finance course business students take is a business finance course. Yet business finance cannot be taught in isolation; it is simply one part of finance. So what is finance?

Finance, in its broadest terms, is the study of how and under what terms savings (money) are allocated between lenders and borrowers. The key term in the definition is *allocated*, and you may recognize the similarity of finance and economics, which studies how scarce resources are allocated in an economy. In many ways, finance is closely related to economics. However, finance is distinct from economics in that finance is not just about how resources are allocated but also under *what terms* and through *what channels*. Whenever funds are transferred, a financial contract comes into existence, and these contracts are called financial securities. As we will discuss in depth in other chapters, exchanging funds (money) for pieces of paper (securities) opens up an enormous number of opportunities for fraud. As a result, the study of finance requires a basic understanding of securities and corporate law and the institutions that facilitate this exchange of funds. In this chapter, we will briefly review the structure of the Canadian financial system and the major agents in the system, so you will understand the place of business finance in the financial system.

1.1 REAL VERSUS FINANCIAL ASSETS

Canada's Balance Sheet

A balance sheet is simply a snapshot of what is owned (*assets*) and what is owed (*liabilities*) at a particular time. The difference between the value of what is owned and what is owed is *net worth* or *equity*—as, for example, the equity in a house. We can estimate balance sheets for individuals and for institutions (both businesses and governments). We will discuss financial statements in detail in Chapter 3.

Table 1-1 aggregates the 2005 market value of the assets and liabilities of the three major domestic groups in our economy: (1) individuals, referred to as the household sector by Statistics Canada (StatsCan), (2) businesses, and (3) government. The Canadian assets and liabilities that are held by non-resident individuals, businesses, and governments compose the balance sheet of the *non-resident* sector, which we generally "net" out to determine what the country owes to or is owed by non-residents.

Table 1-1 shows that as of 2005, Canadians had total assets with a market value of $4,567 billion, or $135,000 for every Canadian. Deducting the net foreign debt in 2005 of $181 billion (4 percent of total assets) produces a net worth of $4,386 billion. Of course, Canadians owed more than $181 billion, but most of that was to other Canadians—that is, individuals owed banks and other financial institutions, banks owed individuals, some businesses owed the government, and so on. Similarly, Canadians owed more than $181 billion to non-residents, but offsetting the *gross* or total debt was what non-residents owed Canadians, so the *net* foreign debt was $181 billion.

Table 1-1 Canada's Balance Sheet ($Billion), 2005	
Residential structures	1,260
Non-residential structures	1,080
Machinery and equipment	425
Consumer durables	371
Inventories	211
Land	1,220
Net foreign debt	−181
Net worth or equity	4,386*

*Rounded
Source: Statistics Canada. *National Balance Sheet Accounts, Quarterly Estimates, Fourth Quarter 2005*. Ottawa: Minister of Industry, 2006 (Catalogue No. 13-214-XIE).

Real Assets

The balance sheet shows all assets according to six major classifications. The assets included under these headings are **real assets**, representing the tangible things that compose personal and business assets. Personal assets are the value of houses (residential structures), the land the houses are on, the major appliances in the houses (televisions, washing machines, etc.), and cars. Major appliances and cars are referred to as consumer durables, because they last many years. For businesses, the major assets are office towers, factories, mines, and so on (non-residential structures), the machinery and equipment in those structures, the land they are on, and the stock or inventories of things waiting to be used or sold.[1]

real assets the tangible things that compose personal and business assets

We have introduced Canada's national balance sheet because *finance is essentially the management of an entity's balance sheet.* This management involves the real asset side and the liability side of the balance sheet. When we look at business finance, we will discuss how firms arrive at the decision to build a new factory, increase the level of their inventory holdings, and make strategic asset acquisition decisions, such as buying another firm (mergers and acquisitions). These are all examples of asset acquisitions, which we will generically refer to as *capital expenditure* (capex) decisions. On the liability side are ways to finance these expenditures, which we will refer to as *corporate financing* decisions. However, these same decisions are made by individuals who are deciding to buy a house or a new car, and by the government, because all entities have a balance sheet.

Financial Assets

Although the national balance sheet presented in Table 1-1 is useful for understanding wealth and types of assets, it removes most of the things that are of interest to students of finance. This is because it nets out all the debts we owe to ourselves, which is almost all of our debts! To understand these financial assets and how the financial system works, we need to disaggregate the data— that is, look at it in greater detail. A useful source of data in this regard is the National Balance Sheet Accounts (NBSA), which is also produced by StatsCan.

---

[1] These assets also include some owned by the different levels of government in Canada.

The basic idea behind the NBSA is to collect financial data on the major agents in the financial system. For example, StatsCan collects data on all persons and unincorporated businesses[2] in Canada and groups them into the household sector account. However, **financial assets** are simply what one individual has lent to another, so one person's positive financial asset is another's *negative* financial asset (or liability). Therefore, StatsCan nets out what one individual owes to another, so that the numbers are the net real assets and the net financial assets of Canadian households. Figure 1-1 provides the overall breakdown of both real and financial assets in Canada for 2005.

financial assets what one individual has lent to another

FIGURE 1-1

Borrowing and Lending: The Big Picture

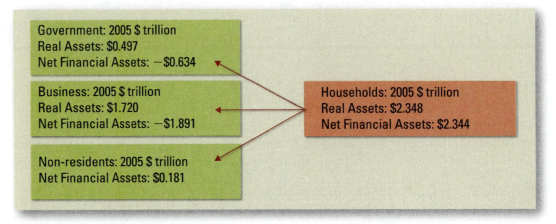

Source: Statistics Canada.

Figure 1-1 shows who owns and owes what in the Canadian economy. If we start with Canadian households and add up all real (physical) assets, like homes and cars, in aggregate, Canadian households owned real assets with a market value at the end of 2005 of $2.348 trillion. In addition to these *real* assets, Canadian households owned *net financial assets* issued by the government, corporations, and non-residents with a market value of $2.344 trillion. So, in aggregate, if we add the two together, Canadian households had total net assets with a 2005 market value of $4.692 trillion, which is slightly greater than the total assets for Canada of $4.567 trillion, as expressed in Table 1-1.

In 2005, all layers of Canadian governments, in aggregate, had real assets worth $497 billion. The bulk of these assets are government office buildings and the machinery and equipment in them, but $100 billion represents the market value of government-owned land. That's the good news. The bad news is that all layers of government in aggregate had net financial assets of –$634 billion, which is the market value of all government debt outstanding. Similarly, Canadian corporations and government Crown corporations had real assets with a market value of $1.720 trillion in 2005, representing the factories, mines, office buildings, and so on, needed to produce the goods and services that we buy. The market value of the financial assets issued by the business sector to finance those real assets, or what we call corporate financing, was –$1.891 trillion.

---

[2] We will discuss business organization in Chapter 2, but unincorporated businesses are basically individuals operating a business that is indistinguishable for tax purposes from themselves.

Notice that if we add up the value of real assets owned by the three domestic sectors, we end up with a total market value of real assets of $4.565 trillion. However, when we add up the total net financial assets of these three sectors, we end up with financial assets of –$181 billion, which equals exactly the net financial assets owned by non-residents. Therefore, the value of the *net* real assets in Canada owned by Canadian residents, or our net worth, equals $4.384 trillion. Also, notice from Figure 1-1 that the net financial assets figure for the household sector equals *positive* $2.344 trillion, while the total net financial assets of the combined government and business sectors equals *negative* $2.525 trillion. This demonstrates that government and business entities obtain most of their financing (i.e., 93 percent) from the domestic household sector (i.e., individuals), with the remaining small proportion of their financing coming from foreign investors.

Although Figure 1-1 shows the flow of savings from households to governments and business with some money flowing in from abroad, it does not show the flows within each sector. However, it does point to the importance of the four major areas of finance: personal finance, government finance, corporate finance, and international finance. Although the main focus of this textbook is on corporate finance, it is important to realize that all these sectors are part of the financial system and are affected by the same types of phenomena; a shock in the government or international sectors can quickly work through the system to affect personal and corporate finance, and vice versa. Because the primary source of savings is the household sector, we will spend some time examining this sector.

Households

Table 1-2 provides a comprehensive listing of the 2005 assets and liabilities of Canadian households.

Table 1-2   Assets and Liabilities of Households, 2005

Assets	$Billion	Liabilities	$Billion
Houses	1,086	Consumer credit	260
Consumer durables	435	Loans	131
Land	827	Mortgages	588
Real Assets	**2,348**	**Total Liabilities**	**979**
Deposits	683		
Debt	114		
Pensions and insurance	1,200		
Shares	1,254		
Foreign and other	72		
Financial Assets	**3,323**		
Total Assets	**5,671**		

Source: Statistics Canada. *National Balance Sheet Accounts, Quarterly Estimates, Fourth Quarter 2005*. Ottawa: Minister of Industry, 2006 (Catalogue No. 13-214-XIE).

In aggregate, the household sector looks much as we would expect from our own experiences. The major real assets are houses, worth $1,086 billion; consumer durables, like washing machines, cars, and so on (plus some other miscellaneous assets), worth $435 billion; and the land on which houses are built, worth $827 billion. The major financial assets are money on deposit, mainly with the banks, worth $683 billion; debt securities, worth $114 billion; the value of pension and insurance assets, worth $1,200 billion; and the market value of the shares in corporations, worth $1,254 billion.

Offsetting these financial assets are $260 billion in consumer credit (credit cards), $131 billion in mainly bank loans and $588 billion in mortgage debt to buy houses. So in aggregate, Canadian households have $979 billion in financial liabilities to offset against the $3,323 billion in financial assets. This leaves net financial assets of $2,344 billion, which is the number reported in Figure 1-1. However, the household sector's liabilities are different forms of debt, which can be netted out against the debt like financial assets, namely, deposits at banks and loans. What is left constitutes the two major financial assets of the household sector: the market value of investments in shares and the market value of investments in insurance and pensions.

It's one thing to tell people that on average each Canadian has $135,000 in wealth, but many of them will respond, "*I* don't have that!" So who does have all that money and is it fair? Answering such questions is a complex matter indeed. However, a good starting point is to examine the retirement problem, which is one of the major challenges of personal finance. So what is the basic problem in retirement planning? We have to finance our non-working or retirement years, when we will be consuming and not earning.

We do not discuss the retirement problem in detail here; however, we note that this problem has important implications for the breakdown of financial assets within the household sector. In particular, we can expect to observe significant differences across the individuals composing this sector, with younger and less wealthy individuals borrowing to buy houses and consumer durables and having a net *negative* financial asset position (i.e., they are in debt). Conversely, older, higher-income individuals save and accumulate financial assets, and thus possess a net *positive* financial asset position. This dynamic was lost when we netted out all the borrowing and lending for the overall household sector in Figure 1-1; however, what it implies is that the people taking out the mortgage debt and consumer credit are generally not the same people as those investing in shares. So there is richness in the financial system that is lost when we aggregate the data. This leads us to the question we explore in the next section: how does this money go from those who have it to those who want it?

CONCEPT REVIEW QUESTIONS

1. What is finance?
2. Distinguish between real and financial assets.
3. Which sector or sectors of the economy are net providers of financing and which are the net users of financing?

1.2 THE FINANCIAL SYSTEM

Overview

Figure 1-2 provides an overview of the financial system of any economy, be it Canada, the United States, or the global economy. In Canada, as we have discussed, the household sector is the primary provider of funds to business and government, with the non-resident sector traditionally being a net provider of funds, despite the fact that all three domestic sectors do invest outside Canada. The basic financial flow is "intermediated" through the financial system, which comprises (1) **financial intermediaries** that transform the nature of the securities they issue and invest in, and (2) market intermediaries that simply make the markets work better. The whole package of institutions is the Canadian financial system. We discuss the various facets of this system in the subsections below.

financial intermediaries entities that invest funds on behalf of others and change the nature of the transactions

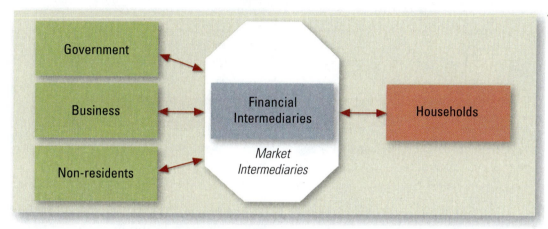

1-2 FIGURE

The Financial System

Channels of Intermediation

Figure 1-2 demonstrates that the financial system transfers funds from lenders to borrowers. This transfer occurs through **intermediation**. One obvious alternative for individuals who need funds is to borrow directly from friends, relatives, and acquaintances. Another is to borrow from a specialized financial institution, like the Royal Bank of Canada (RBC Financial Group). These are two extremes in terms of the transfer of money from lenders to borrowers. In the first case, borrowers obtain funds *directly* from individuals, whereas in the second, they borrow *indirectly* from individuals who have first loaned (deposited) their savings to a *financial institution*, which in turn lends to the ultimate borrowers.

intermediation the transfer of funds from lenders to borrowers

These two patterns of intermediation are demonstrated in Figure 1-3, with the three basic channels represented. In the first channel is *direct* intermediation, where the lender provides money directly to the ultimate borrower. This is a non-market transaction, because the exchange is negotiated directly between the borrower and lender. An example is a relative lending the full amount needed to buy a house. The second channel also represents direct intermediation between the lender and borrower, but in this case, some help is needed because no one

market intermediary an entity that facilitates the working of markets and helps provide direct intermediation but does not change the nature of the transaction; also called a *broker*

individual can lend the full amount needed or because the borrower is not aware of the available lenders. As a result, the borrower needs help to find suitable lenders, which is what market intermediaries do. A **market intermediary** is simply an entity that facilitates the working of markets and helps provide direct intermediation.

FIGURE 1-3

Channels of Savings

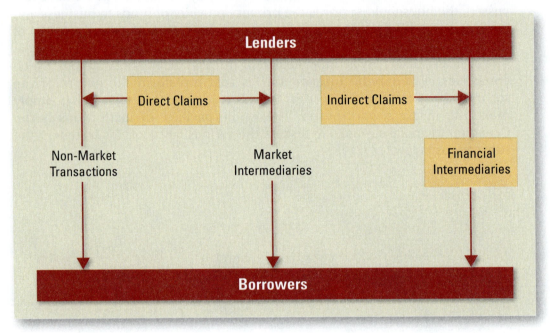

Typically, market intermediaries are called *brokers*. The real estate market has real estate and mortgage brokers, who help with the sale and financing of houses. The insurance market has insurance brokers, who facilitate the sale of insurance, and the stock market has stockbrokers, who facilitate the sale of financial securities. In each case, market intermediaries help to make the market work; their responsibilities are to assist with the transaction and bring borrowers and lenders together, but they do not change the nature of the transaction itself. The most important financial market in Canada is the stock market, or the Toronto Stock Exchange (TSX), which supports a variety of market intermediaries, from stockbrokers who advise clients, through traders who buy and sell securities, to investment bankers who help companies raise capital. In each case, their raison d'être is to make markets work.

The third savings channel is completely different. It represents financial intermediation, where the *financial institution* or *financial intermediary* lends the money to the ultimate borrowers but raises the money itself by borrowing directly from other individuals. In this case, the ultimate lenders have only an *indirect* claim on the ultimate borrowers; their *direct* claim is on the financial institution. In Figure 1-3, the financial intermediary is in a rectangular box to represent that it changes the nature of the transaction, whereas the market intermediary does not. However, ultimately both individuals and financial intermediaries are involved in lending to the ultimate borrowers; it is just that the route to that ultimate borrower differs. Further, market intermediaries help financial intermediaries, as well as individuals, in their dealings with the ultimate borrowers. Commonly, we refer to these two market segments as the "retail" and "institutional" markets. When market intermediaries help individuals, this is retail; when they help financial intermediaries, it is institutional.

Intermediaries

So who are these market and financial intermediaries and how important are they? In terms of financial institutions, let's start with the most familiar ones—the Canadian chartered banks. Table 1-3 provides data from the BMO InvestorLine website for 2005 for the six biggest chartered banks in terms of revenue, assets, and profits.

Table 1-3 Chartered Banks: Financial Statistics, 2005

Bank	Revenue ($million)	Assets ($million)	Profits ($million)
Royal Bank of Canada	29,403	469,521	3,387
Canadian Imperial Bank of Commerce (CIBC)	18,677	280,370	-32
Bank of Nova Scotia	18,332	314,025	3,209
Toronto-Dominion Bank	18,665	365,210	2,229
Bank of Montreal	15,138	297,532	2,400
National Bank	5,320	107,598	855

Source: BMO InvestorLine website: www.bmoinvestorline.com, October 31, 2006.

You may not have a benchmark for these numbers, but it is obvious that the "big" banks are extremely large according to revenue, total assets, and profits. So what do the banks do? Although Canadian banks are involved in almost all areas of the financial system, their core activity is acting as *deposit takers* and *lenders*.

Although the banks are overwhelmingly the most important financial intermediaries, the major insurance companies are also very large. Table 1-4 provides financial data on the top four insurance companies. The big three, Manulife Financial Corporation, Sun Life Financial Inc., and Great-West Lifeco Inc., are all life insurance companies, and each made more than $1 billion in profit in 2005.

Table 1-4 Insurance Companies: Financial Statistics, 2005

Insurer	Revenue ($million)	Assets ($million)	Profits ($million)
Manulife Financial	32,187	322,171	3,294
Sun Life Financial	21,871	171,850	1,867
Great-West Lifeco	23,883	102,161	1,775
ING Canada	4,446	9,926	782

Source: Data from BMO InvestorLine website: www.bmoinvestorline.com, October 31, 2006.

Technically, life insurance is not insurance, because we are all going to die. As a result, in most cases, insurance is a form of savings.[3] Insurance companies are called *contractual savers*, because, in most cases, the premiums are paid on a monthly basis so that the insurers receive a steady flow of money: you buy life insurance and then pay premiums; you die, the policy pays off. Before you die, the insurance company has all the premiums to invest. In contrast, the "pure" insurance companies, which do not have a significant savings component, are the companies that insure houses against fire or cars against collision, for instance. These companies are much smaller than the life insurance companies. ING Canada Inc., for example, is the largest, but with just less than $10 billion in assets, it is dwarfed by the big three life insurers and the major banks.

When we looked at the major financial assets of the household sector in Table 1-2, the two largest components were insurance and pension assets, and direct investments in shares. The funds in pension plans are held directly for their pensioners, and they substitute for having individuals save for themselves for their retirement. Not surprisingly, the data provided in Table 1-5 on the major Canadian pension plans show that they are very large. Like the insurance companies, the pension plans are contractual savers and get a steady flow of money each month. The Caisse de dépôt et placement du Québec is the largest pension fund manager in Canada, with more than $216 billion in assets under management; however, it manages the assets of several Quebec-based pension funds.

Table 1-5   Pension Plan Assets, 2005

Pension Plan Managers	Net Assets ($billion)
Caisse de dépôt et placement du Québec*	216.1
Canada Pension Plan (CPP)†	98.0
Ontario Teachers (Teachers)	96.1
Ontario Municipal Employees (OMERS)	41.6

The Caisse manages the investments of several pension plans.
† As of March 31, 2006.

The three types of financial intermediaries discussed above are financial institutions that change the nature of the financial contract. Chartered banks take in deposits and make loans, insurance companies take in premiums and pay off when an incident occurs, such as a death or a fire, while pension funds take in contributions and provide pension payments after plan members retire. These have traditionally been the three most important types of financial intermediaries. In contrast, mutual funds simply act as a "pass-through" for individuals, providing them with a convenient way to invest in the equity and debt markets. Similar to insurance and pension plans, many mutual funds receive their monies through monthly savings plans, but this is not always the case.

---

[3] Term insurance is insurance in the sense that it pays off only if you die during the life of the policy.

Unlike other financial intermediaries, mutual funds do not transform the nature of the underlying financial security. Mutual funds perform two major functions: (1) they pool small sums of money so that they can make investments that would not be possible for smaller investors, and (2) they offer professional expertise in the management of those funds. We will discuss the relative advantages of paying for professional money management through mutual funds versus simply investing directly in the stock and bond markets later, but the mutual fund business does have enormous amounts of money under management. The dollar amount of mutual fund assets under management has grown dramatically, particularly over the past 20 years, as demonstrated in Figure 1-4. As of December 2005, mutual fund assets totalled $570 billion, versus $17.5 billion in 1986, and a mere $1 billion at the end of 1963.

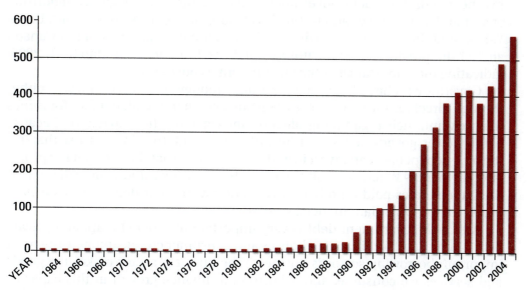

1-4 FIGURE

Canadian Mutual Fund Assets, 1963-2005, ($billion)

Source: Data from Investment Funds Institute of Canada website: www.ific.ca.

This brief look at the major players in the Canadian financial system should help you understand how the system works. At the core of the system are ordinary Canadians who want to buy houses and televisions, save for retirement, and protect themselves from the impact of accidents. We will now turn our attention to the other side of the coin and look at the major issuers of financial securities: the borrowers.

The Major Borrowers

The previous sections introduced the central idea of intermediation—that is, money is transferred from lenders to borrowers either directly though market intermediaries or indirectly through financial intermediaries. Governments are important in this process. For example, the Canada Pension Plan (CPP) and the Quebec Pension Plan (QPP) play large roles in channelling funds from lenders to borrowers. In addition, governments provide many services to Canadians, some of which are paid for out of taxes and some of which are paid for by borrowing. Indeed, the Government of Canada (Canada) had total expenditures of $216 billion for the year ended March 31, 2006 (which is the government's fiscal year end). After the federal government, the next biggest spenders were the Province of Ontario (Ontario) and the Province of Quebec (Quebec) with 2006 expenditures of $89.1 billion and $69.8 billion, respectively. Finally, government-owned **Crown corporations** provide goods and services needed by Canadians. Two of the largest, in terms of company assets, are Hydro-Québec and Ontario Power Generation Inc., with assets of $60.4 billion and $21.6 billion respectively.

Crown corporations
government-owned companies that provide goods and services needed by Canadians

We will talk about debt markets later but note here that the government debt market plays a very important role in the financial system. Even though the federal government has produced a surplus every year since 1997, the amount of Canada debt outstanding sat at $523.3 billion as of March 31, 2005. In other words, the federal government is a net debtor and a significant borrower at that. The provinces and territories are also net debtors, except for Alberta, Yukon, and the Northwest Territories. In fact, the net debt position of Canada and all the provinces and territories was $782.4 billion as of March 31, 2005, indicating the importance of the government as borrowers.

Governments have huge power to raise money from their citizens, either through direct taxation or by monopolizing and charging higher fees for things that we want, such as gambling, alcohol, and cigarettes (the sin taxes).[4] Because of this power, government debt is regarded as default free, in the sense that it is the only debt people can invest in and know for sure that they will get the promised payments.[5] When we look at various financial securities, you will see that the interest rates paid on different types of government debt serve as *benchmarks* for the Canadian financial system.

Although government debt is very important as a benchmark and private debt is important for financing houses and consumer credit, arguably the most important borrowing sector is business. The business sector makes the goods and services we consume, and it borrows to finance growth in this capacity. Indeed, when we looked at Figure 1-1, we noted that the business sector as a whole was a net debtor of $1.891 trillion, approximately three times the net debt position of the government sector ($0.634 trillion).

We conclude this section with a look at the 10 largest non-financial companies in Canada, based on 2005 revenue, shown in Table 1-6. General Motors of Canada Limited is the biggest Canadian company in terms of sales, but as a subsidiary of General Motors in the United States, there are no data for assets or profits. Although revenue is an indicator of size, in that it places a value on what we buy from a company, assets need to be financed and will be reflected in the firm's capital expenditure and corporate financing decisions. You will be studying these topics in business finance. Note that, on average, the profits of the non-financial corporations are significantly less than those of the big five chartered banks. This reiterates the point we made earlier about the important role played by the banks in our financial system.

---

[4] The most important government monopoly is the ability to print banknotes. Anyone who tries to make Bank of Canada banknotes, in competition with the government, goes to jail.

[5] Deposits in banks are also default free up to certain limits because they are in turn insured by the government.

Table 1-6   Non-Financial Canadian Companies: Financial Statistics, 2005

Non-financial Companies	Revenue ($million)	Assets ($million)
General Motors of Canada Ltd.	34,991	Not Available
Loblaw Companies Ltd.	27,812	13,761
Magna International Inc.*	22,873	12,321
Imperial Oil Ltd.	26,936	15,582
Alcan Inc.*	20,408	26,638
BCE Inc.	19,150	40,630
Bombardier Inc.*,†	14,882	17,482
Petro-Canada	17,673	20,655
Onex Corp.	17,626	14,845
EnCana Corp.*	14,322	34,148

* Company reports in U.S. dollars.
† Figures are for the year ended January 31, 2006.

Source: Data from "The Top 1000 in 2005." *Globe and Mail Report on Business* website: www.theglobeandmail.com.

CONCEPT REVIEW QUESTIONS

1. Identify and briefly describe the three main channels of savings.
2. Distinguish between market and financial intermediaries.
3. Discuss how the three most important types of financial intermediaries operate.

1.3 FINANCIAL INSTRUMENTS AND MARKETS

You now know who the biggest borrowers and lenders in Canada are and that financial intermediaries coexist alongside market intermediaries. The next step is to look at the instruments and institutional arrangements that are used to transfer these funds.

Financial Instruments

Financial assets are formal legal documents that set out the rights and obligations of all the parties involved. We discuss the various types of securities in depth at several junctures later on in the text, and so we provide only a brief overview here.

debt instruments legal obligations to repay borrowed funds at a specified maturity date and to provide interim interest payments

equity instruments ownership stakes in a company

common share an equity instrument that represents part ownership in a company and usually gives voting rights on major decisions affecting the company

preferred shares equity instruments that usually entitle the owner to fixed dividend payments that must be made before any dividends are paid to common shareholders

non-marketable financial assets invested funds that are available on demand in instruments that are not tradable

marketable financial assets those assets that can be traded among market participants

money market securities short-term debt instruments

capital market securities debt securities with maturities greater than one year, and equity securities

The two major categories of financial securities are

1. **debt instruments**: These represent legal obligations to repay borrowed funds at a specified maturity date and provide interim interest payments as specified in the agreement. We will discuss these instruments in more detail in Chapter 6 but note here that some of the most common examples are bank loans, commercial paper, bankers' acceptances (BAs), treasury bills (T-bills), mortgage loans, bonds, and debentures.

2. **equity instruments**: These represent an ownership stake in a company. The most common form of equity is the **common share**, which we will discuss at length in Chapter 7 and in later chapters. Companies may also issue **preferred shares**, which usually entitle the owner to fixed dividend payments that must be made before any dividends are paid to common shareholders.

Aside from the debt versus equity distinction, financial instruments can be categorized in several additional ways. One way is to distinguish between **non-marketable** and **marketable financial assets**. The most familiar forms of non-marketable assets are savings accounts or demand deposits with financial institutions, such as chartered banks. The funds invested here are available on demand, which guarantees the liquidity of these investments. Another widely used type of non-marketable financial asset in Canada is the Canada Savings Bond (CSB) and its provincial counterpart, which are issued by the federal or provincial governments. These bonds are non-marketable, unlike traditional bonds, because they are not tradable. However, CSBs can be cashed out by the owner at full par value plus eligible accrued interest at any bank in Canada at any time.

Marketable securities are those that can be traded among market participants. They are typically categorized not only according to whether they are debt or equity securities but by their "term to maturity," or time until the obligation must be repaid. **Money market securities** include short-term (i.e., maturities less than one year) debt instruments, such as T-bills, commercial paper, and BAs. **Capital market securities** include debt securities with maturities greater than one year, such as bonds, debentures, and so on. They also include equity securities, which represent ownership in a company and generally have no maturity date.

Governments raise new financing via the debt markets. They issue T-bills as a source of short-term financing (i.e., less than one year), and they issue traditional bonds and CSBs for long-term financing. Businesses raise short-term financing in the form of debt through loans, or by issuing commercial paper, BAs, and so on (all of which will be discussed in greater detail in later chapters). They raise long-term financing in the form of debt (i.e., through loans, by issuing bonds, or by using other long-term debt instruments) or in the form of equity (i.e., by issuing common shares or preferred shares).

Financial Markets

We have provided a brief overview of the financial instruments that are available to transfer funds from lenders to borrowers. Now we provide a brief description of the financial markets that permit the issue and trading of these instruments. It is important to recognize that financial markets play a critical role in any open economy by facilitating the transfer of funds from lenders to borrowers. In addition, if markets are efficient (which is the topic of Chapter 10), these funds will be allocated to those who have the most productive use for the funds.

For discussion purposes we will begin by distinguishing between primary and secondary markets. **Primary markets** involve the issue of new securities by the borrower in return for cash from investors (or lenders). For example, when the government sells new issues of T-bills or bonds, or when a company sells new common shares to the public, these are primary market transactions; new securities are created and the borrowing entity raises monies it can spend. Chapters 17 and 19 deal extensively with the primary markets.

> **primary markets** markets that involve the issue of new securities by the borrower in return for cash from investors (or lenders)

Primary markets are the key to the wealth transfer process. However, they will not work properly without well-functioning **secondary markets**. Secondary markets provide trading (or market) environments that permit investors to buy and sell existing securities. This service is critical to the functioning of the primary markets, because governments and companies would not be able to raise financing if investors were unable to sell their investments when necessary. Consider how reluctant everyone would be to buy a 20-year corporate bond worth $1,000 or $1,000 worth of a company's common shares, if they were unable to sell these securities even if they had to raise money in a hurry or became nervous about the company's future prospects.

> **secondary markets** trading (or market) environments that permit investors to buy and sell existing securities

There are two major types of secondary markets, although the distinction between them has becoming increasingly blurred over the past few years: (1) **exchanges or auction markets**; and (2) **dealer or over-the-counter (OTC) markets**. Exchanges have been referred to as auction markets because they involve a bidding process that takes place in a specific location (i.e., similar to an auction). Investors (both buyers and sellers) are represented at these markets by **brokers**. In contrast, OTC or dealer markets do not have a physical location, but rather consist of a network of dealers who trade directly with one another. The distinction has become blurred in recent years because trading on most of the major exchanges in the world (and all of the Canadian exchanges) has become fully computerized, making the physical location of the exchanges of little consequence. At the same time, OTC markets have become increasingly automated, reducing the extent of the direct haggling between dealers.

> **exchanges or auction markets** secondary markets that involve a bidding process that takes place in a specific location

> **dealer or over-the-counter (OTC) markets** secondary markets that do not have a physical location and consist of a network of dealers who trade directly with one another

Money market instruments trade in dealer markets. They tend to be very large and are typically issued in sizes of $100,000 or more. As a result, money market trading is dominated by governments, financial institutions, and large corporations. Long-term debt instruments, such as bonds, are also traded primarily through dealer markets, although some are traded on exchanges.

> **brokers** market intermediaries who facilitate the sale of financial securities and help to make the market work

Equity securities, and common shares in particular, represent the major financial asset issued by corporations, and they represent investors' proportionate ownership in a firm. Unlike debt securities, which are normally paid back and result in constant refinancing activity, common shares are generally issued once and then stay outstanding indefinitely.[6] The overwhelming majority of equity security transactions take place on stock exchanges, although there are also OTC markets for equities.

Numerous dramatic changes have taken place in the stock exchanges in recent years, both at home and abroad. At the start of 1999, Canada had five

---

[6] There are occasional share repurchases, but relative to the continuous retirement of debt, the amounts are generally insignificant.

Toronto Stock Exchange (TSX) the major stock exchange in Canada where most equity security transactions take place; it is the official exchange for trading Canadian senior securities

TSX Venture Exchange the stock exchange for trading the securities of emerging companies not listed on the TSX

TSX Group Inc. the company that owns the TSX and the TSX Venture Exchange

TSX Markets the group that performs trading operations for the TSX and the TSX Venture Exchange

market capitalization the total market value of the securities of an entity

Bourse de Montréal the exchange that acts as the Canadian national derivatives market and carries on all trading in financial futures and options

Winnipeg Commodity Exchange the exchange that handles futures trading in commodities

stock exchanges: the **Toronto Stock Exchange or TSX** (formerly called the TSE), the Montréal Exchange (ME), the Vancouver Stock Exchange (VSE), the Winnipeg Stock Exchange (WSE), and the Alberta Stock Exchange (ASE). An overhaul of that structure occurred during 1999 and 2000, resulting in only two Canadian stock exchanges: the TSX and the newly created **TSX Venture Exchange**. Both of these exchanges are owned by the **TSX Group Inc.**, which became the first North American exchange to become publicly listed in November 2002. Trading operations for both the TSX and the TSX Venture Exchange are conducted by **TSX Markets**, also a member of the TSX Group. These two exchanges listed 3,758 issuers as of December 31, 2005, and the total value of securities traded was approximately $1.1 trillion. Indeed, the total market value of the securities composing the TSX markets (which is referred to as the **market capitalization**) was approximately $1.9 trillion, making it the seventh-largest exchange in the world. The TSX is the official exchange for trading Canadian senior securities, that is, big companies with solid histories of profits.

Since March 2000, the **Bourse de Montréal** has functioned as the Canadian national derivatives market, and it now carries on all trading in financial futures and options that previously occurred on the TSX, the ME, and the now-defunct Toronto Futures Exchange. The only other Canadian exchange is the **Winnipeg Commodity Exchange**, which handles futures trading in commodities. The dealer market is also important for derivatives trading as many options trade OTC, in addition to those that are traded on the Bourse de Montréal. Forward contracts also trade in the dealer market and can be viewed as the OTC counterpart of the exchange-traded futures contracts.

Traditionally, stock exchanges were not-for-profit organizations. Membership in a stock exchange (in the form of a "seat") was sold to an individual to allow them to trade on the exchange. However, when the TSX converted into a regular corporation, these seats were exchanged for shares so that now the TSX is a for-profit institution owned by its shareholders. Market intermediaries, like stock brokerages, are now called "participating organizations" or "approved participants" and do not have to own seats in order to trade on the exchange.

The TSX closed its trading floor on April 23, 1997, and all trading is now completely computerized. Brokers enter orders to either buy or sell securities based on their client orders and the computer matches them up. As of January 2006, there were 1,959 firms listed on the TSX and many of the larger ones were also listed on U.S. markets. The total market value of the Canadian firms was $1.8 trillion. The average *daily* trading volume in January 2006 was 321,287 transactions for a value of $5.6 billion, so, on average, shares worth more than $5 billion changed hands every day.

Periodically, companies come to the equity markets and raise money to finance their ongoing activities. As discussed above, these are primary market transactions. In January 2006, $1.42 billion in primary financing was raised on the TSX, of which $282 million was raised by way of initial public offerings (IPOs), where previously private firms sold shares to the general public. The balance consisted of seasoned equity offerings (SEOs), where firms already listed on the TSX raised new money. We will discuss the role of IPOs and SEOs later in the text when we discuss corporate financing issues, because they are an important part of the firm's financing decision.

Finally, as mentioned above, in addition to listing on an organized stock exchange, common shares also trade in the OTC or unlisted markets. Trades in unlisted securities do not need to be reported, except in Ontario, where the **Ontario Securities Commission (OSC)** requires them to be reported on the Canadian Unlisted Board Inc. automated system. The first Canadian quotation and reporting system, the **Canadian Trading and Quotation System Inc. (CNQ)** was launched in July 2003. The CNQ provides an alternative market for very small emerging companies, because the requirements to trade on this market are less stringent than those for the TSX Venture Exchange.

In addition to the primary and secondary markets there are also the third and fourth markets. The **third market** refers to the trading of securities that are listed on organized exchanges in the OTC market. Historically, this market has been particularly important for "block trades," which are extremely large transactions involving at least 10,000 shares or $100,000. Finally, the **fourth market** refers to trades that are made directly between investors (usually large institutions), without the involvement of brokers or dealers. The fourth market operates through the use of privately owned automated systems, with one of the most widely recognized systems being *Instinet* (*Institutional Network*), which is owned by Reuters.

Ontario Securities Commission (OSC) an agency created by the Ontario Government to protect investors in securities transactions

Canadian Trading and Quotation System Inc. (CNQ) an alternative market for small emerging companies

third market the trading of securities that are listed on organized exchanges in the OTC market

fourth market the trading of securities directly between investors without the involvement of brokers or dealers

---

CONCEPT REVIEW QUESTIONS

1. Distinguish among the various types of financial assets.
2. Identify the major sources of financing used by (a) governments and (b) businesses.
3. Distinguish between primary and secondary markets.

1.4 THE GLOBAL FINANCIAL COMMUNITY

In addition to the domestic financial markets discussed above, global financial markets represent important sources of funds for borrowers and provide investors with important alternatives. Indeed, Canadian debt and equity markets represent only a small proportion of the total global marketplace. Therefore, it makes sense for Canadians to borrow and invest abroad, which has become relatively easy to do in today's global business environment.

Table 1-7 demonstrates the importance of global markets to Canadians, and vice versa. In particular, in 2005, Canadians had foreign investments totalling just more than $1 trillion (i.e., the Total Assets figure in the table). Approximately $550 billion of this figure represents investments in financial assets such as foreign stocks, bonds, etc. (i.e., exclude the $465 billion in direct investments). At the same time, foreign investment in Canadian assets exceeded $1.18 trillion (i.e., the Total Liabilities figure), with approximately $770 billion of this amount being in the form of financial securities. Combining the two items, we had a net investment position of –$168.5 billion in 2005. This means that, on aggregate, if we add our foreign borrowings to the amount of direct foreign investment in Canada, it exceeded the sum of what foreigners borrowed from us and the amount that we invested directly abroad.

Table 1-7   Canada's International Investments, 2005

		($million)
Total Assets		**1,016,031**
Canadian direct investments abroad		465,058
Canadian portfolio investments		284,604
Portfolio foreign bonds	82,374	
Portfolio foreign stocks	189,175	
Other portfolio investments	13,055	
Other Canadian investments		266,369
Loans	48,325	
Allowances		0
Deposits	120,694	
Official international reserves	38,030	
Other assets	59,319	
Total Liabilities		**1,184,534**
Foreign direct investments in Canada		415,561
Foreign portfolio investments		508,398
Portfolio Canadian bonds	380,017	
Portfolio Canadian stocks	107,598	
Portfolio Canadian money market instruments	20,783	
Other foreign investments		260,575
Loans	36,107	
Deposits	201,639	
Other liabilities	22,829	
Canada's Net International Investment Position		**−168,503**

Source: Statistics Canada. Figures may be off by 1 due to rounding.

The magnitude of Canadian investment abroad, and foreign investment in Canada, should come as no surprise. In today's financial markets, it is relatively easy for Canadian companies and governments to issue securities in foreign markets. At the same time, it is easy for Canadian investors to invest in foreign markets and for foreign companies to raise funds in Canadian markets. The United States represents a particularly important market for Canadians because of size and its proximity. In fact, as discussed, a large number of Canadian companies are listed on more than one stock market, primarily markets in the United States, such as National Association of Securities Dealers Automated Quotations (Nasdaq) or the New York Stock Exchange (NYSE), which are both discussed below.

Global Financial Markets

The world's money markets and bond markets are very global in nature, with the United States markets representing the world's largest and most active debt markets in the world. As in Canada, global debt markets are primarily dealer markets.

The United States possesses the largest equity markets in the world, which is convenient for Canadians that want to raise money or invest by using these markets. The **New York Stock Exchange (NYSE)** is the world's largest and most famous stock market. Its market capitalization (cap) in 2005 was US$21.2 trillion, which comprised $13.3 trillion in domestic companies' market cap and $7.9 trillion in global listings. There were 2,672 companies listed on the NYSE in 2005 and 403.8 billion shares; an average of 1.6 billion shares per day were traded. The average daily dollar trading value was $56.1 billion.[7]

The second-largest and most important stock market in the United States is the Nasdaq Stock Market, or Nasdaq. Nasdaq is the third-largest stock market in the world, based on its market cap of US$3.6 trillion. In fact, Nasdaq has more listed companies than the NYSE, with approximately 3,200; the average number of shares traded per day (2 billion), exceeds the figure for the NYSE.[8] However, larger firms tend to list on the NYSE, which is why its market cap far exceeds that of Nasdaq. The American Stock Exchange (AMEX) is the only other national organized exchange in the United States; however, it is quite small, as are several U.S. regional exchanges. Finally, thousands of stocks trade in the OTC market in the United States; however, many of these are small companies whose stocks do not trade very actively.

In total, there are approximately 200 stock exchanges in more than 60 nations around the globe. Some of the most important exchanges outside North America include the Tokyo Stock Exchange (TSE), the London Stock Exchange (LSE), the Euronext Market, and the Deutsche Bourse, which reported 2005 market cap figures of US$4.6 trillion, US$3.1 trillion, US$2.7 trillion, and US$1.2 trillion, respectively. Other important exchanges exist in Hong Kong and Australia, as well as in emerging markets, such as South Korea, Singapore, and Mexico. Many exchanges have various sorts of partnerships, as discussed in Finance in the News 1-1.

New York Stock Exchange (NYSE) the world's largest and most famous stock market

TSX NOT LOOKING TO SELL, BUT EXPAND IN U.S.

finance
INTHENEWS1-1

Toronto Stock Exchange Chief Executive Richard Nesbitt said Wednesday he's not considering selling the bourse, and that recent alliances with U.S. derivatives exchanges could one day lead to broader deals.

Nesbitt, in New York to launch a campaign to get more U.S. companies to list on Canada's biggest stock exchange, believes it will remain "a survivor in global exchange consolidation," as bigger exchanges like NYSE Euronext and Nasdaq Stock Market Inc. seek to extend their reach around the world.

"We're not spending any time looking for a buyer," Nesbitt said in an interview with The Associated Press. But, he said, "we wouldn't rule out a deal if we found someone with similar points of view. We'd look at anything that would strengthen the Canadian capital markets."

He's already taken steps toward that goal. Last month, parent company TSX Group announced an alliance with Atlanta-based IntercontinentalExchange Inc. to launch a Canadian derivatives market that will compete with the Montreal Exchange.

It will also partner with New York-based International Securities Exchange Holdings Inc. for trading and clearing natural gas and electricity contracts. TSX also signed a letter of intent with ISE that could see the two exchanges partnering on other projects. And it might explore creating a derivatives platform in Europe and Asia down the line with Intercontinental Exchange.

These alliances might be the first steps to broader arrangements during a period when chief executives at all the world's biggest stock and derivatives markets are worried about competition. But there are no guarantees that anything more concrete will follow.

For instance, the New York Stock Exchange and London Stock Exchange have both signed broader alliances with the Tokyo Stock Exchange.

A big part of TSX's strategy is to lure U.S. companies to list on the Canadian exchange, where there are fewer government regulations to comply with. The exchange is promoting its

---

[7] Source: NYSE 2005 Annual Report.
[8] Source: Nasdaq website at www.nasdaq.com.

U.S. push with Nesbitt on a speaking tour, with stops in Denver, Houston, Dallas and other cities.

Specifically, TSX is looking to attract small to mid-sized companies to the exchange—a direct threat to markets like the American Stock Exchange that specialize in smaller names.

The exchange wants to broaden its niche as a home to the world's large public oil, gas, mining, and energy companies. More than 60 percent of the world's mining companies already have a TSX listing, as do 50 percent of public oil and gas companies.

There are currently 120 U.S. companies listed on the exchange. European exchanges in recent months have attempted to secure U.S. listings, and TSX hopes being in the same time zone as American companies will be an added factor in their favor.

"Canada is so close to the U.S. and so linked that people don't think of us as being international," Nesbitt said. "More and more people are recognizing that the Canadian markets offer strong liquidity. I'm not maligning the approach of U.S. regulators, but we believe in investor protection as well."

Source: Bel Bruno, Joe. "TSX Not Looking to Sell, but Expand in US." *Associated Press*, April 11, 2007, as appeared online at <http://biz.yahoo.com/ap/>. Retrieved April 11, 2007.

CONCEPT REVIEW QUESTIONS

1. Explain why global financial markets are so important to Canadians.
2. Identify and briefly describe the two major stock markets in the United States.

1.5 THE STRUCTURE OF THIS TEXT

We have now introduced how financial systems work in general and have highlighted the importance of global influences and opportunities. In the rest of the textbook, we will focus on the study of business finance, which is introduced in Chapter 2. We will distinguish between **corporate finance**, which focuses on the financing and investment decisions made by corporations, and **investments**, which focuses on the decisions made by the investors in financial securities. In fact, these two areas of finance are merely two sides of the same coin: investors purchase the financial securities that are issued by corporations. But first, we will examine corporate accounting statements in Section II and present some essential tools for financial analysis.

corporate finance the financing and investment decisions made by corporations

investments the decisions made by the investors in financial securities

Sections III, IV, and V focus on the investments side of finance. In particular, we discuss the investment alternatives available to the suppliers of funds and some of the most important factors they need to consider during this investment process. Section III introduces the basic valuation process used in finance and applies it to the valuation of stocks and bonds. Section IV discusses the importance to investors of modern portfolio theory and the notion of efficient markets. Finally, Section V discusses derivative securities, focusing on options and futures contracts in particular.

The second half of the text focuses on the corporate finance side of the coin. Section VI examines corporate investment decisions and provides the framework on which such decisions should be made. We also show how this framework can be used to evaluate potential takeover decisions, as well as the decision of whether or not to enter into a leasing arrangement. In Section VII, we discuss the various long-term financing alternatives available to corporations. We follow this up in Section VIII by examining how firms decide on their long-term financing mix (or capital structure), and we also discuss the main considerations involved in corporate dividend decisions. Finally, Section IX focuses on how firms manage their investment in short-term assets and how they determine their short-term financing mix, which is referred to as working capital management.

Summary

This chapter provides an overview of financial systems in general and the Canadian financial system in particular. We identify the major participants and discuss the different types of financial securities and financial markets. As such, we provide an overview of finance in general.

In the next chapter, and for the balance of the text, we will focus our attention on *business (or corporate) finance*, which is one very important part of the overall financial system. As you develop an understanding of the problems faced by corporations, it is important to realize that business finance is inextricably linked with government finance, personal finance, and international finance—the three other major agents in the financial system—because collectively they determine what happens in the financial system. It is one huge market for borrowing and lending money and what happens in one part of the market affects all other parts of the market.

Key Terms

Bourse de Montréal, p. 18

brokers, p. 17

Canadian Trading and Quotation System Inc. (CNQ), p. 19

capital market securities, p. 16

common share, p. 16

corporate finance, p. 22

Crown corporations, p. 14

dealer or over-the-counter (OTC) markets, p. 17

debt instruments, p. 16

equity instruments, p. 16

exchanges or auction markets, p. 17

finance, p. 4

financial assets, p. 6

financial intermediaries, p. 9

fourth market, p. 19

intermediation, p. 9

investments, p. 22

market capitalization, p. 18

market intermediary, p. 10

marketable financial assets, p. 16

money market securities, p. 16

New York Stock Exchange (NYSE), p. 21

non-marketable financial assets, p. 16

Ontario Securities Commission (OSC), p. 19

preferred shares, p. 16

primary markets, p. 17

real assets, p. 5

secondary markets, p. 17

third market, p. 19

Toronto Stock Exchange (TSX), p. 18

TSX Group Inc., p. 18

TSX Markets, p. 18

TSX Venture Exchange, p. 18

Winnipeg Commodity Exchange, p. 18

QUESTIONS AND PRACTICE PROBLEMS

Multiple Choice Questions

1. According to Canada's national balance sheet, which of the following items is *not* a real asset?

   A. Land
   B. Machinery and equipment
   C. Net worth
   D. Residential structures

2. In business finance, managers make capital expenditure decisions, which may include all of the following except:

   A. Land purchases
   B. Takeovers of another firm
   C. Inventory purchases
   D. Salary payments

3. Consider the following environments. Which one would cause a firm to make different decisions about capital expenditures and corporate financing than it would otherwise?

   A. High unemployment rate
   B. High real gross domestic product (GDP) growth rate
   C. High corporate profits
   D. Low interest rates

4. Which of the following is a correct combination of primary fund lenders and fund borrowers in the financial system?

   A. Households; government
   B. Households; non-residents
   C. Businesses; households
   D. Government; non-residents

5. Which of the following financial intermediaries does not transform the nature of the underlying financial securities?

   A. Banks
   B. Insurance firms
   C. Mutual funds
   D. Pension funds

Practice Problems

6. State the four major financial sectors in the financial system and discuss how they relate to one another.

Medium

7. Explain how banks, pension funds, insurance firms, and mutual funds work in the financial system.

8. Briefly describe why financial and market intermediaries exist in our financial system.

9. List the two main types of primary market transactions and concisely explain them.

Difficult

10. What are secondary market transactions? How do secondary markets facilitate the primary markets?

Corporations

This chapter focuses on the different types of business organizations and what the role of one of these, the corporation, should be. These days, corporations are being called upon more than ever to act in a manner that is socially, economically, and environmentally responsible. However, being a good corporate citizen can put a firm at odds with its fundamental obligation, which is to maximize profits. Home Depot Canada has a solid track record of community involvement. The company uses its resources and expertise to build playgrounds and affordable housing and assists communities affected by natural disasters. It has also developed in-store programs that help customers to identify environmentally preferred products and to dispose of household materials safely.

Sources: Home Depot Canada website
http://www.homedepot.ca

Natural Resources Canada, Corporate Social Responsibility: Lessons Learned.
http://www.nrcan-rncan.gc.ca

Natural Resources Canada, Corporate Social Responsibility: Highlights of Company CSR
Activities. http://www.nrcan.gc.ca

Business (Corporate) Finance

Learning Objectives

After reading this chapter, you should understand the following:

1. The advantages and disadvantages of four different ways to organize a business

2. Some of the pressures exerted on corporations by various stakeholders

3. What the ultimate objective of a firm is and why this is a logical objective

4. Why agency costs arise and how they can reduce shareholder wealth

5. The main types of decisions made by corporations regarding the financial management of their real and financial assets, as well as the associated corporate financing decisions

6. Some of the major types of finance jobs available with financial and non-financial companies

INTRODUCTION

In Chapter 1 we discussed the financial system and provided the context for the discussion of business finance. In this chapter, we discuss the role of the corporation and provide the background that is necessary to analyze how its investment and financing decisions are made. In the process, we discuss the goals of the corporation and how its internal affairs are organized. We conclude with a description of some available jobs in the field.

2.1 TYPES OF BUSINESS ORGANIZATIONS

In Chapter 1 we distinguished between real assets and financial assets, where real assets for the household are tangible things, like houses, dishwashers, computers, and cars, while financial assets are loans in the broadest sense to other people and institutions. However, this discussion of Canadian households was limited by Statistics Canada's (StatsCan's) division of the economy into four main segments: households, business, government, and foreign (non-resident). The reason for this division is that the business sector makes the real investment decisions that *increase* our wealth over time. In contrast, the real investment decisions of households are to buy consumer durables, that is, consumption items that generate value over future periods. Ultimately, we can say that households consume—it's just that some of this consumption is of non-durables, like food, and some of it is of durables, like cars. The business sector, conversely, makes very different real investment decisions, which are intended to increase its ability to make goods and services in the future—that is, to generate future growth in consumption and wealth.

We also noted that the official StatsCan description of Canadian households is of "persons and unincorporated businesses," so some business is conducted within the household, rather than in the business sector. Businesses can be organized in different ways: the four major forms of business organizations are sole proprietorships, partnerships, trusts, and corporations. We discuss each of these below.

Sole Proprietorships

sole proprietorship a business owned and operated by one person

A **sole proprietorship** is a business owned and operated by one person. Starting one is as simple as drumming up business. Many important businesses have been started by someone trying to meet a market need, whether it's the neighbour's daughter who started a lemonade stand one hot summer day or the boy who cleans up yards in his spare time. These people have both started sole proprietorships, in which one person starts working on his or her own rather than for someone else. If these examples seem trivial, think about Bill Gates and Paul Allen (Microsoft Corporation), who started out working on personal computers in their parents' garages.

The big advantage of a sole proprietorship is that setting one up is easy—no paperwork is involved and the owner needs only to start doing business. Of course, if the business begins to grow, the owner might want to register a business name, or even patent a particular business process to keep imitators away or at least make them pay a royalty. Purchasing some business cards is helpful too. However, the critical thing is that the business is almost inseparable from the owner; if that lemonade turns out to be bad, or if part of that yard isn't cleaned up, then the business owner is personally liable. This isn't a big factor for most very small businesses, but if that web page inadvertently damages a client by directing traffic elsewhere, then the owner is personally liable. More to the point, an owner can be sued for damages. If that person has other assets, he or she could lose them or, in extreme cases, be forced into bankruptcy and lose everything because of a bad decision made in that sole proprietorship. This accountability is referred to as **unlimited liability**, because an owner is liable not only to the extent of what is invested in the business but also for any other assets owned. Lawyers generally advise wealthy people not to run a sole proprietorship.

unlimited liability the liability not only for what is invested in the business but also for any other assets owned

Sole proprietorships do have financial implications. The sources of finance available for sole proprietorships are the same ones that are available to individuals. No complicated finance options are available—owners borrow from relatives and friends, or from the bank, through either a loan or a credit card. If businesses create some revenue, owners can use one of the many government programs designed to stimulate small businesses. If a business grows and the owner wants to sell it, it can be problematic, because all the contacts and relationships are personal and belong to the owner, since legally the owner and the business are identical. Selling a profitable window-cleaning business may mean visiting every contact and explaining that someone new is taking over the business and will be serving them in the future. The fact is, there is no continuity in a sole proprietorship, which makes it difficult to sell and, of course, it dies with the owner.

Because legally a sole proprietorship is inseparable from the individual, the owner has to report the income to the Canada Revenue Agency (Revenue Canada) on an annual income tax return. Sole proprietors have to keep the same accounting records as big businesses do and report the income after deducting all reasonable expenses. However, the net income is simply added to any regular salary income and taxed at ordinary tax rates. For this reason, StatsCan cannot separate persons and unincorporated businesses from households, because most of the data come from individual income tax returns.

Partnerships

Suppose you are working on a new web page and need some help from a friend. The two of you start working together. After a while, it becomes a solid relationship and you always work together on jobs for clients. This relationship is a **partnership**, rather than a sole proprietorship. This partnership can be formalized by having a lawyer create a partnership agreement. The agreement formalizes how decisions are made, such as how each partner can buy out the other in the event that one wants to dissolve the partnership. If the partnership grows, then the owners also need to document how new partners enter and their attendant obligations, as well as how others can cash out. The partnership

partnership a business owned and operated by two or more people

agreement further stipulates how the partnership's income is allocated among the partners. Individuals have to be careful with partnerships, since a legal agreement is not required to be considered a partner. Sometimes a partnership can be implied by the actions of a group of people working together. This becomes a problem when a disaffected party sues everyone associated with a business, even people who are not formal partners.

Some very big firms traditionally operated as partnerships, most of which were in the professional services area, such as accounting firms, investment banking firms, doctors' offices, and dentists' offices. Such firms needed more than one person to deliver a full range of services, yet "society" judged it important to hold each member individually responsible for both their own actions and those of their colleagues. However, over time, the increasing complexity of partnership operations, for example, in the accounting and investment banking areas, weakened this argument. With hundreds of partners, it is difficult to justify making all the partners responsible for the actions of one rogue partner. As a result, the importance of traditional partnerships has diminished.

Partnerships are still important, however, for smaller firms, because they maintain the integration of partnership income with other income for each partner. However, newer partnership models have emerged that maintain this tax treatment while removing the unlimited personal liability. The two main partnership forms are *limited liability partnerships* (*LLP*) and *limited and general partnerships*.

LLPs are the new form of organization for professional firms. Each partner has limited liability in the event of a lawsuit against the firm; however, each partner's income is still included as ordinary income and filed by using an individual tax return. Table 2-1 lists the leading accounting and law firms in Canada, according to the *Financial Post* FP500 tables for 2004. Notice that LLP is listed after each firm, indicating a limited liability partnership. Clearly, with the larger firms having hundreds of partners, it is unreasonable to impose unlimited liability on accounting and law firms.

Table 2-1   Canadian Law and Accounting Firms, 2004

Law Firms	Employees	Lawyers	Partners
McCarthy Tétrault LLP	1,250	712	379
Gowling Lafleur Henderson LLP	1,181	698	353
Borden Ladner Gervais LLP	1,290	679	395
Fasken Martineau DuMoulin LLP	936	583	348

Accounting Firms	Sales ($million)	Partners	Professional Staff
Deloitte & Touche LLP	1,024	512	4,603
KPMG LLP	729	433	3,163
PricewaterhouseCoopers LLP	698	430	2,640
Ernst & Young LLP	556	266	2,081
Grant Thornton LLP	315	349	2,166

Source: *Financial Post*, FP500 tables, 2004. Material reprinted with the express permission of: "National Post Company", a CanWest Partnership."

Limited and general partnerships are generally used for tax reasons. In this case, a general partner operates the business and limited partners are passive investors. As long as the limited partners are not active in the business, they have the advantage of **limited liability** in that all they can lose is their initial investment. The general partner, conversely, has unlimited liability as the operator of the business. However, in practice most general partners are corporations (discussed below) and indirectly benefit from limited liability. Limited partnerships are often used in tax shelters and for this reason Canada Revenue Agency looks very carefully at them to make sure they are not a vehicle for tax avoidance; however, there are legitimate reasons to set up a limited partnership.

limited liability the liability for only the initial investment

The largest natural gas distribution company in Quebec is Gaz Métro Limited Partnership (GMIP) with 2004 sales of $1.782 billion and profit of $160 million. Fort Chicago Energy Partners L.P. (Fort Chicago) is another limited partnership that owns half of the Alliance Pipeline, which takes natural gas from Alberta down to U.S. markets. GMIP and Fort Chicago, however, are something of exceptions. In 2005, unincorporated businesses, both sole proprietorships and partnerships, had total real assets of $44 billion, which is a tiny amount compared with the corporate sector with real assets of $1,720 billion. Another form of organization, close to partnerships, has become very important for the organization of Canadian businesses: the trust structure.

Trusts

The trust structure is not new by any means and is, in fact, a standard part of the lawyer's toolkit. **Trusts** are used to separate ownership from control. For example, a standard part of estate planning is transferring assets in trust to children to minimize any tax burden and yet control the use of those assets until death. In this way, ownership has been transferred to one party and yet control stays with the transferring party. Traditionally open-end mutual funds have been organized as trusts. The mutual fund is owned by the unitholders, yet day-to-day control is exercised by the fund manager under the supervision of a board of directors, which appoints the manager. More importantly, as a trust, the income earned by the mutual fund passes through without any tax to the unit owners, who are then subject to taxes on the income received. However, the use of trusts has recently expanded from personal finance and mutual funds to **income and royalty trusts**, which have become very important in the Canadian financial system over the last decade.

trust a legal organization where assets are owned and managed, or controlled by different parties

Income and royalty trusts are set up to invest in the shares and debt obligations of a company. Because it is a trust, all the income passes through without any tax. Further, because the trust owns both the debt and the equity of the company, the use of debt can be maximized to reduce (or eliminate) any corporate income tax, provided the trust pays out most (or all) of its income to unitholders. In the jargon of finance professionals, trusts are "tax efficient." Over the past decade their use has exploded. As of March 31, 2006, there were 238 income trusts listed on the Toronto Stock Exchange (TSX), up from 73 in 2001 and only a handful in the mid 1990s. In fact, the total market capitalization of these instruments grew from $1.4 billion in 1994 to $192 billion by March of 2006, representing approximately 10 percent of the quoted market value of the

income and royalty trusts trusts set up to invest in the shares and debt obligations of a company

TSX.[1] As a result of this growth, the TSX fully incorporated income trusts into the S&P/TSX Composite Index as of March 2006, completing a gradual process that was initiated in November of 2005.

The tax-efficient structure of trusts, along with their popularity among investors, led many corporations to *convert* to the trust structure between 2000 and 2006. This fuelled concerns regarding the loss of corporate tax revenue by the government, because the trust structure eliminates the taxes paid by businesses. In addition, it generated a great deal of worry and speculation regarding the effect that this trend would have on the future growth of businesses in the Canadian economy, since trusts are inclined to pay out their earnings rather than reinvest in the business. All these worries came to a head in the fall of 2006 in response to announcements by Canadian telecommunications giants TELUS Corp. and BCE Inc. that they would be converting to the trust structures. Not only would these conversions add another $50 billion or so in market cap to the income trust market, but their conversion was also taken as a warning sign that many other large corporations could follow suit. As a result of these concerns, on October 31, 2006, Finance Minister Jim Flaherty announced that the distributions made by newly created trusts would be taxed at prevailing corporate tax rates and that this new tax would apply to existing trusts beginning in 2011. Finance in the News 2-1 describes the stock market fallout that followed this announcement on November 1, 2006. In particular, income trust prices dropped about 12.4 percent on average, "wiping out nearly $20 billion in shareholder wealth." The market prices of the shares of BCE Inc. and TELUS Corp. were also hit hard, as the market anticipated they would cancel their plans to convert to the trust structure.

BILLIONS IN VALUE DISAPPEAR AS THIS BOOM TURNS TO BUST

Canada's great income trust boom turned into a bust yesterday as unit prices plunged, erasing billions in market value and sparking outrage from investors who said they were sideswiped by Ottawa's crackdown on the sector.

In a selloff that was as broad as it was deep, the S&P/TSX's capped income trust index sank 12.4 per cent, wiping out nearly $20-billion in shareholder wealth. The rout hammered trusts large and small, from the giant Canadian Oil Sands Trust down to seafood canner Connors Bros. Income Fund.

It also helped slice nearly 300 points from Canada's benchmark stock index—the S&P/TSX composite's biggest setback since June—and drove the dollar down eight-tenths of a cent (U.S.).

Foreign investors fled what had until yesterday been the market's fastest-growing sector.

"I don't think anybody expected it to be this dramatic and this quick," Kate Warne, Canadian market strategist with Edward Jones & Co. in St. Louis said of Ottawa's decision to close the loophole that allows trusts to largely avoid paying income taxes.

Seven of the 10 biggest contributors to the S&P/TSX composite's loss were trusts or would-be trusts, led by TELUS and BCE, whose plans to convert to the structure were widely seen to have forced the federal government to abandon its election promise to leave the sector untouched.

The decision angered investors who have flocked to trusts for their hefty payouts, which have made the $200-billion industry a favourite of seniors and others seeking steady income in an era of low interest rates.

"It makes me feel betrayed," said Cameron Avery, 54, a semi-retired filmmaker

---

[1] Source: TSX website: www.tsx.com.

in Cobble Hill, B.C., whose income trust port-folio is valued in the "higher five figures."

But even as the trust market was collapsing yesterday, some money managers said they were finding bargains amid the carnage. Some trusts are now trading at valuations that make them attractive takeover targets, while the drop has pushed yields on others to tempting levels.

"I think this is a huge buying opportunity," said John Stephenson, who helps manage $1.1-billion at First Asset Investment Management Inc. in Toronto, including more than $500-million in income trusts.

His firm was nibbling at some trusts yesterday and may add to its positions, particularly in the pipeline and power sectors. Among the names he likes are Great Lakes Hydro Income Fund, Innergex Power Income Fund, Royal Utilities Income Fund and Inter Pipeline Fund. All suffered double-digit drops yesterday.

In effect, he said the stock market has already priced in the government's proposed tax on income trust distributions, even though the levy—assuming the legislation is approved—won't come into effect until 2011. That means investors have more than four years to enjoy the juicy distributions. In the meantime, now that the unit prices have tanked, "a lot of private buyers may come in and say these are attractive assets," he said.

Carl Hoyt, who manages the $120-million AGF Monthly High Income Fund, also believes some trusts are trading at attractive valuations. For example, Yellow Pages Income Fund, which tumbled 18.9 per cent yesterday to levels not seen since 2004, is now trading at a multiple that's below that of some takeover deals for similar telephone directory assets in the United States.

"Regardless of the tax legislation, it's possible that a private equity player, of which there are a lot, would look at that and say, hmm, that's an attractive asset," he said of Yellow Pages, whose $6.3-billion market capitalization makes it one of Canada's largest trusts.

For those who lack the stomach for income trusts but still crave income, there's always dividend-paying stocks. Even as trusts were getting clobbered yesterday, shares of many banks, insurers and other dividend stocks were climbing.

Bank of Nova Scotia, Royal Bank of Canada, Canadian Imperial Bank of Commerce and Rogers Communications Inc.—which hoisted its dividend Tuesday—all rose. "The market is hungry for yield," said Marc Lalonde, portfolio manager with Louisbourg Investments Inc. in Moncton.

Source: Heinzl, John. "Billions in Value Disappear as This Boom Turns to Bust." *Globe and Mail*, November 2, 2006, p. B1. Reprinted with permission from the *Globe and Mail*.

Only time will tell what the long-term effect of the October 31 announcement will be on Canada's trust market and on the importance of this business structure going forward. Most of the existing trusts will still be around at least until 2011, because they maintain their tax-preferred status until then. However, the number of conversions from other business structures will be greatly reduced, if not eliminated. In fact, many have suggested that a large number of trusts may convert to the corporation structure, which is discussed below.

Corporations

Corporations are easy to recognize since they have Inc. for incorporated, Ltd. for limited, or, in Europe, PLC for private limited corporation, after their names. In each case, the abbreviations or initials indicate that the owners have the benefit of limited liability in that the maximum they can lose is their investment—that is, they cannot be forced to invest more in the firm to make up for any losses the firm incurs. Unlike a partnership or sole proprietorship, a business that operates as a corporation separates personal assets from any malfeasance or failure at the corporate level. Although the courts have occasionally "pierced the corporate

corporations a business organized as a separate legal entity under corporation law, with ownership divided into transferable shares

veil" and extended that liability, it is very rare and happens only when significant public policy concerns are involved.

How a corporation is formed depends on provincial corporate law; however, it is generally by either a certificate of incorporation or letters patent. The articles of incorporation then indicate the most basic information about the firm, such as its mailing address, name, line of business, number of shares issued, and names and addresses of the officers of the firm—that is, the people who can legally bind the firm by signing cheques and so on. The critical feature is that the corporation is a *distinct legal entity*. For this reason the corporation is entitled to sign contracts in its own name, file its own tax returns, borrow money, make investments, and sue and be sued all in its own name.

As a distinct legal entity, the corporation has significant advantages over a partnership or a sole proprietorship. For one it is *immortal*. Early limited companies had to renew their charter or incorporation periodically, since politicians worried about the public policy implications of having a legal entity with an indefinite life; however, as the operations of corporations have become better understood, these concerns have waned. This indefinite life means that unlike people, corporations can borrow by using debt that will be paid off in 40, and sometimes 50, years' time. Individuals, with finite lives, would have difficulty getting these terms from a bank. It also means that transferring and selling assets is relatively easy because all the contracts go with the company and the share ownership is simply transferred.

The most difficult aspects of corporations are their control and taxation (we will deal with taxes in Chapter 3). In partnerships and sole proprietorships, the owners run the business; in corporations, the owners are the shareholders. For smaller companies, this isn't a problem, but for larger companies, this becomes a serious concern: they usually have a very clear separation of ownership by the shareholders and control by management. This division is the fundamental problem of the governance structure of large companies. We will discuss governance in detail later, because it is integral to the role of mergers and acquisitions and to understanding valuation.

Every company has a set of bylaws that indicate how it is run. Some of the content of the bylaws is determined by corporate law, but most is discretionary and up to the company. What is not discretionary is the requirement that the company have a board of directors (BOD) whose responsibility is to "manage or supervise the management of the business and affairs of the corporation."[2] These directors are appointed at the annual general meeting of the company and serve at the discretion of the shareholders, which means that they can be removed without cause.[3]

In theory, the BOD is elected by the shareholders and acts in their best interests. Their statutory responsibilities are enshrined in the Canada Business Corporations Act (CBCA S122.1) where it states that

> Every director and officer of a corporation in exercising their powers and discharging their duties shall:

---

[2] Section 121 of the CBCA allows the BOD to delegate this responsibility to officers of the corporation.

[3] In the United States, this is not the case; directors can only be removed for cause before the end of their term of appointment. This means that it is technically possible to own 51 percent of the company and yet not be able to immediately remove the board of directors and control the company.

a) act honestly and in good faith with a view to the *best interests of the corporation*; and

b) exercise the care, diligence and skill that a reasonably prudent person would exercise in comparable circumstances.

Essentially, this legal requirement means that members of the BOD cannot fall asleep at a board meeting; they have to exercise the normal standards of professionalism expected of people in their position. This standard is known as the "due diligence" standard, and as long as it is met, members of the BOD cannot be sued for negligence. What should their goals be? The CBCA says only that they must act in the best interests (honestly and in good faith) of the corporation, but what are the best interests of the corporation? To answer this, we have to discuss corporate goals.

CONCEPT REVIEW QUESTIONS

1. Describe the main advantages and disadvantages of sole proprietorships and partnerships.

2. How are trusts distinct from corporations?

3. What are the main advantages and disadvantages of the corporation structure?

2.2 THE GOALS OF THE CORPORATION

You might remember from your economics course that the goal of the firm is to maximize its profits. However, many have challenged this objective and the major reasons are illustrated in Figure 2-1.

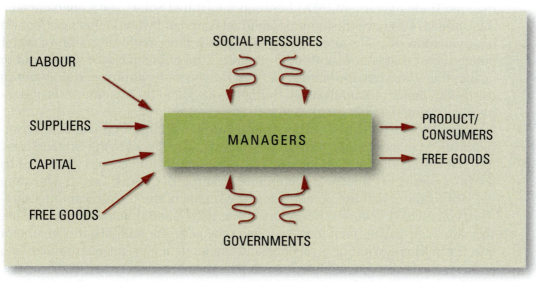

2-1   FIGURE

The Firm As an Input-Output Function

What Figure 2-1 illustrates is that the firm is essentially an input-output mechanism. It takes inputs, such as raw materials, labour, and supplies, and transforms those inputs into something more useful to society when it produces goods or services. For all firms, this activity is regulated both by implicit societal pressures to be good and by laws passed by government to prevent firms from doing things it regards as bad. For example, minimum wage and employment laws prevent firms from using underage labour or paying wages that are too low. Similarly, laws on environmental protection, packaging of goods, and so on, ensure that the firm operates according to what is in consumers' interests. Apart from obeying the law, for sole proprietorships and partnerships, this is the end of the story; those firms are then run in the interests of their owners. Normally, this means that the firms enhance the owners' welfare and make profits.

In finance, we extend the idea of the firm's goal being to maximize its profits, because what the firm should really do is enhance the owner's wealth. Wealth is different from profits, because it reflects the value of all profits, not just today's but also those expected in the future, where profits refer to genuine economic profits and not what the accountant creates (i.e., accounting profits). We will discuss wealth in more detail when we talk about valuation. When this definition of the firm's goal is applied to publicly traded firms, the goal of the firm is to maximize its market value or, alternatively, *maximize shareholder value*: the firm should take resources and create products that society values more highly than it values the inputs. Note that there are two things in Figure 2-1 that we have not discussed: the existence of free goods and the role of managers.

Free goods or *externalities* are things that the firm doesn't pay for or charge for. As a result, the firm creates value without taking into account these other valuable resources and may make decisions that are not in the public's best interests. For example, on the input side is the use of water. Should firms be allowed to use water without paying for it? Water is something that Canada has in abundance, and it would be relatively easy to set up a plant to export water to, say, the U.S. southwest, which is largely desert. In fact, it is possible to reverse the flow of water down the Mackenzie Valley, moving it down the Colorado River to Arizona and California, instead of having it go to the Arctic. This was an issue in the Free Trade Agreement (FTA) between the United States and Canada: would the United States have the right to Canadian water and would refusing a request be a violation of trade under the FTA? Clearly, large-scale diversion of water entails a cost that is not captured in the rates the public pays for water, and to charge this lower rate for large-scale water diversion is almost certainly not in the best interests of Canada, even though it may be in the best interests of people sponsoring the idea.

When Nortel Networks Corporation (Nortel), the largest Canadian telecommunications manufacturer, moved its main executive offices to the United States, it did so despite the fact that the firm had been heavily funded and supported by the Government of Canada. This is another example of externalities. At issue were the jobs involved and the potential loss to Canada of the research and development conducted by Nortel. The argument was that Canada could not afford to lose so many high-paying tech jobs, because they generate spinoffs and incubator effects elsewhere. Without those jobs and the tendency for people to move into and out of Nortel, many other tech companies would relocate away from Canada.

The result of both these input and these output externalities is that very large firms are very visible; their actions often have a significant impact on other firms, and those actions are not necessarily in the best interests of Canada. After all, firms hold privileged status as corporations because they act in *the owners'* interests, so the government has the right to oversee their actions. Consequently, many argue that corporations should act in the "social interest," rather than acting in the interests of their owners.

The social welfare or social interest argument has some validity for the largest firms in Canada because they are the ones that have these spinoff effects on others. However, for most firms, what is good for the firm is also what is good for Canada; there are few spinoffs elsewhere. For this reason, the creation of shareholder value has been widely accepted, not just by academic theorists but also by regulators. In 1994 the TSX issued a report entitled "Where Were the Directors," commonly called the Dey Report after its chairman, Peter Dey. Its mandate was to look at the governance of Canadian companies after the serious recession of the early 1990s. In section 1.1 the Dey Report concluded,

> We recognize the principal objective of the direction and management of a business is to enhance shareholder value, which includes balancing gain with risk in order to enhance the financial viability of the business. (S1.11)

As you will see, this is exactly what finance takes as the objective of the firm. Further, the idea of balancing gain with risk is what we refer to as the *risk-return tradeoff*, and you will become very familiar with it as it comes up in virtually every topic we discuss in this textbook. The Dey Report went on to say,

> A board of directors is not a parliament where elected members represent the best interests of their constituency. Directors have only one constituency and that is the corporation and its shareholders generally. (S4.12)

Here, the Dey Report was explicitly pouring cold water on the social welfare theory that the firm should pay attention to special interests or other stakeholders. The board of directors, in directing the strategy of the firm, should be guided only by what creates shareholder value. What of the other stakeholder interests? The Dey Report suggested,

> Their interests (stakeholders) are generally protected in the terms of the contract establishing their relationship with the corporation and, in many instances by "stakeholder statutes," such as environmental laws, which impose specific duties upon boards of directors in relation to the interests of the particular stakeholder.

In other words, the BOD can ignore stakeholders. The firm has a duty to do the right thing as enshrined in law and the contracts that it signs, for example, with employees. However, beyond these contractual responsibilities, the firm should not be forced to do more. Instead the firm should operate legally, and in compliance with its contractual responsibilities, in the interests of its owners by creating value for them.

2.3 THE ROLE OF MANAGEMENT AND AGENCY ISSUES

Most finance academics, as well as the governance guidelines of the TSX, assess the goal of the firm to be that of the creation or maximization of shareholder value. The problem is that neither group actually runs a firm; that is what managers do.

In smaller firms, managers and owners are often the same people, which solves the problem. Even some quite large Canadian companies have a controlling shareholder to make sure that managers act in the shareholders' best interests. However, for many companies, the shareholders are widely dispersed and the firm's chief executive officer (CEO) is able to pack the BOD with cronies who will not challenge his or her authority. In other words, the firm has poor governance and few checks on management, and it may be run in management's interest rather than in the interests of the shareholders. Further, the interests of managers and shareholders do not necessarily coincide.

As Gordon Donaldson has stated,[4]

> To say that management and shareholders have much in common is only to state the obvious. So do management and the labour force, consumers or any other group having a vested interest in the corporate entity. But to extend this by saying that management, in pursuing the corporate objectives as it sees them, necessarily serves the best interest of the stockholders, in either the short or long run, mis-states the facts in certain important respects. It also leads to confusion in and misinterpretation of financial policy.

agency relationship
managers work on behalf of the shareholders

Managers are employees and we now think of them as *agents* working on behalf of the shareholders—this is referred to as an **agency relationship**. However, how hard managers work to serve the best interests of the shareholders depends on their personal interests and how they are compensated. This is the classic **agency problem** associated with the separation of ownership from management.

agency problems
problems that arise due to potential divergence of interest between managers, shareholders, and creditors

The costs associated with the agency problem are referred to as **agency costs**. There are two major types of agency costs: (1) *direct costs*, which arise because suboptimal decisions are made by managers when they act in a manner that is not in the best interests of their company's shareholders, and (2) *indirect costs*, which are incurred in attempting to avoid direct agency costs. Indirect costs include those that arise because of any restrictions that are placed on the actions of management, those that are associated with monitoring the actions of managers (which includes any compensation paid to the BOD), and those costs associated

agency costs the costs associated with agency problems

---

4 Gordon Donaldson, "Financial Goals: Management vs. Stockholders," *Harvard Business Review* (May/June 1963).

with management compensation schemes that will provide them with incentives to act in the shareholders' best interests. We elaborate on this last topic below.

Suppose you hire the son of a friend to clean up your yard. You could sit on the back porch and watch him to make sure he does a good job. However, this *monitoring* of his work is expensive for you; after all, you probably hired him because your time is valuable and you have other things to do. Monitoring him defeats the purpose. Instead, you can compensate him to try to meet your objectives. Suppose you pay him $10 an hour and think the job will take four hours. What might happen when you come back after four hours? Unless he expects repeat business, so his *reputation* is at stake, he'll probably be only partly done, because with a cost-plus contract, his incentive is to stretch out the job. Conversely, if you agree on a fixed fee, say $40, you'll probably come back after four hours and discover that he left two hours ago. Then you'll have to check everything because he's probably taken short cuts. In this case, his personal incentive is to finish early. What you want to do is align his interests with yours so you don't have to monitor and check his behaviour.

Like your interests and those of your friend's son, the interests of managers and shareholders are usually fundamentally different. For example, shareholders tend to have a short-term interest in the firm and hold the shares and other securities of many entities in a large investment portfolio. If they see the managers acting contrary to what they would like, rather than trying to remove management through a costly proxy fight at the annual general meeting, they will simply sell their shares and go elsewhere.[5] It is simply too costly for most shareholders to try to remove management in a large corporation; however, this is not to say that it doesn't happen. U.S. fund manager Tweedy, Browne Company LLC waged an expensive war to remove Conrad Black from Hollinger International Inc. and eventually succeeded. However, in that case the fund manager was angered by what was perceived as corporate wrongdoing, and at the time of writing, Conrad Black was on trial facing fraud charges brought by U.S. prosecutors.

Managers don't necessarily pursue the best interests of the shareholders because their investment in the corporation goes much deeper than that of a typical shareholder: their careers are inextricably bound up with the firm. For this very reason, managers tend to be more conservative in their decisions than would seem justified by the shareholder approach. Donaldson further analyzed four key areas and found that in each area, managers would make different decisions than the ones that the shareholders would make. These are illustrated in Table 2-2.

Table 2-2   Areas of Disagreement

	Managers	Shareholders
Performance Appraisal	Accounting ROI/cash	Market prices
Investment Analysis	IRR of best division	WACC external
Financing	Retentions Debt New equity	Debt Retentions New equity
Risk	Preservation of firm	Portfolio

---

[5] We will discuss proxy fights later.

For example, when being appraised, managers want to be judged relative to accounting numbers, such as profits and return on investment (ROI), because they can control these numbers. In contrast, shareholders are interested in the stock market performance, because they want managers to create shareholder value. Similarly in investment analysis (choosing projects), managers want to choose the internal rate of return (IRR) of their best project, relative to other divisions of the firm or past performance, because, again, this is what they control.[6] In contrast, shareholders are interested in what they can do with the money, which can be measured by comparing the return on a project with the firm's weighted average cost of capital (WACC). If the firm can't meet the shareholders' criterion, it should give the money to the shareholders so they can invest elsewhere. Obviously managers don't like this idea!

Managers and shareholders also differ in their approach to risk and financing. Donaldson argued that shareholders take a portfolio approach because they hold many securities. This allows them to diversify risk and have the firm be more aggressive, whereas managers see their careers totally tied up with the firm and act conservatively. This approach is carried over to financing, where managers follow a "pecking order": they want to retain earnings first, rather than pay them out in dividends, then use bank debt, and finally issue new equity only as a last resort. In contrast, the shareholders want the firm to use debt, which makes the firm riskier at first, and only then use shareholders' money by retaining earnings, and then lastly issue new equity.

There is no question that Donaldson correctly identified the key differences in the goals of managers and shareholders. But this situation is like hiring your friend's son to work in your yard: it is a question of providing the correct incentive to get managers to do what you want. At the time that Donaldson was writing, most managers were compensated through salary and bonuses, which has changed as BODs have become more aware of the need to make managers act like shareholders.

Table 2-3 lists the 10 highest paid executives in Canada with a breakdown of their compensation. The major components of income are straight salary, annual bonus, share receipts or options, and other. Notice that in all cases, straight salary compensation is relatively low compared with the total package. Annual bonuses are generally somewhat larger, but the largest component by far, with the exception of Nortel, is share compensation. This comes in two forms: grants of restricted stock awarded under incentive plans, and stock options, for which if the company's stock price goes above a certain level, the executive gets the right to buy the stock at a fixed lower price.

The idea behind share incentive plans is simply to have the best interests of CEOs and senior managers coincide with those of shareholders. Often, shares are granted based on reaching certain objectives, such as revenue targets or investment returns. In such cases, the manager has an incentive to get the share price up as high as possible. In the same way, if an executive is given the right to buy shares at a price of $50 when it is selling for $40, then they have incentive to get the share price over $50 to trigger the option. If the share price never reaches $50, the options are worthless. Both types of share programs have the basic objective of aligning the interests of shareholders and managers and traditionally have been used to trump the comments made by management theorists, like Gordon Donaldson.

---

[6] We will discuss IRR and WACC in detail later on.

Table 2-3   Canadian Executive Compensation, 2005

CEO	Company	Salary ($million)	Bonus ($million)	Shares/ Options ($million)	Other ($million)	Total ($million)
Hank Swartout	Precision Drilling Trust	0.84	3.36	55.03	15.59	74.82
Hunter Harrison	Canadian National Railway Co.	1.67	4.67	48.18	1.71	56.22
Mike Zafirovski	Nortel Networks Corp.	0.31	0	8.42	28.70	37.43
John Hunkin	Canadian Imperial Bank of Commerce	0.75	0	28.72	0	29.47
James Buckee	Talisman Energy Inc.	1.10	1.99	20.09	0.15	23.33
William Doyle	Potash Corp. of Saskatchewan Inc.	1.15	1.28	19.53	0.16	22.13
Donald Walker	Magna International Inc.	0.20	6.06	13.26	0.04	19.56
André Desmarais	Power Corp. of Canada	0.91	0.70	16.69	0.55	18.84
Gwyn Morgan	EnCana Corp.	1.48	2.66	13.87	0.16	18.16
Richard Waugh	Bank of Nova Scotia	1.00	1.50	14.40	0.28	17.18

Source: "Executive Compensation 2005." *Report on Business* website: <www.globeandmail.com>.

Whether or not share compensation schemes have successfully met their objectives, however, is doubtful. The stock market peaked in October 2000 and prices subsequently dropped almost 50 percent by the spring of 2002. Technology shares dropped even more: some investors purchased Nortel at $122 and saw it collapse to less than $2, meaning a loss of close to 98 percent. It would be nice to think that the senior management group at Nortel and other tech companies suffered those losses along with their shareholders. However, what happened was that the option grants and share incentive schemes were retooled to continue to provide incentives to management. So if the stock fell 50 percent and made existing options worthless, new ones were granted to continue to provide incentive for managers; the argument was that otherwise management would leave and go elsewhere.

It was never clear why anyone would hire the manager of a company whose stock price had fallen 50 percent. But then, the compensation committees of the BOD granting these options and share grants were not always completely independent of the CEO who received them.[7] However, the important point is that the interests of managers and shareholders are not aligned if, on the downside, managers do not suffer along with the shareholders. In fact, managers have an incentive to use short-sighted measures to pump up the share price so they can exercise their options or share grants. For the managers, this is a heads they win, tails they don't lose strategy.

One final wrinkle in the use of executive stock options is that in the United States this has been linked to outright fraud by senior managers. The U.S. Securities and Exchange Commission investigated 74 firms for "backdating" executive stock options grants.[8] The fraud was that senior managers would get the compensation committee to award them stock options and then date them to an earlier period when the company's stock price was low. Effectively, this meant that on the approval date, the stock was already worth a large amount of money, so there was little incentive value to the grant. This type of fraud was more difficult in Canada, because the rules on reporting executive stock options are much tighter than in the United States. In March 2007, Research In Motion admitted to having "back dated" options, and Jim Balsillie resigned as chairman of the BOD (see Ethic & Corporate Governance 2-1 at the end of this chapter). This demonstrates some of the problems in designing incentive schemes where the people for whom incentives are provided are in charge of the program.

If compensation schemes have largely been used to *reward* management,[9] rather than to provide them with *incentive* to act like shareholders, where does this leave the goal of the firm? Luckily, it does not affect it, because of a more powerful control: the threat of acquisition. Poor management translates into poor stock market performance and a share price that is less than its intrinsic value. If a firm owns assets with an intrinsic value of $50 a share and is selling for $25, because management is incompetent and $25 reflects the value of the profits they are generating, then more efficient managers can afford to bid for the firm to turn it around for a profit. This is termed the *market for corporate control*, because it is based on teams of managers competing for the right to manage corporate assets.

The most important thing Canada can do is make sure that the assets in the country are managed as efficiently as possible so that the country is as wealthy as possible. This requires that the best managers are given the chance to manage assets. In turn, this means that hostile takeovers should be encouraged and managers should be prevented from mounting defensive measures that simply entrench their ability to mismanage our corporate assets. We will talk extensively about mergers and acquisitions later, but this is the reason that finance people believe that the best defence against a takeover is a high stock price. Ultimately, this market for corporate control, not managerial incentives, makes sure that shareholder value creation is the objective of every well-run firm in Canada.

---

[7] The compensation committees of the BOD are supposed to be made up of outside directors to avoid this conflict of interest. However, independent is an elastic term.

[8] David Henry, "How the Options Mess Got So Ugly and Expensive," *Business Week*, September 11, 2006.

[9] Does $75 million really provide managers with that much more incentive than, say, $10 million? Or, alternatively, how many millions does it take to motivate management?

2.4 CORPORATE FINANCE

So what do senior managers do? To answer this question and provide the focus for this textbook, Table 2-4 provides the aggregate balance sheet data for non-financial corporate Canada[10] as estimated by StatsCan.

Table 2-4   Non-Financial Corporate Canada Balance Sheet, 2005

Assets	($billion)	Liabilities	($billion)
Real Assets			
Buildings	815		
Machinery and Equipment	362		
Inventories	191		
Land	281	Payables	203
Financial Assets		Loans	321
Deposits	259	Paper	53
Receivables	249	Mortgages	114
Paper	29	Bonds	321
Debt	22	Claims	296
Claims	509	Shares	1,659
Other	294	Other	44

Source: Statistics Canada. *National Balance Sheet Accounts, Quarterly Estimates, Fourth Quarter 2005.* Ottawa: Minister of Industry, 2006 (Catalogue No. 13-214-XIE).

Real assets are placed first, as is the StatsCan convention, with $815 billion in buildings and land worth $281 billion. This is the value of all the factories and office buildings and the land they are on. There is another $362 billion in machinery and equipment, and $191 billion in inventories, which are things

---

[10] Non-financial means excluding financial companies, like banks and insurance companies.

waiting to be used or sold. When we look at companies, we have to answer some basic questions:

1. How does a firm decide to expand its existing buildings or to construct or buy another building?

2. How does a firm decide to replace machinery and equipment? Just because it still works, does this mean that the firm should still use it?

3. How does a firm decide whether to buy or lease machinery and equipment?

4. How much stock or inventory should a firm carry? Should it keep stocks to meet every contingency or perhaps use just-in-time methods to reduce the investment?

capital budgeting or capital expenditure analysis the framework for analyzing investment or asset decisions

     The framework for analyzing these investment or asset decisions is called **capital budgeting** or **capital expenditure analysis**, and these decisions are some of the most important that a firm can make.

     When we look at the financial assets, firms carry $259 billion on deposit as cash at banks and another $29 billion in short-term investments that can be traded in what StatsCan calls the "paper" market, which we referred to as the money market in Chapter 1. Generally, when these items are combined, they are referred to as cash. Firms then have $249 billion in receivables, which is debt that other firms owe them and for which they are waiting to receive payment. For this reason receivables are often known as trade credit. The remaining assets are claims on other firms and other items. These are mainly investments in other firms that do not represent a controlling interest. In financial terms, the money tied up in financial assets raises another series of questions:

1. How do firms decide to extend credit to customers to purchase their product?

2. How do firms manage their cash? This is a non-interest-bearing asset, so it seems that it should be minimized, but $259 billion is a lot of money on deposit at banks.

3. How do firms manage any temporary surplus cash?

4. Finally, why do firms take minority stakes in other firms, or more generally, how do they decide to buy 100 percent or less of another firm? This question leads us into corporate acquisitions and valuation.

     The combination of the real asset decision and these financial asset acquisition decisions represent acquisition or investment decisions. Generally, we talk about investment decisions in terms of **financial management**.

financial management the process of managing the firm's investment decisions

     So what do the liabilities look like? Just as firms wait for others to pay them, firms are also waiting to pay others. This is the $203 billion of payables, for which firms have received supplies but have yet to pay for them, so this is trade credit on the payables side. The other liabilities represent decisions made by the firm to finance corporate activities. For example, there is $321 billion in loans from banks and other financial institutions, $53 billion in short-term borrowings from the short-term paper (or money) market, $114 billion in mortgage debt, and $321 billion in debt that has been issued under an indenture and sold to major institutions (bonds). We'll talk about these different instruments later, but they are all different types of debt. Finally, there is $1,659 billion of shares outstanding and $296 billion in claims, which are claims that other firms have on these firms. These aggregate liabilities raise the following basic questions in corporate financing:

1. How does a firm decide between raising money through debt or equity?

2. In terms of equity how does it raise the equity: through retaining earnings or through issuing new equity?

3. In fact, how does a firm decide to go public and issue shares to the general public versus remaining a non-traded private company?

4. If it decides to issue debt, what determines whether this is bank debt or bonds issued to the public debt market?

5. What determines whether firms access the short-term money market versus borrowing from a bank?

These basic questions represent the core of liability management for corporations, which we refer to as their **corporate financing** decisions. Taken together, the *financial management of assets* and *corporate financing decisions* represent the area of **corporate finance**.

> **corporate financing** the sources of money for a company, including using debt or equity, retaining earnings or issuing equity, going public, using bank debt or bonds, and using the short-term money market or borrowing from a bank

> **corporate finance** the financial management of assets and corporate financing decisions

---

CONCEPT REVIEW QUESTIONS

1. Describe the two key decision areas with respect to the financial management of assets.

2. What are some of the key corporate financing decisions made by firms?

3. What are the two key topics covered in the study of corporate finance?

> **chief financial officer (CFO)** the top financial manager in a company

> **senior vice-president of finance** in some companies, functions as the CFO

2.5 FINANCE CAREERS AND THE ORGANIZATION OF THE FINANCE FUNCTION

It should be emphasized that every manager should be a financial manager, in the sense that the ideas discussed in this textbook are important for all managers within a firm. However, when we think of finance jobs, we generally distinguish between jobs in corporate finance (i.e., working within the finance function of a non-financial company, like BCE Inc.) and "pure" finance jobs within a financial intermediary, like the Royal Bank of Canada or Manulife Financial Corporation.

Figure 2-2 gives the basic functional breakdown of the finance function within a non-financial corporation. The top person is the **chief financial officer (CFO)**, or in more traditional companies, the **senior vice-president of finance**. Under the CFO are the two main finance jobs: the **treasurer** and the **controller**. Although the breakdown of responsibilities will vary from firm to firm, generally the treasurer does the things that we discuss in this textbook and in the other finance courses normally taught at a university. The controller usually does the things normally discussed in accounting courses. As a result, anyone interested in working for a non-financial company, like Ford Motor Company of Canada, Limited or BCE Inc., should study a lot of accounting, because what these firms regard as finance is heavily accounting influenced.

> **treasurer** one of the two main finance jobs in a non-financial firm; focuses on the finance side: forecasting, pension management, capital budgeting, cash management, credit management, financing, risk management

> **controller** one of the two main finance jobs in a non-financial firm; focuses on the accounting side: compliance, tax management, systems/MIS, internal audit, accounting, and budgeting

FIGURE 2-2

Finance in a Non-Financial Company

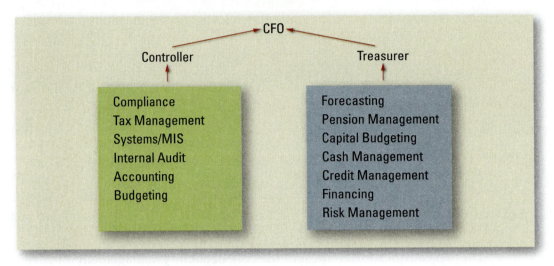

The controller, for example, is responsible for compliance. This entails making sure that the firm meets its statutory legal responsibilities with securities commissions and other regulatory bodies, makes its tax payments to the government, fulfills its responsibility to prepare and file financial statements, and ensures that its internal control systems eliminate fraud so that the financial statements fairly represent the company's financial position. As part of this financial system, the controller is normally responsible for the management information system (MIS), because its main purpose is to collect the data required for internal audits and the preparation of the firm's financial statements. Finally, the system that produces the financial statements is the same system that generates budgets and targets for the upcoming year.

From this brief description of the controller's functions, it follows that finance jobs in the controller's department require training in financial accounting, management accounting, taxes, MIS, and control systems. These are all regarded as "finance" in non-financial companies.

In contrast, the treasurer has the pure finance job in a company. The treasurer's basic function is to manage the treasury, which is the company's cheque book. To do this, the treasurer has to manage the company's cash and decide whom to extend credit to: cash and credit management. They must then pay the bills and make sure that cash is available when needed. This means forecasting the firm's future cash position, determining its capital expenditure plans, and arranging both debt and equity financing. If the firm has a pension plan, the treasurer is also responsible for managing these financial assets the same way as a portfolio manager in a mutual fund would manage them. As we noted in Chapter 1, the largest private pension plans manage billions of dollars. Finally the treasurer is responsible for risk management. Traditionally, this has meant arranging adequate insurance and making sure the firm was covered if a fire burned down the building. However, over the past 30 years, many new techniques have emerged to manage financial risks, such as the risk of serious exchange rate or interest rate movements. These new techniques of financial risk management are the responsibility of the treasurer.

The important thing about finance jobs within a non-financial firm is that the jobs are very broad and need a strong dose of accounting and knowledge developed in other courses in a business school as well as finance. This is still true, but to a lesser extent, for the finance jobs within a financial intermediary.

Generally, in the major financial institutions, people start out as **analysts**, who require an undergraduate degree, and then progress to **associates**. Normally, associates require an MBA or a professional designation, such as chartered accountant (CA), certified general accountant (CGA), certified management accountant (CMA), or chartered financial analyst (CFA), before being promoted to **manager**. As we indicated earlier, the Canadian banks dominate the financial system, and Canadian bank offers different career paths, simply because they are such huge organizations. In the traditional *commercial banking*, or business lending side, the standard job is that of an **account manager** for small and medium-sized businesses. The job entails managing the bank's relationships with companies by extending credit, helping to manage their receivables and cash, and directing them to the bank's more specialized services, such as foreign exchanges services, mergers and acquisitions, and specialized credit. **Banking associates** generate reports on companies, prepare industry reports, and perform the background checks (due diligence) needed before extending credit.

The *investment banking* side of the major chartered banks have three major types of jobs, either in sales or trading, or in "pure" investment banking. The investment banking side of the business is structured as a separate business segment, which is referred to as an *investment dealer* in Canada, whereas such businesses are referred to as investment banks in the United States and in most other countries. The pure investment dealer activities reflect the division of the business into corporate financing, and mergers and acquisitions (M&A). These are the advisory functions that mirror the corporate finance jobs in a non-financial company.

Corporate financing workers, whether analysts, associates, or managers, advise their clients and help them access the capital markets to raise financing. Although a company may raise capital relatively infrequently, investment dealers constantly advise their clients on what is available in the capital market. On the M&A side, investment dealers, whether analysts, associates, or managers, advise their clients on suitable candidates for acquisition, or on how to defend themselves against a hostile acquisition. This often involves restructuring operations, selling off divisions (divestitures), or changing the firm's financial structure.

Investment dealers, whether in corporate financing or M&A, derive part of their expertise from the investment dealer's knowledge of what is happening in the financial markets. Investment dealer **security analysts** monitor the valuations of the companies they follow and make recommendations to buy and sell a company's shares. They are generically referred to as *sell side* analysts because they generally recommend that their clients buy or sell securities. Their expertise in understanding a particular industry and what a company is worth is invaluable to the dealer when considering how much a company would be worth if it were taken public and its shares sold in an initial public offering (IPO). **Sales and trading people** then execute trades on behalf of their clients and conduct proprietary trading for the dealer itself using the bank's own capital. **Private bankers** and **retail brokers** help their clients manage their personal wealth. Retail brokers usually work with the general public and deal with small to medium-sized accounts, advising them on investment strategies to build their wealth. Private bankers deal with larger accounts and generally charge a flat fee of 1.0 percent of the value of the portfolio for their services; retail brokers generally charge per trade.

---

analysts first-level jobs in a financial institution; require an undergraduate degree

associates second-level jobs in a financial institution; require an MBA or a professional designation, e.g., CFA

managers third-level jobs in a financial institution

account managers people who manage a bank's relationships with companies, extending credit, helping to manage receivables and cash, and directing them to the bank's more specialized services

banking associates people who generate reports on companies, prepare industry reports, and perform background checks on credit applicants

security analysts people who monitor the valuations of the companies and make recommendations to buy and sell a company's shares

sales and trading people people who execute trades on behalf of their clients and conduct proprietary trading for the dealer itself by using the bank's own capital

private bankers people who help clients, usually people who have large accounts, manage their personal wealth

retail brokers people who help clients, usually people who have small to medium-sized accounts, manage their personal wealth

financial and investment analysts people who do research, perform detailed analyses of individual investments, and make recommendations on overall financial strategy

portfolio managers professionals in charge of the overall management of a portfolio

fixed income or **equity traders** people who implement the investment strategies and either buy or sell the stakes in companies

corporate finance associates and consultants finance professionals who advise on restructuring, small scale M&A, and corporate financing

The larger insurance companies and pension funds, as we saw earlier, have significant long-term investments. As a result, they employ *buy side* analysts to do research on which particular investments to buy or sell. In supporting these decisions, they have **financial and investment analysts** who do their own in-house research, performing detailed analyses of individual investments and making recommendations on overall financial strategy. **Portfolio managers** are the professionals in charge of the overall management of a portfolio. The analysts report to the portfolio managers, who make the ultimate decisions for their particular portfolio. Because these portfolios are very large, most of the larger companies employ **fixed income** or **equity traders** to implement their investment strategies and either buy or sell their sometimes very large stakes in companies.

The final major group with a significant number of finance jobs are the management consulting and accounting firms. In their consulting practices, these firms need to analyze the financial health of the firm and often their advice contains a corporate finance element. Many of the smaller deals that do not involve significant capital market access are structured by accounting and consulting firms. The finance professionals are normally known as **corporate finance associates and consultants**, and they advise on restructuring, small-scale M&A, and corporate financing.

ethics
AND CORPORATE GOVERNANCE 2-1

RESEARCH IN MOTION TO RESTATE RESULTS BY $250 MILLION

Research In Motion Ltd., maker of the BlackBerry e-mail phone, will restate results to cut earnings by about $250 million and said James Balsillie will give up his post as chairman after a review of its stock-options grants.

Research in Motion didn't find intentional misconduct by its executives, the Waterloo, Ontario-based company said today in a statement. The restatements, which aren't yet complete, cover more than three years of results dating back to 2004.

The adjustment exceeds an earlier prediction by Research In Motion, which forecast in January that restatements would cut past earnings by more than $45 million. In concluding its options probe, the company said Balsillie will remain co-chief executive officer as it separates the roles of chairman and CEO to increase corporate governance.

"The overall financial impact still looks pretty minor," said Tavis McCourt, an analyst at Morgan Keegan & Co. in Nashville, Tennessee. He rates the shares "market perform" and doesn't own any. "My biggest concern is what the impact of

senior management involvement will be going forward."

Balsillie and co-CEO Michael Lazaridis will voluntarily contribute C$10 million ($8.5 million) to cover some costs of the review and the restatement, Research In Motion said. Directors and officers will return any benefit from mispriced options.

Shares of Research In Motion fell $1.45, or 1.1 percent, to $134.52 at 4 p.m. New York time in Nasdaq Stock Market trading. They had gained 90 percent this year before today.

BALSILLIE'S AUTHORITY
Until the options review began, all grants except those to the company's co-CEOs were made "by or under the authority of" Balsillie, Research In Motion said. All options granted prior to February 27, 2002 were accounted for incorrectly because the company didn't use variable accounting, the release said.

Balsillie said in an interview today that the company's options probe "hasn't affected our business one bit." The company also announced it won 1 million BlackBerry subscribers, a record number of additions, in the quarter ended March 3. "Our business is thriving," Balsillie said.

Research In Motion is one of at least 200 companies that have disclosed internal or federal investigations into options. Investigators are trying to determine whether companies inflated the value of employee options by backdating or timing the grants to coincide with days when the stock price was low.

A special committee of the board found the company had "failed to maintain adequate internal and accounting controls with respect to the issuance of options in compliance with the company's stock option plan," according to the statement.

SHAREHOLDERS LOSE

Of the grants the company made between Feb. 28, 2002, and August 2006, 321 awards had incorrect dates, Research In Motion said in its statement. That's about 63 percent of all grants made after Feb. 28 2002, the company said.

"The shareholders here are the losers," said Richard Williams, director of research at ICAP in Jersey City, New Jersey. He rates the shares "sell" and doesn't own any. "Backdating creates greater dilution. More shares had to be created to pay for those greater profits."

As part of changes to management roles, Chief Financial Officer Dennis Kavelman will become chief operating officer and the position of CFO will be eliminated. Controller Brian Bidulka was named chief accounting officer to oversee all financial reporting and compliance activities.

Research In Motion will also expand its board to nine members from seven, adding Royal Bank of Canada COO Barbara Stymiest and John Wetmore, former head of International Business Machines Corp.'s Canadian unit, as directors. The company has yet to appoint a new chairman. The company announced its internal review in September, and said in October that the U.S. Securities and Exchange Commission had begun an informal inquiry.

Source: Fournier, Chris and Heiskanen, Ville. "Research In Motion Restates Results by $250 Million." Bloomberg, March 5, 2007. © 2007 Bloomberg LP. All rights reserved. Reprinted with permission.

DISCUSSION QUESTIONS

1. What is 'option backdating,' and why would Richard Williams say "the shareholders are the losers here"?

2. RIM's executive stock options were granted "by or under the authority of" Balsillie and a special committee found that the Board of Directors failed to maintain adequate internal accounting controls. How would the requirements of Sarbanes-Oxley (SOX), which is discussed in Chapter 3, affect these practices in the future?

3. The article does not mention that RIM is a Canadian company. Under what conditions, if at all, should a Canadian company be subject to the requirements of U.S. legislation like SOX?

4. The article discusses governance changes and that RIM will separate the functions of the Chairman of the Board from the CEO. Why should this improve RIM's governance structure?

5. In Chapter 2 we discussed the typical organization of the finance function. RIM has now abolished the CFO title and the controller has become the chief accounting officer (CAO). Why do you think RIM did this, and what are the advantages and disadvantages of this action?

Summary

In this chapter, we discuss the many different ways of organizing businesses, from sole proprietorships to corporations, and the recent innovations in the use of trusts that dramatically changed the Canadian business landscape. We also discuss some of the pressures exerted on corporations and that although finance people take it for granted that firms should create shareholder value, this is not always the case. One important consideration that can detract from this goal is the agency relationship that exists between owners and company managers, who act as agents on behalf of the company's shareholders (owners). Agency costs arise because managers may not act in the best interests of shareholders or because they must be induced to act optimally. We then discuss the main types of decisions made by corporations involving the financial management of their real and financial assets, as well as the associated corporate financing decisions. We conclude by discussing some of the major types of finance jobs that are available with both financial and non-financial companies. Many of these jobs require a solid background in accounting. This leads us logically to the next section of this text, which reviews some of the most important concepts in financial accounting, at least from a finance point of view.

Key Terms

account managers, p. 47

agency costs, p. 38

agency problems, p. 38

agency relationship, p. 38

analysts, p. 47

associates, p. 47

banking associates, p. 47

capital budgeting or capital expenditure analysis, p. 44

chief financial officer (CFO), p. 45

controller, p. 45

corporate finance, p. 45

corporate finance associates and consultants, p. 48

corporate financing, p. 45

corporations, p.33

financial and investment analysts, p. 48

financial management, p. 44

fixed income or equity traders, p. 48

income and royalty trusts, p. 31

limited liability, p. 31

managers, p. 47

partnership, p. 29

portfolio managers, p. 48

private bankers, p. 47

retail brokers, p. 47

sales and trading people, p. 47

security analysts, p. 47

senior vice-president of finance, p. 45

sole proprietorship, p. 28

treasurer, p. 45

trust, p. 31

unlimited liability, p. 29

QUESTIONS AND PRACTICE PROBLEMS

Multiple Choice Questions

1. Which of the following businesses is the *least likely* to be operated as a partnership?

   A. Accounting firms

   B. Doctors' offices

   C. Dentists' offices

   D. Steel foundry

2. Which of the following statements is *false?*

   A. The limited liability partnership (LLP) is one of the two main partnership forms.

   B. Limited liability partnerships (LLP) are usually set up for tax reasons.

   C. In the limited and general partnerships form, the limited partners are passive investors.

   D. In the limited and general partnerships form, the general partner has unlimited liability.

3. Which of the following are the responsibilities of a corporation?

   A. Operate in the legal sense

   B. Act in the "social interest"

   C. Maximize the wealth of its shareholders

   D. All of the above

4. Which of the following is the main concern from the point of view of a company's shareholders?

   A. IRR of the best division when investment is analyzed

   B. Preservation of the firm when risk is concerned

   C. Accounting return on investment when performance is appraised

   D. Market prices when performance is appraised

5. What is the most important purpose of share incentive plans?

   A. Compensate straight salary

   B. Align the interests of managers and shareholders

   C. Reward management

   D. Boost the share price

6. Which of the following is *not* a concern related to capital budgeting?

    A. The percentage of debt financing in the capital structure
    B. Whether or not to replace old equipment to boost output
    C. Whether to purchase or lease machinery
    D. Inventory level

7. Who is the person in charge of the pure finance job (cash and credit management, risk management, etc.) in a company?

    A. Controller
    B. Treasurer
    C. Chief operating officer
    D. Accountant

8. Which of the following responsibilities does *not* usually belong to the controller?

    A. Compliance
    B. Credit management
    C. Tax management
    D. Budgeting

Practice Problems

Easy

9. List and define the four major forms of a business organization.

10. Summarize the characteristics of the sole proprietorship.

11. State the main differences between corporations and sole proprietorships.

12. List the main responsibilities of the treasurer and the controller.

Medium

13. State the statutory responsibilities of directors that are described in the Canada Business Corporations Act.

14. Provide an example of the conflicts of interest between shareholders and managers.

Difficult

15. Yellow Pages Income Fund is an Income Trust whose units trade on the Toronto Stock Exchange. On October 31, 2006, just before the Government of Canada announced new taxes for businesses organized as trusts, the price of each Yellow Pages unit was $15.12. The firm had been making regular payments to its owners at a rate of $1.03 per year; this means that the owners were getting a yield (or return) of 6.8 percent per year. The day after the government's announcement, the unit price fell to $12.26, but there was no immediate change in the payments to owners. What was the yield on Yellow Pages units on November 1, 2006?

16. Janice borrowed $100,000 from friends and family to start her company (a sole proprietorship). Recently, business has been poor, and Janice has decided to cease operations and liquidate the firm. She expects to obtain $108,000 from selling the assets of the company. How much money will the debt-holders

receive, and how much will be left for Janice? Would these figures be different if the company had been a corporation?

17. Suppose Janice (see Problem 16) only obtains $93,000 when she sells all the assets of the firm. How much money would the debt-holders receive if the business were a corporation? If it were a sole proprietorship? How much would Janice receive in each case?

18. When you hired Dan to manage your business, you agreed to pay him a bonus of 10 percent of profits at the end of each year. The company now has a choice between two projects (it can only take on one of them). Project A will generate profits of $50,000 per year, and the detailed financial calculations show that it will increase the value of the firm by $123,100. Project B will generate profits of $40,000 per year, but will increase the firm's value by $125,500. Which project is Dan likely to choose, and why? Which project would you, the owner of the firm, prefer?

19. As the CFO of your company, it falls to you to make the final decision on large expenditures. Recently, your controller has proposed purchasing a new computer system at a cost of $50,000. He believes the system will deliver savings of $60,000 in the accounting department, and could be useful to other departments as well. Your treasurer takes a decidedly different view of the proposal. She claims that the company will have to borrow money to buy the computer system, and this will cost $10,000 in interest. As well, she is concerned that the amount of savings promised by the controller won't materialize. Should you purchase the computer system?

PART 2

FINANCIAL ANALYSIS TOOLS

Accounting is the language of finance; if that is so what is it saying to us when accounting scandals involving billions of dollars have led to the downfall of mega companies such as Enron and WorldCom. Understanding how financial statements are prepared and what they mean to external investors is a key skill that is necessary for any student of finance. The tools of financial analysis are developed so that external investors can better understand and interpret financial statements. These skills are developed through a detailed analysis of a real Canadian company.

CHAPTER 3
Financial Statements

CHAPTER 4
Financial Statement Analysis and Forecasting

Statement of Responsibility

ANNUAL REPORT

The Sarbanes-Oxley Act (2002), introduced in the United States in the wake of several major accounting scandals in that country, also affects the financial statement reporting requirements of New York Stock Exchange-listed Canadian firms such as Domtar Corporation, a manufacturer of pulp, paper, and forest products. Domtar's compliance with the act is evident in the company's 2005 annual report. In a statement of responsibility, management declares that the consolidated financial statements and all other information contained in the annual report are its responsibility. Management states that a system of internal controls are in place to ensure the reliability of financial information. A group of internal auditors reviews these controls and an Audit Committee made up of independent directors reports to the Board of Directors. The statement of responsibility is signed by Raymond Royer, President and Chief Executive Officer, and Daniel Buron, Senior Vice President and Chief Financial Officer.

Source: Domtar 2005 Annual Report, retrieved February 13, 2007, from www.domtar.com.

3

Financial Statements

Learning Objectives

After reading this chapter, you should understand the following:

1. The importance of preparing financial statements in accordance with a given set of guidelines or principles, and what the most important principles are

2. The fact that preparing accounting statements involves the use of judgement

3. How the basic financial statements for a company are constructed

4. The important information that can be found on a company's balance sheet, income statement, and cash flow statement

5. Why accounting income differs from income for tax purposes

6. How the capital cost allowance (CCA) system works

7. How different forms of investment income are taxed for corporations and for individuals

INTRODUCTION

Accounting is the language of business and one of the most important sources of corporate information. Gaining a good understanding of accounting is essential for any serious student of finance. As we discussed in Chapter 2, many "finance jobs" in non-financial companies require a significant knowledge of accounting. Even finance jobs with financial intermediaries require a good understanding of financial accounting. In this chapter, we will review the salient features of financial accounting. This chapter is no substitute for a course in financial accounting, but it does deal with the issues that are vital to understanding finance. It will also help explain how the accounting scandals of the late 1990s occurred.

3.1 ACCOUNTING PRINCIPLES

At its most basic level, accounting is simply an organized way of summarizing all of a firm's transactions and presenting them in such a way that external users can understand the firm's affairs. Clearly, problems arise when the firm tries to present its accounting statements in a way that does *not* fairly represent its affairs, either to creditors, like the bank, or to the common shareholders. Consequently, external users of the firm's financial statements have to become skilled in analyzing these statements and spotting signs that things may not be quite as management presents them. It is important to realize that management prepares the firm's financial statements, not the firm's auditors. Auditors, like Deloitte & Touche LLP (Deloitte), simply attest to whether or not the financial statements fairly represent the firm's financial position according to **generally accepted accounting principles (GAAP)**.

generally accepted accounting principles (GAAP) the set of basic principles and conventions that are applied in the preparation of financial statements

In Canada, GAAP are contained in the Canadian Institute of Chartered Accountants (CICA) Handbook. The *CICA Handbook* has the force of law in Canada in that financial statements must be prepared in accordance with these principles when the firm raises money from Canadian investors. In the United States, GAAP consist of the principles of the Financial Accounting Standards Board (FASB). Twenty years ago, the differences between U.S. and Canadian GAAP were significant; however, these differences are becoming less important. This convergence is partially due to the growing economic integration between the two countries, the passage of the Free Trade Agreement, and the fact that many Canadian firms now list their securities on U.S. and Canadian stock exchanges and thus have to file their statements using both U.S. GAAP and Canadian GAAP.[1]

The convergence between Canadian and U.S. GAAP is not an isolated incident. In fact, accounting standards around the world are converging as both firms and investors increasingly "shop" the world for capital and investments, respectively. One of the prime instigators of this convergence has been the London-based International Accounting Standards Board (IASB). The economic integration of the European Community (EC) has required harmonization of disparate accounting standards ranging from very conservative tax-based accounting in northern

---

[1] A good example would be financial statements of Canadian banks, which contain a detailed reconciliation of Canadian and U.S. GAAP.

Europe[2] to GAAP-style accounting in the United Kingdom that is very similar to that used in Canada. The IASB issues its own standards, known as international financial reporting standards (IFRS), and has taken the lead on many accounting issues, such as the expensing of executive stock options. It regularly meets with members of the FASB to develop common standards, as well as to have joint meetings of both boards. Recently, the IASB has also met with the Accounting Standards Board of Japan (ASBJ) to encourage convergence with Japanese GAAP. Canadian companies are now moving to adopt the IFRS, as discussed in Finance in the News 3-1.

CHANGING THE RULES

finance
INTHENEWS3-1

Just as they're getting used to changes wrought by the Sarbanes-Oxley Act, accounting departments at Canada's public companies are girding for another upheaval: the switch to international accounting standards.

The Chairman of the Canadian Accounting Standards Board says the transition will require lots of education for accountants and investors, but it will be worth it.

"This is the cost-effective, long-run strategy," Paul Cherry said. "We're confident the benefits will outweigh the transition costs."

Already, 75 countries have adopted the International Financial Reporting Standards (IFRS), including Russia, Australia, and all the European Union nations. The switch will move Canadian standards further from the U.S. system.

Proponents say adopting international standards will make it easier for investors to understand Canadian companies' financial results, thus giving them much better access to global capital markets.

"We're less than 4 percent of global capital markets, by any standard," Mr. Cherry noted. "It's too expensive a proposition for Canada to go and explain to the other 96 percent the details and eccentricities of our system."

Canadian and international standards are similar; they share a principles-based approach, rather than the more detailed and voluminous rules-based system favoured in the U.S.

But there are significant differences in areas such as measuring impairment of long-lived assets, accounting for off-balance-sheet structures, and consolidations.

The international standards and Canadian standards disagree on 80 individual points, said Rafik Greiss, IFRS Canadian market leader at Ernst & Young. Of those points, about half are slight differences while half are significant, he said.

"Companies need to understand this is not just a technical exercise," Mr. Greiss said. The new accounting standards will ripple through whole industries, he said, affecting information technology, performance evaluations, tax planning, even long-term incentive plans for employees. "It's a change-management exercise."

Some are worried about the timing of the change, said Bob Tait, president and CEO of the Canadian Investor Relations Institute.

Accounting departments, for example, are still trying to comply with new regulations on internal controls laid out in the U.S. Sarbanes-Oxley Act, part of the reaction to Enron and other accounting related scandals. Canadian accounting standards were tightened to address the same issues.

"It's not the most ideal time to bring in further changes that are going to tax the accounting department. It's going to be tough," Mr. Tait said.

But he believes the change will be worth it in the long run for businesses and investors, who will have an easier time comparing, say, a Calgary-based mining company with one based in London.

"It just puts everyone on the same playing field," he said. "For those who invest globally, it makes it a lot easier for them to make their investor decisions as opposed to having to do some sort of interpretive dance to figure out who's reporting what."

Source: Dube, Rebecca. "Changing the Rules." *Globe and Mail*, October 19, 2006, pp. B17, B18. Reprinted with permission from the *Globe and Mail*.

---

[2] Many Northern European countries do not allow separate tax and financial accounting; the same statements are presented to investors and tax authorities.

Although significant progress has been made with respect to harmonizing accounting standards, it is a long and painful process because many of the special principles have been developed in response to unique local or regulatory concerns. For example, some of the major differences between U.S. and Canadian GAAP have stemmed from Canada's position as a major exporter of natural resources priced in U.S. dollars: the treatment of foreign exchange gains and losses is much more important for Canadian than for U.S. firms. Similarly, heavily regulated sectors, like banking and insurance, are required by their regulators to follow particular procedures in the preparation of their financial results. Consequently, it is not just the accountants that need to be in harmony—it is also politicians and regulators. Indeed, Finance in the News 3-1 suggests that Canadian and international standards (IFRS) differ on 80 individual points, despite the fact that they are both principle-based, unlike U.S. standards, which are rules-based. As a result, even with all the goodwill in the world, substantial GAAP differences around the world will continue for some time.

The Impact of Recent Accounting Scandals

Whether or not a firm's financial statements fairly represent its financial position became a major issue in the United States after the failure of Enron Corporation (Enron) in 2001. At the time, Enron was a respected and widely admired U.S. company that had been ranked as high as seventh on the Fortune 500 list of U.S. companies. Enron's collapse triggered dozens of lawsuits and criminal charges:

- Sixteen former Enron executives pleaded guilty to securities fraud, insider trading, and conspiracy.

- Four former Merrill Lynch & Co., Inc. (Merrill Lynch) executives and one mid-level Enron finance executive are in jail for misreporting loans.

- Merrill Lynch, J P Morgan & Co., Citigroup Inc., and the Canadian Imperial Bank of Commerce (CIBC) have paid US$400 million to settle allegations that they helped Enron "cook its books," and they have also paid US$6.6 billion to settle a variety of shareholder lawsuits against them.

- The last two CEOs of Enron, Kenneth Lay and Jeffrey Skilling, were found guilty on 29 counts between them. They were on trial for "misleading investors, analysts, auditor and employees through false and sanitised financial statements, empty hype and shady accounting manoeuvres in finance broadband, trading and retail energy units."[3] Kenneth Lay died less than two months after being found guilty. Jeffrey Skilling is serving his sentence of 24 years and 4 months in a U.S. federal prison.

The fallout from Enron's bankruptcy has had enormous implications for accounting and finance. Quite simply, the financial collapse of Enron has changed the accounting landscape and what is expected of a firm's financial statements. So many individuals were hurt by the collapse, and it happened so quickly to such a widely admired firm, that the U.S. Congress had to act to restore public confidence in the U.S. financial system. As a direct consequence,

---

[3] This section is adapted from Kristen Hays, "Trial of Enron Founder Ken Lay and Ex CEO Jeffrey Skilling Starts January 30," *Associated Press*, January 22, 2006.

the U.S. Congress in 2002 passed the Sarbanes-Oxley Act (SOX). The main provisions of this act are as follows:[4]

- the establishment of a Public Company Accounting Oversight Board to register and inspect public accounting firms and establish audit standards

- the separation of audit functions from other services, such as consulting, provided by the big accounting firms, with the auditors rotating every five years so that they do not get too close to the companies they are auditing

- the implementation of much stricter governance standards, including internal controls, with auditors reporting to the company's audit committee, which is to be composed of independent members of the board of directors (BOD) with the power to engage independent consultants

- the requirement that the company's annual report contain an internal control report that indicates the state of the firm's internal controls and assesses their effectiveness

- the requirement that both the chief executive officer (CEO) and the chief financial officer "certify" that the firm's financial statements "fairly present, in all material respects, the operations and financial condition of the issuer"

As the key provisions of SOX indicate, the main targets are the company and its auditors. There was widespread belief that Enron's auditor, Arthur Andersen LLP, was too tight with Enron, as many former Andersen people worked with Enron, and the local auditors overruled head office in several key areas. Rotating the company's auditors every five years will promote their objectivity. Further, separating the non-auditing functions of the major accounting firms from their audit functions will help prevent accounting firms from being in a conflict of interest. Previously, many felt the accounting firms were treating auditing as a "loss leader" to get consulting contracts. Consequently, they were not sufficiently objective in their audit responsibilities. This judgement is confirmed by the fact that the U.S. government set up an oversight body to regulate audit firms and take direct control of many accounting areas.

For U.S. companies, the major change is the requirement of stronger internal controls. One of the failures at Enron was apparently a weak audit committee that did not exercise proper oversight of the company's financial statements. Now, the audit committee has to be composed of independent and unrelated members of the BOD who have the power to engage external consultants and to have the external auditors report to them. Further, management has to report on and the auditor comment on the firm's internal controls, with the CEO and chief financial officer certifying the statements are fair.

SOX has had a major impact in the United States, improving public confidence in the objectivity of the financial statements of U.S. companies. It also affects a significant number of Canadian companies (especially the large ones) that issue securities in the United States and have to comply with U.S. securities laws. Indeed, although Canada has had fewer accounting scandals, and those that have occurred are of a smaller scale than those in the United States, concerns over such misrepresentations and their impact on the business environment have dictated that Canadian regulatory authorities maintain strict controls over the auditing process, similar to those employed in the United States.

---

[4] See the summary on the web page of the American Institute of Certified Public Accountants (AICPA) at www.aicpa.org.

3.2 ORGANIZING A FIRM'S TRANSACTIONS

Bookkeeping

Table 3-1 presents a series of transactions that someone, let's call him Jim, has made in setting up a company to make widgets (for some reason, the examples in accounting textbooks always have people making widgets!).

Table 3-1   Jim's Widget Business

1. December 1: Jim opens a business account with a $50,000 deposit.
2. December 5: Jim purchases a lathe for $30,000 by using $20,000 cash and a $10,000 loan.
3. December 10: Jim buys $10,000 worth of inventory on credit.
4. December 11: Jim pays $5,000 to suppliers (creditors).
5. December 31: Jim sells $20,000 worth of widgets, $15,000 for cash and $5,000 on credit.
6. December 31: Jim recognizes cost of sales (inventory decline) of $8,000.
7. December 31: Jim pays hydro, rent, and so on, of $5,000.
8. December 31: Jim withdraws $10,000 for himself.
9. January 5: Jim pays a further $5,000 to creditors.

The accountant must make sense of these transactions. Before we get into the accounting issues, we will first discuss *bookkeeping*, which is different from accounting. On December 1, Jim opened his business by putting in $50,000 of *capital* (i.e., he *capitalized* his business). The secret in bookkeeping and accounting is to recognize that every transaction is an exchange, so there must be *two* parallel transactions. This parallelism is called *double-entry bookkeeping*. For this transaction, the business received $50,000 in cash and gave Jim ownership rights, or capital, worth $50,000. Jim might decide that as far as his statements are concerned, this $50,000 represents 50,000 shares, each with a book value of $1.

By convention, increases in assets, like cash, are recorded as *debits* on the left side of a balance sheet. In contrast, increases in liabilities, like the capital owed to Jim, are recorded as *credits* on the right side of the balance sheet. So, after this transaction, the balance sheet for Jim's Widgets would look as follows:

Balance Sheet for Jim's Widgets (December 1)

Assets		Liabilities and Equity	
Cash	$50,000	Owner's equity	$50,000
Total assets	$50,000	Total liabilities and equity	$50,000

The **balance sheet** is a snapshot of the firm's financial position, listing assets on the left side, and liabilities and owner's equity on the right side. In practice, the firm's bookkeeper wouldn't make up a balance sheet after every transaction; he or she would record the transaction in a journal or ledger and then post all the transactions to the firm's total balance sheet after a certain period. So balance sheets are for a particular period, like the end of a year or a quarter. Because he is just starting out, Jim will be doing his own bookkeeping. What would the balance sheet look like after Jim purchases a lathe to make his widgets? Well, he has a lathe with a cost of $30,000, so he debits (increases) equipment on the assets side for $30,000, credits (reduces) cash by $20,000, and credits (increases) loans for $10,000, because he paid $20,000 in cash and now owes $10,000.

balance sheet a snapshot of the financial position of a firm, listing assets on the left and liabilities and owner's equity on the right

Balance Sheet for Jim's Widgets (December 5)

Assets		Liabilities and Equity	
Cash	$30,000	Loan	$10,000
Equipment	$30,000	Owner's equity	$50,000
Total assets	$60,000	Total liabilities and equity	$60,000

The second transaction illustrates a couple of things. First, in accounting parlance, "debit" means to increase an asset or decrease a liability, while "credit" means to increase a liability or decrease an asset. Because Jim paid $20,000 in cash, he credited cash for this amount. Second, the balance sheet still balances, but it has now increased by the amount of the equipment ($10,000) that was not paid for in cash.

For the third transaction, Jim buys $10,000 worth of inventory (i.e., stock, wood, and other supplies) that he needs to produce his widgets. Because he has good credit, the suppliers simply ship him the goods with invoices for him to pay. So he debits (increases) inventory for $10,000 and credits (increases) accounts payable to indicate that he has to pay $10,000 to his suppliers. For the fourth transaction, Jim pays $5,000 to his suppliers (creditors), so he credits (reduces) cash for $5,000 and debits (reduces) payables for $5,000. After these transactions on December 11, the balance sheet will look as shown on the following page.

Balance Sheet for Jim's Widgets (December 11)

Assets		Liabilities and Equity	
Cash	$25,000	Payables	$5,000
Inventory	$10,000	Loan	$10,000
Machinery	$30,000	Owner's equity	$50,000
		Total liabilities	
Total assets	$65,000	and equity	$65,000

liquidity the ease with which assets and liabilities are converted to cash

By convention, items on a balance sheets are listed in terms of their **liquidity**, which is how easily they are converted to cash. On the asset side, cash is the most liquid, then inventory, and finally machinery. On the liability side, payables are the most liquid, since they have to be paid in the normal course of business, then loans, and finally owner's equity.

Up to now, Jim has been buying things and getting ready to produce his widgets, so not much happens for the next few weeks. Then at year end, he sells $20,000 worth of widgets, $15,000 for cash and $5,000 to someone who'll pay in 30 days (Jim hopes). He debits (increases) cash for $15,000 and debits (increases) accounts receivables for $5,000, but what about sales (or revenues) of $20,000? For now he will set up an account on the liability side called the IS account. The balance sheet now looks as follows:

Balance Sheet for Jim's Widgets (December 31)

Assets		Liabilities and Equity	
Cash	$40,000	Payables	$5,000
Receivables	$5,000	Loan	$10,000
Inventory	$10,000	Owner's equity	$50,000
Machinery	$30,000	IS	$20,000
		Total liabilities	
Total assets	$85,000	and equity	$85,000

It is now year end. Jim has to prepare his balance sheet, but he faces some special problems. So far, all the transactions have been mechanical and verifiable in that he had the invoices and the receipts to document the transactions. Therefore, the process has been simple bookkeeping, with very little judgement needed. However, Jim recognizes in transaction 6 from Table 3-1 that he has used $8,000 of his inventory, because he does a quick check of what he has on hand and finds that he is short this amount. Jim also recognizes in transaction 7 that some of the $5,000 he has paid in hydro and rent is for the future, because he had to pay two months' rent on moving in and he also had to make a deposit for hydro. Finally, he knows that the $10,000 he took out of his business (transaction 8) can't all be salary, because it is excessive compared with his sales of $20,000. Jim also notices that his lathe is a bit worn, and he realizes that he will have to pay some interest on his loan soon. In short, Jim recognizes that although he could do his own bookkeeping, he can't do the accounting, so he has to set up a meeting to talk to an accountant.

Accounting Conventions: The Basic Principles

What is the difference between an accountant and a bookkeeper? In a crude sense, the bookkeeper manages all the transactions in a firm, while the accountant uses them to create the firm's financial statements. Accountants do this by applying the GAAP that we described above so that other accountants can understand and accept what was done. As noted earlier, the GAAP is a set of basic *principles* and *conventions* applied in preparing financial statements. The CICA Handbook is a compendium of "how to's" for different types of transactions. The principles included in the Handbook are accepted by securities regulators, like the Ontario Securities Commission (OSC), for use in preparing statements for securities offered to the general public.

The most basic principles of GAAP are

1. *the entity concept*: the accounting is for an economic entity, such as a corporation.

2. *the going concern principle*: the statements must reflect the accounts on the basis that the firm is not in imminent threat of bankruptcy, otherwise they have to be qualified.

3. *a period of analysis*: such as a year-end balance sheet.

4. *a monetary value*: in Canada, accountants use historical cost accounting, in which transactions are for the dollars actually involved, with no restatement for inflationary effects.

5. *the matching principle*: the revenues must be matched against the costs that generated those revenues.

6. *revenue recognition*: revenues are only recognized when there is a verifiable sale.

A particular entity's statements are prepared for a specific period, and the entity has to be a going concern (currently in business). The most powerful principle is the *matching* principle, which leads to *accrual* accounting: costs and revenues have to match the period, even if the cash components of the transactions occur in other periods. This is the point at which the accountant's judgement is needed to match up these revenues and costs.

The major conventions of GAAP are

1. *procedures*: assets are on the left and liabilities and equity on the right; when multiple years are shown, assets are on the top and liabilities and equity below.

2. *standards*: in Canada, this is the CICA Handbook.

3. *consistency*: the firm shouldn't constantly switch between different conventions, even if they are acceptable within GAAP.

4. *materiality*: everything that someone could reasonably rely on is disclosed.

5. *disclosure*: the statements should "fully and fairly" disclose the firm's position. *Full disclosure* means that all material data that might be of significance to a reasonably intelligent user should be disclosed. *Objectivity, consistency,* and *conformity* to GAAP are all aspects of full disclosure.

Of particular importance is the convention that requires full disclosure, which means that the statements should be objective, consistent, and conform to GAAP. This convention also reflects the force of securities law in Canada and explains why any material change has to be disclosed to the securities markets by a press release or in filings with the relevant securities commission. It was the obvious failure of Enron and its auditors[5] in this respect that forced the U.S. Congress to act. It used Sarbanes-Oxley to impose a public oversight board to regulate the U.S. accounting profession and force the U.S. Securities and Exchange Commission (SEC) to get tougher with monitoring the internal audit committees of U.S. companies.

CONCEPT REVIEW QUESTIONS

1. Differentiate between debits and credits with respect to assets and liabilities.
2. Explain what is meant by the matching principle. How is this principle related to the use of accrual accounting?
3. Explain what is meant by full disclosure and why it is such an important accounting convention.

3.3 PREPARING ACCOUNTING STATEMENTS

The Balance Sheet and the Income Statement

An accountant, armed with accrual accounting, looked at Jim's business and focused on the matching and revenue recognition principles. For example, the accountant indicated the following:

1. Inventory should be reduced by $8,000, and cost of sales of $8,000 should be expensed against revenues.

2. Of the $5,000 in payments the accountant expensed $300 for hydro for the month, $1,200 for rent, and recorded the balance of $3,500 as a prepaid expense.

3. Of the $10,000 that Jim withdrew, the accountant indicated that $4,000 was a reasonable salary for the month and the balance of $6,000 reflected a reduction or return of capital.

4. The lathe has suffered wear and tear, and its value should be reduced. After looking at similar pieces of equipment, the accountant reduces the lathe's value by $2,000. This cost is offset against revenues.

5. The accountant advises Jim to record an expense of $500 for the interest that he owes but hasn't paid for the period.

6. Finally, the accountant will prepare Jim's tax return and recognize that, for tax purposes, Jim is able to write off $5,000 for wear and tear on the lathe, rather than the actual $2,000, because the government is giving special incentives for firms to buy more modern equipment.

---

[5] Enron's auditor Arthur Andersen LLP, was found guilty of obstruction of justice. The verdict was later overturned, but by then Arthur Andersen had ceased to exist, as few would accept an audit from a firm found guilty of obstruction of justice.

After making these *judgement calls*, the accountant records these transactions to the special IS account that Jim inserted on the balance sheet:

- Inventory is credited (reduced) by $8,000, and the IS account credited (reduced) with cost of sales of $8,000.

- Cash is credited (reduced) by $5,000, of which $1,500 is credited to rent and hydro in the IS account, and $3,500 is debited to a new asset account called prepaid expenses.

- Cash is credited (reduced) by $10,000 for Jim's withdrawal. Capital is credited (reduced) by $6,000, and the IS account is credited (reduced) by $4,000 for Jim's salary.

- The equipment account is credited (reduced) by $2,000 for the wear and tear on the lathe, and the IS account credited (reduced) by $2,000 for equipment wear and tear.

- The IS account is credited (reduced) by $500 for interest expense, and a new account is debited (increased) by $500 for accrued interest payable.

- Finally, the IS account is credited with $2,000 for taxes payable at a 50 percent tax rate, and two new accounts are created and debited $500 for accrued taxes payable and $1,500 for deferred income taxes.

The accountant has made a lot of judgement calls and has used the matching concept to match up Jim's Widgets' revenues and costs over the period, which in this case is from the start of the business until year end. After all this debiting and crediting, the balance sheet looks as follows:

Balance Sheet for Jim's Widgets (December 31)

Assets		Liabilities and Equity	
Cash	$25,000	Payables	$5,000
Receivables	$5,000	Accruals	$1,000
Inventory	$2,000	Loan	$10,000
Prepaids	$3,500	Deferred taxes	$1,500
Machinery	$28,000	Owner's equity	$44,000
		IS	$2,000
Total assets	$63,500	Total liabilities and equity	$63,500

Those of you familiar with accounting will recognize the IS account listed below the owner's equity as the **income statement**. For convenience, let's write out the transactions that Jim made to this account and record the income statement for Jim's Widgets.

While Jim was adding these transactions to the balance sheet account, he was actually making up the income statement. The balance of $2,000 is the *net income* for Jim. Now that the accountant knows that Jim's Widgets made $2,000 in profit or net income, he or she could ask Jim if he wants some of the $10,000 withdrawal as a dividend payment, rather than as salary or a withdrawal of

income statement a firm's financial statement showing the sales, expenses, and net profit for a given period

capital. To make these decisions, Jim has to understand the tax consequences, which we will defer explaining for the moment.

Income Statement for Jim's Widgets

Revenues	$20,000
Cost of sales	8,000
Hydro	300
Rent	1,200
Salaries	4,000
Depreciation (lathe)	2,000
Interest	500
Before-tax income	4,000
Taxes paid	500
Deferred income tax (50%)	1,500
Net income	2,000
Dividends	0
Retained earnings	2,000

The accountant reports one final number to Jim: because Jim capitalized his company with 50,000 shares, each with a $1 book value, his company earned $0.04 per share (i.e. $2,000/50,000). This is the earnings per share (EPS) for Jim's Widgets and is a very important number, as you will see later. However, note that Jim could just as easily have capitalized his company using 10,000 shares with a book value of $5, in which case the $2,000 net income divided by the 10,000 shares would have given an EPS of $0.20. In isolation, the EPS is meaningless; it is only useful when we look at trends over time or compare it with other per share figures, such as the stock price.

What is income? In economics, income is the amount that can be withdrawn from a business while keeping it whole, in the sense of not encroaching on the capital value. However, although this is the guiding principle behind the matching and revenue recognition principles, in practice the correlation between the two is loose. In accounting, income is the highest number consistent with GAAP that the auditor will accept. If this seems cynical, remember how loosely related Enron's net income was with any semblance of economic profit. For this reason, the external analyst must understand how the accountant creates the income statement and balance sheet.

Changing Accounting Assumptions

Suppose that Jim's accountant interpreted three things differently:

1. On reflection, the accountant feels that the lathe has not deteriorated that much and expenses only $1,000 for wear and tear.

2. The accountant talks to Jim and recognizes another $5,000 in sales that corresponds to a customer that has promised to buy some of Jim's widgets. Another $5,000 is added to receivables, because no cash has been received.

3. On reflection, the accountant feels that $2,000 of Jim's salary reflects the development of a unique style and also suggests that Jim patent this style.

Obviously, these new interpretations will influence Jim's balance sheet, as well as his profits. For now, we focus our discussion on the impact that these three decisions have on Jim's profits, which jump to $6,000, as shown below:

Revised Income Statement for Jim's Widgets

Revenues	$25,000
Costs of sales	8,000
Hydro	300
Rent	1,200
Salaries	2,000
Depreciation (lathe)	1,000
Interest	500
Before-tax income	12,000
Taxes paid	4,000
Deferred income tax (50%)	2,000
Net income	6,000
Dividends	0
Retained earnings	6,000

The extra $4,000 comes from the recognition of the extra $5,000 in sales ($2,500 after tax),[6] the reduction (or understatement) of Jim's wear and tear on the lathe by $1,000 ($500 after tax), and the reduction (or understatement) of Jim's salary by $2,000 ($1,000 after tax). These changes certainly make Jim's business look more profitable, and the balance sheet will be stronger as well. There is now an extra $5,000 receivable, the equipment is worth $1,000 more, and there is a new $2,000 account for patents and brand names. All in all, Jim's business looks much better, all because of different judgement calls made by Jim's accountant.

The three areas in which the accountant changed the financial statements are all classic areas of financial statement manipulation. WorldCom Corporation's accounting fraud was a simple case of deciding that the rental payments for telephone lines were an asset, rather than an expense. So instead of deducting them as expenses and reducing income, they were added to the balance sheet as assets, exactly like the $2,000 of Jim's salary. Bristol-Myers Squibb had to restate its financial statements after it was revealed that a significant component of its sales were actually to controlled distributors, where there was an agreement to buy them back under certain circumstances, exactly like the $5,000 in additional sales to someone who had "promised" to buy some of Jim's widgets. The understatement of wear and tear on Jim's lathe is another classic case where conservatism in writing down the value of an asset makes the company's income statement and balance sheet look good.

---

[6] With an assumed 50 percent tax rate, all the changes on an after-tax basis are half the amounts.

What these three examples, along with the other adjustments, indicate is the significant scope for judgement in the preparation of a firm's annual statements and the ongoing need to seriously examine the assumptions underlying these judgements. The examples emphasize the old phrase "figures can lie and liars can figure."

Tax Statements

Let's assume that Jim decides against the *aggressive* adjustments discussed in the section above and keeps to his original statements. We now consider the two tax accounts: taxes payable and deferred taxes. To understand the tax accounts you have to understand that corporations are allowed to say different things to different people. In particular, they are allowed to present one set of accounts to Canada Revenue Agency (the tax authorities) and then another to the investing public. There are limits on how different they can be, but Canada is not like northern European countries, where only one set of statements is used and the accounts given to the tax authorities are the same as those presented to the general public. One of the biggest differences in the statements in Canada is wear and tear.

depreciation/amortization
the reduction in value of an asset over time

What we have been calling "wear and tear" has traditionally been referred to by accountants as **depreciation**, because the asset is depreciating or reducing in value through time. Depreciation is now referred to as **amortization** expense by accountants. For the financial statements, the accountant is allowed to use any reasonable (GAAP-compliant) method for calculating depreciation (amortization). The most common method is to divide a depreciable asset's cost, less an estimated salvage value, by its estimated useful life and expense that amount per year, which is referred to as the *straight-line method*. There are other, more sophisticated methods, such as by machine usage. However, for tax purposes, the government allows a special form of depreciation, which in Canada is called capital cost allowance (CCA). Essentially, every asset is allocated to a CCA asset class and a fixed percentage of the *undepreciated* balance is allowed as an expense each year. So for tax purposes, Jim's income statement may look like the following:

Tax Return for Jim's Widgets

Revenues	$20,000
Costs of sales	8,000
Hydro	300
Rent	1,200
Salaries	4,000
CCA	5,000
Interest	500
Taxable income	1,000
Taxes paid	500

The only difference from Jim's original income statement is that the CCA expense of $5,000 replaces the depreciation expense of $2,000. As a result, the tax bill for Jim's Widgets is only $500, despite the fact that the financial statements report $4,000 in before-tax income. So what is the deferred tax bill of $1,500? It's actually a figment of the accountant's imagination; it is the amount Jim's Widgets would pay if the government didn't allow accelerated depreciation for tax purposes (i.e., CCA). One thing should be made very clear: this is not money that is presently owed to the government. Canada Revenue Agency, similar to tax authorities all around the world, tries to collect all the money owed it. The deferred income taxes are entirely a result of the accountant's judgement in using depreciation for the financial statements that differ from the CCA allowed for tax purposes.

Cash Flow Statements

By now the element of judgement that permeates a firm's financial statements should be obvious. To outsiders, this is extremely annoying because external (non-accounting) observers tend to believe that there is one number that is waiting to be counted by the accountant, but this is not the case. A very good example to the contrary is Nortel Networks Corporation (Nortel). On March 11, 2006, Nortel announced that it was restating its financial results for at least the prior four years. This was Nortel's *third* attempt at preparing its financial statements for those years. Nortel's chief financial officer, Peter Currie, blamed the misstatements on "misapplication of accounting theory."[7] However, an external telecommunications analyst expressed many people's frustration with Nortel by stating, "really how many accountants does it take to screw in a light bulb?"

How then can we assess the element of judgement in a firm's financial statements and how much money Jim has really made? One answer is to look at the third major financial statement: the **cash flow statement**, which essentially undoes the effects of judgement as much as possible and tracks the actual flow of hard cash through a firm. There are two ways to calculate the cash flow statement: (1) by examining the changes in the balance sheet accounts, and (2) by adding back non-cash items to net income.

An increase of cash occurs when you decrease an asset. For example, if Jim sells some of his inventory, all else constant, it generates cash. Alternatively, cash is generated when liabilities increase, for example, if loans go up. So for Jim's Widgets, he can estimate the *sources* of cash from increases in liabilities and decreases in assets, and he can estimate the *uses* of cash as the opposite. Because Jim started out with nothing and he knows what his year-end balance sheet looks like, for this example the changes are easy to estimate because it is just a rearrangement of the balance sheet. This is demonstrated below, where the net change in cash (or net cash flow) is $25,000, which corresponds to the $25,000 in the cash account on the balance sheet for Jim's Widgets. This makes sense, because the beginning cash balance was zero.

cash flow statement a summary of a firm's cash receipts and disbursements over a specified period

Sources and Uses of Funds for Jim's Widgets

Increase in payables	$5,000
Increase in accruals	1,000
Increase in loans	10,000

---

[7] Tyler Hamilton, "Nortel Accounting Woes Continue," *Toronto Star*, March 11, 2006.

Increase in deferred taxes	1,500
Increase in owner's equity	44,000
Increase in retained earnings	$2,000
Total sources of cash	63,500
Increase in receivables	5,000
Increase in inventory	2,000
Increase in prepaid expenses	3,500
Increase in machinery	28,000
Total uses of cash	38,500
Increase in cash	25,000

Another way to arrive at the same result is to start with the net income figure of $2,000 and then add back the non-cash items in the income statement. This version of the cash flow statement is presented below:

Cash Flow Statement for Jim's Widgets

Net income	$2,000
Depreciation	+2,000
Deferred income taxes	+1,500
Traditional cash flow	5,500
Increase in receivables	–5,000
Increase in prepaids	–3,500
Increase in inventory	–2,000
Increase in accruals	+1,000
Increase in payables	+5,000
Increase in net working capital	–4,500
Cash flow from operations	1,000
Capital expenditures	–30,000
Free cash flow	–29,000

In Jim's case, the major *non-cash items* in the income statement are depreciation and deferred income taxes. Remember that depreciation was a non-cash item because the accountant just "charged off" $2,000 to represent the wear and tear on the lathe, but no cash was involved in this. Similarly, the only taxes Jim paid were those that were calculated using CCA, resulting in the $500 tax liability. The deferred or future income taxes were created from the accountant's judgement and do not reflect what is owed to the government. Adding these judgement calls back to net income indicates that Jim's Widgets had cash flow of $5,500. This figure is often referred to as the **traditional cash flow** figure.

Historically, analysts have focused on traditional cash flow, since for many manufacturing firms depreciation is a major non-cash expense. Further, it adjusts for any aggressive choice of depreciation, by adding back whatever was subtract-

traditional cash flow net income plus non-cash expenses such as depreciation and deferred taxes

ed in the income statement. For example, if Jim had followed aggressive accounting practices and used depreciation of $1,000 instead of $2,000, this would have been added back in calculating traditional cash flow. Therefore, focusing on cash flow negates the effect of aggressive accounting for depreciation.

However, other subtle non-cash items are often even more important. For example, Jim's accounts receivables increased by $5,000 because $5,000 of his sales were credit sales and not cash sales. Instead of cash, all Jim got was someone's promise to pay him later. As a result, net income overstates cash flow by assuming that all sales are cash sales. Jim also paid $5,000 for rent and hydro, only $1,500 of which passed through the income statement; another $3,500 was classified as prepaid expenses but still involved cash payments. Similarly, Jim paid $10,000 for inventory but used only $8,000 of it, as $2,000 was still in inventory at the end of the year. Jim has to recognize that he paid $2,000 for this inventory. The sum of these three items is the increase in *working capital* of $10,500. We call this working capital simply because it represents short-term investments that turn over or are constantly "working."

Offsetting this increase in working capital is the fact that some of the expenses in the income statement similarly do not involve cash. For example, Jim recorded $500 in interest and $500 in taxes on the income statement as expenses, because the accountant wanted to match these expenses with Jim's revenues. However, neither the bank nor the government was actually paid, although the expenses have been accrued, and these obligations can be referred to as *accruals*. Similarly, there are still accounts payable of $5,000 outstanding, which means that some of the inventory expenses on the income statement are not yet paid. When these two accounts of $6,000 are subtracted from the working capital of $10,500, *net working capital* increased by $4,500. The net working capital figure indicates that Jim made a cash investment of $4,500 in his widget business, reflecting the difference between what is recorded on the income statement and what went through his cheque book.

When we subtract the increase in net working capital of $4,500 from the traditional cash flow of $5,500, we get **cash flow from operations (CFO)** of $1,000. The value of looking at CFO is that it takes into account changes in net working capital. It brings to light any increases in receivables and inventory, so the analyst can ask why people aren't paying for their sales and why inventory is increasing. If sales are constant and yet the increase in net working capital is significant, it is one sign that the firm's net income numbers might be aggressive. For example, remember Jim's possible use of aggressive accounting in recording $5,000 of sales prematurely. If Jim had done this, then net working capital would have increased by this $5,000, since the sales would have shown up as credit sales and increased receivables. As a result, subtracting this larger increase in net working capital when calculating CFO would have corrected for this aggressive accounting assumption.[8]

cash flow from operations (CFO) the result of subtracting the increase in net working capital from traditional cash flow

The next step in the cash flow statement above was to subtract capital expenditures (capex) of $30,000 from CFO. This gives a figure that is commonly called **free cash flow**, which is −$29,000 in Jim's case. Financial analysts focus on free cash flow to see whether a company is generating or using cash. In Jim's case, he is investing in his company and it is using cash. Free cash flow is important because it picks up the effect of all three of the aggressive accounting practices that Jim

free cash flow the result of subtracting capital expenditures from cash flow from operations

---

[8] However, Jim's figures would be down because he reported and paid more income tax.

could have used. In the final case, where Jim could have claimed that $2,000 of his salary was to develop a brand or patent for his business, this would have been a capital expenditure. In that case, although Jim's income would have been higher, the increased capital expenditures would have been subtracted from CFO and reduced the free cash flow figure.

Financial analysts like to calculate free cash flow because it focuses on the financing of the firm: if the firm is using cash, it has to raise the money from somewhere. As a result, free cash flow indicates the firm's financing problems, or lack thereof. In practice, accountants prepare a variation of the free cash flow statement above that accounts for *cash flow from financing (CFF)* and is referred to as the cash flow statement. For Jim's Widgets, an abbreviated version of the cash flow statement would look like the following:[9]

Cash Flow Statement for Jim's Widgets

Cash flow from operations	$1,000
Cash flow from investing	−30,000
Bank loan	10,000
Capital stock	44,000
Cash flow from financing	$54,000
Change in cash	$25,000

This presentation of the cash flow statement simply takes free cash flow of −$29,000 and adds CFF of +$54,000 to it. Because Jim still owes the bank $10,000 and has invested $44,000 in owner's equity, CFF is $54,000. When this amount is added to the free cash flow deficit of $29,000, we arrive at the net cash flow (or change in cash) figure of $25,000, as calculated in the sources and uses of funds statement above.

Most financial analysts focus on the cash flow statement. However, one problem with this statement is that the same information can be presented in several different ways. In fact, both the name and the presentation of the cash flow statement has changed several times over the past 20 years in response to user concerns.

We now leave our simple example, which was designed to show the basic accounting principles involved in determining financial statements, and look at the actual financial statements of Rothmans Inc.

CONCEPT REVIEW QUESTIONS

1. How is the balance sheet related to the income statement?

2. What happens to the net income figure when a firm's accountants make more aggressive accounting assumptions? Briefly explain.

3. How do cash flow statements alleviate the impact of most major accounting assumptions?

4. Why do income statements differ from tax statements? What is the major difference?

---

[9] This statement is abbreviated because it leaves out the computation of CFO and cash flow from investing (or capex), which were calculated above.

3.4 ROTHMANS INC. ACCOUNTING STATEMENTS

Rothmans Inc. (Rothmans) is one of the big three tobacco companies in Canada, and it owns 60 percent of Rothmans, Benson & Hedges Inc. (RBH). We present and discuss Rothmans' financial statements in this chapter, and in the next chapter, we provide some tools that can be used to analyze these statements.

Accompanying Statements

We begin by looking at the information the company files with the financial statements. Figure 3-1 shows Management's Report for Rothmans' March 2006 fiscal year-end statements.

Management's Report

The consolidated financial statements of Rothmans Inc. and its subsidiary companies have been prepared by management and are in accordance with generally accepted accounting principles in Canada. The significant accounting policies are outlined in note 1. All other financial and operating information in the annual report is consistent with that contained in the consolidated financial statements.

Management is responsible for maintaining a system of internal accounting controls which provides reasonable assurance that assets are safeguarded and that reliable financial information is produced. Management believes that existing internal controls are appropriate in terms of cost and risk to meet these objectives. Internal auditors employed by the Company and its subsidiaries monitor accounting records and related systems.

PricewaterhouseCoopers LLP were appointed by the shareholders at the 2005 annual meeting as independent auditors to examine and report on the Company's consolidated financial statements and their report appears on the following page. As part of their examination, PricewaterhouseCoopers LLP reviewed internal control systems to the extent deemed necessary to support their opinion on such consolidated financial statements.

The Company's Board of Directors has overall responsibility for and has approved the consolidated financial statements and all other information in the annual report. The Board has appointed an Audit Committee consisting of six independent directors to review the audited consolidated financial statements prior to their submission to the full Board. The Committee also meets periodically throughout the year with Company officials, internal auditors and PricewaterhouseCoopers LLP.

John R. Barnett
President and Chief Executive Officer

Michael E. Frater
Vice President Finance and
Chief Financial Officer

May 18, 2006

3-1 FIGURE

*Rothmans Inc.
Management Report*

Source: Rothmans Inc.
Annual Report 2006.
Rothmans' website:
www.rothmansinc.ca.

You should note several things from Figure 3-2. First, the shareholders appointed the auditors PricewaterhouseCoopers LLP (PwC) at the annual general meeting. Although this is technically correct, the fact is that the shareholders simply voted on the company's appointment. Second, management, not the auditors, prepared the financial statements in accordance with Canadian GAAP. The auditors were asked to "examine and report" on these statements, which included (in the spirit of SOX) a review of the company's internal control system. The report then indicates that the BOD is responsible for the statements and (again consistent with SOX) appointed an audit committee composed of "independent" directors who met with management, the internal auditors, and PwC, the external auditors. Finally, the report is signed by both the CEO and the chief financial officer of Rothmans.

Auditors' Report

To the Shareholders of Rothmans Inc.

We have audited the consolidated balance sheets of Rothmans Inc. as at March 31, 2006, 2005 and 2004 and the consolidated statements of earnings, retained earnings and cash flows for the years then ended. These financial statements are the responsibility of the Company's management. Our responsibility is to express an opinion on these financial statements based on our audits.

We conducted our audits in accordance with Canadian generally accepted auditing standards. Those standards require that we plan and perform an audit to obtain reasonable assurance whether the financial statements are free of material misstatement. An audit includes examining, on a test basis, evidence supporting the amounts and disclosures in the financial statements. An audit also includes assessing the accounting principles used and significant estimates made by management, as well as evaluating the overall financial statement presentation.

In our opinion, these consolidated financial statements present fairly, in all material respects, the financial position of the Company as at March 31, 2006, 2005 and 2004 and the results of its operations and its cash flows for the years then ended in accordance with Canadian generally accepted accounting principles.

PricewaterhouseCoopers LLP

PricewaterhouseCoopers LLP
Chartered Accountants
Toronto, Ontario

May 9, 2006

Rothmans Inc. 2006 53

So what did PwC have to say? Its opinion is presented in Figure 3-2.

Note from Figure 3-2 that the auditors' report is addressed to the shareholders of Rothmans and not to the BOD or management. Management prepared the statements, and PwC commented on them for the benefit of the shareholders. So what did PwC do? It indicates that the firm carried out some tests to make sure that things were as management said they were (i.e., that the inventories were there and that people owed Rothmans the amounts they claimed they were owed, etc.). It used to be that the auditor checked everything, but that isn't feasible now, so the auditors do spot checks. Second, PwC checked on the judgement that management used. Remember, a large amount of judgement goes into financial statements. PwC checked that the judgement used in choosing a depreciation rate, recognizing revenue, and so on, was reasonable. Finally, the auditors assessed the overall financial statement presentation. What does this last sentence mean? It says that the statements "fairly present, in all material respects, the financial position of the Company ... in accordance with Canadian GAAP." The audit opinion does not say that the statements fairly present in an absolute sense, simply that the company has chosen a set of accounting principles that are allowed under GAAP and has prepared the statements fairly in conformity with those principles. This difference may seem picky, but sometimes financial statements that fairly present according to GAAP do not fairly present in an absolute sense.

Rothmans' Balance Sheet

Rothmans is a fairly simple company and its financial statements are very straightforward, which is one reason we chose them. Its balance sheet as presented in the 2006 annual report is provided in Table 3-2.

Table 3-2   Rothmans Inc. Balance Sheet

Consolidated Balance Sheets

March 31 (in thousands of dollars)	2006	2005	2004
Assets			
Current Assets:			
Cash and cash equivalents	48,364	23,255	46,978
Short-term investments	81,867	168,740	137,929
Accounts receivable	11,795	32,119	31,993
Inventories (note 4)	206,433	209,819	198,941
Prepaid expenses	1,835	1,322	2,123
Total current assets	350,294	435,255	417,964
Property, plant and equipment (note 5)	76,298	69,149	56,292
Future income taxes (note 10)	6,301	8,831	7,993
Prepaid pension benefit cost (note 9)	13,295	12,003	11,738
Other assets	2,887	3,290	2,770
	449,075	528,528	496,757

Table 3-2   Rothmans Inc. Balance Sheet continued

Liabilities

Current Liabilities:

Accounts payable and accrued liabilities	42,618	47,445	37,021
Excise and other taxes payable	67,680	79,578	77,587
Dividend payable to minority shareholder of subsidiary company	10,761	-	-
Income taxes payable	20,437	21,475	30,178
Total current liabilities	141,496	148,498	144,786
Other long-term liabilities	2,399	2,167	1,468
Other employee future benefits (note 9)	33,444	33,497	30,439
Long-term debt (note 6)	149,751	149,708	150,000
Minority interest in subsidiary company	8,125	950	1,567
	335,215	334,820	328,260
Shareholders' Equity			
Capital stock (notes 7 and 8)	45,347	41,974	38,869
Retained earnings	68,513	151,734	129,628
Total shareholders' equity	113,860	193,708	168,497
	449,075	528,528	496,757

Approved by the Board:

Pierre Des Marais II, O.C.
Director

John Barnett
Director

Source: Rothmans Inc. *Annual Report 2006*. Rothmans' website: www.rothmansinc.ca.

---

current assets assets (cash and equivalents, short-term investments, accounts receivable, inventories, prepaid expenses) that are expected to be converted into cash within a year

Table 3-2 shows that in fiscal 2006 Rothmans had total assets of $449 million, which comprised $48 million in cash and equivalents, $82 million in short-term investments, $12 million in accounts receivable, $206 million in inventories, and $1.8 million in prepaid expenses. The items listed above are all called **current assets**, because they are expected to be converted into cash within a year as receivables are collected, inventories sold, and so on. For longer-term assets, Rothmans had $76 million invested in property, plant, and equipment. Rather than having deferred income taxes, Rothmans reported an income tax asset in the amount of $6.3 million. This asset arises due to timing differences between the tax and reporting values of certain assets and liabilities. Rothmans also had a surplus in its pension plan and therefore reported prepaid pension benefits of $13.3 million.

For liabilities, Rothmans owed suppliers $42.6 million and owed the government excise taxes and income taxes of $88.1 million. Of that $88.1 million, $67.7 million was for excise taxes that Rothmans collected for the government and $20.4 million was for income taxes. Rothmans also owed $10.8 million in dividends to the minority shareholder of a subsidiary company. In total, Rothmans had current liabilities of $141.5 million. Rothmans' long-term liabilities consisted of long-term debt of $150 million and future employee benefits and other liabilities of approximately $36 million, which represent benefits that have been promised but for which Rothmans has not yet set aside cash to pay. Rothmans' equity holders have contributed $114 million in shareholders' equity, either through original contributions, or by having net income retained and reinvested within the business.

In looking at Rothmans' assets and liabilities, you should recognize the similarity to the simple statements prepared for Jim's Widgets. Of course, the preparation of the statements for a firm with $449 million in assets is more complex than for Jim's Widgets, but in principle the same GAAP have been followed. Just as Jim's Widgets does, Rothmans has cash, accruals, receivables, prepaid expenses, and plant and equipment. On the asset side one difference is $82 million in short-term investments, which Rothmans needs in part to pay the $88 million due the government in excise and income taxes. The other major difference is the pension asset. Accounting for pensions is very complex and we do not discuss it here, but note that on the balance sheet are a series of notes that provide details on the calculation of various balance sheet items, such as pensions, which is discussed in note 9. If you want to know exactly what the pension asset consists of, read note 9 that accompanies the statements for a detailed explanation. These notes are usually very informative.

On the liability side, the only new item is the minority interest in a subsidiary company. The entity concept requires the reporting of the overall entity; however, Rothmans owns 60 percent of RBH. Because this is a controlling interest, Rothmans consolidates or reports everything and then separates out the minority amount of equity that the shareholders of Rothmans do *not* own. Essentially the minority interest is equity not owned by Rothmans' shareholders.

Rothmans' Income Statement

How much money did Rothmans make in fiscal 2006? To see this, we look at the income statement (also known as statement of earnings), in Table 3-3.

Table 3-3   Rothmans Inc. Income Statement

Consolidated Statements of Earnings and Retained Earnings

Year ended March 31 (in thousands of dollars, except per share data)	2006	2005	2004
Earnings			
Revenues:			
Sales, net of excise duty and taxes	652,271	636,771	620,104
Investment income	3,351	4,229	3,839
Total revenues	655,622	641,000	623,943
Costs:			
Operating costs excluding amortization	363,545	362,641	355,861
Earnings before interest, taxes and amortization	292,077	278,359	268,082
Amortization (notes 5 and 6)	10,663	9,574	9,880

Table 3-3   Rothmans Inc. Income Statement continued

Interest expense (income)			
- Long-term debt (note 6)	8,328	8,958	7,973
- Other	(1,743)	(1,518)	(2,454)
Earnings before income taxes and minority interest	274,829	261,345	252,683
Income taxes (note 10)			
- Current	106,584	106,589	105,762
- Future	2,530	(838)	(4,177)
Total income taxes	109,114	105,751	101,585
Earnings before minority interest	165,715	155,594	151,098
Minority interest	66,251	62,597	60,821
Earnings for the year	99,464	92,997	90,277
Earnings per common share (notes 3 and 7)			
- Basic	1.47	1.38	1.34
- Diluted	1.45	1.37	1.34
Retained Earnings			
Balance at beginning of year	151,734	129,628	93,969
Earnings for the year	99,464	92,997	90,277
	251,198	222,625	184,246
Dividends paid:			
Common Shares			
(2006 - $2.70 per share*, 2005 - $1.05, 2004 - $0.8125)	(182,685)	(70,891)	(54,618)
Balance at end of year	68,513	151,734	129,628

* Includes special dividend of $1.50 per share paid on June 17, 2005

54   *Rothmans Inc. 2006*

Source: Rothmans Inc. *Annual Report 2006*. Rothmans' website: www.rothmansinc.ca.

We can see from Table 3-3 that in 2006 Rothmans Inc. had sales (after excise taxes) of $652.3 million from operations and $3.3 million in investment income, resulting in total revenues of $655.6 million. Subtracting operating costs of $363.5 million from revenues gave it earnings before interest, taxes, and amortization (EBITDA) of $292.1 million, from which it paid $6.6 million in interest expenses and paid $106.6 million in income tax. Note that the firm also deferred tax payments to Canada Revenue Agency in the amount of $2.5 million. In contrast, during 2004 and 2005 the firm actually paid more in taxes to Canada Revenue Agency than it reported as a tax liability on its financial statements, which can be inferred from the negative figures reported for future income taxes. This is unusual and indicates that Rothmans held a significant amount of "old" plant and equipment that had already been largely depreciated for tax purposes.

Overall, in 2006 Rothmans produced $165.7 million in profits of which $66.2 million (i.e., the minority interest amount) did not belong to Rothmans' shareholders; it belonged to the owners of the 40 percent of RBH that

Rothmans does not own. Once this amount is subtracted, the net income that did belong to Rothmans' shareholders was $99.464 million. So when Rothmans' net income is divided by the average (adjusted) number of shares outstanding, it produced a basic EPS figure of $1.47. Companies are also required to report "diluted" EPS, which is simply the adjusted net income divided by the total possible number of shares that could be outstanding if all potentially "dilutive" securities outstanding were converted into common shares. For example, a company might have some "convertible" bonds out-standing, which, under certain circumstances, could be converted into common shares. The diluted EPS takes into account all the potential shares that could "dilute" the EPS by spreading the net income over a greater number of shares. Rothmans has limited potential for equity dilution, so its diluted EPS figure of $1.45 was very close to its basic EPS figure of $1.47.

Rothmans' Cash Flow Statement

We examine Rothmans' statement of cash flows in Table 3-4. In terms of non-cash items, the biggest item is minority interest, which represents income owned not by the shareholders of Rothmans but by the minority shareholders in RBH. However, this "expense" is not actually paid out to these minority shareholders—the figure merely represents the amount that in some sense "belongs" to them. In fact, the only cash flows these minority shareholders receive is their proportionate share of any dividends paid out by the subsidiary. Therefore, the minority interest is added back to net income as are the other non-cash items, such as amortization, future (deferred) income taxes, and some pension-related accounting items. The net working capital adjustments are also relatively minor so that CFO is very close to net income plus minority interest and amortization. This similarity in numbers essentially indicates that Rothmans is not prematurely recording sales, building up inventory, or avoiding paying its bills. Its net income figure is reliable.

Table 3-4   Rothmans Inc. Cash Flow Statement

Consolidated Statements of Cash Flows

Year Ended March 31 *(in thousands of dollars)*	2006	2005	2004
Cash provided by (used in):			
Operating Activities			
Earnings for the year	**99,464**	92,997	90,277
Adjusted for non-cash items			
Amortization (notes 5 and 6)	**10,663**	9,574	9,880
Minority interest	**66,251**	62,597	60,821
Future income taxes	**2,530**	(838)	(4,177)
Loss on disposal of property, plant & equipment	**44**	150	388
Defined & other employee future benefits expense	**5,014**	7,681	8,240
Defined & other employee future benefits funding	**(6,359)**	(4,888)	(2,145)
Share option compensation cost	**-**	1,030	1,092
	177,607	168,303	164,376
Changes in non-cash operating working capital	**5,607**	(6,281)	61,184
	183,214	162,022	225,560

Table 3-4   Rothmans Inc. Cash Flow Statement continued

Investing Activities			
Additions to property, plant & equipment, net	(17,583)	(21,666)	(11,621)
Proceeds on disposal (purchase) of short-term investments	86,873	(30,811)	(55,841)
	69,290	(52,477)	(67,462)
Financing Activities			
Dividends paid			
By the Company	(182,685)	(70,891)	(54,618)
By a subsidiary company to minority shareholder	(48,315)	(63,214)	(69,138)
Proceeds on issuance of bond	-	149,697	-
Repayment of long-term debt	-	(150,000)	-
Payment of financing charges on issuance of bond	-	(1,634)	-
Proceeds on issuance of common shares	3,373	2,075	1,209
Repayment of bank indebtedness	-	-	(20,447)
Proceeds on other long-term liabilities	232	699	692
	(227,395)	(133,268)	(142,302)
Increase (decrease) in cash and cash equivalents	25,109	(23,723)	15,796
Cash and cash equivalents at beginning of year	23,255	46,978	31,182
Cash and cash equivalents at end of year	48,364	23,255	46,978
Supplementary Disclosures			
Income taxes paid	106,953	115,185	92,534
Interest paid			
- Long-term debt	8,328	5,480	7,921
- Other	347	232	171

■   56   *Rothmans Inc. 2006*

Source: Rothmans Inc. *Annual Report 2006*. Rothmans' website: www.rothmansinc.ca.

In 2006, Rothmans' cash flow from investing (CFI) was $69.3 million, from the net proceeds of $86.9 million from the disposal of short-term investments, which more than offset $17.6 million in capital expenditures on property, plant, and equipment. The positive figure contrasts sharply with the CFI figures for 2004 and 2005, which were −$67.5 million and −$52.5 million, respectively. Firms that are growing and constantly investing in (acquiring) new assets typically have negative CFI figures.

The cash flow from financing (CFF) figure for 2006 of −$227.4 million consisted almost entirely of dividends that were paid by the parent company and a subsidiary, with little impact made by debt and equity financing. This was also the case for the 2004 and 2005 CFF figures. Finally, adding the CFO, the CFI, and the CFF shows that Rothmans generated $25.1 million in net cash flows during the 2006 fiscal year.

The strength of Rothmans can be seen when we use the information from the cash flow statement to estimate its free cash flow, as shown in Table 3-5.

Table 3-5   Rothmans Inc. Free Cash Flow Statement Estimated

Free Cash Flow (For the year ended March 31)	2004 ($million)	2005 ($million)	2006 ($million)
Net income + minority interest	144.885	151.098	165.715
Total cash flow from operations (CFO)	225.560	162.022	183.214
Capital expenditures (capex)	−11.621	−21.666	−17.583
Free cash flow	213.939	140.356	165.631

Source: Rothmans Inc. *Annual Report 2006*. Rothmans' website: www.rothmansinc.ca.

The total company (including the minority interest) had earnings of $165.7 million and cash flow from operations of $183.2 million. After deducting capital expenditures of $17.6 million, the 2006 free cash flow was $165.6 million. The free cash flow can be viewed as the funds available to pay dividends by the company and its subsidiary, which were actually $231 million in 2006, albeit $101 million was in the form of a "special" dividend to shareholders. Overall, Rothmans' financial statements are clean, in the sense that there are very few adjustments that make the statements difficult to understand.

CONCEPT REVIEW QUESTIONS

1. Who is responsible for the preparation of a company's financial statements?
2. What are the scope and purpose of the auditor's opinion?
3. Identify the main components of a firm's balance sheet and income statement.
4. What are the three main categories of the cash flow statement? What is the importance of the information found in each category?

3.5 THE CANADIAN TAX SYSTEM

Canadian taxes are levied on both personal and corporate income, but the government recognizes the potential for double taxation of income earned through a corporation and has designed a partially integrated system. We will explain what we mean by partially integrated as we develop our understanding of taxes. We begin by noting that the United States operates a classical system of double taxation, while Europe, by and large, operates a fully integrated system, which leaves Canada somewhere in the middle. How taxes are levied has important implications for corporate finance, so it is important to realize from the outset that the Canadian tax system differs in some fundamental ways from the U.S. system. As a result, corporate finance strategies that are based on the U.S. tax code are not directly applicable in Canada or Europe.

Corporate Taxes

As we saw in Chapter 2, corporations are distinct legal entities and are taxed as such. We also saw in this chapter that corporations file income tax returns with Canada Revenue Agency that are determined in much the same way as they prepare their income statement for investors. However, we also noted that there are some differences. One main difference that we discussed previously is that different methods are used to calculate amortization expense. Another major difference is in the treatment of investment income and expenses. We elaborate on these two issues below.

As mentioned above, CCA is amortization for tax purposes and the government has designed it to be as simple as possible. First, all assets are allocated to one of a number of CCA asset classes. Four of the major ones are listed below:

Asset Class	Type of Assets	CCA Rate
Class 1	Buildings	4%
Class 8	Office equipment	20%
Class 43	Manufacturing equipment	30%
Class 45	Computers	45%

undepreciated capital cost (UCC) the undepreciated cost of assets, calculated by asset class and written off on a declining balance basis

Class 8 is, in fact, a general catch-all category, so when in doubt use a 20 percent CCA rate! The CCA rate is the rate that is applied to the **undepreciated capital cost (UCC)** of an asset class; the higher the rate, the faster the assets are depreciated. Notice that the general rates make sense in terms of the assets' economic lives. Computers may last a long time, but the rapid pace of technological progress means that you will generally replace them before they wear out. Their economic life is relatively short, and their CCA rate is high. In contrast, buildings last much longer, so their CCA rate of 4 percent is much lower. The asset classes or pools have been designed such that CCA is applied to the balance of the pool at the end of the fiscal year. So rather than calculating CCA for each item separately, it is calculated for the pool as a whole. For most firms, unless they make a special election, their fiscal year is the same as their calendar year.

half-year rule Canada Revenue Agency allows only one-half of the CCA rate to be applied to net acquisitions to an asset class in the first year the assets are acquired

One minor adjustment associated with CCA is that because it is taken on the year-end balance, Canada Revenue Agency allows only one-half of the CCA rate to be applied to net acquisitions to an asset class in the first year the assets are acquired. This is known as the **half-year rule**, which was implemented to reduce the incentive to purchase assets right at the end of the year, and then claim a full year's depreciation on the purchased assets. Remember, CCA is a non-cash expense, but it reduces taxable income and therefore reduces taxes payable. As a result, firms generally want to charge as much CCA as possible.

For example, suppose a company buys a new computer for $5,000. The CCA would be 45 percent of $5,000 or $2,250. Using the half-year rule, only $1,125 can be deducted in the first year. After deducting CCA of $1,125, the balance that remains to be depreciated (i.e., the associated UCC) is $3,875, which equals the asset class's UCC if it were the only asset in that class. For the following year, if no further class 45 assets were acquired, the CCA would be 45 percent of the UCC of $3,875, or $1,744. Notice that although 45 percent seems to be a high depreciation rate, it is applied to the UCC, which declines each year, so the firm will actually be taking CCA on this computer forever, even though its economic life may be only three years. Conversely, most of the asset's value will be depreciated within three years, and virtually all of it will be depreciated after six years, as illustrated in Figure 3-3. Note that although CCA expenses technically go on forever, for practical purposes, they end after six years or so for this asset class. By year 10 the UCC is only $18.

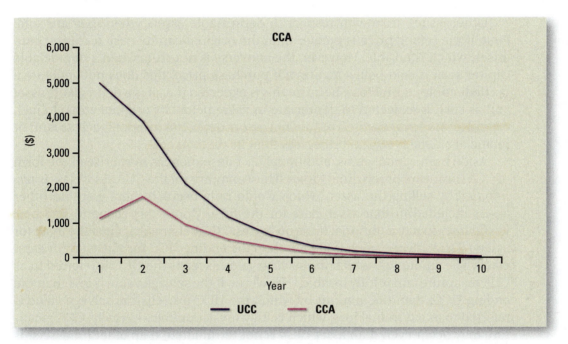

3-3 FIGURE

CCA Expenses Through Time

One advantage of using CCA asset classes or pools is that individual assets are not amortized separately, unless they are the only asset in the pool. This makes it very easy to account for sales of assets: the proceeds are subtracted from, instead of added, to the pool, and the half-year rule comes into play only when the net acquisitions figure for an asset class is positive (i.e., when purchases exceed sales for that asset class). The example below illustrates how to apply the CCA system.

Example 3-1: Estimating CCA

A company purchases equipment for $650,000 that is in asset class 38, which has a CCA rate of 30 percent (declining balance method). Assume this is the only asset in this class. Estimate the CCA associated with this asset class for the year of acquisition and for the subsequent two years.

Solution

For year one, apply the half-year rule, which states that only one-half of the CCA rate is applied in year 1. Therefore, we can estimate CCA in year 1 as

CCA (year 1) = ($650,000) × (0.30) × (1/2) = $97,500

Because the *full* CCA rate is applied to the UCC of the asset class in all years subsequent to the first year, we can estimate the CCA expense in years 2 and 3 as follows:

UCC (beginning of year 2) = UCC (beginning of year 1) − CCA (year 1)
= $650,000 − $97,500 = $552,500

CCA (year 2) = (UCC) × (CCA rate) = ($552,500) × (0.30) = $165,750

UCC (beginning of year 3) = UCC (beginning of year 2) − CCA (year 2)
= $552,500 − $165,750 = $386,750

CCA (year 3) = (UCC) × (CCA rate) = ($386,750) × (0.30) = $116,025

capital gain a taxable gain incurred when an asset is sold at a price greater than its original cost

capital loss a tax deductible loss generated when a non-depreciable asset is sold at a price lower than its original cost

CCA recapture a tax on the amount by which the salvage value (sale price) of an asset exceeds the undepreciated capital cost; occurs only if the asset class is terminated or if an asset is sold for a price that exceeds the remaining UCC for that asset class

terminal loss a tax deduction equal to the amount by which the undepreciated capital cost exceeds the salvage value (sale price); occurs only if the asset class is terminated

Other issues arise with respect to depreciable assets when they are sold. First, if the selling price is greater than the original capital cost, a **capital gain** arises, which is taxable. However, the converse is not true; when a depreciable capital asset is sold below its original purchase price, this does not generate a tax deductible **capital loss**, because this is expected (i.e., it is a depreciable asset and as such is expected to depreciate in value below its original cost). In fact, capital losses are generated only when a non-depreciable asset (such as land or financial assets) is sold at prices less than its original cost.

Aside from capital gains, additional tax consequences may arise in the form of **CCA recapture** or **terminal losses**. These may arise if the CCA asset class is *terminated* by selling the asset, which would only occur if there were no other assets included in that asset class for the firm. Under this scenario, the firm would have to pay additional taxes on "excess" CCA charged against the asset (or assets) if the salvage value is greater than the ending UCC for the asset (or asset class). The amount by which the salvage value exceeds the UCC is referred to as CCA recapture and is fully taxable.[10] However, if the salvage value is less than the ending UCC, then the amount by which the UCC exceeds the salvage value is referred to as a terminal loss, which is fully tax deductible.[11] Finally, CCA recapture may occur even if an asset class is not terminated, if an asset (or assets) is (are) sold for a price that exceeds the remaining UCC for that asset class. The examples below illustrate capital gains, CCA recapture, and terminal losses.

Example 3-2: Capital Gains and CCA Recapture

Assume that, after three years, the company from Example 3-1 sells for $700,000 the equipment it purchased for $650,000. Estimate the tax consequences of this transaction, again assuming that this is the only asset in this class.

---

[10] In other words, it is viewed as if the firm charged too much CCA (amortization), because the asset is sold for more than its depreciated book value for tax purposes (UCC). Therefore, the firm must pay back the amount of taxes it saved by charging too much CCA.

[11] In other words, the firm did not charge enough CCA, because the asset was sold below its book value for tax purposes (UCC). Therefore, the firm is permitted to amortize the asset to its selling price and deduct this charge for tax purposes.

Solution

First, check for capital gains, which do occur in this example:

Capital gains = Selling price − Original cost = $700,000 − $650,000 = $50,000

Next, determine whether a CCA recapture or terminal loss results.

The CCA recapture (terminal loss) will equal the excess (deficit) amount of CCA that the firm charged, which can be determined as the difference between the lower of the selling price and the original cost, and the ending UCC (which was determined in Example 3-1):

CCA recapture (terminal loss) = Lower of selling price and the original cost − UCC

= $650,000 − $386,750 = $263,250

This number is positive, so it represents a CCA recapture of $263,250. The firm must claim this taxable amount on its income tax return.

Example 3-3: Terminal Loss

Ignore Example 3-2, and now assume that, after three years, the company from Example 3-1 sells for $200,000 the equipment it purchased for $650,000. Estimate the tax consequences of this transaction, again assuming that this is the only asset in this class.

Solution

First, check for capital gains, which do not occur in this example, because the selling price of $200,000 is less than the original cost of $650,000.

Next, determine whether a CCA recapture or terminal loss results:

CCA recapture (terminal loss) = Lower of selling price and the original cost − UCC

= $200,000 − $386,750 = −$186,750

The number is negative, so it represents a terminal loss of $186,750.

As we saw with Rothmans, firms often make temporary investments while waiting to pay bills. These assets generate investment income. Similarly, Rothmans has both debt and common shares outstanding, so it paid interest on its debt and dividends on its common shares. How investment income and expenses are treated for tax purposes is very important in finance. The basic rule is that interest is fully taxable when earned and fully deductible when paid. Usually, firms combine these two items into one "net interest" amount that is taxable.

Unlike interest, dividends are not tax deductible when paid; they are paid out of *after-tax income*. In return, when a Canadian corporation receives dividends from another Canadian corporation, they are not taxable, because they are paid out of the after-tax income of the issuing corporation. Otherwise, dividends flowing through multiple companies would attract tax at every stage, thereby increasing the effective tax rate. This represents another difference between accounting income and income for tax purposes. In particular, for accounting purposes, any dividends received are added to income. All else constant, this means that companies prefer to pay interest (issue debt) and receive dividend income. We will return to this preference when we discuss corporate financing issues. In terms of taxable income, it means that firms with significant dividend income and high CCA deductions will appear to pay lower rates of tax on their financial statements.

The basic tax rate for Canadian corporate income for 2005 consisted of a federal and a provincial rate. The basic rate of federal corporate income tax was 28 percent, from which a 7 percent reduction was given for active businesses—that is, non-investment income—and a further 9 percent reduction for small businesses earning less than $300,000. Currently, there is a 1.12 percent surtax, so for small businesses with income up to $300,000, the Canada rate is 13.12 percent; for those with income above that, it is 22.12 percent. In addition there is provincial tax that runs from 2 percent for small businesses in New Brunswick, for an overall rate of 15.12 percent, to 16 percent for larger businesses in Manitoba, for an overall rate of 38.12 percent. The lower small-business rate is removed once taxable income exceeds $10 million. **Operating losses** can also be important for corporations, since they can be used to reduce taxable income. If a company has a loss, it can carry it back five years to restate prior tax returns and get a refund on taxes that have been "overpaid." Alternatively, the operating loss can be stored and carried forward for 10 years to reduce future taxes payable.

operating loss loss generated when a firm's tax deductions are greater than its taxable income; losses can be carried back five years to get a refund on taxes paid or carried forward for 10 years to reduce future taxes payable

Personal Tax

Canada operates a progressive personal tax system in which the rates increase with income. For 2005, the basic federal income tax rates were

- 15 percent on taxable income up to $35,595

- 22 percent on income between $35,596 and $71,190

- 26 percent on income between $71,191 and $115,739

- 29 percent on income above $115,739

In addition, each province operates a separate provincial tax system. It used to be that provincial taxes were a simple multiple of federal taxes, so that Ontario, for example, would add 52 percent (at its peak) of federal taxes. However, things have changed over the past 10 years and most provinces have developed a parallel tax system. For 2005, the combined federal and Ontario tax rates are shown in Table 3-6.

In looking at the tax rates, remember that these rates are marginal rates, which means they are the rates on the next dollar of income. For example, the top rate of 46.41 percent is applied to every dollar of income above $115,740—effectively, the government is almost an equal partner every time someone in Ontario goes looking for work. Remember too that interest income is taxed as ordinary income: the marginal tax rate for investment income differs depending on whether the individual earns interest from debt, dividends from common shares, or capital gains from increases in security prices.

Both cash and stock dividends received by individuals from Canadian corporations are taxable by using the dividend tax credit system. The May 2006

Table 3-6   Ontario Taxable Income

Lower Limit	Upper Limit	Basic Tax	Rate on Excess	Marginal Rate on Dividend Income	Capital Gains
$ — to	$ 8,148	$ —	0.00%	0.00%	0.00%
8,149 to	11,336	—	16.00	3.33	8.00
11,337 to	14,477	510	28.10	5.63	14.05
14,478 to	34,010	1,393	22.05	4.48	11.03
34,011 to	35,595	5,700	25.15	8.36	12.58
35,596 to	59,882	6,098	31.15	15.86	15.58
59,883 to	68,020	13,664	32.98	16.86	16.49
68,021 to	70,559	16,348	35.39	19.88	17.70
70,560 to	71,190	17,246	39.41	22.59	19.70
71,191 to	115,739	17,495	43.41	27.59	21.70
115,740	and up	36,833	46.41	31.34	23.20

Source: Ernst & Young website: www.ey.com.

budget impacted the amount of tax savings associated with dividend income. The system works in the following manner: first, the amount of the dividend is "grossed up" (by 45 percent as per the May 2006 budget, 25 percent before that) to obtain the full taxable amount of dividend income included in taxable income. Then, a dividend tax credit of 18.97 percent (federal—previously 13.33 percent) and 6.50 percent (Ontario—previously 5.13 percent) of the taxable dividend is deducted from taxes paid. We will discuss how this interacts with corporate taxation when we consider how a firm should be financed later in the textbook. However, note for now that the tax rate on dividend income is always lower than that on interest income. This difference used to result in tax rates that were about 15 percent lower on average, but under the new rules the dividend tax rates will be 20 percent to 25 percent lower, depending on an investor's tax category and on how the provinces respond to the federal changes, which had not been finalized at the time of writing.

The final source of investment income is capital gains. These are currently taxed on the basis that 50 percent of the capital gain (i.e. the taxable capital gain) is included as ordinary income. As a result, the effective rate is simply half that of ordinary income. If an individual incurs a capital loss, it can only be used to offset capital gains income, but not ordinary income. That being said, if there is an excess of capital losses, it can be carried back three years, to reduce any taxes paid on previous capital gains, or carried forward indefinitely. Of course, tax rates and tax rules are constantly changing and we suggest that you check the newest tax rules.

Top combined 2007 personal tax rates on ordinary income, interest, capital gains, and dividends are outlined in Table 3-7.

Table 3-7   Top 2007 Personal Tax Rates

Taxable Income	Ordinary Income	Capital Gains	Dividends Eligible	Non-Eligible
Federal Only	29.00%	14.50%	14.55%	19.58%
Alberta	39.00%	19.50%	17.45%	25.21%
British Columbia	43.70%	21.85%	18.47%	31.58%
Manitoba	46.40%	23.20%	23.83%	36.75%
New Brunswick*	46.95%	23.48%	23.18%	35.40%
Newfoundland and Labrador	48.64%	24.32%	32.52%	37.32%
Non-resident	42.92% †	21.46%	21.53% †	28.98% †
Northwest Territories	43.05%	21.53%	18.25%	29.65%
Nova Scotia	48.25%	24.13%	28.35%	33.06%
Nunavut	40.50%	20.25%	22.24%	28.96%
Ontario	46.41%	23.20%	24.64%	31.34%
Prince Edward Island	47.37%	23.69%	24.44%	33.61%
Quebec	48.22%	24.11%	29.69%	36.35%
Saskatchewan	44.00%	22.00%	20.35%	30.83%
Yukon	42.40%	21.20%	17.23%	30.49%

* New Brunswick's 2007 budget revised the top combined rates.

† Non-resident rates for interest and dividends apply only in certain circumstances.

CONCEPT REVIEW QUESTIONS

1. Explain how to calculate the CCA expense for an asset class in a given year.
2. Explain why a firm cannot claim CCA recapture and a terminal loss for the same asset class in the same year.
3. Why would firms prefer to receive dividend income and make interest payments rather than make dividend payments and receive interest payments?
4. What form of investment income has the highest tax rate in Canada?

Summary

This chapter provides a basic overview of accounting statements, beginning with a discussion of the principles on which they are constructed. We discuss the importance of using generally accepted accounting principles (GAAP) to create financial statements that adhere to somewhat uniform standards. We then illustrate how to apply these principles by developing a simple set of financial statements from a series of transactions that an entrepreneur makes in setting up a business. We look at the financial statements of a large company (Rothmans Inc.) to show that these simple principles are the basic ones needed to understand the financial statements of large corporations. Finally, because much accounting revolves around tax issues, we conclude the chapter with a brief discussion of the Canadian tax system.

Key Terms

amortization, p. 70

balance sheet, p. 63

capital gain, p. 86

capital loss, p. 86

cash flow from operations (CFO), p. 73

cash flow statement, p. 71

CCA recapture, p. 86

current assets, p. 78

depreciation, p. 70

free cash flow, p. 73

generally accepted accounting principles (GAAP), p. 58

half-year rule, p. 84

income statement, p. 67

liquidity, p. 64

operating loss, p. 88

terminal loss, p. 86

traditional cash flow, p. 72

undepreciated capital cost (UCC), p. 84

QUESTIONS AND PRACTICE PROBLEMS

Multiple Choice Questions

1. Which of the following is *correct*?

    A. Shareholder's equity = Assets + Liabilities

    B. When a firm pays a bill using cash, the only transaction is a credit to cash.

    C. A debit on the right side of the balance sheet may be an increase to accounts payable.

    D. Debit inventory when there is an increase in inventory.

2. What is the correct book entry when a firm increases its inventories by using its sound credit with the supplier?

    A. Credit inventories and debit cash.

    B. Credit inventories and debit accounts payable.

   C. Debit inventories and credit cash.

   D. Debit inventories and credit accounts payable.

3. Which of the following assets does *not* qualify for capital cost allowance (CCA)?

   A. Land

   B. Manufacturing equipment

   C. Building

   D. Computer

4. Which of the following is a source of cash inflows?

   A. Decrease of inventories

   B. Increase of accounts receivable

   C. Payment of dividends

   D. Decrease of accounts payable

5. Which of the following is a non-cash item?

   A. Receipt of dividends

   B. Payment of interest

   C. Amortization

   D. Purchase of new equipment

6. Which of the following equations represents free cash flow?

   A. Net income + Depreciation + Deferred income taxes

   B. Net income + Depreciation + Deferred income taxes +/− Change in working capital

   C. Net income + Depreciation + Deferred income taxes +/− Change in working capital − Capital expenditures

   D. Net income + Depreciation + Deferred income taxes +/− Change in working capital − Capital expenditures +/− Financing cash flows

7. Which of the following is *not* classified as cash flow from financing?

   A. Issuance of long-term debt

   B. Repurchase of capital stock

   C. Payment of dividends

   D. Purchase of equipment

8. Which of the following firms is most likely to report minority interest in its balance sheet?

   A. A subsidiary firm

   B. A firm that controls 20 percent of another firm

   C. A firm that controls 80 percent of another firm

   D. Government

9. Capital gains occur in which of the following cases?

   A. Selling price of the asset < Initial cost of the asset

   B. Selling price of the asset > Initial cost of the asset

   C. Selling price of the asset < Ending UCC

   D. Selling price of the asset > Ending UCC

10. Which of the following statements is *false*?

   A. Canada operates a progressive personal tax system.

   B. When dividends are paid, they are not taxable.

   C. When interest is earned, it is fully taxable.

   D. Total CCA expense for a firm always exceeds its amortization expense for its accounting statements.

Practice Problems

11. State three of the most basic principles in the *CICA Handbook*.

12. The balance sheet for a small corporation shows total assets of $429,500 and total liabilities of $379,000. What is the value of the shareholders' equity?

Easy

13. The firm in Problem 12 had retained earnings of $5,000 at the beginning of the year. Its net income for the year was $7,500, and it paid out $4,000 in dividends. What is the value of its retained earnings at the end of the year?

14. Using the net income and earnings per common share (EPS) figures from Rothmans Inc.'s income statement (Table 3-3), determine how many shares (approximately) the company had outstanding at the end of 2006.

15. Randy's Rowboats Ltd. purchases and begins to use its first six rowboats for a total cost of $2,400. Randy believes the boats can be used for five years, providing the company with equal value each year. After five years, the boats will be worthless.

   A. Use your best judgement to determine a reasonable amount to charge to amortization expense each year.

   B. Find the book value (cost less amortization) of the boats for each of the five years they will be used.

16. Kash Kow Inc. pays out all its after-tax earnings to shareholders in the form of dividends. Suppose that in 2005 the company earned $1 per share before tax. Corporate income tax was paid at a rate of 25 percent. For a high income earner living in Ontario, the personal tax on dividend income was 31.34 percent. How much of the original $1 per share would such a shareholder have left after all the taxes were paid?

17. List the correct book entries when a firm sells $40,000 of inventories for $70,000 by using credit sales. (Ignore the tax effect.)

18. GG Inc. just bought a computer for $10,000, which belongs to class 45 and has a CCA rate of 45 percent. Calculate the first-year CCA and second-year CCA expenses. (Assume this computer is the only asset in this asset class.)

Medium

19. Based on the figures in Problems 12 and 13, how much money did the shareholders actually invest in the firm (i.e., what is the value of the capital stock)?

Use the following information to answer questions 20 to 24.

Twin brothers, David and Douglas Finn, started a small business from their college dormitory room. Finns' Fridges purchased several small refrigerators to rent to other students for use in their rooms. At the end of their first year of operations, the brothers' records showed the information below.

Current assets (cash and accounts receivable)	$2,000
Interest payable	200
Other current liabilities	800
Property and equipment (net)	4,000
Long-term liabilities	3,200
Owners' equity	1,800
Revenues	2,000
Interest expense	200
Amortization expense	1,000

20. Construct a balance sheet and income statement for the business.

21. Based on the balance sheet you created, how much working capital does Finns' Fridges have?

22. Suppose Finns' Fridges is subject to corporate income tax at a rate of 30 percent. What will be the company's net income after tax?

23. David and Douglas invested $500 each to capitalize Finns' Fridges. To allow for future flexibility (such as selling shares to other investors), they placed a "par value" of $10 on each share; thus each brother owns 50 shares. Based on the net income figure from Problem 20, what were the earnings per share (EPS) of Finns' Fridges for its first year of operations?

24. David Finn notices that the local appliance store is now charging $210 for the same model of refrigerator his company bought for $200. Given that Finns' Fridges purchased 25 of these refrigerators, what should the company's balance sheet show as the value of property and equipment?

25. Corine's Candies Inc. paid dividends of $2.5 million during 2005. However, the company needed extra cash to open new stores, so it issued $1.3 million in new stock. What was Corine's cash flow from financing in 2005?

26. Based on Rothmans' balance sheet as presented in Table 3-2 of the text, Total Current Assets for the firm fell by nearly 20 percent between fiscal 2005 and

2006. Which component of the current assets decreased the most? By what dollar amount, and percentage amount, did it fall?

27. Rothmans Inc. paid $2.70 in dividends for each common share outstanding during 2006. Use the total "Dividends paid by the company" figure from the firm's cash flow statement (Table 3-4) to determine how many shares (approximately) the company had outstanding in 2006. Compare to your answer from Problem 14.

28. The cash flow statement for Rothmans Inc. (Table 3-4) shows proceeds on issue of common shares of $3.373 million for 2006. Is this reflected on the company's balance sheet (Table 3-2)? If so, how?

29. The rowboats Randy purchased (see Problem 15) are a "Class 7" asset, so they have a CCA rate of 15 percent. Determine the amount of the capital cost allowance for each of the five years the boats will be used (for simplicity, you may ignore the "half-year rule").

30. Jason's business purchased several pieces of machinery some time ago for $25,000. At the beginning of the current year this pool of assets had a UCC of $15,000. During the year, Jason decided to sell all of the assets from this pool. For each of the three sale prices below, determine if the firm will report a capital gain, and the amount (if any) of CCA recapture and/or terminal loss.

   A. $30,000
   B. $20,000
   C. $10,000

31. Suppose firms A and B have identical revenues and operating expenses, so that each has earnings before amortization and taxes of exactly $1 million. Both firms will report amortization of $200,000 on their public financial statements. On its tax return, firm A claims $200,000 for CCA, whereas firm B is able to claim $400,000. Based on a tax rate of 30 percent of taxable income, how much tax will each firm pay?

32. Given the income statement for GG Inc. and the following adjustments to be made, rebuild its income statement:

   a. GG Inc. should use the straight-line depreciation method, which incurred only $1,500 depreciation cost.

   b. GG Inc. forgot to book $4,000 salary paid during the year.

   c. GG Inc. should use the new corporate tax rate, which is 35 percent.

Difficult

GG Inc. Income Statement for Y2006 (unadjusted):

Revenue	$90,000
Cost of sales	10,000
Rent	10,000
Depreciation	2,500
Interest	2,000
Income before taxes	65,500
Taxes paid	26,200
Net income	39,300

33. Estimate cash flow from operations for KER Inc. using the following information:

Net income	$90,000
Depreciation	10,000
Deferred income taxes	5,000
Increase in inventories	20,000
Decrease in accounts receivable	1,000
Increase in accounts payable	2,000
Decrease in accruals	2,500
Increase in prepaids	5,000

34. The Finn brothers are getting concerned that the financial statements for Finns' Fridges (see Problem 20) don't properly reflect the true state of affairs. The 25 customers were charged $10 in rent at the end of each month. Now that the academic year is over, five of these customers (students) have vacated their dormitory rooms without paying the last month's rent on the refrigerators. Moreover, one student seems to have taken the refrigerator with him when he left! Douglas doubts the company will ever receive the late rental fees, or retrieve the stolen fridge. Based on this, construct a new balance sheet and income statement for the company.

35. Rothmans Inc. owns 60 percent of its subsidiary firm. If the minority interest on the balance sheet (Table 3-2) shows the value of the equity not owned by Rothmans shareholders, what is the value of the shareholders' equity for the entire subsidiary firm?

36. Repeat Problem 29 to include the "half-year rule."

37. Prince Rupert Fly'n Fish Inc. purchases one small plane in its first year of business for $70,000. In year 2 it purchases another plane for $90,000. Find the UCC at the end of year 3 if the CCA rate for aircraft is 25 percent.

38. Suppose that Prince Rupert Fly'n Fish (see Problem 37) decided to sell its first aircraft for $50,000 in year 2 (purchased for $70,000 in year 1). As before, the second plane costs $90,000 and is bought and put-in-use in year 2. Find the UCC at the end of year 3. The CCA rate is 25 percent.

39. What is the apparent tax rate (tax paid as a percentage of net income) for firms A and B in Problem 31?

Analyzing Financial Statements

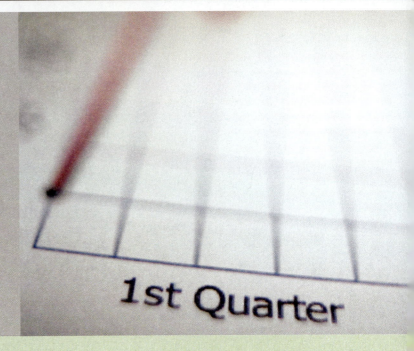

1st Quarter

Companies and the people who analyze them often use ratios or valuation measures that do not conform with generally accepted accounting principles (GAAP). This sometimes makes comparing one firm to another difficult. In its annual report, BCE Inc. reconciles its non-GAAP financial measures (Canadian) with its closest GAAP equivalents. EBITDA, which stands for earnings before interest, taxes, depreciation and amortization, is a commonly used measure of operating performance for certain industries. It can be compared to GAAP operating income before the deduction of amortization expense, net benefit plans cost, and restructuring costs. BCE provides EBITDA for investors interested in the company's ongoing operations and its ability to service debt. Care must be taken when using non-GAAP numbers. The company points out, for example, that the restructuring expenses not included in EBITDA are not necessarily non-recurring ones.

Source: Bell Canada Enterprises 2005 Annual Report, retrieved February 15, 2007, from http://www.bce.ca.

CHAPTER 4

Financial Statement Analysis and Forecasting

Learning Objectives

After reading this chapter, you should understand the following:

1. Why return on equity is one of the key financial ratios used for assessing a firm's performance, and how it can be used to provide information about three areas of a firm's operations

2. Why outsiders and insiders are concerned with a company's ratios related to leverage, efficiency, productivity, liquidity, and value

3. How to calculate, interpret, and evaluate the key ratios related to leverage, efficiency, productivity, liquidity, and value

4. Why financial forecasts provide critical information for both management and external parties

5. How to prepare financial forecasts by using the percentage of sales approach

6. How external financing requirements are related to sales growth, profitability, dividend payouts, and sustainable growth rates

CHAPTER 4 PREVIEW

INTRODUCTION

If accounting is the language of business, what is it saying to us? This chapter answers this question and shows how external interested parties can use financial statements to evaluate a firm. Of course, no one uses financial statements in isolation; they look at additional information on the firm and the macroeconomic environment, and compare the firm's statements across time and with members of its peer group, such as other firms in the same industry or industry averages. Analyzing a firm's statements also depends on *why* it is being done. A bank making a short-term loan will look at different factors than would the same bank making a long-term loan. Further, in both cases, the bank will look at different factors than would an equity analyst trying to value the company's common shares.[1] In turn, both will look at different factors than would another firm interested in buying the first one or possibly lowering its prices to heighten competition. However, in all cases, a major source of information is the firm's financial statements, and financial analysis provides a standard framework of analysis. Once the basics of financial analysis are understood, the same tools can be used to forecast whether the firm is likely to use or need cash over a forecast horizon. This is clearly important, not just for the firm, but also for its creditors, like the bank, and investment dealers who need to advise the firm on its financing issues. In this chapter, we will introduce the basics of financial analysis and forecasting.

4.1 CONSISTENT FINANCIAL ANALYSIS

In Chapter 3, you learned about the significant role that judgement plays in the preparation of a firm's financial statements. It is reasonable to ask whether, with so much judgement involved, financial analysis based on these statements is a bit like building a sand castle. To some extent this is true, and it has led to significant efforts by third parties to reconcile and standardize the financial statements of firms, as discussed in Chapter 3. However, despite efforts to harmonize accounting standards, important differences in generally accepted accounting principles (GAAP) still persist. These GAAP differences have forced users of financial statements to attempt an external reconciliation of GAAP. For example, Morgan Stanley, a major U.S. investment bank, has recently completed an ambitious program of harmonization, not just across U.S. companies but also globally. They did this because users of financial statements need to be able to compare the financial statements of companies in the same industry that are based in different countries. For example, three of the world's largest oil and gas companies include Exxon Mobil Corporation (United States), BP P.L.C. (United Kingdom), and EnCana Corporation (Canada). The problem is how can their financial statements be compared if they are prepared using different forms of GAAP?

---

[1]It is possible for the same investment bank's credit and equity analysts to offer different advice for their debt and equity clients, since their perspectives differ.

The answer that Morgan Stanley came up with was ModelWare.[2] All Morgan Stanley analysts now have to produce their "numbers" on the same basis. This involves both the data and the calculations derived from the data. Figure 4-1 describes the basic process. Morgan Stanley assumed, as we will, that one of the key numbers is **return on equity (ROE)**, which is in the middle of the profitability tree.

return on equity (ROE)
the return earned by equity holders on their investment in the company; net income divided by shareholders' equity

$\frac{NI}{SE}$

4-1 FIGURE

The Morgan Stanley ModelWare Profitability Tree

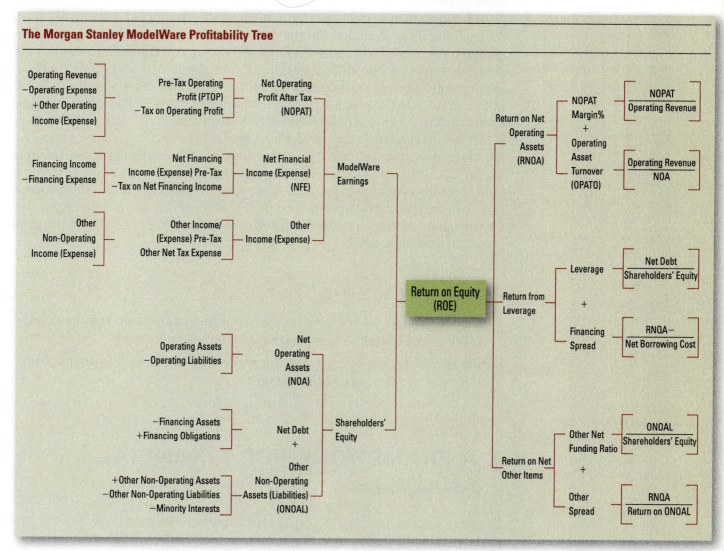

The Morgan Stanley ModelWare Profitability Tree

Morgan Stanley used a consistent set of accounting rules to derive all the basic numbers, such as shareholders' equity and earnings (shown on the left side). To do this, it used a common set of principles. For example, as you may remember from your accounting courses, inventory can be accounted for in several different ways, such as first-in, first-out (FIFO) and last-in, first-out

[2] ModelWare, Morgan Stanley, August 4, 2004.

(LIFO), when describing which cost to include in the income statement when a "widget" is sold. All Morgan Stanley analysts use FIFO. Similarly, operating income has to be calculated in the same way, even if one country (the United Kingdom, for example) requires amortization of certain assets, whereas another country (the United States, for example) does not. By harmonizing the accounting principles employed, the basic ingredients in financial analysis (left side) are estimated on a more consistent basis. Morgan Stanley's second step was to harmonize the actual financial ratios that analysts calculate (shown on the right side). For example, in calculating return on investment (ROI), analysts must follow the same method.

It is too early to say whether Morgan Stanley's attempt at harmonization will do anything more than add another set of standards to confuse investors and analysts. For example, it states, "A key exercise for any energy investor is accurately determining the capital employed and the return potential. There are many permutations on the general concept and competing acronyms (ROIC, ROCE, ROACE, RONA, etc.). To ensure consistency, Morgan Stanley now defines RNOA strictly." However, whether RNOA displaces ROIC, ROCE, ROACE, or RONA when competing companies advocate these other calculations is doubtful. What it does point out is that there are no "generally accepted financial ratios." It is important, when looking at ratios generated by another party, to *always* see how they are calculated. Even some of the most basic ratios, such as ROE, can vary when calculated by different institutions, even if the input data are the same.[3] Acting on the assumption that all ratios are prepared on the same basis can lead to misleading conclusions.

CONCEPT REVIEW QUESTIONS

1. What difficulties do analysts face when trying to compare the financial statements of firms that are based in different countries?

2. Why should people be aware of the precise definition of a financial ratio employed by the source of the ratio?

4.2 A FRAMEWORK FOR FINANCIAL ANALYSIS

Return on Equity (ROE) and the DuPont System

Morgan Stanley put ROE in the centre of their profitability tree for a good reason: ROE measures the return earned by the equity holders on their investment in the company. It is calculated as the net income (NI) divided by shareholders' equity (SE), as shown in Equation 4-1.[4]

---

[3] This is not because they make mistakes, but rather because they employ different definitions of the same ratio.

[4] ROE can also be defined as NI available to the common shareholders (i.e., NI – preferred dividends) divided by common equity (CE). For Rothmans, there is no difference, because it does not have any preferred equity. For some firms, it can make a difference.

$$ROE = \frac{NI}{SE}$$

[4-1]

We calculate the 2006 ROE for Rothmans Inc. (Rothmans) by using the figures reported in Chapter 3, and we will do the same for the other ratios introduced in this chapter. In 2006, NI was $99.464 million, while SE was $113.860 million, so Rothmans' ROE was

We commented earlier about typical ROEs, but 87.36 percent is at the

$$\text{ROE} = \frac{NI}{SE} = \frac{99.464}{113.860} = 87.36\%$$ *upper end profitability*

extreme upper end of corporate profitability in Canada (or anywhere for that matter). As we shall see, Rothmans is not a typical company in many ways.

ROE is not a "pure" financial ratio because it involves dividing an income statement (flow) item by a balance sheet (stock) item.[5] As a result, some people estimate the ROE as NI over the "average" SE, that is, the average of the starting and ending SE. This adjustment acknowledges that NI is earned throughout the year, so it makes sense to divide by an average of SE to recognize that not all of those funds were invested throughout the year. For example, the ending SE is partly the result of the retained earnings for the year, which in turn is dependent on the net income for the year; however, with three years of data, the use of the average SE causes the loss of an observation. As a result, most analysts use the ending SE as the denominator simply to get more estimates of the ROE; that way, they can assess a trend over time. However, this tends to understate a firm's profitability on average, because the ending SE will usually exceed the average for the year if the firm is profitable.[6]

The next step in financial analysis is to understand where Rothmans' ROE came from. The most popular approach to "decomposing" ROE is attributable to the DuPont Corporation (DuPont), which pioneered a variation of the expansion of the ROE shown in Figure 4-2.

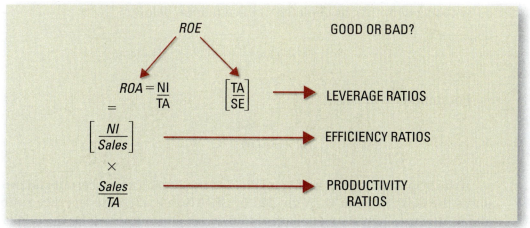

4-2 FIGURE

DuPont System

---

[5] "Pure" ratios involve dividing an income statement item by another income statement item, or dividing a balance sheet item by another balance sheet item.

[6] As we shall see in Rothmans' case, this approach leads to a higher ROE due to the decline in SE that results from the large special dividend paid during 2006.

The DuPont system provides a good starting point for any financial analysis and is commonly included in research reports as a way of summarizing a firm's key financial ratios. Table 4-1 shows the information for Rothmans from 2003 to 2006 as provided by E-Trade Canada Securities Corporation (E-Trade Canada).[7] We do not comment on the items in the table now, but you will see how all the reported figures and ratios are related as you proceed through this section, with particular emphasis on the 2006 numbers.

Table 4-1   E-Trade Canada's Rothmans ROE Analysis

Return on Equity	3/31/2006	3/31/2005	3/31/2004	3/31/2003
(1) Net sales	652,271	636,771	620,104	575,469
(2) Pretax income	274,829	261,345	252,683	240,197
(3) Net income	99,464	92,997	90,277	86,678
(4) Total assets	449,075	528,528	496,757	429,965
(5) Shareholders' equity	113,860	193,708	168,497	130,537
Pretax margin % (2/1)	42.13	41.04	40.75	41.74
× Tax retent % (3/2)	36.19	35.58	35.73	36.09
= Profit margin % (3/1)	15.25	14.60	14.56	15.06
× Assets utilization % (1/4)	145.25	120.48	124.83	133.84
= ROA % (3/4)	22.15	17.60	18.17	20.16
× Leverage (4/5)	394.41	272.85	294.82	329.38
= ROE % (3/5)	87.36	48.01	53.58	66.40

Source: Data from E-Trade Canada

return on assets (ROA) net income divided by total assets

The DuPont approach defines the firm's **return on assets (ROA)** as NI divided by total assets (TA), as depicted in the equation below:

[4-2]

$$ROA = \frac{NI}{TA}$$

leverage ratio total assets divided by shareholders' equity; it measures how many dollars of total assets are supported by each dollar of shareholders' equity, or how many times the firm has leveraged the capital provided by the shareholders into total financing

For Rothmans in 2006,

$$\text{ROA} = \frac{NI}{TA} = \frac{99.464}{449.075} = 22.15\%$$

If the ROA is multiplied by TA and divided by SE, the TA's cancel out and produces the ROE. So what is TA divided by SE? This is called the **leverage ratio**, and it measures how many dollars of total assets are supported by each dollar of SE, or how many times the firm has "leveraged" the capital provided by the shareholders into total financing. It is shown in Equation 4-3.

---

[7] An E-Trade account is required to obtain the data, but every student of finance should take $500, open a discount brokerage account, and really learn about finance.

$$Leverage = \frac{TA}{SE}$$

[4-3]

The 2006 leverage ratio for Rothmans is

$$Leverage = \frac{TA}{SE} = \frac{449.075}{113.860} = 3.944$$

Thus, Rothmans has *leveraged* every dollar of shareholders' equity into $3.944 of total financing by using debt and other forms of liabilities to help finance its operations.

The way to interpret this ratio is that every dollar of total assets earned an ROA of 22.15 percent, but the shareholders didn't provide all this financing. They provided about one-quarter of the money to buy the firm's total assets (i.e., 1/3.94)—that is, the firm leveraged up each dollar of shareholders' equity by 3.944. As a result, the ROE is the ROA of 22.15 percent multiplied by the leverage ratio of 3.944, which gives an ROE of 87.36 percent. What this figure means is that part of the reason for Rothmans' high ROE is that it is extremely profitable and has a high ROA of 22.15 percent. The rest of the story is that Rothmans magnified this ROA by using a significant amount of financial leverage. As a result, when we analyze corporate performance we look at ROE, ROA, and a series of ratios that measure **financial leverage**, since how the firm finances its operations is very important.

We can now decompose ROA into two of its major components: the firm's **net profit margin** and its (asset) **turnover ratio**, which we define below:

financial leverage the use of capital provided by shareholders to increase total financing

net profit margin part of return on assets; net income divided by sales

turnover ratio part of return on assets; sales divided by total assets

$$Net\ profit\ margin = \frac{NI}{Sales}$$

[4-4]

$$Turnover\ ratio = \frac{Sales}{TA}$$

[4-5]

Multiplying the two together cancels the sales figure on the bottom of net profit margin with the sales figure on the top of the turnover ratio, leaving NI/TA, or simply the ROA, as shown below:

$$ROA = \frac{NI}{TA} = \frac{NI}{Sales} \times \frac{Sales}{TA}$$

[4-6]

For Rothmans the 2006 net profit margin or (return on sales) was

$$Net\ profit\ margin = \frac{NI}{Sales} = \frac{99.464}{652.271} = 15.25\%$$

So Rothmans made more than 15 percent on average, on the net amount after excise taxes, for every pack of cigarettes it sold. We look at the net profit margin to determine how *efficiently* the firm converts sales into profits. Later in the chapter, we will expand our analysis to include additional efficiency ratios.

So if every dollar of sales earned Rothmans 15 percent in profits, how many dollars of sales did it generate from each dollar invested in assets, or alternatively what was its turnover ratio?

$$\text{Turnover ratio} = \frac{Sales}{TA} = \frac{652.271}{449.075} = 1.452$$

For 2006, with total assets of $449.075 million, Rothmans generated sales, net of excise duties, of $652.271 million. In other words, each dollar of assets generated about $1.452 in sales. The turnover ratio is a productivity ratio, as it measures how *productive* the firm is in generating sales from its assets. As you will see, several productivity ratios can be calculated to determine the main drivers of this overall productivity.

Now we have the major ratios of the DuPont formula. Putting them all together produces the following equation:[8]

[4-7]

$$ROE = \frac{NI}{SE} = \frac{NI}{Sales} \times \frac{Sales}{TA} \times \frac{TA}{SE}$$
$$= Net\ profit\ margin \times Turnover\ ratio \times Leverage\ ratio$$

For Rothmans in 2006,

$$ROE = \frac{NI}{Sales} \times \frac{Sales}{TA} \times \frac{TA}{SE} = 15.25 \times 1.452 \times 3.944 = 87.33\%$$

(the difference of 0.03 percent is due to rounding)

Each dollar of equity supported $3.944 of assets, which in turn generated $1.452 in sales, which in turn generated a net profit margin of 15.25 percent. In other words, overall the ROE is determined by leverage, turnover, and profit margin. So what does this mean?

Interpreting Ratios

A single ratio on its own provides little information. To judge whether a given ratio is "good" or "bad" requires some basis for comparison. Two bases are commonly used for comparison:

1. the company's historical ratios, or the *trend* in its ratios

2. *comparable* companies—for this purpose, we can use a similar company or use industry average ratios

---

[8] This is the simplest and most commonly used version of the DuPont system. There are other versions, which we do not discuss here, many of which break ROE into five or more components.

Table 4-2 includes Rothmans' DuPont analysis ratios over 2004 to 2006, which are identical to those provided by E-Trade Canada in Table 4-1.

Table 4-2   Rothmans' DuPont Ratios

Rothmans (March 31)

	2004	2005	2006
ROE	0.5358	0.4801	0.8736
ROA	0.1817	0.1760	0.2215
Net profit margin	0.1456	0.1460	0.1525
Turnover	1.2483	1.2048	1.4525
Leverage	2.9482	2.7285	3.9441

Often, unique factors drive a particular firm's ratios and that makes them difficult to compare with the ratios of other firms. For example, if a firm has made a recent large acquisition of another firm, key profitability and turnover ratios often drop. For this reason, it is important to look at a firm's ratios over time. What we can observe from Table 4-2 is that Rothmans is consistently profitable, with ROEs ranging from 48.01 percent to 87.36 percent over this three-year period. Most firms can only hope for this sort of profitability! Notice that the net profit margin over this period showed very little variation, but the turnover ratio and the leverage ratio both increased dramatically during 2006. These increases are primarily attributable to the large "special" dividend of $1.50 per share that Rothmans paid during 2006. This resulted in a significant (approximately $80 million) decrease in shareholders' equity and total assets during the year, despite the fact the company's sales and net income both increased from the previous year. As a result of the large increases in these two ratios, the firm's ROE also increased dramatically, despite the fact that the net profit margin increased only slightly during the year.

So how does Rothmans compare with other tobacco companies? Ideally, we would compare Rothmans to another Canadian tobacco company of similar size, or even an industry average comprising several similar Canadian firms. Certainly, this would be a viable approach if we were comparing the Canadian banks, because they are so similar. However, no other Canadian tobacco companies are comparable to Rothmans. Therefore, we have to look abroad. Larger tobacco companies are based all over the world, but we chose a U.S. company, Altria Group, Inc. (Altria), for comparison. Altria, which used to be called Philip Morris, is the largest tobacco company in the world and is the producer of Marlboro cigarettes. Obviously, this comparison is less than optimal, given the differences in U.S. versus Canadian GAAP discussed previously; however, it is still the best of the limited choices.

Table 4-3 provides the DuPont ROE data for Altria for the 2003 to 2005 period. These ratios are comparable to Rothmans ratios for the 2004 to 2006 period because the Altria figures are as of December 31, while the Rothmans figures are as of March 31.

Table 4-3   Altria's Dupont Ratios

Altria (December 31)

	2003	2004	2005
ROE	0.3670	0.3066	0.2922
ROA	0.0957	0.0926	0.0967
Net profit margin	0.1132	0.1051	0.1066
Turnover	0.8455	0.8816	0.9065
Leverage	3.8352	3.3095	3.0232

The overall ROEs for Altria are in the 29 percent to 37 percent range, which are lower than the figures for Rothmans. In addition, the figures are generated differently. Altria generally has profit margins that are 4 percent to 5 percent lower than Rothmans' are. It also has substantially lower turnover ratios, in the 0.84 percent to 0.91 range, while Rothmans' turnover ratios are in the 1.20 percent to 1.45 percent range. Combining these two results leads to higher ROA figures for Rothmans than for Altria. In fact, Rothmans' ROA is generally about twice as large as the ROA for Altria. During 2003 and 2004, Altria's leverage ratios were larger than those of Rothmans, resulting in greater magnification of the ROA figures as reflected in ROE; however, Rothmans' ROE figures were still much larger than those for Altria. In 2005, Altria's leverage ratio of 3.02 was lower than the figure for Rothmans, leaving Altria's ROE much lower than Rothmans' figure.

On the surface, we could conclude that Rothmans has better operating results than Altria, because Rothmans' profit margins and turnover figures are better. In addition, up until Rothmans' dramatic increase in its leverage ratio in 2006 as a result of the special dividend, it also used less leverage than Altria. However, we should consider any possible contributing factors before reaching any conclusions. For example, Altria has diversified into other areas and its non-tobacco operations could be causing the differences between it and Rothmans. Alternatively, the differences between U.S. and Canadian GAAP could significantly affect the ratios. However, the evidence is so strong that it seems reasonable to conclude that Rothmans is consistently more profitable on a relative basis than is the largest tobacco company in the world. Further, it has done this without significantly over-leveraging itself. To get a better understanding of these results, we can extend the analysis of the leverage, efficiency, and productivity ratios.

CONCEPT REVIEW QUESTIONS

1. What three areas of a firm's operations does the DuPont system provide information about?

2. All else being equal, list three factors that will lead to higher ROE ratios.

3. What can we use as a basis for comparison when looking at financial ratios? What kind of information can we gain from this comparison?

leverage, turnover, profit margin

4.3 LEVERAGE RATIOS

Leverage is synonymous with magnification. It is good when a firm is low risk and earns a healthy ROA, since it magnifies these high ROAs into even higher ROEs, but when the firm loses money, the use of leverage magnifies ROEs on the downside as well. This can get the firm into serious trouble. We will discuss this in detail when we discuss the firm's capital structure in Chapters 20 and 21. But for now we will introduce the major ratios that we look at in discussing financial leverage. There are basically three types: stock ratios, flow ratios, and other ratios.

stock ratios the amounts of debt outstanding at a particular time

Stock ratios indicate the amounts of debt outstanding at a particular time. For leverage, there are three basic stock ratios: the leverage ratio (discussed above), the debt ratio, and the debt-equity ratio. The **debt ratio** is defined as total liabilities (TL) divided by total assets (TA), as shown in the equation below:[9]

debt ratio total liabilities divided by total assets

$$Debt\ ratio = \frac{TL}{TA}$$

[4-8]

For Rothmans in 2006,

$$Debt\ ratio = \frac{TL}{TA} = \frac{335.215}{449.075} = 0.7465$$

The debt ratio is just a rearrangement of the leverage ratio, which for Rothmans was 3.944.[10] The debt ratio confirms that Rothmans makes extensive use of other people's money—or does it? Rothmans' liabilities, as discussed in Chapter 3, include money that it owes suppliers and money that it has collected in excise and income taxes on behalf of the government. As long as it stays in business, Rothmans will continue to generate trade credit as suppliers ship to it and it pays them 30 or 60 days later. Further, as long as smoking is considered socially undesirable, the government will use the tobacco companies to raise tax revenues to help deter smoking. But in a broad sense, these liabilities are not debt in the way that bank debt is debt. These liabilities arise as a result

---

[9] There are many variations of this ratio that include the use of total debt or total long-term debt in the numerator and/or dividing by total capital instead of total assets.

[10] In fact, the leverage ratio is simply one divided by one minus the debt ratio (i.e., 1/(1 − 0.7465) = 3.944).

of normal operations, not from someone deciding to invest or lend money to Rothmans.

To capture the use of "genuine" debt, we estimate the amount of interest-bearing debt the firm has outstanding relative to shareholders' equity. The sum of interest-bearing debt and shareholders' equity is referred to as **invested capital** to distinguish it from total assets, some of which is financed as a result of normal business operations. Rothmans' only interest-bearing debt is $149.751 million of long-term debt, since it repaid its short-term bank loans in 2003. So its **debt-equity (D/E) ratio** is simply debt (D) divided by shareholders' equity (SE) as shown below:

invested capital the sum of interest-bearing debt and shareholders' equity

debt-equity (D/E) ratio debt divided by shareholders' equity

[4-9]

$$D/E \ ratio = \frac{D}{SE}$$

For Rothmans for 2006,

$$D/E \ ratio = \frac{D}{SE} = \frac{149.751}{113.860} = 1.32$$

This means that for every dollar of equity contributed by shareholders, Rothmans borrowed $1.32 in interest-bearing debt.

The D/E ratio's advantage over the debt ratio is that it measures the use of interest-bearing debt. This is important because it is the promise to pay interest that makes debt risky. Rothmans does not face risk as a result of its tax-collecting activities on behalf of the government, because its creditors think well enough of it to ship supplies on credit, or because an accountant has decided to generate accruals in terms of future employee benefits. It does face risk through its interest-bearing debt. In this respect, analysts often "net out" interest-bearing debt by subtracting cash and marketable securities. In Rothmans' case, these two items total $130.231 million, almost equal to the amount of interest-bearing debt it holds. So in some sense Rothmans has very little debt. However, the bulk of cash and marketable securities is used in its operations or held for tax payment to the government. So in Rothmans' case, it would probably be appropriate only to subtract the excess of cash and short-term investments over taxes due (of $67.68 million), which leaves $62.551 million, but even this significantly reduces its true D/E ratio.

This discussion of the role of interest-bearing debt should remind you that not only is it important to determine the amount or stock of debt, but it is also equally, if not more, important to evaluate how much the debt costs. More generally we look at measures that indicate the *flow* of fixed commitments to income, which provides an estimate of a firm's ability to *service* its debt obligations. The most important of these measures is the **times interest earned (TIE)**, or coverage ratio, which is earnings before interest and taxes (EBIT) divided by interest expense (I), as shown in the equation below:

times interest earned (TIE) earnings before interest and taxes divided by interest expense; also called the *coverage ratio*

[4-10]

$$TIE = \frac{EBIT}{I}$$

We estimate the TIE for Rothmans in 2006 as shown below and calculate EBIT (of $281.414 million) by subtracting the amortization expense of $10.663 million from the earnings before interest, taxes, depreciation, and amortization (EBITDA) figure of $292.077 million found in Table 3-3 of Chapter 3.

$$TIE = \frac{EBIT}{I} = \frac{(292.077 - 10.663)}{6.585} = \frac{281.414}{6.585} = 42.736$$

So how do we evaluate the TIE? It means that for every dollar of interest expense, Rothmans' had almost $43 of income available to pay interest and taxes. This emphasizes how little risk Rothmans' debt imposes on its operations in relation to the profits it generates.[11]

A final ratio that is normally calculated is a mixture of the above ratios. The **cash flow to debt ratio** measures how long it would take to pay off a firm's debt (D) from its cash flow from operations (CFO). It is calculated as follows:

cash flow to debt ratio
how long it would take to pay off a firm's debt from its cash flow from operations; cash flow from operations divided by debt

$$Cash\ flow\ to\ debt\ ratio = \frac{CFO}{D}$$

[4-11]

For Rothmans in 2006

$$Cash\ flow\ to\ debt\ ratio = \frac{CFO}{D} = \frac{183.214}{149.751} = 1.22$$

Given its CFO of $183.214 million and its total debt outstanding of only $149.751 million, Rothmans could pay off all its debt within a year if it devoted its operating cash flow to debt repayment. This indicates, once again, Rothmans' very strong credit position.

So what is the overall assessment of Rothmans' leverage position in 2006? The debt ratio and the leverage ratio exaggerate Rothman's indebtedness because its short-term liabilities are inflated by its tax-collecting responsibilities. Its D/E ratio and interest coverage ratios better indicate the risk that interest-bearing debt imposes on the firm. In particular, although the D/E ratio is relatively high, the TIE ratio indicates that Rothmans' earnings can very easily support the required interest payments. This assessment is borne out once we net out interest expense and look at the ability of Rothmans to pay off its interest-bearing debt from cash flow from operations.

To gain additional insight, look at the trend in Rothmans' leverage ratios, and compare them with those of a comparable company or industry average, such as Altria. These ratios are included in Table 4-4.

---

[11] There are other coverage ratios, which are variations of the TIE that are adjusted to include the impact of other fixed charges, such as preferred share dividends, lease obligations, and sinking fund payments, but these will be discussed later when we talk about other contractual commitments attached to different types of securities.

Table 4-4	Leverage Ratios					
	Rothmans (March 31)			Altria (December 31)		
	2004	2005	2006	2003	2004	2005
Leverage	2.9482	2.7285	3.9441	3.8352	3.3095	3.0232
Debt ratio	0.6608	0.6335	0.7465	0.7393	0.6978	0.6692
D/E ratio	0.8902	0.7729	1.3152	0.9785	0.7482	0.6703
TIE	46.7842	36.1270	42.7356	13.7035	12.9082	14.3405
Cash flow to debt	1.5037	1.0823	1.2235	0.4408	0.4739	0.4621

The trend in Rothmans' leverage ratios (Table 4-4) shows that the amount of debt as a percentage of total financing increased substantially during 2006 from its 2004 and 2005 levels. In fact, the actual level of debt and total liabilities did not increase during the year; however, the leverage ratios increased because the amount of equity financing declined during the year as a result of the payment of a special dividend, as discussed above. In any event, the TIE ratio and the cash flow to debt ratio for Rothmans were both extremely high in 2006, as discussed above, and they were both higher than the 2005 figures, indicating that Rothmans can more than adequately cover its debt obligations.

Comparing Rothmans with Altria, Rothmans had a lower percentage of debt financing than Altria during 2004 and 2005 but had a higher percentage during 2006. However, Rothmans' TIE and cash flow to debt ratios indicate it could cover its debt obligations much easier than Altria could, with TIE ratios that were about three times as large as those for Altria and cash flow to debt ratios that were more than double those for Altria. Overall, Rothmans carries a relatively high amount of debt, but it generates more than enough profits and cash flows to easily service its debt obligations.

CONCEPT REVIEW QUESTIONS

1. Why is it important to look at stock and flow leverage ratios to assess a firm's debt situation?
2. Briefly explain what type of information is provided about a firm's leverage position by the debt ratio, the D/E ratio, the TIE ratio, and the cash flow to debt ratio.

4.4 EFFICIENCY RATIOS

efficiency ratios ratios that measure how efficiently a dollar of sales is turned into profits

Efficiency ratios measure how efficiently a dollar of sales is turned into profits, so we start with Rothmans' 2006 net profit margin of 15.25 percent, which is a very healthy figure. However, it is a measure of overall profitability, and frequently it is broken out into its major components. How it is done depends on the type of firm and the amount of data presented in its financial statements. Unfortunately, not all firms present a good breakdown of their cost structure, and this is the case with Rothmans.

When looking at a firm's cost structure, economists like to think in terms of variable and fixed costs, where variable costs vary with the amount of production and sales and fixed costs do not. Suppose a firm has sales of $120 and variable costs of $72 or 60 percent of sales. This means that the firm has a *contribution margin* of 40 percent, or $48 is available to contribute to the firm's fixed costs and profits. With fixed operating costs of $31 and fixed interest costs of $5, the firm has taxable income of $12. With a 50 percent income tax rate, its net income and taxes are both $6, and it has a net profit margin of 5 percent. This example is illustrated in Table 4-5, which also shows what happens with a 10 percent increase and decrease in sales.

Table 4-5   Profit Margin and Sales Variability

Sales	120	132	108
Contribution margin (40%)	48	53	43
Fixed cost	31	51	31
Interest	5	5	5
Tax	6	8.5	3.5
Net income	6	8.5	3.5
Net profit margin	5.0%	6.4%	3.2%

If the firm sells more and sales increase to $132, then only the variable costs increase. The gross profit, which is sales minus variable costs, also increases by 10 percent to $53. However, because the fixed production and interest costs stay the same, the taxable income increases from $12 to $17 or 40 percent, and the net profit margin increases to 6.4 percent. Conversely, if sales decrease by 10 percent to $108, the process works in reverse and the existence of the fixed costs causes net income to drop by 40 percent.[12]

The above example indicates that the more fixed costs the firm has, the greater its income variability. Note that although sales varied by +/−10 percent, net income varied by +/−40 percent. We will discuss this more in Chapters 20 and 21, when we discuss the financial and business risk of the firm. However, we can estimate the **degree of total leverage (DTL)** as the contribution margin (CM) divided by the earnings before taxes (EBT).[13]

degree of total leverage (DTL) contribution margin divided by earnings before taxes

$$DTL = \frac{CM}{EBT}$$

[4-12]

---

[12] The actual numbers are rounded.

[13] We don't use net income to estimate the DTL. With a 50 percent tax rate, half the gain accrues to the government in income taxes because income taxes are not a fixed payment.

For the previous example,

$$DTL = \frac{CM}{EBT} = \frac{48}{12} = 4.0$$

break-even point (BEP)
the level of sales at
which the firm covers all
its operating and finan-
cial costs; total operating
and fixed costs divided
by the contribution
margin ratio

The DTL for our example firm shows a very significant exposure of profits to variability in sales, because every 1 percent change in sales causes a 4 percent change in earnings before taxes. This exposure depends on the firm's cost structure, which is crucial to the risk of the firm. It also allows the firm to estimate its **break-even point (BEP)**, which is the level of sales at which the firm covers all its operating and financial costs. In the above example, the firm needs revenues of $90 to cover these costs; if revenues fall below this level, it loses money.

This $90 break-even point is calculated as the total operating and fixed costs (FC) divided by the contribution margin ratio, as shown below:

[4-13]

$$BEP = \frac{FC}{CM}$$

For our example firm,

$$BEP = \frac{FC}{CM} = \frac{\$31 + \$5}{0.40} = \$90$$

The contribution margin ratio is just the complement of the variable costs as a percentage of sales, so with variable costs at 60 percent of sales, the contribution margin is 40 percent or 0.40. Dividing the fixed operating and financial costs of $36 by 40 percent produces the break-even point of $90.

Clearly, it is important for the firm to know its break-even point and how its profits vary with sales. As a result, internally it will have the information to estimate these important values. However, externally, the firm is not required to present this information in its financial statements. Further, the proxies that are available are often poor. From your managerial cost accounting course, you know that cost of goods sold includes variable production costs, as well as the allocation of factory overhead—that is, it includes fixed costs. If the firm does only one thing, this factory overhead can include almost all of its operating fixed costs, as it does for Rothmans. Unfortunately, what is presented for Rothmans does not allow a break-out of variable and fixed costs, so we cannot estimate its break-even point or contribution margin, or the sensitivity of its profits to sales increases or decreases.

However, consistent with the basic idea of calculating the contribution margin, that is, revenues minus variable costs, we can calculate a variation of it: the **gross profit margin**. This ratio is defined as sales (S) minus the cost of goods sold (CGS) divided by sales, which is shown below:

gross profit margin sales
minus the cost of goods
sold divided by sales

[4-14]

$$Gross\ profit\ margin = \frac{S - CGS}{S}$$

For Rothmans in 2006,[14]

$$Gross\ profit\ margin = \frac{S - CGS}{S} = \frac{652.271 - 363.545}{652.271} = 0.4426$$

---

[14] Note that we did not include Rothmans' investment income as part of sales revenues, because this may be income from temporary investments and we are interested in the profitability of Rothmans' operations.

A gross margin of 44.26 percent indicates that after excise taxes, 44.26 percent of Rothmans' sales is available to cover its non-production costs. Alternatively, only 55.74 percent of Rothmans' sales actually goes to expenses associated with making cigarettes.

The other expenses, apart from cost of goods sold, that firms normally incur are period costs, which are often loosely called fixed costs, because, in the short run, they are unrelated to sales revenues. These costs consist of advertising, research and development, general sales and administrative expenses, and amortization expenses. For Rothmans, these expenses were relatively trivial in 2006 at $10.663 million and represent amortization expenses. Other expenses that might be classified as period costs are included by Rothmans in its cost of goods sold, because all it does is produce cigarettes.[15]

The final ratio is the **operating margin**, which is defined as net operating income divided by sales, as shown below:

operating margin net operating income divided by sales

$$Operating\ margin = \frac{NOI}{Sales}$$

[4-15]

For Rothmans, this ratio is relatively easy to calculate, but this is not always the case. Note that in the income statement for Rothmans, we estimated EBITDA, or earnings before interest, tax, depreciation, and amortization. EBITDA is frequently used as a measure of operating cash flow because it is taken before the non-cash items, depreciation, and amortization are deducted. Many analysts use EBITDA in their calculations, because it is a "harder" number than net operating income as it is less susceptible to the effects of accounting judgement.

The EBITDA figure for Rothmans in 2006 was $292.077 million. However, this figure may not truly reflect Rothmans' operations because it includes investment income, as well as sales revenues. This is a special form of investment income; it is not generated by making short-term investments but by extending credit to customers. If a company provides trade credit, that is, it allows a customer to pay 30 or 60 days after delivery, the customer implicitly pays a slightly higher price than it would for a cash sale. We will talk about trade credit in Chapter 24, but if all Rothmans' sales were cash sales, its EBITDA would be lower by this investment income figure of $3.351 million, leaving $288.726 million. **Net operating income (NOI)** is then calculated as this adjusted version of EBITDA minus the $10.663 million of amortization expense, or $278.063 million. We would note here that EBIT is simply this net operating income figure plus the $3.351 million in investment income, or $281.414 million, which is the figure we used above to calculate the TIE ratio.

net operating income (NOI) the adjusted earnings before interest, taxes, depreciation, and amortization minus amortization

We will be using these different definitions of income frequently in the text, so be sure you know the differences among gross profit, contribution margin, EBITDA, net operating income, EBIT, and net income. We will use net operating income to calculate the operating margin, but note that although conceptually this is correct, in many cases firms do not break out their revenues as diligently as Rothmans. As a result, the operating margin is often calculated by using EBITDA or EBIT as well as NOI. For Rothmans, the operating margin was

$$Operating\ margin = \frac{NOI}{S} = \frac{278.063}{652.271} = 0.4263$$

---

[15] It could also be that the ban on cigarette advertising and the fact that cigarettes are a mature product mean that these costs are not material.

For reference, 42.63 percent is a very high operating margin, but given the way Rothmans presents its financial statements little value is added to what we know from its gross profit margin. In any event, Table 4-6 provides the efficiency ratios for Rothmans and Altria for the past three fiscal years, which allows us to further evaluate Rothmans' efficiency results. We can see that Rothmans has maintained steady profitability, with very little variability in its net profit margins, gross profit margins, and operating margins. Altria also displayed little variability in these ratios, with all of the margins being consistently lower than those for Rothmans. In short, Table 4-6 confirms that Rothmans has displayed consistent, strong profitability.

Table 4-6   Efficiency Ratios

	Rothmans (March 31)			Altria (December 31)		
	2004	2005	2006	2003	2004	2005
Net profit margin	0.1456	0.1460	0.1525	0.1132	0.1051	0.1066
Gross profit margin	0.4261	0.4305	0.4426	0.3519	0.3348	0.3286
Operating margin	0.4102	0.4155	0.4263	0.1938	0.1867	0.1696

CONCEPT REVIEW QUESTIONS

1. What useful information is provided by the contribution margin, the degree of total leverage, and the break-even point?

2. Why is it uncommon to see the three ratios above reported by companies for external users of their financial statements?

3. What useful information is provided by the net profit margin, the gross profit margin, and the operating margin?

4.5 PRODUCTIVITY RATIOS

productivity ratios
measurements of how productive the firm is in generating sales from its assets

receivables turnover
sales divided by accounts receivable

If the efficiency ratios measure how efficiently the firm turns sales into profits, the next question is how productive the firm is in generating sales from its assets. You saw that the turnover ratio is sales divided by total assets, so the key to looking at different **productivity ratios** is to look at variations of the turnover ratio for each major asset class. For example, we can see how productive the firm is in using receivables, inventory, and plant and equipment, because these are the major categories of assets that all firms have.

We begin by defining the **receivables turnover** ratio as sales (S) divided by accounts receivables (AR).

$$Receivables\ turnover = \frac{S}{AR}$$ sales / account receivables.   [4-16]

For Rothmans in 2006,

$$Receivables\ turnover = \frac{S}{AR} = \frac{652.271}{11.795} = 55.30$$

For every dollar invested in receivables (i.e., credit extended to purchasers), Rothmans generated $55.30 in sales. Alternatively, we can say that Rothmans turned its AR account over 55.30 times during the year, on average.

The turnover ratio is useful, but it is common to calculate a variation of it called the **average collection period (ACP)**. To do this, divide the average daily _credit_ sales into the accounts receivable, because only credit sales generate receivables; cash sales, obviously, generate cash! However, Rothmans, like most companies, does not break out sales into cash and credit sales, at least not in its external financial statements. Therefore, it is common to use average daily sales (ADS) in the denominator, which equals annual sales divided by the 365 days in a year. When we define ACP in this manner, ACP is 365 divided by the receivables turnover ratio, because if AR are "turned over" 10 times a year, it implies that the firm takes an average of 36.5 days to collect on its AR. Therefore, we can define the ACP as

average collection period (ACP) accounts receivable divided by the average daily _credit_ sales

$$ACP = \frac{AR}{ADS} = \frac{365}{Receivables\ turnover}$$ [4-17]

For Rothmans in 2006,

$$ACP = \frac{AR}{ADS} = \frac{11.795}{(652.271/365)} = \frac{11.795}{1.787044} = 6.60\ days$$

Notice that 6.60 days also equals 365 divided by the receivables turnover ratio of 55.30. So if Rothmans sales were all on credit, as they probably were since it does not sell direct to retailers, at the end of 2006 its customers were paying on average 6.60 days after purchase. If the collection period lengthened, we would check to see whether Rothmans had changed its credit terms to stimulate sales or whether its customers were simply delaying payment because of poor economic conditions.

The second major current asset category is inventory. For Rothmans, this is $206.433 million in 2006 and consists of leaf tobacco ($95.542 million), finished cigarettes ($88.839 million), and packaging materials ($22.052 million). These amounts reflect the standard division of inventory into finished goods and raw materials. Conceptually, the **inventory turnover** ratio is calculated as the cost of goods sold divided by inventory, because when a widget is sold, its financial cost moves from inventory (INV) and is expensed through cost of goods sold.

inventory turnover the cost of goods sold (or sales) divided by inventory

$$Inventory\ turnover = \frac{CGS}{INV}$$ [4-18]

For Rothmans in 2006,

$$Inventory\ turnover = \frac{CGS}{INV} = \frac{363.545}{206.433} = 1.76$$

As we might expect, Rothmans keeps a significant amount of inventory on hand as tobacco leaf is a seasonal crop, while consumption and sales of cigarettes are not.

For some firms, the data on cost of goods sold is not reliable because of accounting differences in how such items as factory overhead are treated. As a result, the cost of goods sold is often replaced by sales in the inventory turnover ratio, which leaves the following:

[4-19]

$$Inventory\ turnover = \frac{S}{INV}$$

When we calculate Rothmans' 2006 inventory turnover ratio by using this equation,

$$Inventory\ turnover = \frac{S}{INV} = \frac{652.271}{206.433} = 3.16$$

Notice the large difference in the inventory turnover ratio figures, depending on which version of the two equations above are used. This difference makes it very obvious why we have stressed the importance of determining precisely how a ratio is calculated.

average days sales in inventory (ADSI) inventory divided by average daily sales

Similar to what we did with the receivables turnover ratio, it is common to invert the inventory turnover ratio and call it the **average days sales in inventory (ADSI)**:

[4-20]

$$Average\ days\ sales\ in\ inventory\ (ADSI) = \frac{INV}{ADS} = \frac{365}{Inventory\ turnover}$$

For Rothmans in 2006, we obtain the following:

$$ADSI = \frac{INV}{ADS} = \frac{206.433}{(652.271/365)} = 115.52\ days$$

Notice that this equals approximately 365 divided by the inventory turnover ratio calculated by using sales of 3.16. So in 2006, Rothmans had 115.5 days of sales tied up in inventory and only 6.6 in receivables.

fixed asset turnover sales divided by net fixed assets

The final productivity ratio is the **fixed asset turnover** ratio, calculated as sales divided by net fixed assets (NFA), which is simply the depreciated value of the fixed assets:

[4-21]

$$Fixed\ asset\ turnover = \frac{S}{NFA}$$

For Rothmans in 2006,

$$Fixed\ asset\ turnover = \frac{S}{NFA} = \frac{652.271}{76.298} = 8.55$$

For Rothmans, this ratio very high, because the production process for cigarettes is relatively simple, most of its assets are well depreciated, and cigarette manufacturing in North America is not a growth industry. As firms depreciate their assets, the fixed asset turnover ratio automatically increases, so many analysts also look at the fixed asset turnover ratio by using gross assets, which is the undepreciated cost of the fixed assets (i.e., without any depreciation deducted). Rothmans had property, plant, and equipment (fixed assets) with an initial cost in 2006 of $212.474 million but had taken depreciation in previous years of $136.176 million. So its fixed assets are 64 percent depreciated. In fact, given that firms depreciate their assets more quickly for tax purposes than they do for their financial statements, this explains the unusual situation discussed in Chapter 3: Rothmans paid more in actual income taxes in 2004 and 2005 than it reported on its financial statements.[16]

We now provide some context for Rothmans' 2006 ratios as calculated above by reporting its historical ratios, as well as those for Altria, in Table 4-7.

Table 4-7   Productivity Ratios

	Rothmans (March 31)			Altria (December 31)		
	2004	2005	2006	2003	2004	2005
Turnover	1.2483	1.2048	1.4525	0.8455	0.8816	0.9065
Receivables turnover	19.3825	19.8254	55.3006	NA	15.5735	18.2529
ACP	18.8314	18.4108	6.6003	NA	23.4372	19.9968
Inventory turnover (using sales)	3.1170	3.0349	3.1597	8.5241	8.9244	9.2455
ADSI	117.0988	120.2692	115.5165	42.8197	40.8991	39.4788
Fixed asset turnover	11.0158	9.2087	8.5490	5.0613	5.4959	5.8673

There are several things to note from Table 4-7. First, Rothmans' turnover, receivables turnover, and inventory turnover ratios all increased during 2006, with its total asset turnover ratios exceeding those for Altria. Of particular note is the dramatic increase in the receivables turnover ratio, which increased from 19.8 to 55.3, resulting in an ACP of 6.6 days, which is well below the previous

[16] In simple terms, its CCA, or tax depreciation, was less than the depreciation in its financial statements, so it was reporting more income to Canada Revenue Agency (Revenue Canada) than shown in its financial statements.

year's ACP of 18.4 days. As a result, Rothmans' ACP was well below that of Altria in 2006 but had been similar to Altria's in the two previous years. Conversely, while Rothmans' inventory turnover ratio improved slightly in 2006, it remained much lower than Altria's ratios, which is not a good thing.

In addition, Rothmans' fixed asset turnover ratio declined from 2004 to 2006. However, this reflects steady investment in plant and equipment, which exceeded amortization expense during those years, since sales actually increased. Therefore, it would be hard to view this as a negative trend, especially given the fact, as noted, that a large proportion of Rothmans' assets had been depreciated by 2006. In fact, Rothmans' fixed asset turnover exceeded Altria's in all three years, and part of the reason was the amount that Rothmans' assets had depreciated. For example, although Rothmans' fixed assets had been 64 percent depreciated as of 2006, Altria's fixed assets had only been 44 percent depreciated.

CONCEPT REVIEW QUESTIONS

1. What information can be gained from examining a firm's receivables turnover, inventory turnover, and fixed asset turnover ratios?

2. Why is it common to estimate the ACP by using total sales rather than credit sales, and to estimate inventory turnover by using sales rather than cost of goods sold?

4.6 LIQUIDITY

As we discussed previously, DuPont analysis shows that, together, the leverage, efficiency, and productivity ratios help explain a firm's good or poor performance in terms of ROE. However, some financial statement users have a different interest when examining financial statements. Banks, for example, and suppliers shipping to Rothmans on credit, want to know whether it has the means to pay off its debts. This leads to a focus on the liquidity of the company. As we discussed previously, **liquidity** refers to how easily something can be converted into cash.

The focus in analyzing the liquidity of the company is on the overall liquidity of a firm's assets and on the available assets to meet current liabilities. In terms of overall liquidity we look at the ratio of current assets (CA) to total assets (TA). This is referred to as the **working capital ratio**, because current assets are often called **working capital**. This is defined below:

liquidity the ease with which something can be converted into cash

working capital ratio current assets divided by total assets

working capital current assets

[4-22]

$$\text{Working capital ratio} = \frac{CA}{TA}$$

For Rothmans in 2006,

$$\text{Working capital ratio} = \frac{CA}{TA} = \frac{350.294}{449.075} = 0.7800$$

For Rothmans, this ratio indicates that its assets are extremely liquid, with 78 percent supposedly converting to cash within a year. Overall, Rothmans' balance sheet is very liquid, indicating relatively small amounts of net fixed assets and large amounts of current assets. So how liquid are these current assets?

One of the most important liquidity ratios is the **current ratio**, also called the bankers' ratio, which is estimated as current assets divided by current liabilities (CL):

current ratio also called the *bankers' ratio*; current assets divided by current liabilities

$$Current\ ratio = \frac{CA}{CL}$$

[4-23]

For Rothmans in 2006,

$$Current\ ratio = \frac{CA}{CL} = \frac{350.294}{141.496} = 2.48$$

Rothmans has $2.48 in current assets for every dollar in current liabilities. This ratio is important for bankers because bank loans are normally short term and included in current liabilities. So a current ratio of almost 2.48 means that many assets will be soon converted to cash and may be available to help pay off a bank loan. However, if a bank has to seize assets or force a firm to liquidate assets, then it is a sign that some of its assets are probably not worth much. In particular, the inventory of a bankrupt or failing firm is normally not worth its book value, while it is unlikely a creditor could ever recover any funds from prepaid expenses. For this reason banks also look at the **quick ratio**, or **acid test ratio**, which is cash (C) plus marketable securities (MS) plus accounts receivable (AR) divided by current liabilities, as shown below:[17]

quick ratio or **acid test ratio** cash plus marketable securities plus accounts receivable divided by current liabilities

$$Quick\ ratio = \frac{C + MS + AR}{CL}$$

[4-24]

For Rothmans in 2006,

$$Quick\ ratio = \frac{C + MS + AR}{CL} = \frac{48.364 + 81.867 + 11.795}{141.496} = \frac{142.026}{141.496} = 1.00$$

For Rothmans in 2006, the quick ratio is less than half its current ratio. This occurs because its largest current asset is its inventory of more than $200 million, which is close to 60 percent of Rothmans' current assets. When this figure is removed, its liquidity reduces dramatically.

Table 4-8 contains the current and quick ratios for Rothmans and Altria over the 2004 to 2006 period. Rothmans' liquidity ratios deteriorated over this period, but they were still much more liquid than Altria's, according to all three measures. Note here that the reason for the decline in these ratios is the sharp reduction in accounts receivable during 2006, which corresponds to the large increase in receivables turnover noted above. Although this does not look good when reflected in the liquidity ratios included in Table 4-8, collecting receivables faster can hardly be viewed as a negative thing, unless it adversely affects sales or profit margins, which doesn't appear to be the case for Rothmans. This highlights one of the most important facets of ratio analysis that we have already touched on several times—ratios cannot be looked at in isolation!

---

[17] Sometimes the quick ratio is calculated as current assets minus inventory divided by current liabilities, which would include prepaid expenses.

Table 4-8   Liquidity Ratios

	Rothmans (March 31)			Altria (December 31)		
	2004	2005	2006	2003	2004	2005
Current ratio	2.8868	2.9310	2.4756	NA	1.0987	0.9856
Quick ratio	1.4981	1.5092	1.0037	NA	0.4877	0.4442
Working capital ratio	0.8414	0.8235	0.7800	NA	0.2548	0.2388

Before we proceed to the next section, we elaborate on the concept of adjusting book values to realizable values in the event of bankruptcy. We introduced this concept when we treated inventory as worthless in calculating the quick ratio, which is an extreme example of asset adjustment. E-Trade Canada has an interesting way of estimating realizable values, as depicted in Table 4-9.

Table 4-9   E-Trade Canada's Risk Ratings

Growth Rates	2006	2005	2004	2003
Net ROA %	22.15	17.60	18.17	20.16
Long-term debt growth (YTY %)	0.03	(0.19)	0.00	N/A
Asset growth (YTY %)	(15.03)	6.40	15.53	N/A
Components of Net Liquidated Value				
Cash @ 100%	130,231	191,995	184,907	113,270
Marketable securities @ 98%	N/A	N/A	N/A	N/A
Receivables @ 90%	10,616	28,907	28,794	75,373
Other current assets @ 80%	1,468	1,058	1,698	2,027
Inventory @ 50%	103,217	104,910	99,471	76,767
Net plant @ 25%	19,075	17,287	14,073	13,654
Total Liquid Assets	**264,606**	**344,156**	**328,943**	**281,091**
Current liabilities (100%)	141,496	148,498	144,786	110,964
	123,110	195,658	184,157	170,127
Long-term debt (100%)	149,751	149,708	150,000	150,000
	(26,642)	45,950	34,157	20,127
Other liabilities (100%)	10,761	0	0	0
	(37,403)	45,950	34,157	20,127
Net of Liabilities	**(37,403)**	**45,950**	**34,157**	**20,127**
−Preferred stock	0	0	0	0
= Net Liquid Value	**(37,403)**	**45,950**	**34,157**	**20,127**
Average shares	67,745	67,492	33,610	33,299
Net Liquid Value per Share	**(0.55)**	**0.68**	**1.02**	**0.60**

Source: Data from E-Trade Canada.

E-Trade Canada looks at these data as a risk ranking, but the objective is really to estimate a realizable value. It begins by reporting the ROA for Rothmans, because, ultimately, risk stems from winding up the company and profitable companies do not go bankrupt! It then looks at the trend growth rate in debt, which has been virtually zero over the 2004 to 2006 period. Rothmans actually displayed negative asset growth in 2006 as a result of the special dividend discussed previously; however, its asset growth was positive in the prior two years.

Of more importance for our present purposes is the asset adjustment analysis. E-Trade Canada values cash at 100 percent of its book value, because it is cash. Marketable securities are then worth 98 percent; receivables, 90 percent; other current assets, 80 percent; inventory, 50 percent; and net plant, 25 percent. For Rothmans in 2006, the adjusted value of the total assets is $264.606 million. From this, E-Trade Canada subtracts Rothmans' liabilities and long-term debt of $302.008 million to get a net realizable value of −$37.403 million. This produces an answer of −$0.55 per share when divided by the number of shares outstanding.

Several things are important in E-Trade Canada's analysis. First, it uses the same adjustments for all companies, so the analysis allows easy comparisons across companies. Second, as we would expect, the discounts from book value increase as the liquidity of the asset deteriorates; for example, receivables are worth 90 percent; inventories, 50 percent; and fixed assets, only 25 percent. This occurs because a bank seizing the receivables has to wait only 30 or 60 days for customers to pay their bills. In contrast, the inventory of a failed firm is often not worth much, while plant and equipment often entail significant costs in physically removing them from one location and transporting to another. Finally, for Rothmans in 2006, the number is negative, which implies that if the company was shut down, insufficient funds would be generated by a company-wide liquidation to pay off all creditors. In contrast, Rothmans' liquidation values for the previous three years were all positive, albeit quite small, especially in relation to its market price per share.

What is of interest is that Rothmans' share price at the end of March 2006 was $20.25, a full $20.80 above its net liquid value per share of −$0.55. The reason for this is that Rothmans is a going concern and not just any going concern but an extremely profitable one; the value of the assets in use is significantly more than their value to someone else. This leads to the final set of ratios that analysts often consider, which includes valuation ratios. These summarize how the market values the firm's operations.

CONCEPT REVIEW QUESTIONS

1. What type of financial statement user will be most interested in a firm's liquidity ratios?

2. What useful information do we obtain from a firm's working capital, and current, and quick ratios?

3. Why might bankers focus more on the quick ratio than on the current ratio?

4.7 VALUATION RATIOS

We will discuss common share valuation in Chapter 7, but at this stage we introduce some of the standard ratios that people look at to understand the *relative valuation* of a company. We started this by looking at the net liquid value per share of Rothmans, which E-Trade Canada estimated at -$0.55 in 2006. E-Trade Canada put this value on a per share basis so that it can be contrasted with the share price.

Some ratios that are useful in assessing a firm's relative value include the earnings per share (EPS), which has been discussed previously, and the **equity book value per share (BVPS)**, which is the ending shareholders' equity (SE) divided by the ending number of shares outstanding.

equity book value per share (BVPS) shareholders' equity divided by the number of shares outstanding

[4-25]

$$BVPS = \frac{SE}{Number\ of\ shares}$$

For Rothmans in 2006,

$$BVPS = \frac{SE}{Number\ of\ shares} = \frac{\$113.860}{67.856} = \$1.678$$

In 2004, Rothmans doubled the number of shares outstanding from the 33.610 million shares by using a two-for-one share split, which essentially gave every shareholder another share for each one already owned. We will discuss later why Rothmans did this, but it reminds us that analysts should always pay attention to changes in the number of shares outstanding when looking at per share data. For example, the actual diluted EPS figures that were reported each year for 2002 to 2005 were $2.74, $2.58, $2.68, and $1.37. This might lead an unsuspecting analyst to conclude that 2005 was a poor year, when what happened was that each shareholder received another share for each one already held. Usually, reporters of financial information will adjust the previous per share values to reflect any changes in the number of shares outstanding. That is why in Table 3-3 of Chapter 3, we reported diluted EPS figures of $1.34 and $1.37 for 2004 and 2005, respectively; the 2004 EPS figure had been adjusted to reflect the two-for-one split.

dividend yield the dividend per share divided by the share price

In terms of valuation, one of the most basic ratios an analyst can look at is a company's **dividend yield**, which is the current dividend per share (DPS) divided by the current share price (P).

[4-26]

$$Dividend\ yield = \frac{DPS}{P}$$

For Rothmans, the 2006 DPS was $2.70, so at a share price of $20.25,

$$Dividend\ yield = \frac{DPS}{P} = \frac{2.70}{20.25} = 0.1333$$

A dividend yield of 13.33 percent is extremely high, and when we look at Rothmans' historical dividend yields, this figure is out of line with previous yields. The reason for this is that $1.50 of the total DPS of $2.70 was a special one-time dividend. If we replace the $2.70 figure with the regular dividend amount of $1.20, we get the following:

$$Dividend\ yield = \frac{DPS}{P} = \frac{1.20}{20.25} = 0.0593$$

This dividend yield of 5.93 percent is much more reasonable, but even this dividend yield would be regarded as high, because at that time yields on long Canada bonds were less than 5 percent. It is also higher than its 2004 and 2005 values of 4.7 percent and 4.4 percent, respectively. Equation 4-26 tells us that a high dividend yield can be caused by high dividend payouts or low share prices or both. Because investors are concerned about the firm's ability to sustain its dividend payments, one ratio that is useful to assess this ability is the **dividend payout** ratio, which is the DPS divided by the EPS, as shown below:

dividend payout the dividend per share divided by the earnings per share

$$Dividend\ payout = \frac{DPS}{EPS}$$

[4-27]

We will use the diluted EPS in this equation, although it is also common to use the basic EPS figure. For Rothmans in 2006, we obtain the following:

$$Dividend\ payout = \frac{DPS}{EPS} = \frac{2.70}{1.45} = 1.8621$$

This ratio implies that during 2006, Rothmans paid out 186.21 percent of its earnings as dividends, which is obviously not a sustainable long-term policy, because the firm would eventually liquidate itself. However, we must again account for the $1.50 special dividend, which leaves us with a dividend payout of

$$Dividend\ payout = \frac{DPS}{EPS} = \frac{1.20}{1.45} = 0.8276$$

So, this tells us that Rothmans paid out almost 83 percent of its earnings as regular dividends, which is also a very high percentage. We would expect this from a *low-growth* business, such as Rothmans. However, it is still retaining some money within the business, and given its overall low growth rate, there is little reason to retain more or believe that it can't maintain its dividend.

One of the most important and widely followed value ratios is the **price-earnings (P/E) ratio**, which is estimated as the share price (P) divided by the EPS, as shown below:

price-earnings (P/E) ratio the share price divided by the earnings per share

$$P/E = \frac{P}{EPS}$$

[4-28]

Similar to the dividend payout ratio, we use the diluted EPS figure in the denominator, rather than the basic EPS (which is sometimes used).

For Rothmans in 2006,

$$P/E = \frac{P}{EPS} = \frac{20.25}{1.45} = 13.97$$

This means that investors were willing to pay $13.97 for $1 of Rothmans' 2006 earnings. The higher the ratio, the more investors will pay, and vice versa. We will discuss the determinants of P/E ratios at some length in Chapter 7 but will note here that P/E ratios increase when share prices increase or when EPS declines. Usually, analysts focus on prices, which are reflected in the numerator of the P/E, and some would argue that a company's shares become too expensive when its P/E ratio gets too high. Conversely, others might argue that a high P/E ratio is warranted because they expect substantial growth in the company's future earnings or because they feel that the company's shares represent a relatively low-risk investment. In either event, from the firm's point of view, higher P/E ratios are a good thing, because they suggest that the markets have confidence in the firm, all else being equal. Remember, in Chapter 2 we suggested that the goal of the firm is to maximize shareholder wealth, which is reflected in share price.

The P/E ratio estimated above is based on the *trailing*, or last year's, EPS and is sometimes called the trailing P/E ratio. However, Rothmans' fiscal year runs until the end of March, so at the time of writing this EPS was more than six months old. The analysts following Rothmans and making recommendations to investors estimated its 2007 fiscal EPS figure at $1.41, based on the fact that the six-month results had already been reported. When we estimate the P/E ratio based on the current price and by using a forecast or expected EPS (EEPS) figure, we refer to it as the **forward P/E ratio**, as shown below:

forward P/E ratio share price divided by the expected earnings per share

[4-29]

$$Forward\ P/E = \frac{P}{EEPS}$$

At the time of writing, the 2007 EPS estimate for Rothmans was $1.41, while its share price was $20.96, leaving us with a forward P/E ratio of

$$Forward\ P/E = \frac{P}{EEPS} = 14.87$$

Security analysts recommending companies tend to use forward P/E ratios because they normally make shares look cheaper (i.e., as long as EPS continues to increase).

A forward P/E ratio of 14.87 means that if an investor held the stock for almost 15 years and the EPS stayed the same, you would get back in profits the $20.96 that you paid for it. In this sense, the P/E ratio is a simple example of a *payback period*, which will be discussed in Chapter 13. The higher the P/E ratio, the longer the shareholder has to wait to recover the cost of their investment in future profits. Generally, low P/E shares are regarded as *value* stocks, since the payback period is lower and there is less emphasis on any growth in the forecast EPS. In contrast, high P/E shares are generally regarded as *growth* stocks, because investors are relying more heavily on future growth in the EPS.

The P/E ratio and dividend yield are useful value indicators for many firms. However, P/E ratios are meaningless when EPS is negative or is very low, while dividend yields will equal zero for firms that do not pay dividends. In such cases, analysts look for other ratios that provide an indication of a firm's relative value, and many relative value ratios exist. One commonly used ratio is the **market-to-book (M/B) ratio**, which is defined as the market price per share (P) divided by the book value per share (BVPS), as shown below:

market-to-book (M/B) ratio the market price per share divided by the book value per share

$$M/B = \frac{P}{BVPS}$$

[4-30]

Using the 2006 book value and year-end price for Rothmans,

$$M/B = \frac{P}{BVPS} = \frac{20.25}{1.678} = 12.07$$

This ratio indicates that every dollar invested by the shareholders in Rothmans was worth $12.07 as of the end of March 2006. A dollar invested in Rothmans operations is worth $12.07 in part because of Rothmans' ROE of 87.36 percent. This ROE is so good, and so much better than what investors can get elsewhere, that they have bid up the share price to well above its book value. Remember E-Trade Canada's estimate that if liquidated, Rothmans' net liquid assets could not cover its liabilities. Clearly, making cigarettes in Canada continues to be an extremely profitable business.

Finally, another valuation ratio that is often considered is the **EBITDA multiple**, which is calculated as the **total enterprise value (TEV)** divided by EBITDA, which is shown below:

EBITDA multiple the total enterprise value divided by earnings before interest, taxes, depreciation, and amortization

total enterprise value (TEV) equity market value plus the market value of the firm's debt

$$EBITDA\ multiple = \frac{TEV}{EBITDA}$$

[4-31]

The total enterprise value is an estimate of the total market value of the firm, which equals the equity market value plus the market value of the firm's debt. This is the market value of what we called *invested capital* when we looked at the firm's financial statements. For Rothmans, its March 31, 2006, equity market value at a $20.25 share price with 67.856 million shares outstanding was $1,374.084 million. Usually, it is reasonable to assume that the book value of debt provides a sufficient approximation of its market value; although this will not always be the case.[18] We will make this assumption for Rothmans' debt in 2006. Therefore, we add the amount of Rothmans' total debt outstanding of $149.751 million to the market value of its equity and estimate its total enterprise value at $1,523.835 million. Combining this with Rothmans' 2006 EBITDA of $292.077 million,

$$EBITDA\ multiple = \frac{TEV}{EBITDA} = \frac{1,523.835}{292.077} = 5.22$$

This ratio is of particular interest when a firm is considering the takeover or purchase of another firm, since it values the whole firm and not just the common equity. It also recognizes that the firm can always issue or buy back common equity and debt.

For Rothmans, an EBITDA multiple of 5.22 seems to be relatively high, indicating the relatively high market prices that existed in the mid 2000s. However, as with all ratios, it is important to put the ratios in context, and for this purpose, Table 4-10 reports the value ratios for Rothmans and Altria over 2004 to 2006.

---

[18] We will elaborate in Chapter 6 on why this assumption may not be reasonable.

Table 4-10 Value Ratios	Rothmans (March 31)			Altria (December 31)		
	2004	**2005**	**2006**	**2003**	**2004**	**2005**
Dividend yield	0.0474	0.0438	0.1333	0.0485	0.0462	0.0410
Dividend payout	0.6063	0.7664	1.8621	0.5841	0.6184	0.6132
P/E	12.7799	17.5109	13.9655	12.0398	13.3991	14.9739
M/B	6.8451	8.3685	12.0682	4.4208	4.0979	4.3619
EBITDA multiple	4.8535	6.3545	5.2095	7.8436	8.8194	9.7774
Dividend yield (excl. special dividend)	NA	NA	0.0593	NA	NA	NA
Dividend payout (excl. special dividend)	NA	NA	0.8276	NA	NA	NA

By using the dividend ratios in Table 4-10 for Rothmans that exclude the 2006 special dividend, we can see that its 2006 dividend yield of 5.93 percent was higher than its 2004 and 2005 values, and that it also exceeds Altria's 2005 dividend yield of 4.10 percent. These observations are consistent with Rothmans' dividend payout ratio, which increased to 82.76 percent during 2006 and exceeded Altria's payout ratio of 61.32 percent. Rothmans' 2006 P/E ratio was in line with its previous ratios and was slightly less than the one for Altria in 2005. However, Rothmans' M/B ratio increased dramatically during 2006 and was almost three times as large as Altria's 2005 figure. Of course, this difference can be easily explained by the decline in equity that resulted from the large special dividend during 2006. The fact that Rothmans' M/B ratio was also much higher than Altria's in the two prior years is at least partially attributable to the high level of depreciation associated with Rothmans' fixed assets that we noted earlier. Finally, Rothmans' EBITDA multiples were relatively stable in the 4.8 to 6.3 range but were consistently much less than those for Altria. This disparity is likely due to differences in the manner in which each company computes EBITDA.

Overall, we get mixed signals from our analysis of the value ratios provided in Table 4-10. On the one hand, based on the P/E ratios and dividend yield figures, it appears that Rothmans was valued similarly to Altria. On the other hand, the M/B ratios make Rothmans appear to be more expensive than Altria, while the EBITDA multiple makes Rothmans look less expensive. These conflicting conclusions could be the result of the ratios being based on different ending periods (December 2005 versus March 2006), the use of different accounting standards that affect the calculation of EBITDA and BVPS, and so on. On balance, it appears that Rothmans is modestly priced, based on its moderate P/E ratios and high dividend yields, which are lower than, but are also consistent with, its historical ratios and those for Altria.

Concluding Comments on Valuation Ratios

Overall what do we make of Rothmans as a potential investment? Our financial analysis indicates that it has a relatively high absolute level of debt, but that the company can easily service its debt obligations from existing operating profits and cash flows. It also possesses high operating margins and good turnover, so it is exceptionally profitable. Moreover, this profitability is not a sudden aberration; it has been in place for some time and is expected to continue in the future. This constancy is reflected in its stock price, which is a whopping 12 times its book value per share. Despite this very high M/B ratio, Rothmans is selling at a P/E ratio of only 14, mainly because it has very little growth potential. This fact is reflected in its high dividend payout ratio, which exceeds 82 percent, because there is little need to plow back cash into its operations; cigarette production is not a growth industry. As a result, Rothmans would be considered a value stock, based on its high dividend yield of 5.9 percent. To determine what will happen to Rothmans in the future, we have to do some financial forecasting and consider some what-if scenarios.

CONCEPT REVIEW QUESTIONS

1. What useful information do we obtain from the dividend yield, P/E ratio, M/B ratio, and EBITDA multiple?

2. Why are P/E ratios and dividend yields often not useful indicators of value?

3. Why is it so difficult to assess whether a firm is properly valued?

4.8 FINANCIAL FORECASTING

To do a reasonable job of financial forecasting, we first must complete a comprehensive financial analysis to develop a good understanding of the relationships in the firm's financial statements. Financial forecasting is a critical job for the firm, its financial advisors, and its external analysts. The firm cannot decide *how to* finance itself until it first assesses the nature of the financing need to determine whether funds are required in the short or long run, whether the financing needs will grow through time, whether the financing need arises from a problem that is self-correcting, and so on. The firm's financial advisors also need to consider the firm's needs when recommending a financial strategy, just as the bank needs to consider these when structuring a loan or credit facility. Finally, equity investors need to consider the firm's financing needs when buying the company's shares, because the last thing they want is to invest in a company only to find that it has to raise more money.

The Percentage of Sales Method

The most important input in financial forecasting is an accurate sales forecast, because sales growth drives a firm's financing requirements. As a result, financial forecasting requires input from most of the divisional managers of the firm but particularly the marketing managers. This will become evident when we consider the most basic forecasting technique: the **percentage of sales method**. At this point, we will first consider a stylized example and then return to our study of Rothmans. The reason for this is that Rothmans has some very special problems and in many ways is not "typical"; it is best to consider the general principles first.

The percentage of sales method involves the following steps:

1. Determine which financial policy variables you are interested in.

2. Set all the non-financial policy variables as a percentage of sales.

3. Extrapolate the balance sheet based on a percentage of sales.

4. Estimate future retained earnings.

5. Modify and iterate until the forecast makes sense.

Financial policy variables are the variables that the treasurer is concerned with. For example, the treasurer could be concerned with common equity (whether the firm has to issue equity or not), long-term funds (equity plus long-term debt), or the firm's total external financing requirement. To illustrate, we will assume that the treasurer is interested in total **external financing requirements (EFR)**. Let's look at a simple balance sheet for a hypothetical firm (Table 4-11) and see what this means.

Table 4-11   Balance Sheet

Cash	5	Accruals	5
Securities	10	Payables	5
Receivables	10	Bank debt	20
Inventory	25		
Current assets	50	Current liabilities	30
Net fixed assets	100	Long-term debt	40
		Common equity	80
Total assets	150	Total liabilities	150

This firm has total assets of $150 that have been financed with $80 of common equity, $40 of long-term debt, and $20 of short-term debt. Taken together, these are referred to as invested capital, because both the common shareholders and the bank and long-term debt investors have made a decision to invest in the firm. In contrast, the accruals and payables are referred to as **spontaneous liabilities**, because as long as the firm is in business (i.e., a going concern), it will naturally generate payables and accruals: suppliers will ship goods on credit, and workers will work and collect their wages at the end of the month. In this sense, when we generate a five-year financial forecast, these accounts will be assumed to automatically increase with sales and only the financial policy variables will initially be kept constant.[19]

The next step is to convert the non-policy variables to a percentage of sales. For the sake of our example, we will assume that sales are $120 and that the percentages that result from this sales level are reasonable for the future. In practice, we would look at the ratios over the previous five years or so, factor in current business conditions for the firm (e.g., new orders), and assess what values would be reasonable going forward.

The third step is to extrapolate the balance sheet based on the sales forecast by using these percentages of sales. For our purposes, we will assume that sales are forecast to increase by 10 percent a year. The result is the naive initial forecast shown in Table 4-12.

Table 4-12   Initial Forecast

Sales	120	%	132	145	160	
Cash	5	4.2	5.5	6.1	6.7	
Marketable securities	10	8.3	11.0	12.1	13.3	
Accounts receivable	10	8.3	11.0	12.1	13.3	percentages
Inventory	25	20.8	27.5	30.3	33.3	of sales
Net fixed assets	100	83.3	110.0	121.0	133.0	
Total assets	150	125.0	165.0	181.6	199.6	
Accruals	5	4.2	5.5	6.1	6.7	
Accounts payable	5	4.2	5.5	6.1	6.7	
Short-term debt	20	16.7	20.0	20.0	20.0	
Long-term debt	40	33.3	40.0	40.0	40.0	
Equity	80	66.7	80.0	80.0	80.0	
Total liabilities and equity	150	125.0	151.0	152.2	153.4	
Cumulative (EFR)			14.0	29.4	46.2	

The top line is the sales forecast, with sales going from the current level of $120 to $132 one year out, and then $145, and finally $160. Then we express all the asset accounts and the spontaneous liabilities as a percentage of sales, because these are the non-policy variables and are extrapolated based on the sales forecast. Take cash, for example: it is $5 or 4.2 percent of the $120 sales level, so based on a 10 percent sales growth forecast, it increases by 10 percent to $5.50, $6.10, and $6.70. The values of the other assets are also increased by 10 percent per year, resulting in a forecast value of $199.60 for total assets.

---

[19] This is not to say that these amounts are ignored: some financially constrained firms will decide to delay paying bills to meet their financial targets. This means that payables will increase more than proportionally with sales. We will discuss this in Chapter 24.

On the liability side, as discussed, we assume that spontaneous liabilities increase at the rate of sales, so we get a forecasted value of $13.40. Subtracting this figure from the total assets forecast of $199.60, we get the required invested capital figure of $186.20. However, recall that we assumed no change in the amount of invested capital, leaving only $140 in invested capital, which suggests a shortfall of $46.20. This shortfall is the balance sheet *plug*, which we have labelled as the EFR.[20] Notice that this is a cumulative not an annual requirement—that is, the firm needs to raise $46.20 in total financing over the next three years.

However, this forecast is extremely naive or simple. For one thing, it ignores any new equity that the firm will generate simply by retaining some of its future earnings. For another, it assumes that the existing debt will still be there in three years time. In practice, some of it may need to be refinanced, or the bank may refuse to renew the short-term loans. However, we'll assume that all the debt can be renewed and focus on the retained earnings. To do this, we need to look at the firm's income statement (Table 4-13).

Table 4-13   Income Statement

Sales	120
Gross operating profit	48
Fixed costs	31
EBIT	17
Interest	5
Taxes (50%)	6
Net income	6
Dividends	3

If this looks familiar, it is the example we used before when looking at efficiency ratios, where the firm has a cost structure of 60 percent variable costs and fixed costs of $31. So at the current sales level of $120, it has EBIT of $17, from which it subtracts $5 in interest on the $60 of debt and pays 50 percent income taxes or $6. As a result, it has net income of $6 and a net profit margin of 5 percent. However, it pays out 50 percent of its earnings as dividends, so only $3 is retained within the firm. What is important is that the firm's retained earnings as a percentage of sales are its net profit margin, times one minus the dividend payout, which equals 2.5 percent (i.e., 5% × 0.50) in this example.

If we use this information to revise our simple forecast above, we add 2.5 percent of sales each year to retained earnings, which leaves us with our first revision to our naive forecast, depicted in Table 4-14.

---

[20] Remember, the balance sheet has to balance.

Table 4-14   First Revision of Forecast

Sales	120	%	132	145	160
Cash	5	4.2	5.5	6.1	6.7
Marketable securities	10	8.3	11.0	12.1	13.3
Accounts receivable	10	8.3	11.0	12.1	13.3
Inventory	25	20.8	27.5	30.3	33.3
Net fixed assets	100	83.3	110.0	121.0	133.0
Total assets	150	125.0	165.0	181.6	199.6
Accruals	5	4.2	5.5	6.1	6.7
Accounts payable	5	4.2	5.5	6.1	6.7
Short-term debt	20	16.7	20.0	20.0	20.0
Long-term debt	40	33.3	40.0	40.0	40.0
Equity	80	66.7	83.3	86.9	90.9
Total liabilities and equity	150	125.0	154.3	159.1	164.3
Cumulative (EFR)			10.7	22.5	35.3

The only difference between this revision and the initial one is that we have taken into account the future retained earnings of 2.5 percent per dollar of sales, which has reduced the EFR by $10.90. However, this forecast is still relatively naive and does not make use of skills in financial analysis. We can improve on this naive forecast. To do this, we will go through all the non-financial policy assumptions to see whether we can improve on them.

First, we have to recognize that the percentage of sales technique automatically imposes a very strict relationship between the assets and sales. For example, when we assume that cash is 4.2 percent of sales, we assume that it will remain so whether sales are $10 or $1,000. Graphically, we are forcing the relationship between cash and sales to be a straight line going through the origin. A more reasonable assumption would be that there are economies of scale to managing cash and that the *marginal* impact of sales growth is less than the average percentage of sales of 4.2 percent. For example, the true relationship at a sales level of $120 might be $3 plus 2.5 percent of sales so that the marginal impact of sales growth is only 2.5 percent of sales. Figure 4-3 depicts the differences in the cash forecasts that arise by changing this assumption.

How cash varies with sales can be determined by statistically analyzing previous sales levels and cash balances. A linear relationship as graphed in Figure 4-3 can be estimated with or without a constant by using an ordinary least squares (OLS) linear regression. This regression can be done in Excel or by using various other statistical packages. For our forecast, we assume that the treasurer has done this analysis and is satisfied that, over the three-year horizon, operations can be managed from existing cash balances and *no* further investment is required. Cash will be held constant at $5.

FIGURE 4-3

Cash Forecast

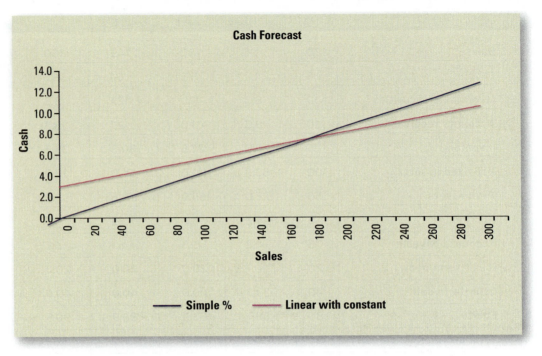

We will temporarily skip marketable securities and consider accounts receivable and address the issue of whether assuming they are a strict percentage of sales is reasonable. In this case, it may be. Previously, when considering the investment in accounts receivable, we showed that the number of days of sales in receivables, or the ACP, gave essentially the same information as the receivables turnover ratio. As long as the firm maintains the same credit policy, the same mix between credit and cash sales, and the economy doesn't crash, then assuming a constant percentage of sales is reasonable. However, if the firm anticipates changing its credit policy and granting more lenient credit terms, then the percentage of sales tied up in receivables will increase, as it will if the proportion of credit to cash sales increases. Both of these events might happen in an economic downtown, where the firm might use more lenient credit as a way of maintaining its level of sales. Understanding the macroeconomic environment that generates the sales forecast will help the treasurer refine the percentage of sales tied up in receivables. For our purposes, we will assume that no slowdown is expected during the forecast period and that estimating receivables at 8.3 percent of sales is reasonable.

We treat inventory in a similar manner to receivables. As long as the inventory turnover ratio is expected to be constant, inventory will increase in line with sales. However, the same qualifications apply in terms of the macroeconomic environment. If a downturn is anticipated, then the firm might plan to increase the level of inventory in order to bolster sales by offering immediate delivery. In contrast, the firm might believe that it can reduce inventory, either because some of it is obsolete or because it plans to adopt new inventory management systems, such as "just-in-time" inventory planning. However, consistent with our treatment of receivables, we assume that using a constant percentage of sales is reasonable.

The last asset item is net fixed assets. Here, whether or not the assumption of a constant percentage of sales is reasonable largely depends on whether the firm is a single-plant or multi-plant firm. In a single-plant firm, the assumption of a constant percentage of sales tied up in net fixed plant and equipment is usually unreasonable; investment in plant and equipment usually lasts many years and the firm does not replace a part of it each year. Instead, investment in plant and equipment is "lumpy." The firm will build its plant and equipment, and then each year the plant and equipment will reduce in value as the firm takes depreciation. After a certain number of years, major refurbishment and replacement is needed, and the cycle begins again. For multi-plant firms, this effect gets smoothed out because the process is occurring over large numbers of plants.

This brings us back to the question of why firms hold marketable securities. Generally, firms do not create value by investing in marketable securities; they hold marketable securities as a temporary resting place for cash until it can be used. Suppose that the treasurer talks to the controller and realizes that the $10 in marketable securities is needed to fund a plant expansion next year, after which there will be no further capital expenditures over the forecast horizon. In this case, it makes no sense to extrapolate marketable securities into the future. Further, after the plant and equipment are expanded, it will decline in the future as the plant and equipment are depreciated. So we'll assume that the firm depreciates the plant and equipment by $10 per year, but in the first year, it spends the $10 in marketable securities to maintain the plant and equipment at $100.

The final items to consider are the spontaneous liabilities. These act very much like accounts receivable, because the major item is accounts payable. As long as the firm does not anticipate changing its payment policy, then its payables will increase in line with sales, so assuming that payables will remain a constant percentage of sales is reasonable. Making the adjustments discussed above, we get the second revision to the forecast, which is shown in Table 4-15.

Table 4-15   Second Revision of Forecast

Sales	120	%	132	145	160
Cash	5	4.2	5.0	5.0	5.0
Marketable securities	10	8.3	0.0	0.0	0.0
Accounts receivable	10	8.3	11.0	12.1	13.3
Inventory	25	20.8	27.5	30.3	33.3
Net fixed assets	100	83.3	100.0	90.0	80.0
Total assets	150	125.0	143.5	137.4	131.6
Accruals	5	4.2	5.5	6.1	6.7
Accounts payable	5	4.2	5.5	6.1	6.7
Short-term debt	20	16.7	20.0	20.0	20.0
Long-term debt	40	33.3	40.0	40.0	40.0
Equity	80	66.7	83.3	86.9	90.9
Total liabilities and equity	150	125.0	154.3	159.1	164.3
Cumulative (EFR)			−11.2	−21.7	−32.7

This revision has profoundly different implications for the treasurer. Whereas before the firm had an external financing requirement, now it would be able to repay some financing obligations because the EFR is negative. The reasons for this are that the firm no longer needs the increase in cash or the marketable securities and, more important, that the plant and equipment don't need new money spent on them during the forecast period.

The final step is to consider changes in the net profit margin. Previously, we assumed that the net profit margin remained the same even when sales changed. However, if the 10 percent sales growth forecast is due to a recovery from a recession, then the firm may be able to achieve this growth without adding to its fixed costs. In this case, the net profit margin may also increase, if the firm's fixed costs are indeed fixed. Table 4-16 reports the income statements that arise if we maintain gross profits at 40 percent of sales but maintain fixed costs at $31.

Table 4-16   Profit Margin and Sales

Sales	120	132	145	160
Gross margin (40%)	48	53	58	64
Fixed costs	31	31	31	31
Interest	5	5	5	5
Tax	6	8.5	11.0	14.0
Net income	6	8.5	11.0	14.0
Net profit margin	5.0%	6.4%	7.6%	8.7%

Notice that the profit margin increases dramatically from 5.0 percent to 8.7 percent over the four-year period. This is the typical "recovery from recession" pattern, in which the firm lowers fixed costs during a recession, through restructuring and cost cutting, so that the immediate impact of a recovery causes greatly improved profit margins.

Finally, as we will discuss in Chapter 22, usually firms do not follow a constant dividend payout policy; they tend to cautiously increase dividends in line with sustainable earnings. We'll assume that the treasurer expects the dividend to stay at $3 for the next three years. This means that retained earnings will increase much more quickly than net income will. If this higher level of retained earnings is added to our forecast, we get the final forecast, as shown in Table 4-17.[21]

---

[21] Note that some "sophisticated" financial planning models build in a further refinement so that as debt changes, so too does the firm's interest charges and net profit margin. This can be done quite easily in Excel by simultaneously solving for all values. However, we find that this extension generally adds little to the usefulness of financial planning, particularly now that interest rates are so low.

Table 4-17   Final Revision of Forecast

Sales	120	%	132	145	160
Cash	5	4.2	5.0	5.0	5.0
Marketable securities	10	8.3	0.0	0.0	0.0
Accounts receivable	10	8.3	11.0	12.1	13.3
Inventory	25	20.8	27.5	30.3	33.3
Net fixed assets	100	83.3	100.0	90.0	80.0
Total assets	150	125.0	143.5	137.4	131.6
Accruals	5	4.2	5.5	6.1	6.7
Accounts payable	5	4.2	5.5	6.1	6.7
Short-term debt	20	16.7	20.0	20.0	20.0
Long-term debt	40	33.3	40.0	40.0	40.0
Equity	80	66.7	85.5	93.5	104.5
Total liabilities and equity	150	125.0	156.5	165.7	177.9
Cumulative (EFR)			−13.0	−28.3	−46.3

The upshot of this final revision is that the surplus is even greater, and the treasurer has to develop a plan for managing these funds, rather than arranging for the firm to raise money. This is quite a different scenario indeed!

In considering how we changed the simple percentage of sales forecast, we have obviously exaggerated certain effects. For example, fixed costs are only fixed in the sense that they do not vary with sales. However, they still tend to increase over time through wage increases and the general tendency to hire more staff as the firm's profits increase. Likewise, it would be difficult for the firm to maintain the dividend at $3 as profits and cash start to pile up. Alternative assumptions about the macroeconomic environment could soon cause the surplus to become a deficit. For example, if a slowdown is forecast, then a stable or declining sales forecast could cause the profit margin to contract while requiring more receivables and inventory as a percentage of sales. However, this is not the point of the exercise, because many different scenarios can be envisioned. What we wanted to demonstrate is how the simple percentage of sales forecasting method, when allied with basic skills in financial analysis, can produce an effective forecast. However, if it is employed "blindly," it may provide misleading results. Moreover, even though the percentage of sale forecasting method can be improved for short-tem forecasts it is very accurate for multi-plant firms over longer periods of time, which brings us to simple formula forecasting techniques.

CONCEPT REVIEW QUESTIONS

1. Why is the sales forecast the most critical component of financial forecasting?

2. Describe the basic percentage of sales approach to financial forecasting. What is the main underlying premise to this forecasting approach?

3. What are some of the major limitations of the percentage of sales approach, and how may they be overcome?

4.9 FORMULA FORECASTING

Let's return to the simple percentage of sales forecasting method, as this works very well for longer periods and for multi-plant firms. From the initial forecast, total assets in our example were 125 percent of sales and spontaneous liabilities were 8.4 percent, so invested capital was the balance of 116.6 percent. As we discussed previously, when we subtract spontaneous liabilities from total assets, we get the firm's invested capital, or net assets, as a percentage of sales. We will denote this by a, which represents the treasurer's financial policy variable, because it is the total invested capital requirement of the firm as a percentage of sales.

Under the assumptions of the percentage of sales method, if the firm doesn't grow, then there is no need for additional net assets. This is because the firm will not need to provide additional credit to customers (accounts receivable) or inventory to meet demand, and the firm's fixed assets should be able to continue to produce enough to meet demand. Consequently, the current level of invested capital is sufficient for the firm. The corollary is that positive EFR mainly arise as a result of sales growth. We represent this sales growth by g, so if current sales are S, next period's sales growth is $S \times g$ and the incremental capital required is $a \times S \times g$. In our previous example, current sales were $120, and the forecast sales growth rate was 10 percent, so incremental sales were expected to be $12. With the net asset requirement of 116.6 percent of sales, the firm will acquire additional invested capital of $14.

From this additional invested capital, we need to subtract the forecast retained earnings. As we noted before, this is the net profit margin times one minus the dividend payout. We represent the net profit margin by PM, and we denote one minus the payout ratio as b, which is commonly referred to as the **retention (or plowback) ratio**. Therefore, we can express the forecast retained earnings as $b \times PM \times (1 + g) \times S$. In our example, with current sales of $120, the forecast sales $[(1 + g) \times S]$ are $132, using a sales growth rate of 10 percent. In this case, the forecast retained earnings are 2.5 percent of $132 or $3.30, since we are assuming a 5 percent net profit margin (PM) and a retention ratio (b) of 50 percent. The EFR of $10.70 is then exactly what we calculated in the first revision of our percentage of sales forecast in Table 4-14.

retention (or plowback) ratio one minus the payout ratio

Algebraically, we can represent this EFR as

$$EFR = a \times S \times g - b \times PM \times (1 + g) \times S$$

[4-32]

This is the invested capital requirement minus the forecast retained earnings. The advantage of the algebraic formulation is that it focuses on the key drivers of the EFR, which are the sales growth rate, the invested capital requirement, and the amount of earnings retained by the firm.

The EFR in our example can also be expressed as a linear function of the sales growth rate (g). We can see this more easily by dividing both sides of Equation 4-32 by the current sales level and rearranging to get

$$\frac{EFR}{S} = -b \times PM + (a - b \times PM)g$$

[4-33]

This line can be graphed with EFR/S along the vertical (y) axis, and with g along the horizontal (x) axis, as shown in Figure 4-4.

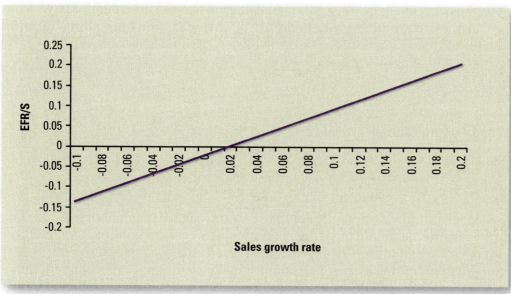

4-4 FIGURE

External Financing Requirements

This is an important graph. It tells us that for negative and low *forecast* sales growth rates, EFR is zero or even negative (i.e., cash is freed up). The reason for this is twofold: first, the firm generates profits from its sales, some of which ($b \times PM$) are retained within the firm; second, it also liberates some of its investment in accounts receivable and inventory, which both decline as sales fall. At this point, it is important to remember that this is the *forecast* growth rate. If the firm plans for positive sales growth, and then sales decline, this often results in more receivables and inventory than planned and generates a positive EFR. In fact, many firms run into severe financing problems when sales decline dramatically and they are not able to cut production quickly enough, so they just produce for inventory.

The graph indicates a basic principle in finance, which is that declining- and low-growth firms tend to be *cash cows*, in that they generate cash. Notice from Equation 4-33 that at a zero growth rate, the firm does not need any new invested capital, so the EFR equals the forecast earnings retained within the business. Further, notice that the coefficient of growth is positive as long as $a > (b \times PM)$, which will almost always be the case. This means that EFR increases as sales growth increases, all else being equal. In our example, $a > (b \times PM)$, because the sales growth causes the firm to increase its net assets by a, which in our example is 116.6 percent, and this is only partially offset by the retained earnings percentage of sales, which in our example is 2.5 percent. The result is that the sales growth generates an external financing need and problems for the treasurer. This is the norm—as sales grow, firms require external financing to support these sales, no matter how profitable they are.

Finance professors like linear relationships like those discussed above, because they generate a line that crosses the horizontal axis. This point is very important, because it measures a break-even point. We have already discussed the break-even point, which is the sales level at which the firm covers its fixed costs. However, there is also a sales growth rate at which the firm neither generates nor needs financing—that is, it breaks even in the financing sense. This is the point in Figure 4-4 at which the line crosses the horizontal axis, which we call the **sustainable growth rate (g*)**.[22] We can find this point by setting EFR/S = 0 in Equation 4-33 and solving for g, which leaves us with

sustainable growth rate (g*) the sales growth rate at which the firm neither generates nor needs financing—that is, it breaks even in terms of financing

[4-34]

$$g^* = \frac{b \times PM}{(a - b \times PM)}$$

For our example, we have:

$$g^* = \frac{b \times PM}{(a - b \times PM)} = \frac{0.50 \times 0.05}{(1.166 - 0.50 \times 0.05)} = 0.0219$$

Sales for the firm in our example can grow at 2.19 percent per year before it needs external financing. The fact that it is forecast to grow at 10 percent generates the EFR in the first revision of our percentage of sales forecast.

If sales for the firm in our example do in fact grow at 10 percent per year and exceed its sustainable growth rate, then one of two things has to happen. Either the firm has to raise external funds or the parameters in our equation have to change. The parameters can be changed by increasing the net profit margin, decreasing the dividend payout rate, or decreasing the net investment in assets. In fact, these factors are those that we altered in our forecast revisions in the previous section. By knowing the sustainable growth rate, as well as the target growth rate given by the marketing people, the treasurer gains valuable information about the nature of the financing problem facing the firm in the future—the rest of the effort is working out the details.

[22] See Robert Higgins, "Sustainable Growth under Inflation," *Financial Management 10* (Autumn 1981), pp. 36–40.

CONCEPT REVIEW QUESTIONS

1. What four variables have a direct impact on a firm's need for external financing?

2. What is the nature of the relationship between EFR and the four variables described above?

3. Explain what the sustainable growth rate is, and why it is important.

4.10 ROTHMANS' EXTERNAL FINANCING REQUIREMENTS

There are some useful lessons to be learned from repeating the forecasting exercise for Rothmans; we will keep the forecast as simple as possible, without making unrealistic assumptions. For this purpose, we begin by expressing Rothmans' 2004–2006 balance sheets accounts as a percentage of sales, which is shown in Table 4-18.

Table 4-18   Rothmans Percentage of Sales

Balance Sheet (March 31)	2004 (%)	2005 (%)	2006 (%)	Average (%)	Use (%)
Cash and equivalents	0.0758	0.0365	0.0741	0.0621	0.0621
Short-term investments	0.2224	0.2650	0.1255	0.2043	0.2043
Accounts receivable	0.0516	0.0504	0.0181	0.0400	0.0400
Inventories	0.3208	0.3295	0.3165	0.3223	0.3223
Prepaid expenses	0.0034	0.0021	0.0028	0.0028	0.0028
Total current assets	0.6740	0.6835	0.5370	0.6315	
Property, plant and equipment	0.0908	0.1086	0.1170	0.1054	0.1054
Future income taxes	0.0129	0.0139	0.0097	0.0121	0.0121
Prepaid pension benefits	0.0189	0.0188	0.0204	0.0194	0.0194
Other assets	0.0045	0.0052	0.0044	0.0047	0.0047
Total assets	0.8011	0.8300	0.6885	0.7732	–
Liabilities and Equity					
Accounts payable and accrued liabilities	0.0597	0.0745	0.0653	0.0665	0.0665
Excise and other taxes payable	0.1251	0.1250	0.1038	0.1180	0.1180

Table 4-18   Rothmans Percentage of Sales continued

Balance Sheet (March 31)	2004 (%)	2005 (%)	2006 (%)	Average (%)	Use (%)
Dividend payable to minority shareholder of subsidiary company	0.0000	0.0000	0.0165	0.0055	0
Income taxes payable	0.0487	0.0337	0.0313	0.0379	0.0379
Total current liabilities	0.2335	0.2332	0.2169	0.2279	
Other long-term liabilities	0.0024	0.0034	0.0037	0.0031	0.0031
Other employee future benefits	0.0491	0.0526	0.0513	0.0510	0.0510
Long-term debt	0.2419	0.2351	0.2296	0.2355	Starting value
Minority interest in subsidiary company	0.0025	0.0015	0.0125	0.0055	0.0055
Total liabilities	0.5294	0.5258	0.5139	0.5230	
Capital stock	0.0627	0.0659	0.0695	0.0660	Starting value
Retained earnings	0.2090	0.2383	0.1050	0.1841	Starting value + RE
Total shareholders' equity	0.2717	0.3042	0.1746	0.2502	
Total liabilities and equity	0.8011	0.8300	0.6885	0.7732	

For most of the items, the percentages are similar for each of the three years, which implies that using the percentage of sales forecasting approach is reasonable. The three notable accounts that are exceptions to the rule are short-term investments, accounts receivable and retained earnings, which are all a much lower percentage of sales in 2006 than they were in previous years. The reduction in short-term investments and retained earnings can be explained by the large special dividend paid during 2006, while the reduction in receivables seems to be out of line with previous years' results.

Table 4-18 also reports the average percentages over this three-year period, as well as an additional column entitled "Use," which shows the assumption we will use to construct our forecast. You will note that we have simply used the three-year average percentage of sales to forecast most of the balance sheet items, which simplifies our forecasting process considerably.

Two exceptions are the long-term debt and capital stock accounts, where we assume no change in the value. This is equivalent to saying that the firm neither issues nor retires any long-term debt or common stock outstanding. If we go back through the actual balance sheets, we see there has been little change in either item, so this seems to be a reasonable enough assumption. In addition, this is a useful assumption for forecasting purposes, because these are two sources of external financing accounts that Rothmans might use.

The only other account that is not estimated as a direct percentage of sales is the retained earnings account, which we estimate by using the procedures described in the preceding two sections. In particular, we have derived an equation that helps us to determine how retained earnings will increase in the future, based on forecasted sales growth, profit margins, and retention rates. We will use three-year averages for Rothmans to estimate future growth, profit margins, and retention ratios. Ignoring the 2006 special dividend, the dividend payout ratio averaged 73.35 percent over this period, implying a 26.65 percent retention ratio. The net profit margin averaged 14.80 percent, and sales grew at an average annual rate of 2.56 percent. All of these estimates seem reasonable, for our purposes.

Based on these assumptions, and using the three-year sales growth rate of 2.56 percent, we construct our financial forecast, which is shown in Table 4-19.

Table 4-19   Rothmans Forecast

	2007 ($million)	2008 ($million)	2009 ($million)
Cash and equivalents	41.571	42.635	43.727
Short-term investments	136.678	140.177	143.765
Accounts receivable	26.785	27.470	28.174
Inventories	215.588	221.107	226.767
Prepaid expenses	1.850	1.898	1.946
Total current assets	422.472	433.287	444.379
Property, plant and equipment	70.542	72.347	74.199
Future income taxes	8.121	8.329	8.542
Prepaid pension benefits	12.969	13.301	13.642
Other assets	3.135	3.215	3.298
Total assets	517.239	530.480	544.060
Accounts payable and accrued liabilities	44.497	45.636	46.805
Excise and other taxes payable	78.905	80.925	82.997
Dividend payable to minority shareholder of subsidiary company	0	0	0
Income taxes payable	25.359	26.008	26.674
Total current liabilities	148.761	152.570	156.475
Other long-term liabilities	2.107	2.161	2.216
Other employee future benefits	34.110	34.983	35.878
Long-term debt	149.751	149.751	149.751
Minority interest in subsidiary company	3.674	3.768	3.864
Total liabilities	338.403	343.232	348.185
Capital stock	45.347	45.347	45.347

Table 4-19   Rothmans Forecast continued

	2007 ($million)	2008 ($million)	2009 ($million)
Retained earnings	94.898	121.959	149.713
Total shareholders' equity	140.245	167.306	195.060
Total liabilities and equity	478.648	510.538	543.245
Cumulative EFR	38.591	19.942	0.815
	2007	**2008**	**2009**
Sales	668.969	686.095	703.659
Net profit (@ 14.80%)	99.007	101.542	104.141
Reinvested profits with *b* = 26.65%	26.385	27.061	27.754

Notice from Table 4-19 that the bottom line is the cumulative EFR, which is positive $38.59 million for 2007, falling to about half that amount in 2008, and then approaching zero in 2009. If we had extended our forecast by using the same assumptions, we would have forecast negative cumulative EFR figures in 2010 and 2011, reflecting surplus funds. As we have indicated before, Rothmans is not a typical company because its shareholders' equity was only $113.86 million in 2006, which was down from $193.71 million in 2005 because of the special dividends of approximately $101.5 million that it paid in 2006. In fact, if we go back further, we would find that it also paid out $150 million as a special dividend to shareholders in 2003, which was much more than *half* its shareholders' equity in that year. In addition, despite consistently paying out more than 75 percent of its earnings as dividends, Rothmans has piled up surplus cash in the past and has paid it out as a special dividend. Our forecast indicates that this pattern will be repeated in another three or four years.

The fact that Rothmans has been able to continually have surplus cash positions is hardly surprising if we look at its sustainable growth rate, which we can estimate by using the approach described above. In 2006, total assets were 68.85 percent of sales and the spontaneous liabilities 20.04 percent, so net assets (*a*) were 48.81 percent, which is much lower than the 116.6 percent figure used in our example above. This reflects Rothmans' relatively small investment in plant and equipment that we noted previously. To estimate the sustainable growth rate, we also need to estimate the retained earnings percentage of sales, which is the profit margin times the retention rate. By using the three-year average figures for Rothmans, we get 14.80 percent times 26.65 percent, or 3.94 percent. By using Equation 4-34, we can estimate its sustainable growth rate as:

$$g^* = \frac{b \times PM}{(a - b \times PM)} = \frac{0.0394}{(0.4881 - 0.0394)} = 0.0879$$

This is a relatively high sustainable growth, reflecting Rothmans' low level of investment and its very high profitability. In fact, very few firms could grow at this rate without needing any external financing. To make things interesting, note that Rothmans' sales increased from $620.104 million in 2004 to only $652.271 million in 2006, translating into a compound annual growth rate of 2.56 percent, which is much less than its sustainable growth rate. In fact, it is also much lower than the growth rate in nominal gross domestic product (GDP) of 5.0 percent, indicating that making cigarettes is not a growth business in Canada. Thus, it is not surprising that Rothmans maintains such a high payout rate and periodically pays substantial special dividends with its excess cash. If it had good growth opportunities that required investment, it would probably use these profits for this purpose.

We will return to Rothmans as an example in subsequent chapters. However, note that it is a company that makes a product that is not only socially undesirable but is also subject to significant litigation risk, as well as to a hostile tax environment. In fact, at the end of its 2005 annual report, Rothmans commented on an ongoing RCMP investigation into tobacco smuggling that occurred in Canada in the late 1980s and early 1990s in response to very high excise taxes, and on a raid the RCMP carried out on the company in 2002. Although it noted that no charges had been laid against it, Rothmans also noted that another Canadian tobacco company was charged and the charges were so severe that it filed for protection from its creditors. We will discuss bankruptcy and insolvency in Chapter 21, but this clearly poses an ongoing risk to the company.

Tobacco companies have been sued in the United States, and this remains a risk, despite the fact that some claims are themselves now being investigated for fraud. More important is the claim by the provinces for reimbursement for health costs linked to tobacco.[23] Under Canadian securities laws, every Canadian company has to issue a material change form if something happens that can materially affect its share price. On September 29, 2005, Rothmans filed such a form (Form 51-102F3), shown in Finance in the News 4-1.

ROTHMANS INC. ANNOUNCES FURTHER DETAILS REGARDING SUPREME COURT OF CANADA DECISION

In the wake of the ruling released yesterday by the Supreme Court of Canada upholding the constitutional validity of the *Tobacco Damages and Health Care Costs Recovery Act* (British Columbia), Rothmans Inc. provided further details concerning the impact of Thursday's Supreme Court of Canada decision on the action commenced by the Province of British Columbia in January of 2001 against Rothmans Inc., Rothmans, Benson & Hedges Inc. (RBH) and other Canadian and foreign tobacco product manufacturers.

Although RBH is disappointed with the result of the Supreme Court decision, RBH believes that it continues to have strong defences to the Province's claim. To date no substantive court hearings have been held regarding the merits of the Province's claim as the action had been stayed pending the outcome of the constitutional challenge. The Supreme Court decision lifted the stay of the Province's action.

Source: Rothmans, Benson & Hedgs Inc. news release, September 30, 2005.

---

[23] It is difficult to see where this type of litigation would end, as presumably similar claims could be levied against brewers, distillers, car companies, and anyone else that manufactures a product that could cause health problems.

off-balance-sheet liabilities liabilities not shown on a firm's balance sheet that may be sources of risk to the firm's future liquidity, capital, or sales

Rothmans may be very profitable, have very clean financial statements, and be forecast to generate significant surplus funds over the foreseeable future, but (and it is a big but) it may not be around in three or four years. Conceivably, it could be subject to new taxes to recover health costs, be forced to pay restitution to people who never read the warnings on cigarette packages, or pay civil damages to the government for not actively discouraging cigarette smuggling. In other words, it faces significant potential **off-balance-sheet liabilities**.

CONCEPT REVIEW QUESTION

1. What is the relationship among the sustainable growth rate, the actual sales growth rate, external financing requirements, and dividend payments?

ethics
AND CORPORATE
GOVERNANCE 4-1

EXPERTS QUESTION DELOITTE'S ROLE IN NORTEL ACCOUNTING PROBLEMS

Court documents filed by the U.S. Securities and Exchange Commission (SEC) against former executives of Nortel Networks Corp. state the company's auditor, Deloitte & Touche LLP, knew about some of the biggest problems at Nortel several years ago.

The documents contain specific allegations against four former Nortel executives for their role in an accounting meltdown at the telecommunications giant that took place over a four-year period. And audit industry experts say the auditors could have done more to raise the alarm.

"There's a huge audit failure here, either of Deloitte or of the audit system," said Karim Jalal, professor and Chartered Accountants' distinguished chair in accounting at the University of Alberta business school.

According to the allegations, Deloitte was aware of some of the problem areas and had discussed them with Nortel's management as early as October, 2000. Deloitte also continued to sign "clean" audit opinions at Nortel despite a series of four financial-statement restatements with adjustments going back to 1999 at the Brampton, Ont.-based company.

Some in the audit industry ask why, if Deloitte knew about the issues at Nortel as the SEC alleges, the auditor did not do more to resolve the problems or to bring them into the open.

"They could have withheld their [audit] opinion," said Anthony Scilipoti, executive vice-president at Veritas Investment

Research. "They could have resigned if they felt [the problems] were material enough."

In the first quarter of 2003, for instance, the SEC alleges Deloitte asked Nortel's management to provide documentation to support the release of US$80-million of reserves—effectively a US$80-million boost to earnings, sufficient to turn Nortel's results from a loss to a profit for that period.

When Nortel's management did not provide supporting documentation for the accounting entry, Deloitte's only action was to let the US$80-million entry stand and recommend the company should provide support for similar entries in the future, the SEC documents state.

Also, in 2000, Deloitte complained to Nortel's management that guidance given to the company's staff on how to account for certain types of controversial transactions was too brief, according to the SEC. However, Nortel's management was able to deflect Deloitte by simply telling the auditor that the guidance was a tool to help raise potential problems to more senior staff, the SEC document says.

The U.S. regulator's version of events shows a "very lax" response from Deloitte and suggests a breakdown in the relationship between the auditor and Nortel's management, Prof. Jalal said. "That's when Deloitte should have resigned."

Instead, Deloitte continued on as Nortel's auditor until December last year, when the telecom company dropped the audit firm in favour of rival KPMG LLP. Deloitte had been Nortel's auditor for 92 years. The auditor was paid fees of about $81-million from Nortel in 2005, more than from any other client on the Toronto Stock Exchange.

A spokesman for Deloitte said it is not appropriate for them to comment on an ongoing investigation. Canada's audit regulator, the Canadian Public Accountability Board, also said it is not appropriate for the organization to comment on whether it is specifically investigating Deloitte's audit of Nortel.

Prof. Jalal said the alleged failures at Nortel show a systemic problem with auditing.

"The problem is in the current system, [the auditor's disagreements with manage-ment] don't get out into the public," he said. "The information never comes out until the shareholder gets wiped out."

One reason the SEC might not have come down hard on Deloitte is because of concerns about the lack of competition in the audit industry, said Tim Leech, principal at governance consultancy Paisley Consulting.

Since the collapse of Arthur Andersen in the wake of the Enron Corp. scandal, the audit profession has been dominated by four firms with global reach, which means there is little choice for multi-national corporations like Nortel.

The SEC would not want to cause the number of global audit firms to fall any lower, Mr. Leech said.

Source: Mavin, Duncan Mavin. "Experts Question Deloitte's Role in Nortel Accounting Problems." *Financial Post*, March 16, 2007. Material reprinted with the express permission of "National Post Company," a CanWest Partnership.

DISCUSSION QUESTIONS

1. Who has traditionally appointed the auditor and how did this change under the provisions of Sarbanes-Oxley (SOX) discussed in Chapter 3?

2. At the time of Nortel's troubles Deloitte, one of the big four accounting firms, was allowed to do consulting for Nortel as well as be its auditor. Why do you think SOX changed this and required a separation of the audit function from consulting activities?

3. Nortel was Deloitte's biggest client with $81 million in fees in 2005, and yet there were suggestions that Deloitte should have resigned the account when its advice was not taken. Discuss the pressures that Deloitte's auditors must have been under and the advantages and disadvantages of resigning.

4. Arthur Andersen collapsed after it was charged with obstruction of justice and the big five became the big four. Discuss the options that the SEC might have considered even had it felt that Deloitte, like Andersen before it, had failed its responsibilities in its audit function.

5. Do you think that the audit opinion is more reliable now after SOX than before. Why or why not?

Summary

Almost all corporate finance questions involve an analysis of macroeconomic conditions, followed by a financial analysis of the firm. It is critical to understand the sources of a firm's profitability or lack of. The basic analysis is to look at the ROE and then break this out into operating profitability, leverage, and efficiency and productivity ratios, with a look at liquidity ratios to see what the firm's financial reserves are. These same skills at financial analysis are then needed in financial forecasting, for which the external financing requirement is essentially the plug in a forecast balance sheet. All forecasts then hinge on a sales forecast. For longer-term forecasts, the sustainable growth rate represents an easy shortcut to estimating the types of financing problems a firm is likely to have.

Key Terms

Formulas/Equations

(4-1) $ROE = \dfrac{NI}{SE}$

(4-2) $ROA = \dfrac{NI}{TA}$

(4-3) $Leverage = \dfrac{TA}{SE}$

(4-4) $Net\ profit\ margin = \dfrac{NI}{Sales}$

(4-5) $Turnover\ ratio = \dfrac{Sales}{TA}$

(4-6) $ROA = \dfrac{NI}{TA} = \dfrac{NI}{Sales} \times \dfrac{Sales}{TA}$

(4-7) $ROE = \dfrac{NI}{SE} = \dfrac{NI}{Sales} \times \dfrac{Sales}{TA} \times \dfrac{TA}{SE}$

$= Net\ profit\ margin \times Turnover\ ratio \times Leverage\ ratio$

(4-8) $Debt\ ratio = \dfrac{TL}{TA}$

(4-9) $D/E\ ratio = \dfrac{D}{SE}$

(4-10) $TIE = \dfrac{EBIT}{I}$

(4-11) $Cash\ flow\ to\ debt\ ratio = \dfrac{CFO}{D}$

(4-12) $DTL = \dfrac{CM}{EBT}$

(4-13) $BEP = \dfrac{FC}{CM}$

(4-14) $Gross\ profit\ margin = \dfrac{S - CGS}{S}$

(4-15) $Operating\ margin = \dfrac{NOI}{Sales}$

(4-16) $Receivables\ turnover = \dfrac{S}{AR}$

(4-17) $ACP = \dfrac{AR}{ADS} = \dfrac{365}{Receivables\ turnover}$

(4-18) $Inventory\ turnover = \dfrac{CGS}{INV}$

(4-19) $Inventory\ turnover = \dfrac{S}{INV}$

(4-20) $Average\ days\ sales\ in\ inventory\ (ADSI) = \dfrac{INV}{ADS} = \dfrac{365}{Inventory\ turnover}$

(4-21) $Fixed\ asset\ turnover = \dfrac{S}{NFA}$

$$\text{(4-22)} \quad \textit{Working capital ratio} = \frac{CA}{TA}$$

$$\text{(4-23)} \quad \textit{Current ratio} = \frac{CA}{CL}$$

$$\text{(4-24)} \quad \textit{Quick ratio} = \frac{C + MS + AR}{CL}$$

$$\text{(4-25)} \quad \textit{BVPS} = \frac{SE}{\textit{Number of shares}}$$

$$\text{(4-26)} \quad \textit{Dividend yield} = \frac{DPS}{P}$$

$$\text{(4-27)} \quad \textit{Dividend payout} = \frac{DPS}{EPS}$$

$$\text{(4-28)} \quad \textit{P/E} = \frac{P}{EPS}$$

$$\text{(4-29)} \quad \textit{Forward P/E} = \frac{P}{EEPS}$$

$$\text{(4-30)} \quad \textit{M/B} = \frac{P}{BVPS}$$

$$\text{(4-31)} \quad \textit{EBITDA multiple} = \frac{TEV}{EBITDA}$$

$$\text{(4-32)} \quad EFR = a \times S \times g - b \times PM \times (1 + g) \times S$$

$$\text{(4-33)} \quad \frac{EFR}{S} = -b \times PM + (a - b \times PM)g$$

$$\text{(4-34)} \quad g^* = \frac{b \times PM}{(a - b \times PM)}$$

QUESTIONS AND PRACTICE PROBLEMS

Multiple Choice Questions

1. The generally accepted accounting principles in Canada are prescribed by:
   - A. GAAP
   - B. CICA
   - C. IFRS
   - D. FASB

2. Which of the following ratios is *not* in the DuPont system?

   A. Net profit margin
   B. Leverage
   C. Asset turnover
   D. Return on investment

3. Which of the following components of the DuPont system for Hill Inc. is *correct*?
   sales = $5,600; earnings before tax (EBT) = $2,090; T = 40 percent; total liability = $30,900; equity = $16,500.

   A. Net profit margin = 37.32 percent
   B. Asset turnover = 11.81 percent
   C. Leverage = 1.87
   D. Leverage = 0.53

4. To increase return on equity (ROE),

   A. increase equity, all else being unchanged.
   B. decrease debt outstanding, all else being unchanged.
   C. decrease corporate tax rate, all else being unchanged.
   D. decrease earnings after tax, all else being unchanged.

   Use the following information to answer Questions 5 to 10.

Balance Sheet as of December 31, 2005

	$million		$million
Cash	400,000	Accounts payable	500,000
Marketable securities	500,000	Accrued liabilities	90,000
Inventory	250,000	Wages payable	150,000
Equipment	1,000,000	Long-term debt	2,000,000
Land	2,500,000		
		Common shares	2,800,000
Patent	980,000	Retained earnings	90,000
Total assets	5,630,000	Total liab. and equity	5,630,000

Income Statement 2005

	$million
Sales	1,090,000
COGS	380,000
Wages	200,000
Interest	150,000
EBT	360,000
Tax	108,000
NI	252,000

5. What is the debt ratio?

    A. 0.36

    B. 0.94

    C. 0.55

    D. 0.49

6. Calculate the debt-equity ratio and times interest earned ratio.

    A. 3.4; 0.36

    B. 0.95; 2.4

    C. 0.69; 3.4

    D. 2.4; 0.95

7. What is the gross profit and the operating margin? (Use EBIT as operating income.)

    A. 60 percent; 35 percent

    B. 65 percent; 47 percent

    C. 55 percent; 30 percent

    D. 70 percent; 49 percent

8. Which of the following is average days sales in inventory?

    A. 84 days

    B. 70 days

    C. 66 days

    D. 80 days

9. Which of the following is the working capital ratio?

    A. 24 percent

    B. 18.5 percent

    C. 20.4 percent

    D. 155 percent

10. Which of the following is invested capital?

    A. $5,630,000

    B. $2,890,000

    C. $4,800,000

    D. $4,890,000

Practice Problems

Finns' Fridges is a company created by twin brothers, David and Douglas Finn, to rent small refrigerators to other students in their college dormitory. Use these statements to answer the questions about Finns' Fridges.

Balance Sheet for Finns' Fridges (End of the year indicated)

	Year 1	Year 2
Assets		
Current assets (cash)	1,150	493
Property and equipment (net)	3,840	3,888
Total assets	4,990	4,381
Liabilities and Owners' Equity		
Interest payable	200	160
Tax payable	177	182
Dividends payable	200	210
Long-term debt	3,200	2,400
Total liabilities	3,777	2,952
Common shares	1,000	1,000
Retained earnings	213	429
Total owners' equity	1,213	1,429
Total liabilities and owners' equity	4,990	4,381

Income Statement for Finns' Fridges (For the full-year indicated)

	Year 1	Year 2
Revenues (net of bad debts)	1,950	2,200
Selling and administrative expenses	0	220
Loss (stolen equipment)	160	0
EBITDA	1,790	1,980
Amortization expense	1,000	1,212
EBIT	790	768
Interest expense	200	160
Earnings before tax	590	608
Tax (30%)	177	182
Net income	413	426
Earnings per share (100 shares)	$4.13	$4.26
Dividends per share	$2.00	$2.10

11. At the end of 2005, Corine's Candies Inc. had total shareholders' equity of $13.8 million. In 2006, the company had net income of $5.2 million and paid out half of this amount in dividends, resulting in shareholders' equity at the end of 2006 of $16.4 million. Use the average amount of shareholders' equity to determine Corine's ROE for 2006.

Easy

12. Find Finns' Fridges' return on equity (ROE) for Years 1 and 2 using the owners' equity figure at the end of each year. Did this ratio improve or get worse between Year 1 and Year 2?

13. Use the definition of the leverage ratio in the DuPont system to determine if Finns' Fridges has become more or less leveraged between Year 1 and Year 2.

14. One key part of ROE in the DuPont system is the return on assets (ROA). Find the ROA for Finns' Fridges and determine if it is increasing or decreasing.

15. The most recent financial statements for a large, Canadian furniture and appliance rental chain show that its debt ratio was 0.256 and its debt-to-equity ratio was 0.073. At the end of Year 2, was Finns' Fridges more or less leveraged than this major competitor? (Remember to use only the interest-bearing liabilities, i.e. long-term debt, when calculating the D/E ratio.)

16. The large competitor firm mentioned in Problem 15 had net operating income of $4.426 million and sales of $30.16 million in its most recent accounting period. Find the operating margin for this competitor. Comment on Finns' Fridges level of operating efficiency compared to this real-world business.

17. Corine's Candies Inc. registered a gross profit margin of 75 percent on sales of $16 million in 2006. What would the company's income statement show for the value of cost of goods sold?

Medium

18. In the DuPont system, there are two components of ROA. Determine whether efficiency or productivity (or both) is responsible for the increase in ROA for Finns' Fridges from Year 1 to Year 2.

19. We can calculate cash flow from operations (CFO) as net income + non-cash expenses + change in working capital. In Year 2, the change in working capital for Finns' Fridges was –$25. Find the CFO, and use this figure to calculate the cash flow to debt ratio. How many years would it take for the company to pay off its entire debt load if it devoted its cash flow to debt repayment?

20. Find the operating margin for Finns' Fridges for both Year 1 and Year 2 (you may assume that the net operating income is equal to the firm's EBIT). Was there an increase or a decrease in the operating margin, and is this a good trend or a bad one?

21. Calculate the fixed asset turnover for Finns' Fridges for Years 1 and 2 (note that net fixed assets corresponds to "property and equipment (net)" on the company's balance sheet). Has the company become more or less productive in terms of generating sales from assets?

22. At the end of its most recent fiscal period, the large appliance rental company in Problem 15 had a working capital ratio of 4.3 percent and a current ratio of 18.2 percent. Calculate these ratios for Finns' Fridges at the end of Year 1 and Year 2. Is the company more or less liquid than its competitor?

23. The Finn brothers are planning their third year of operations. As a first step in the process, create a "Percentage of Sales" balance sheet for Finns' Fridges as of the end of Year 2.

24. A. Suppose the Finns believe they can increase revenues to $2,600 in Year 3. Use this figure and the Percentage of Sales balance sheet (Problem 23) to forecast the company's balance sheet at the end of Year 3. Remember that the "financing" components (long-term debt, and total owners' equity) should be left unchanged from the Year 2 figures.

    B. The forecast balance sheet does not balance! Determine the amount of external financing required by Finns' Fridges based on the initial forecast.

25. To achieve the target level of revenues in Year 3 ($2,600), Finns' Fridges will have to buy some more equipment. This will increase the amortization expense to $1,422. Selling costs will be the same percentage of sales as in Year 2 and the interest expense for the year will be $120. Use this information to determine the amount of net income the company should expect to earn in Year 3.

26. Use the average dividend payout ratio from Years 1 and 2, and the forecast net income figure from Problem 25, to estimate the total amount of dividends that will be paid by the company in Year 3.

27. Suppose that Finns' Fridges will actually pay $270 in dividends in Year 3. Determine the value of the retained earnings account at the end of Year 3 based on the forecast net income in Problem 25.

28. The forecast for retained earnings (Problem 27) changes the Year 3 forecast for total liabilities and owners' equity to $4,770. With total assets forecast to be $5,177 determine how much external financing will be required in Year 3.

29. What is the current ratio and quick ratio for GG Co.? Inventories = 650,000; current assets = $1,200,000; total liabilities = $3,500,096; long-term debt = $2,099,000.

30. Calculate the degree of total leverage (DTL) and break-even point given the following information: sales = $400,088; variable cost = $120,000; NI = $180,000; T = 40 percent; fixed cost (FC) = $80,000.

31. Use the following information to create a revised forecast of the Year 3 balance sheet for Finns' Fridges. Cash will increase by the forecast EBITDA amount (see Problem 25); it will be reduced by $1,050 to purchase new equipment, $552 for Year 2 payables, and $800 for debt repayment. The property and equipment (net) account will increase by $1,050 (new fridges purchased) but must be reduced by the $1,422 amortization expense. Interest and tax payable will reflect the respective expenses on the forecast income statement (again, see Problem 25). Dividends payable will be $270. Long-term debt will be reduced by $800, and the retained earnings figure is $718. With this revised forecast, is any additional external financing required?

Difficult

32. Use the Year 2 financial statements for Finns' Fridges to determine the company's sustainable growth rate.

33. Calculate the receivables turnover, inventory turnover, and average collection period given the following accounting data: accounts receivable (AR) = $500,000; accounts payable = $305,000; inventory = $650,000; gross profit = $550,000; sales = $950,000. Interpret the average collection period.

34. Calculate BVPS, dividend yield, dividend payout, and market-to-book ratio given the following information: shareholders' equity = $945,000; number of shares outstanding = 500,000; total dividend = $150,000; market price of each share = $9.50; net income = $433,000.

35. GG Co. has the following information from its financial statements: interest-bearing debt = $900,000; shareholders' equity (SE) = $2,500,000; sales = $1,050,000; NI = $670,000; dividend = $200,000; sales growth (g) = 5 percent. Calculate EFR/S and discuss the relationship between dividend payout and EFR. Calculate sustainable growth rate for GG Co.

36. Suppose that GG Co. (see Problem 35) would like to grow its sales by 20 percent, which is greater than its sustainable growth rate. If all the other financial information remains unchanged, how much external financing will the company require?

37. The shares of Corine's Candies Inc. are currently trading at $18.20 and there are 4 million shares outstanding. The company's 2006 net income was $5.2 million. Find the market value of equity for the company and the P/E ratio of the shares.

38. Other candy making firms have an average Forward P/E ratio of 12.0 at this time. With a share price of $18.20, what are the expected 2007 EPS for Corine's Candies if its Forward P/E ratio is the same as the industry average?

39. The managers of Corine's Candies like to use the EBITDA Multiple to value the firm. EDITDA was approximately $10 million in 2006. Use the market value of equity from Problem 37 and a debt value of $20 million to find the total enterprise value (TEV). Next, calculate the EBITDA Multiple. Suppose the industry-average EBITDA Multiple for candy producers is 8.65. Is the market valuing Corine's Candies Inc. more or less highly than its competitors?

The three iron laws of finance are the time value, risk value, and tax value of money. In finance, the saying "time is money" is the building block for valuing securities. In this section we develop the basic discounted cash flow model that is the workhorse of finance. We start with the time value of money and apply the basic discounting framework to valuing bonds and equities. In the process, we develop the celebrated Gordon growth model for valuing low risk equities, and discuss fundamental approaches to equity valuation.

Discount Rates

The discount rate used to determine the value of our money today is related to the opportunity cost of that money. So what might be the opportunity cost of pursuing a master's degree in Canada? In a study by Statistics Canada (Statscan), the opportunity cost was defined as tuition + additional fees + books + lost income − part-time income earned during the school year. For the 1995-96 academic year, Statscan estimated the opportunity cost on average was $29,956. The survey indicated that the returns to earning a post-graduate degree appear to outweigh the costs. Five years after 1990 graduation, master's graduates earned on average one-third more than those with bachelor's degrees. The unemployment rate for master's graduates is also lower.

Source: *Education Quarterly Review*, 2002, Vol. 8, No. 4; Culture, Tourism and the Centre for Education Statistics, Statistics Canada. *Pursuing a master's degree: Opportunity cost and benefits*. Statistics Canada Catalogue no. 81-003-XIE. Ottawa.

http://www.statcan.ca

Time Value of Money

Learning Objectives

After reading this chapter, you should understand the following:

1. The importance of the time value of money and how cash flows at different points in time can be compared on a consistent basis

2. How compound interest differs from simple interest

3. How the same compound value formula can be used to solve four different finance problems

4. How special constant payment problems can be valued as annuities, and in special cases as perpetuities, and what the difference is between an ordinary annuity and an annuity due

5. How to apply annuity formulas to value loans and mortgages and how to set up an amortization schedule

6. How to solve simple retirement problems

INTRODUCTION

Section I introduced you to the study of finance, and Section II examined the importance of company financial statements. In Section III, we discuss the basic valuation process, as it applies to financial securities. This valuation process relies heavily on discounting future expected cash flows, one of the tools discussed in this chapter. Mastery of the tools presented in this chapter is necessary for understanding finance.

This chapter will introduce you to everyday problems, such as taking out a loan, setting up a series of payments, and valuing them. The ideas in this chapter are important for all types of financial problems: determining the payments on a weekly versus a monthly mortgage, buying versus leasing a new car, appropriately valuing a bond or stock, determining whether a company should expand production or abandon a product line, and deciding how much a company should be willing to pay for another company. Although each situation involves unique circumstances that will be covered in subsequent chapters, the basic framework used to evaluate them is the same and relies on material covered in this chapter.

5.1 OPPORTUNITY COST

time value of money the idea that money invested today has more value than the same amount invested later

medium of exchange something that can be used to facilitate transactions

In this chapter, we are concerned with the **time value of money**. As we saw in Chapters 1 and 2 the financial system is designed to transfer savings from lenders to borrowers, so that savers have money to spend in the future. We used the problem of saving while working in order to have money when retired to explain this concept. Money, in this sense, represents our ability to buy goods and services, that is, it operates as a **medium of exchange** and has no value in and of itself. Of course, an investor could simply store the dollar bills (tuck them under the mattress!) and spend them in the future; a dollar is always worth at least a dollar in the future.[1] However, this option ignores the fact that the saver has other uses for that dollar, which in economics is called an "opportunity cost" or an "alternative use." This results in a time value of money.

The opportunity cost of money is the interest rate that would be earned by investing it. For this reason, we also call the interest rate the price of money. It helps us to analyze the problem of determining the value of money received at different times. Suppose, for example, a person has three choices: receiving $20,000 today, $31,000 in five years, or $3,000 per year indefinitely. This choice could, for example, be for the payoff from a lottery. We are not advocating gambling, of course, but making a choice among these different options requires knowing how to value the dollars received at different times, that is, the winner needs to adjust for the time value of money.

To make a decision, the person needs to know what the interest rate is. We will use k as a standard notation throughout the textbook for the market inter-

---

[1]This ignores the fact that what we are really concerned about is what that dollar will buy in terms of goods and services, that is, its purchasing power. We discuss this later in the chapter.

est rate. We will also refer to this market interest rate by several other names later in the textbook, such as the **required rate of return** or **discount rate**. The reason for these different names will become clear later, but in all cases we are looking at the investor's opportunity cost, that is, what he or she can do with the money being invested. However, first we have to make some basic distinctions in terms of how this interest rate is earned and distinguish between simple interest and compound interest.

required rate of return or discount rate the market interest rate (*k*) or the investor's opportunity cost

CONCEPT REVIEW QUESTIONS

1. Why does money have a "time value"?
2. What is an "opportunity cost"?

5.2 SIMPLE INTEREST

Simple interest is interest paid or received on only the initial investment (the principal). Although in practice simple interest is used for a limited number of applications, we introduce it first to contrast it with compound interest, which is the norm.

Simple interest interest paid or received on only the initial investment (the principal)

Example 5-1: Simple Interest I

Suppose someone invests $1,000 today for a five-year term and receives 10 percent annual *simple* interest on the investment. How much would the investor have after five years?

Solution

Annual interest = $1,000 × 0.10 = $100 per year.

Year	Beginning Amount	Ending Amount
1	$1,000	$1,100
2	1,100	1,200
3	1,200	1,300
4	1,300	1,400
5	1,400	1,500

The interest earned is $100 every year, regardless of beginning amount, because interest is earned on only the original investment (principal). Interest is *not* earned on the accrued (or earned) interest.

Because the same amount of interest is earned each year, $100 in the example, we can use the following equation to find the value of the investment at any point in time:

$$\text{Value (time } n) = P + (n \times P \times k)$$

where P = principal and n = number of periods. [5-1]

Notice that P × k = interest, so in applying this equation to Example 5-1 means P = 1,000, n = 5, and k = 0.10. The value in year 5 = 1,000 + (5 × 100) = $1,500. This is the amount shown in the table for Example 5-1 at year 5.

Example 5-2: Simple Interest II

We'll repeat the example but assume that the investment is for 50 years.

Solution

Annual interest is still = $1,000 × 0.10 = $100 per year, so using Equation 5-1 we get

$$\text{Value in year 50} = 1,000 + (50 \times 100) = 1,000 + 5,000 = \$6,000$$

The basic point of simple interest is that to get the future value of an investment, we calculate the annual interest, in our case $100, multiply this by the number of years of the investment, and add it to the starting principal.

Recognizing simple interest helps solve our earlier problem. For example, a person offered the choice between $20,000 today and $31,000 in five years can calculate the two annual interest payments. With the same 10 percent interest rate, the annual interest is now $20,000 × 0.10 = $2,000 per year. In five years, it would generate $10,000 in interest, meaning that $20,000 today is worth $30,000 in five years. In this case, given the choice between $20,000 today and $31,000 in five years, with 10 percent simple interest, the correct choice is the $31,000, because it is worth more. However, how do we solve the choice between these two and $3,000 per year forever (indefinitely)?

One way to solve this problem is to assume a very long period, say 100 years. Receiving $3,000 each year for 100 years produces a future value of $3,000 × 100 = $300,000. We then compare this with investing $20,000 for 100 years, which has a future value of $20,000 + ($2,000 × 100) = $220,000. In this case, by assuming that "indefinitely" is 100 years, the solution would be to choose the $3,000 per year. However, apart from the fact that simple interest problems are relatively rare, it turns out that we are missing something very important, particularly when we invest for long periods.

CONCEPT REVIEW QUESTIONS

1. Explain how simple interest payments are determined.
2. Why does simple interest take into account the time value of money?

5.3 COMPOUND INTEREST

Compounding (Computing Future Values)

compound interest interest that is earned on the principal amount invested *and* on any accrued interest

Compound interest is interest that is earned on the principal amount invested *and* on any accrued interest. Compound interest can result in dramatic growth in the value of an investment over time. This growth is directly related to the length of the period, as well as to the level of return earned, which we will demonstrate shortly. Before we get to that, an example will show how compound interest arrangements work.

Example 5-3: Compound Interest I

Suppose someone invests $1,000 today for a five-year term and receives 10 percent annual *compound* interest. How much would the investor have after five years?

Solution

Annual interest is earned on the original $1,000 (principal) *plus* on accrued interest.

Year	Beginning Amount	Interest	Ending Amount
1	$ 1,000	$1,000 \times 0.10 = \$100$	$ 1,100
2	1,100	$1,100 \times 0.10 = \$110$	1,210
3	1,210	$1,210 \times 0.10 = \$121$	1,331
4	1,331	$1,331 \times 0.10 = \$133.10$	1,464.10
5	1,464.10	$1,464.10 \times 0.10 = \$146.41$	1,610.51

Unlike for an investment earning simple interest, the amount of compound interest earned increases every year; the interest rate is applied to the *principal plus interest earned*, so the value of the investment increases. As a result, the interest received increases from $100 in year 1, to $146.41 in year 5; the ending amount of $1,610.51 is much higher than the $1,500 earned with simple interest.

To make the process clear, let's look at the first two years of interest by using a little algebra. For the first year, everything is the same as with simple interest, that is, the ending amount is the starting principal plus the interest or

$$\$1,000 + (\$1,000 \times 0.10) = \$1,100 = \$1,000 \times (1 + 0.10) \text{ or } PV_0(1 + k)$$

where PV_0 = the present value today (i.e., at time 0). We have factored the $1,000 principal value, so to get the future value, we multiply the principal by one plus the market interest rate.

For year 2, the full $1,100 is **reinvested**, that is, we explicitly do not take the $100 of interest out and spend it. As a result, we have the following

reinvest to keep interest earned on an investment fully invested

$$\$1,100 + (\$1,100 \times 0.10) = \$1,210 = \$1,100 \times (1 + 0.10) \text{ or } PV_0(1 + k)^2$$

In this case, $1,100 is invested at the beginning of year 2 and earns the 10 percent interest. The interest earned increases to $110: the $100 interest on the starting principal plus $10 interest earned on the $100 of interest reinvested at the end of the first year. We can again factor the starting value of $1,100 and then factor the $1,000 principal value to get the formula for the future value at the end of year 2. This is the starting principal times one plus the interest rate squared. As we increase the period we get the general formula

[5-2]

$$FV_n = PV_0(1 + k)^n$$

where FV_n = the future value at time n

compound value interest factor (CVIF) a number that represents the future value of an investment at a given rate of interest and for a stated number of periods: $(1 + k)^n$

This equation is called the basic *compounding equation*, and the last term $(1 + k)^n$ is the **compound value interest factor (CVIF)**.

Applying this equation to Example 5-3, we get $FV_5 = 1,000(1 + 0.10)^5 = 1,000(1.61051) = \$1,610.51$. This is $110.51 more than for the investment earning simple interest. Figure 5-1 illustrates what happens with the two types of interest over time. Note that for the first few years, the difference is minimal, but over time it gets bigger and bigger.

FIGURE   **5-1**

Simple vs. Compound Interest

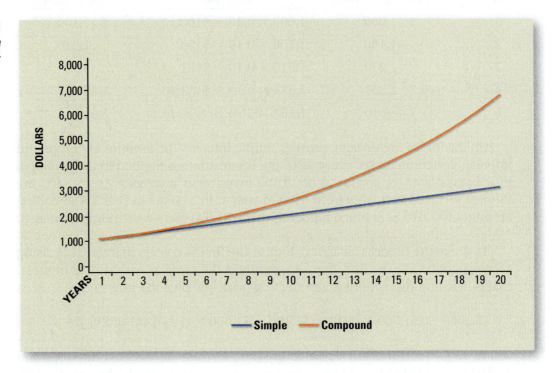

— Simple   — Compound

Example 5-3 can also be solved by using a financial calculator. Although the keystrokes (and variable names) used will vary from one calculator to the next, the basic procedures do not. We will illustrate with one commonly used calculator: the Texas Instrument (TI) BA II Plus.[2]

solution using a financial calculator

(TI BA II Plus)

Input the following variables:

0 → PMT ; −1,000 → PV ; 10 → I/Y ; and 5 → N

---

[2] This is one of only two types of calculators permitted for the Chartered Financial Analyst (CFA) examinations, which are administered by the CFA Institute.

Press (CPT) (Compute) and then (FV)

PMT here refers to regular payments and will be discussed in a later section; FV is the future value; I/Y is the period interest rate; and N is the number of periods. The PV is entered with a negative sign (on this calculator, not on all calculators) to reflect the fact that investors must pay money now to get money in the future. Alternatively, we could have left it positive, which would produce a negative sign in front of the FV, which we could simply ignore. We will do this in some of the ensuing applications.

The answer will be 1,610.51

Time value of money problems can also be solved by using Excel spreadsheets, which have time value of money functions. We illustrate this below solving Example 5-3 by using Excel.

solution using Excel

= FV (rate, nper, pmt, pv, type),

where, rate = interest rate (expressed as a decimal);
nper = number of periods
pmt = the payment amount
pv = present value
type = 0 if it is an ordinary annuity, 1 if it is annuity due. (We will explain what the difference is shortly; for now, our examples will involve ordinary annuities.)

For Example 5-3, we would enter the following in the appropriate cell:

= FV (0.10, 5, 0, −1000, 0) which yields → 1,610.51.

Let us now extend the time horizon for Example 5-3, as we did for the example relating to simple interest.

Example 5-4: Compound Interest II
Repeat Example 5-3, but assume the investment is for 50 years.

Solution
Applying Equation 5-2 to this example, we get

$$FV_{50} = 1,000(1 + 0.10)^{50} = 1,000(117.39085) = \$117,390.85$$

Investing $1,000 for 50 years at an annual interest rate of 10 percent produces $117,390.85. Notice the huge difference between this amount and the future value of $6,000 ($1,000 + [50 × $100]) for the same $1,000 invested for 50 years but earning simple interest!

You might be tempted to ask whether a 50-year term is realistic. It is for many investments. Consider someone who begins investing for retirement in his or her early 20s. Those early investments could earn compound returns for 40 years or so before the individual retires. Further, assuming the individual does not withdraw all the retirement savings on retirement day (which would have severe tax consequences) and assuming that this person lives another 20 to 25 years after retirement, some investment dollars may not be touched for more than 50 years. Finance in the News 5-1 shows just how important it is to begin investing early.

Table 5-1 provides some evidence regarding the power of compound returns. It shows the future values that would have resulted from investing $1,000 at the beginning of 1938 and leaving that money invested for 68 years (until the end of 2005) in various investment assets.

finance
INTHENEWS5-1

GET HEAD START ON RRSP: IT PAYS TO BEGIN SAVING FOR RETIREMENT IN YOUR 20s

Ask any financial adviser when young people should start saving for their retirement. The answer is always the same: they should start socking money away inside a registered retirement savings plan in the same year they begin earning income.

For those leaving high school and not going on to university or college, this can mean starting an RRSP as young as age 18. For others whose education years stretch longer, those first paycheques may not come until the late 20s.

No matter when they start working, however, many people sail clear through their 20s without giving a thought to retirement planning. A survey this year for Royal Trust found the average first-time RRSP contributor is 31 years old.

Yet to earn a healthy nest egg for retirement inside a tax-sheltered plan, it really pays to start early. Popular Canadian investment author Gordon Pape points this out in his 1999 Buyer's Guide to RRSPs.

"The greatest growth takes place in the later years," Pape writes. "So the longer you wait to begin, the less your RRSP will be worth when you retire.

"In fact, if you begin contributions in your early 20s and stop when you reach age 35, leaving the balance in your RRSP, you'll end up with more money at 65 than if you waited until your were 35 to begin and contributed every year thereafter."

Judy Willmer, a certified financial planner with Investors Group Inc. in St. Albert, Alta., has an 18-year old client who just set up an RRSP. But younger people make up only a fraction of her client base; most are between ages 35 and 50.

"Let's say somebody comes in at age 25," Ms. Willmer says. "I'll show them a projection saying if you can save $200 a month up until age 65 you'll have over $1 million. But if you wait 10 years before you save and still want to have that $1-million at age 65, you now have to save $500 a month."

The Royal Trust survey found that first-time RRSP contributors are too cautious in their approach, with only 30% saying they planned to put the majority of their investment money into mutual funds. Others were opting for low-risk, low-growth instruments such as savings accounts. And the survey found that only 47% of first-time RRSP contributors had consulted with a financial adviser, compared to 73% for seasoned investors.

Geoff Anselmo, a 29-year old mutual fund investment specialist with Royal Trust, says it can be difficult to even reach young people to tell them they should start saving for retirement. "You can advertise, but if I'm 21, I'm probably reading the sports section, not the financials," he says.

The young clients who do come his way are often referred to him by their parents. As a way of getting them to see the advantages of investing, he tells them that time is on their side.

Mr. Anselmo illustrates this point with an anecdote about Bill and Linda, who are twins.

At age 22, Bill starts investing $2,000 each year, earning a healthy 12% per year. He continues for six years, then stops and never invests another dime. Linda waits six years, starts investing $2,000 a year at age 28 and continues to do this until she reaches 65. Like her brother, she gets a 12% annual compound rate of return.

At 65, they each have about $1.4-million for their retirement. Yet Bill invested only $12,000 while his sister invested $76,000.

"I find that story in itself is very effective," Mr. Anselmo says. "It talks to people as to why to start early."

Mr. Anselmo generally doesn't develop detailed financial plans for clients in their 20s, mainly because they have a lot of living to do before they can decide what they want their retirement years to look like. Marriage, children, first homes, careers, and career changes all have more importance from where they sit.

"I don't dwell on the things I would dwell on with somebody who is in their prime earning years," he says. "If I talk to somebody young and say, 'At 65, do you want to golf?' they look at me and say, 'I'm worried about tomorrow.'"

Mr. Anselmo encourages the new saver to start with something easy, such as putting $25 or $50 a month into a balanced mutual fund.

Ideally the money gets deducted automatically from their savings accounts, so it is relatively "painless."

As their paycheques get larger, their deductions can increase. Mr. Anselmo finds that after saving up a base of $10,000 or $20,000 and doing some reading on investing, young people can comfortably start to tinker with their investment mixes.

Investors Group's Mrs. Willmer takes a slightly different approach to her younger clients. She always works out cash flow statements, showing them where their money is going. Nights out for beer and pizza can eat up $200 a month if you're not careful, she warns them.

"You can show them that if they are earning $25,000 and they put $1,000 into an RRSP they will pay $250 less income tax that year," she says.

Ms. Willmer always recommends automatic bank withdrawals as a painless way to develop saving discipline. And she does a lot of follow-up to ensure clients keep up with their commitments to themselves even while their lives are undergoing big changes in the years between 20 and 30.

Happily, Ms. Willmer has discovered some of her younger clients do think ahead to retirement. "A lot of the kids are very knowledgeable," she says.

Source: Howell, David. "Get a Head Start on RRSP," as appeared in *Financial Post*, May 20, 1999, p. D4. Material reprinted with the express permission of: "Edmonton Journal Group Inc." a CanWest Partnership.

Table 5-1 Ending Wealth of $1,000 Invested From 1938 to 2005 in Various Asset Classes			
	Annual Arithmetic Average (%)	Annual Geometric Mean (%)	Year-End Value, 2005 ($)
Government of Canada treasury bills	5.20	5.11	29,711
Government of Canada bonds	6.62	6.24	61,404
Canadian stocks	11.79	10.60	946,009
U.S. stocks	13.15	11.76	1,923,692

Source: Data are from the Canadian Institute of Actuaries.

The geometric mean represents the average annual growth rate in the value of $1 invested at the start of the period. The geometric mean is thus the compound rate of return or the interest rate that compounds the starting value to the future value. The compound or geometric return differs from the simple arithmetic average, and we will discuss the difference between the two in detail in Chapter 8. However, aside from this difference, notice the impressive power of compounding over such a long period: $1,000 invested in Canadian equities would have made you almost a millionaire by 2005, and invested in U.S. equities, almost a double-millionaire.

The dramatic difference in ending values results from differences in the rate of return: at a rate of return of 5.11 percent (i.e., the T-bill return) $1,000 would have grown to $29,711, while at 11.76 percent (i.e., the U.S. stock return) it would have grown to $1,923,692—more than 60 times as much! The difference in ending values is significant, even when the differences in returns are small (i.e., consider the difference in ending values of almost $1 million when $1,000 is invested in Canadian stocks at 10.60 percent versus in U.S. stocks at 11.76 percent). These data show why finance professionals struggle to increase the returns on their investments even by very small amounts. In fact, it is normal to look at returns down to 1/100 of 1 percent, which is called a **basis point**. Earning just a few basis points more on one investment causes the future value of the portfolio to compound that much faster.

basis point 1/100 of 1 percent

Let's return to our two choices of $20,000 today or $31,000 in five years' time, assuming the investor now earns *compound* interest of 10 percent. Using the CVIF formula, we get CVIF $= (1 + k)^5 = (1.10)^5 = 1.61051$. The $20,000 compounds to $32,210. So the choice is now $20,000 today, because it will be more than $31,000 in five years if invested at 10 percent with compound interest. However, we still have a problem with comparing either of these single sums with the option of getting $3,000 a year forever. We could compound each of the $3,000 annual payments forward to, say, 100 years in the future, but there are easier ways of doing this.

Discounting (Computing Present Values)

So far we have been concerned with finding future values, but there is a problem with comparing future values: there are many of them! We could choose an arbitrary common period to make the comparisons, which solves this problem. The obvious choice is to compare the values at the *current* time, so instead of calculating future values, we determine *present values*. This process is also called **discounting**. We will explain it with a simple example.

discounting finding the present value of a future value by accounting for the time value of money

Example 5-5: Discounting

An investor estimates that she needs $1 million to live comfortably when she retires in 40 years. How much does she have to invest today, assuming a 10 percent interest rate on the investment?

To solve this example, first start with what is already known: the future value formula Equation 5-2.

$$FV_n = PV_0(1 + k)^n$$

where CVIF = $(1 + k)^n$ is the compound value interest factor. With a starting present value, we multiply by the CVIF to get the future value. Then we can divide the future value by the CVIF to get the present value, or rearranging Equation 5-2 to solve for PV we get

$$PV_0 = \frac{FV_n}{(1+k)^n} = FV_n \times \frac{1}{(1+k)^n}$$

[5-3]

This is the basic *discounting equation*, and the last term, $1/(1 + k)^n$, is called the *discount factor* or **present value interest factor (PVIF)**. Some older textbooks have tables of PVIF and CVIF for various periods and interest rates, although they are simply reciprocals of each other, but the use of computers and calculators makes these tables obsolete.

present value interest factor (PVIF) a formula that determines the present value of $1 to be received at some future time in the future "*n*", based on a given interest rate "*k*"

Solution

So let's return to our example, with FV = 1,000,000; k = 0.10; and n = 40, we get
PV = 1,000,000 × $1/(1.10)^{40}$ = 1,000,000 × (1/45.259256)
= 1,000,000 × 0.02209493 = $22,094.93

An investment of $22,094.93 today, earning a 10 percent return per year, has a future value of $1 million in 40 years. With a 10 percent market interest rate, $22,094.93 today and $1 million in 40 years' time are worth the same, so the two figures are economically equivalent.

Now you know why we call this process *discounting*. If people don't want to pay the full price for something, they ask for a discount, that is, they ask for something off the price. In the same way $1 million in 40 years is not worth $1 million today, so you discount, or take something off, to get it to its true value. Discounting future values to find their present value is the same process, except that when we know the market interest rate, we can use Equation 5-3 to calculate the exact true value.

Notice the following important points from Example 5-5 and Equation 5-3:

- Discount factors (the PVIF) are always less than one (as long as $k > 0$). This means that future dollars are worth less than the same dollars today.

- Discount factors are the reciprocals of their corresponding compound factors and vice versa (PVIF = 1/CVIF).

Example 5-5 could have been solved by using a financial calculator or Excel as follows:

Input the following variables:

0 → PMT ;   −1,000,000 → FV ;   10 → I/Y ; and   40 → N

Press CPT (Compute) and then PV . This will give an answer of 22,094.93

solution using a financial calculator

(TI BA II Plus)

The following function may be used in Excel:

= PV (rate, nper, pmt, fv, type)

For this example, we would enter the following in the appropriate cell:

= PV (0.10, 40, 0, −1000000, 0)

This would yield a PV of 22,094.93.

Determining Rates of Return or Holding Periods

In looking at the discounting problem we noted that we simply divided through by the CVIF, but essentially used the same future value equation, so let's look at this again.

$$FV_n = PV_0(1 + k)^n$$

We have used this equation to solve for future values (FV) and present values (PV), but notice that we can solve for two other values: the interest rate (k) and the period (n). If both the present and future values are known, and we know either the interest rate or the period, we can solve for the last unknown. We illustrate this in the following two examples.

Example 5-6: Finding the Rate of Return

Suppose we modify the lottery example used earlier, and it is now a $20,000 investment that has a payoff of $31,000 in five years. We have the present and future values and the period, and we can solve for the interest rate. This is a very important interest rate, called the *internal rate of return (IRR)*, because it is the rate of return that is *internal* to the values in the problem. Many problems in finance are IRR problems for which we need to compare the rates of return earned on different investments.

Solution

$$FV = 31,000; PV = 20,000; n = 5.$$

Using Equation 5-2, we get $20,000 = 31,000/(1 + k)^5$

We could solve for k in the following manner:

$$31,000/20,000 = 1.55 = (1 + k)^5$$

This is a simple problem, but it is still awkward to solve. One way to solve it is with a calculator through trial and error: Put, say, 1.08 into memory and then enter 1.0 and press "multiply, memory recall, equals" five times. It equals 1.469. Doing the same thing with 10 percent (1.1) produces 1.6105, so we know that the internal rate of return is in between these two numbers and closer to 10 percent than to 8 percent. All that we can then do is iterate to get closer and closer to 1.55; eventually we would end up with 9.161 percent.[3] However, this is a laborious and inefficient process. Using a financial calculator or Excel makes these types of calculations much simpler, as we illustrate below.

Input the following variables:

$0 \rightarrow$ PMT ; $31{,}000 \rightarrow$ FV ; $-20{,}000 \rightarrow$ PV ; and $5 \rightarrow$ N

Press CPT (Compute) and then I/Y . This will give you an answer of 9.161 percent. Notice that either FV or PV needs to be input as a negative number, because to "receive" one cash flow (either today or in the future) you need to "pay" (or invest) either today or in the future.

The following function may be used:

= RATE (nper, pmt, pv, fv, type)

For this example, we would enter the following in the appropriate cell:

= RATE (5, 0, 20,000, −31,000, 0)

This also yields the correct answer of 9.161 percent.

Example 5-7: Solving for Time or "Holding" Periods

In this example, we use the same data as before but change the problem to ask how long we have to invest $20,000 at 10 percent to get $31,000.

Solution

This is a typical mortgage down-payment problem. With our data, we now have to solve the following for n:

$$31{,}000/20{,}000 = 1.55 = (1.1)^n$$

Unfortunately, solving this equation with a simple calculator is even more complicated than the IRR problem was. We could put 1.1 into memory, enter 1.0, and then again press "multiply, memory recall, equals" five times to find that the period is between 4 and 5 years but closer to five. However, we can't be more accurate than this. If you are familiar with logarithms, you can take logs of both sides and solve for n as follows:

$$n = \frac{Ln(FV \,/\, PV)}{Ln(1+k)} = \frac{Ln(1.55)}{Ln(1.1)}$$

---

[3] If you know how to use logarithms, we can take the log of both sides and solve for $Ln(1 + k) = Ln(FV/PV)/n$.

The natural log of 1.55 is 0.438255 and the natural log of 1.1 is 0.09531, so the answer is 4.6 years. However, logarithm tables are rarely used; we used the logarithm function in Excel and typed in =ln(1.55). Using a financial calculator or Excel makes the calculations much easier.

Input the following variables:

0 → PMT ; 31,000 → FV ; −20,000 → PV ; and 10 → I/Y

Press CPT (Compute) and then N . This gives an answer of 4.5982 or 4.6 years.

The following function may be used:

= NPER (rate, pmt, pv, fv, type)

For this example, we would enter the following in the appropriate cell:

= NPER (0.10, 0, −20,000, 31,000, 0)

This would yield an answer of 4.5982 or 4.6 years

We'll summarize what we have learned so far. We have Equation 5-2:

$$FV_n = PV_0(1 + k)^n$$

This equation has four values and if we know any three of them, we can solve for the last one. Therefore, four different types of finance problems can be solved:

- *Future value problems*: how much will I have in w years at x percent if I invest y?

- *Present value problems*: What is the value today of receiving z in w years if the interest rate is x percent?

- *IRR problems*: What rate of return will I earn if I invest y today for w years and get z?

- *Period problems*: How long do I have to wait to get z if I invest y today at x percent?

However, all the problems that we have looked at are single-sum problems, because we were looking at a single investment today and a single payoff in the future. In principle, we can solve almost any problem by using the techniques we have discussed because, for example, valuing a series of receipts in the future can be done by valuing each one individually. However, special formulas exist for standard problems in finance, for which the receipts or payments are the same each period. Think back to our very first example about choosing among $20,000 today, $31,000 in five years, or $3,000 each year forever. The last choice involves valuing a constant $3,000 each year forever and is an example of an *annuity*. In this case, it is a special class of annuity, since it is a perpetual annuity, commonly referred to as a *perpetuity*.

CONCEPT REVIEW QUESTIONS

1. Explain how to compute future values and present values when using compound interest.

2. What is the relationship between CVIFs and PVIFs? Why does this make sense?

3. Why does compound interest result in higher future values than simple interest?

5.4 ANNUITIES AND PERPETUITIES

The Importance of Investing Early

The example below illustrates the power of compound interest as time passes. Consider twins who follow the two different investing approaches described below. Assume each earns a 12 percent annual return:

- Twin 1: At age 21, she begins investing $2,000 per year (at year end) for six years and then she makes no further contributions (total amount invested, $12,000). Note that she invests the same amount each year so this is an example of an annuity. At age 65, she will have accumulated $1.2 million for retirement.

- Twin 2: At age 21, she postpones investing for six years until she reaches age 28 then she invests $2,000 per year for 38 years (total amount invested, $76,000). At age 65 she will have also accumulated $1.2 million for retirement.

Notice that they have the same ending amounts, but Twin 1 invested only $12,000 in total, while Twin 2 invested $76,000. This shows how the compounding effect is magnified as the time horizon increases.

We could solve these problems by *brute force* by valuing each payment the twins make. However, we will solve them after we develop more formally the concept of an annuity.

Ordinary Annuities

So far, we have dealt with PV and FV concepts as they apply to only two cash flows—one today (i.e., the PV), and one in the future (i.e., the FV). In practice, we will often need to compare different series of receipts or payments that occur through time. An **annuity** is a series of payments or receipts, which we will simply call **cash flows**, over some period that are for the *same amount* and paid over the *same interval*, that is, for example, they are paid annually, monthly, or weekly. Annuities are common in finance: the one you may be familiar with is a loan or

annuity regular payments on an investment that are for the same amount and are paid at the same interval

cash flows the actual cash generated from an investment

mortgage payment. This involves an identical payment made at regular intervals for a loan based on a single interest rate.

ordinary annuities equal payments that are made at the end of each period

Ordinary annuities involve *end-of-period* payments. We have the same values as in our earlier discussion: FV, PV, *n*, and *k*. However, now we have another term, PMT, for the regular annuity payment or receipt. The example below demonstrates how to determine the FV and PV of an ordinary annuity.

Example 5-8: FV and PV of an Ordinary Annuity

Suppose someone plans to invest $1,000 at the *end* of each year for the next five years and expects to earn 13 percent per year.

a. How much will the investor have after five years?

b. How much would the investor need to deposit today to have the same results?

Solution

a. We can first depict the series of payments on a timeline diagram, which shows when the cash flows occur:

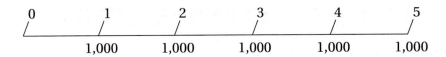

Timelines are very useful in finance, and you should get into the habit of displaying the data in a problem in a timeline. For example, from this diagram we can see that by the end of year five, the first deposit of $1,000 will earn a return for four years, because there are four years from the end of year 1 to the end of the problem in year 5. In contrast, the second payment will earn a return for only three years, the third for only two, the fourth for one year, and the final payment will not earn a return at all. Using this information, we could view this as a five-part problem in which we have to find the future value of each of the five payments.

$$FV_5 = 1,000(1.13)^4 + 1,000(1.13)^3 + 1,000(1.13)^2 + 1,000(1.13)^1 + 1,000$$

$$= 1,000(1.63047) + 1,000(1.44290) + 1,000(1.27690) + 1,000(1.1300) + 1,000(1)$$

$$= 1,000(6.48027) = \$6,480.27$$

The investor would have $6,480.27 after five years.

This would be our brute force calculation, for which we have solved the problem with five separate calculations. This approach is fine for a five-period annuity problem, but it would be tedious for a 25-year monthly-pay mortgage problem that has 300 payments. Fortunately, there is a much quicker way (even without the use of a financial calculator or a spreadsheet). If we look closely at our solution, we can see that we are multiplying $1,000 by the sum of five compound value interest factors (CVIF), based on a 13 percent return (i.e., the CVIF for *k* = 13 percent, with *n* = 4, 3, 2, 1, and 0, respectively).

The *ordinary annuity* equation below adds these CVIFs:

$$FV_n = PMT\left[\frac{(1+k)^n - 1}{k}\right]$$

[5-4]

where PMT is the end-of-period annuity payment. This formula is usually called the compound value annuity formula or CVAF to distinguish it from the single-sum CVIF. The advantage of Equation 5-4 is that it involves only one formula and can easily be solved even on a simple calculator.

Using this equation, we can solve Example 5-8a as follows:

$$FV_5 = PMT\left[\frac{(1+0.13)^5 - 1}{0.13}\right] = 1000(6.48027) = \$6,480.27$$

where we can get the CVIF for five years at 13 percent either by using a simple calculator, putting 1.13 into memory, entering 1.0, and then pressing "times, memory recall, equals" five times, or by using Excel and entering =1.13^5.

(TI BA II Plus)

Input the following variables:

1,000 → PMT ; 5 → N ; 0 → PV (i.e., no deposit today); and

13 → I/Y

Press CPT (Compute) and then FV . This will give you an answer of −6,480.27. Remember, you get a negative value because the calculator is programmed to consider cash outflows and cash inflows.

The following Excel function may be used:

= FV (rate, nper, pmt, pv, type)

For this example, we would enter the following in the appropriate cell:

= FV (0.13, 5, −1000, 0, 0)

This would yield an answer of $6,480.27.

b. To find the present value, we can again view this as a five-part problem for which we have to find the present value of each of the five annual payments:

$$PV_0 = 1000(1/1.13)^5 + 1000(1/1.13)^4 + 1000(1/1.13)^3 + 1000(1/1.13)^2 + 1000(1/1.13)$$
$$= 1000(0.54276) + 1000(0.61332) + 1000(0.69305) + 1000(0.78315) + 1000(0.88496)$$
$$= 1000(3.51724) = \$3,517.24$$

As before, notice that we are using brute force by multiplying $1,000 by the sum of the relevant five PVIF or *discount* factors, which add to 3.51724. Fortunately, the formula for determining the PV of *ordinary annuities* will do this for us:

[5-5]

$$PV_0 = PMT \left[\frac{1 - \dfrac{1}{(1+k)^n}}{k} \right]$$

This formula is usually called the present value annuity formula or PVAF to distinguish it from the PVIF used for valuing single-sum problems.

By using this equation to solve this Example 5-8b we get

$$PV_0 = \$1,000 \left[\frac{1 - \dfrac{1}{(1.13)^5}}{0.13} \right] = 1,000(3.51723) = \$3,517.23$$

The difference of $0.01 is due to rounding errors in the long approach. Again, we can get the PVAF for 5 years at 13 percent by using a simple calculator with memory. For longer-period problems, we can use a financial calculator or Excel.

solution using a financial calculator

(TI BA II Plus)

Input the following variables:

1,000 → PMT ; 5 → N ; 0 → FV ; and 13 → I/Y

Press CPT (Compute) and then PV . This will give an answer of −3,517.23.

solution using Excel

The following Excel function may be used:

= PV (rate, nper, pmt, fv, type)

For this example, we would enter the following in the appropriate cell:

= PV (0.13, 5, −1000, 0, 0)

This would yield an answer of $3,517.23.

We can ensure that our answer is correct by checking that $3,517.23 is the present value of the future value at year 5, calculated earlier, of $6,480.27 with a 13 percent interest rate. We leave this as an exercise for you.

Annuities Due

Sometimes annuities are structured so that the cash flows are paid at the *beginning* of a period, rather than at the end. For example, leasing arrangements are usually set up like this, with the **lessee** making an immediate payment on taking possession of the equipment, such as a car. Such an annuity is called an **annuity due**. The example below demonstrates how to evaluate these cash flows.

lessee a person who leases an item

annuity due an annuity (such as a lease) for which the payments are made at the beginning of each period

Example 5-9: FV and PV of an Annuity Due

We will repeat Example 5-8, except we assume that the payments are made at the *beginning* rather than the end of each year.

a. How much will the investor have after five years?

b. How much would the investor have to deposit today to have the same results?

Solution

a. We begin as before by depicting the data on a timeline:

```
   0          1          2          3          4          5
   |          |          |          |          |          |
 1,000      1,000      1,000      1,000      1,000
```

Notice that as in Example 5-8, we have five cash flows of $1,000 each. However, each cash flow appears one period earlier and thus each receives an extra period of interest at the rate of 13 percent. Using the brute force approach applied in Example 5-8, we can find the future value of each of the five payments.

$$FV_5 = 1,000(1.13)^5 + 1,000(1.13)^4 + 1,000(1.13)^3 + 1,000(1.13)^2 + 1,000(1.13)^1$$

$$= 1,000(1.84244) + 1,000(1.63047) + 1,000(1.44290) + 1,000(1.27690) + 1,000(1.1300)$$

$$= [1,000(6.48027)](1.13) = \$7,322.71$$

Notice that because each flow gets one extra period of compounding at 13 percent, the net result is that we multiply our answer to Example 5-8a by 1.13. In other words, the FV (annuity due) = FV (ordinary annuity)](1 + *k*).

Therefore, we can alter Equation 5-4 to find the FV of an *annuity due* as follows:

$$FV_n = PMT\left[\frac{(1+k)^n - 1}{k}\right](1+k)$$

[5-6]

This is CVAF(1 + *k*), so in practice we don't use a separate formula. However, we can now solve Example 5-9a as follows:

$$FV_5 = PMT\left[\frac{(1+.13)^5 - 1}{0.13}\right](1.13) = [1,000(6.48027)](1.13) = \$7,322.71$$

Note that the value of the annuity due of $7,322.71 is 1.13 times bigger than the value of the ordinary annuity that we calculated earlier of $6,480.27.

There is a "begin" mode on the TI BA II Plus, as there is on most financial calculators. We need to activate begin mode before solving this problem, which can be done as follows for the TI BA II Plus:

Press 2nd BGN 2nd Set . Then input the variables:

1,000 → PMT ;   5 → N ;   0 → PV ; and   13 → I/Y

Press CPT (Compute) and then FV . This gives an answer of −7,322.71. As before, recognize that the negative sign is due to the need for a series of cash inflows matched by a cash outflow.

The following Excel function may be used:

= FV (rate, nper, pmt, pv, type)

Now, we can see what the "type" stands for in the Excel formula. When type is set = 0, as in our previous examples, it refers to an ordinary annuity; when it is set = 1, it refers to an annuity due. So for this example, we would enter the following in the appropriate cell:

= FV (0.13, 5, −1,000, 0, 1)

This yields an answer of $7,322.71.

b. As before, to solve for the present value, we could view this as a five-part problem for which we have to find the present value of each of the five payments.

$$PV_0 = 1,000 \, (1/1.13)^4 + 1,000 \, (1/1.13)^3 + 1,000 \, (1/1.13)^2 + 1,000 \, (1/1.13)^1 + 1,000$$
$$= [1,000 \, (3.51724)](1.13) = \$3,974.48$$

Note that as in Example 5-9a, we are multiplying our answer to Example 5-8a by 1.13, that is (1 + k). Accordingly, we can modify Equation 5-5 to arrive at the formula for determining the PV of an *annuity due*, which is given below:

[5-7]

$$PV_0 = PMT \left[\frac{1 - \dfrac{1}{(1+k)^n}}{k} \right] (1+k)$$

Equation 5-7 is PVAF(1 + k). Using this to solve Example 5-9b, we get

$$PV_0 = \$1,000 \left| \frac{1 - \dfrac{1}{(1.13)^5}}{0.13} \right| (1.13) = [1,000(3.51723)](1.13) = \$3,974.47$$

Again, the difference of $0.01 is due to rounding errors in the long approach.

solution using a financial calculator

Example 5-9b
(TI BA II Plus)

First, activate the Begin (BGN) function. Then input the following variables:

1,000 → PMT ;   5 → N ;   0 → FV ; and   13 → I/Y

Press CPT (Compute) and then PV . This gives an answer of −3,974.47.

solution using Excel

Example 5-9b

The following Excel function may be used:

= PV (rate, nper, pmt, fv, type)

For this example, we would enter the following in the appropriate cell:

= PV (0.13, 5, −1000, 0, 1)

This gives an answer of $3,974.47.

Perpetuities

Perpetuities are special annuities in that they go on forever, so n goes to infinity in the annuity equation. In this case, Equation 5-5 reduces to

perpetuities special annuities that provide payments forever

$$PV_0 = \frac{PMT}{k}$$

[5-8]

   Perpetuities are easy to value because all we do is divide the cash payment or receipt by the interest rate.

Example 5-10: Annuities and Perpetuities

   a. An annuity pays $3,000 per year at year end and earns an annual return of 12 percent per year for 30 years. What is the present value?

   b. What is the PV of a $3,000 per year annuity that goes on forever, that is, in perpetuity, if $k = 12$ percent?

Solution

   a.

$$PV_0 = \$3,000 \left| \frac{1 - \dfrac{1}{(1.12)^{30}}}{0.12} \right| = 3,000(8.05518) = \$24,165.55$$

Input the following variables:

3,000 → PMT ;   30 → N ;   0 → FV ; and   12 → I/Y

Press CPT (Compute) and then PV . This will give an answer of −24,165.55.

The following Excel function may be used:

= PV (rate, nper, pmt, fv, type)

For this example, we would enter the following in the appropriate cell:

= PV (0.12, 30, −3000, 0, 0)

This would yield an answer of $24,165.55.

b. $PV_0 = \dfrac{\$3,000}{0.12} = \$25,000$

Notice the small difference in the present value of these cash streams. This tells you that the PV of the cash flows of $3,000 per year from years 31 to infinity (∞) is only $834.45, that is, $25,000−$24,165.55. This is a very important result and is behind many financial innovations. It means that cash flows far in the future are of very little value because of the discounting involved in the time value of money.[4]

Closing Remarks on Annuities and Perpetuities

We conclude this section by deriving the solution to the investing-early scenario described at the start of this section.

Example 5-11: Investing Early

Solve for Twin 1 from the scenario on page 173.

Solution

This must be solved as a two-part problem, which can then be solved in several ways. We first estimate the future value of the six $2,000 payments at the end of six years.

$$FV_6 = PMT\left[\frac{(1+k)^n - 1}{k}\right] = (2,000)\left[\frac{(1.12)^6 - 1}{0.12}\right] = (2,000)(8.11519) = 16,230.38$$

---

[4] It has also been behind many misleading advertisements for which something is 100 percent backed by a government bond. The small print indicates that the bond pays off in 25 years, so is not worth much today!

Then we estimate the future value of the accumulated savings after 38 years (i.e., from age 27 to age 65):

$$FV_{38} = PV_0(1 + k)^n = (16,230.38)(1.12)^{38} = (16,230.38)(74.17966) = \$1,203,964.13$$

Solve for Twin 2 from the scenario above.

$$FV_{38} = PMT\left[\frac{(1 + k)^n - 1}{k}\right] = (2,000)\left[\frac{(1.12)^{38} - 1}{0.12}\right] = (2,000)(609.83053) = \$1,219,661.06$$

So they both end up with approximately $1.2 million.

CONCEPT REVIEW QUESTIONS

1. Explain how to calculate the present value and future value of an ordinary annuity and an annuity date.

2. Define "perpetuity".

3. Why is the present value of $1 million in 50 years' time worth very little today?

5.5 NOMINAL VERSUS EFFECTIVE RATES

Determining Effective Annual Rates

So far, we have assumed that payments are made annually and that interest is compounded annually, so we have been able to use quoted rates to solve each problem. In practice, in many situations, payments are made (or received) at intervals other than annually (e.g., quarterly, monthly), and compounding often occurs more frequently than annually. We need to be sure that we use the appropriate effective interest rate.

The **effective rate** for a period is the rate at which a dollar invested grows over that period. It is usually stated in percentage terms based on an annual period. To determine effective rates, we first recognize that the annual rates quoted by financial institutions will equal the annual effective rate only when compounding is done on an annual basis. We will use some examples to illustrate the process for determining effective rates.

effective rate the rate at which a dollar invested grows over a given period; usually stated in percentage terms based on an annual period

Example 5-12: Effective versus Quoted Rates

a. Suppose someone invests $1,000 today for one year at a quoted annual rate of 16 percent compounded annually. What is the FV at the end of the year?

b. What if someone invests $1,000 at a quoted rate of 16 percent compounded quarterly?

Solution

a. FV = $1,000(1.16)^1$ = $1,160.

This means that each $1 grows to $1.16 by the end of the period, so we can say that the "effective" annual interest rate is 16 percent.

b. When the rate is "quoted" at 16 percent, and compounding is done quarterly, the appropriate adjustment (by convention) is to charge 16 percent/4 = 4 percent per quarter, so we have

$$FV = 1,000(1.04)^4 = \$1,170$$

Notice that even though the quoted rate is 16 percent, each dollar invested grows to $1.17, that is, by 17 percent by the end of the period. In this case, we say that the "effective" annual interest rate is 17 percent.

We can use the following equation to determine the effective annual rate for any given compounding interval:

[5-9]

$$k = (1 + \frac{QR}{m})^m - 1$$

where k = effective annual rate, QR = quoted rate, and m = the number of compounding intervals per year.

Applying this equation to the previous example, we see the following:

Solution

a. For $m = 1$, QR = 0.16, we get

$$k = (1 + \frac{0.16}{1})^1 - 1 = 0.16 = 16\%$$

so the quoted and effective rates are the same.

b. For $m = 4$, QR = 0.16, we get

$$k = (1 + \frac{0.16}{4})^4 - 1 = 0.1700 = 17\%$$

The effective rate is higher than the quoted rate. This is why it is important to examine the compounding frequency of investments and loans; looking at the rate alone is often not enough.

When compounding is conducted on a continuous basis, we use the following equation to determine the effective annual rate for a given quoted rate:

[5-10]

$$k = e^{QR} - 1$$

where e is the unique Euler number (approximately 2.718) and is found on your calculator and in Excel. It is used frequently in finance. If we use the Excel function, enter =exp(.16), and subtract 1.0, we get 17.351 percent.

The following example shows that as the frequency of compounding increases, the effective annual rate increases.

Example 5-13: Effective Annual Rates for Various Compounding Intervals

What are the effective annual rates for the following quoted rates?

a. 12 percent, compounded annually

b. 12 percent, compounded semi-annually

c. 12 percent, quarterly

d. 12 percent, monthly

e. 12 percent, daily

f. 12 percent, continuously

Solution

a. Annual compounding, $m = 1$: $k = (1 + \frac{0.12}{1})^1 - 1 = 12\%$

b. Semi-annual compounding, $m = 2$: $k = (1 + \frac{0.12}{2})^2 - 1 = 12.36\%$

c. Quarterly compounding, $m = 4$: $k = (1 + \frac{0.12}{4})^4 - 1 = 12.55\%$

d. Monthly compounding, $m = 12$: $k = (1 + \frac{0.12}{12})^{12} - 1 = 12.68\%$

e. Daily compounding, $m = 365$: $k = (1 + \frac{0.12}{365})^{365} - 1 = 12.747\%$

f. Continuous compounding: $k = e^{0.12} - 1 = 12.75\%$

This example shows that as the compounding frequency increases, the quoted rate of 12 percent increases to a maximum effective rate of 12.75 percent, achieved with instantaneous or continuous compounding. However, the daily rate is almost the same at 12.747 percent.

You can, of course, solve effective interest rate problems by using a calculator or Excel.

Example 5-13
(TI BA II Plus)

Perform the following keystrokes:

The screen will show NOM = some value
Make NOM = 12 (this is the nominal rate)
Then

(ENTER) (↓) (↓)

This should show C/Y = some value
For daily compounding, for example, input
C/Y = 365 (this is the number of compounding periods per year)

Then (ENTER) (↓) (↓) , which should show EFF = some value,

Then press (CPT), which gives an answer of 12.747 percent

solution using Excel

Example 5-13

Excel has a special function for solving for effective rates: the Effect(nominal, npery) function, for which nominal is the nominal interest rate and npery is the compounding frequency.[5] For any of the previous periods we would enter

=effect(0.12, n) with n = 1, 2, 4, 12, 365 and by using a very large number to approximate $n = \infty$, and we would get the answers above.

Effective Rates for "Any" Period

In Example 5-12b, the effective quarterly rate is 4 percent, because each dollar grows to $1.04 by the end of one quarter. Similarly, in Example 5-13 (which uses a quoted rate of 12 percent), the effective semi-annual rate for 5-13b is 6 percent (i.e., 12 percent/2), the effective quarterly rate for 5-13c is 3 percent (i.e., 12 percent/4), and the effective monthly rate for 5-13d is 1 percent (i.e., 12 percent/12).

However, suppose we need to know the effective monthly rate associated with the annual effective rate of 12.36 percent from Example 5-13b, perhaps to make monthly payments on a loan. It is not appropriate to divide 12.36 percent by 12, because it is an effective rate, not a quoted rate. Remember, we are looking for the effective monthly rate (i.e., how much $1 would grow by over a given month), based on an annual effective rate of 12.36 percent. In this case, we know that after 12 compounding intervals at a monthly effective rate of $k_{monthly}$, each $1 would have grown to $1.1236. In other words, we have

$$(1 + k_{monthly})^{12} = 1.1236$$

We could solve this equation by taking the 12th root of each side:

$$(1 + k_{monthly}) = (1.1236)^{1/12}$$

So, $k_{monthly} = (1.1236)^{1/12} - 1 = 0.0097588$ or 0.97588%.

We can verify this by compounding $1 at the rate of 0.97588 percent per month for 12 months as follows: $(1.0097588)^{12} = 1.1236$. In other words, investing $1 at 0.97588 percent per month produces the same amount at the end of one year (1.1236) as does investing $1 for one year with semi-annual compounding at 6 percent per six-month period.

The following equation, which is a variation of Equation 5-9, can be used to determine the effective rate for any period, given any quoted rates:

[5-11]
$$k = (1 + \frac{QR}{m})^{\frac{m}{f}} - 1$$

where f = frequency of payments per year (i.e., f = 1 when we are looking for an annual effective rate, f = 12 when looking for monthly effective rate, etc.). Notice that when f = 1, we have Equation 5-9.

---

[5] You may need to add the Analysis ToolPak in Excel, which can be done by clicking on Tools, then Add-Ins, then Analysis ToolPak, and then OK.

There is no specific function to solve for "other than annual" effective rates by using the TI BA II Plus calculator. We could find the effective annual rate for a 12 percent nominal rate with quarterly compounding (as demonstrated in the previous example), and then do the following:

$$(1 + k_{monthly})^{12} = 1.1236$$

$$\text{So, } (1 + k_{monthly}) = (1.1236)^{1/12}, \text{ and}$$

$$k_{monthly} = (1.1236)^{1/12} - 1 = 0.0097588 \text{ or } 0.97588\%$$

In Excel, we can go back to the rate function that we used previously. For example, if the annual rate is 12.36 percent and we want to know the effective monthly rate, then we can use the following:

$$=\text{Rate (nper, pmt, pv ,fv, type)}$$

$$=\text{Rate (12, 0, } -1, 1.1236, 0)$$

Where there are 12 periods and no intervening payments, and we are interested in a \$1 outflow growing to 1.1236. Because we are not interested in annuities, we put in 0 for type. This produces the same answer of 0.975879 percent.

CONCEPT REVIEW QUESTIONS

1. Why can effective rates often be very different from quoted rates?

2. Explain how to calculate the effective rate for any period.

5.6 LOAN OR MORTGAGE ARRANGEMENTS

One common and important application of annuity concepts is with respect to loan or **mortgage** arrangements. Typically, these arrangements involve "blended" payments for equal amounts that include both an interest and a principal repayment component. The loan payments are designed to **amortize** the loan, which means that at the end of the loan term, the balance due (or principal outstanding) will equal zero—in other words, the loan and all associated interest obligations will have been paid off in their entirety. Note that both "amortize" and "mortgage" have the French word *mort* in them, which means death. So a mortgage is killed off over the mortgage period and no money is owed at the end. Similarly, amortize means to kill off financially.

Because these loans involve equal payments at regular intervals, based on one fixed interest rate specified when the loan is taken out, the payments can be viewed as annuities. Therefore, we can determine the amount of the payment, the effective period interest rate, and so on, by using Equation 5-5 and recognizing that the PV equals the amount of the loan.

mortgage a loan, usually secured by real property, that involves "blended" equal payments (both an interest and a principal repayment) over a specified payment period

amortize to retire a loan over a given period by making regular payments

An *amortization* schedule divides the blended payments into the interest portion and the principal repayment portion. This is of importance to businesses, where the interest portion is a deductible expense for tax purposes. The interest portion is determined by applying the effective period interest rate to the principal outstanding at the beginning of each period. The remaining portion of the payment is then used to reduce the amount of principal outstanding. The example below shows the development of an amortization schedule.

Example 5-14: Loan Payments and Amortization Schedule

Determine the required year-end payments for a three-year $5,000 loan with a 10 percent annual interest rate. Complete an amortization schedule.

Solution

First, determine the required payments by solving Equation 5-5 for PMT:

$$PMT = \frac{PV_0}{\left[\dfrac{1 - \dfrac{1}{(1+k)^n}}{k}\right]} = \frac{5,000}{\left[\dfrac{1 - \dfrac{1}{(1.10)^3}}{0.10}\right]} = \frac{5,000}{2.48685} = \$2,010.57$$

$\boxed{\text{FV}} = 0;\ \boxed{\text{PV}} = 5,000;\ \boxed{\text{N}} = 3;\ \boxed{\text{I/Y}} = 10;$

Compute $\boxed{\text{PMT}} = -2,010.57$, or $2,010.57.

Use the Excel payment function (PMT):

=PMT(rate, nper, pv, fv, type)

which for our example gives =PMT(0.10, 3, 5,000, 0, 0), and the same answer of $2,010.57.

Second, determine the loan amortization schedule:

Period	(1)Beg. Princ. Outstanding	(2) PMT	(3) Interest [(1)*k]	(4) Principal Repayment [(2) − (3)]	End Princ. Outstanding [(1) − (4)]
1	5,000.00	2,010.57	500.00	1,510.57	3,489.43
2	3,489.43	2,010.57	348.94	1,661.63	1,827.79
3	1,827.80	2,010.57	182.78	1,827.79	0.00

You need to understand how this amortization table is created. The loan is a simple annual payment loan, so the cost of the loan is the annual interest rate times the outstanding balance, in this case 10 percent times $5,000, or $500. This is the first charge on the loan payments; the residual, which is $1,510.57 in the first year, goes to reduce the amount of the loan.

For the next year, the outstanding balance on the loan is now $3,489.43 and the cost of the loan goes down to $348.94, even though the payment is the same at $2,010.57. As a result, the amount going toward the repayment of the loan increases to $1,661.63.

Note that Excel users can automate the whole process of generating an amortization table by typing amortization into the online help and downloading the amortization template. For our example, Excel produced the information presented in Figure 5-2.

5-2   FIGURE

Mortgage Loan Payments

Mortgage loan payments

Enter values				Loan summary		
Loan amount	$	5,000.00		Scheduled payment	$	2,010.57
Annual interest rate		10.00 %		Scheduled number of payments		3
Loan period in years		3		Actual number of payments		3
Number of payments per year		1		Total early payments	$	-
Start date of loan		06/11/2006		Total interest	$	1,031.72
Optional extra payments	$	-				

Lender Name: [   ]

Pmt No.	Payment date	Beginning balance	Scheduled payment	Extra payment	Total payment	Principal	Interest	Ending balance	Cumulative interest
1	06/11/2007	$ 5,000.00	$ 2,010.57	$ -	$ 2,010.57	$ 1,510.57	$ 500.00	$ 3,489.43	$ 500.00
2	06/11/2008	3,489.43	2,010.57	-	2,010.57	1,661.63	348.94	1,827.79	848.94
3	06/11/2009	1,827.79	2,010.57	-	1,827.79	1,645.02	182.78	0.00	1,031.72

However, even though you can use Excel, you should practise generating your own schedule by using the PMT function and writing out each line separately since Excel sometimes presents the data in a way that your instructor might not accept. Note the heading of the loan amortization schedule and the last line of the schedule compared with the one we developed.

Example 5-15: Determining the Principal Outstanding

Determine the principal outstanding on the loan in Example 5-14 after one year, without making reference to the amortization schedule found in the solution.

Solution

This problem can be solved by recognizing that the principal outstanding at any time on a loan equals the PV of all future payments at that time. For this example, we find the PV for the given payments and interest rate when $n = 2$ (i.e., for the number of payments remaining on the loan after one year):

$$PV_0 = PMT \left[\frac{1 - \frac{1}{(1+k)^n}}{k} \right] = \$2,010.57 \left[\frac{1 - \frac{1}{(1.10)^2}}{0.10} \right] = (\$2,010.57)(1.735537) = \$3,489.42$$

solution using a financial calculator

(TI BA II Plus)

$\boxed{PMT} = 2010.57;$ $\boxed{I/Y} = 10;$ $\boxed{N} = 2;$ $\boxed{FV} = 0;$

Compute $\boxed{PV} = -3,489.42.$

Use the Excel PV function

=PV (rate, nper, pv, fv, type),

which for our example gives =PV (0.10, 2, 2,010.57, 0, 0) and the same answer of $3,489.42.

Notice again that the answers are the same except for $0.01 because of rounding. Remember that the answer will come out as negatives because we are investing money and then receiving a payoff.

Mortgages

In practice, loan repayments are often not made on an annual basis, with many calling for quarterly, monthly, or even weekly repayments. For these arrangements, we need to convert the quoted annual rates into effective period rates that correspond to the frequency of payments, which can be done by using Equation 5-11. This conversion is needed to determine the interest that accrued during the period in question based on the principal outstanding at the beginning of the payment period (i.e., at the beginning of the month, week, etc.), because that amount will be reduced after the payment is made.

Mortgages represent an example of a loan that requires that payments be made more frequently than annually. In fact, mortgage payments must be made at least monthly, but many offer the opportunity to make biweekly or weekly payments. In Canada, mortgages are further complicated by the fact that compounding is done on a semi-annual basis, similar to bonds, which we will discuss in Chapter 6. When we deal with mortgages in Canada, $m = 2$ in Equation 5-11, while $f > 2$ (in fact, f must be greater than or equal to 12, since payments must be made at least monthly).

Finally, there is one other thing to be familiar with: the distinction between the "term" and the "amortization period" associated with long-term loans, such as mortgages. In particular, the term of a loan refers to the period for which investors can "lock in" at a fixed rate. This is usually shorter than the period over which the loan is to be repaid, or amortized, which is called the amortization period. The payments are based on the amortization period. For example, a loan with a 25-year amortization period may be structured so that the investor locks in a fixed rate of 6 percent for five years (which is the term of the loan). The payments for this loan would be determined based on the 6 percent quoted rate, assuming equal payments for 25 years even though after five years the payments will change if the interest rate on the mortgage changes. The example below demonstrates how to apply these concepts in practice.

Example 5-16: Determining Mortgage Payments and Amortization Schedule

Determine the monthly payments and the amortization schedule for the first three months of a $200,000 mortgage loan with an amortization period of 25 years, based on a quoted rate of 6 percent and a 10-year term.

Solution

First, determine the effective period rate.

Because it is a Canadian mortgage, we know that $m = 2$. Since payments are made monthly, we need to find the effective monthly rate, so $f = 12$.

Using Equation 5-11, $k_{monthly} = (1 + \dfrac{0.06}{2})^{\frac{2}{12}} - 1 = 0.4938622\%.$

Second, determine the required monthly payments by using Equation 5-5. There are 300 payments in total, since $n = 25$ years $\times$ 12 months $= 300$. $PV = 200{,}000$ (i.e., the loan amount).

$$PMT = \dfrac{PV_0}{\left[\dfrac{1 - \dfrac{1}{(1+k)^n}}{k}\right]} = \dfrac{200{,}000}{\left[\dfrac{1 - \dfrac{1}{(1.004938622)^{300}}}{0.004938622}\right]} = \dfrac{200{,}000}{156.2972258} = \$1{,}279.61$$

$\boxed{PV} = 200{,}000;$ $\boxed{I/Y} = 0.4938622;$ $\boxed{N} = 300;$ $\boxed{FV} = 0;$

Compute $\boxed{PMT} = -1{,}279.61.$

Third, construct an amortization schedule similar to the one in Example 5-14 above:

Period	(1) Beg. Princ. Outstanding	(2) PMT	(3) Interest $[k \times (1)]$	(4) Principal Reduction $[(2) - (3)]$	End Princ. Outstanding $[(1) - (4)]$
1	200,000.00	1,279.61	987.72	291.89	199,708.11
2	199,708.11	1,279.61	986.28	293.33	199,414.79
3	199,414.79	1,279.61	984.83	294.78	199,120.01

Note that unlike the simple annual payment loan for which the cost of the loan was the annual interest cost, now the cost is the monthly interest rate of 0.4938622 percent because we have a monthly amortization schedule. It is this monthly rate applied to the outstanding balance that determines how much of the mortgage's monthly payments represent the cost of the loan. As is clear from the amortization schedule, very little of the early payments go toward reducing the principal—most of the early payments are for interest. This is true for all long-term loans, because by definition the repayment of the loan is being done over a longer period. As time passes, the interest cost of the fixed payments continues to decrease and the payment of principal correspondingly increases. The reason for this is simply that the interest rate is the cost of borrowing money and this cost has to be subtracted first from the monthly payment.

As before, Excel simplifies the whole process. However, note that Excel reports mortgage costs according to U.S. and not Canadian practice in quoting mortgage rates. In Canada, mortgage rates are quoted equivalent to bonds, so a

6 percent quoted mortgage rate is actually 3 percent every six months and the monthly rate is then determined as the monthly rate that compounds to 3 percent over six months or 0.49386 percent. In the United States, the same 6 percent quote means 0.5 percent per month, that is, the annual rate is simply divided by 12. As a result the same quoted mortgage rate in the United States and Canada will produce different results. The first three months of the Excel amortization table are shown in Figure 5-3:

FIGURE 5-3

Mortgage Loan Payments

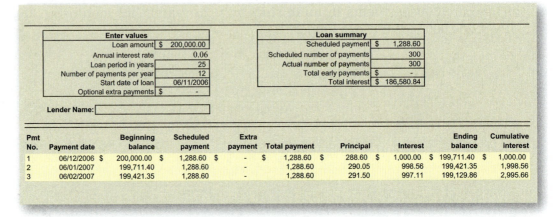

Note that for the first month, the interest payment is simply 0.5 percent times the principal of $200,000, or $1,000, versus $987.72 for the true (Canadian) cost. Also note that the monthly payment is $9 higher at $1,288.60.

Excel is a wonderful software program, but before using the sophisticated functions, always check the answers by using the basic functions first to make sure that the macros written by the programmers are consistent with what you want to estimate. For Canadian mortgages, you can check with a variety of mortgage calculators available free on the Internet that also produce amortization schedules.[6]

One question of interest to a mortgagee would be how much of the loan would be retired after a certain time. We can solve this problem in the same manner that we used for Example 5-15.

Example 5-17: Determining the Principal Outstanding on a Mortgage

Determine the principal outstanding on the mortgage in Example 5-16 at the end of the 10-year term.

Solution

Trying to solve this by constructing an amortization schedule to the end of 10 years would be cumbersome. However, it is easily solved by recognizing that the principal outstanding is the PV of all future payments after 10 years. We find the PV for the payments when n = 15 years $\times$ 12 months = 180 months, that is, for the balance of the payments after 10 years:

$$PV_0 = \$1,279.61 \left[\frac{1 - \dfrac{1}{(1.004938622)^{180}}}{0.004938622} \right] = (\$1,279.61)(119.0642325) = \$152,355.78$$

[6] A well-presented calculator is available on the website of Bankrate.com: www.bankrate.com/goocan/mortgage-calculator.asp.

PMT = 1,279.61; I/Y = 0.4938622; N = 180; FV = 0;

Compute PV = −152,355.78.

=PV (0.004938622, 180, 1,279.61, 0, 0) gives the same answer of −$152,355.78. Note as before that the interest rate is inserted in decimals.

Notice in Example 5-17 that slightly less than 25 percent of the loan has been repaid after 10 years, even though 40 percent of the amortization period (i.e., 10 out of 25 years) has elapsed. This is consistent with our earlier observation with respect to the high proportion of each of the early payments going toward interest versus principal reduction. However, remember that this $152,355.78 is the amount owed after ten years; the present value of this would be a lot less. We leave it as an exercise to work out the present value of the amount of the mortgage still outstanding at the end of 10 years.

CONCEPT REVIEW QUESTIONS

1. Explain how loan and mortgage payments can be determined using annuity concepts.
2. What complications arise when dealing with mortgage loans in Canada?
3. Why is a 6 percent U.S. mortgage not the same as a 6 percent Canadian mortgage?

5.7 COMPREHENSIVE EXAMPLES

We conclude this chapter by providing a few comprehensive examples that involve applying the concepts you have learned to more challenging situations. The second example is a common problem facing investors with respect to planning for retirement.

Example 5-18: Multiple Annuities

a. What is the PV of $1,000 received at year end for the next four years, followed by $2,000 per year end for years 5 to 7, assuming a 10 percent rate of interest, compounded annually?

b. Suppose an investor needed $15,000 at the end of seven years and can only invest $1,000 per year for years 1 to 4 (as above). How much would the investor need to deposit in each of years 5 to 7 to achieve this objective, assuming a 10 percent interest rate as above?

Solution

a. This problem is best solved by first constructing a timeline:

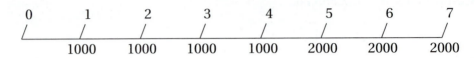

Notice that we can view this problem in several ways. It can be viewed as a four-year annuity of $1,000 followed by a three-year annuity of $2,000, or as a seven-year annuity of $1,000, with a three-year annuity of an "extra" $1,000 beginning at the end of year 5, and so on. Also, we could solve it by finding the future value of both annuities at $t = 7$ and then discounting them, or by finding the PV of the second annuity at $t = 4$ and discounting it back to $t = 0$, which is the approach we have chosen.

Viewing this problem as a four-year ordinary annuity (A1) that pays $1,000 per year, followed by a three-year ordinary annuity (A2) that pays $2,000 per year, we can determine the PV as follows:

$$PV(A1) = 1,000 \left[\frac{1 - \frac{1}{(1.10)^4}}{.10} \right] = 1000(3.16987) = \$3,169.87$$

$$PV(A2) = 2,000 \left[\frac{1 - \frac{1}{(1.10)^3}}{0.10} \right] \left[\frac{1}{(1.10)^4} \right] = 2000(2.48685)(0.683013) = \$3,397.10$$

Notice that for PV(A2), we first determine the PV of the three-year annuity starting at time $t = 4$, (i.e., 4,973.70) then we discount this amount back to today.

(TI BA II Plus)

Enter the following:

0 → [FV] ;   1,000 → [PMT] ;   10 → [I/Y] ;   4 → [N]

Then, [CPT] → [PV] will = −3,169.87

Then, enter the following:

0 → [FV] ;   −2,000 → [PMT] ;   10 → [I/Y] ;   3 → [N]

Then, [CPT] → [PV] will = 4,973.70

This is the PV of the three-year annuity at time $t = 4$, which must be discounted back to time $t = 0$.

Second, enter the following:

4,973.70 → FV ;   0 → PMT ;   10 → I/Y ;   4 → N

then, CPT → PV will = −3,397.10

Using Excel, calculate PV(A1) = PV(0.10, 4,0, −1,000, 0, 0)

We can calculate Excel PV (A2) by first calculation PV of the three-year annuity as

=PV (0.1, 3, −2,000.00, 0, 0)

which gives $4,937.70, and then use

=PV (0.1, 4, 0, −4,937.70, 0)

which gives $3,397.10.

However, we can do this in one step with Excel by recognizing that we can nest Excel functions within each other. In this case, we can write it in one step as

=PV (0.10, 4, 0, PV (0.10, 3, −2,000, 0, 0), 0)

and we would get the same answer.

So the PV(Total) = PV(A1) + PV(A2) = 3,169.87 + 3,397.10 = $6,566.97.

In all these problems, the interest rate need not be the same over the two periods. For our example the interest rate for the second three-year period could be 10 percent, while for the first four periods it could be 5 percent. In this case the Excel solution would be

=PV (0.05, 4, 0, PV (0.10, 3, −2,000, 0, 0), 0)

and the value increases to $4,091.88.

b. This problem can also be best represented by using a timeline:

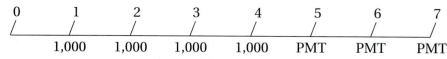

We can solve this problem in several ways. We have chosen to solve it by finding the future value of the first annuity (A1) at $t = 7$, and then determining the FV of the second annuity (A2) at $t = 7$, required to achieve the $15,000 target. Then, knowing the required FV of the three-year annuity, we can determine the payments for years 5 to 7.

Determine the FV of A1 at time $t = 4$:

$$FV_4(A1) = 1,000 \times \left[\frac{(1+0.10)^4 - 1}{0.10}\right] = (1,000)(4.641) = \$4,641$$

Second, determine the FV of A1 at time $t = 7$:

$$FV_7(A1) = 4,641 \times (1.10)^3 = (4,641)(1.331) = \$6,177.17$$

Third, determine the required FV of A2 at time $t = 7$:

Required FV7(A1) = Required amount − FV7(A1) = 15,000 − 6,177.17 = \$8,822.83

Fourth, determine the required payments for A2:

$$PMT = \frac{8,822.83}{\left[\dfrac{(1.10)^3 - 1}{0.10}\right]} = \frac{8,822.83}{3.31} = \$2,665.51$$

solution using a financial calculator

(TI BA II Plus)

First, enter the following:

0 → PV ; −1,000 → PMT ; 10 → I/Y ; 4 → N

then, CPT → FV will = 4,641

Second, enter the following:

4,641 → PV ; 0 → PMT ; 10 → I/Y ; 3 → N

then, CPT → FV will = −6,177.17

Third, enter the following:

8,822.83 → FV ; 0 → PV ; 10 → I/Y ; 3 → N

then, CPT → PMT will = −2,665.51

solution using Excel

=FV (0.1, 4, −1000, 0, 0) gives an answer of \$4,641.

=FV (0.10, 3, 0, 4641, 0) gives an answer of \$6,177.17.

Then we can use the payment function
=PMT (rate, nper, pv, fv, type) so that inserting our values
=PMT (0.10, 3, 0, 8822.83, 0) gives the same answer of \$2,665.51.

If we are really ambitious we can collapse all three Excel functions into a single one and input

=PMT (0.10, 3, 0, 15000+FV(0.10, 3, 0, FV(0.10, 4, −1000, 0, 0), 0), 0)

and get the right answer. However, although this shows the power of Excel, and it is not recommended. Much can be learned by breaking the problem into its three constituent parts because you need to develop an understanding of what is approximately the right answer. This is lost when you collapse it all into one function. Furthermore, you have to be careful because Excel provides a negative present value if the payoff is positive because it treats the values as those from an investment. In our case, we have to add the future value from the annuity since Excel provides a negative value for this.

Example 5-19: Retirement Problem

An investor plans to retire 35 years from today and have sufficient savings to guarantee $48,000 each year for 20 years. Assume retirement withdrawals will be made at the beginning of each of the 20 years. The investor estimates that at the time of retirement, he can sell his business for $200,000. The expectation is that interest rates will be relatively stable at 8 percent a year for the next 35 years. Thereafter, the interest rate is expected to decline to 6 percent forever. The investor wants to make equal annual deposits at the end of each of the next 35 years. How much should be deposited each year in order to meet the stated objective?

Solution

A timeline helps visualize the problem:

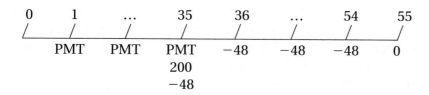

$k = 8$ percent for years 1 to 35 $k = 6$ percent for years 35 to 55

First, Determine how much is needed after 35 years. At this time the investor wants a 20-year *annuity due* of $48,000, because he is drawing down funds immediately on retirement, at a 6 percent interest rate. In other words, find the PV of a 20-year annuity due, when $k = 6$ percent:

$$PV_{35} = 48,000 \left[\frac{1 - \dfrac{1}{(1.06)^{20}}}{0.06} \right] (1.06) = (48,000)(11.46992122)(1.06) = \$583,589.59$$

First, set your calculator to Begin mode and then enter

FV = 0 ; PMT = 48,000 ; I/Y = 6 ; N = 20

and compute PV = −583,589.59 or $583,589.59.

Second, subtract the $200,000 expected from the sale of the business, leaving the amount needed to raise through investments:

Need FV_{35} = 583,589.59 − 200,000 = $383,589.59

Third, determine the required year-end payments over the next 35 years:

$$PMT = \frac{383,589.59}{\left[\dfrac{(1.08)^{35}-1}{0.08}\right]} = \frac{383,589.59}{172.3168037} = \$2,226.07$$

Finally, take your calculator out of Begin mode. Enter

PV = 0 ; FV = 383,589.59 ; I/Y = 8 ; N = 35

then compute PMT = −2,226.07 or $2,226.07.

Or, using Excel,

=PV (0.06, 20, 48000, 0, 1)

gives the same answer of $583,589.59. However, now that we need an annuity due, we have to put a 0 in for the future value to let Excel know that the 1 in the last column refers to an annuity due and is not a future value. If we then use the payment function to calculate the annuity we get
=PMT (0.08, 35, 0, 383,589.59, 0)

We get $2,226.07. As before, we can collapse this into one function as
=PMT (0.08, 35, 0, PV(0.06, 20, −48,000, 0, 1) −200,000, 0)

But this is not advisable until you have more experience with Excel.

Notice that the two problems in this section appear complicated at first but are quite manageable if you break them down into their components. Timelines are very useful for this purpose, because they help you visualize what information you have and what is needed to solve the problem. If you are able to solve these problems, then you have a good understanding of the basic concepts involving the time value of money.

CONCEPT REVIEW

1. Explain how timelines can be used to break a complicated time value of money into manageable components.

2. Demonstrate how to solve a typical retirement problem.

Summary

This chapter demonstrates how to compare cash flows that occur at different points in time, after accounting for the time value of money. This process is applied to virtually every topic that is studied in finance, so it is extremely important. We show how to determine economically equivalent future values from values that occur in previous periods by applying the process of compounding at an appropriate rate of return. Similarly, we show how to determine economically equivalent present values (in today's dollars) for cash flows that occur in the future by discounting them, which is the reciprocal of compounding. These processes can be applied to several cash flows simultaneously.

Annuities represent a special type of cash flow stream that involve equal payments at the same interval, with the same interest rate being applied throughout the period. We see that these kinds of cash flow streams are commonplace in finance applications (e.g., loan payments) and that there are relatively simple formulas that enable us to determine the present value or future value of these cash flows. We also illustrate how to adjust quoted interest rates to find effective rates, which is important because compounding often takes place at other than annual intervals. Finally, we conclude with some more involved applications of the concepts discussed in the chapter.

Key Terms

amortize, p. 185

annuity, p. 173

annuity due, p. 177

basis point, p. 168

cash flows, p. 173

compound interest, p. 162

compound value interest factor (CVIF), p. 164

discount rate, p. 161

discounting, p. 168

effective rate, p. 181

lessee, p. 177

medium of exchange, p. 160

mortgage, p. 185

ordinary annuities, p. 174

perpetuities, p. 179

present value interest factor (PVIF), p. 169

reinvested, p. 163

required rate of return, p. 161

simple interest, p. 161

time value of money, p. 160

Formulas/Equations

[5-1]   Value (time n) = P + ($n \times$ P $\times k$)

[5-2] $FV_n = PV_0(1 + k)^n$

[5-3] $PV_0 = \dfrac{FV_n}{(1+k)^n} = FV_n \times \dfrac{1}{(1+k)^n}$

[5-4] $FV_n = PMT\left[\dfrac{(1+k)^n - 1}{k}\right]$

[5-5] $PV_0 = PMT\left[\dfrac{1 - \dfrac{1}{(1+k)^n}}{k}\right]$

[5-6] $FV_n = PMT\left[\dfrac{(1+k)^n - 1}{k}\right](1+k)$

[5-7] $PV_0 = PMT\left[\dfrac{1 - \dfrac{1}{(1+k)^n}}{k}\right](1+k)$

[5-8] $PV_0 = \dfrac{PMT}{k}$

[5-9] $k = (1 + \dfrac{QR}{m})^m - 1$

[5-10] $k = e^{QR} - 1$

[5-11] $k = (1 + \dfrac{QR}{m})^{\frac{m}{f}} - 1$

QUESTIONS AND PRACTICE PROBLEMS

Multiple Choice Questions

1. What is the total amount accumulated after three years if someone invests $1,000 today with a simple annual interest rate of 5 percent? With a compound annual interest rate of 5 percent?

   A. $1,150, $1,103

   B. $1,110, $1,158

    C. $1,150, $1,158

    D. $1,110, $1,103

2. Which of the following has the largest future value if $1,000 is invested today?

    A. Five years with a simple annual interest rate of 10 percent

    B. 10 years with a simple annual interest rate of 8 percent

    C. Eight years with a compound annual interest rate of 8 percent

    D. Eight years with a compound annual interest rate of 7 percent

Interest rates in the following questions are compound rates unless otherwise stated

3. Suppose an investor wants to have $10 million to retire 45 years from now. How much would she have to invest today with an annual rate of return equal to 15 percent?

    A. $18,561

    B. $17,844

    C. $20,003

    D. $21,345

4. Which of the following is *false*?

    A. The longer the time period, the smaller the present value, given a $100 future value and holding the interest rate constant.

    B. The greater the interest rate, the greater the present value, given a $100 future value and holding the time period constant.

    C. A future dollar is always less valuable than a dollar today if interest rates are positive.

    D. The discount factor is the reciprocal of the compound factor.

5. Maggie deposits $10,000 today and is promised a return of $17,000 in eight years. What is the implied annual rate of return?

    A. 6.86 percent

    B. 7.06 percent

    C. 5.99 percent

    D. 6.07 percent

6. To triple $1 million, Mika invested today at an annual rate of return of 9 percent. How long will it take Mika to achieve his goal?

    A. 15.5 years

    B. 13.9 years

    C. 12.7 years

    D. 10 years

7. Which of the following concepts is *incorrect*?

    A. An ordinary annuity has payments at the end of each year.

    B. An annuity due has payments at the beginning of each year.

C. A perpetuity is considered a perpetual annuity.

D. An ordinary annuity has a greater PV than an annuity due, if they both have the same periodic payments, discount rate and time period.

8. Jan plans to invest an equal amount of $2,000 in an equity fund every year-end beginning this year. The expected annual return on the fund is 15 percent. She plans to invest for 20 years. How much could she expect to have at the end of 20 years?

A. $237,620

B. $176,424

C. $204,887

D. $178,424

9. In Problem 8, what is the present value of Jan's investments?

A. $12,625

B. $12,519

C. $14,396

D. $12,396

10. What is the present value of a perpetuity with an annual year-end payment of $1,500 and expected annual rate of return equal to 12 percent?

A. $14,000

B. $13,500

C. $11,400

D. $12,500

Practice Problems

Easy

11. After a summer of travelling (and not working), a student finds himself $1,500 short for this year's tuition fees. His parents have agreed to loan him the money for three years at a simple interest rate of 6 percent, with interest due at the end of each year.

A. How much interest will he owe his parents after one year?

B. How much will he owe, in total, after three years?

12. Your sister has been forced to borrow money to pay her tuition this year. If she makes annual payments on the loan at year end for the next three years, and the loan is for $2,500 at a simple interest rate of 6 percent, how much will she pay each year?

13. Khalil's summer job has given him $1,200 more than he needs for tuition this year. The local bank pays simple interest at a rate of 0.5 percent per month. How much interest will he earn in one year?

14. A new Internet bank pays compound interest of 0.5 percent per month on deposits. How much interest will Khalil's summer savings of $1,200 earn in one year with this online bank account?

15. History tells us that a group of Dutch colonists purchased the island of Manhattan from the Native American residents in 1626. Payment was made with wampum (likely glass beads and trinkets), which had an estimated value of $24. Suppose the Dutch had invested this money back home in Europe and earned an average return of 5 percent per year. How much would this investment be worth today, 380 years later, using:

A. Simple interest?

B. Compound interest?

16. David has been awarded a scholarship that will pay $2,500 one year from now. However, he really needs the money today, and has decided to take out a loan. If the interest rate is 8 percent, how much can he borrow so that the scholarship will just pay off the loan?

17. Grace, a retired librarian, would like to donate some money to her alma mater to endow a $4,000 annual scholarship. The university will manage the funds, and expects to earn 7 percent per year. How much will Grace have to donate so that the endowment fund never runs out?

18. Grace decides that creating a perpetual scholarship is too costly (see Problem 17). Instead, she would like to support the education of her favourite grand-nephew, Stephen, who plans to begin university in three years. How much will Grace have to invest today, at 7 percent, to be able to give Stephen $4000 at the end of each year for four years?

19. Bank A pays 7.25 percent interest compounded semi-annually, Bank B pays 7.20 percent compounded quarterly, and Bank C pays 7.15 percent compounded monthly. Which bank pays the highest effective annual rate?

20. Jimmie is buying a new car. His bank quotes a rate of 9.5 percent per year for a car loan. Calculate the effective annual rate if the compounding occurs:

A. Annually

B. Quarterly

C. Monthly

21. If Alysha puts $50,000 in a savings account paying 6 percent per year, how much money will she have in total at the end of the first year if interest is compounded:

A. Annually?

B. Monthly?

C. Daily?

22. Tony started a small business and was too busy to consider saving for retirement. Tony sold the business for $550,000 when he was 55 years old. He thought he could fund his retirement, because this was a lot more than his friend had amassed in his account. Tony can invest this total sum and earn 10 percent per year. How much will his investment be worth in five years?

23. Public corporations have no fixed life span; as such, they are often viewed as entities that will pay dividends to their shareholders in perpetuity. Suppose

KashKow Inc. pays a dividend of $2 per share every year. If the discount rate is 12 percent, what is the present value of all the future dividends?

24. Mary-Beth is planning to live in a university residence for four years while completing her degree. The annual cost for food and lodging is $5,800 and must be paid at the start of each school year. What is the total present value of Mary-Beth's residence fees if the discount rate (interest rate) is 6 percent per year?

Medium

25. Calculate the effective annual rates for the following:

   A. 24 percent, compounded daily
   B. 24 percent, compounded quarterly
   C. 24 percent, compounded every four months
   D. 24 percent, compounded semi-annually
   E. 24 percent, compounded continuously
   F. Calculate the effective monthly rate for A to D.

26. On the advice of a friend, Gilda invests $20,000 in a mutual fund which has earned 10 percent per year, on average, in recent years. If this rate of return continues, how much will her investment be worth in:

   A. one year?
   B. five years?
   C. ten years?

27. Your investment research has turned up an interesting mutual fund. It has had an average annual return 0.5 percent greater than the one Gilda's friend recommended (see Problem 26). For each time period from Problem 26, calculate how much better off Gilda would be if she invested $20,000 in this mutual fund.

28. When Jon graduates in three years, he wants to throw a big party, which will cost $800. To have this amount available, how much does he have to invest today if he can earn a compound return of 5 percent per year?

29. In Problem 28, suppose Jon had only $500 to invest. How much can he plan to spend on the graduation party in three years, if the return on the investment will be:

   A. simple interest at 5 percent per year?
   B. compound interest at 5 percent per year?

30. At the age of 10, Felix decided that he wanted to attend a very prestigious (and expensive) university. How much will his parents have to save each year to accumulate $40,000 by the time Felix needs the funds in eight years? Assume Felix's parents can earn 7 percent (compounded annually) on their savings, and that each year's savings are deposited at the end of the year.

31. Felix's parents can only afford to save $3,000 per year for his university education, which begins in eight years. What rate of return would they require on these savings if they must accumulate $40,000?

32. Shortly after John was born, his parents began to put money in a savings account to pay for his post-secondary education. They save $1,000 each year, and earn a return of 9 percent per year. However, the interest income is taxed each year at a rate of 30 percent. How much will John's account be worth after 17 years?

33. John's parents used a regular savings account to save for his post-secondary education. Based on the amount accumulated (from your answer in Problem 32), how much can John withdraw from the account at the beginning of each year for his four years at university? The account will continue to earn 9 percent per year, but interest income is taxed at a rate of 30 percent.

34. Jane's parents save $1,000 per year for 17 years to pay for her university tuition costs. They deposit the money into a Registered Education Saving Plan (RESP) account so that no tax is payable on the interest income. This RESP account provides a return of 6 percent per year.

   A. How much will Jane's account be worth when she begins her university studies?

   B. As an incentive to save for higher education, the government will add 20 percent to any money contributed to an RESP each year. Including these grants, how much will Jane have in her account?

35. Jane's parents used an RESP account to save for her post-secondary education. Based on the amount accumulated (from your answer in Problem 34), Jane would like to withdraw the same amount of money at the beginning of each year of her four-year degree program. All funds (interest and principal) withdrawn from this account are taxed at a rate of 15 percent, and the account will earn 6 percent per year on any remaining funds. How much will Jane have available for tuition each year?

36. Stephen has learned that his great-aunt (see Problem 18) intends to give him $4,000 each year he is studying at university. Tuition must be paid in advance, so Stephen would like to receive his payments at the beginning of each school year. How much will his great-aunt have to invest today at 7 percent, to make the four annual (start-of-year) payments?

37. Rather than give her grand-nephew some money each year while he is studying, Stephen's great-aunt has decided to save the money and pay off Stephen's student loans when he finishes his degree. The total amount owing at that time will be $16,000. How much will she have to save each year until that time if her investments earn a return of 7 percent per year?

38. Jimmie's new car (see Problem 20) will cost $29,000. How much will his monthly car payments be if he obtains a loan that is amortized over 60 months, and the nominal interest rate is 8.5 percent per year with monthly compounding?

39. Create an amortization schedule for Jimmie's car loan (see Problem 38). What portion of the first monthly payment goes towards repaying the principal amount of the loan? What portion of the last monthly payment goes towards the principal?

40. Using the amortization schedule from Problem 39, determine how much Jimmie still owes on the car loan after three years of payments on the five-year loan. What is the present value of this amount?

41. Jimmie would like to pay off his car loan in three years (see Problem 38), but can only afford monthly payments of $594.98. How big a down payment must Jimmie make on the $29,000 car if the nominal interest rate is 8.5 percent with monthly compounding?

42. Jimmie is offered another loan of $29,000 that requires 60 monthly payments of $588.02 (see Problem 38). What is the effective annual interest rate on this loan? What would the quoted rate be?

43. To start a new business, Su Mei intends to borrow $25,000 from a local bank. If the bank asks her to repay the loan in five equal annual instalments of $6,935.24, determine the bank's effective annual interest rate on the loan transaction. With annual compounding, what nominal rate would the bank quote for this loan?

44. The Business Development Bank is willing to loan Su Mei the $25,000 she needs to start her new company. The loan will require monthly payments of $556.11 over five years.

    A. What is the effective monthly rate on this loan?
    B. With monthly compounding, what is the nominal (annual) interest rate on this loan?

45. Compare the loans in Problems 43 and 44. Which is the better deal, and why?

46. After losing money playing on-line poker, Scott visits a loan shark for a $750 loan. To avoid a visit from the "collection agency," he will have to repay $800 in just one week.

    A. What is the nominal interest rate per week? Per year?
    B. What is the effective annual interest rate?

47. Josephine needs to borrow $180,000 to purchase her new house in Yarmouth, Nova Scotia. She would like to pay off the mortgage in 20 years, making monthly payments. For the initial three-year term, Providence Bank has offered her a quoted annual rate of 6.40 percent.

    A. What is the effective annual interest rate?
    B. What is the effective monthly interest rate?
    C. How much will Josephine's monthly mortgage payments be?

48. The Yarmouth Credit Union will provide Josephine with a mortgage at a rate of 6.36 percent, but unlike most Canadian mortgages, the compounding will occur monthly. Should Josephine take out the mortgage loan from the Credit Union, or from Providence Bank (see Problem 47)? Can you answer this question without calculating the monthly mortgage payment?

49. Assume Josephine chose the Providence Bank option (see Problem 47). If Josephine can get the same interest rate for a second three-year term as she did originally, how much will her monthly payments be now?

50. A lakefront house in Kingston, Ontario is for sale with an asking price of $499,000. The real-estate market has been quite active, so the house will almost certainly attract several offers, and may sell for more than the asking price. Charlie is very eager to purchase this house, but is concerned that he may not be able to afford it. He has $130,000 available for a down payment, and can pay up to $1,950.00 per month on a mortgage loan. As a long-time customer, Charlie's bank has offered him a great mortgage rate of 3.90 percent on a one-year term. If the loan will be amortized over 25 years, what is the most that Charlie can afford to pay for the house?

51. Timmy sets himself a goal of amassing $1 million in his retirement fund by the time he turns 61. He begins saving $3,000 each year, starting on his 21st birthday (40 years of saving).

    A   If his savings earn 10 percent per year, will Timmy achieve his goal?

    B.   Will Timmy be able to retire before he turns 60? That is, at what age will the value of his savings plan be worth $1 million?

52. Tommy set the same retirement goal as his friend Timmy (see Problem 51). However, there always seemed to be a reason not to save money, so he put it off for many years. Finally, with just 15 years to retirement, he began to save. Fortunately, Tommy's executive-level job allowed him to save $30,000 per year. If these savings earn 10 percent per year, will Tommy achieve his $1million goal at the desired time?

53. Jack is 28 years old now and plans to retire in 35 years. He works in a local bank and has an annual after-tax income of $45,000. His expected annual expenditure is $36,000 and the rest of his income will be invested at the beginning of each of the next 35 years at an expected annual rate of return of 12.6 percent. Calculate the amount Jack will receive when he retires.

Difficult

54. In Problem 53, if Jack prefers to invest a lump-sum amount today instead of investing annually, but still expects to receive the same amount of money when he retires, how much should he invest today?

55. In Problem 53, if Jack invests the same annual amount at the end of each of the next 35 years instead of at the beginning of the years, how much he will receive when he retires? Explain why this amount is greater or smaller than the result calculated in Problem 53.

56. A.   Determine the month-end payment for a $200,000, 10-year loan with an interest rate of 12 percent, compounded monthly. (Assume there is no down payment)

    B.   Calculate the outstanding loan amount after 18 months.

    C.   Redo part A, assuming it is a mortgage loan with monthly payments.

57. Investor A just turned 20 years old and currently has no investments. She plans to invest $5,500 at the end of each year for eight years, beginning in five years. The rate of return on her investment is 15 percent, continuously compounded. Investor B is 40 years old and he just started to invest at the beginning of every year an equal amount of money starting today. He will invest for 10 years. The

rate of return on his investment is 16 percent, compounded quarterly. Determine the yearly payment Investor B has to make in order to have the same present value as Investor A.

58. Paul and Maria want to have enough money to travel around the world when they retire. They just turned 30 and will retire when they turn 60. They earn a total of $9,000 after taxes each month. Their monthly expenditures include $3,000 in mortgage payments, $850 in car payments and $1,450 in other expenses. They approached a fund manager and decided to invest the rest of their income at the end of each year. They expect to earn a 10 percent expected annual rate of return for each of the next 30 years. When they retire, they will sell their cottage for an expected price of $50,000.

  A. Determine how much they will have when they retire.

  B. How much can Paul and Maria withdraw annually at the beginning of the year for travelling after they retire if they expect to live until they are 90?

59. Veda has to choose between two investments that have the same cost today. Both investments will ultimately pay $1,300 but at different times, as shown in the table below. If Veda doesn't choose one of these investments, she could leave the funds in a bank account paying 5 percent per year. Which investment should Veda choose?

Year	Investment A	Investment B
1	$0	$200
2	$500	$400
3	$800	$700

60. If the cost of each investment in Problem 59 is $1,000, should Veda invest in one of them, or simply leave the money in the bank account? Would her decision change if the investments cost $1,200 each?

61. Instead of a $40,000 lump sum, Felix will need $10,000 per year for four years to pay for tuition (see Problem 30). How much will Felix's parents have to invest at the end of each year for the eight years before he begins his studies if their savings earn compound interest at 7 percent per year? Assume the tuition payments also occur at the end of each year.

62. Repeat Problem 61 assuming the tuition payments occur at the beginning of each year (the savings are still invested at the end of each year).

63. Roger has his eye on a new car that will cost $20,000. He has $15,000 in his savings account, earning interest at a rate of 0.5 percent per month.

  A. How long (to the nearest month) will it be before he can buy the car?

  B. How long will it be before Roger can buy the car if, in addition to his existing savings, he can save $250 per month?

64. How many years will it take for an investment to double in value if the rate of return is 9 percent, and compounding occurs:

A. annually?

B. quarterly?

65. Assume Josephine chose the Providence Bank option (see Problem 47). The three-year term on Josephine's mortgage is now over, and she must renew the loan for another term. How much of the original $180,000 principal amount does she still owe?

66. How much interest did Josephine pay over the three-year term of her mortgage loan (see Problem 47)?

67. A year has passed since Charlie purchased his house (see Problem 50). Assume the original mortgage amount (from your answer in Problem 50) was to be amortized over 25 years, with an initial one-year term at 3.90 percent. If the interest rate on a one-year term has increased to 5.35 percent, what will be Charlie's new monthly mortgage payments?

68. The new and higher mortgage payments calculated in Problem 67 creates a big problem for Charlie, because he can afford to pay only $1,950.00 per month. Rather than sell the house, Charlie has convinced his bank to extend the amortization period on the loan, which will reduce the monthly payments. How long must the amortization period be for this mortgage so that Charlie can afford to make the payments?

69. Céline has just won a lottery. She will receive a payment of $6,000 each year for nine years. As an alternative, she can choose an immediate payment of $50,000.

A. Which alternative should she pick if the interest rate is 5 percent?

B. What would the interest rate have to be for Céline to be indifferent about the two alternatives?

C. The lottery offers a third alternative for lottery prize payments: Céline can opt to receive annual payments of $3,000 per year for the rest of her life. Should Céline choose this option to the $50,000 lump sum payment today, if the interest rate is 5 percent per year?

70. After 20 years, the lottery company in Problem 69 goes out of business, and Céline's payments of $3,000 annually, which were supposed to continue for the rest of her life, stop.

A. What is the present value of the lost payments?

B. How much were these lost payments worth 20 years ago when Céline won the prize?

C. Had she been able to predict that the lottery company would go out of business, should Céline have chosen the perpetual payments, or the $50,000 lump sum?

71. Alysha has decided to use her $50,000 to make a down payment on a house. She will live in the house for the next two years while still at university, and then sell it when she graduates. The bank has offered her a mortgage rate of 5.1 percent compounded semi-annually on a two-year term, with an amortization period of 25 years. The house she is interested in purchasing costs $280,000.

A. If two friends will rent rooms from Alysha for $475 per room, payable at the end of each month, how much additional money must she pay to meet her monthly mortgage payments?

B. In two years, Alysha wants to sell the house for a high enough price to cover the remaining principal amount on the mortgage, and return her down payment. What is the minimum sale price she should accept?

72. How much will Tommy have to earn on his savings (see Problem 52) to be able to amass $1 million in 15 years?

73. KashKow Inc. has just declared that its dividend next year will be $3 per share. That rate of payment will continue for an additional four years, after which the dividends will fall back to their usual $2 per share (see Problem 23). What is the present value of all the future dividends?

74. After one year living in a university residence, Mary-Beth (see Problem 24) decides to rent an apartment for the remaining three years of her degree. She has found a nice location that will cost $450 per month; rent for the first and last month must be paid up front. How much money would Mary-Beth need to have in her bank account right now to be sure she will always have enough for rent? The bank account pays 3.75 percent interest, compounded monthly.

75. Suppose that Mary-Beth plans to return home for four months each summer, and will sub-let her apartment for the same amount she pays in rent (see Problem 74). In other words, she will pay $450 rent, but for only eight months of the year, during each of three years. In this situation, how much would she need to have in her bank account, earning 3.75 percent compounded monthly? (Assume that rent payments are made at the start of each month.)

76. A 65-year-old man intends to use his retirement funds to purchase an annuity from a life insurance company. Given the amount of money the man has available to invest, the insurance company is able to offer two alternatives. The first option is to receive $2,785 each month for as long as he lives; the second option is to receive $3,500 each month, but for only 20 years (payments will be made to his estate if he should die before that time). The relevant interest rate is 6 percent per year, compounded monthly. How long must the man live so that the first option is a better deal?

Bondholders

Bondholders are better protected than shareholders if a company's prospects sour and bankruptcy looms. On the other hand, they do not participate in a company's success when things go well. Recently, however, some bond investors have made profits by paying careful attention to the debt covenants often attached to bond issues. In 2006, Great Canadian Gaming Corporation was forced to redeem $300 million of its senior secured notes after a group of investors claimed the company was in technical default of its covenant obligations. Initially, the company agreed to some new restrictions and to pay an amendment fee to the bondholders. Ultimately, it decided to redeem the bonds, which gave the bondholders a very nice return on their investment.

Source: Great Canadian Gaming Corp. press release, September 26, 2006; Harry Koza, "Great Canadian Gaming calls—bondholders win a sweet pot," *Globe and Mail*, September 1, 2006.

http://www.greatcanadiancasinos.com

http://www.theglobeandmail.com

Bond Valuation and Interest Rates

Learning Objectives

After reading this chapter, you should understand the following:

1. The basic features of different types of bonds

2. How to value bonds given an appropriate discount rate

3. How to determine the discount rate or yield given the market value of a bond

4. How market interest rates or yields affect bond investors

5. How bond prices change over time

6. The factors (both domestic and global) that affect interest rates

INTRODUCTION

Chapter 5 introduced the basic time value of money concepts. In this chapter we discuss bonds, which provide investors with predetermined future payments. As such, the analysis of bonds provides an important application of compounding and discounting.

The bond market is an important part of the capital market and a major source of financing for companies, as well as for governments and financial institutions. Understanding the topics covered in this chapter will deepen your knowledge of applying the tools of valuation as well as your familiarity with financial securities.

We will refer to bonds generically as long-term debt instruments that promise fixed payments to their owners. However, specific terms are used depending on the maturity of the bond. Short-term bonds with a maturity of less than one year are called **bills** or **paper**, those with maturities between one and seven years are called **notes**, and those with terms of longer than seven years are called **bonds**. Because all of these instruments are valued in the same manner, we will refer to them all as bonds in this textbook.

① **bills or paper** short-term bonds with a maturity of less than one year

② **notes** bonds with maturities between one and seven years

③ **bonds** long-term debt instruments that promise fixed payments and have maturities of longer than seven years

6.1 THE BASIC STRUCTURE OF BONDS

The key feature of a bond is that the issuer agrees to pay the bondholder (investor) a regular series of cash payments and to repay the full principal amount by the maturity date. These promises are stipulated in the bond contract and are a fixed contractual commitment; you will hear this phrase again as it is important in corporate financing. Although many payment structures are possible, the traditional "coupon paying" bond provides for identical payments at regular intervals (usually semi-annually or annually), with the full principal to be repaid at the stated maturity date. We call the interest payment a "coupon" because at one time bonds literally had coupons and the investor had to cut the coupon from the bond certificate and send it for payment.[1] Today, almost all bonds in Canada are *registered* and the payments are made directly into individual bank accounts, providing a record of who has paid and who has received the interest. When the principal payment is made in one lump sum at maturity, it is called a **bullet payment** or **balloon payment**.

bullet payment or **balloon payment** a principal payment made in one lump sum at maturity

Bonds are often referred to as fixed income securities because the interest payments and the principal repayment are specified or fixed at the time the bond is issued. In other words, the bond purchaser knows the amount and timing of the future cash payments to be received, barring default by the issuer. However, if the buyer decides to sell the bond before maturity, the price received will depend on the level of interest rates at that time, which we will illustrate shortly.

To understand how bonds are valued, we can use timelines, as developed in Chapter 5. A typical pattern of cash payments is depicted in Figure 6-1. Two things are obvious. First, the structure of the payments differs from that of the loan or

---

[1] The coupons were attached to the bond and could be mailed in by whoever had the bond. Such bonds were called *bearer bonds* and are still widely used in parts of the world where personal tax rates are high.

mortgage discussed in Chapter 5, because those involved "blended" payments that included both interest and principal components. In contrast, a typical bond has interest payments throughout its life and a balloon principal payment at maturity. Second, a bond can be viewed as two separate components: an annuity consisting of the identical and regular interest payments, plus a lump-sum principal payment at maturity. In this way, valuing a traditional bond becomes a straightforward application of the time value of money concepts developed in Chapter 5.

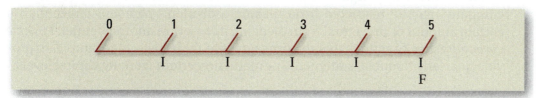

I = interest payments, and F = principal repayment (face value)

6-1 FIGURE

The Cash Flow Pattern for a Traditional Coupon-Paying Bond

Basic Bond Terminology

Before discussing how to value bonds, we will introduce some terminology and institutional features attached to different types of bonds. Most bonds are sold to a variety of investors, and someone must make sure that the payments are made on time. This problem is solved by including all relevant details for a particular bond issue in a **bond indenture** that is held and administered by a trust company. This is a legal document that specifies the payment requirements, all other salient matters relating to the issue (such as any assets that might serve as security or **collateral** for the bond), any protective provisions, and other additional features. The trust company then makes sure that these covenant provisions are observed by the issuer.

   All bond indentures include the basic features attached to the cash payments. The **par value (or face value or maturity value)** represents the amount that is paid at maturity for traditional bonds. The par value of most bonds is $1,000, although bond prices are typically quoted based on a par value of 100. In other words, if the price of a bond is quoted at 99.583, a $1,000 par value bond would be selling for $995.83. The time remaining to the maturity date is referred to as the **term to maturity** of the bond. The regular **interest payments (or coupons)** are determined by multiplying the coupon rate (which is stated on an annual basis) by the par value of the bond. For example, a bond with a coupon rate of 6 percent and a par value of $1,000 would pay coupons of $60 if they are paid annually, or $30 every six months if they are paid semi-annually.

Security and Protective Provisions

Technically, bonds are debt instruments that are secured by real assets; they are often called **mortgage bonds**. However, not all bonds are secured by real property. For example, **debentures** are similar to bonds but are generally unsecured, or are secured by a general floating charge over the company's unencumbered assets, that is, those assets that have not been pledged as security for other debt obligations. Government bonds are debentures because no specific security is pledged as collateral; however, they are referred to as bonds as a matter of convention.

bond indenture a legal document that specifies the payment requirements and all other salient matters relating to a particular bond issue, held and administered by a trust company

collateral assets that can serve as security for the bond in case of default

par value, face value, or maturity value the amount paid at maturity for traditional bonds

term to maturity the time remaining to the maturity date

interest payments (or coupons) the amounts paid on a bond at regular intervals

mortgage bonds debt instruments that are secured by real assets

debentures debt instruments that are similar to bonds but are generally unsecured or are secured by a general floating charge over the company's unencumbered assets

collateral trust bonds bonds secured by a pledge of other financial assets, such as common shares, bonds, or treasury bills

equipment trust certificates a type of debt instrument secured by equipment, such as the rolling stock of a railway

protective covenants clauses in a trust indenture that restrict the actions of the issuer; covenants can be positive or negative

callable bonds bonds that give the issuer the option to "call" or repurchase outstanding bonds at predetermined prices at specified times

call prices prices, generally at a premium over par, at which an issuer can repurchase a bond

retractable bonds bonds that allow the bondholder to sell them back to the issuer at predetermined prices at specified times earlier than the maturity date

extendible bonds bonds that allow the bondholder to extend the bonds' maturity dates

sinking fund provisions the requirements that the issuer set aside funds each year to be used to pay off the debt at maturity

Collateral trust bonds are secured by a pledge of other financial assets, such as common shares, bonds, or treasury bills. **Equipment trust certificates** are secured by equipment, such as the rolling stock of a railway. The assets pledged as security are owned by investors through a lease agreement with the railway until the loan has been retired. The certificates have serial numbers that dictate their maturity date, with a certain amount maturing every year.

Protective covenants are clauses in the trust indenture that restrict the actions of the issuer. *Negative covenants* prohibit certain actions; for example, a company may be restricted from making a dividend payment larger than a certain amount or prevented from pledging its assets to another lender. *Positive covenants* specify actions that the firm agrees to undertake, for example, to provide quarterly financial statements or maintain certain working capital levels.

Additional Bond Features

So far, we have focused our discussion on traditional or regular coupon-paying bonds that provide for full principal repayment at the maturity date. However, some bonds have additional features (or options) that may provide for some, or all, of the principal to be repaid before maturity. We discuss a few of the more common provisions below.

Callable bonds give the *issuer* the option to "call" or repurchase outstanding bonds at predetermined **call prices** (generally at a premium over par) at specified times. These types of bonds create an additional risk for the bondholder. Conversely, **retractable bonds** allow the *bondholder* to sell the bonds back to the issuer at predetermined prices at specified times earlier than the maturity date. In this way, the maturity of the bond is retracted or shortened. In contrast, **extendible bonds** allow the bondholder to extend the maturity date of the bond. Extendibles and retractables provide bondholders with the flexibility of changing the maturity of the bonds to their advantage. We will discuss why they might want to do this after we show how bonds are valued.

Sinking fund provisions require the issuer to set money aside each year so that funds are available at maturity to pay off the debt. Provisions are made in two ways. In the first, the firm repurchases a certain amount of debt each year so that the amount of debt goes down. In the second, the firm pays money into the sinking fund to buy other bonds, usually government bonds, so that money is available at maturity to pay off the debt, although the amount due at maturity is unchanged. Sinking fund provisions benefit the issuer, because they avoid paying the entire face value of the issue at the maturity date. However, if the bonds are actually repurchased, sinking fund provisions are not always beneficial to investors, because their bonds may be randomly called and repaid. Further, the bonds are normally repaid at par value and the investors may suffer a loss if the bonds are worth more. Finally as the amount of the issue declines, there may be a loss in liquidity as the bonds become less attractive. These disadvantages are offset by the operation of a sinking fund in which funds are used to buy government bonds.

Purchase fund provisions are similar to sinking fund provisions, but they require the repurchase of a certain amount of debt only if it can be repurchased at or below a given price. These provisions are generally advantageous to debt holders, since they provide some liquidity and downward price support for the market price of the debt instruments.

Convertible bonds can be converted into common shares at predetermined conversion prices. Convertible bonds may be offered to make debt issues more attractive to investors. These will be discussed in greater depth in Chapters 18 and 19.

From this brief review of the institutional features attached to bonds two things should be very clear: a bond is a contract, and what is in that contract varies from one bond to another. Unlike common shares, which we discuss later, each bond contract has to be reviewed separately, because they differ from one another. Without recognizing this, the differences can come back to haunt investors years after the bond has been issued.[2]

purchase fund provisions the requirements that the repurchase of a certain amount of debt can occur only if it can be repurchased at or below a given price

convertible bonds bonds that can be converted into common shares at predetermined conversion prices

CONCEPT REVIEW QUESTIONS

1. In what ways are bonds different from mortgages?
2. How is a traditional bond structured?
3. What is a bond indenture?
4. What is the difference between a positive and a negative covenant provision?
5. How do sinking funds work?

6.2 BOND VALUATION

We are now ready to examine how bonds are valued. Once investors know the par value, the term to maturity, and the coupon rate, they know both the amount and the timing of all the future promised payments on a bond. The price of a bond is determined by discounting these future payments by using an appropriate discount rate, often referred to as the market rate of interest. We will discuss the factors that affect this discount rate in greater detail later in the chapter, but for now you should be aware that it is a function of market conditions, that is, other market interest rates, as well as of issue and issuer specific factors.

The price of a bond equals the present value of the future payments on the bond, which is the present value of the interest payments and the par value repaid at maturity. By using the concepts developed in Chapter 5, we can use the following equation to price the bond:

$$B = I \times \left[\frac{1 - \frac{1}{(1+k_b)^n}}{k_b} \right] + F \times \frac{1}{(1+k_b)^n}$$

[6-1]

---

[2] In particular, the issuer has to do only what it has contracted to do in the indenture. A famous case involved bonds issued by CP Railway that were redeemable "after 1953." Investors expected the bonds to be redeemed in 1953 and sued the company when it refused. The company won the suit.

where B = the bond price
I = interest (or coupon) payments
k_b = the bond discount rate (or market rate)
n = the term to maturity
F = the face (par) value of the bond

In Equation 6-1, note that the interest or coupon payments are multiplied by the standard present value annuity factor (PVAF) developed in Chapter 5, while the par value is multiplied by the present value interest factor (PVIF). Valuing a traditional bond is an example of applying the time value of money concepts.

Example 6-1: Bond Valuation with Annual Coupons I

Find the price of a $1,000 par value bond that matures in 10 years, if it pays interest annually, based on a 6 percent coupon rate, and if the market rate of interest is 7 percent.

Solution

F = $1,000; I = coupon rate × F = 0.06 × $1,000 = $60; n = 10; k_b = 0.07.

With this information, we can use Equation 6-1 to find the price, or we can solve it by using a financial calculator or Excel.

$$B = 60 \times \left[\frac{1 - \dfrac{1}{(1.07)^{10}}}{0.07} \right] + 1,000 \times \frac{1}{(1 + 0.07)^{10}}$$

$$= [60 \times 7.02358] + [1,000 \times 0.50835] = 421.41 + 508.35 = \$929.76$$

solution using a financial calculator

(TI BA II Plus)

PMT = −60; N = 10; FV = −1,000; I/Y = 7%; compute PV = $929.76

As in Chapter 5, with the calculator solution, we have to be careful with the signs. The calculator program assumes that there is an outflow (negative value) for an investment and then a payoff (positive values).

solution using Excel

Excel contains a range of special functions for valuing bonds. The basic function is the following "price" function:[3]

= PRICE(settlement, maturity, rate, yld, redemption, frequency, basis)

The terms are as follows:

• Settlement is the day on which the bond is paid for or "settled."

---

[3] You may need to add the Analysis ToolPak in Excel, which can be done by clicking on Tools, then Add-Ins, then Analysis ToolPak, and then OK.

- Maturity is the date when the terminal principal is paid.

- Rate is the coupon rate on the bond.

- Yld is the discount rate or yield required on the bond.

- Redemption is the principal amount paid at maturity.

- Frequency indicates how often the coupon is paid, for example, annually.

- Basis we will ignore for now, so we will enter 0.

So to solve this problem in Excel we would enter

= PRICE(date(2006,11,06), date(2016,11,06), .06, .07, 100, 1, 0)

and get the correct answer of $929.76.

The Excel function has several special features. Be careful in entering the dates. In this example, we used date(2006,11,06) to indicate November 6, 2006. The date must be entered in this way for Excel to convert it into a number that can be used for calculations. Then we specified the maturity date as *exactly* 10 years in the future. Excel is sophisticated enough that if we had entered a different maturity date, for example, date(2006,8,6), it would have automatically taken into account that it was nine months to the next interest payment and all of the payments would then be brought forward by three months. With this maturity date, the bond is now worth $930.62, reflecting the fact that the investor is getting all the payments a little earlier.[4] Excel also requires that you enter the par value of the bond in the same way it is quoted, for example, as $100 and not the actual value of $1,000.

As with all problems, you should first solve them by using the basic formula. Then you can determine whether the Excel answer is correct and whether you are inputting the values in the correct way. Errors in inputting the data will produce incorrect answers, and these will be easier to catch if you have used the basic formula first.

In Example 6-1, the bond trades at a **discount** from its par value. This is because the coupon rate is less than the market interest (discount) rate, which means that investors require a return greater than 6 percent on equivalent bonds under current market conditions. Because the future payments are fixed, the only way to get a return higher than the coupon rate on this bond is to pay less than the par value for it. If an investor bought the bond at its par value of $1,000 and held it to maturity, he or she would earn a return equal to the coupon rate of 6 percent. In other words, the person would invest $1,000, get a 6 percent return on that investment per year, that is, $60 in interest each year,

discount (premium) the difference between the bond's par value and the price it trades at, when it trades below (above) the par value

---

[4] In valuing the bond we need to know how many days there are in a year and the time until the interest payment, given that every month does not have 30 days. In Canada, we use the actual number of days in a month and 365 days in a year or actual/365 basis. The U.S. convention is to use 30 days in a month and 360 days in a year, the so-called 30/360 basis. These conventions are called the basis and Excel requires that you enter 0 for the United States and 3 for Canada. There are other conventions used elsewhere in the world and generically these are called the day count convention.

and then receive $1,000 back at maturity. Thus, when market rates = the coupon rate, bonds trade at *par*.[5] Similarly, if market interest rates are below the coupon rate of 6 percent, the bond will trade at a *premium* to par, which we will illustrate in Example 6-2.

Example 6-2: Bond Valuation with Annual Coupons II

Find the price of a $1,000 par value bond that matures in 10 years, if it pays interest annually, based on a 6 percent coupon rate, and if the market rate of interest is 5 percent.

Solution

F = $1,000; I = coupon rate × F = 0.06 × $1,000 = $60; n = 10; k_b = 0.05.

We can use Equation 6-1 to find the price, or we can find it by using a financial calculator or Excel.

$$B = 60 \times \left[\frac{1 - \dfrac{1}{(1.05)^{10}}}{0.05} \right] + 1{,}000 \times \frac{1}{(1+0.05)^{10}}$$

$$= [60 \times 7.72173] + [1{,}000 \times 0.61391] = 463.30 + 613.91 = \$1{,}077.21$$

solution using a financial calculator

(TI BA II Plus)

PMT = −60; N = 10; FV = −1,000; I/Y = 5%; compute PV = $1,077.22

solution using Excel

We enter

= PRICE(date(2006,11,06), date(2016,11,06), .06, .05, 100, 1, 0)

and also get $1,077.22. The difference of $0.01 is due to rounding in the formula solution.

So the bond in Example 6-2 trades at a *premium* over par, because the coupon rate of 6 percent is greater than the market rate of 5 percent.

The two examples assume that interest payments (or coupons) are made on an annual basis. However, in reality, most bonds pay coupons semi-annually. Fortunately, this does not change the valuation process, but we must make the appropriate adjustments to reflect the fact we are dealing with semi-annual periods, rather than annual ones. Specifically, we must divide the annual coupon payments by two to determine the amount of semi-annual coupons and multiply the number of years to maturity by two to obtain the number of semi-annual periods to maturity. Finally, we need a semi-annual discount rate

---

[5] Bonds are often issued at (or very close to) par by setting the coupon rate equal to the market rate at the time of issue.

because that coincides with the frequency of payments. For bonds, as a matter of convention, the appropriate adjustment is to divide the market bond yield by two to obtain the six-month market yield—notice that this implies that the bond yields are not effective rates. Example 6-3 shows how to apply this process.

Example 6-3: Bond Valuation with Semi-Annual Coupons

Determine the price of a 15-year semi-annual pay bond that has a par value of $1,000 and a coupon rate of 5 percent, when the appropriate market rate is 6 percent.

Solution

Semi-annual market rate: $k = 6\% / 2 = 3\%$
Term to maturity (in semi-annual periods): $n = 15$ years $\times 2 = 30$
Semi-annual coupons: $I = $ coupon rate/$2 \times F = 0.05/2 \times \$1,000 = \$25$

$$B = 25 \times \left[\frac{1 - \frac{1}{(1.03)^{30}}}{0.03} \right] + 1,000 \times \frac{1}{(1 + 0.03)^{30}}$$

$$= [25 \times 19.60044] + [1,000 \times 0.41199] = 490.01 + 411.99 = \$902.00$$

$PMT = -25$; $N = 30$; $FV = -1,000$; $I/Y = 3\%$; compute $PV = \$902.00$

solution using a financial calculator

(TI BA II Plus)

solution using Excel

We enter 2 for the frequency of payment:

$= PRICE(date(2006,11,06), date(2021,11,06), .05, .06, 100, 2, 0)$

and we get $901.997 or $902.

Factors Affecting Bond Prices

The examples above illustrate the most important property of fixed income investments, such as bonds: *if interest rates increase, the market prices of bonds decline and vice versa*. This is clear from Figure 6-2, which depicts the bond price-yield curve for a regular coupon-paying bond.

Figure 6-2 demonstrates that bond prices decline when interest rates increase. We can also see that the relationship between market rates and bond price is *not* linear; the curve representing this relationship is *convex*. This fact is evident if we look at the bond pricing equation, in which the discount rate is raised to powers other than one.

The shape of this curve shows two additional factors in the relationship between bond prices and market rates. First, for a given change in interest rates, bond prices will increase more when rates decrease than they will decrease when

FIGURE 6-2

Bond Price-Yield Curve

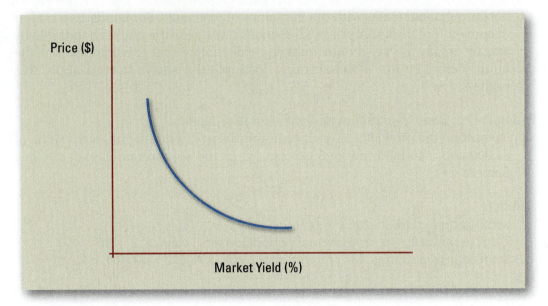

rates increase. Note, for example, that the curve is "steeper" to the left of any point than it is to the right so that the impact of decreasing interest rates is different from the impact of increasing ones. Second, the curve is steeper for lower interest rates, which means that a given change in interest rates will have a much greater impact on bond prices when rates are lower than it will if they are higher.

The second-most important property of bonds is that *the longer the time to maturity, the more sensitive the bond price is to changes in market rates.* Intuitively, this makes sense, because the longer the term to maturity, the longer the investor has "locked in" fixed payments based on the bond's coupon rate. When market rates rise above this rate, the bond price will fall more because the coupon rate is "unattractive" relative to prevailing rates for a longer period. The longer an investor is locked in, the greater the disadvantage and the more the bond price will fall to adjust. Similarly, when rates fall below the coupon rate, the longer an investor is locked in, the greater the attractiveness of the higher coupon. Example 6-4 illustrates this property.

Example 6-4: Estimating Prices for Bonds with Different Terms to Maturity

Consider the semi-annual pay $1,000 par value 5 percent bond examined in Example 6-3, with market rates at 6 percent. Recalculate the price on this bond assuming that the term to maturity is *not* 15 years, but is

a. 5 years.

b. 30 years.

Solution

$k = 3\%$; I = $25; F = 1,000

a. n = 5 years × 2 = 10

$$B = 25 \times \left[\frac{1 - \dfrac{1}{(1.03)^{10}}}{0.03} \right] + 1,000 \times \frac{1}{(1+0.03)^{10}}$$

$$= [25 \times 8.53020] + [1,000 \times 0.74409] = 213.26 + 744.09 = \$957.35$$

$\boxed{\text{PMT}} = -25;\ \boxed{\text{N}} = 10;\ \boxed{\text{FV}} = -1,000;\ \boxed{\text{I/Y}} = 3\%;\ \text{compute}\ \boxed{\text{PV}} = \$957.35$

= PRICE(date(2006, 11, 06), date(2011, 11, 06), .05, .06, 100, 2, 0)

which again gives $957.35.

Notice that this 5-year bond sells at a lower "discount" (higher price) to its par value than does the 15-year bond, reflecting the fact that investors are not locked in to the 5 percent (unattractive rate) for as long.

b. $n = 30\ \text{years} \times 2 = 60$

$$B = 25 \times \left[\frac{1 - \dfrac{1}{(1.03)^{60}}}{0.03} \right] + 1,000 \times \frac{1}{(1+0.03)^{60}}$$

$= [25 \times 27.67556] + [1,000 \times 0.16973] = 691.89 + 169.73 = \$861.62$

$\boxed{\text{PMT}} = -25;\ \boxed{\text{N}} = 60;\ \boxed{\text{FV}} = -1,000;\ \boxed{\text{I/Y}} = 3\%;\ \text{compute}\ \boxed{\text{PV}} = \$861.62$

= PRICE(date(2006,11,06), date(2036,11,06), .05, .06, 100, 2, 0)

which again gives $861.62.

With the longer maturity, the 30-year bond sells at a much bigger "discount" (lower price) to its par value than does the 15-year bond (and the five-year bond), reflecting the fact that investors are locked in to the 5 percent (unattractive rate) for a longer time.

Bond prices' sensitivity to interest rates is directly related to interest rate levels and to the term to maturity. It is also related to the level of the coupon rate associated with the bond (although this factor is much less important than either interest rate levels or the term to maturity). In particular, bond prices will be more sensitive to interest rates for bonds with lower coupon rates than they will be for higher-coupon-paying bonds. This is intuitive, if we recall from Chapter 5 that the compounding (or discounting) effect is accentuated with time, which suggests that a change in the discount rate will have the greatest impact on the most distant cash flows, including the par value to be received at maturity in the case of bonds. For bonds that pay lower coupons, the principal repayment, which occurs at the maturity date, represents a higher proportion of the total payments to be received by the bondholder. As a result, their prices will fluctuate more for a given change in interest rates than will otherwise identical higher-coupon-paying bonds. Example 6-5 illustrates this property.

Example 6-5: Estimating Prices for Bonds with Different Coupon Rates

Consider the semi-annual pay $1,000 par value 5 percent bond examined in Example 6-3 (call it Bond 1). Consider another 15-year bond that pays semi-annual coupons based on a 6 percent coupon rate (Bond 2). Calculate the price of each bond when market rates are

a. 5 percent.

b. 6 percent.

Solution

For both bonds: $F = 1,000$; $n = 30$

For Bond 1: $I = \$25$

For Bond 2: $I = \$30$

a. $k = 5\%/2 = 2.5\%$

Bond 1: B = $1,000 (i.e., it trades at par, since market yield = coupon rate).

Bond 2:

$$B = 30 \times \left[\frac{1 - \dfrac{1}{(1.025)^{30}}}{0.025} \right] + 1,000 \times \frac{1}{(1+0.025)^{30}}$$

$$= [30 \times 20.93029] + [1,000 \times 0.47674] = 627.91 + 476.74 = \$1,104.65$$

b. $k = 6\%/2 = 3\%$

Bond 1:

$$B = 25 \times \left[\frac{1 - \dfrac{1}{(1.03)^{30}}}{0.03} \right] + 1,000 \times \frac{1}{(1+0.03)^{30}}$$

$$= [25 \times 19.60044] + [1,000 \times 0.41199] = 490.01 + 411.99 = \$902.00$$

Bond 2: B = $1,000 (i.e., it trades at par, since market yield = coupon rate).

a. Bond 2:

PMT = –$30; N = 30; FV = –1,000; I/Y = 2.5%; CPT PV = $1,104.65

b. Bond 1:

PMT = –$25; N = 30; FV = –1,000; I/Y = 3%; CPT PV = $902.00

a. For Bond 2:
= PRICE(date(2006,11,06), date(2021,11,06), .06, .05, 100, 2, 0)
which again gives $1,104.65.

b. Bond 1:
= PRICE(date(2006,11,06), date(2021,11,06), .05, .06, 100, 2, 0)
which gives $901.997 or $902.

As we would expect based on our discussion, if we look at the change in the price of each bond in Example 6-5 for a 1 percent change in interest rates, we can see that Bond 1 (with the lower coupon rate) experienced a higher percentage change (decline) in price than Bond 2 (the higher coupon rate bond) did, although the difference is not dramatic:

Percentage change in price of Bond 1
$= (902 - 1,000)/1,000 = -0.0980 = -9.80\%$

Percentage change in price of Bond 2
$= (1,000 - 1,104.65)/1,104.65 = -0.0947 = -9.47\%$

The sensitivity of bond prices to changes in interest rates is generally referred to as **interest rate risk**. All else constant, longer-term bonds with lower coupon rates and with lower market yields will possess greater interest rate risk than will shorter-term, higher coupon bonds with higher market yields. An important measure of interest rate risk, **duration**, incorporates all these factors into a single measure. A discussion of duration is beyond the scope of this textbook; however, note the following:

interest rate risk the sensitivity of bond prices to changes in interest rates

duration an important measure of interest rate risk that incorporates several factors

1. The prices of bonds with higher durations are more sensitive to interest rate changes than are those with lower durations.

2. All else being equal, durations will be higher when (1) market yields are lower, (2) bonds have longer maturities, and (3) bonds have lower coupons.[6]

Bond Quotes

Finance in the News 6-1 shows some typical bond quotes that appear in the financial media.
Let's consider the following quote from the table:

Issuer	Coupon	Maturity	Bid	Yield
Canada	5.500	2009-Jun-01	102.54	4.20

This quote shows the issuer (Canada—that is, the Government of Canada), the associated coupon rate (5.50 percent), the date the bond matures (June 1, 2009), the previous trading day's closing bid price (102.54), and the associated

---

[6] As you might expect, Excel has a duration function—DURATION(settlement, maturity, coupon, yld, frequency, basis)—where all of the same values needed to value a bond are the inputs and the duration function measures the sensitivity of the bond to interest rate changes.

finance
INTHENEWS6-1

CANADIAN BONDS

Canadian Bonds on 2007.05.08

Federal | Provincial | Corporate

Federal

	Coupon	Maturity Date	Bid $	Yield %
Canada	4.250	Dec 01/08	100.00	4.25
Canada	**3.750**	**Jun 01/09**	**99.12**	**4.20**
Canada	**5.500**	**Jun 01/09**	**102.54**	**4.20**
Canada	11.000	Jun 01/09	113.32	4.18
Canada	4.250	Sep 01/09	100.10	4.20
Canada	10.750	Oct 01/09	114.77	4.19
Canada	9.500	Jun 01/10	115.16	4.17
Canada	5.500	Jun 01/10	103.78	4.17
Canada	4.000	Sep 01/10	99.50	4.16
Canada	9.000	Mar 01/11	116.90	4.15
Canada	6.000	Jun 01/11	106.82	4.16
Canada	8.500	Jun 01/11	116.10	4.15
Canada	3.750	Sep 01/11	98.42	4.15
Canada	3.750	Jun 01/12	98.14	4.16
Canada	5.250	Jun 01/12	104.93	4.16
Canada	5.250	Jun 01/13	105.76	4.16
Canada	**10.250**	**Mar 15/14**	**136.09**	**4.14**
Canada	5.000	Jun 01/14	105.09	4.16
Canada	4.500	Jun 01/15	102.18	4.18
Canada	11.250	Jun 01/15	148.04	4.17
Canada	4.000	Jun 01/16	98.62	4.18
Canada	4.000	Jun 01/17	98.31	4.21
Canada	10.500	Mar 15/21	165.20	4.23
Canada	9.750	Jun 01/21	158.01	4.23
Canada	9.250	Jun 01/22	155.45	4.23
Canada	8.000	Jun 01/23	143.36	4.25
Canada	9.000	Jun 01/25	159.32	4.26
Canada	8.000	Jun 01/27	150.18	4.26
Canada	5.750	Jun 01/29	121.47	4.24
Canada	5.750	Jun 01/33	124.20	4.21
Canada	5.000	Jun 01/37	113.99	4.18
CHT	5.100	Sep 15/07	100.25	4.22
CHT	3.700	Sep 15/08	99.18	4.33
CHT	4.100	Dec 15/08	99.67	4.31
CHT	3.550	Mar 15/09	98.69	4.29
CHT	4.650	Sep 15/09	100.82	4.28
CHT	3.750	Mar 15/10	98.61	4.27
CHT	3.550	Sep 15/10	97.81	4.26
CMHC	5.500	Jun 01/12	105.62	4.25
EDC	5.000	Feb 09/09	101.26	4.24
EDC	5.100	Jun 02/14	105.01	4.27

Provincial

Federal | Provincial | Corporate

	Coupon	Maturity Date	Bid $	Yield %
B C	6.000	Jun 09/08	101.72	4.35
B C	6.375	Aug 23/10	106.36	4.28
B C	5.750	Jan 09/12	106.14	4.28
B C	8.500	Aug 23/13	122.81	4.32
B C	6.150	Nov 19/27	120.81	4.58
B C	5.700	Jun 18/29	115.79	4.56
B C MF	5.500	Mar 24/08	100.95	4.37
B C MF	5.900	Jun 01/11	105.85	4.31
HydQue	6.500	Feb 15/11	107.47	4.33
HydQue	10.250	Jul 16/12	127.22	4.33
HydQue	11.000	Aug 15/20	162.57	4.63
HydQue	6.000	Aug 15/31	117.89	4.75
HydQue	6.500	Feb 15/35	127.17	4.73
HydQue	6.000	Feb 15/40	121.13	4.73
Manit	5.750	Jun 02/08	101.42	4.36
Manit	7.750	Dec 22/25	138.51	4.64
NewBr	5.700	Jun 02/08	101.37	4.36
NewBr	6.000	Dec 27/17	112.52	4.50
Newfld	6.150	Apr 17/28	119.43	4.68
NovaSc	6.600	Jun 01/27	125.40	4.64
Ontario	6.125	Sep 12/07	100.59	4.24
Ontario	5.700	Dec 01/08	102.03	4.34
Ontario	4.000	May 19/09	99.40	4.31
Ontario	6.200	Nov 19/09	104.47	4.31
Ontario	4.000	May 19/10	99.18	4.29
Ontario	6.100	Nov 19/10	105.88	4.28
Ontario	6.100	Dec 02/11	107.46	4.28
Ontario	5.375	Dec 02/12	105.24	4.31
Ontario	4.750	Jun 02/13	102.30	4.31
Ontario	5.000	Mar 08/14	103.81	4.35
Ontario	4.500	Mar 08/15	100.75	4.38
Ontario	4.400	Mar 08/16	99.90	4.41
Ontario	4.300	Mar 08/17	98.78	4.45
Ontario	8.100	Sep 08/23	139.76	4.61
Ontario	7.600	Jun 02/27	138.45	4.64
Ontario	6.500	Mar 08/29	125.53	4.63
Ontario	6.200	Jun 02/31	122.53	4.64
Ontario	5.850	Mar 08/33	118.24	4.63
Ontario	5.600	Jun 02/35	115.33	4.62
Ontario	4.700	Jun 02/37	101.32	4.62
OntHyd	5.600	Jun 02/08	101.27	4.36
Quebec	6.500	Oct 01/07	100.85	4.24
Quebec	**5.500**	**Jun 01/09**	**102.26**	**4.34**
Quebec	6.250	Dec 01/10	106.27	4.33
Quebec	6.000	Oct 01/12	107.85	4.35
Quebec	5.250	Oct 01/13	104.78	4.38
Quebec	5.500	Dec 01/14	106.79	4.43
Quebec	5.000	Dec 01/15	103.67	4.48
Quebec	4.500	Dec 01/16	99.81	4.52
Quebec	9.375	Jan 16/23	151.45	4.70
Quebec	8.500	Apr 01/26	146.73	4.73
Quebec	6.000	Oct 01/29	117.34	4.74
Quebec	6.250	Jun 01/32	121.96	4.74
Quebec	5.750	Dec 01/36	116.21	4.73
Saskat	5.500	Jun 02/08	101.17	4.36
Saskat	8.750	May 30/25	150.14	4.62
Toronto	6.100	Aug 15/07	100.46	4.35
Toronto	6.100	Dec 12/17	112.04	4.65

Corporate

Federal | Provincial | Corporate

	Coupon	Maturity Date	Bid $	Yield %
AGT Lt	8.800	Sep 22/25	134.34	5.75
Bell	6.550	May 01/29	93.49	7.14
BMO	6.903	Jun 30/10	106.74	4.57
BMO	6.647	Dec 31/10	106.78	4.60
BMO	4.690	Jan 31/11	100.73	4.47
BMO	6.685	Dec 31/11	108.45	4.64
BNS	4.515	Nov 19/08	100.01	4.51
BNS	3.930	Feb 18/10	98.55	4.49
BNS	7.310	Dec 31/10	109.08	4.57
BNS	4.560	Oct 30/13	99.98	4.56
CIBC	3.750	Sep 09/10	97.66	4.51
CIBC	4.550	Mar 28/11	100.02	4.54
CIBC	4.350	Nov 01/11	99.40	4.50
Domtar	10.000	Apr 15/11	111.28	6.69
Genss	4.002	Mar 15/10	98.74	4.48
Genss	4.245	Sep 15/11	99.06	4.48
GldCrd	4.159	Oct 15/08	99.56	4.48
GrTAA	5.950	Dec 03/07	100.82	4.46
GrTAA	6.450	Dec 03/27	115.10	5.24
GTC Tr	6.200	Jun 01/07	100.09	4.46
Gulf C	6.450	Oct 01/07	106.75	4.39
GWLife	6.750	Aug 10/10	106.72	4.50
GWLife	5.995	Dec 31/12	106.40	4.69
GWLife	6.140	Mar 21/18	111.64	4.75
GWLife	6.740	Nov 24/31	120.56	5.24
GWLife	6.670	Mar 21/33	120.10	5.24
HSBC	7.780	Dec 31/10	110.29	4.67
HydOne	7.150	Jun 03/10	107.62	4.46
HydOne	6.400	Dec 01/11	107.86	4.47
HydOne	5.770	Nov 15/12	106.15	4.50
HydOne	7.350	Jun 03/30	131.10	5.05
HydOne	6.930	Jun 01/32	126.53	5.05
IntrAm	4.400	Jan 26/26	96.74	4.66
IPL	8.200	Feb 15/24	134.68	5.10
Loblaw	6.650	Nov 08/27	106.49	6.09
MLI	6.240	Feb 16/11	105.81	4.54
MLI	6.700	Jun 30/12	109.37	4.63
MolsonC	5.000	Sep 22/15	98.46	5.23
MstrCr	4.444	Nov 21/11	99.84	4.48
Nexen	6.300	Jun 02/08	101.72	4.62
RoyBnk	**4.180**	**Jun 01/09**	**99.34**	**4.52**
RoyBnk	3.700	Jun 24/10	97.66	4.51
RoyBnk	7.288	Jun 30/10	107.86	4.57
RoyBnk	7.183	Jun 30/11	109.48	4.64
RoyBnk	4.580	Apr 30/12	99.98	4.58
RoyBnk	5.450	Nov 04/13	104.41	4.65
SNCLav	7.700	Sep 20/10	109.40	4.64
SunLife	6.865	Dec 31/11	109.25	4.62
SunLife	6.150	Jun 30/12	107.31	4.54
SunLiFi	4.950	Jun 01/16	101.06	4.80
TD Bnk	4.540	Sep 05/08	100.02	4.52
TD Bnk	7.600	Dec 31/09	107.43	4.58
TD Bnk	4.317	Jan 18/11	99.27	4.53
TD Bnk	5.690	Jun 03/13	105.64	4.61
TD Bnk	4.970	Oct 30/15	100.35	4.92
TD Bnk	4.779	Dec 14/16	98.52	4.97
TorHyd	6.110	May 07/13	107.92	4.58
Trizec	7.950	Jun 01/07	111.15	5.36
UniGas	8.650	Nov 10/25	140.60	5.21
WelFarg	4.380	Jun 30/15	97.99	4.68
Wstcoa	6.750	Dec 15/27	115.21	5.51

Source: Data provided by *National Post* and RBC Capital Markets. Retrieved May 9, 2007, from
http://www.canada.com/nationalpost/financialpost/fpmarketdata/bond_trading_summary.html.

yield to maturity (4.20 percent). The ask price is the price the bond could be bought for, based on $100 of face value.[7] For example, if the face value of the bond was $1,000, you would have to pay $1,025.40 ($1,000 × 1.02540) plus accrued interest (discussed below) to purchase the bond. The yields refer to the market (discount) rates that we have been using to value bonds and are discussed in the next section.

Notice that the Government of Canada bond is trading at a premium, because market yields are below the coupon rate of 5.50 percent. Several other bonds listed in Finance in the News 6-1 are trading at discounts from par. This difference is normal because bonds are issued at various points in time, and the coupon rates are set approximately equal to prevailing market rates at that time. Therefore, with different levels of prevailing interest rates, at any given point, we will observe some bonds trading at discounts and others trading at premiums.

Cash Prices versus Quoted Prices

The prices discussed in this section, as well as those reported in the media, such as in Finance in the News 6-1, are typically referred to as *quoted* prices. These differ from the actual prices investors pay for bonds whenever bonds are sold at a date other than the date of a coupon payment. The reason is that interest will accrue to bondholders between such payment dates. For example, an investor who held a bond for 45 days since the last coupon was paid has "earned" 45 days of interest even though he or she will not receive those 45 days of interest if they sell it now because coupons are paid semi-annually—in fact, the bond purchaser will receive those 45 days of interest when he or she receives the next scheduled coupon payment. As a result, a bond purchaser must pay the bond seller the quoted price plus the accrued interest on the bond. This amount is referred to as the *cash price* of the bond.

Example 6-6: The Cash Price of a Bond

Consider the semi-annual pay bond in Example 6-3 that has a $1,000 maturity value and a 5 percent coupon rate and is sold on July 14 at a quoted price of $902. Assume this bond matures on June 30, which implies the semi-annual interest payments on this bond are made on June 30 and on December 31. Calculate the cash price of this bond.

Solution

The cash price for this bond would equal $902 plus 14 days of accrued interest at the coupon rate of 5 percent or

Cash price = Quoted price + Accrued interest
Cash price = $902 + [$1,000 × 0.05 × (14/365)] = $902 + $1.92 = $903.92

Note that we have to choose a convention in terms of how much interest has been earned. Because this is a Canadian bond, we use the Canadian day count, which uses the actual number of days that have elapsed and assumes that there are 365 days in a year.

---

[7] The bid price, which is not reported in this particular bond quote, represents the price the bond could be sold for.

6.3 BOND YIELDS

Yield to Maturity

yield to maturity (YTM)
the discount rate used to evaluate bonds

The discount rate used to evaluate bonds is referred to as the **yield to maturity (YTM)**. It is the yield that an investor would realize if he or she bought the bond at the current price, held it to maturity, received all the promised payments on their scheduled dates, and reinvested all the cash flows received at the YTM. Given the price of a bond and all the details regarding the amount and timing of interest and principal repayments, we can always estimate the bond's YTM, using the following variation of Equation 6-1, which replaces k_b with YTM:

[6-2]

$$B = I \times \left[\frac{1 - \frac{1}{(1+YTM)^n}}{YTM} \right] + F \times \frac{1}{(1+YTM)^n}$$

As we can see from Equation 6-2 the yield to maturity is simply a special form of an internal rate of return, discussed in Chapter 5.

Unfortunately, as we found out in Chapter 5, solving for IRRs is difficult because of the various powers involved in Equation 6-2: solutions require logarithms, a business calculator, Excel, or a lot of time-consuming trial and error. The same problems occur in calculating the YTM on a bond. In fact, an exact algebraic solution for the YTM is not available. Fortunately, financial calculators and Excel are very good at repetitive calculations and can solve the problem very easily. However, if you don't have access to a financial calculator or Excel,[8] you have to use a trial and error approach to estimate the approximate yield that satisfies Equation 6-2.[9] In Example 6-7, we will find the solution by using a financial calculator and Excel first, then use the formula with trial and error.

---

[8] Old-fashioned bond tables, which show yields corresponding to various prices, coupon rates, and maturity dates are also available.

[9] An approximation formula does exist, but it can be off by a significant amount sometimes, especially for longer-term bonds that are trading at prices that are quite different from their par value.

Example 6-7: Estimating the YTM on an Annual-Pay Bond

Estimate the YTM on a 10-year 5 percent bond that pays annual coupons and is selling for $980.

(TI BA II Plus)

(PMT) = 50;   (PV) = −980;   (FV) = 1,000;   (N) = 10

Then compute I/Y will give 5.26 percent, which is an annual rate, so YTM (annual) = 5.26 percent.

Excel has a special function for calculating the YTM.

= YIELD(settlement, maturity, rate, pr, redemption, frequency, basis)

This is the same as the bond pricing formula, except that the yield (yld) has been replaced by the market price (pr). If we input our values, we get

= YIELD(date(2006,11,06), date(2016,11,06) , .05, 98.0, 100, 2, 0)
so we get 5.26 percent, the same as with the calculator. Note that Excel automatically converts the yield to an annual rate.

Notice that this answer appears reasonable, because the bond is trading at a slight discount from par, which implies that the discount rate (YTM) is greater than the coupon rate of 5 percent. Compare the simplicity of this solution to the long trial and error solution, which is provided below.

$B = \$980$; $F = \$1,000$; $I = 0.05 \times 1,000 = \$50$; $n = 10$

$$980 = 50 \times \left[\frac{1 - \dfrac{1}{(1 + YTM)^{10}}}{YTM} \right] + 1,000 \times \frac{1}{(1 + YTM)^{10}}$$

Essentially, we begin by estimating the YTM, trying the coupon even though we know the yield must be greater than 5 percent as the bond is selling at a discount. Substituting this rate into the equation above for YTM gives us a price of $1,000; therefore, the YTM must be above this rate because $1,000 is more than the price we want ($980). Substituting YTM = 6 percent into the equation gives us a corresponding price of $926.40, so 6 percent is too high a discount rate. Therefore we know that the rate we are looking for is between 5 and 6 percent.

We can obtain a close approximation by using linear interpolation, which involves setting up two equivalent ratios, as follows:

Rate	Price
5%	1,000
YTM	980
6%	926.40

We find the YTM by forming one ratio of the rates and putting the corresponding prices in the same position in a ratio of the prices, as follows:

$$\frac{YTM - 5}{6 - 5} = \frac{980 - 1000}{926.40 - 1000}$$

$$\frac{YTM - 5}{1} = \frac{-20}{-73.60} = 0.2717$$

So, YTM = 5.27%

Notice that this is very close to the exact solution of 5.26 percent obtained by using a financial calculator.

We follow the same process to estimate the YTM on a bond that pays semi-annual coupons, except that we first solve Equation 6-2 for a semi-annual rate (denoted YTM_S), and then we convert it to an annual rate by multiplying it by two.[10] Example 6-8 demonstrates this process.

Example 6-8: Estimating the YTM on a Semi-Annual-Pay Bond

Estimate the YTM on a 20-year 6 percent bond that pays semi-annual coupons and is selling for $1,030.

Solution

B = $1,030; F = $1,000; I = 0.06/2 × 1,000 = $30; n = 20 × 2 = 40;

$$1,030 = 30 \times \left[\frac{1 - \dfrac{1}{(1 + YTM_s)^{40}}}{YTM_s} \right] + 1,000 \times \frac{1}{(1 + YTM_s)^{40}}$$

solution using a financial calculator

(TI BA II Plus)

PMT = 30; PV = −1,030; FV = 1,000; N = 40

Then CPT I/Y will give 2.87 percent, which is a semi-annual rate (YTMs), so we multiply by two to find the annual YTM: 2.87% × 2 = 5.74%

---

[10] We multiply the semi-annual rate by two in order to reflect the manner in which bond yields are quoted. As discussed previously, bond yields are not effective annual rates when semi-annual coupons are paid.

We can enter
= YIELD(date(2006,11,06), date(2026,11,06), .06, 103, 100, 2, 0)
and we get 5.746 percent.

Notice that the answers appear reasonable, because the bond is trading at a premium over par, which implies that the discount rate (YTM) is less than the 6 percent coupon rate.

Yield to Call

We mentioned earlier that bonds often have flexible maturity dates, because some bonds are callable by the issuer, and for some, the maturity can be retracted or extended by the investor. This means that we can calculate the yield to maturity for these different dates. Suppose, for example, that the bond in the previous example was callable after five years at par.[11] This means that it is quite possible that the bond will not be outstanding for 20 years, because it may be called after 5 years. This yield, which is associated with a bond's first call date, is called its yield to call (YTC). It can be estimated in the same way as we estimated the YTM by using Equation 6-2, except that we replace the time to maturity (n) with the time to first call (c), and we replace the face value (F) with the call price (CP). This gives us the equation below:

$$B = I \times \left[\frac{1 - \dfrac{1}{(1 + YTC)^c}}{YTC} \right] + CP \times \frac{1}{(1 + YTC)^c}$$

[6-3]

Example 6-9: Estimating the Yield to Call (YTC)

Estimate the YTC on a 20-year 6 percent bond that is callable in five years at a call price of $1,050, if the bond pays semi-annual coupons and is selling for $1,030.

Solution

B = $1,030; CP = $1,050; I = 0.06/2 × 1,000 = $30; n = 5 × 2 = 10

$$1,030 = 30 \times \left[\frac{1 - \dfrac{1}{(1 + YTC_s)^{10}}}{YTC_s} \right] + 1,050 \times \frac{1}{(1 + YTC_s)^{10}}$$

PMT = 30;   PV = −1,030;   FV = 1,050;   N = 10

Then compute I/Y will give 3.081 percent, which is a semi-annual rate (YTC_S), so we multiply by two to find the annual YTC: 3.081% × 2 = 6.16%

---

[11] In practice, many callable bonds may have more than one call date.

We can enter

= YIELD(date(2006,11,06), date(2011,11,06), .06, 103, 105, 2, 0)

and we get 6.16 percent.

Notice that in Example 6-9, the YTC is greater than the coupon rate, because the call price of $1,050 is greater than the bond's current price of $1,030. So what can we say about the 5.75 percent YTM on this bond calculated in Example 6-8, compared with the 6.16 percent YTC? Because the call price is above its current market price, it is unlikely that the bond would be called back by the issuer, so it is selling based on its YTM rather than its YTC. It would trade on its YTC if it was likely that the bond would be called, which would occur if the bond were trading above its call price and, correspondingly, if the YTC < YTM. Generally, the bond trades off whichever of the two is lower. We can confirm this by looking at 5-year and 20-year yields on equivalent non-callable bonds, which takes us into the determination of market interest rates. However, before doing this, we should touch on another simple interest rate measure.

Current Yield

current yield (CY) the ratio of the annual coupon interest divided by the current market price

The **current yield (CY)** is defined as the ratio of the annual coupon interest divided by the current market price. As such, it is not a true measure of the return to a bondholder because it disregards the bond's purchase price relative to all the future cash flows and uses just the next year's interest payment. The current yield is also sometimes referred to as the flat or cash yield. It can be calculated using Equation 6-4:

[6-4]

$$CY = \frac{Annual\ interest}{B}$$

Example 6-10: Current Yield

Determine the current yield for the bond used in Example 6-8, which was trading for $1,030.

Solution

B = 1,030; annual interest = $30 × 2 = $60 (or simply $1,000 × 0.06)

$$CY = \frac{60}{1,030} = 0.0583\ or\ 5.83\%$$

Notice that the current yield does not equal the coupon rate of 6 percent or the YTM of 5.74 percent. This will be the case, unless the bond is trading at its face value and all three rates would be equal. It is clear that whenever bonds trade at a premium, the CY will be less than the coupon rate but greater than the YTM (as in Example 6-10), and whenever they trade at a discount, the CY will be greater than the coupon rate but less than the YTM, as shown here:

Price-Yield Relationships

Bond Price	Relationship
Par	Coupon rate = CY = YTM
Discount	Coupon rate < CY < YTM
Premium	Coupon rate > CY > YTM

CONCEPT REVIEW QUESTIONS

1. Why is there no simple analytical formula for the yield to maturity?

2. When bonds sell above their par value is the yield to maturity greater or less than the coupon rate?

3. Is the yield to call always greater than the yield to maturity?

6.4 INTEREST RATE DETERMINANTS

Base Interest Rates

Interest rates are usually quoted on an annual percentage basis. However, it is common to refer to changes in interest rates in terms of *basis points,* each of which represents 1/100th of 1 percent. For example, a decrease of 10 basis points implies that interest rates declined 0.10 percent.

As we discussed earlier, the interest rate is the price of money and as such is determined by the laws of supply and demand, as for any other commodity. In the case of interest rates, it is the supply and demand for "loanable funds." All else constant, as the demand for loanable funds decreases so does their price, as a result interest rates increase; conversely, interest rates decrease as the supply of loanable funds increases. The interest rates that we have been discussing so far are called **nominal interest rates**, because they are the rates charged for lending today's dollars in return for getting dollars back in the future, without taking into account the purchasing power of those future dollars. One of the most important factors in determining these nominal interest rates is the expected rate of inflation because this determines the purchasing power of those future dollars.

nominal interest rates the rates charged for lending today's dollars in return for getting dollars back in the future, without taking into account the purchasing power of those future dollars

In structuring our discussion of actual interest rates, we will refer to the base rate as the **risk-free rate (RF)**. We will discuss risk at length shortly but the term risk-free, although conventional, is a bit of a misnomer; what it actually refers to is **default free** in that the investors know exactly how many dollars they will get back on their investment. It is common to use the yield on short-term government treasury bills (T-bills), which are discussed in greater detail later in this chapter, as a proxy for this risk-free rate. Federal government T-bill yields are considered risk-free, because they possess no risk of default; the government essentially controls the Bank of Canada and can always have it buy any bonds that are issued with Bank of Canada banknotes. Further government T-bills possess very little interest rate risk because their term to maturity is very short.

risk-free rate (RF) the base interest rate

default free no risk of non-payment

As a result, we have the following approximate relationship:

$$RF = \text{Real rate} + \text{Expected inflation}$$

This relationship is an approximation of the direct relationship between inflation and interest rates that is often referred to as the "Fisher relationship," after Irving Fisher.[12] What the Fisher effect says is that investors attempt to protect themselves from the loss in purchasing power caused by inflation by increasing their required nominal yield. As a result, interest rates will be low when expected inflation is low and high when expected inflation is high.

Table 5-1 of Chapter 5 showed that the average return on Government of Canada T-bills over the 1938 to 2005 period was 5.20 percent. Over the same period, inflation averaged 3.99 percent, which indicates that the average real return over this period was 1.21 percent, or 121 basis points.[13]

Example 6-11: Estimating the Real Rate of Return

If T-bill rates are presently 4.5 percent and the expected level of inflation is 2.0 percent, estimate the real rate of return.

Solution

Real rate = 4.5 − 2.0 = 2.5%

The graph in Figure 6-3 provides the history of the annual inflation rate as measured by the consumer price index (CPI), the yield to maturity on the long Canada bond, and the yield to maturity on 91-day Treasury bills back to 1961.

FIGURE 6-3

Interest Rates and Inflation

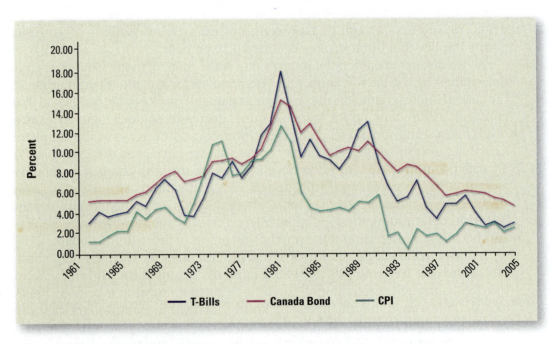

The level of nominal interest rates generally tracked the increase in inflation throughout the 1960s, until inflation peaked at more than 12 percent in 1981.

---

[12] Technically, the correct procedure is to multiply (1 + Real rate) by (1 + Expected inflation) and subtract 1.0. The approximation in Equation 6-5 works very well when levels of inflation are relatively low, as they are today. See Irving Fisher, "Appreciation and Interest," *Publications of the American Economic Association* (August 1896), pp. 1–1001.

[13] Notice that we are looking at returns "after the fact" in this example. In practice, the return is based on expected inflation, which will usually not be the same as actual inflation.

Since then, interest rates have generally declined with the rate of inflation. As we just discussed, one measure of the real rate is the difference between the ongoing expected inflation rate and the level of nominal interest rates. This difference was much larger from 1981 until recently than it was in the 1960s, because the capital market persistently failed to take into account the inflationary pressures in the economy at that time.

Global Influences on Interest Rates

Although interest rate levels vary from one country to the next, global interest rates interact with one another. This occurs because most countries have now removed foreign exchange restrictions, allowing capital to flow from one country to another in search of higher rates of return. As a result, interest rates in Canada are heavily influenced by prevailing rates in other countries, especially those in the United States. This influence is inevitable in today's capital markets because money is the most generic of all commodities; without restrictions, one price will prevail in the capital market.

Exactly how do foreign interest rates affect domestic interest rates? For example, why do investors not invest in the bonds of countries that are offering higher interest rates, and why do companies not issue bonds in countries with lower rates? The answer to these questions lies in the functioning of foreign exchange markets. For example, although it may be tempting to buy bonds in countries offering higher interest rates, the additional gains could be easily cancelled out (and even large losses incurred) as a result of adverse movements in the foreign exchange rates prevailing when funds are converted back into the domestic currency. In other words, investing or issuing debt abroad creates *foreign exchange risk*, which offsets the potential advantages that may arise from inter-country interest rate differentials.

The **interest rate parity (IRP) theory** demonstrates how differences in interest rates across countries are offset by expected changes in exchange rates. If this were not the case, capital would flow from countries with low interest rates to those with high interest rates, increasing the supply of capital in the country with higher rates, which would ultimately drive down borrowing costs. Similarly, the capital outflows from countries with low rates would cause their rates to rise in order to have the supply of funds equal the demand for these funds.

interest rate parity (IRP) theory a theory that demonstrates how differences in interest rates across countries are offset by expected changes in exchange rates

The IRP theory, which is discussed in greater detail in Appendix 6-A, describes the precise relationship between interest rates and currency levels by using forward currency exchange rates, because forward currency contracts can be used to eliminate foreign exchange risk. Essentially, the IRP theory states that forward exchange rates that can be locked in today in order to eliminate foreign exchange risk will be established at levels that ensure the investor would end up with the same amount whether investing at home or in another country (with no foreign exchange risk). Important factors that affect both interest rates and currency exchange rates are inflation and inflation differentials between countries. For example, if Canadian inflation exceeded that in the United States, we would expect that interest rates would be higher in Canada than in the United States. However, the inflation would cause the value of our currency to depreciate versus the U.S. dollar (USD), so that we could remain competitive in international trade. Thus, a U.S. investor who bought Canadian bonds in an attempt to benefit from our higher rates would lose these gains when he or she converted the Canadian dollar (CDN) payments back into USD.

In short, although interest rates are heavily influenced by inflation and other domestic macroeconomic variables, global factors, such as foreign exchange rates and inflation differentials, also play an important role in the level of interest rates at any given time.

The Term Structure of Interest Rates

So far, we have discussed the major factors affecting the base level of interest rates or RF, which we proxy as the yield on short-term government T-bills. The yields on other debt instruments will differ from RF for several reasons. One important factor affecting debt yields is related to its term to maturity. This is obvious if we look at the Canadian bond quotes from Finance in the News 6-1, where we can see various yield levels for bonds with different maturity dates, even though they were issued by the same entity. For example, at the top the Government of Canada benchmarks have yields ranging from 4.14 percent for 7-year bonds, to 4.26 percent for 20-year bonds.

term structure of interest rates the relationship between interest rates and the term to maturity on underlying debt instruments

The relationship between interest rates and the term to maturity on underlying debt instruments is referred to as the **term structure of interest rates**. Finance in the News 6-2 provides a graphical representation of this relationship, which is often referred to as the **yield curve**. The curve must be based on debt instruments that are from the same issuer, or else default risk (discussed below), as well as other risk factors, will affect the difference in yields, in addition to maturity differentials. Therefore, the yield curve is almost always constructed by using federal government issues because they possess the same default risk, as well as similar issue characteristics. In addition, the government tends to have a large number of issues outstanding at any given time; therefore, we can construct a yield curve with rate estimates for a wide variety of maturities.

yield curve the graphical representation of the term structure of interest rates, based on debt instruments that are from the same issuer

finance
INTHENEWS6-2

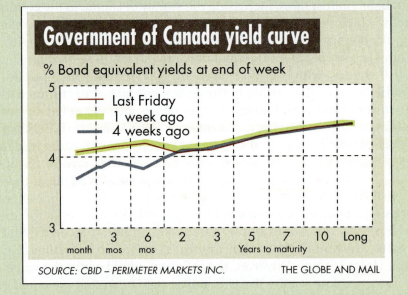

GOVERNMENT OF CANADA YIELD CURVE

Source: "Government of Canada Yield Curve," *The Globe and Mail Report on Business*, May 15, 2006, p. B12.

The yield curve depicted in this Finance in the News 6-2 is slightly *upward sloping*, with one-month rates sitting at just more than 4 percent, and long rates sitting at just more than 4.5 percent; that is, although long-term government bonds are virtually free from default risk in the same manner as short-term government T-bills are, long-term bonds typically yield more than medium-term bonds do, which typically yield more than T-bills do.

Although yield curves are usually upward sloping, they can assume a wide variety of shapes. Figure 6-4 shows four historical Government of Canada yield curves at the end of June in 1990, 1994, 1998, and 2004. Similar to the curve for 2006, those for 1994 and 2004 are upward-sloping curves. However, these three curves vary significantly in terms of their steepness and their starting points. For example, although the long-term rates in 2006 exceed the short-term rates by only 50 basis points, the difference is close to 400 basis points in both 1994 and 2004. In addition, the short-term rates vary from just more than 2 percent in 2004 and just more than 4 percent in 2006, to almost 6 percent in 1994. The *downward-sloping* (or *inverted*) yield curve for 1990 is less common, with short-term rates exceeding long-term rates. These "inverted" yield curves are unusual, and some market participants believe they indicate that short-term rates will fall. In fact, short-term interest rates did decline in the subsequent 1991−93 period. Another less common shape is the relatively flat yield curve in 1998, which indicates that long- and short-term rates are very similar.[14]

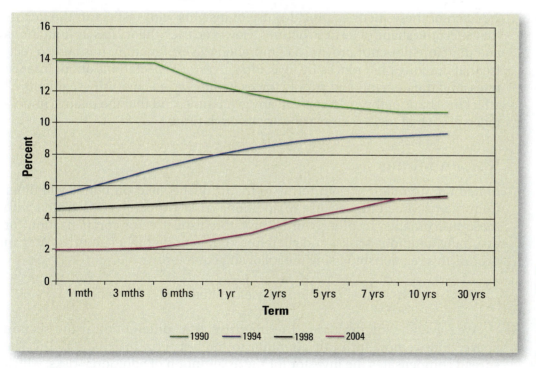

6-4 FIGURE

*Historical Yield Curves
1990, 1994, 1998, 2004*

Several theories attempt to account for the various shapes and movements of the yield curve. We describe three of the most popular theories below:

1. The **liquidity preference theory** suggests that investors prefer short-term debt instruments (i.e., more liquid instruments) because they exhibit less interest rate risk, while debt issuers prefer to lock in borrowing rates for longer periods

liquidity preference theory a theory that suggests that investors prefer short-term debt instruments because they exhibit less interest rate risk, while debt issuers prefer to lock in borrowing rates for longer periods to avoid the risk of having to refinance at higher rates

---

[14] Although the 2006 curve was upward sloping, it too was relatively "flat."

to avoid the risk of having to refinance at higher rates. Therefore, issuers must provide investors with higher yields to induce them to invest in longer-term bonds. As a result, yield curves will generally be upward sloping because long-term rates will be higher than short-term rates. Although this theory is intuitive and does a good job of explaining why yield curves are usually upward sloping, it does not properly account for downward-sloping or flat term structures.

expectations theory a theory that argues that the yield curve reflects investor expectations about future interest rates

2. The **expectations theory** argues that the yield curve reflects investor expectations about future interest rates. Therefore, an upward-sloping yield curve reflects expectations of interest rate increases in the future, and a downward-sloping curve reflects expectations of interest rate decreases in the future. Unlike the liquidity preference theory, this theory provides a reasonable explanation of downward-sloping and flat term structures, as well as for upward-sloping curves. However, it does not account for the predominance of upward-sloping curves, because it is unreasonable to believe that people expect rates to increase most of the time.

market segmentations theory a theory that suggests that distinct markets (or market segments) exist for interest rate securities of various maturities and that rates are determined within these independent market segments by the forces of supply and demand within that market

3. The **market segmentations theory** suggests that distinct markets (or market segments) exist for interest rate securities of various maturities and that rates are determined within these independent market segments by the forces of supply and demand within that market. The resulting term structure merely depicts the consequences of the forces of supply and demand within these markets.

Each of these theories provides useful insights with respect to the factors that affect the shape of term structures. However, each theory has its limitations and therefore does not provide a comprehensive explanation. It is best to realize that liquidity preferences by investors, investor expectations about interest rates, and the demand and supply forces within various maturity segments all affect the shape of the yield curve at any given time, and that the relative importance of each of these factors will vary through time.

Risk Premiums

In addition to differences in terms to maturity, the yield on bonds will differ from the risk-free rate because of additional risks or features associated with these instruments. In other words, investors expect extra compensation for assuming additional risks, and therefore they require higher returns. We can express this relationship using the following equation:

[6-6]

$$k_b = RF +/- \text{ Maturity yield differential} + \text{Spread}$$

spread a difference in yield that compensates the investor for the assumption of additional risks

We have already discussed the maturity yield differential in the section above, and we now turn our attention to the last term in Equation 6-6. The **spread** compensates the investor for the assumption of additional risks, which may include some or all of the following: (1) default or credit risk, (2) liquidity, and (3) issue-specific features. We discuss each of these in turn.

default risk the risk associated with the bond issuer and its ability to pay

The most obvious difference in yield arises because of the different levels of **default risk** associated with the bond issuer. In other words, bondholders require higher yields to compensate them for the possibility that the borrower may default on the promised debt payments. This is obvious in the yields that can be observed in Finance in the News 6-1. For example, if we consider three bond issues that have similar coupon rates and mature on or about the same date, we can observe that their yields differ when they are from separate issuers, which reflects different levels of default risk. For example the 5.50 percent Government of Canada bonds with a June 1, 2009, maturity date were priced to yield 4.20 percent, while the 5.50 percent Government of Quebec bonds with the same maturity date were yielding 4.34 percent, and the 4.18 percent Royal Bank bonds with the same maturity date were yielding 4.52 percent.

Debt ratings are assigned by professional *debt-rating services*, which perform detailed analyses of bond issuers to determine their ability to sustain their required payments of interest and principal repayments. Investment-grade bonds are those with bond ratings of BBB (Dominion Bond Rating Service [DBRS] and Standard & Poor's [S&P]), or Baa (Moody's) or higher. Junk (or high-yield or low-grade) bonds have bond ratings below these. These ratings may be modified by "high" or "low" to indicate the relative ranking within a category. The following are the debt-rating categories for S&P:

debt ratings ratings assigned by professional debt-rating services after detailed analyses of bond issuers to determine their ability to sustain the required interest and principal payments

S&P	
AAA	highest credit quality
AA	very good quality
A	good quality
BBB	medium quality
BB	lower medium quality
B	poor quality
CCC	speculative quality
CC	very speculative quality
D	default
Suspended	rating suspended

Most of the differences in yields for bonds of the same term to maturity that are observed as we move from Government of Canada bonds to provincial government bonds to corporate bonds are due to differences in the default risk associated with the issuers. However, a portion of the difference is also due to the fact that Government of Canada bonds trade more actively than provincial bonds, which trade more actively than most investment-grade corporate bonds, which trade more actively than junk bonds. In other words, some bonds are more liquid than others, which means that they are easier to buy and sell and that the required price concessions are lower. Bonds that are less liquid may have to offer investors a higher yield to compensate them for this illiquidity. This additional yield is referred to as the **liquidity premium**.

Issue-specific premiums arise when bonds have features that cause them to be more or less attractive to investors, relative to straight (option free) bonds. For example, as discussed previously, the call feature is detrimental to bondholders. The reason is that these bonds are likely to be called by the issuer when interest rates are low (so that they can be refinanced at lower rates), which is exactly when the market prices of these bonds are increasing. As a result, investors will not pay as much for a callable bond as they would for an otherwise identical non-callable bond (i.e., they will demand a higher return). Conversely, retractable bonds permit investors to sell the bonds back to the issuer at predetermined prices when interest rates rise (and bond prices fall), which provides protection against rising rates. Similarly, extendible bonds will only be extended by investors if the coupon rates

liquidity premium an additional yield offered on bonds that are less liquid

issue-specific premiums premiums that arise when bonds have features that cause them to be more or less attractive to investors, relative to straight (option-free) bonds

finance
INTHENEWS6-3

TREASURIES VS. CORPORATES

January 1, 2007–Bonds are as integral to a smooth sailing portfolio as a rudder is to a ship. But what kinds of bonds are best? If you're like most financial advisors, this is a question you've grappled with.

High-quality, longer-term bonds with long track records for low correlation and positive real returns come in two varieties: corporate investment-grade and Treasury. These bonds most deserve space in clients' long-term portfolios. But which type gets priority?

No one gets rich off Treasuries. When you buy Treasury bonds, you are not only getting the U.S. government's assurance against default, but there's also no chance of a downgrade (think Ford or GM), no chance of an early call should interest rates fall and the liquidity is downright oceanic. Modest returns are all you can expect for this lack of risk.

According to Lehman Brothers data, corporate investment-grade bonds of all maturities and durations have collectively outperformed their counterpart Treasury issues in 17 of the past 26 years, averaging about 90 basis points more per year. Since 1980, the overall annualized real return on Treasuries, give or take a few basis points, has been about 3%, compared with roughly 4% for corporate investment-grade bonds.

As for volatility, the approximate standard deviation stands at 3.5 for Treasuries, versus 4.0 for corporates. "That's significant added return for only a small amount of additional risk," says David Tiberii, vice president and lead portfolio manager of investment-grade corporate bonds with Baltimore-based T. Rowe Price Associates.

But David Swensen, chief investment officer of Yale University, is no fan of corporate debt. "Many investors purchase corporate bonds hoping to get something for nothing by earning an incremental yield over that available from U.S. Treasury bonds. At the end of the day, excess returns prove illusory as credit risk, illiquidity and optionality work against the holder of corporate obligations, providing less than nothing to the corporate bond investor," he writes in his latest book, *Unconventional Success: A Fundamental Approach to Personal Investment*.

Other investment pros have similarly strong–and often contradictory–feelings about whether a long-term fixed-income portfolio is best cobbled out of government or corporate debt.

"Those people who make unequivocal statements about never buying corporate bonds because the excess return over Treasuries is so paltry are generally not the same people who have to live on a limited fixed income," says Marilyn Cohen, president of Envision Capital Management, an investment advisory firm in Los Angeles that specializes in fixed income. Daniel Fuss, vice chairman of Boston-based Loomis, Sayles & Co., thinks there's nothing wrong with Treasuries; but corporate bonds, despite credit risk and callability features, often offer real opportunity. "Especially for those willing to do some work and uncover value in the market," he adds.

Matthew Gelfand, PhD, a fee-only planner in Bethesda, Maryland., is wary of historical data that shows corporate bonds' relative buoyancy in hard times. "Just because corporates have held up for the past 80 years doesn't mean they necessarily will do so over the next 80," he says. "If there's a major macro event, I'd rather be holding Treasuries."

That said, Gelfand certainly isn't giving up corporate bonds altogether. The extra yield is too sweet to ignore. "I use several actively managed funds where I trust the managers to take maximum advantage of a relatively inefficient market while keeping a close eye on economic conditions," he says. For his Treasury positions, Gelfand uses ETFs and mutual funds; for larger clients, he blends in specific Treasury securities to tailor maturities and interest-rate exposures more precisely.

As much as he likes corporate bonds as a long-term investment, Fuss agrees that right now may not be the best time to load up on corporate debt. He hopes to continue his bond fund's long winning streak with a mix of hand-picked corporates and Treasuries.

on such bonds are competitive; if rates increased, the investors would choose not to extend and could invest in other bonds that offer higher coupon rates. Therefore, extendible and retractable bonds, as well as convertible bonds, offer investors an additional privilege, and so they will trade at higher prices than otherwise identical straight bonds (i.e., they will provide a lower return).

All three of these factors are embedded in what is commonly called the corporate spread over equivalent maturity Canada bonds. In practice, it is very difficult to separate these three components of the corporate spread. Figure 6-5 graphs the weekly historic spreads among AA, A, and BBB bond yields over equivalent maturity long Canada bonds.

6-5 FIGURE

Corporate Spreads

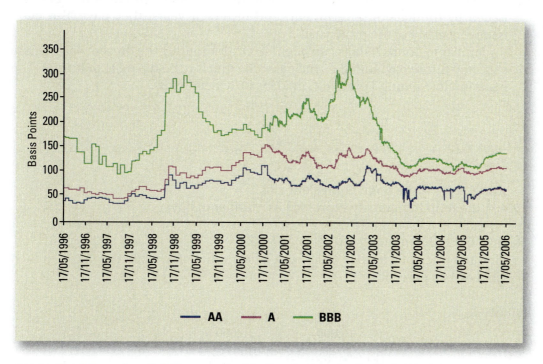

Source: The data are from DataStream and originally came from Scotia Capital Markets.

Notice that as the bond rating deteriorates, the yield spread increases to reflect the greater risks attached to investing in riskier issues as referred to in Finance in the News 6-3. The article discusses the various risks associated with other corporate and high yield debt versus government debt. These spreads vary over time with the business cycle.

CONCEPT REVIEW QUESTIONS

1. How does the expected rate of inflation affect nominal interest rates?
2. Why do interest rates differ between Canada and the United States?
3. Why do interest rates on different-maturity Canada bonds differ?
4. What is a corporate spread?

6.5 OTHER TYPES OF BONDS/DEBT INSTRUMENTS

Treasury Bills

Treasury bills (T-bills) are short-term government debt obligations that mature in one year or less. Partly because of this short term to maturity, they do not make regular interest payments but are sold at a discount from their par (or face) value, which is paid on the maturity date. So the interest earned is the difference between the purchase price and the face value. In Canada, T-bills are issued by the federal government, and in recent years, they have also been issued by many of the provinces.

Similar to bonds, T-bills can be priced by estimating the present value of the expected future payment (i.e., the par value that is to be repaid at maturity). The equation for valuing T-bills in Canada is provided below:

[6-7]

$$P = \frac{F}{(1 + k_{BEY} \times \frac{n}{365})}$$

where, k_{BEY} = the bond equivalent yield
n = the term to maturity expressed as number of days

Example 6-12: Determining the Price of T-bills

Find the price of a 91-day T-bill with a face value of $10,000 that has a quoted yield of 4.20 percent.

Solution

$$P = \frac{10,000}{(1 + 0.0420 \times \frac{91}{365})} = \frac{10,000}{1.010471233} = \$9,896.37$$

Similar to bonds, T-bill prices are usually quoted on the basis of $100 of par value, so the price quote for the T-bill in Example 6-12 would be 98.9637.

Rearranging Equation 6-7, we can determine the yield on T-bills using the following equation:

[6-8]

$$k_{BEY} = \frac{F - P}{P} \times \frac{365}{n}$$

Example 6-13: Estimating the Yield on a T-bill

Estimate the yield on a 182-day T-bill that is presently selling at a price of $98.20.

Solution

$$k_{BEY} = \frac{100 - 98.20}{98.20} \times \frac{365}{182} = 0.018329939 \times 2.005494505 = 0.03676 = 3.676\%$$

In the United States, yields on T-bills are usually quoted based on the *bank discount yield*, which is determined by using a different procedure from that used to calculate the bond equivalent yield in Canada. The differences arise because of the use of face value instead of price in the denominator of the first term and because 360 days is used instead of 365 days to annualize the rate. The resulting equation is given by

$$k_{BDY} = \frac{Face - P}{Face} \times \frac{360}{n} \times 100$$

where k_{BDY} = the bank discount yield.

Zero Coupon Bonds

A **zero coupon bond (or zero)** is structured similarly to a long-term T-bill, in the sense that it does not make regular interest payments but is issued at a discount and repays the par value at the maturity date. The return earned represents the difference between the purchase price and the redemption price. Obviously, the lower the price paid for the bond, the higher the return. "Zeroes" were initially created by financial intermediaries who purchased traditional bonds, "stripped" the cash flows (both the interest and the principal repayment components) from them, and sold these cash flows separately. Today, most zeroes are created this way; however, some are also initially issued as zero coupon bonds. These instruments are very popular with financial institutions, which often use them for hedging purposes with respect to their outstanding liabilities. Zeroes are ideally suited for this purpose because, unlike with traditional bonds, there are no issues with respect to reinvesting interest payments that are received before maturity.

zero coupon bond (or zero) a bond that is issued at a discount, pays no coupons, and repays the par value at the maturity date

Zero coupon bonds are easy to evaluate by using a variation of Equation 6-1 in which we drop the first term (because there are no interest payments to discount). This leaves us with Equation 6-9, shown below.

$$B = F \times \frac{1}{(1 + k_b)^n}$$

[6-9]

Remember that, by convention, we value these bonds by assuming semi-annual discounting periods and convert our quoted yield to a semi-annual yield; therefore, the number of periods should also be expressed in terms of semi-annual periods.

Example 6-14: Valuing Zero Coupon Bonds

Determine the price of a 15-year zero coupon bond with a face value of $1,000 and a market yield of 5 percent.

Solution

$F = 1,000$; $n = 15$ years $\times 2 = 30$; $k_b = 0.05/2 = 0.025$

$$B = 1,000 \times \frac{1}{(1 + .025)^{30}} = 1,000 \times 0.47674 = \$476.74$$

(TI BA II Plus)

$PMT = 0;$ $N = 30;$ $FV = 1,000;$ $I/Y = 2.5;$

compute $PV = -\$476.74$

solution using Excel

We input
$= PRICE(date(2006,11,06), date(2021,11,06), .0, .05, 100, 2, 0)$

and get the same answer of \$476.74. Note that with Excel, the only difference for a regular bond is to enter 0 for the coupon rate.

Notice from Equation 6-9 that if market rates fell, the price of the zero would increase and vice versa, just as is the case for a regular coupon-paying bond. In fact, the market prices of zeroes are even more sensitive to interest rate changes, because they make no coupon payments at all.

Finally, it is relatively straightforward to solve for the YTM on a zero, if we are given the price. In particular, we can rearrange Equation 6-9 to determine an exact solution for the semi-annual YTM_S, as shown in Equation 6-10 below. This value is then doubled to find the annual YTM. Notice that this differs from the coupon-paying bonds, for which there was no finite solution for YTM.

[6-10]

$$YTM_s = \left[\frac{F}{B}\right]^{\frac{1}{n}} - 1$$

Example 6-15: Estimating the YTM on a Zero Coupon Bond

Determine the YTM on a 10-year zero coupon bond with a face value of \$1,000 that is presently selling for \$560.

Solution

$F = 1,000; n = 10 \text{ years} \times 2 = 20; PV = 560$

$$YTM_s = \left[\frac{1,000}{560}\right]^{\frac{1}{20}} - 1 = [1.785714286]^{\frac{1}{20}} - 1 = 1.0294 - 1 = 0.0294 = 2.94\%$$

(TI BA II Plus)

$PMT = 0;$ $N = 20;$ $FV = 1,000;$ $PV = -560$

Compute $I/Y = 2.94\%$

So the annual YTM $= 2.94\% \times 2 = 5.88\%$.

= YIELD(date(2006,11,06), date(2016,11,06), 0, 56, 100, 2, 0)

gives 5.883 percent.

Floating Rate and Real Return Bonds

Floating rate bonds (floaters) have adjustable coupons that are usually tied to some variable short-term rate, such as the T-bill rate, although many variations exist. They differ significantly from traditional fixed income bonds because the coupons increase as interest rates increase and vice versa. Therefore, floaters provide protection against rising interest rates and tend to trade near their par value.

floating rate bonds (floaters) bonds that have adjustable coupons that are usually tied to some variable short-term rate

Government of Canada **Real Return Bonds** provide investors with protection against inflation by providing a real yield of about 4.25 percent. This is achieved by pegging the face value to the rate of inflation (as measured by the CPI) and having the coupon rate of 4.25 percent apply to the inflation-adjusted face value.

Real Return Bonds bonds issued by the Government of Canada that provide investors with protection against inflation

Canada Savings Bonds

Canada Savings Bonds (CSBs) differ significantly from those discussed above. CSBs have no secondary market because they cannot be traded; therefore, their prices do not change over time. They are registered in the name of the investor at the time of purchase and they can be cashed out by the owner, at their full par value plus eligible accrued interest, at any bank in Canada at any time. Presently, they may only be purchased by individuals, estates, and certain trusts. This restriction differs significantly from traditional bonds, which tend to be held mainly by institutional investors.

Canada Savings Bonds (CSBs) bonds issued by the Government of Canada that have no secondary market and can't be traded, so their prices do not change over time

The rates of return on CSBs may vary through time. They are presently available in two forms: (1) regular interest, which pay out the annual interest amounts, and (2) compound interest, which reinvest the interest, so that interest is also earned on accumulated interest (producing the power of compounding, which we discussed in Chapter 5).

CONCEPT REVIEW QUESTIONS

1. How does the formula for determining the price of a T-bill resemble the formula for determining the price of a zero-coupon bond? Why is this so?

2. How do U.S. bank discount yields differ from U.S. bond equivalent yields?

3. How do floaters and real return bonds provide protection against inflation?

Summary

This chapter discussed the nature of bonds as an investment. We examined the standard format of a traditional coupon-paying bond and considered additional features or variations of this structure. We then examined how these instruments can be valued by using the discounting concepts developed in Chapter 5, after we determined an appropriate discount rate. One of the most important factors affecting bond prices is the level of interest rates. The most important property of bond prices is that they increase when interest rates decrease and vice versa. Finally, we considered the various factors, both domestic and global, that affect the basic levels of market interest rates.

Key Terms

balloon payment, p. 212

bills, p. 212

bond indenture, p. 213

bonds, p. 212

bullet payment, p. 212

call prices, p. 214

callable bonds, p. 214

Canada Savings Bonds (CSBs), p. 243

collateral trust bonds, p. 214

collateral, p. 213

convertible bonds, p. 215

coupons, p. 213

current yield (CY), p. 230

debentures, p. 213

debt ratings, p. 237

default free, p. 231

default risk, p. 236

discount (premium), p. 217

duration, p. 223

equipment trust certificates, p. 214

expectations theory, p. 236

extendible bonds, p. 214

face value, p. 213

floating rate bonds (floaters), p. 243

interest payments, p. 213

interest rate parity (IRP) theory, p. 233

interest rate risk, p. 223

issue-specific premiums, p. 237

liquidity preference theory, p. 235

liquidity premium, p. 237

market segmentations theory, p. 236

maturity value, p. 213

mortgage bonds, p. 213

nominal interest rates, p. 231

notes, p. 212

paper, p. 212

par value, p. 213

protective covenants, p. 214

purchase fund provisions, p. 215

Real Return Bonds, p. 243

retractable bonds, p. 214

risk-free rate (RF), p. 231

sinking fund provisions, p. 214

spread, p. 236

term structure of interest rates, p. 234

term to maturity, p. 213

yield curve, p. 234

yield to maturity (YTM), p. 226

zero coupon bond (or zero), p. 241

Formulas/Equations

[6-1] $B = I \times \left[\dfrac{1 - \dfrac{1}{(1 + k_b)^n}}{k_b} \right] + F \times \dfrac{1}{(1 + k_b)^n}$

[6-2] $B = I \times \left[\dfrac{1 - \dfrac{1}{(1 + YTM)^n}}{YTM} \right] + F \times \dfrac{1}{(1 + YTM)^n}$

[6-3] $B = I \times \left[\dfrac{1 - \dfrac{1}{(1 + YTC)^c}}{YTC} \right] + CP \times \dfrac{1}{(1 + YTC)^c}$

[6-4] $CY = \dfrac{Annual\ interest}{B}$

[6-5] RF = Real rate + Expected inflation

[6-6] k_b = RF +/− Maturity yield differential + Spread

[6-7] $P = \dfrac{F}{(1 + k_{BEY} \times \dfrac{n}{365})}$

[6-8] $k_{BEY} = \dfrac{F - P}{P} \times \dfrac{365}{n}$

[6-9] $B = F \times \dfrac{1}{(1 + k_b)^n}$

[6-10] $YTM_s = \left[\dfrac{F}{B} \right]^{\frac{1}{n}} - 1$

[6A-1] $\dfrac{F}{S} = \dfrac{(1 + k_{domestic})}{(1 + k_{foreign})}$

APPENDIX 6A: INTEREST RATE PARITY

Interest rates vary from one country to the next, yet wise investors do not merely invest in the bonds of countries that are offering the highest interest rates. The reason is that trying to exploit such opportunities would expose them to foreign exchange risk, which offsets the potential advantages that may arise from inter-country interest rate differentials. The interest rate parity (IRP) theory demonstrates why the differences in interest rates across countries should be off-set by forward exchange rates. In particular, the IRP states that the following relationship should hold or else *arbitrage opportunities* (i.e., the opportunity to earn riskless profits) will exist:

[6A-1]

$$\frac{F}{S} = \frac{(1 + k_{domestic})}{(1 + k_{foreign})}$$

where F = the current forward exchange rate, expressed in number of units of domestic currency required to purchase one unit of the foreign currency
S = the current spot exchange rate
$k_{domestic}$ = the domestic interest rate
$k_{foreign}$ = the foreign interest rate
    Example 6A-1 uses this equation to determine the predicted forward exchange rate.

Example 6A-1: Using IRP

Assume British interest rates are presently 10 percent on one-year British T-bills. Assume that sterling is quoted at £1 = C$1.7500 and that the interest rate on one-year T-bills in Canada is 6 percent. Find the one-year forward exchange rate.

Solution

Notice that the interest rate differential for the specified one-year term is 4 percent, which implies that the forward exchange rate should be approximately 4 percent lower (in CDN terms) than the spot rate to ensure that IRP holds.
    To be more precise, we can rearrange the IRP equation to solve for the forward rate:

$$F = S \times \frac{(1 + k_{domestic})}{(1 + k_{foreign})} = \$1.75 \times \frac{1.06}{1.10} = \$1.6864$$

The IRP implies that an investor cannot benefit from higher foreign interest rates without assuming risk, which is demonstrated in Example 6A-2.

Example 6A-2: An Arbitrage Opportunity When IRP Does Not Hold

Determine the ending wealth of two Canadian investors with C$1,000 to invest, assuming the conditions depicted in Example 6A-1 exist. Investor 1 invests domestically, while Investor 2 invests in the United Kingdom and eliminates foreign exchange risk using the forward contract.

Solution

Investor 1: Ending wealth = $1,000 × 1.06 = $1,060

Investor 2: First, convert CDN into £: $1,000/1.75 = £571.43
Second, invest £571.43 @ 10%: grows to £628.57
Third, convert £ into CDN through forward contract =
£628.57 × 1.6864 = $1,060.02

Notice that if this is the prevailing forward rate, neither investor is better off by investing in either country (the $0.02 difference is due to rounding error).

Why does this relationship hold? If it didn't then investors could earn arbitrage (riskless) profits without putting up any initial investment. Example 6A-3 demonstrates.

Example 6A-3: An Arbitrage Opportunity When IRP Does Not Hold

In Example 6A-2, if the forward rate was set at $1.700 instead of $1.6864, demonstrate how an investor (arbitrageur) could earn arbitrage (riskless) profit. Assume that anyone can borrow and lend (invest) at the quoted rates.

Solution

When the arbitrageur observes the forward price of $1.700, she would first note that it violates IRP, because F ≠ 1.75[(1.06)/(1.10)] = $1.6864.

This means that the forward rate prices £ too dearly and CDN too cheaply, so she will want to sell £ for CDN through the forward contract. She borrows CDN to buy £ now in the spot market and invests them in the United Kingdom until the maturity date of the forward contract.

Assuming the arbitrageur borrows $2 million, we obtain the following:

1. Borrow $2 million CDN (@6 percent) to buy sterling today.
    Convert $2 million CDN at spot of (1/C$1.75) = £1,142,857.

2. Invest in sterling for one year at 10 percent.
    The total investment at maturity = 1,142,857(1.10) = £1,257,143.

3. Convert back to CDN at the forward rate of 1.70:
    £1,257,143 × C$1.700 = C$2,137,143.
    Pay back loan: ($2 million)(1.06) = $2.12 million.
    Arbitrage profit = $2,137,143 − $2,120,000 = C$17,143.

The arbitrageur would make a riskless (arbitrage) profit (of C$17,143), without assuming any risk and without making any initial investment of her own funds.

The condition in Example 6A-3 could not persist: as investors rushed to exploit such an opportunity, the forward price would quickly fall to $1.6864.[15]

In similar fashion, if the forward rate was $1.66, arbitrageurs would note that this violates IRP because F ≠ £1 = C$1.6864. However, this time the forward rate prices £ too cheaply and CDN too dearly. Investors will want to sell CDN for £ through the forward contract, which means they will borrow £ (at 10 percent), convert them to CDN in the spot market, and invest them in Canada (at 6 percent) until the maturity date of the forward contract.

---

[15] The example above illustrates the existence of an arbitrage possibility; however, it disregards transaction costs and the fact that borrowing and lending rates are not usually equal. Both of these factors affect the potential for arbitrage and explain why IRP need not hold precisely, but rather should hold within reasonable boundaries.

QUESTIONS AND PRACTICE PROBLEMS

Multiple Choice Questions

1. Which of the following statements concerning bonds is *incorrect*?

    A. They involve blended payments of principal and interest.

    B. They have a fixed maturity date at which time the issuer repays the full principal amount.

    C. Bondholders are paid a series of fixed periodic amounts before the maturity date.

    D. The bond indenture is a legal document, specifying payment requirements and so on.

2. Which of the following statements is *incorrect*?

    A. Callable bonds give the bond issuer an option to call the bond at a predetermined price.

    B. All debentures are secured bonds.

    C. Extendible bonds allow bondholders to extend the maturity date.

    D. Convertible bonds give the bondholders an option to convert into common shares at a predetermined conversion ratio.

3. Determine the price of a five-year, 7 percent, annual coupon bond when the market rate is 8 percent. The face value is $100.

    A. $100

    B. $102.50

    C. $96.01

    D. $104.10

4. Which of the following bond prices is most sensitive to market rate changes? The par value = $100 for all.

    A. 5-year, 5 percent coupon rate, yield 5.5 percent

    B. 3-year, 8 percent coupon rate, yield 5.6 percent

    C. 7.5-year, 4.5 percent coupon rate, yield 5.5 percent

    D. 10-year, 4.5 percent coupon rate, yield 5.5 percent

5. Determine the yield to maturity on a six-year, 7 percent, semi-annual-pay bond, which is now priced at $993. Use a financial calculator.

    A. 7.05 percent

    B. 6.98 percent

    C. 3.57 percent

    D. 7.15 percent

6. Which of the following statements is *correct*?

    A. Current yield is the ratio of annual coupon payment divided by the par value.

B. When the coupon rate is higher than the market rate, the bond is priced at a discount.

C. When the market rate is higher than the coupon rate, the bond is priced at a premium.

D. If a bond is at a discount, the coupon rate < current yield < YTM.

7. According to interest rate parity (IRP) theory,

A. differences in interest rates across countries cannot be totally offset by expected changes in exchange rates.

B. forward exchange rates may be locked in today to eliminate foreign exchange risk and ensure investors can profit from moving capital to countries with higher interest rates.

C. the inflation differentials between countries affect both interest rates and currency exchange rates.

D. the country with a higher inflation rate will see its currency appreciate against another country with a lower inflation rate.

8. Which statement is *incorrect*?

A. The liquidity preference theory states that investors prefer short-term debt.

B. According to the expectations theory, a downward-sloping yield curve implies that interest rates are expected to decline in the future.

C. The risk premium in the bond yield reflects default risk, liquidity risk, and issue-specific features.

D. A debt rating of AAA is a worse rating than BB for S&P.

9. Calculate the *quoted* price of a 182-day Canadian T-bill that has a face value of $10,000 and a quoted yield of 5.5 percent.

A. $9,733.07

B. $9,478.67

C. $97.3307

D. $94.7867

10. Which of the following statements is *false*?

A. Zero coupon bonds are deep-discount bonds.

B. Zero coupon bonds are often created when cash flows are stripped from traditional bonds.

C. Floating rate bonds provide protection against decreasing interest rates.

D. There are two forms of return available for Canadian Savings Bond buyers.

Practice Problems

11. State the relationship between market rates and bond prices.

12. Find the price of a bond with FV = $1,000, a coupon rate of 6 percent (paid semi-annually), and three years to maturity when

Easy

A. k_b = 7 percent.

B. k_b = 6 percent.

C. k_b = 5 percent.

13. At maturity, each of the following zero coupon bonds (pure discount bonds) will be worth $1,000. For each bond, find the missing quantity in the table below.

	Price	Maturity (years)	Yield to Maturity
A.	$400	30	
B.	$400		8%
C.		10	12%

14. Suppose that a government of Canada 9 percent annual-pay bond that matures in two years has a yield to maturity of 9.80 percent. If inflation is expected to be 3 percent per year over the next two years, what coupon rate would you expect to find on a Real Return Bond that is otherwise identical?

15. Suppose the inflation rate in Canada, as measured by the CPI, has been averaging 2.5 percent in recent years. The most recent Bank of Canada announcement indicates that it expects 4 percent inflation over the next year. If the real rate of return on Canadian T-bills is 1.75 percent, what is the nominal risk-free rate?

16. The following values are the spread for corporate bond yields:

Bond Rating	Spread over AAA
AA	30 basis points
A	45 basis points
BBB	70 basis points
BB	110 basis points

A. One-year T-bills are trading with a YTM of 6 percent. What yield would you expect to find on A rated corporate bonds maturing in one year?

B. Five-year government bonds have a maturity yield differential of 50 basis points. What yield would you expect to observe on non-investment grade (BB rated) corporate bonds with a five-year maturity?

17. Describe the difference between positive and negative bond covenants.

Medium

18. Calculate the price of the following bond: FV = $1,000; coupon rate = 8 percent, paid semi-annually; market rate = 5 percent; term to maturity = 10 years.

19. State the relationship between bond interest rate risk and the coupon rate, the market yield, and the term to maturity.

20. Using the Fisher relationship, calculate the exact real interest rate and the approximate real rate, given a T-bill rate of 7 percent and an expected inflation rate of 3 percent.

21. Calculate the bank discount yield on a 92-day U.S. T-bill that is currently quoted at $98.0468.

22. A. Value a 10-year $100 zero coupon bond when the market rate is 14 percent.

   B. Calculate the YTM of the above zero coupon bond if the current price is $76.

23. Suppose that, several years ago, the Canadian government issued three very similar bonds: each has a $1,000 face value and a 12 percent coupon rate, and will mature in five years. The only difference among them is the frequency of the coupon payments. If the market yield is now 6.5 percent, what is the price of the bond which pays coupons

   A. annually?

   B. semi-annually?

   C. monthly?

24. You find the following data on two bonds at a time when the market yield is 7 percent:

Bond	Coupon Rate	Price
A	6%	$958.42
B	8%	$1,041.58

   These bonds are otherwise identical (FV = $1,000, five years to maturity, semi-annual coupon payments). Which bond's price will change by more (and by how much) if the market yield falls by 100 basis points?

25. The two bonds below are identical (FV = $1,000, 8 percent coupon rate paid semi-annually) except that they mature at different times:

Bond	Time to Maturity	Price
C	3 years	$1,026.64
D	8 years	$1,060.47

   If the market yield, currently 7 percent, falls by 100 basis points, which bond's price will change more, and by how much?

26. A 10-year bond has just been issued with its coupon rate set equal to the current market yield of 6 percent. How much would the price of the bond change (in percentage terms) if the market yield suddenly fell by 50 basis points? How much would the price change if the yield rose by 50 basis points?

27. Consider a bond with five years to maturity, FV=$1,000, and a coupon rate of 6.50 percent (semi-annual payments). Determine the price of this bond if the market yield is

    A. 7.75 percent.
    B. 5.25 percent.

    In each case, calculate the percentage change in the price of the bond if the market yield rises by 1.0 percent.

28. A zero coupon bond has a par value of $1,000 and will mature in five years. What is the current price of this bond if the market yield is

    A. 7.75 percent?
    B. 5.25 percent?

    In each case, calculate the percentage change in the price of the bond if the market yield rises by 1.0 percent.

29. It is now March 1, 2006, and Peter has just purchased a five-year U.S. government bond (FV = $1,000) whose quoted price is 93.863. This bond has a 5 percent coupon rate, and the last semi-annual coupon payment was made on January 1, 2006.

    A. How much will Peter actually pay for this bond?
    B. Had this been a Canadian government bond, what would the cash price be?

30. A bond with semi-annual coupons at a rate of 10 percent will mature in one year. If the bond's price is $1,010, use the trial-and-error method to find the YTM. Check your answer by using a financial calculator or Excel spreadsheet. What would the YTM be if the bond made annual coupon payments?

31. For each of the YTM figures below, find the price and CY for a two-year, 7 percent annual-pay bond with a face value of $1,000.

    A. YTM = 6 percent
    B. YTM = 7 percent
    C. YTM = 8 percent

32. Sapna would like to receive a real return of 5 percent per year on a bond investment at a time when the expected inflation rate is 2.5 percent. How much would she be willing to pay for a bond maturing in two years if it pays annual coupons at a (nominal) rate of 7 percent? If a real return bond was available with a 4.5 percent coupon (annual payments) and the same two-year maturity, how much would Sapna be willing to pay for it to achieve her desired rate of return?

33. A 90-day U.S. T-bill has a bank discount yield (k_{BDY}) of 4.673 percent. Find the bond equivalent yield (k_{BEY}) on a 90-day Canadian T-bill with the same quoted price.

34. Adam has saved C$1,000 and plans to go surfing in Australia next summer. He won't need the money for a year, so he decides to invest it. Adam could invest the money in Canada, where a T-bill will earn 4.50 percent, and then convert it to Australian dollars (AU) just before he leaves. Alternatively, Adam could con-

vert the funds today and invest in an Australian T-bill earning 5.20 percent. Which approach should he take if the currency spot rate is C$0.90431/AU$ and the one-year forward rate is C$0.89829/AU$?

35. Calculate the price change for a 1 percent increase in market yield for the following bond: par = $1,000; coupon rate = 6 percent, paid semi-annually; market yield = 6 percent; term to maturity = 10 years.

Difficult

36. Calculate the cash price of the following bond sold on September 21: par = $1,000; coupon rate = 4 percent; pays coupons on January 1 and July 1; quoted price = $956. Also explain why the cash price is different from the quoted price.

37. Bower is a Canadian investor. He noticed that the euro spot rate is currently quoted at C$1.4161/euro. The European interest rate is 7 percent on one-year T-bills and the one-year interest rate in Canada is 5 percent. The one-year forward rate is C$1.4090/euro. Determine whether there is an arbitrage opportunity. State the transactions Bower should apply to profit from the arbitrage opportunity if one exits. Explain what will happen if many other investors also seize this arbitrage opportunity.

38. The Slice & Dice Investment Co. needs some help understanding the intricacies of bond pricing. It has observed the following prices for zero coupon bonds that have no risk of default:

Maturity	Price per $1 Face Value
1 year	0.97
2 years	0.90
3 years	0.81

A. How much should Slice & Dice be willing to pay for a three-year bond that pays a 6 percent coupon, assuming annual coupon payments start one year from now?

B. What is the yield to maturity of this three-year coupon bond?

C. Suppose Slice & Dice purchases this coupon bond, and then "un-bundles" it into its four component cash flows: three coupon payments and the par value amount. At what price(s) can they re-sell each of the first three cash flows (the coupon payments) today?

D. The remaining cash flow (the face value amount) is a "synthetic" three-year zero coupon bond. How much must this "strip bond" be sold for if Slice & Dice is to break even on the investment?

E. What is the yield to maturity on the synthetic three-year zero coupon bond?

F. Why are the answers for (b) and (e) different?

39. A bond that matures in 10 years is callable in 3 years at a call price of $1,025. The bond has a semi-annual coupon rate of 8 percent. If the YTM = 7.30 percent and the YTC = 6.92 percent, what is the bond's current price? Is this bond likely to be called?

Price-Earnings Ratio

The price-earnings (P/E) ratio is one of the most commonly used equity valuation measures. P/E ratios vary widely across sectors and are sometimes driven by market sentiment or growth expectations. Some quantitative analysts use valuation screens to pick attractive stocks or sectors and they may use P/E ratios in combination with other valuation metrics, such as return on equity (ROE) growth. Thus, a quantitative specialist might believe a company was worth a second look if its P/E ratio was less than that of the market as a whole, but its ROE was growing at a rate faster than that of the market. The quantitative team at investment dealer Desjardins Securities looks at current key characteristics of the S&P/TSX Composite Index, including ROE, P/E and dividend yield. Its proprietary models then determine the likelihood that a stock will outperform the broader market.

Source: Horvitch, Sonita. "Bay Street's Edge over Wall Street to Narrow," *Financial Post*, February 1, 2007.

Equity Valuation

Learning Objectives

After reading this chapter, you should understand the following:

1. The basic characteristics of equity securities (i.e., preferred shares and common shares)

2. How these securities are valued

3. Some of the major factors that affect stock prices

4. How to relate valuation models to commonly used ratios or "multiples"

INTRODUCTION

In Chapter 6, we discussed how to estimate the value of bonds based on the present value of their expected future cash flows, and how to estimate the implied yield, based on given prices. This chapter applies the same concepts to equity valuation. We began by examining how to evaluate both preferred and common shares based on the present value of their expected future dividend stream. We proceed to show how this approach is related to the *fundamentals* that affect stock prices (i.e., future profitability and dividends, interest rates, and risk). We conclude with a discussion of relative valuation approaches, and show how they too can be related to company fundamentals.

7.1 EQUITY SECURITIES

equity securities
ownership interests in an underlying entity, usually a corporation

Equity securities are ownership interests in an underlying entity, usually a corporation. Generally, equity securities have no fixed maturity date. Equities pay dividends from after-tax earnings, so unlike interest payments, they do not provide the issuer with a tax-deductible expense. However, shareholders pay lower taxes on dividends received from Canadian corporations than they would on interest payments, as discussed in Chapter 3.

common share a certificate of ownership in a corporation; the most common type of equity security

By far, the most common type of equity security is the **common share**, which represents a certificate of ownership in a corporation. A purchaser of 100 shares of common stock owns $100/n$ percent of the corporation (where n is the total number of shares of common stock outstanding). Common shareholders represent the true "owners" of the corporation. They are the residual claimants of the corporation, which means that they are entitled to income remaining only after all creditors and preferred shareholders (discussed below) have been paid. Similarly, in the case of liquidation of the corporation, common shareholders are entitled to the remaining assets only after all other claims have been satisfied. As owners, they can exert control over the corporation through their power to vote, which allows them to elect the board of directors and to vote on major issues, such as takeovers, corporate restructuring, and so on. Chapter 19 discusses the characteristics of common shares in more detail.

preferred share a claim to a fixed dividend rate that is established when the shares are first issued; the other major type of equity security

The other major category of equities is **preferred shares**. These provide the owner with a claim to a fixed amount of equity that is established when the shares are first issued. Most preferred shares have preference over common shares with respect to income and assets (in the event of liquidation), but they rarely have any voting rights. Traditionally, preferred shares had no maturity date, but over the past 30 years preferred shares have been increasingly issued with a fixed maturity date, similar to a bond. The main difference between preferred shares and a bond is that the board of directors declares any dividends and until then, and unlike an interest payment, dividends are not a legal obligation of the firm. Usually, no payments can be made to common shareholders until preferred shareholders have been paid the dividends they are due in entirety. Chapter 19 discusses the characteristics of preferred shares in more detail.

7.2 VALUATION OF EQUITY SECURITIES

A commonly used approach for valuing equity securities follows the discounted cash flow approach used to estimate the value of bonds. In particular, we estimate the expected future cash flows associated with the security, and then determine the discounted present value of those future cash flows, based on an appropriate discount rate (k). The discount rate for equities will equal the risk-free rate of return plus a risk premium (as was the case for bonds). This is shown in Equation 7-1 below:

$$k = RF + \text{Risk premium}$$

[7-1]

where k = the required return on an equity security

RF = the risk-free rate of return

Recall from Chapter 6 that the *risk-free* rate comprises the real rate of return plus expected inflation, and it is proxied by the return on short-term government T-bills. The *risk premium* will be based on an estimate of the risk associated with the security; the higher the risk, the higher the risk premium, because investors will require a higher return as compensation. We will discuss the factors affecting the risk premium and methods for estimating a discount rate for equities in Chapters 8 and 9.

In addition to the discount rate, investors must estimate the size and timing of the expected cash flows associated with an equity security. Making this estimate is straightforward for a bond, because the amount and timing of the coupons and principal repayments is specified in the bond indenture. For equities, this issue is more complex, especially for common shares, as will be discussed shortly. We will first deal with preferred shares because they are easier to value.

7.3 PREFERRED SHARE VALUATION

As mentioned above, traditional preferred shares have no maturity date and pay dividends of a fixed amount at regular intervals indefinitely, as depicted in Figure 7-1.

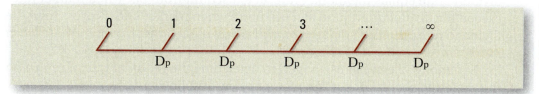

7-1   FIGURE

The Cash Flow Pattern for a Straight Preferred Share

Where D_p = dividend payments

Because the payments are essentially fixed when the preferred shares are issued, they are often referred to as fixed income investments, just as bonds are. The payment of a fixed dividend amount at regular intervals indefinitely means we can view these investments as *perpetuities,* which were discussed in Chapter 5. The value of preferred shares can be estimated by using Equation 7-2, the

4 never ending

equation used to determine the present value of a perpetuity. P_{ps} is the market price (or present value), D_p is the dividend amounts (or payments), and k_p is the required rate of return on the preferred shares (or discount rate).

[7-2]

$$P_{ps} = \frac{D_p}{k_p}$$

The amount of the dividend payments is usually based on a stated par (or face) value and a stated dividend rate, which is similar to the coupon rate on a bond. For example, a preferred share with a par value of $100 and an 8 percent dividend rate would pay an annual dividend of $8 per year. In practice, dividends are paid quarterly; however, for valuation purposes we will assume they are paid annually.[1] This will not have a big influence on the valuation process because of the long time involved (i.e., assuming the dividends are paid to infinity).

Example 7-1: Determining the Market Price of Preferred Shares

Determine the market price of a $50 par value preferred share that pays annual dividends based on a 7 percent dividend rate,

a. when market rates are 7 percent

b. when market rates are 8 percent

c. when market rates are 6 percent

Solution

$$\$50 \times 0.07 = \$3.50/year$$

$D_p = \$50 \times 0.07 = \$3.50$

a. $P_{ps} = \dfrac{D_p}{k_p} = \dfrac{\$3.50}{0.07} = \$50$

b. $P_{ps} = \dfrac{\$3.50}{0.08} = \$43.75$

c. $P_{ps} = \dfrac{\$3.50}{0.08} = \$43.75$

Notice that, similar to bonds, preferred shares will trade at par when the dividend rate equals the market rate, at a discount from par when market rates exceed the dividend rate, and at a premium when market rates are less than the dividend rate. Also note that the *market prices of preferred shares increase when market rates decline, and vice versa.*

Equation 7-2 can be rearranged to determine the required rate of return on the preferred shares for a given market price, as follows:

[7-3]

$$k_p = \frac{D_p}{P_{ps}}$$

---

[1] We will also assume annual dividends when valuing common shares, even though they also usually pay quarterly dividends.

Example 7-2: Estimating the Required Rate of Return on Preferred Shares

Determine the required rate of return on preferred shares that provide a $6 annual dividend if they are presently selling for $70.

Solution

$$k_p = \frac{D_p}{P_{ps}} = \frac{\$6}{\$70} = 8.57\%$$

*holding rights
pd residual before common*

> ## CONCEPT REVIEW QUESTIONS
>
> **1.** In what ways are preferred shares different from bonds?
>
> **2.** How is a traditional preferred share valued?
>
> **3.** How can we estimate the investor's required rate of return for a traditional preferred share?

7.4 COMMON SHARE VALUATION BY USING THE DIVIDEND DISCOUNT MODEL

The Basic Dividend Discount Model

Valuing common shares involves several complications that arise with respect to the appropriate future cash flows that should be discounted. Which cash flows should be discounted? The most popular discounted cash flow valuation model, which is discussed below, uses dividends. However, unlike for bonds or even for preferred shares, there is no requirement that common shares pay dividends at all. In addition, the level of dividend payments is also discretionary, which implies we must make *estimates* regarding the *amount* and *timing* of any dividend payments.

The **Dividend Discount Model (DDM)** assumes that common shares are valued according to the present value of their expected future cash flows. Based on this premise, today's price can be estimated by using Equation 7-4, if we have an *n*-year holding period:

Dividend Discount Model (DDM) a model for valuing common shares that assumes that common shares are valued according to the present value of their expected future dividends

$$P_0 = \frac{D_1}{(1+k_c)^1} + \frac{D_2}{(1+k_c)^2} + \ldots + \frac{D_n + P_n}{(1+k_c)^n}$$

[7-4]

where, P_0 = the estimated share price today

D_1 = the expected dividend at the end of year 1

P_n = the expected share price after n years

k_c = the required return on the common shares

Consider Example 7-3, in which the investor plans to hold the stock for one year.

Example 7-3: Estimating Price for a One-Year Holding Period

An investor buys a common share and estimates she will receive an annual dividend of $0.50 per share in one year. She estimates she will be able to sell the share for $10.50. Estimate its value, assuming the investor requires a 10 percent rate of return.

Solution

$$P_0 = \frac{0.50 + 10.50}{(1 + 0.10)^1} = \$10.00$$

The DDM argues that the selling price at any point (say, time n) will equal the present value of all the expected future dividends from period $n + 1$ to infinity. So the price next year, for example, is the present value of the expected dividend and share price for year 2. By repeatedly substituting for the future share price, we replace it with the present value of the dividend and share price expected the following year. As a result we remove P_n in Equation 7-4 and eventually get the following:

[7-5]

$$P_0 = \frac{D_1}{(1 + k_c)^1} + \frac{D_2}{(1 + k_c)^2} + \ldots + \frac{D_\infty}{(1 + k_c)^\infty} = \sum_{t=1}^{\infty} \frac{D_t}{(1 + k_c)^t}$$

In other words, *the price today is the present value of all future dividends to be received* (i.e., from now to infinity).

Why use dividends? Well, if an investor buys a particular stock, the only cash flows that he or she will receive until the investor sells the stock will be the dividends. Although a firm's residual earnings technically belong to the common shareholders, corporations generally do not pay out all their earnings as dividends. Of course, earnings are important too—without them the corporation could not sustain dividend payments for long. In fact, earnings receive more attention from investors than any other single variable. However, corporations typically reinvest a portion of their earnings to enhance future earnings and, ultimately, future dividends.

Equation 7-5 is the workhorse of share valuation, because it says that the value of a share is the present value of expected future dividends. However, by repeatedly substituting for the share price, we are implicitly making a very important assumption: that investors are rational. We assume that at each time, investors react rationally and value the share based on what they rationally expect to receive the next year. This assumption specifically rules out "speculative bubbles" or what is colloquially known as the "bigger fool theorem."

Suppose, for example, a broker tells a client to buy XYZ at $30. The investor says no, it's only worth $25. The broker replies, "I know, but there is momentum behind it and I am seeing a lot of interest. I think it will go to $40 by next year." The investor is a fool to pay $30 for something he or she thinks is worth $25, but it is not the fool theorem but the bigger fool theorem. If the investor does buy it, he or she *is* a fool, but he or she is also assuming that an even bigger fool will buy it in a year's time for $40.

This type of speculative bubble in which prices keep increasing and become detached from reality is specifically ruled out by the assumption of rational investors coolly calculating the present value of the expected cash flows at each time, so that prices never get detached from these fundamentals. Of course, there have been speculative bubbles when it has been very difficult to estimate these fundamental values. In Appendix 7A, we review the famous bubble involving the South Seas Company in 1720, in which Sir Isaac Newton almost bankrupted himself and then proclaimed, "I can calculate the motions of the heavenly bodies, but not the madness of people." The madness of people was the way in which the share price of the South Seas Company became completely detached from its fundamentals. The Internet bubble of the late 1990s, in which Nortel Networks Corporation (Nortel) share price rose from $20 to $122 and then fell back to less than $2, indicates that the madness of people may not have changed much in almost 300 years. However, we cannot build models based on irrationality, so we will continue with the development of models based on fundamental cash flows.

The Constant Growth DDM

Obviously, it is impractical to estimate and discount *all* future dividends one by one, as required by Equation 7-5. Fortunately, this equation can be simplified into a usable formula by making the assumption that dividends grow at a constant rate (g) indefinitely. Once we make this assumption, we can estimate all future dividends, assuming we know the last dividend paid (D_0):

$D_1 = D_0(1 + g)$

$D_2 = D_1(1 + g) = D_0(1 + g)^2$

$D_3 = D_2(1 + g) = D_0(1 + g)^3$

and so on

Therefore, under the assumption of constant growth in dividends to infinity, Equation 7-5 reduces to the following expression:

$$P_0 = \frac{D_0(1+g)^1}{(1+k_c)^1} + \frac{D_0(1+g)^2}{(1+k_c)^2} + \dots + \frac{D_0(1+g)^\infty}{(1+k_c)^\infty}$$

[7-6]

Constant Growth DDM a version of the dividend discount model for valuing common shares that assumes that dividends grow at a constant rate indefinitely

In Equation 7-6, we are multiplying D_0 by a factor of $(1 + g)/(1 + k_c)$ every period. This represents a *growing perpetuity*, which is easily solved because it represents the sum of a geometric series. In fact, Equation 7-6 reduces to the following expression, which is the Constant Growth version of the DDM, or simply the **Constant Growth DDM**:

$$P_0 = \frac{D_0(1+g)}{k_c - g} = \frac{D_1}{k_c - g}$$

[7-7]

Equation 7-7 has several important points:

1. This relationship holds only when $k_c > g$. Otherwise, the answer is negative, which is uninformative.[2]

2. Only *future* estimated cash flows and estimated growth in these cash flows are relevant.

---

[2] The negative answer occurs because if $g > k$ in Equation 7-6, each future dividend is worth more than the previous one. The value never converges but increases to infinity.

3. It holds only when growth in dividends is expected to occur *at the same rate indefinitely.*

Example 7-4: Using the Constant Growth DDM

Assume a company is currently paying $1.10 per share in dividends. Investors expect dividends to grow at an annual rate of 4 percent indefinitely, and they require a 10 percent return on the shares. Determine the price of these shares.

Solution

$$D_1 = (\$1.10)(1 + 0.04) = \$1.144$$

$$P_0 = \frac{D_1}{k_c - g} = \frac{\$1.144}{0.10 - 0.04} = \$19.07$$

Estimating the Required Rate of Return

The Constant Growth DDM can be rearranged to obtain an estimate of the rate of return required by investors on a particular share as follows:

[7-8]

$$k_c = \frac{D_1}{P_0} + g$$

The first term (D_1/P_0) in Equation 7-8 represents the expected *dividend yield* on the share, which was discussed in Chapter 4. Therefore, we may view the second term, g, as the expected capital gains yield, because the total return must equal the dividend yield plus the capital gains yield. It is important to recognize that this equation provides an appropriate approximation for required return *only* if the conditions of the Constant Growth DDM are met (i.e., in particular the assumption regarding constant growth in dividends to infinity must be satisfied).

Example 7-5: Estimating the Required Rate of Return Using the DDM

The market price of a company's shares is $12 each, the estimated dividend at the end of this year (D_1) is $0.60, and the estimated long-term growth rate in dividends (g) is 4 percent. Estimate the implied required rate of return on these shares.

Solution

$$k_c = \frac{D_1}{P_0} + g = \frac{0.60}{12} + 0.04 = 0.05 + 0.04 = 0.09 = 9\%$$

This result suggests that the expected return on these shares comprises an expected dividend yield of 5 percent and an expected capital gains yield of 4 percent.

Estimating the Value of Growth Opportunities

The Constant Growth DDM can also provide a useful assessment of the market's perception of growth opportunities available to a company, as reflected in its market price. Let's begin by assuming that a firm that has no profitable growth opportunities should not reinvest residual profits in the company, but rather should pay out all its earnings as dividends. Under these conditions, we have $g = 0$, and $D_1 = EPS_1$, where EPS_1 represents the expected earnings per common share in the upcoming year. Under these assumptions, the Constant Growth DDM reduces to the following expression:

$$P_0 = \frac{EPS_1}{k_c}$$

[7-9]

It is unlikely to find a company that has exactly "zero" growth opportunities, but the point is that we can view the share price of any common stock (that satisfies the assumptions of the Constant Growth DDM) as comprising two components: its no-growth component, and the remainder, which is attributable to the market's perception of the growth opportunities available to that company. We denote this as the present value of growth opportunities (PVGO). Therefore, we get Equation 7-10:

$$P_0 = \frac{EPS_1}{k_c} + PVGO$$

[7-10]

Example 7-6: Estimating PVGO

A company's shares are selling for $20 each in the market. The company's EPS is expected to be $1.50 next year, and the required return on the shares is estimated to be 10 percent. Estimate the present value of growth opportunities per share.

Solution

This can be solved by rearranging Equation 7-10 to solve for PVGO:

$$PVGO = P_0 - \frac{EPS_1}{k_c} = \$20 - \frac{\$1.50}{0.10} = \$20 - \$15 = \$5.00$$

Examining the Inputs of the Constant Growth DDM

From Equation 7-7, we can see that the Constant Growth DDM predicts that, all else remaining equal, the price of common shares (P_0) will *increase* as a result of

1. an increase in D_1

2. an increase in g

3. a decrease in k_c

This list illustrates the intuitive appeal of the DDM, because it links common share prices to three important *fundamentals*: corporate profitability, the general level of interest rates, and risk. In particular, expected dividends are closely related to profitability, as is the growth rate of these dividends, while the required rate of return is affected by the base level of interest rates (RF) and by risk (as reflected in the risk premium required by investors). In particular, *all else being equal*, the DDM predicts that common share prices will be higher when profits are high (and expected to grow), when interest rates are lower, and when risk premiums are lower. The effect of these factors on stock prices is discussed in Finance in the News 7-1.

RISING INTEREST RATES, FALLING CORPORATE PROFITS SEND MARKETS INTO DEEP FREEZE

North American stock markets are ending January the same way they started it: bleeding red. Between the mediocre start and the mediocre finish has been an ugly, choppy month of uninspired trading in which the major indexes retreated to two-month lows, obliterating the memory of an upbeat December. The Dow Jones Industrial Average and S&P 500 have fallen 3.3 percent so far this month, the S&P/TSX composite, 1.1 percent, and the NASDAQ composite, 6.4 percent.

It would be tempting to put this down as a short-term cold snap investors will have to weather; after all, stocks hit three-year highs in December and were slated for a pullback. But two big factors suggest this chill could run deeper: Interest rates are heading up, corporate profits are heading down.

Recently, the U.S. Federal Reserve Board has worked to remove doubts in financial markets that it would forge ahead with interest rate rises. Those doubts have been replaced by rumblings it might accelerate the pace of increases.

For stocks, higher interest rates typically mean lower price-earnings multiples, as stock valuations move lower to compete with the rising returns offered by interest paying investments. Price-earnings levels have come down from a year ago, but they are still far from bargain levels (19.6 times trailing 12-month earnings for the S&P 500, 18.7 times for the S&P/TSX composite). They would look awfully rich if the Fed were to launch into more rapid rate increases.

That might not be a big problem if profits were poised to grow enough to offset this so-called "multiple compression." But, with the markets in the midst of the fourth-quarter earning reporting season, many are nervous the profit picture isn't that bright.

According to Thomson First Call, analysts project profits for the S&P 500 companies will rise 9.9 percent in 2005–down from projections of 10.6 percent at the start of the month, and well below the 19 percent growth of each of the past two years. But despite the recent easing of forecasts, "those profit expectations are still too high," says Robert Spector, head Canadian economist and chief strategist at Merrill Lynch in Toronto.

He says to achieve 10-percent profit growth this year, companies will have to continue to expand their margins–something unlikely, given the big margin gains already achieved and the fact their unit labour costs are on the rise.

"Margins aren't going to be expanding, they're going to be contracting," Mr. Spector says. He believes S&P 500 profits will only climb about 5 percent this year.

When you combine sluggish profit growth with lower price-earnings multiples, it doesn't take a genius to see that it doesn't add up to an upturn in the stock market; in fact, it suggests the opposite.

In Canada, interest rates aren't likely to match the Fed's pace (the Bank of Canada is firmly on the sidelines), but that doesn't mean our domestic market will escape the rate impact. BCA Research noted this week that in the past three decades, price-earnings ratios in global stock markets consistently fall when the Fed tightens interest rates–a testament to the dominance of the United States as the world's economic engine.

The Canadian market will also continue to feel the sting of the Canadian dollar. A rule of thumb is that every 3 cents (U.S.) rise in the dollar has the same effect as a one percentage-point rise in rates. With the currency up almost 6 cents against the U.S. dollar in the past year, that's like the Bank of Canada doubling its benchmark rate from its current 2 percent. That creates headwind for stocks.

Are markets ripe for a plunge? Probably not. Mr. Spector says the profits of the past two years have allowed companies to improve their balance sheets, increase dividends and do acquisitions and stock buybacks, which "will put a floor under the markets."

But by the same token, there's little reason to expect an upturn to materialize. The January chill might wear off, but don't expect it to be replaced by a heat wave.

Source: Parkinson, David. "Rising Interest Rates, Falling Corporate Profits Send Markets into Deep Freeze." *Globe and Mail*, January 29, 2005, p. B1. Reprinted with permission of the *Globe and Mail*.

Usually, we can assume that current dividends (D_0) are given, so it is the movements in k_c and g that determine the price of a share (i.e., because $k_c - g$ is the denominator, and because $D_0(1 + g)$ is the numerator). In fact, given the long period involved in the discount process (i.e., to infinity), price estimates are very sensitive to these inputs, as illustrated in Example 7-7 and Example 7-8.

Example 7-7: More Pessimistic Inputs of the Constant Growth DDM

Revisit the company in Example 7-4 that is currently paying $1.10 per share in dividends. This time, revise the expectations for annual growth in dividends to 3 percent (from 4 percent) and revise the estimated required rate of return to 11 percent (from 10 percent). Re-estimate the price of these shares.

Solution

$D_1 = (\$1.10)(1 + 0.03) = \$1.133$

$$P_0 = \frac{D_1}{k_c - g} = \frac{\$1.133}{0.11 - 0.03} = \$14.16$$

Notice the substantial drop in price (i.e., 25.7 percent, from $19.07 to $14.16) that results when we increase the discount rate from 10 percent to 11 percent and lower the growth rate from 4 percent to 3 percent (which are both bad things for stock prices). Similarly, the example below illustrates the large price increase that results from the use of improved estimates for these inputs.

Example 7-8: More Optimistic Inputs of the Constant Growth DDM

Redo Example 7-7 by assuming annual growth in dividends is 5 percent and that the required rate of return is 9 percent.

Solution

$D_1 = (\$1.10)(1 + 0.05) = \$1.155$

$$P_0 = \frac{D_1}{k_c - g} = \frac{\$1.155}{0.09 - 0.05} = \$28.88$$

In this case, the price estimate is 51.4 percent higher than the original estimate of $19.07, yet we only changed each of our inputs by 1 percent! Obviously, we need to be careful when determining these inputs, which are in fact merely estimates.

Estimating DDM Inputs

Estimating the inputs into the Constant Growth DDM generally requires a great deal of analysis and judgement. Assuming we know the most recent year's dividend payment (D_0), we need to estimate k_c and g because $D_1 = D_0(1 + g)$. As discussed earlier, the discount rate for equities will equal the risk-free rate of return plus a risk premium, as depicted in Equation 7-1. We defer further discussion of estimating the discount rate for equities until Chapters 8 and 9.

Several methods can be used to estimate the expected annual growth rate in dividends (g). One of the most common approaches is to determine the company's sustainable growth rate, which can be estimated by using the following equation:

sustainable growth rate the earnings retention ratio multiplied by return on equity

$$g = b \times \text{ROE}$$

[7-11]

where b = the firm's earnings retention ratio = $1 -$ firm's dividend payout ratio

ROE = firm's return on common equity = net profit/common equity (as defined in Chapter 4).

Growth in earnings (and dividends) will be positively related to the proportion of each dollar of earnings reinvested in the company (b) times the return earned on those reinvested funds, which we measure using ROE. For example, a firm that retains all its earnings and earns 10 percent on its equity would see its equity base grow by 10 percent per year. If the same firm paid out all of its earnings, then it would not grow. Similarly, a firm that retained a portion (b) would earn 10 percent on that proportion, resulting in $g = b \times ROE$.[3]

Example 7-9: Estimating a Firm's Sustainable Growth Rate

A firm has an ROE of 12 percent and its dividend payout ratio is 30 percent. Use this information to determine the firm's sustainable growth rate.

Solution

$g = b \times ROE = (1 - 0.30) \times (0.12) = (0.70) \times (0.12) = 0.0840 = 8.40$ percent

Recall from Chapter 4 that we can use the DuPont system to decompose ROE into three factors, as shown in Equation 7-12:

[7-12]

$$ROE = (\text{Net income/Sales}) \times (\text{Sales/Total assets}) \times (\text{Total Assets/equity})$$
$$= \text{Net profit margin} \times \text{Turnover ratio} \times \text{Leverage ratio}$$

The ROE, and hence g, increases with higher profit margins, higher asset turnover, and higher debt (although higher debt implies higher risk and therefore, higher k_c).

Example 7-10: Estimating a Firm's Sustainable Growth Rate by Using the DuPont System

A company just paid an annual dividend of $1.00 per share and had an EPS of $4 per share. Its projected values for net profit margin, asset turnover, and the leverage ratio are 4 percent, 1.25, and 1.40, respectively. Determine the firm's sustainable growth rate.

Solution

ROE = $(0.04)(1.25)(1.40) = 0.07 = 7.00\%$

Payout ratio = DPS/EPS = $1/$4 = 0.25, so $b = 1 - 0.25 = 0.75$

$g = b \times ROE = (0.75)(7.00\%) = 5.25\%$

Another approach to estimating g is to examine historical rates of growth in dividends and earnings levels, including long-term trends in these growth rates for the company, the industry, and the economy as a whole. Predictions regarding future growth rates can be determined based on these past trends by using arithmetic or geometric averages, or by using more involved statistical techniques,

---

[3] A major weakness of this approach is its reliance on accounting figures to determine ROE, because it is based on book values and the accrual method of accounting. As a result, it may not represent the "true" return earned on reinvested funds.

such as regression analysis. Finally, an important source of information regarding company growth, particularly for the near term, can be found in analyst estimates. Investors are often especially interested in "consensus" estimates, because market values are often based to a large extent on these estimates.

It is important to remember in the application of any of these approaches that it is "future" growth being estimated, and the inputs require judgement on the part of the analyst. If researchers believe past growth will be repeated in the future, or want to eliminate period-to-period fluctuations in b and ROE, they may choose to use three- to five-year averages for these variables. Conversely, if the company has changed substantially, or analysts have good reason to believe the ratios for the most recent year are the best indicators of future sustainable growth, they will use these figures. In addition, an analysis of macroeconomic, industry, and company-specific factors may lead researchers to develop predicted values for these variables, independent of their historical levels.

The Multiple Stage Growth Version of the DDM

The Constant Growth DDM relationship holds only when we are able to assume constant growth in dividends from now to infinity. In many situations it may be more appropriate to estimate dividends for the most immediate periods up to some point (t), after which it is assumed there will be constant growth in dividends to infinity. Several situations lend themselves to this structure. For example, it is reasonable to assume that competitive pressures and business cycle influences will prevent firms from maintaining extremely high growth in earnings for long periods. In addition, short-term earnings and dividend estimates should be much more reliable than those covering a longer period, which are often estimated by using some very general estimates of future economic, industry, and company conditions. To use the best information available at any point, it may make the most sense to estimate growth as precisely as possible in the short term, before assuming some long-term rate of growth.

Equation 7-13 can be applied when steady growth in dividends to infinity does not begin until period t:

$$P_0 = \frac{D_1}{(1+k_c)^1} + \frac{D_2}{(1+k_c)^2} + \dots + \frac{D_t + P_t}{(1+k_c)^t}$$

[7-13]

where $P_t = \dfrac{D_{t+1}}{k_c - g}$

Notice that this is Equation 7-4, with n replaced by t and with an estimate for P_t. Figure 7-2 depicts the cash flows associated with this type of a valuation framework.

Growth rate $\neq$ long-term growth rate (g)   Growth rate $= g$ from t to ∞

$$P_t = \frac{D_{t+1}}{k_c - g}$$

7-2   FIGURE

The Cash Flow Pattern for Multiple Stage Growth in Dividends

Essentially, whenever we use multiple period growth rates, we estimate dividends *up to the beginning* of the period in which it is reasonable to assume constant growth to infinity. Then we can use the Constant Growth DDM to estimate of the market price of the share at that time (P_t). Finally, we discount all the estimated dividends up to the beginning of the constant growth period, as well as the estimated market price at that time.[4] This provides us with today's estimate of the share's market price.

Example 7-11: Using the Multi-Stage DDM

A company is expected to pay a dividend of $1.00 at the end of this year, a $1.50 dividend at the end of year 2, and a $2.00 dividend at the end of year 3. It is estimated dividends will grow at a constant rate of 4 percent per year thereafter. Determine the market price of this company's common shares if the required rate of return is 11 percent.

Solution

First, estimate dividends up to the start of constant growth to infinity. In this example, they are all given, so no calculations are required:

$D_1 = \$1.00$

$D_2 = \$1.50$

$D_3 = \$2.00$

Second, estimate the price at the beginning of the constant growth to infinity period:

$D_4 = (\$2.00)(1 + 0.04) = \$2.08$

$$P_3 = \frac{D_4}{k_c - g} = \frac{\$2.08}{0.11 - 0.04} = \$29.71$$

Third, discount back the relevant cash flows to time 0:

$$P_0 = \frac{1.00}{(1+0.11)^1} + \frac{1.50}{(1+0.11)^2} + \frac{2.00+29.71}{(1+0.11)^3} = 0.90 + 1.22 + 23.19 = \$25.31$$

---

solution using a financial calculator

Solution to Third Step:
(TI BA II Plus)

PV (D₁): N = 1; I/Y (or *i*) = 11%; PMT = 0; FV = −1.00; CPT then PV gives 0.90

PV (D₂): N = 2; I/Y (or *i*) = 11%; PMT = 0; FV = −1.50; CPT then PV gives 1.22

PV (D₃+P₃): N = 3; I/Y (or *i*) = 11%; PMT = 0; FV = −31.71; (i.e., 2 + 29.71);

CPT then PV gives 23.19

Then, we add these figures to get $25.31, as above.

A well-known version of the multiple-growth DDM is the two-stage growth rate model, which assumes growth at one rate for a certain period, followed by some steady growth rate to infinity. This is illustrated in Example 7-12.

---

[4] Recall that P_t represents the present value of all the expected dividends from time $t + 1$ to infinity, so we are essentially discounting *all* the expected future dividends associated with the stock.

Example 7-12: Two-Stage Dividend Growth

A company just paid a dividend of $2.00 per share. An investor estimates that dividends will grow at 10 percent per year for the next two years, and then grow at an annual rate of 5 percent to infinity. Determine the market price of this company's common shares if the required rate of return is 12 percent.

Solution

First, estimate dividends up to the start of constant growth to infinity. In this example, we use the first period growth rate of 10 percent:

$$D_1 = (\$2.00)(1.10) = \$2.20$$

$$D_2 = (\$2.20)(1.10) = \$2.42$$

Second, estimate the price at the beginning of the constant growth to infinity period:

$$D_3 = (\$2.42)(1 + 0.05) = \$2.541$$

$$P_2 = \frac{D_3}{k_c - g} = \frac{\$2.541}{0.12 - 0.05} = \$36.30$$

Third, discount back the relevant cash flows to time 0:

$$P_0 = \frac{2.20}{(1.12)^1} + \frac{2.42 + 36.30}{(1.12)^2} = 1.96 + 30.87 = \$32.83$$

PV (D$_1$): N = 1; I/Y (or i) = 12%; PMT = 0; FV = –2.20; CPT then PV gives 1.96

PV (D$_2$+P$_2$): N = 2; I/Y (or i) = 12%; PMT = 0; FV = –38.72; (i.e., 2.42 + 36.30);

CPT then PV gives 30.87

Then, we add these figures to get $32.83, as above.

Limitations of the DDM

Although the DDM provides a great deal of insight into the factors that affect the valuation of common shares, it is based on several assumptions that are not met by a large number of firms, especially in Canada. In particular, it is best suited for companies that (1) pay dividends based on a stable dividend payout history that they want to maintain in the future, and (2) are growing at a steady and sustainable rate. As such, the DDM works reasonably well for large corporations in mature industries with stable profits and an established dividend policy. In Canada, the banks and utility companies fit this profile, while in the United States, there are numerous NYSE-listed companies of this nature. Not surprisingly, the DDM does not work well for many resource-based companies, which are cyclical in nature and often display erratic growth in earnings and dividends. In addition, many of these companies (especially the smaller ones) do not distribute a great deal of profits to shareholders as dividends. The model will also not work well for firms in distress, firms that are in the process of restructuring, firms involved in acquisitions, and private firms. Finally, if a company enters into substantial share-repurchase arrangements, the model will require adjustments, because share repurchases also represent a method of distributing wealth to shareholders.

7.5 USING MULTIPLES TO VALUE SHARES: THE PRICE-EARNINGS (P/E) RATIO

The Basic Approach

Relative valuation approaches determine the value of common shares by comparing the market prices of similar companies, relative to some common variable, such as earnings, cash flow, book value, or sales. Conceptually, these approaches are relatively simple to apply: all we need to do is find a group of comparable firms and then use their financial data and market values to infer the value of the firm in question. However, finding comparable firms is difficult: what firm is similar to Microsoft, for example? Even after we find a group of comparable firms, we have to estimate the appropriate multiple, because values will differ even for comparable firms so the exercise involves substantial analysis and judgement.

price-earnings (P/E) ratio
the share price divided by the earnings per share; the most commonly used relative valuation multiple

We will illustrate the approach by using the most commonly used relative valuation multiple: the **price-earnings (P/E) ratio**. Recall that the P/E ratio, which was introduced in Chapter 4, represents the number of times that investors are willing to pay for a company's earnings, as expressed in the share price, or the share price divided by the earnings per share. The P/E approach is implemented by estimating the firm's earnings per share (EPS) and multiplying it by an appropriate (or justifiable) P/E multiple. The typical P/E formulation uses estimated earnings per share (EPS_1) for the next 12 months. The basic valuation equation can then be expressed as shown in Equation 7-14:

[7-14]

$$P_0 = \text{Estimated } EPS_1 \times \text{Justified P/E ratio} = EPS_1 \times P_0/E_1$$

Notice that the P/E ratio used in Equation 7-14 differs from the one we discussed in Chapter 4, since it is based on expected future earnings (EPS_1) and is called the *leading P/E ratio*. By comparison, when we analyze financial ratios, the reported P/E ratios are based on earnings over the previous 12 months (EPS_0), which are called *lagging P/E ratios*. For valuation purposes, we typically focus on the leading P/E ratio, because market values are based on expectations about the future.

Using the P/E ratio is easy: if the firm's forecast earnings per share are $2 and the P/E ratio for comparable firms is 20X, then the P/E approach would say that a fair share price is $40. We can see from this example why this approach is also called "using multiples." In this case, the multiple of earnings is 20X. What this means is that if this level of earnings stays constant it will take 20 years to earn back the price of the shares. In this sense the multiple is an example of a payback period. The higher the multiple, the longer the payback period and the more the investor is expecting earnings to increase. Alternatively, it could be that the shares are simply more expensive shares.

We can also see why the approach is commonly called **relative valuation**: we are valuing the firm relative to other comparable firms. This means that if the comparable firms are all overvalued, then using the P/E approach will over-value the firm in question. What this means is that if the market is in a "speculative bubble," the P/E approach will not detect it directly. What is then needed is some yardstick or benchmark P/E. We can ballpark this by looking at the P/E ratio for the S&P/TSX Composite Index, which is shown in Figure 7-3.

relative valuation valuing a firm relative to other comparable firms

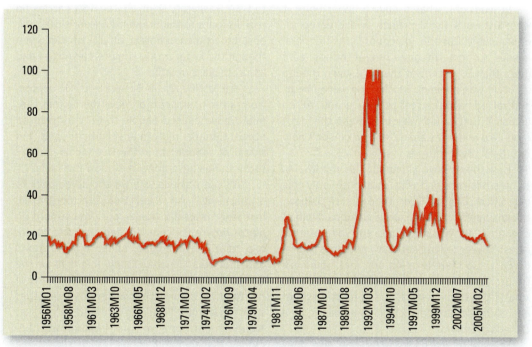

7-3   FIGURE

S&P/TSX Composite P/E

The P/E is based on trailing or lagged earnings for the firms in the S&P/TSX Composite Index, and it vividly demonstrates the problems with the P/E ratio: very low earnings cause the value of the P/E to skyrocket. Despite the fact that the P/E is based on up to 300 companies, these problems are not minimal. In the early 1990s, Canada had a severe recession as a result of high interest rates as well as the costs of adjusting to free trade with the United States, and many Canadian companies incurred very large losses. The earnings for corporate Canada almost disappeared, causing the P/E to increase dramatically. Then

WITH CANADA AT A PREMIUM, WHO WOULDN'T YEARN FOR THE BAD OLD DAYS?

Martin Barnes remembers the bad old days—not fondly, but then, almost nobody does.

It was a dozen years ago that Mr. Barnes, then the freshly minted managing editor of the *Bank Credit Analyst*, published his plea for the nation to wake up. The piece described how Canada was "caught in the vicious grip of a debt trap"; how disastrous government finances "place it firmly in the ranks of the Third World in terms of debt burden"; and how most politicians were in denial about it. "There is no easy or painless escape.

Most Canadians already knew this. But by phrasing it in such dramatic terms, in a respected publication whose audience works in the world's major financial centres, Mr. Barnes helped give the fiscal crisis some international attention. His prophetic conclusion? Despite it all, "the market is massively over sold on a short-term basis and there is scope for a major rally."

In hindsight, what a buying opportunity it was. Ottawa's fiscal crunch had created an enormous "Canada discount" in financial assets. Long-term government bonds paid more than 9 percent at the time, even though inflation was minimal. Stocks, too were cheap, and rallied hard the rest of the decade. All an investor had to do was look past the debt mountain and buy Canada, and he couldn't help but make great returns.

How things have changed. This month, Mr. Barnes has returned with an update—only this one, titled "Can the Good Times Last?" is positively sunny. Canada enjoys a virtuous circle of economic growth, surpluses and low interest rates: 10-year federal debt now pays less than 4 percent. (So there is one group that would like to turn back the clock to 1994: bond investors.) And in the stock market, the Canada discount has disappeared—replaced, in some cases, by a Canada premium.

Start with the banks (everyone else does these days). Though we may all enjoy grumbling about the outrageous fees charged by a comfortable little oligopoly, they are at least giving us something back in return: They've been the main forces lately of TSX's record crunching performance, which this week left the composite index 100 points short of the 13,000 mark.

The banks' rally is driven in part by boffo numbers—CIBC, Bank of Nova Scotia and Toronto-Dominion this week reported annual profits that, combined totalled more than $9-billion. But it's also a story of stock price inflation. Most Canadian bank shares now sell for 13 or 14 times profit, a multiple that strikes some investors as a tad rich. "We're out there buying global banks like ING (of the Netherlands) and HBOS (based in Britain) at 10 or 10 1/2 times earnings," says Tye Bousada, manager of the $5-billion Trimark Fund. "The reality is there's a 35- to 40-percent difference" in valuation.

That may be the starkest example of the Canada premium at play. Canadian energy stocks also trade at higher valuations than their competitors around the world, according to BCA Research. Over all, the TSX carries no real discount to the Standard & Poor's 500, the best broad measurement of U.S. stocks, even though the latter group is more diversified and its profits less volatile.

"Is it justified?" Mr Barnes asks. "I suppose, from a financial point of view, the factors that might have caused people to be very worried about Canada historically—deficits and the threat of separatism in the Québécois nation—those things have gone, really, off the table."

"It's not obvious why we should go back to a discount." All true. But the contrarian investor naturally seeks out investment in places where the mood is negative and assets are, relatively speaking, cheap. Twelve years ago that was Canada. Today, might it be the United States? Mr. Bousada has bet a chunk of his fund on it, and so, too have some other smart investors—firms like Southeastern Asset Management, one of the best-known U.S. money management shops, which scours the world for bargain equities but is finding most of them close to home these days.

"We did not intentionally initiate this shift," Southeastern's managers say in a recent note. "Many of the cheapest international businesses are based in the U.S. today."

Source: DeCloet, Derek. "With Canada at a Premium, Who Wouldn't Yearn for the Bad Old Days?" *Globe and Mail*, December 9, 2006, p. B1. Reprinted with permission of the *Globe and Mail*.

during the slowdown in 2002, after the puncturing of the Internet bubble, two Canadian companies, Nortel and JDS Uniphase Canada Ltd. (JDS Uniphase),[5] lost so much money that the overall earnings of the firms in the TSX Index were not just low but were actually negative. For this reason, the P/E is often set at a maximum of 100.

Recognizing these problems, we can see that typically the P/E is 15X to 20X. When P/E ratios fall to the lower band of this range, we tend to think the stock market is undervalued; when the P/E creeps above 20X, we take it as a warning signal that equities are overvalued. At the time of writing in November 2006, the TSX was at an all-time high, but the P/E was only 16X, since earnings were also at record levels because of very high commodity prices.

The P/E ratio is an attractive (and commonly reported) statistic for investors and analysts for several reasons. First, it relates the price to the earnings owned by the shareholders. Second, it is easy to compute and as a result is commonly available. This makes comparisons relatively straightforward. Third, it is intuitive, as it indicates the payback period and thus can be related to a number of other firm characteristics, such as growth opportunities and risk. The common usage of these ratios is illustrated in Finance in the News 7-2, which discusses the valuation of Canadian shares in general versus U.S. stocks, based on their P/E ratios.

Implementing the P/E Ratio Approach

Equation 7-14 suggests that we need two estimates in order to implement the P/E ratio approach. Unfortunately, obtaining reasonable estimates requires a substantial amount of analysis and also an element of judgement. EPS_1 can be determined by using several approaches, which are similar to those described above for estimating future dividends. In particular, we can analyze historical earnings data, project trends, analyze the company's present situation, and forecast future earnings.[6] In addition, the use of analyst estimates (and consensus estimates) may provide reasonable forecasts of EPS_1.

Estimating justifiable P/E ratios is even more involved, and several approaches are typically used. One commonly used approach is to find *comparable* companies and estimate an appropriate P/E ratio for the company being analyzed, based on a comparison of this company with the others, in terms of risk and growth opportunities. This approach often involves using an industry average P/E ratio, which is then scaled up or down, based on an assessment of whether or not the company is above or below average. Unfortunately, this approach involves a great deal of subjectivity regarding several company-specific characteristics, including risk, potential for growth, and the overall financial health of the company. In addition, this approach may build market errors into the value estimation process. For example, even though a firm may be average within its industry, the industry average P/E ratio may be too high if the market has overvalued this particular industry at a particular time. Another commonly used approach is to examine historical averages for the company or the company's industry. However, using historical averages may be inappropriate if the company has changed substantially and as market and industry conditions change.

---

[5] Most of the losses were due to writing off the value of investments in other firms that no longer had any value.

[6] You can also refer to our discussion of forecasting financial statements in Chapter 4.

Potential problems are associated with the use of industry or historical averages to estimate the appropriate P/E ratio, so it is beneficial to obtain corroborating estimates based on economic, industry, and company fundamentals, if possible. Fortunately, the P/E ratio can be estimated by relating it to the fundamentals in the DDM.[7] We will illustrate this by using the simplest DDM model: the constant growth model:

$$P_0 = \frac{D_1}{k_c - g}$$

Dividing both sides of this equation by expected earnings (EPS$_1$), we get Equation 7-15

[7-15]

$$\frac{P_0}{EPS_1} = \frac{P}{E} = \frac{D_1 / EPS_1}{k_c - g}$$

We are left with the P/E ratio on the left side of Equation 7-15. Notice that D_1/EPS_1 is the expected dividend payout ratio at time 1.

Equation 7-15 indicates that the following fundamental factors affect the justified P/E ratio, and hence share prices:

1. the expected dividend payout ratio (D_1/EPS_1)

2. the required rate of return (k_c)

3. the expected growth rate of dividends (g)

Notice that it is *expected earnings*, not historical earnings, that is the relevant input. Also note that k and g are typically the most important factors in the determination of the P/E ratio because a small change in either can have a large effect on its value.

The following relationships should hold, *all else being equal*:

1. The higher the expected payout ratio, the higher the P/E.

2. The higher the expected growth rate, g, the higher the P/E.

3. The higher the required rate of return, k_c, the lower the P/E.

However, "all else being equal" is a brave assumption, because many of these variables are interrelated. For example, raising the payout ratio and thus increasing the dividend seems to increase the P/E, but raising the payout may also reduce growth, because one estimate of the growth rate is the sustainable growth rate, where $g = (1 - \text{Payout}) \times \text{ROE}$. We might also try to increase the growth rate by taking on risky investment projects that could increase future earnings and dividends, but this could also cause the discount rate k to increase (i.e., recall $k = \text{RF} + \text{Risk premium}$). However, what we can say is that P/E ratios tend to be higher when future growth in earnings and dividends is also expected to be high, and when interest rates or risk premiums are low (because they both affect k_c).

---

[7] Similar to the DDM, this approach for estimating P/E ratios will work best for companies with relatively stable dividend and growth patterns.

Example 7-13: Using the P/E Ratio Approach

Assume that a firm has just reported an EPS of $2.00 and expects to maintain a 40 percent payout ratio. Estimate the firm's P/E ratio and its market price, assuming its ROE is 10 percent and that investors require a 9 percent return on their shares.

Solution

First, estimate $g = (1 - \text{payout})(\text{ROE}) = (1 - 0.40)(10\%) = 6.00\%$.

Second, estimate $\text{EPS}_1 = (\text{EPS}_0)(1 + g) = (2.00)(1.06) = \$2.12$.

Third, estimate $\dfrac{P}{E} = \dfrac{D_1/EPS_1}{k_c - g} = \dfrac{0.40}{0.09 - 0.06} = 13.33$

Fourth, estimate $P_0 = \text{EPS}_1 \times P_0/E_1 = (\$2.12)(13.33) = \$28.26$.

Example 7-14 assumes the payout ratio remains constant at 40 percent, but we vary the main subjective inputs, k_c and g, to assess the effect on the P/E ratio and on price.

Example 7-14: Varying the Inputs of the P/E Ratio Approach

Repeat Example 7-13, assuming the same previously reported EPS of $2.00 and the same payout ratio of 40 percent. However, now assume that the growth rate and required return on the shares are, respectively

a. 5 percent and 10 percent

b. 7 percent and 8 percent

Solution

a. $\text{EPS}_1 = (2.00)(1.05) = \$2.10$

$\dfrac{P}{E} = \dfrac{0.40}{0.10 - 0.05} = 8$

So, $P_0 = (\$2.10)(8.00) = \$16.80$

b. $\text{EPS}_1 = (2.00)(1.07) = \$2.14$

$\dfrac{P}{E} = \dfrac{0.40}{0.08 - 0.07} = 40$

So, $P_0 = (\$2.14)(40.00) = \$85.60$

Notice the wide range of P/E and price estimates in Example 7-14 that arise for relatively small changes in our estimates of k_c and g.

Limitations of P/E Ratios

Aside from the difficulties in estimating an appropriate P/E ratio and in estimating future EPS, there are several other practical concerns regarding the use of P/E ratios. First, P/E ratios are uninformative when companies have negative (or very small) earnings. As we saw for the S&P/TSX Composite, we sometimes get very large or meaningless numbers for the P/E ratio even when we aggregate across all companies. For a particular firm, the possibility of these problems is much higher. Second, the volatile nature of earnings implies a great deal of volatility in P/E multiples. For example, the earnings of cyclical companies fluctuate quite dramatically throughout a typical business cycle.

An example of this is shown in Table 7-1, provided by RBC Dominion Securities Inc. (RBCDS) in their September 2006 Foundations research report where they analyzed the paper and forest products sector.

Table 7-1   P/E Ratios in the Paper and Forest Products Sector

	Price	2006 EPS	Forecast EPS	P/E	P/E forecast	Yield	TSX Symbol
Abitibi	2.72	−0.30	0.12	nm	22.67	0	A
Canfor	11.13	−0.27	0.47	nm	23.68	0	CFP
Cascades	11.54	0.71	0.60	16.25	19.23	1.39	CAS
Canfor Pulp	11.56	1.38	1.20	8.38	9.63	7.51	CFX.UN
Catalyst	3.22	−0.07	0.03	nm	nm	0	CTL
Fraser Papers	7.01	−1.35	−0.41	nm	nm	0	FPS
International	6.60	0.26	0.53	25.38	12.45	0	IFPA
Mercer	9.69	−0.07	0.14	nm	54.35	0	MERC
Norbord	8.41	0.74	0.40	10.24	18.95	4.76	NBD
PRT	11.20	0.69	0.70	16.23	16.0	9.38	PRT.UN
SFK Pulp	4.14	0.64	0.82	6.47	5.05	4.19	SFK.UN
Tembec	1.43	−2.0	−1.11	nm	nm	0	TBC
TimberWest Forest	14.07	0.01	−0.27	nm	nm	7.65	TWF.UN
West Fraser Timber	37.45	0.94	2.35	39.84	15.94	1.5	WFT

Note: nm = not meaningful

Source: RBC Dominion Securities Inc., Foundations Research Report, September 2006.

Notice, first, how many of these securities had negative earnings in fiscal 2006 and were still forecast to have negative earnings for the next year. This made the P/E ratio not meaningful (nm). The reason for this is that the forest products industry is highly cyclical and has been fighting a trade war with the United States in which, despite the Free Trade Agreement, the United States had imposed trade restrictions on lumber imports. Second, notice that even for those firms with forecast earnings, the P/E ratio is highly variable across this industry, ranging from 5.05 to 54.35, even after some firms, such as Catalyst with forecast earnings of 0.03, had the P/E ratio (actually 107) reported as nm.

Also the RBCDS report is a bit misleading, because included in this group of firms are income trusts as well as regular corporations. Note that some TSX symbols have "UN" after them, which indicates an income trust. Usually income trusts have more stable earnings, so their P/E ratios are more stable. For Canfor Pulp Income Fund, PRT Forest Regeneration Income Fund, and SFK Pulp Fund, their P/E ratios are all defined and in the 5 to 16 range, while only TimberWest Forest Corp. has an undefined P/E ratio because of forecast losses.

For these reasons, P/E ratios are normally based on smoothed or normalized estimates of earnings for the forecast year. It is also the reason analysts use other, similar relative value approaches.

Additional Multiples or Relative Value Ratios

The **market-to-book (M/B) ratio**, which was defined in Chapter 4 as the market price per share divided by the book value per share, can also be used to value stocks. This is achieved by multiplying a justifiable M/B ratio times a company's book value per share (which was also defined in Chapter 4). Recall that the book value per share equals the book value of equity (i.e., assets − liabilities) divided by the number of common shares outstanding. As such, valuing stocks relative to their M/B is an attractive approach for several reasons. Book value provides a relatively stable, intuitive measure of value relative to market values, which can be easily compared with those of other companies, provided accounting standards do not vary greatly across the comparison group. It eliminates the problems arising from the use of P/E multiples, because book values are rarely negative and do not exhibit the volatility associated with earnings levels. However, book values may be sensitive to accounting standards and may be uninformative for companies that do not have a large proportion of fixed assets (such as service firms).

market-to-book (M/B) ratio the market price per share divided by the book value per share

The use of the M/B ratio fell out of favour in the 1980s and 1990s because of high rates of inflation that distorted the book value of equity for many firms because of the use of historical cost accounting in an inflationary period. However, the low rate of inflation of the last 10 to 15 years has removed most of these problems, while changes in accounting standards have made the book value of equity more useful.[8]

The **price-to-sales (P/S) ratio** has several properties that make it attractive for valuation purposes. Similar to the P/E and M/B approach, it is implemented by multiplying a justifiable P/S ratio times the sales per share figure. Unlike earnings and book values, sales are relatively insensitive to accounting decisions and are never negative. Sales are not as volatile as earnings levels, hence P/S ratios are generally less volatile than P/E multiples. In addition, sales figures provide useful information about corporate decisions, such as pricing. However, sales do not provide information about expenses and profit margins, which are important determinants of company performance.

price-to-sales (P/S) ratio market price per share divided by sales per share

Another commonly used relative valuation ratio is the **price-to-cash-flow (P/CF) ratio**, where cash flow (CF) is often estimated as Net income + Depreciation and amortization + Deferred taxes.[9] By focusing on cash flow rather

price-to-cash-flow (P/CF) ratio market price per share divided by per share cash flow

---

[8] At one point, firms were required to write off goodwill and this seriously affected both earnings and the book value of equity. Now the goodwill arising from an acquisition is only written off when it is impaired by a drop in value. This is what caused the huge losses to Nortel and JDS Uniphase in 2002.

[9] Some analysts focus on "free" cash flow available to equity holders, which is estimated as Net income + Depreciation + Deferred taxes − Capital spending +/− The change in net working capital − Principal repayments + New external debt financing.

than on accounting income, this ratio alleviates some of the accounting concerns regarding measures of earnings. The **market value to EBIT** or the **market value to EBITDA ratio** can also be used. Using earnings before interest and taxes (EBIT) or earnings before interest, taxes, and depreciation and amortization (EBITDA) instead of net income eliminates a significant proportion of volatility caused in EPS figures by the use of debt and amortization (which is a non-cash expense). We use the market value of the firm's capital (both debt and equity) to reflect the fact that EBIT and EBITDA represents income available to both debt and equity holders. However, although there are many different valuation ratios or "multiples," they are all related to the fundamental valuation drivers, as we now show.

Suppose an investor requires a 15 percent return on his or her shares, expects the firm to pay a $1 dividend, and expects dividends and earnings to grow at 10 percent. In this case, we can use the constant growth model to value the shares at $20.

$$P = \frac{\$1}{0.15 - 0.10} = \$20$$

If 0.5 million shares are outstanding, this firm would have a total market value for the equity or equity market capitalization (cap) of $10 million.

If the firm then has the forecast income statement and financial data shown in Table 7-2, we can link all these valuation multiples.

Table 7-2 Forecast Income Statement

Sales Volume	1 million units
Unit price $10	$10 million
Variable costs	5.0
Fixed cash costs	1.7
EBITDA	3.3
Depreciation	0.8
EBIT	2.5
Interest	0.5
EBT	2.0
Income tax (@50 percent)	1.0
Net income	1.0
Dividends	0.5
Book value of equity	5.0
Book value of debt	5.0

For example, the share price is $20 and the dividend is $1 so the *dividend yield* is 5 percent (i.e., 1/20). In valuing this company, one valuation metric is to simply compare dividend yields across other comparable companies. A high dividend yield relative to other companies might then indicate an undervalued stock. Another way of looking at the dividend yield is to take its reciprocal and look at the dividend multiple, that is, the market price divided by the dividend. In this case, it is selling at 20X its dividend.

In practice, we don't often talk about the dividend multiple because the dividend yield provides the same information and yields on stocks are often compared directly with yields on income trusts, bonds, and other interest-earning securities. However, there is a fundamental problem with using dividend multiples: many firms do not pay dividends! To get around this problem, we can work up the income statement and use the next item, which is earnings. In this case, with an equity market value of $10 million and $1 million in net income, the P/E ratio is 10X. Immediately we can see that although many firms don't have dividends, they should all expect to have some earnings. The problem here is that earnings are cyclical and industry specific, so let's move up the income statement a bit more.

The next item is the earnings before interest and tax (EBIT), which with our example is $2.5 million. The difference between the EBIT and the net income is that the EBIT does not belong to the shareholders, because some flows through to the firm's creditors and some to the government. This is why we usually calculate the total firm value, that is, the value of the debt plus the value of the equity for all the ratios "above" net income. For our example, this comes to $15 million.[10] The EBIT multiple is then 6X, where the EBIT of $2.5 million is divided into the total market value of $15 million.

However, as we know from our accounting discussion, depreciation is a non-cash charge, so we go farther up the income statement and add back depreciation to get EBITDA. This adds back all the accounting items that do not involve cash, of which depreciation of fixed assets is by far the largest component, but there are also some other amortizations, such as issue costs attached to debt, and so on. Again, with a total value of $15 million, the EBITDA multiple is 4.5X. The EBITDA multiple is the most commonly used multiple when firms look at acquiring other firms, because it is a good proxy for the cash flow that the firm generates that can be used by another firm. Another good value is to look at the contribution generated by the firm, which is the EBITDA with all the fixed costs added back. In our example, this is $5 million, giving a 3X multiple. This is useful for firms valuing other firms when they can consolidate operations and remove the fixed costs.

The final valuation multiple is go right to the top line, instead of the bottom line, and look at sales. In our case, the sales multiple is a $10 million common equity value for buying $10 million in revenues or 1.0X. This would be useful if the entire sales of the firm could be switched to another firm and the existing plant and facilities closed down. Another variant on this is to look at the equity value per unit of sales, in our case, $10 million for 1 million unit sales means that the firm's shares are selling for $10 per unit of sales.

If we add to these valuation multiples the market to book ratio, which in our case is 2X (i.e., $10 million/$5 million), and the firm's return on equity (ROE) of 20 percent, we have a comprehensive list of key valuation ratios for the firm, all flowing from the fundamental valuation model.

Not all of these ratios are equally useful for every firm. Cable companies, for example, usually sell on a value per unit of output, in their case, a price per

---

[10] The debt market value is assumed to be the book value of $5 million.

subscriber because the more subscribers a cable company has, the more revenue it can generate. "Old-line" manufacturing firms generally sell on a market to book or P/E ratio basis, because they tend to have stable earnings. Growth companies with large amounts of amortization because of their increasing asset base tend to sell on EBITDA or sales multiples. However, in all cases, these valuation multiples are simply shortcuts for the fundamental discounted cash flow valuation.

A Simple Application: Bennett Environmental

We can illustrate that fundamental valuation and relative valuation are two sides of the same coin, by looking at a realistic valuation of Bennett Environmental Inc. (Bennett) done by TD Securities Inc. (TD Securities). This valuation was conducted as part of a comprehensive valuation exercise when TD Securities initiated coverage of the company in October 17, 2003. The report includes a detailed discussion and history of the company, which operates a treatment plant in Quebec for treating contaminated soil. However, for our purposes we will simply highlight the core valuation.

The analyst produced the data shown in Table 7-3.

Table 7-3   Valuation of Bennett Environmental Inc.

	2003	2004	2005	2006	2007	2008	2009	2010
EBIT	28,873	45,438	70,000	66,372	66,047	63,669	62,236	60,745
Cash Taxes	8,853	12,359	20,825	19,746	19,351	18,941	18,515	18,072
D&A	1,807	3,000	4,000	4,000	4,000	4,000	4,000	4,000
Capex	9,450	17,000	2,000	2,000	2,000	2,000	2,000	2,000
Change in NWC	0	0	0	0	0	0	0	0
Free Cash Flow	**13,376**	**19,079**	**51,175**	**48,626**	**47,695**	**46,728**	**48,720**	**44,673**
Terminal Value								63,8190
TV Growth	3.0							
Discount rate	10.0							

Source: Data from Chris Watkins, *Bennett Environmental: Uniquely Profitable Environmental Treatment Exposure*, October 17, 2003.

The analysis was conducted in 2003 so all the cash flows are forecasts. The table shows seven full forecast years, plus 2003, which was substantially complete. The analyst started with the EBIT and then estimated the cash taxes that would have to be paid (remember that some of the taxes in the financial statements are deferred). The analyst then calculated free cash flows in the way we discussed in Chapters 3 and 4. First, depreciation and amortizations (D&A) were added back and then forecast capital expenditures (capex) were subtracted and adjusted for any changes in net working capital (NWC). This gives the free cash flow that belongs to the firm's creditors and shareholders. Bennett had no significant debt, so these cash flows belonged to the shareholders.

As we discussed earlier, the basic valuation model discounts cash flows to infinity but no spreadsheet has enough columns for that! Typically, the analysis is truncated at some future date. In this case, the terminal value for Bennett was estimated at $638.190 million in 2010, because all the main values had stabilized by then. The analyst assumed that growth would continue at 3.0 percent after that point, so he or she estimated the terminal value by using the constant growth model. The free cash flows and terminal value were then discounted back to the present by using a 10 percent discount rate. The current value of Bennett was then estimated at $601.031 million, composed of three elements: the value of the cash flows until 2010 of $206.494 million, the current value of the terminal value of $360.242 million, and the excess cash on hand of $34.295 million. With 18 million shares outstanding, the analyst estimated Bennett's common shares to be worth $33.21 and, with a current share price of $24.60, recommended the firm as a buy.

TD Newcrest then followed up the discounted cash flow (DCF) analysis by estimating the P/E ratio at 21.1X, 14.2X, and 9.5X, based on current earnings and on forecast earnings for 2004 and 2005, respectively. It also estimated the EBITDA multiple for the same three years at 13.1X, 8.3X, and 5.4 X respectively. These multiples were then used to indicate a trading range based on comparable companies and, TD concluded that using current earnings and EBITDA multiples, Bennett could trade to the $54 to $56 range in two years' time.

To check its valuation TD also did a scenario analysis to see how sensitive this valuation was to some key "drivers." The two key drivers in the DCF are the discount rate and the terminal value growth rate. TD used a range of 9 percent to 12 percent for the discount rate and 1 percent to 4 percent for the terminal growth rate to get a range for Bennett's share value of $23.91 at the low end and $43.15 at the high end. It also looked at other key values, such as the gross margin and selling and general expenses, as well as completing a full financial analysis with all the standard ratios to support its recommendation. Unfortunately, both the United States and Canada reduced their commitment to environmental clean-ups and Bennett did not get enough soil to treat. As of November 2006, BEV's stock price was $0.95, indicating that forecasting is difficult, particularly since it involves the future and that a good spreadsheet model is no substitute for good judgement!

CONCEPT REVIEW QUESTIONS

1. Why can the P/E ratio be viewed as a type of payback period?
2. What drives P/E ratios?
3. Why do P/E ratios differ across even comparable firms?
4. What other relative valuation multiples are useful in valuation?
5. How are multiples linked to a DCF valuation?

IDA MUST TIGHTEN ITS RULES FOR ANALYSTS

There's a situation playing out in the oil patch that raises serious concerns about how research analysts employed by investment dealers are governed by the Investment Dealers Association of Canada.

The plot is simple: A research analyst covering a company for his firm offered to buy a property being sold by that company for his own private company. This particular case involves Roger Serin, who covers the oil patch for TD Newcrest, and Peyto Energy Trust.

Peyto's CEO, Don Gray, recently sent a letter to the IDA calling its attention to Mr. Serin's offer to buy the property from Peyto while publishing opinions on the trust. (The offer itself was made in 2002, when Mr. Serin was covering Peyto for another brokerage, Raymond James. A deal was never done.)

What's interesting—or frightening—is that the IDA, which oversees the activities of brokerage firms, doesn't seem to have a problem with research analysts straddling both sides of the fence. As long as the analyst discloses what's going on, the IDA says the activity is not prohibited. The assumption here is that investors will read the disclosure statements and be able to make up their own minds as to whether the research should or shouldn't be relied on. In fact, the IDA's position is that it's the responsibility of the firm to ensure its analysts are not engaged in deals that could affect their objectivity.

Nonsense. There is no way research analysts should be allowed to both cover a firm and do business with it, too. Period. Full stop.

(I should note here that my husband is an analyst for an investment dealer, and he follows the energy sector.)

Research analysts are not allowed to publish reports on companies if their firms are involved in corporate transactions of any sort. How is it different if the analyst, rather than the firm, is involved in a transaction? In fact, the notion that an analyst may act for their own self interest from time to time is more than a tad frightening because one never knows in whose interest they are acting—theirs or the client's.

By turning a blind eye to this issue, the IDA isn't ensuring a level playing field for investors. It's not reasonable to expect investors to rely on the opinions of individuals who appear just as concerned with looking after their own interests by trying to do business with the companies they are following.

Some might say: "But what about analysts who own shares in the companies they follow?" Well, that is different because they are required to disclose their holdings and once those shares are held in personal accounts, that's where they sit until the analyst puts out a "sell" recommendation; they can't be selling for themselves while having a "buy" recommendation out to clients. Some firms aren't even comfortable with this and don't allow their analysts to hold shares in companies that they cover.

Even so, the most glaring difference is that the buying and selling of shares is done in the public markets and, in the case of analysts, is governed by a bevy of rules and regulations. Property deals, by contrast, are private transactions on which information is not as readily available to the public and which are not governed in the same way as stock transactions.

In this regard, it makes sense to look south of the border, to the Series 87 exams that anyone involved in research for an investment dealer must write—including Canadian analysts with U.S. institutional clients. These exams are run by the National Association of Securities Dealers to test the knowledge of securities rules and regulations of people in the industry.

The regulations specify that any activities that have the potential to compromise the perspective of an analyst—and put the client in second place—are forbidden.

The oil patch has worked hard over the past several years to dispel a widely held notion among investors, primarily in Eastern Canada, that it was an insider's game and the only way anyone made money was if they were in Calgary and plugged in. One of the ways investment dealers opted to handle this perceived disadvantage was to move their research operations westward; back in the early 1990s, many energy analysts followed the sector from Toronto or Montreal. Today, the opposite is true, with only a handful of veterans clinging to their Bay Street perches. And there isn't an investment dealer that regrets the decision to do this because they are, in fact, better plugged in to what is going on.

In a sector as tight as the oil patch, which has been criticized for a bit of "nudge, nudge, wink, wink" behaviour over the years, it's even more important that

there be specific rules governing what analysts can and cannot do beyond disclosing share ownership positions and not publishing opinions when their firm is involved in a transaction.

And an analyst approaching a company he or she follows to do a property deal for private benefit must be on that list. Simply disclosing it doesn't go far enough. Moreover, this is the kind of change in regulations that would be applicable in every sector of the economy that involves investment dealers, investors, opinions and publicly traded companies; this isn't just an oil patch hot button.

What it really comes down to is an issue of transparency and maintaining the integrity of Canada's capital markets. The IDA is a crucial part of making this happen.

Source: Yedlin, Deborah. "IDA Must Tighten Its Rules for Analysts." *Globe and Mail*, April 11, 2006, p. B2.

DISCUSSION QUESTIONS

1. What is the conflict of interest that the article is referring to and how might this damage investors?

2. Former Chief Justice of the U.S. Supreme court Louis Brandeis once stated "Sunlight is said to be the best of disinfectants; electric light the most efficient policeman." Do

you think the IDA's position that transparency is sufficient is adequate?

3. What would be the implications of following U.S. practice and prohibiting "any activities that have the potential to compromise the perspective of an analyst"?

Summary

This chapter reviews the basic approaches to valuing preferred and common shares. It begins by introducing the preferred share valuation process, which is based on estimating the present value of expected future dividends. This approach is then extended to common stock valuation in the form of the Dividend Discount Model (DDM). We show how the constant growth version of the DDM is related to the *fundamentals* that affect stock prices (i.e., future profitability and dividends, interest rates, and risk). We then show how the multiple growth version of the DDM could be used to estimate common share prices. We conclude by examining relative valuation models, and the P/E ratio approach in particular, and how they interact with the DCF model.

Throughout our discussion, we highlight the importance of recognizing the sensitivity of the valuation process to assumptions regarding input variables, such as growth rates, discount rates, and general market conditions, and the fact that valuation is as much an art as it is a science.

Key Terms

common share, p. 256

Constant Growth DDM, p. 261

Dividend Discount Model (DDM), p. 259

equity securities, p. 256

market value to EBIT ratio, p. 278

market value to EBITDA ratio, p. 278

market-to-book (M/B) ratio, p. 277

preferred share, p. 256

price-earnings (P/E) ratio, p. 270

price-to-cash-flow (P/CF) ratio, p. 277

price-to-sales (P/S) ratio, p. 277

relative valuation, p. 271

sustainable growth rate, p. 265

Formulas/Equations

(7-1) $k = \text{RF} + \text{Risk premium}$

(7-2) $P_{ps} = \dfrac{D_p}{k_p}$

(7-3) $k_p = \dfrac{D_p}{P_{ps}}$

(7-4) $P_0 = \dfrac{D_1}{(1+k_c)^1} + \dfrac{D_2}{(1+k_c)^2} + \ldots + \dfrac{D_n + P_n}{(1+k_c)^n}$

(7-5) $P_0 = \dfrac{D_1}{(1+k_c)^1} + \dfrac{D_2}{(1+k_c)^2} + \ldots + \dfrac{D_\infty}{(1+k_c)^\infty} = \sum\limits_{t=1}^{\infty} \dfrac{D_t}{(1+k_c)^t}$

(7-6) $P_0 = \dfrac{D_0(1+g)^1}{(1+k_c)^1} + \dfrac{D_0(1+g)^2}{(1+k_c)^2} + \ldots + \dfrac{D_0(1+g)^\infty}{(1+k_c)^\infty}$

(7-7) $P_0 = \dfrac{D_0(1+g)}{k_c - g} = \dfrac{D_1}{k_c - g}$

(7-8) $k_c = \dfrac{D_1}{P_0} + g$

(7-9) $P_0 = \dfrac{EPS_1}{k_c}$

(7-10) $P_0 = \dfrac{EPS_1}{k_c} + PVGO$

(7-11) $g = b \times \text{ROE}$

(7-12) ROE = (Net income/Sales) × (Sales/Total assets) × (Total Assets/equity)
        = Net profit margin × Turnover ratio × Leverage ratio

$$(7\text{-}13)\quad P_0 = \frac{D_1}{(1+k_c)^1} + \frac{D_2}{(1+k_c)^2} + \dots + \frac{D_t + P_t}{(1+k_c)^t}$$

(7-14) P_0 = Estimated EPS_1 × Justified P/E ratio = EPS_1 × P_0/E_1

$$(7\text{-}15)\quad \frac{P_0}{EPS_1} = \frac{P}{E} = \frac{D_1/EPS_1}{k_c - g}$$

APPENDIX 7A:
A SHORT PRIMER ON BUBBLES[11]

In 1711, the South Seas Company (SSC)[12] was given a monopoly on all English trade to the South Seas, that is, South America. Unfortunately, South America was largely under the control of Spain and England was at war with Spain. Nevertheless, the hope was that in the ensuing peace, England would be able to dictate a freeing up of trade to the company's benefit. As it turns out, the peace would be to England's benefit but not very much to the company's. Meanwhile, John Law, a Scottish promoter in France, had set up the Mississippi Company, which was draining investment from England to France. In response, the South Seas Company offered to have investors convert England's national debt into shares of the company. The company would pay a one-time fee to the government for this conversion and receive the fixed annual payments on the national debt. The certainty of receiving the interest payments would allow the company to borrow to fund its South Seas trade.

It was an audacious plan in an age of optimism and jubilation at England's defeat of both Spain and France. In April 1720, the government accepted the offer, and the stock price took off. It was clear that the plan could only be accepted if the stock price went up enough to encourage investors to convert their national debt into SSC equity. Consequently, the company issued shares on an instalment basis. As the cash came in, the company lent it back so that investors could buy more shares. The stock obviously took off and in doing so sucked in a whole group of neophyte investors.

It also spawned imitators. One of the most interesting of these declared that it was "a company for carrying on an undertaking of great advantage, but nobody was to know what it is." Prices soared, and small investors got in for fear of missing out. Sir Isaac Newton sold his stock in the SSC in April 1720 for a 100 percent gain. However, SSC's stock price rocketed up from 300 pounds to its peak of more than 1,000 pounds and he bought back in. In August the bubble burst and by September prices were back to 300 pounds. The *London Gazette* was full of bankruptcies and Isaac Newton lost 20,000 pounds; philosophically, he made his famous statement, "I can calculate the motions of the heavenly bodies, but not the madness of people."

---

[11] This appendix is based on Laurence Booth, "Investments, 'Alternative' Investments and Bubbles." *Advisor's Guide to New Investment Opportunities*, 2002, pp. 12–19.

[12] See Jim Harrison, "The Damn'd South Sea," *Harvard Magazine*, May–June 1999.

We have learned from this, haven't we? Leaving aside the Great Crash of 1929, there is the little matter of the Crash of 2000, and our recent experience with technology and Internet stocks. The most recent crashes stemmed from the high valuation of the equity market as a result of the long bull markets of the late 1990s.

Long bull markets pull in inexperienced investors who have unrealistic expectations. As we saw in Chapter 5, over long periods, equity market average returns have exceeded 10 percent a year, which is not enough to get investors really excited. However, a couple of 25 percent plus years bring in the people who then come to expect 25 percent plus returns. Moreover, plenty of people are willing to tell them that they can get 25 percent returns and that this time it is different: it is a new world of investing with new metrics.

In the September 1999 issue of *Atlantic Monthly*, James Glassman and Kevin Hassett discuss the advice in their book that the Dow will go to 30,000. They state (page 37), "Stocks were undervalued in the 1980s and 1990s and they are undervalued now. Stock prices could double, triple or even quadruple tomorrow and still not be too high." They go on to suggest (page 42), "A profound change has occurred in the attractiveness of stocks since the early 1980s, as investors have become more rational. The old limits of yields and P/Es do not apply anymore, if they ever did." And finally (page 56), "In truth there is no extra risk in stocks."[13]

It is a familiar refrain during times of speculative bubbles that this time it is different. After all, the little investors get in only after a run-up in prices, so it has to be "different this time," otherwise, they have missed the boat. On May 15, 1929, the *Outlook* and *Independent* remarked, "But apparently there has been a fundamental change in the criteria for judging security values. Widespread education of the public in the worth of equity securities has created a new demand." Similarly, before the correction in 1969, *Barron's* stated, "The failure of the general market to decline during the last three years despite its obvious vulnerability, as well as the emergence of new investment characteristics, has caused investors to believe that the U.S. has entered a new investment era to which old guidelines no longer apply."[14]

The fact is that "old guidelines" are perennial; the only thing that changes is that the old investors die off and a new generation has to learn the same old lessons. Does that 1720 English company that promised, "carrying on of an undertaking of great advantage, but nobody to know what it is," sound familiar? It should. On January 25, 2000, Michael Lewis, the author of *Liar's Poker*, pointed out that there was an Internet company, NetJ.com, that had filed statements with the U.S. Securities and Exchange Commission with the confession that "the company is not currently engaged in any substantial activity and has no plans to engage in any such activity in the foreseeable future." The company had $127,631 in accumulated losses and so little money on hand that the directors would have had to chip in to pay any filing costs to raise capital. The only snag was NetJ.com had a market capitalization of $22.9 million.

---

[13] They also go through an interesting valuation of Cisco (page 52), in which they state, "Using the standard formula for calculating a stock's present value according to the flow of cash it generates over time, we find that Cisco's PRP should be $399 a share. In other words, Cisco's price last June would need to sextuple. Its P/E would rise to 539 (No that's not a misprint)." As we read this, Cisco's price is $19. James Glassman and Kevin Hassett, "Dow 36,000," *Atlantic Monthly*, 284, no. 3 (September 1999).

[14] Quoted in Jim Stack, *The New Paradigm Era or Bubble* (Whitefish, MT: InvesTech Research, 1997).

QUESTIONS AND PRACTICE PROBLEMS

Multiple Choice Questions

1. Jason bought 30,000 shares of CTB Inc. on January 12, 2006. At that time, CTB Inc. had 2 million common shares outstanding. Calculate the portion of CTB Inc. that Jason owns.

    A. 2.3 percent

    B. 1.4 percent

    C. 6.0 percent

    D. 1.5 percent

2. Which of the following is *not* a difference between equity securities and debt securities?

    A. incur a tax-deductible expense

    B. have a fixed maturity date

    C. always involve fixed periodic payments

    D. represent ownership of the security

3. Given that the government short-term T-bill yield is 4 percent, and the risk premium of ABC firm is 6.5 percent, calculate ABC firm's required rate of return.

    A. 8.5 percent

    B. 10.5 percent

    C. 7.25 percent

    D. 11.5 percent

4. Which of the following statements about equities is *correct*?

    A. Every firm pays dividends to common shareholders each year.

    B. Preferred dividends are usually paid annually in practice.

    C. Common shareholders are entitled to a firm's earnings before preferred shareholders.

    D. Common shareholders can vote on issues, such as mergers, election of board members, and so on.

5. Westlake Ltd. just paid a dividend of $2.00 per share, which is expected to grow at a constant rate of 4.5 percent indefinitely. The T-bill rate is 3 percent and the risk premium of Westlake Ltd. is 6.5 percent. Calculate the current share price of Westlake Ltd.

    A. $42.60

    B. $41.80

    C. $46.05

    D. $40.00

6. Grace Holdings recently paid an annual dividend of $1.50 per share, and its estimated long-term growth rate in dividends is 4 percent. The current market price of each share is $26. The implied rate of return on the share is

A. 9.77 percent.

B. 10 percent.

C. 12.5 percent.

D. 13.33 percent.

7. Firestone Co. just paid a dividend of $1.50 per share and its EPS is $9.00. Its book value per share (BVPS) is $36. Calculate Firestone's sustainable growth rate.

A. 20.83 percent

B. 25 percent

C. 4.17 percent

D. 5.25 percent

8. The sustainable growth is *negatively* related to

A. net profit margin.

B. leverage ratio or equity multiplier.

C. payout ratio.

D. retention ratio.

9. Which of the following is *not* a limitation of the DDM model?

A. It cannot be applied to firms without dividend payments.

B. It can only be applied to constant growing firms.

C. It cannot be used to value private firms.

D. It cannot be applied to firms with negative earnings.

10. Which of the following is *false* regarding the relative valuation approach?

A. The most commonly used one is the P/E ratio approach.

B. The M/B ratio may be used instead of the P/E ratio if the firm has negative earnings.

C. We can use the average P/E ratio of the firm's industry when appropriate.

D. The leading P/E ratio can be estimated as: (Payout ratio)$(1 + g)/(k - g)$.

Practice Problems

11. Describe the characteristics of preferred shares.

12. List the elements needed for the calculation of a share price using the Constant Growth DDM.

Easy

13. Describe the Constant Growth DDM valuation method.

14. Describe how to estimate the present value of growth opportunities (PVGO) and what it represents.

15. Fill in the missing information in the following table:

Preferred Shares in Canada					
Company	Price	Par value	Required return	Dividend rate	Dividends paid per share
A		$100	8%	5%	$5.00
B	$60	$50	3%		
C	$70	$75			$8.00
D	$50	$50		14%	
E	$150	$30	7%		
F		$100	4%		$9.50
G			7%	9%	$18.00
H	$18		5%	6%	

16. The preferred shares of Knob and Tube Electrical Company have a par value of $100 and a dividend rate of 8 percent. The current price is $110. If the risk-free rate is 2 percent, what is the risk premium associated with these preferred shares.

17. The Absent Minded Profs purchased a stock for $50. They expect to receive a dividend of $5, and to sell the stock immediately after the last dividend.

   A. If the sale price is $75, what is the expected one-year holding period return?

   B. If the sale price is $35, what is the expected one-year holding period return?

   C. If the actual return was -4 percent, what was the sale price?

   D. If the actual return was 15 percent, what was the sale price?

18. Fill in the missing information in the following table:

Common Shares in Canada					
Company	Price	Required return	Dividend growth	Current dividend	Dividend expected in 1 year
A		15%		$4.50	$5.00
B	$600	3%	1%		
C	$70		5%		$8.00
D	$55			$10.00	$11.00
E		14%	6%	$9.50	
F		15%	0%		$18.00
G	$40	5%	-2%		

19. The ToolWerks Company is expected to earn $10,000,000 next year. There are 2,000,000 shares outstanding and the company uses a dividend payout ratio of 40 percent. The required rate of return for companies like ToolWerks is 8 percent. The current share price of ToolWerks is $75.

A. What are the expected earnings per share for ToolWerks?

B. What are the expected dividends per share for ToolWerks?

C. What is the dividend growth rate expected for ToolWerks?

D. What is the present value of growth opportunities for this firm?

20. Determine the present value of growth opportunities for a company with a leading EPS of $1.85, a required rate of return of 8 percent and a current stock price of $50.

21. The Widget Manufacturing Company's most recent earnings were $300,000. From these earnings, it paid dividends on common equity totaling $175,000. There are 50,000 common shares outstanding. The ROE for Widget is 12 percent. Determine the following:

A. Earnings per share. Which can you calculate: leading or lagging EPS?

B. Dividends per share

C. Earnings retention ratio

D. Sustainable growth rate

Medium

22. State the relationship that the required rate of return, the expected growth rate, and expected dividends have with the market share price, according to the Constant Growth DDM.

23. Star Corporation has issued $1 million in preferred shares to investors with a 7.25 percent annual dividend rate on a par value of $100. Assuming the firm pays dividends indefinitely and the required rate is 10.5 percent, calculate the price of the preferred shares.

24. Calculate the leading P/E ratio, given the following information: retention ratio = 0.6, required rate of return = 10 percent, expected growth rate = 5 percent.

25. You have just been to see your broker at the Fly-by-Night Brokerage Company for advice about investing in the Empire Bank. The broker indicates that the Empire Bank has three different types of securities: debt, preferred stock, and common shares. She states: "Debt is safe because it is a bank and Canadian banks are safe. Empire Bank preferred stock entitles you to vote at the annual general meeting. The Empire Bank has paid a dividend of $2.50 per year for the last 18 years so you are guaranteed to receive $2.50 next year; if you don't, the Bank will go bankrupt". Comment on your broker's statement. Is she correct?

26. The Absent Minded Profs purchased the stock for $50. They expect to hold the stock for two years, and to receive a dividend of $1.50 each year and to sell the stock immediately after the last dividend.

A. If the sale price is $75, what is the expected annual return?

B. If the sale price is $35, what is the expected annual return?

C. If the actual return was -4 percent, what was the sale price?

D. If the actual return was 15 percent, what was the sale price?

(Excel or financial calculator recommended.)

27. The Ibis Company is expected to pay a $1.50 dividend next year. Dividends are expected to grow at 3 percent forever and the required rate of return is 7 percent.

   A. What is the price of Ibis today?
   B. What is the expected dividend yield?
   C. What is the expected capital gains yield?
   D. In one year, immediately after the dividend is paid,
      i)   What is the price of the stock?
      ii) What was the one-year holding period return?
      iii) Looking forward one year, what are the expected dividend and capital gains yields?
   E. In year 10, immediately after the dividend is paid,
      i)   What is the price of the stock?
      ii) What was the one-year holding period return (year 9 to 10)?
      iii) Looking forward one year, what are the expected dividend and capital gains yields?

28. The LMX Company is expected to pay a $2.00 dividend in one year. The required rate of return is 9 percent. The firm uses a dividend payout ratio of 25 percent. Calculate the leading P/E ratio in the following cases:

   A. Expected growth rate = 4 percent
      i) Today
      ii) In one year (immediately after dividend paid)
   B. Expected growth rate = 8 percent
      i) Today
      ii) In one year (immediately after dividend paid)
   C. If a firm is expected to have a constant dividend growth rate, do you expect the P/E ratio to change over time? Explain.

29. The NLF Company currently doesn't pay any dividends but is expected to start paying dividends in 5 years. The first dividend is expected to be $1.00 and to grow at 6 percent thereafter. The required rate of return for the firm is 10 percent. What is the current stock price for NLF?

30. The ExD Company is expected to pay an annual dividend[15] of $5.00 on January 20th. The firm has zero growth and the required rate of return for this type of firm is 10 percent. Calculate the expected stock price for ExD on January 19th and January 21st.

31. Company A's current dividend is $5.00. You expect the growth rate to be 0 percent for years 1 to 5, and 2 percent for years 6 to infinity. The required rate of return on this firm's equity is 10 percent. Determine the following:

   A. The expected dividend at the end of year 5
   B. The expected dividend at the end of year 6

---

[15] Strictly speaking, we should say the ex-dividend date is January 20. If an investor purchases the stock prior to the ex-dividend date, the investor is entitled to the dividend. If the investor purchases on or after the ex-dividend date, the investor is no longer entitled to receive the dividend.

C. The expected price of the stock at the end of year 5 (immediately after the year 5 dividend)

D. The price of the stock today

32. Company B's current dividend is $5.00. You expect the growth rate to be 8 percent for years 1 to 5, and 2 percent from years 6 to infinity. The required rate of return on this firm's equity is 10 percent. Determine the following:

A. The expected dividend at the end of year 5

B. The expected dividend at the end of year 6

C. The expected price of the stock at the end of year 5 (immediately after the year 5 dividend)

D. The price of the stock today

33. Company C's current dividend is $3.60. Dividends are expected to grow by 9 percent for years 1 to 3, 6 percent for years 4 to 7, and, 2 percent thereafter. The required rate of return on the stock is 12 percent. What is the current stock price for Company C?

34. Company D's current dividend is $4.00. Dividends are expected to grow by 25 percent for years 1 to 3 and 10 percent thereafter. The required rate of return on the stock is 15 percent. What is the current stock price for Company D?

35. The Absent Minded Profs are concerned about the impact of errors in their estimates of the future dividend payout ratio for the LCI Company. Assume that the current dividend is $1, ROE is fixed at 10 percent, and the required rate of return is 15 percent. Using Excel, calculate the current stock price for dividend payout ratios ranging between 5 percent and 75 percent in 5 percentage point increments. Is the percentage change in the stock price for a 5 percentage point change in dividend payout ratio constant?

Difficult

36. List three reasons why one firm may have a higher leading P/E ratio than a comparable firm.

37. Firm A has a patent, which will expire in two years. The firm is expected to grow at 10 percent for the next two years and dividends will be paid at year end. It just paid a dividend of $1.00. After two years, the growth rate will decline to 4 percent immediately and the firm will grow at this rate forever. If the required rate of return is 11 percent, value the firm's current share price.

38. DE Inc. just paid a dividend of $4.00 and its current earnings per share is $5. The current T-bill rate is 3 percent and DE's risk premium is 12 percent. The net profit margin, asset turnover, and debt-to-equity (D/E) ratio are 20 percent, 1.5, and 0.67, respectively. Calculate the current share price by using the P/E ratio approach.

39. ABC Company's preferred shares have a par value of $50, a dividend rate of 7 percent, and trade at a price of $70. PWT Company's preferred shares have a par value of $60, a dividend rate of 4 percent, and trade at a price of $45. Which company's preferred stock is riskier?

40. The Xcalibur Sword Company is currently selling for $150. The current dividend is $10 and the required rate of return is 10 percent. What is the expected dividend growth rate?

41. The Absent Minded Profs are interested in investing in the XML Software Company. XML's current dividend is $5.50 and XML shares are selling for $40. The required rate of return for firms like XML is 8 percent. The Profs have conducted an extensive analysis of the company and believe that the dividend growth rate should be 5 percent.

   A. Should the Profs buy the stock at $40? Why or why not?

   B. Do you expect the stock price to stay at $40? Explain.

42. As part of your duties at the Absent Minded Profs, you have been asked to review the analysis carried out by a rival company—the PHD group—of the Frivolous Radio Company. Frivolous has had a constant P/E ratio for the last 5 years. PHD's analyst has made the following statement: "Frivolous' constant P/E ratio is due to zero growth in their earnings and therefore, Frivolous is not a good investment." Comment on PHD's statement.

43. The XYZ Company has an expected profit margin of 10 percent, turnover ratio of 1.8 and a leverage ratio of 0.30. The leading EPS is $2.50 and the firm uses a dividend payout ratio of 35 percent. The required return on firms with XYZ's risk characteristics is 5 percent. Calculate the expected current stock price of XYZ.

44. Company E's current dividend is $4.00. Dividends are expected to decline by 4 percent per year for the next 3 years, and then remain constant thereafter. The required rate of return for this type of company is 15 percent. What is the current stock price for Company E?

45. The Absent Minded Profs have completed a fundamental analysis of the MKL Company. MKL is a young company and expects to invest heavily in facilities and research and development during the next 5 years; it expects to reap the benefits of its research and development during years 6 to 10; however, it expects rivals to enter the market and margins and profitability to stabilize at a lower level after year 10. The details of the analysis are presented below:

Fundamental Analysis of the MKL Company				
Period	Net profit margin	Turnover	Leverage	Dividend payout ratio
Years 1-5	1%	0.75	3.0	.05
Years 6-10	15%	3.00	2.0	.10
Years 11-?	5%	1.40	1.0	.50

The current dividend for MKL is $3.00 and the required rate of return for this type of firm is 15 percent. Determine the current stock price for MKL.

46. The ClearWaters Lobster Company (CWL) is a privately held lobster farming company based in Nova Scotia. It has hired the Absent Minded Profs to help evaluate an offer for the company. Currently CWL has a net income of $150,000 on sales of $350,000—it processes 250,000 lobsters each year. The total assets are $2,500,000 and the book value of equity is $2,000,000. The firm is the sole source of income for the owners, the Wong family, and consequently the dividend payout ratio is 65 percent. The risk free rate is 2 percent and the appropriate risk premium for this firm is 5 percent.

A. StarLobster has approached the Wongs about buying CWL. What is the minimum price the Wongs should consider (using only DCF analysis)?

B. There are three other publicly traded lobster farming companies in Nova Scotia. Summary data on those firms is presented below:

Company	SeaLobster	ToroLobster	AgriLobster
Price per share	$25	$10	$15
Number of shares outstanding	1,000	10,000	500,000
Market value of company per lobster processed	5	7	12
P/E	15	5	35

Given the data on these firms, determine the value of CWL. Discuss the strengths and weaknesses of the comparable firms approach to valuation.

C. StarLobster believes that it can make several changes to the operations of CWL that will increase value. It believes that it can improve the net profit margins to 50 percent without changing the turnover ratio. It will also increase the leverage ratio to 1.50 and will reduce the payout ratio to 40 percent. What is the maximum price StarLobster should consider?

PART 4

PORTFOLIO AND CAPITAL MARKET THEORY

This section of the text discusses the key topics of risk, return, and portfolio theory. We discuss various measures of risk and methods for estimating the required rate of return for securities and portfolios. In the final chapter, we discuss market efficiency and the importance of this issue for both investors and corporations.

Diversification

Diversification by country, industry, or asset class is particularly important for Canadian investors. The universe of investable equities in Canada, as represented by the S&P/TSX Composite Index, is dominated by the energy and financials sectors, which together account for more than 60 percent of the index. The top 10 companies on the S&P/TSX Composite Index are highly concentrated in the energy and financials sectors, and they account for more than 30 percent of the total index compared with approximately 20 percent of the S&P 500 Index by its top 10 constituents. The Canadian market has a significant weighting in resource stocks, whose fortunes are tied to highly cyclical commodity prices. The recent boom in commodity prices helped drive a S&P/TSX Composite Index three-year return of almost 21 percent (at June 30, 2006).

Source: Standard & Poor's website: www.standardpoors.com (April 1, 2007).

Risk, Return, and Portfolio Theory

Learning Objectives

After reading this chapter, you should understand the following:

1. The differences among the most important types of returns

2. How to estimate expected returns and risk for individual securities

3. What happens to risk and return when securities are combined in a portfolio

4. What is meant by an "efficient frontier"

5. Why diversification is so important to investors

INTRODUCTION

This chapter defines risk and return and establishes the relationship between them, with particular emphasis on equity securities. As such, it lays the foundation for Chapter 9, which discusses some of the most important concepts in finance.

8.1 MEASURING RETURNS

In Chapter 7, we discussed the basics of the discounted cash flow (DCF) valuation of equities and finished with an analysis conducted by TD Newcrest (the institutional equities division of TD Securities Inc.) of Bennett Environmental Inc. (BEV). That valuation was done in October 2004, when BEV's share price was $25. It placed BEV's stock price in the $54 to $56 range within two years, based on its earnings, cash flow forecasts, and possible relative valuation multiples, such as the P/E and EBITDA multiples. However, BEV's share price didn't go to $54 to $56; it went down to less than $1. Instead of a capital gain of more than 100 percent ($25 to $55), investors in BEV would have lost about 96 percent.

Risk is typically defined as "the possibility of incurring harm." Purchasing shares in BEV at $25 and then holding them as the stock collapsed caused harm to investors.[1] This chapter is concerned with ways to analyze and manage this risk. First, we develop some basic definitions.

Ex Post versus Ex Ante Returns

ex post returns past or historical, returns

ex ante returns future or expected returns

We have to distinguish between **ex post returns** and **ex ante returns**. Ex post means "after the fact," so ex post returns are past or historical returns. Ex ante means "before the fact," so ex ante returns are expected returns. Advertisements for mutual funds and other investments show historical or ex post returns and then in smaller print have a disclaimer that past returns do not necessarily reflect future, or ex ante, returns. Of course, what investors are interested in are these future or expected returns, but their judgement in terms of what they can reasonably expect is informed by what has happened in the past. The BEV example shows that sometimes what happens is outside of what anyone expects. Even the expert security analysts at TD Newcrest, running all sorts of different scenarios and *stress testing* their models to assess BEV's risk, never anticipated that the share price could drop by 96 percent over a few years.

income yield the return earned by investors as a periodic cash flow

So how can investors measure these ex post or historical returns? As we saw in Chapters 6 and 7, the return on an investment consists of two components: the income yield and the capital gain (or loss) yield. The **income yield** is the return earned in the form of a periodic cash flow received by the investors. These cash flows are interest payments from bonds and dividends from equities. The income

---

[1] BEV's senior management was also under investigation by the Ontario Securities Commission (OSC) because insiders sold shares before informing the market that the soil from a major contract was not shipping in sufficient volumes. On November 23, 2006, the *Toronto Star* reported that the OSC had reached a settlement with John Bennett, the founder of BEV.

yield then measures these cash receipts by dividing them by the purchase price or the beginning of period market price. This is shown in Equation 8-1.

$$\text{Income yield} = \frac{CF_1}{P_0}$$

[8-1]

where CF_1 = the expected cash flows to be received

P_0 = the purchase price (or beginning market price)

The graph in Figure 8-1 shows the dividend yield on the S&P/TSX Composite Index and the yield to maturity on the long Canada bond since 1956.[2]

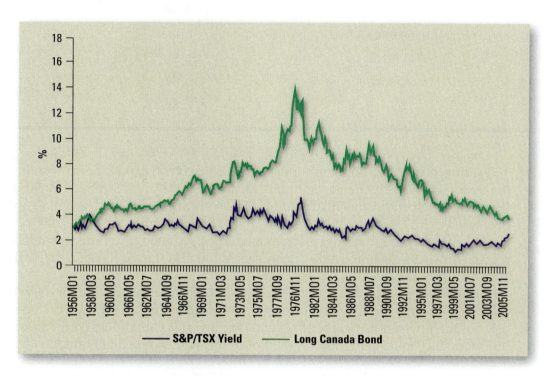

8-1 FIGURE

Market Income Yields

Remember that the yield to maturity on the long Canada bond is the return earned by buying the bond and holding it to maturity. In this sense, it is also an expected return over that very long investment horizon. In contrast, the dividend yield on the S&P/TSX Composite Index (TSX) is the cash that investors can expect to earn if the dividend payments over the next year are the same as they were over the previous period, because the dividend yield is the current dividend payments divided by the current value of the index, not the forecast dividends. Keeping this qualification in mind, the graph in Figure 8-1 illustrates some important points.

The dividend yield on the TSX was very similar to that on long Canada bonds in the mid-1950s. At December 1957, the dividend yield on the TSX was 4.41 percent versus a 3.83 percent yield on the long Canada bond. Obviously, 4.41 percent dominates 3.83 percent, so a piece of the puzzle is missing; otherwise, everyone would buy common shares and no one would buy long Canada bonds. The missing piece is the risk attached to investing in common shares, as

---

[2] The dividend yield depicted here is measured as D_0/P_0, i.e., using dividends paid over the last 12 months, not the expected dividends.

the BEV example indicates.[3] After the late 1950s, the yield gap between common shares and the long Canada bond yield became very significant, as Table 8-1 indicates.

Table 8-1   Average Yield Gap

Average Yield Gap	(%)
1950s	0.82
1960s	2.35
1970s	4.54
1980s	8.14
1990s	5.51
2000s	3.55
Overall	4.58

During the 1950s, Canada bonds yielded, on average, 0.82 percent more than the S&P/TSX dividend yield, and this increased to 2.35 percent in the 1960s, 4.54 percent in the 1970s, and 8.14 percent in the 1980s. The yield gap decreased to 5.51 percent in the 1990s and to 3.55 percent so far in the 2000s.

capital gain (or loss) the appreciation (or depreciation) in the price of an asset from some starting price, usually the purchase price or the price at the start of the year

The main reason that this yield gap has varied so much over time is that the return to investors is not just the income yield but also the capital gain (or loss) yield.

The **capital gain (or loss)** component measures the *appreciation* (or *depreciation*) in the price of the asset from some starting price, usually the purchase price or the price at the start of the year. Dividing this gain or loss by the price produces the capital gain (or loss) yield or return, as expressed in Equation 8-2.

[8-2]

$$\text{Capital gain (loss) return} = \frac{P_1 - P_0}{P_0}$$

where P_1 = the selling price or current market price

The addition of the capital gain or loss yield explains why the yield gap between equities and bonds has varied so much over time. Remember that the yield on the long Canada bond is the fixed return earned by buying and holding the bond to maturity. In contrast, as the firm retains money for reinvestment, the firm should get more valuable over time; investing in common shares should give rise to significant long-term capital gains. In addition, common shares should gain from inflation over the long run as their prices and cash flows are not fixed; in aggregate, they should increase with inflation. As a result, we would expect the yield gap to increase with the rate of inflation, which it generally does. Remember, for example, from Figure 6-3 that the high level of long Canada bond yields coincided with the very high rates of inflation in the 1970s into the 1980s, when the yield gap was the highest.

---

[3] Taxes are also a factor, given the different tax treatment of interest and dividends.

To get the complete picture of the return from investing in bonds versus common shares, we have to add the income yield and the capital gain (or loss) yield together. The **total return** is then as follows:

total return income yield plus the capital gain (or loss) yield

$$\text{Total return} = \text{Income yield} + \text{Capital gain (or loss) yield}$$

$$\frac{CF_1 + P_1 - P_0}{P_0}$$

[8-3]

Example 8-1: Calculating Returns

Estimate the income yield, capital gain (or loss) yield, and total return for the following securities over the past year:

a. A $1,000 par value 6 percent bond that was purchased one year ago for $990 and is currently selling for $995.

b. A stock that was purchased for $20, provided four quarterly dividends of $0.25 each, and is currently worth $19.50.

Solution

a. $CF_1 = 0.06 \times \$1,000 = \$60$; $P_0 = \$990$; $P_1 = \$995$

Income yield = 60/990 = 0.0606 = 6.06%

Capital gain (loss) return = (995 − 990)/990 = 0.0051 = 0.51%

Total return = 6.06% + 0.51% = 6.57%

Or total return = (60 + 995 − 990)/990 = 0.0657 = 6.57%

b. $CF_1 = \$0.25 \times 4 = \$1.00$; $P_0 = \$20$; $P_1 = \$19.50$

Income yield = 1/20 = 0.0500 = 5.00%

Capital gain (loss) return = (19.50 − 20.00)/20 = −0.0250 = −2.50%

Total return = 5.00% − 2.50% = 2.50%

Or total return = (1 + 19.50 − 20)/20 = 0.0250 = 2.50%

In Example 8-1, notice that the bond has not been held to maturity, so the return over one year may be different from the yield to maturity. In this case, the bond has increased in value from $990 to $995, so there is a capital gain of 0.51 percent from holding the bond, in addition to the income yield of 6.06 percent, so the total return is 6.57 percent. This raises an important question: does it matter whether or not the bond is sold in calculating the rate of return? Take part b in Example 8-1, where there is a capital loss of 2.50 percent. This reduces the return from holding the common share from 5.0 percent to 2.5 percent, so it is less than the return from the bond. Should we add this capital loss to the overall return if we don't actually sell the shares?

The answer may seem obvious to most people, but psychologists have observed that people make different decisions if they own something than if they don't. For example, people will keep something for years because it cost $100 and is "valuable," even after they see the identical thing in a flea market selling for $1 and yet wouldn't buy it for $1. Owning assets includes an attachment effect, and with such an attitude, many people refuse to accept capital losses in the total return calculation until they actually sell the asset and realize

paper losses capital losses that people do not accept as losses until they actually sell and realize them

them. Until then, people refer to them as **paper losses**, with the implication that they are not real. This attitude is reinforced by the tax rules: capital gains and losses are only taxable on realization.

A second important point is that whether or not we include paper gains and losses, in part, depends on our *investment horizon*. For example we can look at rates of return over daily, weekly, monthly, annual, or even longer periods. A **day trader** is someone who buys and sells based on intraday price movements. In that case, the total return for a day's trading will include the effect of capital gains and losses daily and sometimes over even shorter periods. In contrast, most people review their investments less frequently, perhaps quarterly or sometimes annually. For them the intraday price variability and total return are not a concern. What is of concern is the total return over, say, a quarter or a year. They are not concerned about rates of return over shorter periods or the paper losses that are involved.[4]

day trader someone who buys and sells based on intraday price movements

mark to market carrying securities at the current market value regardless of whether they are sold

The contrary view is that investors have to **mark to market** the prices of all financial securities over the relevant investment horizon. This means that investors always carry securities at the current market value regardless of whether they sell them. As a result, the total return includes the effect of paper gains and losses on securities not yet sold. This view is based on the basic opportunity cost argument, which asks what the alternative use is for the funds tied up in the investment. Clearly, an investor cannot sell the security at its historical cost; he or she can sell at the current market value, and this is the value that can be reinvested elsewhere. In this textbook, we will always mark to market and consider the total return as including paper gains and paper losses over the relevant investment horizon, because this reflects the economic value of past investment decisions.

Measuring Average Returns

How can we measure these ex post or historical returns? Table 5-1 of Chapter 5 reported the arithmetic and geometric average annual rates of return for various types of investments over 1938 to 2005. These returns assume that the investor buys and holds the security for each year. Part of that table is reproduced in Table 8-2. What is important about the table is that you understand how these returns are calculated.

Table 8-2   Average Investment Returns and Standard Deviations, 1938–2005

	Annual Arithmetic Average (%)	Annual Geometric Mean (%)	Standard Deviation of Annual Returns (%)
Government of Canada treasury bills	5.20	5.11	4.32
Government of Canada bonds	6.62	6.24	9.32
Canadian stocks	11.79	10.60	16.22
U.S. stocks	13.15	11.76	17.54

Source: Data are from the Canadian Institute of Actuaries.

[4] This brings to mind the philosophical question, does a falling tree in a forest make a noise if there is no one there to hear it? Similarly, does a daily total return matter to an investor who only reviews his or her investments once a month?

The **arithmetic mean or average** is the most commonly used value in statistics. It is calculated as the sum of all of the returns divided by the total number of observations, as expressed in Equation 8-4:

$$\text{Arithmetic average (AM)} = \frac{\sum_{i=1}^{n} r_i}{n}$$

[8-4]

where r_i = the individual returns

n = the total number of observations

The **geometric mean**, in contrast, measures the average or compound growth rate over multiple periods, as discussed in Chapter 5. For investments, this is the growth rate in the value invested or equivalently the compound rate of return. Recall that in Chapter 5, Table 5-1 showed that the future value of $1,000 invested in Canadian stocks at the start of 1938 would have grown to $946,009 by the end of 2005 (i.e., after 68 years) if all the income was reinvested each period. In fact, the precise geometric mean return was 10.6020476 percent, which means that $1,000 invested in 1938 compounded at 10.6020476 percent grew to $946,009 after 68 years, or FV = ($1,000)(1.106020476)^{68} = $946,009. In fact, the geometric mean is the rate of return used to find the future value, as discussed in Chapter 5 and calculated as:

[8-5]

$$\text{Geometric mean (GM)} = [(1 + r_1)(1 + r_2)(1 + r_3) \dots (1 + r_n)]^{1/n} - 1$$

Example 8-2: Calculating Arithmetic Average and Geometric Mean

Estimate the arithmetic average and geometric mean for the following returns: 4.3 percent, 3.2 percent, 5.6 percent, 10.5 percent, and −7.6 percent.

Solution

AM = (4.3 + 3.2 + 5.6 + 10.5 − 7.6)/5 = 16/5 = 3.20%

GM = [(1.043)(1.032)(1.056)(1.105)(0.924)]$^{1/5}$ − 1 = (1.1605455)$^{1/5}$ − 1 = 1.0302 − 1

= 0.0302 or 3.02%

In Example 8-2, notice that the geometric mean is less than the arithmetic average. This will always be the case unless the values are all identical. The more the returns vary, the bigger the difference between the AM and GM will be.

We will formally discuss statistical measures of how much returns vary shortly, but note that the last column in Table 8-2 has the standard deviation of the annual returns. The standard deviation measures the "typical" variation of the return: the larger the standard deviation, the more variable the return. When the standard deviation is squared, we get a measure called the variance. Approximately, the difference between the arithmetic and geometric return is half this variance.

For example, the standard deviation of the annual treasury bill (T-bill) returns was 4.32 percent or 0.0432. Squaring this to get the variance gives us 0.0018662, and half this is 0.00093 or 0.093 percent. Note that the difference

---

arithmetic mean or average the most commonly used value in statistics; the sum of all returns divided by the total number of observations

geometric mean the average or compound growth rate over multiple time periods

between the AM and GM T-bill returns is 5.20 percent − 5.11 percent or 0.09 percent! So the approximation is exact. For equities, the standard deviation and variance was 16.22 percent or 0.1622 and 0.0263, so half the variance is 1.31 percent. In this case the difference between the AM and GM equity returns is 11.79 percent − 10.60 percent or 1.19 percent, which is slightly less.

As we indicated before, the more variable the annual returns, the bigger the difference between the AM and GM measures of return. Looking again at Table 8-2, the biggest difference is for the common stock returns and then the long bond returns. The smallest is for the T-bill returns. So when should we use the AM and when the GM to describe the average return from an investment? The answer depends on what we are trying to do.

The AM is appropriate when we are trying to estimate the typical return for a given period, such as a year. So if we wanted to know the best estimate for the rate of return over the next year, we would use the AM of the annual rates of return, because, by definition, this measures the average annual rate of return. We use the GM when we are interested in determining the "true" average rate of return over multiple periods, for instance, if we wanted to know how our investment (and wealth) will grow over time. We use the GM because it measures the compound rate of growth in our investment value over multiple periods. In this sense, the difference between the AM and GM is dependent on the relevant investment horizon.

If the investment horizon is one year, then the AM is the best estimate. If the investment horizon is multiple years, then the GM is better. Example 8-3 below demonstrates why the geometric mean is superior for estimating returns over multiple periods.

Example 8-3: Geometric Mean versus Arithmetic Average

Estimate the annual arithmetic average return and the geometric mean return on an investment that is purchased for $100, rises to $110 after one year, and falls to $100 by the end of the second year. Assume the investment provided no income during the two-year period.

Solution

Total return (Year 1) = (110 − 100)/100 = 0.10 = 10%

Total return (Year 2) = (100 − 110)/110 = −9.09%

AM = (10 − 9.09)/2 = 0.455%

GM = $[(1.10)(0.9091)]^{1/2} - 1 = 0.0000 = 0.00\%$

The annual average arithmetic return is 0.455 percent because this is simply the average of the two annual rates of return. However, to tell an investor that he or she has made on average 0.455 percent, when the investment is worth exactly what it started with, is misleading. In contrast, the geometric mean or compound rate of return provides the correct annual return of 0 percent.

Why the arithmetic average return and the geometric mean return differ in Example 8-3 can now be seen by looking at the two rates of return. As we mentioned before, the annual rates of return have to vary to make a difference between the AM and GM, which they did in Example 8-3. Now notice that the gain of 10 percent is made when the investment is worth $100, whereas the loss of 9.09 percent is made when the investment is worth $110. Clearly, a gain of 10 percent on $100 is $10 and a loss of 9.09 percent on $110 is also $10, which is why the investor ends up with the same $100 that he or she started with. However, the AM simply averages the annual rates of return without taking into account that the amount invested varies across time. For this reason, the GM is a better average return estimate when we are interested in the rate of return performance of an investment over time.[5]

Estimating Expected Returns

Although it is important to be able to estimate the ex post returns realized from past investments, investors are generally interested in the returns they *expect* to realize from an investment made today. In practice, **expected returns** are often estimated based on historical averages, but the problem is that there is no guarantee that the past will repeat itself. For example, 1938 to 2005 included World War II (1939–45), a period of significant inflation (1970s and into the 1980s), and a recession caused, in part, by the passing of the North American Free Trade Agreement among Canada, the United States, and Mexico (early 1990s). For investors interested in expected returns, such events as these can have unexpected effects.

expected returns
estimated future returns

An alternative approach is to use all available information to assess the most likely returns under various future scenarios, and then attach probabilities to the likelihood of each occurring. When this approach is used, the expected return is estimated as the weighted average of the expected returns under each scenario, where the weights correspond to the probabilities of each scenario actually occurring. This is expressed as follows:

$$ER = \sum_{i=1}^{n} (r_i \times Prob_i)$$

[8-6]

where ER = the expected return on an investment

r_i = the estimated return in scenario i

$Prob_i$ = the probability of state i occurring

Example 8-4: Estimating Expected Returns

Suppose you are given the following information for two stocks, A and B, where the return on each varies with the state of the economy:

State of the Economy	Probability of Occurrence	Expected Return on Stock A in This State	Expected Return on Stock B in This State
High growth	10%	60%	5%
Moderate growth	20%	20%	25%
No growth	50%	10%	5%
Recession	20%	–25%	0%

---

[5] Also note that the AM return, estimated over the two years rather than over one year, is 0 because we ignore the intervening rate of return.

Estimate the expected return for each stock.

Solution

$$ER_A = .10(60) + .20(20) + .50(10) + .20(-25) = 10.00\%$$

$$ER_B = .10(5) + .20(25) + .50(5) + .20(0) = 8.00\%$$

The expected return in Example 8-4 is calculated conceptually the same as the AM calculated from historical data; the only difference is how we calculate the probabilities. With Example 8-4, we estimate the probabilities of each event directly. For example, economists might make estimates of different economic growth scenarios for the upcoming year, and then security analysts will estimate the prospects for each firm. This sort of scenario data can then be packaged into the data in the table in Example 8-4. In contrast the AM simply assumes that each observation is equally likely, so the probability of each event is reflected in how many times we observe it in the data. For example, the data from 1938 to 2005 will reflect the historical probabilities of the four different economic scenarios in the table without paying any attention to where we are today.

There are pros and cons to each method for determining expected rates of return. For short-term forecasts the scenario-based approach makes more sense, because where we are today has a huge bearing on what is likely to happen over a short period. However, for longer-run forecasts, the historical approach tends to be better, because like the performance of BEV, it reflects what actually happens even if it was not expected. In the next sections, we will use the scenario-based approach.

CONCEPT REVIEW QUESTIONS

1. What is the difference between ex ante and ex post returns?
2. Why does the income and capital gains component of the total return differ between common shares and bonds?
3. Why is the GM return a better estimate of long-run investment performance than the AM return?
4. Why might a scenario-based expected return be more accurate for a short-run expected return estimate than a historical AM estimate would?

8.2 MEASURING RISK

We have already touched on risk several times. Risk is the probability of incurring harm, and for investors harm generally means losing money or earning an inadequate rate of return. In the rest of this chapter, we will use *risk* to mean the probability that the actual return from an investment is less than the expected return.[6] This means that the more variable the possible returns, the greater the risk. We can see this in Figure 8-2, which graphs the actual returns for various investments from 1938 to 2005 whose averages were reported in Table 8-2. One

---

[6] Often, risk is defined as the probability that the actual return is less than the risk-free rate, because this reflects the alternative investment. However, for our purposes this distinction is not material.

thing that is quite obvious from the graph is the wide variation in returns for Canadian stocks and U.S. stocks relative to those for bonds and T-bills. For example, Canadian stock returns varied from a maximum of 48.43 percent to a minimum of −25.93 percent, while T-bill returns varied much less, with a maximum of 20.37 percent and a minimum of 0.37 percent.

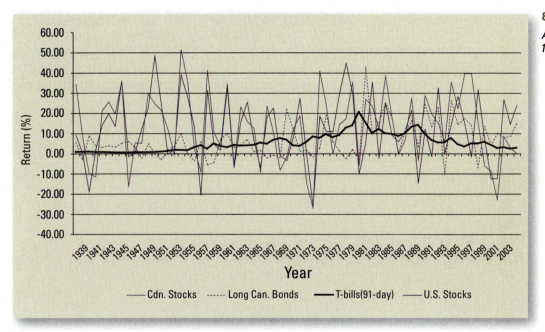

8-2   FIGURE

Annual Returns, 1938-2005

The difference between the maximum and minimum values is called the **range**, so Canadian common stocks had a range of annual returns of 74.36 percent, which is greater than that for T-bills at 20.00 percent. The range summarizes the visual evidence that the returns on common stocks are more variable than those for bonds or T-bills. However, a more accurate measure of risk is the **standard deviation**, because the range only uses two observations, the maximum and minimum, whereas the standard deviation uses all the observations.

range the difference between the maximum and minimum values

standard deviation a measure of risk over all the observations; the square root of the variance; denoted as σ

We reported the standard deviation of the 1938 to 2005 annual returns in Table 8-2 and discussed it when we pointed out the difference between the AM and GM returns. The standard deviation, like the range, clearly shows that common stock returns had a higher standard deviation in their annual returns than did bonds and T-bills over this period. This ranking of investments according to risk is the same ranking in terms of AM and GM returns, and it hints at a basic result in finance: risk and return go hand in hand. In other words, we normally see a tradeoff between risk and return: securities offering higher expected rates of return tend to be riskier. So let's measure this risk by using the standard deviation.

The definition of the standard deviation for a series of historical or ex post returns is as follows:

$$\text{Ex post } \sigma = \sqrt{\frac{\sum_{i=1}^{n}(r_i - \bar{r})^2}{n-1}}$$

[8-7]

where
σ = the standard deviation
$\bar{r}$ = the average return
r_i = the return in year i
n = the number of observations

variance the standard deviation squared; denoted as σ^2 and expressed in units of $\%^2$

The term inside the square root sign in Equation 8-7 is called the **variance**, which is denoted as σ^2. Therefore, the standard deviation is the square root of the variance, and, conversely, the variance is the square of the standard deviation. We focus on the standard deviation, because it is easier to interpret: the standard deviation for a return series is expressed in the same units as the returns, that is, as a percentage. In contrast, the variance is expressed in units of $\%^2$, which makes its interpretation less obvious.

Example 8-5: Calculating the Ex Post Standard Deviation

Estimate the standard deviation of the returns provided in Example 8-2 (i.e., 4.3 percent, 3.2 percent, 5.6 percent, 10.5 percent, and -7.6 percent).

Solution

Recall from Example 8-2 that the arithmetic average for this series of returns was 3.20 percent.

Therefore, we can estimate the standard deviation as follows:

$$\sigma = \sqrt{\frac{(4.3-3.2)^2 + (3.2-3.2)^2 + (5.6-3.2)^2 + (10.5-3.2)^2 + (-7.6-3.2)^2}{5-1}}$$

$$= \sqrt{\frac{1.21 + 0 + 5.76 + 53.29 + 116.64}{4}} = \sqrt{\frac{176.9}{4}} = \sqrt{44.225} = 6.65\%$$

Notice that the variance of this return series is 44.225($\%^2$).

The standard deviation, as we have measured it, estimates the variability of the returns over the sample period. In the case of Example 8-5, this is 6.65 percent. For the investment returns from 1938 to 2005, the standard deviation of the annual returns for common shares was 16.22 percent and that for bonds was 9.32 percent. This raises the question of whether or not this relative risk was constant over the entire period. The graph in Figure 8-3 is the ratio of the standard deviation of the returns on common shares to that on long Canada bonds. To see how this has changed over time, the estimates are based on rolling 10-year periods going back to 1924, so the first estimate is the ratio for 1924 to 1933, the second for 1925 to 1934, and so on.

What is clear is that the relative risk of equities versus bonds has not been constant over this long period. Until the 1960s, the annual rates of return on common shares were about four times more variable than those on bonds. Since then, and increasingly over the last 20 years, they have only been twice as variable. Just as the AM estimate of the annual return reflects the economic circumstances of the period over which it is estimated, so too does the standard deviation. For this reason, we also calculate the scenario-based standard deviation as a measure of risk.

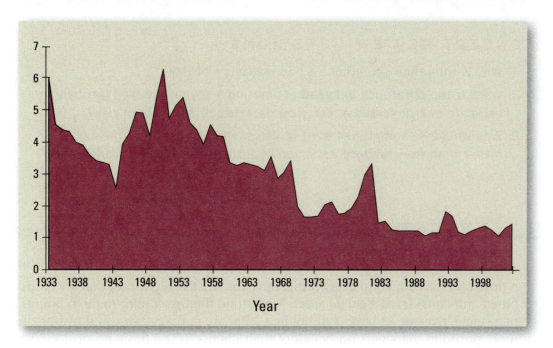

The scenario-based standard deviation can be estimated by using Equation 8-8. We will refer to this as the ex ante measure because we are explicitly taking into account updated probabilities of future events happening (where all variables are as defined in Equation 8-6).

$$\text{Ex ante } \sigma = \sqrt{\sum_{i=1}^{n} (\text{Prob}_i)(r_i - ER_i)^2}$$ [8-8]

Example 8-6: Estimating Ex Ante Standard Deviations

Estimate the standard deviations for stocks A and B from Example 8-4, using the information provided in that example.

Solution

$$\sigma_A = \sqrt{.10(60-10)^2 + .20(20-10)^2 + .50(10-10)^2 + .20(-25-10)^2}$$

$$= \sqrt{250 + 20 + 0 + 245} = \sqrt{515} = 22.69\%$$

$$\sigma_B = \sqrt{.10(5.0-8.0)^2 + .20(25-8.0)^2 + .50(5-8.0)^2 + .20(0-8.0)^2}$$

$$= \sqrt{0.9 + 57.8 + 4.5 + 12.8} = \sqrt{76.00} = 8.72\%$$

Notice that A has the highest standard deviation; therefore, it appears to have the most risk based on the variability of the forecast return around its expected return.

8.3 EXPECTED RETURN AND RISK FOR PORTFOLIOS

portfolio a collection of securities, such as stocks and bonds, that are combined and considered a single asset

modern portfolio theory (MPT) the theory that securities should be managed within a portfolio, rather than individually, to create risk-reduction gains; also stipulates that investors should diversify their investments so as not to be unnecessarily exposed to a single negative event

A **portfolio** is a collection of securities, such as stocks and bonds, that are combined and considered a single asset. A portfolio then may refer to the holdings of a single investor, as well as to holdings that are managed as a unit by one or more portfolio managers on behalf of their clients. It is a basic proposition in finance that securities should be managed within a portfolio rather than individually, because risk-reduction gains are possible by combining securities into a portfolio. The general topic is called **modern portfolio theory (MPT)**, and we will be using the statistical ideas that we have just discussed to explore it. The basic idea is as simple as the old adage "don't put all your eggs in one basket": investors should diversify their investments so that they are not unnecessarily exposed to a single negative event. MPT takes this basic idea and operationalizes it to show how to form portfolios with the highest possible expected rate of return for any given level of risk. First, we examine how to calculate the expected return and risk of a portfolio.

The *expected return* on a portfolio is simply the *weighted average* of the expected returns on the individual securities in the portfolio, as expressed in Equation 8-9. The *portfolio weight* of a particular security is the percentage of the portfolio's total value that is invested in that security. These weights sum to one, because 100 percent of the portfolio must be invested in something, even if it is in cash.

[8-9]

$$ER_P = \sum_{i=1}^{n}(w_i \times ER_i)$$

where ER_P = the expected return on the portfolio
ER_i = the expected return on security i
w_i = the portfolio weight of security i

Example 8-7: Estimating Expected Portfolio Return

Using the data from Example 8-4, estimate the expected return for a portfolio that has $600 invested in stock A and $1,400 invested in stock B.

Solution

Portfolio value = 600 + 1,400 = 2,000
w_A = 600/2,000 = 0.30
w_B = 1,400/2,000 = 0.70
So, $ER_P = w_A ER_A + w_B ER_B$ = (0.30)(10%) + (0.70)(8.0%) = 8.60%

This means that if an investor puts 70 percent of his or her investment in security B, then the remaining 30 percent has to be in A. We can simplify the expected return formula in the two-security case to make it more informative. Let us define w as simply the weight placed on security A, so that $(1 - w)$ is the weight placed on security B. In this case, we can rearrange the expected return for a two-security portfolio formula to get Equation 8-10:

$$ER_p = ER_B + w(ER_A - ER_B)$$

[8-10]

For example, if we place a weight of 0 in A, then by definition 100 percent is invested in B, and we expect to earn 8.0 percent, the expected return on B. Conversely, if we invest 100 percent in A and nothing in B, then we expect to earn 10 percent. Incrementally, as we increase w and put more money (weight) in A, then we pick up the difference in the expected returns between A and B, which, with the numbers from Example 8-7, is 2.0 percent. In financial terms, the cost of investing in A is the lost 8.0 percent expected return from not investing in B, whereas the benefit is its expected return of 10 percent. There is a net advantage in terms of expected return of 2.0 percent.

We graph this relationship in Figure 8-4. Note that the graph sets the base return at 8.0 percent, where everything is invested in B, and then increases to 10 percent as we invest more and more in A.[7]

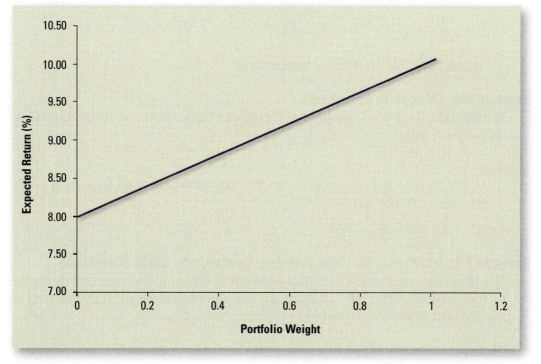

8-4   FIGURE

Expected Portfolio Return

---

[7] For the purposes of this discussion, we have limited the investment weights to a range from 0 percent to 100 percent. However, if we are allowed to *short sell* either security, then the weights can be less than 0 (i.e., negative) and more than 100 percent. Short selling means investors sell shares in a stock that they do not own. This can be done through a broker who "lends" investors shares that they can sell on the condition that the investors agree to "replace" these borrowed shares in the future (i.e., by buying them in the market). Thus, it provides investors with a way to profit from the belief that share prices will decrease. There are several technicalities associated with short selling that we will not discuss here. The main implication of short selling for our present discussion is that investors can maintain a negative position in one of the two stocks, so they can short sell A and use the proceeds to invest in B and vice versa.

Regardless of the number of assets held in a portfolio or the portfolio weights, the expected return on the portfolio is *always* a weighted average of the expected return on each individual asset. However, this is *not* the case for the portfolio standard deviation, because we must account for correlations, or co-movements, among the individual security returns included in the portfolio, which in turn affect the variability in total portfolio returns. Therefore, the standard deviation for a portfolio will reflect the weighted impact of the individual securities' standard deviations and the relationship among the co-movements of the returns on those individual securities.

covariance a statistical measure of the correlation of the fluctuations of the annual rates of return of different investments

The standard deviation of a two-security portfolio can be estimated by using Equation 8-11. Notice that the first two terms inside the square root sign account for the weighted individual security standard deviations (or variances), while the third term accounts for the weighted co-movement of the returns on the two securities. This is denoted by the **covariance** of the returns on A and B (COV_{AB}), which we define below.

[8-11]

$$\sigma_p = \sqrt{(w_A)^2(\sigma_A)^2 + (w_B)^2(\sigma_B)^2 + 2(w_A)(w_B)(COV_{A,B})}$$

where σ_P = the portfolio standard deviation
COV_{AB} = the covariance of the returns on security A and security B

The covariance is calculated as follows:[8]

[8-12]

$$COV_{AB} = \sum_{i=1}^{n} Prob_i(r_{A,i} - \bar{r}_A)(r_{B,i} - \bar{r}_B)$$

where $r_{A,i}$ = the ith return on security A

Example 8-8: Estimating Covariance

By using the data from Example 8-4, estimate the covariance of the returns on securities A and B.

Solution

$COV_{A,B} = .10(60 - 10)(5.0 - 8.0) + .20(20 - 10)(25 - 8.0) + .50(10 - 10)(5 - 8.0)$
$+ .20(-25 - 10)(0 - 8.0)$

$= -15 + 34 + 0 + 56 = 75\%^2$

Example 8-9: Estimating Portfolio Standard Deviation by Using Covariance

Use the covariance estimate in Example 8-8 to estimate the standard deviation of the portfolio described in Example 8-7, which has 30 percent invested in stock A and 70 percent invested in stock B.

Solution

Using Equation 8-11, we get:

$$\sigma_p = \sqrt{(0.30)^2(22.69)^2 + (0.70)^2(8.72)^2 + 2(0.30)(0.70)(75)}$$

$$= \sqrt{46.335 + 37.259 + 31.500} = \sqrt{115.094} = 10.73\%$$

---

[8] The ex post covariance can be calculated as $COV_{AB} = \dfrac{\sum_{i=1}^{n}(r_{A,i} - \bar{r}_A)(r_{B,i} - \bar{r}_B)}{n-1}$

Notice that the portfolio standard deviation of 10.73 percent is *less than* the weighted average of the standard deviations of each individual security, which is 12.91 percent that is, (0.30)(22.69) + (0.70)(8.72). This is always the case, except for one special situation, which we will discuss momentarily. However, before we do, we demonstrate the implication of this difference by graphing the standard deviation of the return on the portfolio as we put a greater share of our investment in the riskier security in Figure 8-5.

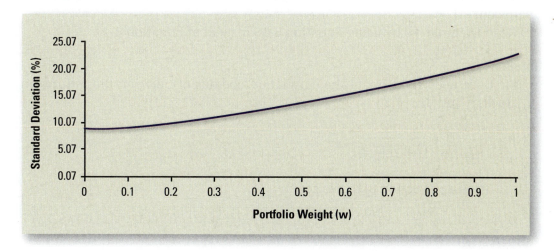

8-5 FIGURE

Portfolio Risk

Notice that we start out with the standard deviation of the portfolio at 8.72 percent because all funds are in B, and we finish up at 22.69 percent because all funds are in A, but in between it is not straight line. In fact, the standard deviation of the portfolio's return barely moves as we move to 20 percent invested in the riskier security, even though we expect to earn a higher rate of return. This is a clear win for the investor: more expected return and virtually the same amount of risk.

The curve that shows the standard deviation of the portfolio's return as we increase the investment in the risky security is distinctly "bowed." To see this, think of rotating the graph counterclockwise and then pulling on the bottom of the bow: you get the shape of the standard deviation of the portfolio return. We will return to this bow shape again as it is one of the most important ideas in MPT. For now, we turn to a discussion of another measure of return co-movements.

Although covariance provides a useful measure of the relationship of the co-movements of returns on individual securities, it is difficult to interpret intuitively because, as was the case with the variance, the unit is percent squared (%^{2}). Fortunately, covariance is related to another statistical measure, the **correlation coefficient** (ρ_{AB}), which can be interpreted more intuitively. The correlation coefficient is related to covariance and individual standard deviations according to the relationship shown in Equation 8-13:

correlation coefficient a statistical measure that identifies how security returns move in relation to one another; denoted by ρ_{AB}

$$\rho_{AB} = \frac{COV_{AB}}{\sigma_A \sigma_B}$$

[8-13]

This equation can be solved for covariance to provide Equation 8-14:

$$COV_{AB} = \rho_{AB} \sigma_A \sigma_B$$

[8-14]

Finally, we can replace the covariance term in Equation 8-11 to produce Equation 8-15, which is commonly used to estimate portfolio standard deviation.

[8-15]

$$\sigma_p = \sqrt{(w_A)^2(\sigma_A)^2 + (w_B)^2(\sigma_B)^2 + 2(w_A)(w_B)(\rho_{A,B})(\sigma_A)(\sigma_B)}$$

Example 8-10: Estimating Portfolio Standard Deviation by Using the Correlation Coefficient

Redo Example 8-9 by using Equation 8-15 instead of Equation 8-11.

Solution

First, we need to estimate the correlation coefficient between the returns on stocks A and B.

$$\rho_{AB} = \frac{COV_{AB}}{\sigma_A\sigma_B} = \frac{75}{(22.69)(8.72)} = 0.379$$

By using Equation 8-15, we get

$$\sigma_p = \sqrt{(0.30)^2(22.69)^2 + (0.70)^2(8.72)^2 + 2(0.30)(0.70)(0.379)(22.69)(8.72)}$$

$$= \sqrt{46.335 + 37.25 + 31.49} = \sqrt{115} = 10.72\%$$

This is the same answer as in Example 8-9, except for a small rounding difference. We can now separate the standard deviation component from the correlation component. This is useful because we already have the standard deviation of both securities in the first two terms, so the correlation coefficient is the only *new* information.

Correlation Coefficient

The correlation coefficient measures how security returns move in relation to one another. It is a relative measure that has a maximum value of +1.0, which denotes *perfect positive correlation*, and a minimum value of −1.0, which denotes *perfect negative correlation*. Positive correlation coefficients imply that the returns on security A tend to move in the *same* direction as those on security B. In other words, when the return on security B goes up, the return on security A also tends to go up, and vice versa. It doesn't mean to say that they always go up together; if they did, they would be perfectly positively correlated. Negative correlation coefficients imply the opposite: the returns on security A tend to move in the *opposite* direction to those on security B. In other words, on average, when the return on security B goes up, the return on security A tends to go down, and vice versa.

The closer the absolute value of the correlation coefficient is to one, the stronger the relationship between the returns on the two securities. In fact, when $\rho_{AB} = +1$, that is, perfect positive correlation, and we know the return on one security, we can predict the return on the other security with certainty.[9] The same applies when we have $\rho_{AB} = -1$, that is, perfect negative correlation, which implies the returns have a perfect negative relationship with each other. When $\rho_{AB} = 0$ (i.e., zero correlation), there is no relationship between the returns on the two securities. Therefore, knowing the return on one security provides no useful information for predicting the return of the second security.

The extreme correlation coefficient values described above do not occur for traditional common shares in practice, because so many different factors influence security returns. Generally, security returns display positive correlations with one another but they are less than one. This is logical because all securities tend to follow the movements of the overall market. As expected, the correlations tend to be higher among securities whose companies are similar in nature, for example, if they are in the same industry, are about the same size, and so on. For example, the correlation coefficient on the common share returns for the Big Six Canadian banks tends to be high in the 0.70 to 0.80 range, while the correlation coefficient between bank stocks and mining stocks tends to be much lower, in the 0.20 to 0.40 range. So the correlation coefficient in our example of 0.379 indicates two securities that are not in the same industry or are not affected similarly by the same economic forces.

Figure 8-6a provides a scatter plot diagram of the returns on Canadian common shares relative to those on U.S. common shares. As expected, these returns possess a high and positive correlation coefficient of 0.69. Indeed, the graph shows that the returns tend to move in the same direction—that is, they both tend to be high or low at similar times. If we attempted to fit a line to these observations, it would be upward sloping, and the points would be relatively close to this line. Figure 8-6b depicts the returns on Canadian common shares relative to those on 91-day T-bills, which display a correlation coefficient that is close to zero (-0.09). The graph shows that knowing the return on one security provides little information about the return on the other: in other words, it would be hard to draw a line through these returns that depicts any kind of relationship.[10]

Finally, we can compare the correlation coefficient with the covariance. As noted in Equation 8-13, the covariance is the correlation coefficient multiplied by the two standard deviations. As a result, the covariance measures the *strength*, or magnitude, of the relationship between two variables. For example, two variables might be perfectly correlated, so that they always move together, but one of them might barely move at all: it might always go up when the other goes up, and vice versa, but not by very much. As a result, the covariance between these two variables might be lower than that between two other variables that are not so highly correlated.

[9] Technically, when $\rho = +1$ or -1 and we plot the returns of one asset on the x-axis and the returns on the other security on the y-axis, we can draw a straight line through the points, and all of them will lie on the line. Such a line would be upward sloping when $\rho = +1$, and it would be downward sloping when $\rho = -1$.

[10] If we did draw a line, it would be downward sloping, as indicated by the slight negative correlation coefficient. However, the small absolute value of the coefficient indicates it would not fit the data very well.

FIGURE 8-6a

*Canadian versus U.S. Stock
Returns (1938-2005)
(correlation coefficient=0.69)*

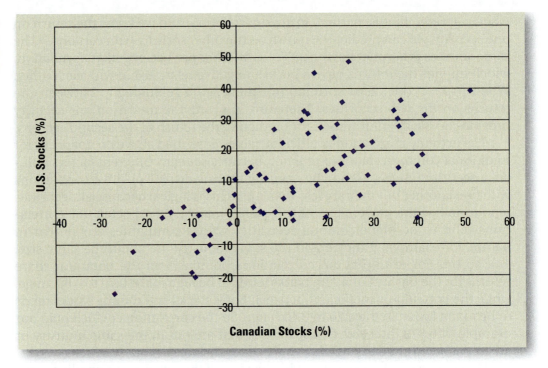

FIGURE 8-6b

*T-Bill Returns versus Canadian
Stock Returns (1938-2005)
(correlation coefficient=-0.09)*

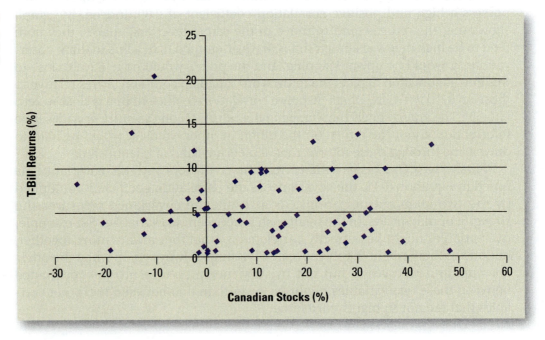

Correlation Coefficients and Portfolio Standard Deviation

Recall that Equation 8-15 showed that the correlation between the returns on the two securities included in a portfolio affected the portfolio standard deviation. Holding the weights and the individual standard deviations constant, it is clear that the lower the correlation coefficient, the lower the standard deviation. Example 8-11 illustrates.

Example 8-11: Estimating Portfolio Standard Deviation as the Correlation Coefficient Changes

Redo Example 8-10 by using Equation 8-15, but now assume that the correlation coefficient between the returns on A and B are

a. −1.0   **b.** 0.0   **c.** 0.60   **d.** 1.0

Solution

a. $\sigma_p = \sqrt{(0.30)^2(22.69)^2 + (0.70)^2(8.72)^2 + 2(0.30)(0.70)(-1.0)(22.69)(8.72)}$

$= \sqrt{46.335 + 37.259 - 83.100} = 0.703\%$

b. $\sigma_p = \sqrt{(0.30)^2(22.69)^2 + (0.70)^2(8.72)^2 + 2(0.30)(0.70)(0.0)(22.69)(8.72)}$

$= \sqrt{46.335 + 37.259 + 0} = 9.143\%$

c. $\sigma_p = \sqrt{(0.30)^2(22.69)^2 + (0.70)^2(8.72)^2 + 2(0.30)(0.70)(0.60)(22.69)(8.72)}$

$= \sqrt{46.335 + 37.259 + 49.860} = 11.552\%$

d. $\sigma_p = \sqrt{(0.30)^2(22.69)^2 + (0.70)^2(8.72)^2 + 2(0.30)(0.70)(1.0)(22.69)(8.72)}$

$= \sqrt{46.335 + 37.259 + 83.100} = 12.911\%$

There are several things to note from Example 8-11. First, the lower the correlation coefficient, the lower the portfolio standard deviation. In fact, the portfolio standard deviation in part a is much lower than either individual standard deviation and is actually very close to zero. Obviously, the benefits will be greater as the correlation coefficient approaches −1. This highlights the importance of security return correlations in determining portfolio risk.

Second, the portfolio standard deviation is *less than* the weighted average of the individual security standard deviations (of 12.911 percent) in parts a to c, as it was in Example 8-10, for which the correlation coefficient was +0.379. Only in part d, for which the correlation coefficient equals +1, which is its highest possible value, was it a weighted average. Because +1 is the maximum value for the correlation coefficient, it must be the case that for all other possible correlation coefficients, we have $\sigma_P < w_A\sigma_A + w_B\sigma_B$. This implies there will be benefits from diversification as long as $\rho_{AB} < +1$, which is virtually always the case.

This result is very important because we have just shown the secret of MPT: by combining securities into portfolios, we can reduce risk. This risk reduction increases as we combine securities that are less than perfectly correlated. It supports the basic finance argument that investors should hold diversified portfolios; otherwise, they are throwing away the magic of diversification: they can lower risk without cost. We will return to this shortly, but we graph the standard deviation of the portfolio return as the correlation coefficient changes in Figure 8-7.

FIGURE   8-7

The Impact of the
Correlation Coefficient

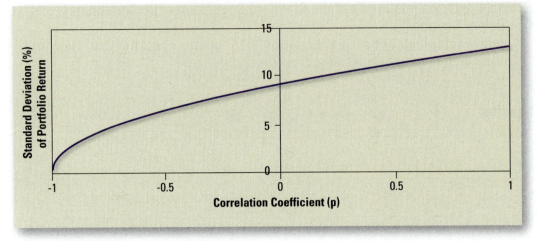

This graph shows several interesting things. First, the slope is not linear, as discussed before. This means that to demonstrate the effect of the correlation coefficient, we can use a zero correlation as an example, because this simplifies the arithmetic. Second, with perfectly negative correlation, the variability of the portfolio is reduced to almost zero, which means there is almost no risk. In fact, whenever the correlation coefficient equals −1, there exists one set of portfolio weights for the two securities such that we can eliminate risk completely. This suggests that to discuss how the standard deviation and expected return of a portfolio varies as we change its composition, we can look at three special cases: when the correlation coefficient between the two securities is zero, plus one, or minus one.

Let's go back to Equation 8-15, which for ease of reference we repeat below.

$$\sigma_p = \sqrt{(w_A)^2(\sigma_A)^2 + (w_B)^2(\sigma_B)^2 + 2(w_A)(w_B)(\rho_{A,B})(\sigma_A)(\sigma_B)}$$

The three special cases produce simplified versions of the standard deviation of the portfolio's return as follows:[11]

If $\rho = 0$ $\sigma_p = \sqrt{(w_A)^2(\sigma_A)^2 + (w_B)^2(\sigma_B)^2}$

If $\rho = +1$ $\sigma_p = \sqrt{(w_A)^2(\sigma_A)^2 + (w_B)^2(\sigma_B)^2 + 2(w_A)(w_B)(\sigma_A)(\sigma_B)}$

If $\rho = -1$ $\sigma_p = \sqrt{(w_A)^2(\sigma_A)^2 + (w_B)^2(\sigma_B)^2 - 2(w_A)(w_B)(\sigma_A)(\sigma_B)}$

The zero correlation coefficient case is obvious as the covariance term disappears. However, in the other two cases, the correlation coefficient also disappears because it is either +1 or −1. We now get a perfect square: for a perfect positive correlation, think $(a + b)^2$, and for a perfect negative correlation, $(a - b)^2$, where a is the standard deviation of security A times its portfolio weight (i.e., $w_A\sigma_A$) and b is the same for security B (i.e., $w_B\sigma_B$). This allows us to simplify the equation for the standard deviation of the portfolio return.

Figure 8-5 showed how the portfolio risk (standard deviation) varied with the composition of the portfolio (i.e., for the weights invested in A and B) for our example case, for which the correlation coefficient was 0.379. Now we can consider how the variability changes with the portfolio composition for these three special cases, because they contain everything of interest. The results are shown in Figure 8-8.

[11] Remember these as they often appear on tests and exams.

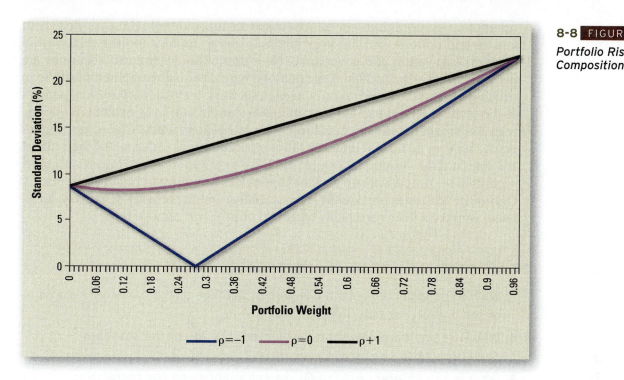

Note that with perfect positive correlation, the variability changes in a linear (straight line) fashion with the portfolio weights. As we discussed before, in this case the standard deviation of the portfolio is a weighted average of each security's standard deviation, similar to the expected return. However, when the correlation is less than perfectly positive, the relationship is "bowed" and it gets more bowed as the correlation decreases until, with a perfect negative correlation, we can remove all risk. In this case, the bow becomes two straight lines that touch the horizontal axis. At this point in the $\rho = -1$ case, we can create a portfolio with a standard deviation of zero and no variability at all.

To calculate the portfolio that removes all risk (i.e., creates a portfolio with no variability), consider the special case of Equation 8-15, which reduces to Equation 8-16 when $\rho = -1$:

$$\sigma_p = w\sigma_A - (1-w)\sigma_B$$

[8-16]

Here, we have set the portfolio weights as w and $(1 - w)$ rather than w_A and w_B because they have to add to 100 percent. If we set the standard deviation of the portfolio equal to zero, we can solve for this weight:

$$w = \frac{\sigma_B}{\sigma_A + \sigma_B}$$

[8-17]

In our case, the weight is 27.76 percent, so if we put 27.76 percent of our investment in security A and 72.24 percent in the lower risk security B, then we get a portfolio that is risk free, that is, it has no variability at all. We can see this point in Figure 8-8, in which the two lines for the perfect negative correlation case cut the horizontal axis at just below 0.3.

The perfect negative correlation case is of great importance in finance, because it is the basis of hedging, which is to take an offsetting position so as to minimize risk. Hedging will be discussed in more detail when we deal with futures and options, but the principle helps us to understand the relationship between correlation and covariance. Note that although the two securities are perfectly negatively correlated, we do not create an equally weighted portfolio in which we invest the same amount in each security. Instead, we put 27.76 percent in the security with the greatest standard deviation and 72.24 percent in the one with the smaller standard deviation. This is because when A goes up, B goes down, but they go up and down by different amounts, as indicated by their different standard deviations. As a result, we have to put *more* in the lower-variability security B to compensate for the fact that it does not move as much as security A. Only if the securities are equally risky, as well as being perfectly negatively correlated, would we form an equally balanced portfolio to remove risk.

CONCEPT REVIEW QUESTIONS

1. Why is the expected return a weighted average of the expected returns of the underlying securities?

2. Why isn't standard deviation a weighted average of the standard deviations of the underlying securities?

3. What is the difference between the covariance and the correlation coefficient?

4. Why can you always remove all risk in a two-security portfolio if the securities are perfectly negatively correlated?

5. In Question 4, is the zero-risk portfolio generally equally weighted in both securities?

8.4 THE EFFICIENT FRONTIER

Two-Security Portfolio Combinations

Figure 8-4 showed how the expected return of a two-security portfolio (with a correlation coefficient of 0.379) changed as we changed the composition by shifting more of our investment toward security A (the riskier security), while Figure 8-5 showed how the portfolio standard deviation changed. Appendix 8A demonstrates how we can vary the weights in each security and determine the resulting portfolio expected returns and standard deviations. If we plot these expected return–standard deviation combinations, with expected return on the vertical axis and standard deviation on the horizontal axis, we get Figure 8-9, which represents all possible portfolio combinations that can be constructed by varying the weights in our two securities, A and B.[12]

The *parabola-shaped* frontier depicted in Figure 8-9 was created using only securities B and A, which had expected returns of 8 percent and 10 percent, standard deviations of 8.72 percent and 22.69 percent, and a correlation coefficient of 0.379. If we had combined two other securities, we would obtain a

---

[12] Note that to construct this entire diagram, we have allowed the weights invested in either security to assume values above 1.0 and below 0 (i.e., we have permitted short selling—refer to footnote 7).

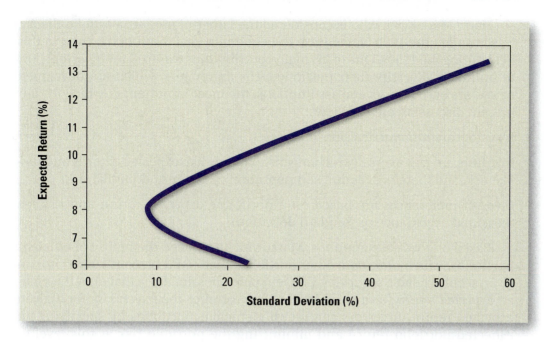

slightly different shape. However, as long as the correlation coefficient is not close to either extreme value (i.e., −1 or +1), this general parabola shape will prevail. Further, because risky securities in general tend to have positive correlation coefficients that are less than one, the shape depicted in Figure 8-9 can be generalized for portfolios formed by using most actual securities.

The Efficient Frontier

We can generalize from the two-security to the *n*-security case, for which the expected return will continue to be a weighted average of the expected returns on the individual securities, regardless of the number of securities in the portfolio. As a result, Equation 8-9 for estimating portfolio expected returns still applies, and the portfolio weights still have to sum to 100 percent. However, calculating the standard deviation on a portfolio of more than two securities becomes cumbersome quite quickly as the number of securities increases. For example, a three-security portfolio can be calculated by using Equation 8-18, which has three weighted variance terms and three weighted co-movement terms:

$$\sigma_p = \sqrt{\begin{aligned}&(w_A)^2(\sigma_A)^2 + (w_B)^2(\sigma_B)^2 + (w_C)^2(\sigma_C)^2 + 2(w_A)(w_B)(\rho_{A,B})(\sigma_A)(\sigma_B)\\&+ 2(w_A)(w_C)(\rho_{AC})(\sigma_A)(\sigma_C) + 2(w_B)(w_C)(\rho_{BC})(\sigma_B)(\sigma_C)\end{aligned}}$$

[8-18]

The four-security portfolio would similarly have four variance terms and six co-movement terms, the five-security portfolio would have five variance terms and 10 co-movement terms, and so on. A 100-security portfolio would have 100 variance terms and 4,950 co-movement terms.[13] Obviously, the more securities in a portfolio, the greater the relative impact of the security co-movements on the overall portfolio risk, and the lower the relative impact of the individual risks.[14]

---

[13] We can represent all these terms in a compact way by using matrix algebra.

[14] We will elaborate on this last point in the next section.

Harry Markowitz, who is considered the father of modern portfolio theory, was awarded the 1990 Nobel Prize in Economics as a result of his work in this field during the 1950s. One of his main contributions was to show investors how to optimally diversify their portfolios. His arguments, which are developed below, are based on several assumptions, the most important of which for our present discussion are as follows:

risk averse to dislike risk, and require compensation to assume additional risk

1. Investors are *rational* decision-makers.

2. Investors are **risk averse** (which means that they like expected returns and dislike risk, and therefore require compensation to assume additional risk).

3. Investor preferences are based on a portfolio's expected return and risk (as measured by variance or standard deviation).

efficient portfolios those portfolios that offer the highest expected return for a given level of risk, or offer the lowest risk for a given expected return

Based on these assumptions, Markowitz introduced the notion of **efficient portfolios**, which *dominate* other portfolios that could be constructed from a given set of available securities. Efficient portfolios are those that offer the *highest expected return* for a given level of risk, or offer the *lowest risk* for a given expected return. Investors can identify efficient portfolios by specifying an expected portfolio return and minimizing the portfolio risk at this level of return, or by specifying a portfolio risk level they are willing to assume and maximizing the expected return given that level of risk.

minimum variance frontier the curve produced when determining the expected return-risk combinations available to investors from a given set of securities by allowing the portfolio weights to vary

The first step in the Markowitz analysis is to determine the expected return-risk combinations available to investors from a given set of securities, by allowing the portfolio weights to vary, just as we did in Figure 8-9 when we considered only two securities. The entire curve is referred to as the **minimum variance frontier**, which is illustrated in Figure 8-10.[15] Although our discussion has focused on plotting expected return against standard deviation, remember that the variance is just the standard deviation squared.

Notice that the shape is virtually identical to the frontier we constructed using only two securities in Figure 8-9. However, although the shape is similar, by using all available securities, we will be able to generate a set of more efficient portfolios, in the sense of offering higher expected return for a given risk level, or lower risk for a given expected return level.

The other difference between Figure 8-9 and 8-10 is the five portfolios marked A through E that we have included in Figure 8-10. All the portfolios that lie along the efficient frontier, including B, E, and D, are attainable by combining the underlying securities. They are referred to as the **attainable portfolios**. Portfolios A and C, conversely, which lie above and below the efficient frontier, are *not* attainable. Portfolio A is not attainable in the sense that there is no way that the underlying securities can be combined in such a way to achieve this combination of expected return and risk. It is simply impossible. Portfolio C is unattainable in a different sense: it can be attained only by deliberately wasting money—that is, by simply not investing some portion of wealth and leaving money to earn zero return. It means that the portfolio is not formed by efficient combinations of the underlying securities.

attainable portfolios portfolios that may be constructed by combining the underlying securities

This leaves us with portfolios B, D, and E, which do lie on the minimum variance frontier. Here we can ignore portfolio D because it is a *dominated* portfolio, even though it lies on the minimum variance frontier. Like portfolio C, which is

---

[15] Although Appendix 8A shows how to solve for all available portfolio weights in the two-security case, this is impractical when a large number of securities are available. However, the problem can be easily solved by using a *quadratic programming model* that chooses optimal *portfolio weights* in the available securities in order to minimize the risk of the portfolio for a given level of expected return. This optimization problem is subject to a wealth constraint (i.e., the sum of the weights in the individual securities must equal total wealth, or 1.0) and is also constrained by the return-risk characteristics of the available set of securities.

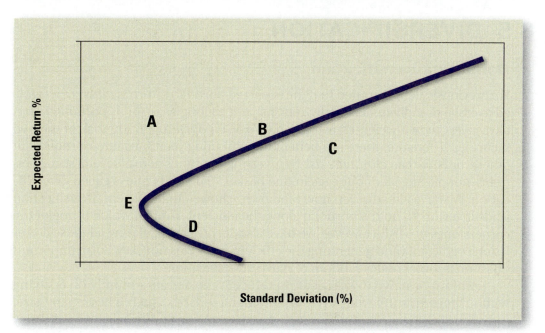

The Efficient Frontier

inefficient (as well as dominated), portfolio D offers a lower expected rate of return for the same risk as another portfolio on the upper half of the minimum variance frontier. We can see this by drawing a vertical line though D. The point where it intersects the top part of the minimum variance frontier indicates a portfolio with the same standard deviation of return but a higher expected rate of return. Portfolio E is a special portfolio: it lies on the efficient frontier and also has the minimum amount of portfolio risk available from any possible combination of available securities. It is referred to as the **minimum variance portfolio (MVP)**.

The importance of the MVP is that portfolios that lie below it on the bottom segment of the minimum variance frontier are *dominated* by portfolios on the upper segment. The segment of the minimum variance frontier above the global minimum variance portfolio, therefore, offers the best risk-expected return combinations available to investors from this particular set of securities. This segment includes the set of efficient portfolios that is commonly referred to as the **efficient frontier**. Rational, risk-averse,[16] investors will be interested in holding only those portfolios, like B, that offer the highest expected return for their given level of risk. In this sense, these portfolios are not dominated by other attainable portfolios. In fact, the efficient frontier is the cornerstone of MPT.

Finally, the particular portfolio chosen by an investor will depend on his or her risk preferences. A more aggressive (i.e., less risk averse) investor might choose Portfolio B in Figure 8-10, while a more conservative (i.e., more risk averse) investor might prefer Portfolio E (i.e., the MVP).

minimum variance portfolio (MVP) a portfolio that lies on the efficient frontier and has the minimum amount of portfolio risk available from any possible combination of available securities

efficient frontier the set of portfolios that offer the highest expected return for their given level of risk that rational; the only portfolios that risk averse investors will want to hold

CONCEPT REVIEW QUESTIONS

1. How do you form the minimum variance frontier in the two-security case?
2. What assumptions about investors underlie Markowitz's theories regarding efficient portfolios?
3. Why is the efficient frontier bowed?
4. What is an unattainable portfolio, and what is a dominated portfolio?

---

[16] We will talk more about risk aversion in the next chapter.

8.5 DIVERSIFICATION

Domestic Diversification

We previously demonstrated that the expected portfolio return is *always* a weighted average of individual security returns, and as long as $\rho_{AB} < +1$, portfolio risk is always *less than* a weighted average (i.e., $\sigma_p < w_A \sigma_A + w_B \sigma_B$) of the risk of the two securities. Therefore, there is a benefit to combining securities into portfolios. In other words, we can *eliminate risk* by investing our funds across several securities, or by "not putting all of our eggs in one basket." This principle is called **diversification**. We have already seen how Markowitz showed that efficient diversification leads investors to hold a portfolio along the efficient frontier, which is one of the cornerstones of MPT. However, we have also seen that calculating all those correlation coefficients and generating the efficient frontier is not easy. So an important question is, how good is random or naïve diversification?

Random or naïve diversification refers to the act of randomly diversifying without regard to relevant investment characteristics, such as company size, industry classification, and so on.[17] An investor randomly selects a relatively large number of securities. Figure 8-11 plots the actual monthly data for Canadian stocks over the 1985 to 1997 period, based on the data reported in Table 8-3, to illustrate naïve diversification in practice. Portfolio risk for a randomly selected portfolio was reduced to approximately 4.5 percent per month over this period. As securities are added to the portfolio, the total risk associated with the portfolio of stocks declines rapidly. The first few stocks cause a large decrease in portfolio risk. Based on this data, 46 percent of portfolio standard deviation is eliminated as we go from 1 to 10 securities.

diversification the elimination of risk by investing funds across several securities

random or naïve diversification the act of randomly buying securities without regard to relevant investment characteristics, such as company size, industry classification, and so on

---

FIGURE   8-11

Diversification with Canadian Stocks

Source: Adapted from Cleary, S. and D. Copp, "Diversification with Canadian Stocks: How Much Is Enough?" Canadian Investment Review (Fall 1999) Figure 1.

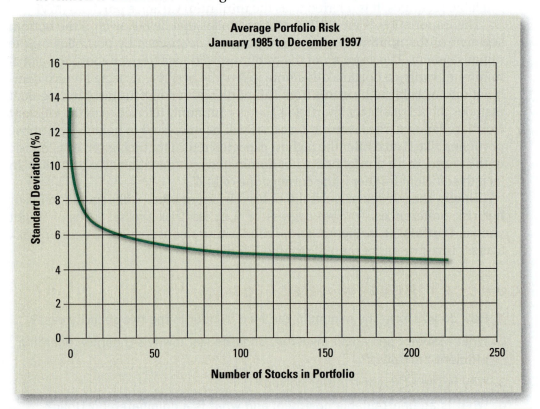

Average Portfolio Risk
January 1985 to December 1997

---

[17] This is commonly represented in cartoons as someone throwing darts into a dartboard to randomly pick stocks. Nowadays we do it with computers.

Table 8-3   Monthly Canadian Stock Portfolio Returns, January 1985 to December 1997

Number of Stocks in Portfolio	Average Monthly Portfolio Return (%)	Standard Deviation of Average Monthly Portfolio Return (%)	Ratio of Portfolio Standard Deviation to Standard Deviation of a Single Stock	Percentage of Total Achievable Risk Reduction
1	1.51	13.47	1.00	0.00
2	1.51	10.99	0.82	27.50
3	1.52	9.91	0.74	39.56
4	1.53	9.30	0.69	46.37
5	1.52	8.67	0.64	53.31
6	1.52	8.30	0.62	57.50
7	1.51	7.95	0.59	61.35
8	1.52	7.71	0.57	64.02
9	1.52	7.52	0.56	66.17
10	1.51	7.33	0.54	68.30
12	1.51	7.03	0.52	71.58
14	1.51	6.80	0.50	74.19
16	1.52	6.63	0.49	76.04
18	1.52	6.51	0.48	77.41
20	1.52	6.39	0.47	78.65
22	1.52	6.25	0.46	80.30
24	1.52	6.15	0.46	81.32
26	1.52	6.07	0.45	82.25
28	1.52	5.99	0.44	83.18
30	1.52	5.91	0.44	84.06
35	1.52	5.76	0.43	85.68
40	1.52	5.62	0.42	87.24
45	1.52	5.50	0.41	88.56
50	1.52	5.41	0.40	89.64
60	1.52	5.25	0.39	91.40
70	1.51	5.12	0.38	92.86
80	1.51	5.02	0.37	94.00
90	1.51	4.93	0.37	94.94
100	1.51	4.86	0.36	95.70
150	1.51	4.64	0.34	98.18
200	1.51	4.51	0.34	99.58
222	1.51	4.48	0.33	100.00

Source: Cleary, S. and Copp, D. "Diversification with Canadian Stocks: How Much Is Enough?" *Canadian Investment Review* (Fall 1999), Table 1.

unique (or non-systematic) or diversifiable risk
the company-specific part of total risk that is eliminated by diversification

market (or systematic) or non-diversifiable risk
the systematic part of total risk that cannot be eliminated by diversification

Figure 8-11 also demonstrates that the benefits of random diversification do not continue indefinitely. As more and more securities are added, the marginal risk reduction per security becomes extremely small, eventually producing an almost negligible effect on total portfolio risk. For example, going from 10 to 20 securities eliminates an additional 7 percent of the monthly portfolio standard deviation, and going from 20 to 30 securities eliminates only 3 percent of the monthly standard deviation. Thus, although a large number of securities are not required to achieve substantial diversification benefits, the monthly portfolio risk levels out as additional securities are added to the portfolio.

The part of the total risk that *is* eliminated by diversification in Figure 8-11 is the company-specific **unique (or non-systematic) or diversifiable risk**. The part that is *not* eliminated by diversification is the **market (or systematic) or non-diversifiable risk**. This portion of the risk cannot be eliminated because all the securities in the portfolio will be directly influenced by overall movements in the general market or economy. Total risk is often divided into these two components, which are additive, as reflected in Equation 8-19:

[8-19]

$$\text{Total risk} = \text{Market (systematic) risk} + \text{Unique (non-systematic) risk}$$

The declining relationship between portfolio risk and the number of securities in a portfolio illustrated in Figure 8-11 for Canadian stocks is a well-known result that holds for diversification among stocks in all developed domestic stock markets around the world. Figure 8-11 highlights the benefits of holding a well-diversified portfolio, in terms of risk reduction, when diversification is achieved by random security selection. Not surprisingly, diversification can be achieved more efficiently when we take a more structured approach to forming portfolios by consciously selecting securities that can be expected to have lower correlations among their returns, that is, to choose them from different industries, and so on.

International Diversification

Our discussion above assumed random diversification in domestic securities only. However, it is reasonable to assume that if domestic diversification is good for reducing risk, international diversification must be better. This is logical, because we would expect the returns among stock returns in different global markets to have lower correlation coefficients than those in the same market. Figure 8-12 demonstrates the benefits of international diversification in reducing portfolio risk, based on evidence provided in a classic research article by Bruno Solnik. Throughout the entire range of portfolio sizes, the risk is reduced when international investing is compared with investing in only domestic stocks (U.S. stocks in this example), and the difference is dramatic—about one-third less. Several studies confirm similar risk-reduction benefits are available to Canadian investors who diversify internationally.

Although almost all experts agree that diversification in general, and international diversification in particular, is one of the most critical components of good portfolio management, recent evidence suggests the benefits of international diversification have been declining in recent years as global equity markets have become more integrated. Finance in the News 8-1 discusses this issue.

8-12 FIGURE

International Diversification

Source: Solnik, Bruno. "Why Not Diversify Internationally Rather Than Domestically?" Financial Analysts Journal (July/August 1994).

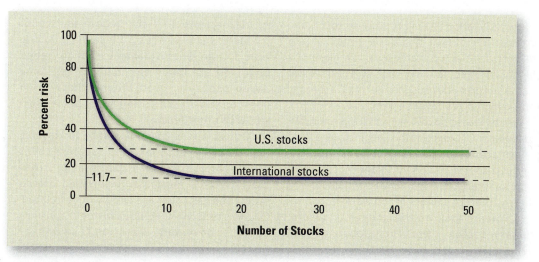

DIVERSIFICATION'S BENEFITS SHRINKING: SPREADING INVESTMENTS ABROAD NOT WHAT IT USED TO BE

finance INTHENEWS8-1

If you've been caught up in the recent wild swings in the stock market, you might be taking another look at your equity portfolio right now: Is it properly diversified to avoid some of the bigger bumps looming ahead?

The problem is, the goal of diversification isn't as easy to achieve as it might sound. In today's globalized environment, an increasing number of companies straddle the world.

"Markets are a little messier than they were 10 years ago," said Eric Kirzner, professor of finance at the Rotman School of Management at the University of Toronto.

Many academics and stock market strategists who have studied this problem have concluded that a number of equity markets are so tightly linked that they don't zig and zag the way they used to. In their industry parlance, international stocks are far more correlated now, often rising and falling like a homogenous bloc.

"All the world cares about the global economy now. Most nations really aren't going their own way," said Larry Speidell, executive vice-president at Laffer Associates, an economic research and consulting firm based in San Diego, CA.

For example, if the U.S. stock market falls over the course of a week, chances are that Canadian and European stock markets will also fall, and by a similar amount. So far in 2006, the S&P/TSX composite index, the Dow Jones industrial average, the UK's FTSE 100 and Germany's DAX index have risen between 1 percent and 2 percent each and have traced a remarkably similar—and volatile—path. They look like one giant market.

Richard Bernstein, chief investment strategist at Merrill Lynch, pointed out in a report earlier this year that rising correlation applies to far more than just international equities.

He found that, as of February, the stocks of small U.S. companies and large U.S. companies moved in the same direction 94 percent of the time; if the S&P 500 was up, an index of small-capitalization stocks was probably up as well. In 2000, the level of correlation was only 62 percent.

Commodities are also moving with U.S. stocks to a greater degree these days. In 2000, the two asset classes tended to move in the opposite direction; when commodities were up, U.S. stocks were usually down, and vice versa—making commodities key to a diversified portfolio.

Now, they frequently move together—and this correlation is at its highest when global stock markets turn rocky.

"There has always been a convergence of global equity markets during downturns in the market," said Wendy Brodkin, practice leader of investment consulting at Watson Wyatt Worldwide. In other words, when investors need the benefits of international diversification most, it lets them down.

Globalization is a big reason for this rising correlation during the good times in the market. Toyota, for example, is now more of a global car manufacturer—not a Japanese car manufacturer—because it derives a bigger proportion of its revenue overseas.

Same goes for Dell Inc., the U.S. computer company, GlaxoSmithKline PLC, the U.K. pharmaceutical firm and Adidas AG, the German sports equipment giant—not to mention hundreds of other large companies in a dozen different sectors of the world economy.

"When I look at the consumer discretionary sector, I find that Japan doesn't behave like Japan; it behaves like the whole world," Mr. Speidell said.

These companies, which operate in many countries, have essentially erased the importance of international boundaries, at least from an investor's perspective. This trend has been developing for some time, but it has never been more pronounced.

As well, low interest rates may also have played a major role in the shrinking benefits of international diversification. The low rates encouraged borrowing among investors, who invested the money in a number of assets, driving up prices. With interest rates on the rise in most countries, the opposite trend is occurring: Investors are withdrawing, causing many markets to turn volatile at the same time.

The need for proper diversification has become a key issue facing Canadian investors in particular. The S&P/TSX composite index has risen nearly 100 percent since its low mark in 2003, largely because of surging energy, mining and banking stocks. These groups now represent a dominant weighting within the benchmark index, leading to warnings that the index is no longer a diversified basket of stocks.

Say this about Canadians: They've been taking these warnings to heart. According to the latest report from the Investment Funds Institute of Canada, investors have been ploughing big bucks into foreign equity mutual funds while pulling money out of Canadian equity funds—a trend that has persisted for six straight months.

Mr. Kirzner noted that this traditional kind of international diversification still makes sense for most investors, even though it's by no means perfect. "I still believe that country-factors are very real," he said. "If you go with, say, an iShares Japan exchange-traded fund, you are definitely going to get some Japan exposure, even though there is no question you are also going to get some overlap [with other funds.]"

Others stress the importance for favouring global industries and sectors over geographical regions. Experts also stress that investors must stay diversified among different assets that are largely uncorrelated.

"In a real panic, equities become correlated in a downward direction," said Blair Falconer, portfolio manager at HSBC Securities (Canada). "That's why you need to be in a number of different asset classes, including gold, commodities, fixed income, real estate, as well as equities."

According to Pacific Investment Management Co., bonds are the key to smooth, long-term performance. For the 20-year period between 1985 and 2005, a portfolio with 60 percent exposure to stocks (the S&P 500) and 40 percent exposure to bonds (the Lehman Aggregate Bond index) delivered 89 percent of the returns of an all-stock portfolio but with 36 percent less volatility.

Although it might seem a bit removed from the concerns of the average Canadian investor, the Iowa Public Employees Retirement System has an excellent online asset allocation calculator at www.ipers.org/sub/calcs/.

Plug in variables such as your age, assets and general view on the economy and the site will generate an instant pie chart giving you a breakdown of how much money should be put into seven asset categories, including large-cap stocks, foreign stocks, bonds and cash.

Using tools like this one can help investors avoid the temptation of chasing after last year's winners—a common mistake among many investors who are seeking diversification.

"You think you're diversifying if you've added something that was the top-performer last year," said Kate Warne, Canadian market strategist at Edward Jones. "I think people may be making the mistake of buying things just because they've heard about them and they think that if they weren't correlated last year, they might not be correlated in the

future—and that will diversify their portfolio." This often is not the case.

Other observers note that investors should be given more investment options to choose from in this day and age of rising correlations. For example, Ms. Brodkin said that better diversification can be gained from alternative investments such as hedge funds, private equity and infrastructure, which tend to be uncorrelated with other assets. Unfortunately, these investments are currently the domain of institutions and well-heeled investors.

"Even though we work with institutional funds, and not retail, we are very concerned about what's happening in the retail market," Ms. Brodkin said. "I think that it's time for us to say in the market that we need to get other things to these investors."

"It's up to the providers in the market to start down the path and look for alternatives."

Source: Berman, David. "Diversification's Benefits Shrinking: Spreading Investments Abroad Not What It Used to Be," *National Post*, July 24, 2006, p. FP1.

CONCEPT REVIEW QUESTIONS

1. What is naïve diversification?
2. What is the difference between diversifiable and non-diversifiable risk?
3. Why is it logical to believe that international diversification will provide benefits to investors?

Summary

This chapter discusses the expected return and risk characteristics of risky securities. We show how the standard deviation is calculated, and how it is commonly used as a measure of risk because it represents the variability in a security's rate of return. We also discuss different definitions of rates of return, including the arithmetic and geometric rates of return and why they differ. We then discuss how portfolios are formed by varying the weight invested in different securities and what happens to the portfolio's expected rate of return and risk. In particular, we emphasize the importance of the correlation coefficient in determining portfolio risk and show how diversification can be used to reduce risk, as well as how to create the efficient frontier.

In Chapter 9, we will further develop these ideas. At the moment, they are mechanical in the sense that we show how a given set of securities can be combined into efficient portfolios. This won Harry Markowitz the Nobel Prize, but it was left to one of his students, William Sharpe, to take these ideas and think through what it means for a capital market dominated by Markowitz-type investors, rationally forming efficient portfolios by using the ideas in this chapter. This led to another seminal idea in finance and another Nobel Prize.

Key Terms

Formulas/Equations

(8-1)   Income yield $= \dfrac{CF_1}{P_0}$

(8-2)   Capital gain (loss) return $= \dfrac{P_1 - P_0}{P_0}$

(8-3)   Total return = Income yield + Capital gain (or loss) yield

$$\dfrac{CF_1 + P_1 - P_0}{P_0}$$

(8-4)   Arithmetic average (AM) $= \dfrac{\sum\limits_{i=1}^{n} r_i}{n}$

(8-5)   Geometric mean (GM) $= [(1 + r_1)(1 + r_2)(1 + r_3) \dots (1 + r_n)]^{1/n} - 1$

(8-6) $ER = \sum\limits_{i=1}^{n}(r_i \times Prob_i)$

(8-7) $\quad$ Ex post $\sigma = \sqrt{\dfrac{\sum\limits_{i=1}^{n}(r_i - \bar{r})^2}{n-1}}$

(8-8) $\quad$ Ex ante $\sigma = \sqrt{\sum\limits_{i=1}^{n}(\text{Prob}_i)(r_i - ER_i)^2}$

(8-9) $\quad ER_P = \sum\limits_{i=1}^{n}(w_i \times ER_i)$

(8-10) $\quad ER_p = ER_B + w(ER_A - ER_B)$

(8-11) $\quad \sigma_p = \sqrt{(w_A)^2(\sigma_A)^2 + (w_B)^2(\sigma_B)^2 + 2(w_A)(w_B)(COV_{A,B})}$

(8-12) $\quad COV_{AB} = \sum\limits_{i=1}^{n}Prob_i(r_{A,i} - \bar{r}_A)(r_{B,i} - \bar{r}_B)$

(8-13) $\quad \rho_{AB} = \dfrac{COV_{AB}}{\sigma_A \sigma_B}$

(8-14) $\quad COV_{AB} = \rho_{AB}\sigma_A\sigma_B$

(8-15) $\quad \sigma_p = \sqrt{(w_A)^2(\sigma_A)^2 + (w_B)^2(\sigma_B)^2 + 2(w_A)(w_B)(\rho_{A,B})(\sigma_A)(\sigma_B)}$

(8-16) $\quad \sigma_p = w\sigma_A - (1-w)\sigma_B$

(8-17) $\quad w = \dfrac{\sigma_B}{\sigma_A + \sigma_B}$

(8-18) $\quad \sigma_p = \sqrt{\begin{array}{l}(w_A)^2(\sigma_A)^2 + (w_B)^2(\sigma_B)^2 + (w_C)^2(\sigma_C)^2 + 2(w_A)(w_B)(\rho_{A,B})(\sigma_A)(\sigma_B) \\ + 2(w_A)(w_C)(\rho_{AC})(\sigma_A)(\sigma_C) + 2(w_B)(w_C)(\rho_{BC})(\sigma_B)(\sigma_C)\end{array}}$

(8-19) $\quad$ Total risk = Market (systematic) risk + Unique (non-systematic) risk

(8A-1) $\quad w = \dfrac{ER_P - ER_B}{(ER_A - ER_B)}$

(8A-2) $\quad \sigma_p = \sqrt{(\dfrac{ER_P - ER_B}{(ER_A - ER_B)})^2(\sigma_A)^2 + (1 - \dfrac{ER_P - ER_B}{(ER_A - ER_B)})^2(\sigma_B)^2 + 2(\dfrac{ER_P - ER_B}{(ER_A - ER_B)})(1 - \dfrac{ER_P - ER_B}{(ER_A - ER_B)})(\rho_{A,B})(\sigma_A)(\sigma_B)}$

APPENDIX 8A: TWO-SECURITY PORTFOLIO FRONTIERS

Figures 8-4 and 8-8 show how the expected return and the standard deviation of a portfolio change as we change the composition by shifting more of our investment toward security A, which is the riskier security. Rather than have two graphs, we combine them into one that implicitly shows all the portfolios. We can do this by noting from Equation 8-10 that rather than writing the expected return as the portfolio weight is varied, we can instead write the portfolio weight as we change our expected return, that is:

[8A-1]

$$w = \frac{ER_P - ER_B}{(ER_A - ER_B)}$$

or with our numbers

$$w = \frac{ER_P - 8\%}{2\%}$$

The way to think about this is to suppose that an investor wants a portfolio with an expected rate of return of 8 percent. In this case, look at the equation above and substitute 8 percent for ER_P, and learn that a zero weight has to be placed in security A, that is, the 8 percent expected return can be met with 100 percent in B. If the expected return on the portfolio is set at 10 percent, then we get 2 percent in the numerator and denominator of Equation 8A-2 and the portfolio weight has to be 100 percent, that is, all the investment has to be placed in security A. Between these two expected returns, we get different portfolio weights as we vary how much is invested in each security.[18]

We can now use Equation 8A-1 to remove the portfolio weights in Equation 8-15 and express the standard deviation of the portfolio solely in terms of the expected returns, standard deviations, and the correlation coefficient as is done in Equation 8A-2:

[8A-2]

$$\sigma_p = \sqrt{(\frac{ER_P - ER_B}{(ER_A - ER_B)})^2 (\sigma_A)^2 + (1 - \frac{ER_P - ER_B}{(ER_A - ER_B)})^2 (\sigma_B)^2 + 2(\frac{ER_P - ER_B}{(ER_A - ER_B)})(1 - \frac{ER_P - ER_B}{(ER_A - ER_B)})(\rho_{A,B})(\sigma_A)(\sigma_B)}$$

Although this is cumbersome, it indicates all the combinations of expected return and risk (standard deviation) created from these two securities.

With our example, we can substitute in and get the following:

$$\sigma_p = \sqrt{(\frac{ER_P - 8\%}{2\%})^2 (22.69\%)^2 + (\frac{10\% - ER_P}{2\%})^2 (8.72\%)^2 + 2(\frac{ER_P - 8\%}{2\%})(\frac{10\% - ER_P}{2\%})(\rho_{A,B})(22.69\%)(8.72\%)}$$

---

[18] As we mentioned before, there is no conceptual reason that the weights can't be more than 100 percent, and we will relax this constraint later.

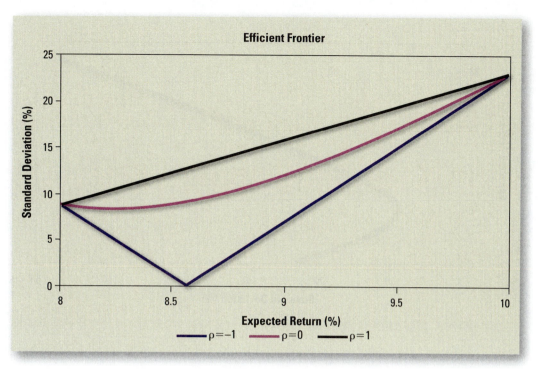

Efficient Frontier

This is a bit simpler, but you need to plug the numbers into Excel to work everything out. If you do this, you can get Figure 8A-1 for our three special cases and anything in between.

As we saw before, if we start out with all investment in security B ($w = 0$), we get an 8 percent expected return and a standard deviation of 8.72 percent. If we move to a portfolio with 100 percent invested in A, we get a 10 percent expected return and a 22.69 percent standard deviation. In between, interesting things happen! Notice that the risk of the portfolio falls, unless the securities are perfectly correlated, as we add the risky security A to the portfolio; this decline is much more dramatic if the securities are negatively correlated. Regardless, adding A to the portfolio increases the expected return and lowers the risk, which means the investor is better off and no one should hold security B in isolation.[19] Eventually, the risk-reduction opportunity from holding A falls and the risk is minimized, after which the standard deviation of the portfolio's return starts to increase.

These diagrams show all the combinations of expected return and standard deviation that result from creating portfolios of the two securities. Now we can return to our example in which the correlation coefficient was 0.379 and graph the efficient frontier with a non-special correlation coefficient. We can also flip the axes because normally in finance, we have the expected return on the vertical axis and the standard deviation or risk on the horizontal axis, as shown in Figure 8A-2.[20]

---

[19] Think about why they might want to hold A in isolation.

[20] Notice that we have also allowed the security weights to go below zero or above one in order to construct Figure 8A-2.

FIGURE 8A-2

Two-Security Portfolios

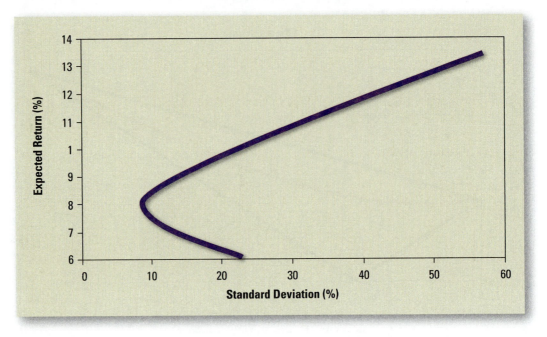

QUESTIONS AND PRACTICE PROBLEMS

Multiple Choice Questions

1. Calculate the capital gain (loss) return for a stock that was purchased at $25 one year ago and is now worth $24. It paid a quarterly dividend of $1 per share throughout the year.

   A. −4 percent

   B. −16 percent

   C. 12 percent

   D. 4 percent

2. In Question 1, what is the total return of the security?

   A. 4 percent

   B. 0 percent

   C. 16 percent

   D. 12 percent

3. Which of the following is *false*?

   A. The income yield of a security that has a $3 cash flow during a period with a beginning price of $15 is 20 percent.

   B. The arithmetic average is always less than the geometric mean of a series of returns.

   C. The geometric mean of 50 percent and −50 percent is −13.4 percent.

   D. The greater the dispersion of a distribution, the greater the spread between the geometric mean and the arithmetic average.

4. Calculate the expected return on a stock that has a 30 percent probability of a 30 percent return, a 20 percent probability of a 40 percent return, and a 50 percent probability of a 15 percent return.

    A. 15 percent

    B. 35.5 percent

    C. 24.5 percent

    D. 20 percent

5. In Question 4, what is the standard deviation?

    A. 11.12 percent

    B. 10.25 percent

    C. 10.11 percent

    D. 12 percent

6. Which of the following is *false*?

    A. The expected return of a portfolio is always the weighted average of the expected return of each asset in the portfolio.

    B. Covariance measures the co-movement between the returns of individual securities.

    C. The standard deviation of a portfolio is always the weighted average of the standard deviations of individual assets in the portfolio.

    D. Standard deviation is easier to interpret than variance as a measure of risk.

7. The correlation coefficient

    A. equals covariance times the individual standard deviations.

    B. measures how security returns move in relation to one another.

    C. may be greater than +1.

    D. shows a stronger relationship between the returns of two securities when its absolute value is closer to 0.

8. Which of the following correlation coefficients will provide the greatest diversification benefits for a given portfolio?

    A. 0

    B. 0.5

    C. 1

    D. −0.9

9. Which of the following is *false*?

    A. The standard deviation of a portfolio that contains two individual securities is the weighted average of individual standard deviations *only* when the correlation coefficient is equal to +1.

    B. It is impossible to eliminate all the risk for a two-security portfolio.

    C. There are $n(n - 1)/2$ co-movement terms and n variance terms for an *n-security* portfolio.

D. The more securities added, the lower the marginal risk reduction per security added.

10. According to the diagram below, which statement is *false*?

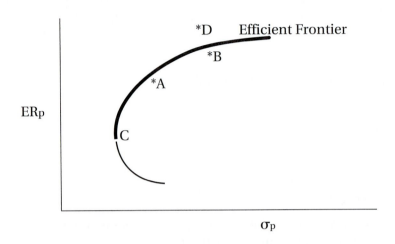

A. Portfolio C is the minimum variance portfolio (MVP).

B. Portfolios on the upper segment above C dominate those on the bottom segment below C.

C. Portfolios A, B, and D are attainable, but C is not.

D. A more risk-averse investor will prefer portfolios on the left side of the efficient frontier.

Practice Problems

Easy

11. Describe when to use the arithmetic average and when to use the geometric mean to describe a return series.

12. State three of the most important assumptions underlying Markowitz's notion of efficient portfolios.

13. The Absent Minded Professors's file on the daily performance of the JellyBean Company has been partially completed. Fill in the missing data.

The JellyBean Company Performance

	Opening price	Dividend	Closing† price	Income Yield	Capital Gain	Total daily return
Monday	$100	$7	$115			
Tuesday	$115	$2			7%	
Wednesday		$8				10%
Thursday				4%	3%	
Friday		$0				15%

† The closing price on one day is assumed to be the opening price for the next day.

14. The Absent Minded Profs have conducted an extensive analysis of the economy and have concluded that the probability of a recession next year is 25 percent, a boom is 15 percent, and a stable economy is 60 percent. Your boss has estimated that the price of the XPK Company will be $60 if there is a recession, $110 if there is a boom, and $85 if the economy is stable. Currently, XPK is trading for $75. Calculate the ex-ante expected return on XPK.

15. You have observed the following returns: 10 percent, –8 percent, 5 percent, 2 percent and –20 percent
    A. Calculate the geometric average return
    B. Calculate the arithmetic average return
    C. Calculate the variance and standard deviation of returns

16. On Monday you invested $175 in the Alligator Dental Floss Company. ADFC has earned daily returns of 7 percent, 19 percent, –45 percent, 3 percent, and 10 percent. What is the value of your investment at the end of the five days?

17. You observed the following daily returns for two companies: ABC and DEF.

	Daily Returns	
	ABC	DEF
Monday	3%	2%
Tuesday	2%	8%
Wednesday	– 8%	14%
Thursday	–10%	12%
Friday	7%	3%

A. Calculate for each stock:

   i) Five day cumulative return
   ii) Geometric average daily return
   iii) Arithmetic average daily return
   iv) Standard deviation of daily returns

B. Calculate the covariance and correlation between the two stocks.

18. The Absent Minded Profs are exploring different portfolio allocations between two stocks. Complete the following table.

	Case 1	Case 2	Case 3	Case 4	Case 5
$ invested in Stock 1	$500			$200	
$ invested in Stock 2	$500		$5000		
Total $ invested		$2000	$5000		$1000
Weight in Stock 1		20%		40%	15%
Weight in Stock 2					
Expected return of Stock 1	8%	3%		5%	2%
Expected return of Stock 2	3%				10%
Expected return of portfolio		8%	6%	7%	

19. Your portfolio consists of two securities: Ice-T and Mr.B. The expected returns for Ice-T is 8 percent while for Mr.B it is 3 percent. The standard deviation is 4 percent for Ice-T and 14 percent for Mr.B. If 15 percent of the portfolio is invested in Ice-T, calculate the portfolio standard deviation if:

A. The correlation between the stocks is .75

B. The correlation between the stocks is –.75

20. The Absent Minded Profs are exploring the risk of different portfolio allocations between two stocks. Complete the following table.

	Case 1	Case 2
Weight in Stock 1		15%
Weight in Stock 2	25%	
Standard deviation of Stock 1	15%	2%
Standard deviation of Stock 2	3%	10%
Covariance between Stocks 1 and 2		
Correlation between Stocks 1 and 2	–.20	.40
Portfolio Variance		
Portfolio Standard Deviation		

21. You have the following return data on six stocks:

Day	XYZ	ABC	DEF	GHI	JKL	MNO
Monday	1%	–18%	3%	6%	7%	3%
Tuesday	2%	–15%	8%	3%	5%	–4%
Wednesday	3%	–12%	13%	1%	3%	8%
Thursday	4%	–9%	18%	3%	2%	–2%
Friday	5%	–6%	22%	–5%	0%	0%

A. Graph the returns of each stock (ABC, DEF, GHI, JKL, and MNO) against the returns of XYZ.

B. Based on the five graphs, which stocks are positively correlated with XYZ?

C. Based on the five graphs, which stocks are negatively correlated with XYZ?

D. Based on the five graphs, which stocks are uncorrelated with XYZ?

E. Calculate the correlation between the five stocks and XYZ to check your results from parts (B)–(D).

22. Calculate the annual arithmetic average and geometric mean return on the following security, and state which method is more appropriate for the situation: purchase price = $30; first-year dividend = $5; price after one year = $35; second-year dividend = $8; selling price after two years = $28.

23. Calculate the ex post standard deviation of returns for the following: 50 percent, 30 percent, 20 percent, 35 percent, 55 percent.

24. An investor owns a portfolio of $30,000 that contains $10,000 in Stock A, with an expected return of 12 percent; $5,000 in bonds, with an expected return of 8

Medium

percent; and the rest in Stock B, with an expected return of 20 percent. Calculate the expected return of his portfolio.

25. On January 1, 2006, the Absent Minded Profs published the following forecasts for the economy:

State of the economy	Probability	Forecasted quarterly returns
Poor	20%	−3%
Average	50%	5%
Boom	30%	8%

During 2006, you observed quarterly returns of 2 percent, −5 percent, 3 percent, and 8 percent.

A. Calculate the ex ante expected quarterly return

B. Calculate the ex ante standard deviation of quarterly returns

C. Calculate the ex post average quarterly return

D. Calculate the ex post standard deviation of quarterly returns

E. Explain the difference between the ex ante and ex post returns

26. On January 1, The Absent Minded Profs completed their analysis of the prospects for the Geriatric Toy Store and concluded that there is a 15 percent chance that the stock price will be $200 in 1 year while there is an 85 percent chance that the stock price will be $45. Six months later, the Profs revised their estimated probabilities to 35 percent chance of the high state (stock price of $200). If the market agrees with the Profs' revised probabilities, what is the expected change in stock price from January 1 to July 1? Assume the discount rate is zero.

27. As an analyst for the Absent Minded Profs, ADFC is one of the firms that you are responsible for. Currently, you have a "hold" recommendation[21] on ADFC. The current price of ADFC is $138.85. You have conducted an extensive analysis of the industry and you feel that the probability that the firm will capture a substantial share of the new market is 35 percent, and the stock price would rise to $250 due to the unusually high growth rate of future earnings. You are expecting earnings to grow at a rate of 45 percent per year for the next five years if the firm is able to capture the new market. However, you feel that there is a 40 percent probability that the firm will face serious difficulties in the near future, in which case the stock price will fall to $14.85 and the earnings growth rate will drop to 3 percent. There is a 25 percent chance that nothing will change for the firm and their earnings growth rate will remain at 12 percent. Should you change your recommendation?

28. The Absent Minded Profs have been using the services of the Scatter Brained Brokerage Company for the last 6 months. SBBC has informed the Profs that the geometric average monthly return was 7 percent, and that over the last six months the Profs earned 16 percent, 19 percent, −23 percent, 14 percent, −8 percent and SBBC can't find the data for the last month. The Profs have given you the task of determining the missing return.

---

[21] Basically you are indicating that you believe that the stock is fairly priced — it isn't a bargain so people who currently don't own it shouldn't buy and it isn't overpriced so people who own it shouldn't sell.

29. The Absent Minded Profs are interested in the tradeoff between investing in two stocks: Xfoot and Ytoe. The expected return on Xfoot is 6 percent and Ytoe is 18 percent.

A. Graph the relationship between the expected return on the portfolio and the weight in Ytoe.

Weight in Ytoe	Portfolio return
0%	6.00%
1%	6.12%
2%	6.24%
3%	6.36%
–	–
–	–
–	–
99%	17.88%
100%	18.00%

B. What is the tradeoff between investing in Xfoot and Ytoe (i.e., if we increase the weight in Ytoe by 1 percent, what is the change in the expected return on the portfolio)?

C. Your boss has just looked at your results and disagrees. He says the tradeoff between Ytoe and Xfoot is negative and therefore, your results are wrong. Explain to your boss how you are both correct.

30. You have observed the following monthly returns for ABC and DEF.

	Monthly returns	
	ABC	DEF
January	6%	1%
February	–3%	3%
March	–2%	5%
April	–1%	7%
May	0%	2%
June	3%	1%
July	4%	–3%
August	8%	–2%
September	5%	–4%
October	3%	–2%
November	4%	1%
December	5%	2%

A. Graph the relationship between the weight in ABC and the portfolio returns (restrict all weights to be greater than or equal to zero)

B. Graph the relationship between the weight in ABC and the portfolio standard deviation (use the same weights as in A).

C. Using the data you have created in A) and B), graph the relationship between the risk and return for the portfolio (put return on the Y axis).

D. Which portfolio weights do you prefer and why?

31. The Absent Minded Profs wish to combine two stocks, Encor and Maestro, into a portfolio with an expected return of 16 percent. The expected return of Encor is 2 percent with a standard deviation of 1 percent. The expected return of Maestro is 25 percent with a standard deviation of 10 percent. The correlation between the two stocks is 0.40.

A. What is the composition (weights) of the portfolio?

B. What is the portfolio standard deviation?

32. The Absent Minded Profs wish to combine two other stocks, Peledon and Mexcor, into a portfolio with a standard deviation of 6 percent. The expected return of Peledon is 2 percent with a standard deviation of one percent. The expected return of Mexcor is 25 percent with a standard deviation of 10 percent. The correlation between the two stocks is 0.40.

A. What is the composition (weights) of the portfolio?

B. What is the expected return on the portfolio?

33. The Grumpy Old Analysts have recently published a study claiming that the benefits to diversification are constant. In other words, adding one more stock to a 3 stock portfolio will have the same impact as adding 1 more stock to a 500 stock portfolio. The Absent Minded Profs are not convinced and give you the task of evaluating the GOA claim.

A. Assume that all the stocks have the same standard deviation, 10 percent, and all are independent (correlation equals 0.00). Create equally weighted portfolios of 1–10 stocks and calculate the portfolio standard deviation for each portfolio. Graph the portfolio standard deviation as a function of the number of stocks. Based on the results of your analysis, evaluate the Grumpy Old Analysts' claim.

B. As the number of firms increases, what do you expect will happen to the risk of the portfolio? Can the risk of the portfolio become close to zero?

34. Calculate the *covariance* and *correlation coefficient* between the two securities of a portfolio that has 40 percent in Stock X, with an expected return of 40 percent and a standard deviation of 12 percent; and 60 percent in Stock Y, with an expected return of 30 percent and a standard deviation of 15 percent. The portfolio standard deviation is 6 percent.

35. Calculate the correlation coefficient (ρ_{AB}) for the following situation:

Difficult

State of the Economy	Probability of Occurrence	Expected Return on Stock A in This State	Expected Return on Stock B in This State
High growth	25%	40%	55%
Moderate growth	20%	20%	25%
Recession	55%	−10%	−20%

36. To achieve a zero standard deviation for a portfolio, calculate the weights of Stock A and Stock B in Problem 35 by assuming the correlation coefficient is -1.

37. An investor purchased 500 shares of Stock A at $22 per share and 1,000 shares of Stock B at $30 per share one year ago. Stock A and Stock B paid quarterly dividends of $2 per share and $1.50 per share, respectively, during the year. One year later, the investor sold both stocks at $30 per share. Calculate the total return of Stock A and Stock B and the total return of the portfolio.

38. In Problem 37, the ρ_{AB} is 0.3 and the standard deviations of Stock A and Stock B are 20 percent and 15 percent, respectively. Calculate the standard deviation of the portfolio.

39. The Absent Minded Profs are exploring the risk of different portfolio allocations between two stocks. Complete the following table.

	Case 1	Case 2
Weight in Stock 1	35%	40%
Weight in Stock 2		
Standard deviation of Stock 1	3%	
Standard deviation of Stock 2	25%	20%
Covariance between Stocks 1 and 2		.022
Correlation between Stocks 1 and 2		
Portfolio Variance	.027	
Portfolio Standard Deviation		26%

40. The Absent Minded Profs are interested in using short-selling in order to increase the possible returns from their portfolio. They have short sold[22] $200 of ABC and invested $1,200 in DEF. The following data is available on ABC and DEF:

	ABC	DEF
Expected return	3%	15%
Standard deviation	7%	35%

The correlation between ABC and DEF is 0.40. Calculate the expected return and standard deviation of the portfolio.[23]

41. The Absent Minded Profs are interested in two stocks: Alcon and Beldon. Both stocks have an expected return of 8 percent. The standard deviation of Alcon is 3 percent and the standard deviation of Beldon is 5 percent. The Absent Minded Profs want the weights to be greater than or equal to zero. What portfolio com-

---

[22] Short selling: Borrow the stock from the broker and sell it. In the future you will have to buy the stock and return it to the broker.

[23] Hint: The total invested is $1,000 and while individual weights can be greater than one or less than zero, the sum of the weights must still be one.

position do you recommend to the Absent Minded Profs if:

A. The correlation between the two stocks is –0.80

B. The correlation between the two stocks is 0.80

42. The Absent Minded Profs are interested in two stocks: Alcon and Beldon. Both stocks have a standard deviation of 8 percent. The expected return of Alcon is 10 percent and the expected return of Beldon is 20 percent. The Absent Minded Profs want the weights to be greater than or equal to zero. What portfolio composition do you recommend to the Absent Minded Profs if:

A. The correlation is 0.00

B. The correlation is 1.0

43. The Absent Minded Profs wish to examine the effect of correlation on the efficient frontier that can be created by investing in ABC and FGI. The expected return of ABC is 6 percent with a standard deviation of 10 percent. The expected return of FGI is 10 percent with a standard deviation of 25% percent. Graph the efficient frontier for:

A. A correlation of 0.00

B. A correlation of –0.50

C. A correlation of 0.50

44. The Absent Minded Profs are interested in seeing the impact of diversification using observed returns on real firms. Obtain monthly returns from January 2006 to December 2006 for the following firms:[24]

Ticker	Name
PFE.TO	Pacific Energy Resources
XMC.TO	Xceed Mortgage Company
CCM.TO	Canarc Resource Corp
NAC.TO	North Atlantic Resources
RCL.TO	Ridley Inc
SMX.TO	SMTC Manufacturing Corp
BH.TO	Brainhunter Inc
CTL.TO	Catalyst Paper Corp
RIM.TO	Research in Motion
TD.TO	Toronto Dominion Bank
RY.TO	Royal Bank
G.TO	Goldcorp Inc
GAR.TO	Garneau Inc
DMC.TO	Data Mirror Corp
K.TO	Kinross Gold Corp

A. For the 15 firms, calculate the return on an equally weighted portfolio consisting of the first firm, first and second, first and second and third ….. until

---

[24] Monthly historical prices, adjusted for dividends, are available from http://ca.finance.yahoo.com. To obtain the data go to the website and type the ticker (don't forget the .TO) in the box labeled "Get Quotes". When you get the page for the firm, on the left hand side you will see a link to "historical prices," click that and you will go to a page containing the historical price data. Download the prices adjusted for dividends and splits. Do this for each firm and then combine the data into one spreadsheet and answer the question.

you have a portfolio with all 15 firms. Calculate the standard deviation of the monthly returns for each portfolio. Plot the portfolio risk against the number of firms. As the number of firms increases, what happens to the risk of the portfolio?

B. Compare your results using the real data with the artificial data used in Problem 33. Do you expect to be able to have a portfolio risk close to zero using real data? Explain your reasoning.

C. Redo your analysis from part (A) with the stocks in a different order. Do you get the same shape of graph? Explain how the shape could be different.

45. The Absent Minded Profs want to examine a "real" efficient frontier involving Research in Motion (RIM.TO) and the Royal Bank (RY.TO).

A. Using monthly data for these two companies from January 2006 to December 2006, graph the relationship between risk and return.

B. Explain the difference between the frontier you developed in part (A) and the efficient frontier.

C. Where do you expect the S&P/TSX index to plot relative to the frontier? Explain.

D. Download the S&P/TSX composite index data for the same period (ticker: ^GSPTSE) and plot the S&P/TSX on your graph.

E. Based on your graph, is the S&P/TSX an efficient portfolio? Explain.

F. What do you expect will happen to the frontier if you increase the number of stocks? Explain your reasoning.

Beta:
Know the Risk

How should investors assess risk in the stocks they buy or sell? As you can imagine, the concept of risk is hard to pin down but it factors into stock analysis and valuation. Is there a rating—some sort of number, letter, or phrase—that will do the trick?

One of the most popular indicators of risk is a statistical measure called beta. Stock analysts use this measure to get a sense of stocks' risk profiles.

Beta is a key component for the capital asset pricing model (CAPM), which is used to calculate cost of equity. Recall that the cost of capital represents the discount rate used to arrive at the present value of a company's future cash flows. All things being equal, the higher a company's beta, the higher its cost of capital discount rate. The higher the discount rate, the lower the present value placed on the company's future cash flows. In short, beta can impact a company's share valuation.

Source: Excerpted from McClure, Ben. "Beta: Know the Risk." Investopedia Advisor website: www.investopedia.com/articles/stocks/04/113004.asp. November 30, 2004. Retrieved May 1, 2007.

The Capital Asset Pricing Model (CAPM)

Learning Objectives

After reading this chapter, you should understand the following:

1. What happens if all investors are rational and risk averse

2. How modern portfolio theory is extended to develop the capital market line, which determines how expected returns on portfolios are determined

3. How to assess the performance of mutual fund managers

4. How the Capital Asset Pricing Model's (CAPM) security market line is developed from the capital market line

5. How the CAPM has been extended to include other risk-based pricing models

INTRODUCTION

This chapter continues the discussion of the relationship between risk and return initiated in Chapter 8.

9.1 THE NEW EFFICIENT FRONTIER

The Efficient Frontier with Risk-Free Borrowing and Lending

In Chapter 8 we introduced the efficient frontier, which is depicted in Figure 9-1. Recall that the portfolios of risky securities that lie along the efficient frontier, that is, on the curve above the minimum variance portfolio (MVP), are efficient and *dominate* all other possible portfolios of risky securities. This means that for a given level of risk, as defined by the standard deviation of their return, these portfolios offer the highest expected rate of return. As we showed in Chapter 8, the derivation of the efficient frontier is a mechanical exercise.

FIGURE 9-1

Efficient Portfolios

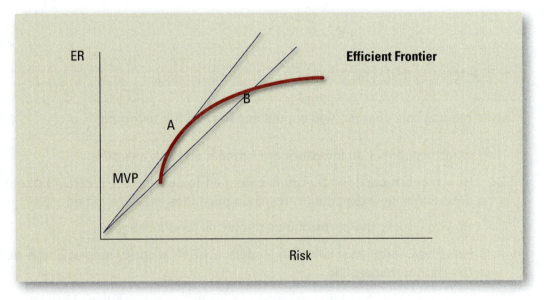

In the two-security case in Appendix 8A, we showed how to generate the efficient frontier from the expected return and standard deviation for each security and the correlation coefficient between their returns. It is slightly cumbersome but we can calculate the expected return on the portfolio and then estimate its standard deviation and graph the efficient frontier, which is what we did for Figure 8A-2. As the number of securities increases, the complexity of this mechanical exercise increases as well, but the general principle doesn't, because it is still mechanical. What we didn't fully explain are the reasons for graphing the efficient frontier.

In considering how investors make decisions among different securities, the assumption is that investors are *risk averse*: they will not willingly undertake fair gambles. Consider a game in which a coin is tossed. If it comes down heads, someone pays the player $100 and if it comes down tails, the player pays $100. The player will likely first wait and see the coin tossed many times to make sure that it is fair and that the odds really are fifty-fifty. In this case, it is called a *fair gamble* because the expected payoff is 0, that is, Expected payoff = 0 = 0.50 × (+$100) + 0.50 × (−$100). If someone turns down a fair gamble, he or she is defined as risk averse. A risk-averse person prefers the risk-free situation, that is, not gambling on a risky situation where there is an equal probability of winning or losing the same amount of money.

The corollary to turning down a fair gamble is that the risk-averse person needs a **risk premium** to be induced to enter into a risky situation. For example, someone might be willing to undertake a gamble if the heads payoff is $150 instead of $100. In this case, the expected payoff increases to $25 and it is no longer a fair gamble because there is a risk premium of $25. Another person might require that the heads payoff increases to $200 before undertaking the gamble, so the risk premium increases to $50. The second individual is more risk averse and requires a larger expected payoff or risk premium to get into the risky situation. Generally, investor behaviour is consistent with risk aversion and the existence of risk premiums to induce individuals to bear risk. We can represent this risk aversion by the required risk premium per unit of risk, with higher risk premiums indicating greater risk aversion.

> **risk premium** the expected pay off to get into a risky situation

We can also reverse the situation and put the individual in a risky situation and ask how much he or she is willing to pay to get out of the risky situation. Suppose, for example, someone is faced with a fair gamble; how much would he or she pay to get out of it? A very risk averse individual would pay a large amount, say $25, to get out of the fair gamble with equally likely payoffs of +/−$100. In this case, instead of calling the increased payoff a risk premium, the payment to get out of a risky situation is called an **insurance premium**.

> **insurance premium** the payment to get out of a risky situation

Recall from Chapter 1 that we discussed the basic institutions in the financial market and listed the major Canadian companies. One set of companies were the insurance companies and Manulife Financial Corporation, Sun Life Financial Inc., and Great-West Lifeco Inc. all had more than $100 billion in assets and $20 billion in revenues. These companies buy these risky situations from individuals and other institutions that do not want to bear them themselves. A house burning down, a car being stolen, and a spouse dying prematurely are all risks that individuals are willing to pay the insurance company to bear so that they reduce the probability of suffering financial harm. In this case, the gross profit margin on most insurance products is about 50 percent, so that only 50 cents of every insurance premium dollar actually goes to pay claims; the remainder ends up in administrative expenses, profits, and taxes. The fact that individuals are willing to pay insurance premiums that generate 50 percent gross margins indicates how risk averse they are.[1]

The existence of insurance markets indicates how risk aversion creates a demand to remove risk, whereas the existence of capital markets indicates how risk aversion generates risk premiums required to induce people to bear risk. In

---

[1] It could also indicate that people do not understand either the probabilities or the payoffs. People seem to be willing to pay very high premiums to remove very low probability risks that even have relatively low payoffs.

the following discussion, we will assume that investors are risk averse, that is, they require a risk premium to bear risk and that the more risk averse they are, the higher the risk premium they require. Further, we will continue to assume that we can represent risk by the standard deviation of the return on the portfolio. These assumptions lead to the result that investors will choose only portfolios on the efficient frontier above the MVP.

We can't say where on the efficient frontier a particular person would be because individuals differ in terms of their risk aversion. But a very risk averse individual might choose portfolio A, and a less risk averse individual might choose portfolio B. Why do we know that the investor choosing A is more risk averse than the investor choosing B? The line going through A to the origin is *steeper* than the line through B and the origin. The slope of the line is the height, which is the expected return on the portfolio divided by the length, which is the standard deviation of the portfolio. Because the line through A is steeper than the line through B, the individual who invests in A requires a *higher* expected rate of return per unit of risk—that is, he or she is more risk averse.

Many lines go through the origin and touch different points on the efficient frontier. The flatter the lines, the less risk averse are the investors. These investors choose a portfolio with a lower expected rate of return per unit of risk and gradually move out along the efficient frontier. Apart from knowing that investors differ in terms of their risk aversion, we know only that their preferred portfolio will lie somewhere along the efficient frontier.[2]

The origin is the point with a zero expected rate of return and zero risk. Zero risk is another way of describing a risk-free asset, such as a treasury bill (T-bill), where the return on the asset is guaranteed with no possibility of earning more or less. We usually use T-bills as the risk-free asset simply because they are obligations of the Government of Canada, which also has a monopoly on issuing Government of Canada bank notes; T-bills are default free because investors know that they will always be paid off in full.[3]

Risk-Free Investing

Consider any point on the efficient frontier in Figure 9-1, such as portfolio A. Now, assume an investor places a portion w of his or her wealth in the risky portfolio A and the remainder $(1 - w)$ in the risk-free asset, the T-bill. Remember that the expected return on a portfolio is always a weighted average of the expected returns on the individual assets, so we can estimate the expected return on this portfolio according to Equation 8-10, reproduced here with RF in place of ER_B as Equation 9-1:

[9-1]

$$ER_P = RF + w(ER_A - RF)$$

---

[2] The previous discussion may be a bit loose for those with extensive economics training. We could represent each individual by his or her indifference curve, symbolizing his or her risk aversion and personal tradeoff between risk and return. However, this adds little to our discussion.

[3] Treasury bills have not always been default free. John Ilkiw, in "The 100% Guarantee—The Reign of the Risk-Free Rate: Past Times, Present Value," *Canadian Investment Review 19*, no. 3 (Fall 2006), p. 7, points out that sovereign debt used to be very risky because monarchs were above the law as it was *their* law and could repudiate debt without recourse. Only with the establishment of the Bank of England and parliamentary assumption of the British national debt in 1688 did the notion of a risk-free asset come into being. Noticeably, interest rates on British debt dropped by 4 percent after this assumption as the default risk of lending to the government disappeared. In some parts of the world, government debt still remains risky.

where ER_P is the expected return on the portfolio that starts out with $w = 0$, because 100 percent is invested in the T-bill. As w increases, more is placed in the risky portfolio, so the investor picks up ER_P at the cost of taking money out of the T-bill. As a result, the expected return on the portfolio increases by the difference: $ER_A - RF$.

We can estimate the standard deviation on this portfolio by using Equation 8-15 from Chapter 8, which is reproduced below:

$$\sigma_p = \sqrt{(w_A)^2(\sigma_A)^2 + (w_B)^2(\sigma_B)^2 + 2(w_A)(w_B)(\rho_{A,B})(\sigma_A)(\sigma_B)}$$

If we replace RF for risky portfolio B, w for w_A, and $(1 - w)$ for w_B, we get the following:

$$\sigma_p = \sqrt{(w)^2(\sigma_A)^2 + (1-w)^2(\sigma_{RF})^2 + 2(1-w)(w)(\rho_{A,RF})(\sigma_A)(\sigma_{RF})}$$

With the risk-free asset, we know exactly what we are going to get from it, so that the standard deviation of its return is zero. Because the return does not vary, the correlation between the return on the risk-free asset and that on the risky portfolio A is also zero. So the standard deviation reduces to

$$\sigma_p = \sqrt{(w)^2(\sigma_A)^2 + (1-w)^2(0)^2 + 2(1-w)(w)(\rho_{A,RF} = 0)(\sigma_A)(0)} = \sqrt{w^2\sigma_A{}^2}$$

Taking the square root of the final term leaves us with Equation 9-2:

$$\sigma_p = w\sigma_A$$

[9-2]

Equation 9-2 is very important as it shows that portfolio risk increases in direct proportion to the amount invested in the risky asset. Therefore, the higher the portfolio allocation (weight) directed to the risky asset, the higher the portfolio risk. Because both the expected return and the standard deviation of a portfolio comprising any risky portfolio and a risk-free asset (RF) can be represented by a line that is based on the weights invested in RF and in the risky asset, all of the expected returns and risks for various portfolio combinations can be expressed as a straight line. We can show this by rearranging Equation 9-2 in terms of the portfolio weight:

$$w = \frac{\sigma_P}{\sigma_A}$$

and substituting for w in Equation 9-1 we get

$$E(R_P) = RF + \left(\frac{E(R_A) - RF}{\sigma_A}\right)\sigma_P$$

[9-3]

Equation 9-3 is the equation of a straight line. It indicates that the line touches the vertical axis at the risk-free rate and then has a constant slope. The slope is the rise over the run, or the increased expected return divided by the increased risk. The increased expected return, as discussed, is the incremental return on the risky portfolio minus the lost return by taking money out of the risk-free asset. We represent this portfolio in Figure 9-2.

FIGURE   9-2

Efficient Portfolios

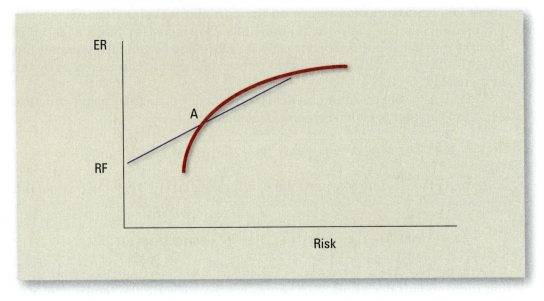

The interpretation of this figure is the same as before: if $w = 0$, all the investment is in the risk-free asset (T-bill), and the portfolio has no risk and earns RF. As w increases, the expected return on the portfolio increases by $(ER_A - RF)$ and its risk by σ_P, until $w = 100$ percent and the portfolio expected return is R_A and its risk is σ_A. Portfolios formed from A and the risk-free asset are portfolios from RF and other portfolios on the efficient frontier. In each case, the equation will be the same as in Equation 9-3. In particular, think about portfolio T in Figure 9-3.

FIGURE   9-3

Efficient Portfolios

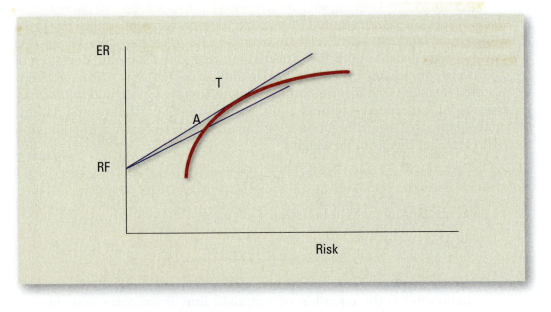

tangent portfolio the risky portfolio on the efficient frontier whose tangent line cuts the vertical axis at the risk-free rate

All portfolios composed of risky portfolio T and the risk-free rate lie along the line RF to T and offer a higher expected rate of return for the same risk as do portfolios composed of the risk-free rate and risky portfolio A. Portfolio T is called the **tangent portfolio**, because it is the risky portfolio on the efficient frontier whose tangent line cuts the vertical axis at the risk-free rate. Portfolios composed of the risk-free rate and portfolio T offer the highest expected rate of return for any given level of risk and represent the **new (or super) efficient frontier**, which is depicted in Figure 9-4.

new (or super) efficient frontier portfolios composed of the risk-free rate and the tangent portfolio that offer the highest expected rate of return for any given level of risk

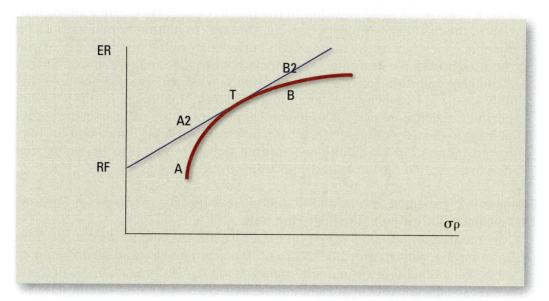

9-4 FIGURE

The New Efficient Frontier

Consider, for example, portfolio A, which was optimal for a very risk averse investor without the risk-free asset. Now this investor could hold a portfolio of the risk-free asset and the risky portfolio T that offers a higher expected rate of return for the same risk as A. This is the new portfolio A2. What this demonstrates is that a portfolio partially invested in the risk-free asset reduces the portfolio risk but can achieve a higher expected rate of return than any portfolio on the efficient frontier of risky assets.

Example 9-1: Expected Return and Standard Deviation for a Two-Asset Portfolio That Includes Investment in a Risk-Free Asset

Assume that portfolio T has an expected return of 10 percent, with a standard deviation of 25 percent, and that the risk-free rate is 4.5 percent. Estimate the expected return and standard deviation for a portfolio that has 30 percent invested in the risk-free asset and 70 percent in T.

Solution

$w = 0.70; (1 - w) = 0.30$

Therefore,

$ER_P = (0.30)(4.5\%) + (0.70)(10\%) = 1.35\% + 7.0\% = 8.35\%$

and

$\sigma_P = (0.70)(25\%) = 17.50\%$

Risk-Free Borrowing

short position a negative
position; the investor
borrows part of the
purchase price from the
stockbroker

Now consider a less risk averse investor who held portfolio B in Figure 9-4. He or she could now hold portfolio B2 and also get a higher expected rate of return for the same level of risk as B. However, getting to portfolio B2 involves having more than 100 percent invested in the risky portfolio T ($w > 100$ percent) and thus a negative or **short position** in the risk-free asset. We create a short position in the risk-free asset by borrowing. One way to do this is to buy stocks on *margin*, which means the investor can borrow part of the purchase price from the stockbroker. For example, some stocks have margin requirements as low as 30 percent, indicating an investor could buy $1,000 worth of stocks by investing only $300 and borrowing the remaining $700 from the broker. In this case, the portfolio weights are $w = 1,000/300$ or 333 percent in the risky asset and -233 percent in the risk-free asset. Of course, investors must pay interest on the borrowed money. For simplicity, we assume that they can also borrow at the risk-free rate.[4] This is illustrated in Example 9-2.

Example 9-2: Expected Return and Standard Deviation for a Two-Asset Portfolio That Includes Borrowing at the Risk-Free Rate

Assume that an investor invests all of her wealth ($1,000) in portfolio T from Example 9-1, with an expected return of 10 percent and a standard deviation of 25 percent. She borrows an additional $700 at the risk-free rate of 4.5 percent, which she also invests in T. Estimate the expected return and standard deviation for this portfolio.

Solution

$w = 1,700/1,000 = 1.70; (1 - w) = 1 - 1.70 = -0.70$

Therefore,

$ER_P = (-0.70)(4.5\%) + (1.70)(10\%) = -3.15\% + 17.00\% = 13.85\%$

$\sigma_P = (1.70)(25\%) = 42.50\%$

The portfolio described in Example 9-2 is similar to B2 and lies on the straight line depicted in Figure 9-4 beyond portfolio T, as would any portfolio formed by borrowing funds at RF and investing them in portfolio T.

The New Efficient Set and the Separation Theorem

We showed above that any point along the tangent line from the risk-free rate is attainable by either investing or borrowing at RF, and then investing all remaining proceeds in the risky portfolio T. From Figure 9-4, we see that all the points along this line *dominate* all the points on the efficient frontier, except for point T. As we showed, A2 is better than A and B2 is better than B. Therefore, allowing for the possibility of risk-free investing and borrowing has expanded the efficient set and provided investors with a *more efficient* set of portfolios from which to choose. This line is often called the new (or super) efficient frontier, or the previous efficient frontier is specifically referred to as the *efficient frontier of*

---

[4] Although borrowing rates are generally higher than the risk-free rate in practice, this assumption can be relaxed without greatly affecting our key results. For more details, refer to any investments text, such as W.S. Cleary and C.P. Jones, *Investments: Analysis and Management*, 2nd Canadian ed. (Toronto: John Wiley & Sons Canada Ltd., 2005), p. 230.

risky portfolios to distinguish it from the efficient frontier of the risk-free asset and the tangent portfolio.

Investors can achieve any point on this new efficient frontier by borrowing or investing desired amounts at RF and investing the remainder in one portfolio of risky assets, which is the tangent portfolio T. Therefore, each investor can choose the point on this line that suits his or her personal risk preferences: more risk averse investors can choose portfolios, like A2, that are heavily invested in the risk-free asset (T-bills), whereas more aggressive investors can choose portfolios, like B2, that involve borrowing.

Something very important arises from this discussion. Suppose investors all agree on the expected rates of return and the risk attached to each security. In that case, the efficient frontier of risky assets is the same for all investors. This would occur, for example, if the investors were clients of an investment company that estimated all these values and then discussed the best portfolio for a particular client. It would no longer be necessary to match each investor's risk preferences with a specific risky portfolio. Instead, the investment company would recommend the same tangent portfolio to all its clients. It might then refer to this portfolio as its *model* portfolio, and some investors would invest in this and the risk-free asset (T-bills), whereas others would borrow to invest in the model portfolio.

Suppose further that all investment companies agreed on the set of expected returns and the risk attached to the securities. In that case, the tangent or model portfolio would also be the same. This result provides the basis for the **separation theorem**, which states that the *investment decision*, that is, how to construct the portfolio of risky assets, is separate from the *financing decision*, that is how much should be invested or borrowed in the risk-free asset. In other words, the tangent portfolio T is optimal for every investor regardless of his or her degree of risk aversion. Further, if everyone holds the same portfolio, it must be the **market portfolio** of all risky securities, because every security has to be held by someone. This is referred to as an *equilibrium condition*, because supply equals demand for all the risky securities, and we replace T with M, which is not just the tangent portfolio but also the market portfolio. This hypothesis is the basis for the most common model we use in finance to price securities, which is discussed in the next section.

separation theorem the theory that the investment decision (how to construct the portfolio of risky assets) is separate from the financing decision (how much should be invested or borrowed in the risk-free asset)

market portfolio a portfolio that contains all risky securities in the market

CONCEPT REVIEW QUESTIONS

1. What is risk aversion and how do we know investors are risk averse?

2. What is the risk of a portfolio consisting of a risk-free asset and a risky security?

3. Why is the tangent portfolio so important?

4. How do we generate a portfolio with a higher expected rate of return than that of the tangent portfolio?

9.2 THE CAPITAL ASSET PRICING MODEL (CAPM)

Capital Asset Pricing Model (CAPM) a pricing model that uses one factor, beta, to relate expected returns to risk

Professor William Sharpe of Stanford University won the Nobel prize for developing the best-known equilibrium asset pricing model, which relates expected returns to risk: the **Capital Asset Pricing Model (CAPM)**. The initial development of the CAPM was based on a number of assumptions that we have already briefly discussed:

1. All investors have identical expectations about expected returns, standard deviations, and correlation coefficients for all securities.

2. All investors have the same one-period time horizon.

3. All investors can borrow or lend money at the risk-free rate of return (RF).

4. There are no transaction costs.

5. There are no personal income taxes so that investors are indifferent between capital gains and dividends.

6. There are many investors, and no single investor can affect the price of a stock through his or her buying and selling decisions. Therefore, investors are price-takers.

7. Capital markets are in equilibrium.

These assumptions may appear unrealistic at first. For example, the assumption of identical expectations is needed so that the efficient frontier of risky portfolios is the same for all investors. However, not all investors matter; the most important are the big institutions that invest most of the money. They all have access to the same information, and they all have expert security analysts analyzing the data. Similarly, borrowing rates differ from lending rates for small investors, but for large institutional investors, the difference is not material. The same applies to transactions costs. The result is that most of the assumptions can be relaxed without significantly affecting the CAPM or its main implications. However, before discussing the CAPM, we discuss what happens to the overall capital market.

The Market Portfolio and the Capital Market Line (CML)

The assumptions for the CAPM listed above give rise to the following very important implications, which have been discussed previously:

1. The "optimal" risky portfolio is the one that is tangent to the efficient frontier on a line that is drawn from RF, as shown in Figure 9-4. This portfolio will be the same for all investors.

2. This optimal risky portfolio will be the *market portfolio* (M), which contains all risky securities. The value of this portfolio will equal the aggregate of the market values of all the individual assets composing it. Therefore, the weights of these assets in the market portfolio will be represented by their proportionate weight in its total value.

As discussed in the previous section, the second implication results from our assumption that market equilibrium exists. This implies that supply equals demand—in other words, all assets are assumed to be bought and sold at the equilibrium price established by supply and demand. Because all assets trade, it must mean that they are correctly priced to adequately compensate investors for the associated risks. For example, if an asset were priced too high so that the expected rate of return was too low, then demand for it would fall, as would its price. Market clearing implies that the price would eventually fall to an equilibrium level so that the asset is held by all investors. Because the market consists of all available assets, and all of these assets are assumed to be priced correctly to reflect adequate compensation for the associated risk, the market portfolio will be the most efficient (or optimal) portfolio, with respect to the weights attached to the individual securities composing it.

Theoretically, the market portfolio should contain all risky assets worldwide, including stocks, bonds, options, futures, gold, real estate, and so on, in their proper proportions. Such a portfolio, if it could be constructed, would be completely diversified. However, in practice, the market portfolio is unobservable, so we use proxies to measure its behaviour. It is common to use common stock market indexes, such as the S&P/TSX Composite Index in Canada and the S&P 500 Composite Index in the United States.

capital market line (CML) a line depicting the highest attainable expected return for any given risk level that includes only efficient portfolios; all rational, risk-averse investors want to be on this line

Figure 9-5 is similar to Figure 9-4, but it does not include the efficient frontier portion and the only portfolio is M, the tangent portfolio, because the market portfolio (M) is the optimal portfolio of risky securities that is combined with RF. Recall that this line produces the highest attainable expected return for any given risk level; therefore, it includes only efficient portfolios. Further, all rational, risk-averse investors will seek to be on this line. In Figure 9-5, it is called the **capital market line (CML)**.

9-5 FIGURE

The Capital Market Line (CML)

$$k_p = RF + \frac{ER_M - RF}{\sigma_M} \sigma_P$$

We can see from Figure 9-5 that the CML has an intercept of RF, just as with any portfolio consisting of the risk-free asset and a risky portfolio. But the risky portfolio is not arbitrary: now it is the market portfolio. So we have a special version of Equation 9-3:

[9-4]

market price of risk the incremental expected return divided by the incremental risk; indicates the additional expected return that the market demands for an increase in risk

$$\text{Slope of the CML} = \frac{ER_M - RF}{\sigma_M}$$

As in Equation 9-3, the slope of the capital market line is the incremental expected return divided by the incremental risk. However, this is a special tradeoff of risk and return called the **market price of risk** for efficient portfolios or the equilibrium price of risk in the capital market. It indicates the additional expected return that the market demands for an increase in a portfolio's risk. Adding the risk-free rate (RF) gives the CML as

[9-5]

$$E(R_P) = RF + \left[\frac{ER_M - RF}{\sigma_M}\right]\sigma_P$$

ER_M = the expected return on the market portfolio M

σ_M = the standard deviation of returns on the market portfolio

σ_P = the standard deviation of returns on the efficient portfolio being considered

required rate of return the rate of return investors need to tempt them to invest in a security

The CML is a special version of Equation 9-3 in another important way. As always, the CML indicates an expected rate of return, just as Equation 9-3 gave the expected return on a portfolio of A and the risk-free rate. However, now we have made enough assumptions to identify the portfolio as the market portfolio and as an equilibrium condition in the capital market, where supply equals demand. As a result, the CML determines not just an expected rate of return but also a **required rate of return**, which we denote as k_P.

Example 9-3: Using the CML

Assume the risk-free rate is 4.5 percent. The expected return on the market is 10 percent and it has a standard deviation of 20 percent. Determine the required rate of return necessary for investors to hold an efficient portfolio with a standard deviation of 25 percent.

Solution

$$k_P = RF + \left[\frac{ER_M - RF}{\sigma_M}\right]\sigma_P = 4.5 + \left[\frac{10 - 4.5}{20}\right](25) = 4.5 + (.275)(25) = 4.5 + 6.875 = 11.375\%$$

Notice that the required return on the portfolio is greater than that expected for the market portfolio, because it has a higher standard deviation.

Having defined the CML and worked through Example 9-3, we can talk in more detail about the difference between expected and required rates of return. Suppose the CML is as graphed in Figure 9-6, and we are looking at three portfolios: A, B, and C. The CML is drawn so that only portfolio B lies on the CML. For this portfolio, the expected rate of return is the same as the required rate of return, so the portfolio is *fairly priced*. Portfolio C is drawn so that the expected portfolio return is higher than that of B. However, this portfolio is below the

CML, which indicates that the required rate of return is higher than this expected rate of return. If we look at just the expected rate of return, C would seem to be a good buy, but this is wrong because it is a very risky portfolio. Given its risk, it is a bad buy and its price would drop, forcing up its expected rate of return until it was fairly priced and the expected and required rates of return were the same. Portfolio A presents the opposite situation: it has a high expected rate of return and relatively low risk. In this case, the expected rate of return exceeds the required rate of return and investors would bid up its price and cause its expected rate of return to fall until it lies on the CML.

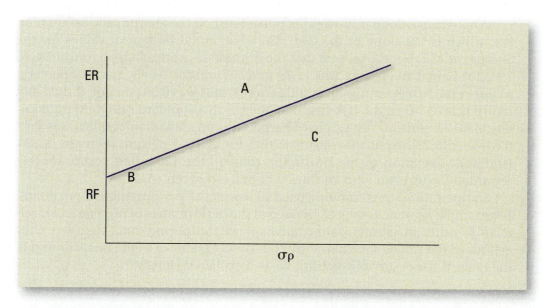

Expected and Required Rates of Return

It is also important to recognize that the CML must always be *upward sloping* because with risk-averse investors, the risk premium must always be positive, and the CML predicts *required* returns. As a result, risk-averse investors will not invest unless they expect to be compensated for bearing risk. The greater the risk, the greater the required rate of return. However, as we discussed in Chapter 8, there is a big difference between ex post and ex ante returns. After the fact (ex post), returns can be (and often have been) less than the T-bill yield. If this were never the case, investing in the equity market would have no risk and no one would hold T-bills. The observation of ex post poor returns on risky securities does not negate the validity of the CML, however; it merely indicates that returns actually realized differed from those that were expected. Another way of saying this is that investors sometimes get it wrong and their expectations are not realized. If investors were never wrong, there would be no risk in the equity market!

The ideas that we have just described have become a critical part of the evaluation of investment performance in a financial system. Consider the slope of the CML in Equation 9-4 again; in equilibrium, all portfolios should lie along the CML, as those offering higher expected than required rates of return have their prices bid up and vice versa. The CML is based on expected rates of return, so it is ex ante. However, if expectations are realized, that is, on average the actual return is what was expected, then we can use the CML to judge the performance of different portfolios ex post, that is, actual portfolio performance.

Sharpe ratio a measure of portfolio performance that describes how well an asset's return compensates investors for the risk taken

Risk-Adjusted Performance and Sharpe Ratios

When the ideas underlying the CML are used in this way, it leads to a discussion of the **Sharpe ratio**, named after William Sharpe of Stanford University, who developed it and first applied it to assessing portfolio performance. The Sharpe ratio is formally defined as

[9-6]

$$\text{Sharpe ratio} = \frac{ER_P - RF}{\sigma_P}$$

When the portfolio is the market portfolio, then the Sharpe ratio is Equation 9-4, which is the slope of the CML. So what would be typical values for the Sharpe ratio? Table 8-2 showed that the arithmetic average return from 1938 to 2005 for Canadian equities was 11.79 percent and for T-bills was 5.20 percent, so the ex post excess return of equities over T-bills was 6.59 percent. If the T-bill return is taken to be the risk-free rate, then with a standard deviation for equities of 16.22 percent, the ex post Sharpe ratio for Canadian equities was 0.41 (i.e., 6.59/16.22). What this means is that for every 1 percent increase in risk (standard deviation of the portfolio's return), the Canadian equity market rewarded the investor with an extra 0.41 percent of return.

Sharpe ratios are commonly used to assess the performance of portfolios. For example Kryzanowski et al.[5] looked at the performance of income trusts relative to other investment alternatives from the period 2002 to 2004. They estimated the values shown in Table 9-1. (Beta (β) shown in the final column of the table, is a measure of volatility. We will explain it shortly.)

Table 9-1   Income Trusts Estimated Values

	Return	σ_P	Sharpe	β
Median income trust	25.83%	18.66%	1.37	0.22
Equally weighted trust portfolio	29.97%	8.02%	3.44	0.28
S&P/TSX Composite Index	8.97%	13.31%	0.49	1.0
Scotia Capital government bond index	9.55%	6.57%	1.08	-0.02

Source: Adapted from L. Kryzanowski, S. Lazrak, and I. Rakita, "The True Cost of Income Trusts," *Canadian Investment Review 19*, no. 5 (Spring 2006), Table 3, p. 15.

Performance over a two-year period is unlikely to be representative of future returns because returns are so volatile, but income trusts are a relatively new investment vehicle and Kryzanowski et al. had limited actual data. In terms of actual returns, the trust sector had very high returns over this period. The median or typical trust earned 25.83 percent, meaning that half the income trusts returned more than that and half less than that. Clearly, 25.83 percent exceeded the 8.97 percent return from the TSX Composite Index and the 9.55 percent from an index of long-term Canada bonds maintained by Scotia Capital. The question is, was this return on trusts earned because they are so risky?

[5] L. Kryzanowski, S. Lazrak and I. Rakita, "The True Costs of Income Trusts," *Canadian Investment Review 19*, no. 5 (Spring 2006), pp. 10–16.

The standard deviation of the typical trust was 18.66 percent. This seems very high, but this is the risk of an individual security, and we saw in Chapter 8 that portfolio diversification reduces the risk of holding individual securities. One solution is to hold a portfolio of income trusts. Kryzanowski et al. showed that the return on a portfolio in which equal amounts were placed in each income trust was 29.97 percent, even greater than the typical income trust return. More importantly, the standard deviation dropped to 8.02 percent because the returns on the trusts were not highly correlated. This standard deviation was lower than that on the S&P/TSX Composite Index and only slightly more than on the Scotia Capital index of government bonds. Higher returns and lower risk sounds like a good deal, and it was, because the Sharpe ratio was 3.44 compared with 1.08 for the government bonds and 0.49 for the S&P/TSX Composite Index.

The Kryzanowski et al. study shows that over this period the Sharpe ratio for income trusts was "off the wall": a value of 3.44 is phenomenally high (remember, the historical ratio for common shares is 0.41), and over this period, the Canadian equity market was not that far off the historical average. It is understandable, from this performance, why investors rushed into income trusts. However, it also indicates the importance of the warning on all investments that *historical performance is no guarantee of future performance*. As discussed in Chapter 2, on October 31, 2006, Finance Minister Jim Flaherty decided to impose a distribution tax on income trusts and limited partnerships. The next day, income trusts dropped in price by approximately 15 percent, wiping out $30 billion in market value. Clearly, this risk never materialized from 2002 to 2004, when Kryzanowski et al. estimated the risk and return properties of income trusts, and so it could not be factored into their Sharpe ratio calculations.

The Sharpe ratio is used by professionals as well as academics. Finance in the News 9-1 is an excerpt from Morningstar Research Inc. (Morningstar), a major provider of data on mutual funds. Mutual funds are portfolios of securities managed by professionals so that individuals don't need to construct their own portfolios. The first part of the definitions describes beta (β), which is in the final column of the Kryzanowski et al. data as well, and which we will discuss shortly, but note the definition of the *Morningstar Risk-Adjusted Returns (MRAR)*. This definition is very similar to the Sharpe ratio in that the numerators in both formulas are the same (excess returns). However, the denominator used in the Sharpe ratio is standard deviation, while the MRAR does not use standard deviation, but instead uses more of a utility function that penalizes downward variation more. This is because Morningstar assumes that investors are more concerned about an unexpected bad outcome than an unexpected good outcome (utility).

CONCEPT REVIEW QUESTIONS

1. Why is the CML an equilibrium model?

2. What is the market price of risk according to the CML?

3. If the expected return on a diversified portfolio lies above the CML, should an investor buy or sell it?

4. When is the expected return equal to the required return?

5. Why is the Sharpe ratio frequently referred to as a "risk-adjusted" measure of performance?

MORNINGSTAR'S RISK-RETURN MEASURES

Beta is a measure of fund performance volatility (risk relative to a market index) over time. It is also referred to as the measure of the "systematic market risk." Beta uses regression analysis to compare the historical price volatility of a security relative to an appropriate benchmark. The actual mathematical formula of beta can be expressed as:

Beta = (Covariance between an investment and the market)/(standard deviation of the market)

One of the most practical ways investors use beta is to determine how volatile a stock or mutual fund is relative to the broader market or an otherwise appropriate benchmark. A beta of 1.0 indicates that a stock has been equally volatile as its benchmark. A beta of 1.25 means it has been 25 percent more volatile than the market, whereas a beta of 0.75 means it's been 25 percent less volatile.

Betas are calculated by Morningstar over the last 36 months. Canadian Equity fund betas are typically calculated relative to members of the S&P/TSX Composite family of indexes, Canadian Bond fund betas are typically calculated relative to the BIGAR Broad Market Composite Index, and U.S. Equity fund betas are typically calculated relative to the S&P 500 Index.

Morningstar Risk-Adjusted Rating

The Morningstar Risk-Adjusted Rating, commonly referred to as the Star Rating, relates the risk-adjusted performance of a fund to its peers in the Morningstar category. Morningstar calculates ratings only for categories with at least 20 funds. To determine a fund's rating, the fund and its peers are ranked by their MRARs. If a fund scores in the top 10 percent of its fund category, it receives five stars (High); if it falls in the next 22.5 percent, it receives four stars

(Above Average); a place in the middle, 35 percent, earns a fund three stars (Neutral or Average); those in the next 22.5 percent receive two stars (Below Average); and the lowest 10 percent get one star (Low).

Morningstar also accounts for instances where a fund is sold in multiple versions, whether multi-class, both trust and segregated, etc. In order to prevent one fund from unfairly taking up many places in a portion of the ratings scale, Morningstar treats multiple versions of a fund as "fractional funds." The multiple versions of a fund are all rated, but they collectively count as one and so leave more room for other deserving funds.

The overall Star Rating for a fund is a weighted combination of its three-, five-, and ten-year ratings. If a fund has less than three years' performance history, it is not rated. If it has at least three but less than five years' history, its overall rating is equal to its three-year rating. If it has at least five but less than ten years' history, its overall rating is equal to 60 percent five-year rating and 40 percent three-year rating. If it has at least ten years' history, its overall rating is equal to 50 percent ten-year rating, 30 percent five-year rating and 20 percent three-year rating.

Morningstar Risk-Adjusted Ratings are recalculated monthly.

Morningstar Risk-Adjusted Returns (MRAR)

MRAR is a measure of a fund's annualized historical excess return (excess is measured relative to risk-free investment in Canadian government T-bills) adjusted for the fund's historical volatility.

Volatility

A measure of risk based on standard deviation in fund performance over 3 years.

Source: Retrieved from Morningstar Research Inc. website at www.morningstar.ca, December 7, 2000. Copyright 2000 Morningstar Research Inc. All Rights Reserved. Neither Morningstar nor its content providers are responsible for any damages or losses arising from any use of this information.

9.3 THE CAPM AND MARKET RISK

The CML provides a method of estimating the required return on equity securities relative to their risk, but it applies only to efficient portfolios and not to individual securities. In addition, the risk premium is based on portfolio risk, as measured by the standard deviation of the return on the portfolio. In corporate finance, we are usually concerned with the risk attached to individual firms and the required return for investing in them. Recall from our discussion in Chapter 8 that as the number of securities included in a portfolio increases, *unique (non-systematic or diversifiable) risk* is eliminated, and only *market (systematic or non-diversifiable) risk* remains. This relationship is depicted in Figure 9-7.

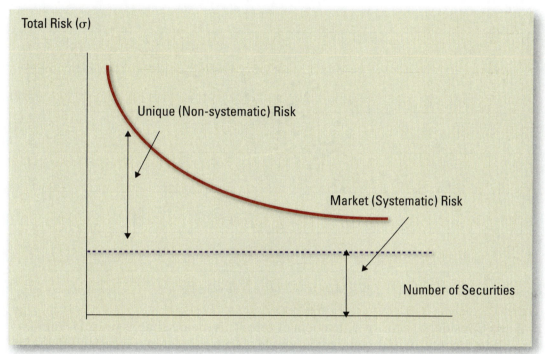

9-7 FIGURE

Portfolio Risk and Diversification

In Figure 9-7, the average risk of an individual security is shown where the curve gets very close to the vertical axis, that is, a one-stock portfolio. Therefore, by randomly building diversified portfolios, the risk of a portfolio falls, until it reaches a baseline and cannot be reduced below this market level. What this means is that part of a security's risk is diversifiable. Further, if it can be diversified away by holding a portfolio of more than, say, 20 securities, it is not important to rational investors. This is the key insight of the CAPM.

The CAPM points out that rational investors should not be compensated for unique or diversifiable risk, because it can be eliminated through diversification. This implies that market risk is the appropriate measure of risk to determine the risk premium required by investors for holding a risky security. We now introduce a new term, **beta (β_i)**, which is a commonly used measure of market risk that relates the extent to which the return on a security moves with that on the overall market. It is typically estimated by first plotting the returns

beta (β_i) a measure of market risk, or performance volatility, that relates the extent to which the return on a security moves with that on the overall market; the covariance between an investment and the market divided by variance of the market

characteristic line a line of best fit through the returns on an individual security, plotted on the vertical axis, relative to the returns for the market, plotted along the horizontal axis

on an individual security on the vertical axis relative to the returns for the market, which are plotted along the horizontal axis, and then fitting a line through the observations, as shown in Figure 9-8. The line is called the **characteristic line** and is determined by using a statistical technique called regression analysis. The slope of the line is the security's beta coefficient. For example, in Figure 9-7, the slope coefficient is 0.85, which indicates that if the market return goes up or down by 1.0 percent, the return on this security is expected to go up or down by 0.85 percent; that is, it changes by 0.85 of the return on the market.[6]

FIGURE 9-8

The Characteristic Line for Security A

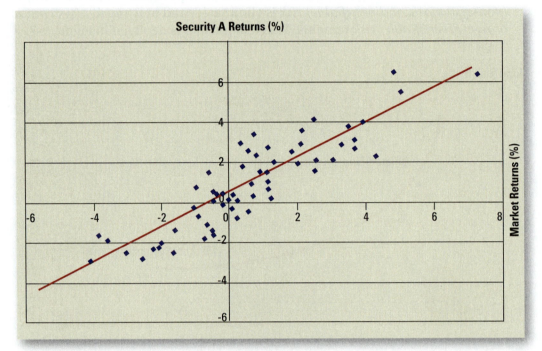

Consider a security with a beta of zero. This means that its return is unrelated to the return on the market as whole. As a result, all of the variability in this security's return is diversifiable by any investor holding a well-diversified portfolio. If this security is added to a diversified portfolio, it has no impact on the portfolio's risk, because all of its risk is diversifiable. In contrast, a security with a beta of, say, 2.0 increases by twice the return on the market portfolio on average. Adding a high-beta security to the portfolio thus increases the risk of the portfolio and makes it more sensitive to market movements.

Estimating beta coefficients is tricky, because we are interested in the extent to which the security moves with the market over a future period. As always, we estimate beta coefficients by using historical data, which assumes that what has happened in the past is a good predictor for the future. Typically, betas are estimated by using 60 months of monthly returns, but sometimes 52 weeks of weekly returns are used. Betas change through time as the risk of the underlying security or portfolio changes. This is particularly important for individual securities, for which betas can change quite dramatically over relatively short periods. Conversely, betas estimated for large portfolios or for industries are

---

[6] The characteristic line is also often estimated by using *excess returns*. The excess return is calculated by subtracting the risk-free rate from both the return on the stock and the return on the market. In excess return form, the same analysis applies.

much more stable because of averaging over many securities. Therefore, estimates of portfolio betas show less change from period to period and are much more reliable than are the estimates for individual securities.

Under some fairly common statistical assumptions, betas can be estimated by using Equation 9-7:[7]

$$\beta_i = \frac{COV_{i,M}}{\sigma_M^2} = \frac{\rho_{i,M}\sigma_i}{\sigma_M}$$

[9-7]

Beta measures the risk of an individual stock or portfolio *relative* to the market portfolio. A beta of 1 implies that if the market increased (or decreased) by 1 percent, the return on the security (or portfolio) would increase (decrease) by 1 percent *on average*. Therefore, the market has a beta of 1. A security with a beta of 1.2 has returns that are 1.2 times as volatile as market returns, both up and down. In other words, if the market increased 10 percent, that security's returns would increase by 12 percent, and so on. Securities with betas greater than 1 are generally considered to be more volatile (or risky) than average. Similarly, securities with betas less than 1 are less volatile (risky). The risk-free asset has a beta of 0, because it has a covariance of zero with the market and has no risk. Finally, negative betas are possible, although they are rare. Equation 9-7 shows that negative betas can only occur if a security has a negative correlation coefficient with market returns, which is uncommon.[8]

Example 9-4: Estimating Beta

The returns on stock X have a standard deviation of 25 percent and a correlation coefficient of 0.70 with market returns, which have a standard deviation of 20 percent. Estimate the beta for stock X.

Solution

$$\beta_X = \frac{\rho_{X,M}\sigma_X}{\sigma_M} = \frac{(0.70)(25)}{(20)} = 0.875$$

Notice that even though stock X has a higher standard deviation than the market, its beta is less than one because of the correlation coefficient of 0.70.

Betas tend to vary a great deal across companies in different industries, because they possess different risk profiles. Although betas tend to be more similar for companies operating in the same industry, they can still vary substantially, because even companies within the same industry can differ substantially across various dimensions, such as financial risk, size, and so on. These comments can be validated by looking at the betas reported in Table 9-2 for several well-known Canadian companies that operate in a variety of industries. Betas range from a low of 0.21 for Sobeys Inc. (a food retailer) to a high of 2.52 for Gammon Lake Resources Inc. (a mining company).

---

[7] The technical assumptions required ensure that ordinary least squares (OLS) is the appropriate regression estimation approach to determine the equation of the characteristic line discussed above.

[8] This is the only way a negative beta is possible, because the standard deviation terms in Equation 9-7 are always positive. Gold stocks have sometimes had negative betas because the price of gold tended to go in the opposite direction of the market; investors would invest in gold when they were nervous about future market movements. However, this relationship is not as strong as it used to be, and negative betas rarely occur, even for gold stocks.

Table 9-2   Canadian BETAS

Company	Industry Classification	Beta
Abitibi Consolidated Inc.	Materials–Paper & Forest	1.37
Algoma Steel Inc.	Materials–Steels	1.92
Bank of Montreal	Financials–Banks	0.50
Bank of Nova Scotia	Financials–Banks	0.54
Barrick Gold Corp.	Materials–Precious Metals & Minerals	0.74
BCE Inc.	Communications–Telecommunications	0.39
Bema Gold Corp.	Materials–Precious Metals & Minerals	0.26
Canadian Imperial Bank of Commerce	Financials–Banks	0.66
Cogeco Cable Inc.	Consumer Discretionary–Cable	0.67
Gammon Lake Resources Inc.	Materials–Precious Metals & Minerals	2.52
Imperial Oil Ltd.	Energy–Oil & Gas: Integrated Oils	0.80
Inco Limited	Materials–Base Metals	1.87
Loblaw Companies Ltd.	Consumer Staples–Food & Drug Retailing	0.25
Magna International	Consumer Discretionary–Auto Parts	1.01
Petro-Canada	Energy–Oil & Gas: Integrated Oils	0.69
Royal Bank	Financials–Banks	0.59
Shell Canada Ltd.	Energy–Oil & Gas: Integrated Oils	0.91
Sobeys Inc.	Consumer Staples–Food & Drug Retailing	0.21
Toronto-Dominion Bank	Financials–Banks	0.97
TSX Group Inc.	Financials–Diversified Financials	1.92
Westjet Airlines Ltd.	Industrials–Transportation: Airlines	0.70
Yellow Pages Income Fund	Consumer Discretionary–Media & Entertainment	0.64

Source: Research Insight, Compustat North American database, June 2006.

Unlike portfolio standard deviations, portfolio betas *are* weighted averages of the betas for the individual securities in the portfolio. Therefore, we can estimate the beta for an *n*-security portfolio by using Equation 9-8:

[9-8]

$$\beta_P = w_A\beta_A + w_B\beta_B + \ldots + w_n\beta_n$$

Example 9-5: Estimating a Portfolio Beta

An investor has a portfolio that consists of $10,000 invested in stock B, which has a beta of 1.2; $20,000 in stock C, which has a beta of 0.8; and $20,000 in stock D, which has a beta of 1.3. Estimate the beta of this portfolio.

Solution

$$w_B = \frac{10{,}000}{(10{,}000 + 20{,}000 + 20{,}000)} = 0.20; \quad w_C = \frac{20{,}000}{50{,}000} = 0.40; \quad w_D = \frac{20{,}000}{50{,}000} = 0.40$$

$$\beta_P = w_B\beta_B + w_C\beta_C + w_D\beta_D = (0.20)(1.2) + (0.40)(0.8) + (0.40)(1.3) = 0.24 + 0.32 + 0.52 = 1.08$$

We can see from this result why diversified portfolios end up with only market risk. First, the beta on the market portfolio, by definition, is 1.0. We can see this from Equation 9-7 by substituting M for the standard deviation of the security and noting that a security is perfectly correlated with itself! So if the average beta is 1.0, as we randomly add securities to a portfolio, we eventually end up with an average risk portfolio with a beta of 1.0, composed of all market risk. This is also why most large portfolios made up of a large number of securities are essentially the same as the market portfolio and earn the same rate of return.[9]

The Security Market Line (SML)

Based on the argument made earlier that investors should be compensated for market risk, as measured by beta, it is easy to use the CML to derive the **security market line (SML)**, which is given in Equation 9-9:[10]

> $$k_i = RF + (ER_M - RF)\beta_i$$

[9-9]

where k_i = the required return on security (or portfolio) i

The SML is the most important and widely used contribution of the CAPM and it is depicted graphically in Figure 9-9. It represents the tradeoff between market risk and the required rate of return for any risky security, whether it is an individual security or a portfolio.

security market line (SML) the tradeoff between market risk and the required rate of return for any risky security, whether an individual security or a portfolio

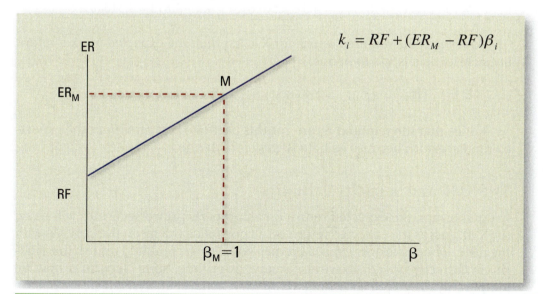

$$k_i = RF + (ER_M - RF)\beta_i$$

9-9   FIGURE

The Security Market Line (SML)

---

[9] This is what is commonly referred to as *closet indexing*, because although they charge large fees, most mutual funds have similar performance.

[10] For a formal derivation of the SML from the CML, refer to any investment textbook. For example, see W.S. Cleary and C.P. Jones, *Investments: Analysis and Management,* 2nd Canadian ed. (Toronto: John Wiley & Sons Canada Ltd., 2005), pp. 248–49.

The SML is upward sloping, which indicates that investors require a higher expected return on riskier, that is, higher-beta, securities. In essence, the SML formalizes the notion discussed previously at several junctures since Chapter 6: the required rate of return on an asset equals the risk-free rate plus a risk premium. According to the SML, the size of the risk premium varies directly with a security's market risk, as measured by beta.

market risk premium
the risk premium as a function of market conditions; the expected return on the market minus the risk-free rate

The risk premium is also a function of market conditions, as reflected in the $ER_M - RF$ term, which is often referred to as the **market risk premium**. The historical averages provided in Table 8-2 of Chapter 8 suggest that the ex post risk premium from 1938 to 2005 in Canada was 6.59 percent (i.e., the average return on the market portfolio of Canadian common stocks was 11.79 percent while the average T-bill return was 5.20 percent).[11]

According to the SML, securities or portfolios with betas greater than the market beta of 1.0 will have larger risk premiums than the "average" stock and will therefore have larger required rates of return. Conversely, securities with betas less than that of the market are less risky and will have lower required rates of return.

Example 9-6: Using the SML

Given that the expected return on the market is 10 percent and the risk-free rate is 4.5 percent, estimate

a. the market risk premium.

b. the required return for security X in Example 9-4, which had a beta of 0.875.

c. the required return for the portfolio in Example 9-5, which had a beta of 1.08.

Solution

a. $ER_M - RF = 10 - 4.5 = 5.5\%$

b. $k_X = RF + (ER_M - RF)\beta_X = 4.5 + 5.5(0.875) = 4.5 + 4.813 = 9.313\%$

Notice that the required return for X is *less than* the expected market return because its beta is *less than* one.

c. $k_p = RF + (ER_M - RF)\beta_p = 4.5 + 5.5(1.08) = 4.5 + 5.94 = 10.44\%$

Notice that the required return for this portfolio is *greater than* the expected market return because its beta is *greater than* one.

The SML and Security Valuation

In equilibrium, the expected return on all properly priced securities will lie *on* the SML, just as the expected return on all portfolios will lie on the CML. As with the CML, when investors expect a return equal to the required return, the security is correctly priced. However, at any given time, some securities may be temporarily mispriced according to CAPM. Whenever analysis suggests that the expected return on a security differs from its required rate of return according to CAPM, then that security is either undervalued or overvalued. Securities or

---

[11] Whether this is a reasonable exante market risk premium is doubtful given market developments since then.

portfolios that have expected returns *greater than* their required rate of return are *undervalued*, because they provide investors with an expected return that is higher than the return required given their risk. Similar to the CML, undervalued securities will lie *above* the SML, reflecting the fact that the expected return exceeds the required return, which is the return along the SML that corresponds to the beta coefficient. Security A in Figure 9-10 represents an example of an undervalued security. Similarly, securities or portfolios whose expected

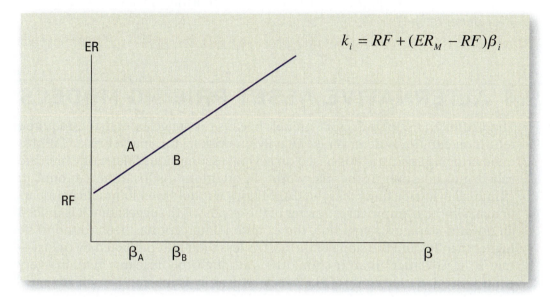

$$k_i = RF + (ER_M - RF)\beta_i$$

9-10 FIGURE

The SML and Security Valuation

returns are *less than* their required rate of return, such as B in Figure 9-10, are *overvalued* and will lie below the SML.

If markets are efficient, we would expect prices to be correct.[12] Therefore, whenever rational investors observe an undervalued security, such as A, they will rush to purchase it because it offers a higher expected return than its required return. As a result of this increase in demand for security A, its price will increase until it eventually equals the price level at which its expected return equals the required return according to the SML. In other words, security A's price will adjust until it lies along the SML. In similar fashion, selling pressure for security B (which is overvalued) would increase, causing B's price to decline until it too lies along the SML.

This discussion of the security market line is very similar to the discussion of the capital market line. The only difference is the measure of risk. For individual securities, the measure of risk is beta, whereas for diversified portfolios, it is the standard deviation. For this reason, Kryzanowski et al. reported the beta for income trusts in their study, which was 0.28. This beta indicated very little correlation between income trusts and the stock market as a whole, so that trusts should be held with common shares in a diversified portfolio. Investors who plunged into income trusts and saw their values drop by 15 percent to 20 percent on November 1, 2006, forgot the basic lesson: diversify, diversify, diversify.[13]

---

[12] We will discuss the notion of market efficiency in Chapter 10.

[13] Morningstar also estimates betas for the mutual funds it rates, as indicated by the definition in Finance in the News 9-1.

9.4 ALTERNATIVE ASSET PRICING MODELS

The CAPM is a "single-factor" model, because it suggests that the required return on equities is determined by only one risk factor: market risk. CAPM is often criticized because it is based on several assumptions, many of which are called into question in the real world. In addition, a substantial amount of empirical evidence finds that the CAPM does not hold well in practice. In particular, although empirical estimates of the ex post SML suggest that it is indeed an upward-sloping straight line, the ex ante y-intercept has been found to be higher than RF, and the slope of the SML is less than that predicted by theory—that is, it is "flatter" than it should be. Although this research remains very controversial, a 1992 study of U.S. stock returns by Fama and French concluded that beta, the sole risk factor in the CAPM, possessed no explanatory power for predicting stock returns.[14] In addition, they found that two other factors (discussed in the next subsection) do a much better job of explaining common stock returns.

An important theoretical problem associated with tests of the CAPM was identified by Richard Roll in 1976 and is commonly referred to as Roll's critique.[15] Roll argued that the CAPM cannot be tested empirically because the market portfolio, which consists of all risky assets, is unobservable. Therefore, researchers are forced to use market proxies, which may or may not be the optimal mean-variance efficient portfolio. In effect, Roll argued that tests of the CAPM are actually tests of the mean-variance efficiency of the chosen market portfolio. He showed that the basic CAPM results will hold whenever the chosen proxy is mean-variance efficient and will not hold if the converse is true. As a result the empirical tests have no power.

Despite the criticisms of the CAPM, it remains the most commonly used method of estimating the required rate of return on individual securities used by both academics and practitioners. One of the main reasons for its staying power is its intuitive appeal for assessing the tradeoff between risk and expected return and the observation that individuals hold diversified portfolios. Further, the contenders have had at least as much difficulty generating statistical support as has the CAPM. However, in response to some of the problems associated with the CAPM, alternative asset pricing models have been developed, and two of the

[14] See E. Fama and K. French, "The Cross Section of Expected Stock Returns," *Journal of Finance 47* (1992), pp. 427–65.

[15] See R. Roll, "A Critique of the Asset Pricing Theory's Tests; Part I: On Past and Potential Testability of the Theory," *Journal of Financial Economics 4* (1976), pp. 129–76.

better-known alternatives are discussed in the next section. In contrast to the CAPM, both of these models are multi-factor models, because they assume that more than one factor affects stock returns.

The Fama-French Model

As mentioned in the previous section, Fama and French found that two additional factors, beyond market returns, affected stock returns. These factors are the market value of a firm's common equity (MVE), and the ratio of a firm's book equity value to its market value of equity (BVE/MVE). Based on this discovery, they developed a three-factor pricing model. Like the CAPM, their model includes an overall market factor; however, it also includes MVE (which is related to firm size) and the BVE/MVE.[16]

The **Fama-French (FF) Model** has become popular over the past decade, because some believe that it does a better job than the CAPM of explaining ex ante stock returns. For example, Ibbotson Associates, Inc. (a major provider of financial information) now gives estimates of the required return on equity for companies based on this model, in addition to estimates determined by the more widely recognized CAPM. However, the FF Model has been criticized because it is not based on sound economic fundamentals while the CAPM is. Further, many believe that the FF Model is simply an example of *data mining*, in which the data have been examined so many times that eventually some variables are bound to be discovered that explain returns better than the CAPM.

The Arbitrage Pricing Theory (APT)

Another well-known multi-factor asset pricing model is the **arbitrage pricing theory (APT)**. The APT holds under very few assumptions, unlike the CAPM. In particular, the APT does not depend on the existence of an underlying market portfolio, and it allows for the possibility that several types of risk may affect security returns. In fact, APT is based on the **no-arbitrage principle**, which states that two otherwise identical assets cannot sell at different prices.

Development of the formal APT assumes that asset returns are linearly related to a set of indexes, which proxy risk factors that influence security returns. The underlying risk factors in the APT represent broad economic forces, which are unpredictable. The APT can be expressed as in Equation 9-10:

$$ER_i = a_0 + b_{i1}F_1 + b_{i2}F_2 + \ldots + b_{in}F_n$$

[9-10]

where ER_i = the expected return on security i

a_0 = the expected return on a security with zero systematic risk

b_i = the sensitivity of security i to a given risk factor

F_i = the risk premium for a given risk factor

Fama-French (FF) Model a pricing model that uses three factors (a market factor, the market value of a firm's common equity, and the ratio of a firm's book equity value to its market value of equity) to relate expected returns to risk

arbitrage pricing theory (APT) a pricing model that uses multiple factors to relate expected returns to risk by assuming that asset returns are linearly related to a set of indexes, which proxy risk factors that influence security returns

no-arbitrage principle the rule that two otherwise identical assets cannot sell at different prices

---

[16] See E. Fama and K. French, "Size and Book-to-Market Factors in Earnings and Returns," *Journal of Finance 50* (1995), pp. 131–55.

Equation 9-10 demonstrates that a security's risk is based on its sensitivity to basic economic factors, while expected return increases proportionately to this risk. The sensitivity measures (b_i) have a similar interpretation to beta in the CAPM, because they measure the relative sensitivity of a security's return to a particular risk premium. In fact, the APT would "collapse" into the CAPM if there were only one risk factor (market returns) influencing security returns.

The main problem with the APT is that the factors are not specified ahead of time. In fact, APT does not even specify the number of risk factors that exist, or state which factors will be the most important. As a result, these factors, as well as their relative importance, must be identified empirically. Most empirical evidence suggests that three to five factors influence security returns and are priced in the market. For example, Roll and Ross identify the following five systematic factors:[17]

1. changes in expected inflation

2. unanticipated changes in inflation

3. unanticipated changes in industrial production

4. unanticipated changes in the default-risk premium[18]

5. unanticipated changes in the term structure of interest rates

CONCEPT REVIEW QUESTIONS

1. Why is the CAPM called a single-factor model?
2. Describe some of the criticisms of the CAPM, including Roll's critique.
3. Briefly describe the strengths and weaknesses of the Fama-French Model and the APT.

Summary

In this chapter we show how the efficient frontier can be expanded by introducing the possibility of risk-free borrowing and lending. Based on certain assumptions that underlie the *capital asset pricing model (CAPM)*, we show that this new *super efficient frontier* can be depicted as a straight line that begins at RF and is tangent to the old efficient frontier at point M, the *market portfolio*. This line is called the *capital market line (CML)* and depicts the required return for *efficient* portfolios based on their standard deviations.

The *security market line (SML)*, which represents the most important contribution of the CAPM, can be derived from the CML. The SML provides a way of estimating the required return for any security or portfolio, based on its market risk, as measured by beta. Criticisms of the CAPM have led to the

---

[17] Richard Roll and Stephen Ross, "An Empirical Investigation of the Arbitrage Pricing Theory," *Journal of Finance* 35, no. 5 (December 1980), pp. 1073–103.

[18] This variable is commonly defined as the yield on long-term corporate bonds minus the yield on long-term government bonds.

development of alternative asset pricing models. We conclude the chapter with a brief description of two of these models: the *Fama-French Model* and the *arbitrage pricing theory (APT)*.

Key Terms

arbitrage pricing theory (APT), p. 371

beta (β_i), p. 363

Capital Asset Pricing Model (CAPM), p. 356

capital market line (CML), p. 357

characteristic line, p. 364

Fama-French (FF) Model, p. 371

insurance premium, p. 349

market portfolio, p. 355

market price of risk, p. 358

market risk premium, p. 368

new (or super) efficient frontier, p. 353

no-arbitrage principle, p. 371

required rate of return, p. 358

risk premium, p. 349

security market line (SML), p. 367

separation theorem, p. 355

Sharpe ratio, p. 360

short position, p. 354

tangent portfolio, p. 352

Formulas/Equations

(9-1) $ER_P = RF + w(ER_A - RF)$

(9-2) $\sigma_p = w\sigma_A$

(9-3) $E(R_P) = RF + (\dfrac{E(R_A) - RF}{\sigma_A})\sigma_P$

(9-4) Slope of the CML $= \dfrac{ER_M - RF}{\sigma_M}$

(9-5) $E(R_P) = RF + \left[\dfrac{ER_M - RF}{\sigma_M}\right]\sigma_P$

(9-6) Sharpe ratio $= \dfrac{ER_P - RF}{\sigma_p}$

(9-7) $\beta_i = \dfrac{COV_{i,M}}{\sigma_M^2} = \dfrac{\rho_{i,M}\sigma_i}{\sigma_M}$

(9-8) $\beta_P = w_A\beta_A + w_B\beta_B + ... + w_n\beta_n$

(9-9) $k_i = RF + (ER_M - RF)\beta_i$

(9-10) $ER_i = a_0 + b_{i1}F_1 + b_{i2}F_2 + ... + b_{in}F_n$

QUESTIONS AND PRACTICE PROBLEMS

Multiple Choice Questions

1. Which of the following statements is *false*?

   A. The standard deviation of a risk-free asset is zero.

   B. Portfolios on the efficient frontier dominate all other attainable portfolios for a given risk or return.

   C. The covariance of any combination of a risky security and a risk-free asset is zero.

   D. The risk measurement associated with the security market line (SML) is the standard deviation of the portfolio.

2. If Portfolio A lies above the SML, Portfolio A is

   A. overvalued.

   B. undervalued.

   C. properly valued.

   D. undetermined.

3. All of the following are *differences* between the CML and SML, *except*

   A. the slope.

   B. the risk measurement.

   C. the *y*-intercept.

   D. the application to the required return on individual securities.

4. What is the *expected return* and *standard deviation* of a portfolio consisting of $2,000 invested in the risk-free asset with an 8 percent rate of return, and $8,000 invested in the risky security with a 20 percent rate of return and a 25 percent standard deviation?

   A. 10.4 percent, 5 percent

   B. 17.6 percent, 20 percent

   C. 5 percent, 10.4 percent

   D. 20 percent, 17.6 percent

5. Which of the following statements is *correct*?

   A. The *new efficient frontier* is a curved line similar to the original efficient frontier.

   B. All of the portfolios along the *new efficient frontier* dominate those along the original efficient frontier.

   C. The weight of the risk-free asset is positive in calculating expected return when investors buy stocks on margin.

   D. Investors who are more risk averse invest to the left of the tangent portfolio.

6. What is the standard deviation of an *efficient portfolio* with a 30 percent expected rate of return, given that RF = 5 percent, ER_M = 10 percent, and σ_M = 24 percent?

A. 50 percent

B. 30 percent

C. 60 percent

D. 120 percent

7. A portfolio with a beta *greater* than 1 is

A. more volatile than the market.

B. less volatile than the market.

C. as volatile as the market.

D. not volatile.

8. Which of the following statements is *false*?

A. Systematic risk cannot be diversified away.

B. The market portfolio includes all risky assets including stocks, bonds, real estate, derivatives, and so on.

C. The market portfolio is observable.

D. The *y*-intercept of both the SML and the CML is RF.

9. Systematic risk (beta)

A. is also called unique risk.

B. equals total risk divided by non-systematic risk.

C. estimates do not change throughout time.

D. measures of portfolios are more stable than those of individual assets.

10. Which of the following firms is expected to have the highest beta?

A. A grocery store

B. A telecommunication firm

C. A bank

D. A mining company

Practice Problems

11. State three of the assumptions underlying the Capital Asset Pricing Model (CAPM).

Easy

12. State Roll's critique concerning the CAPM.

13. The Absent Minded Profs financial services firm is planning to offer several investments to investors and is in the process of designing its marketing materials. Each investment's value in the future will be related to the return on the S&P/TSX Composite Index over the year. The cost and value of the investments are outlined as follows:

		Value of investment if:	
Investment	Cost today	S&P/TSX return <0%	S&P/TSX return $\geq$0%
A	$7	0	$15
B	$12	$15	$15
C	$9	$20	$0
D	$0	- $10	$10
E	$0	$10	- $10

Assume that the probability of the S&P/TSX falling (return <0 percent) is 40 percent and that the risk free rate is zero. Which investments will be preferred by a risk averse investor? Explain your reasoning.

14. Determine if your boss is risk averse or risk loving.[19] For the following decisions, indicate if they are consistent with risk aversion or risk loving:

   a) Buying a lottery ticket
   b) Buying fire insurance on your house
   c) Jaywalking on St. Catherine's Street in Montreal
   d) Backing up your computer

15. The Absent Minded Profs have five clients who have different risk and return preferences. The market portfolio has an expected return of 12 percent with a standard deviation of 7 percent. The risk-free rate is 5 percent. Each client has $1,000 to invest. Fill in the missing information:

Investor	Weight in risk-free asset	$ Amount invested in risk-free asset	Expected portfolio return	Portfolio standard deviation
Charles	20%			
Alger		Borrowed $300		
Fritz			9%	
Eddy			16%	
Nellie				3%

16. Calculate the missing values for the following five efficient portfolios. The expected return on the market is 8 percent with a standard deviation of 5 percent and the risk-free rate is 2 percent.

Portfolio	Expected return	Standard deviation	Sharpe Ratio	Required rate of return
Portfolio 1	14%	9%		
Portfolio 2	9%	3%		
Portfolio 3	3%	10%		

---

[19] A risk-loving investor will pay to undertake a gamble provided the gamble has sufficient upside potential.

Portfolio	Expected return	Standard deviation	Sharpe Ratio	Required rate of return
Portfolio 4	8%	4%		
Portfolio 5	4%	6%		

17. Obtain monthly returns for RIM, the Royal Bank, and the S&P/TSX Composite index for January to December 2006.[20]

   A. Which firm do you expect to have a larger beta? Explain your reasoning.

   B. Calculate the beta for each company.

   C. Create a portfolio consisting of 50 percent in RIM and 50 percent in the Royal Bank.

   i) Calculate the monthly returns for the portfolio and calculate the beta of the portfolio using those monthly returns.

   ii) Using equation 9-8, calculate the beta of the portfolio.

   iii) Compare the two betas.

18. The Absent Minded Profs have obtained the following incomplete information from the Scatter Brained Brokerage Company and have given you the task of completing the table:

	Security 1 beta	Security 2 beta	Weight in Security 1	Portfolio beta
Case 1	.40	1.50	.60	
Case 2		0.45	.80	1.30
Case 3	1.10	1.90		2.10
Case 4	1.25	0.40	.75	
Case 5	1.30		.15	1.90

19. What is the beta of:

   A. The risk-free asset?

   B. The market portfolio?

20. Jackie borrowed $800 at the risk-free rate of 8 percent. She invested the borrowed money and $1,000 in a portfolio with a 15 percent rate of return and a 30 percent standard deviation. What is the expected return and standard deviation of her portfolio?

Medium

21. Stock FM has a standard deviation of 30 percent. It has a correlation coefficient of 0.75 with market returns. The standard deviation of market return is 20 percent and the expected return is 16 percent. The risk-free rate is 6.5 percent. What is the required rate of return of Stock FM? Compare FM's required return to the expected market return.

---

[20] This is the same data you downloaded from Yahoo finance for Chapter 8. Monthly historical prices, adjusted for dividends, are available from http://ca.finance.yahoo.com . To obtain the data go to the website and type the ticker symbol.

22. Estimate the beta of the following stock: market risk premium = 20 percent, RF = 10 percent, P_0 = $10, expected dividend at the end of the year = $2.50, P_1 = $12.50. Assume the market is in equilibrium.

23. There are four risk factors, F_1, F_2, F_3, and F_4, identified to determine the required rate of return, as follows: $ER_i = a_0 + b_{i1}F_1 + b_{i2}F_2 + b_{i3}F_3 + b_{i4}F_4$. Calculate the required rate of return of a portfolio, where b_{i1}, b_{i2}, b_{i3}, b_{i4} are 0.4, 0.5, 1, 1.5, respectively, RF = 5 percent, F_1 = 10 percent, F_2 = 5 percent, F_3 = 9 percent, and F_4 = 12 percent.

24. The Absent Minded Profs have been hired to conduct an investigation of the advice the Shifty Brokerage Company has been giving their clients for a lawsuit. They observe that clients have been placed in the following portfolios:

Investor name	Portfolio	Expected return	Standard deviation
Charles	A	2.00%	0.40%
Laurence	B	4.00%	0.60%
Xiang	C	5.00%	0.30%
Amanda	D	7.00%	0.50%
Amir	E	9.00%	0.45%
Sean	F	10.00%	0.70%

Evaluate the advice the broker has been giving his clients (assume that investors can only invest in one of the six portfolios).

A) Which investors are holding inefficient portfolios?

   i) What changes would you make to their investments—how will this make them better off?

   ii) Mr. Shifty, the broker under investigation, argues that these portfolios are appropriate because these investors are risk-loving. Are inefficient portfolios appropriate for risk-loving investors?

B) Of the investors who are holding efficient portfolios, who is:

   i) The most risk averse

   ii) The least risk averse

25. Three of your friends (Wilma, Fred, and Barney) are having an argument about investments and, because you have taken this course, have come to you for advice. The set of possible investments are (assume you cannot mix risky investments):

Risky portfolio	Expected Returns	Standard Deviation
A	7%	5%
B	13%	7%
C	17%	11%

Wilma says that they should all invest in portfolio A because it has the lowest risk. Fred says that they should all invest in portfolio C because it has the highest return. Barney is just confused.

a) If there is no risk-free asset, can you recommend the same portfolio for each of the friends? Why or why not?

b) If the expected risk-free rate is 2 percent, can you recommend the same set of risky assets for each of the friends? Why or why not?

c) Does the existence of a risk-free asset make the friends better off? Explain your reasoning.

26. Which of the portfolios identified in Question 16 are undervalued, correctly valued, and overvalued? The expected return on the market is 8 percent with a standard deviation of 5 percent and the risk-free rate is 2 percent.

27. The Absent Minded Profs are following five different stocks and need to issue a recommendation (Buy, Hold, or Sell) to their customers. The market return is 7 percent with a standard deviation of 4 percent. The risk-free rate is 3 percent. The CAPM is assumed to hold.

Security	Expected return	Standard deviation	Beta	Recommendation
ABC	5%	9%	1.50	
RTS	10%	3%	1.10	
DKF	6%	10%	.95	
OPL	9%	4%	.75	
WEQ	14%	6%	1.25	

To determine the recommendations, begin by calculating the required returns for each security using the CAPM. Comparing the Expected and Required will indicate which securities are under, over, or correctly priced.

28. If a security's total risk (variance) increases, does that mean the beta must have increased? Explain.

29. The Absent Minded Profs are valuing the Vancouver Rain Making Company and need to calculate the following:

a) The required rate of return. Assume the market risk premium = 8 percent, risk-free rate = 2 percent, beta = 1.2

b) The price of VRM based on the current dividend of $1.25 and a dividend growth rate of 3 percent.

30. Which of the following are examples of systematic (market) and unsystematic (unique) risks:

a) Inflation risk

b) CFO's fraudulent activities

   c) Changes in interest rates

   d) Product tampering

   e) Political risk

   f) CEO's aversion to working on Fridays

Difficult

31. Which security, A, B, or C, will provide the *greatest* return per unit of risk when combined with the risk-free asset with a 5 percent rate of return?

ER_A = 20 percent, σ_A = 5 percent
ER_B = 17 percent, σ_B = 11 percent
ER_C = 28 percent, σ_C = 20 percent

32. The current price of a stock is $20. It is expected to rise to $26 in one year and pay an annual dividend of $1 during the year. RF = 5 percent, ER_M = 9 percent, and the stock's beta = 2.6. Determine whether the stock is overvalued, undervalued, or properly valued. Is the stock above, below, or on the SML?

33. Suppose you have a portfolio now that has $100 in Stock A with a beta of 0.9, $400 in Stock B with a beta of 1.2, and $300 in the risk-free asset. You have another $200 to invest and wish to achieve a beta that is the same as the market beta. In what security should you invest (i.e., what is the market beta of the added security)? Give an example of a firm that may have such a market beta.

34. Portfolio A has a beta of 1.2. Portfolio B has a beta of 0.9. RF = 5 percent, market risk premium = 3 percent. Calculate the required rate of return of A and B. If the expected rate of return of Portfolio A and B are both 8 percent, what investment strategy should apply?

35. Today, you observe the market portfolio has an expected return of 13 percent with a standard deviation of 7 percent and the risk-free rate is 2 percent. If only the risk-free rate increases (no changes to the expected risk and returns of the risky securities), will the composition of the market portfolio change? Will the expected risk and return on the market portfolio change? Explain your reasoning.

36. Your client is confused. He owns shares in the Whistler Snow Making Company and wants you to explain your recommendation. Both of you agree on the following: WSM has an expected return of 12 percent, a standard deviation of 9 percent, and beta of 1.25, the expected return on the market is 8 percent with standard deviation of 3 percent and the risk-free rate is 4 percent.

Your client has a basic understanding of the CAPM and based on the Capital Market Line feels he should sell the stock. However, you are recommending that he buy more of the stock (or at least hold it). Explain your recommendation to your client.

37. Determine the beta of QTax based on the following information:

- Market expected return = 8 percent, standard deviation = 3 percent
- Risk-free rate = 3%
- Current dividend = $4.50
- Dividend growth rate = 5%
- Current stock price = $25

38. The Absent Minded Professors are forecasting the returns for a plumbing supply company: The PVC Company. The PVC Company pays a current dividend of $10 and the dividend is expected to grow at a rate of 3 percent. The Absent Minded Profs have identified two public companies (ABC and VJK) which appear to be comparable to PVC.

   The ABC firm has the same total risk as PVC and a beta of 1.2. The VJK Company, in contrast, has very different total risk than PVC but has the same market risk. VJK's beta is .75. The market risk premium is 5 percent and the risk-free rate is 1 percent. Determine the required return for PVC.

39. The Absent Minded Professors are interested in seeing the relationship between beta and observed returns on real firms. Obtain monthly returns from January 2006 to December 2006 for the following firms and the S&P/TSX Composite index (^GSPTSE).[21]

Ticker	Name
PFE.TO	Pacific Energy Resources
XMC.TO	Xceed Mortgage Company
CCM.TO	Canarc Resource Corp
NAC.TO	North Atlantic Resources
RCL.TO	Ridley Inc
SMX.TO	SMTC Manufacturing Corp
BH.TO	Brainhunter Inc
CTL.TO	Catalyst Paper Corp
RIM.TO	Research in Motion
TD.TO	Toronto Dominion Bank
RY.TO	Royal Bank
G.TO	Goldcorp Inc.
GAR.TO	Garneau Inc
DMC.TO	Data Mirror Corp
K.TO	Kinross Gold Corp

A) Calculate the beta for each firm.

B) Estimate the security market line based on these stocks. Assume that the observed ex post average monthly return equals the expected monthly return. Why do we need this assumption?

C) Based on the estimated security market line, which stocks out-performed,[22] which under-performed?

D) Based on the estimated security market line, what was the monthly risk-free rate for 2006?

E) Based on your results, evaluate the ability of the estimated security market line to explain the sample security returns.

---

[21] This is the same data downloaded from Yahoo finance for Chapter 8. Monthly historical prices, adjusted for dividends, are available from http://ca.finance.yahoo.com . To obtain the data go to the website and type the ticker (don't forget the .TO) in the box labeled "Get Quotes." When you get the page for the firm, on the left hand side you will see a link to "historical prices," click this and you will go to a page containing the historical price data. Download the prices adjusted for dividends and splits. Do this for each firm and then combine the data into one spreadsheet and you will be ready to answer the question.

[22] The security earned a greater return than the return predicted by the CAPM.

Information and Efficiency

The weak, semi-strong, and strong forms of the Efficient Markets Hypothesis (EMH) are introduced in Chapter 10. The strong form assumes that all material information, public and private, is already factored into stock prices, which means there are no gains to be made from trading on insider information. In Canada, insider trading is regulated by the provinces, and these regulations vary. Many people believe a national securities regulator is necessary. Penalties vary by province but generally those found guilty of illegal insider trading may pay fines of $1 million and be jailed for up to two years. Insider trading is often difficult to prove, and convictions in Canada are rare.

Source: "Insider Trading—What's the Problem?" CBC News Online, www.cbc.ca, April 2, 2007.

Source: "Natonal Securities Watchdog Seen Putting Bite into Insider-Trading Laws," My TELUS website: www.mytelus.com, April 2, 2007.

Market Efficiency

Learning Objectives

After reading this chapter, you should understand the following:

1. What is meant by market efficiency
2. How to differentiate among different levels of efficiency
3. How to use the concepts in this chapter to judge corporate decisions
4. How the concepts in this chapter are used in regulating market activity

CHAPTER 10 PREVIEW

INTRODUCTION

This chapter discusses capital market efficiency. This issue is central to most of the topics in finance. For example, the Capital Asset Pricing Model, which was discussed in Chapter 9, is based on the notion that markets are efficient, as are most of the theories and processes discussed throughout the textbook. We will examine some of the evidence on the issue and discuss some of the implications that arise for investors and businesses based on the idea of efficient markets.

10.1 THE IMPORTANCE OF MARKET EFFICIENCY

In Chapters 5 to 9, we talked about valuing different types of securities and how to estimate discount rates or required rates of return. The reason for doing this is that in corporate finance, firms have to know what investors want when they invest in a firm's securities, which is why discount rates are also called required rates of return. Once firms know what investors want, a firm can then make decisions that increase the value of those securities and enhance shareholder value. Never forget that firms have owners and it is the legal requirement, as well as their managerial responsibility, that managers act in the owners' best interests. Correctly estimating discount rates is only part of the problem. A second important element is whether or not market prices reflect the actions of managers. This brings up the question of market efficiency.

There are three elements to market efficiency. The first is that markets have **operational efficiency**. This means that transaction costs are low. If it is very expensive to trade securities, then it will be difficult for firms to raise capital and investment will be lower than it should be. The second element is **allocational efficiency**. This means that there are enough securities to efficiently allocate risk. For example, a capital market in which firms can issue only short-term notes would not be very efficient, even if transaction costs are very low. These two types of efficiency are important for Canadian capital markets but are not the main concern in this chapter. For now, take it that the Canadian markets have a very broad array of financial securities, from short-term treasury bills to common shares and what we will later call hybrids, and these can be issued at relatively low cost. So on most criteria, the Canadian capital markets are both operationally and allocationally efficient. What is important in this chapter is whether the markets have **informational efficiency**.

Suppose, for example, that share prices are chaotic (this is actually a technical term that loosely means they reflect past actions in a predictable way that are magnified many times). If managers then make decisions that they think should increase market values, such as by introducing a new product, they should call a press conference and announce the details. Investors will then analyze all the details of the announcement and market prices will increase. The managers will then have the satisfaction of knowing that their owners (the

operational efficiency
whether transaction costs are low

allocational efficiency
whether there are enough securities to efficiently allocate risk

informational efficiency
whether or not important information is reflected in share prices

shareholders), have reacted positively to their decision. However, if share prices are determined in a chaotic way, then they will not reflect the news in this press announcement; they will reflect these other past actions. If this occurs, managers will have no idea whether their owners agree or disagree with their decisions.

For shareholder value maximization to mean anything, there has to be a connection between the decisions made by managers and the level of share prices. In this way, share prices are like a score sheet used to evaluate management. The closer the link between the actions of managers and this score sheet, the more informationally efficient is the capital market. It is therefore critical in corporate finance to understand how informationally efficient the capital market, and particularly the stock market, is. In this chapter, we will drop the adjective "informational" before efficiency, because our focus is entirely on how to assess whether or not important information is reflected in share prices.

In Chapter 17, we will discuss the basics of securities regulation in Canada. However, the key element is that all **material facts** should be disclosed to the capital market. Material facts are anything that can be expected to affect the share price. In the previous example, we mentioned a press conference, because in Ontario it is a legal requirement for a firm to divulge material facts through a press release that is then filed with the securities commission.[1] If all material facts are disclosed to the stock market, then it is important for managers to know how good this score sheet is, or alternatively how efficient the capital markets are.

> **material facts** anything that can be expected to affect the share price

10.2 DEFINING MARKET EFFICIENCY

An **efficient market** is defined as one in which the prices of all securities accurately reflect all relevant and available information about the securities. This definition implies that security prices, as determined in the capital markets, are "correct." In other words, the current price of a common share reflects all known information, both past and present, about the firm, including information about a company's earnings, financial strength, management strengths and weaknesses, and future plans as announced through press releases and the management discussion and analysis (MD&A) in its financial statements. As discussed in Chapter 7, prices will reflect rational expectations about what will happen in the future and will therefore mirror today's beliefs about future interest rate changes, future profits, potential mergers, and so on. Events that cause these beliefs about the future to change will have a corresponding impact on today's prices.

> **efficient market** a market that reacts quickly and relatively accurately to new public information, which results in prices that are correct, on average

For prices to be correct, the market must react quickly and accurately to new information. Several conditions must exist before markets can operate efficiently. One critical piece of this puzzle is that the integrity of the market is such that all market participants are treated fairly. This requirement is the reason that such a heavy emphasis is placed on **disclosure**, that is, the revelation of all material facts so that everyone in the market is buying and selling based on the same disclosed material facts about the firm.

> **disclosure** the revelation of all material facts so that everyone in the market is buying and selling based on the same material facts about the firm

---

[1] In other provinces, for example British Columbia, the firm has to disclose material facts in a different way, such as by filing a material change form with the provincial securities commission.

securities law the body of law that ensures, through capital market regulations, that all investors have equal access to, and an equal opportunity to react to, new and relevant information and that governs the buying and selling of securities

A lack of disclosure is one reason that *black markets*, and smaller and more loosely regulated markets, tend to be less efficient and that the prices in these markets do not accurately reflect available information. In this case, information is either not disclosed, is disclosed late, or is disclosed in a way such that not all market participants are aware of what is going on. Information disclosure is a very important part of **securities law** and significant attention is devoted to the maintenance and enforcement of these capital market regulations designed to ensure that all investors have equal access to, and an equal opportunity to react to, new and relevant information.[2] For example, insider trading laws prevent "insiders" from acting on private information before that information is made public.[3]

The technical definition of market efficiency suggests that market prices are *always* correct, which requires *instantaneous* and *perfect* price adjustments in response to the arrival of new information in the marketplace. This type of efficiency is not a practical reality; however, efficient markets do react quickly and relatively accurately to new information and therefore prices are correct *on average*. This is a reasonable definition of an efficient market. We can expand on this logic and note that market efficiency is a matter of degree. In other words, more efficient markets process information faster and more accurately than do inefficient ones; therefore, the prices in these efficient markets are closer to the true values.

The following assumptions underlie the existence of efficient markets:

1. A large number of rational, profit-maximizing investors exist, who actively participate in the market by analyzing, valuing, and trading securities. The markets are assumed to be competitive, which means that no one investor can significantly affect the price of a security.

2. Information is costless and widely available to market participants at the same time.

3. Information arrives randomly and therefore announcements are not related to one another.

4. Investors react quickly and fully to the new information, which is reflected in stock prices.

sell side analysts analysts whose job it is to monitor companies and regularly report on their value through earnings forecasts and buy/sell/hold recommendations; they work for the investment banks that underwrite and sell securities to the public

Although these conditions are stringent, and are not met in the strictest sense in the real world, they are not unreasonable today. A large number of market participants actively follow the prices of securities trading in the market and devour information that may affect these prices. For example, all the major investment banks have securities analysts whose job it is to monitor companies and regularly report on their value through earnings forecasts and buy/sell/hold recommendations. These analysts are called **sell side analysts**, because they work for the investment banks that underwrite and sell securities to the public. In Chapters 1 and 2, we saw that there are many institutions in the

---

[2] Securities law in Canada is a provincial responsibility. There has been considerable discussion as to whether or not Canada needs a national regulator, but at the moment, critical provinces are unwilling to give up their responsibilities. As a result, information needs to be disclosed and securities registered in most provinces separately. However, there is a forum for coordination across the provinces and increasingly *national* policies are being developed.

[3] Several definitions exist for "insiders." We suggest the use of a broad definition that includes any party that has access to private information about a security as a result of a special relationship with the underlying entity. For example, this would include anyone who sat on the board of directors for a corporation, as well as that company's officers, lawyers, bankers, and so on.

Canadian capital market that invest in securities, such as insurance companies, mutual funds, and pension funds. These institutions also employ securities analysts to evaluate the research and recommendations produced by the sell side analysts. Because these institutions buy securities, their analysts are commonly referred to as **buy side analysts**.

With all these analysts following firms, we might expect prices to be rationally based on available information and economic fundamentals. In addition, an abundance of free or inexpensive information is available about most actively traded securities, and some would even argue that an overabundance of such information makes it difficult to separate the wheat from the chaff. This information generally arrives randomly and is not predictable, because if it were predictable, the prices would already reflect the information. Therefore, it is reasonable to assume that markets *could* be efficient. However, whether they are efficient or not is another matter, because the analysts and market participants are human and may not process this information efficiently. For example, "group think" may take over and, paraphrasing John Maynard Keynes, it may be better to fail conventionally than succeed unconventionally.[4]

The notion that markets are efficient has been the subject of heated debate for decades. The greatest economist of the twentieth century, John Maynard Keynes, stated,[5]

> It might have been supposed that competition between expert professionals, possessing judgment and knowledge beyond that of the average private investor, would correct the vagaries of the ignorant individual left to himself. It happens, however, that the energies and skill of the professional investor and speculator are mainly occupied otherwise. For most of these persons are, in fact, largely concerned, not with making superior long-term forecasts of the probable yield of an investment over its whole life, but with foreseeing changes in the conventional basis of valuation a short time ahead of the general public. They are concerned, not with what an investment is really worth to a man who buys it "for keeps," but with what the market will value it at, under the influence of mass psychology, three months or a year hence.

Apart from the fact that Keynes was a great investor and substantially increased the endowment of his college at Cambridge University in England, he raised the basic question of whether or not the actions of many specialist investors and analysts made the stock market more or less efficient. Keynes was under no illusions: he believed that their actions destabilized markets. Further, he believed that the stock market should have high transaction costs, that is, be *operationally inefficient*, to keep out small investors who don't know what they are doing and contribute to stock market instability.[6]

buy side analysts securities analysts whose job it is to evaluate the research and recommendations produced by the sell side analysts; they work for institutions in the capital market that invest in securities

---

[4] It used to be a standard phrase that "no one ever got fired for buying IBM," either the computers or the stock. The fact is that the excuse that everyone else did it too, backed by extensive reports from respected security analysts, is very powerful.

[5] One of the best discussions of the role of information in the stock market remains Keynes's *The General Theory of Employment, Interest and Money* (London: Macmillan, 1936), Chapter 12, "The State of Long-Term Expectations," pp. 147–164. Keynes invented what is now called macroeconomics.

[6] This idea was resurrected in the 1990s as a "Tobin" tax, which was a transaction tax suggested by James Tobin of Yale University to reduce short-term speculation.

Keynes's view in part reflected his writing in the 1930s, just after the Great Stock Market Crash of 1929.[7] However, it was a quite common belief: Bernard Baruch, a prominent U.S. investor in the 1920s, reportedly exited the U.S. stock market just before the Great Crash after hearing elevator boys talking about which stocks to invest in. However, as the memories of 1929 and its aftermath receded, the notion that speculation or the actions of specialist investors were stabilizing took hold. In this view, if prices are pushed up too high, then other experts will sell the stocks, driving prices down to an equilibrium level. This is the basic idea we discussed in Chapter 9 in the context of the market portfolio, and it is the dominant view in finance. However, the Internet bubble of the 1990s and the stock market crash of 2000 again had people questioning the stabilizing role of professional investors and market efficiency. It remains an open question as to how informationally efficient the capital markets are.[8]

Finance in the News 10-1 highlights some of these basic questions. We will elaborate on this debate in the sections that follow and discuss some of the empirical evidence.

EFFICIENT MARKET HYPOTHESIS, ACADEMICS AND PRACTITIONERS ARE STILL AT ODDS

If you've ever searched for a pattern in the market's movement, employed fundamental analysis to spot under-or-over valued stocks, or parked your money in an index fund, you've taken a stand on the efficient market hypothesis.

First put forward by Eugene Fama in his landmark doctoral dissertation in 1964, the EMH remains the null hypothesis of academics and active money managers, who have conducted thousands of studies to debunk it. Nothing would challenge the hypothesis more than finding a sustainable anomaly that would lead to an investment strategy. That strategy would enable investors to consistently beat the market to a degree that it would compensate them for the excess risk and transaction costs incurred by trading on the anomaly. Size effect. Day of the week effect. Filter rules. The presidential cycle. Has any research posed a serious challenge to the EMH?

"The momentum effect of Jegadeesh and Titman is the most serious," Fama wrote in response to the question, "though, as they are careful to point out, it cannot be used as the basis of a profitable strategy. Many of the other anomalies are due to bad statistical work, or mistaking rewards for risk with abnormal returns."

Poppycock, says Jeremy Grantham, chairman, of Grantham, Mayo, Van Otterloo & Co. LLC, an active management firm based in Boston, Mass. USA. "I view Fama as the temple guardian. He came out with a theory that carried an enormous amount of weight. It became the dominant academic theory that, indeed, formed part of a culture that clearly suppressed alternative findings. As he's increasingly challenged, he, of course, really admits to nothing.

---

[7] It took investors 30 years to get back to the price level of 1929, and a generation of investors largely ignored the stock market.

[8] The equivalent of Bernard Baruch's elevator boys was the proliferation of day traders in the 1990s. These people gave up their full-time jobs to trade in and out of securities within the day.

CONCEPT REVIEW QUESTIONS

1. What is the diference between the various types of market efficiency?
2. Define market efficiency in terms of information.
3. Discuss the reasonableness of the assumptions underlying market efficiency.

10.3 THE EFFICIENT MARKET HYPOTHESIS (EMH)

The **efficient market hypothesis (EMH)** states that markets are efficient and therefore, in its strictest sense, it implies that prices accurately reflect *all* available information at any point in time. This statement goes well beyond our "weaker" definition of efficient markets proposed in the previous section, where we said that prices in efficient markets are correct *on average*. Because the strictest form of the EMH represents such a high hurdle, it is common to break the EMH down into the following three different, and cumulative, levels that are based on the extent to which prices reflect different types of available information:

> **efficient market hypothesis (EMH)** the theory that markets are efficient and therefore, in its strictest sense, implies that prices accurately reflect all available information at any given time

1. The **weak form EMH** states that security prices fully reflect *all market data*, which refers to all past price and volume trading information. If markets are weak form efficient, historical trading data will already be reflected in current prices and should be of no value in predicting future price changes.

> **weak form EMH** the theory that security prices fully reflect all market data, which refers to all past price and volume trading information

2. The **semi-strong form EMH** states that *all publicly known and available information* is reflected in security prices. This includes information about earnings, dividends, corporate investments, management changes, and so on. It would also include market data, which are publicly available. Therefore, this version of the EMH encompasses the weak form. In other words, if a market is semi-strong efficient, then it must also be weak form efficient. A market that quickly incorporates all publicly available information into its prices is semi-strong efficient. In such a market, it would be futile to analyze publicly available information, such as earnings projections, financial statements, and so on, in an attempt to identify underpriced or overpriced securities.

> **semi-strong form EMH** the theory that all publicly known and available information is reflected in security prices

3. The **strong form EMH** asserts that stock prices fully reflect *all information*, which includes both public and private information. It is obviously the most stringent form of market efficiency, and it encompasses both the weak and semi-strong versions, because market data and all other publicly available information must be reflected in prices, as well as any private information that is possessed by some market participants but not by all. In such a market, no investor could take advantage of the possession of superior information or the superior processing of information to identify mispriced securities, because the prices would already properly reflect all information. Obviously, this is a very strong assertion. For example, it asserts that insiders could not profit from private inside information.

> **strong form EMH** the theory that stock prices fully reflect all information, which includes both public and private information

10.4 EMPIRICAL EVIDENCE REGARDING MARKET EFFICIENCY

A perfectly efficient market is one in which all information is reflected in stock prices quickly and fully. Therefore, all security prices equal their true economic (or intrinsic) value. In practice, not even the strongest supporters of the EMH would claim that markets are perfectly efficient, so it becomes a matter of degree—in other words, exactly how efficient are the markets? Empirical tests of market efficiency tend to be organized around how market prices react to certain kinds of information, and it is common to organize the evidence with respect to the implications about the three different forms of the EMH discussed above.

Countless studies have been conducted to test market efficiency, and we can't discuss them all. However, we will present the general consensus reached on many of the issues involved. Before we begin this discussion, note that the validity of any evidence supporting the existence of market inefficiencies must be *consistent* over reasonably long periods, because random or short-lived inefficiencies may appear from time to time, even in efficient markets. Similarly, many researchers have produced evidence that is *statistically significant*, but it would be difficult to translate these findings into *economically significant* gains, after accounting for risk, trading costs, and so on. Therefore, it makes sense to talk about an *economically efficient market*, in which securities are priced correctly enough so that investors cannot exploit any discrepancies and earn unusual returns after consideration of all risks and trading costs. In fact, it is common for people involved in finance to suggest that "there is no such thing as a free lunch." In such a market, some securities could be priced slightly above their intrinsic values and some slightly below, and time lags could exist in the processing of information, but the discrepancies would be too small to be exploited economically.

Weak Form Evidence

random walk hypothesis
the theory that prices follow a random walk, with price changes over time being independent of one another

If markets are weak form efficient, current market prices will reflect all historical trading data. Therefore, past price *changes* (and total returns) should be unrelated to future price changes. This idea is related to the **random walk hypothesis**, which states that prices follow a random walk, with price changes over time being independent of one another. This hypothesis is logical if information arrives randomly, as it should, and if investors react to it immediately.

Several tests of weak form efficiency are possible. One approach is to test whether price changes are, in fact, independent of one another. This assertion can be statistically tested in many different ways, so we will mention only two of the more commonly cited tests here. *Serial correlation* tests measure the correlation between successive price changes for various lags, such as one day, two days, one month, and so on. There have been numerous variations of these tests performed on Canadian, U.S., and global stock price data throughout the years. The general consensus of these studies has been that the correlations between successive price changes are not related in an economically significant manner, even though some, but not all, studies found *statistically* significant relationships. In other words, the pattern is too weak to be exploited by investors.

Another statistical test of price change independence is called the *runs (or signs) test*. This test involves classifying each price change by its sign (i.e., whether the price change was +, 0, or −), and then examining whether there are any "runs" in the series of signs. The evidence provided by numerous studies that used the signs test also supports return independence. In particular, although "runs" have been documented, they could be consistent with random price changes, because even a truly random series will display some runs.

Although the evidence reported above is far from exhaustive, we can say that for the most part, the evidence supports the notion that price changes in the capital markets are independent of one another.

An alternative approach to test weak form efficiency is to examine specific trading rules that attempt to exploit historical trading data. If any such trading rule could be implemented in a manner that consistently generates abnormal risk-adjusted returns after trading costs, this evidence would contradict weak form efficiency.

Technical analysis involves the analysis of historical trading information to attempt to identify patterns in trading data that can be used to invest successfully. Technical analysts argue that simple statistical tests, such as the ones discussed above, are not conclusive because they are not applied to more sophisticated trading strategies that can be employed. It is difficult to definitively refute this assertion because a virtually unlimited number of possible technical trading rules exist. However, most of the evidence suggests that technical trading rules, on average, have not been able to outperform a simple buy-and-hold strategy, after accounting for risk and trading costs.

> **technical analysis** the analysis of historical trading information to identify patterns in trading data that can be used to invest successfully

In summary, most of the evidence supports the notion that markets are weak form efficient. However, a few important exceptions, or **anomalies**, have been documented.[9] Anomalies are exceptions to a rule or theory—in this case, exceptions to market efficiency. We will discuss a few well-known anomalies; however, there is no guarantee that any trading strategy that is based on exploiting these anomalies would prove fruitful.

> **anomalies** exceptions to a rule or theory

DeBondt and Thaler examined U.S. stock returns and found evidence that people *overreact* to information and that these overreactions lead to stock price "reversals."[10] They found that stocks that had performed poorly over the most recent three- to five-year periods ("losers") tended to outperform in the subsequent three- to five-year periods, while stocks that displayed superior performance in the past ("winners") tended to underperform in the future. Trading strategies that are designed to exploit this pattern are commonly referred to as *contrarian strategies*, because the idea is based on the notion of investing *contrary* to the past performance record of stocks. Several subsequent studies have confirmed these results for U.S. stock returns; however, international evidence has been mixed. Interestingly, Kryzanowski and Zhang find no such pattern for Canadian stocks over a similar period (1950–88) as that studied by DeBondt and Thaler.[11] This tendency for stock prices to reverse contradicts weak form efficiency, because it implies that future stock returns can be predicted merely by examining past trading data.

---

[9] We will also discuss some anomalies with respect to the other forms of market efficiency in the next subsections.

[10] See W. DeBondt and R. Thaler, "Does the Stock Market Overreact?" *Journal of Finance 40*, no. 3 (1985), pp. 793–805.

[11] See L. Kryzanowski and H. Zhang, "The Contrarian Strategy Does Not Work in Canadian Markets," *Journal of Financial and Quantitative Analysis 27* (1992), pp. 389–95.

momentum stocks that have experienced high returns in previous 3- to 12-month periods tend to outperform in the subsequent 3- to 12-month periods

An even more important contradiction of weak form efficiency is the existence of **momentum** in stock returns: stocks that have experienced high returns in previous 3- to 12-month periods tend to outperform in the subsequent 3- to 12-month periods. Notice that this pattern lies in sharp contrast to the longer-term reversal pattern. There is strong empirical support for the existence of momentum in stock returns in most stock markets around the world. Probably the most famous of these studies dealing with U.S. stock returns was conducted by Jegadeesh and Titman in 1993.[12] Jegadeesh and Titman formed portfolios by ranking stocks based on their past 3- to 12-month returns and found that buying the top-performing stocks ("winners") and selling the worst-performing stocks ("losers") produced very significant positive abnormal returns.

Several studies have confirmed the existence of this pattern in Canadian stock returns, as demonstrated in Figure 10-1. This figure shows that from 1980 to 1999, the returns for a "winner" portfolio (based on the most recent six-month performance) averaged 20.76 percent in the subsequent six-month period, well above the returns to the "loser" portfolio (5.99 percent), and the S&P/TSX Composite Index (6.10 percent).[13] Strong international evidence also supports the existence of momentum.[14]

There is evidence also of seasonal patterns in stock returns. The best-known pattern is the *January effect*: stock returns, especially those for smaller compa-

---

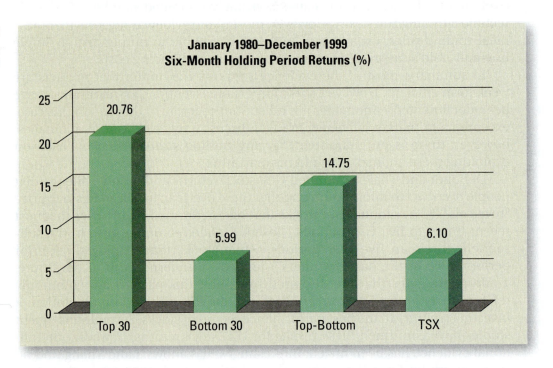

FIGURE 10-1

Momentum in Canadian Stock Returns, 1980-1999

Source: Cleary, S., Schmitz, J., Doucette, D. "Industry Affects Do Not Explain Momentum in Canadian Stock Returns," *Investment Management and Financial Innovations 2* (2005), pp. 49–60.

---

[12] See N. Jegadeesh and S. Titman, "Returns to Buying Winners and Selling Losers: Implications for Stock Market Efficiency," *Journal of Finance 48* (1993), pp. 65–91.

[13] See S. Cleary, J. Schmitz, and D. Doucette, "Industry Affects Do Not Explain Momentum in Canadian Stock Returns," *Investment Management and Financial Innovations* (2005), pp. 49–60.

[14] For example, see K.G. Rouwenhorst, "International Momentum Strategies," *Journal of Finance 53*, no. 1 (February 1998), pp. 267–84.

nies, are statistically higher in January than they are over the other 11 months of the year, with most of these returns arriving in the first five trading days. This pattern has been documented in the Canadian, U.S., and global markets. Other seasonal patterns have been noted, including the day-of-the-week effect, which refers to the fact that the average Monday return has historically tended to be negative and significantly different from the average returns for the other four days, which are all positive. Finally, studies have also found that returns tend to be higher on the last trading day of each month. Although these patterns are interesting to note, it would be difficult and very risky to attempt to exploit them, because the evidence refers to "averages," which means they do not occur all the time, and because of the trading costs involved.

Semi-Strong Form Evidence

Most tests of the EMH focus on the semi-strong version. This is logical, because most analysis of security prices, as well as most corporate finance decisions, involve the use of publicly available information. Most studies support the semi-strong EMH; however, some do not. We discuss two broad categories of approaches to these tests below.

One way of testing for semi-strong market efficiency is to examine the speed of adjustment of stock prices to announcements of significant new information. In a semi-strong efficient market, prices would adjust quickly and accurately to this new information so that investors could not act on it after its announcement and earn abnormally high risk-adjusted returns. In contrast, if the market overreacts or underreacts, or if time lags exist in stock price adjustments, and investors can exploit these flaws, then the market is not semi-strong efficient.

Figure 10-2 illustrates the price adjustment process for an efficient market (A), for an inefficient market that overreacts to new information (B), and for an inefficient market that reacts too slowly to new information (C). Notice that for this example, the stock is trading at $20 on the announcement date of the significant event (t). For market A, the market is efficient and the price adjusts immediately and accurately to the new information, which is obviously good news, because the price increased to $23. Market B overreacts to the new information, which provides investors with a window of opportunity to earn abnormal profits as a result of this information, if this overreaction occurs consistently and is of sufficient magnitude. In this case, investors could sell or short sell the stock shortly after the information becomes public and profit when the price subsequently declines. Market C, conversely, reacts too slowly to the new information, which again provides an opportunity for investors to exploit the information (i.e., by purchasing the stock "after" the information becomes public). Of course, many other possible patterns are displayed by inefficient markets.

There are numerous examples of these types of studies and most of them have taken the form of an **event study**: stock returns are examined to determine the impact of a particular event on stock prices. Most of these studies support the notion that the market adjusts to new public information rapidly and accurately, and that investors could not earn **abnormal returns** based on inefficient market reactions to significant information announcements.[15]

event study an examination of stock returns to determine the impact of a particular event on stock prices

abnormal returns returns that exceed the expected return on a stock, according to a model of stock returns, such as the CAPM

---

[15] Usually, abnormal returns are defined as those that exceed the expected return on a stock according to a model of stock returns, such as the CAPM.

FIGURE 10-2

Efficient and Inefficient Markets

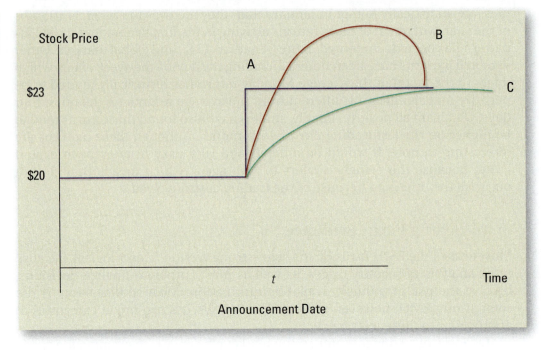

Many event studies have examined the impact of a variety of significant types of information events. For example, researchers have examined the price behaviour surrounding company-specific announcements regarding such events as stock splits, takeover announcements, dividend changes, accounting changes, and so on. Researchers have also examined significant economy-wide announcements, such as unexpected interest rate changes, and so on, that could be expected to influence aggregate price levels. The results of most of these studies are similar: prices begin to react to the event before the announcement is made public, and the final price adjustment occurs rapidly when the actual announcement is made. This is depicted in Figure 10-3, which obviously alludes to the announcement of some positive news. Notice that this evidence supports the semi-strong form of market efficiency because investors could not have earned abnormal returns after the information was made public. This evidence does not provide support for strong form efficiency, because the price increase that occurs before the announcement suggests that some investors are profiting from private information about upcoming price changes, by buying the securities before the information becomes made public.

One exception to the efficient processing of new information has been documented with respect to earnings "surprises." These refer to earnings announcements that either exceed or fall short of consensus earnings estimates. Several studies have confirmed that a lag exists in the adjustment of stock prices to earnings surprises. In particular, companies displaying the largest positive earnings surprises displayed superior *subsequent* performance, while poor *subsequent* performance was displayed by companies with low or negative earnings surprises. Although substantial price adjustments occurred before, and on the date of, the actual announcement, similar to the studies discussed above, the substantial adjustments occurring *after* the announcement date contradict semi-strong efficiency. In addition, stocks that have experienced positive earnings forecast revisions have been found to produce positive abnormal returns subsequent to the revision, on average. The larger the revisions, the greater the excess returns. This also contradicts the semi-strong form of the EMH.

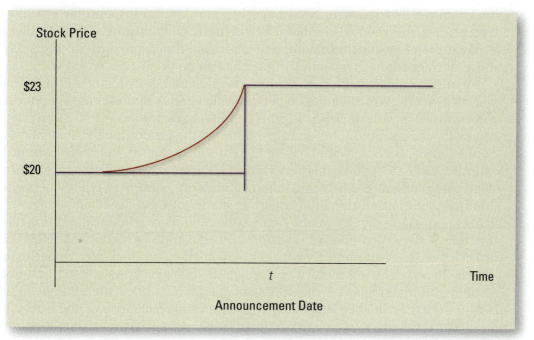

This anomaly may be related to a certain extent to the momentum anomaly discussed in the previous subsection. In particular, it has been argued that the slow reaction of markets to earnings announcements, as well as to other news items, contributes to the price momentum effect. In other words, prices react positively to good news (and negatively to bad news), but the full extent of the reaction is insufficient; therefore, prices will continue to appreciate (depreciate).

A second general approach to testing semi-strong market efficiency is to examine the performance of investors and see if they are able to use publicly available information to consistently generate abnormal risk-adjusted returns over sustained periods. A variety of active strategies have been tested, with most results suggesting that such strategies do not outperform a simple buy-and-hold strategy. Perhaps the strongest evidence of semi-strong market efficiency is the fact that professional fund managers, with all of their training, expertise, technological capability, and access to data, do not outperform the market on a risk-adjusted basis, on average. An abundance of evidence exists that suggests this is the case. In fact, most studies indicate the performance of the average active portfolio manager, after expenses, is actually substantially worse than the performance of their passive benchmarks. Some studies suggest they may underperform their benchmarks by as much as 50 to 200 basis points. Empirical evidence also suggests that pension fund managers consistently underperform their benchmarks.

Although most evidence supports semi-strong efficiency, several exceptions have been noted. Some investment "styles" have been able to produce abnormal returns.[16] One of the most important of these exceptions is that "value" stocks have consistently outperformed "growth" stocks. Value stocks are generally referred to as those that have below-average price-to-earnings (P/E) and market-to-book (M/B) ratios, and that have above-average dividend yields. They are thought to provide good value per dollar of market price. Growth

---

[16] An investment style refers to the forming of portfolios that consist of stocks that have some common underlying characteristics.

stocks, conversely, have above-average P/E and M/B ratios, and have below-average dividend yields. Their name refers to the fact that investors are willing to pay a premium for these companies because they expect them to display above-average future growth in earnings and share price.

Figure 10-4 depicts the performance of value and growth stocks in Canada over the January 1982 to June 2006 period, which demonstrates that value stocks outperformed growth stocks during this period. The figure shows that $1 invested in growth stocks would have grown to $6.06 by the end of June 2006, while $1 invested in value stocks would have grown to $19.91. In fact, the average annual return for value stocks over this period was 14.2 percent, while the average return on growth stocks was 9.5 percent. Although this is only summary-type evidence, it confirms the results of numerous rigorous studies of U.S., Canadian, and global market returns through the years—in fact, the number of studies supporting this assertion is far too comprehensive to even begin to list. Of course, the higher returns could exist in perfectly efficient markets if value stocks are riskier than growth stocks. However, the evidence suggests this is not the case, at least not according to traditional risk measures, such as standard deviation and beta. In fact, most of the evidence suggests that the opposite result arises with respect to risk—that is, value stocks appear to be less risky than growth stocks. This also turns out to be the case for the data used to construct the diagram in Figure 10-4, where the monthly standard deviation for the growth index was 5.25 percent, and the monthly standard deviation for the value index was 4.17 percent.

This value stock anomaly contradicts semi-strong market efficiency, because all the ratios used to categorize stocks in this manner are publicly available. The fact that this pattern has not disappeared in response to its widespread recognition by the investment community is all the more troublesome to efficient market advocates; in efficient markets, when investors recognize this pattern, they

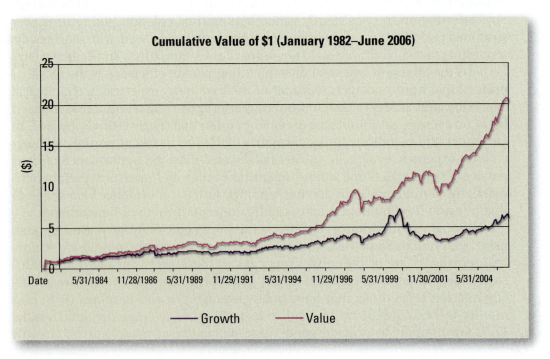

FIGURE 10-4

Growth and Value Stocks in Canada

Source: Data are from MSCI Barra website, Returns for Barra Canadian Equity Style Indexes (Growth and Value Indexes), at www.mscibarra.com.

should increase their demand for value stocks, driving up their prices and causing the excess returns to disappear. Similarly, the prices of growth stocks should decline in response to a decrease in demand for these types of stocks. However, these patterns have persisted. In any event, it is not a foolproof strategy because in any given year, growth stocks could outperform value stocks, even though value stocks have continued to outperform over the long run.

Another commonly used investing style involves forming portfolios based on the "size" of the underlying common stocks. Size is commonly measured by using the stock's market capitalization (or market cap), which equals the number of shares outstanding times the market price per share. This investing style has emerged in response to the **size effect** anomaly, which has been well documented in the finance literature since the early 1980s. The size effect refers to the fact that small market cap stocks tend to outperform large cap stocks, even after adjusting for risk. Interestingly, a large portion (as much as 50 percent) of the size effect has occurred in January. In fact, the January effect noted in the previous section is driven to a large extent by the performance of small stocks in January and is sometimes referred to as the "small firm in January effect."

size effect small market cap stocks tend to outperform large cap stocks, even after adjusting for risk

Figure 10-5 depicts the returns on Canadian small caps, as measured by the Barra Small Cap Index, versus the broad market, as measured by the S&P/TSX Composite Index. Over this period, small caps outperformed the broader index, providing an annual return of 16.25 percent versus 11.91 percent. However, the small cap returns were more volatile, which is shown in Figure 10-5, and which is confirmed by the standard deviation of 24.80 percent versus 15.12 percent. The graph illustrates that although small caps outperformed over a reasonably long period, in some years they underperformed, so it is by no means a "free lunch." In addition, small caps generally have substantially higher trading costs than larger cap stocks because they tend to trade less actively.

10-5 FIGURE

S&P/TSX Composite Index versus Small Cap Stocks in Canada, 1991-2005

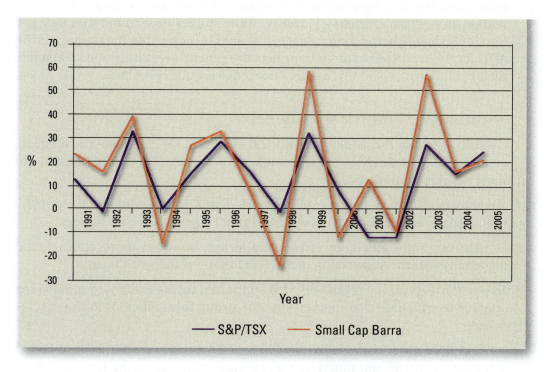

Sources: Data are from the Canadian Institute of Actuaries, S&P/TSX Composite Index returns; and MSCI Barra website, Barra Canadian Small Cap Index returns, at www.mscibarra.com.

Another long-standing semi-strong EMH anomaly is related to the information provided by the Value Line Inc., in its Value Line Investment Survey, which is one of the largest and best-known investment advisory services in the world. Value Line ranks a large universe of stocks from 1 (best) to 5 (worst), based on its expectations regarding the stocks' performance over the next 12 months. Substantial evidence suggests that the performance of stocks categorized in the first two categories has been clearly superior in the subsequent period, while the lower-ranked stocks have performed poorly. Of course, this evidence contradicts semi-strong efficiency, because investors could profit by using these ratings after they have been made public. However, evidence also suggests that it would be hard to exploit this anomaly after trading costs, because the market adjusts relatively quickly to this information.

Strong Form Evidence

The strong form version of the EMH asserts that prices reflect all public *and* private information, which is a very stringent requirement. For example, this suggests that insiders could not profit from inside information that is not known to the public, because prices would already reflect this information. However, it seems impossible that prices could reflect information that is not yet publicly available. Therefore, it is not surprising that, on balance, the evidence does not support this version of the EMH.

Strong form efficiency tests examine whether any group of investors has information (public or private) that allows them to earn abnormal profits *consistently*. Therefore, it is common to examine the performance of groups that are thought to have access to "private" information, such as insiders. Given their access to privileged information, it is not surprising that several studies have found that they have consistently earned abnormal returns on their stock transactions, which refutes strong form efficiency. However, some studies have found that they perform only slightly better than average. It should be noted that the trading activity of insiders is restricted in order to protect the general investing public. Therefore, their potential to exploit this insider knowledge is quite restricted.

Summary of Empirical Evidence

Overall, based on the available empirical evidence, we can make the following conclusions regarding the capital markets of Canada, the United States, and most developed markets:

1. Weak form efficiency is very well supported, and it is reasonable to conclude that markets are weak form efficient, although a few anomalies do exist.

2. Semi-strong form efficiency is well supported; however, more contradictory evidence exists for this version of the EMH than for the weak form.

3. Strong form efficiency is not very well supported by the evidence, and it is reasonable to conclude that markets are not strong form efficient in the strictest sense.

One final observation is that in Chapter 9 we introduced the Fama-French three-factor model and noted that this includes the size of the firm, measured by its equity market value, and the firm's book valued equity divided by its market value of equity as additional "risk" factors. As noted, small firms had to out-perform large ones and value stocks outperform growth stocks. The market value of equity used by Fama-French identifies small and large firms, while the market-to-book ratio identifies value and growth stocks and is the reciprocal of the Fama-French risk factor. It is an ongoing debate as to whether the Fama-French "risk" factors identify riskier firms or simply these stock market anomalies or departures from efficiency. Eugene Fama, as the "temple guardian" of market efficiency, views these as risk factors and the market as efficient. Others are more sceptical.

CONCEPT REVIEW QUESTIONS

1. Is the weak form EMH well supported by empirical evidence? Discuss any exceptions.

2. Is the semi-strong EMH well supported by empirical evidence? Discuss any exceptions.

3. Is the strong form EMH well supported by empirical evidence? Discuss any exceptions.

10.5 IMPLICATIONS

The EMH states that security prices will fully and accurately reflect all available information at any given time. The evidence suggests this strict interpretation of market efficiency does not hold; however, we can conclude that markets react quickly and relatively accurately to new public information. As a result, market prices are correct *on average*. Therefore, we can say that although markets may not be perfectly efficient, they are relatively efficient. This statement has several important implications for investors and for corporate officers.

Some important implications for investors include the following:

1. Technical analysis, which involves examining trading data for patterns, is not likely to be rewarded in the form of substantial abnormal returns, because markets appear to be weak form efficient.

2. Fundamental analysis based on the use of various forms of publicly available information is also likely to be unsuccessful at generating abnormal profits, although some opportunities appear to be available. The implication is that to benefit from the use of such data, the analysis must be of superior and consistent quality. Average, or below-average, analysis will likely be unfruitful. This notion is consistent with the subpar performance reported by the "average" professional portfolio manager.

3. In light of items 1 and 2 above, active trading strategies are unlikely to outperform "passive" portfolio management strategies on a consistent basis. Passive strategies involve buy-and-hold strategies and the purchase of such products as index mutual funds or exchange-traded funds (ETFs) that replicate the performance of a market index. The lack of success for active strategies is partially attributable to the extra costs associated with collecting and processing infor-

mation, as well as to the additional trading costs associated with active strategies. Obviously, these extra costs can be justified only if the approach generates sufficient additional returns to compensate for them. Passive strategies minimize these costs and therefore provide "average" results. Finance in the News 10-2 discusses the benefits of using a passive strategy that the authors label the "couch potato portfolio." They suggest that such a strategy has outperformed 80 percent of actively managed funds through the years.

4. Whether or not investors decide to pursue a passive or active strategy, it is critical that they focus on the basics of good investing by defining their objectives in terms of expected return and acceptable risk levels, and by maintaining an adequately diversified portfolio. When markets are relatively efficient, as they appear to be, paying attention to these factors will do more to promote success than will the analysis of individual security prices.

finance
INTHENEWS10-2

CHILD'S PLAY: THE COUCH POTATO PORTFOLIO

There are people out there, and we've met plenty of them, who spend hours every week sweating over their investments. Some of these investing junkies actually seem to enjoy reading balance sheets and analysts' opinions.

Most of us, though, aren't like that. We want good performance with low risk — but between our jobs and our families we don't have a lot of time to follow the market.

If that sums up your situation, MoneySense has the perfect portfolio for you. It will not only beat the performance of most people who spend hours on their investing, it will beat about 80% of the money managed by professionals. Best of all, like an ideal houseplant, this portfolio thrives on neglect. It performs superbly even if you pay attention to it for only 15 minutes a year.

We call our approach the Couch Potato strategy. It's based on the simple fact that the market is smarter than any single individual. If the market says a stock is worth $20 a share, chances are the stock is probably somewhere close to $20 a share.

This may surprise you. Most market commentary is geared to making you believe that there are scads of undiscovered bargains out there. But think about how the world works and you realize how unrealistic that proposition is.

On any given day, thousands of highly paid, highly competitive mutual fund managers and pension fund experts are scouring the market looking for bargains. When they think a stock is undervalued, they buy it. All that buying forces up the price of the stock until it's trading for what most investors believe is fair value. Similarly, if the pros believe a stock is overvalued, they sell it and keep on doing so until the stock meets their definition of fair value. Thinking that you're going to beat the system and turn up lots of great, undiscovered stocks is a bit like thinking you can wander into a thoroughly explored wilderness and spot a gold mine that all the professional geologists just happened to overlook.

The best proof of the market's intelligence is that even the professionals can't keep pace with it. Over any period of a few years or more, about 80% of actively managed mutual funds lag behind the market. They're weighed down by the salaries of their managers, by research costs, by marketing expenses, by fees paid to financial planners, by trading expenses.

Here's where the Couch Potato strategy comes in. It's based on a simple idea: if active management doesn't beat the market, why not dump it and buy the market instead?

You buy the market by investing in a small collection of low-cost index funds. These funds passively follow the ups and downs of market indexes, such as the S&P/TSX Composite index of Canadian stocks or the Standard & Poor's 500 index of U.S. stocks. Your exact mix of funds can vary (and we'll get to the details in just a second), but the

finance
INTHENEWS10-2

key advantage of the Couch Potato strategy is that it gives you wide diversification among hundreds of stocks and bonds at rock-bottom cost.

Why is this so important? Because low costs are crucial when it comes to investing success. Most investors pay about 2.5% of their assets each and every year to invest in actively managed mutual funds. On the other hand, you can become a Couch Potato for 0.5% a year or less. The couple of percentage points you save go directly to your bottom line and can have a tremendous effect over time.

Let's say you have a $200,000 portfolio. This year alone you would save about $4,000 by becoming a Couch Potato investor rather than an investor in actively managed mutual funds. Over a few years, assuming you reinvested all of your savings, the difference would grow and grow, because the money you would be saving would compound on itself. Assuming typical rates of return, the money you would save by becoming a Couch Potato would be more than enough to buy you a luxury car in 10 years' time even if you were never to invest another cent in your portfolio.

Whenever we lay out the math, people are naturally skeptical. It seems too good to be true. How can the mutual fund industry get away with charging us so much for so little? Doesn't all that expensive professional management accomplish something?

Sadly, no. If you doubt us, click here to see how our Classic Couch Potato portfolio has generated 11% returns over the past 29 years. Or visit Scott Burns' site at Dallasnews.com and see how Burns, the inventor of the original Couch Potato approach, has fared. Compare the Potato's results to what the average actively managed mutual fund has accomplished—we think you'll be impressed. Then, if you want to better understand the reasoning behind

Potato-hood, pick up Unconventional Success. It's a new book by David Swensen, the legendary investor who piloted Yale University's huge endowment fund to record-breaking performance. In his book, Swensen lays out a Couch Potato-like strategy of his own. Coincidence? We think it's merely another affirmation of the Couch Potato's unarguable logic.

The Potato is ultimately about common sense. It rests on three ideas:

The first idea—as we've already seen—is to keep your costs low. This ensures that you, not your financial adviser, reaps most of the rewards from your portfolio.

The second idea is to diversify among different types of assets. By doing so, you ensure that no single blow-up can devastate your portfolio. We usually recommend that Couch Potato investors follow a classic balanced strategy, which consists of putting 60% of your money in stocks and 40% in bonds, but you may want to adjust the stock component upward if you're young and willing to take on additional risk in pursuit of larger returns. Conversely, you may want to dial down the stock portion if you're older and more conservative.

The third idea is to rebalance once a year to get back to your original asset allocation. If your stocks shoot up in value, for instance, you would sell some and put the proceeds into bonds. Doing so ensures you're constantly selling high and buying low.

That's it. If you follow those three ideas, you're going to do well. In fact, you can adapt the Couch Potato strategy to suit your individual situation and preferences. Our Classic Couch Potato Portfolio is a simple strategy that spans Canadian and U.S. markets. Our Global Couch Potato Portfolio takes things a step further and expands your portfolio to span the world. Both are just suggestions and can be tweaked to suit your purposes.

Source: Hood, Duncan and McGugan, Ian "Child's play: the Couch Potato Portfolio," *MoneySense* February/March 2006. Reprinted with permission.

Two of the most important implications for corporate officers are as follows:

1. The timing of security issues or repurchases is unimportant in an efficient market because prices will be correct on average. In other words, prices will not become inflated so there is no optimal time to sell new securities, and securities will not be undervalued so there is no optimal time to repurchase outstanding securities.

2. If short-run momentum and overreaction continue, we would expect the opposite: that firms sell equity after a price run-up and repurchase shares after a price decline. Therefore, management should monitor the price of the company's securities, and see whether price changes reflect new information or short-run momentum and/or overreaction.

CONCEPT REVIEW QUESTION

1. What are the main implications of the EMH for investors? for corporate officers?

ethics
AND CORPORATE
GOVERNANCE 10-1

INCOME TRUSTS

David Dodge, governor of the Bank of Canada, weighed in on the income trust debate yesterday, offering his views on the positive and not-so-positive sides of the investment products.

"An income trust is different in terms of its risk characteristics than either an equity or a bond," he told the Senate's Banking, Trade and Commerce Committee, expanding on why trusts can be a positive addition to Canadian capital markets.

"It may well be that for certain investors that particular risk characteristic that surrounds an income trust can be quite attractive and can fill a niche ... and it may allow some issuers to tap the capital market who couldn't otherwise tap the capital market."

But he added the bank did "worry" on the accounting side of income trusts.

"There are basically no standards for distributable cash and the accounting industry itself and the [Investment Dealers Association] are working on this," he said. This will allow investors to compare income trusts to other investments.

He said the bank was not competent to give a view on whether income trusts, which divert nearly all their profits to distributions, would lead to a reduction of research, development and investment in the economy.

"Certainly, as I said earlier, an income trust is an appropriate vehicle in a number of circumstances as long as the incentive to choose that vehicle is not so strong that an inappropriate vehicle gets chosen. That, I think, is the real issue here. That is difficult for me to comment on."

Companies have been rushing to convert to income trusts because it reduces their tax burden when compared with a traditional corporation. Individual unit holders, however, eventually pay the tax on distributions.

U.S. investors have been getting a break, however, because they pay a mere 15 percent flat tax on the payouts compared with Canadians who pay a full marginal rate. This can be double or triple that of their American counterparts.

"I can not comment on what one might do about that," Mr. Dodge said.

In the morning, he repeated his view that the U.S. economy is undergoing a necessary cyclical correction but it was likely to be short-lived and unlikely to turn into a recession. "In our view, it is likely to be a temporary slowing of growth, not a contraction," Mr. Dodge told the summit in Niagara-on-the-Lake by videoconference from Ottawa.

The Canadian slowdown will also likely be mild and while Ontario may well underperform the rest of the country as its heavy exposure to the slowing U.S. housing and auto sectors hits hard, it should continue to post modest growth.

"When you consider that automotive products made up 44 percent of Ontario's merchandise exports last year, it is clear that the U.S. downturn will likely affect Ontario more severely than other provinces. But I remind you that roughly 70 percent of Ontario's economic activity comes from the service sector and the service sector remains in good shape."

With other countries trying to reduce energy usage in an effort to curb greenhouse gases, Ontario would be wise to make the products it sells energy-efficient, Mr. Dodge also said.

"That's an economic factor that we have to take into account, and we in Ontario, I think it's very important, that we recognize that producing goods and services that economize on the use of energy inputs will, in fact, position us better to sell our goods and services in world markets in 2020 and 2030," he told the summit.

He added the bank had not done any specific research on how the drive to reduce emissions would affect the Canadian economy.

On the long-term structural issues facing Ontario, Mr. Dodge said it was critical the province improve efficiency and productivity by investing in infrastructure and human capital.

He threw his support behind public-private partnerships (PPPs) as a way for Ontario to dig its way out of an infrastructure crunch.

"There is evidence from other countries that public-private partnerships can both increase the efficiency of investments and support their financing," Mr. Dodge said. "Now is the right time to encourage partnerships between the government of Ontario and private providers, given the climate of low, nominal interest rates and the presence of large pension funds that are searching for these kinds of investment opportunities."

Source: Thorpe, Jacqueline. "Income trusts a good thing, Dodge says Accounting is a 'worry': Only way for some issuers to tap capital markets." *National Post*, October 26, 2006, p.FP4. Material reprinted with the express permission of "National Post Company," a CanWest Partnership.

DISCUSSION QUESTIONS

1. Income trusts pay out most of their operating cash as distributions; is Mr. Dodge right to worry that items like distributable cash are not regulated according to Canadian GAAP and thus have no standard definition?

2. U.S. investors pay only a 15 percent Canadian withholding tax on any distributions, whereas Canadians pay full marginal personal tax rates. However, U.S. investors pay U.S. taxes on distributions with a credit for the Canadian withholding taxes. In assessing income trusts, should Mr. Dodge be concerned with the total tax burden of investors or just the Canadian tax burden?

3. Should income trusts be restricted based on the observation that they do not conduct as much research and development as regular corporations?

Summary

In this chapter, we define an efficient market as one that reacts quickly and relatively accurately to new information, and therefore its prices are correct *on average*. The efficient market hypothesis (EMH) suggests that market prices fully and accurately reflect all available information. The EMH is commonly broken down into three cumulative levels that are based on the extent to which prices reflect different types of available information. The weak form EMH states that security prices reflect all market data; the semi-strong form states that prices reflect all publicly known and available information; and the strong form states that prices reflect all public and private information.

Most of the assumptions required for markets to be efficient are reasonable, and the empirical evidence suggests that markets are reasonably efficient, but not perfectly so. In particular, the evidence suggests that markets are weak form efficient, are reasonably semi-strong form efficient, but are not strong form efficient. We discuss several important implications that arise from these conclusions, both for investors and for corporate decision-makers.

Key Terms

abnormal returns, p. 393

allocational efficiency, p. 384

anomalies, p. 391

buy side analysts, p. 387

disclosure, p. 385

efficient market, p. 385

efficient market hypothesis (EMH), p. 389

event study, p. 393

informational efficiency, p. 384

material facts, p. 385

momentum, p. 392

operational efficiency, p. 384

random walk hypothesis, p. 390

securities law, p. 386

sell side analysts, p. 386

semi-strong form efficient market hypothesis (EMH), p. 389

size effect, p. 397

strong form efficient market hypothesis (EMH), p. 389

technical analysis, p. 391

weak form efficient market hypothesis (EMH), p. 389

QUESTIONS AND PRACTICE PROBLEMS

Multiple Choice Questions

1. Which of the following statements about an efficient market is *false*?

   A. It reflects all relevant and available information.

   B. Prices will reflect such information as firm financial strength and earnings.

   C. It reacts to new information quickly and correctly.

   D. Price changes follow predictable patterns through time.

2. Which of the following is *not* a form of the efficient market hypothesis (EMH)?

   A. Semi-strong
   B. Strong
   C. Semi-weak
   D. Weak

3. Which of the following is *useful* in attempting to identify mispriced securities if the semi-strong form of EMH is assumed?

   A. Past stock price changes
   B. Earnings expectations
   C. Past and current published trading volumes
   D. Relevant insider information

4. Which of the following statements is *true*?

   A. The weak form of the EMH encompasses the semi-strong form.
   B. The strong form of the EMH encompasses the semi-strong form.
   C. The semi-strong form of the EMH encompasses the strong form.
   D. The strong form of the EMH does not encompass the weak form.

5. If a test is statistically significant,

   A. it must be economically significant as well.
   B. it cannot be economically significant at all.
   C. it could be economically significant if the test is still significant after accounting for risk, trading costs, and so on.
   D. None of the above.

6. Which of the following conclusions is *false*?

   A. Evidence strongly supports the weak form of EMH.
   B. Evidence strongly supports the semi-strong form of EMH, with more contradictory evidence than for the weak form.
   C. Evidence strongly supports the strong form of EMH.
   D. Evidence does not support the strong form of EMH.

7. An investor is exploiting a contrarian strategy and observes a stock displaying superior performance over the past three to five years. What should the investor do?

   A. Buy more shares of the stock.
   B. Short sell the stock.
   C. Buy the stock on margin.
   D. Do nothing.

8. Which of the following statements is *false*?

   A. Stock returns tend to produce statistically higher returns in January than in the other 11 months of the year.
   B. Average Monday returns tend to be negative, while average returns for the other four trading days tend to be positive.

exchange, not with an individual. Investor A might buy a futures contract and investor B might sell one, but instead of one contract between A and B, there are two contracts involving each individual and the exchange. The exchange then assigns responsibility for reducing the credit risk and making sure that delivery takes place to a **clearing corporation**. In Canada the Canadian Derivatives Clearing Corporation (CDCC) handles these responsibilities for futures contracts, as well as option contracts, which we discuss in Chapter 12.

To make sure that people fulfill their contractual obligations, the CDCC enforces two types of **margins**: an **initial margin** and a **maintenance margin**. The margin is essentially a good faith deposit made by both the buyer and the seller to ensure they complete the transaction. In effect, it is a performance bond. The margin is set by each clearinghouse based on the risk involved in the underlying asset: the more risky the asset, the higher the margin. The initial margin is relatively small and varies between 2 percent and 10 percent of the value of the contract, but it is required of both the buyer and the seller. Usually, the brokerage house managing the transaction for the customer imposes a higher margin, particularly for new or smaller clients, but they are not permitted to impose smaller margins.[7]

All futures contracts are then *marked to market* each day, as the value of the contract changes. This means that all profits and losses on a futures contract are credited to investors' accounts every day to calculate their equity position in the underlying contracts. If the equity position increases, these profits can be withdrawn; losses reduce investors' equity positions. Whenever an investor's equity position drops below the maintenance margin requirement (normally 75 percent of the initial margin), he or she will receive a **margin call** and will be forced to contribute more money to increase the equity position. If he or she fails to make this margin call, the position will automatically be closed out. This process of marking to market is called **daily resettlement**, based on the contract's **settlement price**, which is normally, but not always, the daily closing price.

For example, suppose a futures contract is for 1,000 units of some underlying asset and the starting price is $50; the contract value is $50,000. This is referred to as the **notional amount** of the contract, even though the investor does not have to come up with $50,000 to enter into it. The buyer and seller of this contract both need to deposit the initial margin requirement, which we assume is $2,000 (i.e., 4 percent of $50,000). Assume the maintenance margin is 75 percent of the initial margin (or $1,500). The buyer's commitment is to buy 1,000 units at $50 and the seller's commitment is to sell 1,000 units at $50. If the price closes up $0.25 on the first day, at $50.25, then the futures contract is now worth $250 to the buyer. This is because the buyer has contracted to buy the asset for $50,000 and it is now worth $50,250, so the equity increases from $2,000 to $2,250. Conversely the seller's equity has declined from $2,000 to $1,750. Like all futures contracts, the gains and losses offset each other. In this case, the buyer has gained $250 at the expense of the seller and the clearinghouse will transfer this $250 from the seller's account to the buyer's. The next day, the process starts all over again. If the buyer feels that now that the price has gone up, he or she wants to cancel the contract, the buyer makes an **offsetting** sale and the purchase is cancelled. The buyer can then withdraw the $2,250.[8] In this case the buyer has a $250 profit on the margin deposit of $2,000.

clearing corporation a company that has the responsibility for reducing the credit risk and making sure that delivery takes place for futures contracts and option contracts

margin a good faith deposit with the clearinghouse by both the buyer and the seller to ensure they complete the transaction

initial margin a relatively small deposit made with the clearinghouse, usually between 2 and 10 percent of the value of the contract

maintenance margin a minimum amount that must be maintained in a margin account

margin call a requirement to add money and increase an equity position to a minimum level

daily resettlement marking to market and adjusting investors' equity positions

settlement price the price used to settle futures contracts; usually the daily closing price

notional amount the dollar amount upon which a contract is valued

offsetting cancelling a futures position by making an equivalent but opposite transaction

---

[7] Customers are allowed to post margin by depositing securities, such as T-bills.

[8] Similarly, the investor with the short position in the futures contract could enter into an offsetting purchase to close their position. Entering into offsetting transactions is the most common way of closing futures positions, and actual delivery of the underlying asset occurs very rarely, in less than 5 percent of all futures transactions.

Suppose instead that both parties leave their contract outstanding and the next day the price increases again, only this time it jumps to $51. Now the buyer's equity position has increased by $1,000 from its starting position, and the seller's equity position has correspondingly decreased by $1,000. The clearing corporation will have transferred this amount from the margin accounts and now the seller's equity of $1,000 is below the maintenance margin. This drop in margin would result in the seller getting a call from the broker, telling him or her to post more money or the position will be closed. It is this daily resettling, combined with the enforcement of margin requirements, that ensures that both the buyer and the seller meet their commitments. This is the reason that the margin is viewed as a performance bond: both the buyer and the seller have to post margin to make sure that they deliver on their promise. The result is the elimination of credit risk and individuals can trade futures contracts without worrying about the identity of their *counterparty*, that is, whom they are trading with.

Example 11-7 illustrates the concepts associated with marking to market.

Example 11-7: Daily Marking to Market: Long Position

An investor enters into a long position in 50,000 futures contracts that requires a $50,000 initial margin and has a maintenance margin that is 75 percent of this amount. The futures price associated with this contract is $20. Assume the spot price of the underlying asset closes at the following prices for the next five days: $20.50, $20.75, $21.00, $19.75, and $19.25. Estimate the daily profit (loss) for this investor, as well as the equity position, assuming no cash deposits or withdrawals are made from the account.

Solution

Day	Spot Price	Daily Profit	Equity Position (Margin Balance)
0	$20	—	$50,000
1	$20.50	$0.50 × 50,000 = $25,000	$50,000 + $25,000 = $75,000
2	$20.75	$0.25 × 50,000 = $12,500	$75,000 + $12,500 = $87,500
3	$21.00	$0.25 × 50,000 = $12,500	$87,500 + $12,500 = $100,000
4	$19.75	−$1.25 × 50,000 = −$62,500	$100,000 − $62,500 = $37,500
5	$19.25	−$0.50 × 50,000 = −$25,000	$37,500 − $25,000 = $12,500

Notice that the investor would receive a margin call on day 5, when the equity position fell below the maintenance margin requirement of $37,500.

Example 11-8: Daily Marking to Market: Short Position

An investor enters into a short position in 50,000 futures contracts that requires a $50,000 initial margin and has a maintenance margin that is 75 percent of this amount. The futures price associated with this contract is $20. Assume the spot price of the underlying asset closes at the following prices for the next five days: $20.50, $20.75, $21.00, $19.75, and $19.25. Estimate the daily profit (loss) for this investor, as well as the equity position, assuming no cash deposits or withdrawals are made from the account.

Solution

Day	Spot Price	Daily Profit	Equity Position (Margin Balance)
0	$20	—	$50,000
1	$20.50	$-0.50 \times 50,000 = -\$25,000$	$50,000 - \$25,000 = \$25,000$
2	$20.75	$-0.25 \times 50,000 = -\$12,500$	$25,000 - \$12,500 = \$12,500$
3	$21.00	$-0.25 \times 50,000 = -\$12,500$	$12,500 - \$12,500 = \$0$
4	$19.75	$+\$1.25 \times 50,000 = \$62,500$	$0 + \$62,500 = \$62,500$
5	$19.25	$+\$0.50 \times 50,000 = \$25,000$	$62,500 + \$25,000 = \$87,500$

Notice that the investor would have received a margin call on day 1, when the equity position fell below the maintenance margin requirement of $37,500. Because the price continued to go up and additional losses were incurred, the investor might also have had to contribute on days 2 and 3 as well, depending on how much he or she contributed each day. Therefore, in practice, the margin account numbers after day 1 would reflect these contributions.

Futures Contracts Markets

Producing a standardized contract requires that both the underlying asset and the term of the contract be standardized. The term of the contract is set by the individual exchange, but for financial futures, most exchanges follow the lead of the major markets in Chicago—the Chicago Board of Trade (CBOT) and the Chicago Mercantile Exchange (CME)—and set delivery months as March, June, September, and December. In practice, physical delivery rarely takes place as most positions are closed out with an offsetting transaction before the final day of trading, which is generally a couple of days before delivery. In this way, futures contracts are designed to share the price risk and not actually transfer the underlying asset. Most futures then generally have a rolling 18-month term, so at any point, investors can normally buy and sell futures on the same commodity with six different maturity dates.

To standardize the underlying asset, the exchange specifies precisely what is being traded, so that even though delivery rarely takes place, people know exactly what they are buying or selling. For the rare occasions when delivery does take place, the exchange will specify both the location and how delivery will occur. This is why, for example, the London Metals Exchange keeps a list of recognized warehouses.

Finally, the exchange determines how much of the asset is traded in each contract. In the example above, we used $50,000 as a *notional* contract amount. In practice, the actual amount varies with the needs of the individuals who are trading. So what does all this mean in practice?

Understanding the futures market means understanding the basic distinction between futures on physical commodities and financial futures, and understanding that there is intense competition across different futures exchanges to capture trading. Some of the major assets traded and the location of the trading are shown in Table 11-2.

Table 11-2   Futures Contracts and Markets

Underlying Asset	Exchange
Commodities	
Wheat/oats/soybeans	Chicago Board of Trade (CBOT)
Cattle/pigs/lumber	Chicago Mercantile Exch. (CME)
Crude oil/heating oil/natural gas	New York Mercantile Exchange
Cotton/orange juice	NY Cotton Exchange
Gold/silver/copper	The Commodity Exchange (Comex)
Lead/nickel/tin	London Metal Exchange (LME)
Canola/western barley/wheat	Winnipeg Commodity Exchange
Financial Futures	
Treasury notes and bonds/DJIA	CBOT
S&P index/Nikkei225/C$/£/€	CME
BAs/Canada bonds/TSX/S&P 60 Index	Montreal Exchange
German bonds/European equities	Euronext/Liffe
Other	
Weather derivatives	CME

Note the variety of commodities traded, ranging from traditional agricultural products to newer energy and base metal contracts. Essentially, we see that futures contracts exist on almost any asset that will generate sufficient interest from companies wanting to hedge risk against changes in its price or that will generate sufficient speculative trading activity. Also note the intense competition. Competition appears through new contracts being introduced like weather derivatives and futures contracts on real estate and the consumer price index; some of these survive while others die off through lack of interest. Finance in the News 11-1 discusses the preliminary competition among futures exchanges to introduce a new contract on Canadian crude oil. The discussion also alludes to the benefits in terms of liquidity of having futures contracts trade on exchanges, as opposed to OTC forward contract trading.

There is significant competition across the futures exchanges. Some of the contracts traded are separated by time zones, so the London Metal Exchange contracts do not really compete with the metal contracts traded in New York, because there is a five-hour time difference. However, the dramatic expansion in the trading of financial futures has produced direct competition. The CBOT trades a futures contract on the Dow Jones Industrial Average (DJIA) stock index that competes with the CME's contract on the S&P 500 Composite Index, because both indexes track the performance of the U.S. equity market.

FUTURES CONTRACT SOUGHT FOR CANADIAN CRUDE

finance
INTHENEWS11-1

The growing importance of Canadian oil sands production could soon be rewarded with the ultimate status symbol, at least in oil market terms: a heavy crude futures contract.

Canadian oil producers say they're in negotiations with investment banks and commodities exchanges over the development of a futures contract for their heavy crude output. A contract on the New York Mercantile Exchange or the Intercontinental Exchange (ICE) for Western Canadian Select, a blend of heavy Canadian crudes, could be created in the next year if sufficient liquidity can be attained, these people say.

"We've spoken to the ICE and Nymex many times to see how we can set up a contract," said Walt Madro, senior vice-president of crude oil marketing at EnCana Corp., Canada's largest energy company.

"They're chasing this very aggressively. We wouldn't be surprised if they started providing quotes within the next 12 months."

At present, Canadian firms trade their crude through private, over-the-counter deals with buyers such as refineries. The lack of transparency inherent in such a system means companies don't know what price their future supplies will achieve, creating uncertainty over revenue projections.

That's a problem producers would like to solve, considering crude output from Alberta's oil sands is expected to triple to three million barrels a day in a 2015 and U.S. refiners are showing greater interest in taking Canadian heavy output. ConocoPhillips Co. recently agreed to a huge supply deal with EnCana, while BP PLC and Marathon Oil Corp. have also said they're keen to source supply of more Canadian crude.

"Having a contract provides a great deal more liquidity with respect to moving volumes while providing improved price disclosure," said Rod Wilson, manager of domestic crude supply and natural gas liquids at Petro-Canada. "It's an uncertainty over revenue projections instrument for companies to lay off risk."

Both Nymex and the ICE refused to comment on the possibility of setting up a heavy crude contract. However, Nymex said earlier this month it had obtained authorization to offer the use of its electronic clearing and trading systems in Alberta. Meanwhile, the Toronto Stock Exchange owner, TSX Group Inc., is also mulling the introduction of a Canadian crude oil contract.

To be sure, the strong support in Canada for a heavy crude contract doesn't mean it will happen or be successful. New contracts frequently struggle to take away trading volumes from the traditional West Texas intermediate (WTI) and Brent benchmarks, resulting in an illiquid contract that's unable to attract traders. This month, a heavy crude contract for Russian Export Blend Crude Oil was launched on Nymex, but trading volumes haven't yet taken off.

However, the Canadian producers see a futures contract as a natural progression for their attempts to position Western Canadian Select as a North American benchmark for heavy crude. The blend, which consists of Canadian heavy conventional and bitumen crude oils, blended with sweet synthetic and condensate diluents, was launched by four producers—EnCana, Petrocan, Canadian Natural Resources Ltd. and Talisman Energy Inc.—in late 2004. Production runs are at around 250,000 barrels a day, compared with the WTI and Brent benchmarks, both of which are near 350,000 barrels a day.

The level needed to maintain a contract is open to debate. Both EnCana and Canadian Natural, the largest producers of Western Canadian Select, think production of 300,000 barrels a day could sustain a contract, and could be reached within the next 12 months. However, both Petrocan's Mr. Wilson and Craig James, manager of crude and natural gas liquids marketing at Talisman, said a more realistic target is 400,000 barrels a day, which is unlikely to be reached in 2007.

Source: Scott, Norval. "Futures Contract Sought for Canadian Crude." *Globe and Mail*, November 23, 2006, p. B18. Reprinted with the permission of the *Globe and Mail*.

It is also interesting to note that relatively little trading takes place on Canadian exchanges. Commodity futures trading in Canada is concentrated on the Winnipeg Commodity Exchange (WCE). The WCE trades western barley, canola, and wheat futures and has in the past also had contracts on rapeseed and other agricultural commodities. The WCE's wheat contract is in direct competition with the wheat contract on the CBOT. However, whereas the CBOT contract is priced in U.S. dollars with a contract size of 5,000 bushels, the WCE contract is in Canadian dollars for 20 metric tonnes. As of June 2006, there was *open interest* of fewer than 5,000 contracts on the WCE, but on the CBOT there was *open interest* of more than 500,000 contracts. **Open interest** represents the number of contracts that are outstanding, so when someone buys and another person sells a futures contact, although two transactions are recorded with the exchange, the open interest is just one contract. The open interest, therefore, represents the true amount of futures market activity.

open interest the number of contracts that are outstanding; the true amount of futures market activity

Trading in financial futures was concentrated in Montreal when the Canadian exchanges were reorganized in 2000. This reorganization involved having the Montreal Stock Exchange give up trading in common stocks to the Toronto Stock Exchange, and having the Toronto Futures Exchange close down so that all derivatives trading would be concentrated in Montreal. Today, the major futures contracts traded on the Montreal Exchange (MX) are the Bankers Acceptances' futures contracts (BAX), those on two-year (CGZ) and 10-year (CGB) Government of Canada bonds, and one on the S&P/TSX60 Index (SXF). In total, there is open interest of typically just fewer than 1 million contracts, with the BAX accounting for just more than half the total.

Trading/Hedging with Futures Contracts

For illustrative purposes, let's look at the futures contract on the 10-year Government of Canada bond to see how it works. The *notional* contract is for a $100,000 10-year 6 percent Government of Canada bond. Prices for the contract are quoted in the same way as for a regular bond; that is, they are quoted as a price per $100, such as $92.50 and then move in increments of $10 or 0.01 per $100.

In setting the initial margin requirement, the MX divides purchasers into speculators and hedgers, with the former posting a $1,400 margin and the latter $1,300. The MX classifies everyone as a speculator except for a small list of "institutions, counterparties, regulated entities and bona fide hedgers as defined in its rules and procedures." The maximum position limit for the 10-year Canada bond future is set at 47,500 contracts, and individuals have to report to the MX when they have 250 or more contracts. This is to make sure that no single institution can dominate trading. For reference purposes, the open interest stood at 289,412 contracts at the time these limits were in effect.

With most futures contracts, the underlying asset is clearly specified and the party responsible for delivering the asset has no choice. However, bond futures generally provide a choice. For example, if someone does choose to take delivery of the underlying asset in the CGB contract, the MX has set the underlying asset as one of three outstanding bonds:

- 5 percent   Long Canada with a maturity date of June 1, 2014

- 4.5 percent   Long Canada with a maturity date of June 1, 2015

- 4.0 percent   Long Canada with a maturity date of June 1, 2016

Each of these bonds then has a conversion factor to make it equivalent in value to the notional 6 percent 10-year bond. For example, the 5 percent bond's conversion factor was set at 0.9372 as of June 9, 2006.

So what can an investor do with this bond future? Well, imagine a portfolio manager on December 1, 2006, who owns $1 million in market value of long Canada bonds, plans to sell the bonds in four months, and wants to protect their value in case interest rates increase. Because the fund is *long* the Canada bond, the investor needs to *sell* (i.e., go *short*) long Canada bond futures to protect the value of the underlying bond portfolio. In this case, the manager sells 10 April 2007 10-year Government of Canada bond futures, because each contract has a notional value of $100,000.

If interest rates increase by April 1, 2007, then the market value of the fund's long Canada bonds will fall, causing a loss in their value. At the same time, the price of the futures contract falls, and because the futures have been *sold*, this generates a capital gain. This type of hedge, which we illustrated previously by using forward contracts, is called a *short hedge*, because a futures sale or a short position in the futures contract is hedging a long position in the underlying asset.

Whether the gain on the futures contract exactly equals the loss on the long Canada bond portfolio depends on how sensitive both are to interest rate changes. If the bond portfolio's value changes exactly mimic those of the asset underlying the CGB contract, the portfolio will be completely hedged. However, when this is not the case, the investor will be exposed to **basis risk**. Basis risk is the risk associated with a hedged position that is attributable to the fact that the asset to be hedged is not identical to the asset used as the hedge. As a result, it may be impossible to create a perfectly hedged position because changes in the price of the underlying asset in the contract will not move in a totally predictable manner with respect to changes in the price of the asset position to be hedged. One of the advantages of forward contracts is that they can be structured to minimize (or even eliminate) basis risk. This is because, unlike futures contracts, forwards are not standardized and can therefore be *tailor-made* with respect to underlying assets and maturity dates.

basis risk the risk associated with a hedged position that is attributable to the fact that the asset to be hedged is not identical to the asset used as the hedge

In our example, if the bond portfolio is not exactly the same as the 6 percent notional 10-year Government of Canada bonds used in the futures contract, there is basis risk because their prices will not move identically. For bonds, this risk can be reduced by adjusting the number of bond futures sold to create a *weighted* hedge. In our example, perhaps selling 9.5 contracts would be more accurate than selling 10.[9] However, the principle remains the same—the portfolio manager can sell bond futures to hedge its underlying exposure to long Canada bonds.

We conclude this section by providing an example of hedging foreign exchange risk. The CME trades a futures contract on the Canadian dollar to allow Americans to hedge their Canadian dollar exposure, but where is the U.S. dollar futures contract that Canadians can use to hedge their U.S. dollar exposure? The fact is that it doesn't exist, because the CME futures contract on $100,000 notional Canadian dollars works fine for Canadians as well. Foreign exchange rates are just reciprocals, so selling Canadian dollar futures on the CME is exactly the same as buying U.S. dollar futures—that is, the futures contract involves selling Canadian dollars and buying U.S. dollars. As of June 9, 2006, the open interest on the CME's Canadian dollar futures contracts was just over 100,000 contracts, involving a notional value of C$5 billion. A significant amount of this involved Canadian parties hedging their U.S. dollar exposure, as well as Americans hedging their Canadian dollar exposure.

---

[9] In fact, the appropriate hedge ratio can be determined by calculating the bond's duration, but this is beyond the scope of our discussion.

Summary of Forward and Futures Contracts

We conclude this section by noting the major differences between forward and futures contracts, which are listed in Table 11-3. The bottom line is that forward contracts offer more flexibility because they are customized OTC contracts; however, they possess additional risks because the contracts are not actively traded and because they possess credit risk. In other words, while forwards and futures serve the same basic purposes, one may be preferred over the other in some situations.

Table 11-3   Forwards versus Futures

	Forwards	Futures
• **Contracts**	Customized	Standardized
• **Trading**	Dealer or OTC markets	Exchanges
• **Default (credit) risk**	Important	Unimportant—guaranteed by clearinghouse
• **Initial deposit**	Not required	Initial margin and maintenance margin required
• **Settlement**	On maturity date	Marked to market daily

CONCEPT REVIEW QUESTIONS

1. Define initial margin, maintenance margin, margin call, open interest, and notional amount.
2. Explain what is meant by "marked to market."
3. What is basis risk? Why is it important for hedgers?
4. Compare and contrast forwards and futures.

swap an agreement between two parties to exchange cash flows in the future

counterparties two parties in a swap agreement

interest rate swap an exchange of interest payments on a principal amount in which borrowers switch loan rates

11.3 SWAPS

The final type of linear hedging contract we will discuss is the **swap**. A swap is an agreement between two parties, called **counterparties**, to exchange cash flows in the future. Note at the outset that this is a direct agreement between two parties: there is no formal exchange to guarantee performance, so the situation involves a dealer or OTC market, and there is credit risk. As a result, like forward contracts, swaps have evolved into a bank instrument, with the banks or swap dealers serving as intermediaries between the two counterparties to the swap. As with most things, the initial contracts were the simplest and the easiest to understand, so let's start with a simple **interest rate swap** example from the mid-1980s.[10]

---

[10] The example comes from the Bankers Trust sponsor's supplement to *Euromoney* (January 1986).

Interest Rate Swaps

We illustrate how an interest rate swap can be initiated by considering two hypothetical companies, A and B. Company A is a top-rated AAA company, whereas company B is a lower-rated BBB company. Credit (bond) ratings are discussed briefly in Chapter 6, and again in greater detail in Chapter 17, but AAA is the highest rating a company can have, and although BBB is a good bond rating, it is the lowest grade of "investment grade" bond ratings. Assume that company A wants to raise debt and pay a floating interest rate, which is usually done to finance short-term receivables and credit that earns a short-term interest rate. Company B, conversely, wants long-term fixed rate financing, perhaps to finance the purchase of machinery and equipment. Both companies approach the capital market, and company A is quoted a rate of 10.8 percent for fixed rate financing or a floating rate of 0.25 percent over LIBOR. In contrast, company B is quoted fixed rate financing at 12.0 percent and floating rate financing at a 0.75 percent spread over LIBOR.

As mentioned earlier, corporate borrowing rates are not generally priced with reference to the Government of Canada treasury bill (T-bill) yield. Floating rate financing in Canadian dollars is generally priced relative to the bankers' acceptances (BA) rate, which is why the Montreal Exchange's most popular hedging contract is the BAX. In contrast, floating rate notes in U.S. dollars are normally priced off LIBOR. Why U.S. dollar financing would be based off a rate established in London, rather than New York, is partly a historical accident, but it is a rate that reflects true market activity. In contrast, rates in New York have historically reflected the intervention and credit controls established by U.S. monetary authorities and have not been true market rates.

Regardless of how the rates are determined and quoted, let's consider what these two companies would do. The quotes look reasonable; the BBB-rated borrower is quoted a higher yield in both the fixed rate and the floating rate markets and would have borrowed at 12.0 percent. The AAA company would have borrowed at LIBOR + 0.25 percent. However, 25 years ago, someone asked the basic question: why is the BBB credit quoted a spread of 1.20 percent more than the AAA in the fixed rate market and *only* 0.50 percent more in the floating rate market? This person recognized that although firm A had an *absolute* financing advantage in both the fixed and the floating rate markets, it also had a **comparative advantage** in the fixed rate market, where its costs were 1.20 percent lower than firm B. In contrast, firm B had a comparative advantage in borrowing in the floating rate market, where it paid only 0.50 percent more than A.

comparative advantage a benefit that one firm has relative to another

To take advantage of this difference in spreads, the companies should both borrow where they have a comparative advantage and then *swap* payments to get what they really want. From this, the swap market was born. So firm A should borrow what it doesn't need, which is fixed rate financing, say, $50 million, at 10.80 percent, and B should borrow what it doesn't need, say $50 million, through a floating rate note at LIBOR + 0.75 percent.

Company A then signs a five-year swap contract agreeing to make payments to B at LIBOR, and in return A will receive from B a fixed 10.9 percent rate. Thus, the overall cost to A is LIBOR −0.10 percent, because it pays LIBOR to B, pays 10.80 percent on its direct financing, but receives 10.9 percent from B through the swap. Therefore, A saves 0.35 percent over its direct quote, which was LIBOR + 0.25 percent. Firm B borrows at LIBOR + 0.75 percent, makes payments to A based on a 10.9 percent fixed rate, while receiving payments based on LIBOR from A. The net effect is that it ends up paying an 11.65 percent fixed rate (i.e., 10.9% + 0.75%) for financing and also saves 0.35 percent over its direct quote.[11] Table 11-4 depicts the swap scenario, where borrowings are represented by minus signs in the table.

	A	B
Table 11-4 An Interest Rate Swap		
	A	**B**
Quotes	(AAA)	(BBB)
Floating	LIBOR + 0.25	LIBOR + 0.75
Fixed	10.8	12.0
Initial		
Floating		−(LIBOR + 0.75)
Fixed	−10.8	
Swap	B pays A fixed and A pays B floating	
	+10.9	−10.9
	−LIBOR	+LIBOR
Net	−(LIBOR−0.10)	−11.65
Saving	0.35%	0.35%

plain vanilla interest rate swap the "fixed for floating" interest rate swap; the simplest and most commonly used type of swap

A "fixed for floating" interest rate swap denominated in one currency, such as the one described in Table 11-4, is commonly referred to as a **plain vanilla interest rate swap**, reflecting the fact that it is the simplest and most commonly used type of swap. Although the example was developed to show that both parties gain 0.35 percent, in reality, how much they gain depends on negotiation between the two. However, in principle there is the spread in the spreads, which total 0.70 percent, and which can be shared in a variety of ways between the two parties. [12]

The comparative advantage argument is a basic one in finance: anyone offered a good deal in floating rate funds but who doesn't need them should borrow them anyway and use a swap to exchange it for what is needed and lock in the financing advantage. In addition, although the swap market may have developed in response to such comparative advantages, today's swap markets have evolved beyond that. Today, many firms enter into swap arrangements to convert an existing fixed rate liability into a floating rate liability, and vice versa. We discuss this in more detail later in this chapter.

The swap arrangement above is not without its problems. One main concern is that company A, which is a highly rated AAA company, is relying on the payments from B, a BBB-rated company, to make its fixed rate payments. In this example, firm A is assuming additional credit risk. If B defaults, then A is stuck with its own 10.80 percent fixed rate financing and, depending on legal interpretation, may also have to continue to pay LIBOR to B even after B stops making the 10.90 percent fixed rate payment to A! For this reason, early swap contracts were directly negotiated between the two counterparties based on documentation used for parallel loan transactions and included "set-off"

---

[11] Note this assumes that the 0.75 percent credit spread over LIBOR is fixed, otherwise its "fixed" rate financing will vary with the credit spread.

[12] In practice, swap dealers will also "pocket" some of the spread as payment for their services.

rights. These rights meant that if either party defaulted, then the other party stopped making payments. This was soon changed, as the required payments for interest rate swaps became **net payments**. This meant that instead of exchanging the total interest amounts, interest rate swaps involve exchanging payments representing the *difference* between the fixed and floating rates.

net payments payments representing the difference between the fixed and floating rates

We illustrate in Table 11-5 how this would work for our interest rate swap example based on various values for LIBOR during the first five periods of the swap. The payments are assumed to be made every six months, which is the norm in practice, so the interest payments are half the quoted rates.

Table 11-5 Interest Rate Swap Net Payments

Period	LIBOR (%)	Floating Pay (%)	Fixed Pay (%)	Net Pay (%)
1	8.0	−4.0	+5.45	+1.45
2	9.0	−4.50	+5.45	+0.95
3	9.80	−4.90	+5.45	+0.55
4	11.0	−5.50	+5.45	−0.05
5	12.0	−6.0	+5.45	−0.55

The cash flows depicted in Table 11-5 are from A's point of view. A receives half the fixed rate of 10.90 percent from B each period, or 5.45 percent of the notional value of the swap, and in return A pays LIBOR. For the first six-month period, LIBOR is 8.0 percent, so A pays half this or 4.0 percent and receives 5.45 percent. The net cash payment is that B pays A 1.45 percent of the notional value of the swap, which is why the sign is positive. From B's perspective, all the signs would be reversed, as it pays the difference of 1.45 percent.

Notice from Table 11-5 that the net payments depend on how LIBOR changes, because the fixed rate does not vary. In the above example, LIBOR increases consistently and by period 5 (two-and-a-half years away) LIBOR has increased to 12.0 percent, and A finds that it is making a net payment to B of 0.55 percent of the notional amount.

This example illustrates two important points. First, the table is expressed as a percentage of the notional amount. The actual cash flows would depend on the notional value of the swap—for a $10 million swap, the percentage would be multiplied by $10 million, so the period 1 payment would be $145,000 (i.e., 0.0145 × $10,000,000), payment 2 would be $95,000, and so on. The equation below depicts the semi-annual payments from the fixed rate payee's perspective.[13]

$$\text{Payment (fixed rate payee)} = NP \times (\text{Fixed} - FR) \times 1/2 \qquad [11\text{-}6]$$

where NP = notional principal

FR = floating rate (usually LIBOR)

and Fixed = fixed rate

---

[13] Notice that all we need to do is change the sign of the cash flow to determine what the floating rate payee pays (receives).

Second, when only net payments are required, the credit risk from A's perspective decreases significantly because it no longer relies on B to make the entire fixed rate payment. All that A gets from B is the much smaller difference between the LIBOR and fixed rate, which may be positive or negative. If B does default, A is still at risk but only for this future stream of differences, rather than for the full interest payments.

Example 11-9: Estimating Payments from an Interest Rate Swap

Company C enters into a two-year, $1 million plain vanilla interest rate swap and agrees to pay a fixed rate of 5 percent and receive LIBOR. Payments are exchanged every six months, based on LIBOR at the beginning of the six-month period. Determine the amount of the required semi-annual payments that C must make, assuming that LIBOR has the following values for each six-month period, beginning now: 5%, 5.5%, 5.25%, and 4.75%.

Solution

After six months: Payment = $1m $\times$ (0.05 −0.05) $\times$ 1/2 = $0

After 12 months: Payment = $1m $\times$ (0.05 −0.055) $\times$ 1/2 = −$2,500 (i.e., they will receive $2,500)

After 18 months: Payment = $1m $\times$ (0.05 −0.0525) $\times$ 1/2 = −$1,250 (i.e., they will receive $1,250)

After 24 months: Payment = $1m $\times$ (0.05 −0.0475) $\times$ 1/2 = $1,250 (i.e., they pay $1,250)

The Evolution of Swap Markets

currency swap the exchange of principal and interest in one currency for the same in another currency

As it turns out, the first swap was not an interest rate swap but a **currency swap** that involved IBM and the World Bank. At the time, the World Bank was required to borrow where it was cheapest in absolute dollars, which tuned out to be borrowing in either Swiss francs or German marks. In fact, it borrowed so much in those currencies that it made up the largest holding in most Swiss franc bond portfolios, and it ended up facing higher interest rates as a result. In contrast, it could issue U.S. dollar bonds quite easily, because it was not a large U.S. dollar issuer. IBM in contrast, was a well-known name but had never issued Swiss franc financing and was offered a good borrowing rate. Given our discussion of comparative advantage above, you might guess what happened next. IBM issued Swiss franc bonds and the World Bank issued U.S. dollar bonds, and each got their preferential rates. They then agreed to swap both the principal and the interest payments. In fact, the World Bank continued to make heavy use of currency swaps, and by the early 1980s it was routinely lowering its borrowing cost by a colossal 1.28 percent a year.[14]

The original swap transactions were extremely profitable to both counterparties, as indicated by the fact that the World Bank was able to lower its borrowing cost by 1.28 percent. This was because the credit spreads between risky borrowers and governments in different types of debt markets were largely unconnected. Theoretically, spreads in the floating rate and fixed rate markets should be the same, just as they should be between U.S. dollar or Canadian dollar financing. This is because most bonds have cross-default clauses in their debt contracts, so that default on any debt instrument anywhere in the world means a default on all debt

---

[14] Wallich, Christine. "The World Bank's Currency Swaps," *Finance and Development*, June 1984.

obligations. As a result the credit risk is the same. However, although the swaps market has caused these spreads to narrow considerably, spread differences continue to exist. Swapping still makes sense, but it doesn't make as much money as it used to.

Knowing what a swap is allows us to make sense of some strange things. For example, we may see "tombstone" advertisements in the newspaper, in which a Canadian company announces that it has issued debt in New Zealand or Australian currencies. Taken on its own, this may not make much sense, especially if the company has no operations in New Zealand or Australia. However, once we realize that the company can swap those New Zealand or Australian dollars into Canadian dollars, then we know that it has issued bonds in Australian dollar or New Zealand dollars because it got a "good" deal, and it then swapped the bonds back into what it really needed—Canadian dollars. In fact, it has been estimated that as much as 75 percent of the bond issues in the international Eurobond market have ended up being swapped into something else.

As swap markets have matured, another major change has taken place. Initially the major investment banks would bring two parties together and arrange the swap for a fee. However, as the liquidity in the market grew, the major banks would increasingly act as a *principal*, directly sign a swap with one party, and then "warehouse" the swap until it could do an offsetting transaction with another party. This development was helped by the increasing standardization in the market. The International Swap Dealers Association (ISDA) has developed standard legal documentation so that everyone knows his or her rights and duties under a standard swap agreement. This standardization means that plain vanilla interest rate swaps and currency swaps have become commodities that can be bought and sold through a telephone call to a bank's swaps desk. As such, swaps have become traded commodities and major instruments for managing interest rate and currency exposures.

Consider, for example, the original IBM–World Bank currency swap. This was a *primary market* transaction, because both IBM and the World Bank used it to raise capital as cheaply as possible. In both cases, their intention was to raise the capital and then forget about it. However, once swaps became standardized, it became possible to constantly change the nature of an institution's liability stream.

Recall, for example, the foreign exchange exposure problem discussed earlier. At that time, we considered a firm that had a US$1.0 million receivable due in a year. Let's change this and say that a Canadian company has a five-year US$ bond outstanding, with fixed semi-annual interest payments of $1 million and a principal of US$30 million due in five years. In this case the Canadian company has a US$ liability stream, so it is *short* the US$. Now suppose the company looks at the current exchange rate and feels that it is at an all time high and will depreciate in the future. As the Canadian dollar depreciates, it will cost the company more Canadian dollars to make those U.S. dollar interest and principal payments.

What can the company do? The most obvious thing is to repay the loan, but if this is a bond held by several U.S. institutions, that may not be possible. An alternative is to enter into a currency swap. The structure of currency swaps permits firms to adjust their foreign exchange exposure. In particular, one distinguishing feature of currency swaps is that, unlike interest rate swaps, they require the exchange of *all* cash flows. This is logical because not only do interest rates change but so do exchange rates. Although this feature increases the credit risk associated with currency swaps, it also provides firms with the opportunity to manipulate the underlying currency associated with a series of future cash flows that it expects to pay (or receive).

In this case, the company can talk to the swaps desk at its bank and swap the U.S. dollar liability stream into a Canadian dollar liability stream. Unlike the original IBM–World Bank currency swap, which was arranged by an investment bank between the two counterparties, the bank is now capable of executing a secondary market transaction with itself as a principal—that is, it doesn't need a counterparty. The reason is that a currency swap can be viewed as a series of forward transactions. Think of the firm's five-year bond not as one transaction but as 10 individual transactions. The first nine transactions involve a US$1 million outflow every six months for interest, while the last one is a US$31.0 million outflow for both the final interest payment and the principal payment. So rather than going through a search for a counterparty, the bank could always execute 10 forward sales of Canadian dollars for U.S. dollars and directly change the U.S. dollars liability stream into a Canadian dollars liability stream. Once it has been converted into a fixed Canadian dollar stream, an interest rate swap can convert it into any other Canadian dollar liability, such as a floating rate liability.

If currency swaps have become a bank market through their links to the forward foreign exchange market, what of interest rate swaps? To understand the link with other instruments, let's go back to our circa 1985 interest rate swap example. At that time, all the rates were unique to the issuers and the interest rates in the swap were negotiated. However, the core of the swap was simply a LIBOR-based rate and a fixed rate. To make a *standardized* product, suppose we fix both the floating and the fixed rates so that everyone knows what they are. So let's fix the floating rate at LIBOR and the fixed rate with reference to the government bond rate, with the choice of rate depending on whether it is a five-year, 10-year, or other maturity contract. Suppose the BBB bond issue was a five-year bond, so that we have a five-year interest rate swap. Let's say the five-year government bond rate was 10.65 percent at the time. In this way the swap could be quoted simply as 10.65 percent. In fact, this is the way that swaps are now quoted, and this rate is called the **swap rate**.

swap rate the rate of the fixed portion of a swap that is used for quoting swaps

We revisit our previous example and assume the swap rate had been 10.65 percent at the time. This transaction is depicted in Table 11-6.

Table 11-6　Percent Interest Rate Swap

	A	B
Quotes	(AAA)	(BBB)
Floating	LIBOR + 0.25	LIBOR + 0.75
Fixed	10.8	12.0
Initial		
Floating		−(LIBOR + 0.75)
Fixed	−10.8	
Swap	B pays A fixed and A pays B floating	
	+10.65	−10.65
	−LIBOR	+LIBOR
Net	−(LIBOR + 0.15)	−11.40
Saving	0.10%	0.60%

In this case, unlike our original example, the 0.70 percent difference in spreads has been allocated as 0.10 percent to the AAA, and 0.60 percent to the BBB. This generally has been the trend over time as the gains to the higher-rated AAA are relatively small, given that it has good access to most markets. In contrast, it is the lower-rated issuers that sometimes face very large spread differences across different markets. Further, the AAA-rated firm is often a bank, and banks now make money trading swaps rather than acting as counterparties. In the above example, the swap rate of 10.65 percent would actually be the mid-point of an "ask" or "bid" rate of 10.63 percent and an "offer" rate of 10.67 percent. If a company wants to swap floating for fixed, it would pay the 10.67 percent fixed (offer) rate, but if it wanted to swap fixed for floating, it would receive the 10.63 percent fixed (ask) rate from the bank. The spread between these two rates of 0.04 percent rewards the bank for trading swaps.

Interest rate swaps are now standard around the world. Table 11-7 gives swap rates for the euro, U.S. dollar, and the pound sterling for June 7, 2006, provided by CLP Structured Finance in the UK.[15]

Table 11-7   Interest Rate Swap Quotes

Fixed Rate	Euro(€) Current	US($) Current	UK(£) Current
1 year	3.41%	5.41%	4.95%
2 year	3.61%	5.38%	5.03%
3 year	3.73%	5.38%	5.08%
5 year	3.87%	5.43%	5.09%
7 year	4.00%	5.50%	5.07%
10 year	4.16%	5.57%	5.00%
12 year	4.24%	5.61%	4.96%
15 year	4.34%	5.66%	4.90%
20 year	4.44%	5.70%	4.80%
25 year	4.48%	5.71%	4.70%
30 year	4.49%	5.71%	4.62%

Source: Data from CLP Structured Finance, June 7, 2006.

Notice that the swap rates follow the full spectrum of the yield curve out to 30 years, so interest rate swaps are very useful for managing interest rate exposure. This also provides the link to other interest rate products. The link in this case is to the forward rate agreements (FRAs) that are discussed in Appendix 11A. Appendix 11A notes that by selling a one-year bond and investing in a two-year bond, a bank can create forward contracts on the one-year interest rate for next year. In the same way, it can sell a six-month bond and invest in a one-year bond to create a six-month interest rate forward for hedging LIBOR. Doing the same thing at six-

[15] CLP Structured Finance website at <www.clpuk.com>. U.S. dollar swap rates are also available from the U.S. Federal Reserve website at <www.federalreserve.gov>.

month intervals creates an FRA. The FRA can be seen as a series of forward interest rates equivalent to an interest rate swap. What this means is that the two core products in the swap market, the interest rate and currency swap, are simply combinations of forward contracts—either on exchange rates or on interest rates. Creating swaps is therefore a key component of the skill set of all the major banks.

The integration of the swap markets with the forward market has allowed the enormous expansion of the market. If a company has a banking relationship with an outstanding line of credit, we have already seen that a company can call and buy and sell forward foreign exchange contracts. The same thing now happens in the swap market. If a company wants to change a floating rate liability into a fixed rate liability, it calls the bank and executes an interest rate swap. More than 80 percent of swap transactions are now for around $10 million as secondary market transactions executed against a bank line of credit.

Recent Developments

total return swap an exchange of an interest rate return for the total return on an equity index plus or minus a spread

Interest rate and currency swaps have been the main focus of this section, because they are the major vehicles for managing interest rate and currency exposure. However, the idea has more applications. If an investor doesn't like what's happening in the bond market and wants to increase exposure to the equity market, that investor could sell bonds and buy equities, but the bond market is not very liquid and the transaction costs are high. Instead, the investor could turn to the swap market and enter into a **total return swap**. This can be accomplished by first entering into an interest rate swap to convert the fixed rate bond payments into payments that vary with a floating rate, such as LIBOR, because almost all swaps go through LIBOR. The investor would then enter into a total return swap, paying LIBOR and receiving the total return from the S&P 500 Index or the S&P/TSX 60 Index plus or minus some spread. The existence of futures contracts on stock market indexes on the Montreal Exchange for the S&P/TSX 60 Index, and on the CME for the S&P 500 Index, allows the equity market exposure to be hedged. These types of swaps are not for the small investor, and the notional principal amount involved is usually $100 million.

What the total return swap does indicate is how swaps have emerged as a major vehicle for managing exposure to any traded commodity that can be hedged. The result is a huge proliferation of specialized swap contracts. However, the more specialized the swap, the less tradable it is and the greater the counterparty risk; only the highly standardized swaps are done with the banks.

CONCEPT REVIEW QUESTIONS

1. Explain how plain vanilla interest rate swaps are structured and what purposes they serve.

2. Explain how currency swaps are structured and how they can be used for hedging purposes.

3. Why does it make sense that interest rate swaps involve an exchange of net payments, while currency swaps exchange all cash flows?

4. Briefly explain the important changes that have occurred in the swap markets, and what these changes have meant to market participants.

Summary

In this chapter, we learn how to diagnose long and short positions in foreign currency, and how these positions can be hedged by using forward foreign currency contracts. Interest rate parity is discussed again and used to derive forward interest rates and to show how banks could derive synthetic securities. Futures contracts are then discussed, and we see that they can be viewed as the public market version of forward contacts. We then discuss swap markets and show how basic interest rate and currency swap can be used to lower borrowing costs or to hedge interest rate or foreign currency exposures.

The explosion of activity in the swap, futures, and forwards markets goes together, because they are all derived from the underlying asset, whether it is foreign exchange rates or interest rates. It is in this sense that these contracts are all derivatives. Market participants regularly use the futures market to offset positions in the swap market, the swap market to offset positions in the forward market, and the forward market to offset positions in the futures market.

Key Terms

basis risk, p. 429

clearing corporation, p. 423

commodity, p. 420

comparative advantage, p. 431

convenience yield, p. 420

cost of carry, p. 421

counterparties, p. 430

covering, p. 416

credit risk, p. 415

currency swap, p. 434

daily resettlement, p. 423

forward contract, p. 412

forward interest rate, p. 441

forward rate agreement (FRA), p. 443

futures contract, p. 422

hedging, p. 415

initial margin, p. 423

interest rate swap, p. 430

London Inter-Bank Offered Rate (LIBOR), p. 420

long, p. 413

maintenance margin, p. 423

margin, p . 423

margin call, p. 423

naked position, p. 413

net payments, p. 433

notional amount, p. 423

offsetting, p. 423

open interest, p. 428

plain vanilla interest rate swap, p. 432

settlement price, p. 423

short, p. 413

speculate, p. 413

spot contract, p. 412

storage costs, p. 420

swap, p. 430

swap rate, p. 436

total return swap, p. 438

underlying assets, p. 412

Formulas/Equations

(11-1)   Profit (loss) from long position = $[S_T - F] \times n$

(11-2)   Profit (loss) from short position = $[F - S_T] \times n$

(11-3) $\dfrac{F}{S} = \dfrac{(1 + k_{domestic})}{(1 + k_{foreign})}$

(11-4) $F = \dfrac{(1 + k_{domestic})}{(1 + k_{foreign})} \times S$

(11-5) $F = (1 + c) \times S$

(11-6)   Payment (fixed rate payee) = NP $\times$ (Fixed $-$ FR) $\times$ 1/2

(11A-1) $F_t = \dfrac{(1 + R_t)^t}{(1 + R_{t-1})^{t-1}} - 1$

APPENDIX 11A
FORWARD INTEREST RATES AND FORWARD RATE AGREEMENTS (FRAs)

FORWARD INTEREST RATES

Interest rate parity is a special example of forward pricing simply because the cost of carry is the ratio of one plus the interest rates in both countries. In other words, for IRP,

$$(1 + c) = \dfrac{(1 + k_{domestic})}{(1 + k_{foreign})}$$

For our synthetic forward example in the chapter, the cost of carry is the cost of borrowing in Canadian dollars relative to the investment income earned in U.S. dollars. If the Canadian one-year interest rate is 10 percent and the U.S. interest rate is 5 percent, then the cost of synthetically creating the forward rate is 1.10/1.05 or 4.76 percent. The lost income caused by the Canadian dollar borrowing cost is higher than the income earned on the U.S. investment. As a result, the cost of carry is positive and the forward rate of Canadian dollars for U.S. dollars has to show a 4.76 percent depreciation in the Canadian dollars, that is, if the spot rate is 1.0, the forward rate has to be 1.0476. In this way, the income loss of 4.76 percent is offset by a 4.76 percent capital gain on the exchange rate. Alternatively, if the Canadian borrowing rate is 5 percent and the U.S. rate is 10 percent, then the cost of carry is negative at -4.45 percent. The forward rate has to show a 4.45 percent appreciation of the Canadian dollars to 0.95. In this way, the income gain from borrowing at 5 percent in Canada and investing at 10 percent in the US, that is, a negative cost of carry, is offset by a capital loss from being in U.S. dollars.

Note that in the interest rate parity condition, it is the ratio of one plus the interest rate in both countries that determines whether the forward rate exceeds or is less than the spot rate. However, in Table 11-1 there were forward foreign exchange rates for the Canadian dollar against the U.S. dollar going forward 10 years. This brings up another very important forward rate: **forward interest rate**. In Chapter 6, we discussed the term structure of interest rates and the *yield curve*, where we noted that, in May 2006, the yield curve was slightly *upward sloping*. However, the yield curve moves around all the time based on the state of the economy and expectations about where interest rates are going. Figure 11A-1 shows the yield on 91-day T-bills issued by the Government of Canada and the yield on a portfolio of long Canada bonds with an average maturity exceeding 10 years. The two yields represent the very short and very long end of the yield curve, respectively.

forward interest rate
an interest rate that is specified now for some time in the future

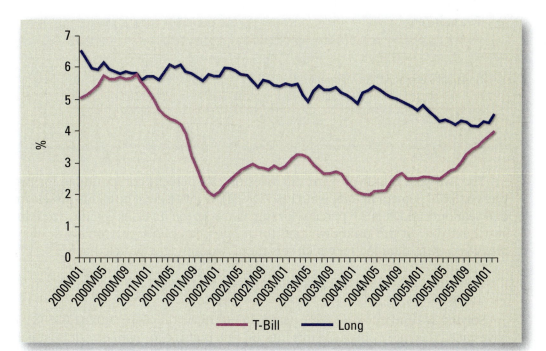

11A-1 FIGURE

Canadian Interest Rates

We can see that near the start of the period, the T-bill yields and those on long Canada bonds were very similar, and, in fact, at the end of 2000 both yielded 5.6 percent. This was an example of a *flat* yield curve, in which interest rates were essentially the same across all maturities. Short-term interest rates then declined to the 2 percent level, where they remained until the end of 2004, when the Bank of Canada started increasing interest rates again, and they consistently increased to reach the 4.2 percent level by mid-2006. For illustrative purposes, let's go back to mid-2004 when T-bill yields were at 2.0 percent and see what the yield curve indicated.

Suppose at that time that the yields on *zero coupon bonds*, which were discussed in Chapter 6, were exactly as follows:

One year:	2.00%	Four year:	3.65%
Two year:	2.75%	Five year:	4.00%
Three year:	3.25%	Ten year:	5.00%

Remember that zero coupon bonds are discount bonds: they do not pay interest explicitly, so the return is earned by buying them at a discount and then selling them at maturity for their par value. Now suppose an investor wanted to invest for two years. There are multiple ways of investing for two years, but let's look at two alternatives: either a two-year bond is bought or a one-year bond is bought and then the investor invests in another one-year bond at whatever interest rate is available in one year. Schematically, we can represent these choices as shown in Figure 11A-2:

FIGURE 11A-2

Zero Coupon Bonds

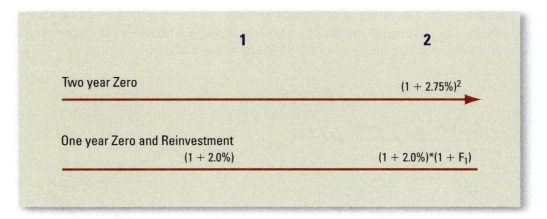

The two-year bond will earn the investor 2.75 percent compounded for two years or 5.576 percent in total (i.e., $(1.0275)^2 - 1$). Conversely, if he or she invests for one year only and gets 2.0 percent for the first year, the investor will have to reinvest next year at the unknown rate for a one-year bond. We can work out a *break-even rate*, denoted F_1, which sets these two strategies equal, that is

$$(1 + 2.75\%)^2 = (1 + 2\%) \times (1 + F_1)$$

Solving, we find that $F = 3.50\%$, because $(1.0275)^2 = 1.05576 = (1.02)(1.0350)$. We have called this rate F_1 because this interest rate is also a *forward rate*. It is actually the forward rate for a one-year bond, *one* year in the future. In fact, embedded in the yield curve are a host of forward rates. For example, we could use the three-year and two-year zero coupon yields to calculate a forward rate for a one-year bond starting in *two* year's time, which would be

$$(1 + 3.25\%)^3 = (1 + 2.75\%)^2 \times (1 + F_2)$$

or 4.25 percent. Equivalently, we could calculate the forward rate for a one-year bond for time period 3 by using the yields on three- and four-year bonds, for time period 4 by using four- and five-year bonds, and so on. In the same way, we could also calculate the forward rate on a two-year bond by using the current yield on the one-year and three-year bonds.

These *break-even interest rates* are also forward rates because a bank can lock in the rate on a one-year bond for one year in the future. It can do this by borrowing by using the current one-year rate and then by using the proceeds to simultaneously invest for two years at the two-year rate. In one year's time, the bank will owe $102 when it has to repay the one-year 2 percent loan. However, the proceeds from that loan will have been invested in the two-year bond and the bank is still owed the $105.576 payoff from this bond next year. As far as the bank is concerned, this is the same as investing $102 next year in a one-year bond that pays off $105.576 at the end of that year, or pays 3.50 percent. As a result, the 3.50 percent break-even rate is also the forward rate for a one-year bond one-year in the future.

The general formula for calculating forward interest rates (F_t) for the one-year bond is as follows:

$$F_t = \frac{(1+R_t)^t}{(1+R_{t-1})^{t-1}} - 1$$

[11A-1]

Equation 11A-1 says (1) find the future value of investing for t periods by investing in the t period discount bond, and (2) then divide by the future value generated by investing for $t-1$ periods by using the $t-1$ bond, and (3) subtract 1.0. This gives the break-even rate as the forward rate for the one-period bond available at the start of time period $t-1$.

Example 11A-1: Estimating Forward Rates

Estimate the one-year forward rate for years 4 and 5, given that zero coupon bonds were yielding the following: three-year, 3.25%; four-year, 3.65%; and five-year, 4.00%.

Solution

Year 4 forward rate $F_4 = \dfrac{(1+.0365)^4}{(1+.0325)^3} - 1 = 0.0486 = 4.86\%$

Year 5 forward rate $F_5 = \dfrac{(1+.0400)^5}{(1+.0365)^4} - 1 = 0.0541 = 5.41\%$

Forward Rate Agreements (FRAs)

Banks actually use these forward rates to offer a product called a **forward rate agreement (FRA)** to manage a firm's exposure to interest rate risk. Suppose, for example, that a firm has issued a floating rate bond for which it is required to pay the one-year T-bill yield plus a 0.50 percent credit spread and the rate adjusts annually with the one-year T-bill yield. The firm may have issued this note in 2000, when it thought short-term interest rates would fall and it wanted to avoid locking in at a higher fixed-term interest rate. But now suppose in 2004 that it thought interest rates were going to increase and it wants *protection* against rising interest rates. This is the same as saying that it wants to *hedge* the interest rate exposure from its floating rate note.

If the firm's floating rate note has two years left before it matures, the first year's interest cost is fixed, and so what it wants to do is fix next year's interest cost. Because this cost is based on the one-year T-bill rate, the bank would offer an FRA based on the one-year forward rate of 3.50 percent. If the T-bill yield is higher than 3.50 percent, at, say, 4.0 percent, then the bank would pay the firm the difference of 0.50 percent. If the T-bill yield is less than 3.50 percent, at, say, 3.0 percent, the firm would pay the bank the difference of 0.50 percent. The cash flows as far as the firm is concerned are shown in Table 11A-1.

forward rate agreement (FRA) an agreement that uses forward rates to manage a firm's exposure to interest rate risk; agreements to borrow or lend at a specified future date at an interest rate that is fixed today

Table 11A-1   FRAs

T-Bill Yield	Spread 0.50%	FRA	Total
3.00	0.50	+0.50	4.00
3.50	0.50	0.00	4.00
4.00	0.50	−0.50	4.00

Regardless of the T-bill yield, the firm has locked in an overall cost of 4.0 percent, which is the forward rate for the one-year T-bill of 3.50 percent plus the 0.50 percent credit spread.

In comparing this interest rate example with our foreign exchange example, we can see that the FRA is a forward contract on the one-year T-bill yield. In this case, the firm starts out with a series of short positions in the one-year T-bill, because it is obligated to *pay* the one-year T-bill yield plus 0.50 percent as long as its floating rate note is outstanding. To cover or hedge this short exposure, it goes long by buying an interest rate forward contract or FRA, which obligates it to pay the difference between the T-bill yield and the forward rate of 3.50 percent.

The example is set out to illustrate that banks offer FRAs to help firms manage their interest rate exposure in the same way that they offer forward foreign exchange contracts to help them manage their foreign exchange exposure. In practice, FRAs are more complex than in our simple example. This is because most floating rate notes have interest rates that fluctuate with LIBOR every six months, not the T-bill yield every year. As a result, FRAs are normally based on six-month LIBOR and not the T-bill yield. The second major difference is that forward foreign exchange contracts are generally one-shot deals to cover a single exposure. However, floating rate notes cover a series of future interest payments extending out to the note's maturity. As a result, FRAs are tailored to the maturity of the note and are equivalent to a series of interest rate forward contracts. However, the basic similarity is the same, because they are both bank instruments designed to help manage a firm's exposure to interest rates and foreign exchange.

QUESTIONS AND PRACTICE PROBLEMS

Multiple Choice Questions

1. Which of the following statements is *false*?

   A. A spot price is a price today for immediate delivery.

   B. If a Canadian firm has to pay U.S. dollars in the future, it worries about the potential depreciation of the U.S. dollar.

   C. The forward price is a price today for future delivery.

   D. We say long U.S. dollar and short Canadian dollar when you buy U.S. dollars and sell Canadian dollars.

2. What is the one year forward rate if the spot rate is C$1.25/US$ and interest rates in Canada and the United States are 5 percent and 4 percent, respectively?

   A. C$1.26/US$
   B. C$1.27/US$
   C. C$1.15/US$
   D. C$1.05/US$

3. Which of the following statements is *false*?

   A. Removing a naked position is called hedging.
   B. To hedge, you take a long position in a U.S. dollar forward contract if you have a long position in U.S. dollars.
   C. There is no initial cash outlay for a forward contract.
   D. Forward contracts could be used to hedge against commodity price changes.

4. Using the interest rates in Question 2, what is the cost of carry of synthetically creating a forward rate by borrowing in Canadian dollars and investing in U.S. dollars?

   A. 1.24%
   B. 0.86%
   C. 0.96%
   D. 1.00%

5. Which of the following statements is *false*?

   A. Cost of carry could be either positive or negative.
   B. The forward rate will change if the spot rate changes.
   C. An income loss is offset by a capital gain on the exchange rate if interest rate parity holds.
   D. The spot rate is not affected by changes in the forward rate.

6. Which of the following statements is *false*?

   A. FRAs are normally based on six-month LIBOR (London Inter-Bank Offered Rate).
   B. FRAs are designed to hedge against interest rates only.
   C. FRAs are tailored to match the maturities of floating rate notes.
   D. FRAs could be viewed as a series of interest rate forward contracts.

7. Which of the following is *false* concerning forwards contracts and futures contracts?

   A. Futures contracts involve credit risk just as forwards contracts do.
   B. The Canadian Derivatives Clearing Corporation (CDCC) takes responsibility for reducing credit risk.
   C. The higher the credit risk, the higher the margin.
   D. Futures contracts are marked to market every day.

8. Suppose a futures contract is for 1,000 units of a certain asset and the starting price is $30. The initial margin is 5 percent. The price closed on the first day at $45. Which of the following statements is *true*?

    A. Only the buyer puts down a $1,500 deposit when he enters the contract.

    B. The futures contract is worth $15,000 to the seller at the end of the first day.

    C. The buyer's commitment is to buy 1,000 units of the asset at $30 on a certain date.

    D. At the end of the first day, the seller's equity increased by $1,500.

9. Which of the following statements concerning futures contracts is *false*?

    A. The initial value of the futures contract is zero.

    B. The values of the buyer and the seller of the futures contract offset each other.

    C. If the buyer gains, the clearinghouse will transfer the gained value from the buyer's account to the seller's account.

    D. If an investor's account falls below the maintenance margin, she will receive a margin call.

10. In practice, most futures contracts are closed out

    A. with an offsetting transaction before the final day of trading.

    B. by actual deliveries of the underlying assets.

    C. by leaving the contracts to expire.

    D. by cash settlement.

11. Which of the following statements concerning Government of Canada bond futures is *false*?

    A. The contract price is quoted per $100.

    B. A maximum position limit is set to prevent a single dominant holding.

    C. Basis risk exists when the underlying asset to be hedged is not identical to the asset used as the hedge.

    D. To hedge, an investor should long a Government of Canada bond futures contract when he has the same bonds to sell in the future.

12. Suppose ABC Inc. pays a fixed rate of 9.5 percent and DEF Inc. pays a floating rate of LIBOR + 1.5 percent. They entered into a swap in which ABC Inc. agrees to pay LIBOR to DEF Inc. and DEF Inc. agrees to pay 9.5 percent to ABC Inc. What is the net paying interest rate for ABC Inc.?

    A. LIBOR + 1%

    B. LIBOR

    C. 12%

    D. LIBOR + 0.5%

13. Suppose ABC Inc. borrows at a fixed rate of 9.5 percent or a floating rate of LIBOR + 1 percent. DEF Inc. borrows at a fixed rate of 12 percent or a floating rate of LIBOR + 1.5 percent. Currently, ABC Inc. borrows at its fixed rate and DEF Inc. borrows at its floating rate. They entered into a swap in which ABC Inc. agrees to pay LIBOR to DEF

Inc. and DEF Inc. agrees to pay 9.5 percent to ABC Inc. How much, in percentage, could ABC Inc. and DEF Inc. save through the swap, respectively?

A. 1% and 1%

B. 0.5% and 1.5%

C. 1.5% and 0.5%

D. 2% and 0%

14. Which of the following statements about interest rate swaps is *false*?

   A. Credit risk exists in interest rate swaps.

   B. The actual cash flows depend on the notional value of the swap.

   C. Net cash settlement increases the credit risk of the interest rate swap.

   D. Interest rate swaps are settled by paying a net amount between the two parties.

15. Which of the following statements about currency swaps is *false*?

   A. The swap rate for currency swaps is the exchange rate.

   B. The swap rate for currency swaps is the interest rate.

   C. The notional amounts of the currency swap are exchanged at the beginning and end of the swap only.

   D. Usually, one party pays a fixed rate, while a counterparty pays a floating rate.

Practice Problems

16. Briefly describe open interest with respect to futures contracts.

17. Briefly describe how total return swaps work.

Easy

18. The Absent Minded Profs have received the following incomplete information about a set of currency forwards. All the forwards are for C$1,000 in one year. Complete the following table:

			Today			In one year		
	Position	Number of Contracts	Spot (C$/US$)	Cost today (C$)	Forward (C$/US$)	Spot (C$/US$) in one year	Payoff (C$)	Profit (Loss) C$
A	Long	1	1.15	$0	1.20	1.40		
B	Short	1	1.15		1.20	1.40		
C	Long	2	.80	$0		.65	$100	
D		3	1.05		1.30	1.20		($300)
E	Long	5	1.10	$0	1.25			$800
F			1.00		1.05	1.30		($2,500)

19. Complete the following table for The Absent Minded Profs. The underlying asset is ounces of gold. Assume no arbitrage.

	Spot	Cost of carry	1 year forward price	1 year interest rate	Annual storage cost
A	$200			8%	4% of spot
B	$235		$285		2% of spot
C			$300	7%	3% of spot
D	$350		$400	4%	
E	$200			9%	$20 per ounce
F			$300	3%	$5 per ounce
G	$250		$285		$15 per ounce

20. Ethel and Egbert have decided to invest in the futures market. Both entered into 1,000 futures contracts which required $30,000 initial margin. The maintenance margin for each investor is $22,500. Ethel and Egbert disagree about the future so Ethel went long while Egbert went short. Estimate each investor's daily profit (loss) and equity position (assuming no cash deposits or withdrawals).

		Ethel		Egbert	
Day	Spot price	Daily profit (loss)	Equity position (margin balance)	Daily profit (loss)	Equity position (margin balance)
0	$100		$30,000		$30,000
1	$75				
2	$50				
3	$80				
4	$130				
5	$100				

21. The Aqua Boat Company has recently issued floating rate debt. The rate is LIBOR + 3 percent, reset semi-annually. The Compost Earth Company has recently issued fixed rate debt. The rate is 5 percent per year. Aqua and Compost have entered into a 2-year interest rate swap with a notional value of $1 million. Aqua agrees to pay 6 percent fixed; Compost agrees to pay LIBOR + 2 percent. Payments are exchanged every six months based on LIBOR at the beginning of the six-month period. Determine the interest rate swap net payments for Aqua:

Start of Period	LIBOR %	Floating pay %	Fixed pay %	Net pay %	Net pay $
1	4%				
2	5%				
3	3%				
4	1%				

22. The Absent Minded Profs are in the process of developing forecasts of short-term interest rates. In order to determine their bond trading strategy, they want to determine the market's short-term (1 year) interest forecasts for different future periods. The Profs have obtained the following data on traded Government of Canada zero coupon bonds of different maturities.

Maturity	Observed YTM%
1 year	3%
2 years	5%
3 years	7%
4 years	6%
5 years	5%

Determine the implied one-year forward rates.

1 year forward rate expected in	Implied one year forward rate %
1 year	
2 years	
3 years	
4 years	
5 years	

23. Calculate the F_1, F_2, F_3, given the following interest rates on zero coupon bonds:

One year:	2.10%	Four year:	3.75%	
Two year:	2.65%	Five year:	4.05%	
Three year:	3.25%			

Medium

24. Briefly describe the process of marking to market for futures contracts.

25. CanComp, a Canadian computer manufacturer, will be delivering a large computer system to a German firm in six months. CanComp expects to receive payment of US $1.5 million at that time. Currently the spot rate is C$/US $1.15 and the six-month forward rate is C$/US $1.25.

   A. What risks does CanComp face with the sale of the computer system?
   B. Describe how CanComp can hedge the currency risk.
   C. What if:
      i) The actual spot rate in six months is C$/US $.75, what is CanComp's profit or loss on the hedge?
      ii) The actual spot rate in six months is C$/US $1.50, what is CanComp's profit or loss on the hedge?
      iii) Given your answers to (i) and (ii), should CanComp hedge? Hint: Remember ex ante versus ex post.

26. CanComp also has a contract to deliver a large computer system to a South African company (RSAComp) in one year and would like to hedge the currency risk. CanComp will receive payment of R3.5 million (the currency of South Africa is the Rand) in one year for the computer system. CanComp can borrow and lend in Canada at 3 percent per annum and can borrow and lend in South Africa at 7 percent per annum. Assume the borrowing and lending is risk free. The current spot exchange rate is C$/Rand .35 and there is no one year forward exchange rate. Describe how CanComp can hedge the currency risk by creating a synthetic forward contract. Demonstrate that your synthetic forward contract hedges the currency risk. Assume all investments are risk free.

27. The HealthBracelet Company will be needing 1,000 kilograms of copper in one year and is trying to decide between buying the copper on the spot market and using a forward contract. The spot price of copper is $15 per kilogram. The forward price is $19 per kilogram. HealthBracelet will need to rent a warehouse space to store the copper at a cost of $100 per month. HealthBracelet is able to borrow and lend at 4 percent per year. Should HealthBracelet buy its copper using the spot market or the forward market? Justify your recommendation.

28. Ethel has decided to invest in the futures market. She entered a long position in 1,000 futures contracts which required $30,000 initial margin. The maintenance margin is $22,500. Assume that Ethel deposits the minimum amount of cash required to satisfy any margin calls and makes no cash withdrawals. Assume that the cash earns no interest. At the end of day 5, Ethel closed her position.

    A. Complete the following table.

				Ethel		
Day	Spot price	Daily profit (loss)	Equity position before cash deposit	Margin call?	Cash deposit	Equity position (margin balance)
0	$100		$0		$30,000	$30,000
1	$92	−$8,000	$22,000	Yes	$500	$22,500
2	$95					
3	$103					
4	$90					
5	$100					

    B. What is Ethel's daily rate of return on her futures position?
    C. If Ethel had used a forward contract, what would her daily rate of return have been?
    D. Why are your answers to B and C different?

29. Simon is managing a large bond portfolio and wishes to hedge against interest rate risk. His portfolio includes Government of Canada bonds and high-grade Canadian corporate bonds. The correlation between the returns on his fund and the Government of Canada 6 percent 10-year bond is 1.00.

A. Describe how Simon can hedge against changes in interest rates.s

B. The Absent Minded Profs' analysis has just shown that the actual correlation between the returns on Simon's portfolio and the 6 percent 10-year Government of Canada bond is only .65. What are the implications for the hedge described in part (A)?

C. Simon strongly believes that interest rates will fall in the near future. Describe how he can speculate on that belief. What risks are inherent in that position (i.e., what happens if interest rates rise?)

30. Hadrian and Boudicca are in the process of renewing their mortgages. Each mortgage is an interest-only mortgage (i.e., the borrower pays only interest and has a balloon payment at the end) for $100,000. Hadrian, having an excellent credit history, is offered the choice between a fixed rate mortgage at 3 percent and a floating rate mortgage at prime + 1 percent ("prime" rate is the domestic version of LIBOR). Boudicca is offered the choice between a fixed rate mortgage at 7 percent and a floating rate mortgage at prime + 3 percent. The current prime rate is 3 percent. Floating rate mortgages are reset at the start of each year.

Hadrian and Boudicca have both recently retired—Hadrian's future income is closely tied to market interest rates (he has his retirement funds invested in bonds) while Boudicca has a fixed retirement income (the Canada Pension Plan).

A. Ignoring interest costs, which mortgage would Hadrian prefer—fixed or floating? Why? Which mortgage would Boudicca prefer—fixed or floating? Why?

B. Assume that Hadrian chose a fixed rate mortgage and Boudicca chose a floating rate mortgage. Design a swap agreement between Hadrian and Boudicca which will make them both better off.

   i) What is this type of swap called?

   ii) What are the risks associated with this swap?

   iii) If the prime rate for the next 4 years is: 3%, 5%, 4%, and 2%, respectively:

      1. Show the cash flows between Hadrian and Boudicca.

      2. Demonstrate that the swap will make Hadrian and Boudicca better off.

31. For Question 13, explain how the spreads are shared between the two parties, and describe the absolute advantage and comparative advantage in the swap.

Difficult

32. The CanGold Mining Company borrowed €100 million in France at an annual interest rate of 3.5 percent. The principal plus interest is due in one year. CanGold used the funds to purchase machine parts in Germany for use in its Indonesian gold mine. In one year, the mine is expected to produce 1 million ounces of gold. Gold is sold on the world market in U.S. dollars. CanGold would like to hedge its currency and commodity risk. The CFO of CanGold has been quoted the following forward contracts:

   i) One year C$/€ forward exchange rate: 1.60

   ii) One year C$/US$ forward exchange rate: 1.05

   iii) One year US$/€ forward exchange rate: 1.10

   iv) One year gold forward contract: US$ 250 per ounce

Design the optimal hedging strategy for CanGold. Hint: Are there any arbitrage opportunities?

33. Bert, the business reporter for the *Sidney Driftwood* (a small regional newspaper on Vancouver Island) has contacted the Absent Minded Profs for information about the oil market. Provide responses to his questions below.

    A. "I understand supply and demand and the difference between the spot and the forward market. I understand that there will be an effect on the forward price of oil if an oil field in Iraq, which is expected to go into production in one year, does not go into production. There will be a decrease in the expected supply so it makes sense that the price expected in the future (the forward price) will increase. What I don't understand is why this causes a change in the spot price—after all the supply of oil today hasn't changed, so why would today's price change?"

    B. "The second thing that puzzled me was the effect of hurricane Katrina on the forward price of oil. The area around New Orleans is a major storage depot for oil in the U.S. and there was extensive damage to the storage facilities in the hurricane. Consequently, there would have been a decrease in the amount of oil available today and, logically, the spot price would have gone up. What I don't understand is why the forward price also rose—future oil production doesn't depend on the availability of storage facilities today."

34. Angela, a reporter with the *Red River Valley Echo*, a local newspaper in Altona, Manitoba, has contacted the Absent Minded Profs with a question about the swap market. Provide a response to Angela's question: "A swap agreement allows two companies to swap payments. Presumably, both parties believe that this agreement will make them better off. If the markets are efficient, how can a swap make the participants better off?" Answer this with respect to both interest rate and currency swaps.

35. At the end of year 0, you observe the following data about Government of Canada pure discount bonds (zero coupon bonds):

Name of Bond Issue	Years to Maturity	YTM%
A	1	5%
B	2	7%
C	3	10%

    A. What price do you expect bond C to sell for at the end of year 2?

    B. The Government of Canada is considering issuing a coupon bond. The bond will pay a 7 percent coupon, paid annually. The face value of the bond will be $1,000. What price would you expect the bond to sell for today?

Granting Options

Companies often grant stock options to employees in an attempt to attract and retain talented workers. In fact, for some of the highest-paid CEOs in Canada, these stock options are a larger component of total compensation than their salaries. However, the manner in which these options are awarded has left the door open for manipulation. In the United States, regulators have focused on the illegal practice of backdating options. Canadian stock exchanges and regulators are keeping an eye out for options abuses as well, and penalties can be severe. One TSX rule stipulates that companies may not issue options based on market prices that do not fully reflect non-public material information.

Source: Torys LLP website: www.torys.com, March 5, 2007.
Source: TSX Group website: www.tsx.com, March 5, 2007.

12

Options

Learning Objectives

After reading this chapter, you should understand the following:

1. The basic nature of options

2. The payoffs associated with long and short positions in call and put options

3. The factors affecting option values, and how those factors influence option values

4. How to use put-call parity to estimate call and put prices, and how it can be used to synthetically create call, put, and underlying positions

5. How options can be used for hedging purposes

6. How to use the Black-Scholes option pricing model to price call options

7. How options are traded, and what is meant by implied volatility

INTRODUCTION

In Chapter 11, we discussed *linear* derivative contracts, where the payoffs directly reflected the behaviour of the underlying asset, so both gains and losses were generated. This chapter discusses *non-linear* payoffs, which may be limited in some way through a maximum gain or loss, or both. The most basic contract is a *call option*, for which the payoff is limited on the downside, so losses are restricted. Working out the value of an asset that in some cases can generate only positive payoffs led to a Nobel Prize for the development of the celebrated Black-Scholes option pricing model (OPM). We show how the OPM can be derived by creating a risk-free asset and show why it is such a powerful model. You will learn what determines the value of options, how to use the option pricing model on the Montreal Exchange's website, and what all those Greek letters mean. This chapter introduces ideas that are often used in business finance, as you will see in Chapter 17, for example, when you learn how options have been used to design innovative new financing instruments.

12.1 CALL OPTIONS

call option the right, but not the obligation, to buy an underlying asset at a fixed price for a specified time

exercise price or strike price the price at which an investor can buy the underlying asset

exercise to implement the rights of options by buying (in the case of call options) or selling (in the case of put options)

expiration date the last date on which options can be converted or exercised

payoff the proceeds that would be generated from the option if today was the expiration date

Call Option Basics

We begin by considering the characteristics of the basic **call option**, which is defined as the *right, but not the obligation*, to *buy* an underlying asset at a fixed price for a specified time. The price at which an investor can buy the underlying asset is called the **exercise or strike price**, and the last date at which the option can be converted or **exercised** is called the **expiration date**.

We begin our discussion by revisiting the example from Chapter 11 in which we had a forward price of $50 on some underlying asset. Now we assume a call option is available on that asset with an exercise price (X) of $50. We set the strike price equal to the forward price to simplify some of the discussion; however, it is not a necessary assumption. For the time being, we will not specify the expiration date of the option. The **payoff** for the *buyer* (*holder*) of this call (i.e., a long call position) for various underlying asset prices is depicted in Figure 12-1. The payoff refers to the proceeds that would be generated from the call option if today was the expiration date and the option holder had to decide whether to exercise the option or not. It does not reflect the investor's *profits*, because it does not account for the purchase price of the option, which we will discuss later. We have also included the payoff from a long position in the underlying asset (i.e., from holding it) in Figure 12-1.

First, think about a long position in the underlying asset. In this case, the payoff is a 45-degree line going through the origin, because the value varies one to one with the price of the underlying asset. In other words, the underlying is worth (or pays off) $1 if the price goes to $1, $2 if it goes to $2, $50 if the price

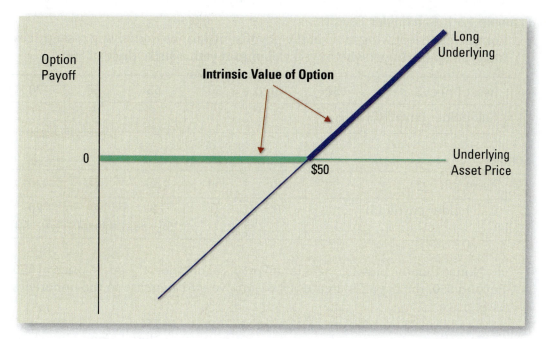

12-1 FIGURE

Call Holder's Payoff

goes to $50, and so on. Now let's shift the 45-degree line over so it cuts the horizontal axis at the strike price, which in this case was the forward price of $50. The result is the payoff from a forward contract, as discussed in Chapter 11. If an investor buys the asset forward, then he or she has a long position; if the asset price exceeds the forward price, the investor has a profit, and if the price is less than the forward price, the investor has a loss. The fact that the payoff on the forward contract is a straight line (which happens to be 45 degrees) is the reason that we previously referred to it as a *linear* payoff.

Now think about the call with the strike price equal to the forward price of $50. If at expiration the underlying asset's price is above $50, say $55, the investor exercises the call. This means that he or she pays $50 and "calls" the asset away from the counterparty, that is, the person who has sold the call. The investor could then obtain a payoff of $5 by selling the asset for $55 in the open market, exactly as we discussed with respect to the forward contract. In this case, we say the call is **in the money**. Conversely, if the underlying asset's price is below $50, the call is worthless and would not be exercised. No one would pay the strike price to call the asset away from its owner for $50 when it can be bought for less in the open market. This is the crucial fact about options: they give the owner the *right*, but not the *obligation*, to do something. Unlike the long position in the forward contract, the investor doesn't incur losses in a long call position when the price of the underlying asset is below the strike price, which we refer to as being **out of the money**.[1] As a result, the investor gets the payoff from the forward contract above the strike price and gets zero below. For this reason, options are examples of securities with non-linear payoffs.[2]

in the money the option would generate a positive payoff if generated today

out of the money the option would generate a negative payoff if exercised today

---

[1] An option is said to be "at the money" whenever the market price of the underlying equals the strike price.
[2] Strictly speaking, the payoffs are piecewise linear.

Example 12-1: Call Holder Payoffs

Complete the following table of the payoffs for various underlying asset prices, for a call option buyer who buys a call option with a strike price of $50.

Asset Price ($)	30	40	50	55	60	70
Call holder payoff ($)						

Solution

Asset Price ($)	30	40	50	55	60	70
Call holder payoff ($)	0	0	0	5 (55−50)	10 (60−50)	20 (70−50)

Notice that the payoff is zero for all prices at or below the strike price of $50. Beyond $50, the payoff increases by $1 for every $1 increase in the underlying asset price.

The discussion above leaves out one important detail—namely, whom investors are buying the option from. In this chapter, we discuss secondary market options, so the supply and trading of such options has no impact on the underlying asset. When an investor buys a call option, he or she buys it from some other market participant unrelated to the underlying asset. Until 30 years ago, investment bankers arranged option contracts directly between two parties, so there was significant credit risk attached to the counterparty; in other words, when the investor exercised the call, he or she couldn't be certain that the counterparty would deliver it. In this way, option markets were similar to the original swap and forward markets. Today, as with the swap markets, option markets now consist of unique over-the-counter (OTC) options that are still arranged between two parties with credit risk. However, a significant number of exchange traded options exist, similar to futures, which have been designed to remove credit risk. In fact, traded options markets are tightly integrated with futures markets. For now, we'll ignore credit risk and consider the payoff for the person who *sells* a call option; such a person is called an **option writer**, because he or she has written the call option that is purchased by someone else. It is common to say that option writers have assumed a **short position** in the option.

option writer the person who sells an option

short position the position taken by the option writer

If someone sells a call option, the payoff is the *mirror image* of that received by the person who buys it, just as the payoff to a short forward position was the mirror image to that of a long forward position. For example, we have already looked at the payoff to the $50 call holder and noted that as the asset price increases, say, to $55, the payoff on the call is $5. This $5 payoff occurs as the asset is called away from the option writer for $50 and sold for $55. The payoff to the call option writer is the opposite, as he or she has to go into the market and buy this asset for $55 and then surrender it for only $50, losing $5. Conversely, when a call expires out of the money and is not exercised, the option writer doesn't lose anything. The payoff for the call option writer of this $50 call is depicted in Figure 12-2.

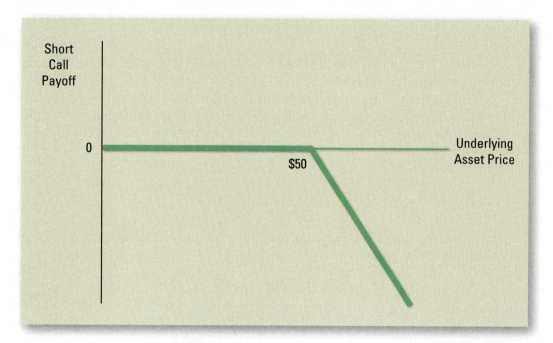

12-2   FIGURE
Call Writer's Payoff

Notice that the payoff from writing the call is the mirror image of that from buying the call, or is the payoff from buying the call "folded" downward at the exercise price.

Example 12-2: Call Writer Payoffs

Complete the following table depicting the payoffs for various underlying asset prices for a call option writer who sells a call option with a strike price of $50.

Asset Price ($)	30	40	50	55	60	70
Call writer payoff ($)						

Solution

Asset Price ($)	30	40	50	55	60	70
Call writer payoff ($)	0	0	0	−5 (50−55)	−10 (50−60)	−20 (50−70)

Notice that the payoff is zero for all prices at or below the strike price of $50. Beyond $50, the payoff decreases by $1 for every $1 increase in the underlying asset price, because the call writer has agreed to sell the asset for $50.

Call Option Values

So what is the value of the call option? At expiration, the value of the option is the asset price minus the strike price when the call is in the money, and zero when it is out of the money. This is the bold line in Figure 12-1, and is called the **intrinsic value (IV)**. We can estimate the intrinsic value of a call option, as shown in Equation 12-1.

intrinsic value (IV) the value of an option at expiration; it is positive when the option is in the money and zero when it is out of the money

[12-1]
$$\text{IV (call)} = \text{Max}(S - X, 0)$$

time value (TV) the difference between the option premium and the intrinsic value

Equation 12-1 states that the IV of a call equals $S - X$ when the call is in the money, and equals 0 otherwise.

The IV is the value of the option on the expiration date. However, before expiration, the value of the call will exceed its intrinsic value because of the option's **time value (TV)**. The market value of the option, commonly known as the **option premium**, is the sum of its IV and its TV. This relationship is given in Equation 12-2:

option premium market value of the option; the sum of an option's IV and TV

[12-2]
$$\text{Option premium} = \text{IV} + \text{TV}$$

We can rearrange this equation to solve for the time value, as shown in Equation 12-3:

[12-3]
$$\text{TV} = \text{Option Premium} - \text{IV}$$

Example 12-3: Estimating Call Option Intrinsic and Time Values

Assume the $50 call option referred to above is selling for $3 in the market. Determine the intrinsic value and time value of this call option, assuming the price of the underlying asset is

a. $48   **b.** $50   **c.** $52

Solution

a. IV = Max(48 − 50, 0) = 0; TV = 3 − 0 = $3

b. IV = Max(50 − 50, 0) = 0; TV = 3 − 0 = $3

c. IV = Max(52 − 50, 2) = 2; TV = 3 − 2 = $1

It has long been known that the option value depends on the price of the underlying asset. However, it was not until Fischer Black and Myron Scholes, two finance professors from the University of Chicago, came up with the Black-Scholes option pricing model that the relationship was clearly understood.[3] We discuss this option pricing model later in the chapter; for now, let's step back and think intuitively about what drives option values.

The option value is influenced by the ratio of the price of the underlying asset to the strike price. Because X is fixed for each call, this essentially means the price of the underlying asset (S). As S falls far below X, not only is the IV of the option zero, but so is the TV. This occurs because there is less chance of the price of the underlying asset recovering to exceed the strike price. At the other extreme, when the price of the underlying asset is far above the strike price, the time value gets smaller, as discussed below. So **deep** in the money and deep out of the money calls are easier to value, because their values get closer to their intrinsic values as their time values get smaller.

deep describes options that are so far in (out of) the money that they are almost certain (not) to be exercised

For example, suppose over the next period it is equally likely that the price of the underlying asset will increase or decrease by $5. If the asset price is currently

---

[3] Robert Merton was also a pioneer in option pricing. Both he and Myron Scholes won Nobel prizes for their work. Unfortunately Fischer Black died before he could be similarly honoured.

$10, the call is deep out of the money. With a decrease in the asset price to $5, the call is still deep out of the money. Even with an increase in the asset price to $15, it is still deep out of the money. With deep out of the money calls, the investor needs a sequence of very positive returns on the underlying asset to generate any value. This makes the time value very small.

Now take the opposite situation, in which the asset price is $100, so the intrinsic value of the call is $50, and it is deep in the money. When the price changes by $5, the intrinsic value of the call also changes by close to $5. If the time value is zero, then the change in the value of the call is exactly the same as the underlying asset. In the extreme case of a call on an asset with a strike price of $0, then the call is deep in the money and exactly the same as the underlying asset.[4]

The impact of the underlying asset price on the call's value means that a curve connects the intrinsic value of the option when it is deep in and deep out of the money. This relationship is illustrated in Figure 12-3, and it means that the call value is related in a non-linear way to the underlying asset price.

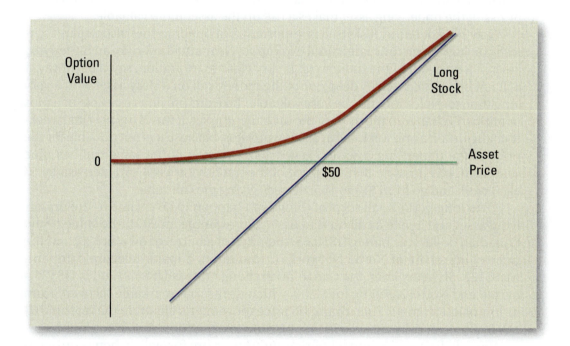

12-3 FIGURE

The Value of a Call Option

The fact that deep in and out of the money call options are relatively easy to value means that the most difficult options to value are those for which the price of the asset is close to the strike price. For options that are at the money (i.e., where $S = X$), the TV is at its largest and by definition the IV is zero. Unfortunately, most options start out with the strike price set close to the price of the underlying asset, so they have lots of time value and little intrinsic value. This factor is what makes option valuation complicated.

The discussion above directs our attention to the most important component of the option value, which is the *risk* of the underlying asset. In most areas of finance, risk is estimated as the variability or standard deviation of an asset's return. However, this is closely related to the range of possible outcomes, and it

---

[4] This assumes that the value of the asset, like a common share, cannot become negative.

was the *range* that we used when we said the outcomes could be plus or minus $5, or a range of $10. Now suppose we are valuing two calls on different assets that both have the same $50 strike price. The first call is on an asset with two equally likely outcomes of plus or minus $5 for a price range of $10, while the second is on a riskier asset with two equally likely outcomes of plus or minus $10 or a range of $20. Which call is the more valuable?

First, consider what happens when the price of the underlying asset falls below X. We know that we are not going to exercise the call and will let it expire worthless, so whether the asset price is $5 or $10 below the strike price doesn't matter. Conversely, it does matter by how much the asset price exceeds X. The call on the low-risk asset will now have an intrinsic value of $5, whereas that on the riskier asset will have an intrinsic value of $10. It is a very important result in option pricing that call options on riskier assets are worth more than those on low-risk assets. The reason for this is that the call protects you from "downside" risk, so how far down you go doesn't matter. All that matters is the upside or how far above the strike price the asset price can get. Anything that expands the range of outcomes or risk of the underlying asset makes a call on the asset more valuable.

Now consider *time*. Risk itself is important, but option values also depend critically on how much time is left until expiration. No matter how risky an underlying asset, if a deep out of the money call is very close to expiration, say, a day away, it will not be worth much. A deep out of the money call on a risky asset with a very long time to expiration may be very valuable. Take our previous example of a plus or minus $5 change in the price of the underlying asset. If this is the possible weekly change, then a one week call at $50 is worthless, because it is not possible for the price of the underlying asset to exceed $50. However, if the same call has nine weeks left, it is possible that the price of the underlying asset can increase by $5 each week and go from $10 to $55, thereby giving the call value.

Over long periods, all sorts of things can happen to give value to the underlying asset and hence a call on that asset. For example, in 2001, the value of the Canadian dollar was barely US$0.65, the price of a barrel of oil was $20, and the price of one share of Nortel Networks Corporation, a major telecom company, was $122. Six years later, the Canadian exchange rate is US$0.91, oil is US$75 a barrel, and Nortel is selling for $2.50, which itself is a remarkable recovery from its low of less than $1. Such dramatic price movements illustrate the reason that call options on risky assets with a long time to expiration are very valuable.

We will discuss the impact of risk and time more formally when we discuss a model of option prices, but risk compounds through time, causing the range of outcomes to increase. This compounding or magnification is greater for high-risk than for low-risk stocks, which makes long-dated call options on risky assets more valuable than similar options on short-dated low-risk assets. For any given call option, all else constant, its value will *decrease* through time. For example, an at the money call starts out with maximum time value and no intrinsic value. If nothing else changes, and it is still at the money at expiration, then it is worthless. Generally, the time value decreases at an increasing rate as the call gets closer to expiration.

Another factor to consider is what drives the underlying asset's price. For example, from Chapter 7, we know that the value of a common share is the present value of a stream of *dividends*, so call options on equities depend on these dividend payments. We will discuss dividend policy in Chapter 22, but suppose a resource company has very large profits because natural resource prices are at an all-time high, and they are not expected to continue. As a result, a company's stock price is $38, consisting of a $26 value for its continuing operations and $12 for its cash. If the firm decides to pay out this cash as a dividend, the stock price will drop by $12, reducing the value of a call on the stock.

Generally, options are not *protected* from any dividend payments made by the underlying asset, so options on high-dividend-paying stocks or assets with large cash distributions are worth less than those on non-dividend-paying stocks. In 1989, Inco Limited, one of the largest nickel producers in the world, was in the above situation and unexpectedly paid out a US$10 dividend, which was worth about C$12 at the time, causing a dramatic drop in its stock price. Paying attention to the dividend payments of the underlying asset is important.

The final factor that affects option prices is the *risk-free interest rate*. Normally, when interest rates go up, the value of securities go down. For example, bond prices always go down when interest rates rise, as discussed in Chapter 6, but equity prices also tend to go down, because the equity discount rate goes up. However, option prices behave differently, because the main effect of increasing interest rates is to decrease the present value of the strike price. An increase in the interest rate has a similar effect on a call price as decreasing the strike price. As a result, call options tend to increase with increases in interest rates.

To summarize our discussion of call option prices,

- They approach their intrinsic value for deep in and deep out of the money calls.
- They increase with the price of the underlying asset.
- They decrease with a higher strike price.
- They increase if the underlying asset is riskier.
- They increase as the time to expiration increases.
- They decrease as the dividend payments of the underlying asset increase.
- They increase as interest rates increase.

That's a lot of factors to consider in a pricing model, and it is important to remember that we considered each of the above factors in isolation, that is, the impact of a change in only one factor at a time. In reality, of course, many of these factors are changing all the time and affect one another. For example, an increase in interest rates or a change in risk may have a negative effect on option prices if the *indirect* effect on the asset price is greater than the *direct* effects discussed above. However, before we consider how to incorporate them into a pricing model we can bracket the value of the call option by considering the characteristics of put options.

CONCEPT REVIEW QUESTIONS

1. Explain why the payoff from a call option is "non-linear."
2. Explain how to estimate the intrinsic value and time value for a call option.
3. Briefly describe the main factors that affect a call option's value, and how they affect the value.

12.2 PUT OPTIONS

Put Option Payoffs

A **put option** is the opposite of a call option: it gives the owner the right, but not the obligation, to *sell* an underlying asset at a fixed price for a specified time. Consider the value of a put on an underlying asset with a strike price equal to the forward price. The payoff for the holder of a put is depicted in Figure 12-4.

FIGURE   12-4

Put Holder's Payoff

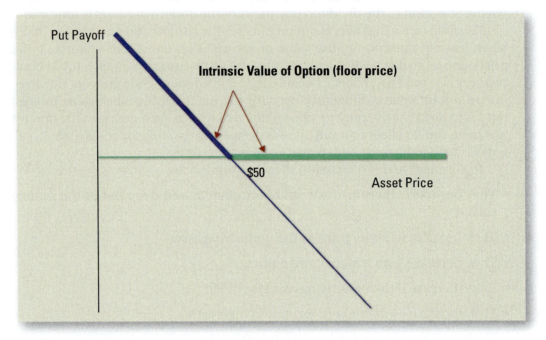

In considering the behaviour of the call option, we first examined a long position in the asset. Because the put is the opposite of a call, we start with the opposite of a long position in the underlying asset, which is a *short position*. When the underlying asset is sold forward and its price exceeds the forward price at $55, the investor loses $5. This occurs because he or she has to go into the market and pay $55 to buy the asset to deliver against the forward contract, for which he or she gets only $50. Conversely, if the asset price falls to $45, the investor generates a $5 profit. He or she buys the asset for $45 and then delivers it to meet the forward commitment and receives the $50 forward price. Graphically, the short position is a 45-degree line going though the forward price of $50, as depicted in Figure 12-4. Notice that this is the mirror image of the long position.

Now consider the payoff on the put option. If the asset price increases, then the investor does not exercise the put option, because there is no reason to sell the asset for $50 when the investor can sell it in the open market for say $55. Conversely, if the asset price drops to $45, the investor exercises the put. It is better to use the put contract and sell it to the counterparty for $50 than to sell it in the open market for $45. The result is the opposite of the call option; put options pay off when the asset price drops *below* the strike price, and they are worthless when it is above. The put allows an investor to take advantage of the downside risk attached to an asset, just as the call allows an investor to take advantage of the upside.

Example 12-4: Put Holder Payoffs

Complete the following table depicting the payoffs for various underlying asset prices for a put option buyer who buys a put option with a strike price of $50.

Asset Price ($)	30	40	50	55	60	70
Put holder payoff ($)						

Solution

Asset Price ($)	30	40	50	55	60	70
Put holder payoff ($)	20 (50−30)	10 (50−40)	0	0	0	0

Notice that the payoff is zero for all prices at or above the strike price of $50. Below $50, the payoff increases by $1 for every $1 decrease in the underlying asset price.

Now we consider the payoff for the *put writer*, who has assumed what is commonly called a *short position* in the put. We know that when the asset price increases above the strike price, the put expires worthless, so the payoff to both the put owner and writer is zero. When the asset price drops below the strike price, say, to $45, then the owner of the put buys the asset for $45 in the open market and sells it to the put writer for $50, making a $5 profit. The put writer's payoff is the opposite of the put holder's, because he or she has to pay $50 for an asset that can be sold for only $45, thereby incurring a $5 loss. The payoff for the put writer is given in Figure 12-5.

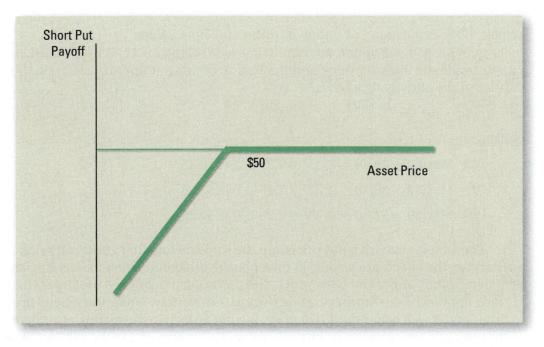

12-5 FIGURE

Put Writer's Payoff

Notice that it is the mirror image of the put holder's payoff, or is the put holder's payoff folded downward.

Example 12-5: Put Writer Payoffs

Complete the following table depicting the payoffs for various underlying asset prices for a put option writer who sells a put option with a strike price of $50.

Asset Price ($)	30	40	50	55	60	70
Put writer payoff ($)						

Solution

Asset Price ($)	30	40	50	55	60	70
Put writer payoff ($)	−20 (30−50)	−10 (40−50)	0	0	0	0

Notice that the payoff is zero for all prices at or above the strike price of $50. Below $50, the payoff decreases by $1 for every $1 decrease in the underlying asset price, because the put writer has agreed to buy the asset for $50.

Put Option Values

We can estimate the intrinsic value of a put option as

[12-4]

$$\text{IV (put)} = \text{Max}(X - S, 0)$$

Equation 12-4 states that IV of a put equals $X - S$ when the put is in the money, and equals 0 otherwise. Equations 12-2 and 12-3 regarding the time value and option premium of an option apply to puts in the same way as they did for calls.

Example 12-6: Estimating Put Option Intrinsic and Time Values

Assume the $50 put option referred to above is selling for $2.25 in the market. Determine the intrinsic value and time value of this put option, assuming the price of the underlying asset is

a. $48   b. $50   c. $52

Solution

a. IV = Max(50 − 48, 0) = 2; TV = 2.25 − 2 = $0.25

b. IV = Max(50 − 50, 0) = 0; TV = 2.25 − 0 = $2.25

c. IV = Max(50 − 52, 0) = 0; TV = 2.25 − 0 = $2.25

The factors that drive put prices are the same factors that affect call prices. However, the effects are usually in the opposite direction. When the asset price is significantly above the strike price, the put is deep out of the money, so the price approaches its intrinsic value of zero. Conversely, when the asset price drops and is well below the strike price, the put is deep in the money, and again the put's price approaches its intrinsic value. This is opposite to the call, but like the call, the put's maximum time value occurs at the strike price, when its intrinsic value is zero. Opposite to the call, an increase in the asset price will decrease the put price, while a higher strike price will increase its value. However, an increase in either the expiration date or the risk (uncertainty) in the underlying asset will increase the put price in the same manner as it would a call price. A decrease in interest rates or an increase in cash dividend payments will increase the put price.

All of the effects discussed above are predictable, given the intuition behind their impact on call prices. However, puts and calls have a major difference when it comes to whether or not an investor can exercise the option before the expiration date. Note that **European options** can be exercised only at maturity, whereas **American options** can be exercised at any time up to and including the expiration date. This distinction is no longer geographic, as the names imply, because European options are traded in North America and vice versa. For call options on non-dividend-paying assets, the distinction is not important; as long as the option can be sold, it should never be exercised before maturity because there is always some time value.[5] However, the distinction is important for put options. Consider what happens if the underlying asset price goes to zero, perhaps because it is a common share and the firm goes bankrupt. Because the underlying asset can never go below zero, the put reaches its maximum value. In this case, all American options would be exercised, because the put holder gets the maximum payoff immediately and that cash can then be reinvested elsewhere.

We can summarize the impact of these basic factors on option prices in Table 12-1.

European options
options that can be exercised only at maturity

American options
options that can be exercised at any time up to and including the expiration date

Table 12-1   Factors Affecting Option Prices

	Call Prices	Put Prices
Higher asset price (S)	↑	↓
Higher strike price (X)	↓	↑
Longer time to expiration	↑	↑
Increased volatility	↑	↑
Increase in interest rates	↑	↓
Increased dividends	↓	↑

CONCEPT REVIEW QUESTIONS

1. Contrast the payoff from a put option with that from a call option.
2. Explain how to estimate the intrinsic value and time value for a put option.
3. Briefly describe the main factors that affect a put and a call option's value, and how they affect the value of each.

---

[5] For interest- or dividend-paying assets, premature exercise may occur in the case of a very large payment that significantly reduces the value of the underlying asset.

12.3 PUT-CALL PARITY

The Four Basic Option Positions

The four basic option positions are (1) long call, (2) short call, (3) long put, and (4) short put, and these positions were diagrammed in Figures 12-1, 12-2, 12-4, and 12-5. Consider these four figures again, and note that if we combine a long call and a short put, we have a 45-degree line going through the strike price, which in our example is also the forward price. This is a long forward contract with gains and losses around the strike price. Similarly if we combine a long put and a short call, we have a 45-degree line going through the forward price. This is a short forward contract with losses and gains around the strike price. The payoffs on these contracts are depicted in Figure 12-6.

FIGURE 12-6

Combining Option Positions

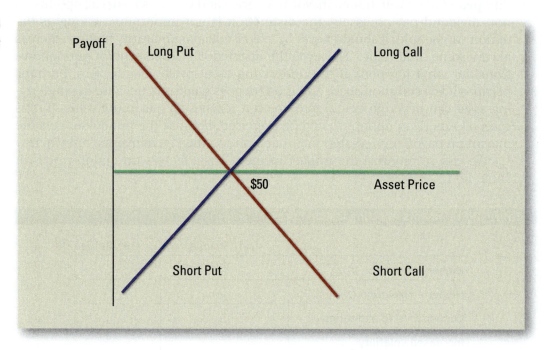

Now we can see why we started with puts and calls with a strike price equal to the forward price. In this special case, the long call and short put add to a forward contract, and the long put and short call is a short forward contract. Examples 12-7 and 12-8 demonstrate.

Example 12-7: Long Call Plus Short Put Payoffs

Complete the following table depicting the payoffs for various underlying asset prices for an investor who simultaneously buys a call and sells a put with a strike price of $50.

Asset Price ($)	30	40	50	55	60	70
Long call payoff ($)						
Short put payoff ($)						
Net payoff ($)						

Solution

Asset Price ($)	30	40	50	55	60	70
Long call payoff ($)	0	0	0	5	10	20
Short put payoff ($)	−20	−10	0	0	0	0
Net payoff ($)	−20	−10	0	5	10	20

Notice that the payoff for the net position is exactly the same as that from a long forward position at a forward price of $50.

Example 12-8: Short Call Plus Long Put Payoffs

Complete the following table depicting the payoffs for various underlying asset prices for an investor who simultaneously sells a call and buys a put with a strike price of $50.

Asset Price ($)	30	40	50	55	60	70
Short call payoff ($)						
Long put payoff ($)						
Net payoff ($)						

Solution

Asset Price ($)	30	40	50	55	60	70
Short call payoff ($)	0	0	0	−5	−10	−20
Long put payoff ($)	20	10	0	0	0	0
Net payoff ($)	20	10	0	−5	−10	−20

Notice that the payoff for the net position is exactly the same as that from a short forward position at a forward price of $50.

If an investor simultaneously established all four basic option positions, then the net position is zero, because in aggregate the four contracts are a *zero sum game*: wealth is not created or destroyed. This is shown in Examples 12-7 and 12-8, because the investor would be combining the two net payoff positions, which add to zero for any underlying asset price. With secondary market options, wealth is simply rearranged among market participants.[6]

Deriving the Put-Call Parity Relationship

Understanding how these four contracts end up looking like long and short forward contracts is the key to understanding **put-call parity**. Consider two portfolios. The first, portfolio A, consists of buying a put (*P*) with *X* = $50 and simultaneously purchasing the underlying asset (*S*). The second, portfolio B, consists of buying a call (*C*) with *X* = $50 and investing the present value of the

put-call parity the relationship between the price of a call option and a put option that have the same strike price and expiry dates; assumes that the options are not exercised before their expiration

---

[6] This ignores the option prices, the fees charged by brokers, and the exchange to make the market. This is why many experts argue that in aggregate, options waste scarce resources in the economy.

exercise price, PV(X), in a risk-free asset paying interest at RF, so that the investor has $50 available to exercise the call option. We assume the options are European so that they can be exercised only at maturity. We also assume the underlying asset provides no dividends or other income. Table 12-2 shows the payoffs from these two portfolios, assuming the underlying asset price can be either $45 or $55.

Table 12-2   Payoff from Combining Calls, Puts, and Underlying Asset Positions

Underlying Price	$55	$45
Portfolio A		
Long put payoff	0	+$5
Long asset payoff	+$55	+$45
Total payoff for A	$55	$50
Portfolio B		
Long call payoff	+$5	0
Invest present value of $50 at RF	+$50	+$50
Total payoff for B	$55	$50

Notice that the payoff from either strategy is the *same* whether the ending share price is $45 or $55. In fact, it is easy to demonstrate that the payoffs for these two portfolios will always be the same, as depicted in Table 12-3.

Table 12-3   Payoff from Combining Calls, Puts, and Underlying Asset Positions: The General

Underlying Price at Expiration Date (S_T)	$S_T > X$	$S_T < X$
Portfolio A		
Long put payoff	0	$X - S_T$
Long asset payoff	S_T	S_T
Total payoff for A	S_T	X
Portfolio B		
Long call payoff	$S_T - X$	0
Invest X at RF short asset payoff	$+X$	$+X$
Total payoff for B	S_T	X

The payoff from either strategy is the *same* no matter what the ending share price is. Because early exercise is not possible, and the payoffs at the expiration date (T) will always be the same, the *cost* of constructing each portfolio must be the same. Denoting the cost of the put as P, the cost of the call as C, and S as the price of the underlying asset, we can therefore say that

$$P + S = C + \text{PV}(X) \qquad [12\text{-}5]$$

Rearranging Equation 12-5, we get the basic put-call relationship:

$$C - P = S - \text{PV}(X) \qquad [12\text{-}6]$$

It is important to recognize that this relationship holds for European options on non-dividend-paying assets. It is also important to recognize that we can solve this equation to determine the call option price, given P, S, X, and RF, and we can also determine the put option price given C, S, X, and RF. Both of these equations are shown below:

$$C = P + S - \text{PV}(X) \qquad [12\text{-}7]$$

$$P = C - S + \text{PV}(X) \qquad [12\text{-}8]$$

Although put-call parity doesn't help us to price the call, unless we know the price of the put and vice versa, it does demonstrate again that these contracts are all derivative, that is, not original, and there is evidence that the basic properties of put-call parity have been known for centuries. We demonstrate how to apply put-call parity in Examples 12-9 and 12-10.

Example 12-9: Finding a Call Price by Using Put-Call Parity
A company's common shares are selling for $20, and a one-year European put option on those shares, with a $20 strike price, is selling for $0.50. If the risk-free rate is 5%, find the value of a one-year European call on the same stock with a $20 exercise price.

Solution
$$C = P + S - \text{PV}(X) = 0.50 + 20.00 - 20/(1.05) = 20.50 - 19.05 = \$1.45$$

Example 12-10: Finding a Put Price by Using Put-Call Parity
A company's common shares are selling for $20, and a six-month European call option on those shares, with a $20 strike price, is selling for $0.90. If the risk-free rate is 5%, find the value of a six-month European put on the same stock with a $20 exercise price.

Solution
Six-month discount rate = 5%/2 = 2.50%
$$P = C - S + \text{PV}(X) = 0.90 - 20.00 + 20/(1.025) = -19.10 + 19.51 = \$0.41$$

The put-call parity equation can also be solved for S, as shown in Equation 12-9.

$$S = C - P + \text{PV}(X) \qquad [12\text{-}9]$$

Equation 12-9 shows that a long position in the underlying asset is equivalent to a long position in a call, a short position in a put with the same strike price, and an investment of PV(*X*) in a risk-free asset. If we multiply this equation by minus one, we can see that a short position in the underlying asset is equivalent to a short position in a call, a long position in a put with the same strike price, and borrowing PV(*X*) at the risk-free rate.

Creating Synthetic Positions by Using Put-Call Parity

The put-call parity relationships are particularly important for hedging purposes. Applying our discussion of how to create synthetic positions by using forward contracts from Chapter 11, we can see how we could use Equations 12-7 through 12-9 to synthetically create long or short positions in puts, calls, or the underlying asset. For our present purposes, we ignore the PV(*X*) term, which involves borrowing or lending at RF, because it does not affect the shape of the net payoff diagram.

We begin by considering a long position in the underlying asset; for example, assume that it is U.S. dollars receivable as we discussed in Chapter 11. We already showed that an investor can sell U.S. dollars forward to remove the exposure completely, but perhaps he or she thinks the Canadian dollar is going to weaken and wants the possibility of getting more Canadian dollars for those U.S. dollars. In other words, the investor wants downside-risk protection if the Canadian dollar strengthens, and wants to maintain upside potential if it weakens. Suppose the contract is priced so that if the Canadian dollar appreciates to $0.90 per US dollar, the investor will break even, but below this, he or she loses money. In this case, the investor might not want to risk a depreciation of the U.S. dollar below C$0.90, so he or she buys a put option to sell U.S. dollars at C$0.90 to fix the minimum Canadian dollars the investor will get out of the contract.

protective put the purchase of a put option to protect a long position in an underlying asset

Buying a put option to protect a long position in an underlying asset is generally referred to as entering into a **protective put**. The purchase of the put option gives the right to sell the U.S. dollar at a fixed price for Canadian dollars, which *insures* the long position against losing money. The net payoff from this overall position resembles that of a *long call* position, as predicted by put-call parity in Equation 12-7 and as depicted by the solid bolded line in Figure 12-7.

FIGURE   12-7

A Protective Put

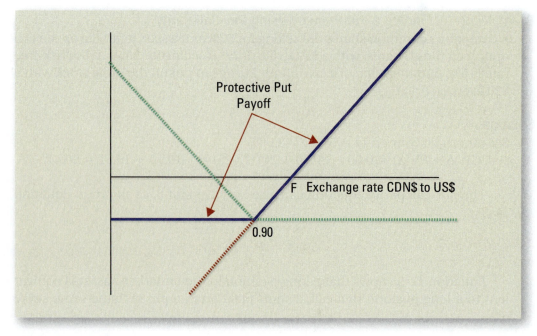

Protective Put
Payoff

F   Exchange rate CDN$ to US$

0.90

The 45-degree line indicates the long position in U.S. dollars from the contract and the green dotted line indicates the long put position we discussed earlier. With a value of the U.S. dollar above C$0.90, the investor does not exercise the put and exchanges U.S. dollars at the spot rate. However, as the U.S. dollar depreciates below C$0.90, say to C$0.80, the investor exercises the put and exchanges the depreciating U.S. dollar for C$0.90 instead of taking the spot rate. The combination is the bold line as indicated in Figure 12-7, which looks like a long call, as predicted by put-call parity. This example indicates a very important result: Although buying puts and calls *naked* is regarded as risky, it is not when the investor already has the asset. In that case, the combination of being long in puts and in the underlying asset is equivalent to being long a call option, so the put acts like *insurance*.

The insurance argument has been used extensively to sell put options. Consider basic house insurance. If homeowners don't have insurance, either nothing happens or they suffer a loss, for example, a house burns down. Buying insurance removes the loss at the cost of the insurance premium. If nothing happens, homeowners are out the insurance premium, but if the house burns down, they sell the ashes to the insurance company in return for a new house. Or consider car insurance: if drivers don't have an accident, nothing happens, but if drivers do, they transfer the loss, that is, vehicle damage and other personal liability, to the insurance company. In both cases, insurance is just a put option, where the buyer has the right to transfer the loss to the insurance company.

Example 12-11: A Protective Put

Complete the following table depicting the payoffs for an investor who buys an underlying asset for $50 and simultaneously buys a put with a strike price of $50.

Asset Price ($)	30	40	50	55	60	70
Long asset payoff ($)						
Long put payoff ($)						
Net payoff ($)						

Solution

Asset Price ($)	30	40	50	55	60	70
Long asset payoff ($)	−20	−10	0	5	10	20
Long put payoff ($)	20	10	0	0	0	0
Net payoff ($)	0	0	0	5	10	20

Notice that the payoff for the net position is exactly the same as that for buying a call at a strike price of $50.

Let's consider another situation where the investor is long the asset but doesn't think the asset is going to increase in value. Normally, he or she would sell the asset. However, suppose the investor is a large pension fund and the asset is a stock market portfolio of $20 billion. In practice, it is difficult to sell that much without causing the price to drop. The investor can sell call options, because he or she doesn't think the price is going to increase to make the calls valuable. The payoff from this strategy is provided below. This is called a **covered call writing**

covered call writing selling call options while owning the underlying asset

FIGURE   12-8
Covered Call Writing

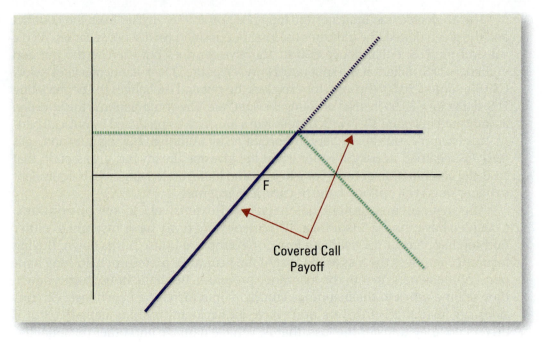

strategy, because the investor has sold a call but owns the underlying asset. As Figure 12-8 indicates, the net payoff position resembles a *short put* position, which is what put-call parity (i.e., Equation 12-8) predicts.

The long position is the 45-degree line, the short call position is the dotted green line, and the combined position is the bold, blue line. If the asset value increases above the call price, it is called away from the investor, so all he or she gets is the strike price, which is set above the forward price. However, below the strike price, the call expires worthless and the investor gets the full value of the long position. Essentially, by selling a call, the investor has sold away some of the upside in the value of the underlying asset. This makes sense if he or she doesn't think there is much upside.

Example 12-12: A Covered Call

Complete the following table depicting the payoffs for an investor who buys an underlying asset for $50 and simultaneously writes a call with a strike price of $50.

Asset Price ($)	30	40	50	55	60	70
Long asset payoff ($)						
Short call payoff ($)						
Net payoff ($)						

Solution

Asset Price ($)	30	40	50	55	60	70
Long asset payoff ($)	−20	−10	0	5	10	20
Short call payoff ($)	0	0	0	−5	−10	−20
Net payoff ($)	−20	−10	0	0	0	0

Notice that the payoff for the net position is exactly the same as that for writing a put at a strike price of $50.

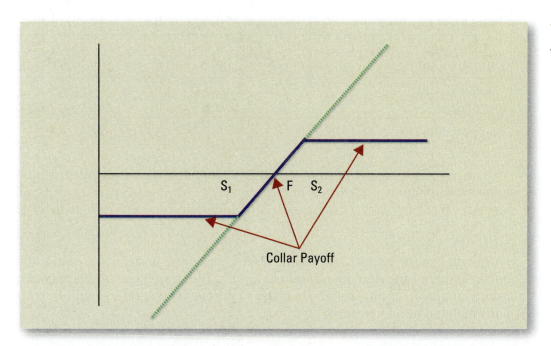

Collar Payoff

If an investor is long the asset, then buying a put places a floor under how much he or she can lose, whereas selling a call places a ceiling on how much he or she can earn. So far, we have talked about how much these options are worth, but clearly they are very valuable, as anyone pricing car insurance (i.e., puts) knows! So buying a put and insuring your asset is costly; one way of financing this is to sell a call, as in Figure 12-9.

Notice that if the asset price goes above S_2, the strike price in the call, the asset is called away, so this is a *ceiling price*. Below S_1, the strike price in the put, the put is exercised, so it is a *floor price*. In between S_1 and S_2 is the payoff from a long position in the underlying asset. The net position is the bold line, and is generically called a **collar**, because the put and call options provide a collar for the price range. In foreign exchange, such contracts have been called flexible forwards or range forwards, while in financing cases, it is referred to as a floor-ceiling loan.

collar a position between the floor and ceiling price

Example 12-13: A Collar

Complete the following table depicting the payoffs for an investor who buys an underlying asset for $50 and simultaneously buys a put with a strike price of $45 and sells a call with a strike price of $55.

Asset Price ($)	30	40	50	55	60	70
Long asset payoff ($)						
Long $45 put payoff ($)						
Short $55 call payoff ($)						
Net payoff ($)						

Solution

Asset Price ($)	30	40	50	55	60	70
Long asset payoff ($)	−20	−10	0	5	10	20
Long $45 put payoff ($)	15	5	0	0	0	0
Short $55 call payoff ($)	0	0	0	0	−5	−15
Net payoff ($)	−5	−5	0	5	5	5

The payoff for the net position equals −$5 for all prices below $45 (the put's strike price), equals +$5 for all prices above $55 (the call's strike price), and increases by $1 for each $1 increase in the underlying asset price between $45 and $55.

Finance in the News 12-1 ties our discussion to the basic tenets of modern portfolio theory and demonstrates how some of the strategies can be applied by using options on equity indexes in order to protect a position in an underlying portfolio held by an investor.

finance
INTHENEWS12-1

TRADING FLOOR SECRETS: COLLARS USING INDEXES

With the markets at all-time highs and the VIX [the Chicago Board Options Exchange's Volatility Index] at all-time lows, it is time to consider if you are making money because you are smart or because the market is at record highs. It is also time to ask yourself if you are going to be the victim of your own greed and ignorance by giving back all your non-actualized profits. Keeping your profits once you have began your options trading education is your responsibility, not the luck and whims of the markets. If you give back all your gains for the year, you have no one to blame but yourself.

That being said, many people know the fundamentals of hedging a stock with that particular underlying asset's options, but what if you have an entire portfolio of stocks and don't want to have to go into each stock to hedge? Hedging 20 stocks with their respective puts is time consuming, costly, and commission intensive. The good news is that when you have a basket of stocks, you have your own little index.

One reader of my articles wrote and inquired about Warren Buffett: "How does Warren Buffett hedge a position like Coke when he has over 300,000,000 million shares?" Mr. Buffett is very secretive about his trading and does not advertise his positions; however, one can make some very educated deductions about what he is doing by looking at the Berkshire annual reports. Specifically, the preponderance of evidence suggests that the Sage of Omaha treats the collective quantity of his stock portfolio as an index and hedges accordingly.

Before I continue, I want to preface that this is not a do-it-yourself kit. I am forced by the constraints of an article this size to leave out so much of the critical information needed to select the best index. An article limited to 1,200 words can only accomplish so much, and is not to be construed as investment advice. Rather, this is education designed to open your eyes and mind to new concepts while at the same time educating.

The key is to find the appropriate index that matches your portfolio. If you are long 15 stocks that are listed on the Nasdaq and one on the NYSE, an appropriate index may be the NDX [Nasdaq-100], MNX [CBOE Mini-NDX Index Options], or such. Going into an index like the DJX [Dow Jones Industrial Average],

finance
INTHENEWS12-1

which represents a price weighted (not cap or geometric weighed) index of the largest companies in America such as 3M, Coca-Cola, Boeing, Citigroup, etc. may not be the most appropriate index, though it will still offer some considerable protection if you chose the index accidentally.

The next thing you will need to do is determine the sum dollar total of all the stocks you are looking to hedge. You may have $40,000 in one account and $53,000 in another. Your IRA also has $50,000 in it, thus your total of all three accounts is $143,000. That is pretty simple, isn't it? Let's move on.

The next step would be to determine how many puts you need. If you had a portfolio that was pretty much loaded with big name NYSE stocks peppered with perhaps a couple of Nasdaq stocks such as MSFT [Microsoft Corporation], then perhaps the SPX (Standard and Poor's 500 Index on the CBOE) would be the appropriate hedge. Because the index today is currently roughly 1,425, and because the index has a $100 multiplier, one SPX put will protect $142,500 (1,425 $\times$ 100 multiplier) worth of stock.

As our imaginary portfolio has roughly $143,000 and one SPX put protects approximately $142,500 of stocks, we are very close to needing one put exactly. Again, I don't have the necessary space to go into more detail, but suffice to say that in most circumstances you will have to be content being slightly over-hedged or under-hedged.

The most complicated step in this whole process is determining which strike put to purchase to protect your portfolio. There is a balance between cost and protection. Like car insurance, you have to determine how much of a deductible you want to absorb. Total coverage offers more protection but comes with a high insurance premium. Notice how options and insurance both use the term "premium."

There are ways of choosing the correct put based on probabilities. One can simply choose to select a put a certain percentage OTM [out of the money].

The last thing to be discussed is the collar. When buying a stock and the stock's put, most experienced traders will sell a call to help offset the cost of the put. This position of long stock, long put and short call is called a collar and is relatively straightforward. The problem with doing this with indexes is the cost associated with selling an index call.

I cannot think of a single broker who will allow a call to be sold in an index and consider it a perfect hedge against a long stock portfolio. There are many reasons for this, mostly the debate between systematic and non-systematic risk. Needless to say, if you sell a call in the index to offset the price of a put, the purchase will require a margin roughly about half the value of the index. So how do you get around this? That too is too much to go into right now, but a more remedial answer is simply go into a few of the stocks and sell enough calls to offset the index puts.

Conclusion

Hedging with an index put is easier, faster and cheaper (usually) than hedging with the corresponding puts associated with the stocks. Empirical studies have proven that if the portfolio is diversified and the appropriate index is selected, then hedging with index options works and compares extremely closely with that of hedging with the stock's puts. Regardless of which technique you elect to implement, the key is to hedge yourself when appropriate to avoid the losses (retraced profits) associated with a market sell-off.

Like most things in life, you get out what you put in. If you train your mind like a professional athlete trains his or her body, you should have professional results. How bad would you feel if the market at Dow 12,500 could be hedged, and some catastrophe occurred causing the market to sell off to 10,000 and you were not hedged? It is one thing not knowing you can protect yourself, and it is a totally different thing not to hedge yourself, knowing you could have been protected at the top and weren't.

Education is the key, so get hungry and do whatever it takes to trade like a pro and get professional results.

Source: Kramer, Scott. "Trading Floor Secrets: Collars Using Indexes," Optionetics.com, December 18, 2006. Retrieved from www.optionetics.com. Reprinted with permission.

The potential option strategies are limited only by an investor's imagination. For example, an investor could have a long position and sell two options instead of one or buy both puts and calls. To make much sense of these strategies we need to discuss how much these options are worth.

CONCEPT REVIEW QUESTIONS

1. Illustrate how to combine the four basic option positions to create a variety of net payoff positions.

2. Explain why the put-call parity relationship should hold if markets are efficient.

3. Explain how to synthetically create long and short positions in calls, puts, and the underlying assets by using put-call parity.

12.4 OPTION PRICING

The Black-Scholes Option Pricing Model

Appendix 12A discusses the binomial option pricing model, which can be used to value complicated securities. The assumption underlying that model is that the underlying asset price can either go up or down to some value over a given period. Although this assumption may seem simplistic, so far, we haven't specified the period involved. We can shorten the period from a month to a week, to a day, to a minute, to a second, and the model still holds. We can then think of a whole sequence of up and down movements as representing the possible movement in the asset price and use numerical procedures,[7] similar to those above, to calculate the option price. Although this is possible, it ignores one of the advantages of the Black-Scholes formula, which reduces to a simple "plug-in" formula, shown in Equation 12-10.

[12-10]

$$C = SN[d_1] - Xe^{-rt}N[d_2]$$

where

$$d_1 = \frac{Ln(S/X) + (r + \sigma^2/2)t}{\sigma\sqrt{t}}$$

$$d_2 = d_1 - \sigma\sqrt{t}$$

Technically speaking, Equation 12-10 applies to European call options on non-dividend-paying stocks; however, variations of this equation exist for calls on dividend-paying stocks, and for puts.

It might be difficult to think of this as a plug-in formula but it is. First, some of the numbers are straightforward, such as S, which is the current asset price, and X, which is the strike price. Recall from Chapter 5 that the term e^{-rt} is the present value formula when we are discounting in continuous time, so just

---

[7] See John Hull, *Options, Futures and Other Derivatives*, 6th ed. (New York: Prentice-Hall, 2006).

think of Xe^{-rt} as the present value of the strike price, where r is the risk-free rate and t is the time to the expiration of the option. If we set $N(d_1)$ and $N(d_2)$ equal to one for now, the Black-Scholes formula says the value of a call is the value of the asset minus the present value of the exercise price. If the asset increases in value at the risk-free rate, then it is in or out of the money at expiration.

The key to option pricing is understanding the $N(d_1)$ and $N(d_2)$ terms, which are the cumulative standard normal density functions for the values d_1 and d_2, because we need to know the cumulative probability that the asset price will exceed the strike price at expiration. To estimate this probability, Black and Scholes assumed that the underlying asset followed a lognormal distribution. This means that the natural logarithm (Ln) of the asset price S is normally distributed, which explains why the term $Ln(S/X)$ is in the equation. To simplify, assume that the call is issued at the strike price, so this is the natural logarithm of 1.0, which is zero. We can also simplify by assuming that this is a single period call option and the risk-free rate is zero, so $r = 0$ and $t = 1$. This leaves a formula for $d_1 = \sigma/2$. Because we are looking for the value of $N(\sigma/2)$, we need the cumulative probability of being half a standard deviation above the mean of the normal distribution. We can look at a table for the standard normal distribution or use Excel and find this value as 0.68. Similarly, $d_2 = -\sigma/2$, which is the cumulative probability of being half a standard deviation below the mean of the distribution, which is 0.32.

To understand d_1, think of it as the number of standard deviations that the call is expected to be in the money, so we will call this the expected *moneyness* of the call. The value for $N(d_1)$ is then the cumulative probability of being in the money. The larger the risk of the underlying asset, the larger is $N(d_1)$ and the moneyness of the call. This reiterates that the more volatile the underlying asset, the more valuable the call. All we are doing is shifting this estimate of the call's expected moneyness. For example, if the asset price is currently above the strike price, $Ln(S/X)$ is no longer zero; instead, it is positive and moneyness increases. Similarly, a higher risk-free rate simply increases the expected moneyness of the call. Finally, the time to expiration of the call increases both the risk-free rate and the standard deviation, so it compounds both, thereby increasing the call's moneyness. We can illustrate all this in Example 12-14.

Example 12-14: Using Black-Scholes I

Assume that an asset is selling for $50 and an investor wants to price a call with an exercise price of $55. The expiration date is 182 days or 182/365 of a year, the risk-free rate is 6%, and the standard deviation of the return on the underlying asset is 30%. What's the value of the call?

Solution

First, we calculate the present value of the strike price:

$$PV(S) = Se^{-rt} \text{ or } \frac{S}{(1+r)^t}$$

We can use either continuous or approximate with discrete compounding. Let's approximate and discount back at 3 percent to get $53.398. With continuous compounding, we would get $53.375.

Next, we calculate d_1 as

$$d_1 = \frac{Ln(50/55) + (.06 + .30^2/2) \times 182/365}{.3 \times \sqrt{182/365}} = -0.2028$$

and $d_2 = -0.4146$. Inserting into the cumulative normal density function, we get $N(d_1) = 0.4197$ and $N(d_2) = 0.3392$ and the call is worth $2.876.

$N(d_1)$ and $N(d_2)$ can be calculated from standard statistical tables. Table 12-4 includes a portion of such a table, and the extended version can be found in Table A-1 at the end of the textbook.

Table 12-4   The Cumulative Probabilities for a Standard Normal Distribution

d	N(d)	d	N(d)	d	N(d)	d	N(d)	d	N(d)
−0.50	.3085	−0.48	.3156	−0.46	.3228	20.44	.3300	−0.42	.3373
−0.40	.3446	−0.38	.3520	−0.36	.3594	20.34	.3669	−0.32	.3745
−0.30	.3821	−0.28	.3897	−0.26	.3974	20.24	.4052	−0.22	.4129
−0.20	.4207	−0.18	.4286	−0.16	.4365	20.14	.4443	−0.12	.4523
−0.10	.4602	−0.08	.4681	−0.06	.4761	20.04	.4841	−0.02	.4920
0.00	.5000	0.02	.5080	0.04	.5160	0.06	.5239	0.08	.5319
0.10	.5398	0.12	.5478	0.14	.5557	0.16	.5636	0.18	.5714
0.20	.5793	0.22	.5871	0.24	.5948	0.26	.6026	0.28	.6103
0.30	.6179	0.32	.6255	0.34	.6331	0.36	.6406	0.38	.6480
0.40	.6556	0.42	.6628	0.44	.6700	0.46	.6773	0.48	.6844
..									
2.00	.9772	2.10	.9821	2.20	.9861	2.30	.9893	2.40	.9918
2.50	.9938	2.60	.9953	2.70	.9965	2.80	.9974	2.90	.9981
3.00	.9986	−	−	−	−	−	−	−	−

We can also determine $N(d_1)$ by using a spreadsheet, such as Excel. In Excel the "Normdist" function calculates the normal distribution function. Entering the following:

$$N(d_1) = Normdist(a1,0,1,true)$$

returns the value for $N(d_1)$. The values to enter in order are a1, which is the spreadsheet cell entry for the value d_1; 0 indicates a zero mean; and 1 is the standard deviation for a unit normal density function. The final value, "true," indicates the cumulative normal distribution; "false" would indicate the individual point estimate of the probability.

Rather than use a spreadsheet, we can use one of several calculators that are available on the Internet. The Montreal Exchange (MX) has an online option pricing calculator at www.m-x.ca/accueil_en.php. By using the MX option pricing model and entering the values for our example, the model produces the output shown in Figure 12-10:

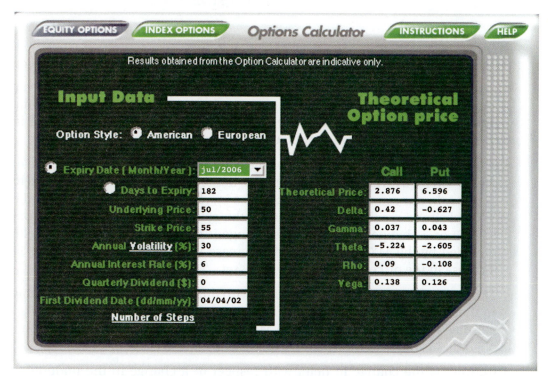

Source: Montreal Exchange website www.m-x.ca/accueil_en.php

12-10 FIGURE

Using Black-Scholes

MX's value for the option is also $2.876, but it provides the price of a $55 put on the same asset at $6.596.[8] It also provides some other values, which we discuss in the next section.

Example 12-15: Using Black-Scholes II

Find the value of a three-month call option with a $20 strike price if the price of the non-dividend-paying underlying asset is $20.50 and its standard deviation is 25 percent. Assume the risk-free rate is 5 percent.

Solution

$S = \$20.50; X = \$20; r = 5\%; t = 3/12 = 0.25; \sigma = 25\%.$

$$d_1 = \frac{Ln(S/X) + (r + \sigma^2/2)t}{\sigma\sqrt{t}} = \frac{Ln(20.50/20) + (.05 + (.25)^2/2)(0.25)}{(0.25)\sqrt{0.25}} = \frac{0.02469 + 0.0203}{0.125} = \frac{0.0450}{0.125} = 0.3600$$

$$d_2 = d_1 - \sigma\sqrt{t} = .3600 - .25\sqrt{0.25} = 0.2350$$

---

[8] The numbers provided in the output are for American options, based on more complicated variations of Black-Scholes equations, which technically apply only to European options. In any event, because the underlying asset in this example does not pay any dividends, the value of a European call option will equal that of an American call option. Conversely, the corresponding European put option would be worth $6.255, approximately $0.34 less than the American put.

From the MX's online option pricing calculator or by using Excel, we can find

$$N[d_1] = 0.6406 \text{ and } N[d_2] = 0.5929$$

$$\text{So, } C = SN[d_1] - Xe^{-rtN}[d_2] = (20.50)(0.6406) - (20)e^{-(0.05)(0.25)}(0.5929) =$$

$$13.13 - 11.71 = \$1.42$$

The "Greeks"

the Greeks the values that give the sensitivity of the option price to changes in the underlying parameters: delta (δ), gamma (γ), theta (θ), rho (ρ), and vega

delta the change in the price of the option for a given change in the price of the underlying asset

theta the change in the option value with time

gamma the change in delta with respect to a change in the underlying asset.

vega the change in the option value with respect to a change in the volatility of the underlying asset

rho the change in the option value with respect to a change in the interest rate

The other values provided by the MX in Figure 12-10—delta, gamma, theta, rho, and vega—give the sensitivity of the option price to changes in the underlying parameters. These Greek letters are commonly referred to as **the Greeks** in option pricing (though vega is not a Greek letter).

- As the stock price increases, so does the call value. The change in the price of the option for a given change in the price of the underlying asset is referred to as **delta**. In our example, if the stock price increases to $50.10 and we use the MX website to recalculate the value of the call, it increases to $2.918 (from $2.876) or a change of $0.042. This change is consistent with the 0.42 delta provided by the MX, so the call will increase in value by $0.42 for every $1 increase in the price of the underlying asset.

- **Theta** is the change in the option value with time. If we move forward one day so that the call has 181 days to expiration, its value drops to $2.862 or $0.014 per day. The theta reported by the MX is approximately this number multiplied by 365 days, so we would get -5.224.

- **Gamma** is the change in delta with respect to a change in the underlying asset. This is important for hedging but we don't include a full discussion of gamma here, as it is beyond the scope of this text.

- **Vega** is the change in the option value with respect to a change in the volatility of the underlying asset. If the standard deviation in our example increases by 1 percent to 31.0 percent, the option value increases to $3.014. A 1 percent increase in volatility increases the option value by $0.138, consistent with the vega reported by the MX.

- **Rho** is the change in the option value with respect to a change in the interest rate. For example, if the interest rate increases from 6 percent to 7 percent in our example, the option value increases to $2.967 (or $0.091), so a 1 percent change in the interest rate causes a $0.091 change in the option, consistent with the rho reported by the MX.

Running the numbers through our Black-Scholes calculator indicates that the call option price behaves the way that it should: it goes up with increases in volatility, the risk-free rate, and the price of the underlying asset, and it falls as time passes.

Finally, what about the extremes? If the current asset price is deep out of the money at $30, the value of the call is $0.0080, and at $25, it is $0.0003, so deep out of the money calls are worthless. Similarly, if the asset price is $100 so that it is deep in the money, the call option is worth $46.628, where $45 is the intrinsic value. So the value of a call mainly reflects its intrinsic value.

12.5 OPTIONS MARKETS

Similar to swaps, options are either traded over the counter, mainly with the major banks, or on organized exchanges. In Canada, options trading is focused on the MX and quotes can be found in the *The Globe and Mail Report on Business*. The MX has a standard practice of listing options on all the constituents of the S&P/TSX 60 Index, as well as on the S&P/TSX MidCap Index. Each option class has to have the interest of two market makers who stand ready to buy and sell the options to create an orderly market. These options follow a short expiration cycle based on the next two months, and there is a minimum daily volume of 40 contracts. If the volume exceeds 80, then longer-dated options are introduced based on months in the next quarterly cycle, and if there is enough interest, long-dated options are introduced with a January expiration date.

On June 9, 2006, the five most active equity options were on Canadian Natural Resources Limited, Royal Bank of Canada (RBC), Suncor Energy Inc., Alcan Inc., and EnCana Corporation. Most open interest was in the RBC options, so let's look at some of the information for these options in Table 12-5.

Table 12-5   RBC Options Quotes

January 07	Strike	Bid	Ask	Last	Volume	Open
	45	3.05	3.20	3.05	10	1043
	45p	2.60	2.75	2.70	10	874
	47.75	1.90	2.00	2.05	24	735
	50p	5.75	5.95	5.80	30	246

The data are for options expiring in January 2007, so these were relatively long options at seven months. As indicated above, most of the options are short dated, out to three months, but where there is sufficient interest, traded options can go out longer. As of June 2006, there were options on several stocks out to January 2008, and new options on BCE Inc., Kinross Gold Corporation, Canadian Natural Resources, and CVRD Inco Limited with January 2009 expiration dates that were set to begin trading on June 28, 2006. However, the longest RBC options were these January 2007 options. Note that there are four contracts, and that the "p" indicates a put option; otherwise, they are calls.

Take the first contract, which is a call on RBC at $45. RBC's stock price closed trading the previous day at $45.15, so the intrinsic value was $0.15, and the time value represented the balance. How much the balance was depended on whether the investor bought or sold the call. If the investor bought the call, the offered or ask price was $3.20, and if the investor sold it, the price was $3.05. The last trade was at $3.05, indicating that someone sold a call to the market maker. The spread between the bid and ask is the market maker's profit for making a market in the calls. On the previous day, 10 calls (i.e., the volume figure from the table) with a strike at $45 were sold, and total trading volume for the four reported options was 74 contracts, with total open interest of 2,898 contracts, where each contract is for 100 shares of RBC.

For the options at other strike prices, the $47.75 call is out of the money and is available at an average price of $1.95. The $45 put is also out of the money, but the $50 put is in the money. For the $50 put, the intrinsic value is $4.85 and the time value is $1.00, based on the midpoint of the bid and ask put prices of $5.85. The time value for put options is generally lower than for calls, because expected rates of return on stocks are positive, so prices are expected to increase.

For option prices, most of the data are objective and verifiable, such as the strike price, the current price of the underlying asset, the risk-free rate, and the expiration date. The only "soft" number is the volatility of the underlying asset's price. However, once we know the price of the option, we can work back and find the volatility that matches this price. For the RBC $45 January 2007 call options, we can use the current quarterly dividend of $0.36 and the MX option calculator to estimate this volatility by trial and error to get about 22 percent. This number is the **implied volatility** of the option.

implied volatility an estimate of the price volatility of the underlying asset based on observed option prices

Implied volatilities provide useful information. Remember from our discussion of the Capital Asset Pricing Model that the volatility of the market portfolio is a key number in deriving expected rates of return. The MX trades options on the S&P/TSX 60 Index exchange traded fund (ETF). ETFs are index funds that are traded like common shares and the S&P/TSX 60 ETF, with ticker symbol XIU, reflects the biggest and most valuable companies in Canada. Every minute of every trading day, the MX calculates the implied volatility of the XIU from the nearest at the money options. These are then used to estimate the implied volatility from an at the money 30-day option, to create a time series of implied volatilities (MVX).

FIGURE 12-11

Implied Volatilities for the S&P/TSX60 Index

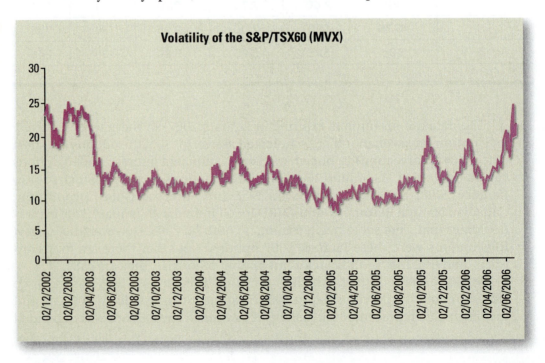

The graph in Figure 12-11 gives the implied volatilities for this index from December 2, 2002, until June 2006. Note that volatility changes over time. In early 2003, it was just less than 25 percent before falling to around 15 percent, where it remained until late 2005, after which it began increasing and reached the 25 percent level again. By June 2006, the options markets were indicating that there was more volatility in the equity market than at any time since the bottom of the stock market crash in the spring of 2003.

CONCEPT REVIEW QUESTIONS

1. Where are options traded?

2. How are implied volatilities calculated? What information do they provide?

AUDIT OPTIONS POLICIES, CSA URGES

ethics
AND CORPORATE
GOVERNANCE 12-1

The Canadian Securities Administrators, or CSA, is recommending that all Canadian public companies assess their policies and controls for stock option grants to ensure they comply with legislation.

The notice comes as a scandal over backdated stock options continues to widen in the United States, where more than 40 companies have already said they will restate earnings or might do so once internal probes are completed. The restatements total at least $2.27 billion (U.S.).

Backdating occurs when a company sets the grant date for stock options retroactively, to a time when the company's stock price was lower, creating an instant paper gain for the executive or employee receiving the options.

Stock options allow recipients to buy shares at a future date, usually at the price on the day they were granted. They are given to managers as an incentive to find ways to boost the stock price.

A University of Michigan study released this week suggests shareholders bear the brunt of the practice, shouldering an average of $510 million per company in losses after the practice is made public. That far outweighs the average $600,000 annual gain for a company's executives.

"If CSA staff become aware, through disclosure reviews, tips or otherwise, of abuses by reporting issuers, they may take enforcement action against the issuers or their directors and officers," the administrators said yesterday.

Regulations in Canada may reduce the opportunity for companies to backdate options here, the CSA said.

Under Toronto Stock Exchange rules, the exercise price for options cannot be less than the market price of the stock when the options are granted, and the exercise price cannot be based on market prices that don't reflect undisclosed material information.

There are similar rules on the TSX Venture Exchange, except issuers are allowed to set the exercise price at a certain discount to the market price.

Securities legislation also requires company insiders to file an insider-trading report within 10 days of receiving options.

Directors are responsible for ensuring that a company prices and discloses options appropriately, the CSA said.

It suggested boards set up a compensation committee that follows national corporate governance guidelines. It also suggested they adopt corporate disclosure and insider-trading policies and establish blackout periods around earnings announcements.

In October, the TSX Group sent a notice to listed companies reminding them of the rules around options.

ethics
AND CORPORATE
GOVERNANCE 12-1

"Staff has become aware that listed issuers may not be adhering to the requirements ... of the manual," the notice said.

In the United States, prosecutors and members of Congress have said backdating grants, or awarding them shortly before good news is announced, subverts their purpose and could involve criminal fraud.

Securities and Exchange Commission chairman Christopher Cox told Congress this week that more than 100 companies are being investigated.

Source: Perkins, Tara. "Audit Options Policies, CSA Urges." *Toronto Star*, September 9, 2006, p. D01. Reprinted with permission of Torstar Syndication Services.

DISCUSSION QUESTIONS

1. Explain what option backdating is and how it hurts shareholders.

2. How do you think the University of Michigan researchers came up with an estimated shareholder loss of $510 million?

3. The CSA staff indicates that action may be taken if they become aware of option backdating. Do you think that they should have the option of not taking action?

Summary

This chapter discusses the Nobel Prize–winning ideas of Fischer Black, Myron Scholes, and Robert Merton. Continuing our discussion from Chapter 11, in which we looked at derivatives with linear payoffs, in this chapter we look at non-linear payoffs, where either the gains or the losses were truncated or changed at some points. We discuss the payoffs from call and put options and how the value of these options are determined by the underlying asset's price and volatility, the strike price and time to expiration of the option, and the conditions in the economy in terms of the risk-free rate. We go on to discuss put-call parity and how options can be used for hedging. We also show how options can be valued by using the Black-Scholes option pricing model and then discuss how options are traded.

Key Terms

American options, p. 467

binomial model, p. 488

call option, p. 456

collar, p. 475

covered call writing, p. 473

deep, p. 460

delta, p. 482

European options, p. 467

exercise, p. 456

exercise price, p. 456

expiration date, p. 456

gamma, p. 482

Greeks, the, p. 482

hedge ratio (h), p. 489

implied volatility, p. 484

in the money, p. 457

intrinsic value (IV), p. 459

option premium, p. 460

option writer, p. 458

out of the money, p. 457

Formulas/Equations

(12-1)   IV (call) = Max$(S - X, 0)$

(12-2)   Option premium = IV + TV

(12-3)   TV = Option Premium − IV

(12-4)   IV (put) = Max$(X - S, 0)$

(12-5) $P + S = C + PV(X)$

(12-6) $C - P = S - PV(X)$

(12-7) $C = P + S - PV(X)$

(12-8) $P = C - S + PV(X)$

(12-9) $S = C - P + PV(X)$

(12-10) $C = SN[d_1] - Xe^{-rt}N[d_2]$

(12A-1) $h = \dfrac{PU - PD}{PU - X}$

(12A-2) $C = \dfrac{1}{h}\left(S - \dfrac{PD}{(1+r)}\right)$

APPENDIX 12A
BINOMIAL OPTION PRICING AND RISK-NEUTRAL PROBABILITIES

BINOMIAL OPTION PRICING

In the chapter, we discussed the Black-Scholes option pricing model, but here we consider a simpler model. Previously, we used an example of an asset selling for $50 with an equal probability of the price going up or down by $5. Now, let's give the price a 60 percent chance of going up to $55, and a 40 percent chance of going

binomial model an option pricing model that uses two numbers, assuming the asset price can go only up or down.

down to $45. We do this to set the expected value on the asset at $51 (i.e., .60 × $55 + .40 × $45) for a 2 percent expected rate of return. For simplicity, let's assume that this refers to a one-month period and that the monthly risk-free rate is 1.0 percent. This is an example of what is termed the **binomial model** (i.e., two numbers), because the asset price can only go up or down.

Now let's think of a one-period call option on this asset with a strike price of $50. In this case, when the asset price is $55, the investor exercises the option and has a $5 payoff, but when the asset price is $45, the option expires worthless. The payoffs on the asset and the call are provided in Figure 12A-1.

FIGURE 12A-1

Binomial Prices

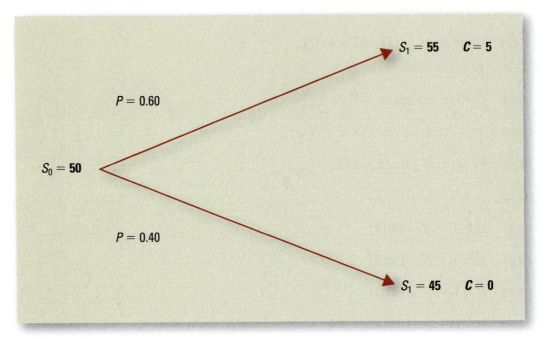

S_0 and S_1 represent the asset prices at times 0 and 1, respectively, C is the payoff on the call, and P is the probability of a given price occurring. To understand how to price the call, we have to take advantage of the fact that it is a derivative and its payoff depends on the underlying asset value. This is the motivation for the central insight of Black and Scholes, which is that although we may not know how to value the call directly, we do know how to value a risk-free asset. Thus, we can derive the value of the call indirectly, if we create a portfolio of the asset and the call that generates the same payoff regardless of the price of the underlying asset. If the payoff of the portfolio is the same, regardless of whether the price of the asset goes up or down, then by definition it is risk-free, and we can value it by discounting at the risk-free rate.

When the price of the asset goes down to $45, the value of the call is zero. So if an investor builds a portfolio of the asset and the call, it doesn't matter how many calls he or she has, the value of the portfolio is still $45. To create a risk-free payoff, we have to think about a portfolio of the asset and the call that generates a payoff of $45, when the price of the asset is $55. For example, suppose the investor has a portfolio of the asset and sells one call, that is, the investor is long the asset and short the call. When the asset is worth $55, the call is exercised against the investor and he or she gets $50 for the asset, which is the payoff from the portfolio. Clearly, this is too high. Suppose the investor sells two calls against the asset. Now when the asset price goes to $55, two calls are exercised against the investor, but he or she has one underlying asset; to deliver against two calls, so the investor has to go and buy another one. The payoff to the portfolio is $45, the same as if the asset value dropped to $45.

What we have discovered is that a portfolio that is long the asset and short two calls gives a payoff of $45 regardless of the price of the underlying asset. This means we have the following:

$$S - 2C = \frac{\$45}{1+r} = \$44.55$$

A portfolio long the asset and short two calls has a payoff of $45, which, given the 1 percent risk-free rate, is worth $44.55 today. However, we know that the asset is worth $50 today, so rearranging we get

$$C = \frac{1}{2}(\$50 - \$44.55) = \$2.725$$

and the call is worth $2.725.

To provide the solution for the general case, we denote the increased price for the asset as PU (price up) and the decreased price as PD. The number of calls that an investor needs to sell to establish the same payoff whether the asset price goes up or down is called the **hedge ratio (h)**, which we can estimate as

hedge ratio (h) the number of calls the investor needs to sell to hedge a long position in the underlying asset

$$PU - h(PU - X) = PD$$

This can be solved to give the following:

$$h = \frac{PU - PD}{PU - X}$$

[12A-1]

In our example, the price can go to either $45 or $55, the hedge ratio is (55 − 45)/(55 − 50), or 2, so two calls have to be sold for every long position in the asset. The value of the call is then estimated by solving the following equation:

$$C = \frac{1}{h}(S - \frac{PD}{(1+r)})$$

[12A-2]

The asset value is $50 and the present value of the asset when the price drops to $45 is $44.55, so the amount in brackets is $5.45, that is, 50 − 45/1.01. With the hedge ratio of 2, that means the call is worth $2.723, that is, 1/2 × $5.45.

The simplicity of the calculation is deceiving: some of the best minds in economics and finance spent decades trying to find the correct formula for valuing a call and couldn't. The reason was that they tried to value it *directly* by estimating the expected cash flow on the call and then using a risk-adjusted discount rate to value that cash flow. Although this is what we do in most areas of finance, no one could derive the correct discount rate. Black and Scholes did not use this approach,[9] and they came up with the central idea of valuing the call *indirectly* by valuing something we knew how to value: a risk-free payoff.

---

[9] See J. Cox, S. Ross, and M. Rubinstein, "Option Pricing: A Simplified Approach," *Journal of Financial Economics* 7, no. 3 (1979), pp. 229–63. The arbitrage argument has also been credited to Robert Merton.

Essentially, Black and Scholes took advantage of the central insight of option pricing, which is that the option is a derivative.

The use of a hedge to generate a risk-free payoff is the central idea of option pricing. With our example, a financial institution selling two calls has to go long the underlying asset to remove or hedge its risk. This is the central reason that the use of derivatives has exploded: rather than selling calls and creating risk for themselves, financial institutions now know how to hedge that exposure. They simply need to calculate the hedge ratio needed to create a risk-free payoff. In our example this hedge ratio is 2: two calls have to be sold to hedge a long position in the asset.

Note also the factors that determine the value of the call in the general formula. The critical three factors are the hedge ratio, the asset value, and the present value of the down payoff on the asset. We will consider the second two first, as the hedge ratio is more complex. So, with our numbers, we have

$$C = \frac{1}{h}(50 - \frac{45}{(1.01)})$$

We make the following observations:

- First, the call is clearly worth more as the asset price goes up. If the current price is $50.25, the call price increases to $2.85.

- Second, the call is worth more as the risk-free rate goes up, because the present value when the price of the asset goes down gets smaller, so less is subtracted from the current asset value. With a 1.5 percent risk-free rate, the call is worth $2.83.

- Third, the call price goes up as the risk of the asset increases. As the range of possible outcomes increases, the asset value falls when the price goes down, making the call worth more. If the range increases to $20, lowering the payoff when the asset goes down to $40, the value of the call increases to $5.10.

- Fourth, as the strike price increases, the denominator in the hedge ratio (12A-1) gets smaller, so the investor has to sell more calls, which reduces the value of the call. At a strike price of $54, the hedge ratio increases to 10 and the call price drops to $0.54.

- Fifth, the call price increases if the up price increases, and the call price decreases if the up price decreases. For example, at $54 the hedge ratio increases to 2.25 and the call price drops to $2.42. We can think of a decrease in the up price as the impact of a dividend payment. Consider two firms, one that pays a dividend and the other that doesn't. In good economic conditions, the dividend-paying firm increases its dividend by $1, so its stock price goes to only $54, whereas the non-dividend-paying stock price goes to $55.[10]

These five observations are consistent with the intuitive results that we discussed in the chapter. The time to expiration, however, can't be applied to this example, because this is a single-period binomial model. We also have not discussed the expected return on the asset as a factor in the option price, or any of the factors that directly affect the market price of risk discussed in the CAPM earlier. In fact, the problem that bedevilled the pricing of options for many decades, the correct discount rate to value the option's payoff, is absent completely. In this case, we have an amazing result: we can behave as if the investor is risk neutral and value the option accordingly.

[10] We discuss dividend policy in Chapter 22, but stock prices tend to fall after payment of a dividend.

Risk-Neutral Probabilities

Let's go back to our simple example in which the payoff is either $55, with a probability of 60 percent, or $45, with a probability of 40 percent, so the expected rate of return is 2 percent, that is, $.60 \times (55 - 50) + .40 \times (45 - 50) = .60 \times 10\% + .40 \times -10\%$. This 2 percent expected rate of return exceeds the risk-free rate of 1 percent because investors are risk averse. However, because the option price does not depend on risk aversion, we will keep things simple and assume the investor is **risk neutral**. In this case, we can calculate the probabilities that will earn a risk-neutral investor the same 1 percent rate of return as the risk-free rate does. We can do this because this is what risk neutrality means: investors ignore the risk involved in determining expected rates of return.

> **risk neutral** the state of ignoring the risk involved in determining expected rates of return

We can calculate the probabilities that will generate a 1 percent return on the asset given the two possible payoffs of $55 and $45. Because a 1 percent return means that the price of the asset has to be $50.50 in the next period, we use the formula of an expected value to get

$$50(1.01) = 55P + 45(1 - P)$$

$$P = \frac{50.5 - 45}{10} = 0.55$$

If instead of a 60 percent chance of going up to $55, there is only a 55 percent chance, then the expected rate of return is 1 percent, the same as the risk-free rate. We can value the option directly as the payoff is still $5 when the asset price is $55. The only difference is that now we use the probability of 55 percent, so the expected payoff is $2.75, while there is a 45 percent chance of getting zero. If this expected cash flow of $2.75 is discounted back one period at the risk-free rate, the result is the option price of $2.72.

As we indicated before this is an amazing result, but to get it, we have derived new probabilities that ensure that the asset price goes up with the risk-free rate, instead of dealing with the *actual* probabilities of the asset going up and down. These probabilities are called the **risk-neutral probabilities**. They are the probabilities that would exist if the investor were risk neutral; of course, they are not the true probabilities, because investors are not risk neutral. However, because the call option can be valued *as if* the investor were risk neutral, we can use these risk-neutral probabilities to determine the expected payoff on the call and value it directly. This insight has generated a huge industry in option pricing, where complicated securities are valued in a *risk-neutral world*, as if the underlying asset always earned the risk-free rate. It has proven to be an incredibly useful construct in solving complex problems and comes directly from the Black-Scholes and binomial option pricing models.

> **risk-neutral probabilities** derived probabilities that ensure that the asset price goes up with the risk-free rate; they would exist if the investor were risk neutral

QUESTIONS AND PRACTICE PROBLEMS

Multiple Choice Questions

1. Which of the following statements about a call option is *false*?

   A. A call option is the right, not the obligation, to buy the underlying asset.

   B. A call option is in the money if the asset price is less than the strike price.

C. A call option is at the money if the asset price is the same as the strike price.

D. On the expiration date, a call option has no time value.

2. Before the expiration of a call option, if its intrinsic value is $12.50 and the market value of the option is $20, what is the time value of the option? What do we call the market value of the option?

　A. $32.50; option premium

　B. $7.50; option premium

　C. $32.50; option price

　D. $7.50; option price

3. Which of the following *increases* the value of a call option?

　A. The price of the underlying asset decreases.

　B. The volatility of the price of the underlying asset decreases.

　C. The remaining time to expiration of the call option increases.

　D. The underlying stock increases its dividend payment.

4. Which of the following *decreases* the value of a put option?

　A. The price of the underlying asset decreases.

　B. The underlying asset becomes riskier.

　C. The interest rate decreases.

　D. The strike price decreases.

5. Which of the following may create a synthetic loan?

　A. Long a put, short the stock, and long a call.

　B. Long a put, long the stock, and long a call.

　C. Short a put, long the stock, and long a call.

　D. Long a put, long the stock, and short a call.

6. What is the intrinsic value (IV) of the following *put*? Underlying asset price (S) = $45, strike price ($X$) = $40. What is the intrinsic value (IV) if it is a *call*?

　A. $0, $5

　B. $5, $0

　C. $5, $5

　D. $0, $0

7. Which of the following positions is the most risky?

　A. Long a call

　B. Short a call

　C. Long a put

　D. Short a put

8. What is the hedge ratio (h) given the following? PU = $55, PD = $48, strike price ($S$) = $45.

   A. 1.95

   B. 2.05

   C. 2.33

   D. 2.50

9. Which of the following is the correct meaning of a hedge ratio of 1/3?

   A. Short one call to hedge a long position of three units of the underlying asset

   B. Short three calls to hedge a long position of the underlying asset

   C. Long one call to hedge a long position of three units of the underlying asset

   D. Long three calls to hedge a long position of the underlying asset

10. Which of the following statements about risk-neutral probabilities is *false*?

   A. They are probabilities that exist if investors are risk-neutral.

   B. They are the actual probability of the asset price going up and down.

   C. They are the probabilities that ensure the asset price goes up with the risk-free rate

   D. They assume the underlying asset earns the risk-free rate

11. Which of the following statements of the Black-Scholes Model is *false*?

   A. It uses a continuously compounded risk-free rate.

   B. d_1 can be thought of as expected moneyness of the call.

   C. $N(d_1)$ is the cumulative probability of being out of the money.

   D. The model assumes that the underlying asset price follows a log normal distribution.

12. Which of the following statements is *correct* given the following information:

January 08	Strike	Bid	Ask	Last
Call A	35	2.85	3.05	2.85
Put B	37	2.10	2.35	2.15
Call C	40.75	1.74	2.0	1.90

   A. The market maker's profit of call A is 0.25.

   B. If the market price of underlying asset is 35, then the time value of put B is 0.10.

   C. The time value for a put is usually higher than that for a call.

   D. By using the market price of an option, we can calculate the implied volatility of the option.

Practice Problems

Easy

13. You are in the process of interviewing for a promotion at the Absent Minded Profs and have to identify the type of security based on the payoff diagrams below. All options expire on January 15th, 200x and the underlying asset is the index. Match the series from the diagrams to the appropriate security and position.

	Position	Series
A	Long Index	
B	Short Index	
C	Long Call	
D	Short Call	
E	Long Put	
F	Short Put	
G	Long Bond	
H	Short Bond	

Diagrams:

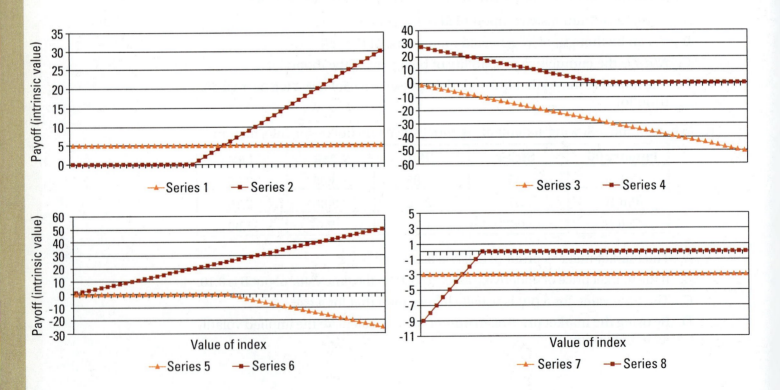

14. Once again The Scatter Brained Brokers have provided the Absent Minded Profs with incomplete information and, again, it is your job to fill in the missing information in the table below:

Long or Short	Call or Put	Strike price	Value of option today	Value of underlying asset	Payoff (intrinsic value)	Profit (loss)
				At expiration		
Long	Call	100	2.50	110		
Short	Call	100	2.50	110		
Long	Put	100	2.50	95		
Short	Put	100	2.50	95		
Long	Call	120	2.50	105		
Short	Call	120	2.50	105		
Long	Put	120	2.50	130		
Short	Put	120	2.50	130		

15. Mr. Cabinet, your boss at the Absent Minded Profs, prefers to have his information presented visually. At his request, graph the payoffs (intrinsic values) and profits at expiration for the following option investments.

A. Long Call, strike = $55, cost today = $10
B. Short Call, strike = $55, cost today = $10
C. Long Put, strike = $55, cost today = $10
D. Short Put, strike = $55, cost today = $10

16. The Scatter Brained Brokers have provided the following partially completed table of information about different securities. All options are written on XCT, a non-dividend paying stock, expire on the same day in one year, and have the same strike price. Fill in the missing information in the following table:

	XCT stock price	Price of call	Price of put	Strike price	Risk-Free rate
A	100		7	95	3%
B	150	30		130	5%
C		3	2	15	6%
D		5	5	25	10%
E	75	25	34	90	
F	130	25	20		5%

17. Fill in the missing information in the following table for a non-dividend paying stock and European call options:

	S	X	r	σ	T	d_1	d_2	$N(d_1)$	$N(d_2)$	Xe^{-rt}	Call value
A	100	98	2%	0.03	1						
B	100	98	2%	0.04	1						
C	100	98	3%	0.03	1						
D	100	99	2%	0.03	1						
E	100	98	2%	0.03	.3						
F	99	98	2%	0.03	1						

18. QBV, a non-dividend paying stock, is currently trading for $100 a share. There is a 25 percent chance that the stock will trade for $85 in one year and a 75 percent chance that the price will increase to $135. The risk-free rate is 5 percent per year. All options expire in one year.

    A. What is the value of a call with a strike of $115?

    B. What is the value of a put with a strike of $98?

19. Briefly state all the factors that affect the value of a call option and a put option.

Medium

20. Does put-call parity hold for the following? RF = 5%, P_0 = $10.50, C_0 = $ 8, stock price (S) = $25, t = 4, strike price (X) = $32. If not, what is the put price according to put-call parity, assuming the others are correct?

21. Briefly explain "the Greeks" delta, theta, vega, and rho, in option pricing.

22. What is the call price (C), given the following information: S = $36, X = $32, r = 5%, t = 2 years, σ = 20%.

23. In Problem 22, if the time value is $4.50, calculate the intrinsic value.

24. Your boss has observed that the call options on XCT and BRG are trading at different prices. Both options have the same strike price and the same time to expiration. Provide two possible explanations for this observation.

25. Mr. Cabinet is also interested in the payoffs to combinations of options. Graph the intrinsic values of the following portfolios (all options expire on the same day and are written on the same, non-dividend paying, underlying asset):

    A. Long 1 call, strike = $25; long 1 put, strike = $20

    B. Short 1 call, strike = $25; long 1 put, strike = $15

    C. Long 1 call, strike = $25; short 1 put, strike =$25

    D. Long 1 call, strike = $25; short 1 share of underlying asset

    E. Long 1 call, strike = $25; short 1 share; $25 in cash

    F. Long 1 put, strike = $25; long 1 share; short $25 in cash (i.e., Repay loan)

26. You have observed that a very smart and successful investor has bought a call and a put on the S&P/TSX index. The options have the same strike prices and expire on the same day. What does the smart investor think is going to happen to the S&P/TSX index? Hint: When will she make money on this investment?

27. QBV, a non-dividend paying stock, is currently trading for $100 a share. There is a 25 percent chance that the stock will trade for $85 in one year and a 75 percent chance that the price will increase to $135. The risk-free rate is 5 percent per year. All options expire in one year.

   A. If the call option on QBV with a strike of $115 is actually trading for $10, show that there is an arbitrage opportunity.

   B. If the put option on QBV with a strike price of $98 is actually trading for $0.50, show that there is an arbitrage opportunity.

28. QBV, a non-dividend paying stock, is currently trading for $100 a share. There is a 25 percent chance that the stock will trade for $85 in one year and a 75 percent chance that the price will increase to $135. The risk-free rate is 5 percent per year. All options expire in one year. You would like to purchase a call with a strike of $125. Unfortunately, it is not available on the market so you will have to create it synthetically. Design a portfolio to create a call with a strike of $125 and demonstrate that it will give the same payoffs as the desired call.

29. DPG, a non-dividend paying stock, is currently trading for $200 a share. There is a 30 percent chance that the stock will trade for $150 in one year and a 70 percent chance that the price will increase to $250. The risk-free rate is 5 percent per year. There is a one-year call with a strike price of $235.

   A. What is the price of the call?

   B. What is the delta of the call? Define and calculate.

30. Calculate the put price (P) according to put-call parity, given the information in Problem 22.

Difficult

31. Complete the following table:

	Long or Short	Call or Put	Strike price	Value of option today	At expiration			
					Value of underlying asset	In/Out of the money	Payoff (intrinsic value of option)	Profit (loss)
A	Long	Put	80	.05				−.05
B	Long	Call	80	2.00				−1
C	Short	Put	80	.05				−.05
D	Short	Call	80	.05				−.05
E	Long	Call		1.00	125			25
F	Short	Put	124		125		-1	1
G			25	2.00	95		0	−2
H			25	2.00	95		70	68
I		Call	75		90			2

J		Put	75		90			2
K		Call	75	5.00	90			−10
L		Put	75		90			−2
M	Short	Call	110				0	2
N		Put	80	3.00			−25	−22

32. Mr. Ken Fused, one of your clients, has been reading his daughter's finance text-book and has a question about options. He says: "If I buy a call option, I have the right to buy the asset at the strike price. If I buy a put option, I have the right to sell the asset at the strike price; and if I sell a put, I have to buy the asset at the strike price. Therefore, buying a call option is the same as selling a put. So if I observe that puts and calls have different prices, I can make money because they should have the same price!" Comment on Mr. Fused's statement—is he correct?

33. Xiang Zhu, a client of the Absent Minded Profs, has phoned you with a question. She has been reading a finance text and can't understand how to use the binomial option pricing model to value a call option. The underlying stock is currently trading for $100, and there is a 30 percent chance that it will increase to $190 and a 70 percent chance that it will fall to $85 in one year. The risk-free rate is 10 percent. There is a call option with a strike price of $170 which, according to the binomial model, should have a value of $4.3290. What has confused Xiang is the following: there is a 30 percent chance that the call will be worth $20 and a 70 percent chance that it will be worth zero so the expected value should be $6. Why is it only worth $4.3290?

   A. Demonstrate that if the call was trading for $6, there would be an arbitrage opportunity.
   B. Calculate the risk neutral probabilities.
   C. Calculate the expected present value of the call option using the risk neutral probabilities.
   D. Why can we value options as if the investors are risk neutral?

34. You have just been appointed manager of the equity portfolio of a large pension plan. The portfolio has a current value of $100 billion and is well diversified and consequently has a beta close to one. The trustees of the pension plan are very risk averse and in order to prevent you from taking on too much risk, they have structured your compensation as follows: if the value of the fund drops below $90 billion in one year, you will be fired with no severance pay. If the fund is between $90 billion and $120 billion, you will be paid $2 million + 0.01 percent of the difference between the fund value and $90 billion (i.e., If the fund is worth $95 billion in 1 year, you will be paid $2 million + $500,000 = $2.5 million). If the fund is worth more than $120 billion, your salary will be capped at $5 million. You are allowed to invest in options on the S&P/TSX. The current value of the S&P/TSX is 1,000 and there are puts and calls traded which expire in one year. The puts and calls both have multipliers of $100. The standard deviation of returns on the S&P/TSX is 10 percent per year and the risk-free rate is 3 percent per year. Assume no dividends for both the portfolio and the S&P/TSX, and that the options are European.

   A. Describe how you can protect your personal interests.
   B. How much will these actions cost the portfolio?

PART 6

LONG-TERM INVESTMENT DECISIONS

Assets are on the left of the balance sheet and liabilities are on the right. In Part 6 we consider the left-hand side: assets. In Chapters 13 and 14 we consider the internal acquisition of assets through capital budgeting and apply the work-horse of finance—discounting future cash flows—to evaluating capital expenditures. In Chapters 15 and 16 we consider special cases: buying another firm's assets (commonly referred to as mergers and acquisitions) and leasing, which combines the asset acquisition and financing decision into one.

Future Considerations

In January 2006, Bombardier Inc. put on hold the launch of its *CSeries* 110-130 seater regional jets because of concerns that the timing was wrong. There appeared to be a lack of interest in the new aircraft by prospective buyers, who were concerned that the launch date meant it would miss out on some new technological advances. Originally slated for a 2010 launch, the new target date is 2013. The company redeployed staff and resources to other projects, keeping a small number of people employed on *CSeries* development. Whether Bombardier will proceed with the *CSeries* remains to be seen. The company, which has spent $120 million to date on the project, faces stiff competition in this market.

Source: Bombardier Inc. Website: www.bombardier.com (March 27, 2007).

CBC News Online website: www.cbc.ca (March 27, 2007).

Financial Times website: www.ft.com (March 27, 2007).

13

Capital Budgeting, Risk Considerations, and Other Special Issues

Learning Objectives

After reading this chapter, you should understand the following:

1. The similarities between corporate investment techniques and the techniques used to value shares

2. The basic capital budgeting process

3. The most important approaches used to determine the value of a firm's capital expenditures (capex)

4. The reasons that firms sometimes use techniques that may seem inconsistent with value maximization

INTRODUCTION

This chapter discusses long-term investment decisions made by firms, that is, investments in real assets, like plants and equipment. In previous chapters, we have seen that a firm's investment decisions are critical to firm value, because market values are based on the expected future growth in company earnings, dividends, and distributable cash flows.

We will revisit several concepts discussed when describing how to value bonds and shares. In particular, we will emphasize that the basic techniques are identical: we have to estimate future cash flows, determine appropriate discount rates, convert those expected future cash flows back into their corresponding present values, and compare them with their cost. The essential difference between valuing shares and valuing projects or companies is not in the approach but in the judgement necessary because of the differing "quality" of the inputs.

13.1 CAPITAL EXPENDITURES

The Importance of the Capital Expenditure Decision

capital expenditures a firm's investments in long-lived assets, which may be tangible or intangible

Capital expenditures are a firm's investments in long-lived assets, which may be *tangible* assets, such as property, plant, and equipment, or *intangible* assets, such as research and development, copyrights, brand names, and franchise agreements. Tangible assets are hard, physical assets while intangible ones are more abstract; it is easier for a firm to borrow against tangible assets than against intangible ones.[1]

These long-term investment decisions determine a company's future direction and can be viewed as the most important decisions a firm can make, because a firm's capital expenditures (capex) usually involve large amounts of money and the decisions are frequently irrevocable. For example, TransCanada PipeLines Limited transmits natural gas from western Canada to central Canada and Chicago. Once these pipeline assets are in place, they are largely unique to that application and have very little alternative use. It is therefore important that the decision to make capex investments is made on sound financial and economic grounds.[2] The irrevocable and unique nature of real investments has its parallel in investments in intangible assets, where a decision to bring out a new soft drink, for example, with the attendant new product development costs and marketing campaign, is also irrevocable. In this case, it is almost impossible to get back the investment costs of a failed new product launch.

---

[1] Under Canadian GAAP, spending to generate intangible assets, such as research and development (R&D) and advertising, is expensed rather than capitalized. They do not appear on the balance sheet as an asset. As a result, most intangible assets that appear on the balance sheet result from a firm taking over another one at a premium to its book value. This premium, called "goodwill," is then allocated to different assets and often results in patent or copyright values or "other" assets appearing on the balance sheet.

[2] These types of decisions are so important that the National Energy Board requires that TransCanada PipeLines gets its approval before it can significantly expand its system. New pipelines have to go through a thorough public examination, as is currently being done for the Mackenzie Valley Pipeline (MVP) to bring natural gas down from the Arctic. The tab for the MVP is approximately $7 billion.

The importance of capex decisions lies in their ability to affect the risk of the firm. In some cases, the very survival of the firm depends on the success of a new product produced from prior capex decisions. Ford, for example, was saved from extinction in the 1980s when it brought out the then revolutionary Ford Taurus, which went on to become the most popular family car in North America.

Capital budgeting refers to the process through which a firm makes capital expenditure decisions by (1) identifying investment alternatives, (2) evaluating these alternatives, (3) implementing the chosen investment decisions, and (4) monitoring and evaluating the implemented decisions. We will focus most of our discussion on the general framework that should be used to evaluate various investment alternatives, because the remaining decisions are firm specific and covered in managerial accounting (which develops the firm's control and audit systems). First, we briefly discuss some important factors in the investment process.

> **capital budgeting** the process through which a firm makes capital expenditure decisions by (1) identifying investment alternatives, (2) evaluating these alternatives, (3) implementing the chosen investment decisions, and (4) monitoring and evaluating the implemented decisions

A firm that does not invest effectively will find itself at a competitive disadvantage, which in the extreme will affect its long-term survival. In the short run, poor investment decisions will make a firm less attractive than those that have better prepared themselves for the future. This will manifest itself in the market price of its debt and equity securities, which will decline, and will hence increase its cost of capital.

Michael Porter has written extensively on the notion that successful companies will create a *competitive strategy* for themselves. Porter identifies five critical factors that determine the attractiveness of an industry: (1) entry barriers, (2) the threat of substitutes, (3) the bargaining power of buyers, (4) the bargaining power of suppliers, and (5) rivalry among existing competitors. These are often called the **five forces**.[3] Porter argues that after inception, firms have little immediate control over the attractiveness of the industry they are in. This implies that industry structure will have a significant input into every firm's investment decisions. However, Porter points out, firms *do* exert control over the manner in which they strive to create a competitive advantage within their industry. Obviously, these decisions will also be closely related to a firm's long-term investment decisions, as discussed below.

> **five forces** the five critical factors that determine the attractiveness of an industry: (1) entry barriers, (2) the threat of substitutes, (3) the bargaining power of buyers, (4) the bargaining power of suppliers, and (5) rivalry among existing competitors

Porter argues that firms can create competitive advantages for themselves by adopting one of the following strategies:

1. *Cost leadership: strive to be a low-cost producer.* This strategy is viable for firms that are able to take advantage of economies of scale, proprietary technology, or privileged or superior access to raw materials. Obviously, investment outlays should be made in accordance with a firm's potential advantage. For example, if economies of scale or technological advantages are possible, firms should invest in a manner that will enable them to exploit these opportunities.

2. *Differentiation: offer "differentiated" products.* Firms can provide products that are differentiated from others in several ways. The most obvious is to have a product that is itself unique by virtue of its physical or technological characteristics. However, firms can also differentiate their products by providing customers with unique delivery alternatives, or by establishing a marketing approach that distinguishes their products from those of their potential competitors.

Either of these strategies can be applied with a broad (industry-wide) focus, or with a narrow (industry-segment) focus, and both have their corollary in

---

[3] Porter, M. "How Competitive Forces Shape Strategy." *Harvard Business Review*, March–April 1979.

capex decisions. As we will discuss, cost leadership usually follows from *replacement* decisions, when firms are constantly striving to use the latest technology to lower the costs of production. Product differentiation usually follows from *new product development* decisions, such as the launch of a new flavoured soft drink or a new model of car.

Porter suggests that it is difficult to sustain a competitive advantage once one has been created. This is particularly true in industries where competition is heated or low barriers to entry exist. Therefore, companies must continually plan (and invest) strategically. This brings up the question of what is the relationship between corporate strategy and the capex decision?

It is a basic premise of finance that when a senior executive justifies a project on non-financial grounds, either the analysis is not rigorous enough, with the advantages not fully developed, or it is a pet project and should not be pursued. Every project is amenable to the analytical techniques that we discuss below—the only difference is that the more qualitative the inputs, the more strategic the analysis. However, this does bring up a basic distinction—the difference between bottom-up and top-down analysis.

bottom-up analysis an investment strategy in which capex decisions are considered in isolation, without regard for whether the firm should continue in this business or for general industry and economic trends

Bottom-up analysis is based on the idea that a firm is simply a set of capex decisions. Equipment replacement is a typical bottom-up analysis, in which an engineer estimates the savings in terms of labour hours, power, material costs, and so on, from replacing one piece of equipment with another. A financial analyst then translates these savings into financial parameters to see whether the replacement savings are worth the cost of the equipment. However, at no point does either the engineer or the financial analyst consider whether the firm should continue in this business. An analogy might be the engineer on the *Titanic* deciding to replace some equipment just after the ship struck the iceberg! In isolation, it might be a good decision, but obviously it is irrelevant on a larger scale.

top-down analysis an investment strategy that focuses on strategic decisions, such as which industries or products the firm should be involved in, looking at the overall economic picture

In contrast, **top-down analysis** focuses on the strategic decisions about which industries or products the firm should be involved in. It is the basic decision of whether Ford should produce passenger cars or trucks, rather than of which passenger cars should be developed. At the time of writing, Ford's F150 trucks were the best-selling vehicles in North America, while its car division was losing money. Consequently, it was seriously being discussed whether or not Ford should "do a Volvo" and sell its car business to someone or shut some plants and become a truck manufacturer.

In looking at bottom-up versus top-down analysis, the capital budgeting framework is identical. What is different is the quality of the estimates. In replacement decisions, the analysis is one of *risk*, in which the analyst can estimate the cost savings with clearly defined probabilities. It may be possible, for example, to estimate that that there is a 30 percent chance of saving $50,000 and a 70 percent chance of saving $100,000 per year. In this way, replacement decisions are similar to the evaluation of equity investments for which there is a long price history and means, variances, and so on, can be estimated to say there is a 50 percent chance of a share going up 15 percent in price and a 50 percent chance of it going down 5 percent. In contrast, top-down or strategic decisions often involve a situation of *uncertainty*, in which it is almost impossible to place probabilities on the possible outcomes. In these situations, as we will discuss later, it is important for the analysis to involve different scenarios, so that the firm can respond to different situations. This flexibility in top-down decision making is an application of the theory of option pricing to capex decisions and is called real option valuation (ROV). ROV is very difficult to implement, but it is one of the hottest areas in financial management, and we will discuss it in detail in Chapter 14.

In Chapter 1 we pointed out that the goal of the firm should be to maximize shareholder wealth. In this chapter, we are developing techniques for making capex decisions that are consistent with this overriding objective. These techniques are generally called **discounted cash flow (DCF) methodologies**, and as their name suggests, they are the capex analogues to the valuation techniques discussed earlier. DCF valuation involves estimating future cash flows and comparing their discounted values with investment outlays required today. In this way, they are technically identical to the approaches used to evaluate bonds in Chapter 6 and preferred and common shares in Chapter 7.

The only practical difference is that whereas the cash flows are fixed in valuing bonds and shares in the sense that the analyst cannot change them, in making capex decisions the analyst can change the underlying cash flows by changing the structure of the project. For example, the firm can decide to defer a project for a year or after the analysis, may decide to change the form of a product. If it is a new car development, for example, some parts may become optional extras to hit a target price point, or a substitute sweetener may be used in a new soft drink. As a result, the application of DCF valuation techniques in capex decisions is by nature more of an *iterative* process than a one-time decision.

In discussing DCF techniques, we defer our discussion of how to estimate cash flows until Chapter 14. In this chapter, we focus on the application of the approaches themselves and discuss their relative advantages, assuming that we already know the expected cash flows. In this way we first focus on the capital budgeting framework.

> **discounted cash flow (DCF) methodologies** techniques for making capex decisions that are consistent with the overriding objective of maximizing shareholder wealth; they involve estimating future cash flows and comparing their discounted values with investment outlays required today

CONCEPT REVIEW QUESTIONS

1. What is a tangible versus an intangible asset?
2. What are irrevocable investment decisions? Why are they important for capital budgeting?
3. Contrast top-down versus bottom-up analysis.
4. In what ways is DCF capex analysis similar to valuing common shares, and in what ways is it different?

13.2 EVALUATING INVESTMENT ALTERNATIVES

Net Present Value (NPV) Analysis

The **net present value (NPV)** of a project is defined as the sum of the present value (PV) of all future after-tax incremental cash flows generated by an initial cash outlay, minus the present value of the investment outlays. The NPV is the

> **net present value (NPV)** the sum of the present value of all future after-tax incremental cash flows generated by an initial cash outlay, minus the present value of the investment outlays; the present value of the expected cash flows net of the costs needed to generate them

present value of the expected cash flows net of the costs needed to generate them. This process is depicted graphically in Figure 13-1, where, for simplicity, there is a single outlay at time zero.

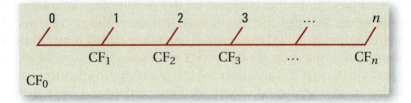

where CF_t = the estimated future after-tax incremental cash flow at time t
CF_0 = the initial after-tax incremental cash outlay

Usually, we use the firm's after-tax marginal cost of capital for projects that are similar to the normal operations of the firm as the appropriate discount rate, because it should reflect the firm's normal financing costs.[4] The NPV of an *n*-year project can therefore be determined by using Equation 13-1.

[13-1]

$$NPV = \frac{CF_1}{(1+k)^1} + \frac{CF_2}{(1+k)^2} + \frac{CF_3}{(1+k)^3} + \ldots - CF_0$$

$$= \sum_{t=1}^{n} \frac{CF_t}{(1+k)^t} - CF_0$$

where CF_t = the estimated future after-tax incremental cash flow at time *t*

CF_0 = the initial after-tax incremental cash outlay

k = the appropriate risk-adjusted after-tax discount rate (which is usually the firm's after-tax marginal cost of capital)

We have discussed previously that the market value of any firm in an efficient market should equal the present value of its expected after-tax cash flows, discounted at an appropriate **risk-adjusted discount rate (RADR)**, which is set based on the overall riskiness of the project. Therefore, we can say that projects that have a *positive NPV* add value to the firm and *should be accepted* because, by definition, a positive NPV implies that the PV of the expected future cash flows exceeds the cash outlay today—that is, it increases the value of the firm. Because the firm's creditors have a fixed claim on the firm's income, regardless of the value of the project, this NPV drops down to the shareholders and increases the market value of the firm's common shares. In this way, accepting positive NPV projects maximizes the firm's market value and creates shareholder value. In contrast, accepting *negative NPV* projects destroys firm value and *should be rejected* because, by definition, the destruction of shareholder value is not in the best interests of the shareholders.

risk-adjusted discount rate (RADR) a discount rate that is set based on the overall riskiness of the project

---

[4] We will revisit the reasonableness of using this discount rate later in this chapter.

We would expect positive NPVs to arise only in situations in which a company has a competitive advantage. Because of the competitive nature of today's business environment, we would not expect to see an abundance of such opportunities, nor would we expect them to persist for very long. Therefore, projects that produce an NPV of zero will be the norm where firms operate in competitive markets. These projects should be accepted, because they provide the appropriate return required to compensate for the financing costs (and risks) associated with the investment.

Example 13-1: Calculating NPV

Suppose a company has an investment that requires an after-tax $12,000 incremental cash outlay today. It estimates that the expected future after-tax cash flows associated with this investment are $5,000 in years 1 and 2, and $8,000 in year 3. Using a 15 percent discount rate, determine the project's NPV.

Solution

$$NPV = \frac{CF_1}{(1+k)^1} + \frac{CF_2}{(1+k)^2} + \frac{CF_3}{(1+k)^3} + \dots - CF_0 = \left[\frac{5,000}{(1.15)^1} + \frac{5,000}{(1.15)^2} + \frac{8,000}{(1.15)^3} \right] - 12,000$$

$$= 13,388.67 - 12,000 = +1,388.67$$

Therefore, the project would be accepted, because it has a positive NPV and would increase firm value by $1,388.67.

solution using a financial calculator

(TI BA II Plus)

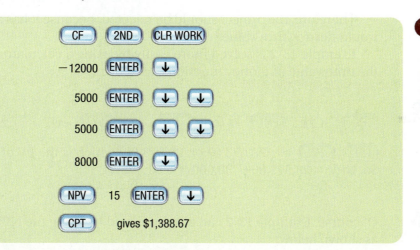

CF	2ND	CLR WORK
−12000 ENTER ↓		
5000 ENTER ↓ ↓		
5000 ENTER ↓ ↓		
8000 ENTER ↓		
NPV 15 ENTER ↓		
CPT	gives $1,388.67	

solution using Excel

The following function can be used to determine the PV of the "future" CFs (not including CF_0):

= NPV (rate, value 1, value 2, …, value n)

where rate = discount rate, value 1 = CF_1, value 2 = CF_2, and so on

For this example, we would enter the following in the appropriate cell:

= NPV (0.15, 5000, 5000, 8000)

This would yield an answer of $13,388.67 for the PV of the future CFs.

When we subtract the initial cash outlay of $12,000 from this amount, this translates into NPV = 13,388.67 − 12,000 = +$1,388.67.[5]

---

[5] If we had the discount rate in our Excel spreadsheet cell B2 and had the year 1, 2, and 3 cash flows in cells B3, B4, and B5, respectively, we could express the Excel function above as follows: = NPV (B2, B3:B5)

Example 13-2: Calculating NPV When Future CFs Represent an Annuity

A project that requires an initial investment of $30,000 is expected to generate after-tax cash flows of $5,000 per year for the next 9 years, and then $6,000 in year 10. Estimate the NPV by using a 12 percent discount rate.

Solution

The "long version" of the solution, involving discounting each of the nine future cash flows separately, is time consuming and unnecessary. This is because the future CFs are all equal at $5,000 (i.e., they form an annuity), except for the ending cash flow of $6,000, which we can view as another $5,000 payment, plus an additional one-time cash flow of $1,000. Therefore, we can solve the PV of the future cash flows by finding the sum of the PV of a 10-year annuity of $5,000 and the PV of a $1,000 cash flow, arriving at $t = 10$, as follows:

$$PV_0 = \$5,000 \left[\frac{1 - \dfrac{1}{(1.12)^{10}}}{.12} \right] + \frac{1,000}{(1.12)^{10}} = 5,000(5.650223) + (1,000)(0.32197)$$

$$= 28,251.12 + 321.97 = \$28,573.09$$

So, NPV = $28,573.09 - 30,000 = -\$1,426.91$

Therefore, the project should be rejected, because it has a negative NPV and would destroy firm value.

Example 13-2 is solved more easily by using a calculator and by using only the time value of money functions, as shown below:

solution using a financial calculator

(TI BA II Plus)

FV $=1,000$; PMT $=5,000$; N $=10$; I/Y $=12$

CPT PV $= -28,573.09$ or, 28,573.09 (which is the PV of future CFs)
So, NPV = $28,573.09 - 30,000 = -\$1,426.91$

solution using a financial calculator

(TI BA II Plus)

Of course, Example 13-2 can also be solved by using the NPV function, as shown below:

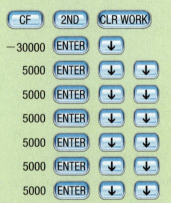

CF   2ND   CLR WORK

−30000 ENTER ↓

5000 ENTER ↓ ↓

5000 ENTER ↓ ↓

5000 ENTER ↓ ↓

5000 ENTER ↓ ↓

5000 ENTER ↓ ↓

5000 ENTER ↓ ↓

5000 ENTER ↓ ↓

5000 ENTER ↓ ↓

5000 ENTER ↓ ↓

6000 ENTER ↓

NPV 12 ENTER ↓

CPT   gives −$1,426.91

In fact, we can use a shortcut when using the NPV function available on the TI BA II Plus calculator:

CF 2ND CLR WORK

−30000 ENTER ↓

5000 ENTER ↓

Because 5,000 occurs 9 times, when F01 shows up on the screen, enter 9, then ENTER ↓
(Then C02 will appear, so just enter 6000, and finish as above).

6000 ENTER ↓

NPV 12 ENTER ↓

CPT gives −$1,426.91

---

solution using Excel

For this example, assuming we have the discount rate in cell B1 and the future cash flows for year 1 through 10 in cells B2 to B11, we would enter the following in the appropriate cell:

= NPV (B1, B2:B11)

This would yield an answer of $28,573.09 for the PV of the future CFs.

When we subtract the initial cash outlay of $30,000 from this amount, this translates into NPV = 28,573.09 − 30,000 = −$1,426.91.

The Internal Rate of Return (IRR)

The **internal rate of return (IRR)** is the same as the yield to maturity (YTM) for a bond that we estimated earlier. In fact, the YTM is the IRR of a bond for a given purchase price. As we showed then, the IRR is the discount rate that makes the NPV equal to *zero* for a given set of cash flows. This implies that it is the discount rate that sets the PV of future CFs equal to the initial cash outlay. In this way, it is a rate of return that is *internal* to this particular set of cash flows; for this reason, it is often called the *economic rate of return* of a given project. We can rearrange Equation 13-1 to obtain Equation 13-2, which can be used to estimate the IRR.

internal rate of return (IRR) the discount rate that makes the present value of future cash flows equal to the initial cash outlay

[13-2]

$$\frac{CF_1}{(1+IRR)^1} + \frac{CF_2}{(1+IRR)^2} + \frac{CF_3}{(1+IRR)^3} + ... = CF_0$$

$$or, \sum_{t=1}^{n} \frac{CF_t}{(1+IRR)^t} = CF_0$$

The general rule for IRR evaluation criteria is that a firm should accept a project whenever the IRR is *greater* than the appropriate risk-adjusted discount rate (k), which is usually the firm's cost of capital. Just like NPV, the IRR represents a discounted cash flow approach; in general, it will lead to the same accept/reject decisions as NPV does. However, note that in Equation 13-2, we could multiply through by $(1 + IRR)^n$ and it then becomes clear that in finding the IRR, we are solving for the roots of an nth order polynomial. Unfortunately, every time the sign of the polynomial changes, that is, the cash flows change from positive to negative, there is a root, so for complex cash flow streams, we often find that there is more than one IRR, or more than one root.[6]

Also note that in solving Equation 13-2, just as for the bond YTM case, there is no finite solution for the IRR. What this means is that solving for the IRR requires a trial and error process similar to the one used to estimate the YTM for a bond. Fortunately, financial calculators or computer spreadsheets make this process very manageable, but be warned that in the case of multiple roots, these procedures give the IRR closest to your starting guess. We didn't worry about this for the bond's YTM because there is only ever one change in cash flow sign: when we buy the bond and there is a cash outflow followed by a series of cash inflows. We illustrate the calculation process in Example 13-3.

Example 13-3: Calculating the IRR

Revisit Example 13-1 and estimate the IRR of the project under consideration.

Solution

The IRR solves the following expression:

$$\left[\frac{5,000}{(1+IRR)^1} + \frac{5,000}{(1+IRR)^2} + \frac{8,000}{(1+IRR)^3} \right] = 12,000$$

Solving by trial and error is very complicated, even for this simple three-period problem. We start by estimating the IRR and try IRR = 20%. Substituting this rate into the equation above gives us a value on the left side of $12,268.52. Therefore, the IRR must be higher than this, because the PV amount is greater than the $12,000 initial outlay. So now we try IRR = 25 percent, which produces a corresponding value on the left side of $11,296. We can conclude that 25 percent is too high. Therefore, we know that the rate we are looking for is between 20 percent and 25 percent, and we can obtain a reasonable approximation by using linear interpolation, which was discussed in Chapter 6:

Discount Rate	PV(LHS)
20%	12,268.52
IRR	12,000
25%	11,296

We find the IRR as follows:

$$\frac{IRR-20}{25-20} = \frac{12,000-12,268.52}{11,296-12,268.52}$$

---

[6] This is a common problem in evaluating leases, which we discuss later in the textbook.

$$\frac{IRR - 20}{5} = \frac{-268.52}{-972.52}$$

$$IRR - 20 = 5 \times \frac{-268.52}{-972.52} = 1.3805$$

So, IRR ≈ 21.38%.

This is one case for which it is worthwhile to use a financial calculator or Excel—and this is only a three-period project; imagine if it were a 20-year project!

(TI BA II Plus)

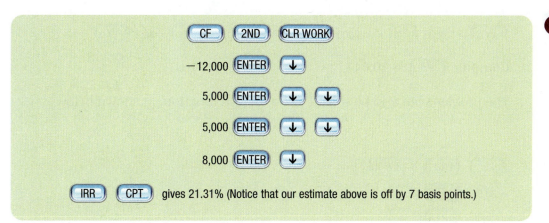

The following function can be used to solve for the IRR:

= IRR (value 0, value 1, value 2, …, guess)

where value 0 = CF_0 (expressed as a negative number), value 1 = CF_1, value 2 = CF_2, and so on, and guess = a guess as to what the IRR is (if nothing is entered, Excel enters 0.10 or 10% as the default). For this example, if we had the year 0, 1, 2, and 3 cash flows in cells B2, B3, B4, and B5, respectively, we could express the Excel function above as follows:

= IRR (B2:B5, 0.20).

Notice in Example 13-3 that the IRR of 21.31 percent exceeded the firm's cost of capital of 15 percent, which implies that the project increases shareholder value and should be accepted. This will always be the case when the NPV is positive, as it was in this case (i.e., recall from Example 13-1 that the NPV for this project was +$1,388.67). In fact, this should be obvious when we look at Equations 13-1 and 13-2, because the NPV will equal zero when the IRR = k. Therefore, when IRR > k, the NPV will be positive because the PV will be higher when we use a *lower* discount rate (i.e., k) than it will when we use the *higher* discount rate (i.e., IRR). This is very intuitive: a positive NPV implies that a project earns a return (IRR) that is higher than the cost of funds (which is reflected in k). Similarly, we can say that a negative NPV implies that IRR < k, and vice versa.

Example 13-4: Calculating the IRR When Future CFs Represent an Annuity

Estimate the IRR for the project in Example 13-2.

Solution

We will skip the long trial and error version of the solution, because it is unnecessary here: the future CFs are equal at $5,000 (i.e., they form an annuity), except for the ending cash flow of $6,000, which we can view as another $5,000 payment plus an extra $1,000 that can be discounted separately. Therefore we can solve the IRR by using a financial calculator.

solution using a financial calculator

(TI BA II Plus)

FV =1,000 ; PMT =5,000 ; PV = –30,000 ; N =10 ; I/Y =12

Compute I/Y = 10.84%

The problem can also be solved using the IRR function, as shown below.

solution using a financial calculator

(TI BA II Plus)

CF   2ND   CLR WORK

−30,000 ENTER ↓

5,000 ENTER ↓

Because 5,000 occurs 9 times, when F01 shows up on the screen, enter 9, then ENTER ↓
(Then C02 will appear, so just enter 6,000, and finish as above.)

6,000 ENTER ↓

IRR CPT gives 10.84%

solution using Excel

For this example, assuming a guess of 10 percent (0.10) for the discount rate and that the cash flows for years 0 through 10 are located in cells B1 to B11, we would enter the following in the appropriate cell:

= IRR (B1:B11, 0.10)

This would yield an answer of 10.84 percent.

Notice that the IRR of 10.84 percent is less than the firm's cost of capital of 12 percent, which implies the project should be rejected. This is consistent with the negative NPV that we calculated in Example 13-2 by using the 12 percent discount rate.

A Comparison of NPV and IRR

The relationship between the NPV and the IRR can be seen from an NPV profile diagram, such as the one shown in Figure 13-2 for two separate projects. NPV profiles depict the NPV of a project for various discount rates.

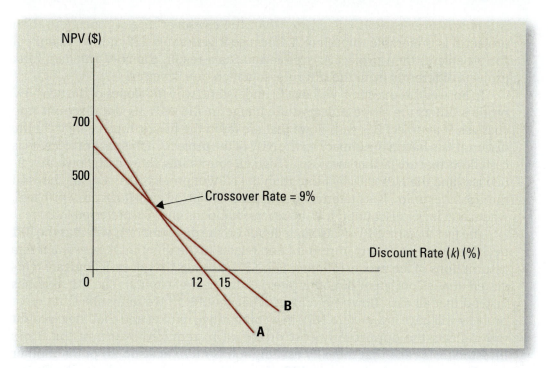

Figure 13-2 graphs the NPV against the discount rate. It shows how the NPV depends critically on the appropriate discount rate—of course, this is obvious from the NPV equation (i.e., Equation 13-1). As the discount rate increases, the NPV decreases and eventually becomes negative for higher discount rates. By definition, we know that the IRR occurs at the discount rate that makes the NPV = 0. This corresponds to the point at which the NPV curve crosses the x-axis in Figure 13-2. For project A, the IRR is 12 percent, while for project B, the IRR is 15 percent. The diagram shows that whenever the discount rate exceeds the IRR, we have a negative NPV, and whenever the discount rate is less than the IRR, we have a positive NPV. We have previously noted these relationships between NPV and IRR.

We can make several useful observations from Figure 13-2. We begin by noting that whether or not the projects should be accepted depends on the discount rate used (k). According to either the NPV or the IRR evaluation criteria, project A should be accepted if $k < 12$ percent, because the NPV will be positive for these discount rates, and because IRR $> k$. Conversely, if $k > 12$ percent, project A should be rejected, because the NPV will be negative, and because IRR $< k$. Similarly, project B should be accepted if $k < 15$ percent, and it should be rejected if $k > 15$ percent. So, if we are independently evaluating a project by using either the NPV or IRR evaluation criteria, we should arrive at the same conclusion.[7]

Figure 13-2 also shows that we can rank projects differently by using NPV versus by using IRR. Suppose, for example, these two were **mutually exclusive projects**, meaning that a firm has to decide between them and can accept only one. Because the IRR of project B is 15 percent, while the IRR of project A is only 12 percent, project B will always appear to be superior, according to the IRR approach. However, by using the NPV approach, we arrive at different rankings depending on the firm's cost of capital (k), because in this example the NPV profiles cross over and have the same NPV at one special discount rate, which

mutually exclusive projects projects for which the acceptance of one precludes the acceptance of one or more of the alternative projects

---

[7] As previously mentioned, this will not be true if we pick the wrong IRR when there are multiple reversals in the signs of the cash flows. This does not happen often in normal projects, but it does happen sometimes, to the surprise of analysts who forget this fact.

crossover rate a special discount rate at which the net present value profiles of two projects cross

is the **crossover rate**. If k is *greater than* the *crossover rate* of 9 percent, then project B is preferable to project A, because it generates a higher NPV, while if $k < 9$ percent, then project A is preferred. As a result, the NPV rule can rank projects differently from the IRR rule, so which one is better?

To answer this question, we have to understand why the slopes of the two NPV profiles differ: the slope reflects the change in the NPV as the discount rate changes. If a project has cash flows that are far in the future, then changes in the discount rate have a big impact on the NPV of the project. In this case project A has cash flows that are farther away, so at high discount rates, these cash flows are valued less and the NPV falls by more than the NPV of project B. As a result, beyond the crossover point, B is preferred to A, because A's far-off cash flows are worth less, whereas at lower discount rates, the reverse happens and A is preferred to B.

The fact that the NPV decision depends on the discount rate, whereas the IRR decision does not, is very important and relates to the different *reinvestment rate* assumptions of the two techniques. The NPV assumes that all cash flows are reinvested at one consistent discount rate (i.e., the cost of capital). The IRR assumes instead that all cash flows are reinvested at the IRR. If we remember that most projects will have low or zero NPV in a competitive market and that the discount rate reflects the opportunity cost or the all-in required return of the firm's investors, it is clear that the NPV assumption is more realistic. To put it another way, if an executive estimates an IRR of, say, 30 percent because he or she finds a wonderful project, the executive is then implicitly assuming that the cash flows generated by this wonderful project can be reinvested in another similarly wonderful project. This means that the executive is assuming that he or she has many wonderful projects, which is not normally a very realistic assumption.

We summarize this discussion by comparing the NPV and IRR criteria in Table 13-1.

Table 13-1   NPV versus IRR

Issue	NPV	IRR
1. Future cash flows change sign	It still works the same for both accept/reject and ranking decisions.	Multiple IRRs may result—in this case, the IRR cannot be used for either accept/reject or ranking decisions.
2. Ranking projects	Higher NPV implies greater contribution to firm wealth— it is an *absolute* measure of wealth.	The higher IRR project may have a lower NPV, and vice versa, depending on the appropriate discount rate, and the size of the project. For example, would analysts prefer an IRR of 100% on $1,000 or 20% on $1 million?
3. Reinvestment rate assumed for future cash flows received	Assumes all future cash flows are reinvested at the discount rate. This is appropriate because it treats the reinvestment of all future cash flows consistently, and k is the investor's opportunity cost.	Assumes cash flows from each project are reinvested at that project's IRR. This is inappropriate, particularly when the IRR is high.

In an important article, Graham and Harvey surveyed the chief financial officers (CFOs) of major U.S. companies as to how they conducted their capital budgeting.[8] Their basic results are reported in Figure 13-3. What is clear is that despite the limitations of the IRR method, it is very widely used in practice and just nudges out the NPV as the most important criterion. This is because, in most cases, the IRR gives the "correct" accept/reject decision and most of the criticisms of the IRR do not often appear in practical applications. More importantly, it holds intuitive appeal because it provides a rate of return on particular investment projects that can be compared with the firm's financing costs. However, as we pointed out earlier, using this approach can cause problems later for the analyst who is unaware of its shortcomings.[9]

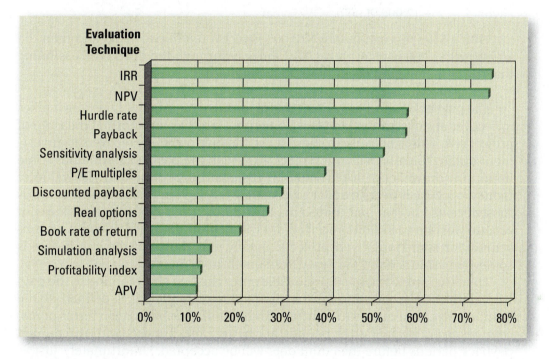

13-3 FIGURE

Evaluation Technique

Source: Data from Graham, John R. and Harvey, Campbell R. "The Theory and Practice of Corporate Finance: Evidence from the Field," *Journal of Financial Economics 60* (2001), p. 187-243.

Payback Period and Discounted Payback Period

The next two most popular techniques mentioned by CFOs were hurdle rates and payback periods. The hurdle rate approach is DCF analysis that uses a discount rate other than the firm's cost of capital, so that conceptually the procedures are the same as NPV and IRR. The **payback period** is defined as the number of years required to fully recover the initial cash outlay associated with the capital expenditure. Shorter payback periods are better, and usually this decision criterion is implemented by choosing a cutoff date and rejecting projects whose payback period is longer than the cutoff period. Example 13-5 illustrates how it is calculated.

payback period the number of years required to fully recover the initial cash outlay associated with a capital expenditure

[8] Graham, John R. and Harvey, Campbell R. "The Theory and Practice of Corporate Finance: Evidence from the Field," *Journal of Financial Economics* 60 (2001), 187–243.

[9] We have sometimes been approached by former students when they have problems with their analysis. Often, these problems occur because they have forgotten the problems with the use of the IRR.

Example 13-5: Calculating Payback Period I

Revisit Example 13-1 and estimate the payback period of the project under consideration.

Solution

Year	Cumulative CFs Recovered
1	5,000
2	10,000
3	18,000

Payback $= 2 + (2{,}000/8{,}000) = 2.25$ years

With a \$12,000 cash outlay, \$10,000 is recovered in two years and then the additional \$2,000 is recovered 1/4 of the way through the third year, assuming that the cash flows are evenly spaced throughout the year.

The payback period provides a useful intuitive measure of how long it takes to recover an investment, and it is sometimes used as an informal measure of project risk. This is because in some sense the quicker a firm recovers its investment outlay, the less risky the project. However, the payback period has some important drawbacks. In particular, it disregards the time and risk value of money, because it treats a dollar of cash flow received in year three the same as those received in year one, and so on. In addition, the payback period does not account for the cash flows received after the cutoff date, which could be substantial for some long-lived projects. Finally, the choice of the cutoff date is somewhat arbitrary and may vary from one firm to the next.

discounted payback period
the number of years required to fully recover the initial cash outlay associated with a capital expenditure, in terms of discounted cash flows

The **discounted payback period** alleviates the first shortcoming of the payback period by accounting for the time value of money. It is defined as the number of years required to fully recover the initial cash outlay in terms of *discounted* cash flows. Shorter periods are better, and projects with discounted payback periods before the cutoff date will be accepted. Unfortunately, just as was the case for the payback period criterion, the discounted payback period ignores cash flows beyond the cutoff date, and the cutoff date is somewhat arbitrary. Example 13-6 shows how the discounted payback period is calculated.

Example 13-6: Calculating Discounted Payback Period

Revisit Example 13-1 and estimate the discounted payback period of the project under consideration.

Solution

Year	Cumulative CFs Recovered	PV(Cumulative CFs Recovered)
1	5,000	$5{,}000/(1.15) = 4{,}348$
2	10,000	$4{,}348 + 5{,}000/(1.15)^2 = 8{,}129$
3	18,000	$8{,}129 + 8{,}000/(1.15)^3 = 13{,}389$

Discounted Payback $= 2 + [(12{,}000 - 8{,}129)/(8{,}000/(1.15)^3)]$

$$= 2 + [3{,}871/5{,}260] = 2.74 \text{ years}$$

In Example 13-6, the discounted payback period is longer than for the simple payback period; the future cash flows are worth less, because they have been discounted for time and risk. If a firm is going to use discounting, it might as well discount all the future cash flows and calculate the NPV. For this reason, the discounted payback period is a sort of compromise between the payback period and the NPV, which is probably why it is not rated highly by CFOs.

Of the other techniques mentioned in the survey, we will discuss sensitivity analysis, simulation analysis, and real options later in the textbook, but they are not really independent techniques; they are more sophisticated implementations of the above techniques. Similarly, P/E multiples and accounting (book) rates of return are important for the way a project will affect the firm's financial statements and important for very large projects. They are rarely looked at for small projects, which leaves the last technique, the profitability index.[10]

profitability index (PI) another discounted cash flow approach used to evaluate capital expenditure decisions; the ratio of a project's discounted net incremental after-tax cash inflows over the discounted cash outflows, which is usually the initial after-tax cash outlay

Profitability Index (PI)

The **profitability index (PI)** is another DCF approach used to evaluate capital expenditure decisions. Like the IRR, the PI is a *relative* measure of project attractiveness. It is defined as the ratio of a project's discounted net incremental after-tax cash inflows divided by the discounted cash outflows, which is usually the initial after-tax cash outlay. Equation 13-3 shows how the PI is calculated:

$$PI = \frac{PV(cash\ inflows)}{PV(cash\ outflows)}$$

[13-3]

It should be obvious from Equation 13-3 that projects with ratios *greater than* 1 should be *accepted*, because by definition they have positive NPVs, while projects with ratios *less than* 1 should be *rejected*. It is also obvious that larger ratios are favoured because their NPVs are higher. The discount rate to be used is the same as the one used for calculating the NPV, and it is usually the firm's cost of capital. Therefore, we observe the following relationship between NPV and PI: when the PI > 1, the NPV > 0 (and vice versa); when the PI < 1, the NPV < 0 (and vice versa).

Example 13-7: Calculating the PI

Revisit Example 13-1 and estimate the PI of the project under consideration.

Solution

$$PI = \frac{PV(cash\ inflows)}{PV(cash\ outflows)} = \frac{\dfrac{5,000}{(1.15)^1} + \dfrac{5,000}{(1.15)^2} + \dfrac{8,000}{(1.15)^3}}{12,000} = \frac{13,388.67}{12,000} = 1.116$$

Therefore, the project should be accepted because the PI > 1. Of course, we knew this already, because we found that its NPV > 0 in Example 13-1, and that its IRR > *k* in Example 13-3.

---

[10] APV can be ignored for our purposes. It is a sophisticated technique that is, in practice, very difficult to implement and rarely used.

We could also have answered Example 13-7 by solving for the NPV (long hand, by using a financial calculator, or by using Excel) and adding the NPV to the initial outlay of 12,000 to find the numerator of the equation above (i.e., 1,388.67 + 12,000 = \$13,388.67), and then proceeding as above.

Example 13-8: Calculating the PI When Future CFs Represent an Annuity

Estimate the PI for the project in Example 13-2 above.

Solution

$$
PI = \frac{\$5,000\left[\dfrac{1-\dfrac{1}{(1.12)^{10}}}{.12}\right] + \dfrac{1,000}{(1.12)^{10}}}{30,000} = \frac{28,573.09}{30,000} = 0.952
$$

Therefore, this project should be rejected because its PI < 1.

As discussed above, the PI produces the same accept/reject decisions as do the NPV and normally the IRR approaches. In addition, the PI does not suffer from two of the weaknesses of the IRR approach, because it uses one consistent and reasonable discount rate, and because it works even when future cash flows change signs. Like the IRR, the PI is attractive because it can be expressed as a percentage, so rather than 1.116 in Example 13-7, we could have said +11.6 percent.

One weakness that the PI measure shares with IRR is that it is a *relative* measure and not an absolute measure of wealth, like NPV. Although it is useful as a *starting point* for ranking projects when some projects must be rejected, final decisions should be based on which projects maximize the total NPV for the firm.[11] In this case, the PI is often used when firms are capital constrained, as we will discuss later.

CONCEPT REVIEW QUESTIONS

1. What discount rate do we use to determine the NPV of a project and why?
2. Why do we sometimes get multiple IRRs for a project?
3. What are the reinvestment rate assumptions underlying NPV and IRR?
4. What is the crossover rate?
5. Why is the payback period a poor evaluation technique?
6. Is the PI rule consistent with the NPV rule?

---

[11] We will elaborate on this point later in this chapter, when we discuss mutually exclusive projects and capital rationing.

13.3 INDEPENDENT AND INTERDEPENDENT PROJECTS

Two or more **independent projects** have no relationship with one another. A firm's decision to accept one project (e.g., purchase a new computerized accounting system) has no impact on the firm's decision to accept another project that is independent of the first one (e.g., replace an aging piece of machinery that is used in the production process). As long as there are no capital spending restrictions,[12] the decision rule is to accept projects that generate a positive NPV (or an IRR > k, or a PI > 1), and reject those that don't. However, many projects have relationships with one another. For example, Finance in the News 13-1 discusses ShawCor Ltd.'s decision to expand its pipe capacity. The company refers to the direct benefits of this investment in reducing lead times and meeting a growing demand. However, the company also alludes to related benefits for its other Alberta operations. Presumably, subsequent investment decisions made by the parent company and by its other Alberta operations will rely on this decision. We must take these relationships into account in our decision process, as discussed below.

independent projects projects that have no relationship with one another; accepting one project has no impact on the decision to accept another project

Net Present value

finance
INTHENEWS13-1

SHAWCOR TO EXPAND PIPE-COATING CAPACITY

Just days after scrapping its proposed acquisition of Nisku, Alta.-based pipeline coatings company Garneau Inc., ShawCor Ltd. says it will invest $30-million to boost its pipe-coating capacity in Western Canada.

The Toronto-based energy services provider said yesterday the investment will occur through its subsidiary, Shaw Pipe Protection Ltd.

"This program, resulting from the termination of the Garneau acquisition, will add the necessary coating capacity required to meet the rapidly growing demand for pipe coatings, including insulation coatings for Alberta tar sands projects as well as large-diameter transmission pipeline projects," ShawCor said in a release.

The investment includes three main components—construction of a new coating plant in Camrose, Alta; a new rail spur at Camrose to double transportation capacity; and upgrades to boost capacity of its existing Camrose coating plant.

"Completion of this program, which is expected by the end of the second quarter 2007, will significantly reduce lead times; meet the growing demand for insulated pipelines in the tar sands region, and also enable other Alberta [operations] of Shaw Pipe Protection to become more focused and efficient," ShawCor added.

On Friday, the company nixed its planned $25.5-million acquisition of Garneau after several regulatory delays linked to a review by the Competition Bureau.

ShawCor chief executive officer Gary Love has said the deal was scrapped because the companies "ran out of time."

In late May, the companies said the deal's closing had been delayed by a pending review in the competition law division of the federal Justice Department. A second and third delay was announced in the summer, putting the deal in doubt.

The bureau's review, Mr. Love said, was centred on the pipe-coating activities of each company, which have very similar operations in Western Canada.

ShawCor, a global energy services company, focuses on technology-based products and services for the pipeline and pipe services industry and petrochemical and industrial markets. It had 5,336 employees in 20 countries at the end of 2005, with annual revenue of more than $1-billion.

ShawCor Class A shares closed down 23 cents to $18.57 yesterday on the Toronto Stock Exchange.

Source: "ShawCor to Expand Pipe-Coating Capacity." Canadian Press as appeared in the *Globe and Mail*, October 11, 2006, p. B6. Reprinted with permission from Canadian Press.

---

[12] This issue is discussed in the next section.

contingent projects
projects for which the acceptance of one requires the acceptance of another, either beforehand or simultaneously

Capital expenditures can represent **contingent projects**. A firm can implement investment A (e.g., purchase the newest accounting software package) only if it also undertakes investment B (e.g., change the operating system to Microsoft Windows). In other words, one project is feasible only if another project is undertaken either beforehand or simultaneously. For these types of investment projects, the rule is to estimate the total NPV of *all* contingent projects and accept them if this total NPV is positive. In such a situation, it is possible that a project on which others are contingent (e.g., the updating of an operating system) can be accepted even if it does not generate a positive NPV on its own. In fact, this is often the case with operating systems. This could occur if the benefits provided by the contingent projects more than offset the losses generated by the initial project.

Mutually exclusive projects, as defined earlier, imply that a firm must choose among two or more alternatives. In other words, if a firm is considering replacing an old computer system with either system A or system B, it would never buy both, even if the analysis suggested that they both generated positive NPVs.[13] In such a case, the firm must decide which project is best. Recall from our previous discussion on IRR versus NPV that whenever a firm has to rank projects, NPV is superior. The decision will be straightforward if the projects have identical time horizons, because the firm will choose the one that produces the highest NPV, assuming the NPV is positive. However, when the projects under consideration have different time horizons, the firm must take this into consideration in its analysis.

chain replication approach a way to compare projects with unequal lives by finding a time horizon into which all the project lives under consideration divide equally, and then assuming each project repeats until it reaches this horizon

Projects with unequal lives can be compared by using two approaches, both of which assume that the project can be replicated at the end of its useful time horizon. The **chain replication approach** involves finding a time horizon into which all the project lives under consideration divide equally and then assuming each project is repeated until they reach this horizon. For example, if a firm is comparing a three-year project with a four-year project, it would assume the three-year project could be replicated four times and that the four-year project could be replicated three times (for a total of 12 years each). It then finds the PV of all the replicated projects for each individual project and chooses the one that generates the highest NPV over the entire period, assuming the NPV is positive. This approach is demonstrated in Example 13-9.

Example 13-9: The Chain Replication Approach

A company is considering three separate, mutually exclusive projects, A, B, and C. Project A requires a $10,000 cash outlay today and is expected to generate after-tax cash flows of $7,000 in year one and $6,000 in year 2. Project B requires a $8,500 cash outlay today and is expected to generate after-tax cash flows of $4,000 in year one and $7,000 in year 2. Project C requires a $10,600 cash outlay today and is expected to generate after-tax cash flows of $5,000 for each of the next three years. Assume that 15 percent is the appropriate discount rate and use the chain replication approach to determine which project the firm should choose.

Solution

Notice that projects A and B both have two-year time horizons, so we can calculate their respective NPVs and choose the one that generates the highest NPV, provided it is positive.

---

[13] If A and B were *independent* projects that generated positive NPVs, a firm would accept both projects.

$$NPV_A = \left[\frac{7,000}{(1.15)^1} + \frac{6,000}{(1.15)^2}\right] - 10,000 = 10,623.82 - 10,000 = +623.82$$

$$NPV_B = \left[\frac{4,000}{(1.15)^1} + \frac{7,000}{(1.15)^2}\right] - 8,500 = 8,771.27 - 8,500 = +271.27$$

Therefore, the firm would choose project A over project B.

Now, the firm would compare project A with project C, which has a three-year life.

First, it would calculate the NPV for project C.

$$NPV_C = \left[\frac{5,000}{(1.15)^1} + \frac{5,000}{(1.15)^2} + \frac{5,000}{(1.15)^3}\right] - 10,600 = 11,416.13 - 10,600 = +816.13$$

Project C is also attractive. Notice that it generates an NPV ($816.13) that is higher than the one A generates ($623.82) over a two-year period. If C produced an NPV that was lower than (or equal to) project A's NPV, which was generated over a shorter period, the firm would accept A over C. However, because this is not the case, the firm needs to determine the project that is best over a six-year period (i.e., because the projects have two- and three-year horizons).

The firm would now estimate the total NPV generated by projects A and C over a six-year time horizon, assuming A is replicated twice and that C is replicated once.

Assuming A generates an NPV at time 0 of $623.82 (over years 1 and 2), the same NPV at time 2 (over years 3 and 4), and the same NPV at time 4 (over years 5 and 6), the total NPV at time 0 is as follows:

$$NPV_A = \left[623.82 + \frac{623.82}{(1.15)^2} + \frac{623.82}{(1.15)^4}\right] = 623.82 + 471.70 + 356.67 = \$1,452.19$$

Similarly, for project C, the total NPV is as follows:

$$NPV_C = \left[816.13 + \frac{816.13}{(1.15)^3}\right] = 816.13 + 536.62 = \$1,352.75$$

Therefore, project A should be accepted instead of project C, because it would generate a higher total NPV over a six-year period than would project C, assuming both projects can be replicated.

The chain replication approach is a reasonable approach for solving Example 13-9, which had to go out to only six years to find a common time horizon for projects A and C. But what if we had to compare a five-year project with a seven-year project? This would force us to go out to 35 years, which would be cumbersome indeed! Fortunately, another approach leads to the same decisions as the chain replication approach but is much more computationally efficient. The **equivalent annual NPV (EANPV) approach** finds the NPVs of the individual projects and then determines the amount of an annual annuity that is economically equivalent to the NPV generated by each project over its respective time horizon. Then, we choose the project that generates the

equivalent annual NPV (EANPV) approach a way to compare projects by finding the net present value of the individual projects, and then determining the amount of an annual annuity that is economically equivalent to the NPV generated by each project over its respective time horizon

highest EANPV, which is defined in Equation 13-4.[14] Example 13-10 demonstrates.

$$EANPV = \frac{Project\ NPV}{\left[\dfrac{1 - \dfrac{1}{(1+k)^n}}{k}\right]}$$

[13-4]

where n = the project's time horizon, and the term inside the brackets in the denominator is the PV annuity factor for an n-year annuity, as discussed in Chapter 5.

Example 13-10: The EANPV Approach

Redo Example 13-9 by using the EANPV approach instead of the chain replication approach.

Solution

We already solved for the NPVs of all three projects in the solution to Example 13-9, so we will not replicate those calculations here. The NPVs for A, B, and C were $623.82, $271.27, and $816.13, respectively, and that would rule out project B, because it has the same life as A but has a lower NPV. Therefore, all we need to do is to compare the EANPV of A with the one for C.

$$EANPV_A = \frac{Project\ NPV_A}{\left[\dfrac{1 - \dfrac{1}{(1+k)^2}}{k}\right]} = \frac{623.82}{\left[\dfrac{1 - \dfrac{1}{(1.15)^2}}{0.15}\right]} = \frac{623.82}{1.625709} = \$383.72$$

$$EANPV_C = \frac{Project\ NPV_C}{\left[\dfrac{1 - \dfrac{1}{(1+k)^3}}{k}\right]} = \frac{816.13}{\left[\dfrac{1 - \dfrac{1}{(1.15)^3}}{0.15}\right]} = \frac{816.13}{2.283225} = \$357.45$$

solution using a financial calculator

(TI BA II Plus)

Project A: FV = 0 ; PV = 623.82 ; N = 2 ; I/Y = 15

Compute PMT = −383.72 or $383.72

Project C: FV = 0 ; PV = 816.13 ; N = 3 ; I/Y = 15

Compute PMT = −357.45 or $357.45

---

[14] It would be incorrect to take the NPV and divide by the number of years required to generate the NPV, because this would disregard the time value of money.

The following function can be used: PMT (rate, nper, pv, fv, type)

For Project A: we would enter the following in the appropriate cell:

= PMT (0.15, 2, −623.82, 0, 0)

This would yield an answer of $383.72.

For Project C: we would enter the following in the appropriate cell:

= PMT (0.15, 3, −816.13, 0, 0)

This would yield an answer of $357.45.

Therefore, the firm would choose project A over project C, just as we determined by using the chain replication approach. The EANPV approach shows that project A generates a higher NPV per year than does project C.

CONCEPT REVIEW QUESTIONS

1. What is the difference between independent and mutually exclusive projects?

2. How can we compare two choices, one involving a wooden bridge lasting 10 years and another involving a steel bridge lasting 25 years that costs more?

13.4 CAPITAL RATIONING

Theoretically, firms should accept all independent projects that generate positive NPVs, which will enhance firm value. However, in practice, firms often face capital budget constraints, which may force them to turn down attractive projects. Theoretically, this constraint should not exist in efficient markets because firms should always be able to source new financing to take advantage of investment opportunities that generate returns (i.e., IRRs) that exceed the cost of raising the required investment funds. However, these constraints may arise because of market inefficiencies, which restrict the firm's ability to raise funds in the capital markets, or because they are imposed internally (i.e., management sets certain budget limits that cannot be exceeded). When firms face capital budget constraints, it is common to say that **capital rationing** prevails—that is, investment capital must be rationed among available investment projects.

We now return to Rothmans Inc. (Rothmans). Figure 13-4 depicts the situation for Rothmans in fiscal 2006. With $177.6 million of internal cash flow and investment of only $11.976 million, Rothmans is the very antithesis of a capital-constrained company. It can accept all the projects listed on its **investment opportunity schedule (IOS)** until the IRR equals its weighted average cost of capital (WACC)—or equivalently until the last project accepted has an NPV of zero. However, suppose Rothmans had only $5 million of internal funds; it could not accept all its projects and would be *capital rationed*, unless it issued new debt or equity.

capital rationing when the total amount of investment capital available is restricted and must be allocated among available investment projects

investment opportunity schedule (IOS) the internal rate of return expected on each potential investment opportunity, ranked in descending order

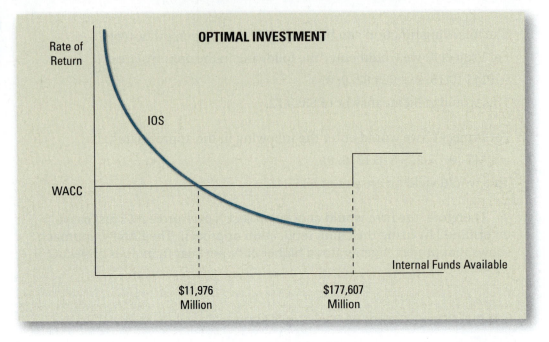

The important point about capital rationing is that the cost of capital is no longer the appropriate opportunity cost. Now cash flows generated by a project can be reinvested at a higher rate than assumed by the cost of capital, because the firm is leaving some positive NPV projects on the table because of lack of financing. The reinvestment rate assumption underlying the IRR has more validity, because the firm can reinvest the cash flows from a project at the IRR of the marginal project, rather than at its cost of capital. The problem is that the IOS schedule is rarely a nice smooth downward sloping function, as shown in Figure 13-4.

When firms have to choose among discrete, lumpy, projects with limited funds, they have to consider the cost of the investment, because this is constrained by the capital budget. In this case, we can first estimate the NPVs and the IRRs, but we can't fully rely on either of them as a criterion, because they ignore the cost of the investment and the capital constraint. The PI is often a useful starting point because it gives the highest present value relative to the initial cash outlay, which is constrained. However, the final decision should be based on which combination of projects generates the highest total NPV while satisfying the capital budget constraint. This is because the PI, like the IRR, may lead to incorrect decisions, because it is a relative measure. Example 13-11 generates the correct procedure for dealing with capital rationing.[15]

Example 13-11: Capital Rationing

A firm is considering the following independent investments

Project	CF_0 (Initial Cash Outlay)	NPV	Project Life	PI
A	$100,000	$13,646	4	1.136
B	50,000	−$3,342	6	0.934
C	80,000	$10,558	3	1.132

[15] This problem can be solved by integer programming techniques, but rarely is the problem difficult enough to justify the analysis.

Project	CF_0 (Initial Cash Outlay)	NPV	Project Life	PI
D	60,000	$4,320	7	1.072
E	75,000	$10,825	5	1.144
F	90,000	$7,225	6	1.080

a. In the absence of capital rationing, which projects should be selected? Determine the size, in total dollars, of the firm's capital budget under this scenario. What is the total NPV of all the projects selected?

b. Now suppose a capital budget constraint of $250,000 is placed on new investments. Determine which projects should be selected? What is total NPV under this scenario? What is the loss to the company from the capital rationing constraint?

Solution

a. In the absence of capital rationing, the firm should select projects A, C, D, E and F because they all have positive NPVs and are assumed to be independent.

Capital budget = 100,000 + 80,000 + 60,000 + 75,000 + 90,000 = $405,000
Total NPV = 13,646 + 10,558 + 4,320 + 10,825 + 7,225 = $46,574

b. The firm should take on the combination of positive NPV projects that maximizes total NPV, within the given budget constraints:

Combination	Total NPV	Capital Budget	Within Budget
A, C, D	28,524	240,000	Yes
A, D, E	28,791	235,000	Yes
C, E, F	28,608	245,000	Yes
A, C, E	35,029	255,000	No

If the capital budget constraint is fixed, then the firm should select only projects A, D, and E.[16] The total NPV is now only $28,791 under capital rationing, and the "loss" to the company = $46,574 − $28,791 = $17,783. Notice that the loss of $17,783 equals the sum of the NPVs of the two forgone positive NPV projects (i.e., C and F). This is detrimental to firm value as it is forced to turn down two "good" positive NPV investments, because the firm lacks the capital to proceed with them. The PI criterion indicates A, C, and E have the highest PIs, but unfortunately they cost more than the budget allows. Although the PIs are a good starting point, they rarely give the optimal solution.

Although we have come up with the maximum NPV given the budget constraint, in reality the firm would conduct further analysis. For example, the company would forecast its budget for the following year and look at the deferral possibilities. It may be, for example, that C can be deferred and it is better to go with A and E this year and roll over the excess in the budget to take C and other projects next year.

---

[16] If there was $5,000 "slack" in the constraint, then the combination of A, C, and E would generate the highest NPV; however, it requires a $255,000 outlay, which exceeds the $250,000 constraint.

13.5 THE APPROPRIATE DISCOUNT RATE

As mentioned above, it is usually appropriate to use a firm's weighted average cost of capital (WACC) as the discount rate to evaluate long-term investment projects. This occurs because it represents the after-tax cost of the average dollar of long-term financing to the firm, and we assume that firms will finance long-term investments by using long-term financing. This is appropriate if the project under consideration is an "average" risk investment project for the company—in other words, if it is a typical investment and will not substantially change the asset mix of the company.

However, if a company is considering a project that is atypical in the sense that it is either more or less risky than the average investment for that company, this fact should be reflected in the discount rate used to evaluate that project. For example, a company could be considering introducing a new product line that entails greater (or lower) risks than its traditional offerings. Under these circumstances, a higher discount rate should be used for projects that possess above-average risk, and a lower discount rate should be used for projects that possess below-average risk. If a firm does not adjust the discount rate under these circumstances and merely uses a constant WACC to select investment projects, it will make inappropriate decisions. In particular, this could lead the firm to reject positive NPV low-risk projects that appear unattractive if evaluated by using a discount rate that is too high. It could also lead the firm to accept negative NPV high-risk projects that appear attractive if evaluated by using a discount rate that is too low.

A good example of this problem was Marathon Oil Corporation in the United States. For a time, the company comprised two divisions: the original oil company and US Steel. Suppose, for example, that the oil company's WACC was 8 percent and the steel company's was 12 percent, while the overall company was composed of 50 percent of each division, so that the company WACC was 10 percent. Applying the company WACC of 10 percent to capital projects would cause some of the steel division's *bad* projects with IRRs of 11 percent to be accepted, even if stand-alone steel companies were rejecting similar projects. Likewise, good oil projects earning 9 percent would be rejected, even if they were being accepted by equivalent oil companies. If Marathon Oil did this over time, it would gradually become a bad steel company, because it would be doing things that good steel companies weren't. Similarly, it would be rejecting many good opportunities that good oil companies would have accepted.

The common response to the Marathon Oil problem is to estimate risk-adjusted discount rates (RADRs) by adjusting the cost of capital up or down based on the risk level and financing of a specific project under consideration. Marathon Oil would use a discount rate of 8 percent in its oil division and 12 percent in its steel division. Estimating these different discount rates involves estimating betas and the risk associated with the investment and the optimal financing. One method of doing this is the **pure play approach**. This approach involves estimating the weighted average cost of capital of firms in an industry associated with the project. Another approach is to estimate beta for the project by regressing the return on assets (ROA) of the project against the ROA of the market index. Similar techniques can be used to estimate the appropriate project cost of debt and then to estimate the appropriate overall cost of capital.

Several practical difficulties are associated with estimating RADRs. For example, it may be difficult to find an appropriate company to use in order to employ the pure play approach, and the regression of project ROA on an index ROA may lead to an inaccurate beta measure. In addition, intuitive adjustments that are made by managers are subjective in nature and prone to error, but this may be no more than in other techniques. However, despite the associated difficulties, estimating risk adjusted discount rates is preferable to blindly applying one constant discount rate to all projects, regardless of their individual risk characteristics.

> **pure play approach** estimating betas and the risk associated with an investment and the optimal financing by estimating the weighted average cost of capital of firms in an industry associated with the project

---

CONCEPT REVIEW QUESTIONS

1. How and why do we adjust the discount rate for multi-divisional firms?
2. What mistakes can occur if firms do not make the appropriate adjustments?

13.6 INTERNATIONAL CONSIDERATIONS

Figure 13-5 depicts a chart of investment in and out of Canada. Portfolio (PORT) flows are investments in financial securities like shares and bonds, whereas foreign direct investment (FDI) is investment in real assets and companies by firms. All types of investments across national boundaries are increasing as the world becomes one giant marketplace. Outbound FDI by Canadian firms has increased in 15 years from 14 percent of gross domestic product (GDP) to more than 30 percent, while inbound FDI has increased from just less than 20 percent to about 26 percent. Firms make these foreign investments for many reasons: they may want to take advantage of cheaper resources, both labour and materials; they may want to enter new markets; or they may want to have access to new technology. To exploit such opportunities, many firms establish foreign subsidiaries or enter into joint ventures with firms that are in foreign countries.

Regardless of the motives, foreign investment is a capex decision and firms have to apply the same criteria as for domestic projects. However, some practical difficulties arise when attempting to apply the NPV evaluation process to foreign investments:

- How do we account for the political risk of expropriation or an insurrection or the imposition of foreign exchange controls so the firm can't get its investment back?

FIGURE   13-5

Investment as a Percentage of GDP

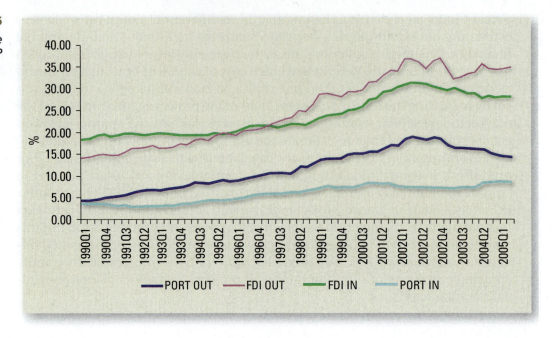

- How do we account for other potential legal and regulatory issues where local competitors may have privileged access to cronies in the government?

- How do we adjust for foreign exchange risk because cash flows are denominated in a foreign currency?

- How do we adjust for the taxes paid in a foreign currency and the possibility that when they are paid back to Canada, they may be taxed again?

- How do we finance a foreign project if the local markets are poorly developed?

These important questions are covered in a multinational business finance course and many large Canadian firms are increasingly dealing with them. The Export Development Corporation of Canada (EDC) helps Canadian firms export and make FDI decisions.[17] EDC is a branch of the Canadian government and offers extensive insurance programs to mitigate some of the risks of FDI. For example, EDC offers political risk insurance (PRI) against

- breach of contract risk

- conversion risk

- expropriation risk (including gradual or creeping expropriation)

- non-payment by a sovereign obligor

- political violence risk

- repossession risk

- transfer risk

The terms of the PRI vary from one country to another depending on the risk, but in evaluating FDI, the PRI can, in part, be removed by charging the project with a 1 percent PRI fee based on the capital committed, which is the normal fee for comprehensive political risk insurance for a typical developing country.

---

[17] Check out EDC's website at <www.edc.ca>.

The techniques developed in Chapters 11 and 12 to manage financial risk are often used to manage foreign exchange risk. Canadian firms routinely use forwards to sell future foreign cash flows forward into Canadian dollars and may also issue foreign currency debt to hedge their investment. Therefore, FDI project analysis involves all the standard domestic problems, plus a variety of complex institutional problems that make it considerably more difficult than domestic project analysis.

CONCEPT REVIEW QUESTIONS

1. What is so different about evaluating FDI compared with domestic projects?
2. Name some unique risks that can arise when evaluating FDI.

Summary

In this chapter, we discuss the capital budgeting process for companies. We focus most of our discussion on the criteria (NPV, IRR, profitability index, payback period, and discounted payback period) that are commonly used to evaluate capital expenditure decisions. We show why NPV is the preferred measure, although the other criteria also provide useful information. Finally, we consider three specific complexities: those caused by capital rationing, those caused by risk differences within multi-divisional firms, and those caused by FDI. In Chapter 14, we will show exactly how to calculate the cash flows and will work through more detailed examples.

Key Terms

bottom-up analysis, p. 504

capital budgeting, p. 503

capital expenditures, p. 502

capital rationing, p. 523

chain replication approach, p. 520

contingent projects, p. 520

crossover rate, p. 514

discounted cash flow (DCF) methodologies, p. 505

discounted payback period, p. 516

equivalent annual NPV (EANPV) approach, p. 521

five forces, p. 503

independent projects, p. 519

internal rate of return (IRR), p. 509

investment opportunity schedule (IOS), p. 523

mutually exclusive projects, p. 513

net present value (NPV), p. 505

payback period, p. 515

profitability index (PI), p. 517

pure play approach, p. 527

risk-adjusted discount rate (RADR), p. 506

top-down analysis, p. 504

Formulas/Equations

(13-1) $$NPV = \frac{CF_1}{(1+k)^1} + \frac{CF_2}{(1+k)^2} + \frac{CF_3}{(1+k)^3} + \ldots - CF_0$$

$$= \sum_{t=1}^{n} \frac{CF_t}{(1+k)^t} - CF_0$$

(13-2) $$\frac{CF_1}{(1+IRR)^1} + \frac{CF_2}{(1+IRR)^2} + \frac{CF_3}{(1+IRR)^3} + \ldots = CF_0$$

$$or, \quad \sum_{t=1}^{n} \frac{CF_t}{(1+IRR)^t} = CF_0$$

(13-3) $$PI = \frac{PV(cash\ inflows)}{PV(cash\ outflows)}$$

(13-4) $$EANPV = \frac{Project\ NPV}{\left[\dfrac{1 - \dfrac{1}{(1+k)^n}}{k}\right]}$$

QUESTIONS AND PRACTICE PROBLEMS

Multiple Choice Questions

1. What will probably happen if a firm does not invest effectively?

   A. The firm could still maintain its competitive advantage.

   B. The cost of capital of the firm will be unchanged.

   C. The long-term survival of the firm will be affected.

   D. The short-term performance will be unaffected.

2. Which of the following is *not* a critical factor that Porter identified in determining industry attractiveness?

   A. Bargaining power of suppliers

   B. Entry barriers

   C. Rivalry among competitors

   D. Bargaining power of government

3. What is the NPV for a project with an after-tax initial investment of $17,000 and five equal cash flows of $8,000 at the start of each year, beginning with the third year? The appropriate discount rate is 20 percent. Should it be accepted or not?

   A. $2,937.41; accept
   B. $6,924.90; accept
   C. −$385.49; reject
   D. $1,998.35; accept

4. Which of the following statements about IRR and NPV is *incorrect*?

   A. NPV and IRR yield the same ranking when evaluating projects.
   B. NPV assumes that cash flows are reinvested at the cost of capital of the firm.
   C. IRR may have multiple IRRs when the sign of cash flow changes more than once.
   D. IRR is the discount rate that makes NPV equal zero.

5. When will NPV and IRR have different rankings when we evaluate two mutually exclusive projects? $IRR_A < IRR_B$.

   A. Discount rate (k) < crossover rate
   B. Discount rate (k) < IRR_A
   C. Discount rate (k) > crossover rate
   D. Discount rate (k) < IRR_B

6. Which project(s) should a firm choose when the projects are independent? When they are mutually exclusive? Suppose both are within the capital budget and $k = 15\%$ for both projects.

   Project A: $CF_0 = \$2,000$; $CF_1 = \$1,000$; $CF_2 = \$2,000$; $CF_3 = \$1,500$
   Project B: $CF_0 = \$2,000$; $CF_1 = \$1,000$; $CF_2 = \$1,000$; $CF_3 = \$4,500$

   A. Both projects; project A
   B. Both projects; project B
   C. Project B; project B
   D. Neither project; neither project

7. What is the IRR of the following project? After-tax initial investment = $6,000; $CF_1 = \$2,500$; $CF_2 = \$4,000$; $CF_3 = \$5,000$. If $k = 20\%$, should you accept the project?

   A. 15%; no
   B. 35.87%; yes
   C. 25.65%; yes
   D. 35.87%; no

8. Which of the following would *not* happen if a firm uses WACC for all projects, regardless of the individual risks of the projects?

   A. Accept a high-risk project with negative NPV
   B. Reject a low-risk project with positive NPV

    C. Accept an average-risk project with positive NPV

    D. Reject a high-risk project with positive NPV

9. To estimate risk-adjusted discount rates, a firm could use all of the following methods, *except*

    A. cost of capital ± risk premium.

    B. regress the ROA of the project on the ROA of the whole firm.

    C. regress the ROA of the project on the ROA of market index.

    D. pure play approach.

10. We should *reject* a project if

    A. NPV > 0.

    B. IRR > required rate of return.

    C. discounted payback period < required period.

    D. PI < 1.

Practice Problems

Easy

11. State the drawbacks of the payback period and discounted payback period.

12. The LargeCo has a capital budget of $100 million to invest in projects. It has evaluated six independent projects and the results of the analysis are summarized below:

Project	Initial investment	NPV	Salvage value
A	$10 million	$5 million	$3 million
B	$90 million	$15 million	$5 million
C	$25 million	$8 million	$2 million
D	$40 million	$7 million	$1 million
E	$25 million	$3 million	$5 million
F	$15 million	$2 million	$8 million

    A. If the company was not capital constrained, which projects should they undertake?

    B. Given their capital constraint, which projects do you recommend that they undertake?

    C. How can the firm increase its capital budget?

13. Bert has just been hired by the Absent Minded Profs as a summer co-op student and has been assigned to assist you. Bert is puzzled about why the Absent Minded Profs are calculating IRR and Payback Periods for investment projects. According to Bert's finance textbook, NPV gives the best measure of the impact of a project on shareholder wealth.

    A. Explain to Bert the advantages and disadvantages of Payback and IRR.

B. Which evaluation techniques are the most popular with companies (i.e., the Absent Minded Profs' clients)?

C. Given the disadvantages and limitations of Payback and IRR, why do you think so many CFOs continue to use them as criteria for evaluating projects?

14. For each pair of investment opportunities, indicate if they are more likely to be mutually exclusive or independent projects. Explain your choices.

   A. Cruise line:

      i) Build a cruise ship to carry 10,000 passengers

      ii) Build two ships each carrying 5,000 passengers

   B. Mining company in Northern Alberta

      i) Use old open pit mine for waste disposal

      ii) Use old open pit mine for fishing and hunting lodge

   C. University

      i) Use classroom for tutorials

      ii) Use classroom for faculty meetings

   D. You:

      i) Latte

      ii) Cappuccino

   E. You:

      i) Salad

      ii) Steak

Use the following information to answer questions 15 to 23.

The Absent Minded Profs have been hired as consultants for the BigCo Manufacturing Company. BigCo is considering several projects and has provided the forecasted annual after-tax cash flows in Table 1.

Table 1

Annual cash flows (all amounts in $millions)

	Project A	Project B	Project C	Project D	Project E	Project F	Project G
Year 0	−1,000	−2,000	−8,000	−5,000	−5,000	−10,000	−3,000
Year 1	500	1,500	2,000	4,800	2,000	3,000	1,500
Year 2	1,000	1,000	2,000	1,000	3,000	2,000	1,200
Year 3	1,200	300	8,000	6,000	5,000	1,000	300
Year 4	2,500	500	2,000	−3,000	1,000	1,000	
Year 5	3,000	200	2,500	−4,000	3,000	3,000	

15. Assume that BigCo's cost of capital for all the projects is 7 percent. Calculate the NPV, IRR, Payback period, Discounted payback, and Profitability index for each project in Table 1. The firm requires a payback period of 2 years and a discounted payback period of 2.5 years.

	Project A	Project B	Project C	Project D	Project E	Project F	Project G
NPV							
IRR							
Payback							
Discounted payback							
Profitability index							

16. If the firm is not capital constrained and the projects in Table 1 are independent, which projects should the firm undertake using the following criteria:

   A. NPV

   B. IRR

   C. Payback period

   D. Discounted payback period

   E. Are any of your recommendations, based on the above criteria, contradictory? Explain how that would be possible.

17. If the firm is not capital constrained and the projects in Table 1 are mutually exclusive, which project should the firm undertake using the following criteria:

   A. NPV

   B. IRR

   C. Payback period

   D. Discounted payback period

   E. Profitability index

   F. Are any of your recommendations, based on the above criteria, contradictory? Explain how that would be possible.

18. The BigCo Manufacturing Company is also debating whether to invest in Project G (a three-year project) or Project D. Determine which project is preferred (assuming that the appropriate cost of capital is 7 percent) using the:

   A. Chain replication approach

   B. Equivalent annual NPV approach

Medium

19. Using Projects A to F in Table 1, construct BigCo's investment opportunity schedule. If BigCo has $8,000 available for investment, which projects should it undertake (assume all projects are independent)? Justify your recommendations to the CEO of BigCo.

20. The CFO of BigCo is concerned about the sensitivity of his decisions to the choice of discount rate. For projects A, C, and E, plot the NPV profiles on the same graph. Does the NPV ranking of the three projects remain the same for every possible discount rate? Explain your observations.

21. Calculate the crossover rate for projects B and C from Table 1.

22. The Absent Minded Profs have conducted an analysis of BigCo and have found that the firm is made up of two different divisions: SatellitesRUs (a satellite launching service) and a bank. Projects A to G are all related to satellite launching technology. The Absent Minded Profs have also examined the industry of each division and have found the following:

Firm	Industry	Cost of capital
Crash'n Burn	Satellite Launching	27%
Liddy's Launchers	Satellite Launching	20%
Reliable Bankers	Banking	5%
Reliance Bank	Banking	4%
VBigCo	Satellite Launching and Banking	10%

   A. What is the appropriate discount rate for projects A to G? Describe your assumptions.

   B. What will be the impact on the shareholder value of BigCo if the firm used 7 percent, the overall WACC, in the valuation of the satellite launching projects (A to G)?

23. The CEO of BigCo has just bought a fancy financial calculator and calculated the IRR and NPV of Project D from Table 1 and is utterly confused. His calculator is telling him that the IRR is 26 percent, but when he uses a cost of capital of 1 percent, the NPV is negative. The CEO expects that if the IRR is greater than the cost of capital then the NPV should be positive. How are the CEO's observations possible? Hint: See the NPV profile of Project D.

24. For the following decisions, indicate whether they are examples of a "bottom-up analysis" or a "top-down analysis"

   A. Replacing the printing press at a newspaper

   B. A newspaper's decision to sell all its print services and move into on-line data services

   C. A pharmaceutical company's research investment in developing a cholesterol drug

   D. A car company's research investment in developing a cholesterol drug

   E. Your decision to take an English literature elective rather than a sociology elective this semester

   F. Your decision to do a degree in business rather than medicine

25. Cutler Compacts will generate cash flows of $30,000 in year one, and $65,000 in year two. However, if they make an immediate investment of $20,000, they can instead expect to have cash streams of $55,000 in year one and $63,000 in year two. The appropriate discount rate is 9 percent.

   A. Calculate the NPV of the proposed project.

B. Why would IRR be a poor choice in this situation?

26. Frank is evaluating two investments—investment 1 has a Profitability Index (PI) of 2.4 while investment 2 has a PI of 1.2. As these investments are mutually exclusive, Frank is recommending investment 1. The Chairman of the Board of BigCo has asked for your comments on Frank's recommendation.

27. Fred is evaluating two investments—investment 1 will produce cash flows for the next 5 years and has an NPV of $1,000. Investment 2 will produce cash flows for the next 15 years and has an NPV of $700. Based on this analysis Fred recommends investment 1. Discuss whether this conclusion is appropriate.

28. Given Project A: $CF_0 = -\$23,000$; $CF_1 = \$6,000$; $CF_2 = \$9,000$; $CF_3 = \$15,600$

   Project B: $CF_0 = -\$20,000$; $CF_1 = \$4,000$; $CF_2 = \$8,000$; $CF_3 = \$15,000$

   What is the crossover rate (r)?

29. If the NPV of a project is $5,090 and its after-tax initial investment is $10,050, what is its PI? Should the firm accept the project? Does the PI yield the same decision as the NPV? (Assume all the cash flows except for the initial investment are inflows.)

30. SK Inc. has two projects as follows:

Projects	Initial CF	CF_1	CF_2	CF_3	CF_4
A	2,500	800	1,200	900	2,000
B	3,000	750	1,500	1,000	4,000

   If SK set 2.6 years as a cutoff period for screening projects, which projects will be selected, using the payback period method?

31. Which project(s) will be selected if a company uses the *discounted* payback period method in Problem 30 and the discount rate is 12 percent?

32. State the decision rules for NPV, IRR, PI, and the discounted drawback period. List two possible consequences of using IRR.

33. What are independent projects? What are mutually exclusive projects?

34. Briefly explain the pure-play method for estimating beta.

Difficult

35. MedCo, a large manufacturing company, currently uses a large printing press in its operations and is considering two replacements: the PDX341 and PDW581. The PDX costs $500,000 and has annual maintenance costs of $10,000 for the first 5 years and $15,000 for the next 10 years. After 15 years, the PDX will be scrapped (salvage value is zero). In contrast the PDW can be acquired for $50,000 and requires maintenance of $30,000 a year for its 10 year life. The salvage value of the PDW is expected to be zero in 10 years. Assuming that MedCo must replace their current printing press (it has stopped functioning), has a 10

percent cost of capital, and all cash flows are after tax, which replacement press is the most appropriate?

36. Malcolm, a very junior reporter, has asked for your help with his first article for a major national newspaper. He has provided you with the following excerpt from his article and would like your comments:

The BathGate Group, one of the few all-equity firms left in Canada, has recently built a Widget manufacturing plant in Whitby. The firm has invested $1 million and according to our sources the promised return on the investment (IRR) is over 27 percent! The shareholders of the firm must be ecstatic—they are currently only receiving a return of 10 percent. Just think—in ten years the value of the plant is expected to be close to $11 million…

   A. What is Malcolm assuming about the reinvestment rate? Does it make sense?

   B. What is Malcolm assuming about the riskiness of the project? Are the shareholders necessarily happy with this decision?

37. The Longlife Company is considering an investment in Ponce Leon Mineral Baths. The investment has the same risk characteristics as the firm. It is assumed that all cash flows are perpetuities and that there are no taxes. Currently the firm has cash flows of $1,000 a year with required debt payments of $300 per year. The current market value of the firm (debt plus equity) is $13,000. The firm is considering an investment of $5,000 in a project that will generate $610 a year forever. Assume that the firm can continue to borrow at 5 percent.

   A. Should the firm undertake the investment?

   B. Demonstrate that the investment will increase/decrease shareholder value (show the impact on cash flows to debt holders and equity holders).

38. The analysis of a two division company (DV2) has indicated that the beta of the entire company is 1.35. The company is 100 percent equity funded. The company has two divisions: Major League TV (MLTV) and Minor League Shipping (MLS) which have very different risk characteristics. The beta of a pure-play company comparable to MLTV is 1.85 while for MLS the beta of a comparable pure-play is only 0.75. The risk-free rate is 3 percent and the market risk premium is 5 percent. Assume all cash flows are perpetuities and the tax rate is zero.

   A. Calculate the cost of capital of the entire company.

   B. The company is evaluating a project that has the same type of risk as MLTV. The project requires an initial investment of $10,000 and pays $1,000 per year forever. Should the company undertake this project? Why or why not?

39. Westlake Corp. has a capital structure that has 60 percent debt at a cost of 12 percent and 40 percent equity. Westlake's stock has a beta of 1.2. Market risk premium = 8% and risk-free rate = 5%. The firm has a potential project on hand, which requires an initial investment of $120,000 and generates an annual year-end cash flow of $37,500 for five years. Calculate the IRR of this project. Decide if the project should be accepted or not, assuming the project is less risky than the firm. $T_C = 40\%$.

40. A project has an NPV of $50,000. Calculate the cost of capital of this project if it generates the following cash flows for 6 years after an initial investment of $200,000:

Year 1: $50,000
Year 2: $50,000
Year 3: $30,000
Year 4: $80,000
Year 5: $60,000
Year 6: $70,000

41. Based on the cash flows given below, calculate the PI of a project that has a required rate of return of 15 percent. Also, indicate whether the project should be accepted.

Year 0: —$90,000
Year 1: $20,000
Year 2: $40,000
Year 3: —$15,000
Year 4: $100,000

42. GiS Inc. has the following four projects on hand:

Project	Initial CF	Accum.CF$_1$	Accum.CF$_2$	Accum.CF$_3$	Accum.CF$_4$
#1	−15,067	3,385	8,965	14,078	21,495
#2	−14,543	2,578	6,865	12,095	19,067
#3	−8,565	3,097	5,674	9,883	15,688
#4	−6,500	2,955	4,985	4,985	12,000

Given R_F = 5%, ER_M = 12%, firm-beta = 1.2, after-tax cost of debt = 6.5%. The firm is financed by 40 percent debt and 60 percent equity. Projects 1, 2, and 3 have the same capital structure as the firm, while project 4 has a 1 percent risk premium. Calculate the cost of capital for the four projects using the following methods:

A. The payback period: If the cut-off period for screening projects 1 and 2 = 3.5 years vs. for project 3 = 2.25 years, which project(s) should be rejected?

B. The discounted payback period method: If the cut-off period for screening project 4 = 3.25 years, should it be accepted?

43. GiS Inc. now has the following two projects available:

Projects	Initial CF	After-tax CF$_1$	After-tax CF$_2$	After-tax CF$_3$
#1	−12,095	5,500	6,000	9,500
#2	−3,080	3,450	3,000	

Assume that R_F = 5%, risk premium = 10%, beta = 1.2. Use the chain replication approach to determine which project(s) GiS Inc. should choose if they are mutually exclusive.

44. Solve Problem 43 using EANPV and assuming market risk premium = 10%.

45. SK Inc. has a project that requires a $50,000 after-tax initial investment and produces these after-tax cash flows at each year-end: $18,000; 20,000; −$5,000; $40,050; $58,000; and $20,000. The appropriate domestic discount rate is 19.4 percent. The project is in another developing country, where extra risk is assumed to be 4.6 percent. Calculate the project's NPV. Should SK Inc. accept or reject the project?

46. Calculate the NPV and IRR of the following project and check whether they produce the same decision. After-tax initial investment = $66,777; after-tax cash flows at each following six year ends are all $20,000. The year-end cash flow at year 7 is $40,000. Assume $k = 18\%$.

47. A firm is considering two mutually exclusive projects, as follows. Determine which project should be accepted if the discount rate is 15 percent. Use the chain replication approach. Assume both projects can be replicated.

Project	Initial CF	CF_1	CF_2	CF_3
A	5,000	2,500	4,050	0
B	3,000	750	1,750	2,000

48. Redo Problem 47 using the EANPV approach.

49. Assume that SK Inc. has a capital budget of $ 200,000. In addition, it has the following projects for evaluation. Determine which project(s) should be chosen, assuming $k = 13\%$.

Project	Initial CF	CF_1	CF_2	CF_3
A	100,000	80,000	80,000	0
B	75,000	50,000	60,000	70,000
C	120,000	55,000	100,000	80,000

Estimating Cash Flow

This chapter discusses estimating cash flow and capital expenditures. How do real-world managers determine the need for new machinery and equipment, and whether or not to expand a firm's operations? In the case of Calgary-based global oilfield services company Precision Drilling Ltd., which had $1,269 million in revenues in 2005, the investment made in the maintenance or expansion of its assets depends on the outlook for the industry in which it operates. Precision Drilling has budgeted approximately $285 million for expansion and "productive capacity maintenance" in 2007. Of this amount, $105 million is earmarked for maintenance, $140 million for the completion of existing expansion programs, and only $40 million for new expansion. In an environment of high natural gas inventories that could lead to weaker natural gas prices, the company aims to preserve cash and maintain low levels of debt. It plans to fund its 2007 capital expenditure program primarily by using cash flow from operations

Source: Precision Drilling Ltd. press release, December 18, 2006. Retrieved from http://pressrelease.precisiondrilling.com/

Cash Flow Estimation and Capital Budgeting Decisions

Learning Objectives

After reading this chapter, you should understand the following:

1. How to estimate the future cash flows associated with potential investments

2. How to determine whether these investments are the result of expansion or replacement decisions

3. How to conduct a sensitivity analysis to see how the value changes as key inputs vary

4. Why real option valuation techniques have become an important trend in project evaluation

5. How mistakes can easily be made in dealing with inflation

INTRODUCTION

Chapter 13 illustrated the capital budgeting process and discussed the most important approaches used to evaluate investment opportunities. However, the inputs to the analysis were largely already specified. This chapter is hands on, and you'll have many opportunities to practise your skills.

14.1 GENERAL GUIDELINES

In Chapter 13, we discussed several capital budgeting evaluation criteria (i.e., NPV, IRR, profitability index, payback period, and discounted payback period). All of these methods require an estimate of the present cash outlay, as well as estimates of the future cash flows associated with the investment opportunity. In this chapter, we discuss how to estimate these important inputs into those evaluation procedures. We will need to draw on our discussions in Chapters 3 and 4 regarding the firm's financial statements, as well as the capital cost allowance (CCA) system in Canada.

We begin by providing some general guidelines for estimating the cash flows associated with capital expenditure decisions:

1. Estimate all cash flows on an *after-tax* basis, because taxes can play an important role in any investment decision, and because we use an after-tax cost of capital to discount these cash flows. As we will show, we have many ways to approach capital budgeting, but one of the most important principles is to compare like with like, that is, use after-tax cash flows with an after-tax discount rate.

2. Use the appropriate cash flow estimates that represent the **marginal or incremental cash flows** arising from capital budgeting decisions, or the changes that result from the firm's decision which generate additional cash flows. For example, a firm is considering introducing a new product line that will generate $100,000 per year in additional after-tax cash flows. However, the introduction of this new product line will "cost" the firm $40,000 in after-tax cash flows as a result of lost sales for an existing product. This is called *cannibalization* and the marginal cash flows that should be used in evaluating the new product line are $60,000 per year (i.e., $100,000 − $40,000).

3. Do *not* include associated interest and dividend payments in estimated project cash flows, because they should already be accounted for in the discount rate (i.e., the appropriate cost of capital). This is why we discount with the weighted average cost of capital (WACC), where *all the financing costs are captured in the discount rate*. The WACC is discussed in detail in Chapter 20.

4. Adjust cash flows (particularly the initial cash outlay and the terminal cash flow at the end of the estimated project life) to reflect any additional *working capital requirements* that are associated with the project. For example, consider a firm that is evaluating a new production process. The process requires the firm to hold additional inventory on hand, which would tie up more funds and is

marginal or incremental cash flows the additional cash flows that result from capital budgeting decisions, generated by new projects

reflected in the firm's level of working capital (as defined in Chapter 3). This represents a drain of cash that should be considered in the capital budgeting decision, because any funds that are tied up have an associated cost. Of course, another firm could be considering a process that requires the firm to hold lower amounts of inventory on hand, and this would represent a source of funds for the firm, which should also be considered in evaluating the implementation of that process.

5. Treat **sunk costs** as irrelevant; we are concerned with *future* cash flows. Suppose a firm has spent $50,000 to try to get a project up and running. If something happens to make the project undesirable, the firm should not proceed any further; otherwise, it will simply be "throwing good money after bad." In other words, it should accept the $50,000 loss, which makes more sense than losing another $100,000 on the project. Obviously, this is easier said than done.

> **sunk costs** costs that have already been incurred, cannot be recovered, and should not influence current capital budgeting decisions

6. Although sunk costs are irrelevant, **opportunity costs** should be factored into cash flow estimates. Opportunity costs represent cash flows that must be forgone as a result of an investment decision. We use the following example to distinguish between sunk costs and opportunity costs. Consider a firm that purchased a piece of land several years ago for $150,000. Today, the firm is considering whether or not to use the land as the location for a new storage facility. In this situation, the original outlay of $150,000 is a sunk cost and should be ignored. However, the land cannot be considered "free," because the firm always has the option of using it for another purpose or selling it. Assuming the firm could sell this land today at a market price of $200,000, this would represent the opportunity cost of using the land for the storage facility; as such, it should be included in the cost of the project.

> **opportunity costs** cash flows that must be forgone as a result of an investment decision

7. Determine the appropriate *time horizon* for the project. We need to know how long a project is likely to continue before it is economic to finish or replace it. In this sense *abandonment decisions* have to be considered because projects are finished when it is economic to do so and not when the engineer says the assets are no longer functioning.

8. Ignore *intangible* considerations that cannot be measured in the financial analysis, unless their impact on cash flows can be estimated. Often, intangible benefits are used to justify poor projects. If there are spinoffs, they should be analyzed and incorporated into the analysis however hard it is to do so.

9. Ignore **externalities** in the calculations. Externalities are the consequences that often result from an investment that may benefit or harm unrelated third parties. As with intangible factors, although we do not account for these effects in the financial analysis, they could have a huge impact on the final investment decision. An example is a project that generates employment in a depressed region: it is the government's job to assess the value of these externalities, not the firm's.

> **externalities** the consequences that result from an investment that may benefit or harm unrelated third parties

10. Consider the effect of all *project interdependencies* on cash flow estimates. This issue was discussed in Chapter 13 for mutually exclusive projects and for contingent projects. Undertaking a project now may mean a negative NPV but give the firm the option to do other things in the future that may generate value.

11. Treat *inflation* consistently. This is back to comparing like with like: discount nominal cash flows with nominal discount rates, and real cash flows with real discount rates.

12. Undertake all *social investments* required by law. This may be obvious but many social and infrastructure projects have negative rates of return or no definable impact on the value of the firm, but they have to be undertaken.

CONCEPT REVIEW QUESTIONS

1. How should we treat taxes and inflation when determining the present value of future cash flows?

2. Why do we not deduct interest costs from the cash flows to be discounted?

14.2 ESTIMATING AND DISCOUNTING CASH FLOWS

initial after-tax cash flow (CF$_0$) the total cash outlay required to initiate an investment project, including the change in net working capital and associated opportunity costs

Sometimes it is convenient to distinguish among three different categories of cash flows and estimate each type of cash flow separately. Each category of cash flow is discussed below.

The Initial After-Tax Cash Flow (CF$_0$)

capital cost (C$_0$) all costs incurred to make an investment operational, such as machinery installation expenses, land-clearing costs, and so on; these can be depreciated for tax purposes

The **initial after-tax cash flow (CF$_0$)** refers to the total cash outlay that is required to initiate an investment project.[1] It includes additional cash flows, such as the change in net working capital and associated opportunity costs, both of which were discussed in the previous section. These items may affect the firm's cash flow, but they cannot be expensed for tax purposes. CF$_0$ differs from the **capital cost (C$_0$)** of an investment, which includes all costs incurred to make an investment operational, such as machinery installation expenses, land-clearing costs, and so on. These can be depreciated for tax purposes. The CF$_0$ can generally be estimated by using Equation 14-1.

[14-1]

$$CF_0 = C_0 + \Delta NWC_0 + OC$$

where $C_0 =$ the initial capital cost of the asset

$\Delta NWC_0 =$ the change in net working capital requirements (as discussed in the previous section)

$OC =$ the opportunity costs associated with the project (as discussed in the previous section)

---

[1] In fact, this could involve a cash *inflow* rather than an outlay for some projects. For example, if a firm is considering selling a division, it will get the cash today (so CF$_0$ will be negative) and will forgo the future cash flows (CF$_t$) associated with that division, which will be recognized as *negative* cash flows for capital budgeting decision-making purposes.

Example 14-1 illustrates how to estimate the CF_0.

Example 14-1: Calculating CF_0

Brennan Co. is evaluating the proposed acquisition of a new milling machine. The machine's base price is $625,000, and it would cost another $25,000 to modify it for special use by the firm. To use the machine, the firm will need to maintain additional raw materials inventory of $100,000. Estimate the firm's associated after-tax cash outlay.

Solution

Capital cost $= C_0 = \$625,000 + \$25,000 = \$650,000$

Initial cash outlay $= CF_0 = C_0 + \Delta NWC_0 + OC = \$650,000 + \$100,000 + \$0 = \$750,000$

Note that the cost of the capital asset is not just the $625,000 purchase price but also all other cash outlays that are needed to get the equipment operational. In this case, the $25,000 in modifications have to be capitalized and then depreciated over the life of the machine, because just like the equipment itself, they generate benefits over the life of the equipment. Generally, in any analysis, costs have to be divided into capitalized costs and expenses. The Canada Revenue Agency (CRA)[2] requires anything that generates future benefits to be capitalized and then the value to be expensed through depreciation expenses over future periods. In contrast, costs that generate no future benefits can be expensed immediately and so are immediately tax deductible.

Expected Annual After-Tax Cash Flows (CF_t)

The **expected annual after-tax cash flows (CF_t)** are those that are estimated to occur as a result of the investment decision. These cash flows comprise the associated expected incremental increase in after-tax operating income (i.e., the operating CFs), as well as any incremental tax savings (or additional taxes paid) that result from the initial investment outlay. The tax savings are associated with the additional depreciation expenses that may be charged for tax purposes as a result of the initial investment. Recall from our discussion in Chapter 3 that the amount of depreciation charged for tax purposes is prescribed by CRA according to the asset class associated with the cash outlay and is called the capital cost allowance (CCA). Because CCA is a non-cash expense and we are trying to estimate cash flows, we have two ways to deal with it. The first approach is to deduct CCA from operating income, then deduct the associated taxes payable, and finally add the amount of the CCA expense back (because it is a non-cash expense). The second approach is to recognize that CCA creates tax savings for the firm in the amount of the CCA expense times the company's effective tax rate (T) and add this amount to the after-tax operating income, which is determined by deducting the taxes associated with the firm's before-tax operating income. These two approaches are shown in Table 14-1.

expected annual after-tax cash flows (CF_t) the cash flows that are estimated to occur as a result of the investment decision, comprising the associated expected incremental increase in after-tax operating income and any incremental tax savings (or additional taxes paid) that result from the initial investment outlay

---

[2] CRA is still often referred to as Revenue Canada.

Table 14-1 Two Ways to Determine Cash Flows After Capital Cost Allowance	
(1) Before-tax operating income (OI)	(2) Before-tax operating income (OI)
−CCA	−Taxes payable on OI
Taxable income	After-tax OI
−Taxes payable	+ CCA tax savings
After-tax income	Net cash flow
+ CCA (non-cash expense)	
Net cash flow	

Example 14-2: Calculating Future Annual CF$_t$

With respect to the milling machine purchase that Brennan Co. was considering in Example 14-1, the firm's production department anticipates the machine will generate an additional $450,000 per year in annual operating revenue, while the associated annual operating expenses are projected to be $325,000 per year. The economic life of the machine is expected to be five years. This milling machine is in asset class 9, which has a CCA rate of 30 percent (declining balance method). Estimate the amount of the annual after-tax cash flow for each year by using both approaches described above.

Solution

For all five years, operating income = operating revenue − operating expense
= $450,000 − $325,000 = $125,000

Recall from Chapter 3 that the half-year rule applies in the first year an asset is acquired, which means that only one-half of the CCA rate is applied in year 1. Therefore, we can estimate CCA in year 1 as:

CCA (year 1) = (C_0) × (CCA rate) × (1/2) = ($650,000) × (0.30) × (1/2) = $97,500

Because the full CCA rate is applied to the undepreciated capital cost (UCC) of the asset in all years subsequent to the first year, we can estimate the CCA expense in years 2 through 5 as follows:

UCC (beginning of year 2) = UCC (beginning of year 1) −CCA (year 1) = $650,000 −$97,500 = $552,500

CCA (year 2) = (UCC) × (CCA rate) = ($552,500) × (0.30) = $165,750

UCC (beginning of year 3) = UCC (beginning of year 2) −CCA (year 2) = $552,500 −$165,750 = $386,750

CCA (year 3) = (UCC) × (CCA rate) = ($386,750) × (0.30) = $116,025

UCC (beginning of year 4) = UCC (beginning of year 3) −CCA (year 3) = $386,750 −$116,025 = $270,725

CCA (year 4) = (UCC) × (CCA rate) = ($270,725) × (0.30) = $81,218

UCC (beginning of year 5) = UCC (beginning of year 4) −CCA (year 4) = $270,725 −$81,218 = $189,507

CCA (year 5) = (UCC) × (CCA rate) = ($189,507) × (0.30) = $56,852

UCC (end of year 5) = $189,507 − $56,852 = $132,655

Combining these estimates with the firm's tax rate of 45 percent, we can estimate CF_t's as follows:

APPROACH 1

	Year 1	Year 2	Year 3	Year 4	Year 5
Operating income	$125,000	$ 125,000	$ 125,000	$125,000	$125,000
−CCA expense	−97,500	−165,750	−116,025	−81,218	−56,852
Taxable income	27,500	(40,750)	8,975	43,782	68,148
−Taxes payable (@45%)	−12,375	+18,338*	−4,039	−19,702	−30,667
After-tax income	15,125	(22,412)	4,936	24,080	37,481
+CCA expense	+97,500	+165,750	+116,025	+81,218	+56,852
Net cash flow	$112,625	$ 143,338	$ 120,961	$105,298	$ 94,333

APPROACH 2

	Year 1	Year 2	Year 3	Year 4	Year 5
Operating income (OI)	$125,000	$125,000	$125,000	$125,000	$125,000
−Taxes payable on OI (@45%)	−56,250	−56,250	−56,250	−56,250	−56,250
After-tax OI	68,750	68,750	68,750	68,750	68,750
+CCA tax savings (CCA × T)	+ 43,875	+ 74,588	+ 52,211	+ 36,548	+ 25,583
Net cash flow	$112,625	$143,338	$120,961	$105,298	$94,333

* In year 2 we assume that the firm can refile the previous year's tax return and get a tax refund so CRA sends the firm a cheque for $18,338. Alternatively, the assumption is that the firm has other taxable income that it can then shield from tax.

Notice the following points from Example 14-2:

1. Both approaches give the same result. Because it is relatively easy to calculate the amount of the associated CCA tax savings, we will use approach 2. This is also important because the use of declining balance CCA means that the tax deductions last forever and the asset is never fully depreciated. This makes it difficult to put all the cash flows into a spreadsheet unless we make some assumptions at the end of the project's life. As a result, we can estimate the annual operating cash flows by using Equation 14-2.

$$CF_t = CFBT_t(1 - T) + CCA_t(T)$$

[14-2]

where $CFBT_t$ = cash flow before taxes (i.e., incremental pre-tax operating income)

CCA_t = the CCA expense for year t

T = the firm's marginal (or effective) tax rate

2. CCA expense is lower in year 1 because of the half-year rule, then is the highest in year 2, declines in year 3, and declines every year thereafter as the UCC continually declines.

3. After-tax OI is the same for each of the five years in Example 14-2, and we could view these cash flows as an annuity. This becomes particularly important, because there is a formula that determines the present value of the CCA tax shield associated with capital investments, which we will introduce shortly.

Example 14-3: Estimating the PV of Future CF$_t$

Determine the present value of the cash flows from years 1 to 5, assuming the firm's cost of capital is 12 percent.

Solution[3]

PV(Future CF$_t$)

$$= \frac{\$112,625}{(1.12)^1} + \frac{\$143,338}{(1.12)^2} + \frac{\$120,961}{(1.12)^3} + \frac{\$105,298}{(1.12)^4} + \frac{\$94,333}{(1.12)^5}$$

$$= \$100,558 + \$114,268 + \$86,098 + \$66,919 + \$53,527 = \$421,370$$

Examples 14-2 and 14-3 deal with future cash flows in which the CCA tax savings cash flows are determined without considering what happens to the machine at the end of its useful economic life. As discussed in Chapter 3, if this asset is sold at that time, its price may affect the CCA expense (and cash flow) in the terminal year of the project. Before proceeding to this issue, we will first deal with the issue of the ending (or terminal) cash flow.

Ending (or Terminal) After-Tax Cash Flows (ECF$_n$)

ending (or terminal) after-tax cash flow (ECF$_n$) the total cash flow that is expected to be generated in the terminal year of a project, aside from that year's expected after-tax cash flow; the estimated salvage value of the asset

The **ending (or terminal) after-tax cash flow (ECF$_n$)** is the total cash flow that is expected to be generated in the terminal year of a project, aside from that year's expected after-tax cash flow, as determined above. It comprises the estimated selling or **salvage value (SV$_n$)** of the asset.

As discussed in Chapter 3, this selling price can have tax consequences. First, if the selling price is greater than the original capital cost, a *capital gain* arises, which is taxable. The converse is not true: when depreciable capital assets are sold below their original purchase price, they do not generate tax-deductible capital losses, because this lower price is expected (i.e., because they are depreciable assets, they are expected to depreciate in value below their original cost).

salvage value (SV$_n$) the estimated sale price of an asset at the end of its useful life

---

[3] Note that the CCA tax savings are as risky as the firm's pre-tax income, because without any pre-tax income, the CCA tax shields are worthless and CRA places restrictions on the transfer of CCA tax shields within different types of firms. For this reason, they are discounted at the firm's WACC. In the United States, where it is easier to file consolidated tax returns and transfer depreciation tax shields between firms, the tax shields are often discounted at the firm's borrowing cost. In practice, this adjustment usually makes very little difference in the final DCF analysis.

Aside from capital gains, additional tax consequences can arise. In particular, *CCA recapture or terminal losses* may be generated by the sale of an asset (or assets), if the CCA asset class is terminated by selling the asset, which would occur only if no other assets were included in that asset class for the firm. Under this scenario, the firm would have to pay additional taxes on "excess" CCA charged against the asset (or assets) if the salvage value is greater than the ending UCC for the asset (or asset class). The amount by which the salvage value exceeds the UCC is referred to as CCA recapture and is fully taxable.[4] However, if the salvage value is less than the ending UCC, then the amount by which the UCC exceeds the salvage value is called a terminal loss, which is fully tax deductible.[5] Finally, CCA recapture may occur even if an asset class is not closed, if an asset (or assets) is sold for a price that exceeds the remaining UCC for that asset class.

In addition to the salvage value and all the associated tax complications, the working capital that was associated with the project will be recaptured at the end of the project, which represents a cash inflow. This means that the people to whom you have extended credit will pay off the debts once the project is finished, and all inventory on hand will be sold, so that the net amount after the firm has paid its suppliers is available to finance other projects.

We can estimate the ending cash flow with tax implications by using Equation 14-3, in which the second-last term is included only if a capital gain arises, and the last term is included only if a terminal loss or CCA recapture occurs.[6]

$$ECF(\text{With Tax Implications})_n = SV_n + \Delta NWC_n - [(SV_n - C_0) \times T]$$
$$- [(SV_n - UCC_n) \times T]$$

[14-3]

where ECF(with tax implications)$_n$ = ending cash flow in year n (i.e., at the end of the project life)

SV_n = the estimated salvage value in year n for the asset purchased

ΔNWC_n = the net working capital "released" upon termination of the project

C_0 = the original capital cost of the asset

UCC_n = the asset (or asset class) ending UCC balance

T = the firm's effective tax rate

Generally, capital gains are rare for depreciable capital assets, because most large firms will have several assets in a given CCA pool, and the pool will remain open after the asset is sold. As a result, the asset cost and UCC will usually be greater than the salvage value of any particular asset, so that capital gains, terminal losses,

---

[4] In other words, it is viewed as if the firm charged too much CCA (depreciation), because the asset is sold for more than its depreciated book value for tax purposes (UCC). Therefore, the firm must pay back the amount of taxes it saved by charging too much CCA.

[5] In other words, the firm did not charge enough CCA, because the asset was sold below its book value for tax purposes (UCC). Therefore, it is permitted to depreciate the asset to its selling price and deduct this charge for tax purposes.

[6] Notice that the last term "self-adjusts" for terminal losses or CCA recapture, because it will be negative if CCA recapture occurs (i.e., because $SV_n > UCC_n$) and it will be positive if a terminal loss occurs (i.e., because $SV_n < UCC_n$).

and CCA recapture will not happen. In such situations, we can estimate the ending cash flow by using Equation 14-4, which eliminates the last two terms of Equation 14-3.

[14-4]

$$ECF_n = SV_n + \Delta NWC_n$$

Example 14-4: Calculating ECF$_n$

Regarding the project being considered by Brennan Co. in Examples 14-1, 14-2, and 14-3, the production department estimated that the $100,000 in additional net working capital requirements will be released after the economic life of the machine. Management estimates that at the end of five years, the milling machine can be sold for $132,655. Assume the asset class remains open after the milling machine is sold. Determine the ending cash flow and the present value of this ending cash flow.

Solution

Notice in this example that no capital gains arise because $SV_n < C_0$. Because the asset class is left open, a terminal loss is not possible. Because $SV_n = UCC_n$, there is no CCA recapture—we do not need to check against the UCC for the entire class. Therefore, we can use Equation 14-4, as follows:

$$ECF_n = SV_n + \Delta NWC_n = \$132,655 + \$100,000 = \$232,655$$

$$PV(ECF_n) = \frac{\$232,655}{(1.12)^5} = \$132,015$$

Putting It All Together

Recall from Chapter 13 that the NPV of an investment equals the present value of the future cash flows minus the initial cash outlay, as was expressed in Equation 13-1, which is replicated below:

$$NPV = \sum_{t=1}^{n} \frac{CF_t}{(1+k)^t} - CF_0 = PV \ (Future \ CFs) - CF_0$$

If we decompose the future CF_t in the equation above into the annual CFs and the ending cash flow, as discussed above, we obtain Equation 14-5.

[14-5]

$$NPV = PV(Annual \ CFs) + PV(ECF_n) - CF_0$$

Referring to Examples 14-1 through 14-4, we can use Equation 14-5 along with the values we calculated to find the NPV of this project for Brennan Co. We do this in Example 14-5.

Example 14-5: Estimating the NPV

Determine the NPV of the project being considered by Brennan Co. by using the information in the solutions to Examples 14-1 through 14-4. Should it accept or reject this project?

Solution

$$NPV = PV(\text{Operating CFs}) + PV(ECF_n) - CF_0 = \$421,370 + \$132,015 - \$750,000$$
$$= -\$196,615$$

Therefore, Brennan Co. should reject the project.

Valuation by Components

The project that was considered in Examples 14-1 through 14-5 was relatively straightforward to evaluate. However, it would take much longer to find the NPV if it were a 20-year project, because we would have to calculate cash flows for each year and then discount them back individually. Obviously, the use of a spreadsheet program, such as Excel, is one way to make the calculations. However, if using Excel is not an option, we can use formulas to simplify the calculations by separating the problem into its different components.

Whenever operating cash flows are assumed to be the same every year, as in Example 14-5, we can view these cash flows as an annuity and find their present value by using the present value of an annuity formula, which was introduced in Chapter 5. This assumption is reasonable for most replacement decisions in which the cash savings are assumed to be the same each year. The example is depicted in Equation 14-6.

$$PV(\text{Operating Cash Flows}) = CFBT(1-T) \times \left[\frac{1 - \dfrac{1}{(1+k)^n}}{k}\right]$$

[14-6]

In addition to the annuity formula for the operating cash flows, we can also separately determine the present value of the tax shield created by the CCA expenses for the investment. The first equation can be used in most circumstances, because it applies when there is no CCA recapture or terminal loss. This situation occurs whenever an asset class is left open or when the salvage value is less than the UCC for an entire class, which happens most frequently for long-term capital expenditures.

$$PV(\text{CCA Tax Shield}) = \frac{(C_0)(d)(T)}{d+k} \times \frac{(1+0.5k)}{(1+k)} - \frac{(SV_n)(d)(T)}{(d+k)} \times \frac{1}{(1+k)^n}$$

[14-7]

where d = the applicable CCA rate

The first part of the first term of Equation 14-7 $\left[\dfrac{(C_0)(d)(T)}{d+k}\right]$ is a variation of the Dividend Discount Model (DDM), which was introduced in Chapter 7, as a method of finding the present value of a growing perpetuity (of dividends). However, in this situation, the starting cash flow in the numerator is the tax savings generated by the CCA expense $[(C_0)(d)(T)]$ instead of D_1 as it is in the DDM. The denominator $(d+k)$ is a variation of $k-g$ in the DDM, where d is positive to reflect the fact that the amount of CCA charged actually declines (or displays negative growth) every year.[7] The second part of the first term in the equation reflects the impact of the half-year rule on the CCA tax savings in the first year. This first term, therefore, estimates the present value of CCA tax savings if the asset were held indefinitely. The second term in Equation 14-7 reflects the fact that the CCA tax savings do not, in fact, go on perpetually, because the asset is assumed to be sold at some estimated salvage value at the end of the project's estimated useful life. Therefore, we subtract the present value of this part of the CCA tax savings that the firm will not realize, because this portion would be generated only if the asset were held indefinitely.

Equation 14-7 applies when there are no terminal losses or CCA recapture. Whenever an asset class is terminated, the possibility exists that one of these items will arise, and we need to use Equation 14-8 to estimate the present value of CCA tax savings. Equation 14-8 would also apply if an asset class was left open and CCA recapture occurred, except that we would replace the UCC for the asset in question with the UCC for the entire asset class in the equation.

[14-8]

$$PV(CCA\ Tax\ Shield) = \frac{(C_0)(d)(T)}{d+k} \times \frac{(1+0.5k)}{(1+k)} - \frac{(UCC_n)(d)(T)}{(d+k)} \times \frac{1}{(1+k)^n}$$
$$- \frac{(SV_n - UCC_n)(T)}{(1+k)^n}$$

The last term in this equation reflects the present value of the cash flow impact of any terminal loss or CCA recapture that arises. Notice that it will be negative when CCA recapture occurs (i.e., when $SV_n > UCC_n$), and it will be positive if a terminal loss occurs (i.e., when $SV_n < UCC_n$).

Finally, whenever capital gains occur, we must also estimate the present value of the cash flow implications arising from the taxable capital gain. We can do so by using Equation 14-9, which estimates the present value of the capital gain times the firm's tax rate and is based on the assumption that the firm pays taxes at the full marginal rate on its taxable gains, which may or may not always be the case.[8]

[14-9]

$$PV(Capital\ Gains\ Taxes\ Paid) = \frac{(SV_n - C_0)(T)}{(1+k)^n}$$

Noting that we have already accounted for the tax implications at the end of the project, we therefore must estimate the present value of the ending cash flow by using ECF_n, as defined in Equation 14-4. Combining all this information, we can express the NPV equation as follows:

[14-10]

$$NPV = PV(Operating\ CFs) + PV(CCA\ Tax\ Shield) + PV(ECF_n)$$
$$- PV(Capital\ Gains\ Taxes\ Paid) - CF_0$$

In this equation, the PV(Operating CFs) term can be estimated by using Equation 14-6 if the operating cash flows are expected to be the same every

---

[7] In other words, it is the same as $k - g$, except that g is negative.

[8] If the firm faces a different tax rate for capital gains (T_{CG}), we can simply replace this rate for T in the equation.

year. The PV(CCA tax shield) can be estimated by using Equation 14-7 or 14-8, depending on whether or not terminal losses or CCA recapture arise, while the PV(Capital gains taxes paid) term applies only if a capital gain arises and can be estimated by using Equation 14-9.

Example 14-6: Finding the NPV by Using the Valuation by Components Approach I

Use Equations 14-6 through 14-10 (as applicable) to estimate the NPV of the Brennan Co. project that was solved by using the longer approach in Examples 14-1 through 14-5.

Solution

$CF_0 = \$750,000$

$$PV(Operating\ Cash\ Flows) = CFBT(1-T) \times \left[\frac{1-\frac{1}{(1+k)^n}}{k}\right] = [\$125,000(1-0.45)] \times \left[\frac{1-\frac{1}{(1.12)^5}}{0.12}\right]$$

$$= (\$68,750) \times (3.604776) = \$247,828$$

Because there is no terminal loss or CCA recapture associated with the termination of this project, we use Equation 14-7 to estimate the present value of the CCA tax shield:

$$PV(CCA\ Tax\ Shield) = \frac{(C_0)(d)(T)}{d+k} \times \frac{(1+0.5k)}{(1+k)} - \frac{(SV_n)(d)(T)}{(d+k)} \times \frac{1}{(1+k)^n}$$

$$= \frac{(\$650,000)(0.30)(0.45)}{0.30+0.12} \times \frac{(1+0.5\times0.12)}{1+0.12} - \frac{(\$132,655)(0.30)(0.45)}{0.30+0.12} \times \frac{1}{(1.12)^5}$$

$$= \$197,736 - \$24,195 = \$173,541$$

$$PV(ECF_n) = \frac{\$232,655}{(1.12)^5} = \$132,015 \text{ (as calculated in Example 14-4)}$$

There are no capital gains, so this term is zero.

Now we can put these items together to determine the NPV of the project.

$$NPV = PV(Operating\ CFs) + PV(CCA\ Tax\ Shield) + PV(ECF_n)$$
$$+ PV(Capital\ Gains\ Taxes\ Paid) - CF_0$$
$$= \$247,828 + \$173,541 + \$132,015 + \$0 - \$750,000 = -\$196,616$$

This is the same answer we obtained when we solved the problem by in Examples 14-1 through 14-5.[9]

Example 14-7: Finding the NPV by Using the Valuation by Components Approach II

Redo Example 14-6 assuming that the asset class is now closed upon termination of the project and that the salvage value is
a. $100,000   **b.** $200,000

---

[9] The $1 difference is due to rounding.

Solution

Notice that changing the salvage value affects only the PV(CCA tax savings) and the PV (ECF_n) terms; therefore, we do not need to re-estimate the other terms.

$CF_0 = \$750,000$

PV(Operating cash flows) = \$247,828

Because there are no capital gains, that term is still zero.

In this example, because the asset class is closed at the termination of the project, we must use Equation 14-8, which accounts for a terminal loss or CCA recapture, to estimate the present value of the CCA tax shield:

a. Now we have $ECF_n = \$100,000 + \$100,000 = \$200,000$

$$PV(CCA\ Tax\ Shield) = \frac{(C_0)(d)(T)}{d+k} \times \frac{(1+0.5k)}{(1+k)} - \frac{(UCC_n)(d)(T)}{(d+k)} \times \frac{1}{(1+k)^n} - \frac{(SV_n - UCC_n)(T)}{(1+k)^n}$$

$$= \frac{(\$650,000)(0.30)(0.45)}{0.30+0.12} \times \frac{(1.06)}{(1.12)} - \frac{(\$132,655)(0.30)(0.45)}{0.30+0.12} \times \frac{1}{(1.12)^5}$$

$$- \frac{(\$100,000 - \$132,655)(0.45)}{(1.12)^5}$$

$$= \$197,736 - \$24,195 + \$8,338 = \$181,879$$

$$PV(ECF_n) = \frac{\$200,000}{(1.12)^5} = \$113,485$$

So

$$NPV = PV(Operating\ CFs) + PV(CCA\ Tax\ Shield) + PV(ECF_n)$$
$$+ PV(Capital\ Gains\ Taxes\ Paid) - CF_0$$
$$= \$247,828 + \$181,879 + \$113,485 + \$0 - \$750,000 = -\$206,808$$

The project is even less attractive because of the lower salvage value, despite the increase in the CCA tax shield through the terminal loss of \$32,655 (i.e., \$132,655 UCC − \$100,000 salvage value).

b. Now we have $ECF_n = \$200,000 + \$100,000 = \$300,000$

$$PV(CCA\ Tax\ Shield) = \frac{(C_0)(d)(T)}{d+k} \times \frac{(1+.5k)}{(1+k)} - \frac{(UCC_n)(d)(T)}{(d+k)} \times \frac{1}{(1+k)^n} - \frac{(SV_n - UCC_n)(T)}{(1+k)^n}$$

$$= \frac{(\$650,000)(0.30)(0.45)}{0.30+0.12} \times \frac{(1.06)}{(1.12)} - \frac{(\$132,655)(0.30)(0.45)}{0.30+0.12} \times \frac{1}{(1.12)^5}$$

$$- \frac{(\$200,000 - \$132,655)(.45)}{(1.12)^5}$$

$$= \$197,736 - \$24,195 - \$17,196 = \$156,345$$

$$PV(ECF_n) = \frac{\$300,000}{(1.12)^5} = \$170,228$$

So,

$$NPV = PV(Operating\ CFs) + PV(CCA\ Tax\ Shield) + PV(ECF_n)$$
$$+ PV(Capital\ Gains\ Taxes\ Paid) - CF_0$$
$$= \$247,828 + \$156,345 + \$170,228 + \$0 - \$750,000 = -\$175,599$$

The project will still be rejected, although it is more attractive because of the higher salvage value, despite the decrease in the CCA tax shield because of the taxable CCA recapture of \$67,345 (i.e., \$132,655 UCC − \$200,000 SV).

Example 14-8: Finding the NPV When k Changes

Redo Example 14-6 by assuming, once again, that the asset class is left open, the salvage value is \$132,655, and all else is as in the original example, except that the discount rate is 10% instead of 12 percent.

Solution

All of the terms, except for the initial cash outlay, will be affected by the change in the discount rate.

$CF_0 = \$750,000$

$$PV(Operating\ cash\ flows) = CFBT(1-T) \times \left[\frac{1 - \frac{1}{(1+k)^n}}{k}\right] = [\$125,000(1-0.45)] \times \left[\frac{1 - \frac{1}{(1.10)^5}}{0.10}\right]$$

$$= (\$68,750) \times (3.79079) = \$260,617$$

Because no terminal loss or CCA recapture is associated with the termination of this project, we use Equation 14-7 to estimate the present value of the CCA tax shield:

$$PV(CCA\ Tax\ Shield) = \frac{(C_0)(d)(T)}{d+k} \times \frac{(1+0.5k)}{(1+k)} - \frac{(SV_n)(d)(T)}{(d+k)} \times \frac{1}{(1+k)^n}$$

$$= \frac{(\$650,000)(0.30)(0.45)}{0.30+0.10} \times \frac{(1+0.5 \times 0.10)}{1+0.10} - \frac{(\$132,655)(0.30)(0.45)}{0.30+0.10} \times \frac{1}{(1.10)^5}$$

$$= \$209,403 - \$27,799 = \$181,604$$

$$PV(ECF_n) = \frac{\$232,655}{(1.10)^5} = \$144,460$$

So,

$$NPV = PV(Operating\ CFs) + PV(CCA\ Tax\ Shield) + PV(ECF_n)$$
$$+ PV(Capital\ Gains\ Taxes\ Paid) - CF_0$$
$$= \$260,617 + \$181,604 + \$144,460 + \$0 - \$750,000 = -\$163,319$$

The project would still be rejected, although the NPV is higher (less negative) because of the use of a lower discount rate, which increases the present value of the future cash flows.

Example 14-9: Finding the NPV When Operating Cash Flows Are Higher

Redo Example 14-7 (again assuming $k = 10\%$), but now assume that all of the annual operating cash flows are 10 percent higher than the original estimates.

Solution

The only term that is affected by this assumption is the present value of the operating cash flows.

$CF_0 = \$750,000$

$$PV(Operating\ Cash\ Flows) = CFBT(1-T)\times \left[\frac{1-\dfrac{1}{(1+k)^n}}{k}\right] = [\$137,500(1-0.45)]\times \left[\frac{1-\dfrac{1}{(1.10)^5}}{0.10}\right]$$

$$= (\$75,625)\times(3.79079) = \$286,678$$

$PV(CCA\ Tax\ Shield) = \$181,604$ (as in Example 14-8)

$PV(ECF_n) = \$144,460$ (as in Example 14-8)

So,

$NPV = PV(Operating\ CFs) + PV(CCA\ Tax\ Shield) + PV(ECF_n)$
$\qquad + PV(Capital\ Gains\ Taxes\ Paid) - CF_0$
$\qquad = \$286,678 + \$181,604 + \$144,460 + \$0 - \$750,000 = -\$137,258$

The project would still be rejected, although the NPV is higher (less negative) because of the increase in estimated operating cash flows.

CONCEPT REVIEW QUESTIONS

1. Why does the initial cash outlay often exceed the purchase price of an asset?

2. How do taxes affect the annual cash flows and terminal cash flows of an investment project?

3. Explain why the valuation by components approach can save computational time and still lead to the correct answer.

14.3 SENSITIVITY TO INPUTS

Examples 14-7 through 14-9 examine the impact of changing one or more inputs into the "base case" project estimates. We did this to illustrate the impact of various estimates on the resulting NPV, as well as to implement various forms of the equations introduced in the previous section. In practice, companies are dealing with estimates of future cash flows, discount rates, and so on. Because any estimate of the future is subject to error, it is often useful to examine the impact on the attractiveness of a project if one or more of the estimates is incorrect. In other words, firms may want to estimate the NPV (or IRR, profitability index, or payback period) of projects by using a *range* of estimates. We briefly discuss some commonly used approaches for doing so.

Sensitivity Analysis

Sensitivity analysis examines how an investment's NPV changes as we change the value of one input at a time, similar to what we did in Examples 14-7 through 14-9. For instance, in Example 14-7, we varied the estimated salvage value and recalculated the NPV, which demonstrated how a change in this estimate could affect the attractiveness of a project. Similarly, in Examples 14-8 and 14-9, we changed the value of the discount rate and then the operating cash flow estimates to isolate how sensitive the NPV is to these inputs. This type of analysis allows firms to determine which of their estimates are the most critical in the final decision. Obviously, the most critical estimates require the greatest amount of scrutiny on the part of the firm.

> **sensitivity analysis** an examination of how an investment's NPV changes as the value of one input at a time is changed

Scenario analysis examines how an investment's NPV changes in response to differing *scenarios* with respect to the values of one or more estimates, such as sales or costs. It is also informative to vary the discount rate used in the NPV calculations, because this variable is hard to estimate precisely and can change substantially through time as market, industry, and company conditions change. It often makes sense to vary more than one input variable at a time, because it allows us to account for interactions among the variables and for the fact that many variables can be related to external variables, such as the overall health of the economy or the company's industry. For example, if interest rates decline, it is reasonable to assume that a firm's discount rate may decline, and if the product it sells is sensitive to interest rates, it is also reasonable to assume that the operating cash flows associated with a particular capital expenditure could increase under this favourable scenario. Similarly, if the price of oil declines, this may reduce the expected operating cash flows from an investment for an oil producer. The decline in oil prices could also cause the market price of the oil producer's common shares to decline, which could increase its cost of capital.

> **scenario analysis** an examination of how an investment's NPV changes in response to varying scenarios in terms of one or more estimates, such as sales or costs

It makes sense to view the impact on all variables of certain scenarios that might arise. Scenario analysis can provide important information, because we know that estimates will rarely be completely accurate and can often be well off the mark.

Scenario analysis is often conducted in the form of a "what if" analysis. For example, a company would typically estimate a *base case* (most likely) scenario. It would then make more optimistic and more pessimistic assumptions to produce, at minimum, an optimistic (or best case) scenario and a pessimistic (or worst case) scenario. In practice, it is common to produce a wide variety of what-if scenarios, which can be easily handled through the use of a spreadsheet program, such as Excel. We provide a simple scenario in Example 14-10.

Example 14-10: Scenario Analysis

A company has a project that requires an initial after-tax cash outlay of $100,000, which is also equal to the capital cost of the assets that are purchased to get the project up and running. The asset class will be left open at the end of the project's useful life, and the applicable CCA rate is 20 percent. The firm's effective tax rate is 40%. It makes the following estimates.

	Base case	Best case	Worst case
Project life	12 years	15 years	9 years
Discount rate (k)	12%	10%	14%
Salvage value	$50,000	$60,000	$30,000
Annual operating after-tax cash flows	$12,000	$15,000	$9,000

Determine the NPV for each scenario.

Solution

$CF_0 = \$100,000$

Base case:

$$PV(Operating\ Cash\ Flows) = [\$12,000] \times \left[\frac{1 - \dfrac{1}{(1.12)^{12}}}{0.12} \right]$$

$$= (\$12,000) \times (6.194374) = \$74,332$$

Because no terminal loss or CCA recapture is associated with the termination of this project, we use Equation 14-7 to estimate the present value of the CCA tax shield:

$$PV(CCA\ Tax\ Shield) = \frac{(C_0)(d)(T)}{d+k} \times \frac{(1+0.5k)}{(1+k)} - \frac{(SV_n)(d)(T)}{(d+k)} \times \frac{1}{(1+k)^n}$$

$$= \frac{(\$100,000)(0.20)(0.40)}{0.20+0.12} \times \frac{(1+0.05 \times 0.12)}{1+0.12} - \frac{(\$50,000)(0.20)(0.40)}{0.20+0.12} \times \frac{1}{(1.12)^{12}}$$

$$= \$23,661 - \$3,208 = \$20,453$$

$$PV(ECF_n) = \frac{\$50,000}{(1.12)^{12}} = \$12,834$$

There are no capital gains, so this term is zero.

$$NPV = PV(Operating\ CFs) + PV(CCA\ Tax\ Shield) + PV(ECF_n) - CF_0$$

$$= \$74,332 + \$20,453 + \$12,834 + \$0 - \$100,000 = +\$7,619$$

The base case NPV suggests that the project should be accepted because it generates a positive NPV.

Best case:

$$PV(Operating\ Cash\ Flows) = [\$15,000] \times \left[\frac{1 - \dfrac{1}{(1.10)^{15}}}{0.10} \right]$$

$$= (\$15,000) \times (7.60608) = \$114,091$$

$$PV(CCA\ Tax\ Shield) = \frac{(\$100{,}000)(0.20)(0.40)}{0.20+0.10} \times \frac{(1+0.5\times0.10)}{1+0.10} - \frac{(\$60{,}000)(0.20)(0.40)}{0.20+0.10} \times \frac{1}{(1.10)^{15}}$$

$$= \$25{,}455 - \$3{,}830 = \$21{,}625$$

$$PV(ECF_n) = \frac{\$60{,}000}{(1.10)^{15}} = \$14{,}364$$

$$NPV = PV(Operating\ CFs) + PV(CCA\ Tax\ Shield) + PV(ECF_n) - CF_0$$

$$= \$114{,}091 + \$21{,}625 + \$14{,}364 + \$0 - \$100{,}000 = +\$50{,}080$$

The best case NPV suggests that the project is extremely attractive and should be accepted.

Worst case:

$$PV(Operating\ Cash\ Flows) = [\$9{,}000] \times \left[\frac{1 - \frac{1}{(1.14)^9}}{0.14} \right]$$

$$= (\$9{,}000) \times (4.94637) = \$44{,}517$$

$$PV(CCA\ Tax\ Shield) = \frac{(\$100{,}000)(0.20)(0.40)}{0.20+0.14} \times \frac{(1+0.5\times0.14)}{1+0.14} - \frac{(\$30{,}000)(0.20)(0.40)}{0.20+0.14} \times \frac{1}{(1.14)^9}$$

$$= \$22{,}085 - \$2{,}171 = \$19{,}914$$

$$PV(ECF_n) = \frac{30{,}000}{(1.14)^9} = \$9{,}225$$

$$NPV = PV(Operating\ CFs) + PV(CCA\ Tax\ Shield) + PV(ECF_n) - CF_0$$

$$= \$44{,}517 + \$19{,}914 + \$9{,}225 + \$0 - \$100{,}000 = -\$26{,}344$$

The worst case NPV suggests that the project is extremely unattractive and should be rejected.

Examining these three scenarios tells the company that although the project seems attractive and has significant upside, it could also turn out to be a losing proposition and is not without risk.

Once we conduct scenario analysis, a final step is to consider a what-if scenario analysis. In Example 14-10, we assumed that a variable changed and yet the firm did not change anything in response. In the extreme, we said that the project is extremely unattractive if the worst case materialized and the operating cash flows were only $9,000 a year for nine years, although the risk of the project increased and the salvage value dropped to $30,000. But a firm would not stand by and watch a project deteriorate without doing anything. In practice, firms respond to changing

real option valuation (ROV) an assessment that takes into account that the firm responds to different circumstances and changes its operating characteristics

circumstances. For example, Finance in the News 14-1 discusses just such a situation involving Canadian Natural Resources Limited's announcement that it would be "slashing its natural-gas drilling plans and putting more money into oil, responding to lower gas and higher oil prices." **Real option valuation (ROV)**, discussed in the next subsection, takes into account that the firm responds to different circumstances and changes its operating characteristics.

finance
INTHENEWS14-1

CNQ CUTS GAS DRILLING PLANS, PUTS MORE MONEY INTO OIL

Canadian Natural Resources Ltd., the country's No. 2 gas producer, is slashing its natural-gas drilling plans and putting more money into oil responding to lower gas and higher oil prices.

Spending on oil wells in North America is increasing by about $150-million or 13 percent to $1.32-billion to capitalize on record crude prices.

"It makes sense to go to oil, "Steve Laut, Canadian Natural president, said in an interview yesterday after the company announced quarterly results and a 374-percent increase in profit.

The cost to drill gas wells and get them ready for production has soared but the price of gas has plunged. EnCana Corp. has suggested several times recently that costs might be reaching a plateau, but Mr. Laut said it is too early to make such a declaration.

Last week, Precision Drilling Trust, which owns the largest fleet of rigs in Canada, said revenue per operating day rose 24 percent from last year, indicative of the soaring costs for producers such as Canadian Natural.

Canada's No. 2 oil and gas company, Canadian Natural decided in May to cut back its gas wells by 150 and yesterday said it was cutting another 308 mostly shallow gas wells and coal-bed methane, both of which produce small returns even when costs are reasonable. The total number of gas wells for 2006 now stands at around 690, about 60 percent of the number set out last Novemeber.

The latest cutback means gas production for the year is expected to be 3 percent lower than previously forecast.

Canadian Natural also cut its oil production forecast by 4 percent for 2006 because of problems in the North Sea and offshore West Africa.

Analysts were still relatively impressed. UBS Securities Canada Inc. said "good second-quarter results [were] tempered by reduced guidance." The price of natural gas plunged by about two-thirds from its December peak because of reduced demand, in part because of a warm winter.

Despite cutting the number of wells drilled, Canadian Natural's budget for gas is still expected to be $1.84-billion, up 3 percent from $1.79-billion in May. About three quarters of the money has already been spent.

The company's second-quarter results were impressive, analysts said. Profit was $1.04-billion or $1.93 a share, almost five times the $219-million or 41 cents booked a year earlier.

The company's Horizon oil sands project is moving along well, the firm said. The $6.8-billion first phase remains on budget and is expected to be producing oil in August, 2008.

But phases two and three, which are budgeted at about $3.9-billion, likely face rising cost pressures. Last week, Shell Canada Ltd. said an expansion of its Athabasca oil sands project could cost $12.8-billion, 75 percent more than an estimate made last year.

Mr. Laut, said Canadian Natural will decide on expansion in 2008,

"If oil stays at $75 [(U.S.)] a barrel to 2008, I'm quite sure the costs to build phases two and three will be higher than what we projected when oil was $45. On the other hand, our balance sheet will be much stronger."

Canadian Natural shares closed at $61.07 (Canadian) on the Toronto Stock Exchange, down 2 cents.

Source: Ebner, Dave. "CNQ Cuts Gas Drilling Plans, Puts More Money into Oil." *Globe and Mail*, August 3, 2006, p.B3. Reprinted with permission from the *Globe and Mail*.

Real Option Valuation (ROV)

ROV places great weight on the *flexibility* involved in a firm's operations. The classic example of ROV is in mining. Suppose a mine costs $150 to get into operation, lasts for one year, and can produce 100 units of production at a fixed cost of $200 and a variable cost of $6. If the price of the ore is expected to be $10 and the discount rate is 12 percent, then the NPV is as follows:

$$NPV = -\$150 + \frac{(\$10 - \$6) \times 100 - \$200}{1.12} = \$28.57$$

where, for simplicity, we have assumed no taxes or CCA

Clearly the mine is a go because it has a positive NPV. Suppose the analyst then conducted a sensitivity analysis with respect to the most important factor, which is the ore price, to see what happens when there is an equal probability of the ore price being either $12 and $8, or $14 and $6, or $16 and $4. We might suppose that the mine becomes less valuable as the ore price volatility increases, yet this is not the case. Table 14-2 shows the cash flow estimates under the three ore-price scenarios.

Table 14-2   Real Options Example

	Scenario 1: Ore Price $12 or $8	Scenario 2: Ore Price $14 or $6	Scenario 3: Ore Price $16 or $4
Good price ($p = .5$)	$12	$14	$16
Cash flow	$400	$600	$800
Bad price ($p = .5$)	$8	$6	$4
Cash flow	$0	−$200	−$200
Expected cash flow	$200	$200	$300

The expected cash flows are highest in scenario 3, in which the ore price variability is highest and the ore price is either $16 or $4. The reason for this is that the cash flow for the bad price scenario remains at −$200, which is the same as in scenario 2 because there is an explicit option available to the firm: to shut down. From basic economics, a firm will operate only when the contribution margin is positive or, said differently, when the price exceeds the variable cost. In the case of the mine, when the ore price is at or below its $6 variable cost, the firm can't lose more than its fixed $200 costs or it will shut down. As a result, in the $16 ore price case, it earns $800, while in the $4 case it loses only $200, so the expected cash flow is a 50 percent chance of $800 and a 50 percent chance of −$200, or $300. Therefore, the value of the mine goes up as the volatility of its ore price increases.

We illustrate this with a **decision tree** in Figure 14-1, in which we map out the two possibilities.

decision tree a schematic way to represent alternative decisions and the possible outcomes

FIGURE 14-1

A Decision Tree

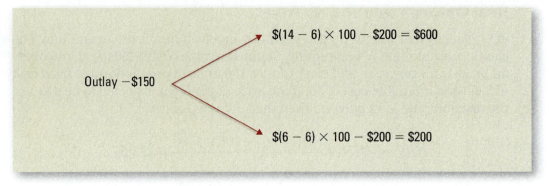

The firm loses the $200 fixed costs regardless of the ore price, because these costs are defined as fixed. However, its contribution depends on the ore price. When the ore price is above $6, there is a positive contribution; when it is below $6, the contribution is zero as the firm shuts down. Although we called this the shutdown option, it is, in fact, a 100 unit *call option* on the ore. If the ore price is above $6, the firm executes its option to go into business and produce ore; if the ore price is below $6, it throws the option away and does not open the mine.

We can use the binomial option pricing model discussed in Appendix 12A to value this option, as long as we have the futures price for the ore. In fact, option pricing is used to value mines producing copper, gold, zinc, and other commodities when there are traded commodities and the cost structure of the mine is clearly defined, as it usually is.

ROV has been applied to other cases, in which the firm has the option to defer or delay a project, abandon a project, or switch the use of the asset from producing one product to another. For example, we started out by saying that capex decisions had the possibility of changing the risk of the firm and were very important if the decisions used irrevocable unique assets. However, if the assets involve generic modern production equipment that can be used to do other things, then the flexibility involved in closing down an unprofitable project and using the assets elsewhere considerably reduces the project's risk. In this case, scenario analysis combined with these event-changing parameters gives a more accurate NPV than assuming that nothing changes as critical values faced by the project change. In this way, ROV and decision tree analysis have dramatically increased our understanding of corporate decision-making and the value of the flexibility and strategic considerations raised by senior management.

NPV Break-Even Analysis

NPV break-even point
the level of annual operating cash flow required for a project to produce an NPV of zero

Because the annual operating after-tax cash flows are so critical to the success or failure of many investment projects, firms may pay particular attention to how variations in these cash flows affect the viability of a project. Sometimes, they will want to know what level of annual operating cash flow is required for a project to "break even" in the sense of producing an NPV of zero. We will denote this as the operating cash flow **NPV break-even point** of a project.[10] The break-even discount rate is the IRR of the project. We calculate the operating cash flow NPV break-even point for the project discussed above in Example 14-11.

---

[10] Firms pay attention to many other break-even points, such as the accounting break-even point, which occurs when the accounting profit equals zero and is typically measured in units of sales.

Example 14-11: NPV Break-Even Analysis

Use the base case estimates for all inputs other than operating after-tax cash flows for the project examined in Example 14-10. Determine the break-even operating after-tax annual cash flow amount.

Solution

$CF_0 = \$100,000$

$PV\ (CCA\ Tax\ Shield) = \$20,453$

$PV\ (ECF_n) = \$12,834$

We can set the NPV = 0 and solve for the value of the PV of the operating CFs that is required, as follows:

$$NPV = PV\ (Operating\ CFs) + PV\ (CCA\ Tax\ Shield) + PV\ (ECF_n) - CF_0$$
$$\$0 = PV\ (Operating\ CFs) + \$20,453 + \$12,834 - \$100,000$$
$$PV\ (Operating\ CFs) = \$66,713$$

Now we can solve for the annual after-tax CF that satisfies this equation as follows:

$$PV\ (Operating\ Cash\ Flows) = [Break\text{-}even\ Operating\ CF] \times \left[\frac{1 - \dfrac{1}{(1.12)^{12}}}{0.12} \right]$$

$$\$66,713 = (Break\text{-}even\ Operating\ CF) \times (6.194374)$$
$$Break\text{-}even\ Operating\ CF = \$10,770$$

Notice that this annual cash flow is less than the $12,000 estimate in the base case, which had produced a positive NPV.

CONCEPT REVIEW QUESTIONS

1. What insights can be gained by using sensitivity analysis, scenario analysis, and NPV break-even analysis?
2. What limitations of scenario analysis does the real option valuation approach address?

14.4 REPLACEMENT DECISIONS

Earlier in this chapter, we introduced 12 guidelines for estimating cash flows. Guideline 2 stated that we should focus on *marginal* or *incremental* cash flows that arise as a result of a capital budgeting decision. This refers to the additional cash flows that will be generated for the firm. So far, this has been relatively easy to deal with, because we have been considering **expansion projects**—that is, projects that would add something extra to the firm in terms of extra sales or cost savings. For these types of projects, the new cash flows that arise from the investment decision represent incremental cash flows.

expansion projects projects that add something extra to the firm in terms of sales or cost savings; their new cash flows are incremental cash flows

replacement projects
projects that involve the
replacement of an exist-
ing asset with a new one

Replacement projects, as their name suggests, involve the replacement of an existing asset (or assets) with a new one. We deal with these types of decisions in the same manner as we deal with expansion problems, except that we must be more aware of focusing on *incremental* cash flows. We demonstrate this point in Example 14-12.

Example 14-12: Evaluating Replacement Decisions

A firm is considering the purchase of a new machine priced at $350,000 to replace an existing machine. The present market value of the existing machine is $50,000, and it is expected to have a salvage value of $15,000 at the end of eight years. Management estimates that the company will benefit from the new machine by reducing annual operating expenses by $50,000 over the life of the project, which is expected to be eight years. This new machine is expected to have a salvage value of $100,000 at the end of eight years. The firm's marginal tax rate is 40 percent, and its marginal cost of capital is 15 percent. Both machines belong to class 10, which has a CCA rate of 30 percent, and the asset class will remain open. Estimate the NPV of replacement and decide whether or not replacement should occur.

Solution

We must first estimate the *incremental* capital cost (ΔC_0), which is the difference between the purchase price of the new machine and the salvage price of the old machine. This will be the addition to the asset class and will determine the additional CCA tax savings generated by the new investment. The incremental capital cost also represents a component of the firm's incremental initial after-tax cash outlay (ΔCF_0).

$$\Delta C_0 = C_0^{New} - C_0^{Old} = 350{,}000 - 50{,}000 = \$300{,}000$$

In this example, there is no mention of opportunity costs arising or of additional working capital being tied up, so we can estimate the initial cash outlay as follows:

$$\Delta CF_0 = \Delta C_0 + \Delta NWC_0 + OC = \$300{,}000 + \$0 + \$0 = \$300{,}000$$

Now, we need to estimate the present value of the annual incremental operating cash flows (ΔOperating CFs).

$$\Delta CFBT = \$50{,}000 \text{ per year in additional cost savings}$$

$$PV(\Delta Operating\ CFs) = (\Delta CFBT)(1-T)\left[\frac{1-\dfrac{1}{(1+k)^n}}{k}\right]$$

$$= (\$50{,}000)(1-0.40)\left[\frac{1-\dfrac{1}{(1.15)^8}}{0.15}\right] = (\$50{,}000)(0.60)(4.487322)$$

$$= \$134{,}620$$

Now we estimate the present value of the incremental CCA tax savings generated by the replacement decision. Because the asset class is left open and there is no CCA recapture or terminal loss, we can use Equation 14-7, making sure to use the incremental capital cost (ΔC_0) as estimated above and also using the incremental salvage value (ΔSV_n), which is estimated below:

$$\Delta SV_n = SV_{New} - SV_{Old} = \$100,000 - \$15,000 = \$85,000$$

$$PV(\Delta CCA \ Tax \ Shield) = \frac{(\Delta C_0)(d)(T)}{d+k} \times \frac{(1+0.5k)}{(1+k)} - \frac{(\Delta SV_n)(d)(T)}{(d+k)} \times \frac{1}{(1+k)^n}$$

$$PV(\Delta CCA \ Tax \ Shield) = \left[\frac{(\$300,000)(0.30)(0.40)}{0.30+0.15}\right]\left[\frac{1+0.5(0.15)}{1+0.15}\right] - \left[\frac{(\$85,000)(0.30)(0.40)}{0.30+0.15}\right]\left[\frac{1}{(1.15)^8}\right]$$

$$= \$67,373$$

Next, we need to estimate the present value of the incremental ending cash flow (ΔECF_n) associated with the replacement decision as follows:

$$\Delta ECF_n = \Delta SV_n + \Delta NWC_n = \$85,000 + \$0 = \$85,000$$

$$PV(\Delta ECF_n) = \frac{\Delta ECF_n}{(1+k)^n} = \frac{\$85,000}{(1.15)^8} = \$27,787$$

We can combine the results above to determine the NPV of the replacement decision, as follows:

$$NPV = PV(\Delta Operating \ CFs) + PV(\Delta CCA \ Tax \ Shield) + PV(\Delta ECF_n) - \Delta CF_0$$

$$= \$134,620 + \$67,373 + \$27,787 - \$300,000 = -\$70,220$$

Therefore, the firm should not go ahead with this replacement project.

CONCEPT REVIEW QUESTION

1. Discuss any differences in the evaluation of a replacement decision versus an expansion decision.

14.5 INFLATION AND CAPITAL BUDGETING DECISIONS

Because capital expenditures typically involve the estimation of cash flows several years in the future, inflation can play an important role in determining these estimates, because it will affect future levels of sales and expenses. In addition, inflation affects the level of interest rates and therefore affects the firm's cost of capital that is to be used in discounting these future cash flows.

Earlier in this chapter, we introduced Guideline 11 for estimating cash flows, which said that we need to treat inflation *consistently*. So far, we have been estimating future cash flows on a *nominal* basis (i.e., estimating the actual cash flow that will result in year 2, etc., without making adjustments for inflation). As a result, we have been discounting these cash flows by using nominal (or actual) discount rates. This approach treats inflation consistently. An alternative is to estimate future *real* (or inflation-adjusted) cash flows and discount these real cash flows by using *real* discount rates (which have also been adjusted for inflation). However, one difficulty with this approach is that the CCA tax savings estimates represent the actual amount of CCA that can be charged in a given year. Therefore, the easiest way to proceed is usually to estimate the nominal cash flows and discount them by using nominal discount rates.

It is important for firms to consider the impact that inflation will have on both sales and expenses, as well as the discount rate. Although it is often reasonable to assume that both items will be equally affected by inflation, this will not be the case for all firms or all situations. Much depends on the industry they are in and on the products they sell. For example, sometimes inflation will have a greater impact on selling prices than it will on expenses, and sometimes the opposite will hold. Example 14-13 demonstrates the impact that such variations in the growth of sales and expenses can have on the NPV of a project.

Example 14-13: The Impact of Inflation

A firm is considering a project with the following forecasts:

- The initial after-tax cash outflow will be $1,000,000, the entire outflow represents a capital cost of $1,000,000, and the appropriate CCA class is asset class 8 (CCA rate 20 percent, declining balance method).

- There is no terminal loss or CCA recapture associated with the project.

- Revenues will be $350,000 in the first year and will grow at 5 percent per year after that.

- Costs will be $75,000 in the first year and will grow at 5 percent per year after that.

- The project will last 10 years, and the equipment has an estimated salvage value of $100,000 at that time.

- The firm's required return is 18 percent.

- The firm pays taxes at a marginal rate of 40 percent.

a. Calculate the NPV of this project.

b. Redo part a. by assuming the first year's revenue is $350,000; however, there is no growth in revenue beyond that. In addition, costs turn out to be $100,000 the first year and grow at 7 percent per year thereafter.

c. Redo part a. by assuming the first year's revenue turns out as expected, but revenue grows at a rate of 7 percent per year thereafter until year 10, while costs are $75,000 in the first year and rise at 3 percent per year thereafter until year 10.

Solution

This problem can be solved much more efficiently by using a spreadsheet program, such as Excel, but we will proceed by using formulas.

The present value of CCA tax savings and the present value of the ending cash flow will be the same for parts a., b., and c., so we solve for these items first.

$$C_0 = \$1,000,000$$

$$CF_0 = C_0 + \Delta NWC_0 + OC = \$1,000,000 + \$0 + \$0 = \$1,000,000$$

$$PV(CCA\ Tax\ Shield) = \left[\frac{(\$1,000,000)(0.20)(0.40)}{0.20+0.18}\right]\left[\frac{1+0.5(0.18)}{1+0.18}\right] - \left[\frac{(\$100,000)(0.20)(0.40)}{0.20+0.18}\right]\left[\frac{1}{(1.18)^{10}}\right]$$

$$= \$194,469 - \$4,022 = \$190,447$$

$$ECF_n = SV_n + \Delta NWC_n = \$100,000 + \$0 = \$100,000$$

$$PV(ECF_n) = \frac{ECF_n}{(1+k)^n} = \frac{\$100,000}{(1.18)^{10}} = \$19,106$$

a. The operating cash flows are expected to grow at a rate of 5 percent per year, because both revenue and expenses are expected to grow at 5 percent per year for 10 years. We *could* estimate all 10 operating cash flows separately and discount each of them. In fact, this would be the appropriate strategy if we were using a spreadsheet. However, when solving this by calculator, a computationally more efficient method is to use a variation of the constant growth version of the DDM, which gives the present value of a "growing perpetuity." The cash flows in this example do not grow at 5 percent forever, but only for 10 years. We can adjust for this fact by subtracting the present value of the growing perpetuity of operating cash flows from years 11 to infinity from the present value of the perpetuity from time 0 to infinity. This leaves us with the PV of the 10-year annuity. In other words,

$$PV(Operating\ CFs) = \frac{CFBT_1(1-T)}{k-g} - \frac{CFBT_{11}(1-T)}{k-g} \times \frac{1}{(1+k)^{10}}$$

$$= \frac{(\$350,000 - \$75,000)(1-0.40)}{0.18-0.05} - \frac{(\$350,000 - \$75,000)(1-0.40)(1.05)^{10}}{0.18-0.05} \times \frac{1}{(1+0.18)^{10}}$$

$$= \frac{\$165,000}{0.13} - \frac{(\$165,000)(1.628895)}{0.13} \times (0.1910645) = \$1,269,231 - \$395,015 = \$874,216$$

Combining the above results, we can find the NPV as follows:

$$NPV = PV(Operating\ CFs) + PV(CCA\ Tax\ Shield) + PV(ECF_n) - CF_0$$

$$= \$874,216 + \$190,447 + \$19,106 - \$1,000,000 = \$83,769$$

Strictly speaking, the firm should go ahead with the project (however, the NPV is not that high, relative to the $1 million required outlay).

b. Revenues display no growth and remain at $350,000 per year for 10 years. Expenses start at $100,000 (not $75,000) and grow at 7 percent per year thereafter.

The beginning cash flow, tax shield, and ending cash flow calculations are not affected, only the operating cash flows, so we redo those here. Notice that revenues and expenses now grow at different rates, so we must consider each separately.
The PV(Operating CFs) = $943,758 − $340,444 = $603,314, which is well below

$$PV(\text{Operating Revenues}) = \frac{Rev_1(1-T)}{k-g} - \frac{Rev_{11}(1-T)}{k-g} \times \frac{1}{(1+k)^{10}}$$

$$= \frac{(\$350{,}000)(1-0.40)}{0.18-0} - \frac{(\$350{,}000)(1-0.40)(1.00)^{10}}{0.18-0} \times \frac{1}{(1+0.18)^{10}}$$

$$= \frac{\$210{,}000}{0.18} - \frac{(\$210{,}000)(1.0)}{0.18} \times (0.1910645) = \$1{,}166{,}667 - \$222{,}909 = \$943{,}758$$

$$PV(\text{Operating Costs}) = \frac{Cost_1(1-T)}{k-g} - \frac{Cost_{11}(1-T)}{k-g} \times \frac{1}{(1+k)^{10}}$$

$$= \frac{(\$100{,}000)(1-0.40)}{0.18-0.07} - \frac{(\$100{,}000)(1-0.40)(1.07)^{10}}{0.18-0.07} \times \frac{1}{(1+0.18)^{10}}$$

$$= \frac{\$60{,}000}{0.11} - \frac{(\$60{,}000)(1.967151)}{0.11} \times (0.1910645) = \$545{,}455 - \$205{,}011 = \$340{,}444$$

the value of \$874,216 calculated in part a. under the previous assumptions. The NPV can now be calculated as

$$NPV = PV(\text{Operating CFs}) + PV(\text{CCA Tax Shield}) + PV(ECF_n) - CF_0$$

$$= \$603{,}314 + \$190{,}447 + \$19{,}106 - \$1{,}000{,}000 = -\$187{,}133$$

Under this scenario, the project would produce a negative NPV and would be unattractive.

c. Revenues grow at 7 percent instead of 5 percent for 10 years. Expenses start at \$75,000 and grow at 3 percent per year thereafter. Once again, the beginning cash flow, the CCA tax shield, and the ending cash flow calculations are not affected. Notice that revenues and expenses now grow at different rates, so we must consider each separately.

$$PV(\text{Operating Revenue}) = \frac{Rev_1(1-T)}{k-g} - \frac{Rev_{11}(1-T)}{k-g} \times \frac{1}{(1+k)^{10}}$$

$$= \frac{(\$350{,}000)(1-0.40)}{0.18-0.07} - \frac{(\$350{,}000)(1-0.40)(1.07)^{10}}{0.18-0.07} \times \frac{1}{(1+0.18)^{10}}$$

$$= \frac{\$210{,}000}{0.11} - \frac{(\$210{,}000)(1.967151)}{0.11} \times (0.1910645) = \$1{,}909{,}091 - \$717{,}537 = \$1{,}191{,}554$$

$$PV(\text{Operating Costs}) = \frac{Cost_1(1-T)}{k-g} - \frac{Cost_{11}(1-T)}{k-g} \times \frac{1}{(1+k)^{10}}$$

$$= \frac{(\$75{,}000)(1-0.40)}{0.18-0.03} - \frac{(\$75{,}000)(1-0.40)(1.03)^{10}}{0.18-0.03} \times \frac{1}{(1+0.18)^{10}}$$

$$= \frac{\$45{,}000}{0.15} - \frac{(\$45{,}000)(1.343916)}{0.15} \times (0.1910645) = \$300{,}000 - \$77{,}032 = \$222{,}968$$

The PV(Operating CFs) = \$1,191,554 −\$222,968 = \$968,586, which is well above the \$874,216 that was calculated under the assumptions in part a.

$$NPV = PV\ (Operating\ CFs) + PV\ (CCA\ Tax\ Shield) + PV\ (ECF_n) - CF_0$$

$$= \$968,586 + \$190,447 + \$19,106 - \$1,000,000 = \$178,139$$

Under this scenario, the project would produce a much larger positive NPV and be more attractive.

CONCEPT REVIEW QUESTIONS

1. Why is it usually more precise to use nominal cash flows and nominal discount rates when evaluating projects?

2. Why might inflation affect cash inflows differently from the way it would affect cash outflows?

Summary

In this chapter, we demonstrate several approaches and guidelines for estimating the future cash flows associated with an investment. The chapter involves a lot of number crunching, because in capex evaluation, there are alternative ways of solving many of the problems. We also introduce several equations that can be used to estimate the present value of future cash flows and differentiate between expansion and replacement decisions. We proceed to discuss how sensitivity analysis, scenario analysis, what-if decision tree analysis, and NPV break-even analysis can be used to determine how variations in estimates can affect the attractiveness of project evaluations. We conclude by illustrating the impact that inflation can have on capital budgeting decisions.

Key Terms

capital cost (C_0), p. 544

decision tree, p. 561

ending (or terminal) after-tax cash flow (ECF_n), p. 548

expansion projects, p. 563

expected annual after-tax cash flows (CF_t), p. 545

externalities, p. 543

initial after-tax cash flow (CF_0), p. 544

marginal or incremental cash flows, p. 542

NPV break-even point, p. 562

opportunity costs, p. 543

real option valuation (ROV), p. 560

replacement projects, p. 564

salvage value (SV_n), p. 548

scenario analysis, p. 557

sensitivity analysis, p. 557

sunk costs, p. 543

Formulas/Equations

(14-1) $CF_0 = C_0 + \Delta NWC_0 + OC$

(14-2) $CF_t = CFBT_t(1 - T) + CCA_t(T)$

(14-3) $ECF(\text{With Tax Implications})_n = SV_n + \Delta NWC_n - [(SV_n - C_0) \times T] - [(SV_n - UCC_n) \times T]$

(14-4) $ECF_n = SV_n + \Delta NWC_n$

(14-5) $NPV = PV(\text{Annual CFs}) + PV(ECF_n) - CF_0$

(14-6) $PV(\text{Operating Cash Flows}) = CFBT(1 - T) \times \left[\dfrac{1 - \dfrac{1}{(1+k)^n}}{k} \right]$

(14-7) $PV(\text{CCA Tax Shield}) = \dfrac{(C_0)(d)(T)}{d + k} \times \dfrac{(1 + 0.5k)}{(1+k)} - \dfrac{(SV_n)(d)(T)}{(d+k)} \times \dfrac{1}{(1+k)^n}$

(14-8) $PV(\text{CCA Tax Shield}) = \dfrac{(C_0)(d)(T)}{d + k} \times \dfrac{(1 + 0.5k)}{(1+k)} - \dfrac{(UCC_n)(d)(T)}{(d+k)} \times \dfrac{1}{(1+k)^n} - \dfrac{(SV_n - UCC_n)(T)}{(1+k)^n}$

(14-9) $PV(\text{Capital Gains Taxes Paid}) = \dfrac{(SV_n - C_0)(T)}{(1+k)^n}$

(14-10) $NPV = PV(\text{Operating CFs}) + PV(\text{CCA Tax Shield}) + PV(ECF_n) + PV(\text{Capital Gains Taxes Paid}) - CF_0$

QUESTIONS AND PRACTICE PROBLEMS

Multiple Choice Questions

1. When making capital expenditure decisions, firms should *not* consider which of the following?

    A. After-tax incremental cash flows

    B. Additional working capital requirements

    C. Sunk costs

    D. Opportunity costs

2. Which of the following will yield the same capital expenditure decisions?

   A. Using nominal cash flows and a real discount rate versus using nominal cash flows and a nominal discount rate

   B. Using nominal cash flows and a nominal discount rate versus using real cash flows and a real discount rate

   C. Using real cash flows and a real discount rate versus using real cash flows and a nominal discount rate

   D. Using nominal cash flows and a nominal discount rate versus using real cash flows and a nominal discount rate

3. What is the initial after-tax cash flow (CF_0) of a project given the following information: initial cost = $400,050; R&D costs associated with the project = $10,000; associated opportunity costs = $90,000; *decrease* in inventory = $15,000; installation costs = $5,000.

   A. $480,050

   B. $510,050

   C. $490,050

   D. $520,050

4. Which of the following items is *not* included in the calculation of the ending (or terminal) cash flow (ECF_n)?

   A. Salvage value

   B. The change in inventory levels

   C. The change in accounts receivable levels

   D. Operating cash flows

5. Oak Inc. is planning to purchase new, faster printers to replace its existing printers. The capital cost of the new printers = $300,000. The current market price of the old printers = $50,000. The applicable CCA rate (d) = 20%, the tax rate = 40%, and k = 20%. It is estimated that the new printers could last for 15 years. What is the second-year incremental CCA expense?

   A. $45,000

   B. $55,000

   C. $25,000

   D. $65,000

6. In Question 5, if the project is expected to generate annual revenue of $50,000, while incurring an annual cost of $18,000, what is the second-year after-tax cash flow?

   A. $20,000

   B. $19,200

   C. $37,200

   D. $18,000

7. In Questions 5 and 6, suppose annual revenue starts at $50,000, annual expenses start at $18,000, and both will grow at a rate of 6 percent from year 2 to year 15. What is the present value of operating cash flows for all 15 years?

A. $120,090

B. $115,811

C. $132,000

D. $109,088

8. Which of the following will *not* decrease the present value of the CCA tax shield associated with an investment project?

A. An increase in the personal income tax rate.

B. A decrease in the corporate tax rate.

C. A decrease in the CCA rate.

D. A decrease in the discount rate.

9. Which of the following statements is *false*?

A. CCA recapture occurs when the salvage value is greater than the ending UCC for the asset or asset class.

B. Capital gains occur when the salvage value is greater than the original cost of the asset.

C. CCA recapture is taxable.

D. A terminal loss occurs when the salvage value is greater than the ending UCC for the asset or asset class.

10. What is the terminal cash flow (ECF_n) based on the following information? The release of additional inventory tied up = $2,000; salvage value = $10,000; UCC = $20,000; initial cost ($C_0$) = $35,000; T = 40%. Assume the asset class will remain open.

A. $12,000

B. $16,000

C. $8,000

D. $14,000

Practice Problems

Easy

11. Jensen's Juice Bar is considering purchasing a new blender. Indicate which of the following statements is a relevant consideration in the "new blender" decision:

A. Last year Jensen's spent $500 on a new blender.

B. Customers would prefer to have their juice made on the new blender and won't buy juice produced on the old one.

C. The manager of the juice bar just got a raise.

D. The juice bar's tax rate is 29 percent.

E. The juice bar's monthly rent is $500.

F.   If Jensen's buys a blender there will be no space for a coffee maker.

G.   The new blender is blue and blue is your favourite colour.

12. The ScatterBrained Consultants, a subsidiary of the ScatterBrained Brokers, have provided the Absent Minded Profs with the following information. Complete the table assuming that the project is in its fifth year.

	Tax rate	Annual Cash flow before taxes	Discount rate	CCA rate	PV of operating cash flows
A	24%	$5,000	5%	35%	
B	43%	$3,000	10%	24%	
C	36%	$8,000	8%	19%	
D	50%	$15,000	15%	30%	
E	15%	$9,000	36%	36%	

13. Prepare a schedule of the annual capital cost allowance for a major project. The initial investment is $50,000, the tax rate is 27 percent, and the CCA rate is 35 percent. Determine the amount of CCA allowed each year. Assume that the item will continue in use for more than four years.

End of Year	Opening UCC balance	CCA	Closing UCC balance
0			
1			
2			
3			
4			

14. Complete the following table provided by the ScatterBrained Consultants. Assume that the asset class is left open, and/or the salvage value is less than the UCC for the entire class.

	CCA rate	Tax rate	Discount rate	Initial investment	Salvage value	Project life (n)	PV(CCA Tax shields)
A	15%	35%	10%	$1,000	$0	5	
B	20%	40%	14%	$1,200	$500	4	
C	25%	35%	5%	$5,000	$1,000	8	
D	40%	45%	12%	$3,000	$200	10	
E	30%	50%	8%	$4,000	$300	14	
F	20%	35%	15%	$1,000	$500	7	
G	10%	27%	6%	$9,000	$0	9	

15. Which of the following items, relating to working capital, would be considered a cash inflow or outflow when evaluating a project (and why):

A. Increase in inventory

B. Increase in accounts payable

C. Increase in accounts receivable

16. The KRZ Company has hired the Absent Minded Profs to help evaluate several projects. The firm's tax rate is 40 percent and the appropriate discount rate is 10 percent. The projects are independent. Each asset class is large and continues after the project terminates. KRZ is not capital constrained. Which of the following projects do you recommend to KRZ and why?

Project	Initial investment	Annual pre-tax operating cash flows	Salvage value	CCA rate	Length of project
A	$4,000	$2,000	$0	30%	3 years
B	$4,000	$3,000	$0	30%	3 years
C	$8,000	$3,000	$500	30%	6 years
D	$8,000	$3,200	$500	30%	4 years
E	$12,000	$1,400	$750	20%	30 years
F	$12,000	$1,600	$750	20%	10 years
G	$16,000	$1,700	$1,500	20%	20 years
H	$16,000	$3,000	$1,000	20%	10 years

17. The Java Cafe Company has hired the Absent Minded Profs to help evaluate several projects. The firm's tax rate is 45 percent and the appropriate discount rate is 8 percent. The projects are independent. Each asset class consists only of the project asset and will be terminated at the end of the project. Java is not capital constrained. Which of the following projects do you recommend to Java and why?

Project	Initial investment	Annual pre-tax operating cash flows	Salvage value	CCA rate	Length of project
A	$40,000	$15,000	$30,000	10%	3 years
B	$40,000	$15,000	$25,000	10%	3 years
C	$90,000	$20,000	$50,000	30%	5 years
D	$85,000	$35,200	$65,000	30%	6 years

18. What is the difference between sensitivity analysis and scenario analysis?

19. The KRZ Company has hired the Absent Minded Profs to help evaluate several projects. The firm's tax rate is 40 percent and the appropriate discount rate is 10 percent. The projects are independent. Each asset class is small and will be terminated at the end of each project. KRZ is not capital constrained. Which of the following projects do you recommend to KRZ and why?

Medium

Project	Initial investment	Annual pre-tax operating cash flows	Salvage value	CCA rate	Length of project
A	$4,000	$2,000	$500	30%	3 years
B	$4,000	$3,000	$500	30%	3 years
C	$8,000	$3,000	$1,500	30%	6 years
D	$8,000	$3,200	$1,500	30%	4 years
E	$12,000	$1,400	$1,750	20%	30 years
F	$12,000	$1,600	$2,750	20%	10 years
G	$16,000	$1,700	$3,500	20%	20 years
H	$16,000	$3,000	$3,000	20%	10 years

20. You are trying to decide whether or not to go to graduate school. If you get a job right after you get your bachelor's degree, you expect to earn $40,000 a year and you expect your salary to increase by 5 percent a year for the next 40 years. If you go to graduate school, you will spend four more years at school. The tuition and books are expected to cost $8,000 a year. Assume living expenses are $15,000 a year. When you graduate you expect to start at a higher salary that will increase by 7 percent a year. However, you will only be able to work for 36 years. Your savings earn 4 percent a year.

   A. What is the minimum post-graduate school starting salary you will require to make going to graduate school a positive NPV project? (Note: we are not considering the non-monetary benefits of a higher education.)

   B. How will your answer change if you have to borrow $40,000 at the start of graduate school to finance your education? Assume that the loan will only have to be repaid after you graduate. The interest rate on the loan is 9 percent and it must be repaid in equal installments over the first 5 years after graduation.

21. You are trying to decide whether to continue renting an apartment or to buy a house. In 20 years you plan on leaving Canada and moving to a warm tropical island and would like to have as much money as possible. You have just won $25,000 on the lottery and will be able to use that money for a down payment. At the moment, your rent is $700 a month and you expect it to increase by 1% a year. The long-term forecast for housing in your area is that house prices are expected to rise at a rate of 5 percent a year for the next 20 years. With $25,000 down, you are able to obtain a 5-year $250,000 mortgage at 7 percent, compounded monthly and amortized over 20 years (the value of the house you are considering is $275,000). Every five years you will have to renegotiate the mortgage and you expect interest rates to increase by 50 basis points (1/2 a percentage point) each time. Assume zero taxes.

   A. If you expect to earn 10 percent on your investments, should you buy a house or continue to rent? (Suggestion: use Excel to solve this problem.)

   B. Would your answer change if you only expected to earn 4 percent on your investments?

22. Your boss is very puzzled by the finance courses in his MBA program. He has learned that "Cash Flow is King," but notices that the capital budgeting problems spend a lot of time and effort dealing with depreciation and CCA but not with interest expenses. He knows that depreciation and CCA are non-cash expenses, and he knows that interest is definitely a cash expense. He would like an explanation of why he needs to bother with depreciation and CCA and not with interest expense.

23. The Absent Minded Profs are competing with the Clueless Consultants for a job. The potential client has provided the following information on a hypothetical project: initial cost = $500,000; building renovation = $600,000; building can not be rented due to the project (currently the building is vacant). Clueless Consultants have made the following statement to the Board of Directors:

    We have conducted an extensive analysis of the project and have concluded that your decision should consider the initial cost of $500,000 only. The $600,000 spent on renovation does not affect future cash flow; therefore we can ignore it. The potential rental revenue should be ignored also, as the building is currently empty and therefore is not a cost of this project.

    The Board of Directors has asked for your comments on Clueless Consultants' statement.

24. The Absent Minded Professors are evaluating a project for a small manufacturing firm. The firm has provided the following data—the initial cost of the project is $2,500; CCA rate is 10 percent; tax rate is 25 percent and the cash flow in the first year is $700. Cash flows are expected to increase at 5 percent a year for four years. At the end of the fourth year, the project will end and the machinery acquired to start the project will be scrapped (zero salvage). The asset class is large and will continue. The appropriate discount rate is 7 percent.

    A. Calculate the NPV of this project.

    B. The Professors have also obtained the following information about the best and worst case scenarios. In the best case, the cash flow in the first year will be $900 and will grow at 8 percent a year. In the worst case, the cash flow in the first year will be $300 and will grow at 2 percent a year. The best case was presented above. The probability of the worst case is 30 percent, best case is 15 percent, and base case is 55 percent. Calculate the expected NPV of the project.

    C. The Professors are not very confident about the growth rate assumption and the initial cash flow estimate. Conduct a sensitivity analysis to assess the impact of possible errors in those estimates.

    D. Using the base case estimates, determine the NPV break-even initial cash flow.

25. Malcolm, the young reporter, has returned with another question. He has observed that the BathGate Company, a shareholder wealth maximizing company, has just made an investment that appears to have a negative NPV. Malcolm is very puzzled about why a company would undertake a negative NPV project. Assume that the NPV of the cash flows is in fact negative and the project is actually shareholder wealth maximizing. What aspect of the project is Malcolm not considering?

26. The BathGate Group has just completed their analysis of a project. The CFO has presented the following information to the Board of Directors:

    The initial cost of the project is $15,000. Sales are expect to be 10,000 units in year one and are expected to grow by 5 percent per year forever. In year one, we expect to sell units for $3 each and foresee no real change in unit price. Variable and fixed costs are zero.

    The firm's required rate of return is 8 percent. The corporate tax rate is 30 percent. Assume the CCA rate is zero.

    A. Calculate the NPV of this project if there is zero inflation forecast.
    B. Calculate the NPV of this project if inflation is forecasted to be 2 percent per year. Assume the required rate of return is nominal.
    C. Calculate the NPV of this project if inflation is forecasted to be 2 percent per year and the firm requires a real rate of return of 8 percent.

27. Summarize all the cash flows that cannot be used in the capital budgeting process and explain the reasons.

28. Calculate the initial cash flows (CF_0) for the following two projects. Which project has a larger CF_0?

    A. Project A: equipment purchase price = $200,000; installation cost = $5,000; extra working capital requirement = $50,500
    B. Project B: machine purchase price = $120,500; shipping cost = $10,000; decrease in working capital = $20,000; opportunity cost = $80,500.

29. Describe how CCA recapture and CCA terminal losses occur.

30. Assuming that the asset class is terminated, calculate the present value of the CCA tax shield using the following information.

    A. C_0 = $300,000; CCA rate (d) = 0.3; T = 0.4; RF = 4.5%; project beta = 1.2; market risk premium = 10%; SV_n = $35,000; UCC_n = $55,000; The project has a 5-year life.
    B. Calculate the PV (CCA tax shield) if the asset class remains open.

31. Calculate the present value of operating cash flows given the following information:

    CFBT = $195,000; T = 40%; the project will last for 6 years. The project has 1.5 percent extra risk premium compared to the firm's cost of capital. The firm has 30 percent debt at a cost of 6 percent, 50 percent common equity at a cost of 12 percent, and the rest of them are preferred shares at 8 percent.

32. Briefly state the application of Real Option Valuation (ROV).

33. Brigid Co. has the following potential project:

    Land purchase price = $1,000,000, machine price = $600,000; Additional working capital requirement = $50,000. Cash flows will be generated at year end. Rev_1 = $250,000 and grows at 5 percent each year for 5 years, while $cost_1$ = $100,000 and grows at 4 percent. At the end of the project, the assets can be sold for $20,000, while the additional inventory that was tied up will be released. The applicable CCA rate = 30 percent. The tax rate = 45%, and RF = 4.5%; $\beta_{project}$ = 1.5; ER_M = 9.5%. The ending UCC = $124,500.

Calculate the NPV of the project if the asset class remains open upon termination of the project. Decide whether or not Brigid Co. should accept the project.

34. Calculate the NPV in Problem 33 assuming a best case of the following: project life = 20 years; $\beta_{project}$ = 0.8; SV_n = $100,000; Rev_1 = $500,000.

Difficult

35. The Clueless Consultants have presented the following statement to the Board of Directors of the BigCo:

When comparing two mutually exclusive projects, we only need to consider the NPV. When the two projects have different lives, we recommend comparing the NPV/life (i.e., NPV divided by the number of years) ratios of the projects and choose the project with the highest ratio. The NPV/life ratio reflects the average annual increase in shareholder value expected from the project.

The Chairman of the Board is not convinced and has asked the Absent Minded Professors to review this statement. Explain to the Chairman why the Clueless' approach to dealing with projects of different lives is incorrect. Provide a numerical demonstration (the Chairman likes numbers!) to support your arguments.

36. Consider the following scenario and decide whether La Presse should replace its current printing press with a new one:

Currently La Presse has a printing press in its plant which costs $5,000 a year in maintenance. The maintenance costs are expected to increase by $1,000 a year for the next 5 years. At the end of the 5 years, the machine will be scrapped and the salvage value will be zero. The press was fully depreciated 8 years ago. The current press has a unique capability to print very large certificates in addition to the regular printing. The revenue from the certificate business is expected to be $1,500 per year for the next 5 years.

A replacement machine is available at a cost of $25,000 with a life expectancy of 5 years. At the end of the 5 years the salvage value is expected to be $5,000. The CCA rate for the machine is 20 percent. Annual maintenance costs of the new machine are $500 per year.

The company is expected to be very profitable in the future. The real risk-free rate is 2 percent, inflation is expected to remain at 3 percent for the next 5 years, and the appropriate real discount rate for risky cash flows is 7 percent. The tax rate is 34 percent.

37. XK Radio has hired the Professors to help in the assessment of a project to launch a satellite to deliver a 24/7 infomercial radio station to the world. The satellite costs $500 million and has a CCA rate of 35 percent. The satellite is expected to last 10 years and then burn up in the earth's atmosphere. XK does not expect to replace the satellite and the asset class will terminate in 10 years. The launch is expected to take place in two years and will cost $5 million. Satellite launches are risky undertakings and there is a 40 percent chance that the rocket taking the satellite into space will explode on take-off. If the launch fails, XK will close the business, as they will only have $50 million of cash left and will be unable to acquire another satellite.

A terrestrial (land-based) infomercial ratio station is expected to generate annual pre-tax operating cash flows of $50 million per year while a satellite-based system is expected to generate operating cash flows of –$25 million for the first 3 years after the satellite goes up, and $150 million per year for the next 7 years. The initial startup costs for both terrestrial and satellite-based stations is the same: $50 million (CCA rate = 45%, zero salvage value). Due to licensing restrictions, XK must decide now whether it will be a satellite-based or land-based infomercial station. Radio stations can only operate in one area—terrestrial or space, not both.

The tax rate for XK is 35 percent. The appropriate discount rate for XK is 20 percent.

A   Do you recommend that XK invest in the satellite launch project?

B. Describe how your analysis would change if the licensing restriction allowed XK to decide terrestrial/space in 2 years.

38. The CFO of the CanGold Company is considering investing in a gold mine in Mongolia. The mine will cost $200 million to get into production and will last for one year. At the end of one year it is expected to produce 1 million ounces of gold. The price of gold is expected to be $500 an ounce in one year (the forward price). The current price of gold is $300 an ounce. Fixed costs of production are $50 million and variable costs are $250 per ounce. Assume no taxes or CCA. The appropriate discount rate for the mine is 15 percent. Risk-free borrowing and lending is available at a rate of 3 percent per year.

A. Based on NPV, should CanGold invest in the Mongolian gold mine?

B. If in one year, we know that the price of gold will be either $200 an ounce or $850 per ounce

   A. Describe how having the choice of closing the mine can change the value of the asset.

   B. Describe how the volatility of the price of gold could increase the value of the mine.

   C. Draw the decision tree for this project.

   D. Value the mine as a call option on gold (hint: use the arbitrage arguments behind the binomial option pricing model. Think of the mine as a financial security).

39. The Absent Minded Professors have been hired as consultants to the XrayGlasses Corp (XGC). XGC is in the process of deciding whether to invest in a new production facility. The new facility will enable it to produce and sell X-ray machines to airports. The manufacturing and marketing process is not very different from their current line of business. The management of XGC has produced certain estimates about the new facility. Review the estimates to:

A. Determine the NPV of this project to the XrayGlasses Corporation.

B. Make a recommendation, with supporting arguments, to the management of XrayGlasses about the project.

   • Cost of the machinery: $45,000; Installation costs: $15,000

   • Life of the project: 5 years; the expected salvage value of the machine is $2,000

- An environmental assessment of the building site: $200,000
- Charles LeCrook has offered XrayGlasses $150,000 for the building. XrayGlasses paid $45,000 for the building 10 years ago and spent $50,000 last month on renovations.
- The CCA rate on the machinery is 25 percent and there are other assets in the pool. At the end the project, we do not expect to close the pool. The firm's tax rate is 35 percent.
- Currently work-in-progress inventory is $65,000. This is expected to increase by $2,000 immediately and to remain at that level for the life of the project. This inventory will be sold at the end of the project.
- Currently accounts receivable are $15,000. This is expected to increase by $3,000 by the end of year 1. The higher level of accounts receivable is expected to continue until the end of the project at which time the accounts will be paid in full.
- Currently accounts payable are $25,000. This is expected to increase by $2,000 by the end of year 1. The higher level of accounts payable is expected to continue until the end of the project at which time the accounts will be paid in full.
- XGC expects to sell 25 machines in the first year, 30 in year 2, and 40 machines per year for years 3 to 4.
- Variable costs are expected to be $5,000 per machine; the expected sales price is $50,000.
- Annual fixed costs for the firm are currently $900,000 per year and will rise to $930,000 during the project.
- Currently the firm sells 400 pairs of X-ray glasses to airport security guards each year. These sales are expected to disappear when the X-ray machines enter service. The price of a pair of glasses is $550 and the cost of production is $50.
- The company will have to borrow to finance the start-up of the project. The expected interest expense is $5,000 per year. Each year the firm will have to repay $3,000 of the principal of the loan. Overall, the firm expects to remain at its optimal capital structure.
- Currently the firm pays $25,000 in dividends. This is expected to increase to $28,000 during the life of the project.
- The YTM of the firm's debt is 5 percent, the cost of equity is 14 percent, and the WACC is 10 percent.

40. GG Inc. has a project that requires purchases of capital assets costing $40,000 and additional raw material inventory of $2,000. Shipping and installation costs are $1,500. GG Inc. estimated that the project would generate an annual operating *after-tax* cash flow of $5,600 for six years at each year end. At the end of the project, the assets can be sold for $4,000, while the additional inventory that was tied up will be released. The assets are in asset class 9, which has a CCA rate of 30 percent. The tax rate = 40%, and $k = 15\%$. The ending UCC = $8,469. Calculate the NPV of the project if the asset class is closed on termination of the project. Decide whether or not GG Inc. should accept the project.

41. Repeat Problem 40 but assume that the project would generate annual revenue of $70,000 and annual costs of $40,000 for six years. Also, assume the asset class will remain open.

42. Repeat Problem 41 by assuming that the asset class will be closed at the end of six years.

43. Calculate the NPV of the project described in Problem 41, but assume that the discount rate has changed based on the following information: RF = 3.4%; project Beta = 1.2; the market risk premium = 5.5%; and the firm is financed entirely by equity. What is the percentage change in the NPV because of the change in the discount rate? Decide whether or not the project should be accepted.

44. Calculate the operating cash flow NPV break-even point for the project defined in Problem 40 by using a 15 percent discount rate.

45. GG Inc. is now considering replacing some old equipment. The market price of the old equipment is $50,000 and the salvage value at the end of five years is $15,000. The new equipment will cost $100,000 and could be sold at the end of five years for $35,000. An additional $4,000 in working capital is required and will be released at the end of five years. The new equipment is estimated to generate $10,000 in before-tax operating income, compared with $6,000 for the old one. Assume that $T = 40\%$ and $k = 15\%$. Both the new and old equipment belong to class 10, which has a CCA rate of 30 percent, and the asset class will remain open at the end of five years. Estimate the NPV of the replacement decision and decide whether or not replacement should occur.

46. Calculate the present value of the operating cash flows if the revenue of a project grows at 5 percent, while expense grows at 4 percent, given that $Revenue_1 = \$15,000$ and $Expense_1 = \$7,000$. Assume the firm is all-equity financed, RF = 8%, project Beta = 0.8, the market risk premium = 5.5%, and $T = 40\%$. The project is expected to last for eight years.

47. A. Describe how CCA expenses change through the life of a project.

    B. Given $C_0 = \$250,000$; CCA rate = 0.2; tax rate = 40%; and Year 2 operating income (OI) = $150,000, calculate the cash flow in Year 2.

Buyer Wanted

Silverwing Energy Inc., an Alberta-based junior exploration and production company, announced on February 6, 2007, that it was actively looking for a buyer, a merger, a recapitalization, or the sale of some of its assets. Silverwing's advisors, Westwind Partners Inc. and Orion Securities Inc., along with a special committee formed by the company's board of directors, will together seek out interested parties. A data room will be available at the company and the company said it plans to issue a confidential information memorandum detailing its operations, finances, and exploration and development opportunities. Silverwing explores for and produces natural gas and crude oil in Alberta and northeastern British Columbia. Junior exploration companies typically look for buyers with more experienced management teams and that are large enough to handle increased production demands.

Source: "Silverwing Initiates Value Maximization Process." Globe Investor website: www.globeinvestor.com, February 6, 2007.

Mergers and Acquisitions

Learning Objectives

After reading this chapter, you should understand the following:

1. The different types of acquisitions
2. How a typical acquisition proceeds
3. What differentiates a friendly from a hostile acquisition
4. Different forms of combinations of firms
5. Where to look for acquisition gains
6. How accounting may affect the acquisition decision

INTRODUCTION

Chapters 13 and 14 discussed the issues surrounding the typical capital expenditure decisions of firms. We focused our discussion on typical investments that would help the existing firm grow "from within." However, firms can also grow by acquiring other firms, or by acquiring selected assets from other firms. Sometimes an entirely new entity is formed, and sometimes the "acquiring" firm simply becomes larger and the "target" firm ceases to exist. In this chapter, we illustrate how decisions about mergers and acquisitions can be evaluated on a financial basis using standard discounted cash flow valuation techniques.

15.1 Types of Takeovers

takeover the transfer of control from one ownership group to another

Few topics generate more interest from the financial media than that of corporate **takeovers**, which refers to the transfer of control from one ownership group to another. Takeovers can occur in several manners, which are described below.

acquisition the purchase of one firm by another

The terms "mergers," "acquisitions," and "takeovers" are often used in different ways. An **acquisition** occurs when one firm (the *acquiring firm* or *bidder*) completely absorbs another firm (the *target* firm). Under this arrangement, the acquiring firm retains its identity, while the acquired firm ceases to exist. Such a situation occurred when the Canadian firm ATI was purchased by the U.S. firm Advanced Micro Devices (AMD) on October 25, 2006. The acquisition of ATI by AMD was announced as a transaction valued at approximately US$5.4 billion. As the AMD news release stated the result is:

> A new and more formidable company, determined to drive growth, innovation and choice for its customers, particularly in the commercial and mobile computing segments and in the rapidly growing consumer electronics market. Combining technologies, people, and complementary strengths, AMD plans to deliver in 2007 customer-centric platforms for the benefit of customers who want to collaborate in the development of differentiated solutions.[1]

Even though the news release announced that the two companies were "joining together" and that it was a "new company," the fact is that AMD purchased ATI. We know this because ATI's shares were delisted from the TSX and on AMD's website, ATI is listed as the "graphics and media processes" division within AMD. Thus the key idea in an acquisition is the disappearance of the purchased firm as all senior management functions reside with the acquirer.

merger the combination of two firms into a new legal entity

In contrast, a **merger** is usually the combination of two firms into a new legal entity. Such a situation notionally occurred when on May 7, 1998, Daimler-Benz and Chrysler announced that they were combining as a "merger of equals" worth

---

[1] "AMD and ATI to Create Processing Powerhouse," AMD press release, July 24, 2006. Retrieved from www.amd.com.

almost US$40 billion. The combination of the third-largest U.S. car company with the prestigious maker of Mercedes Benz cars was obviously big news and the fact that the new company's name was a hybrid of the merging firms' names indicated that it was an integration of the two companies, with neither dominant. For a time it appeared as if nothing had changed, until 2003, when the *Detroit News* announced that the merger was in fact a takeover or acquisition of Chrysler by Daimler. This sparked multiple lawsuits, since it was clear that, like ATI within AMD, Chrysler was becoming a division within Daimler and effective control and decision-making would be in Germany.

What this discussion indicates is the elasticity in the terms "merger," "acquisition," and "takeover." The AMD takeover of ATI was clearly an acquisition right from the start, with ATI ceasing to exist. The furor over the Chrysler acquisition by Daimler was that it was announced as a merger, with the implication that the new company would involve an integration of the two with shared responsibilities and management, when in fact it was an acquisition that left Daimler in charge. Shortly after, most of the senior Chrysler management left.

One key consideration in classifying acquisitions and mergers is how the deal is financed. Most acquisitions are made through **cash transactions** where the shareholders in the target company receive cash for their shares. We will briefly discuss securities laws later. When one company acquires another, the approval of the target company's shareholders is required, since they have to agree to sell their shares. However, in an acquisition, the shareholders of the *acquiring* company do not normally have to give their approval. Buying another company is regarded as the same as buying a new piece of equipment or any other purchase. Only if there is some specific provision in the company's charter do the shareholders of the acquiring firm get to vote on whether or not the company should make the acquisition.

> **cash transaction** the receipt of cash for shares by shareholders in a target company

The alternative to a cash transaction is a **share transaction**, where the acquiring company offers shares or some combination of cash and shares to the target company's shareholders. In contrast to a cash transaction, a share transaction often requires the approval of the acquiring firm's shareholders. Whether it does or does not require approval depends on whether the firm has a limit on the authorized share capital. If the firm's authorized share capital is limited to, say, 3 million shares and it wants to offer shares that exceed this limit, then shareholder approval is needed. To get around this, in recent years most companies have sought and received shareholder approval to issue an unlimited number of shares. However, this does point to the most basic distinction between a merger and an acquisition.

> **share transaction** the offer by an acquiring company of shares or a combination of cash and shares to the target company's shareholders

Since in a merger a new company is created, both sets of shareholders have to agree to exchange their existing shares for shares in the new company. In this way a genuine merger is a transaction that requires both sets of shareholders to approve the transaction. In Canada this process is called an **amalgamation**. The two companies approve an amalgamation agreement and a special meeting of the shareholders is called to vote on the agreement. Under the Canada Business Corporations Act (CBCA), 21 days' notice is given for this special meeting and, since the shareholders have to vote, all the normal rules for proxy statements and other information are invoked. The basic rule is that two-thirds of the shareholders of both amalgamating firms have to approve the special resolution to amalgamate.[2] This can sometimes result in tense battles as dissident shareholders

> **amalgamation** a genuine merger in which both sets of shareholders must approve the transaction

---

[2] Note that this is two-thirds of all the shareholders including groups that do not normally have the right to vote. Moreover, sometimes they have the right to vote as a class, so a small group can defeat an amalgamation proposal.

refuse to support an agreement crafted by the two sets of managers. An amalgamation is also used when the acquirer has purchased all the shares in the target, but in this case, since it owns all the shares, the process is a formality.

An amalgamation can also become a tense situation after a firm has partially completed a takeover. Sometimes the acquirer can end up with a majority of the shares, say 70 percent, so that it knows that it can get the two-thirds majority for an amalgamation and yet there are still 30 percent of the shares outstanding held by dissident shareholders who have not agreed to sell their shares. This is a special form of acquisition called a **going private transaction** or an **issuer bid**.

going private transaction or issuer bid a special form of acquisition where the purchaser already owns a majority stake in the target company

These sorts of transactions have been common in Canada, since there were many Canadian companies where the majority of the shares were owned by another company and only a minority were owned by Canadian shareholders. Imperial Oil, for example, has a majority owner in Exxon. Similarly, companies like Dupont Canada, Shell Oil Canada, Sears Canada, Goodyear Canada, Ford Canada, and so on, all have had a majority of their shares owned by their U.S. parents. In this case, the minority of shares traded in the Canadian market were not the result of failed takeover bids, but the desire of U.S. companies to keep a public "float" of the shares in the hands of Canadian shareholders. This motivation dropped in importance after Canada signed the Free Trade Agreement (FTA) with the United States and the economies became more integrated. A side effect of the FTA was that U.S. multinationals wanted to become more integrated and buying out the Canadian minority shareholders removed an obstacle to this.[3]

Regardless of how a public minority of shareholder is created, the issues and principles are the same. When a controlling shareholder seeks approval for an amalgamation, special rules kick in. The reason for this is the presumption that the controlling shareholder knows much more accurately what the true value of the shares really is and will abuse this position unless safeguards are in place. The critical safeguards are that a "majority of the minority" shareholders has to approve the special resolution to amalgamate the two companies and that there be a **fairness opinion**. A fairness opinion is an opinion by an independent expert about the value of a firm's shares, based on an external valuation. These valuations are particularly difficult given that with a controlling shareholder there is little possibility of any other party buying the shares!

fairness opinion an opinion provided by an independent expert regarding the true value of a firm's shares based on an external evaluation

A good example of this principle is Sears, Roebuck and Co., which on December 5, 2005, announced that it would make a bid for the 46 percent of Sears Canada that it did not own at $16.86 a share. Sears' initial aim was to buy enough shares so that it would own 90 percent, since under Ontario securities law, it can squeeze out less than 10 percent of minority shareholders, who are then forced to accept the offer that has been accepted by the other shareholders. This rule prevents a "holdup" problem that might occur if the last shareholder asks for a ridiculously high price. However, since the offer was an insider bid, Sears Canada set up a committee of six independent members of the board of directors to evaluate the bid. They hired Genuity Capital Markets to do a fairness opinion, which came in at a range of $19.00 to $22.25 a share—well above the offer from Sears Roebuck. On this basis, the independent directors unanimously rejected the offer from their own company's parent and also announced that they would not stand for re-election at the May 2006 annual general meeting.[4]

---

[3] Under the CBCA, directors of a Canadian company have to act in the best interests of the company as a whole, and not just the majority shareholder. This restricted the ability of the U.S. parent to integrate the Canadian subsidiary into its North American operations.

[4] Given the directors' decision, they probably would not have been nominated for re-election.

In March 2006, Sears Roebuck announced that it had received only 9.5 percent of the 46 percent of the Sears Canada shares it did not hold. It also announced that instead of trying to buy the shares directly it would seek a statutory amalgamation at a special meeting of shareholders. In this case all it needed to amalgamate Sears Canada with Sears Roebuck was the two-thirds necessary for an amalgamation plus a majority of the minority shareholders. It also sweetened the price marginally to $18. However, a new valuation by Genuity Capital reiterated its valuation and judgements on both sides.

This situation deteriorated when it was discovered that Sears' Canadian financial advisors had entered into a *lock-up agreement* to sell shares controlled by them to Sears Roebuck without disclosing this. The Ontario Securities Commission (OSC) was asked to rule on this and decided that these shares could not be counted as part of the "majority of the minority" rule, a decision that was upheld by the Ontario Divisional Court. At the time of writing, Sears Roebuck was still trying to buy Sears Canada cheaply, knowing that it controls the Craftsman and Kenmore brand names and there were no other potential buyers. Since Sears Canada's stock price was $4 over the bid price from Sears Roebuck, it was doomed not to succeed.

15.2 Securities Legislation

The previous discussion on takeovers highlights the role of securities legislation in determining what can be done and when it can be done. Securities legislation is relevant since it governs an exchange of shares by the target company's shareholders and their right to receive full value for their shares. We will examine other aspects of securities laws later when discussing new issues of securities, but the main thing to remember is that this is a provincial responsibility and there are slight differences across the provinces. However, the Ontario Securities Act, administered by the OSC, embodies many features that are common to all jurisdictions.

There are several critical shareholder percentages that investors have to be aware of:

1. 10%: early warning

2. 20%: takeover bid

3. 50.1%: control

4. 66.7%: amalgamation

5. 90%: minority squeeze-out

The 10 percent early warning threshold (5 percent in the United States) is the level of shareholding by any one owner that requires a report to be sent to the OSC. This allows the company to know who owns its shares and whether a significant block has been bought by a potential acquirer. Once a shareholder holds 20 percent of shares, they cannot buy any more shares in the open market unless they make a takeover bid (we will discuss this in more detail later). The 50.1 percent ownership level then gives a company control so that it can call a special meeting of the shareholders (5 percent shareholding needed for this) and can change the membership of the board of directors (BOD). Unlike in the United States, members of the BOD can be removed without cause, so the majority shareholder can change management and take control of the firm's affairs.[5]

As we have just seen, a firm can seek a special meeting of shareholders to vote on an amalgamation, which needs support from owners of 67 percent of the shares, but this can be disputed by a majority of the minority shareholders. Finally, following a takeover bid, if the firm owns 90 percent of its shares, it can force the minority of the shareholders to sell their shares at the takeover price. This prevents a small minority from frustrating a bid that is fair since it has been accepted by the majority of shareholders. Otherwise, a few dissidents could wreak havoc by refusing to sell a small number of shares.

The above share percentage milestones explain a lot of takeover behaviour. Initially most firms will acquire under the 10 percent early warning level and possibly up to the 20 percent level of the target's shares in the open market. This is referred to as obtaining a *toehold*. They do this to acquire the shares at the market price without paying a premium. After acquiring 20 percent, buying any more shares requires a takeover bid, which is an offer to purchase outstanding voting shares of a class of securities to any person or company who is in Ontario where together the offeror's securities constitute in aggregate 20 percent or more of the outstanding securities.

This definition applies to individuals alone or "working in concert with others." Otherwise a company could buy 20 percent itself and then get friendly parties or another subsidiary to buy two more blocks of 20 percent and thereby effect a takeover without making a takeover bid.

Unless the purchase is exempt from the Ontario Securities Act, any further takeover bid must then follow strict rules. A takeover circular, describing the bid, financing, and all relevant information, similar to a prospectus, must be sent to all shareholders for review. The target then has 15 days to circulate a letter indicating acceptance or rejection and the bid has to be open for 35 days from its announcement in the newspaper or the mailing of documents to shareholders. Shareholders then **tender** to the offer by signing the authorizations sent to them, but in the event of a competing offer they can withdraw their acceptance while the competing bid automatically increases the takeover window by 10 days.

The takeover bid does not have to be for 100 percent of the shares. If the bid is for, say, 60 percent, and more shares are tendered, then the acquirer prorates the shares tendered so everyone receives an equal proportion. That is, if 80 percent are tendered and 60 percent are bought, then everyone who has tendered gets to sell 75 percent (60 ÷ 80) of the shares tendered. While the tender offer is outstanding, the acquirer can buy another 5 percent of shares through the facilities of the stock exchange as long as it announces that it intends to do so. Finally the tender offer price cannot be for less than the average price that the acquirer has bought shares for in the previous 90 days. This is to prevent a coercive takeover bid where the acquirer offers one price for the shares needed to get control and then a lower price once they have control. This is called a

tender to sign an authorization accepting a takeover bid made to target company shareholders

---

[5] In the United States, directors have a fixed term and cannot be forcibly removed simply because of a change in ownership. The result is that by staggering membership of the BOD, a firm can prevent a majority owner from immediately changing the board and senior management. As a result it may take several years for a majority owner to change directors and senior managers.

two-part tender offer, which is illegal in Canada since it produces a rush to sell into the higher price at the first stage and "coerces" shareholders.[6]

The basic objective of these rules is to make sure that an acquirer treats all the shareholders fairly and everyone gets the same price. Otherwise there is an economic incentive to lock up shares early at a high price, so that an acquirer has control and can then offer a lower price, knowing that no one else can mount a competing bid. In this way, different classes of shareholders are treated differently and the shares are sold below their true value. As the Sears Roebuck example highlights, once you have control, no one else can bid and there is a temptation to try to buy the remaining shares cheaply without paying a premium price.

As indicated before, all takeovers have to abide by these rules unless they are exempt from the Ontario Securities Act for one of the following reasons. Where there is limited involvement by shareholders in Ontario—say a takeover of a Manitoba company, where there are very few Ontario shareholders—securities legislation in another province (in this case Manitoba) will apply. Securities legislation is concerned with the involvement of the public, so takeovers of private firms are exempt. An acquirer can also buy shares from fewer than five shareholders as long as the premium over the market price is not more than 15 percent. This is to allow the sale of blocks of shares. Finally, and most importantly, a normal course tender offer can be made through a stock exchange as long as no more than 5 percent of the shares are purchased through the exchange over a one-year period. This 5 percent rule allows for **creeping takeovers**, where a company acquires a target over a long period of time by slowly accumulating shares.

> **creeping takeovers** the acquisition of a target company over time by the gradual accumulation of its shares

CONCEPT REVIEW QUESTIONS

1. What is the difference between an acquisition and a merger?
2. What is the majority of the minority rule?
3. What is a takeover circular?
4. What is a creeping takeover?

15.3 FRIENDLY VERSUS HOSTILE TAKEOVERS

Friendly Takeovers

With a knowledge of securities legislation, we can now consider whether an acquisition should be hostile or friendly and discuss how a deal is hammered out. To understand this, consider first the difficulty of valuing a company when an external party only has access to public sources of information. How do you value a small biotech company, for example, when you have no direct information on

---

[6] Coercive two-part tender offers are allowed in the United States.

friendly acquisition the acquisition of a target company that is willing to be taken over

offering memorandum a document describing a target company's important features to potential buyers

data room a place where a target company keeps confidential information about itself for serious potential buyers to consult

confidentiality agreement a document signed by a potential buyer guaranteeing it will keep confidential any information it sees in the data room about a target company

due diligence the process of evaluating a target company by a potential buyer

letter of intent a letter signed by an acquiring company scoping out the terms of agreement of its acquisition, including legal terms

no-shop clause a clause in a letter of intent stating that the target agrees not to find another buyer, demonstrating its commitment to close the transaction

break fee a fee paid to an acquirer or target should the other party terminate the acquisition, often 2.5 percent of the value of the transaction

whether recent lab tests were positive or negative? Similarly, for an oil and gas company or mining firm, it may not be obvious how much potential is left in an oil and gas field or mineral reserve. The obvious thing to do, when faced with this uncertainty, is to go to the target company and ask whether it is interested in being acquired. In this way the acquirer hopes for a **friendly acquisition**.

Friendly acquisitions also start out when the target voluntarily puts itself into play. This can occur for many reasons, but often occurs when the founder is no longer playing a part in the business and it is time for the firm to leave the controlling family and be sold to other interests. Such an incident occurred when CHUM Limited was sold to Bell Globemedia on July 12, 2006, for $1.7 billion. In this case the estate of the founder of CHUM Limited, Allan Waters, agreed to sell its controlling 88.6 percent of the voting shares to Bell Globemedia. At the time of writing, the deal was subject to federal government approval.

If a firm decides to sell itself, it normally consults an investment bank to put together an **offering memorandum** describing the most important features of the company to potential buyers. This offering memorandum is much like an abbreviated prospectus, which will be discussed in detail with respect to securities issues in Chapter 17. Regardless of whether it is the company that decides to sell itself, or an acquirer that approaches it, the company that is willing to be sold has to provide more information so that its fair value can be estimated.

The target firm can disclose more information by setting up a **data room** where it can keep confidential information. When serious acquirers express interest, they can access the data room by signing a **confidentiality agreement**. Not all acquirers will want to sign a confidentiality agreement since normally this restricts the acquirer's freedom of action. Typically the acquirer is prohibited from using the information to damage the target, such as by hiring away key employees or approaching key customers. There is also usually a time limit for these restrictions. Clearly the objective of the confidentiality agreement is to restrict access to important information to serious potential acquirers. This process of evaluating the target is called **due diligence** and is an important part of the acquisition process.

Once the confidential data have been evaluated, if the acquirer goes forward, it normally signs a **letter of intent**. This scopes out the terms of an agreement and allows the acquirer to do the third stage of the due diligence process,[7] where its legal team checks the title for property, terms of contracts, and so on, to make sure that all the claims in the data room documents are actually correct and the firm owns the assets that it says it owns. The letter of intent also usually contains a **no-shop clause**, where the target agrees not to try to find another buyer. In this way, the target shows that it is committed to making the transaction work. There is also usually a termination or **break fee** of 2.5 percent of the value of the transaction.

Break fees have become very controversial. In the Bell Globemedia proposal to purchase CHUM Limited, for example, a $41 million break fee (2.4 percent of the transaction) was negotiated. The justification for the break fee is that once companies get into the final round of due diligence, the expectation is that a deal will be completed. However, despite a no-shop clause, sometimes a com-

---

[7] The first phase is the examination of public information that is usually included in the offering memorandum, the second phase is the provision of confidential documents in the data room, and the final phase is the *serious* verification process.

peting bid does come in. Faced with two alternative offers, the BOD has a *fiduciary* duty to act in the best interests of the shareholders and seek the best possible price. It may then be that the firm that started the process and has committed significant resources to negotiating an agreement finds itself the loser. The break fee is designed to compensate the original acquirer for these costs as well as reward it for generating a competing bid and getting the target shareholders a better price.

Once the final due diligence phase has been completed and everything has worked out to the satisfaction of the acquirer, the final sale agreement is reached and ratified or agreed to by both parties. It is then taken to the shareholders for approval. If it is a private company, that is the end of the story, but for a firm with public shareholders, the deal then goes to the shareholders for approval.

This typical process is sketched in Figure 15-1.

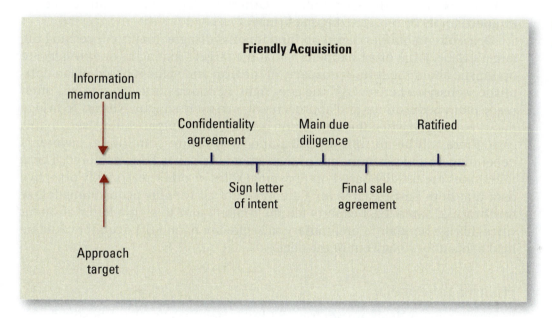

Friendly Acquisition

Information memorandum

Confidentiality agreement

Main due diligence

Ratified

Sign letter of intent

Final sale agreement

Approach target

15-1 FIGURE

Friendly Acquisition

With a friendly transaction there is a lot of scope for structuring the acquisition to the mutual benefit of both parties. The key areas usually involve careful tax planning, legal structuring to avoid certain liabilities, providing milestones for incentive agreements, and the possibility of "cherry picking" for certain more valuable assets. We will discuss each of these in turn.

Careful tax planning is important in any transaction. When an acquisition is made for cash it is always taxable in the hands of the target company shareholders. If the share price has run up significantly, this could mean forcing the shareholders to pay capital gains tax on the appreciation in the value of their shares. On the other hand, a share swap is usually non-taxable. This is why in many smaller acquisitions the target company's shares are swapped for preferred shares in the acquiring company. The target's shareholders, usually the founders, get a steady income from the preferred shares and are relieved from day-to-day concerns about their company. The acquiring firm can then integrate the target into its existing operations.

Tax concerns also often motivate the target company's assets being sold to the acquirer instead of the shares. In an **asset purchase**, the target firm receives

asset purchase a purchase of the firm's assets rather than the firm itself

CAPITAL:

Number of common shares outstanding   0.5m
Invested capital (book values)

Equity	$5m
Debt	$5m

Market value of equity $15m

Valuation Ratios	T1	T1 5-Yr. Avg.	Industry Avg.
Price-earnings (P/E) (trailing)	15.00x	14.5	16.5
Value/EBIT	8.00x	5.5	7.5
Value/EBITDA	6.06x	4.8	6.0
P/Sales	1.50x	1.35	1.6
P/Book value (P/B) (equity)	3.00x	3.00	3.2
Price per unit of output	$15x	14.5	16.0
Return on equity (ROE)	20.00%	16.5%	17.5%

Remember in these ratios that EBIT (earnings before interest and taxes) and EBITDA (earnings before interest, taxes, depreciation, and amortization) belong to all the security holders, not just the shareholders, so these multiples are based on the total market value of the firm; that is, the value of the equity plus the debt. In this case, to get the equity value, we then have to subtract the market value of the debt.[15]

Of course, the actual value ratios for T1 listed above are based on the current market price of T1's common shares, and we cannot use them to value T1 since they just give us back the current value. In order to use the multiples approach to estimate the true value of T1, we would need to estimate "justifiable" P/E ratios drawn from comparables or a bottom-up analysis, as discussed in Chapter 7.

Estimate the value of T1's equity:

a. using the industry averages for the first five valuation ratios presented above

b. using the five-year averages for T1 for the first five valuation ratios presented above

c. using the forward P/E ratio that is calculated based on the assumptions that:

   i. 9 percent is a reasonable cost of equity for T1;
   ii. T1 maintains its present dividend payout ratio; and
   iii. T1's dividends and earnings grow at an annual rate of 6 percent indefinitely

Solution

a. Using P/E ratio: Value = P/E × Net income = 16.5 × $1m = $16.5m

Using V/EBIT ratio: Value = V/EBIT × EBIT − DEBT = 7.5 × $2.5m = $18.75 − $5m = $13.75

Using V/EBITDA ratio: Value = V/EBITDA × EBITDA − DEBT = 6.0 × $3.3m = $19.8m − $5.0m = $14.8m

Using P/Sales ratio: Value = P/Sales × Sales = 1.6 × $10m = $16.0m

Using P/B ratio: Value = P/B × BV = 3.2 × $5m = $16m

---

[15] Often the price-to-sales ratio used may be the total firm market value-to-sales ratio.

The industry average multiples indicate that T1's equity may be currently "undervalued" at $15 million, and it should be valued somewhere around $16 million, depending on which multiple is used.

b. Using P/E ratio: Value = P/E × Net income = 14.5 × $1m = $14.m

Using V/EBIT ratio: Value = V/EBIT × EBIT − DEBT = 6.5 × $2.5m − $5.0 = $8.7m

Using V/EBITDA ratio: Value = V/EBITDA × EBITDA − DEBT = 4.8 × $3.3m −$5.0 = $10.8m

Using P/Sales ratio: Value = P/Sales × Sales = 1.35 × $10m = $13.m

Using P/B ratio: Value = P/B × BV = 3.0 × $5m = $15m

The company's historical (five-year) average multiples indicate that T1's equity should be valued somewhere between $8.75 million and $15.84 million, depending on which multiple is used.

c. The justifiable forward P/E ratio for T1 based on these assumptions can be calculated as follows:

P/E (forward) = Payout ÷ (k − g) = (0.5m ÷ 1.0m) ÷ (0.09 − 0.06) = 0.5 ÷ 0.03 = 16.67

Next year's earnings based on a 6 percent growth rate = ($1m)(1.06) = $1.06m

Value of T1's equity = (P/E)(E_1) = (16.67)($1.06m) = $17.67m

Example 15-1 demonstrates that various valuation models may be used to estimate justifiable multiples, which can then be used to evaluate a target firm. However, in practice, we cannot just "passively" use these ratios, for several reasons. For one thing, the use of different accounting methods can affect many of the items used in the multiples approach. We illustrate how these differences can affect the ratios and the valuation process in the example below.

Example 15-2: Accounting Differences

Consider two companies, A and B, that are identical in sales and profitability, and both have 1 million common shares outstanding. However, their income statements differ significantly as a result of the accounting methods they choose. In particular, their accounting choices differ in the following ways:

i. Firm A uses LIFO to account for inventory, while firm B uses FIFO.[16]

ii. Firm A uses accelerated depreciation method, while firm B uses straight-line depreciation.

iii. Firm A fully funds pension costs, while B reports an unfunded pension liability.

iv. Firm B sells surplus property for a gain to beef up earnings, while A has similar unrealized gains available to it.

---

[16] Canadian firms tend to use FIFO, but U.S. firms tend to use FIFO or LIFO.

The differences in the income statements of A and B are illustrated below:

	A($)	B($)
Sales	10,000,000	10,000,000
Cost of goods sold	6,000,000	6,000,000
Selling & general	1,500,000	1,500,000
LIFO difference[i]	400,000	0
Depreciation[ii]	400,000	300,000
Pension costs[iii]	200,000	50,000
Gain on property sale[iv]		150,000
Earnings before tax	1,500,000	2,300,000
Income tax expense @40%	600,000	920,000
Net income	900,000	1,380,000
Earnings per share	0.90	1.38

Estimate the price of A's and B's shares respectively using a P/E ratio of 15.

Solution

	A	B
Price using P/E ratio of 15×	$13.50	$20.70
Total equity value	$13.5m	$20.7m

Notice that the "only" difference in the companies is their accounting choices, yet we get very different valuations if we blindly use a P/E multiple of 15. This implies the importance of taking such factors into consideration in the valuation process.

Example 15-2 illustrates how different accounting choices can affect income statement items. Of course, a firm's capital structure decisions will also affect valuation ratios, as illustrated in the example below.

Example 15-3: Differing Capital Structures

Consider two companies, C and D, that are identical in sales and operating profitability (as measured by EBIT), but have different capital structures, as depicted below:

	A($)	B($)
EBIT	2,000,000	2,000,000
Interest	500,000	0
EBT	1,500,000	2,000,000
Income taxes (40%)	600,000	800,000
Net income	900,000	1,200,000
Debt (Book value)	10,000,000	0
Equity (Book value)	10,000,000	20,000,000
Equity (Market value)	12,000,000	20,000,000

Calculate the P/E ratio for both companies.

Solution

	A	**B**
P/E ratio	(12,000,000 ÷ 900,000)	(20,000,000 ÷ 1,200,000)
	13.33×	16.66×

Notice the significant difference in P/E ratios that is caused by the fact that A uses $10 million in debt financing while B is all-equity financed. Obviously, capital structure decisions can have a big impact on valuation multiples, as we discuss later when we consider the question of an optimal capital structure.

In order to avoid the problems associated with the multiples approach, we can make adjustments to the financial statements and/or to the multiples we use for valuation purposes. Alternatively, we can use a different valuation framework that avoids some of the problems associated with using multiples. But note that if we have to use a multiple, most corporate valuations focus on the EBITDA and EBIT multiples since they remove the problem with capital structure and focus higher up the income statement and avoid some of the accounting problems that result from firms focusing on the *bottom line* (i.e., net income).

Liquidation Valuation

This approach can be implemented following a process such as the one below:

1. Estimate the liquidation value of current assets based on their "realizable value." For example, if a company's accounts receivables are with good credit-quality firms and most of them are current, it might be reasonable to value them at 80 percent of their book value. This percentage could be lower for firms whose customers were of lower average credit quality, or if they had a large percentage of "overdue" receivables. Similarly, inventory could be valued according to its marketability, etc.

2. Estimate the present market value of tangible assets such as machinery, buildings, and land.

3. Subtract the value of the firm's liabilities from the total estimated liquidation value of all the firm's assets. This represents the liquidation value of the firm.

The liquidation value approach is useful but it can involve several estimates, which may be imprecise at best, especially when a company has a lot of assets. More importantly, it values companies based on existing assets and is not forward-looking. Therefore, we will devote most of our time to the use of discounted cash flow valuation approach, which is discussed below, although it must also overcome several challenges, as we shall see.

Discounted Cash Flow Analysis

The DCF approach was applied to specific securities in Chapters 7 and 8. Now we apply it to the valuation of a company. The first step in this process is to estimate the future after-tax cash flows associated with a company. This step is fraught with difficulties, as alluded to in the quote below, which is referred to as *Professor Finagle's Three Laws of Information*:[17]

---

[17] Hunt, Pearson. "Funds Position: Keystone in Financial Planning." *Harvard Business Review*, May/June 1975.

The information we have is not what we want.
The information we want is not what we need.
The information we need is not available!

Let's examine these three "laws" one at a time, except we will modify the last statement, so that we have a viable way of approaching the issue.

1. *The information we have is not what we want.*

What we *have* (i.e., what we can find from the company's financial statements) is accounting earnings, which represents the bottom line, and which is affected by accounting choices, and which can be manipulated by accounting "trickery."

What we *want* is cash flow; so the typical solution is to add back non-cash items such as depreciation, amortization, and deferred taxes, which leaves us with the *traditional cash flow.*

2. *The information we want is not what we need.*

What we *want*, or what analysts typically try to estimate, is *cash flow from operations (CFO).* Recall from Chapter 3 that CFO may be estimated as traditional cash flow *minus* the increase in accounts receivable and/or inventory, *plus* the increase in accounts payable and/or other accruals.

Using CFO helps eliminate the issues involved with accounting differences such as the use of LIFO/FIFO and different revenue recognition policies. However, CFO does not truly reflect what we *need*, which is discussed below.

3. *The information we need, we can have, if only we look.*

What we really need is an estimate of the cash that can be withdrawn from a business after the firm has made all required investments to sustain its future growth. This is best described as the *free cash flow* of a firm, which was defined in Chapter 3, and can be estimated as: Free cash flow = CFO − "normal" capital expenditure (capex) requirements.

This cash flow estimate not only adjusts for the accounting problems discussed in items 1 and 2 above, but also ensures the firm grows in the long run and does not "run down" its assets to sustain profitability in the short run.

To summarize, the cash flows we will use in the DCF valuation approach will be the company's free cash flows. These free cash flows, which are defined in Equation 15-2 below, are the free cash flows to equity holders, since it represents the cash flows left over after all obligations, including interest payments, have been paid.[18]

> *Free cash flow to equity = net income +/− non-cash items (amortization, deferred taxes, etc.) +/− changes in net working capital (not including cash and marketable securities) − net capital expenditures*

[15-2]

The next step in DCF valuation is to discount all of the future cash flow estimates back to the present, as depicted in Equation 15-3. Notice that this is

---

[18] It also assumes the firm does not issue any new debt, which would be added to the free cash flow amount. We ignore this component of free cash flow to equity for valuing takeover targets, since the new financing would presumably come from the acquiring firm going forward. The free cash flow to the firm (both equity and debt holders) would simply be the free cash flow to equity plus the after-tax amount of the interest payments (less any new debt issued that was added to determine free cash flow to equity).

virtually identical to Equation 7-5 from Chapter 7, which depicted the generalized version of the dividend discount model (DDM); the only difference is that we use cash flows in the numerator instead of dividends. Since we are using free cash flow to equity, the appropriate discount rate (k) will be the risk-adjusted cost of equity for the target firm.[19]

[15-3]

$$V_0 = \frac{CF_1}{(1+k)^1} + \frac{CF_2}{(1+k)^2} + \dots + \frac{CF_\infty}{(1+k)^\infty} = \sum_{t=1}^{\infty} \frac{CF_t}{(1+k)^t}$$

Similar to the constant-growth version of the DDM, this equation can be simplified in the following manner if we assume that these cash flows grow at some constant annual rate (g) to infinity.

[15-4]

$$V_0 = \frac{CF_1}{k-g}$$

In practice, it is common to refine this process so that we can focus on estimating cash flows that will arise in the short- to medium-term, and then make some simplifying assumption about cash flows beyond some terminal date (T). This process is depicted in Figure 15-3.

The DCF Valuation Framework

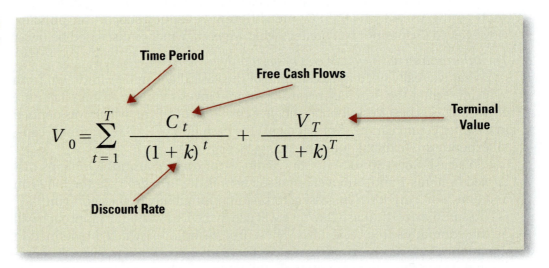

$$V_0 = \sum_{t=1}^{T} \frac{C_t}{(1+k)^t} + \frac{V_T}{(1+k)^T}$$

Time Period · Free Cash Flows · Terminal Value · Discount Rate

The final term in the equation in Figure 15-3 is the terminal value (V_T). This value is the present value of all future cash flows from time T to infinity, and it is usually estimated assuming some reasonable sustainable annual growth rate in cash flows from some time T forward. Notice that this is the same approach that we used when we applied the multiple stage growth DDM in Chapter 7. For future reference, we number and present the equation from Figure 15-3 below.

[15-5]

$$V_0 = \sum_{t=1}^{T} \frac{CF_t}{(1+k)^t} + \frac{V_T}{(1+k)^T}$$

---

[19] If we instead had decided to use free cash flow to the firm, we would need to use the target firm's weighted average cost of capital as the appropriate discount rate. Our discussion in Chapter 20 shows us that this discount rate reflects all financing costs, and therefore we should not include interest payments in our cash flow estimates. By using free cash flow to the firm, we have already made this adjustment since we added back the after-tax interest amount to the free cash flow to equity estimates.

We now illustrate this valuation approach using some simple examples.

Example 15-4: DCF Valuation I

We are given the following information about a potential takeover candidate firm (T2) for next year, based on what it is expected to contribute after it is acquired (i.e., with any arising synergies included): expected EBIT = $2 million; expected interest payments = $200,000; expected depreciation and amortization expense = $100,000; expected deferred taxes = $50,000; tax rate = 42 percent; expected increase in net working capital = $200,000; and expected net capital expenditures = $150,000.

a. Estimate T2's free cash flow to equity next year.

b. Estimate the value of T2's equity in total, and on a per share basis, assuming that next year's free cash flow increases annually at a 5 percent rate indefinitely. The firm has 500,000 shares outstanding. The appropriate beta is 1.2, the expected return on the market is 10 percent, and the risk-free rate is 4 percent.

Solution

a. Net income = $(2,000,000 - 200,000) \times (1 - .42) = \$1,044,000$
Free cash flow to equity = net income + non-cash expenses − increase in net working capital − net capital expenditures = $1,044,000 + 100,000 + 50,000 - 200,000 - 150,000 = \$844,000$.

b. Since we are assuming constant growth in the cash flows to infinity, we can use Equation 15-4.
$k = 4 + (10 - 4)(1.2) = 11.20\%$;
$CF_1 = \$844,000$; $g = 5\%$.

$$V_0 = \frac{CF_1}{k - g} = \frac{844,000}{.112 - .05} = \$13,612,903$$

Therefore, the per share value = $\$13,612,903 \div 500,000 = \$27.23$

Example 15-5: DCF Valuation II

We are given the following information about a potential takeover candidate firm (T3) for the next three years.

$	Year 0	Year 1	Year 2	Year 3
Net income	1,450	1,500	1,550	1,600
Depreciation	100	100	100	100
Deferred taxes	50	50	50	55
Accounts receivable	200	230	250	260
Inventory	150	160	180	190
Accounts payable	210	230	240	250
Capital expenditures	80	70	80	90
Dividends	150	150	160	160

After three years, free cash flow is expected to grow at 6 percent per year indefinitely. Estimate the value of T3's equity using DCF analysis assuming the appropriate discount rate is 12 percent.

Solution

$	Year 1	Year 2	Year 3
Net income	1,500	1,550	1,600
+Depreciation	+100	+100	+100
+Deferred taxes	+50	+50	+55
− Increase in accounts receivable	−30	−20	−10
− Increase in inventory	−10	−20	−10
+ Increase in accounts payable	+20	+10	+10
− Capital expenditures	−70	−80	−90
Free Cash Flow to Equity	1,560	1,590	1,655

$k = 12\%$; $CF_1 = \$1,560$; $CF_2 = \$1,590$; $CF_3 = \$1,655$.

Since we are assuming constant growth after three years, we can use Equation 15-5.

$$V_0 = \sum_{t=1}^{T} \frac{CF_t}{(1+k)^t} + \frac{V_T}{(1+k)^T}$$

Now, we need to estimate the terminal value after three years, which can be estimated using the constant growth version of the DCF formula, since $g = 6\%$ per year from year 3 to infinity.

$$V_T = \frac{CF_{T+1}}{k-g} = \frac{(1,655)(1.06)}{.12 - .06} = \$29,238.33$$

Now, we can estimate the value of T3 today:

$$V_0 = \frac{1,560}{(1.12)} + \frac{1,590}{(1.12)^2} + \frac{1,655}{(1.12)^3} + \frac{29,238.33}{(1.12)^3}$$

$$= 1,392.86 + 1,267.54 + 1,178.00 + 20,811.27 = \$24,649.66$$

The Acquisition Decision

In the section above, we discussed different methods of determining the value of a takeover candidate. This is a critical part of the takeover decision process, since an acquisition will only make sense if the target firm can be acquired for a price that is less than its value to the acquiring firm. For example, the acquiring firm in Example 15-5 should only acquire firm T3 if it can acquire T3 at a cost less than or equal to $24,650. The example below demonstrates that the cost of the acquisition of T3 depends on how the target firm is purchased: by cash or shares.

Example 15-6: The Cost of an Acquisition

Firm A estimates that it can purchase firm T3 from Example 15-5 in one of two ways: (i) by paying $24.00 per share in cash; or (ii) by giving T3's shareholders two shares in the new combined firm A-T3 for each share of T3.

Prior to the merger, T3 had 1,000 shares outstanding, which are trading at $20 per share, and A had 3,000 shares outstanding, trading at $12 per share.

Assuming that A is properly priced prior to the acquisition, should A acquire T3? If so, which method should it use to acquire T?

Solution

We estimate the cost under each method:

a. **Cash:** The cost is $24 \times 1,000 = \$24,000$, which means that purchasing T3 by cash would generate an NPV of $\$24,650 - \$24,000 = +\$650$.

b. **Stock:** Since A is giving T3's shareholders two of its shares (worth $12 each) for every share of T3, and since T3 has 1,000 shares outstanding, the cost appears to be 2,000 shares $\times \$12 = \$24,000$; however, this is not correct since what A is really giving to T3's shareholders is 2,000 shares in the new company A-T3, which is created from the merger.

To estimate the cost we must therefore estimate the value of the new company A-T3 after the merger:

Post-merger value of A-T3 = Value of A + Value of T3 to A

$$= (3,000)(\$12) + 24,650 = \$60,650$$

Since there will be $3,000 + 2,000$ (new shares issued) $= 5,000$ shares outstanding in the new firm, each share will be worth $\$60,650 \div 5,000 = \$12.13$.

So, the actual cost of giving T3's shareholders 2,000 shares equals:

$$\text{Cost} = (2,000 \text{ shares})(\$12.13 \text{ per share}) = \$24,260.$$

Thus, the NPV under this scenario would be $\$24,650 - \$24,260 = +\$390$.

This example highlights the SVAR analysis. Using cash lets the original shareholders keep the expected NPV, whereas using a share swap lets the target firm shareholders share in the NPV. Clearly if the firm is very confident in the NPV, it should use cash, but if the NPV is highly uncertain, then a share swap reduces the risk to the original shareholders.

The Effect of an Acquisition on Earnings per Share

Table 15-1 referred to the earnings per share (EPS) "growth game" as a motive for several M&As during the 1960s. An acquiring firm can increase its EPS if it acquires a firm that has a P/E ratio lower than its own P/E ratio, even if no synergies arise from the merger. This is illustrated in the example below.

Example 15-7: The EPS Effect

Firm A2 acquires firm T4 for cash at T4's present market value, and no synergies arise. The following pre-merger information is provided.

	A2	T4
Total earnings	$10,000	$3,000
Number of common shares outstanding	4,000	2,000
EPS	$2.50	$1.50
Market price per share (P_0)	$20	$9.00
P/E ratio	8 times	6 times
Total market value of equity	$80,000	$18,000

Solution

New firm A2-T4:

Total earnings = $10,000 + $3,000 = $13,000

Total shares outstanding = 4,000 (i.e., the number of shares A2 had outstanding).

Post-merger EPS = $13,000 ÷ 4,000 = $3.25 (well above A2's pre-merger EPS of $2.50).

Notice that if the market were inefficient and the P/E ratio for A2 remained at 8, the value of A2-T4 would equal EPS × P/E ratio = $3.25 × 8 = $26.00.

Therefore, the market value of A2-T4 would equal $26.00 × 4,000 = $104,000.

This is well above what it should be in an efficient market, since we know the combined market value should equal the market value of A2 plus the market value of T4, since we assumed no synergies were created. In other words, the combined market value of A2-T4 should equal 80,000 + 18,000 = $98,000. Total market value of A2 (after paying cash for T4) is $80,000. This implies that the P/E ratio should be: $98,000 ÷ $13,000 = 7.54, and the share price for A2-T4 should equal $3.25 × 7.54 = $24.50, not $26.00.

In an efficient market, the market value of the combined firm should be $98,000 in the example above, and not $104,000. Given full disclosure, analysts are aware of the earnings multiplier game and see through such accounting gimmicks. This would mean that the accounting motivation for M&A is not significant. However, many firms do not seem to disclose the full extent of their acquisitions. For example, Tyco, the large U.S. conglomerate, was the target of much criticism for its disclosure of its M&A activity, with some suspicion that its earnings were in part from accounting and not organic growth.

CONCEPT REVIEW QUESTIONS

1. What is the difference between value and price?
2. What is fair market value?
3. What key multiples are used in valuing companies?

4. Why do differing capital structures cause problems with using P/E multiples?

5. What is free cash flow?

6. When does EPS increase when using a share swap?

15.6 ACCOUNTING FOR ACQUISITIONS

Historically, Canadian companies could use one of two methods to account for business combinations: the **purchase method**, or the *pooling-of-interests method*. However, the CICA worked closely with the Financial Accounting Standards Board (FASB) of the United States to eliminate the pooling-of-interests method of accounting for business combinations as of June 30, 2001. This caused fewer difficulties in Canada than in the United States, since the pooling method was only permitted in the rarest of circumstances in Canada, unlike in the United States, where it had been used more frequently. The International Accounting Standards Board (IASB) also no longer permits the use of the pooling method.

Since the pooling method is no longer used, we will not elaborate on its application. Under the purchase method, one firm basically assumes all of the assets and liabilities of the other (target) firm and all operating results included from the date of acquisition going forward. No restatement of prior periods' results is necessary. At the time of the acquisition, all of the assets and liabilities of the target firm are restated to reflect its FMV as of the acquisition date. Since we know that equity is defined as assets minus liabilities, this implies the difference between the FMV of the target firm's assets and liabilities is the FMV of its equity. If the purchase price exceeds the FMV of the target firm's equity, the excess amount is referred to as **goodwill**, which is reported on the asset side of the balance sheet for the new entity. The example below illustrates the purchase method.

purchase method a method of accounting for business combinations where one firm assumes the fair market value of all of the assets and liabilities of the other (target) firm and all operating results included from the date of acquisition going forward

goodwill the excess amount of a target firm's purchase price over the fair market value of its equity

Example 15-8: The Purchase Method

Assume Company A1 acquires Company T5 for $1,250 in cash on June 30, 2006. The table below provides the balance sheets for A1 and T5 on that date, as well as the estimated market values for T5's assets and liabilities. Construct A1's balance sheet after the acquisition using the purchase method.

$	A1	T5 (Book Value)	T5 (FMV)
Current assets	10,000	1,200	1,300
Long-term Assets	6,000	800	900
Goodwill			
Total	16,000	2,000	2,200
Current liabilities	8,000	800	800
Long-term debt	2,000	200	250
Common stock	2,000	400	1,250
Retained earnings	4,000	600	
Total	16,000	2,000	2,300

Solution

$	A1 (Pre-Merger)	T5 (Book Value)	T5 (FMV)	A1 (Post-Merger)
Current assets	10,000	1,200	1,300	11,300 *
Long-term assets	6,000	800	900	6,900 **
Goodwill				100 ***
Total	16,000	2,000	2,200	18,300
Current liabilities	8,000	800	800	8,800
Long-term debt	2,000	200	250	2,250
Common stock	2,000	400	1,250	3,250
Retained earnings	4,000	600		4,000
Total	16,000	2,000	2,300	18,300

* 10,000 + 1,300 = 11,300
** 6,000 + 900 = 6,900
*** Goodwill = 1,250 (Price paid) − MV (T5's Equity) = 1,250 − [2,200 MV(T5's assets) − 1,050 MV(T5's liabilities)] =1,250 − 1,150 = 100

In addition to the recent accounting rule changes with respect to purchase versus pooling accounting, new rules have also been implemented about the valuation of goodwill and intangibles. One of the most important rule changes is that the goodwill resulting from an acquisition may not be amortized, where-as in prior years, amortization was mandatory. Instead, the market value of goodwill must be assessed annually, and it will be written down and charged directly to earnings per share if the value is deemed to have been permanently "impaired." As a result of this new treatment of goodwill, its fair value will be subjected to an annual impairment test. As discussed above, the value of good-will on the balance sheet is what is left over after properly valuing everything else. As a result, companies will be required to employ common valuation tech-niques, such as detailed discounted cash flow analysis, in order to determine fair value.

CONCEPT REVIEW QUESTIONS

1. Explain how the purchase method gives rise to goodwill.

2. How is goodwill treated for accounting purposes in Canada and the United States?

Summary

In this chapter, we discussed the various forms of business combinations, paying particular attention to mergers and acquisitions. We examined some of the most common motives that exist for takeovers, as well as some desirable characteristics of potential takeover "targets." We then demonstrated how to evaluate a potential takeover candidate using the multiples approach and using discounted cash flow analysis. We concluded with a discussion of how acquisitions should be accounted for in the financial statements, and showed the impact that acquisitions can have on earnings per share.

Key Terms

acquisition, p. 584

amalgamation, p. 585

arbs, p. 593

asset purchase, p. 591

break fee, p. 590

cash transaction, p. 585

confidentiality agreement, p. 590

conglomerate merger, p. 596

creeping takeovers, p. 589

cross-border (international) M&A, p. 596

data room, p. 590

defensive tactic, p. 593

due diligence, p. 590

extension M&A, p. 601

fair market value (FMV), p. 606

fairness opinion, p. 586

friendly acquisition, p. 590

geographic roll-up, p. 600

going private transaction/issuer bid, p. 586

goodwill, p. 619

horizontal merger, p. 595

hostile takeover, p. 592

letter of intent, p. 590

management buyouts (MBOs)/leveraged buyouts (LBOs), p. 607

merger, p. 584

no-shop clause, p. 590

offering memorandum, p. 590

overcapacity M&A, p. 600

proactive model, p. 608

purchase method, p. 619

selling the crown jewels, p. 594

share transaction, p. 585

shareholder rights plan/poison pill, p. 593

synergy, p. 600

takeover, p. 584

tender, p. 588

tender offer, p. 592

vertical merger, p. 595

white knight, p. 594

Formulas/Equations

(15-1) $\Delta V = V_{A-T} - (V_A + V_T)$

(15-2)   *Free cash flow to equity = net income +/− non-cash items (amortization, deferred taxes, etc.) +/− changes in net working capital (not including cash and marketable securities) − net capital expenditures*

(15-3) $V_0 = \dfrac{CF_1}{(1+k)^1} + \dfrac{CF_2}{(1+k)^2} + \ldots + \dfrac{CF_\infty}{(1+k)^\infty} = \displaystyle\sum_{t=1}^{\infty} \dfrac{CF_t}{(1+k)^t}$

(15-4) $V_0 = \dfrac{CF_1}{k-g}$

(15-5) $V_0 = \displaystyle\sum_{t=1}^{T} \dfrac{CF_t}{(1+k)^t} + \dfrac{V_T}{(1+k)^T}$

QUESTIONS AND PRACTICE PROBLEMS

Multiple Choice Questions

1. Which of the following statements about takeovers is *false*?

   A. Mergers create a new firm, while consolidation does not.

   B. Both mergers and consolidations require two-thirds votes from both firms.

   C. In the tender offer, the acquiring firm makes a public offer to purchase shares of the target firm.

   D. Acquisition of assets is one of the types of takeover.

2. Which of the following is *not* one of the three types of M&A?

   A. Vertical M&A

   B. Horizontal M&A

   C. Proxy contest

   D. Conglomerate

3. Which of the following M&As is valid?

   A. $V_{A-T} = \$400,000$; $V_A = \$200,000$; $V_T = \$210,000$

   B. $V_{A-T} = \$390,000$; $V_A = \$200,000$; $V_T = \$190,000$

   C. $V_{A-T} = \$410,000$; $V_A = \$200,000$; $V_T = \$190,000$

   D. $V_{A-T} = \$600,000$; $V_A = \$400,000$; $V_T = \$210,000$

4. Which of the following is a poor motive for M&As as suggested by evidence?

   A. Diversification

   B. Economies of scale

   C. Economies of scope

   D. Complementary strengths

5. Which of the following is *not* a reason for financial synergies?

   A. Increased debt capacity

   B. Reduced average issuing costs

   C. Reduced cash flow volatility

   D. Increased need of external financing

6. What is the market value of the equity of a firm that has a trailing P/E ratio of 4.5 and expected earnings (E_1) of $550,000? The firm is expected to grow at 5 percent.

   A. $2,475,000

   B. $2,357,143

   C. $1,850,000

   D. $2,050,099

7. Which of the following firms will have the *lowest* reported earnings figure, assuming all other information is the same? (Assume increasing prices for inventory.)

   A. A firm using LIFO to account for inventory and accelerated depreciation methods

   B. A firm using FIFO to account for inventory and accelerated depreciation methods

   C. A firm using LIFO to account for inventory and straight-line depreciation methods

   D. A firm using FIFO to account for inventory and straight-line depreciation methods

8. Which of the following cash flow measures should be used in the DCF valuation approach?

   A. Cash flow from operations (CFO)

   B. Free cash flow

   C. Cash flow from investing (CFI)

   D. Traditional cash flow

9. Which of the following statements of liquidation valuation is *false*?

   A. Current accounts receivable with good credit firms should be realized at a relatively high percentage of book value.

   B. Liquidation value equals liquidation value of current assets and market value of tangible assets.

   C. Overdue accounts receivable with bad credit firms should be realized at a relatively low percentage of book value.

   D. Liquidation valuation approach is not forward-looking.

10. Which of the following firm structures is least likely to be the target for a bidder?

A. Common shares are widely held

B. The stock is undervalued

C. Simple corporate structure

D. Many legal problems

Practice Problems

Easy

11. The Buyum Private Equity group has just made a tender offer for at most 60 percent of the Sellum Company. Sellum has 1,000 shares outstanding. Mr. Smith is a shareholder of Sellum and has tendered his shareholdings. For each situation below, indicate how many of Mr. Smith's shares will be accepted by Buyum.

	Total shares tendered by Sellum shareholders	Mr. Smith tendered	Total number of shares accepted by Buyum	Number of Mr. Smith's shares accepted by Buyum
A	1000	400		
B	1000	300		
C	500	400		
D	500	300		
E	500	100		

12. Marcel owns 12 percent of the Steam Forge Company (SFC). SFC trades on the Toronto Stock Exchange and has been the subject of a takeover attempt by the Iron Forge Company (IFC). Assuming that Marcel is the only minority shareholder who will not co-operate with IFC, what is the minimum level of ownership IFC needs in order to:

A. Call a special meeting of the shareholders

B. Replace the board of directors

C. Replace the firm's management

D. Force Marcel to sell at the takeover price

E. Win a vote on amalgamation

Medium

13. Julius is a shareholder in a public corporation, which has recently acquired another company, and the consequences for the bidding firm have been catastrophic. Julius is suing the bidder's board of directors for breach of duty as he believes that they failed in their duties to the shareholders. The board of directors, in their response to the suit, said: "a board member is from British Columbia and he knew about a timber company that was for sale and we could get it cheap. We saw that the profits of lumber companies had increased over the last 2 years, so we bought it. We didn't waste time and money looking at other possible candidates, we had found a good deal. We knew the deal was good because the CEO of the target was the cousin of the board member from BC." The bidding company, prior to the acquisition, was in the business of making sewing machines. The board of directors of the bidding firm has 12 members, 8 of whom are either current or former executives with the company.

Discuss at least three serious problems with the board's approach toward this acquisition.

14. The balance sheets of a bidder and target companies are as follows:

Balance Sheet (BIDDER) as of 31/12/0x

Tangible assets	$50,000		
Accumulated depreciation 32,000		Total debt	$15,000
Net tangible assets	$18,000		
Goodwill	3,000	Equity	6,000
Total assets	$21,000	Total claims	$21,000

Balance Sheet (TARGET) as of 31/12/0x

Tangible assets	$31,000		
Accumulated depreciation 10,000		Total debt	$19,000
Net tangible assets	$21,000		
Goodwill	0	Equity	2,000
Total assets	$21,000	Total claims	$21,000

The tax rate for both companies is 25 percent; amortization of goodwill is carried out over 10 years and is not tax deductible. The acquisition will be accounted for using the purchase method. Prior to the acquisition, the bidding firm had 10,000 shares outstanding with a share price of $20. The target had 5,000 shares outstanding with a market price of $10. The bidder acquired the target by offering 0.80 bidder shares per target share.

After analyzing the target, the bidder has decided that the market value of the targets assets is $65,000 and the market value of the bidder's assets are $45,000.

A. How many shares will be outstanding for the combined firm?

B. What fraction of the combined company will be owned by the original bidder shareholders?

C. How much goodwill was created by this transaction?

D. Show the consolidated balance sheets for BT (fill in the templates provided).

Combined Firm Balance Sheet as of 31/12/0x

Net tangible assets		Total debt	
Goodwill		Equity	
Total assets		Total claims	

15. List and briefly describe the different types of takeovers.

16. Briefly describe three common defensive tactics against a takeover.

Use the following information to answer Problems 17 to 21.

Sales	$1,550,000
CGS	350,000
Depreciation	400,000
Interest	150,000
Income tax	260,000
Dividends	300,000
Common shares outstanding	500,000
P/EBITDA	10X

17. Calculate the market price of the company's common shares using a relative valuation approach.

18. Calculate the trailing and forward P/E ratio using the price calculated in Problem 17. Assume a 6 percent earnings growth.

Difficult

19. Calculate the trailing and forward P/E ratio using the following assumptions: RF = 5%; β= 0.65; market risk premium = 5%; dividends and earnings grow at 6% indefinitely; and the firm maintains its current dividend payout ratio.

20. Calculate the market value of the *firm* given the following additional information: cost of equity = 8.25%, free cash flow to equity grows at 6% indefinitely; total debt outstanding = $1,000,000; increase in current assets = $400,000; increase in current liabilities = $300,000; and capital expenditures = $100,000.

21. In Problem 20, if the free cash flow to equity grows at 8 percent for the first two years and then grows at 5 percent indefinitely, what is the market value of the firm now?

22. ABC Inc. is planning to purchase DEF Inc. in one of two ways: (i) by paying $22 per share in cash; or (ii) by giving DEF's shareholders two shares in the new combined firm ABC-DEF for each share of DEF. Prior to the merger, DEF had 500,000 shares outstanding trading at $20 per share. ABC had 600,000 shares outstanding trading at $18 per share. Assume that ABC is properly priced prior to the acquisition. DEF is valued at $15,875,000 to ABC. Should ABC acquire DEF? If so, which method should it use to acquire DEF?

23. Complete the following balance sheet for the post-merger firm B-T. The bidder acquired the target for $2,000 *in cash*.

$	Bidder	Target (Book Value)	Target (FMV)	B-T (Post-Merger)
Current assets	25,000	3,500	2,900	
Long-term assets	10,000	1,000	1,300	
Goodwill				
Total assets	35,000	4,500	4,200	
Current liabilities	11,000	1,500	1,500	
Long-term debt	5,000	800	1,000	
Common stock	15,000	1,800	2,000	
Retained earnings	4,000	400		
Total	35,000	4,500	4,500	

24. Calculate the post-merger EPS and market value of equity, assuming no synergies arise in this acquisition settled *in cash*. Analyze the difference, if there is any. Further, calculate the *new* P/E ratio and share price for post-merger B-T. Additional information is given as follows:

	Bidder	Target
Total earnings	$25,000	$7,000
Number of common shares outstanding	8,000	3,500
EPS	$3.13	$2.00
Market price per share (P_0)	$29.50	$12.00
P/E ratio	9 times	6 times
Total market value of equity	$236,000	$42,000

25. Carla is the CEO of The Superior Sausage Company (a Canadian firm, listed on the Toronto Stock Exchange) and believes that the best way for the company to grow is through acquisitions. She has identified a likely target, Bunns and Bagels (B&B), which is also listed on the Toronto Stock Exchange.

A. Describe two different possible types of motives for this acquisition.

B. Carla is very uncertain about the value of B&B. Describe how she can structure the deal to reduce the risk to Superior Sausage.

C. Carla has just publicly announced that she feels that the senior management of B&B is not only incompetent, but likely to have been committing fraud.

i) Is a takeover by Superior Sausage more likely to be friendly or hostile? Why?

ii) Is Superior more likely to use a tender offer or a merger offer? Why?

iii) Describe three ways B&B could try to defend itself from Superior.

D. Before the market opened on Monday, Bunns and Bagels announced that it had received a merger offer from Franks' Fine Franks. By the end of trading on Monday, B&B has earned a return of –2 percent (negative 2 percent). The return on the market that day was 4 percent and the daily risk-free rate was close to zero. The beta for B&B is 2, with a standard deviation of the regression of 2 percent.

i) What is the abnormal return for B&B on Monday?

ii) Given the empirical evidence on mergers and acquisitions, is the market's reaction unusual? Why or why not?

26. You are a risk arbitrageur and you observe the following information about a deal: The current price of the target is $20 per share and the current price of the bidder is $15 per share. The bidder is offering 2 bidder shares per target share and you expect the deal to be completed in one year. Neither company is expected to pay dividends over the next year. Assume you can freely short sell and there are no margin requirements. You do not use any leverage.

A. Calculate the following:

    i) The offer premium

    ii) Clearly describe the transaction you will undertake to capture the premium

    iii) Show how your transaction will make money

B. Is it possible that your actual return will not equal the expected return? Describe two situations that can cause the risk in risk arbitrage.

To Lease or Not to Lease?

The Government of Canada, like many corporations, has had to assess the financing of some of its assets. In March 2007, it announced plans for the sale-leaseback of nine properties, located in Vancouver, Edmonton, Calgary, Toronto, Ottawa, and Montreal. The nine office buildings are part of a study of 40 government office buildings to determine whether leasing rather than owning them would make more economic sense. Canada's Minister of Public Works and Government Services, the Honourable Michael M. Fortier, has said that the government's core business does not include owning and managing real estate. These activities should be left to the private sector, which has the experience and the capability to manage the buildings in a cost-effective manner. The government currently leases 43 percent of the office space it uses.

Source: "Canada's New Government Announces Two-Step Strategy for Real Estate Management." CCN Matthews website: www.ccnmatthews.com. Retrieved May 1, 2007.

Leasing

Learning Objectives

After reading this chapter, you should understand the following:

1. The basic characteristics of leases and how to differentiate between operating and financial (or capital) leases

2. The accounting treatment of both operating and financial leases

3. The benefits and disadvantages of leases

4. How the lease decision can be evaluated using the discounted cash flow valuation methods

INTRODUCTION

This chapter discusses leasing arrangements, which may represent attractive alternatives for companies to finance both short- and long-term investments. This chapter deals with basic financial issues faced by Canadian individuals as well as firms; think of this chapter the next time you decide to buy or lease a new car.

16.1 Leasing Arrangements

In earlier chapters we had considered the purchase of a piece of equipment separate from its financing, which will be discussed in later chapters. However, these two decisions are often combined into one decision, which is generically called **asset-based lending**. This definition flows from the fact that the financing is tied directly to a particular asset. It is thus an example of **secured financing**, where the financing is based on an underlying asset that serves as collateral in the event of a default. Examples of asset-based lending are secured loans, conditional sales contracts, and leases. We will talk about the differences between these types of asset-based financing, but the focus is on leases. While most textbooks discuss leasing either as a financing or investment decision, we have chosen to discuss it as a capital budgeting decision because it allows a further chance to develop basic valuation skills in discounting cash flows. Also, a firm may choose to lease, rather than purchase, one of the long-term assets considered in capital budgeting.

First let us step back and discuss the institutional framework for asset-based financing. The Canadian Finance and Leasing Association (CFLA) is the professional body that acts as the umbrella group for asset-based lenders. It contains about 160 members and three broad groups of financial companies. *Independent asset-based finance companies,* such as CIT, represent about 60 percent of the outstanding balances; the **captive finance companies** of the major manufacturers, such as GM, represent about 29 percent of the outstanding balances; and the remainder are with the *chartered banks*. There are restrictions in the Bank Act that prevent the chartered banks from leasing consumer household property, vehicles (except for commercial transportation equipment), and real property (land and buildings). As a result, this is one major segment of the capital market where the banks are not as important as they are elsewhere.[1]

Asset-based financing is always tied directly to some underlying asset. The major assets financed in this way are broadly split among the different types of financial companies. The independents are mainly involved in machinery and equipment financing, where approximately 20 to 25 percent of all machinery and equipment is leased, with 60 percent of their customers being **small and medium-sized enterprises (SMEs)**. Approximately 40 percent of the assets

asset-based lending financing that is tied directly to a particular asset

secured financing financing that is based on an underlying asset that serves as collateral in the event of a default

captive finance companies finance companies that are divisions of major manufacturers to provide loans to purchase or lease their products

small and medium-sized enterprises (SMEs) businesses that generally have fewer than 50 employees

---

[1] Banks are continually lobbying for greater access to this market. Currently, chartered bank leasing has to be done through separate subsidiaries where 80 percent of the assets are leases and the balance are bridge financing to leases.

financed are either transportation equipment, such as buses, trucks, and trailers, or office equipment. As we will discuss, this financing tends to be extremely flexible and is often tailor-made to meet the needs of the original manufacturers and ranges across the whole spectrum of asset-based financing. Often an SME will approach a manufacturer for a piece of equipment and will be offered on-the-spot financing as a pre-arranged package with the asset-based financier.

In contrast, the captive finance companies are subsidiaries of the major manufacturing companies and finance the purchase of the equipment they sell. This sector is dominated by the big vehicle manufacturers like GM, Ford, and DaimlerChrysler, where it is estimated that about a third of all new vehicles are leased, a third paid for by cash, and a third through borrowing. The final group, the chartered banks, are much more restricted since they primarily finance through capital leases, as a direct alternative to a secured loan.

So what is a lease and how is it distinct from other asset-based forms of financing? The CFLA provides the following definition:

> A lease contract is an agreement where the owner conveys to the user the right to use an asset in return for a number of specified payments over an agreed period of time. The owner of the asset is referred to as the **lessor**, the user the **lessee**.[2]

Thus, what leasing does is give the lessee an alternative to purchasing an asset that they need.

As indicated above, there are different types of asset-based financing and unfortunately the definitions differ across accountants, lawyers, and tax authorities. As a result some forms of asset-based financing are specifically structured to get one interpretation for accounting and a different one for tax purposes. However, broadly speaking, we can differentiate between **operating leases** and **financial leases**, which are also commonly referred to as full payout or capital leases.

lessor the owner of the asset; conveys the right to use in return for payment

lessee the party in a lease agreement who pays to obtain the right to use the asset

operating lease a lease where some of the benefits of ownership do not transfer to the lessee and remain with the lessor

financial lease a lease where essentially all the benefits of ownership transfer to the lessee; also known as a capital or full payout lease

Types of Asset-Based Financing

The Canada Revenue Agency (CRA) has released an interpretation bulletin (IT 233R) regarding when a lease is considered to be a lease for tax purposes. CRA decides that a lease is actually a sale of equipment through a *conditional sales agreement* if one of the following occurs:

- the lessee automatically acquires ownership at some point

- the lessee is required to buy the asset at some point or guarantee that the lessor gets a certain value for it

- the lessee has the right to buy the asset at some point for substantially less than the likely fair market value

- the lessee has the right to buy the asset at a price that would cause a reasonable person to conclude that they will buy it

The key feature that the CRA is concerned about is that if any of the above conditions are satisfied, a reasonable person would conclude that the expectation is

---

[2] "The asset based financing, equipment & vehicle leasing industry," CFLA backgrounder for the House of Commons Finance Committee, September 4, 1998.

that ownership of the asset is being transferred to the user of the asset, even though that party has to make a series of future payments that "look like" a loan or lease payment. CRA is interested in this because the owner of the asset has the right to claim capital cost allowance (CCA) for tax purposes. So if any of the above conditions are satisfied, CRA regards the user—and not the party receiving the payments—as having the right to claim CCA.

In contrast, the accounting profession has a slightly different interpretation of a lease. A financial, capital, or full payout lease is similar to the CRA definition in that all the benefits of ownership transfer to the lessee. In this way, the payments to the lessor are to pay for the initial purchase of the equipment and provide the lessor with a financial return. In this case the lease usually:

- requires the lessee to carry out maintenance and insure the asset

- provides the lessee with a fixed purchase option

- covers 75 percent of the economic life of the asset

- is structured so that the present value of lease payments exceeds 90 percent of the cost

- involves fixed rental payments

As with the CRA definition, the lessee is assumed to own the asset and thus claims depreciation on the firm's income statement and records the value of the asset as an asset and the financing obligation as a liability on its balance sheet.

If it is not a capital lease, then it is an operating lease. The critical features of operating leases are that some of the benefits of ownership do not transfer to the lessee and remain with the lessor. As a result, the conditions are the opposite to those for a capital lease.

In comparing capital with operating leases we can see that the criteria are all different ways of saying that the lessor maintains significant residual exposure to the value of the asset. In fact, under the Bank Act, chartered banks cannot write leases where they have significant exposure to the residual value of the asset. Also, but not always, operating leases are usually *full-service* leases in which the *lessor is responsible for maintaining the asset*, providing any insurance and paying property taxes on the asset (if the asset is land or a building). However, even though the accounting definition means that ownership transfers to the lessee, for income tax purposes the CRA criteria may not be met and the lessor may be able to claim the CCA for tax purposes.[3]

sale and leaseback (SLB) agreement an agreement in which the owner of an asset sells it to another party and then leases the asset back

Another type of leasing arrangement is a **sale and leaseback (SLB) agreement**. In an SLB, the owner of an asset sells it (usually to an insurance company or pension fund) and then signs an agreement to lease the asset back. Thus, the lessee retains the use of the asset and receives a large, one-time cash inflow at the time of the sale. This type of arrangement was particularly popular for organizations in very low tax brackets. Universities, for example, pay no tax. They are therefore unable to get any depreciation tax deductions for the assets that they own. The university could sell an asset to someone who does pay taxes and can use the depreciation deduction. When the university leases the asset back, part of the tax savings that the new owner is enjoying could be passed back to the university in the form of lower lease payments.

---

[3] In some cross-border transactions, there is even a suspicion that both parties to the "lease" are able to claim depreciation for tax purposes in their own jurisdiction since these definitions differ across countries. As well, the lessor and lessee can file a joint election to have the lease counted as an operating or a capital lease.

The 1989 federal budget changed the tax rules concerning SLB agreements so that the lessor could deduct depreciation on leased assets only from the income derived from leasing, which has made them less attractive from a tax minimization point of view. As a result of this legislation, SLBs have declined substantially for non-profit organizations such as universities and hospitals.[4]

A **leveraged lease** is a popular financing vehicle in the United States. It is a three-way agreement among the lessee, the lessor, and one or more external lenders. As with other lease arrangements, the lessee uses the asset and makes regular lease payments, while the lessor purchases (or owns) the asset, delivers it to the lessee, and receives lease payments. However, the lessor puts up only a small portion (usually in the 20 to 50 percent range) of the purchase price of the asset, and lenders supply the remaining financing, in return for interest payments from the lessor. The lenders are protected against default because they have a first lien on the leased asset, and because the lease payments go directly to the lenders in the event of a loan default by the lessor.

leveraged lease a three-way agreement among the lessee, lessor, and a third party lender in which the lessor buys the asset with only a small down payment and the lender supplies the remaining financing

The attractiveness of leveraged leases in the United States is that the lessor puts up only a portion of the asset purchase price but receives all of the tax benefits of ownership, and has lease payments available to service the loan payments. Leveraged leases are not popular in Canada since CRA restricts the use of CCA deductions to the party at risk and the deductions cannot be carried over into other income. In the United States, however, they can, and the lessee can benefit in the form of lower lease payments whenever the lessor's costs are reduced.

CONCEPT REVIEW QUESTIONS

1. What is the difference between an operating and a capital lease?
2. What type of leases do chartered banks normally make?
3. What is a sale and leaseback agreement (SLB)?

16.2 ACCOUNTING FOR LEASES

While analysts tend to use the broad definitions of operating and financial leases discussed above, accountants use a more stringent definition of financial leases. This is important because financial leases are included on the balance sheet of the lessee, while operating leases are not, and the lessor retains the leased asset on its balance sheet. Operating leases are an example of **off-balance-sheet financing** (for the lessee) and are included only in the notes to the financial statements. For a financial lease, the present value of all lease payments is entered along with debt on the right side of the lessee's balance sheet. The same amount is entered as the value of the asset that is leased on the left side of the balance sheet.

off-balance-sheet financing a financing arrangement that does not appear in a company's balance sheet, but only in the notes to the financial statements

In addition to the balance sheet differences noted above, the income statement is affected by the classification of a lease as operating or financial. For operating leases, the resulting expense for the lessee is the full amount of the lease payments made to the lessor, which is classified as rental expense for the

---

[4] One prominent Canadian university sold its library and then leased it back. At the time, some observers could understand why they sold it, but not why they leased it back.

lessee, and as rental income for the lessor. Since the lessor retains the asset on its balance sheet, it charges depreciation expense against the asset. For financial leases, the lease payments will be broken down into interest expense and principal repayment, the latter of which is not an expense, but is reflected in the declining value of the liability reported on the balance sheet. As a result, for financial leases, the lessee's associated expenses will be in two forms: interest associated with the financing arrangement and depreciation expense associated with the asset. The lessor reports income in the form of a gain (or loss) on the asset at the time the lease arrangement (i.e., the sale) is initiated, and then it reports periodic interest income based on the interest portion of the lease payments it receives.

These accounting differences are summarized in Table 16-1.

Table 16-1   Operating versus Financial Leases

	OPERATING		FINANCIAL	
	Lessee	Lessor	Lessee	Lessor
Asset	Not on balance sheet (B/S); disclose in footnotes	Report on B/S	Report on B/S	Not on B/S
Lease payments	Expense the full amount as rental expense	Claim as rental income	Decompose into interest and principal repayment, and expense the interest portion	Claim the interest portion of payments received as interest income
Depreciation expense (associated with leased asset)	Cannot claim	Claim	Claim	Cannot claim

Obviously, there are some potential benefits for firms when leases are classified as operating leases rather than financial leases, which we will elaborate on in the next section. However, there are certain guidelines that must be followed. For accounting purposes, leases are classified as financial leases if *at least one* of the following criteria is met:

1. The lease transfers ownership of the property to the lessee by the end of the lease term.

2. The lessee has a bargain purchase option; i.e., it can purchase the asset at a price below fair market value when the lease expires.

3. The lease term is 75 percent or more of the estimated economic life of the asset.

4. The present value of lease payments is 90 percent or more of the asset's fair market value at the inception of the lease.

Financial Statement Effects of Lease Classification

Given our discussion above, it is not surprising that whether or not a lease is classified as operating or financial can have a significant impact on a firm's financial statements. As a result, many of the ratios (discussed in Chapter 4) that analysts use to examine company performance can be affected, as will the firm's cash flow statements. We use the examples below to illustrate some of the major differences that can arise.

Example 16-1: Income Statement and Cash Flow Statement Effects

Assume a company leases an asset with a present fair market value of $317,000. The lease arrangement requires four annual payments of $100,000. The appropriate interest rate is 10 percent. Assume the asset has a zero salvage value at the end of its useful life of four years, and that it can be depreciated using straight-line depreciation. Contrast the income statement and cash flow statement impacts of classifying the lease as financial versus operating. Assume that the firm's expected income and cash flow statements look like the following for the next four years, ignoring the effect of this lease arrangement:

	Year 1	Year 2	Year 3	Year 4
Revenue	$10 million	$10 million	$10 million	$10 million
Net income (excluding lease)	$500,000	$500,000	$500,000	$500,000
Cash flow from operations	$600,000	$600,000	$600,000	$600,000
Cash flow from financing	$100,000	$100,000	$100,000	$100,000
Cash flow from investing	−$300,000	−$300,000	−$300,000	−$300,000
Net cash flows	$400,000	$400,000	$400,000	$400,000

Solution

Operating Lease:

The annual charge to the income statement = Rental expense = $100,000
The annual effect on cash flow from operations (CFO) = $100,000
The annual effect on total cash flow = $100,000

Net effects:

	Year 1	Year 2	Year 3	Year 4
Net income	$400,000	$400,000	$400,000	$400,000
Cash flow from operations	$500,000	$500,000	$500,000	$500,000
Cash flow from financing	$100,000	$100,000	$100,000	$100,000
Cash flow from investing	−$300,000	−$300,000	−$300,000	−$300,000
Net cash flows	$300,000	$300,000	$300,000	$300,000

Financing Lease:

Effect on Income Statement:

Annual depreciation expense = $(317,000 − 0) \div 4 = \$79,250$

Interest expense (year 1) = $\$317,000 \times 0.10 = \$31,700$

Principal repayment (year 1) = $100,000 − $31,700 = $68,300

Principal outstanding (end of year 1) = $317,000 − $68,300 = $248,700

Interest expense (year 2) = $248,700 × 0.10 = $24,870

Principal repayment (year 2) = $100,000 − $24,870 = $75,130

Principal outstanding (end of year 2) = $248,700 − $75,130 = $173,570

Interest expense (year 3) = $173,570 × 0.10 = $17,357

Principal repayment (year 3) = $100,000 − $17,357 = $82,643

Principal outstanding (end of year 3) = $173,570 − $82,643 = $90,927

Interest expense (year 4) = $90,927 × 0.10 = $9,093

Principal repayment (year 4) = $90,927 (i.e., the total principal outstanding at the beginning of the year, which must be fully paid)

Associated Expenses

	Year 1	Year 2	Year 3	Year 4
Depreciation expense	−$79,250	−$79,250	−$79,250	−$79,250
−Interest expense (@10%)	−$31,700	−$24,870	−$17,357	−$9,093
Charges on net income	−$110,950	−$104,120	−$96,607	−$88,343

Effect on Cash Flow Statement

Cash flow from operations (CFO)	Year 1	Year 2	Year 3	Year 4
−Interest expense	−$31,700	−$24,870	−$17,357	−$9,093
Cash flow from financing (CFF)				
−Principal repayment	−$68,300	−$75,130	−$82,643	−$90,927
Net effect on total cash flow	− $100,000	− $100,000	− $100,000	− $100,020*

*The extra $20 is required to fully amortize the purchase price.

	Year 1	Year 2	Year 3	Year 4
Net income	$389,050	$389,050	$403,393	$411,657
Cash flow from operations	$568,300	$575,130	$582,643	$590,907
Cash flow from financing	$31,700	$24,870	$17,357	$9,073
Cash flow from investing	−$300,000	−$300,000	−$300,000	−$300,000
Net cash flows	$300,000	$300,000	$300,000	$300,000

Example 16-1 makes two things obvious:

1. Net income will generally be *higher* for operating leases in the *early* years, and it will generally be *lower* in the *later* years. This is because the interest expense charged for financial leases declines as the liability (lease obligation) is amortized by the lease payments. This means that the expense associated with a financing lease will decrease through time, since the depreciation expense usually is constant, whereas the lease expense for an operating lease remains constant through the years (i.e., it equals the amount of the lease payments).

2. The CFO will be *lower* when a lease is classified as operating, since the full lease payment will be subtracted from CFO, unlike for financial leases where only the interest portion of these payments is subtracted. On the other hand, its CFF will be *higher*, because unlike financing leases, operating leases have no principal repayment component. Even more important to note is that the overall effect on total cash flow will be the *same* as for financial leases. It is merely the classification of the cash flows that is affected.

Example 16-2: Balance Sheet Effects

Assume the company from Example 16-1 decides to lease the asset worth $317,000 considered in that example. The company's balance sheet excluding the lease is given below. Depict the firm's balance sheet after the lease arrangement has been entered into, assuming the lease is classified as: (i) an operating lease; and (ii) a financial lease.

Current assets	$2,000,000	Current liabilities	$1,000,000
Long-term assets	$8,000,000	Long-term debt	$6,000,000
		Equity	$3,000,000
Total assets	$10,000,000	Total liabilities and equity	$10,000,000

Solution

Operating Lease:
The balance sheet remains unchanged—it is exactly the same as the one given above. The only difference is that the firm would have to disclose the lease in the footnotes to the financial statements.

Financial Lease:
The new balance sheet would reflect the $317,000 on both sides of the balance sheet.

The $317,000 on the liability side would be broken down into the current portion of the obligation (i.e., the first year's required principal repayment component of the lease payment), and the remaining part of the lease, which would be classified as long-term debt.

Addition to current liabilities = $68,300 (principal repayment as calculated in Example 16-1).

Long-Term Debt = $317,000 − $68,300 = $248,700

Current assets	$ 2,000,000	Current liabilities	$ 1,068,300
Long-term assets	$ 8,317,000	Long-term debt	$ 6,248,700
		Equity	$ 3,000,000
Total assets	$10,317,000	Total liabilities and equity	$10,317,000

Example 16-2 demonstrates that the firm will appear larger, and will have more debt if a lease is classified as financial, as opposed to operating.

The example below shows the impact of the lease classification on some commonly used ratios that were discussed in Chapter 4.

Example 16-3: Financial Ratio Effects

Calculate the following ratios from Chapter 4 for the company in Examples 16-1 and 16-2 for Year 1, using the balance sheet items from Example 16-2, and using the income statement information from Example 16-1, assuming the lease in question is classified as an operating lease or as a financial lease. Assume the firm has 1 million common shares outstanding, and that its share price is $10 per share regardless of the method of accounting for the lease. Comment on any differences in the ratios.

Ratios: Current; debt; leverage; net income (NI) margin; asset turnover; return on assets (ROA); return on equity (ROE); price-earnings (P/E).

Solution

Ratio	Operating	Financial
Current (CA/CL)	$2,000,000 \div 1,000,000 = 2.0$	$2,000,000 \div 1,068,300 = 1.87$
Debt (TL/TA)	$7,000,000 \div 10,000,000 = 0.70$	$7,317,000 \div 10,317,000 = 0.71$
Leverage (TA/E)	$10,000,000 \div 3,000,000 = 3.33$	$10,317,000 \div 3,000,000 = 3.44$
NI margin (NI/S)	$400,000 \div 10,000,000 = 4.00\%$	$389,050 \div 10,000,000 = 3.89\%$
Asset turnover (S/TA)	$10,000,000 \div 10,000,000 = 1.00$	$10,000,000 \div 10,317,000 = 0.97$
ROA (NI/TA)	$400,000 \div 10,000,000 = 4.00\%$	$389,050 \div 10,317,000 = 3.77\%$
ROE (NI/E)	$400,000 \div 3,000,000 = 13.33\%$	$389,050 \div 3,000,000 = 12.97\%$
P/E (P_0/EPS)	$10 \div 0.40 = 25.00$	$10 \div 0.38905 = 25.70$

It is obvious from the calculations above that when leases are classified as financial leases versus operating leases, the firm will report lower current ratios, higher debt and leverage ratios, lower asset turnover, and lower profitability ratios (at least in the early years). Since the classification of a lease has no impact on a firm's total cash flows, its price should be unaffected; therefore, the P/E ratios should be higher to reflect the lower earnings per share (EPS). However, note that if the P/E ratio remained at 25, the share price would be lower, reflecting the lower EPS. Obviously this is inappropriate, and should not happen in efficient markets.

The example above illustrates that there will be a significant impact on a company's financial ratios depending on the classification of a lease as operating or financial. Thus we can see that managers have an incentive to have leases classified as operating rather than financial, from a financial ratio point of view. Therefore, one might suspect that a manager may try to make sure that her leases are categorized as operating leases in an attempt to "fool" the readers of her company's financial statements. However, while operating leases are not included on the balance sheet, companies are required to disclose the information in the notes to the financial statements. Hence, the information is publicly available, and if markets are efficient, this should be a waste of time, since most analysts would see through this type of manipulation.

CONCEPT REVIEW QUESTIONS

1. What are the cash flow from operations and the free cash flow implications of an operating versus a capital lease?

2. Which type of lease, operating or capital, gives a higher asset turnover ratio?

16.3 EVALUATING THE LEASE DECISION

Leasing provides an alternative to buying an asset. If a company needs an asset and has the opportunity to lease it, it must compare the cash flows from leasing with the cash flows from buying in order to determine which is better. There are four main differences in the cash flows for a company that leases an asset instead of buying it:

1. It does not have to pay for the asset up front.

2. It does not get to sell the asset when it is finished with it, if it is an operating lease, or if title is not transferred through a financial lease.[5]

3. It makes regular lease payments. If the lease is an operating lease, then the full amount of the lease payments is tax deductible; if it is classified as a financial lease, then only the interest portion of the payments is deductible.

4. It does not get to depreciate the asset for tax purposes if it is an operating lease. If it is a financial lease, it does get to charge depreciation.

The example below provides a discounted cash flow (DCF) framework for evaluating the attractiveness of leasing.

Example 16-4: Leasing versus Buying

A firm wishes to obtain a limousine for its executives. The limousine would cost $1 million to buy (it is very luxurious and also bulletproof). The limousine would be depreciated at a rate of $100,000 per year for tax purposes. Assume the limousine could be sold in five years for $500,000. The firm could also sign a five-year operating lease for a limousine with lease payments of $140,000 per year, with each payment due at the beginning of the year.[6] The firm's effective tax rate is 40 percent. Determine whether or not the firm should lease the limo, assuming its before-tax cost of borrowing is 7 percent.

Solution

The following cash flows need to be considered:

- The firm saves $1 million in today's dollars by not buying the asset.

- If the firm buys the limousine, it will get $100,000 per year in depreciation. Each year this will result in a tax savings of (0.40 × $100,000) = $40,000, which can be assumed as an inflow at the end of the year (i.e., when the firm pays its taxes). If the firm leases, it *forgoes* this tax benefit.

- The firm must make regular tax-deductible lease payments at the beginning of each of four years.[7] Using an effective tax rate of 40 percent, these payments translate into after-tax payments of $140,000 (1 − 0.40) = $84,000 per year.[8]

---

[5] Note that in many cases the salvage value would be discounted at a higher rate, reflecting the risk attached to the future value. For simplicity we abstract from this but it is often an important component of the analysis.

[6] We realize that most lease payments are made monthly, and not annually; however, we assume annual payments for simplicity.

[7] Notice that since it is an operating lease, the lessee can deduct the full amount of the lease.

[8] Technically it is not correct to adjust for tax savings to the "beginning" of year lease payments, since the tax savings will result at year end. We do this for simplicity, and demonstrate below that it does not make a substantial difference in our ending answer.

The table below presents the cash flows associated with leasing rather than buying (in $000s):

Year	0	1	2	3	4	5
Initial cost	1000					
After-tax lease payment	−84	−84	−84	−84	−84	
Forgone tax shield	0	−40	−40	−40	−40	−40
Forgone salvage value						−500
Total	916	−124	−124	−124	−124	−540

Now that we have estimated the incremental cash flows that result from leasing instead of buying, the question is how to evaluate these cash flows. It is usually appropriate to consider leasing as a form of debt financing, since it represents a legal obligation to make periodic payments to another party (i.e., the lessor). Viewing the lease arrangement above in this manner, we can say it is like a $1 million loan, and we can estimate the interest rate that the firm is paying on this "loan-like arrangement," which we can then compare with the firm's after-tax borrowing cost. To solve for this rate, we simply treat it like the following IRR problem, with k denoting the IRR:

$$0 = 916 - \frac{124}{1+k} - \frac{124}{(1+k)^2} - \frac{124}{(1+k)^3} - \frac{124}{(1+k)^4} - \frac{540}{(1+k)^5}$$

$$k = 3.32\%$$

Recall from Chapter 13 that we can solve for the IRR by long hand, or more simply as follows:[9]

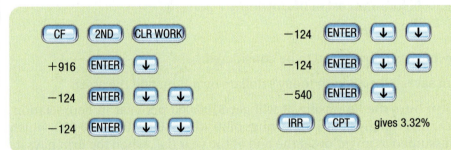

For this example, if we "guessed" an IRR of 10 percent, and we had the year 0, 1, 2, 3, 4, and 5 cash flows in cells B2 through B7, respectively, we could express the required Excel function as follows: = IRR (B2:B7, 0.10). This would also give us an answer of 3.32 percent.

Thus, leasing instead of buying involves receiving financing at an effective rate of 3.32 percent. This rate should be compared with the *after-tax* rate at which the firm can normally borrow.

For this example, we are given that the before-tax cost of borrowing is 7 percent, so:

[9] See Example 13-3 of Chapter 13 for the "long-hand" version.

After-tax cost of borrowing = 7% × (1−.40) = 4.20%.[10]

Therefore, since 3.32% < 4.20%, the firm should lease the limousine, since leasing provides cheaper financing than normal borrowing does.

An easier way to evaluate the lease is to simply use the after-tax borrowing rate as a discount rate and calculate the NPV (net present value) of leasing versus buying.

For this example, we can estimate the NPV of leasing versus buying as follows (numbers in thousands):

$$NPV(leasing) = 916 - \frac{124}{1.042} - \frac{124}{(1.042)^2} - \frac{124}{(1.042)^3} - \frac{124}{(1.042)^4} - \frac{540}{(1.042)^5}$$

$$= +28.41 \text{ (in \$000s)}$$

solution using a financial calculator

(TI BA II Plus)

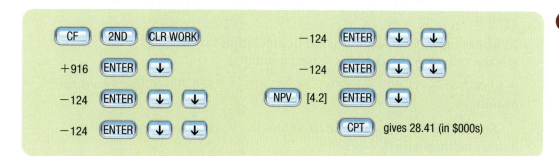

solution using Excel

The following function may be used to determine the PV of the "future" CFs (not including CF_0):

= NPV(rate, value 1:value 5)

If we had the discount rate of .042 in our Excel spreadsheet cell B2, and had the years 1 through 5 cash flows in cells B3 through B7, respectively, we could express the Excel function above as follows:

= NPV(B2, B3:B7), which would give the PV of future CFs as −887.59, which when added to +916 gives an NPV of +28.41 (in $000s).

We could also estimate the NPV of leasing by finding the present value of the various kinds of cash flows, which can be expressed as follows:

NPV(leasing) = CF_0 (i.e., purchase price savings) − PV(forgone depreciation tax savings) − PV(forgone salvage value) − PV(after-tax lease payments)

CF_0 = $1,000,000;

Depreciation tax savings = 0.40 × $100,000 = $40,000 per year end.

---

[10] This approach to estimating the after-tax cost of borrowing is correct if the borrowing is in the form of traditional bonds because they pay interest only, and the interest payments are completely tax deductible. It would not be strictly correct if the before-tax borrowing cost applied to a loan with blended payments of principal and interest, since only the interest portion of these payments is tax deductible. However, for practical purposes, this estimate is close enough.

$$PV\text{(Depreciation tax savings)} = 40,000 \times \left[\frac{1 - \dfrac{1}{(1.042)^5}}{.042}\right] = \$177,077$$

$$PV\text{(Salvage Value)} = 500,000 \times \left[\frac{1}{(1.042)^5}\right] = \$407,035$$

$$PV\text{(After-tax lease payments)} = 84,000 \times \left[\frac{1 - \dfrac{1}{(1.042)^5}}{.042}\right] \times (1.042) = \$387,479$$

Now, we can put all of these factors together to estimate the NPV of leasing:

NPV(leasing) = CF_0 − PV(forgone depreciation tax savings) − PV(forgone salvage value) − PV(after-tax lease payments)

= $1,000,000 − 177,077 − 407,035 − 387,479 = +\$28,409$ (difference due to rounding)

So, the NPV = $28,410, which is positive, so it is better to lease the limousine than buy it.

Note that in the example above, the positive NPV of leasing tells you that leasing is better than buying, but not whether you should acquire the asset in the first place. This question should be answered based on the total NPV of the project, as discussed in Chapters 13 and 14. To incorporate lease financing into an overall NPV problem, simply calculate the NPV of the project assuming that you buy the asset, then add on the NPV of leasing. This gives the NPV of the project including the advantage of financing the asset through leasing.

As mentioned previously, normally leases involve monthly, rather than annual, payments, with each payment due at the beginning of the month. In addition, the tax savings associated with these payments will be realized at year end when the firm pays its taxes. We removed these complications in the example above to make things simpler. The example below addresses these issues, demonstrating that the end result is not greatly affected by the simplifying assumptions employed in Example 16-4.

Example 16-5: Leasing versus Buying with Monthly Payments

Find the NPV of leasing the limousine described in Example 16-4, assuming that everything is the same except that lease payments of $11,667 (i.e., $140,000 ÷ 12) are made monthly, and that we treat the tax benefits of these payments appropriately; i.e., assuming they occur at the end of each *year*.

Solution

We can estimate the NPV of leasing using the following expression, where we have replaced the last term PV(after-tax lease payments) from the formula solution to

Example 16-4, with the following two terms: + PV(tax savings from lease payments) − PV(before-tax lease payments).

NPV(leasing) = CF_0 − PV(forgone depreciation tax savings) − PV(forgone salvage value) + PV(tax savings from lease payments) − PV(before-tax lease payments)

We begin by stating the PV of the cash flows from Example 16-4 that remain unchanged:

CF_0 = $1,000,000;

PV(Depreciation tax savings) = $177,077

PV(Salvage value) = $407,035

Next, we estimate the PV of the tax savings associated with the lease payments.

Annual lease payments = $11,667 × 12 = $140,000

Annual tax savings due to lease payments = $140,000 × 0.40 = $56,000 per year

Assuming these tax savings are realized at year end we get:

$$\text{PV(Tax savings from lease payments)} = 56{,}000 \times \left[\frac{1 - \dfrac{1}{(1.042)^5}}{.042} \right] = \$247{,}907$$

Number of monthly lease payments: n = 5 years × 12 months = 60;

Monthly discount rate = $(1.042)^{1/12} - 1 = 0.3434379\%$;

Before-tax payments = $11,667;

So, assuming beginning of month lease payments we have:

PV(before-tax lease payments)

$$= \$11{,}667 \times \left[\frac{1 - \dfrac{1}{(1.003434379)^{60}}}{.003434379} \right] \times (1.003434379) = \$633{,}798$$

Now, we can put all of these factors together to estimate the NPV of leasing: NPV(leasing) = CF_0 − PV(forgone depreciation tax savings) − PV(forgone salvage value) + PV(tax savings from lease payments) − PV(before-tax lease payments)

= 1,000,000 − 177,077 − 407,035 + 247,907 − 633,798 = +$29,997

This number is slightly larger ($1,587) than the NPV of $28,410 that we calculated under the simplifying assumptions that lease payments were made annually at the beginning of the year, and that the tax savings were realized at the same time. The reason the NPV is larger is because the last two terms in the expression above [i.e., + PV(tax savings from lease payments) − PV(before-tax lease payments)] equal − $385,891, while the last term in the simplified version in Example 16-4 that they replace [i.e., − PV(after-tax lease payments)] equalled −$387,479. This is due to the assumption of beginning of year payments versus beginning of month payments, which translates into a higher PV of the outlay, despite the fact that the tax savings are appropriately valued at year end.

In most cases, it is reasonable to make the assumptions we did in Example 16-4, since the end result was quite close. However, in situations where precision is critical, it will be worthwhile to use the more accurate (and somewhat lengthier) approach that was used in Example 16-5.

We made one other simplification in Example 16-4: we assumed depreciation for tax purposes was a constant amount per year. In practice, we have learned that depreciation that may be charged for tax purposes—the capital cost allowance (CCA)—is calculated using the declining balance method. The following example adjusts for this fact.

Example 16-6: Leasing and CCA Tax Shields

A firm is considering whether to purchase or lease a machine that costs $100,000 and is subject to a 20 percent CCA rate, declining balance method. The required lease payments are $25,000 per year for four years (with beginning of year payments as usual). The lessor has agreed to provide maintenance as part of the lease contract and the firm has estimated $10,000 per year in maintenance expense would be incurred if it decided to purchase the machine. It estimates the asset could be sold for $46,080 after 4 years. The firm's before-tax borrowing rate is 10 percent, and its effective tax rate is 40 percent. Should it purchase or lease the machine, assuming the acquisition of the machine has a positive NPV and that the lease would qualify as an operating lease?

Solution

First, we estimate the cash flows:

After-tax annual lease payments = $25,000 \times (1 - 0.40) = $15,000$

After-tax borrowing cost = $0.10 \times (1 - 0.40) = 6\%$

After-tax annual maintenance savings = $10,000 \times (1 - 0.40) = $6,000$

CCA Tax Shield (CCA × 0.40)

UCC (beginning year 1)	100,000	
CCA (year 1)	(10,000)	$4,000
UCC (beginning year 2)	90,000	
CCA (year 2)	(18,000)	$7,200
UCC (beginning year 3)	72,000	
CCA (year 3)	(14,400)	$5,760
UCC (beginning year 4)	57,600	
CCA (year 4)	(11,520)	$4,608
UCC (end year 4)	46,080	

(Cash flows in 000s)

Year	0	1	2	3	4	5
Initial cost	100					
After-tax lease payment	−15	−15	−15	−15		
After-tax maintenance savings		+6	+6	+6	+6	

Forgone tax shield	0	−4	−7.2	−5.76	−4.608
Forgone salvage value					−46.08
Total	85	−13	−16.2	−14.76	−44.68

We can estimate the NPV of leasing as follows:

$$NPV\ (leasing) = 85,000 - \frac{13,000}{1.06} - \frac{16,200}{(1.06)^2} - \frac{14,760}{(1.06)^3} - \frac{44,688}{(1.06)^4}$$

$$= 85,000 - 12,264 - 14,418 - 12,393 - 35,397$$

$$= +\$10,528$$

solution using a financial calculator

(TI BA II Plus)

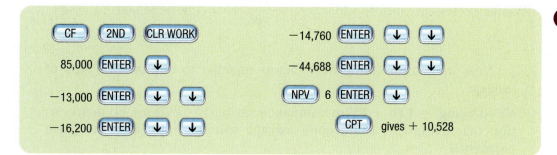

CF   2ND   CLR WORK   −14,760 ENTER ↓ ↓

85,000 ENTER ↓   −44,688 ENTER ↓ ↓

−13,000 ENTER ↓ ↓   NPV 6 ENTER ↓

−16,200 ENTER ↓ ↓   CPT gives + 10,528

solution using Excel

The following function may be used to determine the PV of the "future" CFs (not including CF_0):

= NPV(rate, value 1:value 4)

If we had the discount rate of .06 in our Excel spreadsheet cell B2, and had the years 1 through 4 cash flows in cells B3 through B6, respectively, we could express the Excel function above as follows:

= NPV(B2, B3:B6), which would give the present value of the years 1 – 4 cash flows as −74,472. Adding 85,000 to this amount gives the NPV of +10,528

Similar to our solution to Example 16-4, we could also estimate the NPV of leasing by finding the present value of the various kinds of cash flows, which can be expressed as follows:

NPV(leasing) = CF_0 (i.e., purchase price savings) + PV(maintenance savings) − PV(forgone depreciation tax savings) − PV(forgone salvage value) − PV(after-tax lease payments)

CF_0 = \$100,000;

$$PV(\text{maintenance savings}) = 6,000 \times \left[\frac{1 - \dfrac{1}{(1.06)^4}}{.06} \right] = \$20,791$$

We can estimate the PV of the CCA tax shield using Equation 20-7 from Chapter 20, which applies when there is no terminal loss or CCA recapture. This equation is appropriate here because we assume the salvage value is the ending UCC at the end of four years.

$$PV(CCA\ Tax\ Shield) = \frac{(C_0)(d)(T)}{d+k} \times \frac{(1+.5k)}{(1+k)} - \frac{(SV_n)(d)(T)}{(d+k)} \times \frac{1}{(1+k)^n}$$

$$= \frac{(100,000)(.20)(.40)}{.20+.06} \times \frac{(1+.5\times.06)}{(1+.06)} - \frac{(46,080)(.20)(.40)}{.20+.06} \times \frac{1}{(1.06)^4}$$

$$= 29,898 - 11,231 = \$18,667$$

$$PV(Salvage\ Value) = 46,080 \times \left[\frac{1}{(1.06)^4}\right] = \$36,500$$

$$PV(after\text{-}tax\ lease\ payments) = 15,000 \times \left[\frac{1-\dfrac{1}{(1.06)^4}}{.06}\right] \times (1.06) = \$55,095$$

Now, we can put all of these factors together to estimate the NPV of leasing:

NPV(leasing) = CF0 + PV(maintenance savings) − PV(forgone depreciation tax savings) − PV(forgone salvage value) − PV(after-tax lease payments)

= 100,000 + 20,791 − 18,667 − 36,500 − 55,095 = $10,529 (difference due to rounding)

So, the NPV = +$10,528, which is positive, so it is better to lease than to buy.

We now consider how to evaluate a financial lease in the example below. Two key differences to note are that the firm will likely get to claim the depreciation tax savings, and it may also take ownership of the asset at the end of the lease term, and therefore, will be able to sell it for the estimated salvage value if it so chooses, so this cash flow is not forgone. In addition, the entire amount of the lease payment is not tax deductible, as is the case for operating leases. Rather, just the interest portion may be expensed. However, this is exactly the same as it would be for a loan; i.e., only the interest portion of the loan payment is tax deductible. Therefore, the only real difference between a standard financial lease and a loan is that the lease payments are made at the beginning of the period, while the loan payments are made at the end of the period.[11]

Example 16-7: Entering into a Financial Lease versus Borrowing

A company is given the option of entering into a five-year, $10,000 financial lease arrangement that calls for monthly payments based on a 6 percent lease rate, or borrowing $10,000 through a five-year loan that also calls for monthly payments based on a 6.12 percent lending rate. Which option should the firm choose?

---

[11] In reality, loans require some form of down payment, whereas leases may provide 100 percent financing.

Solution

Notice that we cannot blindly select the lease option just because $6\% < 6.12\%$, since the lease involves beginning of month payments, while the loan involves end of month payments.

First, we calculate the monthly payments for each option.

Leases:
Monthly lease rate $= 6\% \div 12 = 0.5\%$;
Number of monthly payments $= 5$ years $\times 12$ months $= 60$;

$$\text{Monthly lease payments} = \frac{10{,}000}{\left[\dfrac{1 - \dfrac{1}{(1.005)^{60}}}{.005}\right](1.005)} = \$192.37$$

Loan:
Monthly loan rate $= 6.12\% \div 12 = 0.51\%$;

$$\text{Monthly loan payments} = \frac{10{,}000}{\left[\dfrac{1 - \dfrac{1}{(1.0051)^{60}}}{.0051}\right]} = \$193.89$$

Now we need to find the PV of the payments under each option, but which discount rate should we use? It turns out it doesn't matter, but it makes the most sense to use the loan rate, since we are evaluating the lease option.

Trivially, the PV of the loan payments using the monthly loan rate $= \$10{,}000$ (since that is the amount we used to determine the required payments). Now we need to estimate the PV of the beginning of month lease payments using the loan rate.

$$\text{PV(lease payments)} = 192.37 \times \left[\dfrac{1 - \dfrac{1}{(1.0051)^{60}}}{.0051}\right](1.0051) = \$9{,}972.39$$

This implies that the firm should enter into the lease arrangement, since the effective cost of the asset would be *less than* \$10,000, which is the cost under the loan arrangement.[12] Notice that we could have come to the same conclusion if we had used the monthly lease rate to evaluate both options. We would have found that the PV of the lease payments was \$10,000, while the PV of the loan payments was \$10,029.07.

The solution to Example 16-7 may appear somewhat lengthy, but it is a useful framework since it accommodates other variations in the loan versus lease decision, such as differences in required down payments, any services provided through leasing arrangements, and any bargain purchase options.

---

[12] In fact, we could say the NPV of leasing versus borrowing $= 10{,}000 - 9{,}972.39 = +\$27.61$.

CONCEPT REVIEW QUESTIONS

1. Explain how to calculate comparisons in the lease versus buy decision, when the lease in question is an operating lease.

2. How does the analysis change when the lease is a financial lease?

16.4 MOTIVATION FOR LEASING

In the previous section, we showed how leases could, under some circumstances, provide "cheaper" financing than typical loan arrangements. The attraction of leases in such cases is obvious; however, leases provide other benefits to lessees. Below, we provide a description of some of the most common reasons why firms enter into lease arrangements; some are better reasons than others.

1. **Cheaper financing**. This can occur for operating leases because the entire lease payment is tax deductible. In addition, the lessee may end up receiving attractive leasing rates if the lessor is better able to take advantage of the CCA tax savings associated with ownership of the underlying asset, and market conditions induce them to pass these benefits on to the lessee.

2. **Reduce the risks of asset ownership**. Leasing allows companies to acquire needed equipment without assuming the risk of having to resell the asset, or of having it become obsolete. This is particularly important for assets whose technological capabilities are constantly changing, which is one reason many companies lease computers rather than purchase them. Essentially this means that the equipment manufacturer or other lessor, rather than the user, bears the risk of the salvage value of the asset at the end of the lease.

3. **Implicit interest rates**. Leasing usually offers firms fixed rate financing over the life of the lease, whereas small firms in particular are often forced to use variable rate, prime-based lending when borrowing from banks.

4. **Maintenance**. Under a full-service lease arrangement, the lessor will provide maintenance. Often, the lessor will be a specialist in this type of equipment and is therefore better able to provide maintenance than the lessee.

5. **Convenience**. It is often more convenient to lease an asset than to purchase it, especially if it is only needed for a relatively short period of time and/or if it is a very specialized or illiquid asset that may be hard to sell in the future.

6. **Flexibility**. Leases often offer more flexibility. For example, they often include the option to cancel a lease, which may be important where obsolescence is a possibility. Also the CFLA offers the example of a ski-lift operator that financed the lifts with a lease where payments were seasonal to coincide with the winter months for obvious reasons.

7. **Capital budget restrictions**. Since leasing requires a very limited initial capital outlay (just the first lease payment plus any arrangement fees), managers may be able to circumvent capital budget constraints by leasing assets, rather than buying them. This is a dubious reason for leasing, since it allows division managers to circumvent broader-based company policies.

8. **Financial statement effects**. As demonstrated in Examples 16-1 through 16-3, the use of operating leases versus debt or financial leases enhances the "appearance" of the firm's financial statements since they provide "off-balance-sheet" financing. The use of operating leases can also lead firms to report higher net income, lower debt ratios, and higher liquidity ratios. However, this should not affect the firm's value in efficient markets, since it does not affect the level of its cash flows or the nature of the financial risks it faces. It merely changes the way these items are reported in the financial statements. Therefore, this is not a good reason for leasing.

Case Example

The CFLA offers the following example of how a lease is useful for an SME.

> The usual leasing transaction of interest to a business would likely target a particular core asset that will directly contribute to revenue production. For an SME, typically, it would be a "small-ticket" transaction for specific equipment or vehicles between $15,000 and $100,000. The acquisition of new equipment or of new vehicles is an important way for SMEs to grow their businesses and enhance productivity. These acquisitions are building blocks or discrete investment projects that allow for relatively simple business planning: matching projected incremental revenue to the business generated by the investment to incremental expenses and to incremental productivity—on a step-by-step basis.
>
> By way of illustration, consider the possible example of a $50,000 photocopier for a street corner photocopy business. Often, an entrepreneur will know the particular equipment needed by the business. The manufacturer or a dealer/distributor is contacted. Normally the equipment sales representative of the manufacturer or dealer/distributor meets the customer on the customer's premises or at the dealer/distributor's offices. With the long hours put in by entrepreneurs, "house calls" can be very helpful.
>
> The sales representative will likely have been trained by either the manufacturer's finance company or by the independent financing institution associated with the manufacturer to understand how to structure the financing. The sales representative usually has an in-depth knowledge of the equipment in question and the business of the customer. This knowledge base is very helpful in structuring practical financing for SMEs.
> A business customer will usually be offered a financing/leasing package that will include not only the cost of the equipment but also the cost of delivery, installation, servicing and insurance. The credit decision is usually part of a highly automated process that can be concluded very rapidly, often at the point-of-sale.
>
> The single question of greatest interest to most lessees is the amount of the monthly payment. The lease payment schedule can be tailored to the customer's anticipated revenue stream

(example—a lower monthly lease payment in year one of the lease with a sliding scale increasing the amount of the monthly payment over the lease term). The lease payment schedule is fixed at the start of the lease such that the lessee will know the amounts and due dates throughout the lease term.

If, during the term of the lease, the customer decides that a new model of the copier would be to the advantage of the business, the lessor will generally negotiate the replacement of the old technology with the new one, rolling the costs into a new lease with a new payment schedule.

Under Canadian Generally Accepted Accounting Principles (GAAP), an operating lease is not capitalized on the financial statements of the lessee. Lease payments are considered an expense for the lessee. In contrast, typical bank financing or finance leases are capitalized and recorded as a debt liability on the borrower's financial statement thereby affecting the debt/equity ratios impacting the business. This "off-balance-sheet" feature—acquiring needed plant, equipment and vehicles by way of an operating lease—can be a real advantage, particularly to SMEs.

Also for non-production assets, that is, equipment and vehicles not considered as part of the core production of a business—for example, photocopiers in an office (rather than in a photocopy shop) or trucks—if acquired by way of a loan, the total of the GST and PST must be paid upfront by the customer (although the GST will be refunded eventually). The total sales tax plus the down payment can be a significant upfront amount. On the acquisition of non-production assets by way of lease, the sales taxes are levied generally on each monthly lease payment over the full term of the lease rather than as a single lump sum, upfront payment.[13]

The CFLA example highlights the fact that in practice, the leasing decision is not a simple investment versus financing decision, but is an integration of both. In this example, the lease is an operating lease that allows the SME to transfer many of the business risks of ownership to a party—the manufacturer—better equipped to manage those risks.

CONCEPT REVIEW QUESTIONS

1. Why are leases often more flexible than a borrow purchase option?
2. Why do you think that the major market for leasing is often SMEs, rather than large corporations?
3. If you were opening a copy centre, do you think you would lease or borrow to buy the equipment and why?

[13] "The asset based financing, equipment & vehicle leasing industry," CFLA backgrounder for the House of Commons Finance Committee, September 4, 1998.

Summary

In this chapter we discuss leasing as a financing source. In a lease arrangement, the lessor retains ownership rights to an asset, but makes the asset available for use by the lessee, who in turn agrees to make periodic lease payments to the lessor. We discussed the general differences between operating and financial (or capital) leases and how they are treated by the CRA for tax purposes and by companies for accounting purposes. We demonstrated that, as a result of these differences, with all else being equal, classifying a lease as operating rather than financial will result in a company reporting higher net income, lower debt ratios, and higher liquidity ratios. We proceeded to show how firms can evaluate a potential lease decision using the discounted cash flow (DCF) analysis framework. We concluded by discussing various motivations that firms might have for entering into leasing arrangements and focused on the flexibility surrounding writing lease contracts and the close relationship that exists between manufacturers and equipment leasing firms.

Key Terms

asset-based lending, p. 632

captive finance companies, p. 632

financial lease, p. 633

lessee, p. 633

lessor, p. 633

leveraged lease, p. 635

off-balance-sheet financing, p. 635

operating lease, p. 633

sale and leaseback (SLB) agreement, p. 634

secured financing, p. 632

small and medium-sized enterprises (SMEs), p. 632

QUESTIONS AND PRACTICE PROBLEMS

Multiple Choice Questions

1. Which of the following statements about an operating lease is *false*?

   A. It has a shorter term than a capital lease.
   B. The lessee cannot cancel the lease before the operating lease ends.
   C. It's usually a full-service lease.
   D. Payments of one operating lease are usually not enough to fully cover the asset cost.

2. Capital leases are

   A. cancellable before expiration without penalties.
   B. short-term leases.
   C. leases for which the lessors are responsible for maintenance of the assets.
   D. leases for which payments will cover the initial asset costs.

3. Which of the following statements about leveraged leases is *false*?

   A. There is an external lender, lessor, and lessee in the lease.

   B. The lender receives interest payments from the lessee.

   C. The lessee could bargain for lower lease payments if the market is competitive.

   D. The lender has the first lien on the leased asset.

4. Which of the following leases is classified as a financial lease?

   A. The lessee could purchase the asset at $10,000 while the market value of the lease is $9,000 when the lease expires.

   B. The lease term is 5 years and the economic life of the asset is 6 years.

   C. The lease does not transfer the ownership of the asset to the lessee when the lease expires.

   D. In the lease inception, the fair market value of the assets is $60,000 while the present value of the lease payments is $50,000.

5. Which of the following organizations is *most likely* to enter into a sale and lease-back agreement?

   A. Factory

   B. University

   C. Investment firm

   D. Real estate firm

6. What is the asset/liability recognized on the lessee's balance sheet at the beginning of the lease given the following operating lease information? Minimum annual lease payment at the beginning of each year = $12,000; lease term = 7 years; appropriate discount rate = 10 percent; salvage value = 0.

   A. $58,421

   B. $61,000

   C. $0

   D. $58,000

7. What is the lessee's depreciation expense of a capital lease using the straight-line method given the following: salvage value = $0; annual minimum lease payment (MLP) at the beginning of each year = $5,000; lease term = 5 years; appropriate discount rate = 8 percent.

   A. $21,561

   B. $19,964

   C. $20,099

   D. $23,506

8. Which of the following is *higher* under operating leases?

   A. NI and CFO

   B. CFF and NI in the early years

   C. Depreciation and NI

   D. Total cash flow and CFO

9. Under financial leases, the following ratio is *higher*, compared with the operating lease:

   A. Current ratio

   B. Leverage ratio

   C. NI margin

   D. ROE

10. Which of the following financial figures is *unchanged* regardless of the type of lease?

    A. Leverage ratio

    B. P/E ratio

    C. Total cash flow

    D. Asset turnover

Practice Problems

11. Briefly describe three motivations for leasing.

12. The White River Manufacturing Company has just signed several leases and it has hired the Absent Minded Profs to do the initial classification of the leases as operating and financial for accounting purposes. White River could have bought each asset for $1 million instead of leasing. The appropriate discount rate is 10 percent per year; all lease payments are annual and paid at the end of the year. For each of the following leases, classify them as operating or financial and explain your reasoning.

Easy

	Expected economic life of the asset	Annual lease payments	Length of lease	Purchase price at end of lease	Expected market value of asset at end of lease
A	10 years	$150,000	8 years	$10,000	$10,000
B	5 years	$100,000	2 years	$900,000	$700,000
C	10 years	$20,000	5 years	$500,000	$300,000
D	9 years	$185,000	8 years	$1,000	$50,000
E	25 years	$120,000	22 years	$8,000	$25,000
F	10 years	$200,000	5 years	$800,000	$500

13. Charles Zhang, the owner of a small moving company, has decided that economic conditions are perfect for him to expand his business. An expansion of his business will require him to buy five new moving trucks at a total cost of $200,000. Mr. Zhang's company has $5,000 in cash and has a $30,000 line of credit at the bank. Being a small company, it does not have the option of issu-

ing public debt and Mr. Zhang is not comfortable with mortgaging his family home to buy the trucks. Describe two ways Mr. Zhang can acquire the trucks. Discuss the advantages and disadvantages of each.

14. Financial statements for Canadian public corporations are available from the System for Electronic Document Analysis and Retrieval (SEDAR) at www.sedar.com, or from companies' websites.

   A. Review a copy of Air Canada's annual report for fiscal year end 2006 (March 2007), and determine the portion of Air Canada's long-term debt and capital leases that was made up of capital leases. Hint: See Note 7.

   B. Obtain the same ratio for TELUS. Hint: See Note 17.

Medium

15. Igor, the intern at the Absent Minded Professors, has just presented Professor Bleary with his valuation of the Kitchen Gadget Company (KGC). He has identified two other companies (Kitchen Widgets and Kitchen Thingies) in exactly the same line of business as KGC and carried out his valuation using multiples. All three companies use 100 percent equity. Igor presents the following analysis:

	Kitchen Widgets	Kitchen Thingies	Average P/E
P/E ratio	15	20	$17.50

   As the Kitchen Gadget Company has an EPS of $1, Igor has valued KGC at $17.50 per share. Professor Bleary looks at Igor's work, tells him to do it again, and mumbles something about "notes." Igor is utterly confused and has come to you for help. You have quickly reviewed Igor's work and noted that KGC has a policy of buying all its assets; in contrast Kitchen Widgets uses operating leases while Kitchen Thingies uses financial or capital leases.

   A. Explain to Igor what the "notes" are.

   B. Explain how he should have done the valuation.

   C. Is this likely to affect his valuation of KGC?

Difficult

16. Expedic Utility Corp. needs to increase its electricity production capacity. It is interested in a slightly used reactor located in Ontario. It has been offered two alternatives: buy the reactor for $10 billion (will have to hold it for 20 years) or lease it for 10 years at $1.3 billion per year. At the end of 10 years, Expedic would have the option to either buy the reactor for $2 billion or renew the lease at annual payments of $1.8 billion. Expedic has a cost of capital of 7 percent. Assume the economic life of the reactor is 20 years, the CCA rate is $500 million per year, and the tax rate is 40 percent. At the end of 20 years, the reactor will have a salvage value of zero. Assume all lease payments are made at the beginning of the lease, all leases are operating leases, maintenance costs of $10 million per year will be covered by the lessor, and that all CCA is taken at the end of the year (do not apply the half-year rule).

   A. Draw the decision tree for Expedic. What choices does it have to make and when?

B. Ignoring the real options value, what is your recommended course of action to the CEO of Expedic?

17. Malcolm McKee has just been appointed finance minister and is convinced that the leasing business is just a way of avoiding paying taxes. He has hired the Absent Minded Profs to evaluate the cash flow effects to both the lessee and the lessor in financial leases. McKee wants to determine if there is any loss of tax revenue to the government. Use the information given below to answer the following questions.

- Cost of the asset is $1.25 million. Lessor will have to buy asset in order to lease it to lessee.

- Cost of capital for both firms is 10 percent.

- The annual cash flows (before tax) generated by the asset is $500,000 regardless of who uses the asset.

- To acquire the asset, the firm will make annual interest payments at the end of each year and repay the principal of $1.25 million at the end of the 5th year (just like a bond).

- Maintenance and insurance costs = $0

- Economic life of asset = term of lease = 5 years

- CCA of $250,000 claimed at the end of each year (for convenience we are assuming straight line)

- Annual lease payments made at the end of the year: $300,000

- Tax rate of both lessee and lessor: 40 percent

- Assume that both firms make sufficient income to claim any tax benefits.

A. Complete the following table assuming the firm buys the asset instead of leasing it.

	Firm buys asset instead of leasing					
	Year 1	Year 2	Year 3	Year 4	Year 5	Principal repayment
Cash flow from asset						
Interest payments						
Lease payments						
CCA on asset						
Tax payment						
After-tax cash flows						

B. Complete the following table assuming the firm uses a financial lease instead of buying the asset. For simplicity, assume that the entire lease payment is treated as a financing charge (like interest).

	Firm uses financial lease instead of buying (lessee)					
	Year 1	Year 2	Year 3	Year 4	Year 5	Principal repayment
Cash flow from asset						
Interest payments						
Lease payments						
CCA on asset						
Tax payment						
After-tax cash flows						

C. Complete the following table for the lessor in the financial lease. For simplicity, assume that the entire lease payment is treated as a financing charge (like interest).

	Lessor in financial lease					
	Year 1	Year 2	Year 3	Year 4	Year 5	Principal repayment
Cash flow from asset						
Interest payments						
Lease payments						
CCA on asset						
Tax payments						
After-tax cash flow						

D. Are Mr. McKee's suspicions about loss of tax revenue correct?

E. How could the firms (the sum of lessee and lessor) gain from leasing activities? In other words, why would a lessor lease the asset to the operating firm rather than use the asset itself?

18. Estimate the *change* in NI, cash flow from operations (CFO), and cash flow from financing (CFF) at the end of the first year if a firm decided to enter into a lease agreement. The lease term is 4 years while the economic life of the asset is 5 years. The annual lease payment is $10,000 at the beginning of each year and the appropriate discount rate is 8 percent. There is no salvage value at the lease end. The lessee uses the straight-line depreciation method.

19. Estimate the *change* in NI, CFO, and CFF *as opposed to* the results calculated in Problem 18 if the economic life of the lease is 6 years instead of 5 years.

20. What are the changes in current assets, long-term assets, current liabilities, and long-term liabilities at the end of the first year in Problem 18?

21. A firm plans to either lease a piece of equipment or purchase it. The purchase price up front is $500,000 and it is depreciated at $50,000 per year for tax purposes. The equipment could be sold in nine years for $50,000. If the firm leases the equipment under an operating lease, it pays annual lease payments of $25,000 at the beginning of each of nine years. The firm's effective tax rate is 40 percent. Determine whether or not the firm should lease the equipment, assuming the before-tax cost of borrowing is 8 percent.

22. A firm plans to either purchase or lease a machine that costs $250,000 and is subject to a 20 percent CCA rate, declining balance method. The required lease payments are $30,000 at the beginning of each of four years. The lessor has agreed to provide maintenance as part of the lease contract and the firm has estimated $20,000 per year in maintenance expense would be incurred if it decided to purchase the machine. It estimates the asset could be sold for $115,200 (the ending UCC at the end of year 4) after 4 years. The firm's before-tax borrowing rate is 8 percent, and its effective tax rate is 40 percent. Should it purchase or lease the machine, assuming the acquisition of the machine has a positive NPV and that the lease would qualify as an operating lease?

23. Suppose you are going to enter into a six-year, $22,000 financial lease that requires monthly payments based on an 8 percent lease rate. Alternatively, you could borrow $22,000 via a six-year loan that requires monthly payments based on a 7 percent lending rate. Which option should you choose?

PART 7

LONG-TERM FINANCING

Having considered the left hand side of the balance sheet in Part 6, we now consider the right hand side and examine how a firm finances its operations. This involves securities laws, since obtaining funds from the public is heavily regulated due to the possibility of fraud. We discuss the role of provincial securities commissions and how securities are issued to the public. We then discuss the different types of securities that firms issue, how equities differ from debt securities, and the range of securities in between these two extremes—commonly referred to as hybrids. We conclude by examining how to estimate a firm's cost of capital based on its use of the various financing alternatives.

Issues and Investors

Connacher Oil, an oil and natural gas exploration and production company, surprised market participants by cancelling a bought deal. In effect, the company was giving back money that was already in its pocket. On April 17, 2007, Conacher sold $50 million of common stock and flow-through stock to a syndicate of dealers led by GMP Securities. The common stock component of the deal was priced at $4.15 per share. The decision to cancel the share issue was made by the company and the dealers and was good news for investors already committed to the shares, which traded as low as $3.83 once the news of Conacher's increased budget costs was released.

Source: Connacher Oil website: www.connacheroil.com (April 30, 2007).
Globe and Mail Website: www.theglobeandmail.com (April 30, 2007).

Investment Banking and Securities Law

Learning Objectives

After reading this chapter, you should understand the following:

1. That the core problem in raising capital is information asymmetry, which, in extreme cases, can lead to fraudulent activities

2. The importance of securities laws and regulations in financial markets

3. The basic steps included in the initial public offering (IPO) process

4. What is included in a prospectus and why it is critical for IPOs

5. Why continuous disclosure requirements are important for investors, and how they affect secondary offerings

INTRODUCTION

In Chapters 17, 18, and 19 we develop an overview of corporate financing and an understanding of the cost of capital as the overall cost of the funds invested in the firm. To understand how this cost of capital is determined, we need to understand why certain types of securities exist and the basic reasons firms issue debt versus equity securities. In Chapters 6 and 7, we discussed the basics of bonds and equities and how to value them. However, we did not discuss why these securities exist or, just as important, the difference between private and public markets for securities—that is, why some securities are traded while others aren't.

To understand these issues, we discuss some major financial scandals in which investors (both equity and debt investors) lost millions and sometimes billions of dollars. The underlying reasons for these losses are fraud and criminal activity. It is an unfortunate truth that financial markets, by their very nature, are subject to potential abuse, because investors find it difficult to separate frauds from legitimate investments. In this chapter, we discuss the basic problem of raising external capital and separating good from bad investments. The problem arises from asymmetric information: fraudsters know that they are fraudsters, whereas investors do not. Differences in information have a huge impact on the design of financial securities and the practice of corporate financing.

After considering this basic problem and illustrating it with recent and classic frauds, we discuss securities regulation and the reasons that we have all those legal requirements. We then discuss the process of taking a firm public and how to raise capital through both initial public offerings (IPOs) and seasoned equity offerings (SEOs). In the process, we show how this applies to both debt and equity securities. In Chapters 18 and 19, we then discuss how these same types of problems, because of differences in information, cause the firm to choose between issuing different types of securities.

17.1 CONFLICTS BETWEEN ISSUERS AND INVESTORS

The Basic Problem of Asymmetric Information

We begin by considering the most basic case of investors investing in what, unknown to them, is a deliberate fraud. This is an example of **asymmetric information** or information that one side has and the other doesn't. This is an extreme case in which one side knows that the securities being offered are worthless, that is, they are a complete fraud, whereas the investors think it is a legitimate business opportunity.

In Chapters 6 and 7, we discussed the valuation of common stocks (equities) and bonds and developed the discounted cash flow valuation formulas. In all cases, there is an initial outflow to buy the security and then a series of expected future cash inflows. These future inflows are then discounted back to

asymmetric information
information that one party in a deal has and the other doesn't; an extreme example is someone selling securities that the investor doesn't know are worthless

the present to estimate the present value of a security. However, think about an initial issue of securities from the issuer's perspective. It receives an immediate cash inflow based on the assumption that it will in turn pay a series of expected future cash flows. If both the investor and issuer agree on the expected stream of future cash flows, the situation is *symmetric*: what the investor expects to receive is what the issuer expects to pay, so that the investor's expected rate of return is equal to the issuer's cost of raising capital.

This is the basic approach of corporate finance: we look to the capital markets to get an indication of the cost of certain types of financing, which is the reason, in this textbook, we discussed the essentials of capital markets before discussing corporate financing. If the current interest rate on long-term debt is 6 percent, we say that the cost of long-term debt financing to the firm is 6 percent; if we estimate the CAPM required rate of return on equity to be 12 percent, we say the cost of common equity financing is 12 percent. Some nuances here will be dealt with later, but the principal assumption is that the investor and the issuer agree on the value of the expected stream of cash flows and come up with the same estimate. The problem, however, is that capital markets exhibit information asymmetries, which is a fancy way of saying that people frequently have different information about the same future stream of cash flows, and thus they value the securities differently. In fact, they can disagree so much that a market may not exist and a firm cannot find anyone to buy its securities and experiences a "financing gap."[1]

The classic example of market failure in the presence of information asymmetries was demonstrated by Professor George Akerlof, who formalized the notion of a market for lemons. Consider the most familiar *lemons market*, which is that for used cars. Suppose that for a given make and year or used car, there are two types: good cars, which were driven by responsible drivers who regularly maintained them, and lemons, which were driven by people who drove them excessively and never properly maintained them. However, let's assume the lemon looks as good as the good-quality car, because the owner has turned the odometer back and put heavier oil in the transmission. Suppose the true value of the good car to a mechanic who knows it is $15,000 and that for the lemon is $10,000. If there are equal numbers of both types of cars in the market, the average price for the car is $12,500, or more likely less than this amount, taking into account the risk of buying a lemon. So suppose it is $11,000.

At a market price of $11,000, the owner of the good car will not offer it for sale. Instead he or she will sell it privately to someone who trusts the owner, like a relative or close friend. After all, the owner knows the true mileage and the fact that he or she has completed the scheduled maintenance. As a result, the owner will not offer a $15,000 car for sale to the general public for $11,000, so the supply of good cars will go down. For the lemon, the situation is the opposite because its owner knows that it is a lemon and that the going market price exceeds its true value, so he or she will put it up for sale. The result is that there will be an unequal supply of good cars and lemons; the market supply will consist entirely of lemons plus a few cars sold by people with no friends or relatives to sell to. As a result, the overall market for cars fails.

This market for lemons is an example of *Gresham's law*. Sir Thomas Gresham, who coined the phrase "bad money drives out good," observed that

---

[1] Governments are constantly worried about financing gaps and the fact that good companies cannot get financing on reasonable terms. Of course, people disagree profoundly on what constitutes reasonable terms.

in sixteenth-century England, gold and silver coins circulated at their par value; for example, a one-shilling coin was valued at one shilling. However, the metallic value of the coins, based on their gold and silver content, would vary as some coins were "clipped." This was a practice in which people deliberately clipped or shaved off some of the coin and used the gold and silver for other purposes. The result was that faced with owning two coins—a new, fully valued silver coin and a clipped one—the owner would pass on the clipped one and save (or clip) the fully valued coined. Hence the phrase bad money drives out good. Gresham's law applies to any situation in which there is a single market price, and yet the value of the commodity traded differs. Inevitably, it is the inferior-valued commodity that is passed on, as is the case in Akerlof's car example, in which the car market becomes dominated by lemons.[2]

Of course, there are mechanisms to adjust for this market failure. In Gresham's time, people would weigh the coins and refuse to accept badly clipped coins at face value. Similarly, in Akerlof's example, one solution is to get a mechanic's report . However, a buyer may not have any faith in the seller's choice of mechanic, requiring that the buyer also get a mechanic's report, adding two layers of cost. Another solution is to buy from the dealer at which the car was originally sold and serviced, thus relying on the car dealer's reputation. In this case, the lemons would be sold at auction, where only the pros (mechanics and used car dealers) buy. Failing that, a last solution is to buy a used car from someone who clearly has no friends or relatives! The point is that we get a richer set of markets with alternative market mechanisms. This is what happens in financial markets: much of the richness of financial markets is derived from arrangements developed to deal with these information asymmetries.

Let's return to our discussion of an investor who wants to buy a new issue of securities but who doesn't realize the issue is fraudulent. From the issuer's perspective, this is a fantastic deal: for the initial cash received from selling the securities, the criminal promises to make a series of future payments. All he or she has to do for this cash is provide some "legal" documentation and a few certificates, essentially some paper. If the criminal can raise, say, $200 million from a group of investors, he or she needs only to make a few payments before jumping on a plane to a jurisdiction that won't extradite him back to Canada! The criminal enjoys a $200 million inflow in return for printing up a few certificates.

Real-World Examples of Fraudulent Activities

Historically financial markets have been rife with fraud and abuse. A little more than 100 years ago, many of the securities sold to the general public were frauds. However, frauds occur at all levels and not just with the general public. The U.S. Securities Exchange Commission's (SEC) website shows that frauds are still happening. For example, William E. Lyons is accused of trying to sell US$220 million in fraudulently issued zero coupon bonds to Bear Stearns Companies, Inc. (Bear Stearns), a major U.S. investment bank, through what is commonly called the prime bank scam. In the SEC complaint, section 16 alleges that:

---

[2] Gresham's law also explains why coins have traditionally been "milled" with a defined edge: so that everyone knows that the coin has not been tampered with. This practice has continued, even though most coins now have little monetary value.

Lyons' efforts to market the bank guarantee offering to Bear Stearns were designed to persuade representatives of Bear Stearns to tender the $200 million payment for the purchase of a purported $220 million bank guarantee. Such a payment by Bear Stearns would have generated a total of approximately $1 million in compensation to SV Group and Lyons.

Lyons was a former broker at Bear Stearns and the SEC complaint in section 13 further alleges that:

Had Lyons conducted an independent inquiry, he would have discovered that the purported bank guarantees that he was offering and their associated funding and issuing transactions had the hallmarks of a fraudulent prime bank securities scheme.

Bear Stearns rejected Lyons's proposal in December 2002, indicated that the transaction was probably fraudulent, and suggested he check the SEC website. However, apparently Lyons then tried to sell the securities to Merrill Lynch & Co., Inc. (Merrill Lynch), Goldman Sachs Group, Inc., and Chase Manhattan Bank, three other prominent U.S. financial institutions. This is when the SEC intervened.

Lyons' alleged actions illustrate that if a criminal wants to steal, he or she goes where the money is: the major financial institutions. If Lyons had tried to sell these securities to the general public, it would have taken a lot more effort with a lot more publicity to raise US$200 million. It is interesting that he tried to sell zero coupon bonds: if he had sold regular interest-bearing bonds, the fraudsters who originally issued the bonds would have had to pay interest and the lack of interest payments would have caused the purchasers to contact the SEC or police soon after the missed interest payment. In contrast, zero coupon bonds have no payments until maturity, so there is no tip off that they are fraudulent until they are redeemed.

In the same way, most frauds are perpetrated by using **bearer bonds**, which are unregistered bonds and the owner is the person who has the bonds at a particular time. Bearer bonds are popular in Europe, where they are allegedly used often for tax evasion. However, in North America, almost all bonds are registered and maintained as (computer) book entries, with just a tiny number of bearer bonds, which is why most frauds involve foreign, zero coupon bearer bonds.[3]

bearer bonds unregistered bonds that are payable to whomever holds them

One of the biggest frauds in England involved a fraudulent issue of 10-year zero coupon bonds sold into a small regional market, away from the major market in London, where it might have been noticed. The fraud became known only after the bonds were sold and the bearer bonds were warehoused. A lowly clerk happened to notice that the new bonds didn't seem to be as stiff as other bonds that he had previously catalogued and put away. On checking he discovered they all had the same serial number! It turned out the bonds had been copied on reasonably sophisticated copy machines, but the paper was different. The popular novel by Paul Erdman, *Zero Coupon* (1993), was loosely based on this real-life fraud.

---

[3] In Canada, the Canadian Depository for Securities (CDS) is owned by the major banks and handles 77 million transactions a year with $2.7 trillion on deposit. Purchases and sales are then made through computer entries at CDS.

Ponzi scheme a fraud that involves selling enough new fake securities so that the cash inflow can be used to make the interest payments on the earliest fake securities

Zero coupon bonds aren't really needed for fraud; all that is needed is some mechanism for keeping investors happy while the fraudster tries to defraud more people. The classic way of doing this is to sell enough new fraudulent securities so that the cash inflow from their sale can make the interest payments on the earliest fraudulent bonds. This type of fraud is called a **Ponzi scheme**, after Carlo Ponzi, an Italian born in 1882, who immigrated to the United States.

When dealing with a customer in Spain, Ponzi[4] noticed that he received an international postal reply coupon that could be exchanged for U.S. stamps. What he also noticed was that he could buy these coupons in Spain and exchange them for U.S. stamps worth six times as much. In financial terms, we say that he recognized an *arbitrage* opportunity—he could buy something in one market (i.e., Spain and other countries) and resell it for more in another market (i.e., the United States). Technically, arbitrage implies the ability to earn a profit without assuming any risk. In any event, Ponzi subsequently discovered that the cost of the round-trip transaction involved so many administrative details that he could not make a profit. However, his idea was easily understood, and friends and relatives had wanted in on his investment before it occurred to him that it was not profitable. He took their money and issued them notes promising a 50 percent return in six months, ostensibly so he could buy more postal coupons. He then paid off the notes as they came due with the money from new investors as word of his genius spread. The more he bragged about his financial acumen, and the more satisfied customers he had, the more the money rolled in.

Several groups warned investors that something was wrong, but as long as Ponzi paid off on the 50 percent interest-bearing notes, he had an army of satisfied investors who were vociferous in their support of his enterprise. His status was enhanced after he paid off a horde of investors who panicked and demanded their money back. It seemed that Ponzi could do no wrong. However, auditors looking at his books eventually declared that he was bankrupt, and the U.S. federal authorities arrested him on August 13, 1920. It turned out that in order to fulfill his scheme, he needed to buy 180 million postal certificates, and he had bought only two! He was sentenced to five years in jail by the U.S. government, and seven to nine in Massachusetts, but he skipped bail. He was later found selling "underwater" building lots in Florida for $10 and promising investors they could be resold for $5.3 million within two years!

The recent example of Lyons and the classic case of Ponzi illustrate the problems of information asymmetry in issuing securities. In both cases, the issuers knew that what they were selling was not worth what investors were paying. These cases are extreme cases of information asymmetry, and in the face of rampant fraudulent activity, such as this, financial markets cannot survive. Consider, for example, two possible issuers, one a fraudster, like Ponzi, and the other a legitimate company. If the investor cannot distinguish between them, then he or she has to bear this fraud risk and every dollar invested in the fraudulent scheme will be lost. Increasing the interest rate might solve this problem; however, such activity is self-defeating.

Consider a simple case in which the market interest rate is 10 percent for non-fraudulent bonds. If one in five bonds is fraudulent in a given market, then introducing a "fraud premium" would put the interest rate at 37.5 percent,

---

[4] This discussion is based on the article "Charles Ponzi," available at http://home.nycap.rr.com/useless/ponzi/.

based on a one-year investment horizon and assuming the market does not require a risk premium. This rate may be calculated as follows:

$$4 \times (1 + k) = 5 \times (\$1.10)$$

$$k = 37.5\%$$

In other words, the investor wants 10 percent or $1.10 (principal plus interest) on each $5 invested but will only get $(1 + k)$ on the $4 invested in the legitimate businesses and will get $0 from the fraudster. As the amount of fraudulent activity in the market increases, so too does the market interest rate applied to all borrowers.

However, there is a problem with increasing the market interest rate, just as there was in Akerlof's market for lemons. We know that Ponzi was willing to pay 37.5 percent—after all, he actually paid 50 percent on six-month notes—while fraudsters usually have no intention of paying all the money back. As a result, they will *promise* to pay any market interest rate, because they don't expect to pay it anyway. Conversely, legitimate businesses can't normally generate the profits required to pay 37.5 percent and will balk at paying such a high rate when they have no intention of committing fraud. Consequently, they will not issue securities to the general public, just as the owner of a good car doesn't sell to the public. Instead, legitimate businesses will rely on private financing, and the public markets will be left to the fraudsters and inevitably dry up. In this case, the willingness to pay an exorbitant interest rate should be a tipoff to any sensible person not to lend them money.

FRAUDSTER JAILED IN STOCK SCAM

Michael Mitton, known to authorities as one of this country's premier fraud artists, was "coaxed out of retirement" to do one last job—a scheme that could have netted him and his colleagues tens of millions of dollars. But the 48-year-old father of three got caught early this year by the RCMP.

He pleaded guilty to fraud and money laundering in a Bay Street scam known as the "pump and dump," a scheme to drive up the price of Pender International Inc.—a company whose only asset was a partial stake in a worthless, flooded mine in northern Ontario—and then sell the shares to an unsuspecting public.

It was fraud convictions number 104 and 105 for the native of Montreal, who pulled off most of his cons in British Columbia over a 30-year career. Judges there have described him as a "professional swindler," "a consummate liar ... a rogue of the first order."

Had the Mounties and the Ontario Securities Commission not noticed something suspicious was happening at Pender, there could have been "substantial risk to the stock markets of this province and this country and some threat to economic prosperity." Pender's share price rose from thirty cents (U.S.) to $11.25, or more than 3,700 per cent, in a 35-day period on the National Association of Securities Dealers Over-the-Counter Bulletin Board.

Mitton was also ordered to pay back $2.6 million to HSBC Securities, its loss in the scam. Aneillo (Neil) Peluso and Michael Ciavarella, are the two other co-accused facing charges in connection with the fraud.

Prosecutor Randy Schwartz told the judge that Mitton was involved in a "sophisticated, large-scale fraud," and had it been successful it would have "undermined confidence in the public markets."

Schwartz went on to tell the court that despite Mitton's long criminal record he still deserved credit for acknowledging his guilt, adding that Mitton had "made concessions"

finance
INTHENEWS17-1

that would "enable the ongoing prosecution" in the case. Mitton stood to make about $580,000 (Canadian) from his end of the scam, which Addario described as "small" in relation to what it could have netted.

In an agreed statement of facts presented to the court by Schwartz and Addario, Mitton admitted he was the "architect" of the scheme which involved the accumulation of most of Pender's free shares and then ratcheting up the price in trading between related brokerage accounts.

"He was the co-conspirator with sufficient expertise in the capital markets to orchestrate the manipulation" the statement said.

Mitton also settled trades by cheque rather than transferring funds, which delayed settlements and gave him time to recycle money to finance more trading.

In one case, HSBC Securities held an outstanding debit of about $2.6 million (U.S.) on the purchase of Pender shares in an account that had not been settled. Mitton and Ciavarella exercised control over the account.

HSBC ended up with the loss after concluding the Pender shares were being manipulated, but the brokerage refused to sell the stock because of that knowledge.

The statement of facts revealed that when brokerages started to freeze accounts by parties trading in Pender in December 2004, Ciavarella emptied some of them of about $250,000 before they closed.

Despite a regulatory freeze on the accounts and orders directing Mitton to stop trading in Pender stock and any securities that month, he started again a few weeks later. It included trading in Pender shares.

To fuel interest in Pender and jack up the stock price, Mitton also acknowledged in the statement that he wrote numerous news releases containing false or misleading information between July 2004 and April 2005.

Mitton also used aliases to hide his identity.

"Given that Mr. Mitton's true name is notorious within the securities industry, his successful use of aliases was integral to his ability to orchestrate and carry out the fraud in this case," the statement said.

Source: Pron, Nick and Van Alphen, Tony, "Fraudster Jailed in Stock Scam." *Toronto Star*, March 23, 2007, p. F1. Reprinted with permission of Torstar Syndication Services.

This insight is behind almost all securities law. Quite simply, if investors cannot distinguish good investments from lemons offered by fraudsters, they will not invest in the public markets. Investors have to be confident that they are being treated fairly in the capital market, otherwise they will invest offshore where they are treated fairly, or they will invest in real assets, like houses and gold. There is then a social loss from the collapse of financial markets. This explains why there is a direct (positive) correlation between the existence of public capital markets and respect for the "rule of law." In countries where there is no confidence in the enforcement of laws against fraud or there is a belief that markets are rigged, financial transactions are done mostly through private placements in which the borrower and lender know each other. In these cases, there are also usually social enforcement costs to mitigate fraud. These generally involve either social costs, such as being excluded from the best "clubs,"[5] or draconian punishment for criminals.[6]

Like the used car market, alternative market mechanisms have evolved in the financial markets so that investors can invest with some assurance that they are

---

[5] Traditionally, in Canada, like many other countries, fraud was disciplined by the perpetrators being designated as social outcasts and their family being excluded from the best schools, clubs, and so on. The loosening of social bonds has weakened the effectiveness of these types of constraints in Canada but not in more socially cohesive cultures.

[6] In Russia, the capitalists that bought former state owned enterprises at reduced prices have not fared very well. Mikhail Khordovsky is in jail for 10 years for fraud and tax evasion, while Yukos, the oil and gas company he owned and ran, faces a $27.5 billion tax bill and a forced merger with Gazprom, the state-owned oil company.

not buying lemons. The main mechanisms are securities legislation and corporate law, which keep known criminals out of the markets and require that any securities offered to the public are checked to ensure that they are legitimate. This overall process of checking securities offered to the public is called **due diligence**, and can be very expensive and time consuming. It is as a result of fraud that so much checking and legal documentation is required. We will discuss some Canadian cases of fraudulent activity below.

> **due diligence** the process of checking securities offered to the public to ensure they are legitimate

Some Canadian Examples of Fraudulent Activities

In 1908, Carlo Ponzi served 20 months in jail for a similar pyramid scam in Canada. If U.S. securities laws in 1920 had been as tough as they are now, he would never have been allowed to sell securities to the public, because his criminal background would have disqualified him from registration as a securities broker-dealer. Likewise, one of the charges the SEC levied against William Lyons was that he was not registered to sell financial securities. Keeping known criminals out of the business and making sure that those in it understand the basics of the business and abide by professional standards is a necessary, if not sufficient, condition for minimizing fraud in the markets.

In her book *Contrepreneurs* (1988), Diane Francis details how Toronto used to be the "bucket shop" capital of the world. These bucket shops were basically basements in large buildings with banks of dedicated telephones, where salespeople would call wealthy doctors and dentists in the United States, touting junior resource stocks on the then Vancouver Stock Exchange (VSE).[7] The broker-dealers selling these "penny stocks" would often trade among themselves in "wash sales," in which the sum of the external sales activity was zero. By selling among themselves at ever higher prices, the appearance of momentum was generated to attract investors looking at the statistics in the newspaper. These securities were highlighted as emerging "growth" stocks with great potential to attract investors looking for a quick profit. However, once the price had been artificially inflated to attract enough external investors, the insiders sold out and these external investors found out that there was no one else to sell to! This example illustrates the basic proposition that although it is easy to buy securities, they are often difficult to sell. These types of activities have now been shut down by securities regulators.[8]

If buying securities directly from a company, or through a broker-dealer, is considered risky why not buy them through an asset manager selling mutual funds? Buying a mutual fund holding many securities is less risky—right? Not necessarily. In Quebec, Norbourg Asset Management Inc. (Norbourg) was closed down and its founder, Vincent Lacroix, charged by Quebec's main regulator, the Autorité des marchés financiers (AMF), with misappropriating investor funds. The AMF claimed Lacroix stole $84 million from Norbourg and Evolution mutual funds, and it is claiming $10 million in punitive damages. The AMF froze Norbourg's assets in August 2005 and a later audit revealed that $130 million was missing.[9]

---

[7] The Vancouver Stock Exchange (VSE) no longer exists and has been replaced by the TSX Venture Exchange. These salespeople took pains not to sell to Canadians to avoid alerting Canadian authorities.

[8] As late as 2001, the RCMP arrested 30 to 40 people involved in a Nigerian letter scam operating out of Toronto. The scam mainly targeted wealthy Americans, claiming that there was money tied up in Nigeria, and all that was needed was some seed capital to get it out. Some U.S. investors lost up to $5 million.

[9] "Quebec Regulators Sue Norbourg's Founder for $94 Million," *CBC News Online*: www.cbc.ca, October 24, 2005.

Regulators and police try hard to stop criminal activity, but they can never shut it down completely. It's like trying to stop people from speeding—the laws are there, as is the enforcement, but the police can't be everywhere. Investors need to remember the old adage that "if it sounds too good to be true, it probably is."

This warning may be obvious, but it is remarkable how gullible people can be. Moreover, the statistical evidence is that gullible investors tend to be of above-average intelligence and workaholics who consider themselves to be financially literate. This is why doctors and dentists are prime candidates for fraudsters: they have lots of money and are eager to get more, while they are also clever enough to think they understand what's going on and don't need expert advice. It appears that the easiest person to defraud is someone who has a high opinion of himself or herself.

CONCEPT REVIEW QUESTIONS

1. How does the existence of asymmetric information lead to market inefficiencies?

2. Why can increases in interest rates not be used to solve the "lemons problem" in markets?

3. Why are securities legislation and corporate laws essential for markets to perform properly?

17.2 A PRIMER ON SECURITIES LEGISLATION IN CANADA

Securities Legislation—Basic Responsibilities

Canada has no federal securities regulator because it is a provincial and territorial responsibility. There has been a great deal of debate over this format, with many parties pushing for the establishment of a federal securities regulator. Finance in the News 17-2 discusses this topic.

As it stands today, the main regulators in Canada are the Ontario, B.C., and Quebec provincial securities commissions. However, selling securities in other provinces and territories requires that the issue be cleared with their authorities as well. Similarly, in the United States, securities regulation is a state responsibility, but so many issues in the United States are national in scope and cross state lines that the U.S. **Securities and Exchange Commission (SEC)** is, in effect, a national securities regulator. However, issues can be sold within a state if no out-of-state investors are involved. This raises the basic point that securities regulation is designed to protect investors in that jurisdiction, so the provincial and territorial authorities exert authority whenever its citizens are involved. This is the reason that scam artists in Toronto sold into the United States and not in Canada: in this way the Ontario Securities Commission (OSC) was not directly involved. For the same reason, Internet fraud now seems to come from Russia where regulation is lax.

Securities and Exchange Commission (SEC) a U.S. agency that is, in effect, a national securities regulator

FLAHERTY SEES NATIONAL SECURITIES REGULATOR AS A "PRIORITY"

finance INTHENEWS17-2

The Conservative government wants to appoint a national stock market regulator "on a priority basis."

The idea of a single stock market regulator has been tossed around for years, but the many proposals have been lost in interprovincial rivalries.

But Finance Minister Jim Flaherty wants to sit down with the provinces and work out a solution that would suit every stakeholder.

"The minister of finance will engage with provinces and territories on this issue on a priority basis," the budget documents said.

"The government of Canada believes that Canadians would best be served by a common securities regulator that administers a single code, is responsive to regional needs and has a government structure that ensures broad provincial participation," the government said in the federal budget delivered Tuesday.

A common regulator would also foster more responsive policy-making, improve market efficiency, eliminate duplication, provide common standards of investor protection and strengthen Canada's voice in international discussions on regulatory standards.

The provinces of British Columbia, Alberta and Quebec have tended to oppose the idea of a single regulator because they fear that Ontario would run the show.

Source: "Flaherty Sees National Securities Regulator as a 'Priority,'" CBC News Online: www.cbc.ca, May 2, 2006.

A security, according to the Ontario Securities Act (OSA), *includes* "any document, investment or writing commonly known as a security,"[10] such as bonds and common equities. The critical fact is that the list is not exhaustive. In practice, the OSA and other provincial and territorial securities commissions aim to protect investors not just from fraud but also from "the imposition of unsubstantial schemes," that is, misleading and bad investments.

In determining whether a security exists, the OSC looks at several factors. For example, the following are often looked at by a judge in determining the court's authority:

- whether the promoter raises money and leads the investor to expect a profit

- whether the investor has any control on how the money is spent

- whether there is risk involved

Other factors are also important, but these are the major ones, and taking a broad interpretation of these criteria implies that almost any document can be construed as a security. For example, securities have been found to exist when a half interest in a pair of royal chinchillas was sold, where warehouse receipts were sold indicating ownership of casks of whiskey, and where leases were sold that gave drilling rights. The critical point seems to be the protection of the public interest and courts have taken a broad view of what this interest is.

A classic case involved Pacific Coast Coin Exchange of Canada (PCCE), which sold silver on a 35 percent margin (that is, purchasers only put up 35 percent of the money for the silver). Purchasers could then sell the silver back to PCCE; pay interest on the loan, storage, and handling charges; and receive the difference (positive or negative) in the price of silver. PCCE promoted its business, emphasizing silver as a store of value during a highly inflationary

---

[10] See the OSC's website to find their current investigations and rules at www.osc.gov.on.ca. This section is heavily based on Jeffrey MacIntosh and Christopher Nicholls, *Securities Law* (Toronto: Irwin Law, 2002); and Christopher Nicholls, *Corporate Finance and Canadian Law* (Toronto: Carswell, 2000).

period.[11] The OSC shut down PCCE's operations as it was in violation of the OSA, a decision that the Supreme Court of Canada confirmed. Although PCCE's operations did not technically meet the definition of a security as then defined, the Supreme Court stated that the important point is the policy behind the legislation and that "substance not form" dictates whether or not something is a security. All that is necessary for the OSC to claim jurisdiction is that a transaction has an effect on Ontario residents sufficient to prejudice the public interest.

This broad interpretation of what constitutes a security and the application of securities laws means that the OSC is involved in five major areas in which securities are transferred or traded:

- primary market offerings
- secondary market trading
- activities of investment professionals
- insider trading
- takeover bids

The broad definition of a trade is a *sale* of a security for valuable consideration. It also includes the activities of traders on an organized exchange, registrants who take orders to buy and sell securities, and any "act, advert, solicitation, conduct or negotiation to directly or indirectly further a trade." Traders and individuals registered to buy and sell securities (i.e., registrants) are regulated; however, given the broad scope of what constitutes a security, many individuals are traders and do not realize it. For example, lottery tickets sold at the corner store could be regarded as securities and the storekeeper required to register with the OSC. However, the fact that lotteries are well known, with no public interest, means that, in practice, they aren't treated as securities.[12]

Security Offerings

The other main implication of the definition of a trade is the promotion aspect. Anyone who phones someone to generate a sale is involved in trading, as is any website that promotes particular securities. Moreover the OSC has broad powers to restrict such activity before a trade is effected, meaning that documents used to generate sales of securities are highly regulated. The most significant area involves **initial public offerings (IPOs)** of securities, because the assumption is that information asymmetry is greatest with IPOs. IPO trades are *primary offerings*, that is, a first-time *distribution* of securities. Most provinces in Canada, including Ontario, have a closed system for the distribution of securities. What this means is that any distribution of securities has to be accompanied by a **prospectus**, a formal summary of a security that describes the costs, investment objectives, and risks involved. It is illegal to distribute securities without delivering a prospectus to the purchaser. The system is called closed because there are a very limited number of ways of being *exempt* from the prospectus requirement.

initial public offering (IPO) the first sale of a security

prospectus a formal summary of a security that describes the costs, investment objectives, risks, and performance

---

[11] The case was settled in 1978, and the 1970s saw inflation at double-digit levels.

[12] The fact that only about 35 percent of the gross proceeds from lotteries are returned as payoffs should be a concern. In Ponzi's scheme, the eventual liquidation of his "business" resulted in about a 35 percent payout as well.

There are two types of prospectuses: long form and short form. For IPOs, a firm has to have a **long-form prospectus**.[13] It consists of about 70 pages of dense discussion about the firm. The overriding requirement is that the prospectus supply "full, true and plain disclosure of all material facts relating to the securities proposed to be distributed." This definition has important components; the "full, true and plain" means that it has to be understandable (and not in "legalese") and it must correctly portray the situation of the firm. Further, every *material fact* has to be disclosed, where a material fact is something that can reasonably be expected to affect the price of the securities being distributed. This also means that half-truths, while technically correct, and omissions do not represent full, true, and plain disclosure. The prospectus has to be signed by both the chief executive officer (CEO) and the chief financial officer (CFO) on behalf of the issuing firm's board of directors (BOD) and the investment dealer helping to sell the securities. This makes all signatories liable for damages in the event of misrepresentation.[14]

The possibility of being sued is what ensures that the investment dealer and the issuing firm do a comprehensive job of explaining the firm's position. This involves performing their due diligence, defined earlier, and doing a reasonable investigation of the facts to ensure that there has been no material misrepresentation. The standard applied is "that required of a prudent person in the circumstances of the particular case." The investment dealers and the lawyers preparing the prospectus have to check and recheck the statements made by the issuing firm to assure themselves that the prospectus fairly represents the firm's position.[15]

The British Columbia Securities Commission (BCSC) has a 66-page document dictating what has to be included in a prospectus.[16] Broadly speaking, this document says that a prospectus has to contain the following:

- the securities being issued and who can buy them

- the price of the securities, the fees to the investment dealer involved with the distribution, and the net proceeds

- the market for the securities, that is, whether they will be traded

- the business of the issuer and its subsidiaries, with a discussion of the past three-year history

- risk factors involved with buying the securities

- summary financial information

- management's discussion and analysis

Under each of these general groupings is an extensive list of what needs to be discussed, as well as specific requirements for different types of distributions, such as by a mining firm or a mutual fund. It is easy to understand, from reviewing the

long-form prospectus a long document supplying full, honest disclosure of all facts that can reasonably be expected to affect the price of the security, written in plain language; it must be signed by the chief executive officer and chief financial officer

---

[13] All legal documents in Canada can be retrieved from the OSC's SEDAR website at www.sedar.com. Investors can search for both long-form and short-form prospectuses.

[14] Before Sarbanes-Oxley (SOX), discussed in Chapter 3, the standard advice was not to trust the annual report but instead to look to the last prospectus, because an investor could sue for misrepresentation in the prospectus but not in the annual report. This is still true for Canadian companies that are not subject to SOX.

[15] This does not mean that the prospectus includes "full, true and plain disclosure of all material facts." If the firm deliberately wants to commit fraud, then even diligent work by the investment dealer and its lawyers may not uncover it.

[16] BC Securities Commission, *BC Form 41-601F: Information Required in a Prospectus*, on the commission's website at www.bcsc.bc.ca.

BCSC document, why the cost of preparing a prospectus is at least $500,000 for a $20 million offering.

Despite the cost, a prospectus is required for all distributions. The OSC has determined that there are three types of distributions. The first is a distribution by an issuer. The assumption here is that the issuer is raising money in the primary market from investors and by definition knows more about the true value of the securities than the investors do. Hence, the prospectus is designed to remedy this information asymmetry. Imagine, for example, if Carlo Ponzi had had to describe his business by using "full, true and plain" disclosure, and an investment bank and legal firm had to sign off on his prospectus! The second is a distribution being sold from a control block.[17] The assumption here is that someone owning a control block also has privileged access to the firm, and as a result there is an information asymmetry that the prospectus is designed to remedy. In this case, a prospectus has to be prepared even if the firm is raising no money, so that the distribution is a *secondary market* not a *primary market* transaction. Again, the fact the firm has to bear this cost is not a factor. What is important is that investors buying the securities are protected. The third is a distribution in which restricted shares are being sold to the public for the first time.

As indicated above, a prospectus is required for most distributions of securities and in the process the securities are registered. This means that trades in the security can be effected by a securities firm that is registered with the appropriate securities commission. In this way, the Canadian Depository for Securities Limited (CDS) is normally the registered owner of the securities and trades in the securities are effected by means of computer (book) entries. What this means is that the prospectus requirement goes hand in hand with the registration of the securities, which allows them to be subsequently bought and sold in the public markets. Without a prospectus, the securities are not registered and cannot be publicly traded. The market for non-registered securities is called the **exempt market**.

exempt market the unregulated market for non-registered securities that raise money from private investors

If a firm wants to raise a small amount of money, then preparing a $500,000 prospectus and engaging an investment dealer to distribute the securities does not make much sense. As a result, there are exemptions from the prospectus requirement based on smaller issues, the sophistication of the potential investors, and the risk of the securities. To prevent securities that are sold in the exempt market from slipping into the public markets, or so-called "backdoor underwriting," the exempt purchasers can sell only to other exempt purchasers or, under certain circumstances, they can sell the securities in the public market after holding them for certain time,[18] if the issuer has effectively met the prospectus requirements by becoming a "reporting issuer," which will be discussed later.

The three major categories of exempt purchasers that make up the exempt market are based on the sophistication of the purchaser, the low-risk nature of the instrument, and the existence of alternative regulatory protection. For these

[17] Control blocks are not defined in law. Clearly, 50.1 percent effects legal control, but a prospectus may also be required to distribute smaller blocks, even down to 5 percent if there are grounds for believing that there is inside information.

[18] Normal hold periods are four months to two years, after which the securities are regarded as seasoned.

purchasers, the issuer normally prepares an **offering memorandum**, rather than a prospectus. Although both of these documents have the same objective and have to be correct, the amount of information in an offering memorandum is significantly less, which lowers the cost of preparing it.[19]

Sophisticated purchasers are essentially individuals and institutions that can be expected to hire their own experts to conduct their own due diligence. For example, securities can be sold, without a prospectus to accredited investors, such as banks, governments, wealthy investors (net assets of more than $1 million and $300,000 a year in family income), investment dealers, and individuals owning control blocks. Similarly, government debt issues are exempt, as are debt issues by many financial institutions. Finally, securities issued as part of takeovers and corporate reorganizations are exempt, because they are covered by corporate law requirements to provide proxy circulars and similar documents. The only other major exemption is for private firms, now called closely held issuers; as long as no promotion is done and less than $3 million is raised, securities can be sold to no more than 35 individuals with the approval of the BOD. In this case, the issue has to be accompanied by an information statement containing basic information about the issuer.

Securities legislation has come a long way since the days of Carlo Ponzi. The definition of a security is now so broad as to cover any attempt to sell an interest in something to someone with an expectation of making a profit. All such distributions need to be accompanied by a prospectus, unless they are sold into the exempt market by means of what is referred to as a private placement. The prospectus is designed to minimize information asymmetry problems so that Ponzi schemes and other frauds are rare and so that investors will have confidence in the public markets. This confidence is encouraged by the breadth and depth of the information required in a prospectus and the fact that almost everyone involved in its production can be sued if there are material misrepresentations. The restrictions on "hyping" securities while they are being issued and the registration of the professionals involved in their subsequent trading are both designed to enhance the confidence in secondary as well as primary markets. In the sections below, we will discuss why firms choose to go public rather than sell securities through a private placement or the exempt market and how ongoing supervision of firms develops after they have filed their initial long-form prospectus.

offering memorandum a document with the same objectives as a prospectus but providing significantly less information, which lowers the cost of preparing it

CONCEPT REVIEW QUESTIONS

1. What are some of the more important issues arising from the fact that securities regulation is a provincial and territorial, but not a federal, responsibility in Canada?

2. Why are prospectuses so important for public market issues?

3. Differentiate offering memorandums from prospectuses and exempt markets from public markets.

---

[19] In some cases, the OSA requires an offering memorandum, which is delivered to the OSC but is not publicly available. In other cases, the issuer decides, or the investment dealer insists, on the preparation of one to help market the issue.

17.3 IPOs AND INVESTMENT BANKING

The principles that we have discussed apply to all public offerings of securities, whether they are debt or common equity securities and whether or not this is the first time such securities have been offered. In this section, we discuss a particularly important public offering of securities, namely common shares to the public for the first time (i.e., IPOs). Although it is not strictly necessary, such public offerings are almost always listed on an organized exchange, such as the Toronto Stock Exchange (TSX) or TSX Venture Exchange, which allows these shares to be easily traded.

The Motivation for IPOs

Most firms "going public" have had this as a long-term goal for many years before they actually become a publicly traded company. The response to a Conference Board of Canada's survey indicates that firms have several reasons for going public.[20] One of the most frequently cited reasons is the desire on behalf of some investors to "cash out." Sometimes this is a way of paying off private equity investors and other venture capitalists that financed the firm in its earlier stages of development. The founders of the company often want to cash out if they are no longer actively involved in managing the company. The managers then face the choice of either selling the company to someone else privately, or going public and combining a sale of shares by the company with the sale of the founders' shares. In this way an important part of going public is the fact that a market price exists and shareholders can evaluate and liquidate their investment more easily.

Other firms go public because they want access to a more diversified set of financing options. In particular, two often-expressed motives are to escape dependence on bank lending and to increase the use common equity as an acquisition currency. We discussed the closed system of securities regulation in the previous section, but if a firm wants to buy another firm through an exchange of shares, the purchasing firm is restricted unless it is publicly traded, because the shares are not registered and can only be sold to exempt purchasers and not to the general public. This lack of liquidity in the stock makes the firm's shares unattractive as a means of financing takeovers. As discussed in Chapter 15, any firm making extensive acquisitions will find it advantageous to have publicly traded shares.

It is also important to recognize that many private firms are extremely dependent on their bank for financing. Even if they have good relationships with their bank, there is a perception that this improves after they go public. This may be due to the belief that being a "listed company" has significant value. The listing of a firm's shares on a major exchange, coupled with the prospectus requirement, dramatically increases the flow of information about the firm, which the bank may find comforting. Several respondents to the Conference Board of Canada's study reported that the relationships with suppliers and customers did improve as a result of a public listing, which provides a kind of "seal of approval" that the firm has arrived.

The reasons given by the participants in the Conference Board of Canada's eight case studies are broadly consistent with the ideas advanced by Stewart

---

[20] For some case histories see Michael Andrews, *Initial Public Offerings: The Experience of Eight Canadian Growth Companies* (Ottawa: Conference Board of Canada, 1995).

Myers.[21] Myers also emphasizes the use of the stock price as an incentive mechanism to enhance managerial efficiency.

Suppose, for example, we divide a new firm's development into five stages:

1. technological experimentation

2. pilot studies and sales

3. improvement in production and scaling up manufacturing

4. full-scale marketing and production

5. expansion into other lines

These five stages roughly correspond to the product life cycle discussed in strategy classes. What Myers added is the need to provide incentive for the founders and reward them for their industry and innovation, which will vary across the product life cycle.

As we discussed in Chapter 2, an *agency relationship* exists when people hire someone else to execute their wishes. In this respect, managers are agents for the owners of the firm, and the question is when does a firm transfer from being an owner-managed firm to one that has a *separation* of ownership from control, which is what normally happens when a firm goes public? One of the reasons mentioned in the Conference Board of Canada's study is the ability to cash out the founders by allowing them to sell their shares to the public.

In Myers' view, the entrepreneur is essential at stages 1 and 2, valuable at stage 3, useful but replaceable at stage 4, and not needed at all at stage 5. So suppose at stage 1 and 2, the entrepreneur is willing to commit "sweat equity" and all his or her savings into the enterprise but needs some external finance. The company can't raise external equity at this stage, because the informational problems are too large. Instead, the firm raises **private equity or venture capital** from a partner. In this way the funds are provided from the exempt market.

private equity or venture capital money raised from private investors in the exempt market

The entrepreneur, as well as the partner, then needs a commitment to go public at stage 3 and certainly by stage 4, as the proportion of intellectual or human capital versus real capital in the value of the firm goes down. Essentially, if the venture is successful after stage 2, then the entrepreneur's value has been validated by an increase in the value of the firm. Yet at this stage, significant external funds are needed to formalize the firm's business plan and buy real assets. This is the ideal point to take the firm public, so the investment by the entrepreneur or founder and backers can be monetized. Otherwise, the value will be diluted by the new funds raised to take the firm to the next stage. Also, at this stage, the entrepreneur is no longer as important to the firm as it moves into a classic production mode with a formal managerial culture and with less need to provide incentive on the creative side of the business.

Myers was writing at the time of the Internet bubble and was clearly influenced by the large number of hi-tech firms going public at that time. The basic idea is consistent with **agency theory**, the study of relationships between shareholders and a company's managers and the costs of resolving conflicts between them and aligning their interests, and with the observation that private firms involve a higher proportion of "intellectual" capital. They go public when this is less important and when they face increased financing needs. The corollary also follows: firms with little need to provide incentive for management have less need

agency theory the study of relationships between shareholders and a company's managers and the costs of resolving conflicts between them and aligning their interests

---

[21] Myers, Stewart. "Financial Architecture," *European Financial Management* 5, no. 2 (1999), pp. 133–41.

to go public. It is hardly surprising, for example, that utility firms like the local water company are run under private, normally municipal, management; they have less need to motivate management to be efficient and create value.[22]

Agency theory also explains why divisions are sometimes spun off from larger firms. Entrepreneurial activity cannot be properly rewarded within a large firm in which there is little correspondence between the effort expended by entrepreneurial managers and the value they create. In contrast, entrepreneurial activity is often stimulated in a wave of innovation as a division is spun off from a bureaucratic parent company, and the managers start focusing on creating enough value to take the firm public.

Going public can thus be seen as a longer-term objective of many firms to monetize the value created by the founders when their value to the firm starts to wane, and the firm moves to stage 3 or 4. Even before this point, the firm will have been in constant contact with its investment dealer as it sought out different sources of financing.

The Stages of the IPO Process

A typical IPO involves four basic stages and normally involves an investment dealer (or investment bank in the United States) that specializes in raising capital for firms and being their "eyes and ears" on the capital market. The first stage involves the initial discussion with the investment dealer, which then triggers the formal IPO process. The second stage consists of drafting an initial prospectus. The third stage, commonly called the waiting period, involves finalizing the prospectus and obtaining clearance from the securities commission. The final stage involves pricing and distributing the issue, and providing after-market stabilization. The process is illustrated in Figure 17-1.

FIGURE **17-1**

The Stages of an IPO

| Discussion triggers IPO | Preliminary prospectus: three to five months | Waiting period and road shows: one to two months | Pricing, distribution, and after-market stabilization: one month |

Initial filing: red herring

Final clearance

preliminary prospectus a document produced for prospective investors by an underwriter, with the understanding that it may be modified significantly before the final prospectus is published

The Conference Board of Canada survey referred to earlier indicates that in this first phase of going public, the firm will use its existing investment dealer but will frequently add other dealers to broaden the distribution of its shares and increase the number of analysts who will subsequently follow and make recommendations on the firm. At this early stage, the firm will also "clean up" its legal structure by removing different classes of shares, changing its bylaws and its board of directors, and by generally making itself more marketable.

The second phase involves preparing the **preliminary prospectus**,[23] a document produced for prospective investors by an underwriter, with the

---

[22] There may be other reasons, however, such as external monitoring.

[23] The preliminary prospectus is often called a "red herring" because of the notice in red type required by law on the first page, indicating its status.

understanding that it will be modified significantly before the final prospectus is published. It usually takes from three to five months to complete. It is this stage that illustrates the Catch-22. The investment dealer would like to do some pre-marketing to see the amount of interest in the company. However, promoting and discussing the sale of shares is regarded as trading, and this cannot happen without a prospectus being delivered. Consequently, the firm will normally sign a "letter of intent" with its investment dealer indicating that all out-of-pocket costs will be covered as it helps the firm to prepare a preliminary prospectus. During this period, the firm, its lawyers, and the investment dealer are not allowed to hype or promote the stock, and communications with the public have to remain unchanged. Further, the investment dealer has to restrict the flow of information.

It is at this stage that the firm and the investment dealer decide on the broad type and terms of the public offering. They can choose from four different types of public offerings: a **best efforts offering**, a **firm commitment offering**, a **bought deal,** and a **standby or rights offering**. The last two can only be used with seasoned offerings, and most IPOs are firm commitment offerings. In a best efforts offering, the investment dealer signs an agency agreement to do its best to sell the shares, with no guarantee of its success. The investment dealer is rewarded on the basis of the shares that it sells—that is, it is paid a certain amount for each share it sells. Such offerings are rare, because firms do not like the uncertainty attached to the process. If this is the only option that is available to the firm after it contacts several investment dealers, it may be a warning sign that the firm should not go public. Occasionally, a firm commitment offering will be converted into a best efforts offering after the investment dealer discovers there is limited investor interest.

In a firm commitment offering, the investment dealer buys the new securities from the issuer and guarantees the sale of a certain number, while in a bought deal, the underwriter buys all the shares of a seasoned issue to resell later, even before the drafting of the preliminary prospectus. In a standby or rights offering, common shares are offered at a discount to investors who already own shares.

The standard IPO contract is a firm commitment arrangement in which the investment dealer buys the shares for a fixed price and resells them to the public at a slightly higher price, thus earning their profits on this **spread** (i.e., the difference between the purchase and reselling price). In this case the investment dealer **underwrites** or guarantees the offering, which is why investment dealers are commonly referred to as *underwriters*.[24] Larger issues will have a **lead investment dealer** that manages the whole process and a **banking (or dealer) syndicate** that is formed temporarily to sell part of the issue. Both groups underwrite the issue and guarantee the firm the proceeds. However, sometimes an investment dealer joins as part of the **selling group** on a best efforts basis, and any shares it cannot sell are returned to the banking syndicate.

best efforts offering shares that are sold by investment dealers through an agency agreement to do their best, with no guarantee of success; investment dealers are paid an amount for each share they sell

firm commitment offering an offering in which the investment dealer buys the new securities from the issuer and guarantees the sale of a certain number

bought deal an offering in which the underwriter buys all the shares of a seasoned issue to resell later, even before the drafting of the preliminary prospectus

standby or rights offering an offering of common shares at a discount to investors who already own shares; can only be used with seasoned offerings

spread the difference between the price at which an investment dealer buys shares and the slightly higher price at which they are resold to the public

underwrite to assume risk by guaranteeing an offering

lead investment dealer a securities firm that manages the process of selling larger issues

banking (or dealer) syndicate a group formed temporarily to jointly underwrite and sell a new security offering

selling group everyone who works to sell an issue

---

[24] Canadian investment banks are more frequently called investment dealers, as discussed in Chapter 2, and their association is still called the Investment Dealers Association or IDA. This is because the use of the term "bank" was restricted under the Bank Act in Canada. Because most of the dealers are now owned by the chartered banks, the use of the American term "investment bank" is becoming more common, although we still use investment dealer throughout most of our discussion.

Investment Dealers Association (IDA) the national self-regulatory organization of the Canadian securities industry

market or disaster "out" clause a clause that gives the underwriter a way to cancel an issue if financial markets deteriorate so much that the underwriter cannot market the issue profitably

overallotment or greenshoe a clause that gives the underwriter the option of buying more shares from the issuer if investor demand is strong

lock-up period a time in which the founders of the company are prohibited from selling their shares

waiting period the time after the preliminary prospectus has been drafted and has been sent to the securities commission to be examined for deficiencies, during which the investment dealer and the issuer wait for final clearance to sell the securities

The compensation to the investment dealer comes from the standard 4 percent underwriting fee based on the gross proceeds of the issue[25] and the difference between what it buys the shares at from the issuer, and the price it sells them at to the public. The **Investment Dealers Association (IDA)**, the national self-regulatory organization of the Canadian securities industry, enforces rule 29, which expressly prohibits selling securities at a price higher than that provided in the prospectus during the course of the distribution.

The underwriting agreement includes standard clauses that provide the issuer with the authority to issue the securities, require it to prepare a prospectus, prevent it from issuing any other securities while the underwriting is underway, and obligate it to pay the underwriter. The contract also stipulates when the securities will be transferred to the underwriter and when the underwriter will pay the issuer. This payment is normally conditional on a **market or disaster "out" clause**.[26] If the state of the financial markets deteriorates so much that the underwriter cannot market the issue profitably, then the issue can be cancelled. This is clearly a huge safety net for the underwriter, but what is defined as "deterioration" in the state of the market is not clear. The B.C. Supreme Court stated that the market out clause referred to the state of the issuing company's shares and not the market generally. Like many legal interpretations, this one has yet to be tested in other cases, but if this holds, then it lessens the value of a firm commitment offering and brings it closer to a best efforts offering.

Another standard underwriting clause is an **overallotment** (or **"greenshoe"**) option that gives the underwriter the option of buying more shares from the issuer (usually 15 percent more) if investor demand is strong. Finally, many agreements also contain a **lock-up period** that prevents the founders of the company from selling their shares for a given time. Because cashing out by the founding entrepreneur or some other private equity investors' shares is a common motive for going public, as discussed above, the last thing the investment dealer wants is a large number of shares being sold just as it is marketing the issue. For this reason, the investment dealer almost always negotiates a lock-up period so that these shares cannot be sold for six months. The actual lock-up period depends on the investment dealer's assessment of how many of the existing common shares are likely to flood the market. If the number of shares is large, then it might impose a *phased* period in which only a certain percentage of the shares can be sold over certain intervals.

Once the preliminary prospectus has been drafted, it is sent to the securities commission to be examined for any deficiencies. This third phase is generally called the **waiting period**, as the investment dealer and the issuer wait for final clearance to sell the securities. This period usually lasts at least three weeks and is longer for IPOs, because there is less information already available than for seasoned offerings.[27] During the waiting period, the underwriter can market the issue and collect "expressions of interest." However, the final price has not been set, so the underwriter indicates a range of possible prices, usually $2 apart, because it is illegal to sell the securities until the prospectus is final.

---

[25] In the United States, the fee is 7 percent, as there is less competition among the investment banks.

[26] The difference between the two is the extent of deterioration in the markets and the amount of margin that the investment dealer is allowed to post. All the investment dealers finance their inventory of securities with borrowings, mainly from the chartered banks.

[27] It is no longer the practice of the OSC, as it has been in the past, to examine every prospectus in detail.

The marketing of the issue will involve "road" shows (or "dog and pony" shows) to describe the issuer and the issue itself in the major financial cities where the issue will be marketed.[28] Typically, exempt purchasers (i.e., the major financial institutions) will be contacted by different members of the selling group and invited to these presentations by senior management and the lead underwriter. Because it is important to the underwriter to sell the issue as quickly as possible, the focus is on institutional clients that can buy large blocks of shares. Significant retail investors may also be invited to attend, although this is less common now than in the past.

It is important to note that at this stage the "expressions of interest" are not firm orders. In the case of the major institutions, the expressions of interest are usually in the form of **limit orders** in which they indicate that they are willing to buy so much at a certain price. For retail investors, they are generally **market orders**, which means they are for fixed amounts at whatever the final price is. This interaction between the investment dealer and the market is extremely useful for setting the final terms of the issue and confirming that the issue can be sold.

limit orders expressions of interest that are not firm orders but indications from major institutions of how much they are willing to buy at a certain price

If the securities commission finds any deficiencies in the prospectus, the issuer has a minimum of 10 days to rectify them—although it may take longer if the deficiencies are significant. Once the revised prospectus has been accepted by the commission, it becomes a final prospectus. The OSC will then issue a receipt and the prospectus will be sent for printing. It is at this stage that the underwriting contract is finalized between the issuer and the investment dealer as they meet to set the final price and quantity of shares being issued. Normally, the price is set after the market closes early in the week so that the issue can be quickly sold. As a guideline, the underwriter sets the price assuming that the issue will be at least twice over-subscribed, based on the earlier expressions of interest. In this way, the underwriter hopes that the price will rise above the issue price on the first day of trading. The fact that the price is expected to rise and generate short-run profits to the purchasers is partly why IPOs tend to be over-subscribed. The practice of short-term trading by buying IPOs is referred to as "stagging" the new issue and can be very profitable when many attractive issues come to the market.

market orders orders from retail investors for fixed amounts at whatever the final price is

Once the issue is cleared for sale by the OSC, the underwriters go into high gear to convert the "expressions of interest" into firm sales. This is the beginning of the fourth phase and is formally called the **distribution period**. Its length depends on the nature of the issue. Normally, the underwriter has to write a cheque to the issuer within three days or so of the issue as the issuer delivers the shares to the underwriter. The underwriter is under great pressure to sell the shares as quickly as possible. The issuer is under a continuing obligation to amend the prospectus if a material change occurs during the distribution. This obligation continues after the issuer is paid by the underwriter and only finishes when the underwriter has informed the issuer that the shares have been sold. This distribution period usually lasts about a month and, during it, the underwriter is under special restrictions.

distribution period the period after the issue has been cleared for sale by the securities commission and the underwriters convert the expressions of interest into firm sales

The first restriction is that this is the "quiet" period. Essentially, all the relevant information should have been included in the prospectus, so the underwriter and issuer are both prohibited from hyping the stock to help sell it.

---

[28] The prospectus needs to be cleared in each province and territory in which the securities will be sold.

The investment dealer in particular cannot issue an analyst report recommending the shares. Also during this period, the underwriters as a group are normally restricted from reducing the price—otherwise, one member of the group could dump its shares if market conditions deteriorate. Finally, the lead underwriter has the right to trade in the shares to maintain an orderly market and help make the issue successful.[29]

The basic way in which an underwriter supports the share price during the distribution period is through the overallotment option. First, the underwriter will try to sell more shares than are issued and will be short the stock, if it is successful. If so, the underwriter then exercises its option and gets more shares from the company. However, under Canadian (and most other countries') laws, investors have a two-day "cooling off" period and can renege on an offer to purchase the shares. Alternatively, if the issue appears to be having trouble, many of the expressions of interest may disappear and even those that honour their commitment may dump the shares if they learn that the issue is in trouble or will want to take short-term profits.

The underwriter will quickly realize if an issue is trouble as it makes a market in the stock and sees the selling pressure. Because the underwriter is short the stock, it can buy it back in the open market. This constant buying by the underwriter is what supports the price during the distribution period if the issue is "cold" or if shares are being dumped for short-term profits. If this price support is ineffective, then after supporting the price, the underwriter will give up and the price will drift (sometimes quickly) lower. The underwriter will then take a loss or try to exercise its *market out* clause at the cost of their reputation.

Remember that all the investment dealer has before it begins selling the shares are "expressions of interest." Given the common knowledge that there is a first day run-up in the share price for IPOs, many investors order more shares than they want to hold for the long term. As a result, the investment dealer faces the risk that either these expressions of interest do not materialize as actual purchases, or that they are quickly sold into the market. To counter this risk, the investment dealer tries to place as much of the issue as possible in friendly hands that have demonstrated that they will honour their commitments and not cut and run. A corollary is that for cold issues, when large-scale institutional purchases dry up, the banking group is forced to turn to the retail or ordinary investor to try to sell the issue. An investor getting a call from a retail broker selling an IPO is often a signal that the issue is cold and institutions have already turned it down.

IPO Underpricing

underpricing the pricing of an IPO at less than its market value; it is the difference between the initial offering price and the price on the first day of trading

One controversial issue in IPOs is the size of this first-day return earned by investors. If the investment dealer had a fiduciary duty to the issuer to get the best possible price for the issue, then nothing would happen on the issue day. However, the first-day return tends to be very high, meaning that the issuer could have sold at a higher price and instead "left money on the table." In other words, the IPO is priced at less than its market value and the price on the first day of trading is much higher. This is referred to as **underpricing**. Jay Ritter has

---

[29] This is also the reason that the other members can't sell below the stated price; otherwise, they would be selling to the lead underwriter.

surveyed the literature on first-day underpricing in North America versus other counties and reports the first-day returns shown in Table 17-1.

Table 17-1   IPO Underpricing Evidence

Country	Sample	Period	Return
Canada	500	1971-1999	6.3
United Kingdom	3,122	1959-2001	17.4
United States	14,840	1960-2001	18.4
Australia	381	1976-1995	12.1
New Zealand	201	1981-1999	19.1

Source: Jay Ritter, "Differences between European and American IPO Markets," *European Financial Management* 9, no. 4 (2002), pp. 421-434.

These countries were chosen because capital markets are very similar based on external capital and English common law. What is of interest is that Canada's first-day return is by far the lowest at 6.3 percent and is about one-third of first-day returns in the United States. Of the 38 countries sampled by Ritter, the first-day return of 6.3 percent is the lowest of any country except Denmark, where the sample was very limited.

When investment dealers are asked why underpricing is so low in Canada, the answer given is that there is too much competition for business in Canada, and Canadian firms do not need to tolerate high underpricing, because they want the best price for their shares. In contrast, a large number of reasons have been given for the underpricing in the United States, none of them entirely convincing. The most obvious is that it lowers the risk of the underwriter losing money on the issue. However, this answer implies that the U.S. investment banks are more powerful than their equivalents in Canada and although there is anecdotal evidence of this, it is difficult to prove.

Other reasons that have been advanced for the high level of underpricing in the United States is the litigious nature of the U.S. economy. If the share price falls, then the risk is high that someone will mount a class action suit against the underwriter for misleading the purchasers. In support of this is the observation that some U.S. law firms specialize in suing underwriters, and they do this routinely if the share price falls by 20 percent shortly after the IPO, which seems to be the magic number. Another reason that has been advanced is that a well-received public offering paves the way for subsequent offerings by the firm and builds momentum into the share price. However, the relative rarity of equity issues makes this rationale dubious.

A final reason that has been offered is that of **spinning**: the underwriter allocates IPOs to favoured clients, knowing that they will make a large profit on the first day and making some people very wealthy. Spinning was popular among investment dealers during the Internet bubble, when first-day returns on hot Internet stocks were often more than 100 percent. Allocating IPOs to favourite clients was then essentially a way of bribing them with millions of dollars to get future investment banking business. The bribe was then paid at the expense of the issuing firm, which did not receive full value for its securities.

spinning the underwriter allocates IPOs to favoured clients knowing that they will make a large profit on the first day

Spinning is obviously unethical. It was severely criticized after the stock market crashed in 2001 and investors became aware of the corruption in the marketing of Internet stocks in the United States in the 1990s. In April 2003, then U.S. attorney general for New York, Elliot Spitzer, reached a global settlement with most of the major U.S. investment banks in which they agreed to pay US$1.4 billion in restitution. Most of the settlement was related to the biased nature of security analyst reports and how they were used to pump up Internet and technology stock prices. However, part of it was also related to spinning, which became illegal and was banned. In May 2003, Spitzer reached a settlement with Philip Anschutz, former chair of Qwest Communications International, Inc. (Qwest), a major U.S. telecom company. As part of the settlement, Anschutz "disgorged" US$4.4 million in profits on IPO shares he received from Salomon Smith Barney, a major U.S. investment bank. According to Spitzer, the IPO allocations were awarded Anschutz as a reward for investment banking business from Qwest and were never disclosed.

CONCEPT REVIEW QUESTIONS

1. Briefly discuss the possible motivation for firms to enter into IPOs, and relate these motivations to the five stages of firm development discussed by Myers (1999).

2. List and briefly describe the four basic stages of the IPO process.

3. List and briefly describe some possible reasons for the existence of IPO underpricing.

17.4 POST-IPO REGULATION AND SEASONED OFFERINGS

The Post-IPO Market

After the quiet period has ended, the investment dealer's research analyst can initiate coverage on the company, because, by this time, it is assumed that the prospectus no longer contains all relevant information and the analyst may add value. In fact, promising analyst coverage of the firm's shares is a key part of the pitch that an investment dealer makes to win investment banking business. The analyst coverage, plus the investment dealer's agreement to make a market in the firm's shares, offers the firm the possibility of enhancing liquidity in its shares and increasing its recognition within the investment community.

Unfortunately, these practices were also taken to excess in the United States during the Internet bubble. In the settlement that Elliot Spitzer extracted from the major U.S. investment banks, not only did he get the practice of spinning stopped, but he also revealed the depth to which research analysts were compromised in their pursuit of investment banking business. It was routine to reward analysts with a share of the investment banking business they brought in, in effect turning research analysts into promoters of the company's stock, rather than providers of objective research.

In the settlement reached with Elliot Spitzer, two analysts, Jack Grubman of Salomon Brothers and Henry Blodget of Merrill Lynch, were both charged with issuing fraudulent research reports and agreed to pay penalties of US$15 million and US$4 million, respectively. They were both also banned from the securities business for life. The SEC charged Credit Suisse First Boston (CSFB) with issuing *fraudulent* research on two stocks and producing *misleading* research on three others. Allegations were made that investment banks paid other investment banks to provide analyst research coverage to avoid the appearance that the "buy" recommendations were coming from within.

The excesses evident in the United States were not evident in Canada, and regulatory changes in the U.S. have made research analysts independent of investment banking. However, it is obviously difficult to win investment banking business from a company if a research analyst is trashing the stock! Hence, even when a formal separation exists between research and investment banking, it is sensible to discount recommendations from the company's investment dealer. That just leaves the investment dealers who want to win the firm's business in the future.

The other holdover from the IPO is that the lock-up period usually lasts around six months. During the Internet boom, share prices tended to dip sometimes as much as 20 percent after six months, as the lock-ups expired and insiders sold some of their shares. This was particularly evident for technology and Internet stocks, because insiders usually continued to hold more than 80 percent of the shares—that is, the IPOs were so sought-after at the time that only 20 percent were sold on the IPO date. Consequently, insiders were under tremendous pressure to diversify their own portfolios by selling shares. To counter this tendency for prices to drop as the lock-ups expired, research coverage was often initiated with buy recommendations at about the six-month mark.

Continuous Disclosure Requirements

IPOs are not as hot as they were in the late 1990s, so the fraction held by insiders is usually much less than 80 percent. However, common advice is to be wary of IPOs for which the founders are left with a high percentage of the shares, because the likelihood is that the market will have to absorb some of this supply in the future. After the IPO, people who buy the shares in the secondary market do not get a copy of the prospectus. After all, the information in the prospectus rapidly becomes out of date, so requiring that secondary market investors get a copy is of little value. To remedy this, almost all issuers are required to become **reporting issuers** and provide **continuous disclosure**. The main components of continuous disclosure are the filing of quarterly and annual financial statements, annual information forms (AIFs), and proxy and information circulars.

Although firms normally include financial statements within the annual report, in Ontario there is no requirement to include all the material normally included in the annual report, much of which is promotional. Since 1982, the OSC has required larger firms (i.e., those with a market value greater than $75 million or sales of more than $10 million) to file an AIF complete with a comprehensive management discussion and analysis (MD&A) of its operations. The AIF and MD&A provide prospectus-type disclosure for all larger firms with securities traded in Ontario. Under corporate law, an annual proxy statement has to be filed for the annual general meeting in order to change the company's

reporting issuers issuers that are required to provide continuous information disclosure

continuous disclosure the filing of quarterly and annual financial statements, annual information forms, and proxy and information circulars

bylaws and elect members of the BOD, so this is regarded as part of continuous disclosure as well.[30]

Firms are also required to disclose any "material changes" in the affairs of a reporting issuer. Note that material *facts* are also required to be disclosed, but a material *change* is broader and encompasses more than a material fact. A material change can occur even when all the facts are already known. However, the exact definition of a material change is elusive and the interpretation seems to be that "investors should know it when they see it."

The OSC requires that firms issue a press release and file a material change report in its System for Electronic Document Analysis and Retrieval (SEDAR) on the OSC's website, as soon as is practical and within 10 days of a material change. It is important that firms cannot selectively disclose facts, not even to industry professionals, such as security analysts. This first became important in the United States where regulation FD, which stands for **fair disclosure**, mandated that information given to security analysts, such as earnings guidance, had to be made available to all. The result has been a surge in webcasts in which ordinary investors can listen in to hear just how clever some of the security analysts are. Checking a company's website under investor relations usually reveals information about upcoming webcasts.

In Canada, selective disclosure became a hot issue in October 2000 after the CFO of Air Canada instructed staff to leave telephone messages on the answering machines at major investment dealers indicating that its upcoming results would be worse than expected. The next day, it released most of this information in a press release, but by then the share price had already dropped. Air Canada paid both the Ontario and Quebec Securities Commissions $500,000 plus costs in restitution. In October 2001, the recommendations of the Crawford Committee on analyst standards led to the formal adoption of FD in Canada.

fair disclosure the requirement that all information given to security analysts, such as earnings guidance, be made available to everyone

Seasoned Offerings and Short-Form Prospectuses

The upshot of these requirements for continuous disclosure is that the preparation of a long-form prospectus for a seasoned equity issue by a reporting issuer is redundant, because the information should be available already. The result has been the development of the **short-form prospectus**. Essentially, any reporting issuer with an outstanding AIF can issue securities under a short-form prospectus, which indicates the nature and pricing of the securities, omits all corporate information, and incorporates existing documents by reference. As long as the securities are not "novel" they can be cleared by the OSC in a matter of days, so that issues can be brought to market very quickly.[31]

The short-form prospectus has changed the basic way in which firms now raise both debt and equity capital, and it has directly led to the growth of the bought deal, in which the underwriting contract is signed even before the drafting of the preliminary prospectus. The OSC allows this because it knows that the prospectus now only includes details of the offering, rather than of the issuer, and that the prospectus will follow within two days. This allows the investment dealer to market the issue to major institutions and close the transaction usually within two to three days from the initial discussions with the issuer. Often the investment

short-form prospectus a document that indicates the nature and pricing of the securities, omits all corporate information, and incorporates existing documents by reference

---

[30] These requirements also explain why investing in small-cap stocks is so risky. The fact is that these companies do not provide the same level of disclosure as reporting issuers and information asymmetry can be more acute.

[31] Examples of short-form prospectuses are available at www.sedar.com, but long-form prospectuses are now quite rare.

dealer directly approaches the issuer and tells the issuer that based on its knowledge of the market, it can raise a certain amount of money. As a result, it is often the investment dealer that initiates the transaction and not the issuer.

To show how dynamic seasoned equity offerings have become, we consider the $180 million in common equity raised by BC Gas in October 2001. BC Gas (now Terasen Gas Inc.) is primarily a local gas distribution company in the lower B.C. mainland, and as a largely regulated utility, there is little unknown about its operations. In late 2001, it bought the gas distribution assets of another utility company on Vancouver Island from Westcoast Energy Inc. To pay for this acquisition, on the closing of the deal, BC Gas invited bids from a series of investment dealers and then awarded the underwriting contract to RBC Dominion Securities Inc. (RBCDS) and Scotia Capital Inc. Apart from the standard 4 percent underwriting fee, the underwriters agreed to pay BC Gas $36.15 a share. The only snag was that the closing price for the BC Gas shares was $36.10.

The BC Gas financing shows how competitive the investment dealer business has become now that the prospectus requirements have been reduced in favour of continuous disclosure. It has reduced the importance of the other skills provided by the investment dealer in favour of its raw trading and marketing power. In the BC Gas case, the market was so short of deals that both RBCDS and Scotia Capital were willing to incur a trading loss (because they knew the closing price) and eat into their 4 percent commission, simply to generate activity for their investment dealer teams. The example illustrates how seasoned offerings have developed in Canada to enable larger firms to rapidly access markets to raise capital.

Thomson Financial Inc., a Canadian company that supplies data globally, reports the Canadian financings (in U.S. dollars) for the first half of 2006 for the major underwriters in Canada. These results are shown in Table 17-2.

Table 17-2   Canadian Financings (January to June 2006)

Book Runner	Proceeds US$ (million)	Proceeds Rank	Share (%)	Number of Deals
CIBC World Markets	2,468.5	1	20.1	25
RBCDS	1,972.9	2	16.1	23
TD Securities	1,309.5	3	10.7	21
Canaccord Capital	951.3	4	7.8	15
GMP Capital Trust	949.7	5	7.7	19
BMO Nesbitt Burns	693.1	6	5.7	15
Merrill Lynch	583.9	7	4.8	4
Scotia Capital	448.4	8	3.7	7
National Bank Financial	393.7	9	3.2	9
Sprott Securities	309.9	10	2.5	10
Top Ten	10,080.9		82.3	148
Industry	12,276.1		100.0	157

Source: Data from Thomson Financial Inc., *Globe and Mail*, July 12, 2006.

The book runner is the lead investment dealer who manages the transaction. Of the US$12.276 billion raised in the first half of 2006, 82.3 percent was raised by the top 10 underwriters, and almost half by the big three: CIBC World Markets Inc., RBCDS, and TD Securities Inc.. These three had a slightly smaller share of the total number of deals, indicating that they tended to do bigger deals. Most of these underwriters are part of major chartered banks. The major exceptions are Canaccord Capital Inc., GMP Capital Trust, and Sprott Securities Inc., each of which specializes in different areas of the capital market. Merrill Lynch is the lone U.S. investment bank in the top 10. Almost all of these investment dealers compete to be the lead underwriter in security offerings, then participate as part of the banking or selling group, so the investment dealer business exhibits both intense competition and cooperation.

CONCEPT REVIEW QUESTIONS

1. Explain why the lock-up period is an important consideration for investors, especially for issues that are still largely held by issuer insiders.
2. How do continuous disclosure requirements protect investors?
3. Briefly explain why short-form prospectuses are permitted by regulators for a large percentage of seasoned issues, and explain why they have led to the growth in popularity of bought deals.

Summary

A prerequisite to understanding corporate financing is to first understand the basics of securities laws. Investment dealers who assist firms in raising capital must abide by these laws, which severely restrict what they can and cannot do.

We discuss how one of the core problems in raising capital is the existence of information asymmetry—some people have access to privileged information and have a clearer idea of the value of the securities being offered than do others. In the extreme case of fraud, there is a clear asymmetry of information. In fact, it was the existence of fraud in the financial markets that led to the creation of securities commissions and the tight regulation of the offering process. We show how broad the legal definition of a security is, what constitutes a prospectus, and why it takes so much time and effort to raise money through an IPO. In contrast, once the information is available in the capital markets, the requirement for continuous disclosure for larger firms means that secondary offerings in today's markets can be accomplished incredibly quickly at very low cost.

Key Terms

agency theory, p. 679
asymmetric information, p. 664
banking (or dealer) syndicate, p. 681
bearer bonds, p. 667
best efforts offering, p. 681
bought deal, p. 681

QUESTIONS AND PRACTICE PROBLEMS

Multiple Choice Questions

1. Which of the following statements about due diligence is *false*?

    A. It is designed to ensure the legitimacy of securities offered to the public.

    B. It is designed to ensure that there is no misleading information when companies issue shares.

    C. It is expensive to implement.

    D. It is not time consuming.

2. Which of the following regulators in the Canadian securities markets does not exist?

    A. Ontario Securities Commission

    B. British Columbia Securities Commission

    C. Federal Securities Commission

    D. Quebec Securities Commission

3. Which of the following statements is *false*?

    A. An IPO is assumed to have the least information asymmetry.

    B. There are two forms of prospectuses.

    C. An IPO is the first-time distribution of securities.

    D. "Full, true and plain" means every material fact has to be disclosed.

4. The market for non-registered securities is called the

    A. non-registered market.

    B. secondary market.

    C. primary market.

    D. exempt market.

5. Which of the following statements about the exempt market is *false*?

    A. "Backdoor underwriting" refers to the slipping of securities from the exempt market into the public market.

    B. In the exempt market, the issuer prepares a prospectus too.

    C. Only if the issuer becomes a reporting issuer can the issuer sell securities in the public market.

    D. There are three major types of exempt purchasers.

6. Which of the following issuers is *not* exempt?

    A. Government debt issuers

    B. Financial institution debt issuers

    C. Securities issued as part of takeovers

    D. Private firms with a promotion.

7. Which of the following statements about public offerings is *false*?

    A. There are four types of offerings.

    B. Bought deal offerings and standby offerings are used only for seasoned offerings.

    C. Most IPOs are best efforts offerings.

    D. A lead investment dealer and a banking syndicate are involved in larger issues.

8. Which of the following is *not* a main component of continuous disclosure?

    A. Filing of quarterly financial statements

    B. Filing of annual financial statements

    C. Filing of proxy and information circulars

    D. Filing of monthly financial statements.

Practice Problems

Easy

9. In late 2006, Canada Post began issuing "Permanent" Stamps. Purchased at the current first-class letter rate ($0.51 at the time), these stamps may be used indefinitely even if the price of new stamps increases. Arthur Ponzarelli (known to his friends as "Ponzi") is always looking to make a quick buck, and he thinks these stamps present a lucrative opportunity. Expecting the price of postage to increase by $0.01 very soon, he decides to "invest" in 100,000 stamps.

    A. If Canada Post raises the postal rate to $0.52 two weeks later, and Arthur can resell his securities (the stamps) at the new price, how much profit will he make?

B. To avoid running foul of securities laws, Arthur decides to sell his stamps to someone in another province and will have to pay $249 for shipping and insurance. Unfortunately, his reputation for shady deals has preceded him, so the purchaser is only willing to pay $0.5125 per stamp. Will he still make a "quick buck"?

10. Back in their college days, David and Douglas Finn started renting refrigerators to other students for use in their dormitory rooms. Over the years, Finns' Fridges has grown and financed its operations by retaining most of the profits it made. Now, however, the brothers would like to "cash out" by taking the company public through an IPO. Together, the brothers own 1,000,000 shares and will sell half of their holdings. In addition, the company will issue 250,000 new shares as part of the IPO to provide additional growth financing. What percentage of the firm's shares will the Finns own after the IPO?

11. If the IPO for Finns' Fridges (see Problem 10) goes well, the contract with the investment bankers has a "greenshoe" clause which permits them to sell 15% more shares than originally planned. These additional shares would all be issued by the company, not sold by the Finn brothers themselves. How much of the firm will the brothers own if this overallotment option is taken up?

12. Niagara Vineyards and Winery needs to raise $2,000,000 in new equity. If the costs of the share issue are estimated to be 7 percent of gross proceeds, how large does the offering need to be? How much will Niagara pay in flotation costs?

13. Winnipeg Water & Gas Co. recently issued a series of bonds; the gross proceeds were $25,000,000. The underwriting fees were 2 percent, and additional issuance costs were $75,000. How much did the company actually receive from the sale? As a percentage of the gross proceeds, what were the total costs of the bond issue?

14. If the interest rate for non-fraudulent bonds is 12 percent, and chances are that two out of eight bonds are fraudulent bonds, what is the interest rate based on a one-year investment and assuming the market does not require a risk premium?

Medium

15. Briefly state the five major areas in which the Ontario Securities Commission (OSC) is involved.

16. Briefly state three types of distributions of securities determined by the OSC.

17. Briefly describe the basic stages of IPOs.

18. What are limit orders and market orders?

19. What is the quiet period?

20. Lansdowne Ltd. needs to raise $10 million and intends to sell additional shares. The company's existing shares are trading on the Toronto Stock Exchange for $28. However, the investment dealer hired by Lansdowne has cited investors' concerns about information asymmetry to justify an offering price of $25 per share. Underwriting costs charged by the investment dealer are 5 percent of the issue price. How many shares must the firm sell to net $10 million?

Difficult

21. The little company you and your friend started in your parents' garage has grown so much that you are now ready to take the firm public. In your discussions with one of the top investment dealers, you have been given a choice between two alternatives:

Plan I: The investment dealer will underwrite the issue of 1 million shares at $14 per share. There will be an underwriting fee of 6.5 percent of the gross proceeds.

Plan II: The investment dealer will accept the securities on a "best efforts" basis. The price will be $15 per share, and it is believed that 95 percent of the shares will be sold. The investment dealer's fee will be $950,000.

What will the net proceeds be under each plan? Which plan should you accept?

22. Pills4u.com and Drugs-R-Us Co. both sell prescription medications over the Internet. Each company has recently announced an IPO at $15 per share. At this price, one of the companies is undervalued by $1.50, while the other is overvalued by $1.00. Unfortunately, you have no way of knowing which is which, as you have no particular expertise in pharmaceuticals or Internet sales. Nonetheless, you plan to buy 1,000 shares of each company stock at the offer price.

A. If you are allocated the full 1,000 shares of each new issue, how much profit will you make when the shares adjust to their true value?

B. If an issue is undervalued, it will be rationed, and you will only get half your order. What profit do you expect in this situation?

23. Sous-Chefs, Inc. is an employment agency that specializes in the restaurant industry. The company intends to sell 800,000 shares in its IPO and the investment dealers working on the issue have been seeking expressions of interest in the shares from various investors (pension plans, mutual funds, and so on). As the dealers sit down with the company's management to price the issue, the "book" looks like this:

Investor	Number of Shares	Limit Price
A	200,000	$21.00
B	150,000	$20.50
C	300,000	$20.00
D	200,000	$19.25
E	250,000	$19.00
F	350,000	$18.75
G	250,000	$18.50
H	100,000	$18.00
I	150,000	$17.50
J	200,000	$17.00

A. What is the highest issue price that the shares can command if all the investors live up to their intentions as shown in the table?

B. Suppose the investment dealers want to set the price so that the issue is two-times oversubscribed. That is, all the shares will still sell if the investors only purchase half the number of shares indicated. At what price should the shares be issued?

24. The Sous-Chefs, Inc. IPO was priced at $18.50 (see Problem 23) and will trade on the Toronto Stock Exchange. If the amount of underpricing is the same as the historical average for Canadian stocks (refer to page 685), what do you expect the price of the stock to be at the end of its first day of trading? What would its price be if the first day return is the same as typically seen in the United States?

Debt Rating

On April 17, 2007, rating agency DBRS placed the ratings of BCE and its wholly owned subsidiary, Bell Canada, under review with negative implications. The action was prompted by BCE's announcement that it was pursuing strategic alternatives in an attempt to maximize shareholder value. DBRS is concerned that the privatization of the company that may result from this process could have a negative effect on its financial risk profile because of any associated increase in debt. DBRS is monitoring the BCE situation and has stated that an increase in the company's debt to EBITDA ratio to above 4.0 could lead to a cut in its rating to below BBB (low). Debt rated below BBB (low) is no longer investment-grade.

Source: DBRS website: www.dbrs.com, April 24, 2007.

Debt Instruments

Learning Objectives

After reading this chapter, you should understand the following:

1. The basic features of debt financing

2. The main distinctions between short-term funds in the money market and long-term funds in the capital market

3. The types of debt financing that are provided by the banks

4. The requirements that must typically be satisfied for public debt issues

5. How debt ratings are determined, what they mean, and how useful they are in predicting default and recovery rates associated with public debt issues

INTRODUCTION

In Chapter 17, we developed an overview of raising capital and the role of securities regulation in protecting the public through mandatory disclosure. However, no matter how much information is disclosed, investors will disagree on the interpretation of that information and view the firm's prospects differently. Consequently, they will invest in different types of securities. In this chapter, we discuss the implications for one of the two classic types of securities: debt securities. In Chapter 19, we will discuss the implications for equity securities and so-called hybrids, which are part debt and part equity.

Debt is a contract between a lender and a borrower that stipulates the terms of repayment of the loan. As a contract, these terms are limited only by the imagination of the contracting parties. However, a critical component is that the interest on debt securities is fully deductible for tax purposes by the borrower (payer or issuer) and fully taxable for the lender (recipient or investor). As a result, one of the major factors determining whether or not a security is debt is its treatment by the Canada Revenue Agency (CRA). In this sense, debt is what CRA accepts as debt for tax purposes. We will see that many factors determine whether a firm issues debt or equity securities or some form of hybrid, but tax consequences are always a factor.

18.1 WHAT IS DEBT?

It might seem obvious what debt is. After all, many of us have borrowed money from friends, relatives, or financial institutions.[1] For example, someone might borrow $1,000 at 10 percent interest and agree to pay the loan back in one year's time. In this case, the borrower has to pay back $1,100 at the end of the year; 10 percent interest is the cost of "renting" the $1,000 in principal for the year. In this way, the 10 percent interest rate is the cost of borrowing money.

fixed contractual commitments require the parties involved to adhere to specific requirements

All of this is straightforward, but it is important to point out that the interest cost and principal repayment are **fixed contractual commitments**, and failing to honour them has serious implications that we discuss later. The fact that the principal and interest payments are fixed contractual commitments is the essential difference between debt and equity. With equity, an investor is an owner, shares in the profits of the business, and has no "contractual" rights, because equity is not a contract in the way that debt is. Instead, a shareholder owns a share in the business and as an owner has the rights allocated in the company's articles of incorporation and bylaws, as we discussed in Chapter 2, as well as in the general provisions of corporate and securities laws. However, a shareholder does not have a specific contract that details the cash flows he or she can expect to receive from the investment. An owner is a "residual claimant," which means that he or she gets what is left after all the firm's contractual commitments have been met.

---

[1] Preferably not from credit cards, as the interest cost is prohibitive.

The fact that payments on debt are a fixed contractual commitment puts them in the same category as the firm's rental payments on property, its wage bill to its workforce, and its other expenses of doing business. They are legitimate costs of doing business and are tax deductible. In contrast, equity costs are not a cost of doing business in the same sense. Instead, they represent returns to the *owners* of the business after the company has paid all its legitimate expenses. As such, equity securities are treated differently for tax purposes; by investigating this difference, we can understand why and how debt and equity securities differ.

Suppose, for example, that a firm has $10 million in assets and expects to generate 10 percent of this amount (or $1 million) in earnings before interest and tax (EBIT). If the corporate tax rate is 40 percent, then the firm will pay $400,000 in tax, assuming it makes no interest payments. However, if the firm had borrowed $5 million at 7 percent, it would have had a $350,000 interest expense deduction, reducing its taxable income to $650,000 and its tax bill to $260,000. The firm's tax bill drops by $140,000 because of its decision to finance part of its operations with debt instead of equity. The calculations are shown below:

	No Debt	$5 Million in Debt
EBIT	$1,000,000	$1,000,000
Interest	0	350,000
Taxable income	1,000,000	650,000
Tax (40%)	400,000	260,000
Net income	600,000	390,000

Of the $350,000 in interest expense paid by the firm, only 60 percent, or $210,000, is actually paid by the owners of the firm; the other 40 percent or $140,000 is paid through a reduction in income taxes remitted to the government. We can see this in the fact that net income has dropped by $210,000 despite the increased interest payments of $350,000.

This simple example highlights a very important point: the net cost of the firm using debt is the after-tax cost. In our example, this was the 7.0 percent interest rate multiplied by one minus the tax rate $(1 - 0.40)$ or 60 percent. This gives the debt cost as 4.2 percent. Generally, we can use Equation 18-1 to determine this **after-tax cost of debt** (K):

after-tax cost of debt (K) the net costs of the firm using debt, calculated as the before-tax interest cost of the firm's debt multiplied by one minus the corporate tax rate

$$K = K_d (1 - T)$$

[18-1]

where K_d is the before-tax interest cost of the firm's debt, and T is the corporate tax rate.

We will generically use K as the yield, or required return, on a security and indicate what type of security it is by using subscripts; in this case we subscript the yield with d, indicating debt.

The discussion illustrates a basic rule: if a business is taxable, it makes sense to correctly identify all legitimate costs of doing business, because these reduce the taxable income and thus the tax bill. For corporations, it means they legitimately try to ensure that their financing costs are tax deductible, because it reduces their income taxes. Conversely, CRA has to make sure that the Income

Tax Act is enforced and that firms take only legitimate deductions for genuine debt securities.

CRA uses three basic tests to make sure that the interest on debt is tax deductible:

1. Interest is compensation for the use or retention of money owed to another.

2. Interest must be referable to a principal sum.

3. Interest accrues from day to day.

These criteria make sense. Using the example of a $1,000 loan again, the $1,000 is the principal sum, and the interest of 10 percent is referable back to that principal to get the $100 in interest. If the loan is paid off late, then the borrower would expect to pay more than $100 in interest, because he or she has rented the principal for a longer time. This is the way in which the interest accrues as the loan is outstanding: the longer the loan is outstanding the more interest is paid. However, as simple as this appears to be, a huge amount of litigation has been involved in deciding whether these three factors actually hold for a particular security.

For example, Richardson[2] shows that requirement 2 (i.e., that interest is referable to a principal sum) dates to a Supreme Court of Canada decision concerning the Saskatchewan Farm Security Act of 1944. At that time, the Province of Saskatchewan wanted to reduce the debt burden faced by its farming community but could not waive interest payments because they are a federal responsibility and are stipulated in the federal Income Tax Act. Therefore, the province passed a law reducing the principal value associated with the required interest payments but stipulated that the interest payments would not be reduced even though the principal value was! Effectively, the reduction in principal payments was set so that they would offset the interest paid, thereby removing the burden of the interest payments and helping Saskatchewan farmers. However, the Supreme Court of Canada ruled that the interest payments could no longer be regarded as interest, because the principal sum was being reduced and the interest had to be tied back to this principal.

This is a typical pattern in finance. "Innovative" financing vehicles are created to exploit the wording in the Income Tax Act to try to make things tax deductible and appear to be debt, when they really aren't. As the Saskatchewan example highlights, this isn't just a corporate or personal activity; governments do it as well.[3] The CRA responds when it eventually finds out[4] and challenges the deduction, which often then ends up in tax court. The courts rule on whether these securities comply with the definitions of interest and the intent of the Income Tax Act. If the deduction is disallowed, the loophole is then closed until clever financiers find another way of doing the same thing. However, before we talk about some of the *grey area securities* between debt and equity, we will consider *plain vanilla* debt securities. First, we will discuss short-term debt.

---

[2] Stephen Richardson, "New Financial Instruments: A Canadian Tax Perspective," in *New Financial Management* (Toronto: Canadian Tax Foundation, 1993).

[3] Another example of provincial activity was the sale and leaseback of Ontario's GO Transit rolling stock. The provincial government as a non-taxable entity cannot use any tax shields. However, by selling the rolling stock to a private enterprise that can use the tax shields, and then subsequently leasing the equipment back at a favourable rate, the province gained at the expense of the federal government.

[4] It may take years for the CRA to dissect an income statement and challenge a deduction.

CONCEPT REVIEW QUESTIONS

1. Distinguish debt from equity.

2. Explain how to estimate the after-tax cost of debt.

3. What three characteristics does CRA use to determine whether or not interest payments are tax deductible?

18.2 SHORT-TERM DEBT AND THE MONEY MARKET

Government Treasury Bills

The simplest sort of debt contract is one that most of us have made by lending a friend a few dollars and telling him or her to pay us back next week. This is obviously a loan, but it is not backed by anything other than the friend's promise to repay in a week's time. If this promise is documented in a written contract that says, "I promise to pay $X to YYY on April 30," it is called a **promissory note**. Different layers of government issues such as short-term promissory notes, which are called **treasury bills (T-bills)**, because the promise is issued by the treasury department of the government. Generally, any debt instrument with a maturity of less than a year is called a *bill* or *paper*, from one to seven years it is called a *note*, and more than seven years it is a *bond*. All the bills and short-term paper outstanding are then generically referred to as the *money market*.

The federal Government of Canada, at the end of March 2006, had $185.565 billion in T-bills outstanding. The standard reference point in the money market is the 91-day federal government T-bill, for which the implicit interest rate is commonly referred to as "the" T-bill yield. However, the Government of Canada sells T-bills of varying maturities out to one year, depending on its financing needs. It does this by auctioning off a stock of bills and requiring government securities dealers to place minimum bids on these securities.

The Bank of Canada acts as the Government of Canada's fiscal agent in selling these securities and maintaining an orderly auction market. It does this by requiring that all orders for T-bills be submitted through government securities dealers (GSDs) and dividing orders into *competitive bids* and *non-competitive bids*. Competitive bids are orders to buy securities at a particular price at the auction, whereas non-competitive bids are orders to buy them at the average price determined in the auction. A special group of GSDs are the largest and most active dealers, called *primary dealers*, who are given preferential treatment because they are important for the implementation of monetary policy.[5] These primary dealers then have to bid for a certain amount of T-bills at each auction. The Bank of Canada sets special limits on how much of the auction each dealer can buy to avoid market manipulation.[6]

promissory note a written promise to pay back a loan

treasury bills (T-bills) a promissory note issued by a government treasury department

---

[5] Remember from macroeconomics that the Bank of Canada controls interest rates through buying and selling treasury bills and moving government deposits around, so the dealers are important for these processes.

[6] These new procedures were introduced when the number of dealers declined with government financing requirements. In particular, three major U.S. dealers withdrew from the Canadian auction in 2001, as there simply wasn't enough government borrowing.

As discussed in Chapter 6, T-bills, like most money market instruments, are normally sold on a *discount basis*. This means that the Bank of Canada might auction off $500 million in T-bills, but they do not pay a specific interest rate. Instead, they are sold at a discount to their par value, and the "interest" is earned by the investor being paid the full par value at the maturity date. For example, suppose in an auction that the winning bid for a $1,000 par value 91-day T-bill is $990.099. The interest is the difference between the market price of $990.099 and the $1,000 paid back by the government in 91 days, or $9.901. This means the 91-day interest rate is 1.0 percent, which we can calculate as

$$990.099 = \frac{1,000}{(1+K)}$$

We do not deal with T-bill yields and pricing in great detail here because we did so in Chapter 6; however, we can see that if we solve for K, it is 1.0 percent, because $1,000/(1.01) = $990.099. In quoting interest rates, this 1.0 percent is converted to an annual rate by multiplying by the number of 91-day periods there are in a year, which means the rate would be quoted as 4.0110 percent (i.e., 1% × 365/91).[7] Most money market issues are traded on a discount basis but some commercial paper is issued in interest-bearing form.[8]

Although the federal government's T-bill auction plays a pivotal role in the money market, there are other T-bills outstanding. The larger provinces, particularly Ontario and Quebec, sell T-bills through the major investment dealers, as do some of the larger municipalities. As of the end of March 2006, there was $13.942 billion outstanding T-bills issued by the provinces and major municipalities.

Commercial Paper

commercial paper (CP)
short-term debt instruments, usually unsecured, issued by companies

For corporate financing, companies can issue **commercial paper (CP)**, which are instruments that are similar to T-bills. Unlike T-Bills, CP is normally issued with maturities of 30 and 60 days, rather than 91 days. One major problem with CP is that corporations have credit risk: they may default on their obligation to pay investors back in 30 or 60 days. This is a major problem for all corporate debt obligations, but it is particularly acute for CP because it is almost always unsecured, which means the investor has no underlying assets to seize in the event of a default. Further, the dollar amounts involved are frequently very large for reasons we will come to shortly.

To understand the importance of credit risk, consider a 30-day interest-bearing CP issue (instead of a discount issue) of $100 million with the same interest rate as the T-bill yield of 6 percent (or approximately 0.5 percent per 30 days). However, now there is a 1 percent chance of the CP issuer defaulting and if it does, the investor gets nothing. We represent this in Figure 18-1.

Because money market instruments are quoted on an approximate interest rate basis, the 6.0 percent annual rate translates to 0.5 percent per month (i.e., 6%/12). On a $100 million investment, if the issuer does not default, the investor gets $100.5 million after one month; if the issuer defaults, the investor

---

[7] There are many quoting conventions. One of the most common in the United States is to treat each month as if it had 30 days. When the U.S. government then issues 90-day treasury bills, the annual rate is exactly four times the quarterly rate.

[8] For tax purposes, the CRA regards the increase from the purchase price to the par value as interest and not capital gains, because the "gain" is locked in at the time of purchase.

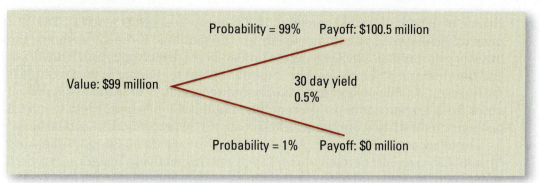

18-1 FIGURE

Commercial Paper Payoffs

gets nothing. The investor has a 99 percent chance of getting $100.5 million and a 1.0 percent chance of getting $0, or $99.495 million (i.e., .99 × $100.5 + .01 × $0). If this expected payoff is discounted back for one month at 0.5 percent, the $100 million CP is worth only $99 million (i.e., $99.495 million/1.005).

This example illustrates a very important point: the quoted interest rates are called **promised yields**. They are the rates investors would get if the issuer does not default and they are paid off on time, as promised. For government issues, where there is virtually no default or credit risk, these promised yields are also expected rates of return. However, for corporate issues, which have default risk, the expected rate of return is always *lower* than the promised yield, because the promised yield is the maximum rate the investor can hope to earn by holding the security to maturity.

promised yields the quoted interest rates received if the issuer does not default and the investor is paid off on time, as promised

In our example, the company could not issue $100 million of CP at the T-bill yield of 6.0 percent, because if it did, the CP would be worth only $99 million. Instead, to raise the $100 million par value, the company would have to increase the promised yield higher than the default-free T-bill yield. The value of the 30-day CP issue can be found from Equation 18-2:

$$V = \frac{PAR(1+R)P + RECOVER(1-P)}{(1+K)}$$

[18-2]

where par value (PAR) is $1,000, R is the promised yield, P the probability of not defaulting, $(1 - P)$ is the probability of defaulting, RECOVER is the recovery rate if the company defaults, and K is the investor's required return.

In our example, we simplified this equation by setting RECOVER equal to zero and the investor's required rate of return equal to the T-bill yield. If we continue with these assumptions, we can find the promised yield necessary for the CP to be issued at PAR, that is, PAR = V:

$$R = \frac{(1+K_{TB})}{P} - 1$$

[18-3]

where K_{TB} is the required return for investing in T-bills. In the absence of default risk ($P = 1$), the promised yield on CP would be the same as that on T-bills. However, with the 1.0 percent chance of default, the promised yield has to be 1.515 percent per month (i.e., (1.005)/.99 − 1), or 18.2 percent per year (i.e., 1.515% × 12).

The difference between the promised yield on CP and the yield on the equivalent maturity T-bill is called the **yield spread**. In this case, given a 1.0 percent

yield spread the difference between the yield on one debt instrument and the yield on another

chance of default, the yield spread is 12.2 percent (i.e., 18.2% − 6.0%). The 12.2 percent yield spread is compensation for the fact that if the CP defaults, the investor gets nothing. Obviously, as the probability of default goes up, P goes down and the yield spread increases. The important point to note from this example is the huge impact that default risk has on promised yields. Even if the risk of default drops from 1.0 percent to 0.1 percent, the monthly CP promised yield is still 0.6 percent (versus 0.5 percent) for a yield spread of 1.20 percent on an annual basis.

For reference purposes, on August 9, 2006, the yields on 30-day T-bills and "prime" CP were 3.99 percent and 4.32 percent, respectively, resulting in a yield spread of 0.33 percent. This indicates the extremely low default risk attached to prime CP in Canada.[9] The actual risk of investing in CP is extremely low, so that only the very best companies can access the CP market. The reason for this is that assessing default risk requires time as well as analytic skills. This outlay may be worthwhile when investing for a long period, but few investors are inclined to do this analysis for an investment with a 30-day maturity. However, as we noted, default risk does have a huge impact on yields. To solve this problem, the market has developed alternative risk-assessment measures. Credit rating agencies have developed the most basic measure, which provides default or credit ratings to investors, thereby relieving investors of the need to do individual analyses.

The most important credit rating agency in Canada is the Dominion Bond Rating Service (DBRS). In addition to DBRS, two U.S. rating agencies, Moody's and Standard & Poor's (S&P), also provide ratings on Canadian firms. However, they mainly provide ratings on longer-term issues, rather than on money market instruments. This may change, as S&P, in particular, is evolving as the major competitor to DBRS since it took over the Canadian Bond Rating Service (CBRS) in 2001.

DBRS rates commercial paper, longer-term bonds, and preferred shares and has separate rating categories for each. Generally, the ratings are very similar but sometimes the short-term risk of investing in CP is less than the longer-term risk of investing in the same company's long-term bonds, so the ratings may differ slightly. For CP, DBRS has three basic rating categories:

R-1 Prime credit quality

R-2 Adequate credit quality

R-3 Speculative

Within these categories, DBRS adds sub-ratings of high, mid, and low, so R-1 (high) is the highest rating, while R-3 (low) is the lowest. In practice, to some extent these rating categories are moot, because as of December 2004, the percentage distribution of CP by rating category was as follows:

	Companies	Securitizations	Total
R-1 (high)	8.8	55.0	63.8
R-1 (mid)	15.5	3.0	18.5
R-1 (low)	17.3	0.4	17.7
Below R-1 (low)	0.0	0.0	0.0

---

[9] Or it indicates the extremely high RECOVER rates in the event of default.

The two rating groups are for CP issued by companies and CP issued as securitizations. These latter issues are for groups of securities with external credit enhancements, which we will discuss when we talk about working capital management in Chapter 24. In 2004, no CP was issued in the Canadian market with other than a prime R-1 rating.

The distribution of DBRS CP ratings confirms the fact that the CP market is only accessible for firms with the very best credit ratings. However, even for these firms, investors are wary of investing in CP unless the companies have **liquidity support**, ensuring that money will be available to pay off the CP if the firms cannot roll it over by selling to new investors. Liquidity support is usually a dedicated backup line of credit from a bank. In this way, the firm can draw down on the credit line to pay off the CP if needed when it comes due. The commitment fee to establish a bank line of credit used for liquidity support is about 0.125 percent per year, which adds to the overall cost of a company issuing CP.

CP is sold directly from the dealing rooms by the major investment banks. The trading or dealing room is a huge room with areas allocated for selling different securities, with each desk flanked by a series of computer screens. The *money market desk* is an area in which traders sell CP. The traders call major institutional investors and sell them the CP that the bank has arranged to sell on behalf of their clients. Usually, the bank charges 0.125 percent as a selling commission, but this is often bid down, depending on market conditions. CP is usually sold on the basis of its credit rating, and an investor will ask, "What do you have R-1 (low)?" This is why the credit ratings are so important, because to a large extent, all the R-1 (low) issues are interchangeable.

liquidity support ensuring money is available to pay off a debt, often in the form of a dedicated backup line of credit from a bank that ensures that companies have money to pay off the CP if the firms cannot roll it over by selling to new investors

Bankers' Acceptances (BAs)

If an issuer does not have a good enough credit rating to access the CP market, it is forced to rely more heavily on its bank for financing. One way of doing this is to have its bank guarantee or "accept" its commercial paper by selling the CP to the bank, which then accepts it by stamping "accepted" on it and selling it from its own money market desk. These accepted CP issues are called **bankers' acceptances (BAs)**. If the issuer defaults, then the bank will pay off the CP at maturity, thereby converting the instrument's credit status into that of the major bank that guarantees it.

In many countries, including the United States, BAs are created as a result of international trade. Typically, an exporter will receive a "bill of exchange" in return for the export of its goods. This bill of exchange is essentially a promissory note issued by the foreign importer, usually guaranteed by its local bank. The exporter will then have this note accepted by its own bank so that it can be sold for cash. In this way, U.S. BAs are created by international trade. Unlike in the United States and most other countries, BAs in Canada have nothing to do with trade. They are a method by which lower-rated companies can issue short-term paper into the money market.

BAs trade as bank CP, and because most Canadian banks are rated R-1 (mid), BA yields are marginally lower than prime commercial paper, which is generally a mixture of R-1 (low) and R-1 (mid). As of August 9, 2006, the following were the yields on T-bills, CP, and BAs.

bankers' acceptances (BAs) short-term paper sold by an issuer to a bank, which guarantees or accepts it, obligating the bank to pay off the debt instrument at maturity if the issuer defaults

	1 Month (%)	3 Month (%)
Treasury bills	3.99	4.15
BAs	4.30	4.32
CP	4.32	4.33

The yields on CP and BAs were very close.

In terms of the cost to a firm, issuing CP involves the actual interest cost plus the bank fees. These fees include the issuing or dealing fee of 0.125 percent and the cost of a line of credit of 0.125 percent, so the total cost of issuing CP as of August 9, 2006, was 4.32 percent plus 0.25 percent, plus any other incidental fees. These incidental fees consist of the costs of computer screens and data services, part of the time the firm devotes to managing the issue, and the costs of actually printing up the CP notes and selling and redeeming them. In total, the cost of a CP issue is usually the CP yield + 0.375% or 4.695 percent. In contrast, the cost to the firm of issuing BAs is the yield on the BA plus the bank's stamping or acceptance fee. This fee is usually 0.50 percent to 0.75 percent, depending on the credit risk involved. As of August 9, 2006, the total cost to the firm of financing by using BAs was 4.80 percent to 5.05 percent. CP tends to be significantly cheaper for the largest creditworthy companies that do not need 100 percent backup from a line of credit and that raise significant amounts of money.

Overall, as of the middle of 2006, the Canadian money market consisted of the amounts outstanding shown in Table 18-1.

Table 18-1 Canadian Money Market (August 2006)

	$ Million
Corporate commercial paper	50,041
Securitizations	91,202
BAs	44,322
Provincial T-bills	13,942
Canada T-bills	185,165
Total	384,672

CONCEPT REVIEW QUESTIONS

1. Explain how interest is received on most money market instruments.
2. Contrast T-bills, commercial paper, and BAs in terms of who issues them, their basic structure and default risk, and the yields they provide.
3. Define yield spreads, and explain how they arise.

18.3 BANK FINANCING

In short-term financing, the chartered banks are very important. For example, when issuing CP, most firms are required to have a backup line of credit to ensure that in the event of a disruption in the money market,[10] funds are available to pay off the CP. Technically, the line of credit is not available if the credit condition of the company deteriorates, and the credit condition is reviewed continually by the bank. Similarly, the banks are critical for the BA market because it is the bank's credit that supports the BA and not that of the firm. However, the CP and BA markets are useful only for companies that have reasonably large and continuous financing needs, because CP and BAs are sold in large amounts, usually of at least $1 million. For smaller, irregular-sized financing requirements, firms rely more on traditional bank financing. These consist of term loans and lines of credit.

Lines of Credit (L/Cs)

We have already mentioned **lines of credit (L/Cs)** in our discussion of CP, because they are a basic financing tool provided by banks. There are different types of L/Cs. The standard L/C is an **operating or demand L/C**. These are lending facilities that are made available by the bank for the firm's operating purposes, and they generally cannot be used to back up a CP program. Technically, operating L/Cs are demand loans that can be cancelled at any time. However, in practice, banks are reluctant to do anything that might trigger financial problems for the firm, because this might leave them legally liable for damages. The structure of L/Cs is a maximum dollar amount that the firm can draw down by electronically transferring funds from the operating line to its chequing (or current) account.

The standard cost of the operating line is the **prime lending rate**. Prime is an example of a **floating interest rate**, because it changes regularly, so the cost of a firm's demand loan will float with the bank's prime lending rate. As prime changes, the bank will inform the firm of the change in the cost of its loan for the upcoming month. Whereas the CP costs about 4.70 percent and the BAs cost about 5.0 percent, on August 9, 2006, prime was 6.0 percent. The bank will make loans available to its most creditworthy customers at rates below prime, particularly if they are large enough to access the money market. However, most firms are "prime plus" borrowers, and borrowing rates may be quoted as prime plus 0.5 percent, prime plus 1 percent, and so on.

The second type of bank line adds more stability to the firm. This is the **term or revolving L/C**. The term is usually at least 364 days and is often out to five years, renewable every six months. Often a five-year "revolver" is renewed at the end of each year, making it an "evergreen" five-year line of credit. Because the revolver is a commitment of credit, the bank has to provide capital against these commitments to ensure the liquidity of the bank. The common 364-day L/C occurs because more capital is required against a one-year or 365-day LC!

Revolving L/Cs are very flexible financing tools for both the bank and the firm. In addition to being used to provide straight borrowings, they are also used to backup CP programs or other commitments, such as forward foreign currency contracts. However, banks have tightened up on the potential uses for

lines of credit (L/Cs) a basic financing tool provided by banks that establishes a loan with a specified limit to a firm based on its creditworthiness

operating or demand L/C lending facilities that are made available by the bank for the firm's operating purposes and that generally cannot be used to back up a CP program; these demand loans can be cancelled at any time

prime lending rate the standard cost of the operating line; the interest rate banks use to calculate their other interest rates

floating interest rate an interest rate that changes regularly

term or revolving L/C a line of credit extended by a bank to a firm for a specific amount that automatically adjusts as payments are made or received

---

[10] Sometimes, external factors, such as an unexpected major default, cause investors to stop buying CP, even though the credit status of an issuer is unchanged.

these bank L/Cs. The general principle banks use is that lines of credit are for "liquidity" and not "credit-enhancement" purposes. This means that the bank will withdraw or adjust the line of credit if a "material adverse change" occurs; that is, if the credit quality of the firm deteriorates. The L/C is outstanding to provide the firm with liquidity that it can draw down only if its credit quality is constant. The Office of the Superintendent of Financial Institutions Canada (OSFI), which regulates the banks, monitors lines of credit to make sure that they are used for liquidity purposes. What the OSFI is worried about is the possibility that a deterioration in credit quality could cause large numbers of poor credit firms to suddenly draw down on their lines of credit, thus endangering the stability of the banking system.

Firms have to meet a variety of restrictions to maintain access to the funds in an L/C. Typically, the maximum value of the L/C is determined by using a standard formula, such as that it cannot exceed 75 percent of a company's receivables plus 50 percent of its inventory. Normally, the firm must provide periodic abbreviated financial statements, sometimes on a monthly basis. The firm may then have to meet certain credit restrictions, or **covenants**, such as maintaining the following:

covenants promises or restrictions in a contract

- a minimum current ratio of 1.4 or net working capital of $100 million

- net worth (shareholders' equity) in excess of $250 million

- a minimum interest coverage ratio (times interest earned) of 1.75

- an asset coverage ratio in excess of 2 and a debt ratio less than 0.75

The covenants in the revolving loan allow the bank to pull the loan (i.e., demand payment) and prevent the firm from drawing it down beyond a certain amount as its credit quality deteriorates. However, the restrictions are only of limited effectiveness, because firms usually have more than one bank account and they know before the bank whether they are going to violate the conditions. In this case, they can simply draw down the line of credit before informing the bank of the violations and transfer the funds to another bank where they have full use of the money. Of course, this will damage their reputation, which could impede their ability to borrow in the future.

In addition to the interest costs, the banks normally charge a commitment fee of around 0.50 percent for setting up the L/C, which is also charged on the unused balance. As with the operating line, most revolvers are based on prime, with less creditworthy firms paying higher spreads above prime. However, increasingly, larger customers who may be able to access the money market directly are being offered lines that can be drawn down in either Canadian or U.S. dollars. The Canadian dollar funds are then based on BA plus 0.50 percent to 75 percent, while the U.S. rate is based on LIBOR. This is consistent with our discussion in Chapter 11, where we saw that the base borrowing rates for banks are the BA rate in Canadian dollars and LIBOR for U.S. dollars.

Term Loans

The idea behind L/Cs is that the funds are used for working capital purposes: financing receivables, inventory, and ongoing corporate activity, such as hedging by using swaps and forwards. In fact, some more traditional banks still require "cleanup" periods in which the firm has a zero balance on its line of credit, to make sure that the bank is not providing "permanent" financing, which should be financed with longer-term funds. **Term loans** differ from lines of credit because they have a fixed maturity, require repayment to be made on a fixed schedule, and are made to finance longer-term requirements such as equipment purchases.

These loans are structured in a variety of ways. They are usually for at least three years and may go out to 10 years or longer. Some involve *bullet* or *balloon* payments, where only interest is paid until maturity, at which time the entire principal is due and payable. Such loans generally provide permanent financing of the firm's operations, rather than financing a particular asset. In contrast, amortizing loans are similar to conventional loans made to individuals, in which a monthly payment consists of both interest and principal payments, similar to a car loan or mortgage, which are valued as annuities, as discussed in Chapter 5.

Similar to other forms of bank financing, term loans may be based on the prime lending rate and thus float with the general level of interest rates. However, term loans are often offered with a fixed interest rate over the term of the loan. In addition, term loans are also offered by insurance companies and specialized business finance companies, often for longer periods than those offered by the chartered banks.

The big advantage of term loans to a borrowing company is that they are easy to arrange. All firms have banking relationships because they need chequing accounts to gain access to the payments system, and they also need banks for short-term financing and to arrange hedging contracts, such as swaps and forwards. Consequently, the firm's bank already has inside knowledge of its activities, and it can readily arrange a term loan if it judges the firm to be creditworthy. Further, the term loan can often be structured to fit with a firm's operating and revolving L/Cs. For example, sometimes a revolver is structured to switch into a term loan at the end of its five-year life.

> **term loans** loans to finance longer-term requirements, such as equipment purchases; they have a fixed maturity and require repayment to be made on a fixed schedule

CONCEPT REVIEW QUESTIONS

1. Briefly describe operating L/Cs, revolving L/Cs, and term loans.
2. Why do banks typically impose debt covenants on their borrowing customers?
3. Why is it reasonable to assume that most firms will have a banking relationship?

18.4 LONG-TERM FINANCING

Long-term financing generally refers to any debt issued with a term longer than one year and is often called *funded* debt. The reason for this is that short-term debt is not regarded as permanent capital; therefore, when a firm accumulates "too much" short-term debt, it funds this debt by issuing long-term debt. As discussed above, banks provide medium-term financing through term loans, which are also provided by insurance companies and other specialized financial companies. These are examples of private financing, because there is no offering of the debt to the general public. For bank financing, the firm generally does not have to provide any extra information, because it already provides information in support of its existing bank relationship. For term loans from other entities, the firm will have to provide an *offering memorandum*. As discussed in Chapter 17, this document contains much the same type of information as that provided in a prospectus, but in less detail.

The remaining forms of financing involve public financing, and here it is important to realize that securities legislation, and the required filing of a prospectus, applies to debt as well as equity offerings. As discussed in Chapter 17, most financing in the capital markets is done by *reporting issuers* who can raise capital, both debt and equity, through the issue of a short-form prospectus. These documents are filed with the provincial or territorial securities commissions and are publicly available. For example, the documents filed with the Ontario Securities Commission (OSC) are available on <www.sedar.com>.

For example, on November 21, 2001, BC Gas (BC Gas now Terasen Gas Inc.) filed a short-form prospectus to raise $500 million in medium-term note debentures (MTNs).[11] The word *debenture* used to mean unsecured bonds but now generically refers to any bond, so that we refer to secured and unsecured debentures. The prospectus indicated that the MTNs would be in either interest-bearing or discount form and would be either registered for sale in Canada or as global debentures. The interest rates were to be determined by the company after consultation with its dealers for an amount of up to $500 million for 25 months from the date of the prospectus, bringing the total MTN borrowing up to $1,400 million.

The short-form prospectus simply gave notice that BC Gas intended to raise $500 million in some form or another over the next two years. The exact terms of any issue would then be documented in a pricing supplement or "term sheet" negotiated between the company and its investment dealers, who would be canvassing major institutional purchasers to work out the most attractive issue at any point in time. As we discussed in Chapter 11, BC Gas could always use the swap market to convert the terms of a particular issue into something more attractive to it.

Apart from the information included in the prospectus, the following was incorporated "by reference":

• annual information form

• audited financial statements

• unaudited six month statements

• any other information filed with the securities commission after the date of the prospectus but before the termination of the offering

Essentially, all the regular documents filed by BC Gas as a reporting issuer were part of the prospectus. The BC Gas short-form prospectus is an example of the new *continuous disclosure* practices that allow larger firms to access the capital markets on an almost continuous basis.

When firms issue securities to the general public, some basic mechanical problems have to be solved. For example, who keeps track of who owns the securities and makes sure that they get their interest or dividends and ensures that the company meets its obligations? Securities offered to the general public

---

[11] The following discussion paraphrases the information in the prospectus.

are normally held by the Canadian Depository for Securities (CDS). CDS physically holds the securities and maintains book entries regarding security ownership, but as we pointed out in Chapter 17, this is usually a major institution rather than the ultimate owner. The day-to-day administration of the securities is done by a **transfer agent**. For the BC Gas MTNs, CIBC Mellon Trust Company (CIBC Mellon) was the transfer agent and registrar, and maintained a record of the individuals who owned the MTNs and who therefore expected to receive interest and principal payments. Payment of interest, for example, could be made by electronic funds transfer or by cheque (dated on the interest date) to the owner in CIBC Mellon's books.

transfer agent a company that handles the day-to-day administration of securities and maintains records, including purchases, sales, and account balances

The transfer agent also makes sure that the legal documentation is satisfied. For example, the BC Gas MTNs were issued under a 1977 indenture between CIBC Mellon and a predecessor company (Inland Gas & Oil, Ltd.). This indenture had been updated many times since, but it stipulated the rights of the MTN holders. For example, it stipulated that BC Gas could issue an unlimited amount of MTNs, but the bonds would rank equally with all other unsecured and unsubordinated debt of the company. So what does this mean?

First, it means that the MTNs ranked behind any secured debt outstanding in the event of default—that is, the secured debt holders had first claim on the particular underlying assets in the event of default. In the case of BC Gas, two different types of secured bonds technically ranked ahead of the MTNs. The first were BC Gas's first *mortgage bonds*. Mortgage bonds are similar to residential mortgage arrangements, in which the lender has registered a claim on the underlying real property that is financed. For BC Gas, this largely consisted of small-diameter pipelines used for distributing natural gas to customers in British Columbia. The *first* indicates that these mortgage bonds have first claim on the underlying assets, whereas *second* would indicate that they rank behind the first mortgage bonds. BC Gas also had $275 million of **purchase-money mortgages** outstanding, which are mortgages that constitute all or part of the compensation received for the sale of property and are used when the seller is also the lender. These were issued for the purchase of gas-distribution assets of another B.C. company.

purchase-money mortgages mortgages that constitute all or part of the compensation received for the sale of property; used when the seller is also the lender

For BC Gas, the impact of these secured bonds was moot, because none of the first mortgage bonds were still outstanding, while the purchase-money mortgages were specialized financing tools. Generally, mortgage bonds have been declining in popularity, because, like a regular mortgage, the claim of the lender has to be registered, which involves significant legal costs, particularly for companies with assets across Canada. Furthermore, what is a creditor going to do if it has to seize kilometres and kilometres of underground gas mains? The problem is that many underlying assets are very specific[12] to the firm; if it does go bankrupt, thus forcing the lender to seize the assets, they have very little value. So, de facto, there were few claims above BC Gas's MTNs.

The term **unsubordinated debt** means that no other unsecured debt ranked ahead of these MTNs. BC Gas did not have any subordinated debt outstanding at the time, but if it did, it would simply mean that this class of unsecured debt ranked behind the MTNs. If BC Gas had "junior" subordinated debt, it would mean that this debt ranked even farther behind. This ranking has the same interpretation as the terms *first* and *second* when used in reference to mortgage bonds.

unsubordinated debt unsecured debt that ranks first with the company; no other unsecured debt ranks ahead of it

---

[12] The alternative uses for underground small-diameter natural gas pipes are rather limited.

The BC Gas trust indenture also indicated the actions of the company that could trigger default:

1. non-payment of principal when due

2. non-payment of interest after 30 days

3. an order for the winding up or liquidation of the firm

4. the company making a general assignment of debts or declaring itself to be bankrupt

5. any execution that is enforced against the property of the company and is not paid after 45 days to the extent that it had not been challenged

6. default on the part of the company's first mortgage bonds or purchase-money mortgages

7. the company violating a covenant provision and failing to make good on such a violation in 60 days

cross-default clause
default on one obligation also constitutes default on another

The first two clauses are clear: failing to make a contractual payment of principal or interest causes default. Clause 6 indicates that default on its other long-term obligations also constitutes default on the MTNs, which is referred to as a **cross-default clause**. Clause 5 indicates that if someone goes to court and is allowed to claim any of the assets of BC Gas, and this claim has not been settled in 30 to 45 days (depending on the type of asset), this also causes default. This clause is similar to the cross-default clause in that it indicates an inability to pay a court order. Clauses 3 and 4 indicate that even if the company has not defaulted on any of its obligations, if it initiates procedures to wind down its business or go into bankruptcy, then this constitutes default.

We will discuss the last clause shortly. All these actions constitute "default," so how does this happen and what does it mean? It is the job of the trustee, CIBC Mellon, to monitor BC Gas's situation and at its discretion, or on the direction of the holders of 25 percent of the outstanding value of the MTN bonds, inform BC Gas that all of the outstanding MTN debt and accrued interest are due immediately. If BC Gas fails to pay on demand the full principal and interest owed, CIBC Mellon at its discretion, or again at the request of holders of 25 percent of the value of the outstanding MTNs, then proceeds to get a court order to enforce payment. It is this movement to enforce payment that usually triggers the defaulting firm to go into bankruptcy protection.

The last major feature of the BC Gas MTN indenture is the covenant provisions, which restrict what BC Gas can do. These particular MTNs were relatively "clean" in that they had few restrictions. The major covenants were as follows:

1. BC Gas will not "mortgage, pledge, charge or otherwise encumber" any of its assets unless the MTNs are given the same security. The only exception is the existing first mortgage bonds and purchase-money mortgages.

2. BC Gas will not guarantee any debt that is not necessary for carrying on its existing business.

3. The company will not issue any additional debt unless its earnings in 12 of the past 23 months satisfy a 2.0 times interest coverage ratio after the new debt has been issued and other debt retired.

4. The company will maintain its facilities for the supply of gas to enable it to carry on its business and not sell shares that cause certain designated subsidiaries to cease to be subsidiaries.

The first covenant is a standard **negative pledge** clause. It means that BC Gas could not create higher-priority debt that ranked above the MTNs without giving the MTN holders the same security. All BC Gas could do was issue more debt under its two existing secured debt indentures. The idea behind the negative pledge is simply to prevent the company from issuing large amounts of senior debt that ranks above the MTNs, thereby making them riskier. The second covenant prevented BC Gas from issuing guarantees. The reason for this restriction was that BC Gas was part of a holding company and the bondholders were worried that its parent might make the company guarantee other assets of the company. If the guarantee was then called, it would endanger the credit of the company, making the MTNs riskier. The fourth covenant was to make sure that BC Gas remained a utility that distributed natural gas.

negative pledge a clause that stipulates that a borrower may not create higher-priority debt without giving the other debt holders the same security

The most interesting covenant provision is the third one, which is standard to most gas-distribution utilities. This is the interest coverage restriction (ICR). Although the company could issue an unlimited amount of MTNs under the indenture, the ICR restricted the issue to make sure that such issues did not make the existing MTNs riskier. As we discussed in Chapter 4, the interest coverage ratio is the earnings before interest and tax (EBIT) divided by the interest payments. What the ICR does is make sure that the firm does not issue too much debt to lower this ratio below 2.0. In doing this, it allows the company to "smooth" its earnings a bit by taking the best 12 out of 23 months. The interest on the new debt is then added to the existing interest costs and the interest on any debt retired is subtracted. The focus on the ICR is common for utilities because their earnings are very stable. For other firms, the restriction is more often in terms of the debt ratio.

An ICR of 2.0 would be very low for a typical firm, but utilities have very low business risk because they are regulated and provide an essential service. The result is that utility debt is also low risk. A critical part of the prospectus for the MTNs was that BC Gas debt was rated A by DBRS, and in the opinion of BC Gas's legal counsel, it was an eligible investment under most of the legislation governing prudent investments for major financial institutions. These rules are often referred to as "legal for life" rules and mean that the BC Gas MTNS could be sold to the widest possible group of investors.[13]

CONCEPT REVIEW QUESTIONS

1. Define mortgage bonds, secured debentures, unsecured debentures, and subordinated debt.

2. Discuss the rationale for including debt covenants in a public issue.

3. Briefly describe the negative pledge and cross-default clauses.

---

[13] These regulations include, for example, the Insurance Companies Act, the Trust and Loan Companies Act, and the Pension Benefits Standards Act (Canada).

18.5 BOND RATINGS

Interpreting Debt Ratings

We have already seen that DBRS rates commercial paper and that a rating is essential to access the CP market. Since investments have such a short maturity it makes credit analysis expensive. For longer-term debt issues, most purchasers, like the major institutions mentioned above, do their own credit analysis. However, bond ratings are still very important. In Chapter 6, we listed Standard & Poor's (S&P) debt-rating categories; here we show DBRS's rating structure for long-term debt:

AAA	Highest credit quality
AA	Superior credit quality
A	Satisfactory credit quality
BBB	Adequate credit quality
BB	Speculative
B	Highly speculative
CCC/CC/C	Very highly speculative

investment grade a bond rating that means the issuer is likely to meet payment obligations

junk bonds speculative bonds with ratings below investment grade; often called high-yield bonds

In addition, each rating may be modified with a high or low rating. The lowest **investment-grade** bond rating is BBB (low), and below this the bonds are commonly referred to as **junk bonds**, although they are more politely referred to as *high-yield bonds*.

The long-term bond ratings are very similar in meaning to the CP ratings we discussed earlier. In fact, normally there is a direct transfer, with R-1 (high) being equivalent to AAA, R-1 (mid) to AA, and R-1 (low) to A.

We previously noted that there is currently no R-2-rated CP outstanding in the Canadian money market, where R-2 is equivalent to a BBB long-term bond rating and is still regarded as investment-grade debt. Similarly, until very recently there was very little BBB-rated original issue long-term debt in Canada. The relatively few issues outstanding were either from smaller regulated utilities or were from issuers that started out as some form of A and then were subsequently downgraded—the so-called "fallen angels." The rule of thumb is that non-investment-grade issuers, below BBB (low), generally raise debt in the U.S. high-yield market and then swap back into the Canadian market, because there are more investors willing to invest in original issue high-yield debt in the United States.

The most common DBRS rating is A, which DBRS describes as:

> Long-term debt rated "A" is of satisfactory credit quality. Protection of interest and principal is still substantial, but the degree of strength is less than that of AA rated entities. While "A" is a respectable rating, entities in this category are considered to be more susceptible to adverse economic conditions and have greater cyclical tendencies than higher-rated securities.[14]

---

14 "Bonds, Long Term Debt and Preferred Share Ratings," DBRS, January 2000.

Determining Bond Ratings

DBRS determines a bond rating after extensive consultation with the company through a site visit, in which the company can state its view of its business and future prospects, and after examining at least five years of historical financial statements. DBRS usually will already have prior knowledge of the company from its extensive industry surveys. DBRS will then issue a draft report to the company to check for any analytic or data errors before issuing a final rating. In determining its rating, DBRS is guided by two basic principles: the stable rating philosophy and the hierarchy principle.

The **stable rating philosophy** is summed up by the idea that the rating is based on structural and not cyclical factors. The fortunes of most companies will fluctuate with the business cycle: when the economy is hot, most companies will make money and, conversely, when it is in recession, most companies will struggle. Holders of 20- or 30-year debt can expect the company to operate though many ups and downs of the business cycle. DBRS aims to see through these predictable effects and change ratings only when a clear structural change occurs in the company's credit. This sounds easier than it is, because, in practice, it is sometimes difficult to maintain ratings when the economy is in deep recession, even though the company is responding to that recession in a predictable manner. This is the stage when many rating agencies put companies on **credit watch**, rather than cutting the rating.

The **hierarchy principle** is based on the fact that DBRS rates debt issues and not companies. Although we think of a rating as applied to a particular company, this is not the case: DBRS generally takes off a level for each class of debt. So the first mortgage bonds of a company might be rated as A (high), unsecured MTNs as A, and junior subordinated bonds as A (low). DBRS departs from this rule when there is very little of the higher-ranked debt outstanding, in which case the next class of debt assumes the rating of the more senior debt. For this reason, it is inappropriate to compare the rating of one company's first mortgage bonds with another firm's junior subordinated debentures.

In determining its rating, DBRS looks at six basic factors:

1. *Core profitability:* This is an assessment based on standard profit measures, such as the return on equity, return on assets, the "quality" of a firm's earnings, its cost structure (i.e., whether it is the low-cost producer, etc.), its growth opportunities, and its pricing structure.

2. *Asset quality:* Assets are made up of many different types, so DBRS looks at the importance of intangibles (for example, how valuable is the goodwill on the firm's balance sheet), the market value of the firm's assets, and its use of derivatives and risk management to see whether it is managing its operational and market risks effectively.

3. *Strategy and management strength:* Ultimately, a firm comprises assets and management, so that an assessment of a firm's credit risk is vitally concerned with the capabilities of the senior management group. This is particularly important if the firm is actively involved in mergers and acquisitions in which a clear strategic approach and skills at integrating acquired companies are valuable.

stable rating philosophy the idea that ratings are based on structural and not on cyclical factors; changes in ratings are made not based on temporary changes in the economy but on clear structural changes in a company's credit

credit watch a status applied to a firm by a rating agency when it is monitoring the firm

hierarchy principle a theory based on the fact that rating agencies rate debt issues and not companies; rating agencies rate each class of debt lower than the previous class, unless there is very little of the higher-ranked debt outstanding

4. *Balance sheet strength:* If the lenders have to initiate bankruptcy proceedings, it is important to understand where they stand in the overall liabilities of the firm, so standard debt ratios, coverage tests, and the amount of financial flexibility available to the firm are important. The latter includes an assessment of the firm's reliance on short-term debt, its commitment to a capital expenditure program that cannot be easily stopped, and the support potentially available from other parties, such as affiliated companies. Size is important because larger firms are usually less risky and have more market power.

5. *Business strength:* This category includes standard issues, such as market share; growth prospects for the industry; a defensible base of diversified operations; up-to-date management information systems; key intangibles, such as the quality of its workforce; and industry issues, such as the degree of unionization and competition.

6. *Miscellaneous issues:* This is a "catchall" category of issues, such as the quality of the firm's accounting statements and whether there have been consistent restatements, the structure of the bond indenture, and the importance of the firm and industry to the province or territory or to Canada.

Overall, the DBRS approach combines standard financial analysis based on the ratios discussed in Chapter 4 with a broader firm and industry analysis. The result is a mixture of quantitative with qualitative factors. Finance in the News 18-1 discusses a possible "downgrade" in Torstar Corporation's (Torstar) ratings by DBRS and Moody's in response to Torstar's rapidly increasing debt load, which is one of the key financial variables considered in determining ratings.

RATING AGENCIES WILL BE ALL OVER TORSTAR RESULTS

Credit rating agencies will be watching Torstar Corp. closely this week when the newspaper publisher reports its latest quarter of financial results, since the company faces a potential downgrade if profits continue to slide.

Torstar's rating was placed under review at Dominion Bond Rating Service Ltd. and Moody's Investors Service Inc. this month owing to the hefty amount of debt it plans to take on through the company's investment in Bell Globemedia.

Torstar is spending $283-million to buy a 20 percent stake in Bell Globemedia, which owns CTV, The Globe and Mail and several specialty television channels. It also plans to borrow up to $100-million to finance its piece of Bell Globemedia's $1.4-billion deal to buy CHUM Ltd., announced this month.

Those transactions would more than double Torstar's debt to $733-million from $350-million, sparking concerns among bond rates.

But the added burden comes as Torstar's operations are also under pressure. Soft adver-tising markets have sapped profits at the Toronto Star and its smaller Ontario newspapers, while the company's Harlequin book unit is getting hammered by the rising dollar.

After CanWest Global Communications Corp. reported sharply lower ad revenue at its newspaper operations this month, analysts are now watching Torstar.

"Not only has [Torstar] levered itself up materially, but because it had a couple of soft quarters, it is possible that might be justification alone to warrant a downgrade," DBRS analyst Martin Stevenson said. "We'll be keeping a close eye to see if the Toronto Star is feeling the same effects [as CanWest]."

CanWest and Torstar have seen their shares drop to three-and four-year lows, respectively, in recent weeks because of debt concerns and a broader selloff by investors in the newspaper sector.

While both companies have raised flags with credit rating agencies, CanWest's situation is more pressing since the company's

bonds are below investment grade and falling earnings have pushed the company close to breaking one of its covenants. Under that arrangement, the company can carry a maximum of $6 in debt for every $1 of cash flow without facing penalties from its bank.

CanWest's leverage sits at 5.87, based on the bank's calculation of cash flow. The Winnipeg-based company and its operations have $2.7-billion in consolidated debt with $1.4-billion in consolidated debt applicable to the covenant. The sale of CanWest's Irish TV assets for $198-million, expected to close this year, should pull that number back to roughly 5.10.

Torstar, meanwhile, has been adding debt to a balance sheet that was once considered underleveraged. If the company borrows the full $100-million to finance its share of the CHUM purchase, it could end up with just over $3 of pro forma debt for every $1 of cash flow at current levels. Though Torstar's bonds remain investment grade, analysts want more clarity on how much the company expects to borrow for the CHUM deal before deciding on any potential downgrade.

"We'd like to address [the rating] as soon as we can get clarification of what the actual amount may be that they put into CHUM and how much, if any, of that, is debt," Moody's analyst Darren Kirk said.

Torstar faces a potential downgrade to the lowest level of investment status at Moody's, while DBRS hasn't been specific.

Bell Globemedia's bid for CHUM was put together quickly after the controlling Waters family decided to sell in late May. Details of the financing have yet to be worked out, Torstar chief executive officer Robert Prichard said. The company's plans have been to finance such purchases in part through debt, which he said is manageable.

"This is exactly what the BGM investment meant," Mr. Prichard said. "The only surprise is that CHUM came available so soon."

Source: Robertson, Grant. "Rating Agencies Will Be All Over Torstar Results," *Globe and Mail*, July 31, 2006, p. B3. Reprinted with permission of the *Globe and Mail*.

Empirical Evidence Regarding Debt Ratings

We can assess the quality of the DBRS ratings by looking at how accurately they correlate with future default rates. In April 2005, DBRS assessed the default experience in Canada[15] by using what is termed a static pool analysis. What this amounts to is looking at the ratings for all the firms, and then tracking the default rates for these classes in the future, ignoring any subsequent changes in rating. The basic results, based on averages in the number of companies (and not on the dollar amounts outstanding), after 5, 10, and 20 years are shown in Table 18-2.

Table 18-2   Average Default Rates (%) in Canada

DBRS Rating	The Number of Years Examined		
	5	10	20
AAA	0.00	0.00	0.00
AA	0.56	0.63	0.63
A	0.95	1.60	2.33
BBB	2.34	3.82	5.03
BB	6.37	8.99	10.11
B	28.33	28.33	28.33
CCC	33.33	33.33	33.33

[15] *DBRS Corporate Default Study*, DBRS, April 2005.

Several points are important from the DBRS analysis. First, the default rates clearly increase as the DBRS rating goes down, so their ratings provide a good indicator of credit risk. Second, for the investment-grade bond ratings, we can see why BBB is the cutoff point between the investment and non-investment-grade ratings. For the AAA, AA, and A ratings, the default rates are very low, with no AAA-rated issuers actually defaulting, and only 0.63 percent of the AA's defaulting. However, there is an exponential increase as credit quality deteriorates, with 2.33 percent of the A's defaulting after 20 years, 5.03 percent of the BBB's, 10.11 percent of the BB's, and 28.33 percent of the B's. From this, we can understand why many major institutional investors restrict their bond portfolios to holding debt with a minimum rating of A, or utilities with BBB. Finally, for the really risky low-rated debt, B and CCC, default either happens quite early or doesn't happen at all, because the default rates are essentially stable beyond five years.

Of course, DBRS does not leave its ratings unchanged when structural changes affect the underlying credit risk. As a result, ratings migrate as the credit quality of a firm deteriorates. DBRS gives the example of Trizec Properties Inc., formerly a major Canadian property developer. Three years before bankruptcy, it was rated AA (low); two years before bankruptcy, it was rated BBB (low); one year before bankruptcy, it was B rated; and three months before bankruptcy, it was CCC.

Of course, defaulting is only part of the story, because an investor wants to know how much it is likely to get in the event of a default. Information on recovery rates is difficult to get because it very much depends on the industry the firm is in and the nature of the underlying assets. However, Gilson[16] reports on a Salomon study that gave the market values for different types of debt after a firm defaulted, shown in Table 18-3. These market prices would reflect these recovery rates.

Table 18-3   Default Recovery Rates

Type	Market Value/Par Value
Senior secured	54.6%
Senior unsecured	40.6
Senior subordinated	31.3
Subordinated	30.1
Junior subordinated	23.0
All bonds	34.2

The Salomon data indicate that after going into default, the average market price to face value was only 34.2 percent. However, this rate clearly declines with the ranking of the debt, because senior secured debt traded for 54.6 percent of face value, while junior subordinated debt traded for only 23 percent of face value.

[16] Gilson, Stuart. "Investing in Distressed Situations: A Market Survey," *Financial Analysts Journal 51*, no. 6 (November–December 1995), pp. 8–27.

The data on default and recovery rates indicate what we would expect: high-risk bonds have both a higher probability of defaulting as well as a lower recovery rate. In Figure 18-2, we indicate the yield spreads between different bond ratings. In each case, the bond yield is from an index of long-term bonds maintained by Scotia Capital Markets and the spread is the difference between the yield on this index and that on an index of long Canada bonds. The spreads are weekly values from May 1996 to May 2006, but in the earlier period, only monthly values are available. For the overall 10-year period, the average AA spread over long Canada bonds was 0.63 percent, the A spread was 0.97 percent, and the BBB spread was 1.72 percent. Unfortunately, there are no longer enough AAA-rated bonds outstanding to make up an index.

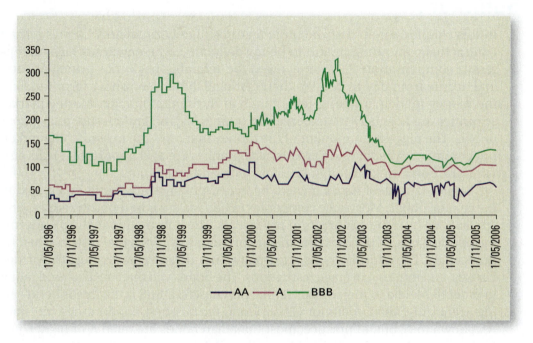

18-2 FIGURE

Canada Bond Yield Spreads

Figure 18-2 reports average yield spreads; however, averages are deceptive. What also matters is the variability. In this case, the standard deviation of the spreads is 0.19 percent (AA), 0.29 percent (A), and 0.57 percent (BBB), respectively, indicating that the spreads are not only higher with the lower-rated debt but also much more variable. We can see this during the slowdown experienced in the Canadian economy after the stock market peaked in October 2000. By 2002, BBB-rated bonds in Canada yielded 3.26 percent more than equivalent-maturity long Canada bonds, and even AA-rated bonds traded similarly to BBB-bonds in normal years.

The spread experience indicates that during economic slowdowns, there is a *flight to quality*, when investors are reluctant to invest in riskier securities and invest more heavily in low-risk investments, like Canada bonds. During these recessionary or slowdown periods, some firms experience financing problems and discover that they cannot access long-term funds on reasonable terms. In fact, these spreads are on **seasoned bond issues** (or actively traded bond issues) and they do not indicate whether or not new funds are available on those terms. For this reason, during these periods, lower-rated companies usually have to finance with shorter-term debt or to rely on bank borrowings.

seasoned bond issues
actively traded bond issues that have been outstanding for some time

CONCEPT REVIEW QUESTIONS

1. Differentiate investment-grade debt from junk debt.
2. Briefly describe the main factors DBRS considers in determining its debt ratings.
3. Briefly summarize the evidence regarding how well debt ratings work.

Summary

In this chapter, we discuss the basic features of debt financing. Debt is a fixed contractual commitment, and to be tax deductible, the payments have to represent compensation for money owed, be referable back to a principal sum, and accrue from day to day. We then distinguish between short-term funds in the money market and long-term funds in the capital market. Money market securities are normally traded on a discount basis and are referred to as paper or bills. The biggest component of the money market is the treasury bill market, but commercial paper and bankers' acceptances are also important. Firms also use bank borrowings through lines of credit and term loans.

Longer-term debt issues have to be issued under a prospectus when sold to the general public. Most large companies in Canada are now reporting issuers and so can issue by using a short-form prospectus. The information in the prospectus includes the type of debt and the major covenant provisions that restrict what the firm can do. The critical clauses are usually cross-default clauses, negative pledge clauses, and interest coverage restrictions. The bonds will then need a bond rating in order to be sold to major institutional purchasers. DBRS is the major bond-rating agency in Canada both for CP and long-term issues. Bond ratings run from AAA down to C, but, in practice, most Canadian bonds are rated A or higher, just as there is currently no CP rated lower than R-1 (low) outstanding. These ratings are very highly correlated with actual default rates and the recovery rates that investors can expect in case of default.

Key Terms

after-tax cost of debt (k), p. 699	investment grade, p. 714
bankers' acceptances (BAs), p. 705	junk bonds, p. 714
commercial paper (CP), p. 702	lines of credit (L/Cs), p. 707
covenants, p. 708	liquidity support, p. 705
credit watch, p. 715	negative pledge, p. 713
cross-default clause, p. 712	operating or demand L/C, p. 707
fixed contractual commitments, p.698	prime lending rate, p. 707
floating interest rate, p. 707	promised yields, p. 703
hierarchy principle, p. 715	promissory note, p. 701

Formulas/Equations

(18-1) $K = K_d (1 - T)$

(18-2) $V = \dfrac{PAR(1+R)P + RECOVER(1-P)}{(1+K)}$

(18-3) $R = \dfrac{(1+K_{TB})}{P} - 1$

QUESTIONS AND PRACTICE PROBLEMS

Multiple Choice Questions

1. Which of the following statements about debt is *incorrect*?

   A. Interest payments and principal payments are fixed commitments.

   B. Interest payments are tax deductible.

   C. Bond issuers are paid a series of fixed periodic amounts before the maturity date.

   D. Debt indenture is a legal document, specifying payment requirements, and so on.

2. What is the after-tax cost of debt? $Tc = 40\%$; before-tax cost of debt = 8%.

   A. 3.2%

   B. 7.5%

   C. 4.8%

   D. 6.0%

3. What is the promised yield to issue at PAR, assuming RECOVER = 0, $P = 90\%$, and $k = k_{TB} = 2\%$?

   A. 12%

   B. 13%

   C. 11%

   D. 10%

4. What is the yield spread, if the promised yield on 30-day CP is 5 percent, the yield on the 91-day T-bill is 3 percent, and the yield on the 30-day T-bill is 2 percent?

A. 2%

B. 3%

C. 4%

D. 5%

5. Which of the following money market instruments could a firm without a very sound credit rating use when seeking financing?

A. Commercial paper

B. Bankers' acceptance

C. Bill of exchange

D. Both A and B

6. Which of the following reflects the negative pledge clause?

A. The issuing firm must make its interest payments.

B. The issuing firm must fulfill its supplies to promised customers.

C. The issuing firm has to maintain a current ratio of more than 2.5.

D. The issuing firm must not issue any new debt with existing assets as collateral.

7. Which of the following statements about lines of credit is *false*?

A. An operating or demand line of credit is the standard type.

B. A revolver has more stability than an operating line of credit.

C. Prime is the cost base of a revolver and is a floating rate.

D. A revolver is usually at least 364 days.

8. Which of the following ratings is the highest?

A. BB

B. CCC

C. A

D. AA

Practice Problems

Easy

9. State the three basic tests the CRA uses to ensure interest payments are tax deductible.

10. Determine the selling price of a Government of Canada Treasury Bill that has a quoted annual interest rate of 2.1 percent and will mature in 180 days. You may assume a par value of $1,000.

11. Collingwood Corp.'s 60-day commercial paper has a promised yield of 9 percent per year, but the expected yield is just 6 percent due to the risk of default. If the current 60-day T-bill yield is 6 percent, what is the yield spread on this commercial paper?

12. As the newly appointed treasurer for Collingwood Corp., you have to decide how to raise $50 million in short-term financing. You believe you could issue commercial paper with a promised yield of 9 percent. However, your bank will

charge a commitment fee of 0.125 percent on the line of credit to back up this paper, as well as 0.125 percent as a selling commission. As an alternative, the bank suggests using bankers' acceptances which would have a lower yield of 8.75 percent. The bank's "stamping" fee for these BAs is 0.625 percent. Which financing alternative should you choose?

13. Collingwood Corp. has a revolving line of credit on which it owes $50 million. One of the restrictions imposed with this financing arrangement is that the company must maintain a minimum interest coverage ratio of 1.75. If this is the only borrowing, and the annual interest rate is 9.75 percent, how much does the company have to earn to live up to the covenant?

14. Calculate the price of the 91-day T-bill if the face value = $1,000,000 and the quoted interest rate = 4.8%.

Medium

15. Calculate the value of the one-month CP given the following: PAR = $500,000; R (promised yield) = 5%; probability of not defaulting = 95%; RECOVER = 0; K = 15%.

16. List and briefly describe the five basic factors used to determine a DBRS rating.

17. Jackie would like to borrow $150,000 to expand her small business, but needs to understand the impact of the 8 percent interest payments. Last year, her company did not pay any interest and had total earnings before tax of $123,500. The tax rate was 30 percent. Determine the company's net income for the year. Assuming that EBIT and the rate of taxation will not change, calculate how much the net income figure will change if Jackie proceeds with the loan. Explain to Jackie why her company's net income does not fall by the amount of the interest payments.

18. The cost (interest rate) of the loan Jackie needs for her business is 8 percent per year. Given that the company's net income will fall by less than the amount of interest paid (see Problem 17) is Jackie correct to think that the after-tax cost of the loan is lower than 8 percent? With a tax rate of 30 percent, what is the after-tax cost of this loan?

19. Collingwood Corp.'s bank is willing to provide it with a 10-year term loan for $50 million. The annual payments on this loan will be $5 million, and there is a "bullet" payment of $50 million at maturity. What is the interest rate being charged by the bank? Does it make sense that this loan would have a higher cost than the alternatives presented in Problem 12?

20. In your job as treasurer of Collingwood Corp., you have to arrange for a line of credit for the firm. The following is taken from the company's most recent balance sheet.

Current Assets	
Cash	$ 1,271,987
Accounts Receivable	18,536,000
Inventory	74,196,000
	94,003,987
Property and Equipment (net)	126,323,000
Goodwill	46,888,000
Total Assets	267,214,987

The bank will provide credit up to 75 percent of the value of receivables, and 50 percent of the inventory value. What is the maximum credit limit that Collingwood can obtain?

Difficult

21. Michael M. specializes in buying high-risk commercial paper; his required return on these investments is 12 percent per year. He is considering buying some 60-day paper from Collingwood Corp. with a promised yield of 9 percent per year. However, Michael believes there is a 1 percent chance that Collingwood will default on this debt, in which case he would only recover 80 percent of the face value. How much will Michael be willing to pay for each $1,000 par value of this paper?

22. Collingwood Corp. is able to issue its 60-day commercial paper at par with a promised yield of 9 percent per year. The current T-bill yield is 6 percent per year (or 1 percent for the 60-day period) which is also the expected return on the commercial paper, as there is some risk of default. If Collingwood were to default, investors will recover 80 percent of the face value of the debt. Based on this information, what is the probability that Collingwood will default on its commercial paper?

23. When Collingwood Corp. issued its 60-day commercial paper the promised yield was 9 percent, whereas the 60-day T-bill yield was 6 percent. There is a 2 percent chance that Collingwood will default on this debt. If investors were willing to pay the full par-value amount to purchase the paper, how much do they expect to recover in the event of a default?

24. Rather than take a term loan from the bank, Collingwood Corp. has decided to issue $50 million of 10-year bonds. DBRS has assigned a rating of "BB" to this bond issue.

    A. Determine the probability that no default occurs during the life of these bonds, based on historical average default rates.

    B. Valuing long-term bonds with default risk is quite difficult. For simplicity, assume that the bonds mature in one year and can be valued in the same manner as commercial paper (Equation 18-2). Collingwood Corp. will pay coupon interest (the promised yield) of 10 percent, whereas the current yield on treasury bonds is 6 percent. Use the estimated default rate from (A) to determine the value of the bonds. You may assume that the bonds are worthless in the event of a default.

25. Sometimes, bonds are completely worthless when a company defaults on payments. However, in practice, bonds typically have some market value (recovery rate) even after a default. Collingwood's bonds are unsecured, but are senior to any other debt. Use this and the information in Problem 24 to determine the value of the bonds.

Warrants

Warrants are an example of the hybrid instruments discussed in Chapter 19. Warrants are similar to options, but they have a longer time horizon (two to five years). They provide excellent leverage for the longer-term investor seeking exposure to a particular security or industry—they trade like the underlying security to which they are attached, but they cost less. The downside to holding warrants is that they may expire with no value if their exercise price remains at or above the stock price. The common shares and warrants of Stelco Inc. saw significant price increases in April 2007, based on takeover rumours sparked by the sale of Algoma Steel to India's Essar Global Ltd. The North American steel industry has experienced significant consolidation, and Stelco is now one of the few remaining independently owned steel manufacturers. The Stelco warrants have an exercise price of $11 per share and are "in the money" warrants.

Source: Stelco Inc. website: www.stelco.com. May 2, 2007.

"Stelco Leads Gainers," Globeinvestor.com website: www.rbcinvest.globeinvestor.com. April 24, 2007.

"Stelco hopes to be takeover target," *Financial Post* website: http://www.canada.com/nationalpost/financialpost/. May 1, 2007.

Equity and Hybrid Instruments

Learning Objectives

After reading this chapter, you should understand the following:

1. The basic rights associated with share ownership

2. How these rights are distributed differently across different classes of shareholders

3. How preferred shares differ from common shares and the different features that may be associated with preferred shares

4. Why combining warrants with debt issues or issuing convertible bonds or debentures can provide firms with attractive financing options

5. The wide variety of hybrid financing options available to firms, and how they are constructed by combining the basic characteristics of debt and equity to various degrees

INTRODUCTION

In Chapter 18, we discussed debt and how it is largely determined by what the Canada Revenue Agency (CRA) regards as interest for tax purposes. In this chapter, we consider non-debt securities. We start out with equity, both common shares and preferred shares, which are part of shareholders' equity. We show that the basic rights provided to common shareholders can be distributed among different classes of common shares, so all common shares are not equal. In particular, some of them have voting rights, others don't, and some of them have larger dividends than others do.

Preferred shares in Canada come in a wide variety of forms because of the way that dividends are taxed. As a result, we have preferred shares that are very similar to commercial paper (CP), midterm notes, or long-term financing, with the major difference being that preferred shares pay dividends rather than interest. We then show how conversion features in warrants and convertibles make convertible bonds part common equity and part debt, depending on the structure of the conversion feature. We look at the non-tax features of different securities and how they are treated by the major rating agencies.

A good understanding of the material in this chapter is necessary to comprehend the range of corporate financing activities undertaken by firms and how firms can mix them to attempt to lower their overall financing cost, which will be discussed in Chapter 20.

19.1 SHAREHOLDERS' EQUITY

In Chapter 7, we defined *equity securities* as ownership interests in an underlying business, usually a corporation. We then defined common shares as certificates of ownership interest in a corporation, so that common shareholders represent the true "owners" of the corporation. Finally, we defined *preferred shares* as those that provide the owners with a claim to a fixed amount of equity that is established when the shares are first issued. However, MacIntosh and Nicholls[1] point out that the terms "common share" and "preferred share" have no statutory definition in Canada; they are used to describe classes of shares. Our discussion distinguishes between the two forms of equity, as well as the implications to investors and to the underlying business.

Shareholder Rights

In Chapter 18, we saw that the basic definition of debt flows from what the CRA determines to be interest and tax deductible. Equity can be regarded as a security for which the payments are not tax deductible. In addition, the Canada Business Corporations Act (CBCA) 24(3) provides that

---

[1] MacIntosh, Jeffrey and Nicholls, Christopher. *Securities Law* (Toronto: Irwin Law, 2002).

Where a corporation has only one class of shares, the rights of the holders thereof are equal in all respects and include the rights

a) to vote at any meeting of shareholders of the corporation;

b) to receive any dividend declared by the corporation; and

c) to receive the remaining property of the corporation on dissolution.

Provincially incorporated companies operate under provincial laws with similar provisions. These three rights then define the basic rights of common shareholders.

The most basic right of common shareholders is the right to vote. Because they own a "share" of the business, shareholders have the right to make important decisions at the annual general meeting. These rights include the right to elect the members of the board of directors (BOD), to appoint the auditors of the firm, to make changes in the articles of incorporation and bylaws of the company, and to vote on major changes in the firm's operations. What constitutes a major or fundamental change in the firm's operations is difficult to define, but it normally includes a major acquisition of another firm through an exchange of shares or the disposition of major assets.

However, even these rights can be severely circumscribed. At one time, most equity holders also had a **pre-emptive right**, which was the right to maintain proportional ownership in a company when new shares were issued. If the firm were to issue, say, 50 percent more shares in a seasoned offering, each shareholder had the right to buy 50 percent more shares to maintain his or her proportional interest. The pre-emptive right meant that most new issues of shares were made by means of a *rights offering* to existing shareholders. However, starting in the early 1950s, Canadian companies changed their corporate structure to remove the pre-emptive right, allowing them to sell shares to new investors. As a result, very few rights offerings are made and shareholders cannot prevent their ownership share being diluted by the sale of new shares to other investors.[2]

pre-emptive right the right of shareholders to maintain proportional ownership in a company when new shares are issued

The loss of the pre-emptive right has been exacerbated by the fact that most companies have now authorized an unlimited number of common shares or have increased the authorized capital so that they no longer need shareholder approval to issue more common shares. This means that for reporting issuers, as we discussed in Chapter 17, firms can sell new shares very quickly by means of a *bought deal* to major institutional investors and thus dilute the ownership share of existing investors.

The two remaining rights, to receive a dividend and to receive any remaining property on the dissolution of the corporation, reflect the equity owners' rights as the **residual owners**. For example, the equity holders have no right to a dividend until it is declared by the company's BOD. Furthermore, there are extensive restrictions on when the company can declare a dividend, the major one being that the firm has to have the resources to pay the dividend without impairing its ability to meet its fixed contractual commitments. In this sense,

residual owners equity owners who receive any remaining cash flows or property (on the dissolution of the corporation) after all other commitments have been satisfied

---

[2] In fact, a standard takeover defence is to sell shares to a friendly investor, thereby reducing the stake of a potentially hostile acquirer. *Poison pills*, discussed in Chapter 15, are another example of the lack of pre-emptive rights and their impact on shareholder dilution.

the payment of the dividend reflects the fact that the equity holders are last in line after all other claims on the firm's earnings stream have been met. In the same way, if the firm is liquidated, all other claimants on the firm's assets have to be met before the equity holders receive any payment.

A right not explicit in the above CBCA description is the right to *limited liability*, which was discussed in Chapter 2. The equity holders commit initial equity to the firm, but they are legally protected from being forced to put more money into the firm. As a result, if the firm cannot meet its fixed commitments to pay interest, and so on, the equity holders cannot be forced to inject more money into the firm to allow it to meet these commitments. If the creditors then put the firm into bankruptcy and there is not enough money to pay off all the claims on the firm, again the equity holders cannot be forced to put more money into the firm. Limited liability ensures that the shareholders can only lose their initial investment, so their *downside* risk is limited, while they have unlimited *upside* potential. In this sense, common shares have some of the characteristics of call options discussed in Chapter 12. We will use this insight when discussing financial strategy.

Different Classes of Shares

The CBCA definition qualifies the three rights of the common shareholders by stating these rights apply "where there is only one class of shares outstanding." It is up to the articles of incorporation of the company to decide how these rights are allocated when multiple classes of shares are outstanding. The only legal requirement is that each of these three rights has to be attached to a class of shares.

For example, a share structure could be set up as follows:

A Shares
- no voting rights as long as dividend payments are made

- a $0.05 dividend in addition to any dividend paid to class B shares, but only if class C dividends are not in arrears

- an equal share with class B shares in any residual receipts on the winding up of the company

B Shares
- full voting rights

- no dividends if dividends on class C shares are in arrears

- an equal share with class A shares in any residual receipts on the winding up of the company

C Shares
- no voting rights unless dividends are in arrears for two years, after which each share gets one vote

- a dividend of $0.30 per share every quarter when declared by the board of directors; no dividends on class A and B shares can be paid if these dividends are in arrears

- payment of $25 par value before any payments to class A and B shares on the winding up of the company

This is a loose description of a possible share structure that meets the CBCA requirements. The voting rights rest with the class B shares, and all shares have clearly specified rights in the event of a dividend payment or the winding up of the company. In this case, the class B shares would be regarded as common shares. The class A shares have no voting rights but have a slight preferential dividend and would commonly be referred to as **non-voting shares** or **restricted shares**. The class C shares are preferred shares, because they have a preferred dividend over both the A and B shares.

non-voting shares or restricted shares common shares that have no voting rights but a slight preferential dividend

This share structure is relatively simple and, in fact, companies have no limitations on designing the share structure. This example of two classes of common shares and one class of preferred shares is quite common for Canadian firms, but it raises the problem of allocating voting rights.

Voting rights mean control and the ability to choose the BOD, and through them, senior management and the strategic direction of the company. This control value is very important, because it means the firm can be taken over only by buying the voting shares. In the event of a takeover, voting shares are more valuable than non-voting shares. A good example of this was Bell Globemedia Inc.'s (Bell Globemedia) takeover offer for CHUM Limited (CHUM) on July 13, 2006.

CHUM had a dual-class share structure, which means that it had A and B shares similar to those described above. In CHUM's case, 90 percent of the class A shares were held by the Waters family, descendants of CHUM's founder Allan Waters, and these shares had normal voting rights. The family also owned 10 percent of the class B non-voting shares which were otherwise widely held. Bell Globemedia (now called CTVglobemedia Inc.) offered $52.50 for the class A shares and $47.50 for the class B shares. In both cases, the offer price was about a 60 percent premium over the average price for CHUM's shares. However, the fact that the A shares received a $5 per share premium rankled many big institutional shareholders.

If the same offer had been made to both classes of shares, the price would have been $48.50. As a portfolio manager at AIC said, "The overall price is not the issue. It's the difference and discrimination, if you will, that's fairly large."[3] The CHUM case was relatively mild compared with previous cases. For example, in 1988, shareholders of the voting shares in Canadian Tire Corporation, Limited (Canadian Tire) received a takeover premium and the non-voting shares did not. The Toronto Stock Exchange (TSX) changed its rules after the Canadian Tire case to prevent this from happening again, by creating "coattail" provisions so that both classes of shares have to be purchased; the non-voting shares ride the coattails of the voting shares, which the acquirer needs to get control. However, the rules apply only to new listings and CHUM, like many companies, was grandfathered because its shares were already outstanding.

The desire to maintain control by establishing or maintaining classes of shares with different voting rights is common to many family-run businesses, in which the founder needs external capital but wants to maintain control. A classic example was the Four Seasons Hotels Limited (Four Seasons), a chain founded by Isadore Sharpe, whose family controlled 67 percent of the votes through multiple voting shares.[4] In September 1996, Four Seasons proposed to reorganize its two main classes of shares. The subordinated voting shares were

[3] Sethi, Chanakya. "CHUM Investors Criticize Dual-Class Discount." *Globe and Mail*, July 13, 2006, p. B4.

[4] Barbara Shecter, "Four Seasons Plan Assailed," *Financial Post*, Friday September 27, 1996.

to be renamed limited voting shares and the multiple voting shares owned by the Sharpe family, which already had 12 votes each, were to be renamed variable voting shares. The plan was to increase the voting power of these shares as more limited voting shares were issued to keep the Sharpe family at 67 percent of the votes. In essence, without putting up any more money, the Sharpe family would always control the company through these variable voting shares. Many institutional investors refuse to invest in limited or non-voting shares, but on the day the Four Seasons plan was announced the stock price went up 55 cents and reached a 52-week high.

What both the CHUM and the Four Seasons examples highlight is the role of the *founder* of the company. When the voting rights are concentrated in the hands of a visionary leader who has built the company, investors are often only too happy to see control concentrated in his or her hands because the company *is* the senior management. For this reason, many institutional investors were relatively indifferent to the Four Seasons' plan. The problems arise when the bloodline "thins out" and the second and third generations of the family do not have the managerial skills evident in the original founder, or when the firm is sold. This was the case with CHUM: when control passed out of the hands of the founder, there was no clear strategic direction for the company. CHUM became a takeover target and investors became upset at the price differential between the voting and the non-voting shares.

The value of these voting rights very much depends on who has control of the company and whether it is good or bad for shareholder value creation. Empirical studies that have estimated the value of these voting rights have produced mixed results, as have studies of the stock market's reaction when firms recapitalize their share structure to create or remove these voting differentials. The problem is that differential voting rights may not affect value when the founder runs the company, but they do when that founder ceases to be involved. Regardless, the limited or non-voting shares usually have a slight premium in terms of the right to a dividend to offset the lost value of control.

Another famous example of the impact of control is Ford Motor Company, in which 71 million B shares, with 40 percent of the voting rights, are in a **family trust**. The problem of what happens after the founder ceases to be involved and gradually the wealth is dispersed over succeeding generations is solved through a trust. Trusts are a standard way of separating ownership from control. For example, inheritances often go to a minor and the wealth is put into a trust. The minor receives the income from the inheritance but cannot control it until he or she reaches a given age, normally 25. In similar fashion, the shares in the Ford family trust ensure that income flows through to the hundreds of individuals descended from Henry Ford, but all the votes are held by the plan trustees.

Family members installed Clay Ford, great grandson of Henry Ford, as president and CEO of Ford in 2001. Since 2001, Ford's stock price has fallen from just more than $20 to less than $7 and things have become so desperate that Ford has hired investment bankers to see how it can be reorganized or broken up. One extreme option being considered is to sell all of Ford's assets, except its truck division, which continues to make record profits. For the last several years, shareholder resolutions to change Ford's share structure have been defeated, but each year the number of votes in favour has increased.

family trust a trust that ensures income flows to the people descended from the company founder, but all the votes are held by the plan trustees

Some Basic Ratios

We now return to our previous example of Rothmans Inc. (Rothmans). Its shareholders' equity figures for fiscal year end of 2004, 2005, and 2006 are presented in Table 19-1.

Table 19-1   Rothmans Inc. Shareholders' Equity

$Million	2004	2005	2006
Preferred stock	0	0	0
Capital stock	38.869	41.974	45.347
Retained earnings	129.628	151.734	68.513
Total shareholders' equity	168.497	193.708	113.860
Total liabilities and equity	496.757	528.528	449.075
Total common equity	168.497	193.708	113.860
Shares outstanding year end (million)	67.351	67.572	67.856
Book value per share ($)	2.5018	2.8667	1.6780
Diluted earnings per common share ($)	1.34	1.37	1.45
Common dividend per share ($)	0.8125	1.05	2.70*

* Includes a special dividend of $1.50

Notice that Rothmans had no preferred shares outstanding, just common shares. Its 2006 common equity figure consisted of $45.347 million in common shares, which had been contributed by shareholders through seasoned and initial public offerings, and $68.513 million of common equity in the form of retained earnings, representing the cumulative earnings that Rothmans reinvested in the firm, rather than paying a dividend. Some firms divide the capital stock into the par value of the shares and additional contributed capital, but Rothmans does not provide this level of detail, and most firms in Canada have no stated or par value for their common shares. In fact, it has not been permissible to issue common shares with a par value since 1975 for firms incorporating under the CBCA.

As of its 2006 fiscal year end, Rothmans had 67.856 million shares outstanding, so that each common share had a book value per share (BVPS) of $1.678, calculated as

$$BVPS = \frac{Common\ equity}{Number\ of\ shares} = \frac{\$113.860}{67.856} = \$1.678$$

Rothmans' BVPS indicates the amount of money that Rothmans' shareholders have invested in the firm. As we discussed in Chapter 4, Rothmans is so profitable that the market price (P) of its shares was $20.25 as of March 2006, which translates into a market-to-book ratio (M/B) of 12.07; calculated as:

$$M/B = \frac{P}{BVPS} = \frac{20.25}{1.678} = 12.07$$

The 2006 M/B figure for Rothmans is much higher than the 2004 and 2005 figures of 6.85 and 8.37. A big reason for this is the decline in the 2006 BVPS figure to $1.678 from the 2005 figure of $2.867, because of the decrease in retained earnings to $68.513 million from its 2005 value of $151.7 million. This reduction in retained earnings can be attributed to the $1.50 per share special dividend paid during the year, which totalled approximately $101.5 million. When combined with the regular dividend of $1.20 per share, the total dividends paid during 2006 were $182.685 million, which far exceeded the 2006 net earnings figure of $99.464 million.

Indeed, Rothmans' 2006 dividend yield was exceptionally high at 13.33 percent when the special dividend of $1.50 per share is included, and it was a healthy 5.93 percent excluding the special dividend. These calculations are shown below:

Including special dividend: $Dividend\ yield = \dfrac{DPS}{P} = \dfrac{2.70}{20.25} = 0.1333$

Excluding special dividend: $Dividend\ yield = \dfrac{DPS}{P} = \dfrac{1.20}{20.25} = 0.0593$

Dividends are very attractive in Canada for tax reasons, both for corporations and for individuals. As we discussed in Chapter 3, dividends received by one Canadian corporation from another Canadian corporation are not taxed to avoid double taxation of income at the corporate level.[5] In contrast, interest income is taxable between corporations because, as we discussed before, interest expense is tax deductible.

Dividend income is also attractive for individuals, because of the dividend tax credit system in Canada. Traditionally, this system was structured so that the effective tax rate paid was the same for owners of a small private corporation whether they withdrew their compensation as dividends or as salary. However, in the May 2006 budget, the federal government reformed the tax rates to reduce the overall tax rate on dividend income from public corporations, and since then most of the provinces have also reformed their taxation of dividend income.

For 2006, Canadian dividend income was grossed up by 45 percent for federal tax purposes and then a tax credit of 0.275 percent was applied against the federal tax. In Ontario, a tax credit of 0.09425 percent is applied against Ontario tax. The combined tax rate on dividend income for someone in the top tax bracket is 25.09 percent, versus 46.41 percent for interest income and 23.2 percent for capital gains income. Further, the Ontario tax credit will gradually increase until 2010, when the overall tax rate will be the same as that on capital gains. Like all tax changes, these proposals may be modified as a result of changes in government revenues and expenses. However, the impact has been to enhance the attractiveness of dividend income in all provinces.

---

[5] Of course, the income is eventually taxed twice in total, because individual investors pay taxes on any dividends received. However, eliminating the tax on dividends paid to other corporations avoids having the same dollar of income taxed three times—twice at the corporate level and once again when received by individual investors.

19.2 PREFERRED SHARE CHARACTERISTICS

The fact that interest and dividend income are taxed differently is well known in the capital market. BMO Nesbitt Burns Inc., the investment dealer arm of the Bank of Montreal, produces a preferred share quarterly report that tracks the performance of the preferred share market. In the December 2005 issue of their *Preferred Share Statistics*, BMO Nesbitt Burns provided the yields on various instruments, as shown in Table 19-2.

Table 19-2   Preferred Share Yields, November 2005

Straight Preferreds (%)	
Dividend yield	5.22
Long Canada yield	4.19
After tax spread (corp.)	2.50
After tax spread (indiv.)	1.34
Retractable Preferreds (%)	
Dividend yield	3.33
Mid Canada yield	3.90
After tax spread (corp)	0.80
After tax spread (indiv)	0.20
Floating Rate Preferreds (%)	
Dividend yield	3.24
BA (3 month)	3.40
After-tax spread (corp)	1.03
After-tax spread (indiv)	0.40

Source: Data from BMO Nesbitt Burns, *Preferred Share Statistics*, December 2005.

Table 19-2 reports the yields on three different types of preferred shares, which we discuss below. Because of the favourable tax treatment accorded dividends in Canada, a variety of different types of preferred shares exist in the capital market.

Many of these issues are designed to mimic different types of bonds and appeal to bond investors who want the more favourable tax treatment. Remember that although preferred shares are a type of equity and the dividends are not legally an obligation until they are declared, for low-risk companies, their payment is virtually assured.

The first type of preferred share reported in Table 19-2 is the traditional **straight preferred share**. These are preferreds that have no maturity date and pay a fixed dividend at regular intervals (usually quarterly). As discussed in Chapter 7, these can be viewed as perpetuities and valued accordingly. These were the most common type of preferreds in the Canadian market until the 1970s. In Table 19-2, the straight preferred yields are 5.22 percent, compared with the 4.19 percent yield for long Canada bonds, implying a positive yield spread of 1.03 percent.

There are several reasons for this spread. The most obvious reason is that bonds issued by the Government of Canada are clearly of lower risk than are preferred shares issued by a firm that may default. In addition, straight preferred shares that have no maturity date have a longer life than even the longest-term government bonds, and so they will have greater maturity risk, as discussed in Chapter 6. These risks, particularly the default risk, are reflected in this yield spread, even before we take taxes into account.

The 1.03 percent spread is based on before-tax yields, so it does not take into account the **tax value of money**: dividends are taxed more favourably than is interest income. To account for the tax differences, BMO Nesbitt Burns also estimates the after-tax spreads, which are based on a corporate investor in the 35 percent tax bracket for which the dividend income is non-taxable, and on a private investor in the highest tax bracket. In this case, the *after-tax spread* would increase to 2.50 percent for a corporate investor, and 1.34 percent for a personal investor.

The second type of preferred share presented in Table 19-2 is the **retractable preferred share**, which gives the investor the right to sell it back to the issuer, thus creating an early maturity date. Retractable preferreds permit early retirement, with the typical retraction date being set at five years. Therefore, even though the preferred shares may end up being outstanding for longer periods, they are valued as if the maturity is five years. For this reason, BMO Nesbitt Burns compares the yields on retractable preferreds with those on midterm bonds. As of the end of November 2005, the retractable preferreds yielded 3.33 percent while the midterm Canada bonds yielded 3.90 percent, producing a negative spread (–0.57 percent) between the yields on the riskier preferred shares and on the less risky bonds. Of course, the reason for this is the different tax treatment of dividends and interest. Indeed, when we look at the after-tax yield spreads, we see that it is +0.80 percent for the corporate investor and +0.20 percent for the individual investor, so that the traditional risk-return relationship prevails on an after-tax basis.

The final type of preferred share reported in Table 19-2 is the **floating rate preferred share**. These shares generally have a long maturity date, but every three or six months their dividend is reset by an auction mechanism so that the dividend yield will be in line with current market interest rates. Alternatively, many of the floating rate preferred shares issued by the major banks have their dividend rate float with 75 percent of the prime rate, usually to some maximum rate. The result is that they always sell very close to their par value, because their dividend rate is always very close to the current market rate. The yield on these

straight preferred share a preferred share that has no maturity date and pays a fixed dividend at regular intervals, usually quarterly

tax value of money accounting for the fact that dividends are taxed more favourably than is interest income

retractable preferred share a share that gives the investor the right to sell it back to the issuer, thus creating an early maturity date

floating rate preferred share a share that has a long maturity date and every three or six months has its dividend reset by an auction mechanism so that the dividend yield is in line with market interest rates

floaters is compared with those on three-month bankers' acceptances (BAs) in Table 19-2 above, which represent an alternative short-term fixed-income investment. The yield on the floaters was 3.24 percent, less than the 3.40 percent yield on the BAs, producing a negative spread of –0.16 percent. Once again, on an after-tax basis, positive spreads of 1.03 percent for corporate investors and 0.40 percent for individual investors are observed.

Three important points about the yield data emerge. First, although the time and risk value of money are important, so too is the tax value of money. Second, the capital market is creative in designing securities to match investor demand: preferred shares have been designed to match similar fixed income debt securities but with the tax advantage of dividends.[6] Finally, the comparisons are never perfect because preferred shares are unambiguously riskier. However, note that the after-tax spreads are smallest for the shorter-term securities, where the risk differences are the lowest, and largest for the infinite-lived straight preferred shares, when compared with long-term Canada bonds.

The basic risk attached to investing in preferred shares is that they have *equity risk* in addition to the investment risks attached to fixed income securities. As mentioned above, equity securities do not provide a contractual right to anything except to the residuals after all others have been paid off. If in any quarter, the BOD decides *not* to pay a dividend, the holders of the preferred shares cannot seek legal action to force payment. This rule gives the firm some flexibility if it runs into serious financial trouble, because it can conserve cash by suspending the dividend payments.

However, because they don't carry a right to receive a dividend, most preferred shares have a **cumulative provision** attached, which means that no dividends can be paid on common shares until preferred share dividends, *both current and arrears*, are paid in full. This ensures that the common shareholders, who have voting rights, don't just suspend payment on the preferred share dividends, while continuing to make dividend payments on the common shares. For some preferred shares, as the arrears accumulate, they give rise to limited voting rights, so that the preferred shareholders can exercise some voting rights over the company. However, like bonds, these rights depend on the structure of the preferred shares.[7]

cumulative provision a stipulation that no dividends can be paid on common shares until preferred share dividends, both current and arrears, are paid in full

A common result for firms experiencing financial trouble is to suspend dividend payments on all classes of shares, including preferred shares, to conserve cash. If the firm then recovers, it then faces the problem of significant cash payments to clear off the preferred dividend arrears. In practice, what happens in these situations is that the arrears are often paid through the issue of common shares or some combination of cash and shares. This allows the firm to clean up its balance sheet and start fresh.

An example of a traditional straight preferred issue is the series F preferred shares issued by Great-West Lifeco Inc. Great-West Lifeco has several series of preferred shares outstanding, each with slightly different features. As with other classes of shares, Great-West Lifeco's authorized capital allows it to issue more of these shares if it wants or it can start another series. As of August 2006, 8 million of the F series were outstanding and each one had a par value of $25. Unlike common shares, preferred shares will have a par value, so that their claim in

---

[6] At one point in the 1980s, there was an attempt to issue 30-day preferred shares to directly mimic BAs, until the CRA closed this down.

[7] Note that many of the short-term preferred shares, particularly those issued by the banks, do not have this cumulative feature, because the risk of non-payment is very low.

bankruptcy is known. In addition, similar to that for bonds, the amount of the dividend payments is sometimes expressed as a percentage of par. In the case of these particular preferred shares, the dividend is $1.48 per year and they are traded on the TSX under the symbol GWO.PR.F, similar to common shares. An interesting feature of Great-West Lifeco's preferred shares is that the series F, G, and H do not have dividends that cumulate, whereas the series A, B, C, D, and E do.

Like many preferred share issues, this series is *callable* by Great-West Lifeco. In this case, they are callable at $26 in September 2008 and at $25.75 in September 2009, and then declining by $0.25 each year until they are callable at par. This means that at Great-West Lifeco's option, it can *call* the preferred shares away from their owners by paying the fixed call price.

From this discussion of Great-West Lifeco's preferred shares, we can see that they have many of the characteristics of bonds. Like bonds, they have many different features that require that each series of preferred shares be evaluated separately. We have discussed retraction features and call features, but some preferred shares are *convertible* into other securities, usually common shares, which we will discuss shortly. Other preferred shares have *purchase funds*, which act like *sinking funds* for debt securities, which were discussed in Chapter 6. Like sinking funds, purchase funds require the company to buy back a certain number of shares each year, which produces a "two-edged" sword: in the short run, it increases the number of purchasers and ensures a ready market for the shares, but in the long run, as the number of shares goes down, it has the opposite effect.

Just like bonds and commercial paper, preferred shares are rated by the rating agencies, such as Dominion Bond Rating Service (DBRS). However, because preferred shares are riskier than either bonds or CP, the rating structure is more limited. PFD-1 is equivalent to both AAA- and AA-rated bonds, PFD-2 to A-rated bonds, PFD-3 to more highly rated BBB bonds, PFD-4 to lower-rated BBB and BB rated bonds, and PFD-5 to B or lower rated bonds.

hybrid security a security that is part debt and part equity

We have discussed preferred shares in the context of shareholders' equity, because legally they are equity securities. However, as the discussion above demonstrates, they share many characteristics with debt and are commonly regarded as a **hybrid security**: part debt and part equity. In fact, there is a continuum of financial securities that run the full range from common shares to what people typically think of as debt. We discuss some of the hybrids in the following sections, because they can be very important for corporate financing. However, before we do so, we briefly discuss income trusts.

CONCEPT REVIEW QUESTIONS

1. Briefly describe the following types of preferred shares: straight, retractable, and floating rate.

2. Briefly describe the following features that may be associated with preferred shares: cumulative provision, callable feature, and purchase funds.

3. Why are preferred shares sometimes called hybrid securities?

19.3 INCOME TRUSTS

In Chapter 2, we introduced *income trusts* and discussed how they are usually structured so that the trust itself invests in the shares and debt obligations of an underlying operating company. Because it is a trust, all the income is passed through to trust unitholders without any tax consequences to the trust. Further, because the trust owns both the debt and the equity of the company, the use of debt can be maximized to reduce (or eliminate) any corporate income tax, provided the trust pays out most (or all) of its income to unitholders. Obviously, this structure provides the businesses with the ultimate incentive to pay out most of their earnings in order to avoid paying taxes, which, in turn, made trusts very popular among investors.

The tax-efficient structure of trusts, along with their popularity among investors, led to dramatic growth in this market. As of March 31, 2006, the TSX listed 238 income trusts, up from 73 in 2001 and only a handful in the mid-1990s. In fact, the total market capitalization of these instruments grew from $1.4 billion in 1994 to $192 billion by March 2006, representing approximately 10 percent of the quoted market value of the TSX.[8] Income trusts became the major source of equity initial public offering (IPOs) in Canada during the 2000s, often accounting for more than half of all new equity IPOs. Some of these trust IPOs provided financing for new businesses, while others were associated with existing companies converting to the trust structure. As a result of this growth, the TSX fully incorporated income trusts into the S&P/TSX Composite Index as of March 2006.

We also noted in Chapter 2 that on October 31, 2006, Finance Minister Jim Flaherty announced unexpectedly, and in contradiction of a key election promise, that the distributions made by newly created trusts would be taxed at prevailing corporate tax rates and that this new tax would apply to existing trusts beginning in 2011. This announcement was made just as Canadian telecommunications giants Telus Corp. and BCE Inc. were preparing to convert from the traditional corporate structure to the income trust structure, which would have added another $50 billion or so in market cap to the income trust market.

Not surprisingly, both BCE Inc. and Telus Corp. subsequently cancelled their plans to convert to the trust structure, and many other planned income trust IPOs were also cancelled. Indeed, the October 31 announcement brought a dramatic end to the growth of income trusts and severely damaged the Canadian equity IPO market, as can be seen in Finance in the News 19-1. The article shows that IPO activity declined significantly in 2006 from its 2004 and 2005 levels, primarily because of the end of income trust IPOs in the fourth quarter of 2006. Despite the fact that there were no income trust IPOs in the fourth quarter, they still accounted for 60 percent of total 2006 IPO activity, down from 75 percent in 2005. Not surprisingly, PricewaterhouseCoopers LLP predicted that the virtual elimination of trust IPOs has provided a "very dim" outlook for 2007 IPO activity.

---

[8] Source: TSX website at <www.tsx.com>.

IPO ACTIVITY SET TO TUMBLE IN WAKE OF TRUST CRACKDOWN

Initial public offerings this year are expected to plunge to their lowest levels since the unravelling of the dot-com boom, dragged down by the government's recent decision to put the brakes on the income trust market, according to a new study.

Accounting firm PricewaterhouseCoopers LLP (PwC) predicted yesterday that IPO activity could dwindle to less than $3-billion in 2007, little more than half of the $5.4-billion in new issues that hit Canadian markets last year, and well below the record $6.8-billion achieved in 2005.

"Without a clear view of where the market for new issues is headed, companies have shelved plans for equity financing through the capital markets," said Ross Sinclair, who heads up the firm's IPO and income trust services group. "Investors are still looking for a place to invest and companies still need capital to grow. They're just not meeting on the [Toronto Stock Exchange]."

The fourth quarter of last year was a case in point. When Finance Minister Jim Flaherty unveiled his income trust crackdown on Halloween and tabled a proposal to tax trusts like regular companies, income trust IPOs were stopped cold.

Only five companies launched IPOs in the last three months of 2006, and none of them were trusts. For the entire year, income trusts accounted for more than $3-billion in IPOs—or roughly 60 percent of the market—versus more than $5-billion, or 74 per cent, in 2005.

Now that small and midsize companies cannot access public money through the tax-efficient trust structure, the IPO outlook for 2007 is "very dim," PwC noted in its study.

This dwindling IPO activity, coupled with an increasing number of going-private transactions, will narrow the choices for investors and exacerbate the already high levels of liquidity in financial markets, industry watchers say.

"You can only own so many banks, insurance companies and oil companies before you start crying for variety," one senior banker said.

Mr. Sinclair, meanwhile, suggested many potential trust candidates will opt for higher valuations from foreign suitors and private equity firms rather than attempt an IPO as a regular corporation.

"I don't think that there's another $200-billion worth of business trusts to roll in over the next five years, but I still think there are a lot of good, Canadian-owned, middle-market companies that will have trouble accessing public markets in this environment," he said.

Last year's largest trust offering was the $700-million IPO for Teranet Income Fund, while the biggest corporate IPO was Air Canada's $525-million deal, announced in the fall.

The value of IPO activity on Canadian stock exchanges has averaged almost $5.8-billion annually over the past five years. But PwC is forecasting this year will be the worst since the dot-com crash of 2001, when issuers raised only $2.1-billion through IPOs.

IPOs in Canada

Gross value of IPOs on Canadian exchanges ($billions CAD)

2000: $5.3	2004: $6.2
2001: $2.1	2005: $6.8
2002: $5.8	2006: $5.4
2003: $4.6	

Source: Stewart, Sinclair. "IPO Activity Set to Tumble in Wake of Trust Crackdown." *Globe and Mail*, January 5, 2007, p. B3. Reprinted with permission of the *Globe and Mail*.

CONCEPT REVIEW QUESTION

1. Why did income trusts become such a popular form of equity financing, and what happened to change that?

19.4 WARRANTS AND CONVERTIBLE SECURITIES

We now consider the last major class of securities issued by companies, which includes warrants, convertible bonds, and convertible preferred shares.

Warrants

Warrants are the corporate finance equivalent of *call options*, with two major differences. First, call options are transactions between two external investors so that what one gains the other loses, but there is *no impact* on the firm. Warrants are issued by firms to raise capital, and when they are exercised, more shares are created. Second, call options are usually issued with very short maturities because they are standardized. Warrants almost always have longer maturities, which makes them more valuable. The data in Table 19-3 come from the *Financial Post* and list the first five warrants outstanding on the Canadian exchanges at the start of August 2006.

warrants the corporate finance equivalent of call options that are issued by firms to raise capital, and when they are exercised, more shares are created; they usually have long maturities, which makes them more valuable

Table 19-3 Warrant Listings

Company	Stock Close	Symbol	Stock Exch.	Exercise Price	Recent Close	Bid/ Ask	Intrinsic Value	Time Value	Years Left	Expiry Date
Agnico-Eagle Mines Ltd	40.420	AEM.WT.U	TSX	US$19.000	US$19.500		18.920	3.147	1.3	Nov. 14, 2007
Ascendant Copper Corp	0.500	ACX.WT	TSX	2.500	0.150	Bid	-2.000	0.150	4.3	Nov. 21, 2010
Aumega Discoveries Ltd	0.090	AUM.WT	TSX-VEN	0.400	0.010	Bid	-0.310	0.010	0.5	Feb. 16, 2007
Avnel Gold Mining Ltd	1.100	AVK.WT	TSX	1.060	0.550	Bid	0.040	0.510	3.9	June 30, 2010
Baja Mining Corp	1.500	BAJ.WT	TSX-VEN	1.150	1.270		0.350	0.920	2.7	Apr. 19, 2009

Source: Data from *Financial Post*, August 29, 2006.

Note that all of these warrants are for mining firms. In fact, most warrants are issued by junior firms looking for equity financing. The company gets initial financing from issuing the warrants, and then if events turn out well, such as after a successful drilling operation, the stock price rises and the firm gets a further infusion of equity as the warrants are exercised. Unlike calls, when the warrants are exercised, the warrant holder pays the exercise price to the company in return for shares. Warrants thus provide *primary* financing because the issuing company raises capital from their sale. Note that the maturities of these warrants run from six months for the Aumega warrants out to 4.3 years for the Ascendant Copper warrants.

The fact that when warrants are exercised it increases the number of shares outstanding means that they can be valued by using a variant of standard option pricing models. We denote the existing number of shares as n and the number of shares issued on exercise of the warrants at an exercise price of X as m. If the value of the firm, without taking into account the warrants, is V, then the payoff if the warrants are exercised can be expressed as shown in Equation 19-1:

[19-1]

$$\text{Payoff to warrant holders} = \frac{m}{n+m}(V + mX) - mX$$

Equation 19-1 says that after the warrants are exercised, the value of the firm must be the value without the warrants (V) plus the proceeds to the firm from the exercise of the warrants (mX), for a total value of $V + mX$. Of this total value, the percentage owned by the warrant holders is $m/(n+m)$, whereas the cost to them is the exercise value of mX. As a result, the payoff to the warrant holders is just the difference between these two values. If we multiply the exercise value mX by $(n+m)/(n+m)$ and simplify, the payoff reduces to Equation 19-2:

[19-2]

$$\text{Payoff to warrant holders} = \frac{m}{n+m}(V - nX)$$

In Equation 19-2, $V - nX$ can be viewed as the standard payoff to n secondary market calls with the same strike price of X—in other words, if we divide both of these terms by n, the first term is the share price (i.e., V/n), and the second term is the exercise price (X). The first term, $m/(n+m)$, is the **dilution factor**, which results from the additional shares that are created as the warrants are exercised. Consequently, however the value of a *secondary* market call is determined, the value of the warrant is this amount multiplied by the dilution factor, whether we use the Black-Scholes or the binomial option pricing models discussed in Chapter 12 and Appendix 12A, respectively.

dilution factor the amount by which ownership is reduced when additional shares are issued

Example 19-1: Estimating Payoffs to Warrants

A company has 10 million shares outstanding that are trading at $20 per share. The company has 1 million warrants outstanding that have an exercise price of $18 each. What is the payoff to the warrant holders of exercising them?

Solution

m = 1 million

n = 10 million

V = $20 × 10 million = $200 million

X = $18

By using Equation 19-2, we can estimate the payoff as

$\text{Payoff} = \dfrac{m}{n+m} = 1/(10+1) \times (200 - (10)(18)) = (1/11) \times (20)$

$= \$1.818$ million

As long-term options, warrants are extremely valuable, and they trade at significant premiums over their *intrinsic value*—that is, they possess a significant *time value*. For example, Avnel Gold Mine's warrants are approximately at the money, because the exercise price of $1.06 is only slightly less than the closing price of $1.10, so the intrinsic value is only $0.04. However, because they have 3.9 years until expiration, the market price of these warrants is $0.55, exactly half the market price for Avnel's common shares.

The fact that warrants are valuable means that they are frequently used as *sweeteners* to make issues more attractive and thereby access financing that would not otherwise be available. For example, junior mines often have significant capital expenditures and limited cash flow to meet interest payments on any financing. If they approach a venture capitalist for debt financing, they may be asked to pay a very high interest rate, given the risks involved. This in turn compounds the problem of a lack of cash flow to make the interest payments. In these circumstances, the combination of a low-cost loan and warrants may allow the firms to raise debt. The low interest rate helps alleviate a firm's cash flow problems, while the warrants make new equity financing available if the firm is successful. Investors may be willing to buy these warrants, which may provide a significant payoff if the firm does well and its share price increases.

Furthermore, the very risk that makes debt financing expensive also makes the warrants valuable. Recall from our discussion in Chapter 12 that call options are more valuable when the underlying asset price is more volatile. This is also true for warrants, which are simply corporate-issued call options. As a general rule, we often see warrants and convertibles (which are discussed below) being issued by firms that face significant uncertainty and possess correspondingly low bond ratings. They have difficulty raising debt capital without resorting to the use of some form of sweetener. For these firms, using warrants or adding convertible features reduces the cash outlay for interest payments, thus lowering the risk of financial distress.[9]

If the warrants are *detachable*, the institution providing the debt may sell the warrants to other investors. If they are not detachable, issuing bonds plus warrants is similar to issuing convertible bonds.

Convertible Securities

Convertible bonds, as described in Chapter 6, are bonds (preferred shares) that are convertible into a specified number of common shares at the option of the convertible holder. In many ways they are similar to bonds (preferred shares) with warrants. The key difference is that when convertibles are converted, the bonds are exchanged for common shares and the bonds are no longer outstanding, whereas for debt with warrants attached, the debt remains outstanding and the exercise price is paid in cash. This means that the firm does not get any new financing when convertibles are converted; all that happens is that the debt is converted into common shares. In contrast, with warrants, the firm gets new financing from the sale of new shares at the exercise price.

At August 29, 2006, the *Financial Post* had the data shown in Table 19-4 for the first five convertible bonds outstanding in Canada.

---

[9] A basic problem of debt financing is that increasing the interest rate for riskier borrowers make the borrowers even riskier.

Table 19-4   Convertible Bond Listings

Issuer	Symbol	Coupon	Maturity	Last Price	Parity	Yield to Maturity	Premium	Conversion Ratio	Conversion Price	Symbol	Share Price Tuesday, August 28, 2006
ACE Aviation	ACE.NT.A	4.25%	1-Jun-2035	94.50	67.19	4.60%	40.66%	2.23	44.88	ACE.A	30.15
Advantage Energy	AVN.DB	10.00%	1-Nov-2007	134.62	132.78	-15.82%	1.33%	7.52	13.30	AVN.UN	17.67
Agricore	AU.DB	9.00%	30-Nov-2007	106.25	102.13	3.81%	4.03%	13.33	7.50	AU	7.66
Alamos Gold	AGI.DB	5.50%	15-Feb-2010	172.00	154.91	-11.05%	9.83%	18.87	5.30	AGI	8.30
Alexis Nihon	AN.DB	6.20%	30-Jun-2014	100.80	93.92	6.07%	7.08%	7.33	13.65	AN.UN	12.85

Source: Data from *Financial Post*, August 29, 2006.

conversion ratio (CR) the number of shares that a convertible security could be exchanged for

Similar to the case for warrants, companies that issue convertible bonds tend to be high risk. The first company listed is ACE Aviation Holdings Inc. (ACE), formerly Air Canada, which emerged from bankruptcy as ACE. Its outstanding convertible bonds have a 4.25 percent coupon and were selling for $94.50. These bonds had a 35-year maturity, a yield to maturity of 4.60 percent, and a reported **conversion ratio (CR)** of 2.23, although the more precise conversion ratio is 2.2284. This means that each bond can be converted into 2.2284 ACE common shares. Remember that bonds have a $1,000 par value but are always quoted as $100, so if we divide the 2.2284 into $100, we can say that the **conversion price (CP)** is $44.88 (i.e., $100/2.2284), as reported in the listing. ACE is effectively selling common shares for $44.88 if the bonds are converted. We depict this relationship in Equation 19-3.

conversion price (CP) the price at which a convertible security can be converted into common shares based on its conversion ratio

[19-3]

$$CP = \frac{Par}{CR}$$

conversion value (CV) the value of a convertible security if it is immediately converted into common shares

At the time, however, the market price (P) of ACE's common shares was only $30.15, so the **conversion value (CV)**, denoted as "Parity" in the listing, for these convertibles was 2.2284 times this current share price, or $67.19. The conversion value is the value of the bonds if they are immediately converted into common shares, as denoted in Equation 19-4.

[19-4]

$$CV = CR \times P$$

Because the bonds were selling for $94.50 at the time, and their value if immediately converted into common shares was only $67.19, the bonds were selling for a premium over their conversion value of 40.65 percent (i.e., 27.31/67.19). Equation 19-5 estimates this conversion premium.

$$\text{Convertible premium} = \frac{(Market\ Value - CV)}{CV} \qquad [19\text{-}5]$$

We can view this 40.65 percent premium as the percentage by which the ACE share price would have to increase before it began to make sense to convert the bonds into common shares. Recall from Chapter 12 that when the stock price is less than the exercise price for call options, we say the option is *out of the money* and has an intrinsic value of zero; no one would exercise the call. Similarly, with the ACE convertible, when the conversion value is less than the bond's market value, no one will voluntarily convert the bonds into common shares.

The stated term to maturity of the bonds is 35 years. However, these particular convertibles provide the holder the option of demanding payment at par value every five years starting June 1, 2010, so effectively they are five-year renewable notes and the yield is based on this shorter maturity. The benchmark five-year Canada bond was yielding 4.06 percent on August 28, 2006, so the spread of the yield on the ACE bonds over the five-year Canada rate was 0.54 percent. Most of ACE's debt consists of aircraft leases and the implicit rate is significantly more than 4.60 percent; the **straight bond value (SBV)** of these ACE convertibles is much less than the current market price. The SBV can be determined by using the standard bond pricing equation that was introduced in Chapter 6, where we use the yield on similar non-callable bonds as the market rate (k_b). We reproduce Equation 6-1 below.

straight bond value (SBV) the price that the convertible bonds would sell for if they could not be converted into common stock

$$SBV = I \times \left[\frac{1 - \frac{1}{(1 + k_b)^n}}{k_b} \right] + F \times \frac{1}{(1 + k_b)^n} \qquad [19\text{-}6]$$

where SBV = the straight bond value

I = interest (or coupon) payments

k_b = the yield on similar non-callable bonds

n = the term to maturity

F = the face (par) value of the bond

Every convertible bond has a **floor value (FV)**, because it will always sell *for no less than* the larger of its straight bond value and its conversion value. This is logical because even if the company's shares are trading at a price well below the conversion price, so that the value of the conversion feature is negligible, the bond would still be held by investors and valued as a straight bond. Therefore, it will never trade below the SBV. Similarly, a convertible bond would never sell below its conversion value because if it did, arbitrageurs would buy the bond, convert it into common stock, and sell the shares, thus earning riskless profits. Therefore, we can estimate the FV of a convertible as shown in Equation 19-7:

floor value (FV) the lowest price a convertible bond will sell for, which is equal to the larger of its straight bond value and its conversion value

$$FV = \text{Max}(SBV, CV) \qquad [19\text{-}7]$$

Of course, in practice, convertibles usually sell at prices higher than their minimum value because of the time value of the conversion option.

Example 19-2: Convertible Bond Values

A 10 percent coupon bond has 10 years to maturity when market rates on similar non-convertible bonds are 8 percent. It is convertible into 50 common shares and has a $1,000 par value. Estimate the following for this convertible:

a. conversion price

b. straight bond value (SBV), assuming it pays annual coupons

c. conversion value (CV), if the shares are trading at $25 per share

d. floor value (FV)

e. conversion premium, if it was trading at $1,350

Solution

a. CP = Par/CR = $1,000/50 = $20

b. Par = $1,000; I = coupon rate × F = 0.10 × $1,000 = $100; n = 10; k_b = 0.08.

With this information, we can use Equation 19-6 to find the price, or we can solve it by using a financial calculator or Excel.

$$SBV = 100 \times \left[\frac{1 - \dfrac{1}{(1.08)^{10}}}{0.08} \right] + 1,000 \times \frac{1}{(1+0.08)^{10}} = \$1,134.20$$

PMT = −100; N = 10; FV = −1,000; I/Y = 8%; compute PV = $1,134.20

=price(date(2006,11,06), date(2016,11,06), .10, .08, 100, 1, 0)
produces $1,134.20

c. CV = CR × P = 50 shares/bond × $25/share = $1,250

d. Floor value (FV) = Max(SBV, CV) = Max(1,134.20, 1,250) = $1,250

The convertible *cannot* trade below this.

e. Convertible premium = (1,350 − 1,250)/1,250 = 8.00%

Conceptually, we can view a convertible bond as a straight bond plus the option to convert the bonds into common shares. When the ACE bonds were issued during the second quarter of 2005, they had a par value of $330 million and a market value of $319 million. At that time, ACE estimated the straight bond value at $236 million, or $71.52 per $100 of par value, by using a 12 percent interest cost for equivalent debt. ACE common shares were selling for $35 at the time, so the conversion value was $77.99 (i.e., 2.2284 × $35). Taking into account some minor issue costs, ACE estimated the option value of the convertibles at $94 million, or $28.48 per $100 value.

ACE therefore regarded the convertibles as 28.5 percent equity and 71.5 percent bonds, which shows the true *hybrid* nature of the convertibles.

The hybrid nature of the convertibles can also be illustrated by assuming that the convertibles mature in 2010, when the purchasers can surrender the convertibles for their par value. Essentially, there are two alternatives: either ACE's share price goes higher than the conversion price, or it doesn't. If the price goes higher than $44.88, then investors will convert the bonds into the common shares, because the conversion value will exceed the bond value of the convertible. To make sure that conversion occurs, most convertible bonds are also *callable* by the issuer. For these particular bonds, ACE can buy them back at any time after June 6, 2008, at par value plus accrued interest. Therefore, if the conversion value exceeds the par value, ACE can state its intention to buy them back at par, thereby *forcing conversion* by the investors—that is, because they will get a higher price by converting than by selling them back at par.

If ACE did not have the right to buy the bonds at $100 plus accrued interest, investors would continue to hold the bonds and would not convert them into common shares, because there would still be *time value* attached to the option to convert. If the ACE share price is less than the conversion value at the maturity date, the holders will simply demand their par value of $100 for the bond, and the conversion privilege will expire worthless, just like an out of the money call option. These two scenarios are illustrated in Figure 19-1.

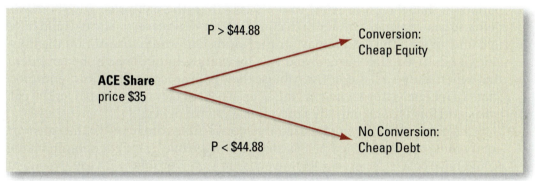

Convertible Scenarios

Note that if the convertibles are converted, ACE ends up with "cheap" equity because the ACE share price when the convertibles were issued was $35 and it has effectively sold equity with a time lag for $44.88. However, suppose the share price is now $60. In this case, an even better strategy, in retrospect, would have been to finance with straight debt and then to have issued shares for $60 five years later; the after-the-fact best financing choices would have been, in order, common shares, convertibles, and debt. However, firms (or investors) do not have the luxury of perfect foresight.

Now consider what happens if the bonds aren't converted. In this case, ACE is forced to redeem the bonds at par value, but it will have had the benefit of having had five-year debt that paid only 4.25 percent, when similar straight debt would have cost it 12 percent. As a result, ACE has ended up with cheap debt financing. However, the stock price only had to increase from $35 to $44.88 over five years, or 5.1 percent annually, at the time of issue. The expected rate of return on ACE's common equity was certainly higher than 5.1 percent because it is so risky, so the original expectation was that the convertibles would be converted. The fact that they are not means that the shareholders have received an inadequate rate of return. Suppose the stock price is $30 and the stock has performed badly over the five-year period. The best scenario would have been for ACE to have sold common shares for $35 in 2005, because the shares are now worth less than this, and the after-the-fact best financing choices would have been common shares, convertibles, and debt.

This what-if scenario analysis indicates that convertibles are rarely the "right" decision, but they are never the "wrong" decision, because the firm gets either cheap debt or cheap equity financing. It is this compromise that makes convertibles popular for many high-risk junior companies that have trouble accessing debt markets because of the high interest rate, and that management believes has a share price that is undervalued and so is reluctant to issue more common shares. In ACE's case, it was so soon after they emerged from bankruptcy that the market would not have been very receptive to a new share issue. In these cases, just like adding warrants to debt issues, convertibles can be sold when the company may not be able to attract conventional debt financing.

The discussion is a simplification of reality, because the ACE convertibles may sell for more than their par value because of their option value and yet ACE may not want to call them. In this situation, they would remain outstanding for another five years. The reason for this is that firms are reluctant to call convertibles unless the conversion value is at least *20 percent more than their call value.* Unlike simple call options, it takes a significant length of time for a firm to go through the legal process of calling the bonds. If the share price falls during this period so that the conversion value is less than the call price, investors will demand cash payment rather than converting. In this case, the firm would have to come up with the cash to pay for the bonds and would lose out on the infusion of equity capital. Firms avoid this by waiting until they can be confident that when they call the convertibles, they will be converted into common shares. Generally, this means having at least a 20 percent premium over the call price, and for riskier shares this premium is often higher.

This discussion has emphasized that convertibles are hybrids: they are part equity and part debt. When ACE issued its convertibles, straight debt financing would have cost it 12 percent. However, issuing convertibles with a 4.25 percent coupon did not mean that it got cheap debt, because at the issue date, the convertibles were 71.5 percent debt and 28.5 percent equity. If the debt cost is taken to be 12.0 percent and the cost of this "equity" 15 percent, then the cost of using the convertibles (ignoring tax shields) is a weighted average of these two financing costs or 12.90 percent. For most companies, the pre-tax cost of the convertibles is more than the straight debt cost because they are part equity, and equity is more expensive to the firm than debt.[10]

As we look at the other convertibles, we note that what the *Financial Post* lists as the "premium" is the market price minus the conversion value, divided by the conversion value. This will always be positive because the convertibles will always sell for more than the higher of their conversion value or bond value because of their option value. However, note that Advantage Energy Income Fund's convertibles are selling for a 1.33 percent premium, that is, the market value is very close to their conversion value, meaning that these convertibles have very little option value left. The market price is significantly above par value and there is only about a year left before the bonds mature. In contrast,

---

[10] There are cases in which the promised interest cost is so high (because of the risk of the firm) that convertibles have a lower cost. This is due to the conventional use of the promised yield as the cost of debt.

the Alamos Gold Inc. convertibles have more option value left because they are 3.5 years away from maturity, which is reflected in their higher premium.

CONCEPT REVIEW QUESTIONS

1. Explain why issuing debt or preferred shares with warrants attached, or issuing convertible bonds or preferred shares, may represent attractive sources of financing for higher-risk firms.

2. Define and explain how to determine the following for a convertible: conversion price, conversion value, straight bond value, floor value, and convertible premium.

19.5 OTHER HYBRIDS

Categorizing Hybrids

Warrants, convertible bonds, and convertible preferred shares are the most obvious type of hybrids. However, there has been enormous innovation in corporate financing aimed at creating hybrids that satisfy multiple objectives. Our focus on hybrids so far has been on the tax definition of what the CRA regards as interest for tax purposes. However, there is also the question of how these securities "look" on the firm's financial statements—that is, whether they are categorized as debt or equity and how the rating agencies treat them. The financial criteria for whether hybrids are debt or equity or some mix are different from the CRA's criteria.

DBRS, for example, looks at four major factors to determine whether a security is debt or equity: (1) the permanence factor, (2) the subordination factor, (3) the legal factor, and (4) the subjective factor.

The **permanence factor** relates to whether or not the security will be outstanding for a long period. Common shares are the gold standard because they have no maturity date and no requirement to redeem them at any point. BAs, conversely, are the ultimate debt instrument because they have a very limited 30- or 60-day life and then have to be redeemed. The **subordination factor** refers to the priority of the claim on the firm's assets and income stream. Again, common shares are the gold standard and BAs are obvious debt because they have an absolute claim to be paid off in 30 or 60 days. The **legal factor** means the legal rights of the investors—that is, whether they have a contractual right to receive income or whether it is in some way discretionary, such as the declaration of a dividend by the BOD. Finally, the major **subjective factor** is the intention of the company when it issues the securities.

Standard & Poors (S&P), one of the two major U.S. bond rating agencies, has gone into the issue of hybrids in more detail because there are more outstanding in the U.S. market. S&P[11] has four criteria that are similar to those of DBRS:

permanence factor the length of time for which the security will be outstanding; a major factor in determining whether a security is debt or equity

subordination factor the priority of the claim on the firm's assets and income stream; a major factor in determining whether a security is debt or equity

legal factor the rights of the investors; a major factor in determining whether a security is debt or equity

subjective factor the intention of the company when it issues the securities; a major factor in determining whether a security is debt or equity

---

[11] Corporate Equity Criteria-Equity Credit, S&P 28, October 2004.

1. Does it have ongoing payments that could lead to default?

2. Does it have a maturity or repayment requirement?

3. Does it provide a "cushion" for creditors in case of distress?

4. Is it expected to remain in the capital structure?

Clearly, S&P criterion 1 is the same as DBRS 3, which is the contractual commitment to pay interest, where failure leads to default. S&P 2 is the same as DBRS 1, which is the question of permanence versus a maturity date. S&P 3 is then similar to DBRS 2, where the deeper the subordination, the more "cushion" provided senior bondholders. Finally, S&P 4 is similar to DBRS 4 where the question is the intention of the company and whether the security is expected to remain part of the firm's long-term financing or its capital structure.

An example illustrating the DBRS and S&P criteria might help. In our discussion of preferred shares, we noted that there are different types of preferred shares to mimic debt but attract the tax treatment of dividends. One class of these preferred shares were retractable preferred shares, which BMO Nesbitt Burns compared with five-year Government of Canada bonds. What we didn't discuss was what these preferred shares were retractable into—that is, when the holders ask for their money back, what do they get?

A **hard retraction** requires that the preferred shares be paid off in cash. In effect, this makes them very bond-like because apart from getting dividends for five years instead of interest at the end of five years, the investor gets cash back. A **soft retraction** allows the preferred shares to be paid off with common shares or other preferred shares. In this case, the firm has no commitment to pay cash, and it simply issues more shares with no cash outlay.

In terms of the S&P/DBRS criteria, preferred shares with a hard retraction are very debt-like, because they are not permanent, have a fixed contractual commitment to pay off at maturity with cash, and are not a permanent part of the firm's capital structure. The soft retractables have no fixed contractual commitments, have no maturity because they are simply replaced with other types of equity, and are more likely to be a permanent part of the firm's capital structure. Hence, they are more equity-like. DBRS and S&P would give them greater equity weight because they do not strain the firm's cash flow.

Creative Hybrids: Some Examples

Another security that looks like debt but is closer to equity is an **income bond**. These bonds are generally issued after a reorganization, so that the "interest" is tied to some cash flow level for the firm. Recently, **cash flow bonds** have been sold in the United States with the same objective. In both cases, the maturity dates have been quite long, usually at least 30 years, and the fact that the "interest" payments are conditional on the firm meeting certain thresholds reduces the contractual commitment to pay interest. As a result, income bonds get significant equity weight. In fact, in Canada, the payments are not tax deductible and are classified as dividends. This significantly reduces their attractiveness as far as the company is concerned, which is why they have mainly been a "desperation play" after a major reorganization (when the company has lots of tax loss carry forwards and little use for tax shields).

Another way of achieving the same type of objective for some firms is the **commodity bond**. Suppose a gold producer has fixed mine costs to produce

---

hard retraction the requirement that the preferred shares be paid off in cash

soft retraction the allowance for preferred shares to be paid off with common shares or other preferred shares

income bonds bonds issued after a reorganization with the interest tied to some cash flow level for the firm and with quite long maturity dates

cash flow bonds bonds sold in the United States that have the same objectives as do income bonds in Canada

commodity bond a bond whose interest or principal is tied to the price of an underlying commodity, such as gold

gold but then faces uncertain revenues because they are tied to the price of gold. One way to manage this gold price risk is by using derivatives that are tied to the price of gold, such as those discussed in Chapter 11, or through long-term fixed-price contracting. However, an alternative is to tie the bond payments to the price of gold. This can be done in two ways: either the interest payment is tied to the price of gold, or the principal is. If the principal is tied to the price of gold, then as the gold price increases, so too does the principal, and because interest is expressed as a percentage of the principal, the investor receives more interest. If the bond payments are structured carefully, the CRA criteria are met and the interest is tax deductible, but the bonds are less risky to the firm because the interest payments are tied to its major risk, which is the price of gold.

Commodity bonds, in which the principal is tied to some external index, are an example of indexed bonds. The most common of these are the *real return bonds* issued by the Government of Canada, which were discussed in Chapter 6. In this case, the principal is tied to the consumer price index (CPI), and as the CPI increases, the principal increases and the interest is expressed as a percentage of this increasing principal. In this way, the investor's income increases with inflation, thereby preserving a real rate of return. As of August 29, 2006, the yield on the real return bond, equivalent to the regular 30-year fixed rate Canada bond, was 1.63 percent. In this instance, the investor could choose between the real return bond yielding 1.63 percent, and the regular bond yielding 4.24 percent. The difference is that with the regular bond, the investor runs the risk that inflation will erode the real purchasing power of both the income and the maturity value of the bond. The difference between these two yields of 2.61 percent is slightly above the Bank of Canada's target inflation band of 1.00 percent to 3.00 percent. However, on a simple comparison basis, if the investor thinks the rate of inflation will be greater than this break-even rate of 2.61 percent or is very worried about inflation, then the investor should buy the real return bond.

The problem with the real return bond is that the increase in the value of the principal is regarded by the CRA as income and taxed as such. As a result, ordinary investors holding these bonds are taxed on this income, even if they do not receive any cash. This makes the bonds unattractive for many investors, unless they can hold them in tax-preferred savings plans, like Registered Retirement Savings Plans (RRSPs). For the same reason, these bonds are popular with non-tax-paying institutional investors, such as pension plans.

Real return bonds are not issued by corporations, but they do have an attractive property, which is that the immediate interest payments are much lower than with regular fixed income bonds. Note for example, that the yield on the real return bond was 1.63 percent versus 4.24 percent for the regular bond. The offset is that, at maturity the firm has to pay a much larger principal back to the investor as the nominal $100 has increased with the CPI. For firms that are short of immediate cash, but have good long-run prospects, this is an attractive proposition because it minimizes immediate cash payments and, it is hoped, defers them to a period when the firm is more valuable. Corporations achieve this same result by issuing **original issue discount bonds (OIDs)** or **low-yield notes** that similarly sell at a discount.

Table 19-5 below shows the time path of the cash payments on a 10-year regular interest bond with a 10 percent annual yield, versus an OID with a 10 percent yield but a zero coupon. The principal for both bonds is set at $42.40 for reasons we will come to in a minute. The regular bond has annual cash outflows of $4.24 and, in year 10, a bullet payment of the principal of $42.40. The zero

original issue discount bonds (OIDs) or low-yield notes bonds that sell at a discount from par value when issued by firms coupon discount bond has no annual interest payments; instead, the 10 percent yield is earned through paying $42.40 today and receiving $100 at maturity in 10 years. As a result, the principal increases each year from $42.40 in year one, to $46.65 in year two, and so on, until it reaches the $100 at the end of year 10.

Table 19-5   OID versus Regular Bond Payments

	Regular Bond	OID Bond Principal	OID Bond "Interest"
2	$4.24	$46.65	$4.24
3	4.24	51.32	4.67
4	4.24	56.45	5.13
5	4.24	62.09	5.64
6	4.24	68.30	6.21
7	4.24	75.13	6.83
8	4.24	82.64	7.51
9	4.24	90.91	8.26
10	46.65	100.00	9.09

From the company's point of view, the discount bond involved no annual payments but a much larger payment at maturity. This time pattern of cash flows is useful for many cash poor, yet opportunity rich, companies. However, from a tax point of view, the CRA regards the discount bond as locking in interest in the same way as an issue of treasury bills on a discount basis. The CRA has several ways of determining interest, but the correct way is to compound the $42.40 forward to the $100 maturity value. This provides the series of "interest" payments that the CRA allows the company to deduct in the fourth column. Unfortunately, like the real return bond, although this cash is not paid, the investor has to pay tax on this imputed interest.

The example of a zero coupon bond is an example of an "off-market" interest rate that causes the market value to deviate from par. Another variant is a low-yield note, in which the coupon is not zero but is less than the going market interest rate. This means that the cash flow pattern is in between the two extremes documented above. In some cases, these low-yield notes are combined with a convertible feature, in which case they are called **Liquid Yield Option Notes (LYONs)**, which are accretive convertibles, because the principal accretes or increases over time. Rogers Communications Inc. issued LYONS when it needed to conserve cash while building its cable network.

To return to the problem of tying interest payments to cash flow, another way is to make the interest payments conditional on prior dividend payments. **Adjustable Rate Convertible Subordinated Securities (ARCS)** do just this. They have fixed principal and maturity, and the interest normally comprises two parts: a fixed interest rate, and some function of the dividend paid in the prior six months. These securities are almost all convertible into common shares, so the dividend is expressed as a percentage of the conversion price. If the conversion price is $50 and the dividend per share is $1, this would be expressed as 2 percent.

Liquid Yield Option Notes (LYONs) low-yield notes that are combined with a convertible feature and are accretive convertibles, because the principal accretes or increases over time

Adjustable Rate Convertible Subordinated Securities (ARCS) securities that have fixed principal and maturity, and interest that normally comprises a fixed interest rate and some function of the dividend paid in the previous six months; typically convertible into common shares

The ARCS would then pay 5 percent plus twice this 2 percent dividend rate, or 9 percent in total. The ARCS are then subordinated to the firm's senior debt.

ARCS combine debt and equity features. Because the interest is represented as a percentage, is tied to the principal value, and legally accrues, it is tax deductible. However, as a deeply subordinated debt issue in which the interest could drop to 5 percent, if the dividend is not declared in the prior six-month period, it has some equity-like features.

Another variant of the debt versus equity is **preferred securities**. Note that these are not preferred shares, because the payments are tax deductible. Texaco Inc. was the first to issue tax-deductible preferred securities in 1991, and since then, they have grown in popularity. Texaco set up a 100 percent owned subsidiary in the Turks and Caicos Islands (a tax haven) to issue preferred shares. The proceeds were then loaned to the parent, for whom the interest was tax deductible. The interest flowed to the subsidiary, where it was not taxed, and all of it was used to make the dividend payments. The key provision was that Texaco would not let a 100 percent owned subsidiary put it into bankruptcy if it failed to make the interest payments. In turn, the preferred shares were sold with a five-year deferral of dividend payments, a 30-year life, and deep subordination.

> **preferred securities** securities generated by a company by creating a 100 percent owned subsidiary that issues the shares and then loans the proceeds to the parent company, for whom the interest is tax deductible; interest flows to the subsidiary, where it is not taxed, and is used to make dividend payments

Subsequently, trusts have been used to sell the preferred shares and they are commonly called trust preferred shares. They have been very popular with Canadian companies. Typically, they are rated BBB, or lower, and have been sold into the U.S. market as there is little appetite in the Canadian market for any type of high-yield debt.

Finally, we consider **Canadian optional interest notes (COINS)**, which are also often referred to as **prepaid bonds**. The firm issues 99-year bonds with a par value of $100 and an interest rate of, say, 10 percent, and these sell at par for $100. Remember that this $100 represents the present value of each interest payment, as well as the $100 par value in 99 years. However, the discounting process means that the value of the par value in 99 years at 10 percent is only $0.008, that is:

> **Canadian optional interest notes (COINS)** or **prepaid bonds** 99-year bonds that are sold at their par values of $100, on which the firm immediately prepays the interest from years 11 to 99 on issue, leaving it with a net inflow and allowing it to continue to deduct annual interest payments of $100, even though it has effectively borrowed less

$$\$0.007982 = \frac{\$100}{1.10^{99}}$$

By the same process, the present value of the interest payments from years 11 to 99 is $38.546, and that for years 1 to 10 is $61.446. The market value of $100 is the sum of these three components.

With COINS, after the bonds are issued, the firm immediately prepays the interest from years 11 to 99 for $38.546, leaving it with a net inflow of $61.454. This is why COINS are also called prepaid bonds. However, the firm has met all the legal requirements to continue deducting annual interest payments of $100, even though it has only effectively borrowed $61.454, not $100. Reportedly, some companies also wrote off the prepaid interest of $38.546 immediately. The CRA has now limited the deduction of interest on these prepaid bonds to the imputed interest, that is, 10 percent of the actual amount raised that is, $61.454. The speedy reaction of the CRA represents the dynamic interplay between innovative financing instruments and the tax authorities.

A Financing Hierarchy

S&P has ranked many types of hybrids according to their debt-equity mix and Table 19-6 shows a synopsis of the main securities that we have discussed. They range from common shares, which are rated at 100 percent, to commercial paper or BAs, which are rated at –100 percent, because they are the most debt-like form of debt.[12]

Table 19-6   S&P Financing Rankings

	Equity Share (%)
Common shares	100
Mandatory convertible preferred shares*	90
Straight preferred shares	50
Trust preferred shares	40
Convertible preferred shares	20
Re-marketed preferred shares†	-10
Normal convertible debt	-50
Accreting convertible bonds (LYONS)	-60
Very long term bonds	-70
Medium term bonds	-80
Auction preferred shares	-60
Commercial paper	-100

* Preferred shares for which conversion into common shares is structured to be automatic.
† Preferred shares that after five to seven years, are repriced and resold.

The basic insight from this ranking by S&P is as we stated at the beginning, that debt and equity are polar extremes. In between is a range of securities that have some features of debt and some features of equity. The goal is always to match the cash flow pattern with what the firm can afford, to make the payments tax deductible, and to get as much equity treatment as possible on the financial statements to enhance the firm's credit rating and access to markets. In doing this, corporate financiers at times have been ingenious in the design of these securities.

As the S&P equity weighting scheme indicates, the risk of these instruments differs according to how much equity weight they have. At one extreme, common shares, as the riskiest security, are the most expensive, because investors require the highest rate of return to compensate them for the risk. At the other extreme, CP has the least equity weight and is the most debt–like, with the lowest risk and lowest required rate of return. The costs of the various securities fall between these extremes. A typical hierarchy of financing cost is shown in Figure 19-2.

In practice, the actual rates depend on the level of interest rates and the state of the economy, but common equity is the most expensive and the cost reduces as the equity share falls.

---

[12] The following is our interpretation of the S&P rankings based on Canadian issues.

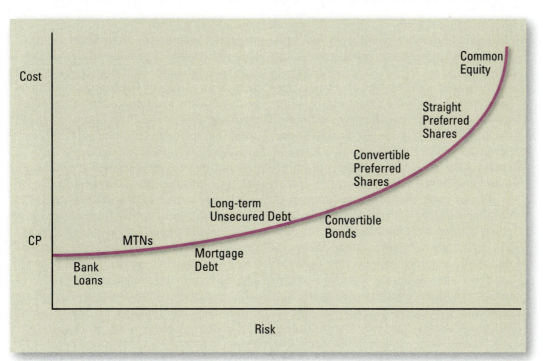

19-2 FIGURE

Financing Hierarchy Costs

CONCEPT REVIEW QUESTIONS

1. Name and discuss the four criteria used by DBRS to classify a security as debt versus equity.

2. Define the following types of hybrids: income bonds, commodity bonds, real return bonds, original issue discount bonds, LYONs, Adjustable Rate Convertible Subordinated Securities, preferred securities, and COINS.

3. Relate the costs of various financing options to their equity-like characteristics.

ONTARIO TEACHERS PENSION PLAN HALTS LENDING OF SHARES TO SHORT SELLERS

ethics
AND CORPORATE
GOVERNANCE 19-1

The Ontario Teachers Pension Plan has taken the rare step of halting the lending of shares to short sellers and plans to set up a new internal lending operation, arguing it wants to maintain tighter control over its voting rights as an investor.

Teachers senior vice-president Brian Gibson said the pension plan halted its lending late last year after two companies in which it held stakes called for shareholder voting on closely contested matters, but Teachers couldn't vote shares that had been borrowed by short sellers.

Mr. Gibson said Teachers had standard arrangements with its securities custodian to allow it to recall shares when necessary, but found the system didn't work well, and the shares could not be retrieved in time for votes.

When shares are lent by an investor for short selling, the voting rights transfer to the borrower. The situation has led some major U.S. companies to criticize the power of hedge funds to sway corporate votes using shares they have only borrowed and do not actually own.

It's not clear that any Canadian votes have been decided by hedge funds using borrowed shares. Mr. Gibson wouldn't identify the cases Teachers encountered, but said that in the end, the missing votes were not needed to clinch a vote. Teachers' move comes as corporate governance experts are increasingly urging institutional investors to get more closely involved in voting their shares and make more in-house decisions about how to vote on key issues.

David Beatty, managing director of the Canadian Coalition for Good Governance, which represents institutional investors, said institutional investors have a fiduciary responsibility to their beneficiaries to ensure the priority is to manage their voting.

In the United States, proposals have been floated to toughen rules on voting borrowed shares, or to require companies to announce the issues that will be up for a vote at a future shareholder meeting when they set the record date for voting. That would allow institutions to see if there are important issues on the ballot and recall their shares before the record date passes.

There has been little public debate of the issue in Canada, where activity has been confined to the internal steps taken by institutional shareholders to control their votes.

Peter Chapman, executive director of the Vancouver-based Shareholder Association for Research and Education says some investors try to control lending during voting periods. "Some institutions don't track it, so they lose their votes. The better practice would be not to lend during the windows when you lose your voting rights."

Doug Pearce, chief executive officer of the B.C. Investment Management Corp., which manages investments for the B.C. government and public sector pension plans, said his fund rarely needs to recall shares for voting. "It is an issue, but we make sure that we secure our vote first, and lending will be secondary to that."

An official at the Ontario Municipal Employees Retirement System said OMERS hasn't had any occasion to recall shares in recent years for voting purposes, and has made no changes to its lending practices.

But Mr. Gibson said Teachers has found the system not only works imperfectly, but has not been economically worthwhile. He said Teachers was earning little income from its lending because most of the proceeds went to the custodian who administered the program.

"Losing votes costs us a lot more economically than the little bit we were making on lending."

He said Teachers has decided to develop an in-house lending program so it can maintain close control over the process.

The extra cost of managing its own lending will be offset by the additional income Teachers will receive by not sharing the revenue with a custodian, Mr. Gibson said.

Source: McFarland, Janet. "Why Teachers Halted Stock Loans to Short Sellers; Seeks to Maintain Tighter Control over Its Voting Rights as Shareholder." *Globe and Mail*, April 3, 2007, p. B11. Reprinted with permission of the *Globe and Mail*.

DISCUSSION QUESTIONS

1. One share equals one vote, so when shares are lent to someone to sell, the new owner gets to vote. Who do you think should get to vote the shares: the underlying owner such as Teachers, or the institution to whom it has lent the shares? Why?

2. Large institutions like Teachers have a lot of influence with their large share holdings, and actively intervene to improve corporate governance. Is Teachers giving up its fiduciary duty to its pensioners by giving up the right to vote through lending its shares?

Summary

This chapter discusses equity and hybrid securities. Securities are financial contracts and how risky they are depends on the design of the contract. The basic issues are how they are treated for tax purposes, and how much equity weight they have, which determines the risk they impose on the firm. Common shares impose the least risk because, according to S&P's criteria, they are a permanent part of the firm's capital structure, impose no commitments that might cause the firm to default, provide a cushion to senior debt that the firm can issue, and have no maturity date. CP and BAs are the opposite in that they have fixed payments, short maturities, a higher priority charge, and are not permanent. However, the interest on CP and BAs is tax deductible, whereas the dividends on common shares are not.

Between these two extremes are all the securities that firms issue. Conventional fixed-rate preferred shares, retractable preferred shares, and floating rate preferred shares all take advantage of the fact that dividends in Canada attract the dividend tax credit and are non-taxable between corporations. Convertible securities and warrants are the most obvious equity-like securities, particularly if they are structured so that conversion is mandatory. They also have the advantage of deferred equity financing or cheap debt financing, depending on what happens to the firm's share price.

This chapter describes the menu of corporate financing opportunities available. How firms choose between them is the topic of Chapter 20.

Key Terms

Adjustable Rate Convertible Subordinated Securities (ARCS), p. 752

Canadian optional interest notes (COINS), p. 753

cash flow bonds, p. 750

commodity bond, p. 750

conversion price (CP), p. 744

conversion ratio (CR), p. 744

conversion value (CV), p. 744

cumulative provision, p. 737

dilution factor, p. 742

family trust, p. 732

floating rate preferred share, p. 736

floor value (FV), p. 745

hard retraction, p. 750

hybrid security, p. 738

income bonds, p. 750

legal factor, p. 749

Liquid Yield Option Notes (LYONs), p. 752

low-yield notes, p. 751

non-voting shares, p. 731

original issue discount bonds (OIDs), p. 751

permanence factor, p. 749

pre-emptive right, p. 729

preferred securities, p. 753

prepaid bonds, p. 753

residual owners, p. 729

restricted shares, p. 731

retractable preferred share, p. 736

soft retraction, p. 750

straight bond value (SBV), p. 745

straight preferred share, p. 736

subjective factor, p. 749

subordination factor, p. 749

tax value of money, p. 736

warrants, p. 741

Formulas/Equations

(19-1) Payoff to warrant holders $= \dfrac{m}{n+m}(V + mX) - mX$

(19-2) Payoff to warrant holders $= \dfrac{m}{n+m}(V - nX)$

(19-3) $CP = \dfrac{Par}{CR}$

(19-4) $CV = CR \times P$

(19-5) Convertible premium $= \dfrac{(Market\ Value - CV)}{CV}$

(19-6) $SBV = I \times \left[\dfrac{1 - \dfrac{1}{(1+k_b)^n}}{k_b}\right] + F \times \dfrac{1}{(1+k_b)^n}$

(19-7) $FV = Max(SBV, CV)$

QUESTIONS AND PRACTICE PROBLEMS

Multiple Choice Questions

1. Which of the following does not appear in the share structure of a firm?

   A. Preferred shares

   B. Common shares

   C. Restricted shares

   D. None of the above

2. Which of the following statements about preferred shares is *false*?

   A. Retractable preferred shares allow the shareholders to bring forward the maturity date.

   B. The most common preferred shares in Canada are straight preferred shares.

   C. Straight preferred shares have maturity dates.

   D. Floating rate preferred shares dividends are reset periodically.

3. Which of the following statements is *false*?

   A. Bonds are exchanged for common shares when convertibles are converted.

   B. The exercise price is paid in cash when warrants are exercised.

   C. Debt is exchanged for common shares when its attached warrant is exercised.

   D. A conversion ratio is specified in convertibles.

4. Which of the following is a correct ranking of after-the-fact best financing choices, assuming that the share price increases beyond the conversion price?

   A. Debt, common shares, and convertibles

   B. Common shares, debt, and convertibles

   C. Convertibles, common shares, and debt

   D. Debt, convertibles, and common shares

5. Which of the following is *not* one of the factors used to judge whether a security is debt or equity?

   A. Subordination

   B. Legal

   C. Subjective

   D. Claim priority

6. Which of the following statements is *false*?

   A. A hard retractable means preferred shares must be paid off in cash.

   B. Commodity bonds help commodity producers to control the commodity price risks.

   C. Real return bonds are tied to the CPI.

   D. Preferred securities are another name for preferred shares.

7. What is the correct ranking of cost from the highest to the lowest?

   A. Common shares, convertible preferred shares, straight preferred shares

   B. Convertible preferred shares, convertible bonds, long-term unsecured debt

   C. medium-term note debentures, bank loans, mortgage debt

   D. Common shares, medium-term note debentures, mortgage debt

Practice Problems

8. State the three basic rights of common shareholders.

Basic

9. The hot Internet stock you bought last year doesn't look so hot anymore; in fact, the company has just declared bankruptcy. The creditors, such as equipment suppliers and employees, are owed $1.5 million. How much will the equity holders receive if, when liquidated, the firm's assets are worth:

   A. $1.7 million

   B. $1.2 million

   C. Suppose that equity holders did not have "limited liability." How much would they receive for each asset value above?

10. Collingwood Corp. has decided to invest some of its excess cash in straight preferred shares issued by other companies. It will earn a yield of 6.5 percent on the $10 million investment. How much net income will Collingwood earn if its corporate tax rate is 30 percent?

11. HMF Financial Group has issued convertible preferred shares with a $50 par value. The conversion price for these shares is $12.50 (per common share). What is the conversion ratio?

12. HMF Financial Group's preferred shares (see Problem 11) also have a call feature which permits the company to re-purchase the shares at par value (or, in effect, force the conversion into common shares). Usually, the common stock will be trading at least 20 percent above the conversion price before the call feature is invoked. At what price of its common stock will HMF consider calling the preferred shares?

13. What are the differences between call options and warrants?

Medium

14. Calculate the conversion price and conversion value of the convertible bonds given the following: selling price = $95; each bond is convertible into 4 common shares. Current common share price = $40. Will the convertible bonds be converted?

15. With the savings from your summer job you were able to buy 500 shares of a hot new Internet company last year. A few months after your purchase, the company was low on cash and needed to raise more equity capital. The company's charter provided a "pre-emptive" right to shareholders, so you were offered the chance to buy 1 additional share for each 5 owned.

   A. What percentage of the firm's equity will you own after your initial purchase if there are 500,000 shares outstanding?

   B. How much of the company's equity will you own if you buy the extra shares being offered?

   C. If you decline to buy the additional shares (but they are sold to other investors), how much of the firm's equity will you own?

16. When Finns' Fridges needed to raise capital to expand, the founding brothers, David and Douglas Finn, were concerned about losing control of the firm if they sold too many shares. The solution devised by their investment banker was to create two different classes of shares. The brothers would each retain 250,000 "Class A" shares which are entitled to two votes apiece. 750,000 "Common Shares" with one vote would be sold to the IPO investors. What percentage of the company's equity will the brothers own? How much control (percentage of the votes) will the Finns maintain?

17. HMF Financial Group has 50,000,000 common shares outstanding, on which it pays a quarterly dividend of $0.20 per share. The firm's capital structure also includes 2,000,000 cumulative preferred shares with a $25 par value that yield 8 percent per year (or 2 percent per quarter). After making some bad loans in the sub-prime mortgage market, HMF suffered a big loss, and suspended its dividend payments on all forms of equity. Six months later, the company is once again in the black having earned $6,000,000 (after tax), which it intends to pay as dividends. How much will the common shareholders receive?

18. The common stock of HMF Financial is currently trading at $10.00, while its preferred shares trade at par (see Problem 11). Calculate the convertible premium on the preferred shares. What does this premium mean?

19. Jack and Jill Inc. very nearly tumbled into bankruptcy last year. To refinance the firm, they issued $25 million worth of 30-year Income Bonds. These bonds have an 8 percent coupon that is payable only if the firm achieves earnings before interest and tax (EBIT) of $3 million. Suppose the firm does achieve its target

and pays out the full coupon interest amount. Determine the company's net income if the tax rate is 30 percent.

20. Calculate the payoff of fully exercising warrants given the following: 500,000 existing shares outstanding (n); 80,000 warrants (m) are outstanding and are exercisable at $15 ($X$). The firm is valued at $10,000,000 ($V$) before warrants are exercised. Identify the dilution factor.

21. Kash Cow Inc. is considering converting from a corporation to an income trust. Its earnings before tax were $1.00 per share last year, and this level of income is expected to continue for the foreseeable future. As a corporation, the firm pays 30 percent tax on its earnings, and then distributes all after-tax income to shareholders in the form of dividends. As an income trust, the company would not pay any tax itself; all earnings would be paid to the equity holders, but CRA will deem these distributions to be interest payments, not dividends.

   A. If the personal tax rate on interest income is 45 percent, and the rate on dividends is 25 percent, which business form, corporation or trust, will leave more money in the equity holders' pockets?

   B. Pension funds can receive dividend and interest income on a tax-free basis (income tax is eventually paid by the pensioners on the income they receive from the plan, but this still leaves a very long period of tax-deferral). How much tax revenue will the government lose from each share of Kash Kow owned by a pension plan if the company converts to an income trust?

22. The financial data for Rothmans Inc. presented in Table 19-1 shows a figure for "Diluted Earnings per Common Share". This number is based on increasing the shares outstanding figure to account for any new shares that will likely be issued (e.g., when warrants are exercised, or convertible bonds are converted to common shares). First, determine the total net income that is consistent with the diluted earnings per share figure and the reported number of shares outstanding. If the company actually reported $99.464 million in earnings, calculate how many extra shares the company may have to issue.

23. Orion's Belt Mining Co. has 12,000,000 common shares outstanding, which are currently trading for $4.75 apiece. In addition, the company has issued 3,000,000 share purchase warrants with a strike price of $4.00 that are just about to expire.

   A. Determine the equity value of the firm before the warrants are exercised.

   B. What is the total cost to the warrant holders to purchase the new shares?

   C. Calculate the value of the shares that the holders of the warrants will own after they are exercised.

   D. How much would you be willing to pay for each warrant?

24. Straight preferred shares of similar risk to the convertibles issued by HMF Financial Group (see Problem 11) are yielding 8 percent per year, whereas these shares are yielding 6 percent on the $50 par value. Determine the "Straight Preferred Value" (or SPV), and the Floor Value for the convertible preferred shares. You may assume the shares have no maturity and can therefore be valued as a perpetuity.

Cost of Capital

This chapter looks at the firm's cost of capital, which is the overall cost of the funds invested in the firm. Firms need this in order to maximize shareholder value, since if the firm doesn't know what investors want, it cannot satisfy them. BASF Group, a chemical company, interprets value-based management as follows: "We aim to earn a premium on our cost of capital in order to further increase BASF's value...Our value-based management is a comprehensive approach that includes all functions within the company, and challenges and encourages all employees to act in an entrepreneurial manner." BASF goes on to state that "Earnings before interest and taxes (EBIT) after cost of capital is the key performance and management indicator for our operating divisions and business units." For 2007, BASF lowered its cost of capital from 10 percent to 9 percent, since it adjusted its capital structure and increased its use of debt. In this chapter, we examine how firms estimate this key management value.

Source: BASF Group website: www.corporate.basf.com. Retrieved April 27, 2007.

Cost of Capital

Learning Objectives

After reading this chapter, you should understand the following:

1. How ROE and the required return by common equity investors are related to a firm's growth opportunities

2. How to apply the steps involved in estimating a firm's weighted average cost of capital, including how to estimate the market values of the various components of capital, and how to estimate the various costs of these components

3. How operating and financial leverage affect firms

4. The advantages and limitations of using growth models and/or risk models to estimate the cost of common equity

In Chapters 17 to 19 we discussed securities legislation; the differences among debt, equity, and hybrid securities; and how securities are issued. We finished by describing a risk hierarchy that essentially corresponded to how a particular security moves from being 100 percent debt, such as commercial paper, to 100 percent equity. This risk hierarchy then corresponds to a *cost hierarchy* as far as the firm is concerned, since investors require compensation for additional risk, which translates into higher costs for the firm. In this chapter, we discuss how firms synthesize this information into their overall cost of funds, called the cost of capital.

The cost of capital is the most basic piece of information a firm needs, since it determines how the firm is valued and is often the appropriate "hurdle rate" to be used for making corporate investment decisions.[1] In this chapter you will learn what the cost of capital means, how to calculate it, and how to avoid some basic and yet common mistakes in corporate financing. During the process, we will discuss some of the problems that result when using the discounted cash flow models discussed in Chapter 7 for valuing equities, and in using the capital asset pricing model (CAPM) discussed in Chapter 9. These two models are the "workhorses" of corporate finance for estimating the cost of capital.

After you master the material on the cost of capital, Chapter 21 discusses how firms should and do determine their financing decisions.

20.1 FINANCING SOURCES

Capital Structure

We begin by returning to the balance sheet to review the major accounts, as depicted in Table 20-1.

Table 20-1 Main Balance Sheet Accounts	
Cash and marketable securities	Accruals
Accounts receivable	Accounts payable
Inventory	Short-term debt
Prepaid expenses	Current liabilities
Current assets	Long-term debt
Net fixed assets	Shareholders' equity
Total assets	Total liabilities and shareholders' equity

On the asset side, we have current (short-term) assets consisting of cash and marketable securities, accounts receivable and inventory, plus there are usually some accounting items, such as prepaid expenses. When the current assets are added to the net fixed assets (i.e., gross fixed assets less accumulated depreciation), we have total assets. We call the financing of total assets the

---

[1] As noted in Chapter 13, the firm's cost of capital is the appropriate discount rate for evaluating projects that possess "average" risk for the company.

financial structure decision, which reflects all of the firm's liabilities. These liabilities include invested capital and other liabilities.

For our purposes, it is useful to distinguish between debt and other types of liabilities that do not represent debt contracts in the strictest sense. In particular, many accruals are strictly accounting items required to prepare the statements according to generally accepted accounting principles (GAAP). As such, they do not represent a decision on the part of an investor or creditor to finance the firm. For example, both the authors are paid by their universities with a two-week to one-month lag, which would show up as wages payable on their university's balance sheet. However, neither of us would consider this delay in getting paid as a financial investment in the university on our part. It is just that the university does not pay us on a daily cash basis, so the accountant accrues a liability. Similarly as long as a firm's credit is good, accounts payable arise as a result of a telephone or computerized order, where the invoice arrives with the order. Again, in most cases the supplier is not explicitly thinking of the value of its shipment as an investment in the company.[2] It is simply the way that business is done between companies. In this sense, the only current liability items that do reflect a creditor actually investing in the company are bank debt, other short-term debt, and the current portion of any long-term debt that is due within a year.

With long-term liabilities, the basic distinction is again between accounting items and money that has been invested within the firm. In the simple balance sheet presented in Table 20-1, all of the liabilities are invested capital, since we do not have any strictly accounting items. However, firms often report the value of benefits owing to workers as a liability since they customarily pay health benefits after retirement even when they are made on a "pay-as-you-go" basis. Also there are often deferred income taxes, as discussed in Chapter 3, as well as other accounting items that do not reflect invested capital. In almost all cases, these "non-debt" accounting items are ignored in estimating firm capital. Apart from explicit debt and the shareholders' equity accounts, the only other item that is included as capital is minority interest, since this reflects the amount of shareholders' equity of a subsidiary that is not owned by the shareholders of the parent firm.[3] The **capital structure** of the firm is then how this invested capital is financed, determining what proportion will be financed through debt and what proportion through equity. How the firm arrives at these decisions is the focus of Chapter 21.

capital structure how a firm finances its invested capital

We now take as an example the simplified balance sheet in Table 20-2.

Table 20-2 A "Simplified" Balance Sheet

Cash and marketable securities	50	Accruals	100
Accounts receivable	200	Accounts payable	200
Inventory	250	Short-term debt	50
Prepaid expenses	0	Current liabilities	350
Current assets	500	Long-term debt	650
Net fixed assets	1,500	Shareholders' equity	1,000
Total assets	2,000	Total liabilities and shareholders' equity	2,000

---

[2] Note that this is not always the case. For firms in serious financial trouble, a shipment may be seen as an investment with an explicit interest charge.

[3] Minority interest arises when a firm reports consolidated financial statements. GAAP requires consolidated statements even when a subsidiary is not 100 percent owned (usually more than 50 percent). As a result, all of the subsidiary's debt and assets are included on the consolidated statements, and the part of the subsidiary's equity that is not owned is shown as minority interest.

debt-to-equity ratio
interest bearing debt to
shareholders' equity plus
minority interest

The financial structure is $2,000, while the capital structure components total $1,700, consisting of $1,000 in shareholders' equity, and total interest-bearing debt of $700 (i.e., $50 + $650), producing a **debt-to-equity ratio** of 0.70 (i.e., $700 ÷ $1,000). This hypothetical capital structure is typical of Canadian firms. The Investment Dealers Association of Canada (IDA) reported that the average debt-to-equity ratio of Canadian companies peaked at 0.78 in 1999, and due to the strong economy it had subsequently dropped to 0.53 by 2005, representing its lowest level in 20 years.

The above numbers come from the firm's financial statements and represent historical book values. For our purposes we can convert them to market values. So suppose the book and market values of the firm's debt are very close, which is often the case now since interest rates have been relatively stable in Canada for the last six years.[4] However, suppose that the firm's equity is selling for 2.5 times its book value, so that its **market-to-book (M/B) ratio**, defined in Chapter 4, is 2.5. For the example above, the total market value of the equity would then be $2,500 (i.e., $1,000 × 2.5), and the total market value of the firm would be $3,200 (i.e., $700 + $2,500). Therefore, the firm's "market valued" debt-to-equity ratio is 0.28 (i.e., $700 ÷ $2,500), which again is fairly typical of Canadian non-financial firms. The key issues in corporate finance are then seeing if we can increase this market value by changing the mix of debt and equity, and in determining the minimum rate of return we have to earn to maintain this market value.

**market-to-book (M/B)
ratio** the market price
per share divided by the
book value per share

Three Ways of Using the Valuation Equation

Before answering these questions, let's review the most basic implication of the simple perpetuity valuation problem as discussed in Chapter 5. Recall that the present value of perpetuity is found by dividing the amount of the regular payment by the appropriate discount rate. For our purposes let's assume the perpetuity is future estimated earnings, which are expected to remain at the same level indefinitely, thus experiencing no growth. We can discount these earnings using the investors' required rate of return to find the present value of those future earnings, as shown in Equation 20-1.

[20-1]

$$S = \frac{X}{K_e}$$

Where X is the forecast earnings, S is the value of the perpetuity, and K_e is the investors' required rate of return, where it is subscripted e for equity.

So if a firm's common shares are expected to earn and pay out $1 in perpetuity and investors require a 10 percent rate of return, the value of this perpetuity (which in this example is the value of the firm's common equity) is simply $10, that is:

$$S = \frac{X}{K_e} = \frac{1}{0.1} = \$10.0$$

We often use perpetuities in finance since they are easy to value and the results almost always hold with more complicated patterns of earnings.

---

[4] Recall that long-term debt will usually be issued at coupon rates that are approximately equal to prevailing market rates so that they are sold at close to their face value. If the interest rates do not change very much, then the market value of such debt will remain close to the book value.

However, note that this is one equation and we can easily rearrange it to solve for any of the three values: we just happened to have focused on the *valuation problem*, which tells us what the perpetuity is worth. When we valued securities in Chapters 5 to 7, we focused on estimating the values of different securities, such as common shares and bonds. In order to do this, we took the investors' required rate of return as given.

However, if we rearrange the same equation to solve for K_e we get:

$$K_e = \frac{X}{S}$$

[20-2]

Given a $10 market price and forecast perpetual earnings of $1 per year, we can estimate the investors' required rate of return as:

$$K_e = \frac{X}{S} = \frac{1}{10} = 10\%$$

This estimate of the investors' required rate of return, or the cost of equity capital to the firm, is called the **earnings yield**, since it is just the forecast earnings divided by the market price, similar to the dividend yield.[5] In practice, the earnings yield is rarely used as an estimate of K_e, since most firms have some expectation for growth, so the stock price reflects these growth opportunities as well as the current earnings. However, the earnings yield was commonly used in the 1950s when inflation and growth expectations were minimal. On the other hand, the basic approach of estimating the discount rate that sets the forecasted stream of earnings or cash equal to the current price is used for all discounted cash flow (DCF) methods of estimating the cost of equity capital. We will discuss this in more detail later, but this way of rearranging the valuation equation solves the *corporate financing* issue of estimating what return investors require. In this example, we estimate that investors require a 10 percent return for holding this perpetuity.

earnings yield the estimate of the investors' required rate of return

Finally we can rearrange the same equation and solve for the forecast earnings, as shown in Equation 20-3.

$$X = K_e \times S$$

[20-3]

So if the security is worth $10 and the investor requires a 10 percent rate of return, then we have to generate forecast earnings of $1, as shown below:

$$X = K_e \times S = 0.1 \times 10 = \$1$$

This explicitly tells the firm's managers what their earnings targets have to be to support the current valuation. This last approach is common in regulated industries where regulators have to determine how much profit a company like Terasen Gas Utility, the TransCanada Mainline, or Enbridge Gas Distribution should earn. Each of these companies is regulated to earn a fair return and the regulator has to determine what prices they can charge to do this. In setting these prices the regulators explicitly use this last version of the valuation equation. So this version is used in regulating utilities as well as in basic corporate finance applications.

---

[5] Notice that it is also the reciprocal of the firm's forward P/E ratio, which was discussed at length in Chapters 4 and 7.

The same equation can therefore be used in three different ways. To illustrate the principle of the cost of capital, we will use this third approach and for the time being assume that the firm's earnings are perpetual, and that the required rates of return are known. So let's assume that the yield on our example firm's debt is 6.0 percent, whereas equity holders require a rate of return of 12.0 percent. We already know that the debt is worth $700 and the equity is worth $2,500, so with this data we can estimate the following:

Interest for the bond holders $= K_d \times D = 0.06 \times \$700 = \$42$

Return to the shareholders $= K_e \times S = 0.12 \times \$2,500 = \$300$

What this tells us is that with a $700 market value for the debt (D) and a 6 percent yield or required return on debt (K_d), the firm has to earn $42 to pay the bond holders. Similarly with the firm's common shares worth $2,500 ($S$), and the shareholders requiring a 12 percent return (K_e), the firm has to earn $300 to meet these expectations. So in total with this mix of debt and equity and a $3,200 current market value, the firm has to earn $342.

Deriving the *Required* Income Statement

Once we have this information we can *work up* the firm's income statement. Suppose, for example, that the firm has a 40 percent corporate income tax rate and its operating costs are $458, composed of $300 of variable costs and $158 of fixed costs. The forecast income statement in this case is presented in Table 20-3.

Table 20-3   A Forecasted Income Statement

Sales	$1,000
Variable costs	300
Fixed costs	158
EBIT	542
Interest	42
Tax (40%)	200
Net Income	300

If the firm has 1,000 shares outstanding, its *earnings per share (EPS)* are $0.30 (i.e., $300 ÷ 1,000).

Note that rather than starting with sales and working down the income statement, we have done the opposite. This is exactly what regulators do in setting prices. They first start with a fair return to the common shareholders, and then add in these other forecast costs to set the firm's revenue or sales requirement, from which they set individual prices. This approach is common in all "rate of return regulated" industries with the exception that they use book values for invested capital instead of market values.[6] Since regulated industries are very capital intensive and firms tend to have relatively high amounts of debt, these financial costs are a very important part of their cost structure. The ideas

[6] Regulators use book values based on the rationale that investors require a fair return on the money that they have invested in the utility.

that we develop in this chapter have been used to set your telephone, water, gas, and electric bills.

We now have a lot of information about the firm. Given its total market value and investor return requirements, the firm has to have sales of $1,000. We also note that the firm's total assets are $2,000, so its **asset turnover ratio**, defined in Chapter 4 as sales divided by total assets, has to be 0.50 (i.e., $1,000 ÷ $2,000), and its **return on assets (ROA)**, defined in Chapter 4 as net income divided by total assets, is 15 percent (i.e., $300 ÷ $2,000). We also note that the book value of its invested capital is $1,700, and its EBIT is $542, so its **return on invested capital (ROIC)**, defined as EBIT divided by the book value of invested capital (IC), is 31.88 percent. This *ROIC*, often referred to as simply *ROI*, is often expressed on an after-tax basis by multiplying by $(1 - T)$, which in our case is 0.60, producing an after-tax ROI of 19.13 percent. The firm's **return on equity (ROE)**, defined as net income divided by the book value of equity, is then $300 divided by $1,000, or 30 percent, which is very high.

The very high *ROE* explains the firm's M/B ratio. Remember that the earnings per share equals the *ROE* times the book value per share (BVPS), as shown below:

$$EPS = \frac{NI}{\# shares} = \frac{NI}{Equity} \times \frac{Equity}{\# shares} = ROE \times BVPS$$

With our example, the BVPS is $1 ($1,000 shareholders' equity divided by 1,000 shares) and the EPS equals this $1 times the 30 percent *ROE*, or $0.30.

Since we are dealing with a perpetuity, the price per share can be expressed as follows:

$$P = \frac{EPS}{K_e} = \frac{ROE \times BVPS}{K_e}$$

[20-4]

Using the numbers from above, the share price is just the $0.30 EPS discounted in perpetuity at the investors' required rate of return or cost of equity capital of 12 percent.

$$P = \frac{EPS}{K_e} = \frac{ROE \times BVPS}{K_e} = \frac{0.30 \times \$1}{0.12} = \$2.50$$

If we divide both sides of Equation 20-4 by the BVPS, we get the basic relationship that drives the M/B ratio:

$$\frac{P}{BVPS} = \frac{ROE}{K_e}$$

[20-5]

For the numbers in this example, we get:

$$\frac{P}{BVPS} = \frac{ROE}{K_e} = \frac{0.30}{0.12} = 2.50$$

Equation 20-5 simply says that if what the firm earns (*ROE*) exceeds what investors require (K_e), then the price goes above the book value of the investment. This is a basic relationship in finance: if you exceed investor expectations, prices go up.

asset turnover ratio sales divided by total assets

return on assets (ROA) net income divided by total assets

return on invested capital (ROIC) earnings before interest and taxes divided by the book value of invested capital

return on equity (ROE) net income divided by the book value of equity

Remember that in Chapter 6, we discussed the pricing of bonds and how when interest rates increase, the price of bonds goes down, and vice versa. Further we indicated that if the current interest rate exceeds the coupon rate on a bond, then it sells at a discount from par value, but if it is less than the coupon rate, it sells at a premium. The current interest rate is another way of saying the investors' required return for investing in bonds. As a result, saying that bonds sell at a discount or a premium to par value, when required returns exceed or are less than the coupon rate, is another way of saying their M/B ratio is less than or greater than 1.0. Similarly in our example, the equity M/B ratio exceeds 1.0 because the ROE of 30 percent significantly exceeds the investors' required rate of return on equity of 12 percent.

Now that we have drawn the link between book values and market values, we proceed to discuss the concept of the cost of capital.

CONCEPT REVIEW QUESTIONS

1. Why is the earnings yield not usually an adequate measure of the required return by equity investors?

2. How are the ROE and K_e related to a firm's growth opportunities and its M/B ratio?

20.2 THE COST OF CAPITAL

Determining the Weighted Average Cost of Capital (WACC)

So far we have considered only the equity market value, so now let's look at the overall market value of the firm; that is, the value of the debt plus the value of the equity (D + S), which for our example is $3,200. We also know that the firm's after-tax *ROI* on its $1,700 book value is 19.13 percent, based on EBIT(1 − T) of $325.2 (i.e., $542(1 − 0.40)). This is an important number because EBIT(1 −T) indicates the net income of the firm if it is financed 100 percent with equity; that is, if there is no deduction for interest payments on the firm's debt. Except for a few items like income from investments and capital gains and losses, it is also equal to a firm's net operating income.

We now have two of the three numbers needed in a valuation equation. We know the overall firm value is $3,200 and the EBIT(1 −T) is $325.20, so we can find the discount rate that sets them equal. First we rewrite EBIT minus taxes as ROI × IC, and re-express the valuation equation above as shown below:

[20-6]

$$V = \frac{ROI \times IC}{K_a}$$

Here we have replaced S (the value of the firm's equity) with V, which stands for the value of the firm, and have denoted the required return as K_a, denoting the average, or overall, required rate of return. For the numbers in this example, ROI × IC = 0.1913 × $1,700 = $325.20, so we get:

$$V = \frac{ROI \times IC}{K_a} = \frac{325.2}{K_a} = \$3{,}200$$

Similar to what we did with the earnings yield previously, we can rearrange to find this overall required rate of return, which is given below:

$$K_a = \frac{ROI \times IC}{V}$$

[20-7]

For the numbers in this example we get:

$$K_a = \frac{ROI \times IC}{V} = \frac{325.2}{3200} = 10.16\%$$

So if we discount the EBIT minus taxes figure using this average required rate of return, we get the overall market value of the firm.

This is obviously a very important number. To understand where it comes from, remember that the total amount needed for the equity holders is $300 or $K_e \times S$, whereas the total amount needed for the bond holders is $42 or $K_d \times D$. This exceeds the amount the firm has to earn of $325.20 by $16.80. This $16.80 is the reduction in the firm's corporate income taxes due to the fact that interest is tax deductible. The exact amount needed to pay the bond holders is $K_d(1 - T) \times D$ or $0.06 \times 0.60 \times 700 = \$25.20$. It is this $25.20 that gives us the EBIT minus taxes of $325.20, when we add it to the required earnings for the equity holders. If we substitute these definitions into the equation for the average required return we get:

$$K_a = \frac{ROI \times IC}{V} = \frac{K_e S + K_d (1-T) D}{V} = K_e \frac{S}{V} + K_d (1-T) \frac{D}{V}$$

[20-8]

where the average required rate of return is a **weighted average cost of capital (WACC)**, which is commonly referred to as just the **cost of capital**.

The cost of capital is a way of calculating the overall required rate of return needed to meet investor expectations. There are three steps involved in estimating the WACC:

weighted average cost of capital (WACC) or **cost of capital** an estimate of a firm's average cost of $1 of financing

1. Estimate market values for the sources of capital, since our focus is on how to increase the market value of the funds invested in the firm and we need these to estimate the weights of the different sources of capital in the total firm value.

2. Estimate the current required rates of return for the various sources of capital invested in the firm.

3. Put them all on the same corporate tax basis to recognize that interest on debt is tax deductible, whereas the return to the equity holders is not.

So with our example, we have the market valued debt ratio at $700 ÷ $3,200 or 21.875 percent, and the market valued equity ratio as 78.125 percent (i.e., $2,500 ÷ $3,200). We then assumed a required return on equity of 12 percent and on debt of 6 percent. Finally the interest cost is tax deductible so on an after-tax basis, it is 3.6 percent or 6.0% × (1 − .40), where the corporate income tax rate is 40 percent. Putting this all together we get:

$$K_a = K_e \frac{S}{V} + K_d(1-T)\frac{D}{V} = 0.12 \times 0.78125 + 0.06 \times (1-.40) \times 0.21875 = 0.1016 = 10.16\%$$

The key result is that the cost of capital is just a *weighted average* of the after-tax costs of the different sources of capital, where the weights are the proportion of each in the total market value of the firm.

Before we proceed, we note that Equation 20-8 is incomplete whenever a firm uses preferred share financing. We also replace the term $K_d(1 - T)$ with K_i to denote the after-tax cost of debt. In this case, we have the following equation:

[20-9]

$$WACC = K_e \frac{S}{V} + K_p \frac{P}{V} + K_i \frac{D}{V}$$

where, P is the market value of the firm's preferred shares, and K_p is the cost of preferred shares, and the value of the firm V now equals $S + P + D$. Notice that we do not need to adjust K_p for taxes, since preferred shares pay dividends out of after-tax income, just like common shares.

Estimating Market Values

Estimating the market value of a firm's common equity (S) is quite straightforward whenever a firm has shares that are traded publicly. We simply multiply the firm's market price per common share (P_0) by the number of shares outstanding (n), as shown below:[7]

[20-10]

$$S = P_0 \times n$$

Estimating the market value of a firm's preferred shares is also quite straightforward if it has preferred shares outstanding that are publicly traded, in which case we can simply use Equation 20-10, replacing the common share information with the market price of the preferred shares (P_p) and the number of preferred shares outstanding. In the event that the firm's preferred shares are not actively traded, we can estimate the market value of each of its preferred shares using the following equation, which was first introduced in Chapter 7, for valuing straight preferred shares:

[20-11]

$$P_p = D_p \div k_p$$

Estimating the market value of a firm's debt can be somewhat more complicated. As mentioned earlier, if interest rates have not changed too much since the debt was first issued by the firm, then the book value of the firm's long-term debt is close to its market value, so we can use the book value. When a firm has bonds outstanding, we can be more precise and use the following bond valuation equation introduced in Chapter 6 to estimate the market value of those bonds.

---

[7] Notice that in the example above we accomplished the same result by multiplying the firm's book value of common equity figure by its M/B ratio.

$$B = I \times \left[\frac{1 - \frac{1}{(1+k_b)^n}}{k_b} \right] + F \times \frac{1}{(1+k_b)^n}$$

[20-12]

where,

B = the bond price;

I = interest (or coupon) payments;

k_b = the bond discount rate (or market rate);

n = the term-to-maturity; and,

F = the face (par) value of the bond.

If the firm has more than one series of bonds or other types of long-term debt issues outstanding, we can repeat this process and add up all of the calculated market values to determine the total market value of the firm's debt outstanding.

We illustrate how to combine these concepts in the following example.

Example 20-1: Estimating Market Values

Suppose firm ABC has the following balance sheet figures:

	Book Value
Debt (D): 8% coupon rate, annual coupons	$1.0 million
10 years to maturity	
Preferred shares (P): 10% dividend rate	$1.0 million
Common equity (CE):	
Common shares (C/S) − 100,000 shares	
(originally issued at $15/share)	$1.5 million
Retained earnings (RE)	$0.5 million
Total	$4.0 million

Assume the marginal tax rate (T) = 40%.

Present market conditions are such that:

Debt: The present market rate on similar risk 10-year bonds is 6 percent.

Preferred shares: Similar risk preferred shares are providing yields of 8 percent.

Common equity: Common share price is currently $25.

Find the market value proportions of these components assuming the firm wants to raise new funds in order to maintain its present capital structure based on these market value proportions.

Solution

Long-term debt (D):

$$B = \$80{,}000 \times \left[\frac{1 - \dfrac{1}{(1+.06)^{10}}}{.06} \right] + \$1m \times \left[\frac{1}{(1+.06)^{10}} \right] = \$1{,}147{,}202$$

Preferred Shares:

$$P = \frac{D_p}{k_p} = \frac{(\$1m)(.10)}{.08} = \frac{\$100{,}000}{.08} = \$1{,}250{,}000$$

Common Equity:

$$S = P_0 \times n = (\$25)(100{,}000\, shares) = \$2.5m.$$

So, according to the "market" value of the firm's balance sheet, we obtain:

$$V = D + P + SE = 1{,}147{,}202 + 1{,}250{,}000 + 2{,}500{,}000 = \$4{,}897{,}202$$

$$and\ \frac{D}{V} = 0.234,\ \frac{P}{V} = 0.255,\ and\ \frac{CE}{V} = 0.511$$

CONCEPT REVIEW QUESTIONS

1. Why is the weighted average cost of capital (WACC) so important?
2. What are the steps involved in estimating a firm's WACC?
3. How can we estimate the market value of common equity, preferred equity, and long-term debt?

20.3 ESTIMATING THE COMPONENT COSTS

Flotation Costs and the Marginal Cost of Capital (MCC)

In the example in the previous section, we were given the cost of equity, as well as the before-tax cost of debt, which we can adjust to determine the after-tax cost of debt. In this section, we show how to calculate the cost of debt and preferred equity if we do not know them, and we discuss estimating the cost of common equity in the following sections. One complication that arises with respect to all sources of capital, except for internally generated funds, is that the firm incurs **issuing** or **flotation costs** when new securities are issued. These include any fees paid to the investment dealer and/or any discounts provided to investors to entice them to purchase the securities. As a result, the cost of issuing new securities will be *higher* than the return required by investors, since the net proceeds to the firm from any security issue will be lower than that security's market price.

issuing or **flotation costs** costs incurred by a firm when it issues new securities

Being aware of this fact is particularly important when we consider the cost of common equity to the firm. In particular, remember that there are two sources of common equity financing: reinvested earnings, which show up on the firm's balance sheet in the retained earnings figure, and new common share issues. When the common equity portion of financing comes entirely from reinvested earnings, the firm's cost of equity will equal the return required by its shareholders, as discussed previously. However, when the firm is forced into issuing new common shares, it must pay flotation costs for issuing these shares, so the cost to the firm is higher than the cost of using internally generated funds.

At this point, it is useful to introduce the concept of the **marginal cost of capital (MCC)**, which may be defined as the weighted average cost of the *next dollar* of financing to be raised. Sometimes the WACC and the MCC are used interchangeably, although they are not really the same, since the WACC represents the weighted average cost of each dollar raised in total. The two tend to be the same for most levels of financing. However, they will differ when, at some financing level, the firm's cost of raising new money increases, causing the MCC to exceed the WACC. Given the discussion in the paragraph above, the most common cause of this increase in the MCC occurs when the firm cannot supply all of its required common equity financing from reinvested earnings (i.e., internal funds). Therefore, it must issue new common shares and bear the brunt of issuing costs, in addition to providing common shareholders with their required rate of return. This causes the cost of common equity to increase, meaning the MCC increases at this point. The reason that MCC and WACC are often identical is that many firms restrict their investment outlays so that all of the common equity finance portion can be provided by internal funds.[8]

In short, the MCC often exceeds the WACC due to the costs of raising additional funds. For large firms, the changes in securities regulation have led to a drop in these issuing costs, so that for firms like Rothmans Inc., they are relatively minor. However, for small firms, these issue costs can be very significant, causing the MCC to jump dramatically.

Currently, these issue costs are approximately as shown in Table 20-4.

> **marginal cost of capital (MCC)** the weighted average cost of the next dollar of financing to be raised

Table 20-4 Average Issuing Costs	
Commercial paper	0.125%
Medium-term notes	1.0%
Long-term debt	2.0%
Equity (large)	5.0%
Equity (small)	5.0%—10.0%
Equity (private)	10.0% and up

What the issue costs mean is that there is a *financing wedge* between what the investor pays and what the firm recieves, the difference being the money that is lost to these issue costs.

---

[8] Recall from Chapter 13 that this procedure is referred to as capital rationing.

Debt

We can determine the cost of debt to the firm by using a variation of Equation 20-12, where we replace the bond price with the net proceeds (NP) the firm receives when it issues new bonds, after paying its flotation costs. We would note here that flotation costs are tax deductible immediately.[9] We must then make one more adjustment to Equation 20-12 to reflect the fact that the interest payments are tax deductible, whereas the principal repayment (i.e., the face value) is not. After making these substitutions, we merely solve for the firm's after-tax cost of debt (K_i) in the same manner as which we solved for the yield-to-maturity (YTM) in Chapter 6. This equation is given below:

[20-13]

$$NP = I \times (1-T) \times \left[\frac{1 - \frac{1}{(1+K_i)^n}}{K_i} \right] + F \times \frac{1}{(1+K_i)^n}$$

Example 20-2: Determining the Cost of Debt

Suppose firm ABC from Example 20-1 can issue new 10-year bonds at par value, which pay 6 percent annual coupons, and that the before-tax issuing costs are 2.5 percent of par. Estimate the firm's before- and after-tax cost of debt.

Solution

Using $100 par value, we get the following values that can be substituted into Equation 20-13:

$NP = 100 - 100(.025)(1 - .40) = 100 - 1.50 = \$98.50; I = (.06)(\$100) = \$6.$

So we have:

$$98.50 = 6 \times (1 - .4) \left[\frac{1 - \frac{1}{(1+K_i)^{10}}}{K_i} \right] + 100 \times \frac{1}{(1+K_i)^{10}}$$

Solving for K_i, using a financial calculator as shown in Chapter 6, we get:[10]

PMT = 6 (1−.40) = \$3.60; PV = −98.50; FV = 100; N = 10.

Then CPT I/Y will give 3.78 percent.
So, the firm's after-tax cost of debt is 3.78 percent.

Preferred Shares

The cost of preferred shares can also be determined by accounting for flotation costs by replacing NP for P_p in Equation 20-11, and then solving the equation for K_p, as shown in the equation below:

---

[9] On the other hand, when debt securities are issued at a discount from their face value, this cost will be amortized over the life of the debt.

[10] Students who have not yet mastered the financial calculator can solve using the trial and error method as illustrated in Chapter 6.

$$K_p = D_p/NP$$

[20-14]

Example 20-3: Determining the Cost of Preferred Equity

Suppose firm ABC from Example 20-1 can issue new preferred shares at par value of $100, which pay annual dividends at an 8 percent rate, and that the net after-tax flotation costs are 2 percent of par. Estimate the firm's before- and after-tax cost of preferred equity.

Solution

Based on their $100 par value, we get the following values that can be substituted into Equation 20-14:

$NP = \$100 (1 - .02) = \$98.00; D_p = (.08)(\$100) = \$8.$

So we have:

$K_p = D_p/NP = \$8 / \$98 = 8.16\%$

Estimating the cost of common equity is more complicated, and we elaborate on various approaches in the sections below.

CONCEPT REVIEW QUESTIONS

1. How do flotation costs affect the cost of capital sources for a firm?

2. Explain how to estimate the cost of debt and preferred equity for a firm.

20.4 THE EFFECTS OF OPERATING AND FINANCIAL LEVERAGE

Sales Changes and Leverage

Before we formally consider how to estimate a firm's cost of common equity, we return to the firm from Table 20-3, which had to generate sales of $1,000 to cover its operating and financing costs. We now consider what might happen if things changed. Suppose, for example, that the firm issued a report that sales potential had increased and it now expected to sell 20 percent more widgets, so that sales revenues was expected to be $1,200, all else constant (see Table 20-5).

Table 20-5 The Income Statement after a 20% Sales Increase	
Sales	$1,200
Variable costs	360
Fixed costs	158
EBIT	682
Interest	42
Tax (40%)	256
Net income	384

operating leverage the
increased volatility in
operating income caused
by fixed operating costs

In this example, the firm's variable costs increase by the same 20 percent that sales increase to $360, but EBIT increases by 26 percent to $682. This is due to **operating leverage**, because some of the firm's operating costs are fixed and do not increase with sales. In addition to the operating fixed costs, the firm's interest costs of $42 are also fixed. As a result, the firm's net income increases by 28.0 percent from $300 to $384. If this $384 is viewed as a perpetuity as before and discounted back at the 12 percent cost of equity, the market value of the equity also increases by 28 percent to $3,200 from $2,500.

We might also ask what happens to the market value of the firm's debt. One indication for this is to go back and look at the times interest earned (TIE) or interest coverage ratio, which was defined in Chapter 4 as EBIT divided by interest expense. At sales of $1,000, if we divided the EBIT of $542 by the interest expense of $42, the TIE ratio was 12.90, which is very high. This means that there was $12.90 of EBIT available for every dollar of interest payments, so the firm's EBIT could drop precipitously and still be able to cover the interest payments. At the new sales and EBIT levels, the coverage ratio increases to 16.24 (i.e., $682 ÷ $42), which means the debt is even safer.

This might mean that the debt is marginally less risky, but as we discussed earlier, debt is normally issued under a trust indenture that indicates how much the firm can issue. For example, with the Terasen Gas Utility indenture discussed in Chapter 18, it could issue as much debt as it wanted provided it satisfied the new issue interest coverage ratio test. As a result, with a higher coverage ratio, the bond holders would expect the firm to issue more debt, so that the required return on the debt would stay the same and all the increased value *drops through* to the common shareholders.[11] So with a constant market value for the firm's debt, the overall firm value increases from $3,200 to $3,700.

Now let's consider what happens if sales drop by 20 percent to $800. Table 20-6 illustrates how the income statement would appear in this case.

Table 20-6 The Income Statement after a 20% Sales Decrease	
Sales	$800
Variable costs	240
Fixed costs	158
EBIT	402
Interest	42
Tax (40%)	144
Net income	216

Now the effect of fixed operating and financial costs works in reverse. With fixed operating costs of $158, the firm's EBIT drops by 26 percent to $402 and then with fixed interest costs the net income drops by 28 percent to $216. If this net income is expected to continue in perpetuity, then discounting it at 12 percent gives an equity market value of $1,800.

With the lower sales level, the TIE ratio drops from 12.90 to 9.57. This is still very high, so the sales drop would not unduly concern the firm's bond holders

---

[11] Note that some drops through to the government since with a proportional corporate income tax, the government is a compulsory shareholder in all private sector activity.

and the market value of the debt may stay the same. The result is that the overall firm value drops from $3,200 to $2,500 and is again fully borne by the shareholders.

This example illustrates the basic proposition that risk *drops down* through the income statement. The first claim on the firm's sales is the variable costs. Remember from microeconomics that the firm will not produce anything unless it covers its variable costs; otherwise, it is increasing its losses as it produces more. The next claim is the fixed operating costs such as leases on cars and equipment and space rentals. These costs are not tied to the level of sales and are incurred regardless of the level of sales. Once the EBIT is determined, the first financial claim is that of the debt holders since it is a fixed contractual commitment. The last and residual claimant is that of the equity holders. When times are good and sales increase, net income increases proportionately more than sales, depending on the size of the firm's fixed operational and financial commitments. This sensitivity was referred to in Chapter 4 as the degree of total leverage (DTL), which in our example is 1.4, indicating that for every 1 percent variation in sales, net income varied by 1.4 percent (i.e., a 20 percent change in sales caused a 28 percent change in net income).

The example also indicates the residual nature of the common shareholders and the fact that they are last in line. As the firm's sales drop, everyone has a higher priority claim than that of the common shareholders, so they see much greater volatility in their return than either the debt holders or others with a stake in the firm's operations.

Revisiting Rothmans Inc.

To show how realistic this example is, we revisit the balance sheet of Rothmans Inc., which was first introduced in Chapter 3 (it is also reproduced with accompanying notes in Appendix I at the end of the textbook).

Table 20-7   Rothmans Inc. Balance Sheet

Consolidated Balance Sheets

March 31 *(in thousands of dollars)*	2006	2005	2004
Assets			
Current Assets:			
Cash and cash equivalents	48,364	23,255	46,978
Short-term investments	81,867	168,740	137,929
Accounts receivable	11,795	32,119	31,993
Inventories (note 4)	206,433	209,819	198,941
Prepaid expenses	1,835	1,322	2,123
Total current assets	350,294	435,255	417,964
Property, plant and equipment (note 5)	76,298	69,149	56,292
Future income taxes (note 10)	6,301	8,831	7,993
Prepaid pension benefit cost (note 9)	13,295	12,003	11,738
Other assets	2,887	3,290	2,770
	449,075	528,528	496,757

Liabilities

Current Liabilities:

Accounts payable and accrued liabilities	42,618	47,445	37,021
Excise and other taxes payable	67,680	79,578	77,587
Dividend payable to minority shareholder of subsidiary company	10,761	-	-
Income taxes payable	20,437	21,475	30,178
Total current liabilities	141,496	148,498	144,786
Other long-term liabilities	2,399	2,167	1,468
Other employee future benefits (note 9)	33,444	33,497	30,439
Long-term debt (note 6)	149,751	149,708	150,000
Minority interest in subsidiary company	8,125	950	1,567
	335,215	334,820	328,260
Shareholders' Equity			
Capital stock (notes 7 and 8)	45,347	41,974	38,869
Retained earnings	68,513	151,734	129,628
Total shareholders' equity	113,860	193,708	168,497
	449,075	528,528	496,757

Approved by the Board:

Pierre Des Marais II, O.C.
Director

John Barnett
Director

For 2006, Rothmans' financial structure was $449.075 million. However, if we ignore non-interest-bearing liabilities or more generally liabilities that are not explicitly an investment in the firm, the invested capital in Rothmans equals the long-term debt of $149.751 million and the common equity of $113.860 million. However, we also add to this common equity figure the minority interest figure of $8.125 million, to get a total common equity figure of $121.985 million. Remember from our discussion of accounting that the financial statements are *consolidated*, so that all of the subsidiary's debt is included on Rothmans Inc.'s balance sheet even if Rothmans Inc. does not own 100 percent of a subsidiary. To make sure we don't bias the statements by including all the debt and only part of the shareholders' equity, the equity in a subsidiary that is not 100 percent owned is included as minority interest. All the other accounting items such as the payables and the potential health liability and other benefits that may be payable in the future to employees are ignored. So Rothmans' book debt-equity ratio is 149.751 ÷ 121.985 or 1.228, which is slightly above average for Canadian companies. As discussed in Chapter 4, Rothmans' 2006 debt-equity ratio figure is significantly higher than the 2005 figure of 0.769. Since the debt figures are virtually identical for Rothmans in both years, this increase can be largely attributed to the dramatic decline in its equity figure during 2006 due to the payment of a large special dividend during that year.

However, as we noted before, Rothmans' share price is significantly higher than its book value per share of $1.678. With 67.856 million shares outstanding

---

[12] Rothmans has some stock options outstanding, but they are not material in terms of equity market value.

at the end of 2006 and a $20.25 share price, the market value of its equity is approximately $1,374.084 million (i.e., $20.25 × 67.856 million).[12] Rothmans' long-term debt carries a 5.32 percent coupon and sells for very close to its book value, so for simplicity reasons we will assume the market value of its debt equals the book value of $149.751 million. Therefore, Rothmans' total market value of debt plus equity is $1,523.835 million, and its market valued debt and equity ratios are approximately 10.90 percent and 89.10 percent, respectively. What these financing weights mean is that estimating the WACC for Rothmans Inc. is almost the same thing as estimating its cost of equity capital, since it is overwhelmingly equity financed in terms of market value weights.

As before, we can ask what is driving this market value and can note from the calculations in Chapter 4 that Rothmans' ROE in 2006 was 87.36 percent, which as we noted before is incredibly high, and was inflated in 2006 due to the decline in Rothmans' equity value. We can also note that its market-to-book ratio was 12.07 (i.e., $20.25 ÷ $1.678), which indicates that this ROE is significantly higher than what investors require given the risk of investing in Rothmans. So if we plug into our market-to-book formula (Equation 20-5), we get the following:

$$\frac{P}{BVPS} = \frac{ROE}{K_e} = \frac{0.8736}{K_e} = 12.07$$

So, $K_e = 0.8736 \div 12.07 = 0.0724 = 7.24\%$

This suggests an estimate of the required return by Rothmans' equity investors of 7.24 percent, which appears reasonable. However, this is probably just a coincidence since the 2006 ROE that we used to determine this rate was abnormally high. Unfortunately this approach to estimating K_e is inadequate because this market-to-book equation was derived assuming that the income available for the common equity holders is a perpetuity and does not grow. While this is a useful assumption in discussing the general idea of the cost of capital, in reality there are few firms that fit the perpetuity (i.e., no-growth) model. As a result, we have to consider more general equity valuation models and what they mean for estimating the cost of common equity. These models either explicitly adjust for risk or take into account a firm's future growth prospects.

CONCEPT REVIEW QUESTIONS

1. Distinguish between operating and financial leverage.

2. Why do we say that equity holders bear the brunt of the effects of leverage?

20.5 GROWTH MODELS AND THE COST OF COMMON EQUITY

The Importance of Adjusting for Growth

When we talk of adjusting for growth, we are referring to forecasting a firm's future earnings and dividends. One way of assessing the importance of a firm's growth prospects is to look at the stock market's time horizon and to estimate the value of the firm's current dividend when viewed as a perpetuity, and then compare this value with the stock price. If the values are significantly different, then it means that the stock market is valuing something other than the firm's current earnings and dividends. Table 20-8 breaks down the stock price for a number of stocks into this no-growth perpetuity value and the remaining percentage of the stock price, which is attributed to future growth opportunities.

Table 20-8 Stock Prices and Growth Prospects

	Stock Market Time Horizon				
Company	Price ($)	DPS ($)	Dividend Yield (%)	Perpetuity ($)	Growth Value (%)
AGF	25.75	0.283	1.10	5.66	78.0
BC Gas	30.60	1.13	3.70	22.60	26.0
CAE	11.50	0.161	1.40	3.22	72.0
Dennings	3.50	0.102	2.90	2.04	42.0
EL Financial	285	0.570	0.2	11.40	96.0
GSW(A)	26.75	0.428	1.6	8.56	68.0
Hammersen	14.05	0.197	1.4	3.94	72.0
Intrawest	6.95	0.292	4.2	5.84	16.0
Jannock	29.60	0.148	0.5	2.96	90.0
Average			1.89		62.22

Source: Booth, Laurence. Table 1 from "What Drives Shareholder Value." *Financial Intelligence* IV-6, Spring 1999.

The firms in Table 20-8 were chosen randomly as the first firm in each alphabetical group that paid a dividend, according to the stock market pages of the *Financial Post*. The first column gives the share price, the second the dividend yield, and the third the dividend per share (DPS). The fourth column gives the perpetuity value of the dividend using the yield on conventional preferred shares (which was 5 percent at the time) to value each firm's dividend. This is the value of the shares if nothing changed and the firm paid this dividend forever. The final column gives the proportion of the share price not explained by the dividend, which by definition is the value attributed to the firm's growth prospects. Overall, an average of 62.22 percent of the market value of this sample of firms could be attributed to growth opportunities and the remaining 37.78 percent to the present value of the current dividend. However, there is huge variation: from a low for Intrawest of only 16 percent attributed to growth, to a high for EL Financial with 96 percent of the share price attributed to growth. The important point of the data in the table is that the simple perpetuity model only works for firms with no growth prospects and the data show that this is only a valid assumption for a limited number of firms, if any.[13]

[13] Note that the data also show why the stock market reacts so quickly to news about a firm's future prospects. With so much of the value of most firms' share price coming from future growth, small changes in these future prospects have a huge impact on the share price. It also indicates how "far-sighted" the stock market is.

In Chapter 7, we discussed how to value common shares when the earnings were not expected to be constant in perpetuity. The general equation was that the value of a common share was equal to the present value of its dividends. In order to make this equation practical, we had to impose some assumptions, otherwise we would be forced into discounting dividends to infinity, since common shares have no maturity date. One of the most important models that we discussed at that time was the constant growth version of the dividend discount model (DDM), as expressed in Equation 7-7, which determines the present value of a *growing* perpetuity. We discuss this model in the next subsection.

The Constant Growth Model

The constant growth DDM is commonly referred to as the Gordon model after Professor Myron Gordon of the University of Toronto. The basic valuation equation was introduced in Chapter 7, and is reproduced below:

$$P_0 = \frac{D_1}{K_e - g}$$

[20-15]

where, the price of a share (P_0) equals the expected dividend (D_1) divided by the required return by common share investors, minus the forecast *long-run growth rate* (g) in dividends and earnings.

As discussed in Chapter 7, we can rearrange this equation to estimate the common equity investors' discount rate or required rate of return. This process is called the DCF method for estimating the investors' required rate of return. The equation for doing so is:

$$K_e = \frac{D_1}{P_0} + g$$

[20-16]

In this equation, the required rate of return is composed of the expected dividend yield (D_1/P_0) plus the expected long-run growth rate (g). The long-run growth rate is then the estimate of the increase in the share price and the investors' capital gain. As discussed previously, this is the appropriate cost of equity capital for the firm when the firm can raise the required funds internally (i.e., using reinvested profits). We illustrate how to use this equation in the following example.

Example 20-4: Determining the Cost of Common Equity—Internal Funds

Let's revisit firm ABC from Examples 20-1 through 20-3, and assume the firm paid a dividend per share last year of $1.00, which is expected to grow at 5 percent per year indefinitely. Recall that its share price is $25. Estimate the cost of common equity using internal funds.

Solution

First, we need to find D_1:

$D_1 = D_0 (1 + g) = \$1.00 (1.05) = \$1.05$

Now we can use Equation 20-16 to estimate K_e:

$$K_e = \frac{D_1}{P_0} + g = \frac{1.05}{25} + .05 = .042 + .05 = .0920 = 9.20\%$$

The equation above shows how we can estimate the cost of common equity for a firm if it does not need to issue new common equity, since it is simply the return required by common equity investors. However, what if ABC needs to raise new common equity financing through a share issue? In this case, we need to account for the share issuance costs as discussed previously, and it turns out that the adjustment to Equation 20-16 is quite straightforward. We simply replace the share price (P_0) with the net proceeds (NP) received by the firm. This accounts for the fact that the firm does not receive the full share price that investors are willing to pay, since a portion of these funds goes to pay for issuing costs. We provide the equation below, where we denote the cost of issuing new common equity as K_{ne}.

[20-17]

$$K_{ne} = \frac{D_1}{NP} + g$$

Example 20-5: Determining the Cost of Common Equity—New Issues

We revisit firm ABC from Example 20-4, and assume the firm can issue new shares with net after-tax flotation costs of 5 percent of the share price. Estimate the cost of new common equity to the firm.

Solution

First, we need to find NP:

$$NP = P_0 (1 - .05) = \$25 (0.95) = \$23.75$$

Now we can use Equation 20-17 to estimate K_{ne}:

$$K_{ne} = \frac{D_1}{NP} + g = \frac{1.05}{23.75} + .05 = .0442 + .05 = .0942 = 9.42\%$$

So, we can see that the firm's cost of equity is 0.22 percent higher for new share issues than when it uses internal funds.

Before we proceed further, it is important to note that Equations 20-15 and 20-16 are the same; therefore, if Equation 20-15 does not hold, then neither does Equation 20-16, nor does Equation 20-17. The reason for mentioning this is that Equations 20-16 and 20-17 are commonly used to estimate the cost of equity capital, but the assumptions used to derive them are often forgotten. As a result, it is easy to misuse them.

Consider the case of a firm that pays no dividends and is growing at 20 percent per year and this growth rate is expected to continue for the foreseeable future. A simple application of Equation 20-16 would suggest the cost of equity capital (internal funds) is 20 percent. Yet if we go back to Equation 20-15 and plug in 20 percent as a growth rate for a zero dividend paying firm, we get results that make no sense. The reason for this is that 20 percent *cannot* be a long-run growth rate, since in deriving Equation 20-15, it is assumed that the growth rate is constant forever and that the dividends start from a positive amount. If nominal GDP is growing at 5 to 6 percent a year, a firm that is growing at 20 percent will be capturing an ever bigger share of GDP. In fact, it is easy to show that such a firm would eventually be bigger than the whole economy. In this case, the assumption of constant growth used to derive Equation 20-15 is implausible, so that using Equation 20-16 or 20-17 to estimate the cost of equity capital is *wrong*.

Unfortunately what often happens is that people try to squeeze the data used in Equations 20-16 and 20-17 to try to make them work; for example, by assuming a small dividend, and then reducing the short-run growth forecast to bring it more in line with what is possible in the long run. However, you cannot torture a model that doesn't fit the assumptions of a particular firm. Instead, you need to use a model that better fits the firm, such as the multi-stage growth models that were discussed in Chapter 7. Before discussing how to use these models, let's explore the constant growth model a bit more.

Growth and ROE

In Chapter 7 we pointed out that one way of estimating growth was the sustainable growth method, where the growth rate was the product of the firm's retention rate (b), defined as 1 minus the firm's payout ratio, times its forecast ROE as shown below:

$$g = b \times ROE$$

[20-18]

Here it becomes obvious that even if the firm retains all of its profits and reinvests within the firm, it is not plausible that it can earn a 20 percent ROE on this investment forever. Such an assumption would imply that no other firm can enter the industry and compete with the firm to also earn these high ROEs. If other firms can enter the market, which will normally be the case, then these high ROEs will be reduced to normal levels due to competitive pressures.

What has to be remembered is that Professor Gordon developed this model for use in public utility regulation where the allowed ROEs should be reasonable and we do not get the problem of rapid growth rates. Further it is a product of regulation that all common equity earns virtually the same regulated ROE. In this case, the average and marginal ROE is exactly the same and every dollar the firm retains earns the same ROE. In contrast, many extremely profitable firms cannot reinvest at the same ROE since they cannot find opportunities as good as their existing ones. In determining the growth rate, the ROE is the future growth rate on incremental investment and this may be greater or smaller than what the firm is currently earning.

However, let's return to the constant growth DDM with the assumption of a constant ROE for the time being. Substituting the sustainable growth rate as expressed in Equation 20-18 (i.e., b $\times$ ROE) into the constant growth DDM in place of g, we get:

$$P_0 = \frac{D_1}{K_e - b \times ROE}$$

[20-19]

Further, we can then recognize that the expected dividend per share (D_1) is the expected earnings per share (X_1) times the dividend payout rate (i.e., one minus the retention rate), since a dollar can either be paid out or retained and reinvested within the firm. Making this substitution for D_1 we get:

$$P_0 = \frac{X_1(1-b)}{K_e - b \times ROE}$$

[20-20]

This equation shows that the price per share is determined by the firm's forecast earnings per share, its dividend payout $(1 - b)$, its ROE, and the required return by common equity shareholders (K_e).

One important use of Equation 20-20 is to see how growth and the firm's ROE affects its share price. Suppose, for example, that the firm's retention rate is 50 percent, its cost of equity capital is 12 percent, and its forecast earnings per share figure is $2. If the firm's ROE is 12 percent, then the forecast growth rate is 6 percent (i.e., 12% × 0.5) and the forecast dividend per share is $1 using the 50 percent payout ratio. In this case, the shares are worth $16.67; that is, $1 divided by 6 percent (i.e., $K_e - g = 12\% - 6\%$). Now suppose instead of a 12 percent ROE, the firm is expected to earn 10 percent or 14 percent. At a 10 percent ROE, the firm's forecast growth rate drops to 5 percent and its share price is only $14.29, whereas at a 14 percent ROE, the firm's growth rate is 7 percent and its shares are worth $20.

What this example illustrates is that the higher the growth rate, the higher the share price, since investors will forecast larger future dividends and earnings. If we rearrange Equation 20-20, we get the following variation of the constant growth DDM, which is:

[20-21]

$$K_e = \frac{D_1}{P_0} + g = \frac{X_1(1-b)}{P_0} + b \times ROE$$

In this equation, the first term is the forecast dividend yield and the second the sustainable growth rate. However, note what happens when we use this equation to estimate the cost of equity capital (internal) for our three growth scenarios, as depicted in Table 20-9.

Table 20-9   Growth and K_e

ROE	P_0	Expected Dividend Yield	Sustainable Growth Rate	K_e
10%	14.29	7%	5%	12%
12%	16.67	6%	6%	12%
14%	20.00	5%	7%	12%

Since the shares were valued using a constant 12 percent discount rate, when we "reverse engineer" from the share price we get the same 12 percent back as the estimate of the cost of equity capital. In this case, the higher forecast growth rate leads to a higher market price and a lower dividend yield. Generally firms with high dividend yields have lower forecast growth rates and vice versa. However, there is no reason for the cost of equity capital to be the same, since the composition of the return between dividends and growth changes. This is a question of the firm's dividend policy, which will be discussed in detail in Chapter 22.

However, note that the firm's retention rate, and thus its dividend payout ratio, is reflected in the constant growth DDM as "b." Table 20-10 gives the share price if this retention rate changes under the three scenarios where the firm's ROE is 10, 12, or 14 percent.

Table 20-10   Retention Rates, ROE, and Share Prices

	ROE		
b	0.14	0.12	0.10
0.40	18.75	16.67	15.00
0.41	18.85	16.67	14.94
0.42	18.95	16.67	14.87
0.43	19.06	16.67	14.81
0.44	19.18	16.67	14.74
0.45	19.30	16.67	14.67
0.46	19.42	16.67	14.59
0.47	19.56	16.67	14.52
0.48	19.70	16.67	14.44
0.49	19.84	16.67	14.37
0.50	20.00	16.67	14.29
0.51	20.16	16.67	14.20
0.52	20.34	16.67	14.12
0.53	20.52	16.67	14.03
0.54	20.72	16.67	13.94
0.55	20.93	16.67	13.85
0.56	21.15	16.67	13.75
0.57	21.39	16.67	13.65
0.58	21.65	16.67	13.55
0.59	21.93	16.67	13.44
0.60	22.22	16.67	13.33

Let's look at the last column in the table, where the ROE = 10% first. We already saw that at a 50 percent retention rate, its share price was $14.29, but now we see that its share price *decreases* as the firm retains more money and reinvests within the firm. In contrast, when ROE = 14%, the share price increases as the firm retains more, while for the 12 percent ROE firm, the share price is independent of the retention rate.

The reason for the above results is that when the firm's ROE is 10 percent, it is less than the investors' required rate of return of 12 percent. As a result, as the firm invests more by increasing its retention rate, the shareholders are unhappy. Why would they invest in a firm where they require a 12 percent rate of return and be happy with the firm investing at 10 percent? In this case the share valuation model is telling the firm's management to reduce investment and return the funds saved as a larger dividend. The shareholders can then take these funds and invest them elsewhere to earn their 12 percent required rate of return. Conversely where the firm is expected to earn 14 percent, the shareholders are saying the opposite: "Don't give us a dividend since we can only earn 12 percent elsewhere, please reinvest more and earn 14 percent." As a result, the share price increases as the firm invests more. Finally, for the 12 percent ROE case, the shareholders are saying: "We don't care what you do, since you are not doing anything for us if you invest or give us a dividend." As a result, there is no impact on the share price.

The above example is very important in finance. For a long time it was felt the above result was due to the firm's *dividend policy*, since the firm's retention rate and dividend payout are changing. However, this is not true. What is really changing is the amount of investment the firm is making and the stock market is valuing whether the firm is creating or destroying value. When $ROE>K_e$, the firm is creating value when it reinvests and when $ROE<K_e$, it is destroying value. This result is independent of how much the firm decides to pay out as a dividend since it can always raise money to pay a dividend. This points out another aspect to the cost of capital: not only is it important to value the firm's shares, but it is also a **hurdle rate** for making investment decisions. This is the meaning of the phrase *required return*: unless an investment jumps this hurdle, it destroys value and should not be undertaken. We will discuss this more at the end of the chapter.

hurdle rate the return on an investment required to create value; below this rate, an investment would destroy value

The example with the different ROEs and different retention rates also emphasizes another key point in finance: there is a big difference between a *growing* firm and a *growth* firm. When $ROE=K_e$, the share price was independent of how much the firm reinvested. If the firm paid out all its earnings and did not grow at all ($b = 0$), the share price is $16.67, whereas if it reinvests all of its earnings ($b = 1$) and grows at 12 percent per year, the share price is still $16.67 (This ignores taxes, which were discussed in Chapter 18.) This is an example of a growing firm where if it simply reinvests at its cost of capital it is "not doing anything" for the shareholders and they don't care whether it is growing or not. Note also that the earnings yield for this growing firm at a 50 percent retention rate is 12 percent, which equals its forecast earnings per share divided by its stock price (i.e., $2 ÷ $16.67). So for growing firms, the earnings yield is a good estimate of their cost of equity capital.

On the other hand, when $ROE>K_e$, the firm is doing something that the shareholders cannot do, which is reinvest at 14 percent. We call these firms growth firms, and say they have growth opportunities. In this case, note that the earnings yield is $2 ÷ $20 or 10 percent, which underestimates the required return by common shareholders. Finally, there are some firms that destroy shareholder value by investing where $ROE<K_e$. For these firms, the earnings yield is $2 ÷ $14.29 or 14 percent, which overestimates their cost of internal equity. These results confirm that the reason the earnings yield is not a good estimate of a firm's cost of internal equity capital is not whether or not its dividends or earnings are growing, but whether it is investing at rates of return that are either greater or less than its cost of equity capital, and whether growth opportunities exist.

Multi-Stage Growth Models

multi-stage growth DDM a version of the DDM that accounts for different levels of growth in earnings and dividends

Another version of the DCF model to consider is the **multi-stage growth DDM**, which was also discussed in Chapter 7. In practice there is no limit to the extent of the growth stages, but let's consider a very simple case in which the firm has some investment today, which we assume equals the firm's book value per share (*BVPS*), which is earning a return (ROE_1) in perpetuity. The firm is expected to invest a similar amount next year (*Inv*), which will again earn a return (ROE_2) in perpetuity. This particular version of the multi-stage model can be expressed as:

$$P_0 = \frac{ROE_1 \times BVPS}{K_e} + \frac{Inv}{(1 + K_e)}(\frac{ROE_2 - K_e}{K_e})$$

[20-22]

The first term in this equation equals the perpetuity value of the current earnings, as discussed previously, where the firm is expected to earn an $ROE = ROE_1$. The second term represents further investment (Inv), which we assume is invested at ROE_2, and is discounted back one period, since it is one period further off in the future, but adds a perpetual amount represented by the difference between the firm's ROE on this investment of ROE_2 minus K_e. As before, if $ROE_2 = K_e$, then this future investment adds nothing to the value of the firm, since it does not create value, and the second term will equal zero. However, if $ROE_2 > K_e$ then this future investment adds value, with the amount of value depending on the amount of investment (Inv) that can be invested at this rate, and by how much ROE_2 exceeds K_e. Equation 20-22 is a basic approach to valuation that breaks out the value of shares into the **present value of existing opportunities (PVEO)**, the first term, and the **present value of growth opportunities (PVGO)**, the second term.

present value of existing opportunities (PVEO) the value of the firms current operations assuming no new investment

We apply this equation by setting the investment amount arbitrarily at $20 for both periods and use a discount rate of 12.0 percent to value this stock. We now consider four scenarios:

present value of growth opportunities (PVGO) the net present value today of the firm's future investments

A. In this scenario, PVEO is high, with $ROE_1 = 20\%$, BVPS = $20, and PVEO= $33.33. The expected ROE next period is expected to remain high at 20%, so PVGO = $11.90. Thus, the share price would be $45.23.

B. In this scenario, $ROE_2 \leq 12\%$, so the firm has no PVGO, but we assume it has the same high ROE for current earnings of 20 percent, so its share price would be $33.33.

C. In this scenario, the firm has very poor current earnings, with $ROE_1 = 2\%$, but it has the same great future prospects as under scenario A. Thus, its PVEO equals $3.33, and its PVGO would be $11.90, translating into a share price of $15.23.

D. In the final scenario, the firm has the same poor current prospects as under scenario C, so its PVEO would be $3.33. On top of that, it is destroying value by reinvesting in the future at an ROE_2 of 10%, so PVGO is $-$2.98$, and its share price would be a trivial $0.35 (i.e., $3.33 - $2.98)!

If we classify these four cases as types of firms, we have the following:

A: High PVEO and high PVGO

B: High PVEO and low PVGO

C: Low PVEO and high PVGO

D: Low PVEO and low PVGO

We can put them into a two-by-two matrix and classify them according to a conventional corporate description pioneered by the Boston Consulting Group as shown in Figure 20-1.

FIGURE   20-1

*Growth
Opportunities and
Firm Type*

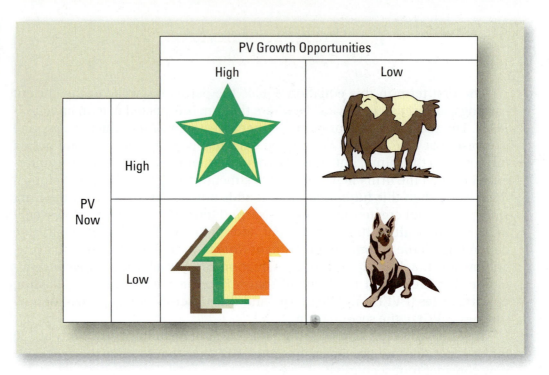

star a firm with high
PVEO and high PVGO

cash cow a firm with
high PVEO but low PVGO

turnaround a firm with
low PVEO and high PVGO

dog a firm with low
PVEO and low PVGO

Firm A would be classified as a **star** in Figure 20-1, having everything going for it, both very good PVEO and excellent PVGO. Firm B would be the **cash cow**, generating significant cash flows from its current opportunities and thus possessing a high PVEO, but it has no good investment opportunities, so its PVGO is zero. Firm C is the **turnaround** candidate, where its current operations are a drag on performance so PVEO is low, but everything is about the future so its PVGO is high. Finally, Firm D is the **dog**, with poor current operations so that its PVEO is low, and on top of that it has been investing in projects that provide returns that are lower than its cost of internal equity, so that it possesses a negative PVGO.

We developed these four stylistic views of firm valuation to show that for every firm, there is a "story" that has to match its valuation. If you can understand this, then estimating its cost of equity capital becomes easier as you then know the biases in using DCF estimates. For example, A has the highest market price since both PVEO and PVGO are high. This could be a large capitalization stock (large cap) such as General Electric where everything is going right. The cash cow would be a utility like TransCanada Pipelines with an excellent profitable core business, but limited growth prospects. The cash cow might also be called a value stock, depending on its price. The turnaround company could be a pure growth stock, with very limited current value, but great growth potential. Classic examples of turnarounds or growth stocks would be the Internet and tech stocks of the late 1990s or companies like Google and Yahoo! today, where investors are paying a huge premium for the PVGO. Finally, dogs *should* be scarce, since they are candidates for hostile takeovers. Regardless of the poor quality of their current operations (low PVEO), their value could be increased just by stopping them from throwing good money after bad by investing at less than its equity cost.

Note that we valued these four firms using the same 12 percent discount rate so the cost of equity capital is exactly the same. However, the market-to-book ratio and earnings yield are different for each, as shown in Table 20-11.

Table 20-11	**The Impact of Growth Opportunities on Share Prices**	
	Earnings Yield (%)	**Market-to-Book**
Star	8.84	2.26
Cash cow	12.00	1.67
Turnaround	2.63	0.76
Dog	114.29%	0.02

The actual numbers are not that important but the critical feature is that the star and the turnaround have very low earnings yields (or high P/E ratios). Both of these types of companies would be regarded as growth firms, since much of the value comes from PVGO. In the case of the turnaround company, its PVEO actually depresses its stock price. For both of these types of companies, DCF estimation methods are quite unreliable due to the importance of PVGO. The cash cow gives back the true discount rate, since there is no PVGO, and it may be viewed as a perpetuity. For the dog, the earnings yield is very high and exceeds 100 percent, since it is forecast to lose value from its future investments, which depresses the share price and thus increases the earnings yield.

The point of these examples is that you have to understand the firm before mechanically applying the DCF formulas, since otherwise it is very easy to make mistakes. The DCF models work best for non-growth firms and for the market as a whole, where growth opportunities are moderate and easiest to estimate. A good example of the latter is the application of the constant growth model by the U.S. Federal Reserve System in what is known as the "Fed model," which is discussed next.[14]

The Fed Model

The Fed model was used to estimate whether the stock market was over- or undervalued and whether the U.S. Fed should "talk down" market values that might be excessive and cause problems if they collapsed. The exact equation used was:

$$\frac{V_{actual}}{V_{Fed}} = \frac{V_{actual}}{Exp(EPS)/(K_{TBond} - 1.0\%)}$$

[20-23]

In this equation, V_{actual} was the actual value for the U.S. stock market, and V_{Fed} was the estimate from the Fed's model, which was the expected earnings per share on the Standard and Poor's 500 Index as reported by security market analysts ($Exp(EPS)$), divided by the yield on the long-term U.S. Treasury Bond (K_{TBond}) minus 1.0 percent. That is,

$$V_{Fed} = \frac{Exp(EPS)}{(K_{TBond} - 1.0\%)}$$

[20-24]

Valuation is easier when you aggregate across all securities since you remove the *unsystematic risk* attached to individual securities, which was

---

[14] Edward Yardeni, "US Stock Valuation Models," Deutsche Bank, October 4, 2000.

discussed in Chapters 8 and 9. In the case of the market as a whole, after-tax earnings should grow at approximately the long-run real growth rate of GDP plus inflation, while the cost of equity for the market as whole should be the Treasury Bond yield plus a market risk premium. We will talk about risk premiums later, but with inflation running at about 1.0 percent, if the market risk premium is close to the real GDP growth rate we get the denominator of the Fed model.

The actual "performance" of the Fed model is illustrated in Figure 20-2, where we can see that the model tracked the U.S. equity market quite well for much of the period until the late 1990s, when actual market values deviated significantly from the values implied by the Fed model. The stock market actually peaked in August 2000, and then went into a freefall that lasted almost three years. This suggests that investors who used the signals provided by the Fed model and decided to get out of the stock market in 2000, when it indicated significant overvaluation, would have saved themselves from large losses.

FIGURE 20-2

Fed's Stock Valuation Model

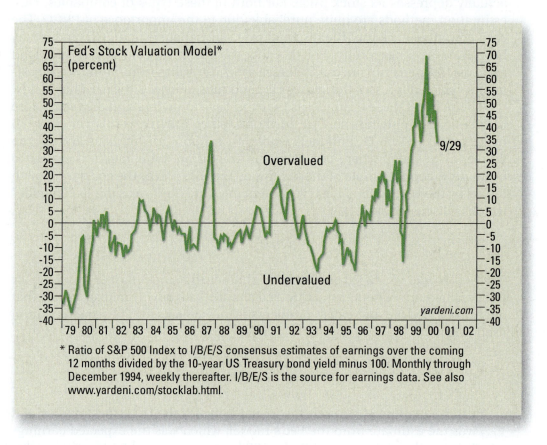

* Ratio of S&P 500 Index to I/B/E/S consensus estimates of earnings over the coming 12 months divided by the 10-year US Treasury bond yield minus 100. Monthly through December 1994, weekly thereafter. I/B/E/S is the source for earnings data. See also www.yardeni.com/stocklab.html.

Denoting $E(EPS)$ as X, we can see that if the Fed model is rearranged it also indicates that the market is fairly valued when the following condition exists:

[20-25]

$$\frac{X}{P_{S\&P\,500}} = K_{Tbond} - 1.0\%$$

This equation says that the earnings yield on the S&P 500 is equal to the long-term Treasury Bond yield minus 1.0 percent. As discussed previously, the earnings yield is the appropriate discount rate for the no-growth case (i.e., for perpetuities), whereas we would expect the market as a whole to grow at the nominal GDP growth rate. So if this nominal GDP growth rate is 5.0 percent, then another way of interpreting the Fed model is that the required return on the equity market as whole averages the long-term Treasury Bond Yield plus a 4.0 percent risk premium (i.e., the 5% nominal GDP growth rate − 1%). With U.S. Treasury Bonds yielding 5 percent in August 2006, this would indicate an overall cost of equity for the U.S. market of 9.0 percent, which seemed reasonable at the time.

CONCEPT REVIEW QUESTIONS

1. Explain how we can use the constant growth DDM to estimate the cost of firms' internal common equity, as well as the cost of new common share issues.

2. Explain the relationship among ROE, retention rates, and firm growth.

3. How can we relate the existence of multiple growth stages to four commonly used firm classifications?

4. Describe the Fed model and how it may be used to estimate the required rate of return of the market as a whole.

20.6 RISK-BASED MODELS AND THE COST OF COMMON EQUITY

Using the CAPM to Estimate the Cost of Common Equity

risk-based models models that estimate costs based on the associated risks

The previous section showed that the DCF model could be rearranged to estimate the investors' required return on a firm's common shares. However, we also discussed how the model performs poorly when applied to growth stocks, which pay low dividends and/or display high growth rates. In these situations, it makes sense to rely more heavily on **risk-based models**. The most important risk-based model is the **capital asset pricing model (CAPM)**, which was discussed in detail in Chapter 9.

capital asset pricing model (CAPM) a pricing model that uses one factor, beta, to relate expected returns to risk

We can represent the central equation of the CAPM, the *security market line (SML)*, as follows:

$$K_e = R_F + MRP \times \beta_e$$

[20-26]

In this equation, the required return by common shareholders (K_e) is composed of three terms:

1. The **risk-free rate of return** (R_F), which represents compensation for the time value of money.

risk-free rate of return compensation for the time value of money

2. The **market risk premium** (MRP), which is compensation for assuming the risk of the market portfolio, and is defined as $E(R_M) - R_F$, where $E(R_M)$ is the expected return on the market.

market risk premium compensation for assuming the risk of the market portfolio

beta coefficient a measure of a firm's systematic or market risk

3. The **beta coefficient** (β_e) for the firm's common shares, which measures the firm's systematic or market risk, and which represents the contribution that this security makes to the risk of a well-diversified portfolio.

The CAPM is derived as a single period model, but just what is meant by a single period is an unresolved issue, since investment horizons differ across investors. In testing the CAPM, it is common use a 30-day time horizon and yet in making corporate finance decisions, such a short time horizon is rarely useful. In fact, when we talked about the characteristics of common equity, one of the most important was the absence of a maturity date. While an individual investor may invest for 30 days, at that time, they will sell the shares to another investor, so the security is still outstanding. In addition, as we will see when we discuss corporate investment decisions, the cost of capital or WACC is used to evaluate long-term investment decisions made by the firm. For this reason, the risk-free rate used in *corporate* applications of the CAPM is usually the yield on the longest maturity Government of Canada bond, which is currently the 30-year bond.

In order to estimate the market risk premium, we generally use long-run averages supplemented by knowledge of the prevailing economic scenario. The basic idea is that over long periods of time, what people expect to happen should eventually be realized, otherwise they are biased in forming their expectations. In contrast, over short periods of time, it is unlikely that expectations are realized. It's like tossing a die: you may get three consecutive 1s, but if you throw it enough times, eventually one sixth of the time you will get 1s, one sixth of the time you will get 2s, and so on. Similarly, we can consider the performance of the S&P/TSX Composite Index over the 2000 to 2005 period, as reported in Table 20-12.

Table 20-12   Returns on the S&P/TSX Composite Index

	Returns (%)
2000	7.507214
2001	−12.57219
2002	−12.43793
2003	26.72485
2004	14.47972
2005	24.12654

Clearly it is difficult to argue that in any one particular year, the performance of the S&P/TSX Composite Index was what had been expected. For example, nobody would have held shares in either 2001 or 2002 if they expected the stock market to go down! Similarly the performance in 2003 and 2005 was exceptional; indeed, if you consistently earned returns of more than 20 percent, then you would become very rich very quickly!

Table 20-13 (formerly Table 8-2 in Chapter 8) shows estimates of average investment returns over the period 1938 to 2005.

Table 20-13 Average Investment Returns and Standard Deviations (1938 to 2005)			
	Annual Arithmetic Average (%)	Annual Geometric Mean (%)	Standard Deviation of Annual Returns (%)
Government of Canada Treasury Bills	5.20	5.11	4.32
Government of Canada Bonds	6.62	6.24	9.32
Canadian Stocks	11.79	10.60	16.22
U.S. Stocks	13.15	11.76	17.54

Source: Data from Canadian Institute of Actuaries

Over this long period of time, the difference between the average return on bonds and the average return on common equities in Canada was 5.17 percent (i.e., 11.79% − 6.62%), which would represent our long-term risk premium.[15] However, if we use the period since 1956, after which there were some major changes in the structure of Canadian capital markets, the risk premium estimate is smaller. Generally most people believe that the Canadian market risk premium over the long-term bond yield is between 4.0 and 5.5 percent. Therefore, with the 4.3 percent long Canada bond yield that prevailed at the time of writing, the Canadian stock market could be expected to earn around 8.3 percent to 9.8 percent going forward over long periods.

The overall estimate of the stock market's expected return is very important since it is broadly consistent with the result of the Fed model for the United States. Recently TD Economics[16] came up with forward-looking estimates, as presented in Table 20-14.

Table 20-14 Long-Run Financial Projections	
Financial Forecasts	Average Annual Percent Return
Bank of Canada Overnight Rate	4.50
Cash: 3-Month T-bills	4.40
Income: Scotia Universe Bond Index	5.60
Canadian Equities: S&P/TSX Composite Index	7.30
U.S. Equities: S&P 500 Index	7.80
International Non-U.S. Equities: MSCI EAFE Index	7.50

Source: TD Economics

[15] Notice that this figure differs from the market risk premium over the T-bill rate of 6.59 percent, which was alluded to in Chapter 9.

[16] TD Economics, "Rates of Return for the Long Haul," January 26, 2006.

The Scotia Universe Bond Index is a portfolio of long-term bonds maintained by Scotiabank and is riskier than the long Canada bond, since some of the bonds are corporate bonds with default risk. Even so, the TD Economics estimate of the market risk premium is about 3.0 percent over the long Canada bond yield of 4.3 percent. However, remember the discussion in Chapter 8 of arithmetic mean (AM) vs. geometric mean (GM) returns, where we suggested that arithmetic mean returns (or simple averages) are always higher than geometric mean (or compound) returns, and that this difference increases with the variability in the arithmetic returns. In fact, the approximate relationship is provided below:

$$AM = GM + \frac{\sigma^2}{2}$$

With annual stock market returns having a standard deviation of 16 percent as provided in Table 20-13, half of their variance is 1.3 percent, so the long-run market risk premium estimated by TD Economics is consistent with an arithmetic market risk premium of 4.3 percent (i.e., 3.0% + 1.3%). This figure is slightly below the long-run average market risk premium of 5.17 percent since 1938, but is consistent with the post-1956 performance.

Estimating Betas

The final piece of information needed to use the SML to estimate required returns is the beta coefficient, which adjusts the risk of the market to the risk of an individual security, so it is an absolute number like 0.50 for a low-risk security and 1.5 for a high-risk security. The beta coefficient measures the degree to which securities move in relation to market movements: the more they move together, the less diversification gains there are and the riskier the security. Betas are normally estimated using the prior five years' monthly return data, but it is important to realize that if nothing happened during this period, then that will be reflected in the estimate. Conversely if something special happened during this period, then the beta

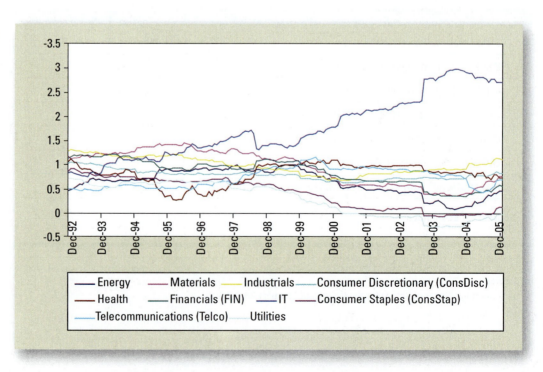

FIGURE 20-3

Estimated Betas for Major Sub Indexes of the S&P/TSX Composite Index

Table 20-15	S&P/TSX Sub Index Beta Estimates									
	Energy	Materials	Industrials	ConsDisc	ConsStap	Health	Fin	IT	Telco	Utilities
1995	0.93	1.41	1.19	0.82	0.68	0.36	0.92	1.25	0.53	0.67
1996	0.93	1.28	1.10	0.83	0.66	0.39	1.02	1.36	0.61	0.65
1997	0.98	1.33	0.97	0.82	0.62	0.60	0.93	1.56	0.62	0.53
1998	0.85	1.12	0.94	0.80	0.60	1.02	1.11	1.40	0.92	0.55
1999	0.91	1.04	0.78	0.73	0.43	1.00	1.00	1.55	1.11	0.30
2000	0.67	0.74	0.73	0.69	0.23	1.10	0.79	1.78	0.92	0.14
2001	0.50	0.60	0.82	0.68	0.10	0.98	0.67	2.12	0.94	−0.03
2002	0.43	0.57	0.86	0.73	0.11	0.99	0.67	2.27	0.92	−0.06
2003	0.27	0.42	0.91	0.74	−0.04	0.85	0.39	2.75	0.82	−0.26
2004	0.17	0.42	1.04	0.81	−0.02	0.84	0.41	2.89	0.55	−0.14
2005	0.48	0.78	1.12	0.84	0.14	0.74	0.58	2.71	0.71	−0.01

Source: Data from *Financial Post* Corporate Analyzer Database

will reflect this.[17] For this reason, we tend to go back over long periods of time and again analyze what happened during the estimation period.

Figure 20-3 gives the beta coefficients estimated for the major sub indexes of the S&P/TSX Composite Index, using the prior five years of monthly data.

Since it is difficult to read the betas of all the major sub indexes from the graph, we also report them in Table 20-15.

What is striking about the estimates and the graph is that one sub index shows rapidly increasing beta coefficients (the IT sub index), whereas most of the other beta coefficients show a constant or decreasing trend. In fact, Consumer Staples and Utilities actually had negative beta estimates, indicating that they moved in the opposite manner to the stock market as a whole, and reduced the risk of a diversified portfolio.

As discussed in Chapter 9, if we sum up all the beta coefficients, their value weighted average has to equal 1.0, which is the beta of the market as a whole. What these estimates indicate is that the IT sub index was very important during this period and as it increased, by definition the other betas *had* to decrease on average. In fact the more recent beta estimates are anomalous, since they reflect the Internet bubble of the late 1990s and subsequent burst in the early 2000s. Figure 20-4 summarizes this phenomenon, showing the stock price of Nortel.

Nortel used to be a telecommunications manufacturer controlled by BCE Inc. However, in the Internet mania of the late 1990s, investor interest shifted to companies making the equipment for the backbone of the Internet. Two Canadian companies, Nortel and JDS Uniphase, attracted a huge amount of interest. As can be seen from Figure 20-4, Nortel's stock price jumped from the $20 to $40 range to peak at over $170, before collapsing to the penny stock range. The prices of JDS and other IT companies followed similar patterns over this time. At one point, Nortel and JDS combined to make up more than one third of the market value of the S&P/TSX Composite Index, and they pushed it up along with them when they soared, and dragged it back down again when they crashed. This is why the IT sub index beta increased so dramatically: it was essentially dictating the major market movements.

---

[17] In other words, beta estimates, particularly those for individual stocks, tend to be very sensitive to the chosen estimation period.

FIGURE 20-4

Nortel Stock Price
(1987-2005)

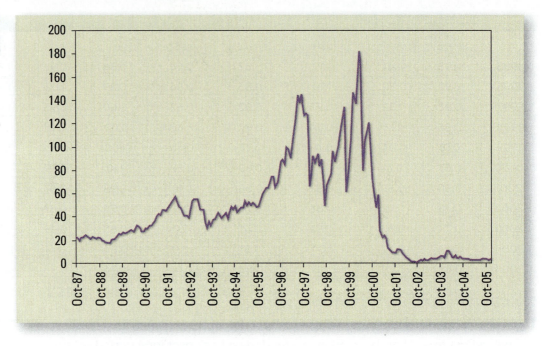

FIGURE 20-4

Nortel Stock Price
(1987-2005)

What this means is that if a repeat of the IT-driven stock market boom and bust is expected again, then these beta estimates are good estimates. If this is not expected to be the case, then these estimates are of little value. Going forward, more reasonable estimates for different sub indexes are those prior to 1998, and the subsequent Internet bubble and bust. During these prior periods, the low-risk sectors like Consumer Staples and the Utilities had betas in the 0.50 to 0.70 range; Consumer Discretionary and Energy betas were slightly higher in the 0.80 to 0.95 range; IT, Materials, and Industrials had betas above 1; and Financials had about "average" risk (i.e., betas close to 1).

FIGURE 20-5

Rothmans Inc. Beta
Estimates

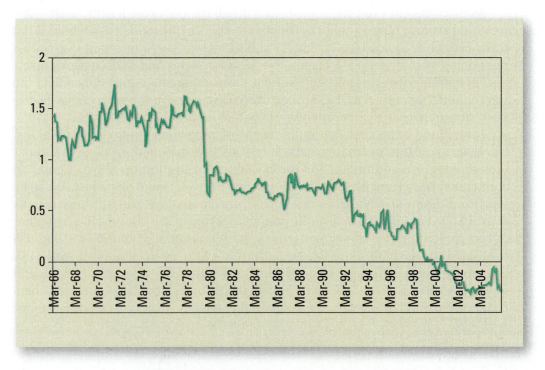

To estimate the risk of an individual company, we could then take the industry grouping as a major input, plus the individual beta estimate. For Rothmans, as a consumer products company, its beta estimates going back to the early 1960s are shown in Figure 20-5.

The Rothmans Inc. (TSX Ticker Symbol: ROC) beta clearly shows a declining trend over time. This decline is exaggerated by the Internet bubble effect since 1998. Prior to that time, its beta had been in the 0.40 to 0.60 range throughout most of the 1990s, indicating a low-risk consumer products company. Using the current long-term Canada bond yield of 4.3 percent, the lower bound of Rothmans' beta estimates of 0.40, and using the lower bound of the estimate for the market risk premium of 4 percent, we estimate Rothmans' cost of equity capital (internal) using the CAPM as:

$$K_e = 4.3 + (4.0) \times (0.40) = 5.90\%$$

If we then use the upper range of the beta estimate of 0.60, and the upper estimate of the MRP of 5.5%, we get:

$$K_e = 4.3 + (5.5) \times (0.60) = 7.60\%$$

This range of 5.90 to 7.60 percent is based on both the low and high ends of the market risk premium and beta ranges. The average of these two estimates of 6.75 percent is consistent with Rothmans' position as a low-risk company.

Now, let's assume that we can use 6.75 percent as the cost of equity for Rothmans and that we can also use the 5.3 percent mentioned previously as its cost of debt. Further, we can estimate its tax rate by returning to its income statement, where we see that for 2006 it had earnings before taxes of $274.829 million and income tax expense of $109.114 million, implying a tax rate of 39.70 percent (i.e., $109.114 ÷ $274.829). Combining these estimates with the estimates of S/V and D/V of 89.10 percent and 10.90 percent determined earlier, we get the following WACC estimate for Rothmans Inc.:

$$\text{WACC} = (0.8910)(6.75) + (0.1090)(5.3)(1 - .3970) = 6.36\%$$

Finally, we conclude this section by revisiting firm ABC from Examples 20-1 through 20-5, and bringing things together for that firm.

Example 20-6: Determining the Cost of Internal Common Equity Using CAPM

Assume the beta for firm ABC from Examples 20-1 through 20-5 is 1.15 and that the risk-free rate is 4.5 percent while the market risk premium is 4.5 percent. Estimate the firm's cost of equity for internal funds using CAPM.

Solution

$$K_e = 4.5 + (4.5) \times (1.15) = 9.68\%$$

Notice that with the CAPM approach, the equity share price is not explicitly considered, which adds a complication if we wanted to estimate the cost of new common equity to the firm. There are two common ways of dealing with this issue. The first is to take the premium over the cost of internal funds that was estimated using the constant growth DDM approach, which does include the price. For this company, the premium was 0.22 percent, since the cost of internal equity was estimated at 9.20 percent, while the cost of new common equity was estimated to be 9.42 percent. However, this will not work when we are unable to use the DDM, which is exactly the time when we will want to use a risk-based approach such as the CAPM, as discussed previously. In this case, we can merely "scale" our estimate of K_e by the following factor, which relates the share price to the net proceeds after flotation costs: P_0/NP. This adjustment leads to the following estimate of the cost of new common equity (K_{ne}):

[20-27]

$$K_{ne} = K_e \times P_0/NP$$

Example 20-7 applies both approaches.

Example 20-7: Determining the Cost of External Common Equity Using CAPM

Use the estimate of internal common equity for firm ABC obtained in Example 20-6 to estimate the firm's cost of external equity.

Solution

Approach #1:

Use the premium determined using the DDM approach, which equals:

$$K_{ne} - K_e = 9.42 - 9.20 = 0.22\%$$

Adding this premium to the estimated K_e of 9.68%, we get:

$$K_{ne} = K_e + 0.22\% = 9.68 + 0.22 = 9.90\%$$

Approach #2:

Adjust K_e:

$$K_{ne} = K_e \times P_0/NP = 9.68\% \ (25/23.75) = 10.19\%$$

So using this approach we get a much larger premium of 0.39 percent.

Example 20-8: Determining the WACC

Use the estimates for firm ABC determined in Examples 20-1 through 20-7. Assume that based on your analysis, you decide to use the common equity costs as determined using the constant growth DDM.

a. Estimate ABC's WACC and MCC assuming it has more than sufficient internal funds to provide the required common equity financing.

b. Estimate ABC's MCC if it needs to issue new common shares to provide the required amount of financing.

Solution

a. Since the firm raises all its common equity internally, we can assume that its WACC equals its MCC.

$$WACC = MCC = K_e \frac{S}{V} + K_p \frac{P}{V} + K_i \frac{D}{V}$$

$$= (9.20)(.511) + (8.16)(.255) + (3.78)(.234) = 7.67\%$$

b. If the firm has to raise new common equity financing, its cost of common equity will rise, as will its MCC.

$$MCC = (9.42)(.511) + (8.16)(.255) + (3.78)(234) = 7.78\%$$

20.7 THE COST OF CAPITAL AND INVESTMENT

If investors in Rothmans want an overall cost of capital of 6.36 percent as calculated in the previous section, this suggests that Rothmans should not reinvest funds within its operations that earn a rate of return less than this *hurdle rate*.[18] Consequently the WACC is not just a valuation tool—it is also used going forward as a tool to evaluate investments. A stylized version of this investment decision is shown in Figure 20-6.

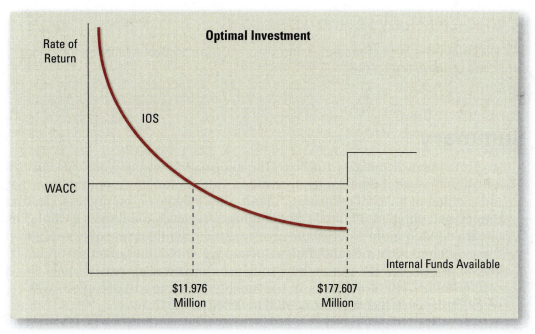

20-6 FIGURE

Rothmans Inc. IOS Schedule (2006)

investment opportunities schedule (IOS) the ranking of a firm's investments from highest to lowest profitability according to the rate of return they are expected to earn

We have previously discussed how to evaluate firm investment decisions in Chapters 13 and 14. Recall that the firm can look at its investments and rank them from highest to lowest profitability according to the rate of return they are expected to earn. This provides us with the downward sloping line in Figure 20-6, indicating the firm's **investment opportunities schedule (IOS)**. This curve

---

[18] This of course assumes that the investments being evaluated are average risk investments for Rothmans.

represents the firms' *demand curve for funds*. Corresponding to this is the firm's *supply curve for funds*, which is initially represented assuming all common equity is supplied by internal funds.

Remember from Chapter 3 that traditional cash flow is net income plus amortization and deferred taxes (i.e., net income plus the non-cash items in the firm's income stream). For Rothmans we indicated in Chapter 3 that cash flow from operations (CFO) less the change in working capital in 2006 was $177.607 million. This is the amount of money that Rothmans had to invest at its WACC of 6.36 percent, and is indicated by the horizontal line. In 2006, Rothmans actually had $5.607 million in net working capital released and made $17.583 million in capital expenditures, for an investment total of $11.976 million. This is shown where Rothmans' IOS intersects its WACC for the optimal investment.[19] For 2006, Rothmans' total investment is significantly below the amount of internal cash flow it generates, which is why Rothmans is a cash cow: it cannot profitably invest all the funds from its operations, since cigarette manufacturing is not a growing industry.[20]

If Rothmans' IOS shifted to the right (very far to the right in Rothmans' case) so that its internal demand for funds outstripped its supply of funds, then eventually it would have to raise additional capital and in this case its MCC would increase above its WACC. This is indicated by the vertical jump in its supply of funds schedule. As discussed previously, under this scenario the MCC would be above the WACC simply due to the costs of raising additional funds.

CONCEPT REVIEW QUESTION

1. Explain the importance of using the WACC as a hurdle rate for making investment decisions.

Summary

In this chapter, we have synthesized the information on the types of securities a firm may issue to finance its operations. In Chapter 19 we pointed out that these different types of securities differ in their degree of "equityness," so that they all had different required rates of return. However, the firm as a whole has to earn enough money to pay the investors their required rate of return. From these different securities and their associated required rates of return and market values, we can determine how much the firm has to earn to meet these commitments. This is the basis for the weighted average cost of capital (WACC), which is the overall cost of the capital invested in the firm.

The WACC is a market value weighted average of the after-tax costs of all these securities. If the firm earns its WACC, then its present market values are supported, but if it is expected to earn less (more) than its WACC then its market value will fall (increase). In most cases, this change in market value drops through to the common shareholders, who are the residual claimant and as a result they are the riskiest of all the securities issued by the firm. In this sense, risk increases as we drop down the income statement.

---

[19] The WACC estimates are not provided by Rothmans; only the cash flow and investment numbers are provided.

[20] It also explains why Rothmans made a large special dividend payment during 2006, which will be discussed further in Chapter 22.

We then showed that the most difficult estimate in the WACC is that for the cost of common equity capital. In estimating this, we discussed the discounted cash flow model that "reverse engineers" the valuation equation to use the current market price in order to estimate the discount rate used by the investor. In doing so, we emphasized that since there are many different types of DCF models, there are many different ways of estimating the cost of common equity. While the constant growth DDM is by far the most popular model, it also leads to serious errors for high growth companies. To understand which model to use, we discussed a simple characterization of types of firms based on the present value of existing and growth opportunities.

Alternatively, rather than using DCF models, the CAPM can be used to minimize estimation errors as we know that the market risk premium has averaged between 4.0 and 5.5 percent historically, so the discount rate on the stock market as a whole is currently in the 8 to 10 percent range, with long-term Canada bond yields of around 4.3 percent. In adjusting for the risk of individual securities, we showed how beta estimates are critically dependent on the time period over which they are estimated. Without making appropriate adjustments for what has happened in the stock market over the last 10 years, we showed that recent beta estimates are seriously misleading. As with the use of the DCF model, use of the CAPM requires judgement, common sense, and an understanding of recent financial history.

Key Terms

asset turnover ratio, p. 769

beta coefficient, p. 794

capital asset pricing model (CAPM), p. 793

capital structure, p. 765

cash cow, p. 790

cost of capital, p. 771

debt-to-equity ratio, p. 766

dog, p. 790

earnings yield, p. 767

hurdle rate, p. 788

investment opportunities schedule (IOS), p. 801

issuing (or flotation) costs, p. 774

marginal cost of capital (MCC), p. 775

market-to-book (M/B) ratio, p. 766

market risk premium, p. 793

multi-stage growth DDM, p. 788

operating leverage, p. 778

present value of existing opportunities (PVEO), p. 789

present value of growth opportunities (PVGO), p. 789

return on assets (ROA), p. 769

return on equity (ROE), p. 769

return on invested capital (ROIC), p. 769

risk-based models, p. 793

risk-free rate of return, p. 793

star, p. 790

turnaround, p. 790

weighed average cost of capital (WACC), p. 771

Formulas/Equations

(20-1) $S = \dfrac{X}{K_e}$

(20-2) $K_e = \dfrac{X}{S}$

(20-3) $X = K_e \times S$

(20-4) $P = \dfrac{EPS}{K_e} = \dfrac{ROE \times BVPS}{K_e}$

(20-5) $\dfrac{P}{BVPS} = \dfrac{ROE}{K_e}$

(20-6) $V = \dfrac{ROI \times IC}{K_a}$

(20-7) $K_a = \dfrac{ROI \times IC}{V}$

(20-8) $K_a = \dfrac{ROI \times IC}{V} = \dfrac{K_e S + K_d(1-T)D}{V} = K_e \dfrac{S}{V} + K_d(1-T)\dfrac{D}{V}$

(20-9) $WACC = K_e \dfrac{S}{V} + K_p \dfrac{P}{V} + K_i \dfrac{D}{V}$

(20-10) $S = P_0 \times n$

(20-11) $P_p = D_p \div k_p$

(20-12) $B = I \times \left[\dfrac{1 - \dfrac{1}{(1+k_b)^n}}{k_b} \right] + F \times \dfrac{1}{(1+k_b)^n}$

(20-13) $NP = I \times (1-T) \times \left[\dfrac{1 - \dfrac{1}{(1+K_i)^n}}{K_i} \right] + F \times \dfrac{1}{(1+K_i)^n}$

(21-14) $K_p = D_p/NP$

(20-15) $P_0 = \dfrac{D_1}{K_e - g}$

(20-16) $K_e = \dfrac{D_1}{P_0} + g$

(20-17) $K_{ne} = \dfrac{D_1}{NP} + g$

(20-18) $g = b \times ROE$

(20-19) $P_0 = \dfrac{D_1}{K_e - b \times ROE}$

(20-20) $P_0 = \dfrac{X_1(1-b)}{K_e - b \times ROE}$

(20-21) $K_e = \dfrac{D_1}{P_0} + g = \dfrac{X_1(1-b)}{P_0} + b \times ROE$

(20-22) $P_0 = \dfrac{ROE_1 \times BVPS}{K_e} + \dfrac{Inv}{(1+K_e)}\left(\dfrac{ROE_2 - K_e}{K_e}\right)$

(20-23) $\dfrac{V_{actual}}{V_{Fed}} = \dfrac{V_{actual}}{Exp(EPS)/(K_{TBond} - 1.0\%)}$

(20-24) $V_{Fed} = \dfrac{Exp(EPS)}{(K_{TBond} - 1.0\%)}$

(20-25) $\dfrac{X}{P_{S\&P\,500}} = K_{Tbond} - 1.0\%$

(20-26) $K_e = R_F + MRP \times \beta_e$

(20-27) $K_{ne} = K_e \times P_0/NP$

QUESTIONS AND PRACTICE PROBLEMS
Multiple Choice Questions

1. Which of the following statements is *false*?

    A. Financing total assets is called the financial structure decision.
    B. Capital structure is how invested capital is financed.
    C. The financial structure is $34,000 if the total assets are $34,000.
    D. The invested capital is $50,000 if the total assets are $50,000.

2. If an all-equity firm is expected to earn and pay out a $5.50 dividend forever (in perpetuity), what is the value of the firm's stock given a cost of equity of 15 percent?

    A. $37
    B. $36
    C. $38
    D. $40

3. What is the earnings yield given a $40,000 earnings figure, a $10 market price per share, and 10,000 shares outstanding?

    A. 0.5
    B. 0.4
    C. 0.3
    D. 4,000

4. What does a firm have to earn given the following? MV of debt = $40,000; MV of equity = $69,000; k_e = 12.5%; k_d = 7%

   A. $11,425

   B. $2,800

   C. $8,625

   D. $10,099

5. Which of the following statements is *true*?

   A. When ROE < k_e, management is adding value to the firm.

   B. When ROE > k_e, management is decreasing the firm's value.

   C. When ROE > k_e, the market price goes above the book value of the investment.

   D. When ROE = k_e, the market price goes above the book value of the investment.

6. Which of the following is *not* an input in the calculation of WACC?

   A. Book values of equity and debt

   B. Market values of equity and debt

   C. Cost of equity

   D. Corporate tax rate

7. To increase the stock price of a firm that is assumed to grow at a constant rate g,

   A. increase the cost of equity.

   B. increase the constant growth rate.

   C. decrease the dividend payout ratio.

   D. increase the retention ratio.

8. Star Inc. just paid a $9.45 dividend, which is expected to grow at a constant rate. Recent EPS is $10.50 and net income is $550,000. Total equity is $1,100,000 and the cost of equity is 12 percent. What is the share market price?

   A. $142.50

   B. $135.70

   C. $130.90

   D. $129.90

9. Which of the following firms is a *growth* firm?

   A. ROE > k_e

   B. ROE < k_e

   C. ROE = k_e

   D. Net income = k_e

10. Which of the following statements is *false*?

    A. Star firms have both high PVGO and PVEO.

    B. Google and Yahoo are examples of turnarounds.

    C. Cash cows could be called growth stocks as well.

    D. Utility firms are examples of cash cows.

Practice Problems

Use the information below to answer Problems 11 to 13.

BALANCE SHEET

Cash	$140,000	Accounts payable	$200,000
Marketable securities	200,000	Wages payable	100,000
Accounts receivable	40,000	Short-term debt	250,000
Inventory	1,000,000	Long-term debt	690,000
		Total liabilities	**$1,240,000**
Fixed assets	900,000	Common stock	950,000
		Retained earnings	90,000
Total assets	**$2,280,000**	**Total Equity & Liabilities**	**$2,280,000**

INCOME STATEMENT

Sales	$1,200,000
CGS	400,000
Amortization	90,000
Interest	56,400
EBT	$653,600
Taxes	$261,440
NI	$392,160
Shares outstanding	300,000

11. What is the cost of equity (K_e) given RF = 5%, beta (β) = 1.2, expected market return (ER_M) = 10%?

12. What is the market price and market-to-book ratio assuming the firm's stock is a perpetuity and the retention ratio (b) = 0?

13. Calculate invested capital and before-tax ROI.

14. Provide two reasons why the cost of a security to a company differs from its required return in capital markets.

15. A firm is going to finance a new project 100 percent with debt, through a new bond issue. Since the firm is using only debt to finance the project, the NPV of the project should be calculated using the cost of debt as the discount rate. Is this statement true, false, or uncertain? Explain.

16. Calculate the WACC (Weighted Average Cost of Capital). The market values of equity and debt are $500,000 and $600,000, respectively. The before-tax cost of debt = 6%; RF = 4%; beta (β) = 1.5; the market risk premium = 10%; and the tax rate = 40%.

17. What is V_{Fed} given the expected earnings per share on the S&P 500 is $10 and the long-term U.S. bond rate is 5 percent?

18. AB Inc. just announced its EPS of $3. Retention ratio (b) = 0.7. The earnings are expected to grow at 10 percent for one year and then grow at 4 percent indefinitely. Given that K_e = 15%, what is the market price?

19. Calculate the cost of issuing new equity for a firm assuming: issue costs are 5 percent of the share price after taxes; market price per share = $20; current dividend = $3.50; and the constant growth rate in dividends is 5 percent.

20. A small brokerage firm and a software development company are both separately considering developing and marketing a new software package. Neither party is aware that the other is considering this project and it is NOT at any point going to become a joint venture. These new software packages will organize mutual fund data into a new type of database and then run a series of complicated algorithms on that new database. The beta of the brokerage firm is 0.8 and the beta of the software firm is 1.4. The risk-free rate is 5 percent and the market risk premium is 10 percent. The NPV of the project, using a 13 percent discount rate, is +$1 million. However, using a 19 percent discount rate, the project has a –$500,000 NPV. Should either or both parties go ahead with the project?

21. Suppose a firm uses a constant WACC to calculate the NPV of all of its capital budgeting projects, rather than adjusting for risk of the individual projects. What errors will the firm make in its capital budgeting decisions?

22. A firm has common shares outstanding with a market capitalization rate of 12 percent. The current market price is $13.80, and dividend payments for this year are expected to be $0.28 What is the per share implied growth rate?

Difficult

23. A firm's earnings and dividends are expected to grow at a constant rate indefinitely, and it is expected to pay a dividend of $9.20 per share next year. Expected EPS and BVPS next year are $10.50 and $30, respectively. The cost of equity is 12 percent and there are 10,000 shares outstanding. Calculate the firm's value assuming that the retention ratio stays the same and the market value of debt is $500,000.

24. Calculate the cost of equity using the constant growth DDM given the following: current dividend = $2.50; payout ratio = 0.7 (assuming it is not changing); ROE = 15%; and the current market price of the stock = $11.50. Is the current management adding to or reducing the shareholders' value?

25. Calculate PVGO and PVEO given the following information: ROE_1 = 20%; ROE_2 = 25%; further investment (Inv) = $50; BVPS = $10; and K_e = 15%. Is this firm a star? If not, what is it according to Boston Consulting Group?

26. A firm has the following capital structure based on market values: equity 65 percent and debt 35 percent.

The current yield on government T-bills is 10 percent, the expected return on the market portfolio is 15 percent, and the firm's beta is approximated at 0.85. The firm's common shares are trading at $25, and the current dividend level of $3 per share is expected to grow at an annual rate of 3.5 percent. The firm can issue debt at a 2 percent premium over the current risk-free rate. The firm's tax rate is 40 percent, and the firm is considering a project to be funded out of internally generated funds that will not alter the firm's overall risk. This project requires an initial investment of $11.5 million and promises to generate net annual after-tax cash flows of $1.4 million perpetually. Should this project be undertaken?

27. A firm has the following balance sheet items:

Common stock: 300,000 shares at $8 each	$2,400,000
Retained earnings	900,000
Debt: 15% coupon, 15 years to maturity	1,800,000
Preferred shares: 12% dividend	1,200,000

The before-tax interest cost on new 15-year debt would be 10 percent, and each $1,000 bond would net the firm $975 after issuing costs. Common shares could be sold to net the firm $8 per share, a 12 percent discount from the current market price. Current shareholders expect a 15 percent return on their investment. Preferred shares could be sold at par to provide a yield of 9 percent, with after-tax issuing and underwriting expenses amounting to 5 percent of par value. The firm's tax rate is 45 percent, and internally generated funds are insufficient to finance anticipated new capital projects. Compute the firm's marginal cost of capital.

28. A company can issue new 20-year bonds at par that pay 10 percent annual coupons. The net proceeds to the firm (after taxes) will be 95 percent of par value. They estimate that new preferred shares providing a $2 annual dividend could be issued to investors at $25 per share to "net" the firm $22 per share issued (after taxes). The company has a beta of 1.20, and present market conditions are such that the risk-free rate is 6 percent, while the expected return on the market index is 12 percent. The firm's common shares presently trade for $30, and they estimate the net proceeds from a new common share issue would be $26 per share (after tax considerations). The firm's tax rate is 40 percent.

   A. Determine the firm's cost of long-term debt, preferred shares, and common equity financing (internal AND external sources) under the conditions above.

   B. What is the firm's weighted average cost of capital assuming that they have a "target" capital structure consisting of 30 percent debt, 10 percent preferred equity, and 60 percent common equity. Assume that they have $2 million in internal funds available for reinvestment and require $3 million in total financing.

   C. Suppose everything remains as above, except that the company decides it needs $5 million in total financing. Calculate the firm's marginal cost of capital.

29. A. Company ABC plans to issue 20-year bonds with a 12.80 percent coupon rate, with coupons paid semi-annually and a par value of $1,000. After-tax flotation costs (issuing & underwriting costs) amount to 2.5 percent of par value. The firm's tax rate is 50 percent. Determine the firm's effective annual after-tax cost of debt.

   B. Company ABC plans to issue $50 par preferred shares (P/S) with annual dividends of $6 (i.e., a 12 percent dividend yield). They estimate flotation costs to be $2 per share after taxes. Find the firm's cost of P/S.

   C. Company ABC wishes to make a new issue of common shares (C/S). The current market price (P_0) is $25, D_1 = $1.75 (expected dividend at the end of this year), while g = 9 percent per year indefinitely. Flotation costs and discounts amount to $1 per share after taxes. Find the firm's cost of issuing new common shares:

      i) Using the dividend valuation approach.
      ii) Using CAPM, given that the risk-free rate is 11 percent, the expected return on the market is 18 percent, and the beta for ABC is 0.95.

   D. Find the cost of internally generated common equity:

      i) Using the dividend model approach
      ii) Using the CAPM approach.

   E. Find the WACC if the firm wishes to raise funds in the following proportions: 30 percent debt, 20 percent P/S, and 50 percent CE (common equity) and it believes all of the CE component can be raised using internally generated funds. Assume the cost of internally generated funds is 17.5 percent.

F. Now suppose the firm wants to raise $10 million for investment purposes and it only has $2 million of internally generated funds available. Determine the "break point" of the CE component.

G. Determine the marginal cost of capital (MCC) if the firm must raise funds beyond the break point. Assume the cost of new common equity issues is 18 percent.

PART 8

FINANCIAL POLICIES

Having discussed the range of financial securities available to the firm, this section considers the critical aspects of financial policy: how can the firm combine its outstanding securities to find an optimal financing policy and how it decides its dividend policy. These are two of the most contentious areas of corporate finance and lead to Franco Modigliani and Merton Miller, Nobel Prize winners in finance, who surprisingly showed that there is no optimal financial policy.

CHAPTER 21
Capital Structure Decisions

CHAPTER 22
Dividend Policy

Finding the Optimal Capital Structure

TELUS is a major Canadian telecommunications company. In its 2006 annual report TELUS states that its objectives when managing capital are: "(i) to maintain a flexible capital structure which optimizes the cost of capital at acceptable risk; and (ii) to manage capital in a manner which balances the interests of equity and debt holders." How does it do this? TELUS manages the capital structure "in light of changes in economic conditions and the risk characteristics of the underlying assets. In order to maintain or adjust the capital structure, the Company may adjust the amount of dividends paid to shareholders, purchase shares for cancellation pursuant to normal course issuer bids, issue new shares, issue new debt, issue new debt to replace existing debt with different characteristics, and/or increase or decrease the amount of sales of trade receivables to an arm's-length securitization trust." It was this quest for a lower cost of capital that led TELUS to consider its conversion to an income trust structure before the federal minister of finance closed that option in 2006. The search for an optimal capital structure as highlighted by TELUS is an important financial objective for firms, since financial cost reductions through the cost of capital enhance shareholder value as much as operating cost reductions. In this chapter you will learn the basic techniques firms use to manage their capital structure.

Source: TELUS 2006 Annual Report available at www.about.telus.com/investors/annualreport2006.

Capital Structure Decisions

Learning Objectives

After reading this chapter, you should understand the following:

1. How business risk and financial risk affect a firm's ROE and EPS

2. How indifference analysis may be used to compare financing alternatives based on expected EBIT levels

3. Modigliani and Miller's (M&M) irrelevance argument, as well as the key assumptions upon which it is based

4. How the introduction of corporate taxes affects M&M's irrelevance argument

5. How financial distress and bankruptcy costs lead to the static trade-off theory of capital structure

6. How informational asymmetry problems and agency problems may lead firms to follow a pecking order approach to financing

7. How other factors such as firm size, profitability and growth, asset tangibility, and market conditions can affect a firm's capital structure

INTRODUCTION

In Chapter 20 we discussed how the firm can estimate the cost of each source of funds and average them to estimate its overall cost of capital. This is what we refer to as the weighted average cost of capital or WACC. In this chapter we discuss how the firm may attempt to minimize its WACC through its financing choices. Just as a firm can increase its value by lowering its production costs, it can increase its value by lowering its capital costs as measured by its WACC. In this chapter, we will discuss how firms attempt to do so, which is much more difficult than lowering production costs and involves sophisticated concepts that have been hotly debated for almost 50 years and are still to some extent unsettled.

In discussing these issues you will learn how firms may use *OPM: other people's money*, and its impact on the common shareholder. You will also learn how to assess the limits placed on a firm's ability to issue debt as creditors and bond-rating agencies assess the risk attached to corporate debt issues. You will then learn how this qualitative assessment conflicts with the celebrated Modigliani and Miller (M&M) proposition that under some simplifying assumptions, the capital structure decision does not affect firm value.

The chapter finishes by showing how issuing debt may create value when we relax the two critical assumptions of M&M: that there are no taxes and that there are no bankruptcy or financial distress costs. You will learn that there are tax advantages to issuing debt and that this leads the firm to do so up to the point where the associated risks of financial distress and bankruptcy outweigh these gains. The result is the static tradeoff model that indicates the general determinants of a firm's target or optimal debt ratio. Firms may then depart from this target by using a pecking order, where they are reluctant to issue equity until they are forced to do so, or when the markets are particularly receptive.

invested capital (IC) a firm's capital structure consisting of shareholders' equity and short- and long-term debt

return on invested capital (ROI) the return on all the capital provided by investors; EBIT minus taxes divided by invested capital

return on equity (ROE) the return earned by equity holders on their investment in the company; net income divided by shareholders' equity

financial leverage the effect of using debt as a source of capital

21.1 FINANCIAL LEVERAGE

Risk and Leverage

We begin by returning to the example we used in Chapter 20 where the firm had a capital structure of $1,700 composed of $1,000 of shareholders' equity and $700 of short- and long-term debt, so this capital structure represented the firm's **invested capital (IC)**. We used this example to motivate a discussion of the cost of capital, but we also worked out the required income statement, where the firm had the financial charges in Table 21-1.

From this data we indicated that the firm's **return on invested capital (ROI)** equalled its EBIT minus taxes figure of $325.20 divided by the invested capital of $1,700, or 19.13 percent, and its **return on equity (ROE)** equalled its net income of $300 divided by shareholders' equity of $1,000, or 30 percent. The manner in which this ROE varies with changes in ROI is due to its **financial leverage**.

Table 21-1 Example Income Statement	
Sales	$1,000
Variable costs	300
Fixed costs	158
EBIT	542
Interest	42
Taxable income	500
Tax (40%)	200
Net income	300

To understand how financial leverage works, consider the equation for the ROE:

$$ROE = \frac{(EBIT - R_D B)(1 - T)}{SE}$$

[21-1]

This simply says we work down the income statement from *EBIT*. First we subtract the interest expense, which is the interest cost of the firm's debt (R_D) times the book value of the firm's debt. As before we use R's to indicate actual costs and now since we are looking at book values, we use B to represent the book value of the firm's debt (bonds or B).[1] We then pay taxes, so ($1 - T$) flows through to the common shareholders, where we represent the book value of equity by *SE* for shareholders' equity.

We now use the definition of the ROI from Chapter 20, which is shown below:

$$ROI = \frac{EBIT(1 - T)}{SE + B}$$

[21-2]

It can be shown that if we re-express *EBIT*(1–T) in the ROE equation, we get the following:

$$ROE = ROI + (ROI - R_D(1 - T))\frac{B}{SE}$$

[21-3]

We refer to this as the financial leverage equation.

The importance of the financial leverage equation is that the ROI measures the return that the firm earns from its operations and does not explicitly consider how the firm is financed.[2] This is because it uses EBIT minus taxes in the numerator and the *total* invested capital in the denominator. It is for this reason that we think of the firm's ROI as reflecting its **business risk**, which was discussed in Chapter 20, while the ROE reflects this business risk, as well as its

business risk variability of a firm's operating income caused by operational risk

---

[1] Notice the difference from Chapter 20 where we used D to denote the market value of the firm's debt.

[2] While it does not explicitly consider how the firm is financed, the interest expense does affect the taxes paid by the firm.

financial risk the variability in a firm's net income caused by the use of financial leverage

financial risk. The financial leverage equation then shows the combination of these two risk factors on the ROE; that is, how much is due to its operations and how much is due to the way that the firm is financed.

Consider our example again where we found that ROI = 19.10 percent. In this case, the interest cost was 6.0 percent, which is 3.6 percent after tax (i.e., $6 \times (1 - .40)$), and the book debt-to-equity (D/E) ratio was $700 \div 1,000$ or 0.70. Substituting into Equation 21-3, we get:

$$ROE = 19.1 + (19.1 - 3.6) \times 0.70 = 30.0\%$$

This is exactly what we calculated directly from the firm's net income and the shareholders' equity (i.e., $\$300 \div \$1,000$). If we get the same answer you might ask why we went through the trouble of calculating the ROE through this roundabout method. The answer is that doing so allows us to examine the impact of how the firm is financed.

It has to be remembered that each dollar invested in the firm earns the same ROI; that is, for investment purposes a dollar is a dollar: there is no such thing as an equity dollar or a debt dollar. It is the corporate financing or capital structure decision that allocates the ROI to different claimants and causes differences in the returns to equity and debt holders. In our example, the debt holders want a fixed 6 percent return and since this cost is tax deductible, it only costs the firm's shareholders 3.6 percent after taxes. So each dollar borrowed from the debt holders earns the firm the ROI of 19.13 percent at a cost of 3.6 percent, and the spread of 15.5 percent drops through to the common shareholders. The only question is then how many dollars of debt are carried by each dollar of equity and this is answered by the D/E ratio of 0.70.

What is happening is that each dollar of equity earns 19.13 percent directly, but in addition, each dollar of equity also supports $0.70 of debt, which earns the spread of 15.5 percent. So indirectly the shareholders earn another 10.87 percent, which is the spread of 15.5 percent times 0.70. The ROE of 30 percent is the direct return from investing at the ROI of 19.13 percent, plus the indirect return of 10.87 percent by *"trading on the equity"* and borrowing money at 3.6 percent while investing it at 19.13 percent. Previously, we used the term OPM to refer to the option pricing model. However, historically, OPM meant this process of using "other people's money," or financial leverage.

In our example, financial leverage is extremely favourable for the firm since it adds another 10.87 percent to the common shareholders' ROE. However, remember that the cost of the debt is a fixed contractual commitment of 6.0 percent before tax, whereas the ROI reflects the business risk of the firm and can vary. If we rearrange Equation 21-3 to group the terms involving the ROI we get:

[21-4]

$$ROE = ROI \left(1 + \frac{B}{SE}\right) - R_D(1-T)\frac{B}{SE}$$

We express the financial leverage equation in this way to show that the second term in Equation 21-4 is fixed, whereas the first term depends on the firm's uncertain ROI. This means we can graph the ROE against the firm's ROI as a straight line. This is what we do in Figure 21-1, with ROE plotted along the y-axis, and ROI plotted along the x-axis.

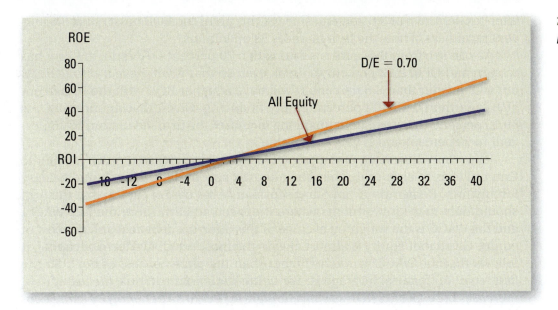

Figure 21-1 maps out the ROEs that result from different levels of ROI for two financing strategies. The first strategy, labelled ROI, is to simply finance using 100 percent equity and not use any debt. In this case, the financial leverage equation suggests that *ROI=ROE*. The second strategy is the one employed by our example firm, where the firm's D/E ratio is 70 percent, which we will refer to as the 70 percent strategy in our further discussion.

The Rules of Financial Leverage

In understanding Figure 21-1, you should work through several important points. Since the graph is a straight line, there are two *break-even points*. The first is where each financial strategy cuts the horizontal axis. For the 100 percent equity financing strategy, this point occurs where the ROI and ROE are zero, since if the firm's ROI is zero, so, too, is its ROE. However, for the 70 percent D/E strategy, when the ROI is zero, the ROE is –2.52 percent. This –2.52 percent is the product of the 0.70 D/E ratio times the 3.6 percent after-tax debt cost. The reason for this is that even if the ROI is zero, the firm still has to pay the debt holders their 6.0 percent interest rate, so with a 70 percent D/E ratio, each dollar of equity loses 4.2 percent. Assuming that the firm can use this loss to recapture previous income taxes paid, the after-tax cost is 2.52 percent.[3] If the firm cannot go back and reclaim previous taxes paid then the loss would be 4.2 percent. These break-even points are often called the **financial break-even points**.

The second break-even point is where the two financing strategies give the same ROE. This point is often called the **indifference point** on the basis that at this point the ROE is the same regardless of how the firm is financed. We can calculate this point by setting the two ROEs to be the same using Equation 21-3. For the 100 percent equity financing strategy, this point is where the ROI equals the

financial break-even points points at which a firm's ROE is zero

indifference point point at which two financing strategies provide the same ROE

---

[3] Remember from our discussion of corporate income tax in Chapter 3 that the firm can carry back losses from the current year to recapture previous income taxes paid. If it has not paid taxes in the past few years, it can carry this loss forward and hope to offset future profits.

after-tax debt cost of 3.6 percent, since at this point the ROE must equal 3.6 percent regardless of how the firm finances its operations.[4]

We can see from this analysis that with a 70 percent D/E ratio, the firm has to earn an ROI of 2.52 percent to break even so that it will have a zero ROE. At any ROI greater than 3.6 percent, it will have a higher ROE with the 70 percent D/E ratio than with 100 percent equity financing. Given that the firm's ROI is 19.13 percent, the use of debt financing increases the firm's ROE from 19.13 percent to 30 percent and is very favourable.

This result illustrates that using OPM tends to increase the ROE since the firm only has to earn more than the after-tax cost of debt. This should be easy for any firm! Remember from our discussion of the cost of capital that the firm should only make investments where it expects to earn more than its WACC, and the WACC is the weighted average of this after-tax debt cost and the cost of equity. Given that equity is almost always the most expensive form of capital, it follows that the WACC is *always* higher than the after-tax cost of debt. So the first "rule" of financial leverage is: ***For value-maximizing firms, the use of debt increases the expected ROE so shareholders expect to be better off by using debt financing, rather than equity financing***. In this way the firm expects to be to the right of the indifference point and the further to the right the firm expects to be, the greater the value of using debt financing.

This is a very important result but it can also be misleading, since it implies that the firm should always finance with debt. Hence, we should consider what we are ignoring since we get a result that says we always have to make the same decision, when in practice firms make multiple decisions. This leads us to consider the second principle of finance, which is the **risk value of money**.

Remember that the behaviour of the ROI reflects the business risk of the firm. The expected ROI can be represented by a point estimate, such as 19.13 percent in our example. However, we have to take into account the business risk of the firm, which is the *variability* in the ROI. Suppose, for example, the forecast ROI was expected to be between 10 and 30 percent. Would this affect the judgement that debt financing increases the ROE? We can examine this by looking at the ROE under the 100 percent equity and 70 percent D/E choices on the graph in Figure 21-1 at the 10 percent and 30 percent ROI levels. These values are calculated in Table 21-2.

risk value of money the principle that future cash flows (money) involving different amounts of risk have different present values

Table 21-2   Varying ROI Values

	70% D/E Ratio	100% Equity
ROI (%)	ROE (%)	
10	14.48	10
30	48.48	30
Range	34	20

At an ROI of 10 percent or 30 percent, the 100 percent equity choice leads to the same ROEs, generating a range of 20 percent. In contrast, the 70 percent

[4] Generally, the indifference point is close to the after-tax cost of debt. It will differ depending on the firm's historical financing rates (costs of debt).

D/E ratio choice leads to ROE values of 14.48 percent and 48.48 percent, for a range of 34 percent. Thus, the range or variability of the ROE increases with debt financing. This simply reflects the fact that the financial leverage line is *steeper* with the 70 percent D/E choice, since the D/E ratio is higher.

Would this increase in risk affect the firm's shareholders? In this example, the answer is no, since the minimum ROI of 10 percent exceeds the indifference point of 3.6 percent. As a result, at all forecast levels of ROI, the firm's ROE is higher with the use of debt financing. However, the important point is that the variability of the ROE always increases as the firm finances with more debt since there are fixed financial charges that the firm has to pay, which are independent of the firm's ROI. If we increase the range of ROI possibilities to −10 to 40 percent then we would get the ROE values in Table 21-3 with the two financing plans.

Table 21-3   Wider Variation in ROI Values

	70% D/E Ratio	100% Equity
ROI (%)	ROE (%)	
−10	−19.52	−10
40	65.48	40
Range	85	50

Now with this wider range in ROI values, the ROE with the 70 percent D/E ratio is −19.52 percent on the low end, which is much lower than that with no debt, while as before, the range of ROE values is much higher for the leveraged position.

This leads to the second rule of financial leverage: ***Financing with debt increases the variability of the firm's ROE, which usually increases the risk to the common shareholders***.

As the above example illustrates, the range of ROE values always increases with debt financing, but depending on the numbers, this does not necessarily mean that risk increases. Sometimes, as in the first example, the firm is better off at all ROI levels with debt financing regardless of the greater variability in the ROE.

Since the range of ROE values increases with debt financing, the firm has to find the cash to cover the fixed interest payments. In the above worst case scenario where the firm has an ROI of −10 percent, it still has to cover the 3.6 percent after-tax and 6.0 percent before-tax interest payments. If the firm's underlying health remains sound it can borrow from the bank or use up some of its cash reserves to make these payments. However, sometimes a series of poor operating results can cause serious financial problems for a highly indebted firm. This situation can compound as the firm's owners might then change their operating procedures once there is a significant risk of financial distress or bankruptcy. We will discuss this in more detail later in the chapter, but at this point we simply note the third rule of financial leverage: ***Financing with debt increases the likelihood of the firm running into financial distress and possibly even bankruptcy***.

Figure 21-2 illustrates this proposition.

FIGURE 21-2

*Investing Using
Leverage*

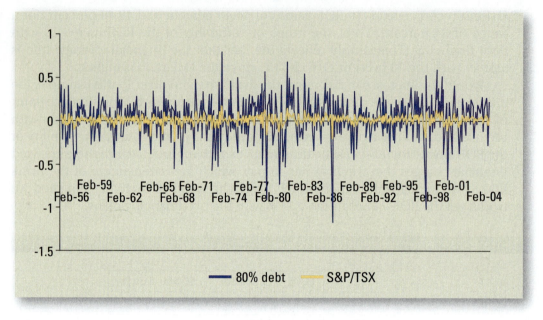

Figure 21-2 graphs the monthly returns from investing in the S&P/TSX Composite Index using two different financing strategies. The first (denoted TSX) is simply the monthly return generated from investing in the index. The second (denoted 80 percent debt) assumes that the individual borrows 80 percent on margin; that is, they put up $1 for every $4 borrowed. For this strategy we assume they pay the treasury bill rate plus 1.2 percent per year (0.1 percent per month). You should notice two things about the graph. The first is the increased variability in the return from the highly leveraged strategy; which is the second rule of financial leverage. The second is that on some occasions the return from the highly leveraged strategy is over –100 percent. For example, in October 1987 the S&P/TSX Composite Index dropped 22.5 percent, but with the 80 percent debt financing strategy the return was –117 percent, which means the "leveraged" investor would have been wiped out. In fact, before that happened, they would have received a margin call from their broker insisting they put up more capital.

Figure 21-2 illustrates that the effects of financial leverage are not confined to corporations. In fact they apply to any economic entity, whether a firm, an individual, or a government. Financial leverage tends to increase returns at the expense of increased variability and increased risk of financial distress. Consequently the amount of debt a firm or individual can carry very much depends on the underlying business risk of the asset being financed. As we saw in Figure 21-2, financing an investment in the stock market with 80 percent debt financing is very risky. In contrast, Canadians are happy to finance their house purchase with 80 percent debt financing. Indeed with high-ratio mortgages, frequently the amount of debt financing is as high as 95 percent. In this case, the asset being financed is perceived to be lower risk than the stock market so that it can be financed with more debt. However, even here there have been times when 80 percent mortgage financing has been risky.

Indifference Analysis

Before leaving our discussion of financial leverage, we examine one more set of financial leverage charts, which relate to the firm's earnings per share (EPS). We noted in our example that the firm has 1,000 shares outstanding so the definition of the EPS in relation to the firm's EBIT is as follows:

$$EPS = \frac{(EBIT - R_D B)(1 - T)}{\#}$$

[21-5]

This is identical to the ROE-ROI relationship except that instead of the book value of equity in the denominator, we now have the number of shares (#). As a result, we can rearrange the definition of the EPS and show how it varies with the EBIT:

$$EPS = \frac{-R_D B(1 - T)}{\#} + \frac{EBIT(1 - T)}{\#}$$

[21-6]

Note that this is also a simple linear relationship.

If the firm has no debt, the first term is zero and the EPS is simply the EBIT minus taxes divided by the number of shares. As the firm finances with debt, it incurs the fixed after-tax interest expense per share and then has fewer shares outstanding. The result is that the EPS-EBIT line pivots and gets steeper as debt is used, so that the same increase in the EBIT causes a bigger impact on the EPS. We can illustrate this in Figure 21-3, where the firm is assumed to have 1,280 shares outstanding in the no debt situation.

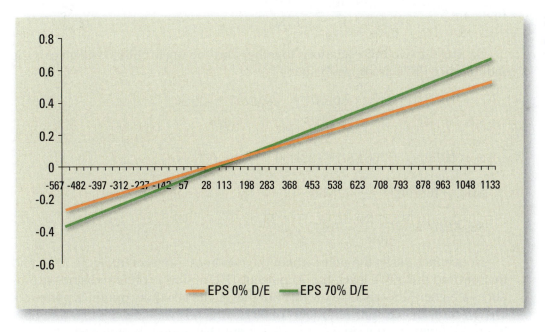

21-3 FIGURE

EPS-EBIT Charts

Note that similar to the ROE-ROI charts, the 0 percent D/E line has a lower intercept since there are no after-tax fixed interest payments to make and is not as steep as the other line. In the EPS-EBIT chart, the 70 percent D/E line is steeper since there are fewer shares outstanding, whereas in the ROE-ROI chart it was steeper because of the larger D/E ratio. Either way the result is the same: as the firm finances with more debt, its EPS and ROE are more sensitive to its operating results; that is, to its EBIT and ROI. All firms look at the impact of financing on their ROE and EPS and these charts are often called **profit planning charts**.

profit planning charts charts showing ROE-ROI and EPS-EBIT for firms to analyze the impact of financing on their profits

EPS indifference point
the EBIT level at which
two financing alterna-
tives generate the same
EPS

Similar to the ROE indifference point discussed with respect to Figure 21-2, the **EPS indifference point** is depicted in Figure 21-3 at the point where the two lines intersect. We can solve for this indifference point in terms of EBIT by setting the EPS, as expressed in Equation 21-5, equal for two alternative financing plans under consideration. Then we merely solve for this indifference EBIT level, which we denote as EBIT*. This will provide the firm with some useful direction in choosing between financing alternatives since firms will generally want to maximize their "bottom line" as measured by EPS, and they will usually have an estimate of their expected EBIT. Example 21-1 below illustrates.

Example 21-1: EPS Indifference Analysis

Calculate the EPS indifference EBIT* level for the firm discussed above assuming it maintains its present 70 percent D/E ratio, and then assuming it was all equity financed. Its pre-tax cost of debt is 6 percent under the present structure, and there are 1,000 common shares outstanding. Further, assume that under the all equity plan, the firm has 1,280 shares outstanding.[5] Which plan is preferable at the current level of sales and EBIT?

Solution

$$EPS_{70\%D/E} = \frac{(EBIT - R_D B)(1-T)}{\#} = \frac{(EBIT - (.06)(\$700))(1-.40)}{1,000} = \frac{.60 EBIT - 25.20}{1,000}$$

$$EPS_{0\%D/E} = \frac{(EBIT - 0)(1-.40)}{1,280} = \frac{.60 EBIT}{1,280}$$

Setting the two EPS equations together and solving for EBIT* will give us the indifference EBIT, as shown below:

$$\frac{.60 EBIT*}{1,280} = \frac{.60 EBIT* - 25.20}{1,000}$$

So, $600 EBIT* = 768 EBIT* - 32,256$

And, $-168 EBIT* = -32,256$

So, $EBIT* = \frac{-32,256}{-168} = \$192$

Notice that this is the point where the two lines intersect in Figure 21-2, and that beyond this EBIT level, the 70 percent D/E option is preferred since it produces a higher EPS, while below this EBIT level, the all equity option is preferred. Therefore, at the current EBIT level of $542, which is well above $192, the more leveraged financing option (i.e., the 70 percent D/E option) is preferred.

Conducting EPS-EBIT indifference analysis is a useful beginning point for firms when trying to evaluate potential financing plans. We will discuss some of the additional issues, which are considerable, in the sections below.

---

[5] We "guesstimate" this figure by assuming the firm can retire the $700 worth of debt by issuing 280 shares at $2.50 (i.e., $700 ÷ $2.50 = 280), using the market share price used in Chapter 20 for this firm.

CONCEPT REVIEW QUESTIONS

1. Define business risk and financial risk.

2. How does financial leverage affect the relationship between ROI and ROE?

3. What are the three rules of leverage?

4. Explain how we determine the ROE and EPS indifference points for a firm under various financing alternatives, and why this analysis provides the firm with useful information.

21.2 DETERMINING CAPITAL STRUCTURE

In 1990, the Conference Board surveyed 119 U.S. companies to determine how they set their capital structures. The survey provided the results in Table 21-4.

Table 21-4   Determinants of Capital Structure

1.	Analysis of cash flows	23.0%
2.	Consultations	18.3%
3.	Risk considerations	16.5%
4.	Impact on profits	14.0%
5.	Industry comparisons	12.0%
6.	Other	3.4%

Source: Data from Conference Board, 1990

In looking at the answers, it is clear that firms will consult with their advisors (#2) and look at other firms in their industry (#5) to check on what is reasonable. However, neither of these are primary methods of determining their capital structure since they do not indicate how their advisors or other firms are determining their capital structure. The three primary methods are impact on profits (#4), risk (#3), and analysis of cash flows (#1). The profit planning charts just discussed under financial leverage are the basic way of assessing the impact on profits, and by varying EBIT and the ROI, they can also be used to assess the impact of risk. What is left to discuss is cash flow.

However, let's first consider some standard financial ratios that are often used. We can think of these ratios as *stock* or *flow* ratios. Stock ratios are measures like the D/E and debt ratios. These ratios measure the stock of outstanding debt relative to the total capital structure of the firm or the amount of equity. These ratios are clearly useful: they are used by the bond-rating agencies and others as a quick check on the firm's financing and they are also often used to limit the amount of debt the firm can raise through its trust indenture. However, we must consider just how useful these ratios really are.

In Chapter 18 we discussed some of the features of different types of debt. For example, we noted that bankers' acceptances had a maturity of 30 days whereas long-term bond issues were typically for 20 or 30 years. Clearly it matters a great deal to the firm if the debt has a 30-day versus a 30-year maturity. For one thing, if the firm has to "roll over" its debt every 30 days, it has to be very confident that it has the cash to pay off this debt if the lenders refuse to renew it. Similarly, if the debt has sinking fund payments, where the firm is contractually obliged to pay off a certain amount of debt each year, this increases the firm's commitments to the debt holders and requires that it have the cash ready to fulfil this commitment. In both cases it is not the *stock* of debt outstanding that matters so much as the *maturity* of the debt. This is why this information is required to be provided in the notes to the firm's financial statements. Further, it suggests that the stock ratios are not completely adequate, since they ignore some of the cash flow commitments attached to debt.

In the same way, consider the flow variables that we discussed previously in Chapter 18, where we placed great emphasis on the interest coverage ratio, defined as EBIT divided by interest expense. Remember that often this is explicitly written into the trust indenture where the firm cannot issue any more debt unless it has an interest coverage ratio of 2.0 or more. However, again this does not include all of the firm's commitments. The most basic limitation is that interest payments are made from cash and not from accounting earnings. Further, similar to the problems with the stock ratios, the interest coverage ratio does not include the impact of any sinking fund payments or other commitments, such as dividends to the preferred shareholders.

fixed burden coverage ratio an expanded interest coverage ratio that looks at a broader measure of both income and the expenditures associated with debt; EBITDA divided by a firm's fixed financing payment requirements

We can get around some of these problems by modifying the times interest earned ratio by including these other commitments. One way is to estimate the **fixed burden coverage ratio**, which is defined below:

[21-7]

$$Fixed\ Burden\ Coverage = \frac{EBITDA}{I + (Pref.\ Div. + SF)/(1 - T)}$$

In the numerator, instead of EBIT, we have EBITDA, which equals EBIT before subtracting out the non-cash deductions for depreciation and amortization. As such, it is a "better" estimate of the firm's cash flow.[6] In contrast, in the denominator we have added to interest the firm's commitment to make sinking fund payments (*SF*) on its debt, and its preferred share dividends (*Pref. Div.*). Since both dividends and sinking fund payments are made out of after-tax income, we "gross them up" by dividing by one minus the corporate tax rate (*1– T*) to get their pre-tax equivalent, which is then comparable to the interest payments. We ignore the common share dividends since these can be cut more easily than the dividends to the preferred shareholders.

cash-flow-to-debt ratio (CFTD) a direct measure of the cash flow over a period that is available to cover a firm's stock of outstanding debt

Another way of modifying the flow and stock variables is to combine them. One key ratio that does this is the **cash-flow-to-debt ratio (CFTD)**, which measures directly the cash flow over a period that is available to cover the firm's stock of outstanding debt. This ratio may be calculated as follows:

[21-8]

$$CFTD = \frac{EBITDA}{Debt}$$

---

[6] Some analysts simply add depreciation to net income.

Again, as with many ratios, cash flow is measured either by net income plus non-cash charges like amortization, or simply by EBITDA.

As the financial ratios depart more and more from standard GAAP values, they become more analyst specific; but the general point is simply that there are serious drawbacks to using either stock or flow variables based on the firm's financial statements as a measure of how much debt a firm can handle. The best measure is for the firm to generate its own forecast of expected cash flows over a short- to medium-term horizon, and then work out internally what level of fixed commitments the firm can handle without seriously exposing it to harm. This "scenario-based" approach to determining capital structure was pioneered by Gordon Donaldson.[7] However, the key question is whether the lenders will lend to the firm based on its internal scenario-based assessment of how much debt it can carry. This requires that sensitive information be divulged to lenders and that the lenders believe the data. Consequently there is still heavy reliance on standard ratios.

Moody's periodically provides data on the most commonly used credit ratios and how they are correlated with their credit ratings. Recently it provided the data in Table 21-5.

Table 21-5   Moody's Average Credit Ratios

	IG	Non-IG
Coverage	4.01	1.45
Leverage (%)	46.2	67.4
Cash flow-to-debt (%)	18.3	8.10
Liquidity (%)	3.66	4.45
Profit margin (%)	6.26	1.39
Return on assets (%)	8.41	6.92
Sales stability	7.14	5.60
Total assets ($billion)	6.31	1.19
Altman Z score	2.17	1.62

Source: Data from Moody's Investor Services, "The Distribution of Common Financial Ratios by Rating and Industry for North American Non-Financial Corporations," December 2004.

Moody's defines these ratios in its own way, but they broadly conform to our previous discussion. Investment grade (IG) companies—firms with at least a BBB bond rating—have higher coverage, less debt (leverage), larger cash flow to debt, less liquidity (cash plus marketable securities as a percentage of total assets), higher profit margins, and higher ROAs than firms with non-investment grade (non-IG) bond ratings. IG firms also tend to have more stable sales and are much larger than non-IG firms.

All of these ratios make sense. Firms with better credit ratings tend to be larger, more profitable, generate more cash, and have more stable sales, meaning lower business risk. The only "outlier" is that they tend to have less liquidity—they hold fewer marketable securities and cash. However, even this makes sense once you realize that better quality firms with more ready access to financial markets generally need to have fewer emergency financial resources on hand because they have that access. It is the poor quality firms without many sources of funds that have to hold more cash for emergency purposes.

The final value in Moody's set of ratios is the Altman Z score. This is due to the work of Professor Ed Altman, and is a weighted average of several key ratios that he found were useful for predicting a firm's probability of bankruptcy.[8] His prediction equation is as follows:

[21-9]

$$Z = 1.2X_1 + 1.4X_2 + 3.3X_3 + 0.6X_4 + 0.999X_5$$

Where,

$X_1 =$ working capital divided by total assets
$X_2 =$ retained earnings divided by total assets
$X_3 =$ EBIT divided by total assets
$X_4 =$ market values of total equity divided by non-equity book liabilities
$X_5 =$ sales divided by total assets

Note that most of the variables are scaled by total assets to standardize them, so we will refer to them by the numerator. However, they all have simple intuitive meanings.

High working capital generally means more receivables and inventory, which are usually more liquid than fixed assets. The existence of retained earnings generally means that the firm has earned money in the past, and therefore it proxies for age and past profitability, among other things. EBIT is a measure of operating profitability. The market value of equity divided by the non-equity book liabilities is another way of saying a *market-valued* debt ratio. Finally, sales divided by assets is the turnover ratio, so it measures how productively the firm is using its assets.

The Altman Z score was the first of many such measures that attempt to summarize a large number of financial ratios into a simple score. In the case of the Z score, the larger the better. Altman estimated it using a sample of 66 U.S. manufacturing firms equally divided between firms that did and did not go bankrupt, and his bankrupt firms had an average Z score of about 1.5. What is interesting is that even though Altman estimated this function more than 40 years ago, Moody's (and many other debt analysis reports) still report Altman's Z score, and it is still working in the sense that the IG firms have higher Z scores than the non-IG firms.

So what we know about capital structure is that firms pay a lot of attention to the impact of issuing debt on their future profit levels and risk, so assessing their underlying business risk is very important. As firms issue more debt, most of their key ratios covered by Moody's deteriorate. As a result, their credit rating weakens and they pay higher interest charges and have to submit to more trust indenture provisions to lessen the risk involved. Knowing how issuing debt affects the firm's credit rating is consequently very important. However, the key question is: does it affect the firm's market value? That is, the previous discussion simply indicates whether the firm can issue debt or not, and on what

---

[8] Altman, E. "Financial Ratios, Discriminant Analysis and the Prediction of Corporate Bankruptcy," *Journal of Finance* 23, 1968.

terms. It does not answer the question of whether it *should* issue debt. This is the question that is addressed in one of the most famous papers in finance, which is discussed in the next section. Surprisingly, the authors answered the question by saying that capital structure is irrelevant!

CONCEPT REVIEW QUESTIONS

1. What are the main determinants of capital structure?

2. Explain how ratios may be used to assess a company's ability to assume more debt.

3. What is Altman's Z score and what does it measure?

21.3 THE MODIGLIANI AND MILLER (M&M) IRRELEVANCE THEOREM

M&M and Firm Value

What we will discuss in this section is a theorem. That is, it is a result based on a series of assumptions about how financial markets work. It is in fact a very powerful theorem for which (in part) the authors, **Franco Modigliani and Merton Miller** (also known as M&M), won the Nobel Prize in Economics.[9] Unfortunately, the "M&M results" are only as good as their assumptions, and most of them have been shown to poorly reflect the "real" world. However, in looking at how their assumptions affect their result, their research has pointed the way for many of the significant developments in corporate finance theory and practice over the last 50 years.

> Franco Modigliani and Merton Miller (M&M) devised a proposition that under some simplifying assumptions, the capital structure decision does not affect firm value

M&M's key assumptions are as follows:

- There exist two firms in the same "risk class" with different levels of debt.

- The earnings of both firms are perpetuities.

- Markets are perfect in the sense that there are no transaction costs or asymmetric information problems.

- There are no taxes.

- There is no risk of costly bankruptcy or associated financial distress.

Of these five assumptions, two are modelling assumptions and three are assumptions about the real world. In 1958, relatively little was known about the pricing of risk, so M&M finessed this by assuming two firms with the same business risk. We could get M&M's result now by using the CAPM (or some other risk adjustment model) to adjust for risk, so this is a simple modelling assumption. Similarly, we have already seen that assuming perpetuities makes valuation easy, since we just divide the expected cash flows by the required rate of return.

---

[9] Modigliani, Franco and Miller, Merton "The Cost of Capital, Corporation Finance and the Theory of Investment," *American Economic Review* 48, 1958.

Again, we can get the M&M results if we assume some growth in the underlying earnings, but at the expense of needless complexity. The critical assumptions are the last three: markets are perfect, with no transaction costs and perfect information availability; there are no taxes; and there is no costly bankruptcy or financial distress risk. Later in the chapter, we will discuss what it means to relax these assumptions, but right now we will discuss the basic M&M model.

M&M proved their proposition by means of an *arbitrage argument*. As we discussed, with respect to the option pricing model, arbitrage arguments are the strongest in finance since they only rely on the assumption that there is no such thing as *"free money"* and that investors prefer more money to less. So let's think about what this means to two firms with the same business risk, but different levels of debt. We assume the first firm has no debt, and we will refer to it as the unlevered firm (U), while the second firm has debt and we refer to it as the levered firm (L), since it uses financial leverage. If we buy some arbitrary percentage of the unlevered firm, say, α, we simply get this percentage of the firm's earnings, which is paid out as a dividend. Since there is no interest paid by an unlevered firm, and since M&M assumed there were no taxes, the firm's EBIT is also its net income. Therefore, our share of the firm's earnings and dividends equals αEBIT, which we have assumed will be paid out as a perpetuity.

If we buy the same share of the equity of the levered firm, we have to subtract the interest payments, so we receive a smaller amount as a dividend. In this case, our share is $\alpha(EBIT - K_D D)$, where the interest cost is the market value of the debt times the required return on debt. The values for the "payoff" from buying the equity of the levered versus the unlevered firms are identical except for the interest charges, since we assumed that the two firms were in the same risk class. In other words, it would be like buying shares in two very similar steel companies or two drug companies. M&M then asked the following question: if the levered firm sold at a discount to the unlevered firm (i.e., investors did not like the effects of financial leverage), what could an investor do? To answer this question, they drew up the M&M arbitrage table as depicted in Table 21-6.

Table 21-6   M&M Arbitrage Table I

Portfolios (Actions)	Cost	Payoff
Portfolio A:	αV_U	$\alpha EBIT$
Buy α of unlevered firm		
Portfolio B:		
Buy α of levered firm's equity	αS_L	$\alpha(EBIT - K_D D)$
Buy α of levered firm's debt	αD	$\alpha K_D D$
Total Portfolio	$\alpha(S_L + D)$	$\alpha EBIT$

The first row, Portfolio A, is the cost and payoff to investing in the unlevered firm. The second two rows are the cost and payoff to buying the same proportion of the equity and debt of the levered firm, where the levered firm's equity is subscripted L for levered (αS_L). The final row is the cost and payoff from this portfolio B, which is composed of buying the same percentage of the levered firm's debt and equity. Note that what the levered firm pays as interest just goes to the investor since they buy the levered firm's debt. Therefore, a portfolio of debt and equity in the levered firm ends up with the same amount of EBIT (i.e., $\alpha EBIT$) as if we had invested in the unlevered firm. Notice that the share of the levered and unlevered firm that you buy makes no difference as α can be any number.

This is a powerful result. If you don't like the negative effects of financial leverage (e.g., the increased variability of returns), you can remove them by effectively *unlevering* the levered firm's equity by buying some of the firm's debt. This is where the arbitrage comes in: if the payoff is exactly the same, these two sets of cash flows must sell for exactly the same value, so their cost must be the same. That is:

$$V_U = S_L + D = V_L$$

[21-10]

This equation says that the value of the levered firm (V_L) is the value of its debt plus the value of its equity ($S_L + D$), and this must equal the value of the unlevered firm (V_U). What this proof says is that under M&M's assumptions, adding debt cannot destroy value, since the investor can undo the negative effects.[10]

If debt cannot destroy value, the next logical question is whether or not it can create value. So suppose the levered equity sells at a premium because of the favourable effects of financial leverage—what can the investor do then? M&M had an answer to this as well, which is that they can create the effects of *corporate leverage* through the use of *personal leverage*. Remember that the effects of leverage are the same whether it is a firm, an individual, or a government borrowing money. In each case, it is simply the effect of using other people's money. So M&M came up with the arbitrage table shown in Table 21-7.

Table 21-7   M&M Arbitrage Table II

Portfolios (Actions)	Cost	Payoff
Portfolio C:	αS_L	$\alpha(EBIT - K_D D)$
Buy α of levered firm's equity		
Portfolio D:		
Buy α of unlevered firm	αV_U	$\alpha EBIT$
Borrow α of levered firm's debt	$\underline{\alpha D}$	$\underline{-\alpha K_D D}$
Total Portfolio	$\alpha(V_U - D)$	$\alpha(EBIT - K_D D)$

Now portfolio (strategy) C is to buy the levered firm's equity at a cost of αS_L, with a payoff of $\alpha(EBIT–K_D D)$. The individual can replicate this payoff, as in Portfolio D, and see whether it can be bought more cheaply. First the payoff to the unlevered firm at a cost of αV_U is $\alpha EBIT$. As before, the only difference is the absence of interest payments and this is one thing everyone knows how to create: all you have to do is borrow money! Now the individual borrows enough to pay the same interest payments of $-\alpha K_D D$, where the negative sign indicates

---

[10] This result underpins the income trust market where the trust owns both the equity and the debt of the operating company. Clearly if you are both the creditor and the debtor, the amount of debt does not matter.

that these are an outflow (i.e., a payment). This is where the perfect market assumption comes in, since M&M assumed that the individual pays the same interest rate when borrowing against the unlevered firm's assets as the levered firm pays. In this case, the cost of generating these interest payments is the same as the money borrowed by the levered firm (i.e., –D).

The cost to the portfolio that replicates the payoff from the levered firm's equity is then $V_U - D$, which has to equal the levered firm's equity value S_L. Rearranging Equation 21-10, we get the same result as before: the levered firm's total value, equity plus debt, has to equal that of the unlevered firm. Therefore, the capital structure decision has no value. So now we have M&M's second proof. If you like the effects of financial leverage, you don't have to pay for them, since you can create the same effect through personal leverage. This is often referred to as M&M's **homemade leverage** result.

homemade leverage the creation of the same effect of a firm's financial leverage through the use of personal leverage

M&M's two results suggest that you can undo the effects of financial leverage if you don't like them, and that you can create them if you do like these effects. These results rely heavily on the perfect capital markets assumptions. They require that individuals can buy both the debt and the equity of the levered firm to undo the effects, and that they can borrow on margin to create homemade leverage. Further, the interest rate that they pay for their debt has to be the same as that paid by the firm. However, nowhere do we define what the individual is. It could be a large financial institution or a hedge fund facing the same type of transaction costs faced by the firm. For this reason most of the focus of the academic literature has been on the key assumptions of no taxes, no costly bankruptcy or financial distress costs, and no asymmetric information or agency costs. However, before considering these assumptions, we should first work through what the initial M&M irrelevancy result means for the cost of capital.

M&M and the Cost of Capital

The M&M results assume that the firm's earnings represent a perpetuity, so we can value the firm's equity as the present value of these earnings, as shown below:

[21-11]
$$S_L = \frac{(EBIT - K_D D)}{K_e}$$

In this case, the cost of equity capital is simply the earnings yield, as we discussed in Chapter 20. As a result, we can estimate the equity cost as follows:

[21-12]
$$K_e = \frac{(EBIT - K_D D)}{S_L}$$

In Equation 21-12, the perpetual earnings (dividends) are simply divided by the market value of the common shares.

Since M&M proved that the value of the firm is unchanged by leverage, we can define the unlevered value (V_U) by discounting the firm's expected *EBIT* by its unlevered equity cost (K_U), so we have:

[21-13]
$$V_U = \frac{EBIT}{K_U} = S_L + D = V_L$$

Example 21-2: M&M's First Model and Firm Value

a. An unlevered firm (U) has an expected EBIT of $2 million, which is expected to remain constant indefinitely. Its cost of capital is 10 percent. What is the market value of this firm?

b. An identical risk levered firm (L) has $5 million in debt outstanding. What is the value of this firm, and what is the value of its equity?

Solution

a. $V_U = \dfrac{EBIT}{K_U} = \dfrac{\$2}{.10} = \$20 \text{ million}$

b. $V_L = V_U = \$20$ million.

$S_L = V_L - D = 20 - 5 = \$15$ million.

Returning to Equation 21-13, we can solve for EBIT, substitute it for the *EBIT* in the leveraged equity cost equation (Equation 21-12), and rearrange to determine how the equity cost varies with the debt-equity ratio.[11] This equation is shown below:

$$K_e = K_U + (K_U - K_D)\frac{D}{S_L}$$

[21-14]

This is referred to as the **M&M equity cost equation**. It states that if the firm has no debt in its capital structure, the investor requires a cost of equity of K_U, which is referred to as the cost of unlevered equity. This cost reflects the *business risk* of the firm, and will depend on the risk class of the firm. As the firm uses debt, the equity cost increases due to the **financial leverage risk premium**, which is the difference between the unlevered equity cost and the cost of debt, times the D/E ratio.

Note that M&M's equity cost equation is NOT the same as the financial leverage equation (Equation 21-3). The financial leverage equation is based on book values and it is always the case that the sum of the debt plus equity equals the invested capital. However, the M&M equation holds because under their assumptions, the sum of the market value of debt plus equity equals the unlevered firm value. As we will see later, this is not the case when we relax M&M's assumptions. What this means is that M&M's equity cost equation (Equation 21-14) is a corollary of their constant value result (Equation 21-10).

A final implication of the M&M result applies to the cost of capital. If value is independent of financial leverage, we can ignore it and simply discount the EBIT cash flows with the unlevered equity cost. The problem is how to estimate this discount rate, since if the firm uses debt, all we observe is the *levered* equity cost (K_e). The answer to this is to go back to Equation 21-14 and rearrange to solve for K_U. If we do this,[12] we get:

M&M equity cost equation an equation to determine how the equity cost varies with the debt-equity ratio

financial leverage risk premium difference between the unlevered equity cost and the cost of debt, times the D/E ratio.

---

[11] From Equation 21-13, we can find EBIT = $K_U(S_L + D)$, which we substitute into Equation 21-12 to get: $K_e = [K_U(S_L + D) - K_D D)] / S_L = K_U + (K_U - K_D) \times D/S_L$.

[12] Dropping the "L" subscripts and rearranging Equation 21-14 to group the unlevered equity cost terms, we get: $K_U + K_U(D/S) = K_e + K_D(D/S)$, or $K_U(1 + D/S) = K_e + K_D(D/S)$. Substituting S/S into the left-hand side for 1, we have $K_U[(S + D)/S]$ on the left, which can also be expressed as $K_U(V/S)$, since $V = S + D$. This leaves us with: $K_U(V/S) = K_e + K_D(D/S)$. Multiplying both sides by S/V leaves: $K_U = K_e(S/V) + K_D(D/V)$.

[21-15]

$$K_U = K_E \frac{S}{V} + K_D \frac{D}{V}$$

This is of course the weighted average cost of capital (WACC), as discussed in Chapter 20. However, there is one difference from the equation we provided there, which is that we have not adjusted K_D for taxes above, since of course in this ideal M&M world, there are no taxes.

Example 21-3: M&M's First Model and the Cost of Capital

Estimate the cost of equity and the WACC for the levered firm in Example 21-2, assuming that its cost of debt is 6 percent.

Solution

$$K_e = K_U + (K_U - K_D)\frac{D}{S_L} = 10 + (10 - 6)(5/15) = 11.33\%$$

$$WACC = 15/20(11.33) + 5/20(6) = 10\%$$

So M&M's results are really quite simple. The value of the firm is *unaffected* by the use of debt. This means that as the firm uses debt, the equity cost increases, and does so by enough to exactly offset the advantage of using "cheap" debt. The result is that the firm's weighted average cost of capital is constant. This is illustrated in Figure 21-4.

FIGURE 21-4

M&M and the Cost of Capital

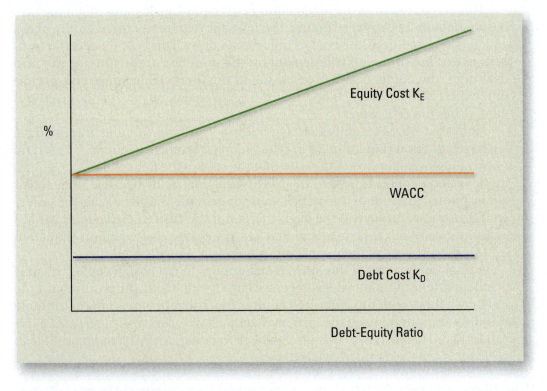

This is a very important figure. M&M were the first to logically analyze the capital structure decision and derive the relationship between the WACC and the firm's financing decision. Previously people had talked loosely about it without imposing any logical structure. Even now when first confronted with the M&M argument people still say that the firm's WACC *must* fall if the unlevered equity cost is, say, 10 percent and debt only costs 6 percent. Obviously 6 percent is less than 10 percent, so the WACC must fall! The error in this logic is that the equity becomes riskier due to the financial leverage risk premium. With the M&M argument, the equity cost rises by exactly enough to offset the cheap debt, leaving the WACC unchanged.

Another faulty argument is to go back to the financial leverage equation and say that the EPS must increase as long as the ROI exceeds the cost of debt so that is the correct cutoff rate for evaluating investments, not the firm's WACC. This, too, is faulty since the use of debt financing will increase the equity cost so that the value of the shares may fall, even if the expected EPS goes up. Further, it is the firm's objective to maximize market values, not EPS.

Consider an unlevered firm with an expected EBIT of $10 million and an unlevered equity cost (K_U) of 10 percent. This means that its value is $100 million (i.e., $10 million ÷ 0.10). If it has 10 million shares outstanding, the share price is $10. Now suppose the firm finds a $10 million project with an ROI of 8 percent. Clearly with a 10 percent equity cost, this project should not be accepted. However, suppose someone says we can borrow debt at a cost of 6 percent, so let's accept it, since the expected EPS will go up. This statement is partly true since we can work out the new higher expected EPS as follows:

$$EPS = \frac{\$10 + .08 \times \$10 - .06 \times \$10}{10} = \$1.02$$

This is higher than the original EPS of $1.00 (i.e., $10 million ÷ 10 million shares). The new EPS reflects the existing $10 million EBIT plus the new EBIT from the project of $0.8 million (8 percent times $10 million) minus the new interest charges of $0.6 million (6 percent times $10 million).

However, the critical value is what happens to the share price, and for this we need to know what the new equity cost is. We can first find the net present value (NPV) of the new project using the 10 percent discount rate. That is:

$$NPV = \frac{0.08 \times \$10}{0.10} - \$10 = -\$2$$

The present value of the project's earnings is $8 million, but since its cost is $10 million, the net present value is –$2 million. So after taking this project, the firm's equity market value will drop from $100 million to $98 million. We can then estimate the new equity cost using Equation 21-14 as:

$$K_e = 0.10 + (0.10 - 0.06){}^{10}\!/_{98} = 10.41\%$$

Thus, the use of $10 million in debt has increased the variability in the EPS and ROE, causing the equity cost to increase from 10 to 10.41 percent.

The new equity price is then the new expected EPS in perpetuity discounted at the new equity cost, or:

$$P = \frac{1.02}{0.1041} = \$9.80$$

Just as the value of the equity drops by $2 million, so the share price drops by $0.20 despite the increase in the expected EPS.

Remember that financial leverage has three effects: increased expected ROE, increased ROE variability, and increased risk of financial distress and bankruptcy. M&M's assumptions rule out the third effect, so we are left with one favourable and one unfavourable effect. In this example, the favourable increase in expected EPS is outweighed by the unfavourable effect of increased financial leverage. As a result, financing an 8 percent project with 6 percent debt increases the expected EPS, but when the WACC is 10 percent the stock price still falls due to the higher financial leverage. *Only if the expected ROI of a project exceeds the WACC will the share price go up.*

CONCEPT REVIEW QUESTIONS

1. State the assumptions underlying the M&M irrelevance theory.
2. Explain the importance of this theory.
3. What is the basic argument that M&M use to arrive at the irrelevancy result?
4. In this ideal M&M world, what will affect firm value?

21.4 THE IMPACT OF TAXES

Introducing Corporate Taxes

Even back in 1958 there were taxes, and the impact of government on corporate investment and financing decisions still exists. Unfortunately, tax is amazingly complex and a full discussion is beyond the scope of this text. However, one key feature we emphasized in Chapter 18 is that the interest on debt is tax deductible. This has a profound impact on the M&M results, since debt is favoured for tax reasons in Canada.[13] We will incorporate taxes into our discussion simply by making all the payments to the equity holders after corporate income taxes in the M&M arbitrage table. What this means is that we multiply all values by (1–T).

The first thing to note is that the value of any firm will be reduced as taxes are introduced, since this reduces the earnings available to the shareholders. For example, the value of the unlevered firm, assuming perpetual *EBIT*, reduces to:

[21-16]

$$V_U = \frac{EBIT(1-T)}{K_U}$$

Notice that for the same level of EBIT, the firm value (as reflected in the numerator of this equation) is reduced as taxes are introduced. Further, the higher the tax rate, the lower the firm value, all else being equal.

---

[13] Although debt is not as much favoured as in the United States, as we shall see when we discuss the dividend tax credit system in Chapter 22.

We now focus on the value of the levered equity since this is what decreases in value for the levered firm when we consider corporate income taxes.

Table 21-8   M&M with Taxes

Portfolios (Actions)	Cost	Payoff
Portfolio E:	αS_L	$\alpha(EBIT-K_DD)(1-T)$
Buy α of levered firm's equity		
Portfolio D:		
Buy α of unlevered firm	αV_U	$\alpha EBIT(1-T)$
Borrow α of levered firm's debt	$\alpha D(1-T)$	$-\alpha K_DD(1-T)$
Total Portfolio	$\alpha(V_U-D)(1-T)$	$\alpha(EBIT-K_DD)(1-T)$

Everything is as before, except now buying the levered equity results in an after-tax net income and dividend of $\alpha(EBIT–K_DD)(1–T)$; similarly the payoff to the unlevered equity is $\alpha EBIT(1–T)$. Under this scenario, getting the same payoff to the homemade leverage portfolio formed by borrowing to invest in the unlevered equity requires interest payments of $\alpha K_DD(1–T)$. If these interest payments are discounted at the cost of debt then $-\alpha D(1–T)$ has to be borrowed in order to generate these interest payments.[14] As a result, to avoid arbitrage the value of the firm must equal: $V_U - D(1-T) = S_L$. Noting that $V_L = S_L + D$, we can rearrange the equation above to get the following:

$$V_L = V_U + DT$$ [21-17]

Equation 21-17 is M&M's valuation equation extended to recognize that interest payments are tax deductible by the corporation, and is sometimes referred to as M&M's second model. The value of the firm with leverage is the value without leverage plus the **corporate debt tax shield** from debt financing.

Remember that interest is tax deductible so in our cost of capital example where the interest rate was 6.0 percent and the corporate tax rate 40 percent, the after-tax cost to the firm was only 3.6 percent. This means that 40 percent of the cost of the interest was paid for by a reduction in the firm's tax bill. If the firm is a perpetuity this debt is outstanding forever, so that discounting this reduction in the interest cost to perpetuity gives the tax shield value TD. This is the implication of the M&M arbitrage argument.

Another way of thinking about this is to remember that the value of the firm is the value of the equity and the value of the debt. If the firm has no debt outstanding, the value is split between the government in tax revenues and the equity market value, since the taxes are proportional to the firm's taxable income. If the corporate income tax rate is 40 percent, then the government is getting 40 percent of the overall value and the shareholders, 60 percent. However, if the firm raises debt, then the government share of the pie falls as its tax revenue falls. Consequently the value of the debt plus the equity goes up. This is illustrated in Figure 21-5.

corporate debt tax shield the value added when a firm uses debt that is attributable to the associated tax benefits

---

[14] In this example we ignore personal taxes and whether the individual borrowing the money gets a tax deduction.

FIGURE   21-5

*Firm Value with
Corporate Taxes*

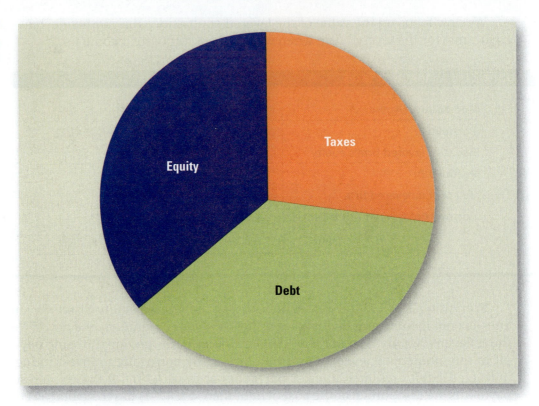

The tax subsidy to using debt explains why in Chapter 18 so many corporate financing vehicles are designed with the intention of making the associated payments tax deductible as interest.

If the value of the firm now goes up with the use of debt as it generates a bigger tax shield value and reduces the government share of the value of private enterprise, then the WACC must go down. To see this we can substitute the M&M tax value (Equation 21-17) into the earnings yield and get the new tax-corrected value of Equation 21-14, which is given below.

[21-18]

$$K_e = K_U + (K_U - K_D)(1 - T)\frac{D}{S_L}$$

In this case, the financial leverage premium is reduced by $(1-T)$. If the government pays for 40 percent of the debt through a reduction in taxes, then the effective debt-equity ratio is only $(1-T)D/S_L$. As a result, the equity cost does not increase by the same amount as it would if there were no taxes paid. This is illustrated in Figure 21-6.

The key differences in this diagram when compared with Figure 21-4 are that the interest cost and the financial leverage risk premium on the equity cost are both reduced by $(1-T)$. As a result, as more debt is used, the cost of equity does not increase enough to offset the use of the cheaper debt. Therefore, the WACC declines continuously with the use of debt financing. Notice also that the equation to determine the WACC would also need to be adjusted to reflect taxes, and would now be the same as the WACC equation introduced in Chapter 20 (ignoring preferred shares). This is shown in Equation 21-19.

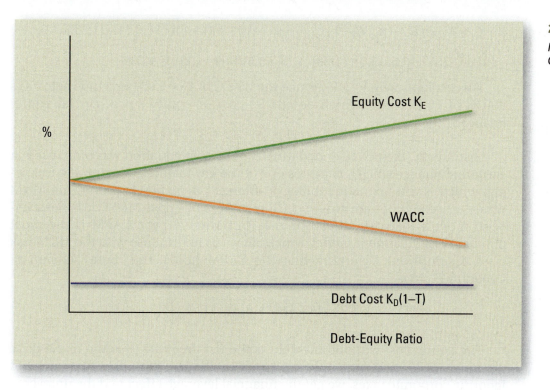

$$WACC = \frac{S}{V}K_e + \frac{D}{V}K_D(1-T)$$

[21-19]

Example 21-4: M&M with Corporate Taxes

Let's revisit the firms in Examples 21-2 and 21-3 and now assume that both U and L face a corporate tax rate of 30 percent, and that they still generate an expected EBIT of $2 million perpetually.

a. Find the value of the unlevered firm (U) assuming their cost of capital is 10 percent.

b. Find the value of the identical risk levered firm (L), which has $5 million in debt outstanding.

c. Find the cost of L's equity and its WACC.

Solution

a. $V_U = \dfrac{EBIT(1-T)}{K_U} = \dfrac{\$2(1-.30)}{.10} = \$14$ million

Notice the decline of $6 million in U's market value. This is the present value of the future tax payments made to the government.

b. $V_L = V_U + TD = \$14 + (.30)(5) = \$15.5$ million.

$S_L = V_L - D = 15.5 - 5 = \$10.5$ million.

Notice that L is worth $1.5 million more than U due to the tax shield value of debt (*TD*).

c. $K_e = K_U + (K_U - K_D)(1-T)\frac{D}{S_L} = 10 + (10-6)(1-.30)(5/10.5) = 11.33\%$

$WACCL = (10.5/15.5)(11.33) + (5/15.5)(6)(1-.30) = 9.03\%$

This explains why $V_L > V_U$, since the WACC of L of 9.03 percent is below U's WACC of 10 percent (which equals its cost of equity since it is all equity financed).

Historically, the tax-extended M&M equity cost equation was often used in corporate finance since it captures one of the key features of corporate financing, which is the tax deductibility of interest payments. However, the M&M equity cost equations are rarely used any more, since post-M&M we have developed models that can adjust for risk. In particular, the CAPM is the most popular risk adjustment model, which allows us to dispense with the M&M risk class assumption. Assuming that the CAPM holds, the "beta" version of Equation 21-18 is:

[21-20]

$$K_e = RF + MRP \times \beta_U (1 + (1-T)\frac{D}{S_L})$$

The equity cost without any debt is the risk-free rate plus the market risk premium (MRP) times the unlevered beta coefficient. With debt financing but ignoring corporate taxes, we get the financial leverage effect and the unlevered beta is multiplied by one plus the debt-equity ratio. However, with corporate income taxes, as before, we multiply the debt by ($1 - T$) to reflect that not all of the debt costs are paid by the shareholders.

Given the importance of the CAPM in estimating the equity cost, Equation 21-20 is more often used than the M&M equations from which it is derived.[15] Given the simplicity of the adjustment, it is relatively easy to *unlever* betas to get the unlevered equity cost and then *relever* them to account for changes in the firm's financial leverage. Although this is common practice, it contains a crucial flaw, which is that the adjustment is based on the M&M equation, which implies that 100 percent debt financing is optimal: since there is always more tax shield value to using more debt, why stop? While it seems obvious on an intuitive level that firms should not finance with 100 percent debt, we can address the issue more formally by relaxing M&M's assumptions that there are no costs related to the risk of financial distress or bankruptcy. We discuss these issues in detail in the next section. The conclusion that 100 percent debt is optimal in the presence of corporate taxes also ignores the impact of personal taxes. We discuss the impact of personal taxes on M&M's conclusions regarding capital structure in the Appendix to this chapter.

CONCEPT REVIEW QUESTIONS

1. How do taxes affect the M&M argument?
2. What are the practical difficulties associated with the implications of M&M's corporate tax model?

---

[15] R. Hamada, "The Effect of the Firm's Capital Structure on the Systematic Risk of Common Stocks," *Journal of Finance*, May 1972.

21.5 FINANCIAL DISTRESS, BANKRUPTCY, AND AGENCY COSTS

The problem with M&M's corporate tax model is that it recognizes the benefits of using debt (i.e., the tax shield DT), but disregards the associated risks, which include the increased risk of bankruptcy or financial distress. The important thing about financial distress and bankruptcy costs is that there is a flow of value away from both the debt holders and the equity holders. In the simple M&M world, anyone can buy both the firm's debt and equity and what the equity holder loses, the debt holder gains, so this is an example of a *zero-sum game*. All that is happening is that value is being rearranged but none is being destroyed. The key feature of bankruptcy and financial distress is that value is destroyed. In this way, while the use of debt creates value by reducing the government's share of taxes, it also destroys value by causing increased risk of financial distress and bankruptcy. In discussing this we must first explain what we mean by distress and bankruptcy.

Bankruptcy is a legal definition. It can occur in two ways: (1) when the firm commits an act of bankruptcy, such as the non-payment of interest, and creditors enforce their legal rights as a result; or (2) when the firm voluntarily declares bankruptcy. Under either scenario, in Canada, the firm is reorganized either under the Companies Creditors Arrangements Act (CCAA) or the Business Insolvency Act (BIA). The CCAA is primarily for larger, more complicated firms (as the debt must exceed $5 million) and is exceedingly flexible. Essentially the court appoints a monitor, who is normally a trustee in bankruptcy working for one of the larger accounting firms, who then reports back to the court. The monitor has considerable flexibility in preventing creditors from exercising their claims against the firm, in restructuring contracts, and in allowing the management of the firm to develop a plan to reorganize in the hope of continuing operations. During this period, the firm is allowed to raise new financing, called debtor in possession (DIP) financing, with a higher priority over existing unsecured claims. It is this financing that provides the firm with some breathing space to reorganize and present a plan to all creditors, which the court can impose, providing enough of them agree.

The BIA is much more rigid. There is very limited scope for preventing creditors from seizing assets, the firm cannot raise DIP financing, and there is no provision for imposing a settlement on all creditors even if a significant majority agree. If a restructuring plan is rejected, then creditors can seize their assets and the firm is liquidated, with anything left after payment to the secured creditors being proportionally allocated to the unsecured creditors. The BIA is much simpler and more predictable than the CCAA and is used mainly by smaller companies where the major creditor is a commercial bank, and as a result it is a lot easier to negotiate a settlement. In contrast, the CCAA is mainly used for large companies with many creditors, where a "stay" or breathing space is needed to sort things out.

Either way, a reorganization is expensive, particularly under the CCAA, where there are much more significant legal, accounting, and court fees. All of these fees represent an outflow of value that goes to neither the debt holders nor the equity holders. If the firm is actually wound up and liquidated, there are even more costs, as the major asset of a failing firm is usually a history of tax losses. These losses can be carried forward and used against future profits and are thus valu-

bankruptcy a state of insolvency that occurs when a firm either commits an act of bankruptcy, such as the non-payment of interest, and creditors enforce their legal rights to recoup money, or when a firm voluntarily declares bankruptcy in an effort to be protected while reorganizing to become solvent again

direct costs of bank-ruptcy costs incurred as a direct result of bank-ruptcy, including liquidation of assets, the loss of tax losses, and legal and account-ing fees

indirect costs of bank-ruptcy, or financial distress costs losses to a firm prior to declaring bankruptcy

financial distress a state of business failing where bankruptcy seems imminent if dra-matic action is not taken

agency costs the costs associated with agency problems

able to the firm. However, if the firm is wound up, these losses disappear and the major beneficiary is the government. In addition, the process of winding up a firm usually results in sales of assets to third parties at "bargain" prices that are less than their value in place, so again there is a value loss to the firm.

Firms try hard to reorganize prior to a formal bankruptcy and liquidation because of these deadweight losses to liquidation from reduced asset prices in distress sales, the loss of tax losses, and the costs of a liquidation in terms of legal and accounting fees. These costs are often referred to as the **direct costs of bankruptcy**.

While the direct costs above can be substantial, even greater losses in value can occur prior to the firm deteriorating into a bankruptcy situation. These losses are often referred to as the **indirect costs of bankruptcy**, or more simply **financial distress costs**. Financial distress is a situation where the firm has yet to commit the act of bankruptcy, yet it knows that unless something dramatic happens it will like-ly go bankrupt. Suppose, for example, the firm still has $10 million in cash and yet its business is failing and is worth only $20 million, but it has a $50 million loan coming due in a year. Clearly if the firm doesn't do anything, in a year's time its creditors will insist on payment and the $20 million business and the $10 million in cash will belong to the creditors. Ignoring any fees and other associated costs, the creditors will get $0.60 on the dollar for their debt and the shareholders will lose everything. This is a situation of **financial distress**.

During periods of financial distress, there is an increase in the **agency costs** due to the increase in the divergence of interests between equity holders and debt holders. In the example discussed in the previous paragraph, the debt holders have a chance of getting $0.60 on the dollar back, while the equity hold-ers' stake in the firm is zero. Therefore, the equity holders (who get to vote) may undertake measures to try to get something for themselves, at the expense of the debt holders. For example, one obvious thing for the shareholders to do is to pay out the $10 million in cash as a dividend. At least this gives them some cash now and in a year's time it simply means that the creditors will only get $20 million instead of $30 million when they seize the firm's assets. However, as well as being unethical, this is illegal.

The responsibility of the board of directors (BOD) is to act in the best interests of the company. For a solvent company this statement means pursuing the best interests of the shareholders. However, for an insolvent company, the responsibil-ity of the BOD shifts to all the stakeholders in the firm, including the creditors. In particular, once the firm is reorganized under the CCCA or BIA, all the dividend decisions of at least the past year and sometimes as far back as three years are reviewed to see whether they were prudent and reasonable at the time. A sudden cash dividend of $10 million shortly before becoming bankrupt would immedi-ately make the board members at the time they were declared personally liable, and would cause the court to order the payments reversed.[16]

However, just because something is illegal doesn't mean there are not other ways of achieving the same result. Funny things happen in failing firms: assets are sometimes sold to related companies owned by the shareholders at "knock down" prices, or the firm pays for joint venture activities for which there seems on the surface to be little benefit. In all cases, they are simply more sophisticat-ed ways of trying to strip cash out of the company before it goes bankrupt, since

---

[16] Note that this is also why directors usually resign as the firm gets into serious financial trouble. There have been times when all the directors have tried to resign, but the CCCA requires at least one director.

when it does, these assets belong to the creditors and not the shareholders. Part of the expense of reorganizing or liquidating a company is simply working out what has happened in the previous few years and whether any assets have been fraudulently stripped out of the company.

A more subtle problem than outright fraud is to recognize that the shareholders essentially have a one-year call option on the underlying firm, where the exercise price is the value of the debt. In one year's time, either the value of the firm exceeds $50 million or it doesn't. If it does, then the firm can refinance and pay off its creditors, and the shareholders will have some residual value. On the other hand, if the value of the firm is less than $50 million, the shareholders are protected by *limited liability* and can simply walk away and hand over the firm to the creditors. It is the existence of limited liability and the fact that shareholders are only exposed up to the value of their investment that creates this call option. We depict the shareholders' value in Figure 21-7.

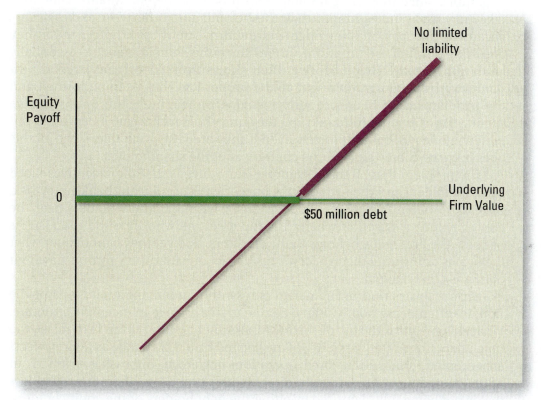

21-7   FIGURE

The Firm as a Call Option for Shareholders

If there is no limited liability, the shareholders have to pay off the $50 million in debt regardless, so they gain (lose) if the underlying firm value (the unlevered value) is greater (less) than the face value of the debt. However, with limited liability they can't be forced to make up the losses if the value of the firm is less than the face value of the debt that is due. As a result the value of the equity behaves like a call option with the minimum value represented by the heavy intrinsic value line depicted in Figure 21-7. The importance of understanding the change in the characteristics of the shares in a firm in financial distress is that options react differently than ordinary common shares. For example, two major factors increasing the value of a call option are time and risk—both of which increase the option value. So with $10 million in cash, the shareholders have the possibility of increasing the risk of the firm and extending the time until they go bankrupt in a year.

Whether or not they can extend the time period will depend on the type of debt that they have outstanding. In this example, all $50 million is due next year. But if instead, it were long-term debt with only the interest payments due next year, then the firm could continue to make the interest payments until all $10 million in cash is used up. During this period, the firm could devote all its time and energy to survival. This means that normal maintenance may be skipped, machines not replaced, advertising and R&D stopped, and generally the operations allowed to run down. The hope on the part of the shareholders is that something happens to give value to the firm, while the worst that can happen is that bankruptcy is delayed. For the creditors, this is a nightmare scenario where they are seeing the value of the operations, as well as the $10 million in cash, go down period by period until by the time they can finally force bankruptcy, they don't get $30 million—they get much less.

The second major problem is that there is an incentive for the shareholders to gamble, since they are gambling with the debt holders' wealth. They may take poor risky investments that they would not otherwise make simply because if they pay off, they might get the firm out of bankruptcy, and if they don't pay off, it doesn't matter to them since the shareholders are essentially bankrupt anyway! This incentive often shows up in poorly researched new product introductions where not all the proper R&D has been performed and the product hasn't been properly tested. Unfortunately the opposite also occurs: if the firm is going bankrupt, the equity holders have no incentive to put in new money for minor projects even if they are very profitable, since all this does is create more value for the creditors, not the shareholders.

The problem that all these examples introduce is that the incentives faced by shareholders and the firm change once there is significant bankruptcy risk. Instead of making positive NPV decisions, where the equity holders bear the risk, they face a situation where it is the creditors who bear the risk. This is because the firm really belongs to the creditors, and yet they cannot alter what the firm is doing until the firm commits the act of bankruptcy by non-payment of interest or principal.

During this period of financial distress, the underlying operations of the firm are often being poorly managed due to this change in incentive structure. What this means in terms of the M&M argument is that if the firm raises too much debt, the underlying EBIT of the levered firm will change as poor projects are accepted, good ones ignored, operations neglected, and cash is stripped out of the company. Again similar to direct bankruptcy costs, there is a value loss that is not being fully captured by either the debt holders or the equity holders.

Creditors are well aware of these types of actions by distressed firms, which is why they take offsetting measures. One standard way is not to lend long term to risky firms. Instead, debt is short-term or includes sinking fund payments that create a continuous cash payment to the creditors, thereby reducing the maturity of the call option. This also explains all the red ink in the trust indenture we discussed in Chapter 17, where the firm agrees to insure its assets, to maintain them in good order, not to sell them unless it meets certain tests, not to exceed a particular debt ratio, and to maintain certain levels of working capital. In all cases, the lender is simply trying to reduce the value of this call option and give it greater control over the affairs of the firm.

The result is that there are significant costs attached to raising too much debt, since too much debt increases the risks of financial distress and bankruptcy, and the associated value outflows to third parties. This leads to a theory that is referred to as the **static tradeoff** model, where the firm uses debt to maximize its tax advantages up to the point where these benefits are outweighed by the associated estimated costs of financial distress and bankruptcy. The model is illustrated in Figure 21-8.

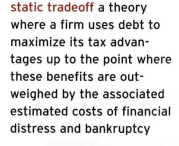

static tradeoff a theory where a firm uses debt to maximize its tax advantages up to the point where these benefits are outweighed by the associated estimated costs of financial distress and bankruptcy

21-8   FIGURE

Firm Value and Financial Distress Costs

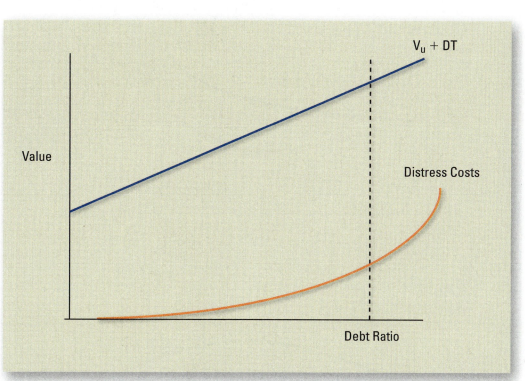

The straight line in Figure 21-8 is the M&M value of the levered firm under the existence of corporate taxes. In other words, it is the value of the unlevered firm plus the tax shield value, where the slope of the line is determined by the tax rate *T*, since value increases with debt by the corporate tax rate. The second curved line is the expected value loss from financial distress and bankruptcy. Notice that the slope of this line is increasing with the debt ratio. This is because at low levels of debt there is little risk of distress or bankruptcy, but this risk and its consequences increases with the debt level. The optimal level of debt occurs where the slope of the financial distress curve is the same as that of the tax-corrected value line because at this point, the marginal tax shield benefit equals the marginal cost of financial distress and bankruptcy. In this way the tax advantages of debt are traded off against the distress and bankruptcy disadvantages.

The conclusions of the static trade-off model are depicted in Figure 21-9. The top diagram shows that the cost of equity increases throughout as more debt is added as expected. Initially, the effect of this increase on the WACC is more than offset by the use of the cheaper debt. As a result, the WACC initially declines as more debt is added. However, beyond a certain point, depicted as D/E*, the WACC begins to increase, reflecting the higher costs of both debt and equity in response to the increased risk of financial distress and bankruptcy. So, the WACC is minimized at D/E*. As a result, as can be seen in the bottom diagram in Figure 21-9, the value of the firm is maximized at this same point. This point, D/E*, represents the optimal capital structure according to the static trade-off model.

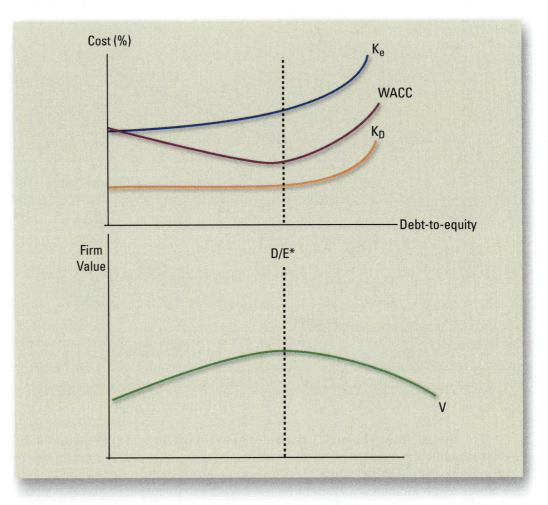

FIGURE 21-9

The Static Trade-Off Model

CONCEPT REVIEW QUESTIONS

1. Explain the impact of financial distress and agency costs on M&M's conclusions regarding capital structure.
2. Why can the firm's debt be viewed as the exercise price to the shareholders' option to purchase the firm?
3. Explain the static trade-off theory.

21.6 OTHER FACTORS AFFECTING CAPITAL STRUCTURE

How well does the static trade-off model explain capital structures? It certainly captures the main effects. However, it ignores two important issues:

1. **Information asymmetry problems:** the effect of informational differences among shareholders, creditors, and management

2. **Agency problems:** the fact that managers make these decisions on behalf of the shareholders, but they have their own interests at stake as well

First let's consider the impact of information differences. Suppose a firm has a market value of $20 million and after careful consideration decides to undertake a new project that costs $5 million and has a $5 million NPV. The firm has 1 million shares outstanding so the share price prior to undertaking the new project is $20. What should it do and how should it finance this project? Theoretically the CEO should call a news conference and announce this great new investment, the media and security analysts in attendance should clap their hands, and the market value of the firm should go up by $5 million to $25 million, and the stock price should rise to $25. The firm should then issue 200,000 shares at $25 each to finance the project, and spend the $5 million so the total value increases to $30 million and the stock price remains at $25 (i.e., $30m ÷ 1.2m).

However, the "real" world does not react like this. Investors will yawn, bombard the CEO with questions, and generally be extremely critical, since they have heard this story before and cannot distinguish between good firms telling the truth and poor firms spinning a story to boost the stock price. So more likely what will happen is that the stock price will stay at $20, forcing the firm to issue 250,000 shares at $20 to finance the project. Then when the truth is revealed and the project does add value, the firm value will later increase to $30 million. So the firm value still gets to $30 million, but this time there are 1.25 million shares outstanding and the stock price only reaches $24.

In fact the situation may be even worse than this since stock prices often drop when the firm announces a new share issue since investors suspect that management thinks the stock price is overvalued and that the company is trying to issue common shares while they are trading at inflated prices! Suppose, for example, that the stock price drops to $18 on the announcement of the share issue. Then the firm will have to issue 277,777 shares to raise the $5 million, and even if the market value gets back up to $30 million, the stock price will only rise to $23.50. In both of these cases, the ownership of this positive NPV project is being shared between the existing shareholders and the new shareholders who are buying in at a below "true" market price.

How can the firm handle this problem of information asymmetry? The obvious answer is to raise $5 million in debt. In this case, when the value of the firm does rise to $30 million after the profits flow from the new investment, the equity is worth $25 million and the debt $5 million, but there are still only 1 million shares outstanding, so the stock price rises to $25.

pecking order order in which firms prefer to raise financing, starting with internal cash flow, then debt, and finally, issuing common equity

What this suggests is that firms only issue equity as a last resort; instead they finance using internal cash flow, then debt and, finally, common equity, in what Stewart Myers[17] refers to as a **pecking order**.

Myers' argument that firms follow a pecking order is based on divulging information. If the firms use internal cash flow then they do not need anyone's permission. For example, even the shareholders can't force the firm to pay a dividend. Similarly the firm can talk to a bank and divulge privileged information to secure a loan. However, when it issues new common shares, as we have seen, the firm has to file a prospectus and reveal all material facts that affect the share price. In the process, the firm has to be careful not to reveal facts to a competitor that may give it a jump start and allow it to compete away the NPV benefits of the project.

The pecking order was also discussed in a different context by Gordon Donaldson.[18] Donaldson justified the pecking order through what we would now call *agency arguments*. He showed that managers' commitment to the firm was through their human capital, versus the "short-term" financial commitment of shareholders. As a result, they were more concerned about the long-term survival of the firm and less inclined to take risks. For these agency reasons, he also argued that managers had a preference for internal cash flow (retained earnings), then debt, and finally issuing new common equity. In an agency model, this financing hierarchy imposes the least risk on the firm and requires the least justification by managers.

Regardless of whether it is for agency reasons or information problems, or some combination of the two, we do see firms using the pecking order in that profitable firms tend to have the least debt simply because they don't need it and have more than enough internal funds. Leveraged recapitalizations involve issuing debt and using the funds to buy back shares. These tend to address these issues over time, but only with a significant lag. The real puzzle is that there are some firms that simply don't use much debt and could. Microsoft, for example, is relatively low risk, hugely profitable, and has no significant debt. It could undoubtedly lower its tax bill by using debt financing and buying back shares, and yet it hasn't.

CONCEPT REVIEW QUESTION

1. Explain how the existence of informational asymmetries and agency costs may lead firms to follow a pecking order to financing.

21.7 CAPITAL STRUCTURE IN PRACTICE

So what do we make of all these factors? First we can say that the static trade-off theory says that you should take advantages of the tax shields from debt, so the first question is: *Is the firm profitable?*

If the firm has no profits then it can't use the tax shields from debt and it might as well finance with equity, or more to the point it has no ability to make interest payments.

---

[17] Myers, S. "The Capital Structure Puzzle," *Journal of Finance*, July 1984.

[18] Donaldson, G. "Financial Goals: Manager versus Stockholders," *Harvard Business Review*, May/June 1963.

The second question deals with whether or not the firm can issue debt. As we saw, lenders make credit evaluations and won't lend if they fear financial distress. In particular, if firms have hard tangible assets that can be sold elsewhere then lenders may lend to them even if they are worried about the survival prospects of the firm. This is because they can always seize their assets, sell them, and recover most of their principal. This leads to the second question: *What type of assets does the firm have? If they are tangible assets that can be used elsewhere they can be used as collateral for a secured loan*.

If the firm's assets are not good collateral, then the lender has to look to the firm's cash flow rather than its assets for security. In this case it will be concerned about its business risk and the variability of its operations. This leads to the third question: *How risky is the firm's underlying business?*

It is a basic law of finance based on our discussion of financial leverage that you do not layer significant financial risk on top of significant business risk.

Generally, financial markets are size constrained. What this means is that preparing a prospectus and so on is time-consuming and costly, so only larger firms access the public markets. Further, larger firms tend to have more diversified operations and more market power. This is not an absolute, but it tends to be the case that larger firms are less risky than smaller firms, so we ask the question: *How big is the firm?*

Finally there is the basic question of whether the firm needs the money and then it becomes very much a function of its profitability and its growth rate. Growing firms need cash, whereas profitable firms generally spin off cash, so we ask: *What is the firm's growth rate and how profitable is it?*

The questions above go a long way to determining how much debt a firm can carry and what its optimal debt ratio will be. Of course firms deviate from their target capital structure when they are offered a good deal. Like everyone else, we may do something we didn't intend to if someone offers us a good deal. In terms of financing, this means that if the firm observes attractive interest rates for debt financing it might lean more heavily on debt financing. This pattern is discussed in Finance in the News 21-1, which alludes to firms' taking advantage of so-called "cheap money" in the long-term risky debt market.

RISK TAKERS REJOICE IN TIDE OF CHEAP MONEY

finance
INTHENEWS21-1

Teresa Cascioli, Paul Desmarais Jr., Ben Bernanke: It's hard to imagine a trio with less in common than these three. Yet each gave us a taste this week of why the unsinkable Canadian stock market smashed another record, and why it may continue to rise.

Start with Ms. Cascioli and Mr. Desmarais. She runs a discount beer outfit; he runs the most powerful corporate entity in the country. She appears in her own radio advertisements; he talks softly and carries a big wallet. She's the blue-collar CEO from Hamilton; he is corporate royalty from Montreal.

This week, she was a seller—handing over control of her company, Lakeport Brewing, to InBev, one of the largest beer companies in the world. And Mr. Desmarais was a buyer, finally sealing the long-rumoured purchase of Putnam Investments for $4.6-billion through Great-West Lifeco.

Why would InBev take out a tiny competitor for nearly three times what it would have cost two years ago? Why would the Desmarais group want to own a tainted, scandal-ridden company—and pay a price for it that some analysts consider rich? At least part of the answer lies in cheap and easy money, the kind that now seems likely to be with us for a while.

It's not simply that interest rates are modest, or that the U.S. Federal Reserve Board

finance
INTHENEWS21-1

indicated this week that it's not likely to raise them any time soon. It's also the kind of money that's cheap.

First, long-term money is inexpensive, thanks in part to Mr. Bernanke's apparent success in snuffing out any hint of inflation without suffocating the economy. The yield curve remains Prairie-flat. An investor who buys two-year U.S. Treasuries today gets a piece of paper that yields 4.9 percent. And if she buys the 30-year government bond instead, she still gets 4.9 percent. Investors get paid nothing extra for taking the longer term.

Second, risky money is cheap. There are many ways to illustrate this, but we'll pick on General Motors (since everyone else does). A year ago, an investor willing to lend his money to the Detroit auto maker for the next 25 years—and accept the bankruptcy risk that comes with that—could expect a 12-percent yield for his trouble. Now it's about 9 percent. Yields on Abitibi-Consolidated's debt plunged in similar fashion this week after the newsprint maker announced its cross-border marriage to Bowater.

Junk bond spreads—the extra yield an investor receives for taking on more risk—are exceedingly thin by historical standards. It's enough to make even the most experienced bond investors wonder how long it can last.

"The risk markets . . . if not drunk, are definitely not walking a very straight line," Pimco managing director Bill Gross said in a commentary this week.

The source of the intoxication is liquidity: Too much cash is chasing too few assets. And if it's worrisome to people like Mr. Gross, it's manna for CEOs, who can be assured that they'll be able to fund their expansion plans with ease and at low cost. Great-West's deal for Putnam is a decent example: Of the $4.6-billion purchase price, just $1.4-billion will be funded through new equity, with a larger chunk coming through bank loans, bond issues and other forms of financing.

And why not? If you can borrow money for a decade or longer and pay interest rates that are barely higher than government bonds, the decision becomes easy. In the long run, the Desmarais clan figures it can improve Putnam to the point where it's generating a 7-percent "earnings yield" (that is, $7 in profit for every $100 in purchase price). Borrow at 5 percent, earn 7? That's the kind of arithmetic that works in any business.

An awful lot of CEOs are doing the same math and figuring out that it shouldn't be too hard to buy their way to better earnings—if not through acquisitions, then through large share buybacks, funded with borrowed money. The debt-fuelled M&A boom isn't about to stop, and until it does, neither will this bull market.

Source: DeCloet, Derek. "Risk Takers Rejoice in Tide of Cheap Money." *Globe and Mail*, February 3, 2007, p. B1. Reprinted with the permission of the *Globe and Mail*.

Similarly, if a firm's share price is very high and increasing and it believes it to be "overvalued," then it may decide to take advantage of this window of opportunity to issue common shares. This is why we observe more equity financing in a strong equity market than a weak one.[19] Therefore, the last question we ask is: ***How high is the stock price and how much has it appreciated over the last year?***

These are the basic questions that are asked in determining a firm's financing decisions.

To see how important these issues are, Table 21-9 reports the book debt-to-equity ratios for the firms in the S&P/TSX 60 Index, which includes the largest publicly traded firms in Canada. The range in the average D/E ratios is from essentially 0 to 3.15, where Husky Energy's average of 9.0, which is driven by two extreme values in 1998 and 1999, is ignored so as not to distort the results. The

---

[19] In fact, firms often issue equity when they think it is overvalued. This opportunistic financing causes significant departures from their long-run "target" debt ratios.

lows of essentially zero are for large rapid growth firms with low levels of profit, whereas the 3.15 is for ACE Aviation, the former Air Canada, which has largely tangible and saleable assets. In between, we have large debt levels for regulated utilities like TransCanada, Enbridge, and TransAlta, and low levels for more risky resource and exploration firms like Teck-Cominco, Talisman, and Suncor. From this grouping of firms, we can see that basic factors like the nature of a firm's assets, its profitability, and growth rate are similar among firms within an industry. This is why industry averages are useful proxies for benchmarking capital structure, but they are not the end of the story.

Table 21-9   Debt-to-Equity Ratios—S&P/TSX 60 Index

	1996	1997	1998	1999	2000	2001	2002	2003	2004	2005	Average
ACE Aviation Holdings Inc.	...	...	...	...	...	...	...	...	...	3.15	3.15
Agnico-Eagle Mines Limited	0.66	1.03	0.72	0.91	1.34	0.71	0	0.01	0.31	0.2	0.59
Agrium Inc.	0.68	0.87	0.71	0.89	0.94	1.32	1	0.9	.053	0.4	0.82
Alcan Inc.	0.32	0.31	0.33	0.27	0.51	0.47	0.45	0.88	0.87	0.67	0.51
ATI Technologies Inc.	0.07	0	0	0	0	0.01	0.04	0.04	0.03	0.03	0.02
Barrick Gold Corporation	0.15	0.16	0.14	0.13	0.22	0.15	0.14	0.14	0.33	0.47	0.20
BCE Inc.	0.89	0.99	0.85	0.56	1.02	0.96	1.05	0.91	0.86	0.85	0.89
Biovail Corporation	0.19	0.06	2.48	0.32	0.52	0.03	0.58	0.64	0.35	0.32	0.55
Bombardier Inc.	1.26	1.47	1.55	2.05	2.47	2.87	5.16	3.09	3.69	2.28	2.59
Brookfield Asset Management Inc.	0.32	0.58	0.66	0.66	0.64	1.56	1.74	1.47	1.65	1.83	1.11
Cameco Corporation	0.15	0.17	0.32	0.19	0.17	0.19	0.12	0.11	0.21	0.32	0.20
Canadian National Railway Company	0.64	0.49	0.97	0.77	0.76	0.93	0.84	0.72	0.7	0.55	0.74
Canadian Natural Resources Limited	0.55	0.94	1.12	1.14	0.77	0.69	0.84	0.46	0.51	0.4	0.74
Canadian Oil Sands Trust	...	...	...	...	0.25	0.77	0.65	0.69	0.64	0.51	0.59
Canadian Pacific Railway Limited	...	...	0.47	0.53	0.64	1.19	0.98	0.91	0.84	0.68	0.78
Canadian Tire Corporation, Limited	0.43	0.6	0.79	1.1	0.76	0.7	0.63	0.48	0.43	0.49	0.64
Celestica Inc.	1.6	1.43	0.16	0.08	0.04	0.03	0	0	0.25	0.34	0.39
Cognos Incorporated	0.02	0.02	0.01	0.01	0	0	0	0	0	0	0.01
Cott Corporation	0.93	1.93	5.16	3.1	2.5	2.28	1.53	0.96	0.71	0.85	2.00
Domtar Inc.	0.54	0.75	0.76	0.63	0.6	1.23	1.01	0.98	1.02	1.45	0.90
Enbridge Inc.	2.49	2.33	2.66	2.24	2.27	2.68	1.63	1.63	1.86	1.95	2.17
EnCana Corporation	0.38	0.43	0.52	0.37	0.33	0.56	0.62	0.57	0.55	0.42	0.48
George Weston Limited	0.77	0.75	0.92	0.94	1.01	1.46	1.15	1.21	1.22	1.08	1.05
Glamis Gold Ltd.	0	0	0	0	0	0	0	0	0.07	0.16	0.02
Goldcorp Inc.	0.04	0	0	0	0	0	0	0	0	0	0.00
Husky Energy Inc.	...	...	43.5	26.58	0.59	0.48	0.47	0.3	0.29	0.25	9.06
Imperial Oil Limited	0.34	0.34	0.37	0.28	0.3	0.31	0.3	0.25	0.23	0.22	0.29
Inco Limited	0.36	0.44	0.45	0.36	0.22	0.16	0.44	0.35	0.33	0.33	0.34
IPSCO Inc.	0.49	0.45	0.42	0.42	0.41	0.5	0.38	0.42	0.29	0.18	0.40
Kinross Gold Corporation	0.15	0.16	0.25	0.32	0.34	0.25	0.14	0.02	0.11	0.16	0.19
Loblaw Companies Limited	0.89	0.87	0.97	0.94	1.05	1.04	0.98	0.99	0.86	0.82	0.94
Magna International Inc.	0.31	0.09	0.16	0.21	0.18	0.15	0.13	0.12	0.17	0.14	0.17

	1996	1997	1998	1999	2000	2001	2002	2003	2004	2005	Average
Manulife Financial Corporation	...	0.26	0.23	0.18	0.18	0.24	0.23	0.18	0.15	0.19	0.20
MDS Inc.	0.56	0.44	0.49	0.35	0.48	0.43	0.44	0.37	0.33	0.32	0.42
Nexen Inc.	0.49	1.71	1.18	0.71	1.09	0.81	0.79	1.15	1.52	0.9	1.04
Nortel Networks Corporation	0.38	0.4	0.17	0.16	0.08	0.88	0.98	0.75	0.84	2.48	0.71
NOVA Chemicals Corporation	0.6	0.63	0.99	0.86	0.84	1.07	0.89	0.65	1.02	1.67	0.92
Novelis Inc.											
Petro-Canada	0.46	0.44	0.46	0.42	0.39	0.28	0.53	0.29	0.3	0.31	0.39
Potash Corporation of Saskatchewan Inc.	0.45	0.55	0.42	0.47	0.45	0.73	0.72	0.73	0.57	0.71	0.58
Research In Motion Limited	0.04	0	0	0.02	0.01	0.01	0.02	0	0	0	0.01
Rogers Communications Inc.	-3.32	-3.42	-3.93	7.6	2.87	2.54	4.89	3.35	2.8	2.22	1.53
Royal Bank of Canada											
Shaw Communications Inc.	2.25	2.58	0.95	0.81	0.75	0.91	1.24	1.17	1.07	1.34	1.31
Shoppers Drug Mart Corporation	...	...	...	0.12	1.88	0.77	0.59	0.44	0.32	0.4	0.65
Sun Life Financial Inc.	...	...	0.28	0.27	0.24	0.2	0.18	0.16	0.14	0.27	0.22
Suncor Energy Inc.	0.34	0.58	0.87	0.63	0.91	1.13	0.78	0.56	0.46	0.5	0.68
Talisman Energy Inc.	0.43	0.8	0.94	0.61	0.47	0.71	0.67	0.44	0.51	0.74	0.63
Teck Cominco Limited	0.4	0.5	0.54	0.41	0.43	0.53	0.47	0.53	0.19	0.37	0.44
TELUS CorporatioN	...	...	0.44	0.45	0.51	1.27	1.32	1.01	0.9	0.67	0.82
The Bank of Nova Scotia											
The Thomson Corporation	1.2	1	0.41	0.36	0.39	0.61	0.48	0.47	0.44	0.43	0.58
The Toronto-Dominion Bank											
Tim Hortons Inc.											
TransAlta Corporation	1.38	1.27	0.85	0.96	1.07	1.12	1.09	0.97	1.06	0.9	1.07
TransCanada Corporation	1.98	2.13	2.34	2.26	1.98	1.92	1.74	1.55	1.55	1.57	1.90
Yellow Pages Income Fund	...	...	...	...	...	...	...	...	0.34	0.4	0.37

Source: Data from *Financial Post* Corporate Analyzer Database

Summary

This chapter has discussed some of the most important issues in corporate finance. Long before OPM stood for the option pricing model, it stood for *other people's money* and was at the heart of financing activities. In this chapter, we have shown the three effects of financial leverage: expected ROE tends to increase, the variability of the ROE increases, and the risk of financial distress increases. These principles apply to the use of OPM regardless of who the borrower is: they are simply the effects of financial leverage. However, this text is concerned with corporate decisions and the Conference Board showed that the major determinants of the firm's capital structure decision are its impact on profits, risk, and cash flows. These impacts can be assessed by profit planning charts or financial break-even (indifference) analysis, as well as by the use of standard ratios calculated by the major rating agencies. However, they do not indicate *how* the use of debt creates value.

The classic M&M arguments assess whether the capital structure decision creates value. Their startling conclusion was that under some simplifying assumptions, issuing debt does not create value. This is because the firm is not doing anything that others can't do just as well; that is, borrow money. In essence, the M&M argument is that firms should stick to doing things where they have a comparative advantage and it is difficult to see how borrowing money is such, since we can all do it. However, what this means is that the WACC is independent of the debt ratio, and simple statements like saying that debt is cheaper than equity, and that its use lowers the WACC, are fundamentally wrong.

However, once we introduce the fact that interest on debt is tax deducible, whereas dividends to the common shareholders are not, it means that there is a tax shield value to raising debt. At a 40 percent tax rate, the fact that interest is tax deductible as a cost of doing business means that for a profitable firm, 40 percent of the value of the debt is effectively being paid by the government in reduced taxes. Hence, there is a transfer of wealth to the private sector from the government as the firm finances with debt. This tax incentive to using debt is offset by the resulting financial distress and bankruptcy costs, as discussed in the static trade-off model.

As its name implies, the static trade-off model does not take into account dynamic effects. The pecking order theory, on the other hand, does account for these dynamic effects as firms tend to first use internal cash flow, then debt, and will only raise new common equity as a last resort. The result is that firms depart from the static trade-off optimal debt ratio over time, and then refinance to bring their debt ratio back in line with their target ratio. Therefore, actual capital structures are constantly changing as firms take advantage of market conditions.

Key Terms

agency costs, p. 840

bankruptcy, p. 839

business risk, p. 815

cash flow-to-debt ratio (CFTD), p. 824

corporate debt tax shield, p. 835

direct costs of bankruptcy, p. 840

EPS indifference point, p. 822

financial break-even points, p. 817

financial distress, p. 840

financial leverage, p. 814

financial leverage risk premium, p. 831

financial risk, p. 816

fixed burden coverage ratio, p. 824

homemade leverage, p. 830

indifference point, p. 817

indirect costs of bankruptcy or financial distress costs, p. 840

invested capital (IC), p. 814

M&M equity cost equation, p. 831

Modigliani and Miller (M&M), p. 827

pecking order, p. 846

profit planning charts, p. 821

return on equity (ROE), p.814

return on invested capital (ROI), p. 814

risk value of money, p. 818

static tradeoff, p. 843

Formulas/Equations

(21-1) $ROE = \dfrac{(EBIT - R_D B)(1 - T)}{SE}$

(21-2) $ROI = \dfrac{EBIT(1 - T)}{SE + B}$

(21-3) $ROE = ROI + (ROI - R_D(1 - T))\dfrac{B}{SE}$

(21-4) $ROE = ROI(1 + \dfrac{B}{SE}) - R_D(1 - T)\dfrac{B}{SE}$

(21-5) $EPS = \dfrac{(EBIT - R_D B)(1 - T)}{\#}$

(21-6) $EPS = \dfrac{-R_D B(1 - T)}{\#} + \dfrac{EBIT(1 - T)}{\#}$

(21-7) $Fixed\ Burden\ Coverage = \dfrac{EBITDA}{I + (Pref.\ Div. + SF)/(1 - T)}$

(21-8) $CFTD = \dfrac{EBITDA}{Debt}$

(21-9) $Z = 1.2X_1 + 1.4X_2 + 3.3X_3 + 0.6X_4 + 0.999X_5$

(21-10) $V_U = S_L + D = V_L$

(21-11) $S_L = \dfrac{(EBIT - K_D D)}{K_e}$

(21-12) $K_e = \dfrac{(EBIT - K_D D)}{S_L}$

(21-13) $V_U = \dfrac{EBIT}{K_U} = S_L + D = V_L$

(21-14) $K_e = K_U + (K_U - K_D)\dfrac{D}{S_L}$

(21-15) $K_U = K_E \dfrac{S}{V} + K_D \dfrac{D}{V}$

(21-16) $V_U = \dfrac{EBIT(1 - T)}{K_U}$

(21-17) $V_L = V_U + DT$

(21-18) $K_e = K_U + (K_U - K_D)(1 - T)\dfrac{D}{S_L}$

(21-19) $WACC = \dfrac{S}{V}K_e + \dfrac{D}{V}K_D(1-T)$

(21-20) $K_e = RF + MRP \times \beta_U\left(1 + (1-T)\,D\big/S_L\right)$

(21A-1) $V_L = V_U + D\left[1 - \dfrac{(1-T_C)(1-T_D)}{(1-T_P)}\right]$

APPENDIX 21-A
PERSONAL TAXES AND CAPITAL STRUCTURE

Recall from our discussion of taxation in Chapter 3 that dividend income and interest income are taxed differently at the personal level, with dividends receiving preferential tax treatment. Since investors will base their valuations of securities on the after-tax cash flows they expect to receive from them, it is reasonable to assume that individual taxes may affect firm value and thus capital structure decisions.

One popular model dealing with personal taxes was introduced by Merton Miller (one of the Ms of M&M).[20] He argues that a firm should strive to minimize all taxes (both corporate and personal) paid on corporate income. By doing so, the firm maximizes total cash flows after corporate and personal taxes available to security holders. Based on a number of technical assumptions, Miller arrived at the following valuation equation, which is a variation of the M&M valuation model, except it also accounts for personal tax rates:

$$V_L = V_U + D\left[1 - \frac{(1-T_C)(1-T_D)}{(1-T_P)}\right]$$

[21A-1]

Where, T_C 5 the corporate tax rate;

T_P 5 the individual's personal tax rate on ordinary income (which also applies to interest income); and,

T_D 5 the individual's tax rate on dividend income.

Technically, we can note several things from this equation.

1. If $(1 - T_P)$ 5 $(1 - T_C)(1 - T_D)$, then V_L 5 V_U, and we get the M&M irrelevancy proposition. This is referred to as an *integrated* tax system and has historically been the tax system in use in Western Europe where individuals get a tax credit for the corporate taxes paid on their behalf. Obviously in this case there are no tax advantages to using debt.

---

[20] Miller, M. "Debt and Taxes," *Journal of Finance* (May 1977), pp. 261–75.

2. If $(1 - T_P) < (1 - T_C)(1 - T_D)$, then $V_L < V_U$, which suggests the firm loses value by issuing debt. In this case there is an incentive for individuals rather than the firm to borrow money since they generate larger tax shields.

3. If $(1 - T_P) > (1 - T_C)(1 - T_D)$, then $V_L > V_U$, which suggests the firm enhances value by issuing debt since there are more debt tax shields at the corporate than the personal level. This is the system we have in Canada and is referred to as a *partially integrated* tax system.

4. If the personal tax rate on dividends (T_D) equals the tax rate on interest income (T_P), then we have what is referred to as a *classic* tax system where all personal income is taxed at the same rate. This is historically the U.S. system and the ratio $(1 - T_D)/(1 - T_P)$ equals one and the M&M corporate tax shields holds even with personal taxes; that is, $V_L = V_U + T_C D$.

Generally, the third case tends to hold; that is $(1 - T_P) > (1 - T_C)(1 - T_D)$, so that $V_L > V_U$. It is the case in Canada that $T_D < T_P$, so the amount by which V_L exceeds V_U is less than the "$T_C D$" term included in M&M's corporate tax model. In other words, there are usually gains to firm value associated with the use of debt, but the gains are not as great as that predicted by M&M's corporate tax valuation model.

For example, based on 2006 federal and provincial tax rate estimates, the combined federal and provincial corporate tax rate for a company operating in Ontario that does not qualify for the small business tax deduction is 36.12 percent. Further assume an Ontario individual in the highest federal and provincial tax brackets with a personal tax rate of 46.41 percent on personal income and 25.09 percent on dividend income.[21] Using these rates, we have the following:

$$(1 - T_P) > (1 - T_C)(1 - T_D)$$
$$(1 - .4641) > (1 - .3612)(1 - .2509)$$
$$0.5359 > 0.4785$$

Notice that these numbers imply the following gains to using debt:

$$V_L = V_U + D[1 - (.4785/.5359)], \text{ or } V_L = V_U + 0.11\,D.$$

Notice that the last term $(0.11D)$ in this expression is lower than that suggested by M&M's second model, which would be $0.3612D$ based on the corporate tax rate above.

While these results might appear very useful at first glance, the model itself is based on several assumptions and is subject to several difficulties. First, as we have discussed several times throughout the text, the financial markets, and hence securities prices, are heavily influenced by the investing behaviour of institutional investors like pension funds, insurance companies, and mutual funds, and most of these are non-taxable. Second, individual investors will face a variety of different marginal tax rates on both ordinary income and dividend income. As a result, the estimates of the tax advantages of using debt are a lower bound. In fact the dividend tax credit system was originally set up to fully integrate the tax system for small businesses based on their lower tax rate. The reason for this is that they have considerable discretion in paying out funds

---

[21] A good site for current tax rates is the Ernst and Young website at
http://www.ey.com/global/content.nsf/Canada/Tax_-_Calculators_-_Overview

from a controlled corporation as dividends or interest or salary and the government wanted to remove any incentive for them to do one thing rather than another. However, if the system is neutral for a small business it can't also be neutral for a larger business facing a higher corporate tax rate.

What we can say is that the Canadian tax system favours corporate debt financing, and that firms get a corporate tax shield from using debt. When we consider personal taxes, the advantage is not as large as that predicted from the corporate tax shield alone, since the government has set personal tax rates to reduce the double taxation of equity income in Canada. As a result, the tax advantages to using debt are between the value implied using personal taxes of 11 percent and that assuming no differential taxes at the individual level of 36 percent.

QUESTIONS AND PRACTICE PROBLEMS

Multiple Choice Questions

1. Which of the following will result in a *decrease* in the weighted average cost of capital (WACC)?

    A. A decrease in T_C

    B. An increase in the cost of debt

    C. An increase in the cost of equity

    D. A decrease in the weight of equity

2. What is the invested capital given the following? Accounts receivable = $40,000; current assets = $200,000; total assets = $500,000; shareholders' equity = $290,000; accounts payable = $10,000; short-term debt = $50,000; and long-term debt = $150,000.

    A. $500,000

    B. $510,000

    C. $490,000

    D. $290,000

3. Which of the following statements is *false*?

    A. ROE is affected by financial risk.

    B. ROI is affected by business risk.

    C. Each dollar invested in the firm earns the same ROI.

    D. There is no such thing as an equity dollar or a debt dollar.

4. Which of the following statements is *false*?

    A. The slope of the financial leverage line is (1 + debt-equity ratio).

    B. ROE = ROI if a firm is 100 percent financed by debt.

    C. The intercept of the financial leverage line is the debt-equity ratio times the after-tax cost of debt.

    D. One of the break-even points is when two financial strategies have the same ROE.

5. Which of the following statements of rules of financial leverage is *false*?

    A. The use of debt normally decreases the expected ROE.

    B. The higher the debt-equity ratio, the steeper the financial leverage line.

    C. Debt financing increases the risk to common shareholders.

    D. Debt financing increases the chances of financial distress.

6. The EPS-EBIT line:

    A. is steeper if there are more shares outstanding.

    B. has a slope equal to $EBIT(1 - T)/\#$.

    C. has an intercept equal to $R_D \, B \, (1 - T)/\#$.

    D. indicates that if $EBIT = 0$, $EPS = - R_D \, B \, (1 - T)/\#$.

7. Which of the following is *not* an assumption of M&M's irrelevance theorem?

    A. Two firms exist with different level of debt.

    B. There is no tax.

    C. Transactions costs are minimal.

    D. There is no risk of costly bankruptcy.

8. In the M&M's irrelevance world, which of the following is *false*?

    A. The cost of equity increases as the debt-equity ratio increases.

    B. If the expected ROI of a project >WACC, the share price will go up.

    C. The firm's objective is to increase the market value of the share price, not EPS.

    D. The WACC always increases as the debt-equity ratio increases.

9. What is the cost of equity for a levered firm given the following? $K_u = 11\%$; $K_D = 6\%$; $T = 40\%$; and $D/S_L = 0.6$.

    A. 11%

    B. 12.8%

    C. 13%

    D. 13.5%

10. Which of the firms below is the *least* likely to raise debt in the capital market?

    A. A profitable firm that has a risky underlying business

    B. A large and profitable firm

    C. A less profitable firm that has a non-risky business

    D. A small firm that has seen its share price decrease in the past

Practice Problems

11. Briefly state the two rules of financial leverage.

12. What is the pecking order according to Myers' argument?

Easy

13. In order for the M&M Irrelevance Theorem to hold, what key assumptions must be met?

Medium

14. Calculate ROE and ROI given the following.

Sales	$168,000
COGS	$ 40,000
Amortization	$ 25,000
SG&A	$ 16,000
Taxes	$ 25,200
R_d	12%
SE	$500,000
Book value of debt (B)	$200,000

15. Calculate ROE if ROI = 15%, R_D = 10%, B = $150,000, SE = $600,000, and T = 0.4. Identify the business risk and financial risk.

16. What is the intercept and slope of the financial leverage (ROE-ROI) line in Problem 15? Explain the meaning of the slope.

17. What is the ROE indifference point of the two strategies of Reg. Inc. as follows? T_c = 40%, Strategy 1: debt-equity ratio = 0.7. Strategy 2: debt-equity ratio = 0.5. Reg. Inc.'s after-tax cost of debt is 7.5 percent.

18. In the M&M no-tax world, calculate the value of the levered firm (V_L). Cost of unlevered equity (K_u) = 12%. Cost of debt (K_D) = 9.5%. Debt (D) = $400,000. NI = $520,000. What is the cost of levered equity?

19. In the M&M corporate tax world, what is the value of levered firm (V_L) in Problem 18 if the tax rate is 40 percent? What is the cost of levered equity? What is the market risk premium (MRP) given β_U = 0.9 and RF = 4.5%?

20. Use two different methods to calculate ROI given the following information for Lili Inc. Sales = $540,000; Cost of goods sold = $90,050; Interest cost = $28,000; T_c = 40%. The firm's debt (B = $300,000) accounts for 25 percent of the invested capital. After-tax cost of debt is 5.6 percent.

21. Calculate the fixed burden coverage and cash-flow-to-debt ratio given the following: EBIT = $550,000; depreciation and amortization = $60,000; preferred dividend = $50,000; sinking fund payments = 0; tax rate = 40%; debt = $100,000. Briefly explain why analysts use EBITDA more often than EBIT.

22. According to the M&M irrelevance theorem, calculate the market value of the unlevered firm (U) and of an identical risk levered firm (L). The expected EBIT of the unlevered firm (U) = $1,500,000, which will remain constant indefinitely. The cost of capital is 15 percent. If the levered firm (L) has $8.5 million debt outstanding, what's the market value of the equity?

23. In the M&M tax world, calculate the value of the unlevered firm (U) and the identical risk levered firm (L). Corporate tax rate = 40%. Perpetual EBIT for U and L = $1,500,000; cost of capital of U = 18%; L has $2 million debt outstanding. Pre-tax cost of debt = 5%. What is the WACC of L?

24. Briefly state the two possible ways bankruptcy can occur. What is the role of a monitor appointed by the court under the Companies Creditors Arrangements Act (CCAA)? Compare the difference of recognizing firm bankruptcy under CCAA and BIA.

Difficult

25. Describe the relationship between the debt ratio and firm value when we consider the existence of bankruptcy costs. How do you view the agency costs when bankruptcy occurs?

26. Calculate Altman's Z score for SS Inc. and then compare with Moody's rating chart. Is SS Inc. an IG or non-IG?

Current assets	CA	$250,000
Current liabilities	CL	$ 50,000
Non-equity book liability	BL	$210,000
Total assets	TA	$600,000
Retained earnings	RE	$190,000
EBIT	EBIT	$ 96,000
Market value of equity	MVE	$400,000
Sales	S	$390,000

27. Explain the elements of Altman's Z score as used in Problem 26.

28. In the M&M no-tax world, an unlevered firm has a cost of equity of 13.5 percent and expected EBIT of $285,000. The firm decided to issue $700,000 debt at a cost of 8 percent to finance a project, which has an ROI of 15 percent. It has 500,000 shares outstanding. Calculate the new share price of the firm after issuing the debt.

29. Calculate the EPS indifference EBIT* level given the following information. Tax rate is 40 percent. Under a 75 percent D/E ratio, the number of common shares outstanding is 30,000; pre-tax cost of debt is 8 percent and outstanding debt is $550,000. Under a 30 percent D/E ratio, the number of common shares outstanding is 65,000; pre-tax cost of debt is 5 percent and outstanding debt is $380,000. Discuss the implication of the indifference EBIT* and indicate which option is better given an EBIT of $35,000.

30. Summarize the main factors you need to consider if the CFO of your firm asks you to evaluate your firm's capital structure.

31. Susan and Celia are twins but have very different attitudes toward debt. Susan believes that firms should have a D/E ratio of .2 while Celia believes that the D/E ratio should be 1.2. Both sisters have agreed that the NotQuiteRight Company (NQR) is an excellent investment. However, the D/E of .5 is not quite right. NQR has an EBIT of $500,000 per year and pays interest of $100,000 per year. The cost of debt is 8 percent and the twins can also borrow and lend at that rate. All cash flows are permanent and there are zero taxes. Show the sisters how they can invest in NQR and still obtain their desired cash flows through borrowing and lending.

32. The SnapDragon Botanicals Company expects a free cash flow of $800,000 every year forever. SnapDragon currently has no debt, and its cost of equity is 20 percent. The corporate tax rate is 35 percent. The firm can borrow at 10 percent. All cash flows are perpetual. SnapDragon has 1,000,000 shares outstanding.

A. What is the value of the firm with zero debt?

B. If SnapDragon issues $2,000,000 of debt and uses the proceeds to repurchase stock, determine the number of shares outstanding and the price per share after the repurchase.

C. What is SnapDragon's cost of equity after the debt issue?

D. Value SnapDragon's equity using the cost of equity. What is the cash flow to equity?

33. The Silver Nugget is currently unlevered and is valued at $5 million. The company is considering including debt in its capital structure and would like to know the likely impact on its value and cost of capital. The current cost of equity is 12 percent. The firm is considering offering $2 million of new debt with an interest rate of 7 percent. The Silver Nugget will use the proceeds of the debt issue to repurchase stock. There are currently 1,000,000 shares outstanding and the marginal tax rate is 34 percent. What is the:

A. New value of the Silver Nugget?

B. New WACC for the Silver Nugget?

34. The Globe Theatre Company has an EBIT of $500,000 per year. The WACC of the firm is 10 percent and the before-tax cost of debt is 5 percent. The debt is risk free and all cash flows are perpetual. The current D/E ratio is 2/3. The corporate tax rate is 40 percent. The new CEO of the Globe, Mr. W. Shakespeare, believes that the D/E ratio is too high and would like to reduce it to 1/3. He will issue stock to repay the debt.

A. What is the impact on the EPS of the Globe Theatre of this change in the D/E ratio?

B. What is the impact on the cost of equity for the Globe Theatre?

35. Your cousin has just started his MBA and is confused. He understands that without taxes, capital structure is irrelevant. He also understands that with taxes, firms should use 100 percent debt. However, his professor is saying that with taxes there are times that the investor will prefer an unlevered firm. How is this possible?

36. Edmund Fitzgerald, a local shipping tycoon, is very confused. He has issued stock to finance a positive NPV investment. He expected the stock price to rise as positive NPV projects are supposed to increase shareholder value. However, the stock price fell! Explain how this is possible in an efficient market.

37. Fitz's Fine Feathers makes excellent down jackets. The company has been in business for over 100 years, but the arrival of personal heaters has had a severe effect on the business. Assume that Fitz has $500 in cash (its only asset) and ignore the time value of money. Fitz has two investment opportunities:

Project	Cost	Probability of success	Value in one year if:	
			Success	Fail
Comforters	$500	.5	520	510
Duck Soup	$500	.1	1,000	0

A. If Fitz has zero debt in its capital structure, which investment is preferred and why?

B. If Fitz has debt in its capital structure and the debt matures in one year and requires a repayment of $800, which investment is preferred and why?

Special Dividends

Special dividends are a way for cash-rich companies to reward shareholders. These dividends are often popular with investors. Husky Energy paid a special dividend of $0.50 per share on April 3, 2007, to its common shareholders. The company said it wanted shareholders to benefit from its strong balance sheet and earnings. The Montreal Exchange also paid a special dividend of $1.00 per common share on March 13, 2007. Investors briefly drove up the stock price of Tim Hortons in mid-April 2007 on speculation by a UBS securities analyst that it would pay a special dividend. The share price declined again after an analyst from RBC Capital suggested the tax consequences of such a move could be negative, and that Tim Hortons might be better off sticking to share buybacks.

Source: Husky Energy Inc. website: www.huskyenergy.ca (April 30, 2007).

Montreal Exchange website: www.m-x.ca (April 30, 2007).

"Tim Hortons: Special Dividend on the Way?" Yahoo! Finance website: http://biz.yahoo.com (April 30, 2007).

"Tim Hortons' Special Dividend Grows Stale." Globeandmail.com website: www.theglobeandmail.com (May 1, 2007).

Dividend Policy

Learning Objectives

After reading this chapter, you should understand the following:

1. The mechanics of dividend payments and why they are different from interest payments

2. The difference between a stock split and a stock dividend

3. Under what assumptions a dividend payment is irrelevant and what a homemade dividend is

4. Why dividend payments generally reflect the business risk of the firm

5. How transactions costs, taxes, and information problems give value to corporate dividend policies

6. How a share repurchase program can substitute for a dividend payout policy

INTRODUCTION

In Chapter 21 we discussed how the firm decides on its capital structure; that is, the mix between debt and equity securities. The second major topic in corporate financing is how to decide on a payout policy: how much of earnings to pay out to common shareholders and how to do this. Payout policy is more commonly referred to as dividend policy, but as we will see, there are several ways of paying out cash to the shareholders apart from paying a cash dividend. It might seem obvious that dividends matter, since we have previously discussed how to value common shares by discounting the expected future dividends. Yet it turns out that this may not be necessarily true. Having challenged conventional wisdom in terms of capital structure, Modigliani and Miller (M&M) went on to challenge the notion that dividends matter, and derived their second irrelevance theorem: that under certain assumptions, how much a firm pays out in dividends is completely irrelevant.

In this chapter you will learn why dividends may be irrelevant and what critical assumptions are needed to get this result. In the process you will understand what "realities" M&M assumed away and how they can affect dividend policy. We will show how dividends are paid out, what type of dividends there are, and why a share repurchase is sometimes seen as a substitute for a regular cash dividend.

22.1 DIVIDEND PAYMENTS

The Mechanics of Cash Dividend Payments

As we discussed in connection with common shares, there is no legal obligation for firms to pay common shareholders a dividend. A dividend has to be declared by the board of directors (BOD), after which it is announced and then becomes a contractual commitment. However, shareholders cannot force the members of the BOD to declare a dividend. Further, there are legal restrictions on whether or not the firm can declare a dividend. As we discussed in connection with bankruptcy in Chapter 21, the BOD cannot declare a dividend if in doing so it causes financial distress and makes the firm unable to fulfil its contractual commitments. If it does, the members of the BOD can be personally liable for damages. The Canada Business Corporations Act (CBCA) also expressly states that after the dividend payment, the value of the firm's assets has to exceed the total of its liabilities plus stated share capital. This is another way of saying that the dividend cannot be used to strip cash out of a firm in a period of financial distress.

On July 25, 2006, Rothmans Inc. issued a press release announcing its first quarter results, stating:

> **Dividend Declared**
> The Board of Directors of Rothmans Inc. declared a quarterly dividend of $0.30 per share payable on September 17, 2006 to shareholders of record at the close of business on September 1, 2006.

In this case, July 25, 2006, is the **declaration date**; afterwards, Rothmans is legally obliged to pay a dividend of $0.30 per share. At this point the amount of the dividend is transferred from retained earnings to an accrued liability. The press release also indicates the **holder of record** date, which is September 1, 2006. This means whoever is the owner of record of Rothmans shares on September 1, 2006, will be entitled to receive the dividend. The dividend will then be paid on September 17 to all those owners.

One question is then, "When can I buy the shares and get the dividend?" Or alternatively, "When can I sell them and not receive the dividend?" The answer is that on most exchanges, common share transactions are settled three business days after the trade. For this reason, most exchanges, as well as most investment dealers for the over-the-counter market, establish an **ex-dividend date** two business days prior to the record date. From this date on, the shares trade without the right to receive the dividend (i.e., ex-dividend). So for Rothmans, the ex-dividend date would be August 30: if you sold the shares on August 29, you would not receive the dividend, since the shares would be registered to the new owner by September 1. However, if you sold them on August 30, you would receive the dividend, since you would still be the holder of record on September 1.

In the case of Rothmans Inc., its current dividend per share is a quarterly dividend of $0.30. However, on page 33 of its 2006 annual report, Rothmans Inc. includes the following diagram, shown in Figure 22-1.

declaration date the date on which the Board of Directors decides that the firm will pay a dividend.

holder of record person who officially owns a share or shares on a given date

ex-dividend date date after which shares trade without the right to receive a dividend

22-1 FIGURE

Rothmans Inc. Dividend Payments

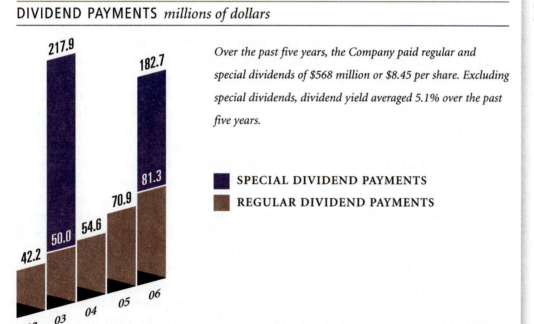

DIVIDEND PAYMENTS *millions of dollars*

217.9   182.7

Over the past five years, the Company paid regular and special dividends of $568 million or $8.45 per share. Excluding special dividends, dividend yield averaged 5.1% over the past five years.

81.3   70.9   54.6   50.0   42.2

■ SPECIAL DIVIDEND PAYMENTS
■ REGULAR DIVIDEND PAYMENTS

02   03   04   05   06

This shows the regular dividend increasing from $42.2 million in 2002 to $81.3 million in 2006, which represents the $0.30 per quarter regular dividend. In addition, Rothmans Inc. periodically pays a **special dividend**. As discussed in Chapters 3 and 4, in 2006, this amounted to an additional $1.50 per share or

special dividend dividend paid in addition to the regular dividend

$101.4 million, which was significantly more than the regular dividend. Further, Rothmans also paid a special dividend in 2003 that amounted to $157.9 million, which was over three times its then-regular dividend of $50 million. Rothmans is quite unusual in its tendency to pay both a very high regular dividend as well as a quite frequent special dividend. We will discuss later why firms pay a special dividend rather than incorporating this amount into their regular dividend.

Dividend Reinvestment Plans (DRIPs), Stock Dividends, and Stock Splits

dividend reinvestment plan (DRIP) plan allowing the use of dividends to buy new shares

If the investor does not want to receive a dividend, many Canadian firms offer the option of using the cash dividend proceeds to buy new shares by way of a **dividend reinvestment plan (DRIP)**. These shares are then issued by the company without any brokerage fees or transactions costs. Generally, DRIPs will buy as many shares as the cash dividend allows, with the residual deposited as cash. At one time, firms used to allow the shares to be purchased at a 5% discount to the closing market price as an incentive for investors to reinvest, but many companies, such as BCE, have now phased out the discount.

odd lots amounts of shares purchased that are in odd numbers, instead of a multiple of 100

DRIPs are popular with both investors and companies. For the company, it means that shares are issued continuously at no cost while they are also seen to be paying a regular dividend. It also fosters a more ongoing relationship with investors, who often end up holding **odd lots** of shares, so that their total share holdings are in odd numbers like 123 shares, instead of a round lot of some multiple of 100. This has become less important in recent years as trading has become more efficient and is no longer done in round lots of 100 shares each. For the long-term investor who is not reliant on income from their portfolio, the automatic reinvestment averages their investment, since they are buying shares at a range of prices. It also removes the problem of accumulating funds to reinvest. However, even though less cash is received by the investor, the full cash dividend is still taxable, which represents an obvious disadvantage.

stock dividend a dividend paid in additional shares rather than cash

A cash dividend along with a DRIP is similar to a **stock dividend**. In this case, rather than giving the investor cash and then taking it back for shares, the company simply gives more shares. A stock dividend is defined as any share distribution where the number of shares issued is less than 25 percent of the outstanding shares. So a company may give a 10 percent stock dividend where each investor gets 10 percent more shares. In terms of accounting, it is treated like a regular cash dividend, so that the value of the shares issued is transferred from retained earnings into the capital stock account. As a result, stock dividends are limited by the available retained earnings.

However, there is one very significant difference between a cash dividend plus a DRIP, and a stock dividend. With the cash dividend plus DRIP, the cash is distributed first and it is up to the investor to decide whether they want to buy more shares. Regardless of the investors' decisions, the firm has to have the cash to make the distribution. With the stock dividend, on the other hand, firms often do not have the cash and simply issue a stock dividend to give the investor "something." Whether the investor pays attention to getting more pieces of paper is another question, since all that is happening is that the value of the common shares is being divided among more shares, which will cause the stock price to fall. In addition, the amount of the stock dividend is fully taxable, despite the fact that no cash is received. Finally, the fact that retained earnings have decreased reduces the firm's ability to subsequently pay cash dividends, which also have to be paid out of retained earnings.

An extreme version of a stock dividend is a **stock split**. In this case, there is a greater than 25 percent increase in the number of shares outstanding. For example a 50 percent increase in the shares outstanding would be referred to as a "3 for 2" stock split rather than a 50 percent stock dividend. This simply means that the investor gets 3 shares for every 2 they already held, or 50 percent more. There are some accounting advantages to this since the retained earnings account is not altered, but the number of shares outstanding is simply increased (in this example by 50 percent). In addition, unlike stock dividends, investors face no tax implications arising from a stock split, except that the average purchase price will be adjusted downward to reflect the split.

stock split a greater than 25 percent increase in the number of shares outstanding

Both stock dividends and stock splits simply divide the value of the common shares among more shares and all else constant, reduce the price per share. Why firms do this is something of a mystery, since there is no underlying change in the firm. One reason often advanced is that by increasing the number of shares, the price per share falls and this may be useful if there is an *optimal trading range* for the share price. This allows the shares to be traded in round lots at a reasonable value. For example, 100 shares at a price of $30 each means a $3,000 trade, but if the share price is $300 then it means a $30,000 trade, which may be too big for small investors.

This argument had some validity when there were significant costs attached to trading shares and round lots of 100 shares meant something. However, trading costs are now deregulated and odd lots of 50 shares and so on can be traded without excessive transactions costs. Further, if the share price gets too high, then what constitutes a round lot changes. For example, shares of Berkshire Hathaway (whose largest shareholder and CEO is Warren Buffet, the second-richest man in the world) closed trading on October 4, 2006, at $97,699 per share. These shares trade in round lots of 1 share and have no trouble attracting investors. On the other hand, foreign securities are often repackaged into bundles of shares as *American Depository Receipts (ADRs)* to get their U.S. dollar price in New York into the $50 range. UK stocks are repackaged for the U.S. market, for example, because they trade in the United Kingdom in pence and would be regarded as penny stocks in New York if they weren't bundled.

It is difficult to know whether these effects have any economic significance, but exchanges do have different rules for shares that trade for under $2 than for those above $2. These rules affect the requirements for listing status as well as brokerage commission rates. This became a problem for Nortel when its stock price collapsed from US$122 down to the $2 range. Nortel's stock price bounced around the $2 level for over two years and it was an embarrassment for Canada's premier technology company to be regarded as a penny stock. In response, at the company's annual shareholder meeting on June 29, 2006, the shares were consolidated in a "one for ten" reverse split. Nortel explained the move as follows:

> The transaction was implemented to increase investors' visibility into the Company's profitability on a per share basis, reduce share transaction fees for investors and certain administrative costs for Nortel and broaden interest to institutional investors and investment funds.[1]

---

[1] The information is available in Nortel's filings with the Ontario Securities Commission at http://www.sedar.com; this quote comes from the Nortel website at http://www.nortel.com/corporate/investor/faq.html.

If investors hadn't paid attention, they might have thought that the 1990s Nortel stock price boom had happened all over again, as once the consolidation took place on December 1, 2006, Nortel's stock price was miraculously above $30 for the first time in six years. However, all that had happened was that the number of Nortel shares that they owned had been cut by 90 percent.

As mentioned above, with stock splits and stock dividends, the firm's value is being divided by a greater number of shares, which means the share price should fall. If there is an optimal trading range it might be that the share price does not decrease proportionally with the greater number of shares. This is easy to test. In a pioneering study, Fama et al.[2] examined 940 stock splits in the United States from 1927–1959 and found no significant wealth change in the month of the split. However, there were two important results. First, they found that firms that split their stock did so after exceptionally good stock market performance. Consistent with the optimal trading range idea, they split their stock in order to bring the stock price back to a "normal" range. Second, they found that two thirds of the firms in their sample increased their aggregate dividend payments, and for those firms the shares performed better for the next year. In contrast, for the one third of the sample of firms that kept their aggregate dividend constant, the share price underperformed the market.

The Fama et al. study has been repeated several times since and the basic message is the same. North American firms do not like to keep their share price in a "normal" trading range and use stock dividends and stock splits to avoid this. If the price run-up that causes the split results in higher dividends, then the stock price continues to outperform the market, but if there is no change, then the share price slips back. This leads to the conclusion that it is not the stock split or dividend itself that is causing the price behaviour but expectations about the firm's future performance, and investors take the stock split as a "signal" that management agrees with this assessment. This *signalling role* for dividends will be discussed in more detail after we consider some data on dividends.

CONCEPT REVIEW QUESTIONS

1. Define four important dates that arise with respect to dividend payments.
2. Explain the similarities and differences among DRIPs, stock dividends, and stock splits.

22.2 CASH DIVIDEND PAYMENTS

We can look at dividends from both a macro and a micro level perspective. At the macro level, dividends are income and data are collected on tax returns. These data then end up in the National Income Accounts and are included as part of the gross domestic product (GDP). Figure 22-2 shows the after-tax profit and dividends paid by corporate Canada divided by GDP since 1961.

---

[2] E. Fama, L. Fisher, M. Jensen, and R. Roll, "The Adjustment of Stock Prices to New Information," *International Economic Review*, Vol. 10, No. 1 (Feb. 1969), pp1–21.

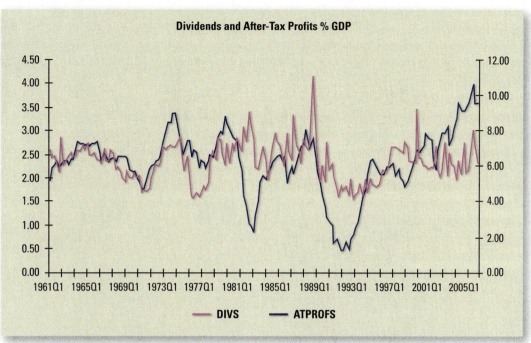

22-2 FIGURE

Aggregate Dividends and Profits

Source: Data from Statistics Canada

The graph shows that after-tax profits generally run at about 6 percent of GDP but are highly variable. During recessions, when GDP weakens, firms lose money because their sales decline, while their fixed operating and financing costs do not drop proportionally. We can see the impact of the recessions in the early 1980s and early 1990s when after-tax profits dropped to just below 3 percent and then barely 1 percent of GDP. The recession in the early 1990s was particularly painful due to the adjustment to the Free Trade Agreement (FTA) with the United States, when corporate Canada had to learn how to compete against larger, more competitive U.S. firms. Finally, we can see the surge in profits earned by corporate Canada in the early to mid 2000s as natural resource prices hit record levels. So in recent years, after-tax profits have been at all-time highs, in the 10 percent range.

In contrast to the volatility in after-tax profits, dividends have remained relatively stable. Note that while dividends roughly tracked after-tax profits from 1961–1980, they were not cut during the recession of 1981–1982, or during the deeper recession of 1991–1993. Further, since 2000 we have seen a large increase in after-tax profits, which has not been matched by an equivalent increase in dividends. We can see these effects more clearly when we look at the aggregate dividend payout, which is aggregate dividends divided by aggregate after-tax profits.

Figure 22-3 indicates that the payout rate is normally around 40 percent, but increased to over 100 percent during the two recessions when profits dropped so dramatically but dividends remained relatively stable. Further, we have seen the payout rate trending downwards since 2000 to an all-time low of 24 percent, due to recent record high profits. This naturally raises an important question (1): *Why are dividends smoothed and not matched to profits? Or another way of saying this is: why don't firms just pay a constant proportion of profits out as dividends and cut them when their profits and cash flows drop as they do during recessions?*

It is also interesting to look at the micro level; that is, the dividends paid by individual companies. Table 22-1 contains the **dividend yields** (defined in Chapters 4 and 7 as the annual dividend per share divided by the share price) for the firms in the S&P/TSX 60 Index from 1996–2005.

dividend yield annual dividend per share divided by the share price

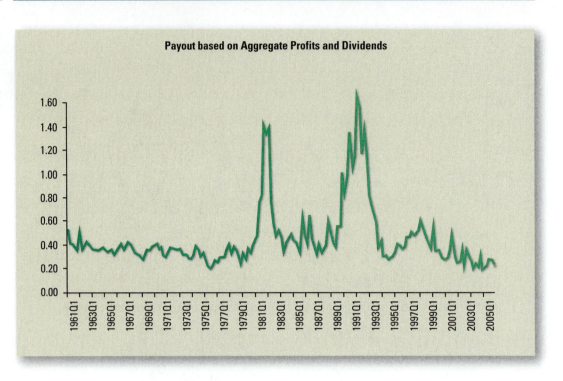

Payout based on Aggregate Profits and Dividends

Table 22-1   S&P/TSX 60 Index Dividend Yields

	1996 %	1997 %	1998 %	1999 %	2000 %	2001 %	2002 %	2003 %	2004 %	2005 %	Average
ACE Aviation Holdings Inc.	...	...	...	...	...	...	...	...	...	0	0.00
Agnico-Eagle Mines Limited	0.61	0.21	0.38	0.2	0.21	0.15	0.14	0.16	0.17	0.16	0.24
Agrium Inc.	0.57	0.64	0.62	0.82	0.69	0.61	0.72	0.62	0.56	0.44	0.63
Alcan Inc.	1.38	1.29	1.56	1.26	1.1	1.03	1.16	1.16	1.03	1.28	1.23
ATI Technologies Inc.	0	0	0	0	0	0	0	0	0	0	0.00
Bank of Montreal	4.17	3.28	2.54	3.16	3.52	2.83	3.35	3	2.77	3.12	3.17
Barrick Gold Corporation	0.36	0.53	0.64	0.64	0.91	0.87	0.77	0.86	0.79	0.71	0.71
BCE Inc.	4.69	3.42	2.52	1.41	1.07	3.15	3.99	4.08	4.29	4.44	3.31
Biovail Corporation	0	0	0	0	0	0	0	0	0	2.01	0.20
Bombardier Inc.	0.94	1.04	0.92	0.87	0.67	1.07	1.93	2.07	2.03	0	1.15
Brookfield Asset Management Inc.	5.51	4.17	4.03	4.86	5.05	3.94	3.06	3	1.49	1.2	3.63
Cameco Corporation	0.79	1	1.37	1.63	2.34	1.5	1.36	1.13	0.65	0.43	1.22
Canadian Imperial Bank of Commerce	3.67	3.07	2.85	3.37	3.17	2.9	3.48	3.28	3.31	3.57	3.27
Canadian National Railway Company	1.53	1.46	1.33	1.35	1.69	1.29	1.2	1.41	1.24	1.23	1.37
Canadian Natural Resources Limited	0	0	0	0	0	0.91	1.09	1.07	0.92	0.55	0.45
Canadian Oil Sands Trust	...	...	...	...	8.28	9.13	5.12	5.13	3.69	1.95	5.55
Canadian Pacific Railway Limited	...	...	0	0	0	0	1.57	1.53	1.47	1.27	0.73
Canadian Tire Corporation, Limited	2.13	1.51	1.08	1.02	1.54	1.71	1.39	1.14	0.99	0.92	1.34
Celestica Inc.	0	0	0	0	0	0	0	0	0	0	0.00
Cognos Incorporated	0	0	0	0	0	0	0	0	0	0	0.00
Cott Corporation	0.23	0.53	0.54	0	0	0	0	0	0	0	0.13

	1996 %	1997 %	1998 %	1999 %	2000 %	2001 %	2002 %	2003 %	2004 %	2005 %	Average
Domtar Inc.	1.29	1.25	1.43	1.02	0.88	1.02	0.86	1.39	1.52	1.85	1.25
Enbridge Inc.	5.51	4.05	3.46	3.68	3.79	3.52	3.36	3.49	3.41	3.08	3.74
EnCana Corporation	1.58	1.56	2	1.96	1.29	11.45	0.92	0.82	0.66	0.54	2.28
George Weston Limited	1.56	1.02	0.82	0.78	1.05	0.88	0.87	1.22	1.44	1.47	1.11
Glamis Gold Ltd.	0	0.61	0	0	0	0	0	0	0	0	0.06
Goldcorp Inc.	0	0	0	0	0	1.42	0.71	0.82	1.59	3.26	0.78
Husky Energy Inc.	...	...	0	0	0	2.11	2.25	6.9	3.43	3.23	2.24
Imperial Oil Limited	3.64	2.9	2.88	2.6	2.27	2.05	1.91	1.72	1.35	0.92	2.22
Inco Limited	0.89	1.06	0.48	0	0	0	0	0	0	0.63	0.31
IPSCO Inc.	1.41	0.93	1.4	1.72	2.41	2.57	0.98	1.12	0.64	0.77	1.40
Kinross Gold Corporation	0	0	0	0	0	0	0	0	0	0	0.00
Loblaw Companies Limited	0.96	0.73	0.67	0.59	0.83	0.8	0.84	1	1.16	1.3	0.89
Magna International Inc.	1.77	1.47	1.32	1.15	1.84	1.63	1.36	1.43	1.49	1.74	1.52
Manulife Financial Corporation	...	0	0	0	1.26	1.16	1.61	2.01	1.86	1.88	1.09
MDS Inc.	0.69	0.41	0.44	0.46	0.35	0.37	0.42	0.49	0.4	0.7	0.47
National Bank of Canada	4.04	3.46	2.59	3.24	3.6	3	3.15	3.05	3.2	3.17	3.25
Nexen Inc.	1.29	0.96	1.26	1.33	0.84	0.86	0.83	0.86	0.78	0.47	0.95
Nortel Networks Corporation	0.69	0.49	0.42	0.16	0.09	0.11	0	0	0	0	0.20
NOVA Chemicals Corporation	0	0	0.39	1.45	1.35	1.31	1.17	1.34	0.88	0.79	0.87
Novelis Inc.	...	...	...	...	...	...	...	0	0	...	0.00
Petro-Canada	1.1	1.07	1.54	1.68	1.39	1.04	0.95	0.73	0.95	0.87	1.13
Potash Corporation of Saskatchewan Inc.	1.44	1.3	1.35	1.52	1.1	1.02	1.06	1.02	0.68	0.54	1.10
Research In Motion Limited	0	0	0	0	0	0	0	0	0	0	0.00
Rogers Communications Inc.	0	0	0	0	0.14	0	0	0.56	0.38	0.31	0.14
Royal Bank of Canada	3.59	2.52	2.35	2.62	3	2.91	2.92	2.91	3.26	3.18	2.93
Shaw Communications Inc.	0.83	0.7	0.32	0.18	0.14	0.16	0.21	0.58	0.78	1.31	0.52
Shoppers Drug Mart Corporation	...	...	...	0	0	0	0	0	0	0.98	0.14
Sun Life Financial Inc.	...	...	0	0	0.46	1.46	1.91	2.32	2.35	2.31	1.35
Suncor Energy Inc.	2.52	1.65	1.42	1.32	1.01	0.8	0.65	0.69	0.61	0.42	1.11
Talisman Energy Inc.	0	0	0	0	0	1.07	0.99	1.09	1.02	0.72	0.49
Teck Cominco Limited	0.68	0.75	1.28	1.48	1.68	1.45	1.58	1.24	1.04	1.66	1.28
TELUS CorporatioN	...	...	0	3.89	3.49	3.94	3.96	2.85	2.06	2.06	2.78
The Bank of Nova Scotia	3.67	2.71	2.37	2.66	2.79	2.82	2.95	3	3.1	3.27	2.93
The Thomson Corporation	2.24	1.77	1.67	1.52	1.35	1.41	1.52	2.74	1.72	1.87	1.78
The Toronto-Dominion Bank	3.68	2.7	2.35	2.15	2.32	2.71	3.19	3.21	3	3.01	2.83
Tim Hortons Inc.	...	...	...	...	...	...	...	...	0	0	0.00
TransAlta Corporation	6.22	5.16	4.52	5.35	5.59	4.06	4.92	5.73	5.88	4.51	5.19
TransCanada Corporation	5.1	4.28	4.24	6.46	5.91	5	4.66	4.38	4.16	3.65	4.78
Yellow Pages Income Fund	...	...	...	...	...	...	...	...	7.34	7.09	7.22

Source: Data from *Financial Post* Corporate Analyzer Database

Looking at the average dividend yields we see that they range from a low of zero for many firms, to a high of 7.22 percent for the Yellow Pages Income Fund. Even discounting Yellow Pages as an income trust, we still see highs of 5.19 percent for TransAlta, a major Alberta energy generator. This raises another important question (2): *Why is there such a substantial difference in dividend yields (and payouts) across major Canadian companies? Why do some firms have very high dividends and some very low or non-existent?*

To answer these two questions (1 and 2), we consider the second major contribution of Modigliani and Miller and consider what value is created by paying a dividend.

CONCEPT REVIEW QUESTIONS

1. What obvious question arises when we examine historical patterns in aggregate dividend payouts?

2. What obvious question arises when we examine cross-sectional patterns in individual company dividend payouts?

22.3 MODIGLIANI AND MILLER'S DIVIDEND IRRELEVANCE THEOREM

M&M, Dividends, and Firm Value

After "proving" in 1958 that under certain circumstances a firm's capital structure did not matter, Modigliani and Miller (M&M) went on in 1961[3] to "prove" that dividend policy did not matter either, thereby showing that two of the major activities of corporate finance were irrelevant. Needless to say, this was then and remains today highly controversial. However, the importance of the M&M argument is not that it is actually correct, but that it points the way to finding where value can be created with dividend policy, and why.

It might seem obvious that dividends matter; after all, one of the most basic equations used to value common shares is the following:

[22-1]

$$P_0 = \frac{D_1 + P_1}{(1 + K_e)}$$

The price of a share today (P_0) is the present (discounted) value of next period's expected dividend per share (D_1) and price per share (P_1). There is the dividend per share in the valuation equation, so dividends must be important, or that is what it seems. However, M&M showed that all is not what it seems.

To understand the M&M proof, first multiply the price per share by the *current* number of shares outstanding (m). This simply converts the price per share equation into an equation that values the total amount of common equity, or the **equity market capitalization** (V_0).

equity market capitalization total common equity market value

---

[3] M. Miller and F. Modigliani, "Dividend policy, growth and the valuation of shares," *Journal of Business*, October 1961.

$$mP_0 = V_0 = \frac{m(D_1 + P_1)}{(1 + K_e)}$$

[22-2]

Similar to their capital structure argument, M&M then made some very important assumptions:

1. There are no taxes.

2. Markets are perfect.

3. All firms maximize value.

4. There is no debt.

The last assumption is there simply because they proved in 1958 that debt is irrelevant so that in this paper they could concentrate on dividend policy; it also helps to simplify their use of the sources and uses of funds constraint. Remember from accounting that the cash flow statement, like all financial statements, always balances. Therefore, without any debt, the sources and uses of funds identity (i.e., sources = uses) can be expressed as:

$$X_1 + nP_1 = I_1 + mD_1$$

[22-3]

Here X represents cash flow from operations and I investment, so $X - I$ is what we termed **free cash flow** in Chapter 3. This free cash flow is then either paid out as a dividend to the current shareholders (mD_1), or new funds are raised by selling new shares (n) to investors next period at the price P_1.

It is important to realize that Equation 22-3 is not an assumption; it is just a constraint that the sources and uses of funds have to balance given the absence of debt financing. Consequently we can solve for the dividends paid out (mD_1) to get:

$$mD_1 = X_1 + nP_1 - I_1$$

free cash flow the result of subtracting the capital expenditures from the cash flow from operations

Notice that this relationship implies that if the firm pays out dividends that exceed its free cash ($X - I$), then it must issue new common shares to pay for these dividends. When we substitute this term into the valuation Equation 22-2 for mD_1, we get the following:

$$V_0 = \frac{X_1 - I_1 + [(m + n)P_1 = V_1]}{(1 + K)}$$

[22-4]

So the value of the firm is simply the value of next period's free cash flow ($X_1 - I_1$) plus next period's equity market value (V_1, which equals $(m + n) P_1$). By repeatedly substituting this to find the value of the firm at all future points in time, we get the fundamental equity valuation formula below:

$$V_0 = \sum_{t=1}^{\infty} \frac{X_t - I_t}{(1 + K)^t}$$

[22-5]

Equation 22-5 is the basic equation we use to value the total market value of the firm's equity as opposed to the price per share. It says that firm value is determined as the present value of the free cash flows to the equity holders.

It is important to realize that Equation 22-1 says that to value a share of common stock we simply discount all the future expected dividends, since this is the cash received by the investor. Yet Equation 22-5 says that to value the aggregate of all the shares (i.e., the total market value of equity), what is important is that we value the free cash flows to all the equity holders. Obviously these two approaches must give exactly the same value, which implies that the dividend is equal to the free cash flow each period. In this way the dividend is the residual that remains after the firm has taken care of all of its investment requirements, so we call this the **residual theory of dividends**.

So what does all this mean? To answer this let's return to the investment opportunity schedule (IOS) for Rothmans Inc. for 2006, previously depicted in Figure 20-6 of Chapter 20, and which is reproduced here.

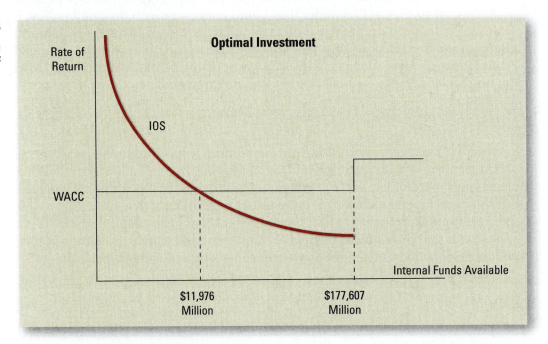

In this figure, we had Rothmans' 2006 cash flow from operations of $177.607 million and its investment of $11.976 million. Clearly in the case of Rothmans,

$$X - I = \$165.631$$

So we can say that Rothmans is a **cash cow**. Another way of saying this is that the residual theory of dividends suggests that it should pay a high dividend, which it has, since it routinely pays out 70 percent of its earnings as dividends and then pays periodic special dividends as well. If on the other hand these numbers were reversed and Rothmans had cash flow from operations of $11.976 million and investment of $177.607 million, it would be classified as a growth stock. In this case, the residual theory of dividends would indicate that it should not pay out a dividend since it would have to raise equity through new share issues to finance its investment.

The key insight from the M&M argument is that the firm always accepts the optimal amount of investment, so investment is *independent* of the firm's dividend policy. The key assumptions that generate this conclusion are that firms maximize value and that markets are perfect. This means they can always raise the necessary capital to undertake all positive NPV projects, so they are not financially constrained. If firms are financially constrained, this irrelevance of dividend policy falls apart, as we will show shortly.

With investment fixed and cash flow from operations being determined by the firm's real operations, it is clear from the sources and uses of funds constraint, Equation 22-3, that new share issues and dividend payments are the opposite of each other. All else constant, an increase in cash dividends paid means the firm has to raise more cash by selling new shares.

Example 22-1: Dividends and Free Cash Flow

A firm has cash flow from operations of $100 million and needs $90 million for investment purposes, leaving $10 million of free cash flow. Assume the firm has 10 million shares outstanding and its shares are presently trading at $20 per share. How many new shares must be issued if they plan to pay out a dividend per share of $2?

$$= nP_1 = mD_1 - (X_1 - I_1) = (10)(2) - (100 - 90) = \$10m$$

Solution

New proceeds required = $20m

Since its share price is $20 with 10 million shares outstanding, we can say that the value of the firm's equity = ($20)(10m) = $200m

When it issues new shares, this $20m must be divided among the new shareholders (n) as well as the existing shareholders (m), so the new share price at time 1 will be:

$$P_1 = \frac{V}{m+n} = \frac{\$200}{10+n}$$

This reduces to:

$$10P_1 + nP_1 = \$200$$

Since we know that nP_1 = $10m, we know that
$$10P_1 = \$200 - \$10 = \$190,$$

So, the new P_1 = $190 ÷ 10 = $19

This implies the firm will need to issue the following number (n) of new shares:

$$n = \$10m \div \$19 = 526{,}316 \text{ new shares.}$$

Notice that the firm value remains the same at $200 million in M&M's world, since it is simply the present value of the firm's future free cash flows to infinity. There are simply more shares outstanding (10,526,316), which are each worth $19.

Example 22-2: Residual Dividend Policy

Consider the firm from Example 22-1.

a. How much would it pay out in dividends per share if they were all equity financed, and the firm followed a strict residual dividend policy?

b. Redo part (a) but assume the firm plans to finance its future investments (including this year's total investment outlay of $90 million) using 30% debt financing.

Solution

a. Dividends per share = Free cash flow per share = $10m/10m shares = $1

b. In this case, only $63 million of the required investment is from operations (i.e., 70% of the $90 million in total investments), since the other $27m (i.e., 30% of $90 m) will be financed using debt. Therefore:

Dividends per share = free cash flow per share = $(100 − 63) ÷ 10m = \$3.70$

M&M's Homemade Dividend Argument

homemade dividends
"dividends" created or eliminated by investors through their own behaviour

M&M's argument is often illustrated using the concept of **homemade dividends**. This refers to the ability of individuals to create (or eliminate) dividends through their behaviour in a perfect M&M world, with no taxes, transactions costs, or other market imperfections. In essence, under M&M's assumptions, investors will buy shares regardless of the firm's underlying dividend policy, since they can create any dividend policy they want. The example below illustrates.

Example 22-3: Homemade Dividends in an M&M World

Consider a no-growth company (NG) whose shares are presently trading at $10 per share. The company has just announced that it plans to pay out all of its free cash flow of $1 per share in the form of a $1 dividend per share at the end of the year, and that these dividends will be maintained indefinitely.

a. Estimate the expected value of the company's shares after one year (P_1), assuming investors require a 10 percent return on these shares.

b. Investor A holds 1,000 NG shares and does not want to receive any dividends next year, but then wishes to sell all her shares and collect all her investment income from NG. Explain what she can do and show how much she will receive after two years.

c. Investor B also holds 1,000 NG shares, but wishes to receive $6,000 in income from his shares at the end of this year, and collect his remaining investment income at the end of the second year, at which time he wishes to sell all his shares. Explain what he can do and show how much he will receive after two years.

d. Explain why the sums of the income received by the two investors differs.

Solution

a. $P_1 = \$1 ÷ .10 = \$10$ per share

b. Investor A can take the $1,000 in dividends she receives (i.e., $1 × 1,000 shares) and buy new shares in NG at the end of the year. Assuming the shares are trading at $10 per share as calculated in part (a), the investor can purchase an additional 100 shares (i.e., $1,000 ÷ $10 per share) with the $1,000 in dividends she receives. At the end of two years, assuming the $1 free cash flow per share and the 10 percent discount rate remain constant, the shares will still be trading at $10 per share. Therefore, she will receive $11,000 for selling her 1,100 shares at $10 apiece, plus $1,100 in dividends, for a total of $12,100.

c. Investor B can take the $1,000 in dividends he receives, and sell an additional 500 shares at $10 each to generate an additional $5,000 in investment income, for a total of $6,000. At the end of two years, assuming the $1 free cash flow per share and the 10 percent discount rate remain constant, the shares will still be trading at $10 per share. Therefore, he will receive $5,000 for selling his remaining 500 shares, plus $500 in dividends (i.e., 500 shares × $1 per share), for a total of $5,500.

d. Investor A receives a total of $12,100 at the end of year two. Notice that investor B receives $6,000 at the end of year one, and $5,500 at the end of year two, for a total of only $11,500. The difference of $600 represents the forgone return of 10% on the $6,000 that investor B withdraws at the end of year one, which investor A leaves invested in firm NG. Recall that our firm share price calculations are based on the assumption that the firm's shares provide investors with a 10 percent return.

The example above illustrates that investors can buy or sell shares in an underlying company to create their own cash flow patterns, or simulated dividend streams. In fact in answering (b) above you were simply using a "homemade" dividend reinvestment plan, which we discussed earlier. Investors who don't like dividends can sign up for a DRIP and undo the effects of a firm's dividend policy. Conversely, in answering part (c) the investor has created a cash flow from the firm simply by selling part or all of their shares.

What the example illustrates is that under the M&M assumptions, the investor is indifferent as to a firm's dividend policy. However, in the real world, there are several practicalities to consider, such as transactions costs, risk, taxes, and other market imperfections. We will elaborate on these matters in the following sections.

CONCEPT REVIEW QUESTIONS

1. Explain how and under what assumptions M&M show that dividends are irrelevant.

2. Explain the relationship between M&M's argument and the use of a residual dividend policy.

3. Briefly describe the notion of homemade dividends as it relates to M&M's irrelevancy argument.

22.4 THE "BIRD IN THE HAND" ARGUMENT

M&M's dividend irrelevance proposition was as controversial in 1961 as it remains today, since it seems to conflict with the intuition that firms that pay cash dividends are less risky than ones where the investors' return comes by way of a capital gain. It then seems to follow that firms that do not pay a cash dividend will be seen as riskier, causing the cost of equity capital to increase and the stock price to fall. This idea is called the **bird in the hand argument** on the basis that a "bird in the hand" (cash dividend) is worth more than "two in the bush" (twice as much in capital gains).

bird in the hand argument the notion that a cash dividend is worth more than an equivalent capital gain

In thinking through this argument, remember in Chapter 20 we used the following version of the two-stage growth model, as expressed in Equation 20-22:

[22-6]

$$P = \frac{ROE_1 \times BVPS}{K_e} + \frac{Inv}{(1+K_e)}(\frac{ROE_2 - K_e}{K_e})$$

The idea was to motivate a discussion of the value of the firm being split between the present value of existing opportunities (PVEO), as measured by the first term in Equation 22-1, and the present value of growth opportunities (PVGO), as measured by the second term. We then used this to discuss four stereotypes of firms: the cash cow, the star, the dog, and the turnaround. These different stereotypes usually are perceived to be different in risk, since PVEO is generally regarded as less risky than PVGO.

Think for a moment about where PVGO comes from: it requires that the firm earn a rate of return (ROE) that exceeds its cost of equity capital (K_e), so in the second term of Equation 22-6 we are adding the present value of all these future net present values. However, from basic economics we know that there will be new entrants to a market when firms earn more than a "normal" level of profits, where "normal" is defined as a fair rate of return on the funds invested, or the cost of equity capital. As a result, if PVGO is high, we can expect other firms to try to enter the market and compete for these excess profits. This makes the PVGO part of the firm's market value extremely vulnerable, as future competition could see it diminish, if not disappear completely.

Of course PVEO can also be subject to market entry and competition if it, too, is partly derived from excess profits. However, for PVEO there is more information about potential entry and new competition for existing operations than there is from PVGO, which may often stretch far into the future. Further, there is more information about the stability of PVEO, since the firm has an earnings history. For these basic reasons, capital gains, or expected increases in the share price, are generally regarded as riskier than current dividends. This is the basic idea that the bird in the hand argument captures: that investors value current dividends more highly than future capital gains. The implication is that investors perceive non-dividend-paying firms to be riskier and they apply a higher discount rate to value them, causing share prices to fall. The "answer" then seems to be for these firms to pay a dividend.

The "dividends-are-better" theory is normally associated with Myron Gordon, developer of the Gordon growth model.[4] It captures the intuition that

---

[4] M. Gordon, "Optimal Investment and Financing Policy," *Journal of Finance*, May 1963.

dividends are more stable than capital gains and as a result more highly valued. It is commonly accepted that cash cows like utilities and banks are less risky than high tech firms like Biovail and ATI Technologies. Further, if you look back at the dividend yields that were provided in Table 22-1, you will see that low-risk utilities and banks do indeed have high dividend yields and high-risk tech firms rarely pay a dividend. So intuitively, the dividends-are-better argument seems to make sense. In addition, in practice, the share prices of high-dividend-paying stocks have tended to perform as well or better than stocks with low dividend payouts, which indicates that investors need not sacrifice growth for income. Finance in the News 22-1 elaborates on this point, suggesting that if investors choose the "right" high-dividend-paying stocks, they can "have it all"—both yield and capital gains.

LOOKING FOR A SURE THING? DIVIDENDS POINT THE WAY

finance
INTHENEWS22-1

There are no sure things in investing, but a select few dividend stocks come awfully close.

Great-West Lifeco Inc. is one, and so is Royal Bank of Canada. Empire Co. is also in the club, as is Transcontinental Inc. What all these stocks have in common is a track record of regularly and substantially increasing their quarterly dividends. This is crucial because however much the dividends at these companies have increased over the past decade, that's pretty close to how much their share price has risen.

Dividend investing is often viewed as a conservative—some might say boring—strategy where you sacrifice first-rate share price gains for income through quarterly dividends. But it appears that if you buy the shares of companies that steadily crank up their dividends, you can have it all.

In this edition of the Portfolio Strategy column, we look at stocks listed on the Toronto Stock Exchange that exhibit this little-studied correlation between dividend and share price increases. Our co-conspirators for this exercise are Tom Connolly, dividend guru and publisher of my personal favourite investing newsletter (the subscription list is closed, sorry), and Globeinvestor.com analyst Pierre Javad.

Mr. Connolly began studying the relationship between dividend increases and share price gains just recently and mentioned it in a recent edition of his newsletter, Connolly Report, which he has published since 1981. To help test the theory, Mr. Javad found all the TSX-listed common stocks that have paid a dividend for the past 10 years and then compared their dividend and share price growth.

In several sectors, notably financials and utilities, it's almost a given that dividends and shares are highly correlated. Great-West's 10-year compound average annual growth rate for its common shares is 20.18 per cent, while its dividend growth rate is 20.19 per cent a year. RBC's shares were up an average annual 15.59 per cent, and its dividend rose an average annual 15.77 per cent.

Several industrial and consumer staple stocks showed the same tendency. Transcontinental shares rose 15.35 per cent and its dividend increased 16.44 per cent. Empire, which controls the Sobeys grocery chain, posted share price growth of 18.06 per cent and dividend growth of 18.49 per cent.

Mr. Connolly said he has long been casually aware that the share price of dividend stocks went up as these companies increased the amount of cash they paid out. But he only realized the full extent of this linkage when a subscriber to his newsletter sent him some personal portfolio information with data for share price gains and dividend increases side by side.

"I said, my gosh, look at that, and I've been working on it ever since," Mr. Connolly said. "It's rather fascinating."

His theory on what's happening here starts with the concept of dividend yield, which is calculated by dividing a company's share price into the total of its four quarterly dividends multiplied by 100. Dividend yields fall if a company's shares rise in price, and they rise if the price drops. A rising dividend

finance
INTHENEWS22-1

should also push up the yield, but this often doesn't happen with the stocks that Mr. Connolly follows. Instead, the rising dividend pushes up the share price enough to keep the yield more or less where it was before. It's as if the stock becomes a bit more valuable as a result of an increased dividend, so investors buy in and move up the price.

This is why a stock that increases its dividends is a stock that should increase in value. Mind you, none of this happens immediately or in a straight line. Mr. Connolly said it takes years—at least five years, most likely—for average share price gains to approximate average dividend increases. He believes this is why many people never notice this phenomenon is actually occurring.

Here are some other observations about the linkage between share price gains and dividend increases.

1. **Oil and metals stocks are usually, but not always, exempt.**
   Suncor Energy Inc. shares rose an average 27.5 per cent a year over the past 10 years, but the company's dividend rose 6.49 per cent. This is because energy stocks trade mainly off the price of oil, just as metals and gold stocks trade off the price of copper, zinc and gold.

   Mr. Connolly said he doesn't even look at dividend-paying resource stocks—"Too cyclical," he said. However, there are a few stocks in this sector that do exhibit a strong correlation between share price gain and dividend increases.

   One is Alcan Inc., where the 10-year average share price gain is 3.84 per cent and the dividend rose an averaged 2.92 per cent. A more interesting example is Petro-Canada, where the share price rose 16.39 per cent and the dividend rose 14.87 per cent.

2. **Solid dividend growth does not always mean a rising share price.**
   Let's call this the Loblaw effect. Despite a sterling record for dividends, a company's share price can lag because of corporate issues that scare away investors. Impressively, Loblaw Cos. Ltd. has jacked up its quarterly payout an average 21.48 per cent annually on average over the past decade. But a big decline in its share

price over the past two years has reduced the 10-year average annual gain to a still reasonable 10.63 per cent.

There's a similar pattern with George Weston Ltd., the holding company that owns a controlling interest in Loblaw. Weston has cranked up its dividend by 25.66 per cent a year over the past decade, while the share price has risen 11.8 per cent annually.

3. **Companies that increase their dividend by small amounts often have tepid share price growth.**
   A good example of this pattern is the utility play TransAlta Corp., where the dividend has risen an average of 0.2 per cent annually and the shares are up 4.4 per cent a year. Maple Leaf Foods Inc. hasn't increased its dividend in the past decade, and its shares have gained an average annual 2.26 per cent.

   Financials are the best examples of how dividend growth trickles down to share price gains, but Laurentian Bank shows there are exceptions even in this sector. With average annual dividend increases of just 2.35 per cent, Laurentian shares have gained an average annual 5.13 per cent.

   Note that a static dividend doesn't necessarily kill share price gains. Onex Corp. hasn't raised its tiny dividend in the past decade and its shares are up a very nice 18.17 per cent a year.

   While some stocks have nearly identical 10-year growth rates in share price and dividend payments, there are others that are just vaguely similar. What do we make of these stocks? One theory is that a stock is undervalued if its 10-year share price gain is less than its dividend gain, and overvalued if the shares have outpaced the dividend.

   Shares of AGF Management Ltd., Bank of Nova Scotia, Transcontinental, ShawCor Ltd. and Toromont Industries Ltd. all lag dividend growth over the past 10 years. So does Loblaw, but here's something to chew on if you're following this stock and hoping that dividend growth will help refloat the stock in the years ahead. The last time Loblaw bumped up its quarterly payout was early 2005.

finance
INTHENEWS22-1

PREDICTING THE FUTURE

One way to get a sense of a stock's price gain potential is to look at how much its dividend has increased over the years. For many dividend stocks, there is a close correlation between dividend growth and share price gains. Here are some examples from the TSX with a 10-year track record.

Company name	Symbol	Recent Yield (%)	10-year share price return (%)	10-year dividend growth rate (%)	Difference (%)
Great-West Lifeco	GWO	2.93	20.18	20.19	0.01
National Bank	NA	3.46	15.69	15.76	0.07
Atco Ltd.	ACO.X	1.87	13.98	14.06	0.08
RBC	RY	3.20	15.59	15.77	0.18
Empire Co.	EMP.A	1.50	18.06	18.49	0.43
Alcan Inc.	AL	1.54	3.84	2.920	0.92
Bank of Nova Scotia	BNS	3.16	15.31	16.34	1.03
Transcontinental Inc.	TCL.A	1.31	15.35	16.44	1.10
Power Financial	PWF	2.74	19.57	18.38	1.19
Magna International	MG.A	1.02	3.61	4.83	1.23

Source: Carrick, Rob. "Looking for a sure thing? Dividends point the way." *Globe and Mail*, April 7, 2007, p. B6.

We can illustrate the difference between the M&M and Gordon arguments with the following diagram in Figure 22-5.

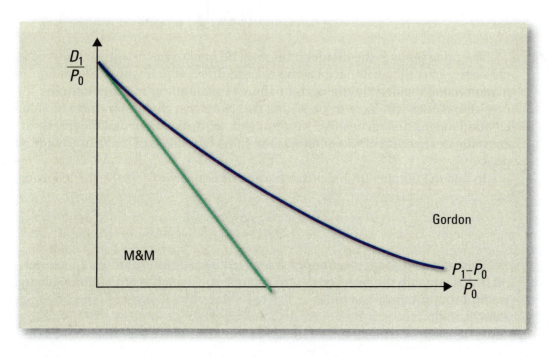

22-5 FIGURE

M&M versus Gordon's Bird in the Hand Theory

The M&M argument is that dividends and capital gains are perfect substitutes. So if the investor wants a 10 percent rate of return they can get this as a 10 percent dividend yield (D_1/P_0), or they can cut the dividend and reinvest more, which they receive as a capital gain ($(P_1 - P_0)/P_0$.) The slope of the line as they cut the dividend is then -1, indicating that the investors' required rate of return or discount rate is constant. Gordon, on the other hand, argues that if the investor wants a 10 percent return from a 10 percent dividend yield, then as the dividend payout is cut they will want an ever higher required rate of return due to the increase in risk. As a result they might want a 15 percent required return if there is no dividend since all of the return is coming from risky capital gains.

So how do we balance the obvious intuition of the "bird in the hand argument" against the formal "proof" offered by M&M? The easiest way is to work through an example. Suppose that a firm has a market value of $50 million, and has $5 million in cash flow that equals its required investment level. Using Equation 22-4, we can see that this firm has zero residual cash and generally should not pay a cash dividend according to the residual theory of dividends. Further, if the discount rate is 10%, the market value of its equity is $45.45 million, as shown below:

$$\$45.45 = \frac{\$50 + \$5 - \$5}{(1.1)}$$

If we further assume there are 1 million shares currently outstanding (m), the price per share is $45.45. In this case, the investor expects to get a zero dividend and a 10% capital gain ($4.55 ÷ $45.45).

Now suppose the firm pays out the $5 million in a $5 per share cash dividend. In this case, M&M assume that the firm still has to find $5 million to pay for the required level of investment, since value creation requires that all positive NPV projects are undertaken.

As a result, the firm will have to issue more shares next period at the then-market price (P_1). We can designate these new shares as (n), so the price per share is

$$P_0 = \frac{5m + {50m}/{1+n}}{1.1}$$

The price today is the dividend that will be paid to the existing owners of $5 per share, plus they will have the new share price, which is the $50 million in market value divided by the current shares outstanding of 1 million plus the new shares that will have to be issued (n). Note that the assumption of value creation means that all positive NPV projects are undertaken and the total market value next period of $50 million is the same regardless of the firm's dividend policy.

To find the number of shares that have to be issued we can solve the following:

$$n\left[P_1 = \frac{\$50}{(1+n)}\right] = \$5\,million$$

This means that the number of shares (n) issued times the price next period (P_1) is equal to the proceeds of the share issue, which is $5 million. Solving, we find that the firm has to issue 111,111 shares at $45 a share. The price per share is then

$$P_0 = \frac{5 + 50/1.1111}{1.1} = \$45.45$$

Notice that this is the same as in the no cash dividend case.

In this case, the shareowners will get an expected dividend yield of 11.0 percent (\$5 ÷ \$45.45), but due to the extra shares being issued their ownership in the firm is *diluted* and they will actually suffer a capital loss of 1 percent as the share price declines from \$45.45 to \$45. Therefore, they still obtain a 10 percent return. By varying the cash dividend amount, we can come up with different numbers for the expected dividend yield and capital gain (loss), but under the M&M assumptions, the investors' return stays the same.

Now that we can see that the M&M argument "works," we can see how to reconcile it with Gordon's argument. First, note that the capital gain in our M&M example is not far off in the future as it is with risky high tech stocks—it is *immediate* when the dividend is paid. As soon as the \$5 million in cash is paid out as a dividend, the firm has to issue 111,111 shares at \$45 to fund its investment. Second, with the M&M assumptions, the underlying operations of the firm are unaffected by the dividend—this is the meaning of the constant value of \$50 million next period. What this means is that by changing from a 0 percent dividend yield to an 11 percent dividend yield firm, as in our example, the firm is not changing itself from a Biovail into a BCE or TransCanada. The firm stays exactly the same. What is important to recognize is that *Biovail is riskier than BCE due to its business risk, not because of its lack of a dividend.*

Gordon is right in arguing that the dividend yield does indicate the risk of the firm and firms that pay large amounts of dividends are less risky than non-dividend-paying firms. However, M&M are also right because changing the dividend cannot change the underlying risk of the firm; this comes from its underlying operations. In this sense, the dividend should reflect the firm's operations through the residual value of dividends and the firm cannot change these underlying operational characteristics by merely changing the dividend.

CONCEPT REVIEW QUESTIONS

1. Explain the "bird in the hand" theory of dividends.

2. Reconcile the predictions of M&M with those of Gordon's arguments about dividend policy.

22.5 DIVIDEND POLICY IN PRACTICE

Accepting the M&M argument as a valid description of the real world leads to some problems. One is that if dividend policy doesn't matter, why is it we see such stability in dividend policy? The M&M proof indicates that the firm is valued based on the residual or free cash flows, so that paying a dividend just means more share issues and lower capital gains. If this is true then the firm can cut the dividend if it is short of cash and increase it when it has surplus cash. However, we saw in Figure 22-1 that dividends are much more stable than earnings (and cash flow) so that firms smooth their dividends. However, there is nothing in M&M's proof that indicates that there is any value to dividend smoothing. Further, M&M's concern was with dividend policy in general and they indicate no difference between a regular and a special dividend, so why is it that firms declare both regular and special dividends?

Table 22-2 reports the dividends per share (DPS) of the firms included in the S&P/TSX 60 Index. What is most remarkable is that the dividends are so stable. While firms do cut their dividend (TransCanada, for example, cut its dividend in both 1999 and 2000), these cuts are rare. Over the entire period, only 8% of the dividends were cut in the following year, while 46% remained constant and 46% increased. It is obvious that in practice, firms are very reluctant to cut their dividend.

Table 22-2   Dividends per Share for the S&P/TSX 60 Index

	1996 $	1997 $	1998 $	1999 $	2000 $	2001 $	2002 $	2003 $	2004 $	2005 $
ACE Aviation Holdings Inc	...	...	...	...	...	...	...	...	...	0
Agnico-Eagle Mines Limited	0.19	0.04	0.04	0.03	0.03	0.03	0.05	0.04	0.04	0.04
Agrium Inc.	0.15	0.15	0.16	0.16	0.16	0.17	0.17	0.15	0.14	0.13
Alcan Inc.	0.82	0.83	0.89	0.89	0.89	0.93	0.94	0.84	0.78	0.73
ATI Technologies Inc.	0	0	0	0	0	0	0	0	0	0
Bank of Montreal	0.74	0.82	0.88	0.94	1	1.09	1.2	1.32	1.51	1.8
Barrick Gold Corporation	0.19	0.22	0.27	0.3	0.33	0.34	0.35	0.31	0.29	0.27
BCE Inc.	1.49	1.49	1.49	1.49	1.36	1.31	1.31	1.31	1.31	1.44
Biovail Corporation	0	0	0	0	0	0	0	0	0	0.61
Bombardier Inc.	0.05	0.08	0.09	0.11	0.14	0.18	0.18	0.09	0.09	0
Brookfield Asset Management Inc.	0.44	0.44	0.44	0.44	0.44	0.44	0.44	0.45	0.48	0.48
Cameco Corporation	0.08	0.08	0.08	0.08	0.08	0.08	0.08	0.1	0.1	0.12
Canadian Imperial Bank of Commerce	0.85	1.05	1.2	1.2	1.29	1.44	1.6	1.64	2.2	2.66
Canadian National Railway Company	0.13	0.15	0.18	0.2	0.23	0.26	0.29	0.33	0.39	0.5
Canadian Natural Resources Limited	0	0	0	0	0	0.1	0.13	0.15	0.2	0.24
Canadian Oil Sands Trust	...	...	...	...	0.47	0.65	0.4	0.4	0.4	0.4
Canadian Pacific Railway Limited	...	...	0	0	0	0	0.51	0.51	0.52	0.58
Canadian Tire Corporation Limited	0.4	0.4	0.4	0.4	0.4	0.4	0.4	0.4	0.48	0.56
Celestica Inc.	...	0	0	0	0	0	0	0	0	0
Cognos Incorporated	0	0	0	0	0	0	0	0	0	0
Cott Corporation	0.03	0.08	0.05	0	0	0	0	0	0	0
Domtar Inc.	0.14	0.14	0.14	0.14	0.14	0.14	0.14	0.22	0.24	0.18
Enbridge Inc.	0.51	0.53	0.56	0.6	0.64	0.7	0.76	0.83	0.92	1.04
EnCana Corporation	0.2	0.2	0.2	0.2	0.2	2.5	0.2	0.2	0.26	0.33
George Weston Limited	0.29	0.32	0.4	0.44	0.7	0.8	0.96	1.2	1.44	1.44
Glamis Gold Ltd.	0	0.07	0	0	0	0	0	0	0	0
Goldcorp Inc.	0	0	0	0	0	0.15	0.17	0.22	0.36	0.82
Husky Energy Inc.	...	...	0	0	0	0.36	0.36	1.38	1	1.65
	1996	1997	1998	1999	2000	2001	2002	2003	2004	2005

	$	$	$	$	$	$	$	$	$	$
Imperial Oil Limited	0.23	0.24	0.25	0.25	0.26	0.28	0.28	0.29	0.29	0.31
Inco Limited	0.55	0.55	0.15	0	0	0	0	0	0	0.36
IPSCO Inc.	0.32	0.32	0.5	0.5	0.5	0.5	0.2	0.2	0.25	0.56
Kinross Gold Corporation	0	0	0	0	0	0	0	0	0	0
Loblaw Companies Limited	0.12	0.15	0.2	0.22	0.35	0.4	0.48	0.6	0.76	0.84
Magna International Inc.	1.08	1.14	1.29	1.32	1.84	2.11	2.14	1.9	1.93	1.84
Manulife Financial Corporation	...	0	0	0	0.2	0.24	0.3	0.39	0.47	0.58
MDS Inc.	0.05	0.05	0.06	0.07	0.08	0.09	0.09	0.1	0.08	0.13
National Bank of Canada	0.49	0.57	0.66	0.7	0.75	0.82	0.93	1.08	1.42	1.72
Nexen Inc.	0.15	0.15	0.15	0.15	0.15	0.15	0.15	0.16	0.2	0.2
Nortel Networks Corporation	0.09	0.1	0.11	0.11	0.11	0.06	0	0	0	0
NOVA Chemicals Corporation	0	0	0.1	0.4	0.4	0.4	0.4	0.4	0.4	0.4
Novelis Inc.	...	...	...	...	...	...	...	0	0	0.44
Petro-Canada	0.1	0.13	0.16	0.17	0.2	0.2	0.2	0.2	0.3	0.35
Potash Corporation of Saskatchewan Inc.	0.72	0.72	0.72	0.99	0.74	0.77	0.79	0.7	0.68	0.73
Research In Motion Limited	0	0	0	0	0	0	0	0	0	0
Rogers Communications Inc.	0	0	0	0	0.05	0	0	0.1	0.1	0.13
Royal Bank of Canada	0.33	0.38	0.44	0.47	0.57	0.69	0.76	0.86	1.01	1.18
Shaw Communications Inc.	0.04	0.04	0.04	0.04	0.05	0.05	0.05	0.09	0.16	0.31
Shoppers Drug Mart Corporation	...	...	...	0	0	0	0	0	0	0.4
Sun Life Financial Inc.	...	...	0	0	0.12	0.48	0.56	0.68	0.86	0.99
Suncor Energy Inc.	0.16	0.17	0.17	0.17	0.17	0.17	0.17	0.19	0.23	0.24
Talisman Energy Inc.	0	0	0	0	0	0.07	0.07	0.08	0.1	0.11
Teck Cominco Limited	0.2	0.2	0.2	0.2	0.2	0.2	0.2	0.2	0.3	0.8
TELUS Corporation	...	...	0	1.4	1.4	1.2	0.6	0.6	0.6	0.88
The Bank of Nova Scotia	0.33	0.37	0.4	0.44	0.5	0.62	0.73	0.84	1.1	1.32
The Thomson Corporation	0.76	0.82	0.93	0.98	1.02	1.08	1.11	1.61	0.98	0.96
The Toronto-Dominion Bank	0.5	0.56	0.66	0.72	0.92	1.09	1.12	1.16	1.36	1.58
Tim Hortons Inc.	...	...	...	...	...	...	...	...	0	0
TransAlta Corporation	0.98	0.98	0.99	1	1	1	1	1	1	1
TransCanada Corporation	1.1	1.18	1.18	1.12	0.8	0.9	1	1.08	1.16	1.22
Yellow Pages Income Fund	...	...	...	...	...	...	...	...	0.91	1.04

Source: Data from *Financial Post* Corporate Analyzer Database

The standard way of explaining this observed dividend behaviour is to suggest that firms smooth their dividends over time as they move toward a new target level of dividends. The original work was by John Lintner,[5] who suggested using the partial adjustment model specified below in Equation 22-7:

$$\Delta D_t = \beta (D_t^* - D_{t-1})$$

[22-7]

[5] J. Lintner, "Distribution of Incomes of Corporations among Dividends, Retained Earnings and Taxes," *American Economic Review* 46, 1956.

This equation simply says that the change in the dividend at time t (ΔD_t) is equal to an adjustment factor (β) times the difference between the target dividend for the period (D_t^*) and the dividend for the prior period (D_{t-1}). If the firm adjusts immediately to the target dividend, then the adjustment coefficient (β) is equal to 1.0, and the cash dividend is always optimal. If it doesn't adjust at all, then the dividend is constant and β is equal to zero.

Lintner took the target dividend (D_t^*) to be a function of the firm's optimal payout rate of the firm's underlying earnings (E_t), which leads to the following model in Equation 22-8:

[22-8]

$$D_t = a + (1 - b)D_{t-1} + cE_1$$

This equation suggests that dividends are a function of the previous period's dividends, and current earnings. Lintner estimated the coefficient on lagged dividends to be 0.70 indicating an adjustment speed (b) coefficient of 0.30. He also estimated the coefficient on current earnings (c) of 0.15. When the adjustment to the target dividend is complete, Linter's estimates imply an optimal payout ratio for U.S. companies of 50 percent (b/c). This is consistent with the aggregate evidence that U.S. companies do pay out about 50 percent of their earnings as dividends and is slightly higher than the 40 percent normal payout of corporate Canada.

Lintner's results have been replicated many times and their importance is twofold. First, the speed of adjustment is only 30 percent, which means that each period, the average firm only moves 30 percent of the way toward its target dividend. Alternatively, this means firms are very reluctant to fully adjust, so their dividends are *sticky*. The second is that the coefficient on earnings is only 15 percent, so that firms do not follow a policy of paying a constant proportion of earnings out as dividends.

The fact that actual dividend policy does not accord with the irrelevance theorem of M&M means obviously (and not surprisingly) that some of their assumptions are not realistic. The critical suspect assumptions are that markets are perfect and that there are no taxes.

CONCEPT REVIEW QUESTION

1. What does real world evidence imply about how firms manage their dividend payments?

22.6 RELAXING THE M&M ASSUMPTIONS: WELCOME TO THE REAL WORLD!

The perfect markets assumption contains a number of aspects, the most important of which are the absence of transactions costs and that all information is freely available and understood.

Transactions Costs

Transactions costs are important because in the M&M model, it is assumed that the firm can pay a dividend and then issue shares to raise the money needed to make the required level of investment.[6] Let's take an extreme situation where transactions costs are very high and the firm cannot raise new capital. In this case the payment of the cash dividend reduces the amount of money available to invest and causes the firm to forgo positive NPV projects. The value of the firm would go down since it is not creating value by accepting positive NPV projects.

Faced with significant costs attached to raising new money, cash-poor, growth firms have little incentive to pay a dividend, since all they are doing is compounding their financing problems. Similarly, firms that face volatile earnings so that their cash fluctuates significantly from year to year will attempt to "store" cash from one period to another. As a result, they will conservatively maintain their dividend payments at a level that minimizes the need to constantly access the capital markets. This brings us to a second aspect of the perfect markets assumption, which is that everyone has the same amount of information.

Dividends and Signalling

M&M assumes perfect markets where all market participants have access to the same information. In practice, however, capital markets are rife with information asymmetries where some parties know more than others. Despite the main focus of securities regulation that aims to make all material facts public information, agents in the capital market often have widely different views about the firm's future prospects and value.

For example, management usually knows more than external investors so the firm has to have some way of *signalling* to investors that their press releases can be believed, since as we discussed in Chapter 21, investors tend to view such information with a great deal of scepticism. One way of doing this is to only increase the dividend when the firm believes that it will not have to cut it in the future. The fact that paying the cash dividend reduces the funds available to the firm means that they will only do so when they think that their internal funds are increasing and are enough to support the dividend payment.[7] Otherwise, as we just discussed, it will impose more transactions costs on the firm in having to raise more funds in the future. This *signalling model* explains why share prices tend to increase on unexpected dividend initiations or increases. In both cases the dividend increase indicates good news because it suggests that management believes it can support the dividend out of future earnings.

Another explanation for the favourable stock market reaction associated with dividend increases is provided by **agency theory**. Many investors are very wary of senior management, since they tend to view the firm as *their* firm and not as belonging to the shareowners. The fear is that senior management may waste corporate resources in over-investing in poor (negative NPV) projects, since it is not "their" money but the shareowners'. This view is supported by the very fact that Donaldson argued that for agency reasons, senior management

agency theory the recognition of conflicts of interest whereby managerial decision making may not be in the best interests of shareholders

---

[6] Or alternatively, it is assumed that investors can create homemade dividends by buying or selling shares without cost to generate any desired cash flows, which makes the firm's dividend decision irrelevant.

[7] It also means that it is expensive for poor-quality firms to mimic this cash dividend payment.

follows a pecking order when raising capital. It means, for example, that share-holders would prefer cash be disgorged as a dividend and then have management explain why it needs the money back by filing a prospectus and issuing new common shares.[8] From an agency perspective, paying a large dividend and forcing the firm to justify future expenditures creates value by controlling management. However, while an agency perspective justifies the stock market's reaction to dividends, it cannot explain the dividend smoothing phenomena.

The signalling model can be explained by examining Figure 22-6.

FIGURE 22-6

The Signalling Model

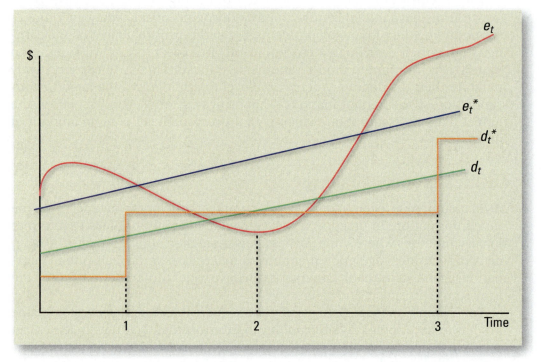

The starred values in Figure 22-6 represent management's view of the underlying or permanent earnings (e_t^*) and dividends (d_t^*) per share, whereas the unstarred values are the actual values. Note that the underlying earnings and dividends are increasing through time so the firm has some long-run target payout. However, actual earnings vary with "predictable" factors such as the state of the economy or the inflation rate. So when the actual earnings increase in line with underlying earnings, the firm increases the dividend per share as at time 1. However, when there are poor earnings at time 2, the firm does not cut its dividend, since to do so would signal to the market that this is not temporary, but permanent. At this point in time, the firm cannot cover its dividend from its earnings, but signals to investors that this earnings drop is expected to be temporary by maintaining the dividend. Figure 22-1 illustrates that this is what many Canadian companies did during the recessions in the early 1980s and 1990s. Then at time 3, the firm increases its dividend again to signal that the earnings increase this time is in line with the firm's underlying earnings increase.

---

[8] In fact this argument has been cited as one factor contributing to the popularity of income trusts, which pay out virtually all of their earnings, forcing them to access capital markets for future financing needs.

This signalling model indicates that dividend changes have *information content*, which provides an important role for dividend policy. This signalling model, when combined with the residual theory of dividends, provides the major theories that explain actual dividend policy. The residual theory of dividends explains generally which types of firms should pay a dividend and the general level of their payout. The signalling model explains how these dividends should be paid out as a slowly adapting dividend per share, as modelled by Lintner.

Taxes

The final imperfection that affects all financial policy is the impact of taxes. Working out how taxes affect financial policy is very difficult because different classes of investors have different tax brackets, so with taxes the general rule is that "one size does not fit all." As discussed in Chapter 19, corporations pay no tax on dividend income if it is received from another Canadian corporation. This is because it is taxed when paid out to an individual and to do otherwise would result in a cascading tax, where the rate could end up as greater than 100 percent.[9] As a result, there is a corporate preference for receiving dividend income. For individuals, on the other hand, the preference for dividend versus capital gains income will depend on the province of residence and on their income level.[10]

Table 22-3 provides 2006 marginal tax rates for dividend versus capital gains income for five provinces as reported by Ernst&Young.[11]

Table 22-3   Individual Tax Rates (%) on Dividends and Capital Gains

	Income Level	$25,000	$50,000	$75,000	$100,000
British Columbia	Dividends	2.52	6.19	15.69	20.04
	Capital gains	12.45	15.58	18.85	20.35
Alberta	Dividends	3.63	8.03	13.83	13.83
	Capital gains	12.63	16.0	18.0	18.0
Ontario	Dividends	0	8.24	20.74	20.74
	Capital gains	10.65	15.58	21.71	21.71
Quebec	Dividends	5.95	15.42	26.06	26.06
	Capital gains	14.37	19.19	22.86	22.86
Nova Scotia	Dividends	0	8.75	17.05	19.06
	Capital gains	12.02	18.48	21.34	22.63

As a general rule, marginal tax rates are lower on dividend income than on capital gains income since the capital gains tax rate is half the marginal tax rate,

[9] This is because tax would be paid every time a dividend passed between different companies.

[10] Therefore it is obvious that M&M's homemade dividend argument is negated by the existence of differential tax rates, as well as by the existence of transactions costs.

[11] http://www.ey.com/global/Content.nsf/Canada/Tax_-_Calculators_-_2006_Personal_Tax

whereas dividend income attracts the dividend tax rate. This differential narrows as the amount of taxable income increases due to the progressive nature of our tax system, but the system still gives rise to **tax clienteles**. High dividend yield stocks are often referred to as "widows and orphans stocks," since they are often held by lower tax rate investors (often retirees), who rely on the dividends for income. In contrast, low dividend yield stocks tend to be held by younger investors who have longer term horizons and are intent on holding for a long time to defer taxes. So although the payment of a dividend may not have an impact on the general level of share prices, it will be an important influence on the type of investors that a firm attracts. The general advice that flows from this is not to drastically change dividend policy since it upsets the existing ownership base.

tax clienteles the fact that investors in different tax brackets have different preferences for reveiving dividend income

Repackaging Dividend-Paying Securities

The tax clienteles identified above are interested in different parts of the return generated by the firm. The problem is that the return comes packaged in one security so that each group gets part of what it wants and part of what it doesn't want. This has lead to some interesting security repackaging products and **income stripping**.

income stripping the process of repackaging securities to provide different types of income based on different parts of the returns

Stripping is common in finance and is entirely respectable. It refers to separating the different parts of the return from owning a security and selling them to different investors. Take BCE, for example, whose major asset is Bell Canada, which has a history of being a reasonably stable firm paying a high dividend. However, the telecommunications revolution of the past 20 years has also provided BCE with growth prospects. As a result, it attracts both growth investors and dividend yield investors, but they both have to buy the same package of returns from BCE. McLeod Young Weir (MYW), a company that is now owned by the Bank of Nova Scotia, found a way around this problem in 1986.

MYW bought $454 million in BCE common shares and repackaged them. The shares were placed in a trust company named "B" corporation, which raised the $454 million by issuing two classes of securities backed by the BCE shares. One class of securities were special preferred shares that had the right to receive all the dividends on these shares for six years. Then at the end of six years they either got the minimum of $30, or the BCE share price minus $1. MYW then sold these preferred shares for $330 million. The second class of securities they issued were referred to as Instalment Receipts (IR), and provided investors with the right to purchase the BCE shares at the end of six years on payment of the minimum of $30, or the BCE share price minus $1. MYW then sold these securities for $143 million.

The pattern of the securities is illustrated below, but the upshot is that $454 million of BCE shares were repackaged and sold for $473 million and MYW pocketed $19 million in fees to cover expenses.

The top box in Figure 22-7 is the valuation of the BCE shares at $454 million. This is the present value of six years of dividends plus the share price at the end of the six years. The bottom two boxes are the values of the preferred share and instalment receipts. Note that if you add the payoffs from the two securities together they sum to the payoff from the BCE shares. So we are just stripping the BCE shares into two new securities.

One interesting feature of these shares is the instalment receipts. Whenever you see minimums or maximums you should think options. In this case, the IR

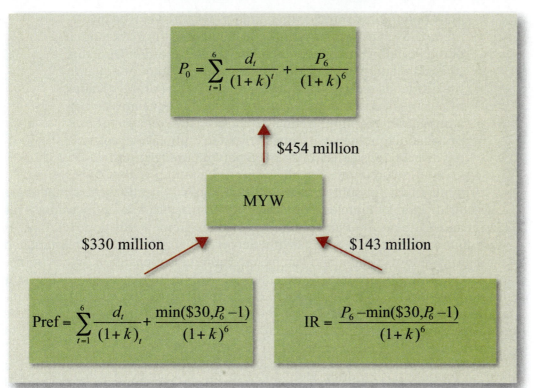

MYW's B Corporation Shares

holders will only pay $30 to buy the BCE shares if the share price is above $30, so this is a straight call option. If the BCE share price is less than $30, they will pay $1 less than the shares are worth. Either way the IR holders end up owning the shares at the end of six years, and the preferred shareholders simply get the dividends on all the shares for the previous five years and either $30 or the BCE share price minus $1. Effectively, the IRs are long-term "in the money" call options on BCE common shares.

So instead of holding BCE shares and getting a package of dividends and capital gains, investors can buy the preferred shares and get more dividends than they can buy directly for $330, or they can buy the IRs and get all capital gains through a long-term call option. The fact that MYW made $19 million in fees indicates that the parts were worth more than the whole and that investors would prefer to own a pure dividend or pure capital gains stream of cash flows. In turn, this implies that tax clienteles do exist.

"B" Corporation was the first dividend strip of common shares in Canada. Since then there have been many examples of what are now termed **split shares**. The Bank of Nova Scotia now has the largest split share mutual fund, where instead of stripping the income on one company, such as BCE, they split it on a pool of companies. Allbanc Split Corporation II has a market value of $300 million and splits the dividends and capital gains from a portfolio of bank shares, which, like BCE, have high dividends. The investor can either buy the preferred shares, which have a fixed dividend (ALB.PR.A), or they can buy the *capital shares*, which receive any increase in dividends plus the capital appreciation (ALB). The shares are issued in the ratio of two capital shares for one preferred share as a unit, but they trade separately.

Allbanc describes its two classes of shares in its 2006 annual report as follows:

split shares shares sold as their dividends and capital gains parts

The Capital Shares provide their holders with a leveraged investment, the value of which is linked to changes in the market price
of the Portfolio Shares. It is the policy of the Board of Directors
to declare and pay quarterly dividends in an amount equal to
the dividends received by the Company on the Portfolio Shares
minus the distributions payable on the Preferred Shares and all
administrative and operating expenses. The Preferred Shares
provide their holders with quarterly fixed cumulative preferential distributions equal to $0.26563 per Preferred Share.

The popularity of split shares has two major implications. First, there are
investor dividend clienteles and dividends do matter to some investors. This
emphasizes the need for companies to consider dramatic dividend changes as
a serious event not to be taken lightly. Second, the capital shares are marketed
as a leveraged investment and can be considered an application of the "homemade" leverage theorem advanced by M&M. In this case, given investor
preference for leverage and dislike of dividends, they can buy the Allbanc capital shares, for example. In this way, the financial policies of the six banks in the
Allbanc portfolio are being changed to the benefit of the capital shareowners in
exactly the way advanced by M&M.

There are now almost 40 families of split shares traded on the TSX with a
market value of $4.2 billion. These firms strip the dividends from the capital
gains for a wide class of common shares ranging from bank and utility stocks to
global telecom stocks. The existence of these families of split shares is an example of the M&M theorems being applied in action, as well as the efficiency with
which financial markets adapt to "imperfections" that provide an opportunity
to create value.

CONCEPT REVIEW QUESTIONS

1. Explain why dividend policy will be relevant in the presence of transactions costs, informational asymmetry and agency problems, and taxes.

2. Describe split shares, and explain what their popularity implies about
   investor preferences for dividends in the real world.

22.7 SHARE REPURCHASES

The final aspect of dividend policy we consider is that of share repurchases.
Note that in the sources and uses of funds constraint expressed in Equation
22-3, we can always set the dividends equal to zero. What this means is that if
the free cash flow is negative, the firm issues shares, and if it is positive, instead
of paying a cash dividend, it repurchases shares.

Let's return to our example of the firm with a $50 million value in the next
period with 1 million shares outstanding. Further assume that it has an expected free cash flow of $5 million in the next period. So its value with a $5 a share
cash dividend is now $50, as below:

$$P_0 = \frac{\$5m + \$50m}{(1+.10)} /1,000,000 = \$50$$

However, if instead the firm used the $5 million in free cash flow generated during the year to buy back 90,909 shares at $55 each at the end of the year, then next period the market value of the shares is:

$$P_1 = \frac{\$50m}{909,090} = \$55$$

Therefore, the present value of $55 today using the 10% discount rate is once again $50.

What this example illustrates is that the firm can use the $5 million in cash either to pay a cash dividend or repurchase shares, and either way with perfect capital markets the shares are worth $50 today. The example also illustrates that share repurchase is simply another form of payout policy. It is an alternative to a cash dividend where the objective is to increase the price per share rather than paying a dividend and forcing the shareholders to immediately pay tax on the dividend.

Of course in this example, the firm has to buy back the shares at $55, which is the ongoing value of the firm of $50 plus the $5 million in cash on hand divided by the current 1 million shares outstanding. If it offers to buy the shares at $60 then all the shareowners should tender their shares as they are only worth $55. Similarly if it offers $50 a share, no one should tender them. The advantage for the shareholder is that they can either hold their shares and receive a larger capital gain in the future or sell out now. Such a persistent policy of share repurchase is technically illegal since there are rules against the improper accumulation of funds within the firm.[12] Consequently what sometimes happens is that firms adopt a policy of large infrequent share repurchase programs. Often at these points, insiders hold on to their shares so that they defer any capital gains and associated taxes.

This example shows that a share repurchase program can act like a cash dividend by providing a payout of funds to the shareholders. However, unlike a dividend, share repurchases can be motivated by several other factors, so it is easy to think that it is part of a payout policy when in fact it is not.

Several other reasons may motivate share repurchases, including:

- *Offsetting the exercise of executive stock options (ESOs)*. ESOs are call options granted to senior executives. When exercised, they result in more shares outstanding. Frequently firms repurchase shares to meet these exercise requirements, thereby leaving the number of shares outstanding constant.

- *Leveraged recapitalizations*. Often debt is raised and the proceeds used to repurchase shares to move the firm back to its optimal capital structure.

- *Information or signalling effects*. Management often indicates that it repurchases shares to signal to the market that it thinks the stock is undervalued.

- *Repurchase dissident shares*. Often there is substantial disagreement among shareholders about the future of the firm. A substantial share repurchase program gives the dissidents an opportunity to sell their shares without depressing the market price, thereby removing an "overhang" of shares.

- *Removing cash without generating expectations for future distributions*. Similar to special dividends, a large share repurchase can return cash to the

[12] Until the late 1940s, the U.S. treasury investigated any firm that did not pay out 70% of its earnings as dividends for improper accumulation of funds. The onus was on the firm to justify a reinvestment rate above 30 percent of earnings.

shareholders without generating expectations about receiving similar distributions in the future.

- *Take the firm private.* A share repurchase to buy all the outstanding firm's shares takes the firm out of the public markets.

CONCEPT REVIEW QUESTIONS

1. Why can share repurchases be viewed as an alternative to paying a cash dividend?

2. What factors may influence a firm's decision to enter into share repurchases?

ethics
AND CORPORATE GOVERNANCE 22-1

MARRIOTT RESTRUCTURING PLAN

The Marriott Corporation said yesterday that it was holding talks about changing the terms of its restructuring plan with bondholders who are suing the company. Marriott, based in Bethesda, Maryland, said on October 5 it would separate its lucrative hotel management business from its real estate, airport and toll-road concessions, leaving Marriott International Inc. free of debt and Host Marriott with $2.9 billion of debt. While the company's shares soared 20 percent, its bonds fell as much as 30 percent. Bondholders filed federal lawsuits to block the plan. Marriott was expected to file a motion to dismiss the suits yesterday, but instead asked the filing deadline be moved to January 11, a spokesman for the company said.

Source: Company News, *New York Times*, December 30, 1992.

DISCUSSION QUESTIONS

1. Marriott Corporation put its "lucrative" hotel services division into a separate company and spun this division off to its shareholders, leaving the bulk of its debt with the existing company, which it re-titled "Host Marriott." Why did the value of the shares soar 20 percent while that of the bonds dropped 30 percent?

2. Shareholder value creation assumes that no one else loses; is it ethical for management to pursue a plan whereby the shareholders gain at the expense of the bondholders?

3. What legal protection does a bond holder have in the face of such a plan?

Summary

This chapter has looked at different types of dividends, including regular and special cash dividends, stock dividends, stock splits, as well as share repurchases. Similar to our discussion of capital structure theory, we present the major argument of M&M, which suggests that in perfect markets the payment of a cash dividend should not affect the value of the firm. This is because according to the M&M assumptions, the value of the firm is determined by real factors such as the firm's free cash flow. Therefore, all a dividend does is create a greater financing need that has to be met by selling more common shares. This leads us to look at the role of M&M's assumptions.

One common argument that justifies the importance of dividends is that they create value because they are safer than capital gains. However, we saw that while dividend-paying firms are generally lower risk than capital gains oriented ones, this is more a reflection of the risk of their basic operations, as well as the residual theory of dividends. A more substantial critique is that transactions costs make it expensive for firms to follow the residual dividend policy implicit in the M&M argument since it is expensive to raise capital.

The existence of transactions costs also leads firms to increase or initiate dividend payments to signal a higher level of earnings. As a result, dividends have information content and the unexpected payment of a dividend generally causes stock prices to increase. Agency theory also results in the same prediction, but cannot explain the most salient feature of actual dividend policy, which is that firms tend to smooth their dividends.

We also saw that there are tax clienteles since investors' preference for dividends versus capital gains is dependent on their tax bracket and level of income. This provides a tax motivation for firms to use share repurchases as a means of payout policy, since this leads to an increase in share prices and capital gains rather than dividends. However, there are many other reasons why firms might want to repurchase their shares.

Key Terms

agency theory, p. 885

bird in the hand argument, p. 876

cash cow, p. 872

declaration date, p. 863

dividend reinvestment plan (DRIP), p. 864

dividend yield, p. 867

equity market capitalization, p. 870

ex-dividend date, p. 863

free cash flow, p. 871

holder of record, p. 863

homemade dividends, p. 874

income stripping, p. 888

odd lots, p. 864

residual theory of dividends, p. 872

special dividend, p. 863

split shares, p. 889

stock dividend, p. 864

stock split, p. 865

tax clienteles, p. 888

Formulas/Equations

(22-1) $P_0 = \dfrac{D_1 + P_1}{(1 + K_e)}$

(22-2) $mP_0 = V_0 = \dfrac{m(D_1 + P_1)}{(1 + K_e)}$

(22-3) $X_1 + nP_1 = I_1 + mD_1$

$$(22\text{-}4) \quad V_0 = \frac{X_1 - I_1 + [(m+n)P_1 = V_1]}{(1+K)}$$

$$(22\text{-}5) \quad V_0 = \sum_{t=1}^{\infty} \frac{X_t - I_t}{(1+K)^t}$$

$$(22\text{-}6) \quad P = \frac{ROE_1 \times BVPS}{K_e} + \frac{Inv}{(1+K_e)}\left(\frac{ROE_2 - K_e}{K_e}\right)$$

$$(22\text{-}7) \quad \Delta D_t = \beta(D_t^* - D_{t-1})$$

$$(22\text{-}8) \quad D_t = a + (1-b)D_{t-1} + cE_1$$

QUESTIONS AND PRACTICE PROBLEMS

Multiple Choice Questions

1. When is the ex-dividend date if the holder of record date is April 14, 2006?

    A. April 15
    B. April 16
    C. April 12
    D. April 13

2. Which of the following statements about M&M assumptions is *false*?

    A. There are no taxes.
    B. Not all firms maximize value.
    C. There is no debt.
    D. Markets are perfect.

3. What is the market value of equity if next-period cash flow from operations and investment are $400,000 and $200,000, respectively, and k = 15%?

    A. $173,913
    B. $347,826
    C. $175,000
    D. $359,499

4. What is the change in dividends if the firm adjusts dividends immediately? The target dividend is $4.50 and the prior-period dividend is $3.

    A. 0
    B. – $1.50
    C. $0.750
    D. $1.50

5. Which of following has a *negative* impact on the share price?

    A. Unexpected dividend increase

B. Unexpected dividend initiation

C. Unexpected dividend decrease

D. None of the above

6. Which of the following statements regarding motivation for a stock repurchase is *wrong*?

A. Firms could be privatized using stock repurchases.

B. Investors consider a firm's stock overvalued when a stock repurchase occurs.

C. Firms use stock repurchase to move capital structure back to some optimum level.

D. Stock repurchases are sometimes used to satisfy dissident shareholders.

Practice Problems

7. Briefly state the underlying idea of the "bird in the hand" argument.

8. Briefly state the tax clientele argument.

9. Briefly describe the difference between a stock dividend and a cash dividend plus a DRIP.

Easy

10. Explain the implications of M&M's homemade dividend argument.

11. Briefly describe the implications of releasing the assumptions of no transaction costs.

12. What is the market price per share if the next period's dividend is $2.50 and $P_1 = \$25$? $k = 15\%$.

Medium

13. Describe possible reactions from the market of the following dividend payout changes: dividend initiation, dividend increase, and dividend decrease.

14. List the main reasons why firms repurchase shares.

15. According to equity market capitalization, what is the cost of capital for the stock of the following firm? Current market value of the equity is $1,200,000 with 100,000 shares outstanding. The stock price is expected grow 5% in a year and the firm is expected to pay out a $1.50 dividend per share at the end of the first year.

16. Explain why firms don't simply pay out dividends as a portion of their profits. What do most firms do in terms of dividend policy?

17. How many new shares does the firm have to issue if it is expected to pay out a dividend of $2.50 per share? Currently the firm has an operating cash flow of $350 million and there is a promising project available, which costs $200 million. There are 100 million shares outstanding with a current price of $40 per share.

18. Sanya Inc. follows a strict residual dividend policy. The firm will have profits of $500,000 this year. After screening all available investment projects, Sanya has decided to take three out of the ten projects and those three will cost $410,000. What dividends will Sanya pay to its shareholders this year? Its current equity

market value is $5,000,500 and the current market price of its shares is $45.60. What is the shortcoming of this policy?

Difficult

19. What is the change in share price if a firm spends its extra $600,000 to buy back stocks at $31 per share instead of paying $600,000 in cash dividends? The next-period market value of equity is $2,500,000 and there are currently 100,000 shares outstanding, with k = 15%.

20. According to John Lintner, what is the adjustment factor β? Interpret the calculated adjustment factor.

21. The current stock price of Abacus Industries is $50. For the last 20 years, the firm has paid an annual dividend of $5. On June 26, they announced a dividend of $6 payable on September 10 to shareholders of record at the close of business on September 1.

    A. What do you expect to happen to the price of Abacus stock on June 26?

    B. If the shareholders of Abacus pay no taxes on dividends, what do you expect to happen to the price of Abacus on the ex-dividend date?

    C. If the shareholders of Abacus pay taxes on dividends, do you expect the stock price reaction on the ex-dividend date to be greater, the same, or less than in (B)?

22. The Mortal Coil Company (MCC) currently has cash flow from operations of $10 million, capital expenditures of $8 million, and pays a dividend of $2 million (all are perpetuities). The company has no growth prospects, debt and shareholders expect an annual return of 5 percent. The total number of shares outstanding is 1,000. For the following investors, describe how they can achieve their desired cash flow patterns and the value of their strategy (future value) at the end of the second year. Each investor owns 10 percent of the company and there are no taxes or transaction costs.

    A. Marie lives in a very high-cost city and would like to receive a dividend of $400,000 at the end of Year 1. She needs this money to finance her lifestyle.

    B. Charlie has found another investment opportunity that will pay him 15 percent and would also like to receive $400,000 at the end of Year 1.

    C. Frank is very frugal and would rather not receive dividends at the end of Year 1.

23. The Safe-n-Secure Company (SNS) is a dividend paying company; its current dividend yield is 8 percent. Current stock price is $100. The company has paid the same dividend for the last 15 years and it is not expected to change. Alice believes that the company is an excellent investment opportunity for her clients and has been contacting them. Here are some of the responses she has received:

    Client A: I need income, I don't trust capital gains—they aren't real, just paper. I'm not interested in this stock; I'd rather just have a bond and get a nice fixed income.

    Client B: Who cares about dividends? I pay more taxes on the dividends so I want capital gains where I can control the timing of the tax bill. The dividend is too high and I will pay too much tax so I'm not interested in the stock.

    A. Which investor's statement is consistent with the "bird in the hand" argument about dividends?

B. Describe how income stripping would allow Alice to satisfy the needs of both Client A and Client B.

24. The Cautious George Company (CGC) is considering its dividend policy. Currently CGC pays no dividends, has cash flows from operations of $10 million per year (perpetual), and needs $8 million for capital expenditures. The firm has no debt and there is no tax. The firm has 2 million shares outstanding, which are currently trading at $50 per share. George, the majority owner of CGC (owns 60 percent), would like to take $20 million of cash out of the company to fund his various charities. The Absent Minded Profs have been hired by CGC to consider different alternatives.

A. George could sell stock to raise the $20 million he requires. What are the advantages and disadvantages of this strategy (impact on the value of CGC and George's control)?

B. CGC could pay a dividend so that George will receive $20 million.

i) Describe how the company can issue stock to create the dividend.

ii) What is the effect on the value of CGC?

iii)What is the effect on George's level of control of the firm?

25. Edmund Fitzgerald, a shipping tycoon, expected his firm to earn $1,000 per year forever, with no growth. Given a cost of capital of 10 percent, the value of the firm is $10,000. Edmund identified a new project, which costs $1,000 but would earn 11 percent per year forever. To invest in this project, Edmund cancelled this year's dividend. Given that he is investing in a positive NPV project, he expected his stock to rise. However, it fell dramatically. Edmund has asked the Absent Minded Profs to explain what happened. Does this mean that investors do not like positive NPV projects?

PART 9

WORKING CAPITAL MANAGEMENT

Last, but certainly not least, is the management of working capital. This topic may appear at the end of the textbook, but most new financial recruits in nonfinancial companies start their careers in managing working capital. These new finance professionals will need to learn whether to extend credit to a trade customer, whether to invest surplus cash balances in marketable securities, and how to decide how much inventory a firm really needs. All of these decisions involve interacting with that most important institution: the Canadian chartered bank, which frequently lends against these working capital assets.

Managing Working Capital

Chapter 23 tells us why managing working capital efficiently is critical to a firm's survival and success. Finning International sells, services, and rents heavy equipment manufactured by Caterpillar Inc. The company's first quarter 2007 results were accompanied by an increase in guidance earnings for the rest of the year, based on a strong order book. However, this increase in demand for its products has put some pressure on Finning's cash flow: "The Company's Canadian and South American operations continue to experience a significant increase in equipment inventories as a result of strong demand for product and in order to meet customer delivery requirements in 2007. Throughout all operations, management continues to focus on improving cash cycle times and operating efficiencies." Finning depends on Caterpillar for parts and equipment deliveries and must sometimes increase inventory levels in order to fulfill expected future demand.

Source: Finning International website: www.finning.com. Retrieved May 10, 2007.

Working Capital Management: General Issues

Learning Objectives

After reading this chapter, you should understand the following:

1. Why the management of net working capital is critical for the survival of the firm

2. How managing receivables, inventory, and payables is related in an integrated approach to net working capital management

3. How the financing and current asset investment decisions interact to determine a company's overall working capital position

4. How some key financial ratios can be used to analyze a firm's net working capital policies

INTRODUCTION

This chapter introduces the concept of working capital management. We discuss various methods firms can use to make these decisions.

In Chapter 4, we defined *working capital* as the sum of the firm's current assets, and in Chapter 3, we talked about **net working capital (NWC)** as the difference between a firm's current assets and its current liabilities. **Working capital management** refers to the way in which a firm manages both its current assets (i.e., cash and marketable securities, accounts receivable, and inventories) and its current liabilities (i.e., accounts payable, notes payables, and short-term borrowing arrangements).

Managing working capital (W/C) effectively is critical to both the short-term and the long-term viability of any firm. In fact, W/C *mismanagement* can often cause liquidity problems, which, in the extreme case, can force a firm into bankruptcy. Many entry-level jobs for finance graduates are in the field of working capital management because every firm has to manage its working capital on a day-to-day basis, whereas the decisions regarding capital structure, dividend policy, and capital budgeting are often episodic decisions that are made quite infrequently by many firms. Consequently, this chapter covers "bread-and-butter" topics that everyone working in a finance capacity in a non-financial company has to know.

What constitutes good W/C management? The answer is complicated; however, we can say that good W/C management is characterized by

1. the maintenance of optimal cash balances
2. the investment of any excess liquid funds in marketable securities that provide the best return possible, considering any liquidity or default-risk constraints
3. proper management of accounts receivables
4. an efficient inventory management system
5. maintaining an appropriate level of short-term financing, in the least expensive and most flexible manner possible

We deal with these points in Chapter 24. In this chapter, we address the concept of W/C management in general. However, before discussing these topics, read the excerpt from *Business Week* on April 28, 1956, in Finance in the News 23-1. This topic was as important then as it is now.

net working capital (NWC) the difference between a firm's current assets and its current liabilities

working capital management the way in which a firm manages both its current assets (cash and marketable securities, accounts receivable, and inventories) and its current liabilities (accounts payable, notes payables, and short-term borrowing arrangements)

23.1 AN INTEGRATED APPROACH TO NET WORKING CAPITAL (NWC) MANAGEMENT

A Classic Working Capital Problem

The *Business Week* article in Finance in the News 23-1 is a classic, because it highlights a basic problem: profits are not cash and a firm can only pay its bills

HOW TO GO BROKE...WHILE MAKING A PROFIT

As the year started, Mr. Jones of the ABC Co. was in fine shape. His company made widgets—just what the customer wanted. He made them for 75¢ each, sold them for $1. He kept a 30-day supply in inventory, paid his bills promptly, and billed his customers 30-days net. Sales were right on target with the sales manager predicting a steady increase. It felt like his lucky year, and it began this way:

Jan. 1 Cash $1,000 Inventory $750 Receivables $1,000

In January, he sold 1,000 widgets; shipped them at a cost of $750; collected his receivables—winding up with a tidy $250 profit.

Feb. 1 Cash $1,250 Inventory $750 Receivables $1,000

This month sales jumped, as predicted, to $1,500. With a corresponding step-up in production to maintain his 30-day inventory, he made 2,000 units at a cost of $1,500. All receivables from January sales are collected. Profit so far: $625.

Mar. 1 Cash $750 Inventory $1,125 Receivables $1,500

March sales were even better: 2,000 units.

Collections: On time. Production to adhere to his inventory policy: 2,500 units. Operating result for the month: $500 profit. Profit to date: $1,125.

Apr. 1 Cash $375 Inventory $1,500 Receivables $2,000

In April, sales jumped another 500 units to 2,500—and Jones patted his sales manager on the back. His customers were paying right on time. Production was pushed to 3,000 units, and the month's business netted him $625 for a profit to date of $1,750. He took off for Florida before he saw the accountant's report.

May 1 Cash $125 Inventory $1,875 Receivables $2,500

May saw Jones' company really hitting a stride—sales of 3,000 widgets, production of 3,500, and a five-month profit of $2,500. But, suddenly he got a phone call from his treasurer: "Come home! We need money!" His books had caught up with him.

June 1 Cash $000 Inventory $2,250 Receivables $3,000

He came home—and hollered for his banker.

Source: "How to Go Broke...While Making a Profit." *Business Week*, April 28, 1956, p. 46.

with cash. In this example, Mr. Jones's "books caught up with him" and he had to come home from his Florida vacation after getting a phone call from his accountant/treasurer. ABC's rapid growth was causing cash flow problems even though it was very profitable. Let's analyze what went wrong—or more accurately, what was going right and what the treasurer should have done to head off an entirely predictable problem.

First, look at the cash flow statement as of June 1, shown in Table 23-1 to find out what happened. Recall from Chapter 3 that firms produce three statements: the income statement, the balance sheet, and the cash flow statement. Of the three, financial analysts tend to look at the cash flow statement the most, because the other two frequently have accounting adjustments that make it difficult to find the firm's problems. The ABC example helps us contrast the usefulness of the income statement with the cash flow statement.

Table 23-1   ABC Company: Sources and Uses of Funds

Income Statement	January – June 1
Sales	$10,000
Cost of goods sold	7,500
Profit	2,500
Operating cash flow	2,500
(No depreciation)	
Increase in accounts receivable	2,000
Inventory	1,500
Change in working capital	3,500
Change in cash	−1,000

We know that Mr. Jones was running a profitable company. When we add up the sales from January to May, we see that he sold $1,000 worth of widgets in January and $500 more each month, so by the end of May, he has cumulative sales of $10,000. These widgets had a $0.75 cost, so he had $7,500 in cost of goods sold. The operating profit was $2,500. We have not included any depreciation charge for wear and tear on his machines, and even if we had, we would just add it back to get operating cash flow, because depreciation is a non-cash charge. So if ABC has cash flow of $2,500, why the telephone call telling Mr. Jones to hurry back?

The problem is the change in ABC's working capital. Mr. Jones sells his widgets on credit with his customers paying him with a 30-day lag. This is typical of **trade credit**, in which a customer orders ABC's widgets and the firm ships them out, along with an invoice indicating the terms of payment, which in this case is 30 days. By June 1, ABC's accounts receivable has increased from $1,000 to $3,000, an increased investment in receivables of $2,000. The reason for the increase is the increased sales level from $1,000 in January to $3,000 in May, meaning that more credit was being granted to ABC's customers, even though ABC's credit policy had not changed.

Similarly, ABC has an inventory policy of keeping a 30-day supply on hand so that when customers place an order, it can be boxed and sent out immediately. In January, Mr. Jones had $750 of widgets on hand, and by June 1 this had increased to $2,250, as ABC's sales level had increased. ABC had increased inventory of $1,500. Again, the reason for the increased inventory was the increase in sales level from $1,000 to $3,000. ABC requires a similar increase in inventory of $2,000 worth of widgets, because the firm keeps one month's sales on hand. However, the widgets are carried in inventory at the "lower of cost and market," so the inventory investment is the $0.75 cost rather than the $1 selling price. ABC has an increased inventory investment of $1,500.

ABC pays its bills immediately, so there are no accounts payable. The change in net working capital is the change in receivables plus inventory minus

trade credit a customer orders a product or service and the firm delivers it, along with an invoice indicating the terms of payment

the change in payables: −$3,500. When the change in NWC is added to the operating cash flow, we get *cash flow from operations* of −$1,000. Because ABC started with $1,000 cash in the bank, by the end of May, the cash has been depleted, and ABC has run out of cash to finance its operations. At this point, ABC's cheques would bounce.

It is important to note that cash flow from operations is the correct measure of the cash-generating ability of the firm. All finance instructors emphasize that depreciation and amortizations are non-cash charges and need to be added to net income to get cash flow, but this is only part of the story; other cash items need to be considered in determining cash flow. If ABC had a cash-only sales policy and did not extend credit, then with the same level of sales, the firm would have $10,000 in cash. However, the fact that sales were on credit with a 30-day payment period means that ABC did not get any cash from the $3,000 of sales in May. The receivables did not increase by this $3,000, because the firm did get the $1,000 from the receivables that were outstanding in January. When firms sell on credit, they have to make sure that they are actually collecting the cash from those sales. Similarly, the income statement includes only the cost of producing items that are sold. If production is unsold, it goes into inventory, but the firm has still paid to produce it, so there is still a cash outflow. The increase in receivables and inventory, net of payables, are the most important net working capital items.

The Cash Budget

If Mr. Jones had estimated ABC's cash flow statement for May, he would have realized that he had a cash flow problem. However, he would need to do a cash flow statement for every month to know exactly when this problem would become acute. Firms do project a **cash budget**, which is essentially a cash flow statement for each month.

So let's think through ABC's problem. The sales level was $1,000 and Mr. Jones was forecasting a $500 increase every month. We can start the sales at $1,000 for month 1 and then increase by $500 for every future month. Mr. Jones could forecast the cash inflow from these sales, which for ABC with a 30-day credit policy, would mean that each month the firm receives as an inflow the previous month's credit sales. In practice, things are slightly more complicated, as we will discuss later.

Remember that the only source of cash from operations is from sales; all the other items are uses of cash. ABC spends $0.75 producing every widget. Two types of widgets are produced: those that are sold and those that are held in inventory. For each month, ABC has a cash outflow for the cost of the widgets produced and sold, which for month 1 is $750, for month 2 is $1,000, and so on. However, in month 2, in addition to production for sales, there is an additional $375 outflow for the 500 widgets produced for inventory, because sales have increased by 500 units and ABC has a one-month supply policy for inventory. In reality for month 2 at a sales level of $1,500, ABC is receiving only the $1,000 from the previous month's sales, while it is paying $1,125 to produce for the current month's sales and an additional $375 to increase inventory, translating into a net cash outflow of $500.

cash budget a cash flow statement for each month

The cash inflows and outflows record the change in the cash budget each month. ABC started with $1,000 in cash, which increased to $1,250 after month 1 and then decreased to $750 after month 2. If Mr. Jones had decided that ABC needed 20 percent of sales in cash "just in case," then the excess cash in month 1 was $1,050. This excess cash could have been invested for a month. However, by month 2 the drop in cash flow from operations means that the excess cash has dropped precipitously to $450. By month 3, the cash budget would have indicated to Mr. Jones that ABC had no excess cash and was now below its desired holding of cash. This was two month's *before* ABC actually ran out of cash and would have given Mr. Jones plenty of time to talk to the bank about arranging some short-term credit. Table 23-2 provides ABC's cash budget for the next six months.

Table 23-2   ABC's Six-Month Cash Budget

$	1	2	3	4	5	6
Sales	1,000	1,500	2,000	2,500	3,000	3,500
Cash inflow	1,000	1,000	1,500	2,000	2,500	3,000
Cash outflow						
Current sales	750	1,125	1,500	1,875	2,250	2,625
Inventory	0	375	375	375	375	375
Operating cash	250	−500	−375	−250	−125	0
Start cash	1,000	1,250	750	375	125	0
End cash	1,250	750	375	125	0	0
Required cash	200	300	400	500	600	700
Surplus/deficit	1,050	450	(25)	(375)	(600)	(700)

The important thing about the cash budget is that it forecasts cash inflows and outflows over a forecast horizon and their cumulative impact on the firm's cash balances. All the problems we discuss in this chapter and Chapter 24 revolve around the cash budget. Typically, firms prepare a cash budget for at least the upcoming year, on at least a monthly (and sometimes even a weekly or daily) basis. These cash budgets are important planning tools for the firm. For example, they indicate when and for how long a firm can expect to have excess cash balances that can be invested in marketable securities. For ABC, this was the first two months of the year. Cash budgets also show when and for how long a firm may require some additional borrowing to cover any cash shortfalls, so it can arrange for some short-term borrowing.

Banks often require a cash budget as part of the documentation for a loan application, because they need to see whether the loan is needed for a short period or is, in fact, permanent financing. A careful look at Table 23-2 indicates that the operating cash flow shortfall is declining: it peaks at −$500, declines to $0 by month 6. If Mr. Jones presented this cash flow forecast to the bank at the beginning of the year, the lending officer would have requested he complete it for the whole year instead of just the first six months. This 12-month budget is presented in Table 23-3.

Table 23-3   ABC's 12-Month Cash Budget

$	1	2	3	4	5	6	7	8	9	10	11	12
Sales	1,000	1,500	2,000	2,500	3,000	3,500	4,000	4,500	5,000	5,500	6,000	6,500
Cash inflow	1,000	1,000	1,500	2,000	2,500	3,000	3,500	4,000	4,500	5,000	5,500	6,000
Cash outflow												
Current sales	750	1,125	1,500	1,875	2,250	2,625	3,000	3,375	3,750	4,125	4,500	4,875
Inventory	0	375	375	375	375	375	375	375	375	375	375	375
Operating cash	250	−500	−375	−250	−125	0	125	250	375	500	625	750
Start cash	1,000	1,250	750	375	125	0	0	125	375	750	1,250	1,875
End cash	1,250	750	375	125	0	0	125	375	750	1,250	1,875	2,625
Required cash	200	300	400	500	600	700	800	900	1,000	1,100	1,200	1,300
Surplus/deficit	1,050	450	(25)	(375)	(600)	(700)	(675)	(525)	(250)	150	675	1,325

By completing the cash budget for the whole year, it becomes apparent that with the $500 increase in sales each month, ABC's cash flow problems peak in May/June and then correct themselves. By month 7 (July), operating cash flow is positive at $125 and from then on the operating cash flow increases every month. By month 10, ABC has surplus funds again and can start to invest the excess in marketable securities.

Mr. Jones would not have enhanced his reputation with the people at the bank if he had gone to see them in May, saying, "Please help me. I am out of cash." At the very least it would have indicated very poor cash management, and the lending officer would have paid very close attention to any loans made to ABC. Instead, if Mr. Jones had completed the cash budget and explained that he needed to set up a facility whereby he could invest surplus funds at the start and end of the year, and that he needed some short-term borrowing in the middle months, the bank could have designed a borrowing and lending facility for ABC. Establishing a good reputation with the bank lending officer is critical, especially for small firms, and the tool for doing this is the cash budget, because it enhances an understanding of the cash inflows and outflows through the firm.

The key components of a cash budget are sales forecasts, estimated production schedules, and estimates of the size and timing of any other major inflows (e.g., from the sale of an asset) or outflows (e.g., capital expenditures, dividend payments) that the firm expects. Example 23-1 provides a simplified example of how to construct a cash budget.

Example 23-1: Cash Budget

A firm has estimated its sales, purchases from suppliers, and wages and miscellaneous operating cash outlays for the first four months of next year as follows:

Month	Sales	Purchases	Wages and Miscellaneous
January	$10,000	$6,000	$3,000
February	$12,000	$7,500	$3,500
March	$15,000	$5,500	$4,000
April	$11,000	$5,000	$3,000

The firm estimates that 50 percent of its sales will be for cash and that 80 percent of its credit sales will be collected one month after the sale, with the remainder being collected in the following month. It also estimates that 50 percent of its purchases will be paid 30 days from the purchase date, while the remaining 50 percent will be paid in 60 days. Assume that sales and purchases were the same in November and December as they are estimated to be in January. Finally, the firm plans to pay dividends of $3,000 in March and expects to receive $1,500 in January from the sale of a used truck. The beginning cash balance is $1,000, which is the minimum cash balance the firm wants to maintain. Estimate the firm's cash budget for the first four months of next year.

Solution

	January	February	March	April
Cash inflows ($)				
Sales				
Current month sales	5,000	6,000	7,500	5,500
Previous month's sales	4,000	4,000	4,800	6,000
Sales from two months ago	1,000	1,000	1,000	1,200
Total sales receipts	10,000	11,000	13,300	12,700
Other cash inflows	1,500*			
Total cash inflows	11,500	11,000	13,300	12,700

	January	February	March	April
Cash outflows ($)				
Purchases				
Previous month	3,000	3,000	3,750	2,750
Two months ago	3,000	3,000	3,000	3,750
Total purchase outflows	6,000	6,000	6,750	6,500
Wages and miscellaneous	3,000	3,500	4,000	3,000
Other cash outflows			3,000†	
Total cash outflows	9,000	9,500	13,750	9,500

How much a firm holds in cash and cash equivalents is also partly determined by its ability to borrow on an operating line of credit or to run an overdraft. In fact, most firms will hold more *liquidity* in borrowing facilities than they will in cash and equivalents, because the cost of standby lending facilities is relatively cheap compared with the opportunity cost of raising capital from the firm's shareholders to invest in marketable securities. In particular, motives 2 through 4 can all be satisfied by using near-cash items, such as investments in marketable securities, and by maintaining additional short-term borrowing capacity.

As individuals, we are certainly familiar with the concept of the importance of "near-cash" as a substitute for cash in our pockets. We can purchase almost anything by using debit or credit cards, which have greatly reduced the need to carry actual cash. In addition, writing cheques is becoming outdated, as most of us pay our bills via automatic debit from our accounts, or by using the Internet or automated banking machines (ABMs). From now on, for exposition purposes, when we refer to cash, we are talking about both cash and near-cash, unless we make the distinction clear.

Determining the Optimal Cash Balance

Now we turn to the question of how to determine the optimal amount of cash to maintain on hand? Like most decisions in finance, it comes down to a classic tradeoff between risk and expected return. In general, cash and near-cash provide very low returns relative to investments in other assets; however, by definition, they provide the ultimate in liquidity and usually have minimal additional risks (i.e., usually cash and near-cash items are virtually default free). So, it is appropriate to assume that cash is low-risk, low-expected return.

A firm can always take a *conservative* approach and choose to maintain a large amount of its assets in cash and near-cash. It will minimize the risk of not being able to satisfy its liquidity requirements. Unfortunately, this approach sacrifices potential returns, which may not be optimal.[2] Another firm may choose to take an *aggressive* approach to cash management and maintain minimal balances. This approach may lead to higher returns; however, it also increases the firm's risk of becoming illiquid and its risk of having to generate liquidity in a hurry. Creating liquidity quickly is often very expensive, because the firm may have to negotiate short-term loans with higher borrowing rates. In more extreme situations, the firm may be forced to sell less liquid assets, such as inventory or even fixed assets, at discounted prices.

Given our discussion above, it is reasonable to conclude that the **optimal cash balance** is the one that balances the risks of illiquidity against the sacrifice in expected return that is associated with maintaining cash. Therefore, the optimal cash balance, as a percentage of total assets, for example, will differ substantially across firms; some firms have *lower* and *more predictable* cash requirements than others—these firms will require proportionately lower amounts of cash. Other firms with higher cash requirements for transactions purposes, or with less predictable cash flows (and therefore a greater need for precautionary liquidity), will hold higher levels of cash.

optimal cash balance the amount of cash that balances the risks of illiquidity against the sacrifice in expected return that is associated with maintaining cash

---

[2] In addition, it may make the firm an attractive takeover candidate, because the acquiring firm can use some of this cash to pay down its takeover financing.

Near-cash items provide a method for alleviating the problem of the low returns associated with holding cash without sacrificing too much in the way of liquidity. For example, a firm can create excess borrowing capacity in the form of an operating line of credit. However, these credit lines often charge fees on the unused portion of the line, which may offset the advantage of requiring the firm to hold less in cash. In addition, firms often maintain a large portion of their liquidity requirements in money market instruments, which provide a higher return than does cash held in a traditional bank account. The level of investment in marketable securities is dictated to a large extent by the firm's liquidity urgency and by how accurately it is able to forecast its future cash requirements. The latter will be a function partly of the volatility of the firm's cash flows, and partly of how well designed a firm's cash budgeting system is. Firms that have well-developed *cash management systems*, and more predictable cash flows, will be able to maintain a higher portion of their liquidity in marketable securities and less in cash.

Cash Management Techniques

The general approach to good cash management is to speed up inflows *as much as possible* and delay outflows *as much as possible*. We discussed this in Chapter 23 in terms of increasing α in the cash budget and decreasing β. The qualifier "as much as possible" is important because firms always face constraints that will delay inflows and prevent them from delaying outflows too much. For example, a firm can always speed up its inflows from sales by refusing to give credit to customers—of course, this will likely have a large impact on its sales, so this may not be a viable strategy. Similarly, a firm may delay making payments to suppliers; however, if the firm is perpetually late in making payments, it will develop a poor relationship with the suppliers. In the extreme, suppliers may end up selling to the firm on a *cash only* basis, which would, in fact, speed up cash outflows, rather than delay them.

An important part of speeding up inflows is the establishment of an efficient credit policy, which specifies the policies for collecting receivables from customers—we will discuss this later in this chapter. Once the payment procedures for customers have been specified, it is important that firms process the payments as efficiently as possible. One objective at this stage should be to minimize **float** time, which can be defined as the time that elapses between the time the paying firm initiates payment, for example, mails the cheque, and when the funds are available for use by the receiving firm. During this float period, the receiving firm does not have the funds available for use.

Float has three major sources:

float the time that elapses between the time the paying firm initiates payment, and the time the funds are available for use by the receiving firm

1. the time it takes the cheque to reach the firm after it is mailed by the customer

2. the time it takes the receiving firm to process the cheque and deposit it in an account

3. the time it takes the cheque to clear through the banking system so that the funds are available to the firm

Historically, the first source of float time has been the longest. Of course, firms can always obtain *postdated cheques* or stipulate that they *require payment by a certain date*, both of which minimize the float associated with mail and processing times. However, over the past decade in particular, firms have made great strides in eliminating float time by making payment options available to (or mandatory for) customers that eliminate the need to mail cheques. Today, most retailers accept *debit cards*, which automatically debit the customer's accounts. This eliminates the problems associated with accepting cheques (i.e., checking for identification, risking the account not having sufficient funds, taking the time to process and deposit the cheque). Many firms also make use of *preauthorized payments*, whereby customer accounts are automatically debited by the bank on the payment date. Other companies use more advanced electronic collection systems, such as *electronic funds transfer (EFT)* and *electronic data interchange (EDI)* systems.

Although many advancements have occurred, many firms still do things the "old-fashioned way": they bill their customers, and their customers pay by cheque. However, even these firms can take steps to speed up the process and reduce float time. Many firms establish centralized or *concentrated banking* arrangements. Under these arrangements, local offices receive customer payments and deposit them into a local bank account, which is combined with similar local accounts into one central account. This minimizes mail float. A similar strategy that can be used concurrently with the concentrated bank account option is to establish *lock box* banking arrangements. These arrangements involve setting up local post office boxes for customers to mail their payments to and authorizing the local bank to empty these boxes and deposit the cheques into the company's account.

Although float works to a firm's disadvantage with respect to collections, it works to the firm's benefit with respect to disbursements. It is reasonable to assume that many of the firm's suppliers will employ the strategies discussed to minimize their float, which implies there is little benefit in trying to maximize disbursement float. In addition, as discussed above, trying to delay making payments may cause poor relations with suppliers. However, firms can still take steps to improve the efficiency of their cash outflows, and minimize the cash they need to maintain on hand for required disbursements. Just as it makes sense for firms to have a *centralized system* to monitor collections, it also does for payments. This will ensure that payments are made on time, but not early (or late), to the greatest extent possible. In addition, most firms establish *zero-balance accounts*, which are centralized accounts that combine the cash balances of many individual accounts into one central account. Under this system, funds are transferred from this account to cover cheques written against the individual accounts as required. This system reduces the need for cash at the aggregate firm level, because it effectively transfers funds from individual accounts that have excess cash to those that need it. In addition, firms usually tie their operating loans to this central account, reducing the total amount of borrowing required by the firm.

Firms can use these methods to speed up cash inflows and slow down outflows to the greatest extent possible. However, another critical component in any cash management system is the actual tracking of the cash requirements through time. This can be especially important for planning and for assessing short-term financing requirements. As demonstrated in Chapter 23, an important tool that firms use to forecast cash balances and borrowing requirements is the *cash budget*. Cash budgets are important planning tools. For example, they tell firms when and for how long they can expect to have excess cash balances that can be invested in marketable securities. They also show firms how much they may require in excess borrowing capacity to cover any shortfalls, and the firms can arrange their short-term lending facilities accordingly. In fact, banks often require cash budgets as a part of any loan application package.

CONCEPT REVIEW QUESTIONS

1. Why do firms hold cash?
2. What is float and why is it important to the firm?

24.2 ACCOUNTS RECEIVABLE

As soon as a firm decides to extend credit to its customers, it has consciously made a decision to allow some of its funds to be tied up in accounts receivable. This decision should be based on a cost-benefit analysis, just as the decision to have funds tied up in cash, or any other asset for that matter, should be. The expected benefits of extending credit are expanded sales and perhaps even improved relationships with customers. The costs may include losses because of an increase in non-payment by customers, as well as the costs of financing the receivables. The financing costs are those associated with the time the firm has to do without the cash payment for goods that have already been sold and whose production costs have already been paid (or at least partially paid, depending on its own ability to delay paying its suppliers and employees).

Although it is technically true that all firms face the decision of whether or not to provide credit for their customers, as a practical matter, many firms really do not have much of a choice. For example, it is hard to imagine a furniture retailer or car dealer that could remain competitive within its industry if it did not provide customers with financing options. However, these types of companies typically provide financing for their customers through a finance subsidiary of the parent company or through arrangements made with one or more banks or financial institutions. Many companies extend credit to their customers by providing them with additional time to make payment on purchases. For these companies, the first decision they need to make is whether or not to extend credit at all. The second decision is to decide which customers will be granted credit. Next, the firms must determine the credit terms to be offered to customers (which may vary across customers). Finally, they must decide on the details of the collection process.

The Credit Decision

credit analysis a process designed to assess the risk of non-payment by potential customers, which involves collecting information about potential customers with respect to their credit history, their ability to make payments as reflected in their expected cash flows, and their overall financial stability

For most companies, the decision of whether or not to extend credit will be largely determined by the nature of the product they sell, the industry they are in, and the prevailing policy used by competitors. This decision is called the *trade credit* decision. Assuming the firm decides to extend credit, it must then determine which of its customers will qualify for it. This decision is often based on a formal **credit analysis** process, which is designed to assess the risk of non-payment by potential customers. The process involves collecting information about potential customers with respect to their credit history, their ability to make payments as reflected in their expected cash flows (which is closely related to income), and their overall financial stability (as reflected in their net worth and their level of existing debt obligations).

Before considering how firms make these decisions, it is important to note that the firm's decision to extend trade credit is subtly different from that of a bank making a loan. Suppose, for example, a firm is considering a $10,000 order for widgets, for which the customer promises to pay in 60 days. If the cost of trade credit is 12 percent per year, the firm might sell the widgets for $10,200 due in 60 days. We will talk about trade credit terms later, but this is similar to a bank lending the customer $10,000 to buy the widgets for cash, and then charging 2 percent interest on the loan so that it is paid $10,200 in 60 days. In both cases, the purchaser owes $10,200, either to the company or to the bank. The bank's profit from the loan is limited to the interest rate,[3] and if the customer defaults, the bank could be out the full $10,000 loan. The firm is in a slightly different position.

First, the firm's cost is not the $10,000 it charges for the widgets, because it has to factor a profit margin into the calculation. If the firm's profit margin is 10 percent and it can't sell the widgets to other customers, then its decision involves a potential loss of $9,000 if the customer does not pay, rather than the $10,000 the bank would lose. If the customer does pay, it becomes an established customer that may make further purchases, generating further profit margins for the firm. The fact that the firm thinks in terms of future profit margins from developing a good customer and loses only its production cost in the case of default means that trade credit is granted to customers who could not secure credit from a bank on the same terms.

In making these decisions, firms can use a number of sources of information to assess the creditworthiness of a particular customer. Usually, firms begin by turning to professional credit agencies, such as Dun & Bradstreet (D&B) Canada Limited, which provide credit ratings and comprehensive credit reports on companies. These reports are based on available financial data, the firm's competitive position, and also the company's credit history. In many cases, this report will provide sufficient information to make a credit decision; however, for larger accounts or for arrangements that are expected to last for a long time, the firm may decide to do some additional investigation. An important source of information can be the company's financial statements. Firms may also ask the company to provide a letter from its main banker. Finally, firms can always look for information regarding a company's past credit relationships from a variety of sources, such as trade associations, other firms that have had prior dealings with the company, and so on.

The evaluation of the credit information that has been gathered can vary significantly from one company to the next. Some companies will have very detailed and mechanical evaluation systems, while others will rely more on judgement. In either case, the key thing that potential creditors are assessing is the likelihood of the customer paying the bills as they come due. There are two sides to this coin.

The first side is the potential customer's *ability to pay*. This is often referred to as the **capacity** of the firm to pay. As discussed in Chapters 3 and 4, two of the most important things affecting a firm's ability to meet future obligations are the amount of cash flow it expects to generate, and how many other obligations

capacity the customer's ability to pay

---

[3] More likely in this situation, the bank would let the company advance the trade credit to the customer and then buy the receivable for $9,803.92, and make its 2 percent interest when the customer pays off the $10,000 debt. This is called factoring.

it has to satisfy. Thus, it is important to examine a firm's expected future *profitability*, as well as the level of *debt* and the amount of debt payments it has accumulated. In addition, because most, if not all, trade credit is of a short-term nature, potential creditors are particularly interested in a potential customer's *liquidity*. As a last resort, creditors can always turn to the assets pledged as security for a loan. In this way, the firm's ability to offer *collateral* enhances its ability to secure credit. In many cases, items are sold on an **open account** basis, which means that the collateral is simply the assets that it sold to the customer. In such situations, the creditor must be wary because some assets do not hold their value. In addition, creditors may have difficulty getting the assets from the customer if it defaults on its obligation.

> **open account** credit in which the collateral is the assets sold to the customer

This leads us to the other side of the coin referred to above—how willing the firm is to pay. This is often referred to as the **character** of the firm. In other words, how reliable and trustworthy is the firm? This is an important question, because even if a firm is *able* to make the required payments, this makes little difference if it chooses not to. Creditors look for clues as to the character of the customer's management team by examining, among other things, its payment history and details about the customer's past dealings.

> **character** how willing the firm is to pay, and how reliable and trustworthy the firm is

These two sides to the credit decision are often referred to as the two C's of credit, with collateral representing the third C. In addition, both capacity and character are often affected by the state of the economy. In a recession, the firm's capacity to pay is often tested as cash flow dries up and finances are under pressure. So economic **conditions** affect the credit decision, and analysts include it as the fourth C of credit: capacity, character, collateral, and conditions. All four are interrelated.

> **conditions** the state of the economy

Because the process of checking creditworthiness can be lengthy and costly, firms tend to prioritize the amount of time and effort devoted to the analysis. For example, all else being equal, larger orders require more scrutiny than do smaller ones.

Credit Policies

> **terms of credit** the due date, and the discount date and discount amount, where applicable, offered to customers

Once a firm has decided to grant credit, it then chooses what **terms of credit** to offer its customers, such as the due date, and the discount date and discount amount, where applicable. In practice, the terms a firm offers can vary from one customer to the next, based on credit analysis and on the importance of the account. In other words, key accounts with an impeccable credit rating will likely demand, and receive, better credit terms than smaller accounts or those with weaker credit ratings. For ease of exposition in our discussion, we will assume that most customers receive the same credit terms.

Credit terms of *2/20 net 45* offer customers a 2 percent discount if they pay the full amount due by day 20, with the full amount being due by day 45. Terms of net 30 require full payment by day 30 and provide no discount options. We use these credit terms to work out how much taking trade credit costs. For example, 2/10 net 45 means that the customer pays either 98 percent after 10 days or 100 percent after 45 days. The cost is 2/98 for getting an extra 35 days to pay, so the effective annual interest rate for not paying on time is

$$k = (1 + \frac{2}{98})^{365/35} - 1 = 23.45\%$$

We express the 2 percent discount in terms of a simple interest rate (2/98 or 2.05 percent) and then express it on an annual basis by working out how many 35-day periods are in a year.

In this example the real cost is 98 percent of the quoted price if the customer pays immediately on receipt of the widgets, during the 10-day grace period. After that, the invoice has to be paid by 45 days and the cost of getting this extra 35 days credit is 23.45 percent. Most firms can borrow from their banks more cheaply than at 23.45 percent, so as a basic rule, firms always take those discounts. If a customer doesn't take the discount, the full 100 percent comes due. It is best to pay by 45 days and avoid the payment reminder telephone calls. Paying on time lowers the effective cost to a more reasonable level.

Generally, when firms decide to extend more *lenient* credit terms, they expect revenues to increase because they will increase the number of units sold and possibly because they will charge higher prices. The costs include the increase in financing costs and the increased risk of non-payment by customers. Conversely, when firms adopt a more *restrictive* policy, it results in collections being accelerated, at the possible expense of sales. Firms can evaluate such decisions by using the now-familiar net present value (NPV) framework, as given in Equation 24-1:

$$NPV = PV(\text{Future CFs}) - CF_0$$

[24-1]

The future cash flows (CFs) will generally be positive when firms loosen their credit terms and will be negative when they tighten them. CF_0 will represent an outlay when the credit terms are loosened, because that requires an additional investment in receivables; and it will represent an inflow when the terms are tightened, because that will reduce the level of receivables. The after-tax cost of short-term debt is usually the appropriate discount rate to use, because receivables are low-risk and are generally financed by using short-term debt (and the operating line of credit, in particular). Example 24-1 demonstrates how this framework can be utilized.

Example 24-1: The NPV of Extending Additional Credit

Suppose a firm that currently does not grant credit is considering adopting a credit policy that permits its customers to pay the full price for purchases (with no penalties) within 40 days of the purchase (i.e., the credit terms are net 40). The firm estimates that it can increase the price of the product by $1 per unit as a result of the new policy, which results in a new price per unit of $111. The firm expects that unit sales will increase by 1,000 units per year (to 11,000 units) and that variable costs will remain at $99 per unit. It also estimates that bad debt losses will amount to $6,000 per year. The firm will finance the additional investment in receivables by using its line of credit, which charges 6 percent interest. The firm's tax rate is 40 percent. Should the firm begin extending credit under the terms described?

Solution

Because the firm did not previously have any receivables, the initial investment (CF_0) can be viewed as the amount of additional funds that will be tied up in receivables, which equals the number of days that sales must be financed times the estimated sales per day: 40 days × sales per day = 40 × [($111 × 11,000 units)/365 days] = 40 days × $3,345.21/day = $133,808.

Now, we need to estimate the PV(Future CFs), which equals the present value of the incremental after-tax cash flows generated by extending credit.

Incremental before-tax annual CFs = (1,000 extra units sold) $\times$ [($111 $-$ $99) profit per unit] + (10,000 units sold) $\times$ ($1 increase in price per unit sold) $-$ ($6,000 in bad debt losses) = (1,000)($12) + (10,000)($1) $-$ $6,000 = $12,000 + $10,000 $-$ $6,000 = $16,000

The appropriate after-tax discount rate = 6% $\times$ (1 $-$ 0.40) = 3.60%

If we assume the firm reaps the benefits of this change in policy indefinitely, we can find the present value of the future benefits by viewing the incremental after-tax annual CFs as a perpetuity:

$$\text{PV(Future CFs)} = \text{Annual after-tax incremental CFs}/k$$

$$= [\$16,000 \times (1 - 0.40)]/0.0360 = \$266,667$$

$$\text{NPV} = \text{PV(Future CFs)} - \text{CF}_0 = \$266,667 - \$133,808 = +\$132,859$$

Thus, the firm should begin extending credit under the terms described above.

In Example 24-1, we considered a firm that decided to extend credit, thus adopting a more lenient credit policy. Of course, firms can always choose to adopt a more stringent credit policy. In this case, the firm will free up cash by reducing the amount of receivables it has outstanding, and the cost will be the forgone additional future cash flows that may result if the firm loses sales or has to reduce its selling price as Example 24-2 demonstrates.

Example 24-2: Adopting a More Stringent Credit Policy

Suppose the firm from Example 24-1 adopts the net 40 credit policy, but one year later, it considers changing the terms to net 30. The firm estimates that it can maintain the same price for the product (i.e., $111 per unit) but that unit sales will decline by 500 units per year (to 10,500 units). Variable costs will remain at $99 per unit. The firm estimates that bad debt losses will be reduced by $2,000 per year (to $4,000) as a result of the new policy. As in Example 24-1, the appropriate after-tax discount rate is 3.60 percent and the tax rate is 40 percent. Should the firm switch to the new policy?

Solution

The initial investment (CF$_0$) in this case can be viewed as the reduction in the amount of accounts receivable (A/R) that need to be financed: A/R(new) $-$ A/R(old) = {30 days $\times$ [($111 $\times$ 10,500 units)/365 days]} $-$ {40 days $\times$ [($111 $\times$ 11,000 units)/365 days]} = [30 days $\times$ $3,193.15/day] $-$ [40 days $\times$ $3,345.21/day] = $95,795 $-$ $133,808 = $-$$38,013.

Now, we need to estimate the PV(Future CFs), which equals the present value of the incremental after-tax cash flows generated by changing the credit policy. In this case, it will be negative because the firm *loses* future cash flows as a result of tightening its credit policy.

Incremental before-tax annual CFs = (500 less units sold) $\times$ ($111 $-$ $99 profit per unit) + ($2,000 reduction in bad debt losses) = ($-$500)($12) + $2,000 = $-$$4,000.

If we assume the firm reaps the benefits of this change in policy indefinitely, we can find the present value of the future CFs (forgone CFs, in this case), by viewing the incremental after-tax annual CFs as a perpetuity:

$$PV(\text{Future CFs}) = \text{Annual after-tax incremental CFs}/k =$$
$$[-\$4,000 \times (1 - 0.40)]/0.0360 = -\$66,667.$$

$$NPV = PV(\text{Future CFs}) - CF_0 = -\$66,667 + \$38,013 = -\$28,654.$$

Thus, the firm should not switch from its existing credit policy to the new one.

When firms offer discounts to customers, two things happen as a result: (1) they lose profits when customers take advantage of the discounts, and (2) they receive payment sooner, so less money is tied up in receivables. The decision to offer discounts (or eliminate them) can be evaluated by using the NPV framework. Example 24-3 demonstrates.

Example 24-3: Offering a Discount

Suppose the firm from Examples 24-1 and 24-2 is maintaining the net 40 credit policy evaluated in Example 24-2. It is now considering adopting a new policy that would involve a discount. In particular, it is considering adopting a 2/10 net 40 policy. The firm estimates that 60 percent of customers will take advantage of the discount, while the remaining 40 percent will pay on day 40. The firm expects that it can maintain the same price for the product (i.e., $111 per unit), that unit sales will remain at 11,000 per year, that variable costs will remain at $99 per unit, and that bad debt losses will not be affected. As in Example 24-1, the after-tax discount rate is 3.60 percent and the tax rate is 40 percent. Should the firm switch to the new policy?

Solution

The initial investment (CF_0) in this case can be viewed as the reduction in the amount of accounts receivable (A/R) that need to be financed.

The average collection period (ACP) under the new policy will be reduced to $[0.60 \times 10 \text{ days} + 0.40 \times 40 \text{ days}] = 22$ days.

The old ACP was assumed to be the net date (i.e., 40 days).

The change (reduction) in receivables $= (22 - 40) \times [(\$111 \times 11,000 \text{ units})/365 \text{ days}] = (-18 \text{ days}) \times (\$3,345.21/\text{day}) = -\$60,214$.

Now, we need to estimate the PV(Future CFs), which equals the present value of the incremental after-tax cash flows generated by changing the credit terms. In this case, it will be negative because the firm *loses* future cash flows as a result of customers taking advantage of the discount.

Incremental after-tax annual CFs = (number of units sold at a discount) $\times$ (discount amount per unit) $\times$ (1 − tax rate) = (60 percent of customers taking discount $\times$ 11,000 annual sales in units) $\times$ (0.02 discount amount $\times$ \$111 per unit) $\times$ (1 − 0.40) = (6,600 units) $\times$ ($2.22) $\times$ (0.60) = −\$8,791.

So, $PV(\text{Future CFs}) = \text{Annual after-tax incremental CFs}/k = [-\$8,791]/0.0360 = -\$244,200$.

$$NPV = PV(\text{Future CFs}) - CF_0 = -\$244,200 + \$60,214 = -\$183,986.$$

Thus, the firm should not offer the discount.

The Collection Process

Firms have many options when deciding how their customers will pay for their purchases. As discussed, several electronic methods are available, such as automatic debit of their bank accounts, or the use of EFT or EDI systems. These approaches not only reduce payment processing time but also reduce (or eliminate) the risk of late payment. These obviously represent attractive collection systems for many firms. However, some firms still invoice their customers at the time of sale, and then collect and deposit cheques as they are received.

When firms are forced to wait for payments from customers, several issues arise. First, they must closely monitor their collections and receivables to avoid having many late payments or, worse yet, non-payments. Second, they must determine what to do when late payments occur. Usually, firms establish a systematic process to deal with such accounts. As a start, most firms will charge interest on overdue accounts as a deterrent. After a predetermined interval, companies will usually notify the customer that the account is in arrears and ask the customer to "settle up." This notification can be done by mail, e-mail, or by phone. If payment is still not received, firms will generally issue a follow-up reminder (or two). Eventually, if they still have not received payment from the customer, firms must decide what to do next. One of the first things they will do, if they have not already done so, is to not allow that customer to make any more purchases on credit. They must then decide whether to hand the bill over to a collection agency, or take legal action against the customer. Both of these options can be costly, so in many cases, firms will just write off the debt and inform the credit agency. This decision will be influenced by the amount that is due, among other things.

factoring arrangements
the sale of a firm's receivables, at a discount, to a financial company called a factor, which specializes in collections, or the outsourcing of the collections to a factor

Sometimes firms avoid the collection process by entering into **factoring arrangements**, whereby they sell their receivables at a discount to a financial company called a factor, which specializes in collections. Alternatively, many factors do not actually purchase the receivables but agree to handle the collections, for a fee of course.

It can be difficult to assess how well a firm manages its accounts receivable. In Chapter 4, we identified some common ratios that do provide useful insight into this issue: the average collection period (ACP) and the receivables turnover ratio. All else being equal, it is preferable to have a lower ACP and higher receivables turnover. However, firms can always make improvements in these ratios by sacrificing sales growth and or profit margins, so it is not as simple as merely examining these ratios. In addition, these ratios do not tell us a great deal about the *quality* of a firm's receivables. One tool that is useful for this purpose is the *aged accounts receivable report*, which categorizes the balances in receivables according to how long they have been outstanding. For example, a firm might provide a list that shows how much of its receivables are outstanding before the due date, after the due date, a month after the due date, and so on. Generally, receivables that have not been outstanding that long are regarded as higher quality than those that have been outstanding well beyond their due date. In fact, banks often require that borrowing firms provide them with this list on a monthly basis to support any financing the banks provide in support of receivables. However, this report also has its limitations. For example, it would be preferable to have many receivables due from high-quality customers (such as government agencies) that are 30 days late than it would be to have many 10-day-old receivables from low-credit-quality customers. In fact, to accurately assess the quality of a company's receivables, it would help to have a list of the customers underlying the receivables and perhaps even a credit analysis of these customers, at least for the larger accounts.

24.3 INVENTORY

The level of inventory that firms decide to hold is based on a tradeoff between benefits and costs, similar to the decisions about investments in cash, marketable securities, and accounts receivable. One reason firms hold large amounts of inventory is that they may have received discounts on large-volume purchases. However, the more important benefits of holding inventory are that holding sufficient levels of raw materials minimizes disruptions in the production process, while maintaining adequate levels of finished goods on hand helps minimize lost sales (and lost customer goodwill) because of shortages.

The benefits of holding inventory do not come without significant costs. Aside from the obvious cost of financing the funds tied up in inventory, a number of other costs are important, including storage, handling, insurance, spoilage, and the risk of obsolescence. Thus, inventory decisions are critical to the firm's performance. In fact, the field of operations management devotes a great deal of attention to modelling efficient inventory control systems. We provide a brief discussion of some of the more common approaches to inventory management, but we do not elaborate on the technical details.

Inventory Management Approaches

Most inventory control systems used by large companies employ highly automated computerized systems that can easily track all kinds of inventory items as they flow into and out of the company. These systems control inventory levels by relating them to the production process, which in turn is related to the firm's projected sales levels.

Any approach to inventory management must balance the benefits of holding inventory and the costs, as discussed above. We briefly describe four of these approaches.:

1. **The ABC approach**: This approach divides inventory into several categories based on the value of the inventory items, their overall level of importance to the firm's operations, and their profitability. The higher the priority of the inventory item, the more time and effort devoted to its management.

2. **The Economic Order Quantity (EOQ) Model**: The EOQ model defines (and determines) the optimal inventory level as the one that minimizes the total of *shortage costs* and *carrying costs*. As such, it determines the inventory level that balances out the benefits (i.e., reduced shortage costs) against the carrying costs (i.e., financing, storage, insurance, spoilage, obsolescence). The model

The ABC approach the division of inventory into several categories based on the value of the inventory items, their overall level of importance to the firm's operations, and their profitability, to determine the time and effort devoted to their management

The Economic Order Quantity (EOQ) Model an approach that defines and determines the optimal inventory level as the one that minimizes the total of shortage costs and carrying costs; it determines the inventory level that balances the benefits (reduced shortage costs) against the carrying costs (financing, storage, insurance, spoilage, obsolescence)

materials requirement planning (MRP) a detailed computerized system that orders inventory in conjunction with production schedules to determine the level of raw materials and work-in-process that must be on hand to meet finished goods demand

just-in-time (JIT) inventory systems a way to fine-tune the receipt of raw materials so that they arrive exactly when they are required in the production process and thereby reduce inventory to its lowest possible level

shows that under certain assumptions, the minimum total cost occurs at the point at which carrying costs equal shortage costs. One of the key assumptions of the EOQ model is that items are sold relatively evenly throughout the year, so it works well for inventories that follow this pattern and not as well when they don't.

3. **Materials Requirement Planning (MRP):** MRP is a detailed computerized system that orders inventory in conjunction with production schedules. The central idea is to determine the exact level of raw materials and work-in-process that must be on hand to meet finished goods demand. With this capability and good sales forecasts, a company can run on extremely low levels of inventory.

4. **Just-in-time (JIT) inventory systems**: JIT systems fine-tune the receipt of raw materials so that they arrive exactly when they are required in the production process. The objective is to reduce inventory to its lowest possible level. JIT systems require close relationships with suppliers in order to work properly.

Evaluating Inventory Management

Although effective inventory management is critical to the success of most firms, just as accounts receivable management is, inventory management is difficult to evaluate. In Chapter 4, we introduced two ratios—the inventory turnover ratio, and the days inventory ratio—that outsiders commonly use to evaluate inventory management. Generally, high inventory turnover is recognized as a good sign, while lower or declining turnover is a warning sign. In particular, a declining inventory turnover ratio indicates that sales are declining, inventory levels are accumulating, or both. The greater the inventory buildup, the greater the financing, storage, spoilage, and insurance costs, and the greater the risk of obsolescence.

Although the inventory turnover ratio is a useful indicator, it is far from comprehensive. For example, it does not measure shortage costs or explicitly measure financing costs, and so on. As discussed above, these are critical considerations in the implementation (and evaluation) of any inventory management system. In addition, turnover ratios cannot be compared across companies that use different methods of accounting for inventory (i.e., LIFO, FIFO, average cost), because the reported inventory levels will differ substantially. Finally, inventory turnover says nothing about the breakdown of inventory in terms of raw materials, work-in-process inventory, and finished goods, which can make a big difference in establishing the market value of inventory.

CONCEPT REVIEW QUESTIONS

1. Identify the costs and benefits of holding inventory.

2. What are the drawbacks to using the turnover ratio to measure inventory policy?

24.4 SHORT-TERM FINANCING CONSIDERATIONS

A common trait among investments in current assets, such as cash, accounts receivable, and inventory, is that they all tend to increase automatically as sales increase. The same cannot be said for short-term financing, with the exception of trade credit. Therefore, it is critical that firms forecast their short-term financing requirements as accurately as possible and ensure they have adequate financing in place.

Because there are many potential sources of short-term financing, firms need to assess the cost effectiveness of alternative financing mechanisms. We use the following variation of Equation 5-9, which was introduced in Chapter 5, to estimate the annual effective rate of return or cost (k) associated with any financing alternative:

$$k = (1 + \frac{n - Day\ financing\ cost}{Purchase\ price})^{365/n} - 1$$

[24-2]

Firms also need to consider any additional benefits or risks associated with these alternatives. We discuss below the most common short-term financing options available to firms.

Trade Credit

Trade credit is usually one of a firm's most important sources of short-term financing. Many firms finance their purchases through the credit terms offered to them by their suppliers, which permits them to delay payments to the supplier. In essence, a firm is *borrowing* from its suppliers when it purchases materials on account. This is the only form of short-term financing that automatically increases with sales, and as such, it is often referred to as a *spontaneous* source of funds.[4] Trade credit provides firms with many advantages: it is generally readily available, convenient, and flexible, and it usually does not entail any restrictive covenants or pledges of security. In addition, it is usually inexpensive. It can, however, be expensive to forgo discounts, as demonstrated in Example 24-4.

Example 24-4: Trade Credit and Discounts

A firm is considering the purchase of one of its inputs from supplier A. The selling price = $1,200 and the credit terms are 2/10 net 40.

a. What is the effective annual cost of forgoing the discount?

b. Another supplier (B) offers the same product for a price of $1,205 on credit terms of net 60. What is the effective annual cost of this option?

c. If the firm can finance these purchases by using a loan that has an effective annual cost of 8 percent, should it take the credit terms or the loan?

---

[4] Although it is true that the amount borrowed on an operating line of credit will increase with the borrowing requirement (which tend to rise with sales), the credit limit on these lending facilities *do not automatically* increase with sales—they have to be renegotiated. Therefore, they do not represent a truly spontaneous source of funds.

Solution

a. We need to recognize that forgoing the discount costs 2% of the $1,200 purchase price, or $24.

In essence, the "true" price = $1,200 − $24 = $1,176, and the $24 is the 30-day financing cost.

So, we can estimate the cost of forgoing the discount by using Equation 24-2:

$$k = (1 + \frac{n - Day\ financing\ cost}{Purchase\ price})^{365/n} - 1 = (1 + \frac{24}{1176})^{365/30} - 1 = (1.02040816)^{12.166667} - 1$$

$$= 0.2786 = 27.86\%$$

We could also solve this by replacing the discount percentage 2/98 for the actual dollar amounts of 24/1,176, because the two ratios must be equal. In other words,

$$k = (1 + \frac{2}{98})^{365/30} - 1 = 0.2786 = 27.86\%$$

Forgoing the cash discount is an expensive decision.

b. Because we know from part a. that the "true" cost is $1,176, we can see that firm B is charging $29 (i.e., $1,205 − $1,176) in financing charges for 60 days of financing. We can estimate the effective annual cost of this option as

$$k = (1 + \frac{29}{1176})^{365/60} - 1 = 0.1597 = 15.97\%$$

This option is less expensive than forgoing the discount, but is still not cheap.

c. We know what the firm should not do—that is, it should not choose supplier A and forgo the discount, because this costs 27.86 percent.

This leaves us with two purchase/financing options: (1) buy through supplier A and pay on day 10 using the 8 percent loan to take advantage of the discount, or (2) buy through supplier B.

We have already calculated that the cost of using supplier B would be 15.97 percent.

The cost of going with supplier A and paying the amount due on day 10 to take advantage of the discount is 8 percent, because the firm can use a loan with a cost of 8% to finance the purchase.

Therefore, the preferred option is to buy through supplier A and pay on day 10 to take advantage of the discount by using a loan at 8 percent.

Bank Loans

Several short-term loan arrangements are available through financial institutions. Generally, they are variable rate (or prime-based) loans that are tied to the prime lending rate (which is the rate offered to the bank's best customers). The most common arrangement for businesses is to establish *operating loans* (or lines of credit). As discussed previously, these loans are usually linked to the firm's current account (i.e., their chequing account), and they enable the business to borrow up to a predetermined amount to finance temporary cash deficits. Operating loans are generally set up so that the firm makes "interest only" payments. The amount of borrowing can be reduced at the firm's discretion, and many companies will have the bank automatically "revolve" the loan for them (for a fee). This involves paying down the amount of the loan whenever there is sufficient cash in the current account, or increasing the borrowing level when there is insufficient cash. Having the bank revolve the loan therefore reduces unnecessary interest costs, because the loan will be paid down whenever the firm has sufficient funds available.

As discussed in Chapter 23, cash budgets can be used to estimate the amount of borrowing that should be arranged. This is important, because firms do not want to have to go back to the bank to arrange additional financing when the need for funds is urgent. Therefore, firms will try to arrange to have the necessary amount of funds available and maintain a little extra cushion. However, firms will want to avoid arranging unnecessary borrowing capacity, because banks normally charge a commitment fee against the unused portion of credit.

Operating loans are typically secured by accounts receivable and inventory, because these are the assets they are usually intended to finance. The "standard" is for banks to offer an operating line for a certain amount that does not exceed 70 percent to 75 percent of the firm's good accounts receivable under 90 days plus up to 50 percent of the firm's inventory value.

Operating loans provide firms with an opportunity to develop a solid banking relationship, which can be important. They also offer a fair degree of flexibility and the costs are usually quite low. Examples 24-5 and 24-6 illustrate how to estimate the costs associated with operating loans.

Example 24-5: Bank Loans

A firm is offered a one-year variable rate loan at a rate of prime plus 1% at a time when the bank's prime lending rate is 5.25 percent. The loan is to be repaid in monthly instalments. Assuming there are no other fees associated with this loan, what is the effective annual cost of this loan?

Solution

The annual quoted rate = 5.25% + 1% = 6.25%.

Now, we need to estimate the effective annual rate associated with this arrangement. We can use Equation 5-9 from Chapter 5:

$$k = (1 + \frac{Quoted\ rate}{million})^{million} - 1 = (1 + \frac{0.0625}{12})^{12} - 1 = 0.0643 = 6.43\%$$

Alternatively, we could estimate the one-month interest cost on a $1,000 loan for example, as

$$\text{One-month interest cost} = (1/12) \times (0.0625) \times (\$1,000) = \$5.21$$

Then we could use a monthly (rather than daily) variation of Equation 24-2 to estimate the cost as

$$k = (1 + \frac{n - Month\ financing\ cost}{Purchase\ price})^{12/n} - 1 = (1 + \frac{5.21}{1000})^{12/1} - 1 = 0.0643 = 6.43\%$$

Example 24-6: Operating Line of Credit

A firm arranges a one-year $800,000 operating line of credit, which carries an 8 percent quoted interest rate and a 0.5 percent commitment fee on the unused portion of the line. The loan calls for monthly payments. The firm uses the line to borrow $600,000 in the first seven months of the year, and then reduces the loan amount to $400,000 for the remainder of the year. What is the effective annual cost (rate) of this loan arrangement?

Solution

First, we determine the effective monthly rate = 0.08/12 = 0.0066667 = 0.66667%.

Now we can determine the total interest paid over the first seven months and over the remaining five months.

$$\text{Interest (months 1-7)} = \$600,000 \times 0.0066667 \times 7 = \$28,000$$

$$\text{Interest (months 8-12)} = \$400,000 \times 0.0066667 \times 5 = \$13,333$$

$$\text{Total interest} = \$28,000 + \$13,333 = \$41,333$$

We then need to estimate the commitment fees throughout the year:

$$\text{Commitment fee (months 1-7)} = (\$800,000 - \$600,000) \times 0.0050 \times 7 = \$7,000$$

$$\text{Commitment fee (months 8-12)} = (\$800,000 - \$400,000) \times 0.0050 \times 5 = \$10,000$$

$$\text{Total commitment fees} = \$7,000 + \$10,000 = \$17,000$$

$$\text{Total costs} = \$41,333 + \$17,000 = \$58,333$$

We then estimate the average amount of financing throughout the year, which can be related to the total annual costs. Notice that we need to take a weighted average to determine the appropriate figure.

$$\text{Average net financing} = [(7/12) \times \$600,000] + [(5/12) \times \$400,000] = \$516,667$$

Now, we can use Equation 24-2 to estimate the effective annual cost:

$$k = (1 + \frac{58,333}{516,667})^1 - 1 = 0.1129 = 11.29\%$$

Notice that the exponent is 1 because we were using annual costs and annual average financing amounts (i.e., if we were using 30-day figures, then the exponent would be 365/30).

Factor Arrangements

As described earlier, a *factor* is an independent company that acts as an outside credit department for its clients. It checks the credit of new customers, authorizes credit, handles collections and bookkeeping, and sometimes will purchase a firm's receivables (at a discount). In practice, various arrangements are possible, with factors providing various combinations of the services listed above. Factors provide the ultimate in convenience; however, as with most things, there is a cost, and the costs are typically quite high. Example 24-7 demonstrates how we can estimate the costs associated with a particular type of factoring arrangement.

Example 24-7: Factor Arrangement

A company has daily credit sales of $40,000 and an average collection period (ACP) of 45 days. A factor offers a 45-day accounts receivable loan equal to 75 percent of accounts receivable. The quoted interest rate is 10 percent and there is a commission fee of 1 percent of accounts receivable. The firm estimates that it will save $2,000 in collection costs and will experience a 0.5 percent reduction in bad debt losses (as a percentage of sales) as a result of the factoring arrangement. What is the effective annual cost of the arrangement?

Solution

$$\text{Accounts receivable (A/R)} = \text{ACP} \times \text{daily credit sales} = 45 \times \$40,000 = \$1,800,000$$

$$\text{Loan amount} = 0.75 \times \text{A/R} = 0.75 \times \$1,800,000 = \$1.35 \text{ million}$$

$$\text{Commission} = 0.01 \times \text{A/R} = 0.01 \times \$1.8 \text{ million} = \$18,000$$

$$\text{Interest} = 0.10 \times 45/365 \times 1.35 \text{ million} = \$16,644$$

$$\text{Savings} = \$2,000 + (0.005 \times 45\text{days} \times \$40,000/\text{day}) = 2,000 + 9,000 = \$11,000$$

$$\text{Net cost} = 18,000 + 16,644 - 11,000 = \$23,644$$

$$k = (1 + \frac{23,644}{1,350,000})^{\frac{365}{45}} - 1 = 15.12\%$$

Money Market Instruments

Larger firms with good credit ratings that require large amounts of short-term financing may be able to issue money market instruments. These securities provide the firm with a cost advantage over other short-term financing options; however, the conditions may be somewhat restrictive. Firms generally have two major types of money market instruments available to them: commercial paper (CP) and bankers' acceptances (BAs).

As discussed in Chapter 18, commercial paper is essentially a short-term promissory note issued by firms, which is rated by external debt agencies in a similar fashion as bonds. Only large firms with top-notch credit ratings can issue CP. It is usually issued at a discount from face value, providing purchasers with an implicit yield. CP is issued in large amounts (usually more than $100,000), and the most common maturity dates are 30, 60, and 90 days. Usually, CP is backed by a bank line of credit.

Bankers' acceptances are similar to CP in many regards—they are issued at a discount from face value in large denominations, with common maturity dates of 30, 60, and 90 days. They differ from CP because they are "stamped" by a bank as accepted in return for a fee that is usually 0.25 percent to 1 percent of the face value of the BAs. In return, the bank guarantees the payments associated with these instruments. Therefore, BAs carry the credit risk of the bank that stamps them and not the company that borrows by using them. Most of the firms that issue BAs are large, well-known firms with excellent credit ratings. However, because of the bank guarantee, some firms that are not able to issue CP may be able to borrow by using BAs—provided they can find a bank that is willing to guarantee their payments.

The yield on CP and BAs is usually quoted based on an approximate annual yield by using Equation 24-3.

[24-3]

$$\text{Approximate annual yield} = \frac{Discount}{Market\ price} \times \frac{365}{Days\ to\ maturity}$$

To estimate the effective annual cost to the firm, we can use Equation 24-2, as we did for the other financing options, where the discount amount represents the major part of the financing cost. Examples 24-8 and 24-9 demonstrate how a firm estimates the cost associated with borrowing by using CP or BAs.

Example 24-8: Commercial Paper

a. Estimate the effective annual cost to a firm of issuing $10 million face value of 90-day commercial paper for net proceeds of $9.85 million. The firm must maintain a $10 million credit line, on which it must pay a standby fee of 0.1%.

b. Determine the quoted yield for the commercial paper.

Solution

a. Discount = $10 million − $9.85 million = $0.15 million

Standby fee = 0.001 × $10 million = $50,000 = $0.01 million

Total financing cost = $0.15 million + $0.01 million = $0.16 million

$$k = (1 + \frac{n - Day\ financing\ cost}{Purchase\ price})^{365/n} - 1 = (1 + \frac{0.16\ million}{9.85\ million})^{365/90} - 1 = 6.75\%$$

b. Approximate annual (quoted) yield

$$\text{Approximate annual (quoted) yield} = \frac{Discount}{Market\ price} \times \frac{365}{Days\ to\ maturity}$$

$$= \frac{0.15m}{9.85m} \times \frac{365}{90} = 0.0618\ \text{or}\ 6.18\%$$

Example 24-9: Bankers' Acceptances

Estimate the effective annual cost to a firm that issues $100 million (face value) of 90-day BAs at a quoted rate of 6.25 percent, if the bank charges a 0.30 percent stamping fee.

Solution

We estimate the selling price of the BAs, by rearranging Equation 24-3:

$$6.25\% = \frac{Discount}{Market\ price} \times \frac{365}{Days\ to\ maturity} = \frac{Face - Price}{Price} \times \frac{365}{90}$$

$0.0625 \times 90/365 = (\$100\ \text{million} - Price)/Price$

$0.015411 = (\$100\ \text{million} - Price)/Price$

$0.015411 \times Price = \$100\ \text{million} - Price$

$1.015411 \times$ Price $= \$100$ million

Price $= \$100$ million$/1.015411 = \$98.482289$ million

Discount $= \$100$ million $- \$98.482289$ million $= \$1.517711$ million

Stamping fee $= 0.003 \times \$100$ million $= \$300{,}000 = \$0.3$ million

Total financing cost $= \$1.517711$ million $+ \$0.3$ million $= \$1.817711$ million

$$k = (1 + \frac{n - Day\ financing\ cost}{Purchase\ price})^{365/n} - 1 = (1 + \frac{1.817711\ million}{98.482289\ million})^{365/90} - 1 = 7.70\%$$

Securitizations

A more recent innovation in financing trade credit is the use of **special purpose vehicles (SPVs)**. SPVs are conduits for packaging portfolios of receivables and selling them to investors in the money market. In this way, the purchaser relies on the credit of the SPV, rather than that of the company selling the receivables. For example, General Motors Corporation of Canada (GM) finances the purchase of its vehicles. It can do this by using any of the previously mentioned instruments. It can take out a bank loan or issue commercial paper or bankers' acceptances, and then use the proceeds to finance car loans. However, such is the volume of car financing that GM's balance sheet would quickly look like that of a financial institution with large amounts of short-term borrowing financing short-term car loans. To avoid this, GM can sell its car loans directly to the capital market through an SPV so that neither the loans nor the financing appear on its balance sheet. This process is called **securitization**.

The essence of securitization is that the credit risk of the seller of the receivables or loans is not directly involved. For example, when GM packages its car loans, the buyers of these loans look primarily to the loans held in the SPV and evaluate their credit, rather than that of GM, which is what would happen if GM issued commercial paper to finance its car loans. However, as we saw in Chapter 18, the money market is very credit conscious because investments are very short term and in practice any money market instrument has to be very good investment grade. This poses a problem because, as we have seen above, many firms will extend credit in situations where a bank would not. This occurs because the firm makes a profit margin on the sale and is anticipating a long-term relationship involving future sales and future profits. If a portfolio of receivables or loans is simply sold to investors, in all likelihood the credit quality would not be high enough to get an investment-grade rating. As a result **credit enhancements** have to be made, such as requiring collateral, insurance, or other agreements, to reduce credit risk.

To access the Canadian money market, a Dominion Bond Rating Service (DBRS) credit rating is required. In generating its credit ratings, DBRS looks to the seller, the collateral, and the structure of the securitization. Although the primary credit concern is for the pool of receivables or loans, the financial health of the seller is still important for several reasons. The most obvious one is that the seller may sell poor-quality loans into the SPV so that over time the quality of the SPV deteriorates.[5] Also, the seller still services the loans; when the creditor makes payments on the loan, or someone pays off the receivable, it is the seller who has to service those payments and pass them to the SPV to be distributed to investors.

special purpose vehicles (SPVs) conduits for packaging portfolios of receivables and selling them to investors in the money market; a recent innovation in financing trade credit

securitization the process of packaging loans and/or receivables together to create new securities

credit enhancements actions taken to reduce credit risk, such as requiring collateral, insurance, or other agreements

---

[5] There is also a slim possibility of fraud.

The collateral in the SPV depends on the particular issue. In the case of GM, the underlying asset is car loans. Other securitizations have been made by Deere & Company (John Deere) and Bombardier Inc. with equipment loans, while Receivables Acquisition and Management Corporation and its clones have been used by CIBC to package receivables from a number of Canadian companies. In each case, DBRS looks at the historical *default rates* on the loans and the history of **prepayments**, because frequently loans are paid off early. By pooling a large number of loans in an SPV, these financial characteristics are fairly stable, but DBRS will stress test the effect of changing historical rates to see how it affects the ability of the SPV to pay off on its securities. For example, for GM car loans the annual default rate is about 1.0 percent and tends to be highest in the first two years, so the credit quality can be improved by taking more seasoned loans that have been outstanding longer. However, the problem is then that they are more likely to be prepaid.

The most important aspects of the SPV are usually the credit enhancements because, as mentioned earlier, usually the credit quality of the underlying assets needs to be enhanced to get an AAA credit rating. For the sale of the loans to be taken off the seller's balance sheet, accounting standards require that the SPV can go back to the seller for no more than 10 percent of the assets. As a result there are usually external as well as seller credit enhancements. These credit enhancements often take several forms:

- having 5 percent of the losses absorbed by the seller—this is often referred to as over-collateralization

- having the next 10 percent of losses on trade receivables absorbed by a third party, such as a major bank like the Union Bank of Switzerland

- issuing subordinated debt to absorb further defaults on termination of the SPV

- creating or issuing different classes of securities so that the prepayment risks are allocated to different securities, as is often the case with mortgage SPVs

Securitization has been a dramatic growth business in Canada. In Chapter 18, we saw that almost a quarter of the Canadian money market is now made up of securitization issues. This means that investors can buy Government of Canada treasury bills, BAs, commercial paper issued by an SPV backed by car loans, equipment loans, trade receivables, and so on. In these cases, besides T-bills, the credit enhancements have upgraded the credit of the seller so that the paper sells on very similar yields to investment-grade issuers, even though the underlying loans are to non-investment-grade creditors.

In practice, firms use some combination of the short-term financing options mentioned to provide them with the desired mix of flexibility and cost effectiveness. Usually, trade credit and bank loans are the predominant sources of short-term financing, especially for smaller companies that do not have the option of accessing the money market.

prepayments the payment of a debt before its due date

CONCEPT REVIEW QUESTIONS

1. What is the cost of 3/15 net 60 trade credit?
2. What is the difference between a bank operating line of credit and a traditional loan?
3. What additional services does a factor provide over a bank?
4. What is the difference between a BA and commercial paper?
5. Why do securitizations require credit enhancements?

Summary

In the first part of this chapter we demonstrate that the optimal level of investment in cash, receivables, and inventory occurs when the benefits balance the costs. In the case of cash, the benefit is the reduced risk of insolvency, while the cost is the opportunity costs of having funds tied up in assets that provide a relatively low return. For receivables, the benefits tend to be increased sales and profitability, while the costs include the financing costs and the increased risk of non-payment by customers. Finally, for inventory, the benefits may be improved production processes or reduced risk of stockouts, which result in forgone revenue and can also damage customer goodwill. The costs include financing, storage, spoilage, obsolescence, and insurance. Successful companies employ effective systems to maximize the benefits of these assets while minimizing the costs.

In the second part of this chapter, we examine the most common short-term financing options available to companies—namely, trade credit, bank loans, factoring arrangements, and money market instruments. We discuss the benefits and disadvantages of each method, and show how we can estimate the associated effective annual costs.

Key Terms

ABC approach, p. 941
capacity, p. 935
character, p. 936
conditions, p. 936
credit analysis, p. 934
credit enhancements, p. 949
Economic Order Quantity (EOQ) Model, p. 941
factoring arrangements, p. 940
finance motive, p. 930
float, p. 932
just-in-time (JIT) inventory systems, p. 942

materials requirement planning (MRP), p. 942
open account, p. 936
optimal cash balance, p. 931
precautionary motive, p. 930
prepayments, p. 950
securitization, p. 949
special purpose vehicles (SPVs), p. 949
speculative motive, p. 930
terms of credit, p. 936
transactions motive, p. 930

Formulas/Equations

(24-1) $NPV = PV(\text{Future CFs}) - CF_0$

(24-2) $k = (1 + \dfrac{n - Day\ financing\ cost}{Purchase\ price})^{365/n} - 1$

(24-3) Approximate annual yield $= \dfrac{Discount}{Market\ price} \times \dfrac{365}{Days\ to\ maturity}$

QUESTIONS AND PRACTICE PROBLEMS

Multiple Choice Questions

1. Which of the following is *not* near-cash?

   A. T-bills
   B. Commercial paper
   C. Bankers' acceptances
   D. Long-term debt

2. Which of the following descriptions about near-cash is *false*?

   A. Low returns
   B. Great liquidity
   C. Minimal additional risk
   D. Credit risk

3. Which of the following statements about float time is *false*?

   A. Historically, mailing time is the shortest.
   B. An efficient credit policy speeds up inflows.
   C. Cheque-processing time is one source of float.
   D. Using preauthorized payment is one way to shorten float time.

4. If the current credit policy is 3/30 net 45, which of the following *tightens* the credit policy?

   A. 3/30 net 40
   B. 3/35 net 50
   C. net 45
   D. 3/40 net 50

5. A firm is offered by its supplier the following credit terms: 3/15 net 60. The sales price of the products is $2,000. What is the effective annual cost of forgoing the discount?

   A. 28%
   B. 32%
   C. 20%
   D. 35%

6. Which of the following statements about bank loans is *false*?

    A. The rate is normally variable.

    B. Lines of credit usually link to the firm's chequing account.

    C. Operating loans are usually secured by accounts receivable and inventory.

    D. The cost of operating loans is quite high.

7. Suppose a firm is offered a two-year variable rate monthly pay loan at prime plus 1 percent, with a prime rate of 6.5 percent. What is the effective annual cost of the loan regardless of other fees?

    A. 7.58%

    B. 7.76%

    C. 7.78%

    D. 8.01%

8. Which of the statements about money market instruments is *false*?

    A. They provide large amounts of short-term financing for firms with good credit ratings.

    B. Two main types available are: commercial paper and bankers' acceptances.

    C. They are similar to bonds.

    D. CP can be issued by any firm that needs large amounts of short-term financing.

9. Which of the following statements about factor arrangements is *false*?

    A. A factor is an independent company.

    B. A factor often checks the credit of new customers.

    C. Factor arrangements can be costly.

    D. A factor does not purchase accounts receivable from its clients.

Practice Problems

10. What are three major sources of float? What are some common methods that address float?

Easy

11. Briefly explain the function of a factor in working capital management.

12. What is the purpose of credit analysis and how is it accomplished?

13. When deciding whether or not to extend credit to an applicant, what two things need to be established about the applicant?

14. What are captive finance companies?

Medium

15. What are some of the advantages of carrying inventories?

16. What are some of the disadvantages of carrying inventories?

17. Briefly explain the transactions motive.

18. Briefly state the principle of the optimal cash balance.

19. A. Calculate the effective annual cost of forgoing discount of credit terms of 3/15 net 50. The selling price is $600.

   B. Another supplier offers $612 on credit terms of net 60. If you could finance the purchase by using loans at an effective annual cost of 10 percent for part A, which option should you choose?

20. What are special purpose vehicles (SPVs)? What is the main advantage of SPVs? List a few forms of credit enhancement that are critical to SPVs.

21. Suppose Sio Inc. has 60 days of accounts receivable (A/R) of $900,000 on its books. A factor offers a 60-day A/R loan equal to 80 percent of A/R. The quoted interest rate is 8 percent, and there is a commission fee of 0.5 percent. The factoring will result in a reduction of $8,000 in bad debt losses. What is the effective annual cost?

22. What is the effective annual cost if a firm issues $1,500,000 face value of 90-day commercial paper for net proceeds of $1,450,000? The firm pays a standby fee of 0.2 percent on the face value.

23. Briefly state four main motives firms have to hold cash.

24. Briefly describe the four inventory management approaches.

Difficult

25. Calculate the effective annual cost of issuing 180-day BAs at a quoted rate of 7.5 percent with a face value of $10,000,000. The bank charges a 0.4 percent stamping fee.

26. ABC Inc. currently grants no credit, but it is considering offering new credit terms: net 30. As a result, the price of its product will increase by $1.50 per unit. The original price per unit is $50. Expected sales will increase by 1,000 units per year. The original sales are 10,000 units. Variable costs will remain at $26 per unit and bad debt losses will amount to $3,000 per year. The firm will finance the additional investment in receivables by using a line of credit, which charges 5 percent interest. The firm's tax rate is 40 percent. Should the firm begin extending credit under the terms described? (Assume ABC benefits from the credit policy change indefinitely.)

27. In Problem 26, assume ABC is switching to 2/10 net 30. It is estimated that 80 percent of customers will take advantage of the discount, while the remaining 20 percent will pay on day 30. The price will remain the same at $51.50 per unit, unit sales will remain at 11,000 per year, and variable costs will remain at $26 per unit. Bad debt losses will not be affected. Use a 40 percent tax rate and a 5 percent discount rate. Should the firm switch to the new policy?

28. There are two suppliers of one input for a factory. Supplier A offers a selling price of $500 with terms of 2/10 net 30, while Supplier B offers $520 with net 60. Which supplier offers the lower effective annual cost?

29. A firm engaged a one-year monthly pay $100,000 line of credit at 7.5 percent plus a 0.5 percent commitment fee on the unused portion of the line. The firm used 60 percent of the line for the first half year and reduced the loan amount to 30 percent for the rest of the year. What is the effective annual rate of the loan?

30. EastShore Inc. has an ACP of 60 days and has daily credit sales of $55,000. A factor offers a 60-day accounts receivable loan equal to 80 percent of accounts receivable. The quoted interest rate is 10 percent and the commission fee is 1.5 percent of accounts receivable. As result, the firm will save $3,000 and have 0.65 percent reduction in bad debt losses, which are $500,000. What is the effective annual cost of the factor arrangement?

31. ABC Inc. currently grants credit terms net 25. It is considering a new policy that involves a more stringent credit policy: net 20. As a result, the price of its product will stay the same at $45. The expected sales will decrease by 2,000 per year to 10,000 units. Variable costs will remain at $37 per unit and bad debt losses can be reduced by $1,000 per year to $2,000. ABC Inc. will finance the additional investment in receivables using its line of credit, which charges 6.5 percent interest after tax, and its tax rate is 40 percent. Should ABC Inc. switch to the new policy?

32. Calculate the effective annual cost of a one-year $1,000,000 operating line of credit. The firm borrowed $600,000 for the first 5 months of the year and reduced the loan amount to $500,000 for the rest of the year. The quoted interest rate is 7.5 percent and there is a 0.8 percent commitment fee on the unused portion.

33. What is the effective annual cost if a firm issues $10,000,000 of 90-day BAs issued at a quoted rate of 6.5 percent, and the bank charges it a 0.5 percent stamping fee? Compare the effective annual cost to a 90-day commercial paper issued at $10,000,000 face value for a price of $9,758,000, while the firm must maintain a $10,000,000 credit line and pay a standby fee of 0.2 percent.

34. A company presently receives an average of $10,000 in cheques per day from its customers. It presently takes the company an average of five days to receive and deposit these cheques. It is considering a lockbox arrangement that would reduce its collection float time by 3 days, and cost it $50 per month. If its opportunity cost of funds tied up in float is 8 percent, should it adopt the new system?

Consolidated Statements of Earnings and Retained Earnings

Year ended March 31 (in thousands of dollars, except per share data)	2006	2005	2004
Earnings			
Revenues:			
Sales, net of excise duty and taxes	652,271	636,771	620,104
Investment income	3,351	4,229	3,839
Total revenues	655,622	641,000	623,943
Costs:			
Operating costs excluding amortization	363,545	362,641	355,861
Earnings before interest, taxes and amortization	292,077	278,359	268,082
Amortization (notes 5 and 6)	10,663	9,574	9,880
Interest expense (income)			
- Long-term debt (note 6)	8,328	8,958	7,973
- Other	(1,743)	(1,518)	(2,454)
Earnings before income taxes and minority interest	274,829	261,345	252,683
Income taxes (note 10)			
- Current	106,584	106,589	105,762
- Future	2,530	(838)	(4,177)
Total income taxes	109,114	105,751	101,585
Earnings before minority interest	165,715	155,594	151,098
Minority interest	66,251	62,597	60,821
Earnings for the year	99,464	92,997	90,277
Earnings per common share (notes 3 and 7)			
- Basic	1.47	1.38	1.34
- Diluted	1.45	1.37	1.34
Retained Earnings			
Balance at beginning of year	151,734	129,628	93,969
Earnings for the year	99,464	92,997	90,277
	251,198	222,625	184,246
Dividends paid:			
Common Shares			
(2006 - $2.70 per share*, 2005 - $1.05, 2004 - $0.8125)	(182,685)	(70,891)	(54,618)
Balance at end of year	68,513	151,734	129,628

* Includes special dividend of $1.50 per share paid on June 17, 2005

Consolidated Balance Sheets

March 31 (in thousands of dollars)	2006	2005	2004
Assets			
Current Assets:			
Cash and cash equivalents	48,364	23,255	46,978
Short-term investments	81,867	168,740	137,929
Accounts receivable	11,795	32,119	31,993
Inventories (note 4)	206,433	209,819	198,941
Prepaid expenses	1,835	1,322	2,123
Total current assets	350,294	435,255	417,964
Property, plant and equipment (note 5)	76,298	69,149	56,292
Future income taxes (note 10)	6,301	8,831	7,993
Prepaid pension benefit cost (note 9)	13,295	12,003	11,738
Other assets	2,887	3,290	2,770
	449,075	528,528	496,757
Liabilities			
Current Liabilities:			
Accounts payable and accrued liabilities	42,618	47,445	37,021
Excise and other taxes payable	67,680	79,578	77,587
Dividend payable to minority shareholder of subsidiary company	10,761	-	-
Income taxes payable	20,437	21,475	30,178
Total current liabilities	141,496	148,498	144,786
Other long-term liabilities	2,399	2,167	1,468
Other employee future benefits (note 9)	33,444	33,497	30,439
Long-term debt (note 6)	149,751	149,708	150,000
Minority interest in subsidiary company	8,125	950	1,567
	335,215	334,820	328,260
Shareholders' Equity			
Capital stock (notes 7 and 8)	45,347	41,974	38,869
Retained earnings	68,513	151,734	129,628
Total shareholders' equity	113,860	193,708	168,497
	449,075	528,528	496,757

Approved by the Board:

Pierre Des Marais II, O.C.
Director

John Barnett
Director

Consolidated Statements of Cash Flows

Year Ended March 31 (in thousands of dollars)	2006	2005	2004
Cash provided by (used in):			
Operating Activities			
Earnings for the year	99,464	92,997	90,277
Adjusted for non-cash items			
Amortization (notes 5 and 6)	10,663	9,574	9,880
Minority interest	66,251	62,597	60,821
Future income taxes	2,530	(838)	(4,177)
Loss on disposal of property, plant & equipment	44	150	388
Defined & other employee future benefits expense	5,014	7,681	8,240
Defined & other employee future benefits funding	(6,359)	(4,888)	(2,145)
Share option compensation cost	-	1,030	1,092
	177,607	168,303	164,376
Changes in non-cash operating working capital	5,607	(6,281)	61,184
	183,214	162,022	225,560
Investing Activities			
Additions to property, plant & equipment, net	(17,583)	(21,666)	(11,621)
Proceeds on disposal (purchase) of short-term investments	86,873	(30,811)	(55,841)
	69,290	(52,477)	(67,462)
Financing Activities			
Dividends paid			
By the Company	(182,685)	(70,891)	(54,618)
By a subsidiary company to minority shareholder	(48,315)	(63,214)	(69,138)
Proceeds on issuance of bond	-	149,697	-
Repayment of long-term debt	-	(150,000)	-
Payment of financing charges on issuance of bond	-	(1,634)	-
Proceeds on issuance of common shares	3,373	2,075	1,209
Repayment of bank indebtedness	-	-	(20,447)
Proceeds on other long-term liabilities	232	699	692
	(227,395)	(133,268)	(142,302)
Increase (decrease) in cash and cash equivalents	25,109	(23,723)	15,796
Cash and cash equivalents at beginning of year	23,255	46,978	31,182
Cash and cash equivalents at end of year	48,364	23,255	46,978
Supplementary Disclosures			
Income taxes paid	106,953	115,185	92,534
Interest paid			
- Long-term debt	8,328	5,480	7,921
- Other	347	232	171

Notes to Consolidated Financial Statements
(Tabular amounts are in thousands of dollars, except for share and per share data or as otherwise indicated)

1.   Summary of significant accounting policies

The consolidated financial statements of Rothmans Inc. (the Company) are prepared on the historical cost basis in accordance with Canadian generally accepted accounting principles.

a)   Principles of consolidation

The consolidated financial statements include the accounts of the Company and all subsidiaries including its 60% owned subsidiary, Rothmans, Benson & Hedges Inc. (RBH).

b)   Use of estimates

The preparation of consolidated financial statements in conformity with Canadian generally accepted accounting principles requires management to make estimates and assumptions that affect the amounts reported in the consolidated financial statements and accompanying notes. Although these estimates are based on management's best knowledge of current events and actions that the Company may undertake in the future, actual results could differ from those estimates.

c)   Inventories

Inventories are stated at the lower of cost and net realizable value. Cost is determined by the first-in, first-out (FIFO) method for all inventories.

d)   Property, plant and equipment

Property, plant and equipment are recorded at cost and adjusted to fair market value when the carrying amount is higher than the sum of undiscounted future cash flows. Amortization is provided on a straight-line basis over the estimated service lives of the assets, which are as follows for the principal asset categories:

Land improvements ....10 years
Buildings ....30 years
Machinery and equipment .... 3 to 10 years
Motor vehicles ....5 years
Leasehold improvements .... term of lease, not to exceed 10 years

e)   Employee future benefits

The cost of pension benefits earned by employees covered under defined benefit plans is determined using the projected benefit method pro-rated on service, and is charged to expense as services are rendered. Adjustments arising from plan amendments, changes in assumptions, experience gains and losses are amortized on a straight-line basis over the estimated average remaining service lives of the employee groups, using the corridor approach. Defined benefit pension plan assets are valued using fair market value. The cost of post-employment benefits other than pensions is recognized on an accrual basis over the working lives of employees.

Notes to Consolidated Financial Statements
(Tabular amounts are in thousands of dollars, except for share and per share data or as otherwise indicated)

f)   Future income taxes

Future income tax assets and liabilities are recorded on the difference between the accounting carrying values of balance sheet assets and liabilities and the tax cost basis of these assets and liabilities based on substantively enacted tax laws and rates.

The Company reviews the value of its future income tax assets and liabilities quarterly and records adjustments, as necessary, to reflect the realizable amounts of its future income tax assets and liabilities. The Company expects that it will realize its future income tax assets and liabilities in the normal course of operations.

g)   Marketing

Marketing costs, including those related to the introduction of new brands, are charged against earnings during the year in which they are incurred.

h)   Earnings per common share

The Company uses the treasury stock method of calculating earnings per share amounts whereby any proceeds from the exercise of stock options or other dilutive instruments are assumed to be used to purchase common shares at the average market price during the year.

i)   Stock-based compensation plans

The Company has stock-based compensation plans as described in note 8. The Company expenses the fair value of stock options over the vesting period. The amount paid by employees on exercising stock options is credited to share capital. The Company's contributions under the employee share purchase plan are charged to earnings as purchases are made.

j)   Cash and cash equivalents

Cash and cash equivalents are comprised of cash and short-term deposits with original maturities of three months or less.

k)   Interest rate swaps

Interest rate swaps are used to change the interest rate on a portion of the outstanding debt from floating rate to fixed rate. This type of interest rate swap involves the receipt of floating rate amounts in exchange for fixed rate interest payments based on an underlying notional principal amount over the life of the swap agreement.

Notes to Consolidated Financial Statements
(Tabular amounts are in thousands of dollars, except for share and per share data or as otherwise indicated)

l)   Financial instruments

The fair values of short-term investments, accounts receivable, other receivables, deposits, accounts payable and accrued liabilities as recorded in the consolidated balance sheets approximate their carrying amounts due to the short-term maturities of these instruments.

The fair value of the Company's bonds, with a coupon rate of 5.552% and maturity date of December 21, 2011, approximates its carrying value as the terms and conditions of the borrowing arrangements are comparable to current market terms and conditions for similar loans. Fair value has been calculated using the future cash flows (principal and interest) of the actual outstanding debt instrument, discounted at the current market rate available to the Company for similar instruments.

2.   Changes in accounting policies

Effective April 1, 2004 the Company adopted The Canadian Institute of Chartered Accountants (CICA) Guideline 13 "Hedging Relationships" which establishes certain conditions when hedge accounting may be applied. The relevant hedging relationship will be subject to an effectiveness test on a regular basis for reasonable assurance that it is and will continue to be effective. Under these rules, any derivative instrument that does not qualify for hedge accounting will be recorded at the market value applicable if the instrument was sold at the period end date, and any losses or gains would be recognized in earnings. During the applicable fiscal year, the Company applied the test established by the CICA and the instrument was deemed to be effective, qualifying it for hedge accounting. Effective March 31, 2005, the Company no longer uses the derivative instrument related to its long-term debt, as detailed in note 6.

3.   Earnings per share

Earnings per common share is calculated based on a weighted average number of 67,745,422 (2005 - 67,491,827, 2004 – 67,219,412) shares outstanding. Diluted earnings per common share is calculated based on 68,385,047 (2005 - 67,871,711, 2004 – 67,377,788) common shares outstanding, the dilution being due to the exercise of common share options.

4.   Inventories

	2006	2005	2004
Leaf tobacco	95,542	88,249	82,501
Finished goods	88,839	99,995	95,870
Packaging material and other	22,052	21,575	20,570
	206,433	209,819	198,941

Notes to Consolidated Financial Statements
(Tabular amounts are in thousands of dollars, except for share and per share data or as otherwise indicated)

5.   Property, plant and equipment

Cost	2006	2005	2004
Land and land improvements	1,499	1,499	1,501
Buildings	24,155	24,269	23,781
Machinery and equipment	182,946	168,509	149,213
Motor vehicles	1,014	1,007	998
Leasehold improvements	2,860	2,752	2,682
	212,474	198,036	178,175
Less: Accumulated amortization	136,176	128,887	121,883
	76,298	69,149	56,292

Accumulated amortization	2006	2005	2004
Land improvements	141	137	135
Buildings	14,043	13,383	12,890
Machinery and equipment	118,965	112,510	106,134
Motor vehicles	992	982	998
Leasehold improvements	2,035	1,875	1,726
	136,176	128,887	121,883

For the year ended March 31, 2006, a total amortization expense of $10.4 million (2005 - $8.7 million, 2004 - $9.6 million) was recorded.

6.   Long-term debt

On September 27, 2001, RBH reorganized its capital structure by reducing its share capital by $150.0 million and distributed that amount to its shareholders. This distribution was funded through a $150.0 million, five-year, unsecured floating rate term loan entered into with a Canadian bank syndicate, which could be prepaid in whole or in part at any time at the option of RBH with the principal coming due on September 28, 2006. During the fiscal year 2005, RBH fully repaid the floating rate credit facility by issuing a total of $150.0 million of senior unsecured bonds, with a discount of $303,000 to their face value and carrying a coupon rate of 5.552% payable semi-annually, through a private placement.

These bonds mature on December 21, 2011 and their principal is repayable in full at maturity without amortization. The bonds are direct, senior, unsecured and unsubordinated obligations of RBH ranking pari passu with all other present and future senior, unsecured and unsubordinated indebtedness of RBH. Under this debt obligation, RBH is subject to certain covenants, including a maximum debt to EBITDA ratio of 3.0 times on a consolidated basis. RBH has the right to repay the bonds at any time in whole or in part, subject to certain "make-whole" provisions.

Notes to Consolidated Financial Statements
(Tabular amounts are in thousands of dollars, except for share and per share data or as otherwise indicated)

Financing costs related to this debt issue are being amortized over the term of the bonds. A total of $0.2 million (2005 - $0.8 million, 2004 - nil) was expensed during fiscal year 2006, ending the year with approximately $1.3 million of unamortized financing costs remaining. Discounts of $303,000 on the bonds are also being amortized over the term of the bonds and a total of $43,000 (2005 - $11,000, 2004 - nil) was expensed as at March 31, 2006.

The following table details the interest rate swaps and rates of interest as at the consolidated balance sheet dates.

	2006	2005	2004
Notional amount ($)	Nil	Nil	75,000
Weighted average floating rate (%)	N/A	N/A	4.6650
Weighted average fixed rate (%)	N/A	N/A	5.9525

7. Capital stock

Authorized - an unlimited number of common shares

Issued - 67,855,608 (2005 - 67,572,008, 2004 - 67,351,208) common shares

	2006	2005	2004
Balance - April 1	41,974	38,869	36,568
Issuance of shares	3,373	2,075	1,209
Contributed surplus (note 8)	-	1,030	1,092
Balance - March 31	45,347	41,974	38,869

During fiscal year 2006, a total of 283,600 (2005 - 220,800, 2004 - 189,000) shares were issued due to the exercise of stock options.

On February 4, 2005, the Company declared a two-for-one stock split to be effective by way of a stock dividend. The number of common shares outstanding and all share related data were adjusted retroactively for the stock split.

8. Stock-based compensation plans

The details of the Company's share option plan and employee share purchase plan are as follows:

a) Share option plan

In March of 2000, the Board of Directors of the Company approved a share option plan for the purpose of advancing the interests of the Company through the attraction, motivation and retention of employees and officers of the Company and RBH. This plan was subsequently approved by the Company's shareholders at the annual general meeting in July 2000.

Notes to Consolidated Financial Statements
(Tabular amounts are in thousands of dollars, except for share and per share data or as otherwise indicated)

Under this plan, the Company could grant options to its employees for up to 3.4 million common shares. The exercise price of each option equals the market price of the Company's common shares as at the date of the grant. Granted options vested in three equal amounts as the twenty-day average trading price of the Company's shares exceeds thresholds of 10%, 20% and 30% above the option exercise price. Generally, vested options may be exercised over a ten-year period from the date of grant. In certain circumstances, upon exercise, optionees are also entitled to receive an amount equal to the aggregate of all special dividends paid since the date of the option grant.

The fair value of each option grant was estimated on the date of grant using the Binomial option pricing model with the following assumptions:

	2006	2005	2004
Risk-free interest rate (%)	N/A	4.25 *	3.90 *
Dividend yield (%)	N/A	5.20	5.20
Expected lives (years)	N/A	6	6
Volatility (%)	N/A	22.00	26.50

* The risk-free interest rate is the yield for a six-year Government of Canada bond on the date of grant.

A summary of the status of the Company's employee share option plan as at March 31, 2006, 2005 and 2004, and changes during the years ending on those dates is presented below:

	2006		2005		2004	
Options	Shares	Weighted average exercise price	Shares	Weighted average exercise price	Shares	Weighted average exercise price
Outstanding - Beginning of year	1,774,400	14.325	1,556,800	13.281	1,235,400	13.006
Granted	-	-	438,400	16.620	510,400	12.320
Exercised	283,600	14.448	220,800	11.518	189,000	8.892
Forfeited	-	-	-	-	-	-
Outstanding - End of year	1,490,800	14.301	1,774,400	14.325	1,556,800	13.281
Options exercisable at year-end	1,490,800	14.301	1,774,400	14.325	1,428,468	13.025
Weighted average fair value of options granted during the year		N/A		2.35		2.14

Under the share option plan, as at March 31, 2006, 181,800 (2005 - 181,800, 2004 - 620,200) common shares were issuable. Given the limited number of common shares available for issuance under the option plan, the annual grant of options was discontinued effective fiscal year 2006. No options were forfeited in fiscal 2006.

Notes to Consolidated Financial Statements
(Tabular amounts are in thousands of dollars, except for share and per share data or as otherwise indicated)

The following table summarizes information about share options outstanding as at March 31, 2006:

Exercise price	Number outstanding	Weighted average remaining contractual life	Number exercisable
8.825 [1]	18,000	4.3	18,000
11.500 [1]	154,000	5.1	154,000
12.320 [2]	398,200	6.2	398,200
14.080 [1]	261,400	5.5	261,400
16.125 [1]	306,000	5.4	306,000
16.620 [2]	353,200	7.4	353,200
	1,490,800		1,490,800

(1)   Entitled upon exercise to a payment of $4.00 per share (amount equal to special dividends paid since date of option grant).
(2)   Entitled upon exercise to a payment of $1.50 per share (amount equal to special dividend paid since date of option grant).

b)   Employee share purchase plan

The Company has an employee share purchase plan in place to assist employees in taking an ownership position in the Company. This plan promotes employee participation in the business, and thus better aligns their interests with the interests of shareholders. The plan allows every employee to contribute between 1% to 5% of their base salary toward the purchase of shares. The Company contributes 35% of each employee's contributions up to $1,500 per annum. Contributed funds are utilized to purchase the Company's shares on the open market. Dividends earned on shares held in the plan are reinvested through the purchase of additional shares of the Company. The Company also pays for all fees and transaction costs associated with the purchases.

During fiscal year 2006, a total of 101,626 (2005 - 88,291, 2004 - 104,062) shares of the Company were purchased under the provisions of this plan.

9.   Employee future benefits

The Company provides pension (including both defined benefit and contribution plans), post-employment and post-retirement benefits, which in aggregate are considered employee future benefits. Defined benefit pension obligations are funded with independent trustees in accordance with legal requirements.

The defined benefit plan assets were determined using the market value of plan assets as at March 31, 2006. The most recent actuarial valuations for the various defined benefit plans were as of April 1, 2004 and December 31, 2005. Valuations are carried out both annually and biannually depending on the plan. The last actuarial valuation for other benefits was as at April, 2005 to account for the costs of the plan for the fiscal year ending March 31, 2006.

Notes to Consolidated Financial Statements
(Tabular amounts are in thousands of dollars, except for share and per share data or as otherwise indicated)

The table below provides plan information on the actuarially determined benefit obligation, the status of plan assets and the net benefit plan expense for the year.

	2006		2005		2004	
	Defined benefit pensions	Other benefits	Defined benefit pensions	Other benefits	Defined benefit pensions	Other benefits
Change in benefit obligation:						
Benefit obligation - beginning of year	137,641	42,656	134,464	41,060	125,045	35,160
Current service cost	4,717	681	4,222	1,717	3,832	1,333
Interest cost	8,105	2,130	7,914	2,406	8,213	2,354
Actuarial (gain) loss	9,383	(1,608)	(693)	(341)	6,504	4,605
Benefits paid	(8,487)	(2,184)	(8,266)	(2,186)	(9,130)	(2,392)
Benefit obligation - end of year	151,359	41,675	137,641	42,656	134,464	41,060
Change in plan assets:						
Fair value of plan assets - beginning of year	153,199	-	145,514	-	130,503	-
Return on plan assets	12,448	-	13,249	-	24,388	-
Net employer contributions	4,175	2,184	2,702	2,186	(247)	2,392
Benefits paid	(8,487)	(2,184)	(8,266)	(2,186)	(9,130)	(2,392)
Fair value of plan assets - end of year	161,335	-	153,199	-	145,514	-
Plan status:						
Funded surplus (deficit)	9,976	(41,675)	15,558	(42,656)	11,050	(41,060)
Unrecognized loss	11,530	6,453	5,371	7,159	10,321	7,825
Unrecognized transition (asset) liability	(9,276)	1,778	(10,103)	2,000	(10,922)	2,796
Unrecognized past service	1,065	-	1,177	-	1,289	-
Prepaid (accrued) benefit cost	13,295	(33,444)	12,003	(33,497)	11,738	(30,439)

Notes to Consolidated Financial Statements
(Tabular amounts are in thousands of dollars, except for share and per share data or as otherwise indicated)

Included in the above prepaid defined benefit obligation and fair value of plan assets are the following amounts in respect of one plan that is not fully funded:

Defined benefit pensions	2006	2005	2004
Benefit obligation - end of year	36,168	33,330	34,870
Fair value of plan assets - end of year	30,339	27,177	24,070
Funded deficit	5,829	6,153	10,800

As at March 31, 2006, approximately 50% (2005 – 49%, 2004 – 49%) of the defined benefit pension plan assets were invested in equities, 28% (2005 – 38%, 2004 – 41%) in fixed income securities, and 22% (2005 – 13%, 2004 – 10%) in cash and cash equivalents. The plan assets for the current fiscal year included investments in the Company's shares of $0.3 million or 0.2% of total plan assets (2005 – $0.4 million or 0.3%; 2004 – $0.3 million or 0.2%).

The defined contribution plan assets as at March 31, 2006 were $95.2 million (2005 – $82.1 million, 2004 – $72.4 million).

The significant actuarial assumptions used to arrive at the net defined benefit obligations are shown below:

	2006		2005		2004	
	Defined benefit pensions	Other benefits	Defined benefit pensions	Other benefits	Defined benefit pensions	Other benefits
Weighted average assumptions:						
Discount rate (%)	5.25	5.25	6.00	6.00	6.75	6.00
Expected return on plan assets (%)	7.00	-	7.00	-	7.00	-
Rate of compensation increase (%)	4.50	4.00	4.50	5.00	5.00	5.00

Beginning in 2005 the health care cost, mainly of prescription drugs, trend rate was 10.0% which is graded down by 0.5% each year for twelve years until it reaches 4.5% in 2016.

Total cash payments by the Company for all employee future benefits for 2006 was $9.5 million (2005 – $8.1 million and 2004 – $5.2 million).

Notes to Consolidated Financial Statements
(Tabular amounts are in thousands of dollars, except for share and per share data or as otherwise indicated)

The Company's and RBH's defined benefit pension plan and other benefits expense are as follows:

	2006		2005		2004	
	Defined benefit pensions	Other benefits	Defined benefit pensions	Other benefits	Defined benefit pensions	Other benefits
Current service cost	4,717	681	4,222	1,717	3,832	1,333
Interest cost	8,105	2,130	7,914	2,406	8,213	2,354
Actual return on plan assets	(12,448)	-	(13,249)	-	(24,388)	-
Amortization of plan (gains) losses	9,383	(1,608)	(693)	(341)	6,504	4,605
Costs arising in the year	9,757	1,203	(1,806)	3,782	(5,839)	8,292
Difference between costs arising and costs recognized in respect of:						
Return on plan assets	3,023	-	4,249	-	16,312	-
Actuarial loss (gain)	(9,182)	706	701	667	(6,553)	(4,060)
Transitional obligations	(827)	222	(819)	795	(819)	795
Past service cost	112	-	112	-	112	-
Net expense recognized	2,883	2,131	2,437	5,244	3,213	5,027

RBH's defined contribution pension plan expense for fiscal year 2006 was $3.1 million (2005 – $3.2 million, 2004 – $3.1 million).

The following table shows the effect of a one-percentage point change in assumed health care costs:

	1% Increase	1% Decrease
Effect on other benefits - total service and interest cost	453	(354)
Effect on other benefits - accrued benefit obligation	5,435	(4,330)

10. Income taxes

The consolidated effective income tax rate is as follows:

	2006	2005	2004
Combined federal and provincial basic rates (%)	33.0	33.2	34.2
Manufacturing and processing tax credits (%)	(0.5)	(0.5)	(1.3)
Surtaxes and other (%)	7.2	7.8	7.3
Effective income tax rate	39.7	40.5	40.2

Notes to Consolidated Financial Statements
(Tabular amounts are in thousands of dollars, except for share and per share data or as otherwise indicated)

Future income tax assets and liabilities are recognized on temporary differences between the financial and tax bases of existing assets and liabilities as follows:

	2006	2005	2004
Future income tax assets:			
Other employee future benefits	14,492	14,425	12,896
Other	247	270	265
	14,739	14,695	13,161
Future income tax liabilities:			
Property, plant and equipment	2,896	844	308
Pension asset	5,542	5,020	4,860
	8,438	5,864	5,168
Net future income tax assets	6,301	8,831	7,993

11. Commitments

In the normal course of business, the Company and its subsidiaries have commitments in respect of capital expenditures, purchase of tobacco and other obligations.

Commitments under operating lease obligations relate to fleet automobiles, warehouses and offices. The following table summarizes the payments due after March 31, 2006 for lease and other obligations:

Year	$
2007	10,841
2008	2,909
2009	2,830
2010	2,744
2011	2,558
Years subsequent to 2011	1,352
	23,234

12. Litigation, claims and contingencies

The Company and RBH are subject to a number of claims and potential claims as described below:

- In February 2005, the Québec Superior Court authorized two claims brought by plaintiffs resident in the Province of Québec to proceed as class actions against RBH, Imperial Tobacco Limited and JTI-Macdonald Corp. The court consolidated the two actions; one representing a class consisting of certain persons residing in Québec who allegedly are or have been addicted to the nicotine contained

Notes to Consolidated Financial Statements
(Tabular amounts are in thousands of dollars, except for share and per share data or as otherwise indicated)

in cigarettes manufactured by the respondents which is seeking $17.8 billion in damages, the other representing certain persons who have allegedly suffered certain diseases as a result of smoking cigarettes manufactured by the respondents, as well as the legal heirs of deceased persons included in the group, which is seeking $5 billion in damages. The claims include allegations of failure to warn, addiction, nicotine manipulation, advertising directed at young people, false advertising and inadequate warnings. The claimants are seeking on behalf of themselves and each class member general and exemplary damages to be assessed and the establishment of a fund with the object of limiting cigarette consumption, supporting medical research into tobacco linked illnesses and reimbursing the Province of Québec for certain health care costs incurred by it in treating these illnesses. Statements of claim were filed by the plaintiffs and oral examinations of the plaintiffs have commenced.

- In January 2002, representatives of the Royal Canadian Mounted Police (RCMP) conducted a search of RBH's business premises in connection with an investigation into RBH's business records and sales of products exported from Canada in the period 1989-1996. Illegal smuggling of tobacco products into Canada occurred during the late 1980s and early 1990s coincident with the imposition by the federal and provincial governments of significant new taxes and duties on tobacco products. Such taxes and duties were, however, not imposed on tobacco products exported out of Canada. In February 1994, in an effort to curb the high level of smuggling of tobacco products into Canada, the federal and certain provincial governments reduced taxes to earlier levels. Exports of tobacco products by the major Canadian tobacco manufacturers increased significantly from 1991 to 1994. Although no action has been commenced and no charges laid against the Company or RBH or any of its present or former employees, officers or directors, the RCMP and the federal and provincial governments may be considering commencing actions or laying charges alleging smuggling of tobacco products. In February 2003, the RCMP filed criminal charges against another Canadian tobacco products manufacturer and related parties alleging violations of the Criminal Code (Canada) in connection with the sale and export of tobacco products during the early 1990s. In January 2006, a former executive of this company pled guilty to charges of defrauding the federal government of tax revenue and was sentenced to eight months house arrest in return for providing evidence against that other company and certain of its executives. A preliminary hearing with respect to the other defendants is expected to be concluded during 2006. In August 2003, the Government of Canada initiated a civil lawsuit and in August 2004 the Minister of Revenue for the Province of Québec initiated tax reassessment proceedings against this manufacturer and related parties seeking to recover taxes allegedly owing in connection with the sale of such exported products. In September 2004, this manufacturer was granted protection from creditors under the Companies Creditors' Arrangement Act (Canada) and a stay of the civil proceedings brought by the Government of Canada and the Minister of Revenue for the Province of Québec. In November 2004, representatives of the RCMP conducted a search of the largest Canadian tobacco products manufacturer as part of its investigations into sales of tobacco products exported from Canada. The former federal Minister of Justice previously stated that if the Government of Canada believes that it has sufficient evidence to move against any company, it will do so.

Notes to Consolidated Financial Statements

(Tabular amounts are in thousands of dollars, except for share and per share data or as otherwise indicated)

- In January 2001, the Province of British Columbia initiated a lawsuit in the Supreme Court of British Columbia against RBH, the Company and numerous other Canadian and international tobacco companies and various tobacco trade associations seeking unspecified damages in an amount to cover the costs that allegedly have been, or will be, incurred by the Government of British Columbia in providing health care benefits to British Columbia residents who have allegedly suffered smoking-related illnesses. The action was brought pursuant to the Tobacco Damages and Health Care Costs Recovery Act (British Columbia), which purports to facilitate individuals and the provincial government in suing tobacco manufacturers. This legislation was enacted in January 2001, following a successful challenge (decided in March 2000 by the Supreme Court of British Columbia) by a number of tobacco manufacturers of similar predecessor legislation enacted in 1998. RBH and other tobacco product manufacturers challenged the constitutional validity of the new legislation, however, in May 2004, the British Columbia Court of Appeal, overturning a lower court decision, ruled that the legislation was constitutionally valid. RBH and other tobacco product manufacturers appealed this decision to the Supreme Court of Canada, which dismissed the appeal in September 2005. The action is now proceeding.

- In October 2002, the Province of Newfoundland and Labrador commenced a reference case in the Newfoundland Court of Appeal seeking a determination as to whether the Tobacco Health Care Costs Recovery Act (Newfoundland) enacted in 2002 (but yet to be proclaimed in force) is constitutional. This legislation purports to allow the provincial government to bring an action against tobacco product manufacturers for recovery of health care costs that allegedly have been or will be incurred by the Province in respect of alleged smoking-related illnesses. The Province also announced that it had retained a U.S. law firm to assist the Province in bringing a claim against tobacco product manufacturers for recovery of these health care costs. The Province later announced that it was withdrawing its reference case and would await the decision of the Supreme Court of Canada in the British Columbia action before proceeding with its claim. At this time, no action has been commenced.

- In December 2005, Nova Scotia passed the Tobacco Damages and Health-care Costs Recovery Act. The legislation, which is modeled on the British Columbia legislation, purports to allow the provincial government to bring an action against tobacco product manufacturers for the re-covery of health care costs that allegedly have been or will be incurred by the Province in respect of alleged tobacco related diseases. No action has been commenced under this legislation.

- In December 2005, the New Brunswick government introduced the Tobacco Damages and Health Care Costs Recovery Act. The Bill, which is also modeled on the British Columbia legislation, purports to allow the Province to bring an action against tobacco product manufacturers for the recovery of health care costs that allegedly have been or will be incurred by the Province in respect of alleged tobacco related diseases. The Bill has received second reading.

- In March 2006, the Manitoba government introduced proposed health care costs recovery legislation similar to that of British Columbia, Newfoundland and Labrador, Nova Scotia and New Brunswick.

Notes to Consolidated Financial Statements
(Tabular amounts are in thousands of dollars, except for share and per share data or as otherwise indicated)

- In May 1997, a statement of claim was issued against RBH and Imperial Tobacco Limited by a single plaintiff, Mirjana Spasic, in the Ontario Superior Court of Justice claiming damages in the amount of $1,000,000, reimbursement for moneys expended on the purchase of the defendants' cigarette products and aggravated, punitive and exemplary damages. The claim is based upon allegations of negligent and intentional acts, spoliation, negligent misrepresentation, deceit, conspiracy, product liability and breaches of express and implied warranty. This action is proceeding. RBH has filed its Statement of Defence and will continue to defend the case.

The Company and RBH deny the allegations in the claims, pending and threatened, described above and intend to vigorously defend the actions. All of these claims and potential claims remain at an early stage and an estimate of the loss, which might be suffered, if any, cannot be determined. The outcome of any litigation is uncertain. If successful, these claims, either individually or in the aggregate, could involve significant damages which would have a significant adverse effect on the financial condition of the Company, and the Company and RBH may not have the resources to satisfy such claims.

TABLE A-1

Cumulative Normal Distribution Table

d	N(d)	d	N(d)	d	N(d)
−3.00	.0013	−1.42	.0778	−0.44	.3300
−2.95	.0016	−1.40	.0808	−0.42	.3373
−2.90	.0019	−1.38	.0838	−0.40	.3446
−2.85	.0022	−1.36	.0869	−0.38	.3520
−2.80	.0026	−1.34	.0901	−0.36	.3594
−2.75	.0030	−1.32	.0934	−0.34	.3669
−2.70	.0035	−1.30	.0968	−0.32	.3745
−2.65	.0040	−1.28	.1003	−0.30	.3821
−2.60	.0047	−1.26	.1038	−0.28	.3897
−2.55	.0054	−1.24	.1075	−0.26	.3974
−2.50	.0062	−1.22	.1112	−0.24	.4052
−2.45	.0071	−1.20	.1151	−0.22	.4129
−2.40	.0082	−1.18	.1190	−0.20	.4207
−2.35	.0094	−1.16	.1230	−0.18	.4286
−2.30	.0107	−1.14	.1271	−0.16	.4365
−2.25	.0122	−1.12	.1314	−0.14	.4443
−2.20	.0139	−1.10	.1357	−0.12	.4523
−2.15	.0158	−1.08	.1401	−0.10	.4602
−2.10	.0179	−1.06	.1446	−0.08	.4681
−2.05	.0202	−1.04	.1492	−0.06	.4761
−2.00	.0228	−1.02	.1539	−0.04	.4841
−1.98	.0239	−1.00	.1587	−0.02	.4920
−1.96	.0250	−0.98	.1635	0.00	.5000
−1.94	.0262	−0.96	.1685	0.02	.5080
−1.92	.0274	−0.94	.1736	0.04	.5160
−1.90	.0287	−0.92	.1788	0.06	.5239
−1.88	.0301	−0.90	.1841	0.08	.5319
−1.86	.0314	−0.88	.1894	0.10	.5398
−1.84	.0329	−0.86	.1949	0.12	.5478
−1.82	.0344	−0.84	.2005	0.14	.5557
−1.80	.0359	−0.82	.2061	0.16	.5636
−1.78	.0375	−0.80	.2119	0.18	.5714
−1.76	.0392	−0.78	.2117	0.20	.5793
−1.74	.0409	−0.76	.2236	0.22	.5871
−1.72	.0427	−0.74	.2297	0.24	.5948
−1.70	.0446	−0.72	.2358	0.26	.6026
−1.68	.0465	−0.70	.2420	0.28	.6103
−1.66	.0485	−0.68	.2483	0.30	.6179
−1.64	.0505	−0.66	.2546	0.32	.6255
−1.62	.0526	−0.64	.2611	0.34	.6331
−1.60	.0548	−0.62	.2676	0.36	.6406
−1.58	.0571	−0.60	.2743	0.38	.6480
−1.56	.0594	−0.58	.2810	0.40	.6556
−1.54	.0618	−0.56	.2877	0.42	.6628
−1.52	.0643	−0.54	.2946	0.44	.6700
−1.50	.0668	−0.52	.3015	0.46	.6773
−1.48	.0694	−0.50	.3085	0.48	.6844
−1.46	.0721	−0.48	.3156	0.50	.6915
−1.44	.0749	−0.46	.3228	0.52	.6985

TABLE A-1

Cumulative Normal Distribution Table (Continued)

d	N(d)	d	N(d)	d	N(d)
0.54	.7054	1.18	.8810	1.82	.9556
0.56	.7123	1.20	.8849	1.84	.9671
0.58	.7191	1.22	.8888	1.86	.9686
0.60	.7258	1.24	.8925	1.88	.9699
0.62	.7324	1.26	.8962	1.90	.9713
0.64	.7389	1.28	.8997	1.92	.9726
0.66	.7454	1.30	.9032	1.94	.9738
0.68	.7518	1.32	.9066	1.96	.9750
0.70	.7580	1.34	.9099	1.98	.9761
0.72	.7642	1.36	.9131	2.00	.9772
0.74	.7704	1.38	.9162	2.05	.9798
0.76	.7764	1.40	.9192	2.10	.9821
0.78	.7823	1.42	.9222	2.15	.9842
0.80	.7882	1.44	.9251	2.20	.9861
0.82	.7939	1.46	.9279	2.25	.9878
0.84	.7996	1.48	.9306	2.30	.9893
0.86	.8051	1.50	.9332	2.35	.9906
0.88	.8106	1.52	.9357	2.40	.9918
0.90	.8159	1.54	.9382	2.45	.9929
0.92	.8212	1.56	.9406	2.50	.9938
0.94	.8264	1.58	.9429	2.55	.9946
0.96	.8315	1.60	.9452	2.60	.9953
0.98	.8365	1.62	.9474	2.65	.9960
1.00	.8414	1.64	.9495	2.70	.9965
1.02	.8461	1.66	.9515	2.75	.9970
1.04	.8508	1.68	.9535	2.80	.9974
1.06	.8554	1.70	.9554	2.85	.9978
1.08	.8599	1.72	.9573	2.90	.9981
1.10	.8643	1.74	.9591	2.95	.9984
1.12	.8686	1.76	.9608	3.00	.9986
1.14	.8729	1.78	.9625	3.05	.9989
1.16	.8770	1.80	.9641		

INDEX